FEB 5 1986

D0944539

DISCARDED

DISCARDED

CORNELL STUDIES IN CIVIL LIBERTY

Milton R. Konvitz, *General Editor*

BOOKS BY MILTON R. KONVITZ

On the Nature of Value
The Alien and the Asiatic in American Law
The Constitution and Civil Rights
Civil Rights in Immigration
Fundamental Liberties of a Free People: Religion, Speech, Press, Assembly
A Century of Civil Rights (with Theodore Leskes)
Expanding Liberties
Religious Liberty and Conscience

EDITOR OF

Freedom and Experience (with Sidney Hook)
Essays in Political Theory (with Arthur E. Murphy)
Law and Social Action: Selected Essays of Alexander H. Pekelis
Education for Freedom and Responsibility by Edmund Ezra Day
Liberian Code of Laws
Liberian Code of Laws Revised
Liberian Law Reports
Aspects of Liberty (with Clinton Rossiter)
Bill of Rights Reader: Leading Constitutional Cases
The American Pragmatists (with Gail Kennedy)
Emerson: A Collection of Critical Essays (with Stephen E. Whicher)
First Amendment Freedoms: Selected Cases on Freedom of Religion, Speech, Press, Assembly
Judaism and Human Rights
The Recognition of Ralph Waldo Emerson

BILL OF RIGHTS READER

Leading Constitutional Cases

MILTON R. KONVITZ

FIFTH EDITION, REVISED

CORNELL UNIVERSITY PRESS | ITHACA AND LONDON

Ref.
342.73
K82b

First edition copyright 1954, second edition copyright © 1960, third edition copyright © 1965, fourth edition copyright © 1968, fifth edition copyright © 1973 by Cornell University.

All rights reserved. Except for brief quotations in a review, this book, or parts thereof, must not be reproduced in any form without permission in writing from the publisher. For information address Cornell University Press, 124 Roberts Place, Ithaca, New York 14850.

First edition 1954
Second edition 1960
Third edition 1965
Fourth edition 1968
Fifth edition 1973
Third printing 1978

Published in the United Kingdom by Cornell University Press Ltd., 2-4 Brook Street, London W1Y 1AA.

International Standard Book Number 0-8014-0783-4
Library of Congress Catalog Card Number 73-8671

Printed in the United States of America by York Composition Co., Inc.

Librarians: Library of Congress cataloging information
appears on the last page of the book.

For Josef, my son

Let a man learn to look for the permanent
in the mutable and fleeting;
let him learn to bear the disappearance of things
he was wont to reverence
without losing his reverence.—EMERSON

86-01300

Preface to Fifth Edition

When the first edition of this work was published in 1954, it had the character of a pioneering undertaking. It stood almost alone. Few courses in civil liberties or civil rights were then offered in colleges or law schools. The book, then, was in search of a market.

Today, less than two decades later, the situation is quite different. Many law schools and departments of government offer courses or seminars in the Bill of Rights or in civil liberties or civil rights, and it is gratifying to see that even some secondary schools have begun to show an interest in these subjects; and now the market is in search of books. The fact that there is a demand for a fifth edition of the *Bill of Rights Reader* is some warrant for thinking that perhaps the book has made a contribution to the changes that we have seen, and that it has a meritorious place even in a field that has become competitive.

Publication of the first edition in 1954 coincided with the start of the Warren era of the United States Supreme Court; fortunately we were able to include the Court's unanimous decision in *Brown* v. *Board of Education*. Chief Justice Warren's opinion in that case was the only opinion bearing his name included in that volume. When Earl Warren succeeded Fred M. Vinson as Chief Justice in 1953, no one—and least of all President Eisenhower, who appointed him—foresaw the emergence of the Warren era in the history of the Supreme Court and in the history of the American people and their institutions. The three successive editions of this book—in 1960, 1965, and 1968—are cumulatively a record of the great constitutional—and political and social—changes that were effected by the Supreme Court in a period of about fifteen years.

In June 1969, Warren Earl Burger succeeded Chief Justice Warren, and a new chapter in the history of the Supreme Court began. Now, with the passage of some five years since the fourth edition, a new edition has become necessary in order to bridge the years and the changes in the Court. The extent of the changes may in part be measured by the fact that this edition contains 48 new cases—40 percent of the total number. Included are the cases dealing with the Pentagon Papers, the death penalty, tax exemption of church property, compulsory secondary education for Amish children, the so-called parochaid legislation, symbolic speech, obscenity for minors, obscenity and the right of privacy, the rights of the poor, the rights of prisoners, the rights of illegitimate children, and some affirmative-action aspects of school desegregation. Some of the decisions were by the Warren Court, and some by the Burger Court. One will find in the cases both continuity and newness, old divisions and new alignments. "Time," said Justice Holmes in his dissenting opinion in *Abrams,* "has upset many fighting faiths." But time has also sustained many fighting faiths. No institution more easily and fully demonstrates both sides of the coin than does the Supreme Court.

Cornell University   M. R. K.
January 2, 1973

Contents

Table of Cases

Bill of Rights Reader

LEADING CONSTITUTIONAL CASES

I. Bill of Rights in the United States Constitution

First Ten Amendments

AMENDMENT I

Congress shall make no law respecting an establishment of religion, or prohibiting the free exercise thereof; or abridging the freedom of speech, or of the press; or the right of the people peaceably to assemble and to petition the Government for a redress of grievances.

AMENDMENT II

A well regulated Militia, being necessary to the security of a free State, the right of the people to keep and bear Arms, shall not be infringed.

AMENDMENT III

No Soldier shall, in time of peace be quartered in any house, without the consent of the Owner, nor in time of war, but in a manner to be prescribed by law.

AMENDMENT IV

The right of the people to be secure in their persons, houses, papers, and effects, against unreasonable searches and seizures, shall not be violated, and no Warrants shall issue, but upon probable cause, supported by Oath or affirmation, and particularly describing the place to be searched, and the persons or things to be seized.

AMENDMENT V

No person shall be held to answer for a capital, or otherwise infamous crime, unless on a presentment or indictment of a Grand Jury, except in cases arising in the land or naval forces, or in the Militia, when in actual service in time of War or public danger; nor shall any person be subject for the same offence to be twice put in jeopardy of life or limb; nor shall be compelled in any criminal case to be a witness against himself, nor be deprived of life, liberty, or property, without due process of law; nor shall private property be taken for public use, without just compensation.

AMENDMENT VI

In all criminal prosecutions, the accused shall enjoy the right to a speedy and public trial, by an impartial jury of the State and district wherein the crime shall have been committed, which district shall have been previously ascertained by law, and to be informed of the nature and cause of the accusation; to be confronted with the witnesses against him; to have compulsory process for obtaining witnesses in his favor, and to have the Assistance of Counsel for his defence.

AMENDMENT VII

In suits at common law, where the value in controversy shall exceed twenty dollars, the right of trial by jury shall be preserved, and no fact tried by a jury, shall be otherwise re-examined in any Court of the United States, than according to the rules of the common law.

AMENDMENT VIII

Excessive bail shall not be required, nor excessive fines imposed, nor cruel and unusual punishments inflicted.

AMENDMENT IX

The enumeration in the Constitution, of certain rights, shall not be construed to deny or disparage others retained by the people.

AMENDMENT X

The powers not delegated to the United States by the Constitution, nor prohibited by it to the States, are reserved to the States respectively, or to the people.

Other Amendments

AMENDMENT XIII

Sec. 1. Neither slavery nor involuntary servitude, except as a punishment for crime whereof the party shall have been duly convicted, shall exist within the United States, or any place subject to their jurisdiction.

Sec. 2. Congress shall have power to enforce this article by appropriate legislation.

AMENDMENT XIV

Sec. 1. All persons born or naturalized in the United States, and subject to the jurisdiction thereof, are citizens of the United States and of the State wherein they reside. No State shall make or enforce any law which shall abridge the privileges or immunities of citizens of the United States; nor shall any State deprive any person of life, liberty, or property, without due process of law; nor deny to any person within its jurisdiction the equal protection of the laws. . . .

Sec. 5. The Congress shall have power to enforce, by appropriate legislation, the provisions of this article.

AMENDMENT XV

Sec. 1. The right of citizens of the United States to vote shall not be denied or abridged by the United States or by any State on account of race, color, or previous condition of servitude.

Sec. 2. The Congress shall have power to enforce this article by appropriate legislation.

AMENDMENT XIX

The right of citizens of the United States to vote shall not be denied or abridged by the United States or by any State on account of sex.

Congress shall have power, by appropriate legislation, to enforce the provisions of this article.

AMENDMENT XXIV

Sec. 1. The right of citizens of the United States to vote in any primary or other election for President or Vice President, for electors for President or Vice President, or for Senator or Representative in Congress, shall not be denied or abridged by the United States or any State by reason of failure to pay any poll tax or other tax.

Sec. 2. The Congress shall have the power to enforce this article by appropriate legislation.

AMENDMENT XXVI

Sec. 1. The right of citizens of the United States, who are 18 years of age or older, to vote shall not be denied or abridged by the United States or any state on account of age.

Sec. 2. The Congress shall have the power to enforce this article by appropriate legislation.

Provisions from Original Constitution

ARTICLE I

Sec. 9. . . . The Privilege of the Writ of Habeas Corpus shall not be suspended, unless when in Cases of Rebellion or Invasion the public Safety may require it.

No Bill of Attainder or ex post facto Law shall be passed.

Sec. 10. No State shall . . . pass any Bill of Attainder, ex post facto Law, or Law impairing the Obligation of Contracts. . . .

ARTICLE III

Sec. 2. . . . The trial of all Crimes, except in cases of Impeachment, shall be by Jury. . . .

ARTICLE IV

Sec.2. The Citizens of each State shall be entitled to all Privileges and Immunities of Citizens in the several States.

ARTICLE VI

. . . No religious Test shall ever be required as a Qualification to any Office or public Trust under the United States.

II. The Rule of Law

1. The United States Constitution Is the Supreme Law of the Land

COOPER v. AARON
358 US 1 (1958)

[Following the decison of the Court in *Brown* v. *Board of Education, post,* the school board of Little Rock, Arkansas, formulated a school desegregation program, which was judicially approved as compliance with the decision in *Brown.* Then the governor and the legislature of Arkansas took the position that they were not bound by the Supreme Court decision, and the school board applied to the federal District Court for permission to suspend for two and a half years its desegregation program, and the court granted the petition. The Court of Appeals reversed this action, and the Supreme Court unanimously affirmed the judgment of the latter court.

[The opinion of Chief Justice Warren is far-reaching in significance, for the case was a challenge by a state to federal authority, the United States Constitution, and the rule of law. The concurring opinion of Justice Frankfurter underscores the gravity of the decision and of the Court opinion.]

Opinion of the Court by The Chief Justice [Warren], Mr. Justice Black, Mr. Justice Frankfurter, Mr. Justice Douglas, Mr. Justice Burton, Mr. Justice Clark, Mr. Justice Harlan, Mr. Justice Brennan, and Mr. Justice Whittaker:

As this case reaches us it raises questions of the highest importance to the maintenance of our federal system of government. It necessarily involves a claim by the Governor and Legislature of a State that there is no duty on state officials to obey federal court orders resting on this Court's considered interpretation of the United States Constitution. Specifically it involves actions by the Governor and Legislature of Arkansas upon the premise that they are not bound by our holding in *Brown* v. *Board of Education,* 347 US 483. . . . That holding was that the Fourteenth Amendment forbids States to use their governmental powers to bar children on racial grounds from attending schools where there is state participation through any arrangement, management, funds or property. We are urged to uphold a suspension of the Little Rock School Board's plan to do away with segregated public schools in Little Rock until state laws and efforts to upset and nullify our holding in *Brown* v. *Board of Education* have been further challenged and tested in the courts. We reject these contentions.

The case was argued before us on September 11, 1958. On the following day we unanimously affirmed the judgment of the Court of Appeals for the Eighth Circuit, . . . which had reversed a judgment of the District Court for the Eastern District of Arkansas. The District Court had granted the application of the petitioners, the Little Rock School Board and School Superintendent, to suspend for two and one-half years the operation of the School Board's court-approved desegregation program. In order that the School Board might know, without doubt, its duty in this regard before the opening of school, which had been set for the following Monday, September 15, 1958, we immediately issued the judgment, reserving the expression of our supporting views to a later date. This opinion of all of the members of the Court embodies those views.

The following are the facts and circumstances so far as necessary to show how the legal questions are presented.

On May 17, 1954, this Court decided that enforced racial segregation in the public schools of a state is a denial of the equal protection of the laws enjoined by the Fourteenth Amendment. *Brown* v. *Board of Education.* . . . The Court postponed, pending further argument, formulation of a decree to effectuate this decision. That decree was rendered May 31, 1955. *Brown* v. *Board of Education,* 349 US 294. . . . In the formulation of that decree the Court recognized that good faith compliance with the principles declared in *Brown* might in some situations "call for elimination of a variety of obstacles in making the transition to school systems operated in accordance with the constitutional principles set forth in our May 17, 1954, decision." The Court went on to state:

Courts of equity may properly take into account the public interest in the elimination of such obstacles in a systematic and effective manner. But it should go without saying that the vitality of these constitutional principles cannot be allowed to yield simply because of disagreement with them.

While giving weight to these public and private considerations, the courts will require that the defendants make a prompt and reasonable start toward full compliance with our May 17, 1954, ruling. Once such a start has been made, the courts may find that additional time is necessary to carry out the ruling in an effective manner. The burden rests upon the defendants to establish that such time is necessary in the public interest and is consistent with good faith compliance at the earliest practicable date. To that end, the courts may consider problems related to administration, arising from the physical condition of the school plant, the school transportation system, personnel, revision of school districts and attendance areas into compact units to achieve a system of determining admission to the public schools on a nonracial basis, and revision of local laws and regulations which may be necessary in solving the foregoing problems.

Under such circumstances, the District Courts were directed to require "a prompt and reasonable start toward full compliance," and to take such action as was necessary to bring about the end of racial segregation in the public schools "with all deliberate speed." *Ibid.* Of course, in many locations, obedience to the duty of desegregation would require the immediate general admission of Negro children, otherwise qualified as students for their appropriate classes, at particular schools. On the other hand, a District Court, after analysis of the relevant factors (which, of course, excludes hostility to racial desegregation), might conclude that justification existed for not requiring the present nonsegregated admission of all

qualified Negro children. In such circumstances, however, the Court should scrutinize the program of the school authorities to make sure that they had developed
arrangements pointed toward the earliest practicable completion of desegregation, and had taken appropriate steps to put their program into effective
operation. It was made plain that delay in any guise in order to deny the constitutional rights of Negro children could not be countenanced, and that only a prompt
start, diligently and earnestly pursued, to eliminate racial segregation from the
public schools could constitute good faith compliance. State authorities were thus
duty bound to devote every effort toward initiating desegregation and bringing
about the elimination of racial discrimination in the public school system.

On May 20, 1954, three days after the first *Brown* opinion, the Little Rock District School Board adopted, and on May 23, 1954, made public, a statement of
policy entitled "Supreme Court Decision—Segregation in Public Schools." In this
statement the Board recognized that

It is our responsibility to comply with Federal Constitutional requirements and we
intend to do so when the Supreme Court of the United States outlines the method to be
followed.

Thereafter the Board undertook studies of the administrative problems confronting the transition to a desegregated public school system at Little Rock. It
instructed the Superintendent of Schools to prepare a plan for desegregation, and
approved such a plan on May 24, 1955, seven days before the second *Brown*
opinion. The plan provided for desegregation at the senior high school level (grades
10 through 12) as the first stage. Desegregation at the junior high and elementary
levels was to follow. It was contemplated that desegregation at the high school
level would commence in the fall of 1957, and the expectation was that complete
desegregation of the school system would be accomplished by 1963. Following the
adoption of this plan, the Superintendent of Schools discussed it with a large number of citizen groups in the city. As a result of these discussions, the Board
reached the conclusion that "a large majority of the residents" of Little Rock were of
"the belief . . . that the Plan, although objectionable in principle," from the point
of view of those supporting segregated schools, "was still the best for the interests
of all pupils in the District."

Upon challenge by a group of Negro plaintiffs desiring more rapid completion of
the desegregation process, the District Court upheld the School Board's plan. . . .
The Court of Appeals affirmed. . . . Review of that judgment was not sought
here.

While the School Board was thus going forward with its preparation for desegregating the Little Rock school system, other state authorities, in contrast, were
actively pursuing a program designed to perpetuate in Arkansas the system of racial
segregation which this Court had held violated the Fourteenth Amendment. First
came, in November 1956, an amendment to the State Constitution flatly commanding the Arkansas General Assembly to oppose "in every Constitutional manner the
Un-constitutional desegregation decisions of May 17, 1954 and May 31, 1955 of
the United States Supreme Court," Ark. Const. Amend. 44, and, through the initiative, a pupil assignment law. . . . Pursuant to the constitutional command, a law

relieving school children from compulsory attendance at racially mixed schools. . . . and a law establishing a State Sovereignty Commission . . . were enacted by the General Assembly in February 1957.

The School Board and the Superintendent of Schools nevertheless continued with preparations to carry out the first stage of the desegregation program. Nine Negro children were scheduled for admission in September 1957 to Central High School, which has more than two thousand students. Various administrative measures, designed to assure the smooth transition of this first stage of desegregation, were undertaken.

On September 2, 1957, the day before these Negro students were to enter Central High, the school authorities were met with drastic opposing action on the part of the Governor of Arkansas who dispatched units of the Arkansas National Guard to the Central High School grounds, and placed the school "off limits" to colored students. As found by the District Court in subsequent proceedings, the Governor's action had not been requested by the school authorities, and was entirely unheralded. The findings were these:

Up to this time [September 2], no crowds had gathered about Central High School and no acts of violence or threats of violence in connection with the carrying out of the plan had occurred. Nevertheless, out of an abundance of caution, the school authorities had frequently conferred with the Mayor and Chief of Police of Little Rock about taking appropriate steps by the Little Rock police to prevent any possible disturbances or acts of violence in connection with the attendance of the 9 colored students at Central High School. The Mayor considered that the Little Rock police force could adequately cope with any incidents which might arise at the opening of school. The Mayor, the Chief of Police, and the school authorities made no request to the Governor or any representative of his for State assistance in maintaining peace and order at Central High School. Neither the Governor nor any other official of the State government consulted with the Little Rock authorities about whether the Little Rock police were prepared to cope with any incidents which might arise at the school, about any need for State assistance in maintaining peace and order, or about stationing the Arkansas National Guard at Central High School. *Aaron* v. *Cooper*, 156 F. Supp. 220, 225.

The Board's petition for postponement in this proceeding states: "The effect of that action [of the Governor] was to harden the core of opposition to the Plan and cause many persons who theretofore had reluctantly accepted the Plan to believe that there was some power in the State of Arkansas which, when exerted, could nullify the Federal law and permit disobedience of the decree of this [District] Court, and from that date hostility to the Plan was increased and criticism of the officials of the [School] District has become more bitter and unrestrained." The Governor's action caused the School Board to request the Negro students on September 2 not to attend the high school "until the legal dilemma was solved." The next day, September 3, 1957, the Board petitioned the District Court for instructions, and the court, after a hearing, found that the Board's request of the Negro students to stay away from the high school had been made because of the stationing of the military guards by the state authorities. The court determined that this was not a reason for departing from the approved plan, and ordered the School Board and Superintendent to proceed with it.

On the morning of the next day, September 4, 1957, the Negro children attempted to enter the high school but, as the District Court later found, units of the Arkansas National Guard "acting pursuant to the Governor's order, stood shoulder to shoulder at the school grounds and thereby forcibly prevented the 9 Negro students . . . from entering," as they continued to do every school day during the following three weeks. . . .

That same day, September 4, 1957, the United States Attorney for the Eastern District of Arkansas was requested by the District Court to begin an immediate investigation in order to fix responsibility for the interference with the orderly implementation of the District Court's direction to carry out the desegregation program. Three days later, September 7, the District Court denied a petition of the School Board and the Superintendent of Schools for an order temporarily suspending continuance of the program.

Upon completion of the United States Attorney's investigation, he and the Attorney General of the United States, at the District Court's request, entered the proceedings and filed a petition on behalf of the United States, as *amicus curiae,* to enjoin the Governor of Arkansas and officers of the Arkansas National Guard from further attempts to prevent obedience to the court's order. After hearings on the petition, the District Court found that the School Board's plan had been obstructed by the Governor through the use of National Guard troops, and granted a preliminary injunction on September 20, 1957, enjoining the Governor and the officers of the Guard from preventing the attendance of Negro children at Central High School, and from otherwise obstructing or interfering with the orders of the court in connection with the plan. . . . The National Guard was then withdrawn from the school.

The next school day was Monday, September 23, 1957. The Negro children entered the high school that morning under the protection of the Little Rock Police Department and members of the Arkansas State Police. But the officers caused the children to be removed from the school during the morning because they had difficulty controlling a large and demonstrating crowd which had gathered at the high school. . . . On September 25, however, the President of the United States dispatched federal troops to Central High School and admission of the Negro students to the school was thereby effected. Regular army troops continued at the high school until November 27, 1957. They were then replaced by federalized National Guardsmen who remained throughout the balance of the school year. Eight of the Negro students remained in attendance at the school throughout the school year.

We come now to the aspect of the proceedings presently before us. On February 20, 1958, the School Board and the Superintendent of Schools filed a petition in the District Court seeking a postponement of their program for desegregation. Their position in essence was that because of extreme public hostility, which they stated had been engendered largely by the official attitudes and actions of the Governor and the Legislature, the maintenance of a sound educational program at Central High School, with the Negro students in attendance would be impossible. The Board therefore proposed that the Negro students already admitted to the school be withdrawn and sent to segregated schools, and that all further steps to carry out the Board's desegregation program be postponed for a period later suggested by the Board to be two and one-half years.

After a hearing the District Court granted the relief requested by the Board. Among other things the court found that the past year at Central High School had been attended by conditions of "chaos, bedlam and turmoil"; that there were "repeated incidents of more or less serious violence directed against the Negro students and their property"; that there was "tension and unrest among the schools' administrators, the class-room teachers, the pupils, and the latters' parents, which inevitably had an adverse effect upon the educational program"; that a school official was threatened with violence; that a "serious financial burden" had been cast on the School District; that the education of the students had suffered "and under existing conditions will continue to suffer"; that the Board would continue to need "military assistance or its equivalent"; that the local police department would not be able "to detail enough men to afford the necessary protection"; and that the situation was "intolerable." . . .

The District Court's judgment was dated June 20, 1958. . . . The Court of Appeals . . . after convening in special session on August 4 and hearing the appeal, reversed the District Court. . . .

In affirming the judgment of the Court of Appeals which reversed the District Court we have accepted without reservation the position of the School Board, the Superintendent of Schools, and their counsel that they displayed entire good faith in the conduct of these proceedings and in dealing with the unfortunate and distressing sequence of events which has been outlined. We likewise have accepted the findings of the District Court as to the conditions at Central High School during the 1957–1958 school year, and also the findings that the educational progress of all the students, white and colored, of that school has suffered and will continue to suffer if the conditions which prevailed last year are permitted to continue.

The significance of these findings, however, is to be considered in light of the fact, indisputably revealed by the record before us, that the conditions they depict are directly traceable to the actions of legislators and executive officials of the State of Arkansas, taken in their official capacities, which reflect their own determination to resist this Court's decision in the *Brown* case and which have brought about violent resistance to that decision in Arkansas. In its petition for certiorari filed in this Court, the School Board itself describes the situation in this language: "The legislative, executive, and judicial departments of the state government opposed the desegregation of Little Rock schools by enacting laws, calling out troops, making statements villifying federal law and federal courts, and failing to utilize state law enforcement agencies and judicial processes to maintain public peace."

One may well sympathize with the position of the Board in the face of the frustrating conditions which have confronted it, but, regardless of the Board's good faith, the actions of the other state agencies responsible for those conditions compel us to reject the Board's legal position. Had Central High School been under the direct management of the State itself, it could hardly be suggested that those immediately in charge of the school should be heard to assert their own good faith as a legal excuse for delay in implementing the constitutional rights of these respondents, when vindication of those rights was rendered difficult or impossible by the actions of other state officials. The situation here is in no different posture because the members of the School Board and the Superintendent of Schools are local officials; from the point of view of the Fourteenth Amendment, they stand in this litigation as the agents of the State.

The constitutional rights of respondents are not to be sacrificed or yielded to the violence and disorder which have followed upon the actions of the Governor and Legislature. As this Court said some 41 years ago in a unanimous opinion in a case involving another aspect of racial segregation: "It is urged that this proposed segregation will promote the public peace by preventing race conflicts. Desirable as this is, and important as is the preservation of the public peace, this aim cannot be accomplished by laws or ordinances which deny rights created or protected by the federal Constitution." *Buchanan* v. *Warley,* 245 US 60. . . . Thus law and order are not here to be preserved by depriving the Negro children of their constitutional rights. The record before us clearly establishes that the growth of the Board's difficulties to a magnitude beyond its unaided power to control is the product of state action. Those difficulties, as counsel for the Board forthrightly conceded on the oral argument in this Court, can also be brought under control by state action.

The controlling legal principles are plain. The command of the Fourteenth Amendment is that no "State" shall deny to any person within its jurisdiction the the equal protection of the laws. "A State acts by its legislative, its executive, or its judicial authorities. It can act in no other way. The constitutional provision, therefore, must mean that no agency of the State, or of the officers or agents by whom its powers are exerted, shall deny to any person within its jurisdiction the equal protection of the laws. Whoever, by virtue of public position under a State government . . . denies or takes away the equal protection of the laws, violates the constitutional inhibition; and as he acts in the name and for the State, and is clothed with State's power, his act is that of the State. This must be so, or the constitutional prohibition has no meaning." *Ex parte Virginia,* 100 US 339. . . . Thus the prohibitions of the Fourteenth Amendment extend to all action of the State denying equal protection of the laws; whatever the agency of the State taking the action. . . . In short, the constitutional rights of children not to be discriminated against in school admission on grounds of race or color declared by this Court in the *Brown* case can neither by nullified openly and directly by state legislators or state executive or judicial officers, nor nullified indirectly by them through evasive schemes for segregation whether attempted "ingeniously or ingenuously." . . .

What has been said, in the light of the facts developed, is enough to dispose of the case. However, we should answer the premise of the actions of the Governor and Legislature that they are not bound by our holding in the *Brown* case. It is necessary only to recall some basic constitutional propositions which are settled doctrine.

Article VI of the Constitution makes the Constitution the "supreme Law of the Land." In 1803, Chief Justice Marshall, speaking for a unanimous Court, referring to the Constitution as "the fundamental and paramount law of the nation," declared in the notable case of *Marbury* v. *Madison,* 1 Cranch 137, that "It is emphatically the province and duty of the judicial department to say what the law is." This decision declared the basic principle that the federal judiciary is supreme in the exposition of the law of the Constitution, and that principle has ever since been respected by this Court and the country as a permanent and indispensable feature of our constitutional system. It follows that the interpretation of the Fourteenth Amendment enunciated by this Court in the *Brown* case is the supreme law of the land, and Art. VI of the Constitution makes it of binding effect on the States, "any Thing in the Constitution or Laws of any State to the Contrary notwithstanding." Every state legislator and executive and judicial officer is solemnly committed by oath taken pursuant to Art. VI, ¶3 "to support this Constitution," Chief Justice Taney, speaking for a unanimous Court in 1859, said that this requirement reflected the framers' "anxiety to preserve it [the Constitution] in full force, in all its powers, and to guard against resistance to or evasion of its authority, on the part of a State." *Ableman* v. *Booth,* 21 How. 506. . . .

No state legislator or executive or judicial officer can war against the Constitution without violating his undertaking to support it. Chief Justice Marshall spoke for a unanimous Court in saying that: "If the legislatures of the several states may, at will, annul the judgments of the courts of the United States, and destroy the rights acquired under those judgments, the Constitution itself becomes a solemn mockery. . . ." *United States* v. *Peters,* 5 Cranch 115. A Governor who asserts a power to nullify a federal court order is similarly restrained. If he had such power, said Chief Justice Hughes, in 1932, also for a unanimous Court, "it is manifest that the fiat of a state Governor, and not the Constitution of the United States, would be the supreme law of the land; that the restrictions of the Federal Constitution upon the exercise of state power would be but impotent phrases. . . ." *Sterling* v. *Constantin,* 287 US 378.

It is, of course, quite true that the responsibility for public education is primarily the concern of the States, but it is equally true that such responsibilities, like all other state activity, must be exercised consistently with federal constitutional requirements as they apply to state action. The Constitution created a government dedicated to equal justice under law. The Fourteenth Amendment embodied and emphasized that ideal. State support of segregated schools through any arrangement, management, funds, or property cannot be squared with the Amendment's command that no State shall deny to any person within its jurisdiction the equal protection of the laws. The right of a student not to be segregated on racial grounds in schools so maintained is indeed so fundamental and pervasive that it is embraced in the concept of due process of law. *Bolling* v. *Sharpe,* 347 US 497. The basic decision in *Brown* was unanimously reached by this Court only after the case had been briefed and twice argued and the issues had been given the most serious consideration. Since the first *Brown* opinion three new Justices have come to the Court. They are at one with the Justices still on the Court who participated in that basic decision as to its correctness, and that decision is now unanimously reaffirmed. The principles announced in that decision and the obedience of the States to them, according to the command of the Constitution, are indispensable for the protection of the freedoms guaranteed by our fundamental charter for all of us. Our constitutional ideal of equal justice under law is thus made a living truth.

Concurring opinion of Mr. Justice Frankfurter:

While unreservedly participating with my brethren in our joint opinion, I deem it appropriate also to deal individually with the great issue here at stake.

By working together, by sharing in a common effort, men of different minds and tempers, even if they do not reach agreement, acquire understanding and thereby tolerance of their differences. This process was under way in Little Rock. The detailed plan formulated by the Little Rock school board, in the light of local circumstances, had been approved by the United States District Court in Arkansas as satisfying the requirements of this Court's decree in *Brown* v. *Board of Education.* . . .

The Little Rock school board had embarked on an educational effort "to obtain public acceptance of its plan." Thus the process of the community's accommodation to new demands of law upon it, the development of habits of acceptance of the right of colored children to the equal protection of the laws guaranteed by the Constitution, had peacefully and promisingly begun. The condition in Little Rock before this process was forcibly impeded by those in control of the government of Arkansas was thus described by the district court, and these findings of fact have not been controverted:

> Up to this time, no crowds had gathered about Central High School and no acts of violence or threats of violence in connection with the carrying out of the plan had occurred. Nevertheless, out of an abundance of caution, the school authorities had frequently conferred with the mayor and chief of police of Little Rock about taking appropriate steps by the Little Rock police to prevent any possible disturbance or acts of violence in connection with the attendance of the nine colored students at Central High School. The mayor considered that the Little Rock police force could adequately cope with any incidents which might arise at the opening of school.
>
> The mayor, the chief of police, and the school authorities made no request to the Governor or any representative of his for State assistance in maintaining peace and order at Central High School. Neither the Governor nor any other official of the State government consulted with the Little Rock authorities about whether the Little Rock police were prepared to cope with any incidents which might arise at the school, about any need for State assistance in maintaining peace and order, or about stationing the Arkansas National Guard at Central High School.

All this was disrupted by the introduction of the State militia and by other obstructive measures taken by the State. The illegality of these interferences with the constitutional right of Negro children qualified to enter the Central High School is unaffected by whatever action or non-action the Federal Government had seen fit to take. Nor is it neutralized by the undoubted good faith of the Little Rock school board in endeavoring to discharge its constitutional duty.

The use of force to further obedience to law is in any event a last resort and one not congenial to the spirit of our nation. But the tragic aspect of this disruptive tactic was that the power of the State was used not to sustain law but as an instrument for thwarting law. The State of Arkansas is thus responsible for disabling one of its subordinate agencies, the Little Rock school board, from peacefully carrying out the board's and the State's constitutional duty. Accordingly, while Arkansas is not a formal party in these proceedings and a decree cannot go against the State, it is legally and morally before the Court.

We are now asked to hold that the illegal, forcible interference by the State of Arkansas with the continuance of what the Constitution commands, and the consequences in disorder that it entrained, should be recognized as justification for undoing what the board of education had formulated, what the district court in 1955 had directed to be carried out, and what was in process of obedience. No explanation that may be offered in support of such a request can obscure the inescapable meaning that law should bow to force. To yield to such a claim would be to enthrone official lawlessness, and lawlessness if not checked is the precursor of anarchy.

On the few tragic occasions in the history of the nation, North and South, when law was forcibly resisted or systematically evaded, it has signaled the breakdown of constitutional processes of government on which ultimately rest the liberties of all. Violent resistance to law cannot be made a legal reason for its suspension without loosening the fabric of our society. What could this mean but to acknowledge that disorder under the aegis of a State has moral superiority over the law of the Constitution.

For those in authority thus to defy the law of the land is profoundly subversive not only of our constitutional system but of the presuppositions of a democratic society. The State "must . . . yield to an authority that is paramount to the State." This language of command to a State is Mr. Justice Holmes', speaking for the Court that comprised Mr. Justice Van Devanter, Mr. Justice McReynolds,, Mr. Justice Brandeis, Mr. Justice Sutherland, Mr. Justice Butler, Mr. Justice Stone. *Wisconsin* v. *Ilinois,* 281 US 179.

When defiance of law, judicially pronounced, was last sought to be justified before this Court, views were expressed which are now especially relevant:

> The historic phrase "a government of laws and not of men" epitomizes the distinguished character of our political society. When John Adams put that phrase into the Massachusetts Declaration of Rights he was not indulging in a rhetorical flourish. He was expressing the aim of those who, with him, framed the Declaration of Independence and founded the Republic. "A government of laws and not of men" was the rejection in positive terms of rule by fiat, whether by the fiat of governmental or private power.
>
> Every act of government may be challenged by an appeal to law, as finally pronounced by this Court. Even this Court has the last say only for a time. Being composed of fallible men, it may err. But revision of its errors must be by orderly process of law. The Court may be asked to reconsider its decisions, and this has been done successfully again and again throughout our history. Or, what this Court has deemed its duty to decide may be changed by legislation, as it often has been, and, on occasion, by constitutional amendment.
>
> But from their own experience and their deep reading in history, the founders knew that law alone saves a society from being rent by internecine strife or ruled by mere brute power however disguised. "Civilization involves subjection of force to reason, and the agency of this subjection is law." (Pound, "The Future of Law," 47 *Yale L. J.* 1, 13 [1937]).
>
> The conception of a government by laws dominated the thoughts of those who founded this nation and designed its Constitution, although they knew as well as the belittlers of the conception that laws have to be made, interpreted and enforced by men. To that end, they set apart a body of men, who were to be the depositories of law, who by their disciplined training and character and by withdrawal from the usual temptations of private interest may reasonably be expected to be "as free, impartial, and independent as the lot of humanity will admit."
>
> So strongly were the framers of the Constitution bent on securing a reign of law that they endowed the judicial office with extraordinary safeguards and prestige. No one, no matter how exalted his public office or how righteous his private motive,

can be judge in his own case. That is what courts are for. *United States* v. *United Mine Workers*, 330 US 258.

The duty to abstain from resistance to "the supreme law of the land," US Const., Art. VI § 2, as declared by the organ of our Government for ascertaining it, does not require immediate approval of it nor does it deny the right of dissent. Criticism need not be stilled. Active obstruction or defiance is barred. Our kind of society cannot endure if the controlling authority of the law as derived from the Constitution is not to be the tribunal specially charged with the duty of ascertaining and declaring what is "the supreme law of the land." See President Andrew Jackson's message to Congress of Jan. 16, 1833, 2 Richardson, *Messages and Papers of the Presidents,* 610, 623.

Particularly is this so where the declaration of what "the supreme law" commands on an underlying moral issue is not the dubious pronouncement of a gravely divided Court but is the unanimous conclusion of a long-matured deliberative process.

The Constitution is not the formulation of the merely personal views of the members of this Court, nor can its authority be reduced to the claim that State officials are its controlling interpreters. Local customs, however hardened by time, are not decreed in heaven. Habits and feelings they engender may be counteracted and moderated. Experience attests that such local habits and feelings will yield, gradually though this be, to law and education. And educational influences are exerted not only by explicit teaching. They vigorously flow from the fruitful exercise of the responsibility of those charged with political official power and from the almost unconsciously transforming actualities of living under law.

The process of ending unconstitutional exclusion of pupils from the common school system—"common" meaning shared alike—solely because of color is no doubt not an easy, overnight task in a few States where a drastic alteration in the ways of communities is involved. Deep emotions have, no doubt, been stirred. They will not be calmed by letting violence loose—violence and defiance employed and encouraged by those upon whom the duty of law observance should have the strongest claim—nor by submitting to it under whatever guise employed. Only the constructive use of time will achieve what an advanced civilization demands and the Constitution confirms.

For carrying out the decision that color alone cannot bar a child from a public school, this Court has recognized the diversity of circumstances in local school situations. But is it a reasonable hope that the necessary endeavors for such adjustment will be furthered, that racial frictions will be ameliorated, by a reversal of the process and interrupting effective measures toward the necessary goal?

The progress that has been made in respecting the constitutional rights of the Negro children, according to the graduated plan sanctioned by the two lower courts, would have to be retraced, perhaps with even greater difficulty because of deference to forcible resistance. It would have to be retraced against the seemingly vindicated feeling of those who actively sought to block that progress.

Is there not the strongest reason for concluding that, to accede to the board's request, on the basis of the circumstances that gave rise to it, for a suspension of the board's nonsegregation plan, would be but the beginning of a series of delays calculated to nullify this Court's adamant decisions in the *Brown* case that the Constitution precludes compulsory segregation based on color in State-supported schools?

That the responsibility of those who exercise power in a democratic government is not to reflect inflamed public feeling but to help form its understanding, is especially true when they are confronted with a problem like a racially discriminating public-school system. This is the lesson to be drawn from the heartening experience in ending enforced racial segregation in the public schools in cities with a Negro population of large proportion.

Compliance with decisions of this Court, as the constitutional organ of the supreme law of the land, has often, throughout our history, depended on active support by State and local authorities. It presupposes such support. To withhold it, and, indeed, to use political power to try to paralyze the supreme law, precludes the maintenance of our federal system as we have known and cherished it for 170 years.

Lincoln's appeal to "the better angels of our nature" failed to avert a fratricidal war. But the compassionate wisdom of Lincoln's first and second inaugurals bequeathed to the union, cemented with blood, a moral heritage which, when drawn upon in times of stress and strife, is sure to find specific ways and means to surmount difficulties that may appear to be insurmountable.

2. *The Executive Is under Law Made by Congress: The Steel Seizure Case*

YOUNGSTOWN SHEET & TUBE CO. *v.* SAWYER
343 US 579 (1952)

[This is the *Steel Seizure Case* of 1952. Government officials tried to settle the labor dispute between the steel industry and its employees. When these efforts failed, President Truman issued an order directing the Secretary of Commerce to seize the steel mills and to operate them. The order was not based upon any statutory authority but on a claim that seizure was necessary to avoid a national catastrophe, for American armed forces were then fighting in Korea. The steel companies procured from the United States District Court an injunction restraining the Secretary of Commerce from acting under the authority of the executive order. The Supreme Court in a 6-to-3 decision upheld the injunction on the ground that the President's order was not within his constitutional powers. In the Court's opinion by Justice Black emphasis is on the theory that the President is without constitutional power to seize private property even when an emergency exists. Justice Dogulas in a concurring opinion also emphasized this point. Justices Frankfurter, Jackson, Clark, and Burton, however, in concurring opinions placed emphasis on the fact that Congress had placed on the books statutory provisions (as in the Labor Management Relations Act of 1947) designed to meet emergency situations. Chief Justice Vinson and Justices Reed and Minton dissented on the ground that the statutes of Congress did not prohibit the seizure and that the President had the constitutional duty to execute and preserve the congressional defense program.

[The essential difference between the majority and minority members of the Court was over the question whether the President had attempted to *make* law or had used his judgment as to how best to *execute* the laws made by Congress. The minority position was that the President had only attempted to execute the laws of Congress relating to the defense program of the United States, while the majority view was that he had attempted to by-pass the laws that provide procedures in case of labor disputes that create national emergencies and had tried to impose his own law.

[In a case in which seven separate opinions have been written it is hazardous to state that there was any one significant proposition on which all Justices agreed; still it would appear that all of them did agree that the Constitution rejects the notion that the President is a lawmaker. Laws are made by Congress and executed by the President. The Government of the United States is one with "distributed authority." This scheme may retard action at times, until Congress should decide what measures to enact, but the doctrine of the separation of powers was adopted "not to promote efficiency but to preclude the exercise of arbitrary power . . . , to save the people from autocracy."

[This is an essential meaning of "the rule of law," of the theory of "a government of laws and not of men."]

Mr. Justice Black delivered the opinion of the Court:

We are asked to decide whether the President was acting within his constitutional power when he issued an order directing the Secretary of Commerce to take possession of and operate most of the Nation's steel mills. The mill owners argue that the President's order amounts to lawmaking, a legislative function which the Constitution has expressly confided to the Congress and not to the President. The Government's position is that the order was made on findings of the President that his action was necessary to avert a national catastrophe which would inevitably result from a stoppage of steel production, and that in meeting this grave emergency the President was acting within the aggregate of his constitutional powers as the Nation's Chief Executive and the Commander in Chief of the Armed Forces of the United States. The issue emerges here from the following series of events:

In the latter part of 1951, a dispute arose between the steel companies and their employees over terms and conditions that should be included in new collective bargaining agreements. Long-continued conferences failed to resolve the dispute. On December 18, 1951, the employees' representative, United Steelworkers of America, C.I.O., gave notice of an intention to strike when the existing bargaining agreements expired on December 31. Thereupon the Federal Mediation and Conciliation Service intervened in an effort to get labor and management to agree. This failing, the President on December 22, 1951, referred the dispute to the Federal Wage Stabilization Board to investigate and make recommendations for fair and equitable terms of settlement. This Board's report resulted in no settlement. On April 4, 1952, the Union gave notice of a nation-wide strike called to begin at 12:01 A.M. April 9. The indispensability of steel as a component of substantially all weapons and other war materials led the President to believe that the proposed work stoppage would immediately jeopardize our national defense and that governmental seizure of the steel mills was necessary in order to assure the continued availability of steel. Reciting these considerations for his action, the President, a few hours before the strike was to begin, issued Executive Order 10340. . . . The order directed the Secretary of Commerce to take possession of and operate most of the steel mills throughout the country. The Secretary immediately issued his own possessory orders, calling upon the presidents of the various seized companies to serve as operating managers for the United States. They were directed to carry on their activities in accordance with regulations and directions of the Secretary. The next morning the President sent a message to Congress reporting his action. . . .

Twelve days later he sent a second message. . . . Congress has taken no action.

Obeying the Secretary's orders under protest, the companies brought proceedings against him in the District Court. Their complaints charged that the seizure was not authorized by an act of Congress or by any constitutional provisions. The District Court was asked to declare the orders of the President and the Secretary invalid and to issue preliminary and permanent injunctions restraining their enforcement. Opposing the motion for preliminary injunction, the United States asserted that a strike disrupting steel production for even a brief period would so endanger the well-being and safety of the Nation that the President had "inherent power" to do what he had done—power "supported by the Constitution, by historical precedent, and by court decisions." The Government also contended that in any event no preliminary injunction should be issued because the companies had made no showing that their available legal remedies were inadequate or that their injuries from seizure would be irreparable. Holding against the Government on all points, the District Court on April 30 issued a preliminary injunction restraining the Secretary from "continuing the seizure and possession of the plant . . . and from acting under the purported authority of Executive Order No. 10340." . . . On the same day the Court of Appeals stayed the District Court's injunction. . . . Deeming it best that the issues raised be promptly decided by this Court, we granted certiorari on May 3 and set the cause for argument on May 12. . . .

The President's power, if any, to issue the order must stem either from an act of Congress or from the Constitution itself. There is no statute that expressly authorizes the President to take possession of property as he did here. Nor is there any act of Congress to which our attention has been directed from which such a power can fairly be implied. Indeed, we do not understand the Government to rely on statutory authorization for this seizure. There are two statutes which do authorize the President to take both personal and real property under certain conditions. However, the Government admits that these conditions were not met and that the President's order was not rooted in either of them. The Government refers to the seizure provisions of one of these statutes (§ 201 (b) of the Defense Production Act) as "much too cumbersome, involved, and time-consuming for the crisis which was at hand."

Moreover, the use of the seizure technique to solve labor disputes in order to prevent work stoppages was not only unauthorized by any congressional enactment; prior to this controversy, Congress had refused to adopt that method of settling labor disputes. When the Taft-Hartley Act was under consideration in 1947, Congress rejected an amendment which would have authorized such governmental seizures in cases of emergency. Apparently it was thought that the technique of seizure, like that of compulsory arbitration, would interfere with the process of collective bargaining. Consequently, the plan Congress adopted in that Act did not provide for seizure under any circumstances. Instead, the plan sought to bring about settlements by use of the customary devices of mediation, conciliation, investigation by boards of inquiry, and public reports. In some instances temporary injunctions were authorized to provide cooling-off periods. All this failing, the unions were left free to strike if the majority of the employees, by secret ballot, expressed a desire to do so.

It is clear that if the President had authority to issue the order he did, it must be found in some provision of the Constitution. And it is not claimed that express constiutional language grants this power to the President. The contention is that presidential power should be implied from the aggregate of his powers under Article II of the Constitution. Particular reliance is placed on the provisions which say that "the executive Power shall be vested in a President . . ."; that "he shall take Care that the Laws be faithfully executed"; and that he "shall be Commander in Chief of the Army and Navy of the United States."

The order cannot properly be sustained as an exercise of the President's military power as Commander in Chief of the Armed Forces. The Government attempts to do so by citing a number of cases upholding broad powers in military commanders engaged in day-to-day fighting in a theater of war. Such cases need not concern us here. Even though "theater of war" be an expanding concept, we cannot with faithfulness to our constitutional system hold that the Commander in Chief of the Armed Forces has the ultimate power as such to take possession of private property in order to keep labor disputes from stopping production. This is a job for the Nation's lawmakers, not for its military authorities.

Nor can the seizure order be sustained because of the several constitutional provisions that grant executive power to the President. In the framework of our Constitution, the President's power to see that the laws are faithfully executed refutes the idea that he is to be a lawmaker. The Constitution limits his functions in the lawmaking process to the recommending of laws he thinks wise and the vetoing of laws he thinks bad. And the Constitution is neither silent nor equivocal about who shall make laws which the President is to execute. The first section of the first article says that "All legislative Powers herein granted shall be vested in a Congress of the United States. . . ." After granting many powers to the Congress, Article I goes on to provide that Congress may "make all Laws which shall be necessary and proper for carrying into Execution the foregoing Powers and all other Powers vested by this Constitution in the Government of the United States, or in any Department or Officer thereof."

The President's order does not direct that a congressional policy be executed in a manner prescribed by Congress—it directs that a presidential policy be executed in a manner prescribed by the President. The preamble of the order itself, like that of many statutes, sets out reasons why the President believes certain policies should be adopted, proclaims these policies as rules of conduct to be followed, and again, like a statute, authorizes a government official to promulgate additional rules and regulations consistent with the policy proclaimed and needed to carry that policy into execution. The power of Congress to adopt such public policies as those proclaimed by the order is beyond question. It can authorize the taking of private property for public use. It can make laws regulating the relationships between employers and employees, prescribing rules designed to settle labor disputes, and fixing wages and working conditions in certain fields of our economy. The Constitution did not subject this lawmaking power of Congress to presidential or military supervision or control.

It is said that other Presidents without congressional authority have taken possession of private business enterprises in order to settle labor disputes. But even if this be true, Congress has not thereby lost its exclusive constitutional authority to make laws necessary and proper to carry out the powers vested by the Constitution "in the Government of the United States, or any Department or Officer thereof."

The Founders of this Nation entrusted the lawmaking power to the Congress alone in both good and bad times. It would do no good to recall the historical events, the fears of power and the hopes for freedom that lay behind their choice. Such a review would but confirm our holding that this seizure order cannot stand.

The judgment of the District Court is affirmed.

3. Fair Notice of What Acts the Law Will Punish

PAPACHRISTOU v. JACKSONVILLE
405 US 156 (1972)

[There can hardly be "the rule of law" if a person may be held to have violated "a statute which either forbids or requires the doing of an act in terms so vague that men of common intelligence must necessarily guess at its meannig and differ as to its application. . . ." Such a statute, the Supreme Court has said, "violates the first essential of due process of law." *Connelly* v. *General Construction Co.*, 269 US 385 (1925). "The Constitution requires that a statute must not be too vague to allow the citizen to ascertain what course of conduct he must follow to put himself safely within the bounds of the law." The certainty required is not tested from the would-be violator's standpoint; "the test is rather whether adequate guidance is given to those who would be law-abiding." *United States* v. *Five Gambling Devices*, 346 US 441 (1953), dissenting opinion of Justice Clark.

[In the instant case, eight defendants were convicted of violating the vagrancy ordinance of the city of Jacksonville, Florida. The Supreme Court unanimously reversed the convictions and held that the vagrancy ordinance was unconstitutional for vagueness: it failed to give a person of ordinary intelligence fair notice that his contemplated action was forbidden; it encouraged arbitrary and erratic police action and convictions; and it made criminal activities which today are normally considered innocent. The Court's opinion was by Justice Douglas. Justices Powell and Rhenquist did not participate in the case.]

Mr. Justice Douglas delivered the opinion of the Court:

This case involves eight defendants who were convicted in a Florida municipal court of violating a Jacksonville, Florida, vagrancy ordinance.* Their convictions,

---

* Jacksonville Ordinance Code § 26–57 provided at the time of these arrests and convictions as follows:

"Rogues and vagabonds, or dissolute persons who go about begging, common gamblers, persons who use juggling or unlawful games or plays, common drunkards, common night walkers, thieves, pilferers or pickpockets, traders in stolen property, lewd, wanton and lascivious persons, keepers of gambling places, common railers and brawlers, persons wandering or strolling around from place to place without any lawful purpose or object, habitual loafers, disorderly persons, persons neglecting all lawful business and habitually spending their time by frequenting houses of ill fame, gaming houses, or places where alcoholic beverages are sold or served, persons able to work but habitually living upon the earnings of their wives or minor children shall be deemed vagrants and, upon conviction in the Municipal Court shall be punished as provided for Class D offenses."

[Continued.]

entailing fines and jail sentences (some of which were suspended), were affirmed by the Florida Circuit Court in a consolidated appeal, and their petition for certiorari was denied by the District Court of Appeals, . . . The case is here on a petition for certiorari, which we granted. . . . For reasons which will appear, we reverse.

At issue are five consolidated cases. Margaret Papachristou, Betty Calloway, Eugene Eddie Melton, and Leonard Johnson were all arrested early on a Sunday morning, and charged with vagrancy—"prowling by auto."

Jimmy Lee Smith and Milton Henry were charged with vagrancy—"vagabonds."

Henry Edward Heath and a codefendant were arrested for vagrancy—"loitering" and "common thief."

Thoms Owen Campbell was charged with vagrancy—"common thief."

Hugh Brown was charged with vagrancy—"disorderly loitering on street" and "disorderly conduct—resisting arrest with violence."

The facts are stipulated. Papachristou and Calloway are white females. Melton and Johnson are black males. Papachristou was enrolled in a job-training program sponsored by the State Employment Service at Florida Junior College in Jacksonville. Calloway was a typing and shorthand teacher at a state mental institution located near Jacksonville. She was the owner of the automobile in which the four defendants were arrested. Melton was a Vietnam war veteran who had been released from the Navy aften nine month in a veterans' hospital. On the date of his arrest he was a part-time computer helper while attending college as a full-time student in Jacksonville. Johnson was a tow-motor operator in a grocery chain warehouse and was a lifelong resident of Jacksonville.

At the time of their arrest the four of them were riding in Calloway's car on the main thoroughfare in Jacksonville. They had left a restaurant owned by Johnson's uncle where they had eaten and were on their way to a night club. The arresting officers denied that the racial mixture in the car played any part in the decision to make the arrest. The arrest, they said, was made because the defendants had stopped near a used-car lot which had been broken into several times. There was, however, no evidence of any breaking and entering on the night in question.

Of these four charged with "prowling by auto" none had been previously arrested except Papachristou who had once been convicted of a municipal offense.

Jimmy Lee Smith and Milton Henry (who is not a petitioner) were arrested between 9 and 10 A.M. on a weekday in downtown Jacksonville, while waiting for a friend who was to lend them a car so they could apply for a job at a produce company. Smith was a part-time produce worker and part-time organizer for a Negro political group. He had a common-law wife and three children supported by him and his wife. He had been arrested several times but convicted only once. Smith's

---

Class D offenses at the time of these arrests and convictions were punishable by 90 days imprisonment, $500 fine, or both. . . . The maximum punishment has since been reduced to 75 days or $450. . . . We are advised that that downward revision was made to avoid federal right-to-counsel decisions. The Fifth Circuit case extending right to counsel in misdemeanors where a fine of $500 or 90-days imprisonment could be imposed is *Harvey* v. *Mississippi*, 340 F.2d 263 (CA5 1965).

companion, Henry, was an 18-year-old high school student with no previous record of arrest.

This morning it was cold, and Smith had no jacket, so they went briefly into a dry cleaning shop to wait, but left when requested to do so. They thereafter walked back and forth two or three times over a two-block stretch looking for their friend. The store owners, who apparently were wary of Smith and his companion, summoned two police officers who searched the men and found neither had a weapon. But they were arrested because the officers said they had no identification and because the officers did not believe their story.

Heath and a codefendant were arrested for "loitering" and for "common thief." Both were residents of Jacksonville, Heath having lived there all his life and being employed at an automobile and body shop. Heath had previously been arrested but his codefendant had no arrest record. Heath and his companion were arrested when they drove up to a residence shared by Heath's girl friend and some other girls. Some police officers were already there in the process of arresting another man. When Heath and his companion started backing out of the driveway, the officers signaled to them to stop and asked them to get out of the car, which they did. Thereupon they and the automobile were searched. Although no contraband or incriminating evidence was found, they were both arrested, Heath being charged with being a "common thief" because he was reputed to be a thief. The codefendant was charged with "loitering" because he was standing in the driveway, an act which the officers admitted was done only at their command.

Campbell was arrested as he reached his home very early one morning and was charged with "common thief." He was stopped by officers because he was traveling at a high rate of speed, yet no speeding charge was placed against him.

Brown was arrested when he was observed leaving a downtown, Jacksonville, hotel by a police officer seated in a cruiser. The police testified he was reputed to be a thief, narcotics pusher, and generally opprobrious character. The officer called Brown over to the car, intending at that time to arrest him unless he had a good explanation for being on the street. Brown walked over to the police cruiser, as commanded, and the officer began to search him, apparently preparatory to placing him in the car. In the process of the search he came on two small packets which were later found to contain heroin. When the officer touched the pocket where the packets were, Brown began to resist. He was charged with "disorderly loitering on the street" and "disorderly conduct—resisting arrest with violence." While he was also charged with a narcotics violation, that charge was *nolled*.

Jacksonville's ordinance and Florida's statute were "derived from early English law," . . . and employ "archaic language" in their definitions of vagrants. The history is an often-told tale. The break-up of feudal estates in England led to labor shortages which in turn resulted in the Statutes of Laborers, designed to stabilize the labor force by prohibiting increases in wages and prohibiting the movement of workers from their home areas in search of improved conditions. Later vagrancy laws became criminal aspects of the poor laws. The series of laws passed in England on the subject became increasingly severe.* But "the theory of the Elizabethan

* See 3 Stephen, *History of the Criminal Law of England,* pp. 203–206, 266–275; 4 *Blackstone Commentaries* (Lewis, ed., 1902), 169. [Continued.]

poor laws no longer fits the facts," *Edwards* v. *California,* 314 US 160. The conditions which spawned these laws may be gone, but the archaic classifications remain.

This ordinance is void-for-vagueness, both in the sense that it "fails to give a person of ordinary intelligence fair notice that his contemplated conduct is forbidden by the statute," . . . and because it encourages arbitrary and erratic arrests and convictions. . . .

Living under a rule of law entails various suppositions, one of which is that "All [persons] are entitled to be informed as to what the State commands or forbids." *Lanzetta* v. *New Jersey,* 306 US 451.

Lanzetta is one of a well-recognized group of cases insisting that the law give fair notice of the offending conduct. . . . In the field of regulatory statutes governing business activities, where the acts limited are in a narrow category, greater leeway is allowed. . . .

The poor among us, the minorities, the average householder are not in business and not alerted to the regulatory schemes of vagrancy laws; and we assume they would have no understanding of their meaning and impact if they read them. Nor are they protected from being caught in the vagrancy net by the necessity of having a specific intent to commit an unlawful act. . . .

The Jacksonville ordinance makes criminal activities which by modern standards are normally innocent. "Nightwalking" is one. Florida construes the ordinance not to make criminal one night's wandering, . . . only the "habitual" wanderer or as the ordinance describes it "common night walkers." We know, however, from experience that sleepless people often walk at night, perhaps hopeful that sleep-inducing relaxation will result.

Luis Munoz-Marin, former Governor of Puerto Rico, commented once that "loafing" was a national virtue in his Commonwealth and that it should be encouraged. It is, however, a crime in Jacksonville.

"Persons able to work but habitually living on the earnings of their wives or minor children"—like habitually living "without visible means of support"—might implicate unemployed pillars of the community who have married rich wives.

"Persons able to work but habitually living on the earnings of their wives or

---

Ledwith v. *Roberts,* 1 K.B. 232, 271, gives the following summary:
"The early Vagrancy Acts came into being under peculiar conditions utterly different to those of the present time. From the time of the Black Death in the middle of the 14th century till the middle of the 17th century, and indeed, although in diminishing degree, right down to the reform of the Poor Law in the first half of the 19th century, the roads of England were crowded with masterless men and their families, who had lost their former employment through a variety of causes, had no means of livelihood and had taken to a vagrant life. The main causes were the gradual decay of the feudal system under which the labouring classes had been anchored to the soil, the economic slackening of the legal compulsion to work for fixed wages, the break up of the monasteries in the reign of Henry VIII, and the consequent disappearance of the religious orders which had previously administered a kind of 'public assistance' in the form of lodging, food and alms; and, lastly, the economic changes brought about by the Enclosure Acts. Some of these people were honest labourers who had fallen upon evil days, others were the 'wild rogues,' so common in Elizabethan times and literature, who had been born to a life of idleness and had no intention of following any other. It was they and their confederates who formed themselves into the notorious 'brotherhood of beggars' which flourished in the 16th and 17th centuries. They were a definite and serious menace to the community and it was chiefly against them and their kind that the harsher provisions of the vagrancy laws of the period were directed."

minor children" may also embrace unemployed people out of the labor market, by reason of a recession or disemployed by reason of technological or so-called structural displacements.

Persons "wandering or strolling" from place to place have been extolled by Walt Whitman and Vachel Lindsay. The qualification "without any lawful purpose or object" may be a trap for innocent acts. Persons "neglecting all lawful business and habitually spending their time by frequenting . . . places where alcoholic beverages are sold or served" would literally embrace many members of golf clubs and city clubs.

Walkers and strollers and wanderers may be going to or coming from a burglary. Loafers or loiterers may be "casing" a place for a holdup. Letting one's wife support him is an intrafamily matter, and normally of no concern to the police. Yet it may, of course, be the setting for numerous crimes.

The difficulty is that these activities are historically part of the amenities of life as we have known it. They are not mentioned in the Constitution or in the Bill of Rights. These unwritten amenities have been in part responsible for giving our people the feeling of independence and self-confidence, the feeling of creativity. These amenities have dignified the right of dissent and have honored the right to be nonconformists and the right to defy submissiveness. They have encouraged lives of high spirits rather than hushed, suffocating silence.

They are embedded in Walt Whitman's writings especially in his *Song of the Open Road.* They are reflected too, in the spirit of Vachel Lindsay's *I Want to Go Wandering* and by Henry D. Thoreau.*

This aspect of the vagrancy ordinance before us is suggested by what this Court said in 1875 about a broad criminal statute enacted by Congress: "It would certainly be dangerous if the legislature could set a net large enough to catch all possible offenders, and leave it to the courts to step inside and say who could be rightfully detained, and who should be set at large." *United States* v. *Reese,* 92 US 214.

While that was a federal case, the due process implications are equally applicable to the States and to this vagrancy ordinance. Here the net cast is large, not to give the courts the power to pick and choose but to increase the arsenal of the police. In *Winters* v. *New York,* 333 US 507, the Court struck down a New York statute

---

* "I have met with but one or two persons in the course of my life who understood the art of Walking, that is, of taking walks,—who had a genius, so to speak, for *sauntering:* which word is beautifully derived 'from idle people who roved about the country, in the Middle Ages, and asked charity, under pretense of going *a la Sainte Terre,*' to the Holy Land, till the children exclaimed, "There goes a *Sainte-Terrer,*' a Saunterer,—a Holy-Lander. They who never go to the Holy Land in their walks, as they pretend, are indeed mere idlers and vagabonds; but they who do go there are saunterers in the good sense, such as I mean. Some, however, would derive the word from *sans terre,* without land or a home, which, therefore, in the good sense, will mean, having no particular home, but equally at home everywhere. For this is the secret of successful sauntering. He who sits still in a house all the time may be the greatest vagrant of all; but the saunterer, in the good sense, is no more vagrant than the meandering river, which is all the while sedulously seeking the shortest course to the sea. But I prefer the first, which, indeed, is the most probable derivation. For every walk is a sort of crusade, preached by some Peter the Hermit in us, to go forth and reconquer this Holy Land from the hands of the Infidels." *Excursions,* pp. 161–162 (1875).

that made criminal the distribution of a magazine made up principally of items of criminal deeds of bloodshed or lust so massed as to become vehicles for inciting violent and depraved crimes against the person. The infirmity the Court found was vagueness—the absence of "ascertainable standards of guilt" (*Id.,* 515, 68 S.Ct. 670) in the sensitive First Amendment area. Mr. Justice Frankfurter dissented. But concerned as he, and many others, had been over the vagrancy laws, he added:

> Only a word needs to be said regarding *Lanzetta* v. *New Jersey,* 306 US 451. . . . The case involved a New Jersey statute of the type that seeks to control "vagrancy." These statutes are in a class by themselves, in view of the familiar abuses to which they are put. Definiteness is designedly avoided so as to allow the net to be cast at large, to enable men to be caught who are vaguely undesirable in the eyes of police and prosecution, although not chargeable with any particular offense. In short, these "vagrancy statutes" and laws against "gangs" are not fenced in by the text of the statute or by the subject matter so as to give notice of conduct to be avoided.

Where the list of crimes is so all-inclusive and generalized* as that one in this ordinance, those convicted may be punished for no more than vindicating affronts to police authority. . . .

Another aspect of the ordinance's vagueness appears when we focus, not on the lack of notice given a potential offender, but on the effect of the unfettered discretion it places in the hands of the Jacksonville police. Caleb Foote, an early student of this subject, has called the vagrancy-type law as offering "punishment by analogy." Such crimes, though long common in Russia, are not compatible with our constitutional system. We allow our police to make arrests only on "probable cause," a Fourth and Fourteenth Amendment standard applicable to the States as well as to the Federal Government. Arresting a person on suspicion, like arresting a person for investigation, is foreign to our system, even when the arrest is for past criminality. Future criminality, however, is the common justification for the

---

* President Roosevelt in vetoing a vagrancy law for the District of Columbia said:

"The bill contains many provisions that constitute an improvement over existing law. Unfortunately, however, there are two provisions in the bill that appear objectionable.

"Section 1 of the bill contains a number of clauses defining a 'vagrant.' Clause 6 of this section would include within that category 'any able-bodied person who lives in idleness upon the wages, earnings, or property of any person having no legal obligation to support him.' This definition is so broadly and loosely drawn that in many cases it would make a vagrant of an adult daughter or son of a well-to-do family who, though amply provided for and not guilty of any improper or unlawful conduct, has no occupation and is dependent upon parental support.

"Under clause 9 of said section 'any person leading an idle life . . . and not giving a good account of himself' would incur guilt and liability to punishment unless he could prove, as required by section 2, that he has lawful means of support realized from a lawful occupation or source. What constitutes "leading an idle life" and "not giving a good account of oneself" is not indicated by the statute but is left to the determination in the first place of a police officer and eventually of a judge of the police court, subject to further review in proper cases. While this phraseology may be suitable for general purposes as a definition of a vagrant, it does not conform with accepted standards of legislative practice as a definition of a criminal offense. I am not willing to agree that a person without lawful means of support, temporarily or otherwise, should be subject to the risk of arrest and punishment under provisions as indefinite and uncertain in their meaning and application as those employed in this clause.

"It would hardly be a satisfactory answer to say that the sound judgment and decisions of the police and prosecuting officers must be trusted to invoke the law only in proper cases. The law itself should be so drawn as not to make it applicable to cases which obviously should not be comprised within its terms." H. Doc. 392, 77th Cong., 1st Sess.

presence of vagrancy statutes. . . . Florida has indeed construed her vagrancy statute "as necessary regulations," *inter alia,* "to deter vagabondage and prevent crimes," . . .

A direction by a legislature to the police to arrest all "suspicious" persons* would not pass constitutional muster. A vagrancy prosecution may be merely the cloak for a conviction which could not be obtained on the real but undisclosed grounds for the arrest. . . .

Those generally implicated by the imprecise terms of the ordinance—poor people, nonconformists, dissenters, idlers—may be required to comport themselves according to the life-style deemed appropriate by the Jacksonville police and the courts. Where, as here, there are no standards governing the exercise of the discretion granted by the ordinance, the scheme permits and encourages an arbitrary and discriminatory enforcement of the law. It furnishes a convenient tool for "harsh and discriminatory enforcement by prosecuting officials, against particular groups deemed to merit their displeasure." . . . It results in a regime in which the poor and the unpopular are permitted to "stand on a public sidewalk . . . only at the whim of any police officer." . . .

A presumption that people who might walk or loaf or loiter or stroll or frequent houses where liquor is sold, or who are supported by their wives or who look suspicious to the police are to become future criminals is too precarious for a rule of law. The implicit presumption in these generalized vagrancy standards—that crime is being nipped in the bud—is too extravagant to deserve extended treatment. Of course, vagrancy statutes are useful to the police. Of course, they are nets making easy the round-up of so-called undesirables. But the rule of law implies equality and justice in its application. Vagrancy laws of the Jacksonville type teach that the scales of justice are so tipped that that even-handed administration of the law is not possible. The rule of law, evenly applied to minorities as well as majorities, to the poor as well as the rich, is the great mucilage that holds society together.

The Jacksonville ordinance cannot be squared with our constitutional standards and is plainly unconstitutional.

Reversed.

* The table below contains nationwide data on arrests for "vagrancy" and for "suspicion" in the three-year period 1968–1970.

Year	Vagrancy		Suspicion		Combined Offenses	
	Total rptd. arrests	Rate per 100,000	Total rptd. arrests	Rate per 100,000	Total rptd. arrests	Rate per 100,000
1968	99,147	68.2	89,986	61.9	189,133	130.1
1969	106,269	73.9	88,265	61.4	194,534	135.3
1970	101,093	66.1	70,173	46.3	171,266	113.0
3 year averages ..	102,170	69.6	82,808	56.5	184,978	126.1

Source: FBI Annual Crime Reports, 1968–1970. Reporting agencies represent population of: 1968—145,306,000; 1969—143,815,000; 1970—151,604,000.

III. Freedom of Religion

1. Freedom to Believe and Freedom to Act

REYNOLDS v. UNITED STATES
98 US 145 (1878)

[The Constitution permits unlimited freedom of religious belief. There may be few absolutes in constitutional law, but freedom of religious belief is such an absolute.

[When it comes, however, to acting out one's belief, religious belief will not always exempt one from the provisions of the criminal law. The state may punish a person who handles a live copperhead snake even if he does this in the course of a religious or church service. *Bunn* v. *North Carolina*, 336 US 942 (1949), dismissing appeal of *State* v. *Massey*, 229 NC 734.

[For Mormons, polygamous marriages were at one time a religious duty. When Utah was a Territory, Congress enacted a statute making polygamy a criminal offense. This led to the *Reynolds Case* in the Supreme Court, which at once became a leading case. The opinion of Chief Justice Waite has often been cited and quoted. His opinion is notable also for his quotation from Jefferson's famous wall-of-separation letter, which was used effectively by the Court some seventy years later in the *Everson Case,* which is also given in this chapter.]

Mr. Chief Justice Waite delivered the opinion of the Court:

This is an indictment for bigamy under Section 5352, Revised Statutes, which, omitting its exceptions, is as follows: "Every person having a husband or wife living, who marries another, whether married or single, in a Territory, or other place over which the United States have exclusive jurisdiction, is guilty of bigamy, and shall be punished by a fine of not more than $500, and by imprisonment for a term of not more than five years." . . .

On the trial, the plaintiff in error, the accused, proved that at the time of his alleged second marriage he was, and for many years before had been, a member of the Church of Jesus Christ of Latter-Day Saints, commonly called the Mormon Church, and a believer in its doctrines; that it was an accepted doctrine of that church "That it was the duty of male members of said Church, circumstances permitting, to practice polygamy: . . . that this duty was enjoined by different books which the members of said Church believed to be of divine origin, and among others the Holy Bible, and also that the members of the Church believed that the practice of polygamy was directly enjoined upon the male members thereof by the

26

Almighty God, in a revelation to Joseph Smith, the founder and prophet of said Church; that the failing or refusing to practice polygamy by such male members of said Church, when circumstances would admit, would be punished, and that the penalty for such failure and refusal would be damnation in the life to come." He also proved "That he had received permission from the recognized authorities in said Church to enter into polygamous marriage; . . . that Daniel H. Wells, one having authority in said Church to perform the marriage ceremony, married the said defendant on or about the time the crime is alleged to have been committed, to some woman by the name of Schofield, and that such marriage ceremony was performed under and pursuant to the doctrines of said Church."

Upon this proof he asked the court to instruct the jury that if they found from the evidence that he "was married as charged (if he was married) in pursuant of and in conformity with what he believed at the time to be religious duty, that the verdict must be 'not guilty.' " This request was refused, and the court did charge "That there must have been a criminal intent, but that if the defendant, under the influence of a religious belief that it was right—under an inspiration, if you please, that it was right—deliberately married a second time, having a first wife living, the want of consciousness of evil intent, the want of understanding on his part that he was committing a crime, did not excuse him; but the law inexorably in such case implies the criminal intent."

Upon this charge and refusal to charge the question is raised, whether religious belief can be accepted as a justification of an overt act made criminal by the law of the land. The inquiry is not as to the power of Congress to prescribe criminal laws for the Territories, but as to the guilt of one who knowingly violates a law which has been properly enacted, if he entertains a religious belief that the law is wrong.

Congress cannot pass a law for the government of the Territories which shall prohibit the free exercise of religion. The first amendment to the Constitution expressly forbids such legislation. Religious freedom is guaranteed everywhere throughout the United States, so far as congressional interference is concerned. The question to be determined is, whether the law now under consideration comes within this prohibition.

The word "religion" is not defined in the Constitution. We must go elsewhere, therefore, to ascertain its meaning, and nowhere more appropriately, we think, than to the history of the times in the midst of which the provision was adopted. The precise point of the inquiry is, what is the religious freedom which has been guaranteed?

Before the adoption of the Constitution, attempts were made in some of the Colonies and States to legislate not only in respect to the establishment of religion, but in respect to its doctrines and precepts as well. The people were taxed, against their will, for the support of religion, and sometimes for the support of particular sects to whose tenets they could not and did not subscribe. Punishments were prescribed for a failure to attend upon public worship, and sometimes for entertaining heretical opinions. The controversy upon this general subject was animated in many of the States, but seemed at last to culminate in Virginia. In 1784, the House of Delegates of that State having under consideration "A bill establishing provision for teachers of the Christian religion," postponed it until the next session, and directed that the bill should be published and distributed, and that the People be requested "to signify their opinion respecting the adoption of such a bill at the next session of Assembly."

This brought out a determined opposition. Amongst others, Mr. Madison prepared a "Memorial and Remonstrance," which was widely circulated and signed, and in which he demonstrated "that religion, or the duty we owe the Creator," was not within the cognizance of civil government. At the next session the proposed bill was not only defeated, but another, "for establishing religious freedom," drafted by Mr. Jefferson, was passed. In the preamble of this Act religious freedom is defined; and after a recital "That to suffer the civil magistrate to intrude his powers into the field of opinion, and to restrain the profession or propagation of principles on supposition of their ill tendency, is a dangerous fallacy which at once destroys all religious liberty," it is declared "that it is time enough for the rightful purposes of civil government for its officers to interfere when principles break out into overt acts against peace and good order." In these two sentences is found the true distinction between what properly belongs to the Church and what to the State.

In a little more than a year after the passage of this statute the convention met which prepared the Constitution of the United States. Of this convention Mr. Jefferson was not a member, he being then absent as minister to France. As soon as he saw the draft of the Constitution proposed for adoption, he, in a letter to a friend, expressed his disappointment at the absence of an express declaration insuring the freedom of religion, but was willing to accept it as it was, trusting that the good sense and honest intentions of the people would bring about the necessary alterations. Five of the States, while adopting the Constitution, proposed amendments. Three, New Hampshire, New York and Virginia, included in one form or another a declaration of religious freedom in the changes they desired to have made, as did also North Carolina, where the convention at first declined to ratify the Constitution until the proposed amendments were acted upon. Accordingly, at the first session of the first Congress the amendment now under consideration was proposed with others by Mr. Madison. It met the views of the advocates of religious freedom, and was adopted. Mr. Jefferson afterwards, in reply to an address to him by a committee of the Danbury Baptist Association, took occasion to say: "Believing with you that religion is a matter which lies solely between man and his God; that he owes account to none other for his faith or his worship; that the legislative powers of the Government reach actions only, and not opinions, I contemplate with sovereign reverence that act of the whole American people which declared that their Legislature should 'make no law respecting an establishment of religion or prohibiting the free exercise thereof,' thus building a wall of separation between Church and State. Adhering to this expression of the Supreme will of the Nation in behalf of the rights of conscience, I shall see, with sincere satisfaction, the progress of those sentiments which tend to restore man to all his natural rights, convinced he has no natural right in opposition to his social duties." Coming as this does from an acknowledged leader of the advocates of the measure, it may be accepted almost as an authoritative declaration of the scope and effect of the amendment thus secured. Congress was deprived of all legislative power over mere opinion, but was left free to reach actions which were in violation of social duties or subversive of good order.

Polygamy has always been odious among the Northern and Western Nations of Europe and, until the establishment of the Mormon Church, was almost exclusively a feature of the life of Asiatic and African people. At common law, the second marriage was always void, and from the earliest history of England polygamy has been treated as an offense against society. After the establishment of the ecclesiastical courts, and until the time of James I., it was punished through the instrumentality of those tribunals, not merely because ecclesiastical rights had been violated, but because upon the separation of the ecclesiastical courts from the civil, the ecclesiastical were supposed to be the most appropriate for the trial of matrimonial causes and offenses against the rights of marriage; just as they were for testamentary causes and the settlement of the estates of deceased persons.

By the Statute of I James I., ch. 11, the offense, if committed in England or Wales, was made punishable in the civil courts, and the penalty was death. As this statute was limited in its operation to England and Wales, it was at a very early period reenacted, generally with some modifications, in all the Colonies. In connection with the case we are now considering, it is a significant fact that on the 8th of December, 1788, after the passage of the Act establishing religious freedom, and after the convention of Virginia had recommended as an amendment to the Constitution of the United States the declaration in a Bill of Rights that "All men have an equal, natural and unalienable right to the free exercise of religion, according to the dictates of conscience," the Legislature of that State substantially enacted the Statute of James I., death penalty included, because as recited in the preamble, "It hath been doubted whether bigamy or polygamy be punishable by the laws of this Commonwealth." From that day to this we think it may safely be said there never has been a time in any State of the Union when polygamy has not been an offense against society, cognizable by the civil courts and punishable with more or less severity. In the face of all this evidence, it is impossible to believe that the constitutional guaranty of religious freedom was intended to prohibit legislation in respect to this most important feature of social life. Marriage, while from its very nature a sacred obligation, is, nevertheless, in most civilized nations, a civil contract, and usually regulated by law. . . . There cannot be a doubt that, unless restricted by some form of constitution, it is within the legitimate scope of the power of every civil government to determine whether polygamy or monogamy shall be the law of social life under its dominion.

In our opinion the statute immediately under consideration is within the legislative power of Congress. It is constitutional and valid as prescribing a rule of action for all those residing in the Territories, and in places over which the United States have exclusive control. This being so, the only question which remains is, whether those who make polygamy a part of their religion are excepted from the operation of the statute. If they are, then those who do not make polygamy a part of their religious belief may be found guilty and punished, while those who do must be acquitted and go free. This would be introducing a new element into criminal law. Laws are made for the government of actions, and while they cannot interfere with mere religious belief and opinions, they may with practices. Suppose one believed that human sacrifices were a necessary part of religious worship, would it be seriously contended that the civil government under which he lived could not interfere to prevent a sacrifice? Or if a wife religiously believed it was her duty to burn herself upon the funeral pyre of her dead husband, would it be beyond the power of the civil government to prevent her carrying her belief into practice?

So here, as a law of the organization of society under the exclusive dominion of the United States, it is provided that plural marriages shall not be allowed. Can a man excuse his practices to the contrary because of his religious belief? To permit this would be to make the professed doctrines of religious belief superior to the law of the land, and in effect to permit every citizen to become a law unto himself. Government could exist only in name under such circumstances.

A criminal intent is generally an element of crime, but every man is presumed to intend the necessary and legitimate consequences of what he knowingly does. Here the accused knew he had once been married, and that his first wife was living. He also knew that his second marriage was forbidden by law. When, therefore, he married the second time, he is presumed to have intended to break the law. And the breaking of the law is the crime. Every act necessary to constitute the crime was knowlingly done, and the crime was, therefore, knowingly committed. Ignorance of a fact may sometimes be taken as evidence of a want of criminal intent, but not ignorance of the law. The only defense of the accused in this case is his belief that the law ought not to have been enacted. It matters not that his belief was a part of his professed religion; it was still belief, and belief only.

In *Regina* v. *Wagstaffe,* 10 Cox, Cr. Cas., 531, the parents of a sick child, who omitted to call in medical attendance because of their religious belief that what they did for its cure would be effective, were held not to be guilty of manslaughter, while it was said the contrary would have been the result if the child had actually been starved to death by the parents, under the notion that it was their religious duty to abstain from giving it food. But when the offense consists of a positive act which is knowingly done, it would be dangerous to hold that the offender might escape punishment because he religiously believed the law which he had broken ought never to have been made. No case, we believe, can be found that has gone so far. . . .

[Judgment of conviction affirmed.]

2. *Free Exercise and Establishment Clauses: School Cases*

a. Bus Fares for Parochial School Pupils

EVERSON *v.* BOARD OF EDUCATION OF TOWNSHIP OF EWING
330 US 1 (1947)

[In the preceding case, *Reynolds* v. *United States,* the Supreme Court quoted from Jefferson's wall-of-separation letter, but this was done only in passing. In the *Everson Case,* however, the Supreme Court for the first time spelled out the doctrine of the separation of church and state and held that the First Amendment clause against an establishment of religion was intended to erect, in Jefferson's words, "a wall of separation between Church and State." The Court also held that this meaning and intention of the First Amendment apply to both the Federal Government and the states.

[With respect to these issues there was unanimity in the Court; four Justices, however—Jackson, Frankfurter, Rutledge, and Burton—held that the majority of the Court were in error when they decided that the wall of separation had not been breached when tax money was used to reimburse parents for the transportation by bus of their children to and from Roman Catholic parochial schools. Such use of public money, said the dissenting Justices, is a violation by the state of the provision of the First Amendment that no law shall be made "respecting an establishment of religion."

[This case was sharply attacked by the Roman Catholic bishops of the United States in a public statement published on November 21, 1948. The statement argued that Jefferson's "metaphor" specifies only that there shall be no "established Church," no state religion; that the First Amendment means only that the Federal Government may not prefer one religion over another; that this amendment is no limitation on the powers of the states; that the decision pointed up the "impending danger of a judicial 'establishment of secularism' that would ban God from public life."

[Much use has been made of the decision of the Court and of the attacks on the decision in the controversy over congressional bills to use federal funds to aid elementary and secondary education—a controversy that has often agitated and divided the American people.

[Justice Black wrote the opinion for the Court. Justice Jackson wrote a dissenting opinion in which Justice Frankfurter joined. Justice Rutledge wrote a dissenting opinion in which Justices Frankfurter, Jackson, and Burton joined.]

Mr. Justice Black delivered the opinion of the Court:

A New Jersey statute authorizes its local school districts to make rules and contracts for the transportation of children to and from schools. The appellee, a township board of education, acting pursuant to this statute, authorized reimbursement to parents of money expended by them for the bus transportation of their children on regular busses operated by the public transportation system. Part of this money was for the payment of transportation of some children in the community to Catholic parochial schools. These church schools give their students, in addition to secular education, regular religious instruction conforming to the religious tenets and modes of worship of the Catholic faith. The superintendent of these schools is a Catholic priest.

The appellant, in his capacity as a district taxpayer, filed suit in a State court challenging the right of the Board to reimburse parents of parochial school students. . . .

The only contention here is that the State statute and the resolution, insofar as they authorized reimbursement to parents of children attending parochial schools, violate the Federal Constitution. . . .

The New Jersey statute is challenged as a "law respecting the establishment of religion." The First Amendment, as made applicable to the states by the Fourteenth, . . . commands that a state "shall make no law respecting an establishment of religion, or prohibiting the free exercise thereof." . . . These words of the First Amendment reflected in the minds of early Americans a vivid mental picture of conditions and practices which they fervently wished to stamp out in order to preserve liberty for themselves and for their posterity. Doubtless their goal has not been entirely reached; but so far has the Nation moved toward it that the expression, "law respecting the establishment of religion," probably does not so vividly remind present-day Americans of the evils, fears, and political problems that caused that expression to be written into our Bill of Rights. Whether this New Jersey law is one respecting an "establishment of religion" requires an understanding of the meaning of that language, particularly with respect to the imposition of taxes. Once again, therefore, it is not inappropriate briefly to review the background and environment of the period in which that constitutional language was fashioned and adopted.

A large proportion of the early settlers of this country came here from Europe to escape the bondage of laws which compelled them to support and attend government favored churches. The centuries immediately before and contemporaneous with the colonization of America had been filled with turmoil, civil strife, and persecutions, generated in large part by established sects determined to maintain their absolute political and religious supremacy. With the power of government supporting them, at various times and places, Catholics had persecuted Protestants, Protestants had persecuted Catholics, Protestant sects had persecuted other Protestant sects, Catholics of one shade of belief had persecuted Catholics of another shade of belief, and all of these had from time to time persecuted Jews. In efforts to force loyalty to whatever religious group happened to be on top and in league with the government of a particular time and place, men and women had been fined, cast in jail, cruelly tortured, and killed. Among the offenses for which these punishments had been inflicted were such things as speaking disrespectfully of the views of ministers of government-established churches, non-attendance at those churches, expressions of non-belief in their doctrine, and failure to pay taxes and tithes to support them.

These practices of the old world were transplanted to and began to thrive in the soil of the new America. The very charters granted by the English Crown to the individuals and companies designated to make the laws which would control the destinies of the colonials authorized these individuals and companies to erect religious establishments which all, whether believers or nonbelievers, would be required to support and attend. An exercise of this authority was accompanied by a repetition of many of the old-world practices and persecutions. Catholics found themselves hounded and proscribed because of their faith; Quakers who followed their conscience went to jail; Baptists were peculiarly obnoxious to certain dominant Protestant sects; men and women of varied faiths who happened to be in a minority in a particular locality were persecuted because they steadfastly persisted in worshipping God only as their own consciences dictated. And all of these dissenters were compelled to pay tithes and taxes to support government-sponsored churches whose ministers preached inflammatory sermons designed to strengthen and consolidate the established faith by generating a burning hatred against dissenters.

These practices became so commonplace as to shock the freedom-loving colonials into a feeling of abhorrence. The imposition of taxes to pay ministers' salaries and to build and maintain churches and church property aroused their indignation. It was these feelings which found expression in the First Amendment. No one locality and no one group throughout the Colonies can rightly be given entire credit for having aroused the sentiment that culminated in adoption of the Bill of Rights' provisions embracing religious liberty. But Virginia, where the established church had achieved a dominant influence in political affairs and where many excesses attracted wide public attention, provided a great stimulus and able leadership for the movement. The people there, as elsewhere, reached the conviction that individual religious liberty could be achieved best under a government which was stripped of all power to tax, to support, or otherwise to assist any or all religions, or to interfere with the beliefs of any religious individual or group.

The movement toward this end reached its dramatic climax in Virginia in 1785–86 when the Virginia legislative body was about to renew Virginia's tax levy for the support of the established church. Thomas Jefferson and James Madison led the fight against this tax. Madison wrote his great Memorial and Remonstrance against the law. In it, he eloquently argued that a true religion did not need the support of law; that no person, either believer or nonbeliever, should be taxed to support a religious institution of any kind; that the best interest of a society required that the minds of men always be wholly free; and that cruel persecutions were the inevitable result of government-established religions. Madison's Remonstrance received strong support throughout Virginia, and the Assembly postponed consideration of the proposed tax measure until its next session. When the proposal came up for consideration at that session, it not only died in committee, but the Assembly enacted the famous "Virginia Bill for Religious Liberty" originally written by Thomas Jefferson. The preamble to that Bill stated among other things that

Almighty God hath created the mind free; that all attempts to influence it by temporal punishments or burthens, or by civil incapacitations, tend only to beget habits of hypocrisy and meanness, and are a departure from the plan of the Holy author of our religion, who being Lord both of body and mind, yet chose not to propagate it by coercions on either . . . ; that to compel a man to furnish contributions of money for the propagation of opinions which he disbelieves, is sinful and tyrannical; that even the forcing him to support this or that teacher of his own religious persuasion, is depriving him of the comfortable liberty of giving his contributions to the particular pastor, whose morals he would make his pattern. . . .

And the statute itself enacted

That no man shall be compelled to frequent or support any religious worship, place, or ministry whatsoever, nor shall be enforced, restrained, molested or burthened in his body or goods, nor shall otherwise suffer on account of his religious opinions or belief. . . .

This Court has previously recognized that the provisions of the First Amendment, in the drafting and adoption of which Madison and Jefferson played such leading roles, had the same objective and were intended to provide the same protection against governmental intrusion on religious liberty as the Virginia statute. . . . Prior to the adoption of the Fourteenth Amendment, the First Amendment did not apply as a restraint against the states. Most of them did soon provide similar constitutional protections for religious liberty. But some states persisted for about half a century in imposing restraints upon the free exercise of religion and in discriminating against particular religious group[s]. In recent years, so far as the provision against the establishment of a religion is concerned, the question has most frequently arisen in connection with proposed state aid to church schools and efforts to carry on religious teachings in the public schools in accordance with the tenets of a particular sect. Some churches have either sought or accepted state financial support for their schools. Here again the efforts to obtain state aid or acceptance of it have not been limited to any one particular faith. The state courts, in the main, have remained faithful to the language of their own constitutional provisions designed to protect religious freedom and to separate religions and governments. Their decisions, however, show the difficulty in drawing the line between tax legislation which provides funds for the welfare of the general public and that which is designed to support institutions which teach religion.

The meaning and scope of the First Amendment, preventing establishment of religion or prohibiting the free exercise thereof, in the light of its history and the evils it was designed forever to suppress, have been several times elaborated by the decisions of this Court prior to the application of the First Amendment to the states by the Fourteenth. The broad meaning given the Amendment by these earlier cases has been accepted by this Court in its decisions concerning an individual's religious freedom rendered since the Fourteenth Amendment was interpreted to make the prohibitions of the First applicable to state action abridging religious freedom. There is every reason to give the same application and broad interpretation to the "establishment of religion" clause. . . .

The "establishment of religion" clause of the First Amendment means at least this: Neither a state nor the Federal Government can set up a church. Neither can pass laws which aid one religion, aid all religions, or prefer one religion over another. Neither can force nor influence a person to go to or to remain away from church against his will or force him to profess a belief or disbelief in any religion. No person can be punished for entertaining or professing religious beliefs or disbeliefs, for church attendance or non-attendance. No tax in any amount, large or small, can be levied to support any religious activities or institutions, whatever they may be called, or whatever form they may adopt to teach or practice religion. Neither a state nor the Federal Government can, openly or secretly, participate in the affairs of any religious organizations or groups and vice versa. In the words of Jefferson, the clause against establishment of religion by law was intended to erect "a wall of separation between Church and State." . . .

We must consider the New Jersey statute in accordance with the foregoing limitations imposed by the First Amendment. But we must not strike that state statute down if it is within the State's constitutional power even though it approaches the verge of that power. . . . New Jersey cannot consistently with the "establishment of religion" clause of the First Amendment contribute tax-raised funds to the support of an institution which teaches the tenets and faith of any church. On the other hand, other language of the amendment commands that New Jersey cannot hamper its citizens in the free exercise of their own religion. Consequently, it cannot exclude individual Catholics, Lutherans, Mohammedans, Baptists, Jews, Methodists, Non-believers, Presbyterians, or the members of any other faith, *because of their faith, or lack of it,* from receiving the benefits of public welfare legislation. While we do not mean to intimate that a state could not provide transportation only to children attending public schools, we must be careful, in protecting the citizens of New Jersey against state-established churches, to be sure that we do not inadvertently prohibit New Jersey from extending its general state law benefits to all its citizens without regard to their religious belief.

Measured by these standards, we cannot say that the First Amendment prohibits New Jersey from spending tax-raised funds to pay the bus fares of parochial school pupils as a part of a general program under which it pays the fares of pupils attending public and other schools. It is undoubtedly true that children are helped to get to church schools. There is even a possibility that some of the children might not be sent to the church schools if the parents were compelled to pay [for] their children going to and from church [schools out of their own] pockets when transportation to a public school would have been paid for by the State. The same possibility exists where the state requires a local transit company to provide reduced fares to school children including those attending parochial schools, or where a municipally owned transportation system undertakes to carry all school children free of charge. Moreover, state-paid policemen, detailed to protect children going to and from church schools from the very real hazards of traffic, would serve much the same purpose and accomplish much the same result as state provisions intended to guarantee free transportation of a kind which the state deems to be best for the school children's welfare. And parents might refuse to risk their children to the serious danger of traffic accidents going to and from parochial schools, the approaches to which were not protected by policemen. Similarly, parents might be reluctant to permit their children to attend schools which the state had cut off from such general government services as ordinary police and fire protection, connections for sewage disposal, public highways and sidewalks. Of course, cutting off church schools from these services, so separate and so indisputably marked off from the religious function, would make it far more difficult for the schools to operate. But such is obviously not the purpose of the First Amendment. That Amendment requires the state to be a neutral in its relations with groups of religious believers and non-believers; it does not require the state to be their adversary. State power is no more to be used so as to handicap religions than it is to favor them.

This court has said that parents may, in the discharge of their duty under state compulsory education laws, send their children to a religious rather than a public school if the school meets the secular educational requirements which the state has power to impose. . . . It appears that these parochial schools meet New Jersey's requirements. The State contributes no money to the schools. It does not support them. Its legislation, as applied, does no more than provide a general program to help parents get their children, regardless of their religion, safely and expeditiously to and from accredited schools.

The First Amendment has erected a wall between church and state. That wall must be kept high and impregnable. We could not approve the slightest breach. New Jersey has not breached it here.

Affirmed.

Mr. Justice Jackson, dissenting:

I find myself, contrary to first impressions, unable to join in this decision. I have a sympathy, though it is not ideological, with Catholic citizens who are compelled by law to pay taxes for public schools, and also feel constrained by conscience and discipline to support other schools for their own children. Such relief to them as this case involves is not in itself a serious burden to taxpayers and I had assumed it to be as little serious in principle. Study of this case convinces me otherwise. The Court's opinion marshals every argument in favor of state aid and puts the case in its most favorable light, but much of its reasoning confirms my conclusions that there are no good grounds upon which to support the present legislation. In fact, the undertones of the opinion, advocating complete and uncompromising separation of Church from State, seem utterly discordant with its conclusion yielding support to their commingling in educational matters. The case which irresistibly comes to mind as the most fitting precedent is that of Julia who, according to Byron's reports, "whispering 'I will ne'er consent,'—consented."

The Township of Ewing is not furnishing transportation to the children in any form; it is not operating school busses itself or contracting for their operation; and it is not performing any public service of any kind with this taxpayer's money. All school children are left to ride as ordinary paying passengers on the regular busses operated by the public transportation system. What the Township does, and what the taxpayer complains of, is at stated intervals to reimburse parents for the fares paid, provided the children attend either public schools or Catholic Church schools. This expenditure of tax funds has no possible effect on the child's safety or expedition in transit. As passengers on the public busses they travel as fast and no faster, and are as safe and no safer, since their parents are reimbursed as before. . . .

Whether the taxpayer constitutionally can be made to contribute aid to parents of students because of their attendance at parochial schools depends upon the nature of those schools and their relation to the Church. The Constitution says nothing of education. It lays no obligation on the states to provide schools and does not undertake to regulate state systems of education if they see fit to maintain them. But they cannot, through school policy any more than through other means, invade rights secured to citizens by the Constitution of the United States. . . . One of our basic rights is to be free of taxation to support a transgression of the constitutional command that the authorities "shall make no law respecting an establishment of religion, or prohibiting the free exercise thereof." . . .

The function of the Church school is a subject on which this record is meager. It shows only that the schools are under superintendence of a priest and that "religion is taught as part of the curriculum." But we know that such schools are parochial only in name—they, in fact, represent a world-wide and age-old policy of the Roman Catholic Church. Under the rubric "Catholic Schools," the Canon Law of the Church, by which all Catholics are bound, provides:

> 1215. Catholic children are to be educated in schools where not only nothing contrary to Catholic faith and morals is taught, but rather in schools where religious and moral training occupy the first place. . . .
> 1216. In every elementary school the children must, according to their age, be instructed in Christian doctrine.

The young people who attend the higher schools are to receive a deeper religious knowledge, and the bishops shall appoint priests qualified for such work by their learning and piety.

1217. Catholic children shall not attend non-Catholic, indifferent, schools that are mixed, that is to say, schools open to Catholics and non-Catholics alike. The bishop of the diocese only has the right, in harmony with the instructions of the Holy See, to decide under what circumstances, and with what safeguards to prevent loss of faith, it may be tolerated that Catholic children go to such schools.

1224. The religious teaching of youth in any school is subject to the authority and inspection of the Church.

The local Ordinaries have the right and duty to watch that nothing is taught contrary to faith or good morals, in any of the schools of their territory.

They, moreover, have the right to approve the books of Christian doctrine and the teachers of religion, and to demand, for the sake of safeguarding religion and morals, the removal of teachers and books. . .

It is no exaggeration to say that the whole historic conflict in temporal policy between the Catholic Church and non-Catholic comes to a focus in their respective school policies. The Roman Catholic Church, counseled by experience in many ages and many lands and with all sorts and conditions of men, takes what, from the viewpoint of its own progress and the success of its mission, is a wise estimate of the importance of education to religion. It does not leave the individual to pick up religion by chance. It relies on early and indelible indoctrination in the faith and order of the Church by the word and example of persons consecrated to the task.

Our public school, if not a product of Protestantism, at least is more consistent with it than with the Catholic culture and scheme of values. It is a relatively recent development dating from about 1840. It is organized on the premises that secular education can be isolated from all religious teaching so that the school can inculcate all needed temporal knowledge and also maintain a strict and lofty neutrality as to religion. The assumption is that after the individual has been instructed in worldly wisdom he will be better fitted to choose his religion. Whether such a disjunction is possible, and if possible whether it is wise, are questions I need not try to answer.

I should be surprised if any Catholic would deny that the parochial school is a vital, if not the most vital, part of the Roman Catholic Church. If put to the choice, that venerable institution, I should expect, would forego its whole service for mature persons before it would give up education of the young, and it would be a wise choice. Its growth and cohesion, discipline and loyalty, spring from its schools. Catholic education is the rock on which the whole structure rests, and to render tax aid to its Church school is indistinguishable to me from rendering the same aid to the Church itself.

It is of no importance in this situation whether the beneficiary of this expenditure of tax-raised funds is primarily the parochial school and incidentally the pupil, or whether the aid is directly bestowed on the pupil with indirect benefits to the school. The state cannot maintain a Church and it can no more tax its citizens to furnish free carriage to those who attend a Church. The prohibition against establishment of religion cannot be circumvented by a subsidy, bonus or reimbursement of expense to individuals for receiving religious instruction and indoctrination.

The Court, however, compares this to other subsidies and loans to individuals and says, "Nor does it follow that a law has a private rather than a public purpose because it provides that tax-raised funds will be paid to reimburse individuals on account of money spent by them in a way which furthers a public program. . . ." Of course, the state may pay out tax-raised funds to relieve pauperism, but it may not under our Constitution do so to induce or reward piety. It may spend funds to secure old age against want, but it may not spend funds to secure religion against skepticism. It may compensate individuals for loss of employment, but it cannot compensate them for adherence to a creed.

It seems to me that the basic fallacy in the Court's reasoning, which accounts for its failure to apply the principles it avows, is in ignoring the essentially religious test by which beneficiaries of this expenditure are selected. A policeman protects a Catholic, of course—but not because he is a Catholic; it is because he is a man and a member of our society. The fireman protects the Church school—but not because it is a Church school; it is because it is property, part of the assets of our society. Neither the fireman nor the policeman has to ask before he renders aid "Is this man or building identified with the Catholic Church?" But before these school authorities draw a check to reimburse for a student's fare they must ask just that question, and if the school is a Catholic one they may render aid because it is such, while if it is of any other faith or is run for profit, the help must be withheld. To consider the converse of the Court's reasoning will best disclose its fallacy. That there is no parallel between police and fire protection and this plan of reimbursement is apparent from the incongruity of the limitation of this Act if applied to police and fire service. Could we sustain an Act that said the police shall protect pupils on the way to or from public schools and Catholic schools but not while going to and coming from other schools, and firemen shall extinguish a blaze in public or Catholic school buildings but shall not put out a blaze in Protestant Church schools or private schools operated for profit? That is the true analogy to the case we have before us and I should think it pretty plain that such a scheme would not be valid. . . .

There is no answer to the proposition, more fully expounded by Mr. Justice Rutledge, that the effect of the religious freedom Amendment to our Constitution was to take every form of propagation of religion out of the realm of things which could directly or indirectly be made public business and thereby be supported in whole or in part at taxpayers' expense. That is a difference which the Constitution sets up between religion and almost every other subject matter of legislation, a difference which goes to the very root of religious freedom and which the Court is overlooking today. This freedom was first in the Bill of Rights because it was first in the forefathers' minds; it was set forth in absolute terms, and its strength is its rigidity. It was intended not only to keep the states' hands out of religion, but to keep religion's hands off the state, and, above all, to keep bitter religious controversy out of public life by denying to every denomination any advantage from getting control of public policy or the public purse. Those great ends I cannot but think are immeasurably compromised by today's decision.

This policy of our Federal Constitution has never been wholly pleasing to most religious groups. They all are quick to invoke its protections; they all are irked when they feel its restraints. . . .

I cannot read the history of the struggle to separate political from ecclesiastical affiars, well summarized in the opinion of Mr. Justice Rutledge in which I generally concur, without a conviction that the Court today is unconsciously giving the clock's hands a backward turn.

Mr. Justice Frankfurter joins in this opinion.

b. Released Time

McCOLLUM *v.* BOARD OF EDUCATION
333 US 203 (1948)

[The question considered in this case was whether there was a breach in the wall of separation between church and state when, under a "released time" arrangement, religious instruction classes were conducted during regular school time within a public school building by denominational teachers. Eight Justices held that this arrangement violated the First Amendment as made applicable to the states by the Fourteenth Amendment. They reaffirmed the broad principles that were formulated the previous year in the *Everson Case,* only this time they found that the constitutional guaranty had been violated.

[Justice Reed alone dissented—not, however, with respect to the broad principles involved, but with respect to their application to the facts in the case. He dissented on the ground that the "released time" arrangements constituted no violation of the provisions of the First Amendment.]

Mr. Justice Black delivered the opinion of the Court:

This case relates to the power of a state to utilize its tax-supported public school system in aid of religious instruction insofar as that power may be restricted by the First and Fourteenth Amendments to the Federal Constitution.

The appellant, Vashti McCollum, began this action for mandamus against the Champaign Board of Education in the Circuit Court of Champaign County, Illinois. Her asserted interest was that of a resident and taxpayer of Champaign and of a parent whose child was then enrolled in the Champaign public schools. Illinois has a compulsory education law which, with exceptions, requires parents to send their children, aged seven to sixteen, to its tax-supported public schools where the children are to remain in attendance during the hours when the schools are regularly in session. Parents who violate this law commit a misdemeanor punishable by fine unless the children attend private or parochial schools which meet educational standards fixed by the State. District boards of education are given general supervisory powers over the use of the public school buildings within the school district. . . .

Appellant's petition for mandamus alleged that religious teachers, employed by private religious groups, were permitted to come weekly into the school buildings during the regular hours set apart for secular teaching, and then and there for a period of thirty minutes substitute their religious teaching for the secular education provided under the compulsory education law. The petitioner charged that this joint public-school religious-group program violated the First and Fourteenth Amendments to the United States Constitution. The prayer of her petition was that the Board of Education be ordered to "adopt and enforce rules and regulations prohibiting all instruction in and teaching of religious education in all public schools in Champaign School District Number 71, . . . and in all public school houses and buildings in said district when occupied by public schools." . . .

Although there are disputes between the parties as to various inferences that may or may not properly be drawn from the evidence concerning the religious program, the following facts are shown by the record without dispute. In 1940 interested members of the Jewish, Roman Catholic, and a few of the Protestant faiths formed a voluntary association called the Champaign Council on Religious Education. They obtained permission from the Board of Education to offer classes in religious instruction to public school pupils in grades four to nine inclusive. Classes were made up of pupils whose parents signed printed cards requesting that their children be permitted to attend; they were held weekly, thirty minutes for the lower grades, forty-five minutes for the higher. The council employed the religious teachers at no expense to the school authorities, but the instructors were subject to the approval and supervision of the superintendent of schools. The classes were taught in three separate religious groups by Protestant teachers, Catholic priests, and a Jewish Rabbi, although for the past several years there have apparently been no classes instructed in the Jewish religion. Classes were conducted in the regular classrooms of the school building. Students who did not choose to take the religious instruction were not released from public school duties; they were required to leave their classrooms and go to some other place in the school building for pursuit of their secular studies. On the other hand, students who were released from secular study for the religious instructions were required to be present at the religious classes. Reports of their presence or absence were to be made to their secular teachers.

The foregoing facts, without reference to others that appear in the record, show the use of tax-supported property for religious instruction and the close cooperation between the school authorities and the religious council in promoting religious education. The operation of the state's compulsory education system thus assists and is integrated with the program of religious instruction carried on by separate religious sects. Pupils compelled by law to go to school for secular education are released in part from their legal duty upon the condition that they attend the religious classes. This is beyond all question a utilization of the tax-established and tax-supported public school system to aid religious groups to spread their faith. And it falls squarely under the ban of the First Amendment (made applicable to the States by the Fourteenth) as we interpreted it in *Everson* v. *Board of Education.* . . . The majority in the *Everson Case,* and the minority . . . , agreed that the First Amendment's language, properly interpreted, had erected a wall of separation between Church and State. They disagreed as to the facts shown by the record and as to the proper application of the First Amendment's language to those facts.

Recognizing that the Illinois program is barred by the First and Fourteenth Amendments if we adhere to the views expressed both by the majority and the minority in the *Everson Case,* counsel for the respondents challenge those views as *dicta* and urge that we reconsider and repudiate them. They argue that historically the First Amendment was intended to forbid only government preference of one religion over another, not an impartial governmental assistance of all religions. In addition they ask that we distinguish or overrule our holding in the *Everson Case* that the Fourteenth Amendment made the "establishment of religion" clause of the First Amendment applicable as a prohibition against the States. After giving full consideration to the arguments presented we are unable to accept either of these contentions.

To hold that a state cannot consistently with the First and Fourteenth Amendments utilize its public school system to aid any or all religious faiths or sects in the dissemination of their doctrines and ideals does not, as counsel urge, manifest a governmental hostility to religion or religious teachings. A manifestation of such hostility would be at war with our national tradition as embodied in the First Amendment's guaranty of the free exercise of religion. For the First Amendment rests upon the premise that both religion and government can best work to achieve their lofty aims if each is left free from the other within its respective sphere. Or, as we said in the *Everson Case,* the First Amendment has erected a wall between Church and State which must be kept high and impregnable.

Here not only are the state's tax-supported public school buildings used for the dissemination of religious doctrines. The State also affords sectarian groups an invaluable aid in that it helps to provide pupils for their religious classes through use of the state's compulsory public school machinery. This is not separation of Church and State. . . .

Reversed. . . .

c. Released Time: The McCollum Case Limited

ZORACH *v.* CLAUSON
343 US 306 (1952)

[In the *McCollum Case* religious instruction was given *within* the public school building. The New York City "released time" program called for the religious courses to be operated *outside* the public school building. The pupils who did not choose to attend the religious courses of their respective denominations were required to remain in their public school classrooms. Six Justices found this system sufficiently different from that presented in the *McCollum Case* to conclude that it violated no constitutional provision.

[Justices Black and Jackson dissented, maintaining that there was no essential difference between this case and the previous one. Justice Frankfurter's dissent emphasized that the state courts had not permitted proof that the New York City program involved coercion of pupils to join the sectarian classes. He also sharply differentiated a "dismissed time" from a "released time" system. Under the former *all* students are dismissed and are free to do with their "dismissed time" as they or their parents may see fit; some of them may go to their church schools, others may go home. This system would involve no coercion. The "released time" system may, however, involve coercion of the reluctant. If it is coercive, it should be declared unconstitutional.

[Again all Justices avowed belief in the principle of separation of church and state. The dissenters, however, maintained that the principle was, in this case, honored in the breach rather than in the observance.]

Mr. Justice Douglas delivered the opinion of the Court:

New York City has a program which permits its public schools to release students during the school day so that they may leave the school buildings and school grounds and go to religious centers for religious instruction or devotional exercises. A student is released on written request of his parents. Those not released stay in the classrooms. The churches make weekly reports to the schools, sending a list of children who have been released from public school but who have not reported for religious instruction.

This "released time" program involves neither religious instruction in public school classrooms nor the expenditure of public funds. All costs, including the application blanks, are paid by the religious organization. The case is therefore unlike *McCollum* v. *Board of Education,* 333 US 203, which involved a "released time" program from Illinois. In that case the classrooms were turned over to religious instructors. We accordingly held that the program violated the First Amendment which (by reason of the Fourteenth Amendment) prohibits the states from establishing religion or prohibiting its free exercise.

Appellants, who are taxpayers and residents of New York City and whose children attend its public schools, challenge the present law, contending it is in essence not different from the one involved in the *McCollum Case.* Their argument, stated elaborately in various ways, reduces itself to this: the weight and influence of the school is put behind a program for religious instruction; public school teachers police it, keeping tab on students who are released; the classroom activities come to a halt while the students who are released for religious instruction are on leave; the school is a crutch on which the churches are leaning for support in their religious training; without the cooperation of the schools this "released time" program, like the one in the *McCollum Case,* would be futile and ineffective. . . .

The briefs and arguments are replete with data bearing on the merits of this type of "released time" program. Views *pro* and *con* are expressed, based on practical experience with these programs and with their implications. We do not stop to summarize these materials nor to burden the opinion with an analysis of them. For they involve considerations not germane to the narrow constitutional issue presented. They largely concern the wisdom of the system, its efficiency from an educational point of view, and the political considerations which have motivated its adoption or rejection in some communities. Those matters are of no concern here, since our problem reduces itself to whether New York by this system has either prohibited the "free exercise" of religion or has made a law "respecting an establishment of religion" within the meaning of the First Amendment.

It takes obtuse reasoning to inject any issue of the "free exercise" of religion into the present case. No one is forced to go to the religious classroom and no religious exercise or instruction is brought to the classrooms of the public schools. A student need not take religious instruction. He is left to his own desires as to the manner or time of his religious devotions, if any.

There is a suggestion that the system involves the use of coercion to get public school students into religious classrooms. There is no evidence in the record before us that supports that conclusion. The present record indeed tells us that the school authorities are neutral in this regard and do no more than release students whose parents so request. If in fact coercion were used, if it were established that any one or more teachers were using their office to persuade or force students to take the religious instruction, a wholly different case would be presented. Hence we put aside that claim of coercion both as respects the "free exercise" of religion and "an establishment of religion" within the meaning of the First Amendment.

Moreover, apart from that claim of coercion, we do not see how New York by this type of "released time" program has made a law respecting an establishment of religion within the meaning of the First Amendment. There is much talk of the separation of Church and State in the history of the Bill of Rights and in the decisions clustering around the First Amendment. . . . There cannot be the slightest doubt that the First Amendment reflects the philosophy that Church and State should be separated. And so far as interference with the "free exercise" of religion and an "establishment" of religion are concerned, the separation must be complete and unequivocal. The First Amendment within the scope of its coverage permits no exception; the prohibition is absolute. The First Amendment, however, does not say that in every and all respects there shall be a separation of Church and State. Rather, it studiously defines the manner, the specific ways, in which there shall be no concert or union or dependency one on the other. That is the common sense of the matter. Otherwise the state and religion would be aliens to each other—hostile, suspicious, and even unfriendly. Churches could not be required to pay even property taxes. Municipalities would not be permitted to render police or fire protection to religious groups. Policemen who helped parishioners into their places of worship would violate the Constitution. Prayers in our legislative halls; the appeals to the Almighty in the messages of the Chief Executive; the proclamations making Thanksgiving Day a holiday; "so help me God" in our courtroom oaths—these and all other references to the Almighty that run through our laws, our public rituals, our ceremonies would be flouting the First Amendment. A fastidious atheist or agnostic could even object to the supplication with which the Court opens each session: "God save the United States and this Honorable Court."

We would have to press the concept of separation of Church and State to these extremes to condemn the present law on constitutional grounds. The nullification of this law would have wide and profound effects. A Catholic student applies to his teacher for permission to leave the school during hours on a Holy Day of Obligation to attend a mass. A Jewish student asks his teacher for permission to be excused for Yom Kippur. A Protestant wants the afternoon off for a family baptismal ceremony. In each case the teacher requires parental consent in writing. In each case the teacher, in order to make sure the student is not a truant, goes further and requires a report from the priest, the rabbi, or the minister. The teacher in other words cooperates in a religious program to the extent of making it possible for her students to participate in it. Whether she does it occasionally for a few students, regularly for one, or pursuant to a systematized program designed to further the religious needs of all the students does not alter the character of the act.

We are a religious people whose institutions presuppose a Supreme Being. We guarantee the freedom to worship as one chooses. We make room for as wide a variety of beliefs and creeds as the spiritual needs of man deem necessary. We sponsor an attitude on the part of government that shows no partiality to any one group and that lets each flourish according to the zeal of its adherents and the appeal of its dogma. When the state encourages religious instruction or cooperates with religious authorities by adjusting the schedule of public events to sectarian needs, it follows the best of our traditions. For it then respects the religious nature of our people and accommodates the public service to their spiritual needs. To hold that it may not would be to find in the Constitution a requirement that the government show a callous indifference to religious groups. That would be preferring those who believe in no religion over those who do believe. Government may not finance religious groups nor undertake religious instruction nor blend secular and sectarian education nor use secular institutions to force one or some religion on any person. But we find no constitutional requirement which makes it necessary for government to be hostile to religion and to throw its weight against efforts to widen the effective scope of religious influence. The government must be neutral when it comes to competition between sects. It may not thrust any sect on any person. It may not make a religious observance compulsory. It may not coerce anyone to attend church, to observe a religious holiday, or to take religious instruction. But it can close its doors or suspend its operations as to those who want to repair to their religious sanctuary for worship or instruction. No more than that is undertaken here.

This program may be unwise and improvident from an educational or a community viewpoint. That appeal is made to us on a theory, previously advanced, that each case must be decided on the basis of "our own prepossessions." . . . Our individual preferences, however, are not the constitutional standard. The constitutional standard is the separation of Church and State. The problem, like many problems in constitutional law, is one of degree. . . .

In the *McCollum Case* the classrooms were used for religious instruction and the force of the public school was used to promote that instruction. Here, as we have said, the public schools do no more than accommodate their schedules to a program of outside religious instruction. We follow the *McCollum Case*. But we cannot expand it to cover the present released time program unless separation of Church and State means that public institutions can make no adjustments of their schedules to accommodate the religious needs of the people. We cannot read into the Bill of Rights such a philosophy of hostility to religion.

Affirmed [constitutionally sustained].

d. Prayer in Public Schools

ENGEL *v.* VITALE
370 US 421 (1962)

[The Court, in a 6-to-1 decision, held that the "non-denominational" prayer used in some of the public schools in New York State, on the recommendation of the Board of Regents, was unconstitutional as a violation of the Establishment Clause of the First Amendment, as read into the Fourteenth Amendment. The Court held that the recital of the prayer was a religious activity. The fact that nonobserving pupils may be excused did not save the constitutionality of the practice, since the practice was found to constitute an "establishment" in the constitutional sense. Justice Douglas wrote a concurring opinion. Justice Stewart dissented and contended that the decision denied the pupils who wished to recite the prayer "the opportunity of sharing in the spiritual heritage of our Nation."]

Mr. Justice Black delivered the opinion of the Court:

The respondent Board of Education of Union Free School District No. 9, New Hyde Park, New York, acting in its official capacity under state law, directed the School District's principal to cause the following prayer to be said aloud by each class in the presence of a teacher at the beginning of each school day:

Almighty God, we acknowledge our dependence upon Thee, and we beg Thy blessings upon us, our parents, our teachers and our country.

This daily procedure was adopted on the recommendation of the State Board of Regents, a governmental agency created by the State Constitution to which the New York Legislature has granted broad supervisory, executive, and legislative powers over the State's public school system. These state officials composed the prayer which they recommended and published as a part of their "Statement on Moral and Spiritual Training in the Schools," saying: "We believe that this Statement will be subscribed to by all men and women of good will, and we call upon all of them to aid in giving life to our program."

Shortly after the practice of reciting the Regents' prayer was adopted by the School District, the parents of ten pupils brought this action in a New York State Court insisting that use of this official prayer in the public schools was contrary to the beliefs, religions, or religious practices of both themselves and their children. Among other things, these parents challenged the constitutionality of both the state law authorizing the School District to direct the use of prayer in public schools and the School District's regulation ordering the recitation of this particular prayer on the ground that these actions of official governmental agencies violate that part of the First Amendment of the Federal Constitution which commands that "Congress shall make no law respecting an establishment of religion"—a command which was "made applicable to the State of New York by the Fourteenth Amendment of the said Constitution." The New York Court of Appeals, over the dissents of Judges Dye and Fuld, sustained an order of the lower state courts which had upheld the power of New York to use the Regents' prayer as a part of the daily procedures of its public schools so long as the schools did not compel any pupil to join in the prayer over his or his parents' objection.* We granted certiorari to re-

* 10 N.Y. 2d 174, 176 N.E. 2d 579. The trial court's opinion, had made it clear that the Board of Education must set up some sort of procedures to protect those who objected to reciting the prayer: "This is not to say that the rights accorded petitioners and their children under the 'free exercise' clause do not mandate safeguards against such embarrassments and pressures. It is enough on this score, however, that regulations, such as were adopted by New York City's Board of Education in connection with its released time program, be adopted, making clear that neither teachers nor any other school authority may comment on participation or nonparticipation in the exercise nor suggest or require that any posture or language be used or dress be worn or be not used or not worn. Nonparticipation may take the form

view this important decision involving rights protected by the First and Fourteenth Amendments.

We think that by using its public school system to encourage recitation of the Regent's prayer, the State of New York has adopted a practice wholly inconsistent with the Establishment Clause. There can, of course, be no doubt that New York's program of daily classroom invocation of God's blessings as prescribed in the Regents' prayer is a religious activity. It is a solemn avowal of divine faith and supplication for the blessings of the Almighty. The nature of such a prayer has always been religious, none of the respondents has denied this and the trial court expressly so found:

The religious nature of prayer was recognized by Jefferson and has been concurred in by theological writers, the United States Supreme Court and State courts and administrative officials, including New York's Commissioner of Education. A committee of the New York Legislature has agreed.

The Board of Regents as *amicus curiae,* the respondents and intervenors all concede the religious nature of prayer, but seek to distinguish this prayer because it is based on our spiritual heritage. . . .

The petitioners contend among other things that the state laws requiring or permitting use of the Regents' prayer must be struck down as a violation of the Establishment Clause because that prayer was composed by governmental officials as a part of a governmental program to further religious beliefs. For this reason, petitioners argue, the State's use of the Regents' prayer in its public school system breaches the constitutional wall of separation between Church and State. We agree with that contention since we think that the constitutional prohibition against laws respecting an establishment of religion must at least mean that in this country it is no part of the business of government to compose official prayers for any group of the American people to recite as a part of a religious program carried on by government.

It is a matter of history that this very practice of establishing governmentally composed prayers for religious services was one of the reasons which caused many of our early colonists to leave England and seek religious freedom in America. The Book of Common Prayer, which was created under governmental direction and which was approved by Acts of Parliament in 1548 and 1549, set out in minute detail the accepted form and content of prayer and other religious ceremonies to be used in the established, tax-supported Church of England. The controversies over the Book and what should be its content repeatedly threatened to disrupt the peace of that country as the accepted forms of prayer in the established church changed with the views of the particular ruler that happened to be in control at the time.

---

either of remaining silent during the exercise, or if the parent or child so desires, of being excused entirely from the exercise. Such regulations must also make provision for those nonparticipants who are to be excused from the prayer exercise. The exact provision to be made is a matter for decision by the board, rather than the court, within the framework of constitutional requirements. Within that framework would fall a provision that prayer participants proceed to a common assembly while nonparticipants attend other rooms, or that nonparticipants be permitted to arrive at school a few minutes late or to attend separate opening exercises, or any other method which treats with equality both participants and nonparticipants." . . .

Powerful groups representing some of the varying religious views of the people struggled among themselves to impress their particular views upon the Government and obtain amendments of the Book more suitable to their respective notions of how religious services should be conducted in order that the official religious establishment would advance their particular religious beliefs. Other groups, lacking the necessary political power to influence the Government on the matter, decided to leave England and its established church and seek freedom in America from England's governmentally ordained and supported religion.

It is an unfortunate fact of history that when some of the very groups which had most strenuously opposed the established Church of England found themselves sufficiently in control of colonial governments in this country to write their own prayers into law, they passed laws making their own religion the official religion of their respective colonies. Indeed, as late as the time of the Revolutionary War, there were established churches in at least eight of the thirteen former colonies and established religions in at least four of the other five. But the successful Revolution against English political domination was shortly followed by intense opposition to the practice of establishing religion by law. This opposition crystallized rapidly into an effective political force in Virginia where the minority religious groups such as Presbyterians, Lutherans, Quakers and Baptists had gained such strength that the adherents to the established Episcopal Church were actually a minority themselves. In 1785–1786, those opposed to the established Church, led by James Madison and Thomas Jefferson, who, though themselves not members of any of these dissenting religious groups, opposed all religious establishments by law on grounds of principle, obtained the enactment of the famous "Virginia Bill for Religious Liberty" by which all religious groups were placed on an equal footing so far as the State was concerned. Similar though less far-reaching legislation was being considered and passed in other States.

By the time of the adoption of the Constitution, our history shows that there was a widespread awareness among many Americans of the dangers of a union of Church and State. These people knew, some of them from bitter personal experience, that one of the greatest dangers to the freedom of the individual to worship in his own way lay in the Government's placing its official stamp of approval upon one particular kind of prayer or one particular form of religious services. They knew the anguish, hardship and bitter strife that could come when zealous religious groups struggled with one another to obtain the Government's stamp of approval from each King, Queen, or Protector that came to temporary power. The Constitution was intended to avert a part of this danger by leaving the government of this country in the hands of the people rather than in the hands of any monarch. But this safeguard was not enough. Our Founders were no more willing to let the content of their prayers and their privilege of praying whenever they pleased be influenced by the ballot box than they were to let these vital matters of personal conscience depend upon the succession of monarchs. The First Amendment was added to the Constitution to stand as a guarantee that neither the power nor the prestige of the Federal Government would be used to control, support or influence the kinds of prayer the American people can say—that the people's religions must not be subjected to the pressures of government for change each time a new political administration is elected to office. Under that Amendment's prohibition against governmental establishment of religion, as reinforced by the provisions of the Fourteenth Amendment, government in this country, be it state or federal, is without power to prescribe by law any particular form of prayer which is to be used as an official prayer in carrying on any program of governmentally sponsored religious activity.

There can be no doubt that New York's state prayer program officially establishes the religious beliefs embodied in the Regents' prayer. The respondents' argument to the contrary, which is largely based upon the contention that the Regents' prayer is "non-denominational" and the fact that the program, as modified and approved by state courts, does not require all pupils to recite the prayer but permits those who wish to do so to remain silent or be excused from the room, ignores the essential nature of the program's constitutional defects. Neither the fact that the prayer may be denominationally neutral, nor the fact that its observance on the part of the students is voluntary can serve to free it from the limitations of the Establishment Clause, as it might from the Free Exercise Clause, of the First Amendment, both of which are operative against the States by virtue of the Fourteenth Amendment. Although these two clauses may in certain instances overlap, they forbid two quite different kinds of governmental encroachment upon religious freedom. The Establishment Clause, unlike the Free Exercise Clause, does not depend upon any showing of direct governmental compulsion and is violated by the enactment of laws which establish an official religion whether those laws operate directly to coerce nonobserving individuals or not. This is not to say, of course, that laws officially prescribing a particular form of religious worship do not involve coercion of such individuals. When the power, prestige and financial support of government is placed behind a particular religious belief, the indirect coercive pressure upon religious minorities to conform to the prevailing officially approved religion is plain. But the purposes underlying the Establishment Clause go much further than that. Its first and most immediate purpose rested on the belief that a union of government and religion tends to destroy government and to degrade religion. The history of governmentally established religion, both in England and in this country, showed that whenever government had allied itself with one particular form of religion, the inevitable result had been that it had incurred the hatred, disrespect and even contempt of those who held contrary beliefs. That same history showed that many people had lost their respect for any religion that had relied upon the support of government to spread its faith. The Establishment Clause thus stands as an expression of principle on the part of the Founders of our Constitution that religion is too personal, too sacred, too holy, to permit its "unhallowed perversion" by a civil magistrate. Another purpose of the Establishment Clause rested upon an awareness of the historical fact that governmentally established religions and religious persecutions go hand in hand. The Founders knew that only a few years after the Book of Common Prayer became the only accepted form of religious services in the established Church of England, an Act of Uniformity was passed to compel all Englishmen to attend those services and to make it a criminal offense to conduct or attend religious gatherings of any other kind—a law which was consistently flouted by dissenting religious groups in England and which contributed to widespread persecutions of people like John Bunyan who persisted in holding "unlawful [religious] meetings . . . to the great disturbance and distraction of the good subjects of this kingdom. . . ." And they knew that similar persecutions had received the sanction of law in several of the colonies in this country soon after the establishment of official religions in those colonies. It was in large part to get completely away from this sort of systematic religious persecution that the Founders brought into being our Nation, our Constitution, and our Bill of Rights with its prohibition against any governmental establishment of religion. The New York laws officially prescribing the Regents' prayer are inconsistent with both the purposes of the Establishment Clause and with the Establishment Clause itself.

It has been argued that to apply the Constitution in such a way as to prohibit state laws respecting an establishment of religious services in public schools is to indicate a hostility toward religion or toward prayer. Nothing, of course, could be more wrong. The history of man is inseparable from the history of religion. And perhaps it is not too much to say that since the beginning of that history many people have devoutly believed that "More things are wrought by prayer than this world dreams of." It was doubtless largely due to men who believed this that there grew up a sentiment that caused men to leave the cross-currents of officially established state religions and religious persecution in Europe and come to this country filled with the hope that they could find a place in which they could pray when they pleased to the God of their faith in the language they chose. And there were men of this same faith in the power of prayer who led the fight for adoption of our Constitution and also for our Bill of Rights with the very guarantees of religious freedom that forbid the sort of governmental activity which New York has attempted here. These men knew that the First Amendment, which tried to put an end to governmental control of religion and of prayer, was not written to destroy either. They knew rather that it was written to quiet well-justified fears which nearly all of them felt arising out of an awareness that governments of the past had shackled men's tongues to make them speak only the religious thoughts that government wanted them to speak and to pray only to the God that government wanted them the pray to. It is neither sacrilegious nor antireligious to say that each separate government in this country should stay out of the business of writing or sanctioning official prayers and leave that purely religious function to the people themselves and to those the people chose to look to for religious guidance.*

It is true that New York's establishment of its Regents' prayer as an officially approved religious doctrine of that State does not amount to a total establishment of one particular religious sect to the exclusion of all others—that, indeed, the governmental endorsement of that prayer seems relatively insignificant when compared to the governmental encroachments upon religion which were commonplace 200

* There is of course nothing in the decision reached here that is inconsistent with the fact that school children and others are officially encouraged to express love for our country by reciting historical documents such as the Declaration of Independence which contain references to the Deity or by singing officially espoused anthems which include the composer's professions of faith in a Supreme Being, or with the fact that there are many manifestations in our public life of belief in God. Such patriotic or ceremonial occasions bear no true resemblance to the unquestioned religious exercise that the State of New York has sponsored in this instance.

years ago. To those who may subscribe to the view that because the Regents' official prayer is so brief and general there can be no danger to religious freedom in its governmental establishment, however, it may be appropriate to say in the words of James Madison, the author of the First Amendment:

[I]t is proper to take alarm at the first experiment on our liberties. . . . Who does not see that the same authority which can establish Christianity, in exclusion of all other Religions, may establish with the same ease any particular sect of Christians, in exclusion of all other Sects? That the same authority which can force a citizen to contribute three pence only of his property for the support of any one establishment, may force him to conform to any other establishment in all cases whatsoever?

The judgment of the Court of Appeals of New York is reversed and the cause remanded for further proceedings not inconsistent with this opinion.

e. Bible Reading in Public Schools

ABINGTON SCHOOL DISTRICT *v.* SCHEMPP
MURRAY *v.* CURLETT
374 US 203 (1963)

[Many states permit or require teachers in the public schools to read passages from the Bible or from the Old Testament. Some also permit or require recitation of the Lord's Prayer. Most of the statutes have been adopted in the twentieth century. The *Schempp Case* involved a Pennsylvania act; the *Murray Case* involved a Maryland act. The Supreme Court, by an 8-to-1 vote, held the statutes unconstitutional as a violation of the First Amendment, made applicable to the states by the Fourteenth Amendment. The opinion for the Court was by Justice Clark. Justices Brennan and Goldberg wrote concurring opinions. Justice Stewart wrote a dissenting opinion, in which he contended that the records in both cases were inadequate for the decisions and that both cases should have been remanded for further hearings.]

Mr. Justice Clark delivered the opinion of the Court:

Once again we are called upon to consider the scope of the provision of the First Amendment to the United States Constitution which declares that "Congress shall make no law respecting an establishment of religion or prohibiting the free exercise thereof. . . ." These companion cases present the issues in the context of state action requiring that schools begin each day with readings from the Bible. While raising the basic questions under slightly different factual situations, the cases permit of joint treatment. In light of the history of the First Amendment and of our cases interpreting and applying its requirements, we hold that the practices at issue and the laws requiring them are unconstitutional under the Establishment Clause, as applied to the states through the Fourteenth Amendment.

I

The Facts in Each Case: No. 142. The Commonwealth of Pennsylvania by law, 24 Pa. Stat. § 15–1516, as amended, Pub. Law 1928 (Supp. 1960) Dec. 17, 1959, requires that "at least ten verses from the Holy Bible shall be read, without comment, at the opening of each public school on each school day. Any child shall be excused from such Bible reading, or attending such Bible reading, upon the written request of his parent or guardian." The Schempp family, husband and wife and two of their three children, brought suit to enjoin enforcement of the statute, contending that their rights under the Fourteenth Amendment to the Constitution of the United States are, have been, and will continue to be violated unless this statute be declared unconstitutional as violative of these provisions of the First Amendment. They sought to enjoin the appellant school district, wherein the Schempp children attend school, and its officers and the Superintendent of Public Instruction of the Commonwealth from continuing to conduct such readings and recitation of the Lord's Prayer in the public schools of the district pursuant to the statute. A three-judge statutory District Court for the Eastern District of Pennsylvania held that the statute is violative of the Establishment Clause of the First Amendment as applied to the states by the Due Process Clause of the Fourteenth Amendment and directed that appropriate injunctive relief issue. . . .

The appellees Edward Lewis Schempp, his wife Sidney, and their children, Roger and Donna, are of the Unitarian faith and are members of the Unitarian Church in Germantown, Philadelphia, Pennsylvania, where they, as well as another son, Ellory, regularly attend religious services. The latter was originally a party, but having graduated from the school system *pendente lite,* was voluntarily dismissed from the action. The other children attend the Abington Senior High School, which is a public high school operated by appellant district.

On each school day at the Abington Senior High School between 8:15 and 8:30 A.M., while the pupils are attending their home rooms or advisory sections, opening services are conducted pursuant to the statute. The exercises are broadcast into each room in the school building through an intercommunications system and are conducted under the supervision of a teacher by students attending the school's radio and television workshop. Selected students from this course gather each morning in the school's workshop studio for the exercises, which include readings by one of the students of 10 verses of the Holy Bible, broadcast to each room in the building. This is followed by the recitation of the Lord's Prayer, likewise over the intercommunications system, but also by the students in the various classrooms, who are asked to stand and join in repeating the prayer in unison. The exercises are closed with the flag salute and such pertinent announcements as are of interest to the students. Participation in the opening exercises, as directed by the statute, is voluntary. The student reading the verses from the Bible may select the passages and read from any version he chooses, although the only copies furnished by the school are the King James version, copies of which were circulated to each teacher by the school district. During the period in which the exercises have been conducted the King James, the Douay and the Revised Standard versions of the Bible have been used, as well as the Jewish Holy Scriptures. There are no prefatory statements, no questions asked or solicited, no comments or explanations made and no interpretations given at or during the exercises. The students and parents are advised that the student may absent himself from the classroom or, should he elect to remain, not participate in the exercises.

It appears from the record that in schools not having an intercommunications system the Bible reading and the recitation of the Lord's Prayer were conducted by the home-room teacher, who chose the text of the verses and read them herself or had students read them in rotation or by volunteers. This was followed by a standing recitation of the Lord's Prayer, together with the Pledge of Allegiance to the flag by the class in unison and a closing announcement of routine school items of interest.

At the first trial Edward Schempp and the children testified as to specific religious doctrines purveyed by a literal reading of the Bible "which were contrary to the religious beliefs they held and to their familial teaching." . . . The children testified that all of the doctrines to which they referred were read to them at various times as part of the exercises. Edward Schempp testified at the second trial that he had considered having Roger and Donna excused from attendance at the exercises but decided against it for several reasons, including his belief that the children's relationships with their teachers and classmates would be adversely affected. . . .

The trial court, in striking down the practices and the statute requiring them, made specific findings of fact that the children's attendance at Abington Senior High School is compulsory and that the practice of reading 10 verses from the Bible is also compelled by law. It also found that

The reading of the verses, even without comment, possesses a devotional and religious character and constitutes in effect a religious observance. The devotional and religious nature of the morning exercises is made all the more apparent by the fact that the Bible reading is followed immediately by a recital in unison by the pupils of the Lord's Prayer. The fact that some pupils, or theoretically all pupils, might be excused from attendance at the exercises does not mitigate the obligatory nature of the ceremony for . . . Section 1516 . . . unequivocally requires the exercises to be held every school day in every school in the Commonwealth. The exercises are held in the school buildings and perforce are conducted by and under the authority of the local school authorities and during school sessions. Since the statute requires the reading of the "Holy Bible," a Christian document, the practice . . . prefers the Christian religion. The record demonstrates that it was the intention of . . . the Commonwealth . . . to introduce a religious ceremony into the public schools of the Commonwealth. . . .

No. 119. In 1905 the Board of School Commissioners of Baltimore City adopted a rule pursuant to Art. 77, § 202 of the Annotated Code of Maryland. The rule provided for the holding of opening exercises in the schools of the city consisting primarily of the "reading, without comment, of a chapter in the Holy Bible and/or the use of the Lord's Prayer." The petitioners, Mrs. Madalyn Murray and her son, William J. Murray, III, are both professed atheists. Following unsuccessful attempts to have the respondent school board rescind the rule this suit was filed for mandamus to compel its rescission and cancellation. It was alleged that William was a student in a public school of the city and Mrs. Murray, his mother, was a taxpayer therein; that it was the practice under the rule to have a reading on each school morning from the King James version of the Bible; that at petitioners' insistence the rule was amended to permit children to be excused from the exercise on request of the parent and that William had been excused pursuant thereto; that nevertheless the rule as amended was in violation of the petitioners' rights "to freedom of religion under the First and Fourteenth Amendments" and in violation of "the principle of separation between church and state, contained therein. . . ." The petition particularized the petitioners' atheistic beliefs and stated that the rule, as practiced, violated their rights

in that it threatens their religious liberty by placing a premium on belief as against nonbelief and subjects their freedom of conscience to the rule of the majority; it pronounces belief in God as the source of all moral and spiritual values, equating these values with religious values, and thereby renders sinister, alien and suspect the belief and ideals of your Petitioners, promoting doubt and question of their morality, good citizenship and good faith.

The respondents demurred and the trial court, recognizing that the demurrer admitted all facts well pleaded, sustained it without leave to amend. The Maryland Court of Appeals affirmed, the majority of four justices holding the exercise not in violation of the First and Fourteenth Amendments, with three justices dissenting.

II

It is true that religion has been closely identified with our history and government. As we said in *Engel* v. *Vitale,* 370 US 421, 434 (1962), "The history of man is inseparable from the history of religion. And . . . since the beginning of that history many people have devoutly believed that 'More things are wrought by prayer than this world dreams of,' . . ." In *Zorach* v. *Clauson,* 343 US 306, 313 (1952), we gave specific recognition to the proposition that "[w]e are a religious people whose institutions presuppose a Supreme Being." The fact that the Founding Fathers believed devotedly that there was a God and that the unalienable rights of man were rooted in Him is clearly evidenced in their writings, from the Mayflower Compact to the Constitution itself. This background is evidenced today in our public life through the continuance in our oaths of office from the Presidency to the Alderman of the final supplication, "So help me God." Likewise each House of the Congress provides through its Chaplain an opening prayer, and the sessions of this Court are declared open by the crier in a short ceremony, the final phrase of which invokes the grace of God. Again, there are such manifestations in our military forces, where those of our citizens who are under the restrictions of military service wish to engage in voluntary worship. Indeed, only last year an official survey of the country indicated that 64% of our people have church membership, Bureau of Census, U.S. Department of Commerce, Statistical Abstract of the United States, 48 (83d ed. 1962), while less than 3% profess no religion whatever. *Id.,* at p. 46. It can be truly said, therefore, that today, as in the beginning, our national life reflects a religious people who, in the words of Madison, are "earnestly praying, as . . . in duty bound, that the Supreme Lawgiver of the Universe . . . guide them into every measure which may be worthy of his . . . blessing. . . ."

III

Almost a hundred years ago in *Minor* v. *Board of Education of Cincinnati,* Judge Alphonzo Taft, father of the revered Chief Justice, in an unpublished opinion stated the ideal of our people as to religious freedom as one of absolute equality before the law of all religious opinions and sects. . . .

The government is neutral, and, while protecting all, it prefers none, and it disparages none.

Before examining this "neutral" position in which the Establishment and Free Exercise Clauses of the First Amendment place our government it is well that we discuss the reach of the Amendment under the cases of this Court.

First, this Court has decisively settled that the First Amendment's mandate that "Congress shall make no law respecting an establishment of religion, or prohibiting the free exercise thereof" has been made wholly applicable to the states by the Fourteenth Amendment. Twenty-three years ago in *Cantwell* v. *Connecticut,* 310 US 296, 303 (1940), this Court, through Mr. Justice Roberts, said:

The fundamental concept of liberty embodied in that [Fourteenth] Amendment embraces the liberties guaranteed by the First Amendment. The First Amendment declares that Congress shall make no law respecting an establishment of religion or prohibiting the free exercise thereof. The Fourteenth Amendment has rendered the legislatures of the states as incompetent as Congress to enact such laws. . . .

In a series of cases since *Cantwell* the Court has repeatedly reaffirmed that doctrine, and we do so now. . . .

Second, this Court has rejected unequivocally the contention that the establishment clause forbids only governmental preference of one religion over another. Almost 20 years ago in *Everson,* the Court said that "[n]either a state nor the Federal government can set up a church. Neither can pass laws which aid one religion, aid all religions, or prefer one religion over another." . . . The same conclusion has been firmly maintained ever since that time . . . and we reaffirm it now.

While none of the parties to either of these cases has questioned these basic conclusions of the Court, both of which have been long established, recognized and consistently reaffirmed, others continue to question their history, logic and efficacy. Such contentions, in the light of the consistent interpretation in cases of this Court, seem entirely untenable and of value only as academic exercises.

IV

The interrelationship of the Establishment and the Free Exercise Clauses was first touched upon by Mr. Justice Roberts for the Court in *Cantwell* v. *Connecticut,* where it was said that their "inhibition of legislation" had

a double aspect. On the one hand, it forestalls compulsion by law of the acceptance of any creed or the practice of any form of worship. Freedom of conscience and freedom to adhere to such religious organization or form of worship as the individual may choose cannot be restricted by law. On the other hand, it safeguards the free exercise of the chosen form of religion. Thus the Amendment embraces two concepts—freedom to believe and freedom to act. The first is absolute but, in the nature of things, the second cannot be.

A half dozen years later in *Everson* v. *Board of Education,* this Court, through Mr. Justice Black, stated that the "scope of the First Amendment . . . was designed forever to suppress" the establishment of religion or the prohibition of the free exercise thereof. In short, the Court held that the Amendment

requires the state to be a neutral in its relations with groups of religious believers and nonbelievers; it does not require the state to be their adversary. State power is no more to be used so as to handicap religions than it is to favor them. . . .

Finally, in *Engel* v. *Vitale,* only last year, these principles were so universally recognized that the Court without the citation of a single case and over the sole dissent of Mr. Justice Stewart reaffirmed them. The Court found the 22-word prayer used in "New York's program of daily classroom invocation of God's blessings as prescribed in the Regents' prayer . . . [to be] a religious activity." It held that "it is no part of the business of government to compose official prayers for any group of the American people to recite as a part of a religious program carried on by the government." In discussing the reach of the Establishment and Free Exercise Clauses of the First Amendment the Court said:

Although these two clauses may in certain instances overlap, they forbid two quite different kinds of governmental encroachment upon religious freedom. The Establishment Clause, unlike the Free Exercise Clause, does not depend upon any showing of direct governmental compulsion and is violated by the enactment of laws which establish an official religion whether those laws operate directly to coerce non-observing individuals or not. This is not to say, of course, that laws officially prescribing a particular form of religious worship do not involve coercion of such individuals. When the power, prestige and financial support of government is placed behind a particular religious belief, the indirect coercive pressure upon religious minorities to conform to the prevailing officially approved religion is plain.

And in further elaboration the Court found that the "first and most immediate purpose [of the Establishment Clause] rested on a belief that a union of government and religion tends to destroy government and to degrade religion." When government, the Court said, allies itself with one particular form of religion, the inevitable result is that it incurs "the hatred, disrespect, and even contempt of those who held contrary beliefs."

V

The wholesome "neutrality" of which this Court's cases speak thus stems from a recognition of the teachings of history that powerful sects or groups might bring about a fusion of governmental and religious functions or a concert or dependency of one upon the other to the end that official support of the State or Federal Government would be placed behind the tenets of one or of all orthodoxies. This the Establishment Clause prohibits. And a further reason for neutrality is found in the Free Exercise Clause, which recognizes the value of religious training, teaching and observance and, more particularly, the right of every person to freely choose his own course with references thereto, free of any compulsion from the state. This the Free Exercise Clause guarantees. Thus, as we have seen, the two clauses may overlap. As we have indicated, the Establishment Clause has been directly considered by this Court eight times in the past score of years and, with only one Justice dissenting on the point, it has consistently held that the clause withdrew all legislative power respecting religious belief or the expression thereof. The test may be stated as follows: what are the purpose and the primary effect of the enactment? If either is the advancement or inhibition of religion then the enactment exceeds the scope of legislative power as circumscribed by the Constitution. That is to say that to withstand the strictures of the Establishment Clause there must be a secular legislative purpose and a primary effect that neither advances nor inhibits religion. . . . The Free Exercise Clause, likewise considered many times here, withdraws from legislative power, state and federal, the exertion of any restraint on the free exercise of religion. Its purpose is to secure religious liberty in the individual by prohibiting any invasions thereof by civil authority. Hence it is necessary in a free exercise case for one to show the coercive effect of the enactment as it operates against him in the practice of his religion. The distinction between the two clauses is apparent—a violation of the Free Exercise Clause is predicated on coercion while the Establishment Clause violation need not be so attended.

Applying the Establishment Clause principles to the cases at bar we find that the States are requiring the selection and reading at the opening of the school day of verses from the Holy Bible and the recitation of the Lord's Prayer by the students in unison. These exercises are prescribed as part of the curricular activities of students who are required by law to attend school. They are held in the school buildings under the supervision and with the participation of teachers employed in those schools. None of these factors, other than compulsory school attendance, was present in the program upheld in *Zorach* v. *Clauson*. The trial court in No. 142 has found that such an opening exercise is a religious ceremony and was intended by the State to be so. We agree with the trial court's finding as to the religious character of the exercises. Given that finding the exercises and the law requiring them are in violation of the Establishment Clause.

There is no such specific finding as to the religious character of the exercises in No. 119, and the State contends (as does the State in No. 142) that the program is an effort to extend its benefits to all public school children without regard to their religious belief. Included within its secular purposes, it says, are the promotion of moral values, the contradiction to the materialistic trends of our times, the perpetuation of our institutions and the teaching of literature. The case came up on demurrer, of course, to a petition which alleged that the uniform practice under the rule had been to read from the King James version of the Bible and that the exercise was sectarian. The short answer, therefore, is that the religious character of the exercise was admitted by the State. But even if its purpose is not strictly religious, it is sought to be accomplished through readings, without comment, from the Bible. Surely the place of the Bible as an instrument of religion cannot be gainsaid, and the State's recognition of the pervading religious character of the ceremony is evident from the rule's specific permission of the alternative use of the Catholic Douay version as well as the recent amendment permitting nonattendance at the exercises. None of these factors is consistent with the contention that the Bible is here used either as an instrument for nonreligious moral inspiration or as a reference for the teaching of secular subjects.

The conclusion follows that in both cases the laws require religious exercises and such exercises are being conducted in direct violation of the rights of the appellees and petitioners. Nor are these required exercises mitigated by the fact that individual students may absent themselves upon parental request, for that fact furnishes no defense to a claim of unconstitutionality under the Establishment Clause. . . . Further, it is no defense to urge that the religious practices here may be relatively minor encroachments on the First Amendment. The breach of neutrality that is today a trickling stream may all too soon become a raging torrent and, in the words of Madison, "it is proper to take alarm at the first experiment on our liberties.". . .

It is insisted that unless these religious exercises are permitted a "religion of secularism" is established in the schools. . . . We do not agree, however, that this decision in any sense has that effect. In addition, it might well be said that one's education is not complete without a study of comparative religion or the history of religion and its relationship to the advancement of civilization. It certainly may be said that the Bible is worthy of study for its literary and historic qualities. Nothing we have said here indicates that such study of the Bible or of religion, when presented objectively as part of a secular program of education may not be effected consistent with the First Amendment. But the exercises here do not fall into those categories. They are religious exercises, required by the States in violation of the command of the First Amendment that the Government maintain strict neutrality, neither aiding nor opposing religion.

Finally, we cannot accept that the concept of neutrality, which does not permit a State to require a religious exercise even with the consent of the majority of those affected, collides with the majority's right to free exercise of religion. While the Free Exercise Clause clearly prohibits the use of state action to deny the right of free exercise to *anyone,* it has never meant that a majority could use the machinery of the State to practice its beliefs. . . .

The place of religion in our society is an exalted one, achieved through a long tradition of reliance on the home, the church and the inviolable citadel of the individual heart and mind. We have come to recognize through bitter experience that it is not within the power of government to invade that citadel, whether its purpose or effect be to aid or oppose, to advance or retard. In the relationship between man and religion, the State is firmly committed to a position of neutrality. Though the application of that rule requires interpretation of a delicate sort, the rule itself is clearly and concisely stated in the words of the First Amendment. Applying that rule to the facts of these cases, we affirm the judgment in No. 142. In No. 119, the judgment is reversed and the cause remanded to the Maryland Court of Appeals for further proceedings consistent with this opinion.

It is so ordered.

f. Textbooks for Parochial School Pupils
BOARD OF EDUCATION OF
CENTRAL SCHOOL DISTRICT NO. 1 *v.* ALLEN
392 US 236 (1968)

[A New York State statute required school districts to purchase, and then to lend, textbooks to students enrolled in parochial as well as in public and other private schools. By 6-3 vote, the Supreme Court upheld this law as constitutional within the Religion Clauses of the First Amendment (and the Fourteenth Amendment). The Court's opinion was by Justice White. Justice Harlan wrote a concurring opinion. Separate dissenting opinions were written by Justices Black, Douglas, and Fortas.]

Mr. Justice White delivered the opinion of the Court:

A law of the State of New York requires local public school authorities to lend textbooks free of charge to all students in grades seven through twelve; students attending private schools are included. This case presents the question whether this statute is a "law respecting the establishment of religion or prohibiting the free exercise thereof," and so in conflict with the First and Fourteenth Amendments to the Constitution, because it authorizes the loan of textbooks to students attending parochial schools. We hold that the law is not in violation of the Constitution.

Until 1965, § 701 of the Education Law of the State of New York authorized public school boards to designate textbooks for use in the public schools, to purchase such books with public funds, and to rent or sell the books to public school students. In 1965 the Legislature amended § 701, basing the amendments on findings that the "public welfare and safety require that the state and local communities give assistance to educational programs which are important to our national defense and the general welfare of the state." Beginning with the 1966–1967 school year, local school boards were required to purchase textbooks and lend them without charge "to all children residing in such district who are enrolled in grades seven to twelve of a public or private school which complies with the compulsory education law." The books now loaned are "text-books which are designated for use in any public, elementary, or secondary schools of the state or are approved by any boards of education," and which—according to a 1966 amendment—"a pupil is required to use as a text for a semester or more in a particular class in the school he legally attends."*

Appellants, the members of the Board of Education of Central School District No. 1 in Rensselaer and Columbia Counties, brought suit in the New York courts against appellee James Allen. The complaint alleged that § 701 violated both the State and Federal Constitutions; that if appellants, in reliance on their interpreta-

---

* New York Education Law § 701 (1967 Supp.):

"1. In the several cities and school districts of the state, boards of education, trustees or such body or officer as perform the functions of such boards, shall designate text-books to be used in the schools under their charge.

"2. A text-book, for the purposes of this section shall mean a book which a pupil is required to use as a text for a semester or more in a particular class in the school he legally attends.

"3. In the several cities and school districts of the state, board of education, trustees or such body or officers as perform the function of such boards shall have the power and duty to purchase and to loan upon individual request, to all children residing in such district who are enrolled in grades seven to twelve of a public or private school which complies with the compulsory education law, text-books. Text-books loaned to children enrolled in grades seven to twelve of said private schools shall be text-books which are designated for use in any public, elementary or secondary schools of the state or are approved by any boards of education, trustees or other school authorities. Such text-books are to be loaned free to such children subject to such rules and regulations as are or may be prescribed by the board of regents and such boards of education, trustees or other school authorities." . . .

tion of the Constitution, failed to lend books to parochial school students within their counties appellee Allen would remove appellants from office; and that to prevent this, appellants were complying with the law and submitting to their constituents a school budget including funds for books to be lent to parochial school pupils. Appellants therefore sought a declaration that § 701 was invalid, an order barring appellee Allen from removing appellants from office for failing to comply with it, and another order restraining him from apportioning state funds to school districts for the purchase of textbooks to be lent to parochial students. After answer, and upon cross-motions for summary judgment, the trial court held the law unconstitutional under the First and Fourteenth Amendments and entered judgment for appellants. The Appellate Division reversed, ordering the complaint dismissed on the ground that appellant school boards had no standing to attack the validity of a state statute. On appeal, the New York Court of Appeals concluded by a 4–3 vote that appellants did have standing but by a different 4–3 vote held that § 701 was not in violation of either the State or the Federal Constitution. The Court of Appeals said that the law's purpose was to benefit all school children, regardless of the type of school they attended, and that only textbooks approved by public school authorities could be loaned. It therefore considered § 701 "completely neutral with respect to religion, merely making available secular textbooks at the request of the individual student and asking no question about what school he attends." Section 701, the Court of Appeals concluded, is not a law which "establishes a religion or constitutes the use of public funds to aid religious schools." We noted probable jurisdiction.

Everson v. *Board of Education,* 330 US (1947), is the case decided by this Court that is most nearly in point for today's problem. New Jersey reimbursed parents for expenses incurred in busing their children to parochial schools. The Court stated that the Establishment Clause bars a State from passing "laws which aid one religion, aid all religions, or prefer one religion over another," and bars too any "tax in any amount, large or small . . . levied to support any religious activities or institutions, whatever they may be called, or whatever form they may adopt to teach or practice religion." Nevertheless, said the Court, the Establishment Clause does not prevent a State from extending the benefits of state laws to all citizens without regard for their religious affiliation and does not prohibit "New Jersey from spending tax-raised funds to pay the bus fares of parochial school pupils as part of a general program under which it pays the fares of pupils attending public and other schools." The statute was held to be valid even though one of its results was that "children are helped to get to church schools" and "some of the children might not be sent to the church schools if the parents were compelled to pay their children's bus fares out of their own pockets." As with public provision of police and fire protection, sewage facilities, and streets and sidewalks, payment of bus fares was of some value to the religious school, but was nevertheless not such support of a religious institution as to be a prohibited establishment of religion within the meaning of the First Amendment. . . .

Abington School District v. *Schempp* . . . fashioned a test ascribed to by eight Justices for distinguishing between forbidden involvements of the State with religion and those contacts which the Establishment Clause permits:

The test may be stated as follows: what are the purpose and the primary effect of the enactment? If either is the advancement or inhibition of religion then the enactment exceeds the scope of legislative power as circumscribed by the Constitution. That is to say that to withstand the strictures of the Establishment Clause there must be a secular legislative purpose and a primary effect that neither advances nor inhibits religion. *Everson* v. *Board of Education.*

This test is not easy to apply, but the citation of *Everson* by the *Schempp* Court to support its general standard made clear how the *Schempp* rule would be applied to the facts of *Everson.* The statute upheld in *Everson* would be considered a law having "a secular legislative purpose and a primary effect that neither advances nor inhibits religion." We reach the same result with respect to the New York law requiring school books to be loaned free of charge to all students in specified grades. The express purpose of § 701 was stated by the New York Legislature to be furtherance of the educational opportunities available to the young. Appellants have shown us nothing about the necessary effects of the statute that is contrary to its stated purpose. The law merely makes available to all children the benefits of a general program to lend school books free of charge. Books are furnished at the request of the pupil and ownership remains, at least technically, in the State. Thus no funds or books are furnished to parochial schools, and the financial benefit is to parents and children, not to schools. Perhaps free books make it more likely that some children choose to attend a sectarian school, but that was true of the state-paid bus fares in *Everson* and does not alone demonstrate an unconstitutional degree of support for a religious institution.

Of course books are different from buses. Most bus rides have no inherent religious significance, while religious books are common. However, the language of § 701 does not authorize the loan of religious books, and the State claims no right to distribute religious literature. Although the books loaned are those required by the parochial school for use in specific courses, each book loaned must be approved by the public school authorities; only secular books may receive approval. The law was construed by the Court of Appeals of New York as "merely making available secular textbooks at the request of the individual student," *supra,* and the record contains no suggestion that religious books have been loaned. Absent evidence we cannot assume that school authorities, who constantly face the same problem in selecting textbooks for use in the public schools, are unable to distinguish between secular and religious books or that they will not honestly discharge their duties under the law. In judging the validity of the statute on this record we must proceed on the assumption that books loaned to students are books that are not unsuitable for use in the public schools because of religious content.

The major reason offered by appellants for distinguishing free textbooks from free bus fares is that books, but not buses, are critical to the teaching process, and in a sectarian school that process is employed to teach religion. However this Court has long recognized that religious schools pursue two goals, religious instruction and secular education. In the leading case of *Pierce* v. *Society of Sisters,* 268 US 510 (1925), the Court held that although it would not question Oregon's power to compel school attendance or require that the attendance be at an institution meeting State-imposed requirements as to quality and nature of curriculum, Oregon had not shown that its interest in secular education required that all children attend publicly operated schools. A premise of this holding was the view that the State's interest in education would be served sufficiently by reliance on the secular teaching that accompanied religious training in the schools maintained by the Society of Sisters. Since *Pierce,* a substantial body of case law has confirmed the power of the States to insist that attendance at private schools, if it is to satisfy state compulsory-attendance laws, be at institutions which provide minimum hours of instruction, employ teachers of specified training, and cover prescribed subjects of instruction. Indeed, the State's interest in assuring that these standards are being met has been considered a sufficient reason for refusing to accept instruction at home as compliance with compulsory education statutes. These cases were a sensible corollary of *Pierce* v. *Society of Sisters:* if the State must satisfy its interest in secular education through the instrument of private schools, it has a proper interest in the manner in which those schools perform their secular educational function. Another corollary was *Cochran* v. *Louisiana State Board of Education,* 281 US 370 (1930), where appellants said that a statute requiring school books to be furnished without charge to all students, whether they attended public or private schools, did not serve a "public purpose," and so offended the Fourteenth Amendment. Speaking through Chief Justice Hughes, the Court summarized as follows its conclusion that Louisiana's interest in the secular education being provided by private schools, made provision of textbooks to students in those schools a properly public concern: "[The State's] interest is education, broadly; its method, comprehensive. Individual interests are aided only as the common interest is safeguarded."

Underlying these cases, and underlying also the legislative judgments that have preceded the court decisions, has been a recognition that private education has played and is playing a significant and valuable role in raising national levels of knowledge, competence, and experience. Americans care about the quality of the secular education available to their children. They have considered high quality education to be an indispensable ingredient for achieving the kind of nation, and the kind of citizenry, that they have desired to create. Considering this attitude, the continued willingness to rely on private school systems, including parochial systems, strongly suggests that a wide segment of informed opinion, legislative and otherwise, has found that those schools do an acceptable job of providing secular education to their students.* This judgment is further evidence that parochial schools are performing, in addition to their sectarian function, the task of secular education.

Against this background of judgment and experience, unchallenged in the meager record before us in this case, we cannot agree with appellants either that all teaching in a sectarian school is religious or that the processes of secular and religious training are so intertwined that secular textbooks furnished to students by the public are in fact instrumental in the teaching of religion. This case comes to us after summary judgment entered on the pleadings. Nothing in this record supports the proposition that all textbooks, whether they deal with mathematics, physics, foreign languages, history, or literature, are used by the parochial schools to teach religion. No evidence has been offered about particular schools, particular

* In 1966 in New York State, almost 900,000 students, or 21.5% of total state enrollment, attended nonpublic schools. . . .

courses, particular teachers, or particular books. We are unable to hold, based solely on judicial notice, that this statute results in unconstitutional involvement of the State with religious instruction or that § 701, for this or the other reasons urged, is a law respecting the establishment of religion within the meaning of the First Amendment.

Appellants also contend that § 701 offends the Free Exercise Clause of the First Amendment. However, "it is necessary in a free exercise case for one to show the coercive effect of the enactment as it operates against him in the practice of his religion," . . . and appellants have not contended that the New York law in any way coerces them as individuals in the practice of their religion.

The judgment is affirmed.

Mr. Justice Douglas, dissenting:

We have for review a statute which authorizes New York State to supply textbooks to students in parochial as well as in public schools. . . .

The statute on its face empowers each parochial school to determine for itself which textbooks will be eligible for loans to its students, for the Act provides that the only text which the State may provide is "a book which a pupil is required to use as a text for a semester or more in a particular class in the school he legally attends." N.Y. Education Law § 701(2). This initial and crucial selection is undoubtedly made by the parochial school's principal or its individual instructors, who are, in the case of Roman Catholic schools, normally priests or nuns.

The next step under the Act is an "individual request" for an eligible textbook (§ 701(3)), but the State Education Department has ruled that a pupil may make his request to the local public board of education through a "private school official." Local boards have accordingly provided for those requests to be made by the individual or "by groups or classes." And forms for textbook requisitions to be filled out by the head of the private school are provided.

The role of the local public school board is to decide whether to veto the selection made by the parochial school. This is done by determining first whether the text has been or should be "approved" for use in public schools and second whether the text is "secular," "nonreligious," or "nonsectarian."* The local boards apparently have broad discretion in exercising this veto power.

Thus the statutory system provides that the parochial school will ask for the books that it wants. Can there be the slightest doubt that the head of the parochial school will select the book or books that best promote its sectarian creed?

If the board of education supinely submits by approving and supplying the sectarian or sectarian-oriented textbooks, the struggle to keep church and state separate has been lost. If the board resists, then the battleline between church and state will have been drawn and the contest will be on to keep the school board independent or to put it under church domination and control.

---

* The State Court of Appeals used the phrases "secular textbooks" and "nonreligious textbooks" without any elaboration as to what was meant. 20 N.Y.2d, at 109, 281 N.Y.S.2d, at 805, 228 N.E.2d, at 794–795. The legislature, in its "statement of policy" to the Act (Laws of 1965, c. 320 § 1) speaks of aiding instruction in "nonsectarian subjects," and gives as examples "science, mathematics, [and] foreign languages." The State Department of Education has stated that "it is necessary that . . . [t]he textbooks be nonsectarian (this eliminates denominational editions and those carrying the 'imprimatur' or 'nihil obstat' of a religious authority). . . ." Opinion of Counsel No. 181. There are no other definitions to be found. . . .

Whatever may be said of *Everson,* there is nothing ideological about a bus. There is nothing ideological about a school lunch, nor a public nurse, nor a scholarship. The constitutionality of such public aid to students in parochial schools turns on considerations not present in this textbook case. The textbook goes to the very heart of education in a parochial school. It is the chief, although not solitary, instrumentality for propagating a particular religious creed or faith. How can we possibly approve such state aid to a religion? A parochial school textbook may contain many, many more seeds of creed and dogma than a prayer. Yet we struck down in *Engel* v. *Vitale,* 370 US 421 an official New York prayer for its public schools, even though it was not plainly denominational. For we emphasized the violence done the Establishment Clause when the power was given religious-political groups "to write their own prayers into law." That risk is compounded here by giving parochial schools the initiative in selecting the textbooks they desire to be furnished at public expense.

Judge Van Voorhis, joined by Chief Judge Fuld and Judge Breitel, dissenting below, said that the difficulty with the textbook loan program "is that there is no reliable standard by which secular and religious textbooks can be distinguished from each other." The New York Legislature felt that science was a nonsectarian subject. Does this mean that any general science textbook intended for use in grades 7–12 may be provided by the State to parochial school students? May John M. Scott's *Adventures in Science* (1963) be supplied under the textbook loan program? This book teaches embryology in the following manner:

To you an animal usually means a mammal, such as a cat, dog, squirrel, or guinea pig. The new animal or embryo develops inside the body of the mother until birth. The fertilized egg becomes an embryo or developing animal. Many cell divisions take place. In time some cells become muscle cells, others nerve cells or blood cells, and organs such as eyes, stomach, and intestines are formed.

> The body of a human being grows in the same way, but it is much more remarkable than that of any animal, for the embryo has a human soul infused into the body by God. Human parents are partners with God in creation. They have very great powers and great responsibilities, for through their cooperation with God souls are born for heaven. (Pp. 618–619.)*

Comparative economics would seem to be a nonsectarian subject. Will New York, then, provide Arthur J. Hughes' general history text, *Man in Time* (1964), to parochial school students? It treats that topic in this manner:

> Capitalism is an economic system based on man's right to private property and on his freedom to use that property in producing goods which will earn him a just profit on his investment. Man's right to private property stems from the Natural Law implanted in him by God. It is as much a part of man's nature as the will to self-preservation. (P. 560.)
>
> The broadest definition of socialism is government ownership of all the means of production and distribution in a country. . . . Many, but by no means all, Socialists in the nineteenth century believed that crime and vice existed because

---

* Although the author of this textbook is a priest, the text contains no imprimatur and no nihil obstat. Although published by a Catholic press, the Loyola University Press, Chicago, it is not marked in any manner as a "denominational edition," but is simply the general edition of the book. Accordingly, under Opinion of Counsel No. 181, the only document approaching a "regulation" on the issue involved here, *Adventures in Science* would qualify as "nonsectarian."

poverty existed, and if poverty were eliminated, then crime and vice would disappear. While it is true that poor surroundings are usually unhealthy climates for high moral training, still, man has the free will to check himself. Many Socialists, however, denied free will and said that man was a creation of his environment. . . . If Socialists do not deny Christ's message, they often ignore it. Christ showed us by His life that this earth is a testing ground to prepare man for eternal happiness. Man's interests should be in this direction at least part of the time and not always directed toward a futile quest for material goods. (Pp. 561–564.) . . .

Even where the treatment given to a particular topic in a school textbook is not blatantly sectarian, it will necessarily have certain shadings that will lead a parochial school to prefer one text over another.*

The Crusades, for example, may be taught as a Christian undertaking to "save the Holy Land" from the Moslem Turks who "became a threat to Christianity and its holy places," which "they did not treat . . . with respect" (Wilson, Wilson, Erb and Clucas, *Out of the Past,* 284 (1954)), or as essentially a series of wars born out of political and materialistic motives (see Leinwand, *The Pageant of World History,* 136–137 (1965)).

Is the dawn of man to be explained in the words, "God created man and made man master of the earth" (Furlong, *The Old World and America,* 5 (1937)), or in the language of evolution (see Wallbank, *Man's Story,* 32–35 (1961))?

Is the slaughter of the Aztecs by Cortes and his entourage to be lamented for its destruction of a New World culture (see Caughey, Franklin, & May, *Land of the Free,* 27028 (1965)), or forgiven because the Spaniards "carried the true Faith" to a barbaric people who practiced human sacrifice (see Furlong, Margaret, & Sharkey, *America Yesterday,* 17, 34 (1963))?

Is Franco's revolution in Spain to be taught as a crusade against anti-Catholic forces (see Hoffman, Vincitorio, & Swift, *Man and His History,* 666–667 (1958)) or as an effort by reactionary elements to regain control of that country (see Leinwand, *The Pageant of World History, supra,* at 512)? In the expansion of communism in select areas of the world a manifestation of the forces of Evil campaigning against the forces of Good? See Hughes, *Man in Time, supra,* at 565–568, 666–669, 735–748.

It will be often difficult, as Mr. Justice Jackson said, to say "where the secular ends and the sectarian begins in education." . . . But certain it is that once the so-called "secular" textbook is the prize to be won by that religious faith which selects the book, the battle will be on for those positions of control. Judge Van Voorhis expressed the fear that in the end the state might dominate the church. Others fear that one sectarian

---

* Some parochial schools may prefer those texts which are liberally sprinkled with religious vignettes. This creeping sectarianism avoids the direct teaching of religious doctrine but keeps the student continually reminded of the sectarian orientation of his education. In Furlong, Margaret, and Sharkey's American history text, *America Yesterday* (1963), for example, the student is informed that the first mass to be said in what is now the United States was in 1526 near Chesapeake Bay, that eight French missionaries to Canada in the early 1600's were canonized in 1930, that one of the men who signed the Declaration of Independence and two who attended the Constitutional Convention were Catholic, and that the superintendent of the Hudson Bay Company's outpost in the Oregon country converted to Catholicism in 1842. And Scott's *Adventures in Science* (1963), in teaching the atmospheric conditions prevailing at the top of Mount Everest, informs the student that when Sir Edmund Hillary first scaled this peak he placed there a "tiny crucifix" which a Benedictine monk had supplied.

America Yesterday, supra, is another example of a text written by the clergy (here a priest and nun together with one layman) that contains no imprimatur and no nihil obstat and is not a denominational edition.

group, gaining control of the state agencies which approve the "secular" textbooks, will use their control to disseminate ideas most congenial to their faith. It must be remembered that the very existence of the religious school—whether Catholic or Mormon, Presbyterian or Episcopalian—is to provide an education oriented to the dogma of the particular faith.* . . .

The challenged New York law leaves to the Board of Regents, local boards of education, trustees, and other school authorities the supervision of the textbook program. . . .

In general textbooks are approved for distribution by "boards of education, trustees or such body or officer as performs the functions of such boards. . . ." N.Y. Education Law § 701(1). These school boards are generally elected, §§ 2013, 2502(2), though in a few cities they are appointed. § 2553. Where there are trustees, they are elected. §§ 1523, 1602, 1702. And superintendents who advise on textbook selection are appointed by the board of education or the trustees. §§ 1711, 2503(5), 2507.

The initiative to select and requisition "the books desired" is with the parochial school. Powerful religious-political pressures will therefore be on the state agencies to provide the books that are desired.

These then are the battlegrounds where control of textbook distribution will be won or lost. Now that "secular" textbooks will pour into religious schools, we can rest assured that a contest will be on to provide those books for religious schools which the dominant religious group concludes best reflect the theocentric or other philosophy of the particular church.

The stakes are now extremely high—just as they were in the school prayer cases (see *Engel* v. *Vitale, supra*)—to obtain approval of what is "proper." For the "proper" books will radiate the "correct" religious view not only in the parochial school but in the public school as well.

Even if I am wrong in that basic premise, we still should not affirm the judgment below. Judge Van Voorhis, dissenting in the New York Court of Appeals, thought that the result of tying parochial school textbooks to public funds would be to put nonsectarian books into religious schools, which in the long view would tend toward state domination of the church. That would, indeed, be the result if the school boards did not succumb to "sectarian" pressure or control. So, however the case be viewed—whether sectarian groups win control of school boards or do not gain such control—the principle of separation of church and state, inherent in the Establishment Clause of the First Amendment, is violated by what we today approve. . . .

---

* The purpose of the parochial school in the beginning is clear beyond peradventure. The generally held Roman Catholic position in the matter of education in public and parochial schools has been well summarized by the late Monsignor John A. Ryan (1869-1945):

" '. . . As a matter of fact, the State maintains a system of schools which is not completely satisfactory to Catholics, inasmuch as no place is given to morality and religion. Since the Church realizes that the teaching of religion and instruction in the secular branches cannot rightfully or successfully be separated one from the other, she is compelled to maintain her own system of schools for general education as well as for religious instruction.' " 2 Stokes, *Church and State in the United States*, 654 (1950).

"The education in the parochial schools follows in general the curriculum in the public schools, the main differences being that about 15 per cent of the time is given to religious instruction, and that the Catholic point of view is brought out in the treatment of historical and other subjects, just as the Protestant point of view might be emphasized in a Protestant school." *Ibid.*

Some, however, think that some parochial schools are changing their character under practical pressures of educational competition. . . .

g. Salaries for Parochial School Teachers

LEMON *v.* KURTZMAN
EARLEY *v.* DiCENSO
403 US 602 (1971)

[Rhode Island and Pennsylvania provided for the partial payment of salaries of teachers in parochial schools. To be eligible, these teachers must teach only courses in secular subjects and meet certain other requirements. Both statutes were held unconstitutional as involving excessive entanglement between government and religion in violation of the Religion Clauses of the First Amendment. Chief Justice Burger delivered the Court's opinion. As to the Pennsylvania case, the judgment was unanimous; Justice Marshall did not participate in the case. As to the Rhode Island case, the decision was 8–1, with Justice White dissenting. Justice Douglas filed a concurring opinion, in which Justice Black joined (and also Justice Marshall, limited to the Rhode Island case). Justice Brennan filed a concurring opinion. Justice White filed an opinion in which he concurred as to the Pennsylvania case but dissented as to the Rhode Island case.]

Mr. Chief Justice Burger delivered the opinion of the Court:

These two appeals raise questions as to Pennsylvania and Rhode Island statutes providing state aid to church-related elementary and secondary schools. Both statutes are challenged as violative of the Establishment and Free Exercise Clauses of the First Amendment and the Due Process Clause of the Fourteenth Amendment.

Pennsylvania has adopted a statutory program that provides financial support to nonpublic elementary and secondary schools by way of reimbursement for the cost of teachers' salaries, textbooks, and instructional materials in specified secular subjects. Rhode Island has adopted a statute under which the State pays directly to teachers in nonpublic elementary schools a supplement of 15% of their annual salary. Under each statute state aid has been given to church-related educational institutions as well as other private schools. We hold that both statutes are unconstitutional.

I
The Rhode Island Statute

The Rhode Island Salary Supplement Act was enacted in 1969. It rests on the legislative finding that the quality of education available in nonpublic elementary schools has been jeopardized by the rapidly rising salaries needed to attract competent and dedicated teachers. The Act authorizes state officials to supplement the salaries of teachers of secular subjects in nonpublic elementary schools by paying directly to a teacher an amount not in excess of 15% of his current annual salary. As supplemented, however, a nonpublic school teacher's salary cannot exceed the maximum paid to teachers in the State's public schools, and the recipient must be certified by the state board of education in substantially the same manner as public school teachers.

In order to be eligible for the Rhode Island salary supplement, the recipient must teach in a nonpublic school at which the average per-pupil expenditure on secular education is less than the average in the State's public schools during a specified period. Appellant state Commissioner of Education also requires eligible schools to submit financial data. If this information indicates a per-pupil expenditure in excess of the statutory limitation, the records of the school in question must be examined in order to assess how much of the expenditure is attributable to secular education and how much to religious activity.

The Act also requires that teachers eligible for salary supplement must teach only those subjects that are offered in the State's public schools. They must use "only teaching materials which are used in the public schools." Finally, any teacher applying for a salary supplement must first agree in writing "not to teach a course in religion for so long as or during such time as he or she receives any salary supplements" under the Act.

Appellees are citizens and taxpayers of Rhode Island. They brought this suit to declare the Rhode Island Salary Supplement Act unconstitutional and to enjoin its operation on the grounds that it violates the Establishment and Free Exercise Clauses of the First Amendment. Appellants are state officials charged with administration of the Act, teachers eligible for salary supplements under the Act, and parents of children in church-related elementary schools whose teachers would receive state salary assistance.

A three-judge federal court was convened pursuant to 28 U.S.C. §§ 2281, 2284, It found that Rhode Island's nonpublic elementary schools accommodated approximately 25% of the State's pupils. About 95% of these pupils attended schools affiliated with the Roman Catholic church. To date some 250 teachers have applied for benefits under the Act. All of them are employed by Roman Catholic schools.

The court held a hearing at which extensive evidence was introduced concerning the nature of the secular instruction offered in the Roman Catholic schools whose teachers would be eligible for salary assistance under the Act. Although the court found that concern for religious values does not necessarily affect the content of secular subjects, it also found that the parochial school system was "an integral part of the religious mission of the Catholic Church."

The District Court concluded that the Act violated the Establishment Clause, holding that it fostered "excessive entanglement" between government and religion. In addition two judges thought that the Act had the impermissible effect of giving "significant aid to a religious enterprise." We affirm.

The Pennsylvania Statute

Pennsylvania has adopted a program which has some but not all of the features of the Rhode Island program. The Pennsylvania Nonpublic Elementary and Secondary Education Act was passed in 1968 in response to a crisis that the Pennsylvania legislature found existed in the State's nonpublic schools due to rapidly rising costs. The statute affirmatively reflects the legislative conclusion that the State's educational goals could appropriately be fulfilled by government support of "those purely secular educational objectives achieved through nonpublic education. . . ."

The statute authorizes appellee state Superintendent of Public Instruction to "purchase" specified "secular educational services" from nonpublic schools. Under the "contracts" authorized by the statute, the State directly reimburses nonpublic schools solely for their actual expenditures for teachers' salaries, textbooks, and instructional materials. A school seeking reimbursement must maintain prescribed accounting procedures that identify the "separate" cost of the "secular educational service." These accounts are subject to state audit. The funds for this program were originally derived from a new tax on horse and harness racing, but the Act is now financed by a portion of the state tax on cigarettes.

There are several significant statutory restrictions on state aid. Reimbursement is limited to courses "presented in the curricula of the public schools." It is further limited "solely" to courses in the following "secular" subjects: mathematics, modern foreign languages, physical science, and physical education. Textbooks and instructional materials included in the program must be approved by the state Superintendent of Public Instruction. Finally, the statute prohibits reimbursement for any course that contains "any subject matter expressing religious teaching, or the morals or forms of worship of any sect."

The Act went into effect on June 19, 1968, and the first reimbursement payments to schools were made on September 2, 1969. It appears that some $5 million has been expended annually under the Act. The State has now entered into contracts with some 1,181 nonpublic elementary and secondary schools with a student population of some 535,215 pupils—more than 20% of the total number of students in the State. More than 96% of these pupils attend church-related schools, and most of these schools are affiliated with the Roman Catholic church.

Appellants brought this action in the District Court to challenge the constitutionality of the Pennsylvania statute. The organizational plaintiffs-appellants are associations of persons resident in Pennsylvania declaring belief in the separation of church and state; individual plaintiffs-appellants are citizens and taxpayers of Pennsylvania. Plaintiff Lemon, in addition to being a citizen and a taxpayer, is a parent of a child attending public school in Pennsylvania. In addition, Lemon alleges that he purchased a ticket at a race track and thus had paid the specific tax which supports the expenditures under the Act. Appellees are state officials who have the responsibility for administering the Act. In addition seven church-related schools are defendants-appellees.

A three-judge federal court was convened pursuant to 28 U.S.C. §§ 2281, 2284. The District Court held that Lemon alone had standing to challenge the Act since he alone had paid the tax that financed the statutory scheme. The organizational plaintiffs-appellants were denied standing under *Flast* v. *Cohen,* 382 US 83 (1967).

The court granted Pennsylvania's motion to dismiss the complaint for failure to state a claim for relief. It held that the Act violated neither the Establishment nor the Free Exercise Clauses, Chief Judge Hastie dissenting. We reverse.

II

In *Everson* v. *Board of Education,* 330 US 1 (1947), this Court upheld a state statute which reimbursed the parents of parochial school children for bus transportation expenses. There Mr. Justice Black, writing for the majority, suggested that the decision carried to "the verge" of forbidden territory under the Religion

Clauses. Candor compels acknowledgement, moreover, that we can only dimly perceive the lines of demarcation in this extraordinarily sensitive area of constitutional law.

The language of the Religion Clauses of the First Amendment is at best opaque, particularly when compared with other portions of the Amendment. Its authors did not simply prohibit the establishment of a state church or a state religion, an area history shows they regarded as very important and fraught with great dangers. Instead they commanded that there should be "no law *respecting* an establishment of religion." A law may be one "respecting" the forbidden objective while falling short of its total realization. A law "respecting" the proscribed result, that is, the establishment of religion, is not always easily identifiable as one violative of the Clause. A given law might not *establish* a state religion but nevertheless be one "respecting" that end in the sense of being a step that could lead to such establishment and hence offend the First Amendment.

In the absence of precisely stated constitutional prohibitions, we must draw lines with reference to the three main evils against which the Establishment Clause was intended to afford protection: "sponsorship, financial support, and active involvement of the sovereign in religious activity." *Walz* v. *Tax Commission,* 397 US 664 (1970).

Every analysis in this area must begin with consideration of the cumulative criteria developed by the Court over many years. Three such tests may be gleaned from our cases. First, the statute must have a secular legislative purpose; second, its principal or primary effect must be one that neither advances nor inhibits religion, *Board of Education* v. *Allen,* 392 US 236 (1968); finally, the statute must not foster "an excessive government entanglement with religion." *Walz, supra,* at 674.

Inquiry into the legislative purposes of the Pennsylvania and Rhode Island statutes affords no basis for a conclusion that the legislative intent was to advance religion. On the contrary, the statutes themselves clearly state that they are intended to enhance the quality of the secular education in all schools covered by the compulsory attendance laws. There is no reason to believe the legislatures meant anything else. A State always has a legitimate concern for maintaining minimum standards in all schools it allows to operate. As in *Allen,* we find nothing here that undermines the stated legislative intent; it must therefore be accorded appropriate deference.

In *Allen* the Court acknowledged that secular and religious teachings were not necessarily so intertwined that secular textbooks furnished to students by the State were in fact instrumental in the teaching of religion. The legislatures of Rhode Island and Pennsylvania have concluded that secular and religious education are identifiable and separable. In the abstract we have no quarrel with this conclusion.

The two legislatures, however, have also recognized that church-related elementary and secondary schools have a significant religious mission and that a substantial portion of their activities are religiously oriented. They have therefore sought to create statutory restrictions designed to guarantee the separation between secular and religious educational functions and to ensure that State financial aid supports only the former. All these provisions are precautions taken in candid recognition that these programs approached, even if they did not intrude upon the forbidden areas under the Religion Clauses. We need not decide whether these legislative precautions restrict the principal or primary effect of the programs to the point where they do not offend the Religion Clauses, for we conclude that the cumulative impact of the entire relationship arising under the statutes in each State involves excessive entanglement between government and religion.

III

In *Walz* v. *Tax Commission, supra,* the Court upheld state tax exemptions for real property owned by religious organizations and used for religious worship. That holding, however, tended to confine rather than enlarge the area of permissible state involvement with religious institutions by calling for close scrutiny of the degree of entanglement involved in the relationship. The objective is to prevent, as far as possible, the intrusion of either into the precincts of the other.

Our prior holdings do not call for total separation between church and state; total separation is not possible in an absolute sense. Some relationship between government and religious organizations is inevitable. *Zorach* v. *Clauson,* 343 US 306, 312 (1952); *Sherbert* v. *Verner,* 374 US 398, 422 (1963) (Harlan, J., dissenting). Fire inspections, building and zoning regulations, and state requirements under compulsory school attendance laws are examples of necessary and permissible contacts. Indeed, under the statutory exemption before us in *Walz,* the State had a continuing burden to ascertain that the exempt property was in fact being used for religious worship. Judicial caveats against entanglement must recognize that the line of separation, far from being a "wall," is a blurred, indistinct and variable barrier depending on all the circumstances of a particular relationship.

This is not to suggest, however, that we are to engage in a legalistic minuet in which precise rules and forms must govern. A true minuet is a matter of pure form and style, the observance of which is itself the substantive end. Here we examine the form of the relationship for the light that it casts on the substance.

In order to determine whether the government entanglement with religion is excessive, we must examine the character and purposes of the institutions which are benefited, the nature of the aid that the State provides, and the resulting relationship between the government and the religious authority. Mr. Justice Harlan, concurring in *Walz, supra,* echoed the classic warning as to "programs whose very nature is apt to entangle the state in details of administration. . . ." Here we find that both statutes foster an impermissible degree of entanglement.

(a) *Rhode Island program*

The District Court made extensive findings on the grave potential for excessive entanglement that inheres in the religious character and purpose of the Roman Catholic elementary schools of Rhode Island, to date the sole beneficiaries of the Rhode Island Salary Supplement Act.

The church schools involved in the program are located close to parish churches. This understandably permits convenient access for religious exercises since instruction in faith and morals is part of the total educational process. The school buildings contain identifying religious symbols such as crosses on the exterior and crucifixes, religious paintings, and statues either in the classrooms or hallways. Although only approximately 30 minutes a day are devoted to direct religious instruction, there are religiously oriented extracurricular activities. Approximately two-thirds of the teachers in these schools are nuns of various religious orders. Their dedicated efforts provide an atmosphere in which religious instruction and religious vocations are natural and proper parts of life in such schools. Indeed, as the District Court found, the role of teaching nuns in enhancing the religious atmosphere has led the parochial school authorities to attempt to maintain a one-to-one ratio between nuns and lay teachers in all schools rather than permitting some to be staffed almost entirely by lay teachers.

On the basis of these findings the District Court concluded that the parochial schools constituted "an integral part of the religious mission of the Catholic Church." The various characteristics of the schools make them "a powerful vehicle for transmitting the Catholic faith to the next generation." This process of inculcating religious doctrine is, of course, enhanced by the impressionable age of the pupils, in primary schools particularly. In short, parochial schools involve substantial religious activity and purpose.

The substantial religious character of these church-related schools gives rise to entangling church-state relationships of the kind the Religion Clauses sought to avoid. Although the District Court found that concern for religious values did not inevitably or necessarily intrude into the content of secular subjects, the considerable religious activities of these schools led the legislature to provide for careful governmental controls and surveilance by state authorities in order to ensure that state aid supports only secular education.

The dangers and corresponding entanglements are enhanced by the particular form of aid that the Rhode Island Act provides. Our decisions from *Everson* to *Allen* have permitted the States to provide church-related schools with secular, neutral, or nonideological services, facilities, or materials. Bus transportation, school lunches, public health services, and secular textbooks supplied in common to all students were not thought to offend the Establishment Clause. We note that the dissenters in *Allen* seemed chiefly concerned with the pragmatic difficulties involved in ensuring the truly secular content of the textbooks provided at state expense.

In *Allen* the Court refused to make assumptions, on a meager record, about the religious content of the textbooks that the State would be asked to provide. We cannot, however, refuse here to recognize that teachers have a substantially different ideological character than books. In terms of potential for involving some aspect of faith or morals in secular subjects, a textbook's content is ascertainable, but a teacher's handling of a subject is not. We cannot ignore the dangers that a teacher under religious control and discipline poses to the separation of the religious from the purely secular aspects of precollege education. The conflict of functions inheres in the situation.

In our view the record shows these dangers are present to a substantial degree. The Rhode Island Roman Catholic elementary schools are under the general supervision of the Bishop of Providence and his appointed representative, the Diocesan Superintendent of Schools. In most cases, each individual parish, however, assumes the ultimate financial responsibility for the school, with the parish priest authorizing the allocation of parish funds. With only two exceptions, school principals are nuns appointed either by the Superintendent or the Mother Provincial of the order whose members staff the school. By 1969 lay teachers constituted more than a third of all teachers in the parochial elementary schools, and their number is growing. They are first interviewed by the superintendent's office and then by the school principal. The contracts are signed by the parish priest, and he retains some discretion in negotiating salary levels. Religious authority necessarily pervades the school system.

The schools are governed by the standards set forth in a "Handbook of School Regulations," which has the force of synodal law in the diocese. It emphasizes the role and importance of the teacher in parochial schools: "The prime factor for the success or failure of the school is the spirit and personality, as well as the professional competence, of the teacher. . . ." The Handbook also states that "Religious formation is not confined to formal courses; nor is it restricted to a single subject area." Finally the Handbook advises teachers to stimulate interest in religious vocations and missionary work. Given the mission of the church school, these instructions are consistent and logical.

Several teachers testified, however, that they did not inject religion into their secular classes. And the District Court found that religious values did not necessarily affect the content of the secular instruction. But what has been recounted suggests the potential if not actual hazards of this form of state aid. The teacher is employed by a religious organization, subject to the direction and discipline of religious authorities, and works in a system dedicated to rearing children in a particular faith. These controls are not lessened by the fact that most of the lay teachers are of the Catholic faith. Inevitably some of a teacher's responsibilities hover on the border between secular and religious orientation.

We need not and do not assume that teachers in parochial schools will be guilty of bad faith or any conscious design to evade the limitations imposed by the statute and the First Amendment. We simply recognize that a dedicated religious person, teaching in a school affiliated with his or her faith and operated to inculcate its tenets, will inevitably experience great difficulty in remaining religiously neutral. Doctrines and faith are not inculcated or advanced by neutrals. With the best of intentions such a teacher would find it hard to make a total separation between secular teaching and religious doctrine. What would appear to some to be essential to good citizenship might well for others border on or constitute instruction in religion. Further difficulties are inherent in the combination of religious discipline and the possibility of disagreement between teacher and religious authorities over the meaning of the statutory restrictions.

We do not assume, however, that parochial school teachers will be unsuccessful in their attempts to segregate their religious beliefs from their secular educational responsibilities. But the potential for impermissible fostering of religion is present. The Rhode Island Legislature has not, and could not, provide state aid on the basis of a mere assumption that secular teachers under religious discipline can avoid conflicts. The State must be certain, given the Religion Clauses, that subsidized teachers do not inculcate religion—indeed the State here has undertaken to do so. To ensure that no trespass occurs, the State has therefore carefully conditioned its aid with pervasive restrictions. An eligible recipient must teach only those courses that are offered in the public schools and use only those texts and materials that are found in the public schools. In addition the teacher must not engage in teaching any course in religion.

A comprehensive, discriminating, and continuing state surveillance will inevitably be required to ensure that these restrictions are obeyed and the First Amendment otherwise respected. Unlike a book, a teacher cannot be inspected once so as to determine the extent and intent of his or her personal beliefs and subjective acceptance of the limitations imposed by the First Amendment. These prophylactic contacts will involve excessive and enduring entanglement between state and church.

There is another area of entanglement in the Rhode Island program that gives concern. The statute excludes teachers employed by nonpublic schools whose average per-pupil expenditures on secular education exceed the comparable figures for public schools. In the event that the total expenditures of an otherwise eligible school exceed this norm, the program requires the government to examine the school's records in order to determine how much of the total expenditures are attributable to secular education and how much to religious activity. This kind of state inspection and evaluation of the religious content of a religious organization is fraught with the sort of entanglement that the Constitution forbids. It is a relationship pregnant with dangers of excessive government direction of church schools and hence of churches. The Court noted "the hazards of government supporting churches" in *Walz* v. *Tax Commission, supra,* at 675, and we cannot ignore here the danger that pervasive modern governmental power will ultimately intrude on religion and thus conflict with the Religion Clauses.

(b) *Pennsylvania program*

The Pennsylvania statute also provides state aid to church-related schools for teachers' salaries. The complaint describes an educational system that is very similar to the one existing in Rhode Island. According to the allegations, the church-related elementary and secondary schools are controlled by religious organizations, have the purpose of propagating and promoting a particular religious faith, and conduct their operations to fulfill that purpose. Since this complaint was dismissed for failure to state a claim for relief, we must accept these allegations as true for purposes of our review.

As we noted earlier, the very restrictions and surveillance necessary to ensure that teachers play a strictly nonideological role give rise to entanglements between church and state. The Pennsylvania statute, like that of Rhode Island, fosters this kind of relationship. Reimbursement is not only limited to courses offered in the public schools and materials approved by state officials, but the statute excludes "any subject matter expressing religious teaching, or the morals or forms of worship of any sect." In addition schools seeking reimbursement must maintain accounting procedures that require the State to establish the cost of the secular as distinguished from the religious instruction.

The Pennsylvania statute, moreover, has the further defect of providing state financial aid directly to the church-related school. This factor distinguishes both *Everson* and *Allen,* for in both those cases the Court was careful to point out that state aid was provided to the student and his parents—not to the church-related school. . . . In *Walz* v. *Tax Commission, supra,* at 675, the Court warned of the dangers of direct payments to religious organizations:

Obviously a direct money subsidy would be a relationship pregnant with involvement and, as with most governmental grant programs, could encompass sustained and detailed administrative relationships for enforcement of statutory or administrative standards. . . .

The history of government grants of a continuing cash subsidy indicates that such programs have almost always been accompanied by varying measures of control and surveillance. The government cash grants before us now provide no basis for predicting that comprehensive measures of surveillance and controls will not follow. In particular the government's post-audit power to inspect and evaluate a church-related school's financial records and to determine which expenditures are religious and which are secular creates an intimate and continuing relationship between church and state.

IV

A broader base of entanglement of yet a different character is presented by the divisive political potential of these state programs. In a community where such a large number of pupils are served by church-related schools, it can be assumed that state assistance will entail considerable political activity. Partisans of parochial schools, understandably concerned with rising costs, and sincerely dedicated to both the religious and secular educational missions of their schools, will inevitably champion this cause and promote political action to achieve their goals. Those who oppose state aid, whether for constitutional, religious, or fiscal reasons, will inevitably respond and employ all of the usual political campaign techniques to prevail. Candidates will be forced to declare and voters to choose. It would be unrealistic to ignore the fact that many people confronted with issues of this kind will find their votes aligned with their faith.

Ordinarily political debate and division, however vigorous or even partisan, are normal and healthy manifestations of our democratic system of government, but political division along religious lines was one of the principal evils against which the First Amendment was intended to protect. . . . The potential divisiveness of such conflict is a threat to the normal political process. . . . To have States or communities divide on the issues presented by state aid to parochial schools would tend to confuse and obscure other issues of great urgency. We have an expanding array of vexing issues, local and national, domestic and international, to debate and divide on. It conflicts with our whole history and tradition to permit questions of the Religion Clauses to assume such importance in our legislatures and in our elections that they could divert attention from the myriad issues and problems which confront every level of government. The highways of church and state relationships are not likely to be one-way streets, and the Constitution's authors sought to protect religious worship from the pervasive power of government. The history of many countries attests to the hazards of religion intruding into the political arena or of political power intruding into the legitimate and free exercise of religious belief.

Of course, as the Court noted in *Walz,* "adherents of particular faiths and individual churches frequently take strong positions on public issues." . . . We could not expect otherwise, for religious values pervade the fabric of our national life. But in *Walz* we dealt with a status under state tax laws for the benefit of all religious groups. Here we are confronted with successive and very likely permanent annual appropriations which benefit relatively few religious groups. Political fragmentation and divisiveness on religious lines is thus likely to be intensified.

The potential for political divisiveness related to religious belief and practice is aggravated in these two statutory programs by the need for continuing annual appropriations and the likelihood of larger and larger demands as costs and populations grow. The Rhode Island District Court found that the parochial school system's "monumental and deepening financial crisis" would "inescapably" require larger annual appropriations subsidizing greater percentages of the salaries of lay teachers. Although no facts have been developed in this respect in the Pennsylvania case, it appears that such pressures for expanding aid have already required the state legislature to include a portion of the state revenues from cigarette taxes in the program.

V

In *Walz* it was argued that a tax exemption for places of religious worship would prove to be the first step in an inevitable progression leading to the establishment of state churches and state religion. That claim could not stand up against more than 200 years of virtually universal practice imbedded in our colonial experience and continuing into the present.

The progression argument, however, is more persuasive here. We have no long history of state aid to church-related educational institutions comparable to 200 years of tax exemption for churches. Indeed, the state programs before us today represent something of an innovation. We have already noted that modern governmental programs have self-perpetuating and self-expanding propensities. These internal pressures are only enhanced when the schemes involve institutions whose legitimate needs are growing and whose interests have substantial political support. Nor can we fail to see that in constitutional adjudication some steps, which when taken were thought to approach "the verge," have become the platform for yet further steps. A certain momentum develops in constitutional theory and it can be a "downhill thrust" easily set in motion but difficult to retard or stop. Development by momentum is not invariably bad; indeed, it is the way the Common Law has grown, but it is a force to be recognized and reckoned with. The dangers are increased by the difficulty of perceiving in advance exactly where the "verge" of the precipice lies. As well as constituting an independent evil against which the Religion Clauses were intended to protect, involvement or entanglement between government and religion serves as a warning signal.

Finally, nothing we have said can be construed to disparage the role of church-related elementary and secondary schools in our national life. Their contribution has been and is enormous. Nor do we ignore their economic plight in a period of rising costs and expanding need. Taxpayers generally have been spared vast sums by the maintenance of these educational institutions by religious organizations, largely by the gifts of faithful adherents.

The merit and benefits of these schools, however, are not the issue before us in these cases. The sole question is whether state aid to these schools can be squared with the dictates of the Religion Clauses. Under our system the choice has been made that government is to be entirely excluded from the area of religious instruction and churches excluded from the affairs of government. The Constitution decrees that religion must be a private matter for the individual, the family, and the institutions of private choice, and that while some involvement and entanglement is inevitable, lines must be drawn.

The decision of the Rhode Island District Court in No. 569 and No. 570 is affirmed. The decision of the Pennsylvania District Court in No. 89 is reversed, and the case is remanded for further proceedings consistent with this opinion.

h. Buildings for Church-related Colleges

TILTON *v.* RICHARDSON
403 US 672 (1971)

[The Higher Education Facilities Act of 1963 provided federal construction grants for college and university facilities, excluding any facility to be used for sectarian instruction or religious worship. The Supreme Court, by 5–4, upheld the act as constitutional. It found that the act had neither the purpose nor the effect of promoting religion. The Court, however, held one provision of the act unconstitutional; namely, that after 20 years, the facility would revert to the institution without limitation as to its religious use. The Court's majority consisted of Chief Justice Burger and Justices Harlan, Stewart, Blackmun, and White. There was, however, no majority opinion, for Justice White did not join in the opinion of Chief Justice Burger but wrote a concurring opinion. Justice Brennan filed a dissenting opinion; and Justice Douglas wrote a dissenting opinion in which Justices Black and Marshall joined.]

Mr. Chief Justice Burger announced the judgment of the Court and an opinion in which Mr. Justice Harlan, Mr. Justice Stewart, and Mr. Justice Blackmun join:

This appeal presents important constitutional questions as to federal aid for church-related colleges and universities under Title I of the Higher Education Facilities Act of 1963, 20 U.S.C. §§ 701–758, which provides construction grants for buildings and facilities used exclusively for secular educational purposes. We must determine first whether the Act authorizes aid to such church-related institutions, and if so, whether the Act violates either the Establishment or Free Exercise Clauses of the First Amendment.

I

The Higher Education Facilities Act was passed in 1963 in response to a strong nationwide demand for the expansion of college and university facilities to meet the sharply rising number of young people demanding higher education. The Act authorizes federal grants and loans to "institutions of higher education" for the construction of a wide variety of "academic facilities." But § 751(a)(2) expressly excludes

> any facility used or to be used for sectarian instruction or as a place for religious worship, or . . . any facility which . . . is used or to be used primarily in connection with any part of the program of a school or department of divinity. . . .

The Act is administered by the United States Commissioner of Education. He advises colleges and universities applying for funds that under the Act no part of the project may be used for sectarian instruction, religious worship, or the programs of a divinity school. The Commissioner requires applicants to provide assurances that these restrictions will be respected. The United States retains a 20-year interest in any facility constructed with Title I funds. If, during this period, the recipient violates the statutory conditions, the United States is entitled to recover an amount equal to the proportion of its present value which the federal grant bore to the original cost of the facility. During the 20-year period, the statutory restrictions are enforced by the Office of Education primarily by way of on-site inspections.

Appellants are citizens and taxpayers of the United States and residents of Connecticut. They brought this suit for injunctive relief against the officials who administer the Act. Four church-related colleges and universities in Connecticut receiving federal construction grants under Title I were also named as defendants. Federal funds were used for five projects at these four institutions: (1) a library building at Sacred Heart University; (2) a music, drama, and arts building at Annhurst College; (3) a science building at Fairfield University; (4) a library building at Fairfield; and (5) a language laboratory at Albertus Magnus College.

A three-judge federal court was convened under 28 U.S.C. § 2282 and § 2284. Appellants attempted to show that the four recipient institutions were "sectarian" by introducing evidence of their relations with religious authorities, the content of their curricula, and other indicia of their religious character. The sponsorship of these institutions by religious organizations is not disputed. Appellee colleges introduced testimony that they had fully complied with the statutory conditions and that their religious affiliation in no way interfered with the performance of their secular educational functions. The District Court ruled that Title I authorized grants to church-related colleges and universities. It also sustained the constitutionality of the Act, finding that it had neither the purpose nor the effect of promoting religion. We noted probable jurisdiction.

II

We are satisfied that Congress intended the Act to include all colleges and universities regardless of any affiliation with or sponsorship by a religious body. Congress defined "institutions of higher education," which are eligible to receive aid under the Act, in broad and inclusive terms. Certain institutions, for example, institutions which are neither public nor nonprofit, are expressly excluded, and the Act expressly prohibits use of the facilities for religious purposes. But the Act makes no reference to religious affiliation or nonaffiliation. Under these circumstances "institutions of higher education" must be taken to include church-related colleges and universities.

This interpretation is fully supported by the legislative history. Although there was extensive debate on the wisdom and constitutionality of aid to institutions affiliated with religious organizations, Congress clearly included them in the program. The sponsors of the Act so stated, . . . and amendments aimed at the exclusion of church-related institutions were defeated.

III

Numerous cases considered by the Court have noted the internal tension in the First Amendment between the Establishment Clause and the Free Exercise Clause. *Walz* v. *Tax Commission,* 397 US 664 (1970), is the most recent decision seeking to define the boundaries of the neutral area between these two provisions within which the legislature may legitimately act. There, as in other decisions, the Court treated the three main concerns against which the Establishment Clause sought to protect: "sponsorship, financial support, and active involvement of the sovereign in religious activity."

Every analysis must begin with the candid acknowledgment that there is no single constitutional caliper which can be used to measure the precise degree to which these three factors are present or absent. Instead, our analysis in this area must begin with a consideration of the cumulative criteria developed over many years and applying to a wide range of governmental action challenged as violative of the Establishment Clause.

There are always risks in treating criteria discussed by the Court from time to time as "tests" in any limiting sense of that term. Constitutional adjudication does not lend itself to the absolutes of the physical sciences or mathematics. The standards should rather be viewed as guidelines with which to identify instances in which the objectives of the Religion Clauses have been impaired. And, as we have noted in *Lemon* v. *Kurtzman* and *Earley* v. *DiCenso,* decided today, candor compels the acknowledgment that we can only dimly perceive the boundaries of permissible government activity in this sensitive area of constitutional adjudication.

Against this background we consider four questions: First, does the Act reflect a secular legislative purpose? Second, is the primary effect of the Act to advance or inhibit religion? Third, does the administration of the Act foster an excessive government entanglement with religion? Fourth, does the implementation of the Act inhibit the free exercise of religion?

(a)

The stated legislative purpose appears in the preamble where Congress found and declared that

the security and welfare of the United States require that this and future generations of American youth be assured ample opportunity for the fullest development of their intellectual capacities, and that this opportunity will be jeopardized unless the Nation's colleges and universities are encouraged and assisted in their efforts to accommodate rapidly growing numbers of youth who aspire to a higher education.

This expresses a legitimate secular objective entirely appropriate for governmental action.

The simplistic argument that every form of financial aid to church-sponsored activity violates the Religion Clauses was rejected long ago in *Bradfield* v. *Roberts,* 175 US 291 (1899). There a federal construction grant to a hospital operated by a religious order was upheld. Here the Act is challenged on the ground that its primary effect is to aid the religious purposes of church-related colleges and universities. Construction grants surely aid these institutions in the sense that the construction of buildings will assist them to perform their various functions. But bus transportation, textbooks, and tax exemptions all gave aid in the sense that religious bodies would otherwise have been forced to find other sources from which to finance these services. Yet all of these forms of governmental assistance have been upheld. . . . The crucial question is not whether some benefit accrues to a religious institution as a consequence of the legislative program, but whether its principal or primary effect advances religion.

A possibility always exists, of course, that the legitimate objectives of any law or legislative program may be subverted by conscious design or lax enforcement. There is nothing new in this argument. But judicial concern about these possibilities cannot, standing alone, warrant striking down a statute as unconstitutional.

The Act itself was carefully drafted to ensure that the federally subsidized facilities would be devoted to the secular and not the religious function of the recipient institutions. It authorizes grants and loans only for academic facilities that will be used for defined secular purposes and expressly prohibits their use for religious instruction, training, or worship. These restrictions have been enforced in the Act's actual administration, and the record shows that some church-related institutions have been required to disgorge benefits for failure to obey them.

Finally, this record fully supports the findings of the District Court that none of the four church-related institutions in this case has violated the statutory restrictions. The institutions presented evidence that there had been no religious services or worship in the federally financed facilities, that there are no religious symbols or plaques in or on them, and that they had been used solely for nonreligious purposes. On this record, therefore, these buildings are indistinguishable from a typical state university facility. Appellants presented no evidence to the contrary.

Appellants instead rely on the argument that government may not subsidize any activities of an institution of higher learning which in some of its programs teaches religious doctrines. This argument rests on *Everson* where the majority stated that the Establishment Clause barred any "tax . . . levied to support any religious . . . institutions . . . whatever form they may adopt to teach or practice religion." In *Allen,* however, it was recognized that the Court had fashioned criteria under which an analysis of a statute's purpose and effect was determinative as to whether religion was being advanced by government action. . . .

Under this concept appellants' position depends on the validity of the proposition that religion so permeates the secular education provided by church-related colleges and universities that their religious and secular educational functions are in fact inseparable. The argument that government grants would thus inevitably advance religion did not escape the notice of Congress. It was carefully and thoughtfully debated, but was found unpersuasive. It was also considered by this Court in *Allen.*

There the Court refused to assume that religiosity in parochial elementary and secondary schools necessarily permeates the secular education that they provide.

This record, similarly, provides no basis for any such assumption here. Two of the five federally financed buildings involved in this case are libraries. The District Court found that no classes had been conducted in either of these facilities and that no restrictions were imposed by the institutions on the books that they acquired. There is no evidence to the contrary. The third building was a language library at Albertus Magnus College. The evidence showed that this facility was used solely to assist students with their pronunciation in modern foreign languages—a use which would seem peculiarly unrelated and unadaptable to religious indocrtination. Federal grants were also used to build a science building at Fairfield University and a music, drama, and arts building at Annhurst College.

There is no evidence that religion seeps into the use of any of these facilities. Indeed, the parties stipulated in the District Court that courses at these institutions are taught according to the academic requirements intrinsic to the subject matter and the individual teacher's concept of professional standards. Although appellants introduced several institutional documents which stated certain religious restrictions on what could be taught, other evidence showed that these restrictions were not in fact enforced and that the schools were characterized by an atmosphere of academic freedom rather than religious indoctrination. All four institutions, for example, subscribe to the 1940 Statement of Principles on Academic Freedom and Tenure endorsed by the American Association of University Professors and the Association of American Colleges.

Rather than focus on the four defendant colleges and universities involved in this case, however, appellants seek to shift our attention to a "composite profile" that they have constructed of the "typical sectarian" institution of higher education. We are told that such a "composite" institution imposes religious restrictions on admissions, requires attendance at religious activities, compels obedience to the doctrines and dogmas of the faith, requires instruction in theology and doctrine, and does everything it can to propagate a particular religion. Perhaps some church-related schools fit the pattern that appellants describe. Indeed, some colleges have been declared ineligible for aid by the authorities that administer the Act. But appellants do not contend that these four institutions fall within this category. Individual projects can be properly evaluated if and when challenges arise with respect to particular recipients and some evidence is then presented to show that the institution does in fact possess these characteristics. We cannot, however, strike down an Act of Congress on the basis of a hypothetical "profile."

(b)

Although we reject appellants' broad constitutional arguments we do perceive an aspect in which the statute's enforcement provisions are inadequate to ensure that the impact of the federal aid will not advance religion. If a recipient institution violates any of the statutory restrictions on the use of a federally financed facility, § 754(b)(2) permits the Government to recover an amount equal to the proportion of the facility's present value which the federal grant bore to its original cost.

This remedy, however, is available to the Government only if the statutory conditions are violated "within twenty years after completion of construction." This 20-year period is termed by the statute as "the period of Federal interest" and reflects Congress' finding that after 20 years "the public benefit accruing to the United States" from the use of the federally financed facility "will equal or exceed in value" the amount of the federal grant.

Under § 754(b)(2), therefore, a recipient institution's obligation not to use the facility for sectarian instruction or religious worship would appear to expire at the end of 20 years. We note, for example, that under § 718(b)(6)(C), an institution applying for a federal grant is only required to provide assurances that the facility will not be used for sectarian instruction or religious worship "during at least the period of the Federal interest therein (as defined in section 754 of this title)."

Limiting the prohibition for religious use of the structure to 20 years obviously opens the facility to use for any purpose at the end of that period. It cannot be assumed that a substantial structure has no value after that period and hence the unrestricted use of a valuable property is in effect a contribution of some value to a religious body. Congress did not base the 20-year provision on any contrary conclusion. If, at the end of 20 years the building is, for example, converted into a chapel or otherwise used to promote religious interests, the original federal grant will in part have the effect of advancing religion.

To this extent the Act therefore trespasses on the Religion Clauses. The restrictive obligations of a recipient institution under § 751(a)(2) cannot, compatible with the Religion Clause, expire while the building has substantial value. This circumstance does not require us to invalidate the entire Act, however. "The cardinal principle of statutory construction is to save and not to destroy." . . . In *Champlin Rfg. Co.* v. *Commission,* 286 US 210 (1932), the Court noted

The unconstitutionality of a part of an Act does not necessarily defeat . . . the validity of its remaining provisions. Unless it is evident that the legislature would not have enacted those provisions which are within its power, independently of that which is not, the valid part may be dropped if what is left is fully operative as a law.

Nor does the absence of an express severability provision in the Act dictate the demise of the entire statute. . . .

We have found nothing in the statute or its objectives intimating that Congress considered the 20-year provision essential to the statutory program as a whole. In view of the broad and important goals which Congress intended this legislation to serve, there is no basis for assuming that the Act would have failed of passage without this provision; nor will its excision impair either the operation or administration of the Act in any significant respect.

IV

We next turn to the question of whether excessive entanglements characterize the relationship between government and church under the Act. . . Our decisions today in *Lemon* v. *Kurtzman* and *Robinson* v. *DiCenso* have discussed and applied this independent measure of constitutionality under the Religion Clauses. There we concluded that excessive entanglements between government and religion were fostered by Pennsylvania and Rhode Island statutory programs under which state aid was provided to parochial elementary and secondary schools. Here, however, three factors substantially diminish the extent and the potential danger of the entanglement.

In *DiCenso* the District Court found that the parochial schools in Rhode Island were "an integral part of the religious mission of the Catholic Church." There, the record fully supported the conclusion that the inculcation of religious values was a substantial if not the dominant purpose of the institutions. The Pennsylvania case was decided on the pleadings, and hence we accepted as true the allegations that the parochial schools in that State shared the same characteristics.

Appellants' complaint here contains similar allegations. But they were denied by the answers, and there was extensive evidence introduced on the subject. Although the District Court made no findings with respect to the religious character of the four institutions of higher learning, we are not required to accept the allegations as true under these circumstances, particularly where, as here, appellants themselves do not contend that these four institutions are "sectarian."

There are generally significant differences between the religious aspects of church-related institutions of higher learning and parochial elementary and secondary schools. The "affirmative, if not dominant, policy" of the instruction in pre-college church-schools is "to assure future adherents to a particular faith by having control of their total education at an early age." *Walz* v. *Tax Commission, supra,* at 671. There is substance to the contention that college students are less impressionable and less susceptible to religious indoctrination. Common observation would seem to support that view, and Congress may well have entertained it. The skepticism of the college student is not an inconsiderable barrier to any attempt or tendency to subvert the congressional objectives and limitations. Furthermore, by their very nature, college and postgraduate courses tend to limit the opportunities for sectarian influence by virtue of their own internal disciplines. Finally, many church-related colleges and universities seek to evoke free and critical responses from their students and are characterized by a high degree of academic freedom.

The record here would not support a conclusion that any of these four institutions departed from this general pattern. All four schools are governed by Catholic religious organizations, and the faculties and student bodies at each are predominantly Catholic. Nevertheless, the evidence shows that non-Catholics were admitted as students and given faculty appointments. Not one of these four institutions requires its students to attend religious services. Although all four schools require their students to take theology courses, the parties stipulated that these courses are taught according to the academic requirements of the subject matter and the teacher's concept of professional standards. The parties also stipulated that the courses covered a range of human religious experiences and are not limited to courses about the Roman Catholic religion. The schools introduced evidence that they made no attempt to indoctrinate students or to proselytize. Indeed, some of the required theology courses at Albertus Magnus and Sacred Heart are taught by rabbis. Finally, as we have noted, these four schools subscribe to a well-established set of principles of academic freedom, and nothing in this record shows that these principles are not in fact followed. In short, the evidence shows institutions with admittedly religious functions but whose predominant higher education mission is to provide their students with a secular education.

Since religious indoctrination is not a substantial purpose or activity of these church-related colleges and universities, there is less likelihood than in primary and secondary schools that religion will permeate the area of secular education. This reduces the risk that government aid will in fact serve to support religious activities. Correspondingly the necessity for intensive government surveillance is diminished and the resulting entanglements between government and religion lessened. Such inspection as may be necessary to ascertain that the facilities are devoted to secular education is minimal and indeed hardly more than the inspections that States impose over all private schools within the reach of compulsory education laws.

The entanglement between church and state is also lessened here by the nonideological character of the aid which the government provides. Our cases from *Everson* to *Allen* have permitted church-related schools to receive government aid in the form of secular, neutral, or nonideological services, facilities, or materials that are supplied to all students regardless of the affiliation of the school which they attend. In *Lemon* and *DiCenso,* however, the state programs subsidized teachers, either directly or indirectly. Since teachers are not necessarily religiously neutral, greater governmental surveillance would be required to guarantee that state salary aid would not in fact subsidize religious instruction. There we found the resulting entanglement excessive. Here, on the other hand, the government provides facilities that are themselves religiously neutral. The risks of government aid to religion and the corresponding need for surveillance are therefore reduced.

Finally, government entanglements with religion are reduced by the circumstance that, unlike the direct and continuing payments under the Pennsylvania program, and all the incidents of regulation and surveillance, the government aid here is a one-time, single-purpose construction grant. There are no continuing financial relationships or dependencies, no annual audits, and no government analysis of an institution's expenditures on secular as distinguished from religious activities. Inspection as to use is a minimal contact.

No one of these three factors standing alone is necessarily controlling; cumulatively all of them shape a narrow and limited relationship with government which involves fewer and less significant contacts than the two state schemes before us in *Lemon* and *DiCenso.* The relationship therefore has less potential for realizing the substantive evils against which the Religion Clauses were intended to protect.

We think that cumulatively these three factors also substantially lessen the potential for divisive religious fragmentation in the political arena. This conclusion is admittedly difficult to document, but neither have appellants pointed to any continuing religious aggravation on this matter in the political processes. Possibly this can be explained by the character and diversity of the recipient colleges and universities and the absence of any intimate continuing relationship or dependency between government and religiously affiliated institutions. The potential for divisiveness inherent in the essentially local problems of primary and secondary schools is significantly less with respect to a college or university whose student constituency is not local but diverse and widely dispersed.

V

Finally, we must consider whether the implementation of the Act inhibits the free exercise of religion in violation of the First Amendment. Appellants claim that the Free Exercise Clause is violated because they are compeled to pay taxes, the proceeds of which in part finance grants under the Act. Appellants, however, are unable to identify any coercion directed at the practice or exercise of their religious beliefs. *Board of Education* v. *Allen, supra.* Their share of the cost of the grants under the Act is not fundamentally distinguishable from the impact of the tax exemption sustained in *Walz* or the provision of textbooks upheld in *Allen.*

We conclude that the Act does not violate the Religion Clauses of the First Amendment except that part of § 754(b)(2) providing a 20-year limitation on the religious use restrictions contained in § 751(a)(2). We remand to the District Court with directions to enter a judgment consistent with this opinion.

Vacated and remanded.

Mr. Justice Douglas, with whom Mr. Justice Black and Mr. Justice Marshall concur, dissenting:

The correct constitutional principle for this case was stated by President Kennedy in 1961 when questioned as to his policy respecting aid to private and parochial schools:

> . . . the Constitution clearly prohibits aid to the school, to parochial schools. I don't think there is any doubt of that.
>
> The Everson case, which is probably the most celebrated case, provided only by a 5 to 4 decision was it possible for a local community to provide bus rides to non-public school children. But all through the majority and minority statements on that particular question there was a very clear prohibition against aid to the school direct. The Supreme Court made its decision in the Everson case by determining that the aid was to the child, not to the school. Aid to the school is—there isn't any room for debate on that subject. It is prohibited by the Constitution, and the Supreme Court has made that very clear. And therefore there would be no possibility of our recommending it. . . .

The public purpose in secular education is, to be sure, furthered by the program. Yet the sectarian purpose is aided by making the parochial school system viable. The purpose is to increase "student enrollment," and the students obviously aimed at are those of the particular faith now financed by taxpayers' money. Parochial schools are not beamed at agnostics, atheists, or those of a competing sect. The more sophisticated institutions may admit minorities; but the dominant religious character is not changed.

The reversion of the facility to the parochial school at the end of 20 years is an outright grant, measurable by the present discounted worth of the facility. A gift of taxpayers' funds in that amount would plainly be unconstitutional. The Court properly bars it even though disguised in the form of a reversionary interest. . . .

But the invalidation of this one clause cannot cure the constitutional infirmities of the statute as a whole. The Federal Government is giving religious schools a block grant to build certain facilities. The fact that money is given once at the beginning of a program rather than apportioned annually as in *Lemon* and *DiCenso* is without constitutional significance. The First Amendment bars establishment of a religion. And as I noted today in *Lemon* and *DiCenso,* this bar has been consistently interpreted from *Everson* v. *Board of Education* through *Torcaso* v. *Watkins,* as meaning: "No tax in any amount, large or small, can be levied to support any religious activities or institutions, whatever they may be called, or whatever form they may adopt to teach or practice religion." Thus it is hardly impressive that rather than giving a smaller amount of money annually over a large period of years, Congress instead gives a large amount all at once. The majority's distinction is in effect that small violations of the First Amendment over a period of years are unconstitutional (see *Lemon* and *DiCenso*) while a huge violation occurring only once is *de minimus*. I cannot agree with such sophistry.

What I have said in *Lemon* and in the *DiCenso* cases decided today is relevant here. The facilities financed by taxpayers' funds are not to be used "for sectarian" purposes. Religious teaching and secular teaching are so enmeshed in parochial schools that only the strictest supervision and surveillance would insure compliance with the condition. Parochial schools may require religious exercises, even in the classroom. A parochial school operates on one budget. Money not spent for one purpose becomes available for other purposes. Thus the fact that there are no religious observances in federally financed facilities is not controlling because required religious observances will take place in other buildings. Our decision in *Engle* v. *Vitale*, 370 US 421, held that a requirement of a prayer in public schools violated the Establishment Clause. Once these schools become federally funded they become bound by federal standards . . . and accordingly adherence to *Engle* would require an end to required religious exercises. That kind of surveillance and control will certainly be obnoxious to the church authorities and if done will radically change the character of the parochial school. Yet if that surveillance is not searching and continuous, this federal financing is obnoxious under the Establishment and Free Exercise Clauses all for the reasons stated in the companion cases.

In other words, surveillance creates an entanglement of government and religion which the First Amendment was designed to avoid. Yet after today's decision there will be a requirement of surveillance which will last for the useful life of the building and as we have previously noted, "[it] is hardly lack of due process for the Government to regulate that which it subsidizes." . . . The price of the subsidy under the Act is violation of the Free Exercise Clause. Could a course in the History of Methodism be taught in a federally financed building? Would a religiously slanted version of the Reformation or Quebec politics under Duplessis be permissible? How can the Government know what is taught in the federally financed building without a continuous auditing of classroom instruction? Yet both the Free Exercise Clause and academic freedom are violated when the Government agent must be present to determine whether the course content is satisfactory.

As I said in the *Lemon* and *DiCenso* cases, a parochial school is a unitary institution with subtle blending of sectarian and secular instruction. Thus the practices of religious schools are in no way affected by the minimal requirement that the government-financed facility may not "be used for sectarian instruction or as a place of worship." Money saved from one item in the budget is free to be used elsewhere. By conducting religious services in another building, the school has—rent free—a building for nonsectarian use. This is not called Establishment simply because the government retains a continuing interest in the building for its useful life, even though the religious schools need never pay a cent for the use of the building.

Much is made of the need for public aid to church schools in light of their pressing fiscal problems. Dr. Eugene C. Blake of the Presbyterian Church, however, wrote in 1959:

> When one remembers that churches pay no inheritance tax (churches do not die), that churches may own and operate business and be exempt from the 52 percent

corporate income tax, and that real property used for church purposes (which in some states are most generously construed) is tax exempt, it is not unreasonable to prophesy that with reasonably prudent management, the churches ought to be able to control the whole economy of the nation within the predictable future. That the growing wealth and property of the churches was partially responsible for revolutionary expropriations of church property in England in the sixteenth century, in France in the eighteenth century, in Italy in the nineteenth century, and in Mexico, Russia, Czechoslovakia and Hungary (to name a few examples) in the twentieth century, seems self-evident. A government with mounting tax problems cannot be expected to keep its hands off the wealth of a rich church forever. That such a revolution is always accompanied by anticlericalism and atheism should not be surprising.

The mounting wealth of the churches* makes ironic their incessant demands on the public treasury. I said in my dissent in *Walz* v. *Tax Commission:*

> The religiously used real estate of the churches today constitutes a vast domain. . . . Their assets total over $141 billion and their annual income at least $22 billion. And the extent to which they are feeding from the public trough in a variety of forms is alarming. . . .

It is almost unbelievable that we have made the radical departure from Madison's Remonstrance memorialized in today's decision.

I dissent not because of any lack of respect for parochial schools but out of a feeling of depair that the respect which through history has been accorded the First Amendment is this day lost.

It should be remembered that in this case we deal with federal grants and with the command that "Congress shall make no law respecting an establishment of religion or prohibiting the free exercise thereof." The million-dollar grants sustained today put Madison's miserable "three pence" to shame. But he even thought, as I do, that even a small amount coming out of the pocket of taxpayers and going into the coffers of a church was not in keeping with our constitutional ideal.

I would reverse the judgment below.

i. Teaching of Evolution in Public Schools

EPPERSON *v.* ARKANSAS
393 US 97 (1968)

[A teacher in an Arkansas school brought an action for a declaration that the State's antievolution statutes were void and to enjoin her dismissal for violation

---

* Churches that owned an unrelated business enjoyed until recently a special tax advantage. Other charitable organizations were taxed on their "unrelated business income" derived from businesses regularly carried on by them. § 512 of the Int. Rev. Code of 1954. That tax was the normal tax and surtax. Thus in the case of income derived from corporations it was 22% on the first $25,000 and 48% on any additional income. § 11. Churches were exempted from this "unrelated business income" tax. § 511(a)(2). Thus they paid no federal taxes on any of their revenues. Under the Tax Reform Act of 1969, 83 Stat. 487, the tax advantage for unrelated business income as respects all businesses owned by churches (prior to May 27, 1969) will be terminated after January 1, 1976. . . .

of these statutes. The Supreme Court unanimously held that these statutes violated the First Amendment and the Fourteenth. The Court's opinion was by Justice Fortas. Justice Black wrote a concurring opinion.]

Mr. Justice Fortas delivered the opinion of the Court:

I

This appeal challenges the constitutionality of the "antievolution" statute which the State of Arkansas adopted in 1928 to prohibit the teaching in its public schools and universities of the theory that man evolved from other species of life. The statute was a product of the upsurge of "fundamentalist" religious fervor of the twenties. The Arkansas statute was an adaption of the famous Tennessee "monkey law" which that State adopted in 1925. The constitutionality of the Tennessee law was upheld by the Tennessee Supreme Court in the celebrated *Scopes* case in 1927.*

The Arkansas law makes it unlawful for a teacher in any state-supported school or university "to teach the theory or doctrine that mankind ascended or descended from a lower order of animals," or "to adopt or use in any such institution a textbook that teaches" this theory. Violation is a misdemeanor and subjects the violator to dismissal from his position.

The present case concerns the teaching of biology in a high school in Little Rock. According to the testimony, until the events here in litigation, the official textbook furnished for the high school biology course "did not have a section on the Darwinian Theory." Then, for the academic year 1965–1966, the school administration, on recommendation of the teachers in biology in the school system, adopted and prescribed a textbook which contained a chapter setting forth "the theory about the origin . . . of man from a lower form of animal."

Susan Epperson, a young woman who graduated from Arkansas school system and then obtained her master's degree in zoology at the University of Illinois, was employed by the Little Rock school system in the fall of 1964 to teach 10th grade biology at Central High School. At the start of the next academic year, 1965, she was confronted by the new textbook (which one surmises from the record was not unwelcome to her). She faced at least a literal dilemma because she was supposed to use the new textbook for classroom instruction and presumably to teach the statutorily condemned chapter; but to do so would be a criminal offense and subject her to dismissal.

She instituted the present action in the Chancery Court of the State, seeking a declaration that the Arkansas statute is void and enjoining the State and the defendant officials of the Little Rock school system from dismissing her for violation of the statute's provisions. H. H. Blanchard, a parent of children attending the public schools, intervened in support of the action.

The Chancery Court, in an opinion by Chancellor Murray O. Reed, held that

---

* *Scopes v. State of Tennessee,* 154 Tenn. 105, 289 S.W. 363 (1927). The Tennessee court, however, reversed Scopes' conviction on the ground that the jury and not the judge should have assessed the fine of $100. Since Scopes was no longer in the State's employ, it saw "nothing to be gained by prolonging the life of this bizarre case." It directed that a *nolle prosequi* be entered, in the interests of "the peace and dignity of the state."

the statute violated the Fourteenth Amendment to the United States Constitution. The court noted that this Amendment encompasses the prohibitions upon state interference with freedom of speech and thought which are contained in the First Amendment. Accordingly, it held that the challenged statute is unconstitutional because, in violation of the First Amendment, it "tends to hinder the quest for knowledge, restrict the freedom to learn, and restrain the freedom to teach." In this perspective, the Act, it held, was an unconstitutional and void restraint upon the freedom of speech guaranteed by the Constitution.

On appeal, the Supreme Court of Arkansas reversed. Its two-sentence opinion is set forth in the margin.* It sustained the statute as an exercise of the State's power to specify the curriculum in public schools. It did not address itself to the competing constitutional considerations.

Appeal was duly prosecuted to this Court under 28 U.S.C. § 1257(2). Only Arkansas, Mississippi, and Tennessee have such "antievolution" or "monkey" laws on their books. There is no record of any prosecutions in Arkansas under its statute. It is possible that the statute is presently more of a curiosity than a vital fact of life in these States. Nevertheless, the present case was brought, the appeal as of right is properly here, and it is our duty to decide the issues presented.

II

At the outset, it is urged upon us that the challenged statute is vague and uncertain and therefore within the condemnation of the Due Process Clause of the Fourteenth Amendment. The contention that the Act is vague and uncertain is supported by language in the brief opinion of Arkansas' Supreme Court. That court, perhaps reflecting the discomfort which the statute's quixotic prohibition necessarily engenders in the modern mind, stated that it "expresses no opinion" as to whether the Act prohibits "explanation" of the theory of evolution or merely forbids "teaching that the theory is true." Regardless of this uncertainty, the court held that the statute is constitutional.

On the other hand, counsel for the State, in oral argument in this Court, candidly stated that, despite the State Supreme Court's equivocation, Arkansas would interpret the statute "to mean that to make a student aware of the theory . . . just to teach that there was such a theory" would be grounds for dismissal and for prosecution under the statute; and he said "that the Supreme Court of Arkansas' opinion should be interpreted in that manner." He said "If Mrs. Epperson would tell her students that 'Here is Darwin's theory, that man ascended or descended from a

---

* "Per Curiam. Upon the principal issue, that of constitutionality, the court holds that Initiated Measure No. 1 of 1928, Ark.Stat.Ann., § 80–1627 and § 80–1628 (Repl. 1960), is a valid exercise of the state's power to specify the curriculum in its public schools. The court expresses no opinion on the question whether the Act prohibits any explanation of the theory of evolution or merely prohibits teaching that the theory is true; the answer not being necessary to a decision in the case, and the issue not having been raised.

"The decree is reversed and the cause dismissed.

"*Ward, J., concurs. Brown, J., dissents.*

"Concurrence. I agree with the first sentence in the majority opinion.

"To my mind, the rest of the opinion beclouds the clear announcement made in the first sentence.

"Paul Ward, Associate Justice."

lower form of being,' then I think she would be under this statute liable for prosecution."

In any event, we do not rest our decision upon the asserted vagueness of the statute. On either interpretation of its language, Arkansas' statute cannot stand. It is of no moment whether the law is deemed to prohibit mention of Darwin's theory, or to forbid any or all of the infinite varieties of communication embraced within the term "teaching." Under either interpretation, the law must be stricken because of its conflict with the constitutional prohibition of state laws respecting an establishment of religion or prohibiting the free exercise thereof. The overriding fact is that Arkansas' law selects from the body of knowledge a particular segment which it proscribes for the sole reason that it is deemed to conflict with a particular religious doctrine; that is, with a particular interpretation of the Book of Genesis by a particular religious group.

III

The antecedents of today's decision are many and unmistakable. They are rooted in the foundation soil of our Nation. They are fundamental to freedom.

Government in our democracy, state and national, must be neutral in matters of religious theory, doctrine, and practice. It may not be hostile to any religion or to the advocacy of no religion; and it may not aid, foster, or promote one religion or religious theory against another or even against the militant opposite. The First Amendment mandates governmental neutrality between religion and religion, and between religion and nonreligion.

As early as 1872, this Court said: "The law knows no heresy, and is committed to the support of no dogma, the establishment of no sect." *Watson* v. *Jones,* 13 Wall. 679, 728, 20 L.Ed. 666. This has been the interpretation of the great First Amendment which this Court has applied in the many and subtle problems which the ferment of our national life has presented for decision within the Amendment's broad command.

Judicial interposition in the operation of the public school system of the Nation raises problems requiring care and restraint. Our courts, however, have not failed to apply the First Amendment's mandate in our educational system where essential to safeguard the fundamental values of freedom of speech and inquiry and of belief. By and large, public education in our Nation is committed to the control of state and local authorities. Courts do not and cannot intervene in the resolution of conflicts which arise in the daily operation of school systems and which do not directly and sharply implicate basic constitutional values. On the other hand, "The vigilant protection of constitutional freedoms is nowhere more vital than in the community of American schools," *Shelton* v. *Tucker,* 364 US 479 (1960), and "This Court will be alert against invasions of academic freedom. . . ." *Barenblatt* v. *United State,* 360 US 109 (1959). As this Court said in *Keyishian* v. *Board of Regents,* the First Amendment "does not tolerate laws that cast a pall of orthodoxy over the classroom." 385 US 589 (1967). . . . There is and can be no doubt that the First Amendment does not permit the State to require that teaching and learning must be tailored to the principles of prohibitions of any religious sect or dogma. . . .

These precedents inevitably determine the result in the present case. The State's undoubted right to prescribe the curriculum for its public schools does not carry with it the right to prohibit, on pain of criminal penalty, the teaching of a scientific theory or doctrine where that prohibition is based upon reasons that violate the First Amendment. It is much too late to argue that the State may impose upon the teachers in its schools any conditions that it chooses, however restrictive they may be of constitutional guarantees. . . .

In the present case, there can be no doubt that Arkansas has sought to prevent its teachers from discussing the theory of evolution because it is contrary to the belief of some that the Book of Genesis must be the exclusive source of doctrine as to the origin of man. No suggestion has been made that Arkansas' law may be justified by considerations of state policy other than the religious views of some of its citizens. It is clear that fundamentalist sectarian conviction was and is the law's reason for existence. Its antecedent, Tennessee's "monkey law," candidly stated its purpose: to make it unlawful "to teach any theory that denies the story of the Divine Creation of man, as taught in the Bible, and to teach instead, that man has descended from a lower order of animals." Perhaps the sensational publicity attendant upon the *Scopes* trial induced Arkansas to adopt less explicit language. It eliminated Tennessee's reference to "the story of the Divine Creation of man" as taught in the Bible, but there is no doubt that the motivation for the law was the same: to suppress the teaching of a theory which, it was thought, "denied" the divine creation of man.

Arkansas' law cannot be defended as an act of religious neutrality. Arkansas did not seek to excise from the curricula of its schools and universities all discussion of the origin of man. The law's effort was confined to an attempt to blot out a particular theory because of its supposed conflict with the biblical account, literally read. Plainly, the law is contrary to the mandate of the First, and in violation of the Fourteenth, Amendment to the Constitution.

The judgment of the Supreme Court of Arkansas is reversed.

Reversed.

j. Liberty of Teaching in Private Schools

MEYER *v.* NEBRASKA
262 US 390 (1923)

[During and immediately after World War I some state legislatures and local school boards sought to prohibit the teaching of the German language. In some instances the prohibition had a special impact on the Lutheran parochial schools, which used German extensively in their teaching program. The supreme courts of Iowa, Ohio, and Nebraska upheld such prohibiting acts as constitutional on the broad ground that the legislature alone could decide what the common welfare demanded. These laws and decisions were challenged before the Supreme Court of the United States in the *Meyer Case*. The Court reversed all the state decisions by declaring the Nebraska statute unconstitutional as violative of the teacher's right to teach and of the parents' right to engage him. "Mere knowledge of the German language," said the Court, "cannot reasonably be regarded as harmful." The teacher of German engages, therefore, in a legal profession—a calling which cannot be outlawed by mere legislative fiat. The act also interfered wrongfully "with the opportunities of pupils to acquire knowledge, and with the power of parents to control the education of their own."

[A state may make reasonable regulations for all schools and may require that instruction be in English. But it may not prohibit the teaching of subjects in addition to those in the curriculum required by the state, when the teaching of such subjects will not be injurious to the health or morals of the child.

[Justices Holmes and Sutherland dissented. Holmes contended that reasonable minds might differ as to the wisdom of the Nebraska law, and therefore he was "unable to say that the Constitution of the United States prevents the experiment being tried." His dissent appears in *Bartels* v. *Iowa,* 262 US 404 (1923), a companion case to the *Meyer Case.*]

Mr. Justice McReynolds delivered the opinion of the Court:

Plaintiff in error was tried and convicted in the district court for Hamilton County, Nebraska, under an information which charged that on May 25, 1920, while an instructor in Zion Parochial School, he unlawfully taught the subject of reading in the German language to Raymond Parpart, a child of ten years, who had not attained and successfully passed the eighth grade. The information is based upon "An Act Relating to the Teaching of Foreign Languages in the State of Nebraska," approved April 9, 1919, which follows:

Sec. 1. No person, individually or as a teacher, shall, in any private, denominational, parochial or public school, teach any subject to any person in any language other than the English language.

Sec. 2. Languages, other than the English language, may be taught as languages only after a pupil shall have attained and successfully passed the eighth grade as evidenced by a certificate of graduation issued by the county superintendent of the county in which the child resides.

Sec. 3. Any person who violates any of the provisions of this act shall be deemed guilty of a misdemeanor and upon conviction, shall be subject to a fine of not less than twenty-five ($25) dollars, nor more than one hundred ($100) dollars or be confined in the county jail for any period not exceeding thirty days for each offense.

Sec. 4. Whereas, an emergency exists, this act shall be in force from and after its passage and approval.

The supreme court of the state affirmed the judgment of conviction. It declared the offense charged and established was "the direct and intentional teaching of the German language as a distinct subject to a child who had not passed the eighth grade," in the parochial school maintained by Zion Evangelical Lutheran Congregation, a collection of Biblical stories being used therefor. And it held that the statute forbidding this did not conflict with the 14th Amendment, but was a valid exercise of the police power. . . .

The problem for our determination is whether the statute, as construed and applied, unreasonably infringes the liberty guaranteed to the plaintiff in error by the 14th Amendment. "No state . . . shall deprive any person of life, liberty, or property without due process of law."

While this court has not attempted to define with exactness the liberty thus guaranteed, the term has received much consideration, and some of the included things have been definitely stated. Without doubt, it denotes not merely freedom from bodily restraint, but also the right of the individual to contract, to engage in any of the common occupations of life, to acquire useful knowledge, to marry, establish a home and bring up children, to worship God according to the dictates of his own conscience, and, generally, to enjoy those privileges long recognized at common law as essential to the orderly pursuit of happiness by free men. . . . The established doctrine is that this liberty may not be interfered with, under the guise of protecting the public interest, by legislative action which is arbitrary or without reasonable relation to some purpose within the competency of the state to effect. Determination by the legislature of what constitutes proper exercise of police power is not final or conclusive, but is subject to supervision by the courts. . . .

The American people have always regarded education and acquisition of knowledge as matters of supreme importance, which should be diligently promoted. The Ordinance of 1787 declares: "Religion, morality and knowledge being necessary to good government and the happiness of mankind, schools and the means of education shall forever be encouraged." Corresponding to the right of control, it is the natural duty of the parent to give his children education suitable to their station in life; and nearly all the states, including Nebraska, enforce this obligation by compulsory laws.

Practically, education of the young is only possible in schools conducted by especially qualified persons who devote themselves thereto. The calling always has been regarded as useful and honorable,—essential, indeed, to the public welfare. Mere knowledge of the German language cannot reasonably be regarded as harmful. Heretofore it has been commonly looked upon as helpful and desirable. Plaintiff in error taught this language in school as part of his occupation. His right thus to teach and the right of parents to engage him so to instruct their children, we think, are within the liberty of the Amendment.

The challenged statute forbids the teaching in school of any subject except in English; also the teaching of any other language until the pupil has attained and successfully passed the eighth grade, which is not usually accomplished before the age of twelve. The supreme court of the state has held that "the so-called ancient or dead languages" are not "within the spirit of the purpose of the act." . . . Latin, Greek, Hebrew are not proscribed; but German, French, Spanish, Italian, and every other alien speech are within the ban. Evidently the legislature has attempted materially to interfere with the calling of modern language teachers, with the opportunities of pupils to acquire knowledge, and with the power of parents to control the education of their own.

It is said the purpose of the legislation was to promote civic development by inhibiting training and education of the immature in foreign tongues and ideals before they could learn English and acquire American ideals; and "that the English language should be and become the mother tongue of all children reared in this state." It is also affirmed that the foreign-born population is very large, that certain communities commonly use foreign words, follow foreign leaders, move in a foreign atmosphere, and that the children are thereby hindered from becoming citizens of the most useful type, and the public safety is imperiled.

That the state may do much, go very far, indeed, in order to improve the quality of its citizens, physically, mentally, and morally, is clear; but the individual has certain fundamental rights which must be respected. The protection of the Constitution extends to all,—to those who speak other languages as well as to those born with English on the tongue. Perhaps it would be highly advantageous if all had ready understanding of our ordinary speech, but this cannot be coerced by methods which conflict with the Constitution,—a desirable end cannot be promoted by prohibited means.

For the welfare of his Ideal Commonwealth, Plato suggested a law which should provide

that the wives of our guardians are to be common, and their children are to be common, and no parent is to know his own child nor any child his parent. . . . The proper officers will take the offspring of the good parents to the pen or fold, and there they will deposit them with certain nurses who dwell in a separate quarter; but the offspring of the inferior, or of the better when they chance to be deformed, will be put away in some mysterious, unknown place, as they should be.

In order to submerge the individual and develop ideal citizens, Sparta assembled the males at seven into barracks and intrusted their subsequent education and training to official guardians. Although such measures have been deliberately approved by men of great genius, their ideas touching the relation between individual and state were wholly different from those upon which our institutions rest; and it hardly will be affirmed that any legislature could impose such restrictions upon the people of a state without doing violence to both letter and spirit of the Constitution.

The desire of the legislature to foster a homogeneous people with American ideals, prepared readily to understand current discussions of civic matters, is easy to appreciate. Unfortunate experiences during the late war, and aversion toward every characteristic of truculent adversaries, were certainly enough to quicken that aspiration. But the means adopted, we think, exceed the limitations upon the power of the state, and conflict with rights assured to plaintiff in error. The interference is plain enough, and no adequate reason therefor in time of peace and domestic tranquility has been shown.

The power of the state to compel attendance at some school and to make reasonable regulations for all schools, including a requirement that they shall give instructions in English, is not questioned. Nor has challenge been made of the state's power to prescribe a curriculum for institutions which it supports. Those matters are not within the present controversy. . . . No emergency has arisen which renders knowledge by a child of some language other than English so clearly harmful as to justify its inhibition, with the consequent infringement of rights long freely enjoyed. We are constrained to conclude that the statute as applied is arbitrary, and without reasonable relation to any end within the competency of the state.

As the statute undertakes to interfere only with teaching which involves a modern language, leaving complete freedom as to other matters, there seems no adequate foundation for the suggestion that the purpose was to protect the child's health by limiting his mental activities. It is well known that proficiency in a foreign language seldom comes to one not instructed at an early age, and experience shows that this is not injurious to the health, morals, or understanding of the ordinary child. . . .

Reversed.

k. The Parochial School and Compulsory School Attendance Laws

PIERCE *v.* SOCIETY OF THE SISTERS OF THE HOLY NAME
268 US 510 (1925)

[Oregon by statute attempted to prohibit parochial and private schools for children between eight and sixteen by requiring their attendance at public schools only. The Supreme Court unanimously held the statute unconstitutional; children, said the Court, are not mere creatures of the state. A state may not attempt to standardize its children by forcing them to accept public school instruction only.]

Mr. Justice McReynolds delivered the opinion of the Court:

The challenged act, effective September 1, 1926, requires every parent, guardian, or other person having control or charge or custody of a child between eight and sixteen years to send him "to a public school for the period of time a public school shall be held during the current year" in the district where the child resides; and failure so to do is declared a misdemeanor. There are exemptions—not specially important here—for children who are not normal, or who have completed the eighth grade, or whose parents or private teachers reside at considerable distances from any public school, or who hold special permits from the county superintendent. The manifest purpose is to compel general attendance at public schools by normal children, between eight and sixteen, who have not completed the eighth grade. And without doubt enforcement of the statute would seriously impair, perhaps destroy, the profitable features of appellees' business, and greatly diminish the value of their property.

Appellee the Society of Sisters is an Oregon corporation, organized in 1880, with power to care for orphans, educate and instruct the youth, establish and maintain academies or schools, and acquire necessary real and personal property. It has long devoted its property and effort to the secular and religious education and care of children, and has acquired the valuable good will of many parents and guardians. It conducts interdependent primary and high schools and junior colleges, and maintains orphanages for the custody and control of children between eight and sixteen. In its primary schools many children between those ages are taught the subjects usually pursued in Oregon public schools during the first eight years. Systematic religious instruction and moral training according to the tenets of the Roman Catholic Church are also regularly provided. All courses of study, both temporal and religious, contemplate continuity of training under appellee's charge; the primary schools are essential to the system and the most profitable. It owns valuable buildings, especially constructed and equipped for school purposes. The business is remunerative—the annual income from primary schools exceeds $30,000—and the successful conduct of this requires long-time contracts with teachers and parents. The Compulsory Education Act of 1922 has already caused the withdrawal from its schools of children who would otherwise continue, and their income has steadily declined. The appellants, public officers, have proclaimed their purpose strictly to enforce the statute.

After setting out the above facts, the Society's bill alleges that the enactment conflicts with the right of parents to choose schools where their children will receive appropriate mental and religious training, the right of the child to influence the parents' choice of a school, the right of schools and teachers therein to engage in a useful business or profession, and is accordingly repugnant to the Constitution and void. And, further, that unless enforcement of the measure is enjoined, the corporation's business and property will suffer irreparable injury.

Appellee Hill Military Academy is a private corporation organized in 1908 under the laws of Oregon, engaged in owning, operating, and conducting for profit an elementary, college preparatory, and military training school for boys between the ages of five and twenty-one years. The average attendance is one hundred, and the annual fees received for each student amount to some $800. The elementary department is divided into eight grades, as in the public schools; the college preparatory department has four grades, similar to those of the public high schools; the courses of study conform to the requirements of the state board of education. Military instruction and training are also given, under the supervision of an Army officer. It owns considerable real and personal property, some useful only for school purposes. The business and incident good will are very valuable. In order to conduct its affairs long-time contracts must be made for supplies, equipment, teachers, and pupils. Appellants, law officers of the state and county, have publicly announced that the Act of November 7, 1922, is valid, and have declared their intention to enforce it. By reason of the statute and threat of enforcement, appellee's business is being destroyed and its property depreciated; parents and guardians are refusing to make contracts for the future instruction of their sons, and some are being withdrawn. . . .

No question is raised concerning the power of the state reasonably to regulate all schools, to inspect, supervise, and examine them, their teachers and pupils; to require that all children of proper age attend some school, that teachers shall be of good moral character and patriotic disposition, that certain studies plainly essential to good citizenship must be taught, and that nothing be taught which is manifestly inimical to the public welfare.

The inevitable practical result of enforcing the act under consideration would be destruction of appellees' primary schools, and perhaps all other private primary schools for normal children within the state of Oregon. Appellees are engaged in a kind of undertaking not inherently harmful, but long regarded as useful and meritorious. Certainly there is nothing in the present records to indicate that they have failed to discharge their obligations to patrons, students, or the state. And there are no peculiar circumstances or present emergencies which demand extraordinary measures relative to primary education.

. . . The fundamental theory of liberty upon which all governments in this

Union repose excludes any general power of the state to standardize its children by forcing them to accept instruction from public teachers only. The child is not the mere creature of the state; those who nurture him and direct his destiny have the right, coupled with the high duty, to recognize and prepare him for additional obligations.

Appellees are corporations, and therefore, it is said, they cannot claim for themselves the liberty which the 14th Amendment guarantees. Accepted in the proper sense, this is true. . . . But they have business and property for which they claim protection. These are threatened with destruction through the unwarranted compulsion which appellants are exercising over present and prospective patrons of their schools. And this court has gone very far to protect against loss threatened by such action. . . .

[Decrees enjoining enforcement of the statute affirmed.]

1. Compulsory School Attendance Laws and the Rights of Parents: The Amish School Case

WISCONSIN *v.* YODER
406 US 205 (1972)

[The Wisconsin compulsory school attendance law required parents to send their children to a public or private school until they reach the age of 16. The Old Order Amish religion forbade attendance at school beyond the eighth grade. The Supreme Court unanimously reversed the conviction of Amish parents who had violated the compulsory attendance law. The Court held that, as applied to these Old Order Amish parents, the law violated the Free Exercise Clause of the First Amendment. The opinion for the Court was by Chief Justice Burger. In a concurring opinion by Justice Stewart, joined by Justice Brennan, stress was placed on the point that the case did not involve the claims of the children, but only those of the parents; that there was nothing in the record to indicate any religious differences between the parents and the children. A concurring opinion of Justice White was joined by Justices Brennan and Stewart. Justice Douglas, dissenting in part, emphasized the religious rights of children, independent of the rights of their parents; and he argued, too, that the constitutional principle involved in the case should apply not only to the Amish but to anyone who could show that the compulsory school attendance law conflicts with his conscience. Justices Powell and Rehnquist did not participate in the case.]

Mr. Chief Justice Burger delivered the opinion of the Court:

On petition of the State of Wisconsin, we granted the writ in this case to review a decision of the Wisconsin Supreme Court holding that respondents' convictions for violating the State's compulsory school attendance law were invalid under the Free Exercise Clause of the First Amendment to the United States Constitution made applicable to the State by the Fourteenth Amendment. For the reasons hereafter stated we affirm the judgment of the Supreme Court of Wisconsin.

Respondents Jonas Yoder and Adin Yutzy are members of the Old Order Amish

Religion, and respondent Wallace Miller is a member of the Conservative Amish Mennonite Church. They and their families are residents of Green County, Wisconsin. Wisconsin's compulsory school attendance law required them to cause their children to attend public or private school until reaching age 16, but the respondents declined to send their children, ages 14 and 15, to public school after completing the eighth grade. The children were not enrolled in any private school, or within any recognized exception to the compulsory attendance law, and they are conceded to be subject to the Wisconsin statute.

On complaint of the school district administrator for the public schools, respondents were charged, tried, and convicted of violating the compulsory attendance law in Green County Court and were fined the sum of $5 each.* Respondents defended on the ground that the application of the compulsory attendance law violated their rights under the First and Fourteenth Amendments. The trial testimony showed that respondents believed, in accordance with the tenets of Old Order Amish communities generally, that their children's attendance at high school, public or private, was contrary to the Amish religion and way of life. They believed that by sending their children to high school, they would not only expose themselves to the danger of the censure of the church community, but, as found by the county court, endanger their own salvation and that of their children. The State stipulated that respondents' religious beliefs were sincere.

In support of their position, respondents presented as expert witnesses scholars on religion and education whose testimony is uncontradicted. They expressed their opinions on the relationship of the Amish belief concerning school attendance to the more general tenets of their religion, and described the impact that compulsory high school attendance could have on the continued survival of Amish communities as they exist in the United States today. The history of the Amish sect was given in some detail, beginning with the Swiss Anabaptists of the 16th century who rejected institutionalized churches and sought to return to the early, simple, Christian life de-emphasizing material success, rejecting the competitive spirit, and seeking to insulate themselves from the modern world. As a result of their common heritage, Old Order Amish communities today are characterized by a fundamental belief that salvation requires life in a church community separate and apart from the world and worldly influence. This concept of life aloof from the world and its values is central to their faith.

* Prior to trial, the attorney for respondents wrote the State Superintendent of Public Instruction in an effort to explore the possibilities for a compromise settlement. Among other possibilities, he suggested that perhaps the State Superintendent could administratively determine that the Amish could satisfy the compulsory attendance law by establishing their own vocational training plan similar to one which has been established in Pennsylvania. Under the Pennsylvania plan, Amish children of high school age are required to attend an Amish vocational school for three hours a week, during which time they are taught such subjects as English, mathematics, health, and social studies by an Amish teacher. For the balance of the week, the children perform farm and household duties under parental supervision, and keep a journal of their daily activities. The major portion of the curriculum is home projects in agriculture and homemaking. See generally, Hostetler and Huntington, *Children in Amish Society; Socialization and Community Education*, c. 5 (1971). A similar program has been instituted in Indiana. . . .

The Superintendent rejected this proposal on the ground that it would not afford Amish children "substantially equivalent education" to that offered in the schools of the area.

A related feature of Old Order Amish communities is their devotion to a life in harmony with nature and the soil, as exemplified by the simple life of the early Christian era which continued in America during much of our early national life. Amish beliefs require members of the community to make their living by farming or closely related activities. Broadly speaking, the Old Order Amish religion pervades and determines the entire mode of life of its adherents. Their conduct is regulated in great detail by the *Ordnung,* or rules, of the church community. Adult baptism, which occurs in late adolescence, is the time at which Amish young people voluntarily undertake heavy obligations, not unlike the Bar Mitzvah of the Jews, to abide by the rules of the church community.

Amish objection to formal education beyond the eighth grade is firmly grounded in these central religious concepts. They object to the high school and higher education generally because the values it teaches are in marked variance with Amish values and the Amish way of life; they view secondary school education as an impermissible exposure of their children to a "worldly" influence in conflict with their beliefs. The high school tends to emphasize intellectual and scientific accomplishments, self-distinction, competitiveness, worldly success, and social life with other students. Amish society emphasizes informal learning-through-doing, a life of "goodness," rather than a life of intellect, wisdom, rather than technical knowledge, community welfare rather than competition, and separation, rather than integration with contemporary worldly society.

Formal high school education beyond the eighth grade is contrary to Amish beliefs not only because it places Amish children in an environment hostile to Amish beliefs with increasing emphasis on competition in class work and sports and with pressure to conform to the styles, manners and ways of the peer group, but because it takes them away from their community, physically, and emotionally, during the crucial and formative adolescent period of life. During this period, the children must acquire Amish attitudes favoring manual work and self-reliance and the specific skills needed to perform the adult role of an Amish farmer or housewife. They must learn to enjoy physical labor. Once a child has learned basic reading, writing, and elementary mathematics, these traits, skills, and attitudes admittedly fall within the category of those best learned through example and "doing" rather than in a classroom. And, at this time in life, the Amish child must also grow in his faith and his relationship to the Amish community if he is to be prepared to accept the heavy obligations imposed by adult baptism. In short, high school attendance with teachers who are not of the Amish faith—and may even be hostile to it—interposes a serious barrier to the integration of the Amish child into the Amish religious community. Dr. John Hostetler, one of the experts on Amish society, testified that the modern high school is not equipped, in curriculum or social environment, to impart the values promoted by Amish society.

The Amish do not object to elementary education through the first eight grades as a general proposition because they agree that their children must have basic skills in the "three R's" in order to read the Bible, to be good farmers and citizens and to be able to deal with non-Amish people when necessary in the course of daily affairs. They view such a basic education as acceptable because it does not significantly expose their children to worldly values or interfere with their development in the Amish community during the crucial adolescent period. While Amish accept compulsory elementary education generally, wherever possible they have established their own elementary schools, in many respects like the small local schools of the past. In the Amish belief, higher learning tends to develop values they reject as influences that alienate man from God.

On the basis of such considerations, Dr. Hostetler testified that compulsory high school attendance could not only result in great psychological harm to Amish children, because of the conflicts it would produce, but would, in his opinion, ultimately result in the destruction of the Old Order Amish church community as it exists in the United States today. The testimony of Dr. Donald A. Erickson, an expert witness on education, also showed that the Amish succeed in preparing their high school age children to be productive members of the Amish community. He described their system of learning-through-doing the skills directly relevant to their adult roles in the Amish community as "ideal" and perhaps superior to ordinary high school education. The evidence also showed that the Amish have an excellent record as law-abiding and generally self-sufficient members of society.

Although the trial court in its careful findings determined that the Wisconsin compulsory school attendance law "does interfere with the freedom of the defendants to act in accordance with their sincere religious belief" it also concluded that the requirement of high school attendance until age 16 was a "reasonable and constitutional" exercise of governmental power, and therefore denied the motion to dismiss the charges. The Wisconsin Circuit Court affirmed the convictions. The Wisconsin Supreme Court, however, sustained respondents' claim under the Free Exercise Clause of the First Amendment and reversed the convictions. A majority of the court was of the opinion that the State had failed to make an adequate showing that its interest in "establishing and maintaining an education system overrides the defendants' right to the free exercise of their religion."

I

There is no doubt as to the power of a State, having a high responsibility for education of its citizens, to impose reasonable regulations for the control and duration of basic education. See, *e.g., Pierce* v. *Society of Sisters,* 268 US 510, 534 (1925). Providing public schools ranks at the very apex of the function of a State. Yet even this paramount responsibility was, in *Pierce,* made to yield to the right of parents to provide an equivalent education in a privately operated system. There the Court held that Oregon's statute compelling attendance in a public school from age eight to age 16 unreasonably interfered with the interest of parents in directing the rearing of their offspring including their education in church-operated schools. As that case suggests, the values of parental direction of the religious upbringing and education of their children in their early and formative years have a high place in our society. . . . Thus, a State's interest in universal education, however highly we rank it, is not totally free from a balancing process when it impinges on other fundamental rights and interests, such as those specifically protected by the Free Exercise Clause of the First Amendment and the traditional interest of parents with respect to the religious upbringing of their children so long as they, in the words of *Pierce,* "prepare [them] for additional obligations."

It follows that in order for Wisconsin to compel school attendance beyond the eighth grade against a claim that such attendance interferes with the practice of a legitimate religious belief, it must appear either that the State does not deny the free exercise of religious belief by its requirement, or that there is a state interest of sufficient magnitude to override the interest claiming protection under the Free Exercise Clause. Long before there was general acknowledgment of the need for universal formal education, the Religion Clauses had specifically and firmly fixed the right to free exercise of religious beliefs, and buttressing this fundamental right was an equally firm, even if less explicit, prohibition against the establishment of any religion by government. The values underlying these two provisions relating to religion have been zealously protected, sometimes even at the expense of other interests of admittedly high social importance. The invalidation of financial aid to parochial schools by government grants for a salary subsidy for teachers is but one example of the extent to which courts have gone in this regard, notwithstanding that such aid programs were legislatively determined to be in the public interest and the service of sound educational policy by States and by Congress. *Lemon* v. *Kurtzman,* 403 US 602 (1971); *Tilton* v. *Richardson,* 403 US 672 (1971). . . .

The essence of all that has been said and written on the subject is that only those interests of the highest order and those not otherwise served can overbalance legitimate claims to the free exercise of religion. We can accept it as settled, therefore, that however strong the State's interest in universal compulsory education, it is by no means absolute to the exclusion or subordination of all other interests. . . .

II

We come then to the quality of the claims of the respondents concerning the alleged encroachment of Wisconsin's compulsory school attendance statute on their rights and the rights of their children to the free exercise of the religious beliefs they and their forbears have adhered to for almost three centuries. In evaluating those claims we must be careful to determine whether the Amish religious faith and their mode of life are, as they claim, inseparable and interdependent. A way of life, however virtuous and admirable, may not be interposed as a barrier to reasonable state regulation of education if it is based on purely secular considerations; to have the protection of the Religion Clauses, the claims must be rooted in religious belief. Although a determination of what is a "religious" belief or practice entitled to constitutional protection may present a most delicate question, the very concept of ordered liberty precludes allowing every person to make his own standards on matters of conduct in which society as a whole has important interests. Thus, if the Amish asserted their claims because of their subjective evaluation and rejection of the contemporary secular values accepted by the majority, much as Thoreau rejected the social values of his time and isolated himself at Walden Pond, their claim would not rest on a religious basis. Thoreau's choice was philosophical and personal rather than religious, and such belief does not rise to the demands of the Religion Clause.

Giving no weight to such secular considerations, however, we see that the record in this case abundantly supports the claim that the traditional way of life of the

Amish is not merely a matter of personal preference, but one of deep religious conviction, shared by an organized group, and intimately related to daily living. That the Old Order Amish daily life and religious practice stems from their faith is shown by the fact that it is in response to their literal interpretation of the Biblical injunction from the Epistle of Paul to the Romans, "Be not conformed to this world. . . ." This command is fundamental to the Amish faith. Moreover, for the Old Order Amish, religion is not simply a matter of theocratic belief. As the expert witnesses explained, the Old Order Amish religion pervades and determines virtually their entire way of life, regulating it with the detail of the Talmudic diet through the strictly enforced rules of the church community.

The record shows that the respondents' religious beliefs and attitude toward life, family, and home have remained constant—perhaps some would say static—in a period of unparalleled progress in human knowledge generally and great changes in education. The respondents freely concede, and indeed assert as an article of faith, that their religious beliefs and what we would today call "life style" have not altered in fundamentals for centuries. Their way of life in a church-oriented community, separated from the outside world and "worldly" influences, their attachment to nature and the soil, is a way inherently simple and uncomplicated, albeit difficult to preserve against the pressure to conform. Their rejection of telephones, automobiles, radios, and television, their mode of dress, of speech, their habits of manual work do indeed set them apart from much of contemporary society; these customs are both symbolic and practical.

As the society around the Amish has become more populous, urban, industrialized, and complex, particularly in this century, government regulation of human affairs has correspondingly become more detailed and pervasive. The Amish mode of life has thus come into conflict increasingly with requirements of contemporary society exerting a hydraulic insistence on conformity to majoritarian standards. So long as compulsory education laws were confined to eight grades of elementary basic education imparted in a nearby rural schoolhouse, with a large proportion of students of the Amish faith, the Old Order Amish had little basis to fear that school attendance would expose their children to the worldly influence they reject. But modern compulsory secondary education in rural areas is now largely carried on in a consolidated school, often remote from the student's home and alien to his daily home life. As the record so strongly shows, the values and programs of the modern secondary school are in sharp conflict with the fundamental mode of life mandated by the Amish religion; modern laws requiring compulsory secondary education have accordingly engendered great concern and conflict. The conclusion is inescapable that secondary schooling, by exposing Amish children to worldly influences in terms of attitudes, goals, and values contrary to beliefs, and by substantially interfering with the religious development of the Amish child and his integration into the way of life of the Amish faith community at the crucial adolescent state of development, contravenes the basic religious tenets and practice of the Amish faith, both as to the parent and the child.

The impact of the compulsory attendance law on respondents' practice of the Amish religion is not only severe, but inescapable, for the Wisconsin law affirmatively compels them, under threat of criminal sanction, to perform acts undeniably at odds with fundamental tenets of their religious beliefs. . . . Nor is the impact of the compulsory attendance law confined to grave interference with important Amish religious tenets from a subjective point of view. It carries with it precisely the kind of objective danger to the free exercise of religion which the First Amendment was designed to prevent. As the record shows, compulsory school attendance to age 16 for Amish children carries with it a very real threat of undermining the Amish community and religious practice as it exists today; they must either abandon belief and be assimilated into society at large, or be forced to migrate to some other and more tolerant region.*

In sum, the unchallenged testimony of acknowledged experts in education and religious history, almost 300 years of consistent practice, and strong evidence of a sustained faith pervading and regulating respondents' entire mode of life support the claim that enforcement of the State's requirement of compulsory formal education after the eighth grade would gravely endanger if not destroy the free exercise of respondents' religious beliefs.

III

Neither the findings of the trial court nor the Amish claims as to the nature of their faith are challenged in this Court by the State of Wisconsin. Its position is that the State's interest in universal compulsory formal secondary education to age 16 is so great that it is paramount to the undisputed claims of respondents that their mode of preparing their youth for Amish life, after the traditional elementary education, is an essential part of their religious belief and practice. Nor does the State undertake to meet the claim that the Amish mode of life and education is inseparable from and a part of the basic tenets of their religion—indeed, as much a part of their religious belief and practices as baptism, the confessional, or a sabbath may be for others.

Wisconsin concedes that under the Religion Clauses religious beliefs are absolutely free from the State's control, but it argues that "actions," even though religiously grounded, are outside the protection of the First Amendment. But our decisions have rejected the idea that religiously grounded conduct is always outside the protection of the Free Exercise Clause. It is true that activities of individuals, even when religiously based, are often subject to regulation by the States in the exercise of their undoubted power to promote the health, safety, and general welfare, or the Federal Government in the exercise of its delegated powers. . . . But to agree that religiously grounded conduct must often be subject to the broad police power of the State is not to deny that there are areas of conduct protected by the Free Exercise Clause of the First Amendment and thus beyond the power of the State to control, even under regulations of general applicability. . . . This case, therefore, does not become easier because respondents were convicted for their "actions" in refusing to send their children to the public high school; in this con-

* Some States have developed working arrangements with the Amish regarding high school attendance. . . . However, the danger to the continued existence of an ancient religious faith cannot be ignored simply because of the assumption that its adherents will continue to be able, at considerable sacrifice, to relocate in some more tolerant State or country or work out accommodations under threat of criminal prosecution. Forced migration of religious minorities was an evil which lay at the heart of the Religion Clauses. . . .

text belief and action cannot be neatly confined in logic-tight compartments. . . .

Nor can this case be disposed of on the grounds that Wisconsin's requirement for school attendance to age 16 applies uniformly to all citizens of the State and does not, on its face, discriminate against religions or a particular religion, or that it is motivated by legitimate secular concerns. A regulation neutral on its face may, in its application, nonetheless offend the constitutional requirements for governmental neutrality if it unduly burdens the free exercise of religion. . . . The Court must not ignore the danger that an exception from a general obligation of citizenship on religious grounds may run afoul of the Establishment Clause, but that danger cannot be allowed to prevent any exception no matter how vital it may be to the protection of values promoted by the right of free exercise. By preserving doctrinal flexibility and recognizing the need for a sensible and realistic application of the Religion Clauses

we have been able to chart a course that preserved the autonomy and freedom of religious bodies while avoiding any semblance of established religion. This is a "tight rope" and one we have successfully traversed. *Walz* v. *Tax Commission*, 397 US 672.

We turn, then to the State's broader contention that its interest in its system of compulsory education is so compelling that even the established religious practices of the Amish must give way. Where fundamental claims of religious freedom are at stake, however, we cannot accept such a sweeping claim; despite its admitted validity in the generality of cases, we must searchingly examine the interests which the State seeks to promote by its requirement for compulsory education to age 16, and the impediment to those objectives that would flow from recognizing the claimed Amish exemption. . . .

The State advances two primary arguments in support of its system of compulsory education. It notes, as Thomas Jefferson pointed out early in our history, that some degree of education is necessary to prepare citizens to participate effectively and intelligently in our open political system if we are to preserve freedom and independence. Further, education prepares individuals to be self-reliant and self-sufficient participants in society. We accept these propositions.

However, the evidence adduced by the Amish in this case is persuasively to the effect that an additional one or two years of formal high school for Amish children in place of their long-established program of informal vocational education would do little to serve those interests. Respondents' experts testified at trial, without challenge, that the value of all education must be assessed in terms of its capacity to prepare the child for life. It is one thing to say that compulsory education for a year or two beyond the eighth grade may be necessary when its goal is the preparation of the child for life in modern society as the majority live, but it is quite another if the goal of education be viewed as the preparation of the child for life in the separated agrarian community that is the keystone of the Amish faith. . . .

The State attacks respondents' position as one fostering "ignorance" from which the child must be protected by the State. No one can question the State's duty to protect children from ignorance but this argument does not square with the facts disclosed in the record. Whatever their idiosyncrasies as seen by the majority, this record strongly shows that the Amish community has been a highly successful social unit within our society even if apart from the conventional "mainstream." Its members are productive and very law-abiding members of society; they reject public welfare in any of its usual modern forms. The Congress itself recognized their self-sufficiency by authorizing exemption of such groups as the Amish from the obligation to pay social security taxes.*

It is neither fair nor correct to suggest that the Amish are opposed to education beyond the eighth grade level. What this record shows is that they are opposed to conventional formal education of the type provided by a certified high school because it comes at the child's crucial adolescent period of religious development. Dr. Donald Erickson, for example, testified that their system of learning-by-doing was an "ideal system" of education in terms of preparing Amish children for life as adults in the Amish community, and that "I would be inclined to say they do a better job in this than most of the rest of us do." As he put it, "these people aren't purporting to be learned people, and it seems to me that the self-sufficiency of the community is the best evidence I can point to—whatever is being done seems to function well."

We must not forget that in the Middle Ages important values of the civilization of the western world were preserved by members of religious orders who isolated themselves from all worldly influences against great obstacles. There can be no assumption that today's majority is "right" and the Amish and others like them are "wrong." A way of life that is odd or even erratic but interferes with no rights or interests of others is not to be condemned because it is different.

The State, however, supports its interest in providing an additional one or two years of compulsory high school education to Amish children because of the possibility that some such children will choose to leave the Amish community, and that if this occurs they will be ill-equipped for life. The State argues that if Amish children leave their church they should not be in the position of making their way in the world without the education available in the one or two additional years the State requires. However, on this record, that argument is highly speculative. There is no specific evidence of the loss of Amish adherents by attrition, nor is there any showing that upon leaving the Amish community Amish children, with their practical agricultural training and habits of industry and self-reliance would become burdens on society because of educational shortcomings. Indeed, this argument of the State appears to rest primarily on the State's mistaken assumption, already noted, that the Amish do not provide any education for their children beyond the eighth grade, but allow them to grow in "ignorance." To the contrary, not only do the Amish accept the necessity for formal schooling through the eighth grade level, but continue to provide what has been characterized by the undisputed testi-

* The law, 26 U.S.C. § 1402(h), authorizes the Secretary of Health, Education, and Welfare to exempt members of "a recognized religious sect" existing at all times since December 13, 1950, from the obligation to pay social security taxes if they are, by reason of the tenets of their sect, opposed to receipt of such benefits and agree to waive them, provided the Secretary finds that the Sect makes reasonable provision for its dependent members. The history of the exemption shows it was enacted with the situation of the Old Order Amish specifically in view. H.R.Rep.No.213, 89th Cong., 1st Sess. 101–102 (1965).

The record in this case establishes without contradiction that the Green County Amish had never been known to commit crimes, that none had been known to receive public assistance, and that none were unemployed.

mony of expert educators as an "ideal" vocational education for their children in the adolescent years.

There is nothing in this record to suggest that the Amish qualities of reliability, self-reliance, and dedication to work would fail to find ready markets in today's society. Absent some contrary evidence supporting the State's position, we are unwilling to assume that persons possessing such valuable vocational skills and habits are doomed to become burdens on society should they determine to leave the Amish faith, nor is there any basis in the record to warrant a finding that an additional one or two years of formal school education beyond the eighth grade would serve to eliminate any such problem that might exist.

Insofar as the State's claim rests on the view that a brief additional period of formal education is imperative to enable the Amish to participate effectively and intelligently in our democratic process, it must fall. The Amish alternative to formal secondary school education has enabled them to function effectively in their day-to-day life under self-imposed limitations on relations with the world, and to survive and prosper in contemporary society as a separate, sharply identifiable and highly self-sufficient community for more than 200 years in this country. In itself this is strong evidence that they are capable of fulfilling the social and political responsibilities of citizenship without compelled attendance beyond the eighth grade at the price of jeopardizing their free exercise of religious belief.* When Thomas Jefferson emphasized the need for education as a bulwark of a free people against tyranny, there is nothing to indicate he had in mind compulsory education through any fixed age beyond a basic education. Indeed, the Amish communities singularly parallel and reflect many of the virtues of Jefferson's ideal of the "sturdy yeoman" who would form the basis of what he considered as the ideal of a democratic society.† Even their idiosyncratic separateness exemplifies the diversity we profess to admire and encourage.

The requirement for compulsory education beyond the eighth grade is a relatively recent development in our history. Less than 60 years ago, the educational requirements of almost all of the States were satisfied by completion of the elementary grades, at least where the child was regularly and lawfully employed.‡ The

---

* All of the children involved in this case are graduates of the eighth grade. In the county court, the defense introduced a study by Dr. Hostetler indicating that Amish children in the eighth grade achieved comparably to non-Amish children in the basic skills. . . .

† While Jefferson recognized that education was essential to the welfare and liberty of the people, he was reluctant to directly force instruction of children "in opposition to the will of the parent." Instead he proposed that state citizenship be conditioned on the ability to "read readily in some tongue, native or acquired." Letter, T. Jefferson to J. Cabell, Sept. 9, 1817, 17 *Writings of Thomas Jefferson*, 417, 423–424 (Mem., ed., 1904). And it is clear that, so far as the mass of the people were concerned, he envisaged that a basic education in the "three R's" would sufficiently meet the interests of the State. He suggested that after completion of elementary school, "those destined for labor will engage in the business of agriculture, or enter into apprenticeships to such handicraft art as may be their choice." Letter from T. Jefferson to P. Carr, Sept. 17, 1814, in *Thomas Jefferson and Education in a Republic*, 93–106 (Arrowwood, ed., 1930). . . .

‡ See Dept. of Interior, Bureau of Education, Bulletin No. 47, Digest of State Laws Relating to Public Education, 527–559 (1915); Joint Hearings on S. 2475 and H.R. 7200 before the Senate Committee on Education and Labor and the House Committee on Labor, 75th Cong., 1st Sess., pt. 2, at 416. [Continued.]

independence and successful social functioning of the Amish community for a period approaching almost three centuries and more than 200 years in this country is strong evidence that there is at best a speculative gain, in terms of meeting the duties of citizenship, from an additional one or two years of compulsory formal education. Against this background it would require a more particularized showing from the State on this point to justify the severe interference with religious freedom such additional compulsory attendance would entail.

We should also note that compulsory education and child labor laws find their historical origin in common humanitarion instincts, and that the age limits of both laws have been coordinated to achieve their related objectives. In the context of this case, such considerations, if anything, support rather than detract from respondents' position. The origins of the requirement for school attendance to age 16, an age falling after the completion of elementary school but before completion of high school, are not entirely clear. But to some extent such laws reflected the movement to prohibit most child labor under age 16 that culminated in the provisions of the Federal Fair Labor Standards Act of 1938. It is true, then, that the 16-year child labor age limit may to some degree derive from a contemporary impression that children should be in school until that age. But at the same time, it cannot be denied that, conversely, the 16-year education limit reflects, in substantial measure, the concern that children under that age not be employed under conditions hazardous to their health, or in work that should be performed by adults.

The requirement of compulsory schooling to age 16 must therefore be viewed as aimed not merely at providing educational opportunities for children, but as an alternative to the equally undesirable consequence of unhealthful child labor displacing adult workers, or, on the other hand, forced idleness. The two kinds of statutes—compulsory school attendance and child labor laws—tend to keep children of certain ages off the labor market and in school; this in turn provides opportunity to prepare for a livelihood of a higher order than that children could perform without education and protects their health in adolescence.

In these terms, Wisconsin's interest in compelling the school attendance of Amish children to age 16 emerges as somewhat less substantial than requiring such attendance for children generally. For, while agricultural employment is not totally outside the legitimate concerns of the child labor laws, employment of children under parental guidance and on the family farm from age 14 to age 16 is an ancient tradition which lies at the periphery of the objectives of such laws.* There

---

Even today, an eighth grade education fully satisfies the educational requirements of at least six States. . . . (Mississippi has no compulsory education law.) A number of other States have flexible provisions permitting children aged 14 or having completed the eighth grade to be excused from school in order to engage in lawful employment. . . .

An eighth grade education satisfied Wisconsin's formal education requirements until 1933. See Wisc.Laws 1927, c. 425, § 97; Laws 1933, c. 143. (Prior to 1933, provision was made for attendance at continuation or vocational schools by working children past the eighth grade, but only if one was maintained by the community in question.) . . .

* The Federal Fair Labor Standards Act of 1938 excludes from its definition of "oppressive child labor" employment of a child under age 16 by "a parent . . . employing his own child . . . in an occupation other than manufacturing or mining or an occupation found by the Secretary of Labor to be particularly hazardous for the employment of children between the ages of sixteen and eighteen years or detrimental to their health or well-being." 29 U.S.C. § 203(*l*).

is no intimation that the Amish employment of their children on family farms is in any way deleterious to their health or that Amish parents exploit children at tender years. Any such inference would be contrary to the record before us. Moreover, employment of Amish children on the family farm does not present the undesirable economic aspects of eliminating jobs which might otherwise be held by adults.

IV

Finally, the State, on authority of *Prince* v. *Massachusetts,* argues that a decision exempting Amish children from the State's requirement fails to recognize the substantive right of the Amish child to a secondary education, and fails to give due regard to the power of the State as *parens patriae* to extend the benefit of secondary education to children regardless of the wishes of their parents. Taken at its broadest sweep, the Court's language in *Prince,* might be read to give support to the State's position. However, the Court was not confronted in *Prince* with a situation comparable to that of the Amish as revealed in this record; this is shown by the Court's severe characterization of the evils which it thought the legislature could legitimately associate with child labor, even when performed in the company of an adult. The Court later took great care to confine *Prince* to a narrow scope in *Sherbert* v. *Verner* when it stated:

On the other hand, the Court has rejected challenges under the Free Exercise Clause to governmental regulation of certain overt acts prompted by religious beliefs or principles, for "even when the action is in accord with one's religious convictions, [it] is not totally free from legislative restrictions." *Braunfeld* v. *Brown,* 366 US 599. The conduct or actions so regulated have invariably posed some substantial threat to public safety, peace or order. . . .

This case, of course, is not one in which any harm to the physical or mental health of the child or to the public safety, peace, order, or welfare has been demonstrated or may be properly inferred. The record is to the contrary, and any reliance on that theory would find no support in the evidence.

Contrary to the suggestion of the dissenting opinion of Mr. Justice Douglas, our holding today in no degree depends on the assertion of the religious interest of the child as contrasted with that of the parents. It is the parents who are subject to prosecution here for failing to cause their children to attend school, and it is their right of free exercise, not that of their children, that must determine Wisconsin's power to impose criminal penalties on the parent. The dissent argues that a child who expresses a desire to attend public high school in conflict with the wishes of his parents should not be prevented from doing so. There is no reason for the Court to consider that point since it is not an issue in the case. The children are not parties to this litigation. The State has at no point tried this case on the theory that respondents were preventing their children from attending school against their expressed desires, and indeed the record is to the contrary. The State's position from the outset has been that it is empowered to apply its compulsory attendance law to Amish parents in the same manner as to other parents—that is, without regard to the wishes of the child. That is the claim we reject today.

Our holding in no way determines the proper resolution of possible competing interests of parents, children, and the State in an appropriate state court proceeding in which the power of the State is asserted on the theory that Amish parents are preventing their minor children from attending high school despite their expressed desires to the contrary. Recognition of the claim of the State in such a proceeding would, of course, call into question traditional concepts of parental control over the religious upbringing and education of their minor children recognized in this Court's past decisions. It is clear that such an intrusion by a State into family decisions in the area of religious training would give rise to grave questions of religious freedom comparable to those raised here and those presented in *Pierce* v. *Society of Sisters.* On this record we neither reach nor decide those issues.

The State's argument proceeds without reliance on any actual conflict between the wishes of parents and children. It appears to rest on the potential that exemption of Amish parents from the requirements of the compulsory education law might allow some parents to act contrary to the best interests of their children by foreclosing their opportunity to make an intelligent choice between the Amish way of life and that of the outside world. The same argument could, of course, be made with respect to all church schools short of college. There is nothing in the record or in the ordinary course of human experience to suggest that non-Amish parents generally consult with children up to ages 14–16 if they are placed in a church school of the parents' faith.

Indeed it seems clear that if the State is empowered, as *parens patriae,* to "save" a child from himself or his Amish parents by requiring an additional two years of compulsory formal high school education, the State will in large measure influence, if not determine, the religious future of the child. Even more markedly than in *Prince,* therefore, this case involves the fundamental interest of parents, as contrasted with that of the State, to guide the religious future and education of their children. The history and culture of western civilization reflect a strong tradition of parental concern for the nurture and upbringing of their children. This primary role of the parents in the upbringing of their children is now established beyond debate as an enduring American tradition. If not the first, perhaps the most significant statements of the Court in this area are found in *Pierce* v. *Society of Sisters,* in which the Court observed:

Under the doctrine of *Meyer* v. *Nebraska,* 262 US 390, we think it entirely plain that the Act of 1922 unreasonably interferes with the liberty of parents and guardians to direct the upbringing and education of children under their control. As often heretofore pointed out, rights guaranteed by the Constitution may not be abridged by legislation which has no reasonable relation to some purpose within the competency of the State. The fundamental theory of liberty upon which all governments in this Union repose excludes any general power of the State to standardize its children by forcing them to accept instruction from public teachers only. The child is not the mere creature of the State; those who nurture him and direct his destiny have the right, coupled with the high duty, to recognize and prepare him for additional obligations.

The duty to prepare the child for "additional obligations," referred to by the Court, must be read to include the inculcation of moral standards, religious beliefs and elements of good citizenship. *Pierce,* of course, recognized that where nothing more than the general interest of the parent in the nurture and education of his children is involved, it is beyond dispute that the State acts "reasonably" and constitutionally in requiring education to age 16 in some public or private school meeting the standards prescribed by the State.

However read, the Court's holding in *Pierce* stands as a charter of the rights of parents to direct the religious upbringing of their children. And, when the interests of parenthood are combined with a free exercise claim of the nature revealed by this record, more than merely a "reasonable relation to some purpose within the competency of the state" is required to sustain the validity of the State's requirement under the First Amendment. To be sure, the power of the parent, even when linked to a free exercise claim, may be subject to limitation under *Prince* if it appears that parental decisions will jeopardize the health or safety of the child, or have a potential for significant social burdens. In this case, the Amish have introduced persuasive evidence undermining the arguments the State has advanced to support its claims in terms of the welfare of the child and society as a whole. The record strongly indicates that accommodating the religious objections of the Amish by forgoing one, or at most two, additional years of compulsory education will not impair the physical or mental health of the child, nor result in an inability to be self-supporting, or to discharge the duties and responsibilites of citizenship, or in any other way materially detract from the welfare of society.

In the fact of our consistent emphasis on the central values underlying the Religion Clauses in our constitutional scheme of government, we cannot accept a *parens patriae* claim of such all-encompassing scope and with such sweeping potential for broad and unforeseeable application as that urged by the State.

V

For the reasons stated we hold, with the Supreme Court of Wisconsin, that the First and Fourteenth Amendments prevent the State from compelling respondents to cause their children to attend formal high school to age 16.* Our disposition of this case, however, in no way alters our recognition of the obvious fact that courts are not school boards or legislatures, and are ill-equipped to determine the "necessity" of discrete aspects of a State's program of compulsory education. This should suggest that courts must move with great circumspection in performing the sensitive and delicate task of weighing a State's legitimate social concern when faced with religious claims for exemption from generally applicable educational requirements.

---

* What we have said should meet the suggestion that the decision of the Wisconsin Supreme Court recognizing an exemption for the Amish from the State's system of compulsory education constituted an impermissible establishment of religion. In *Walz* v. *Tax Commission,* the Court saw the three main concerns against which the Establishment Clause sought to protect as "sponsorship, financial support, and active involvement of the sovereign in religious activity." 397 US 668. Accommodating the religious beliefs of the Amish can hardly be characterized as sponsorship or active involvement. The purpose and effect of such an exemption are not to support, favor, advance, or assist the Amish, but to allow their centuries-old religious society, here long before the advent of any compulsory education, to survive free from the heavy impediment compliance with the Wisconsin compulsory education law would impose. Such an accommodation "reflects nothing more than the governmental obligation of neutrality in the face of religious differences, and does not represent that involvement of religious with secular institutions which it is the object of the Establishment Clause to forestall." *Sherbert* v. *Verner,* 374 US at 409.

It cannot be over-emphasized that we are not dealing with a way of life and mode of education by a group claiming to have recently discovered some "progressive" or more enlightened process for rearing children for modern life.

Aided by a history of three centuries as an identifiable religious sect and a long history as a successful and self-sufficient segment of American society, the Amish in this case have convincingly demonstrated the sincerity of their religious beliefs, the interrelationship of belief with their mode of life, the vital role which belief and daily conduct play in the continued survival of Old Order Amish communities and their religious organization, and the hazards presented by the State's enforcement of a statute generally valid as to others. Beyond this, they have carried the even more difficult burden of demonstrating the adequacy of their alternative mode of continuing informal vocational education in terms of precisely those overall interests that the State advances in support of its program of compulsory high school education. In light of this convincing showing, one which probably few other religious groups or sects could make, and weighing the minimal difference between what the State would require and what the Amish already accept, it was incumbent on the State to show with more particularity how its admittedly strong interest in compulsory education would be adversely affected by granting an exemption to the Amish. *Sherbert* v. *Verner.*

Nothing we hold is intended to undermine the general applicability of the State's compulsory school attendance statutes or to limit the power of the State to promulgate reasonable standards that, while not impairing the free exercise of religion, provide for continuing agricultural vocational education under parental and church guidance by the Old Order Amish or others similarly situated. The States have had a long history of amicable and effective relationships with church-sponsored schools, and there is no basis for assuming that, in this related context, reasonable standards cannot be established concerning the content of the continuing vocational education of Amish children under parental guidance, provided always that state regulations are not inconsistent with what we have said in this opinion.*

Affirmed.

3. Sunday Observance Laws

McGOWAN v. MARYLAND
366 US 420 (1961)

[Employees of a large discount department store located on a highway were convicted in Maryland state courts of making sales on Sunday in violation of the state's Sunday closing laws. The Supreme Court affirmed the conviction. It upheld the constitutionality of the laws against the charges that they were unconstitutionally

---

* Several States have now adopted plans to accommodate Amish religious beliefs through the establishment of an "Amish vocational school." These are not schools in the traditional sense of the word. As previously noted, respondents attempted to reach a compromise with the State of Wisconsin patterned after the Pennsylvania plan, but those efforts were not productive. There is no basis to assume that Wisconsin will be unable to reach a satisfactory accommodation with the Amish in light of what we now hold, so as to serve its interests without impinging on respondents' protected free exercise of their religion.

vague and that they violated the Equal Protection Clause of the Fourteenth Amendment. The Court held that the laws did not violate the Establishment Clause of the First Amendment, for the purpose and effect of the statutes were not to aid religion or Christianity but to set aside Sunday as a secular day of rest and recreation.

[Justice Frankfurter wrote a concurring opinion, joined by Justice Harlan.

[Justice Douglas was the only dissenter. For his opinion see *Braunfeld* v. *Brown, post.*

[This case is to be read with the next case that follows, decided the same day, when the Court also decided *Gallagher* v. *Crown Kosher Super Market,* 366 US 617 (1961), and *Two Guys From Harrison* v. *McGinley,* 366 US 582 (1961).]

Mr. Chief Justice Warren delivered the opinion of the Court:

The issues in this case concern the constitutional validity of Maryland criminal statutes, commonly known as Sunday Closing Laws, or Sunday Blue Laws. The statutes, with exceptions to be noted hereafter, generally proscribe all labor, business and other commercial activities on Sunday. The questions presented are whether the classifications within the statutes bring about a denial of equal protection of the law, whether the laws are so vague as to fail to give reasonable notice of the forbidden conduct and therefore violate due process, and whether the statutes are laws respecting an establishment of religion or prohibiting the free exercise thereof.

Appellants are seven employees of a large discount department store located on a highway in Anne Arundel County, Maryland. They were indicted for the Sunday sale of a three-ring loose-leaf binder, a can of floor wax, a stapler and staples, and a toy submarine in violation of Md. Ann. Code, Art. 27, § 521. Generally, this section prohibited, throughout the State, the Sunday sale of all merchandise except the retail sale of tobacco products, confectioneries, milk, bread, fruits, gasoline, oils, greases, drugs and medicines, and newspapers and periodicals. Recently amended, this section also now excepts from the general prohibition the retail sale in Anne Arundel County of all foodstuffs, automobile and boating accessories, flowers, toilet goods, hospital supplies and souvenirs. It now further provides that any retail establishment in Anne Arundel County which does not employ more than one person other than the owner may operate on Sunday.

Although appellants were indicted only under § 521, in order properly to consider several of the broad constitutional contentions, we must examine the whole body of Maryland Sunday laws. Several sections of the Maryland statutes are particularly relevant to evaluation of the issues presented. Section 492 of Md. Ann. Code, Art. 27, forbids all persons from doing any work or bodily labor on Sunday and forbids permitting children or servants to work on that day or to engage in fishing, hunting and unlawful pastimes or recreations. The section excepts all works of necessity and charity. Section 522 of Md. Ann. Code, Art. 27, disallows the opening or use of any dancing saloon, opera house, bowling alley or barber shop on Sunday. However, in addition to the exceptions noted above, Md. Ann. Code, Art. 27, § 509 exempts, for Anne Arundel County, the Sunday operation of any bathing beach, bathhouse, dancing saloon and amusement park, and activities incident thereto and retail sales of merchandise customarily sold at, or incidental to, the operation of the aforesaid occupations and businesses. Section 90 of Md. Ann. Code, Art. 2B, makes generally unlawful the sale of alcoholic beverages on Sunday. However, this section, and immediately succeeding ones, provide various immunities for the Sunday sale of different kinds of alcoholic beverages, at different hours during the day, by vendors holding different types of licenses, in different political divisions of the State—particularly in Anne Arundel County. . . .

The remaining statutory sections concern a myriad of exceptions for various counties, districts of counties, cities and towns throughout the State. Among the activities allowed in certain areas on Sunday are such sports as football, baseball, golf, tennis, bowling, croquet, basketball, lacrosse, soccer, hockey, swimming, softball, boating, fishing, skating, horseback riding, stock car racing and pool or billiards. Other immunized activities permitted in some regions of the State include group singing or playing of musical instruments; the exhibition of motion pictures; dancing; the operation of recreation centers, picnic grounds, swimming pools, skating rinks and miniature golf courses. The taking of oysters and the hunting or killing of game is generally forbidden, but shooting conducted by organized rod and gun clubs is permitted in one county. In some of the subdivisions within the State, the exempted Sunday activities are sanctioned throughout the day; in others, they may not commence until early afternoon or evening; in many, the activities may only be conducted during the afternoon and late in the evening. Certain localities do not permit the allowed Sunday activity to be carried on within one hundred yards of any church where religious services are being held. Local ordinances and regulations concerning certain limited activities supplement the State's statutory scheme. In Anne Arundel County, for example, slot machines, pinball machines and bingo may be played on Sunday.

Among other things, appellants contended at the trial that the Maryland statutes under which they were charged were contrary to the Fourteenth Amendment for the reasons stated at the outset of this opinion. Appellants were convicted and each was fined five dollars and costs. The Maryland Court of Appeals affirmed. . . .

I

Appellants argue that the Maryland statutes violate the "Equal Protection" Clause of the Fourteenth Amendment on several counts. First, they contend that the classifications contained in the statutes concerning which commodities may or may not be sold on Sunday are without rational and substantial relation to the object of the legislation. Specifically, appellants allege that the statutory exemptions for the Sunday sale of the merchandise mentioned above render arbitrary the statute under which they were convicted. Appellants further allege that § 521 is capricious because of the exemptions for the operation of the various amusements that have been listed and because slot machines, pinball machines, and bingo are legalized and are freely played on Sunday.

The standards under which this proposition is to be evaluated have been set forth many times by this Court. Although no precise formula has been developed, the Court has held that the Fourteenth Amendment permits the States a wide scope of discretion in enacting laws which affect some groups of citizens differently than others. The constitutional safeguard is offended only if the classification rests on grounds wholly irrelevant to the achievement of the State's objective. State legislatures are presumed to have acted within their constitutional power despite the fact that, in practice, their laws result in some inequality. A statutory discrimination will not be set aside if any state of facts reasonably may be conceived to justify it. . . .

It would seem that a legislature could reasonably find that the Sunday sale of exempted commodities was necessary either for the health of the populace or for the enhancement of the recreational atmosphere of the day—that a family which takes a Sunday ride into the country will need gasoline for the automobile and may find pleasant a soft drink or fresh fruit; that those who go to the beach may wish ice cream or some other item normally sold there; that some people will prefer alcoholic beverages or games of chance to add to their relaxation; that newspapers and drug products should always be available to the public.

The record is barren of any indication that this apparently reasonable basis does not exist, that the statutory distinctions are invidious, that local tradition and custom might not rationally call for this legislative treatment. . . . Likewise, the fact that these exemptions exist and deny some vendors and operators the day of rest and recreation contemplated by the legislature does not render the statutes violative of equal protection since there would appear to be many valid reasons for these exemptions, as stated above, and no evidence to dispel them.

Secondly, appellants contend that the statutory arrangement which permits only certain Anne Arundel County retailers to sell merchandise essential to, or customarily sold at, or incidental to, the operation of bathing beaches, amusement parks et cetera is contrary to the "Equal Protection" Clause because it discriminates unreasonably against retailers in other Maryland counties. But we have held that the Equal Protection Clause relates to equality between persons as such, rather than between areas and that territorial uniformity is not a constitutional prerequisite. With particular reference to the State of Maryland, we have noted that the prescription of different substantive offenses in different counties is generally a matter for legislative discretion. We find no invidious discrimination here. . . .

Thirdly, appellants contend that this same statutory provision, Art. 27, § 509, violates the "Equal Protection" Clause because it permits only certain merchants within Anne Arundel County (operators of bathing beaches and amusement parks et cetera) to sell merchandise customarily sold at these places while forbidding its sale by other vendors of this merchandise, such as appellant's employer. Here again, it would seem that a legislature could reasonably find that these commodities, necessary for the health and recreation of its citizens, should only be sold on Sunday by those vendors at the locations where the commodities are most likely to be immediately put to use. Such a determination would seem to serve the consuming public and at the same time secure Sunday rest for those employees, like appellants, of all other retail establishments. In addition, the enforcement problems which would accrue if large retail establishments, like appellants' employer, were permitted to remain open on Sunday but were restricted to the sale of the merchandise in question would be far greater than the problems accruing if only beach and amusement park vendors were exempted. Here again, there has been no indication of the unreasonableness of this differentiation. On the record before us, we cannot say that these statutes do not provide equal protection of the laws.

II

Another question presented by appellants is whether Art. 27, § 509, which exempts the Sunday retail sale of "merchandise essential to, or customarily sold at, or incidental to, the operation of" bathing beaches, amusement parks et cetera in Anne Arundel County, is unconstitutionally vague. We believe that business people of ordinary intelligence in the position of appellants' employer would be able to know what exceptions are encompassed by the statute either as a matter of ordinary commercial knowledge or by simply making a reasonable investigation at a nearby bathing beach or amusement park within the county. . . . Under these circumstances, there is no necessity to guess at the statute's meaning in order to determine what conduct it makes criminal. . . .

III

The final questions for decision are whether the Maryland Sunday Closing Laws conflict with the Federal Constitution's provisions for religious liberty. First, appellants contend here that the statutes applicable to Anne Arundel County violate the constitutional guarantee of freedom of religion in that the statutes' effect is to prohibit the free exercise of religion in contravention of the First Amendment, made applicable to the States by the Fourteenth Amendment. But appellants allege only economic injury to themselves; they do not allege any infringement of their own religious freedoms due to Sunday closing. In fact, the record is silent as to what appellants' religious beliefs are. Since the general rule is that "a litigant may only assert his own constitutional rights or immunities," . . . we hold that appellants have no standing to raise this contention. . . . Furthermore, since appellants do not specifically allege that the statutes infringe upon the religious beliefs of the department store's present or prospective patrons, we have no occasion here to consider the standing question of *Pierce* v. *Society of Sisters,* 268 US 510, 535–536. Those persons whose religious rights are allegedly impaired by the statutes are not without effective ways to assert these rights. Cf. *N.A.A.C.P.* v. *Alabama,* 357 US 449; *Barrows* v. *Jackson,* 346 US 249. Appellants present no weighty countervailing policies here to cause an exception to our general principles. . . .

Secondly, appellants contend that the statutes violate the guarantee of separation of church and state in that the statutes are laws respecting an establishment of religion contrary to the First Amendment, made applicable to the states by the Fourteenth Amendment. If the purpose of the "establishment" clause was only to insure protection for the "free exercise" of religion, then what we have said above concerning appellant's standing to raise the "free exercise" contention would appear to be true here. However, the writings of Madison, who was the First Amendment's architect, demonstrate that the establishment of a religion was equally feared because of its tendencies to political tyranny and subversion of civil authority. Thus, in *Everson* v. *Board of Education,* the Court permitted a district taxpayer to challenge, on "establishment" grounds, a state statute which authorized district boards of education to reimburse parents for fares paid for the transportation of their children to both public and Catholic schools. Appellants here concededly have suffered direct economic injury, allegedly due to the imposition on them of the tenets of the Christian religion. We find, in these circumstances, these appellants have standing to complain that the statutes are laws respecting an establishment of religion.

The essence of appellant's "establishment" argument is that Sunday is the Sabbath day of the predominant Christian sects; that the purpose of the enforced stoppage of labor on that day is to facilitate and encourage church attendance; that the purpose of setting Sunday as a day of universal rest is to induce people with no religion or people with marginal religious beliefs to join the predominant Christian sects; that the purpose of the atmosphere of tranquility created by Sunday closing is to aid the conduct of church services and religious observance of the sacred day. In substantiating their "establishment" argument, appellants rely on the wording of the present Maryland statutes, on earlier versions of the current Sunday laws and on prior judicial characterizations of these laws by the Maryland Court of Appeals. Although only the constitutionality of § 521, the section under which appellants have been convicted, is immediately before us in this litigation, inquiry into the history of Sunday Closing Laws in our country, in addition to an examination of the Maryland Sunday closing statutes in their entirety and of their history, is relevant to the decision of whether the Maryland Sunday law in question is one respecting an establishment of religion. There is no dispute that the original laws which dealt with Sunday labor were motivated by religious forces. But what we must decide is whether present Sunday legislation, having undergone extensive changes from the earliest forms, still retains its religious character.

Sunday Closing Laws go far back into American history having been brought to the colonies with a background of English legislation dating to the thirteenth century. In 1237, Henry III forbade the frequenting of markets on Sunday; the Sunday showing of wools at the staple was banned by Edward III in 1354; in 1409, Henry IV prohibited the playing of unlawful games on Sunday; Henry VI proscribed Sunday fairs in churchyards in 1444 and, four years later, made unlawful all fairs and markets and all showings of any goods or merchandise; Edward VI disallowed Sunday bodily labor by several injunctions in the mid-sixteenth century; various Sunday sports and amusements were restricted in 1625 by Charles I. . . . The law of the colonies to the time of the Revolution and the basis of the Sunday laws in the States was 29 Charles II, c. 7 (1677). It provided, in part:

For the better observation and keeping holy the Lord's day, commonly called Sunday: be it enacted . . . that all the laws enacted and in force concerning the observation of the Lord's day, *and repairing to the church thereon,* be carefully put in execution; and that all and every person and persons whatsoever shall upon every Lord's day apply themselves to the observation of the same, by exercising themselves thereon in the duties of piety and true religion, publicly and privately; and that no tradesman, artificer, workman, laborer, or other person whatsoever, *shall do or exercise any worldly labor or business or work* of their ordinary callings upon the Lord's day, or any part thereof (works of necessity and charity only expected); . . . and that no person or persons whatsoever shall publicly cry, show forth, or expose for sale any wares, merchandise, fruit, herbs, goods, or chattels, whatsoever, upon the Lord's day, or any part thereof. . . . (Emphasis added.)

Observation of the above language, and of that of the prior mandates, reveals clearly that the English Sunday legislation was in aid of the established church.

The American colonial Sunday restrictions arose soon after settlement. Starting in 1650, the Plymouth Colony proscribed servile work, unnecessary traveling, sports, and the sale of alcoholic beverages on the Lord's day and enacted laws concerning church attendance. The Massachusetts Bay Colony and the Connecticut and New Haven Colonies enacted similar prohibitions, some even earlier in the seventeenth century. The religious orientation of the colonial statutes was equally apparent. For example, a 1629 Massachusetts Bay instruction began, "And to the end the Sabbath may be celebrated in a religious manner. . . ." A 1653 enactment spoke of Sunday activities "which things tend much to the dishonor of God, the reproach of religion, and the profanation of his holy Sabbath, the sanctification whereof is sometimes put for all duties immediately respecting the service of God. . . ." . . . These laws persevered after the Revolution and, at about the time of the First Amendment's adoption, each of the colonies had laws of some sort restricting Sunday labor. . . .

But, despite the strongly religious origin of these laws, beginning before the eighteenth century, nonreligious arguments for Sunday closing began to be heard more distinctly and the statutes began to lose some of their totally religious flavor. In the middle 1700's, Blackstone wrote, "[T]he keeping one day in the seven holy, as a time of relaxation and refreshment as well as for public worship, is of admirable service to a state considered merely as a civil institution. It humanizes, by the help of conversation and society, the manners of the lower classes; which would otherwise degenerate into a sordid ferocity and savage selfishness of spirit; it enables the industrious workman to pursue his occupation in the ensuing week with health and cheerfulness.". . . A 1788 English statute dealing with chimney sweeps, 28 Geo. III, c. 48, in addition to providing for their Sunday religious affairs, also regulated their hours of work. The preamble to a 1679 Rhode Island enactment stated that the reason for the ban on Sunday employment was that "persons being evill minded, have presumed to employ in servile labor, more than necessity requireth, their servants. . . ." . . . The New York law of 1788 omitted the term "Lord's day" and substituted "the first day of the week commonly called Sunday." . . . Similar changes marked the Maryland statutes, discussed below. With the advent of the First Amendment, the colonial provisions requiring church attendance were soon repealed. . . .

More recently, further secular justifications have been advanced for making Sunday a day of rest, a day when people may recover from the labors of the week just passed and may physically and mentally prepare for the week's work to come. In England, during the First World War, a committee investigating the health conditions of munitions workers reported that "if the maximum output is to be secured and maintained for any length of time, a weekly period of rest must be allowed. . . . On economic and social grounds alike this weekly period of rest is best provided on Sunday."

The proponents of Sunday closing legislation are no longer exclusively representatives of religious interests. Recent New Jersey Sunday legislation was supported by labor groups and the trade associations . . . ; modern English Sunday legislation was promoted by the National Federation of Grocers and supported by the National Chamber of Trade, the Drapers' Chamber of Trade, and the National Union of Shop Assistants. . . .

Throughout the years, state legislatures have modified, deleted from and added to their Sunday statutes. As evidenced by the New Jersey laws mentioned above, current changes are commonplace. Almost every State in our country presently has some type of Sunday regulation and over forty possess a relatively comprehensive system. . . . Some of our States now enforce their Sunday legislation through Departments of Labor, e.g., S.C. Code Ann. (1952), § 64–5. Thus have Sunday laws evolved from the wholly religious sanctions that originally were enacted.

Moreover, litigation over Sunday closing laws is not novel. Scores of cases may be found in the state appellate courts relating to sundry phases of Sunday enactments. Religious objections have been raised there on numerous occasions but sustained only once, in *Ex parte Newman,* 9 Cal. 502 (1858); and that decision was overruled three years later, in *Ex parte Andrews,* 18 Cal. 678. A substantial number of cases in varying postures bearing on state Sunday legislation have reached this Court. Although none raising the issues now presented have gained plenary hearing, language used in some of these cases further evidences the evolution of Sunday laws as temporal statutes. Mr. Justice Field wrote in *Soon Hing* v. *Crowley* (113 US 703):

Laws setting aside Sunday as a day of rest are upheld, not from any right of the government to legislate for the promotion of religious observances, but from its right to protect all persons from the physical and moral debasement which comes from uninterrupted labor. Such laws have always been deemed beneficent and merciful laws, especially to the poor and dependent, to the laborers in our factories and workshops and in the heated rooms of our cities; and their validity has been sustained by the highest courts of the States.

While a member of the California Supreme Court, Mr. Justice Field dissented in *Ex parte Newman, supra,* saying:

Its requirement is a cessation from labor. In its enactment, the Legislature has given the sanction of law to a rule of conduct, which the entire civilized world recognizes as essential to the physical and moral well-being of society. Upon no subject is there such a concurrence of opinion, among philosophers, moralists and statesmen of all nations, as on the necessity of periodical cessations from labor. One day in seven is the rule, founded in experience, and sustained by science. . . . The prohibition of secular business on Sunday is advocated on the ground that by it the general welfare is advanced, labor protected, and the moral and physical well-being of society promoted.

This was quoted with approval by Mr. Justice Harlan in *Hennington* v. *Georgia* (163 US 299), who also stated:

It is none the less a civil regulation because the day on which the running of freight trains is prohibited is kept by many under a sense of religious duty. The legislature having, as will not be disputed, power to enact laws to promote the order and to secure the comfort, happiness and health of the people, it was within its discretion to fix the day when all labor, within the limits of the State, works of necessity and charity excepted, should cease. . . .

Before turning to the Maryland legislation now here under attack, an investigation of what historical position Sunday Closing Laws have occupied with reference to the First Amendment should be undertaken. . . .

This Court has considered the happenings surrounding the Virginia General Assembly's enactment of "A Bill for Establishing Religious Freedom," . . . written by Thomas Jefferson and sponsored by James Madison, as best reflecting the long and intensive struggle for religious freedom in America, as particularly relevant in the search for the First Amendment's meaning. . . . In 1776, nine years before the bill's passage, Madison co-authored Virginia's Declaration of Rights which provided, *inter alia,* that "all men are equally entitled to the free exercise of religion, according to the dictates of conscience. . . ." . . . Virginia had had Sunday legislation since early in the seventeenth century; in 1776, the laws penalizing "maintaning any opinons in matters of religion, *forbearing to repair to church,* or the exercising any mode of worship whatsoever . . ." (emphasis added), were repealed, and all dissenters were freed from the taxes levied for the support of the established church. The Sunday labor prohibitions remained; apparently, they were not believed to be inconsistent with the newly enacted Declaration of Rights. Madison had sought also to have the Declaration expressly condemn the existing Virginia establishment. This hope was finally realized when "A Bill for Establishing Religious Freedom" was passed in 1785. In this same year, Madison presented to Virginia legislators "A Bill for Punishing . . . Sabbath Breakers" which provided, in part:

If any person on Sunday shall himself be found labouring at his own or any other trade or calling, or shall employ his apprentices, servants or slaves in labour, or other business, except it be in the ordinary household offices of daily necessity, or other work of necessity or charity, he shall forfeit the sum of ten shillings for every such offence, deeming every apprentice, servant, or slave so employed, and every day he shall be so employed as constituting a distinct offence.

This became law the following year and remained during the time that Madison fought for the First Amendment in the Congress. It was the law of Virginia, and similar laws were in force in other States, when Madison stated at the Virginia ratification convention:

Happily for the states, they enjoy the utmost freedom of religion. . . . Fortunately for this commonwealth, a majority of the people are decidedly against any exclusive establishment. I believe it to be so in other states. . . . I can appeal to my uniform conduct on this subject, that I have warmly supported religious freedom.

In 1799, Virginia pronounced "A Bill for Establishing Religious Freedom" as "a true exposition of the principles of the bill of rights and constitution," and repealed all subsequently enacted legislation deemed inconsistent with it. . . . Virginia's statute banning Sunday labor stood.

In *Reynolds* v. *United States,* 98 US 145, the Court relied heavily on the history of the Virginia bill. That case concerned a Mormon's attack on a statute making bigamy a crime. The Court said:

In connection with the case we are now considering, it is a significant fact that on the 8th of December, 1788, after the passage of the Act establishing religious freedom, and after the convention of Virginia had recommended as an amendment to the Constitution of the United States the declaration in a Bill of Rights that "All men have an equal, natural, and unalienable right to the free exercise of religion, according to the dictates of conscience," the Legislature of that State substantially enacted the Statute of James I., death penalty included, because as recited in the preamble, "It hath been doubted whether bigamy or polygamy be punishable by the laws of this Commonwealth." From that day to this we think it may safely be said there never has been a time in any State of the Union when polygamy has not been an offense against society, cognizable by the civil courts and punishable with more or less severity. In the face of all this evidence, it is impossible to believe that the constitutional guaranty of religious freedom was intended to prohibit legislation in respect to this most important feature of social life.

In the case at bar, we find the place of Sunday Closing Laws in the First Amendment's history both enlightening and persuasive.

But in order to dispose of the case before us, we must consider the standards by which the Maryland statutes are to be measured. Here, a brief review of the First Amendment's background proves helpful. The First Amendment states that "Congress shall make no law respecting an establishment of religion. . . ." U.S. Const., Amend. I. The Amendment was proposed by James Madison on June 8, 1789, in the House of Representatives. It then read, in part:

The civil rights of none shall be abridged on account of religious belief or worship, *nor shall any national religion be established,* nor shall the full and equal rights of conscience be in any manner, or on any pretext, infringed. (Emphasis added.) I Annals of Congress 434.

We are told that Madison added the word "national" to meet the scruples of States which then had an established church. . . . After being referred to committee, it was considered by the House, on August 15, 1789, acting as a Committee of the Whole. Some assistance in determining the scope of the Amendment's proscription of establishment may be found in that debate.

Mr. Boudinot proposed the insertion of the language, "no religion shall be established by law." . . . Mr. Gerry "said it would read better if it was, that no religious doctrine shall be established by law." . . . Mr. Madison "said, he apprehended the meaning of the words to be, that Congress should not establish a religion, and enforce the legal observation of it by law, nor compel men to worship God in any manner contrary to their conscience. . . . He believed that the people feared one sect might obtain a pre-eminence, or two combine together, and establish a religion to which they would compel others to conform." . . .

The Amendment, as it passed the House of Representatives nine days later, read, in part:

Congress shall make no law establishing religion. . . .

It passed the Senate on September 9, 1879, reading, in part:

Congress shall make no law establishing articles of faith, or a mode of worship. . . .

An early commentator opined that the "real object of the amendment was . . . to prevent any national ecclesiastical establishment, which should give to an hierarchy the exclusive patronage of the national government." 3 Story, *Commentaries on the Constitution of the United States,* 728. But, the First Amendment, in its final form, did not simply bar a congressional enactment *establishing a church;* it forbade all laws *respecting an establishment of religion.* Thus, this Court has given the Amendment a "broad interpretation" . . . "in the light of its history and the evils it was designed forever to suppress. . . ." . . . It has found that the First and Fourteenth Amendments afford protection against religious establishment far more extensive than merely to forbid a national or state church. Thus, in *McCollum* v. *Board of Education,* 333 US 203, the Court held that the action of a board of education, permitting religious instruction during school hours in public school buildings and requiring those children who chose not to attend to remain in their classrooms, to be contrary to the "Establishment" Clause.

However, it is equally true that the "Establishment" Clause does not ban federal or state regulation of conduct whose reason or effect merely happens to coincide or harmonize with the tenets of some or all religions. In many instances, the Congress or state legislatures conclude that the general welfare of society, wholly apart from any religious considerations, demands such regulation. Thus, for temporal purposes, murder is illegal. And the fact that this agrees with the dictates of the Judaeo-Christian religions while it may disagree with others does not invalidate the regulation. So too with the questions of adultery and polygamy. . . . The same could be said of theft, fraud, etc., because those offenses were also proscribed in the Decalogue.

Thus, these broad principles have been set forth by this Court. Those cases dealing with the specific problems arising under the "Establishment" Clause which have reached this Court are few in number. The most extensive discussion of the "Establishment" Clause's latitude is to be found in *Everson* v. *Board of Education.* . . .

In light of the evolution of our Sunday Closing Laws through the centuries, and of their more or less recent emphasis upon secular considerations, it is not difficult to discern that as presently written and administered, most of them, at least, are of a secular rather than of a religious character, and that presently they bear no relationship to establishment of religion as those words are used in the Constitution of the United States.

Throughout this century and longer, both the federal and state governments have oriented their activities very largely toward improvement of the health, safety, recreation and general well-being of our citizens. Numerous laws affecting public health, safety factors in industry, laws affecting hours and conditions of labor of women and children, weekend diversion at parks and beaches, and cultural activities of various kinds, now point the way toward the good life for all. Sunday Closing Laws, like those before us, have become part and parcel of this great governmental concern wholly apart from their original purposes or connotations. The present purpose and effect of most of them is to provide a uniform day of rest for all citizens; the fact that this day is Sunday, a day of particular significance for the dominant Christian sects, does not bar the State from achieving its secular goals. To say that the States cannot prescribe Sunday as a day of rest for these purposes solely because centuries ago such laws had their genesis in religion would give a constitutional interpretation of hostility to the public welfare rather than one of mere separation of church and State.

We now reach the Maryland statutes under review. The title of the major series of sections of the Maryland Code dealing with Sunday closing—Art. 27, §§ 492–534C—is "Sabbath Breaking"; § 492 proscribes work or bodily labor on the "Lord's day," and forbids persons to "profane the Lord's day" by gaming, fishing et cetera; § 522 refers to Sunday as the "Sabbath day." As has been mentioned above, many of the exempted Sunday activities in the various localities of the State may only be conducted during the afternoon and late evening; most Christian church services, of course, are held on Sunday morning and early Sunday evening. Finally, as previously noted, certain localities do not permit the allowed Sunday activities to be carred on within one hundred yards of any church where religious services are being held. This is the totality of the evidence of religious purpose which may be gleaned from the face of the present statute and from its operative effect.

The predecessors of the existing Maryland Sunday laws are undeniably religious in origin. The first Maryland statute dealing with Sunday activities, enacted in 1649, was entitled "An Act concerning Religion." . . . It made it criminal to "profane the Sabbath or Lord's day called Sunday by frequent swearing, drunkenness or by an uncivill or disorderly recreation, or by working on that day when absolute necessity doth not require it." A 1692 statute entitled "An Act for the Service of Almighty God and the Establishment of the Protestant Religion within this Province," . . . after first stating the importance of keeping the Lord's day holy and sanctified and expressing concern with the breach of its observance throughout the State, then enacted a Sunday labor prohibition which was the obvious precursor of the present § 492. There was a re-enactment in 1696 entitled "An Act for Sanctifying & keeping holy the Lord's Day Commonly called Sunday." . . . By 1723, the Sabbath-breaking section of the statute assumed the present form of § 492, omitting the specific prohibition against Sunday swearing and the patently religiously motivated title. . . .

There are judicial statements in early Maryland decisions which tend to support appellants' position. In an 1834 case involving a contract calling for delivery on Sunday, the Maryland Court of Appeals remarked that "Ours is a christian community, and a day set apart as the day of rest, is the day consecrated by the resurrection of our Saviour, and embraces the twenty-four hours next ensuing the midnight of Saturday." *Kilgour* v. *Miles,* 6 Gill and Johnson 268. This language was cited with approval in *Judefind* v. *State,* 78 Md. 510 (1894). It was also stated there:

It is undoubtedly true that rest from secular employment on Sunday does have a tendency to foster and encourage the Christian religion—of all sects and denominations that observe that day—as rest from work and ordinary occupation enables many to engage in public worship who probably would not otherwise do so. But it would scarcely be asked of a Court, in what professes to be a Christian land, to declare a law unconstitutional because it requires rest from bodily labor on Sunday (except works of necessity and charity), and *thereby* promotes the cause of Christianity. If the Christian religion is, incidentally or otherwise, benefited or fostered by having this day or rest, as it undoubtedly is, there is all the more reason for the enforcement of laws that help to preserve it. Whilst Courts have generally sustained Sunday laws as "civil regulations," their decisions will have no less weight if they are shown to be in accordance with divine law as well as human.

But it should be noted that, throughout the *Judefind* decision, the Maryland court specifically rejected the contention that the laws interfered with religious liberty and stated that the laws' purpose was to provide the "advantages of having a weekly day of rest, 'from a mere physical and political standpoint.' "

Considering the language and operative effect of the current statutes, we no longer find the blanket prohibition against Sunday work or bodily labor. To the contrary, we find that § 521 of Art. 27, the section which appellants violated, permits the Sunday sale of tobaccos and sweets and a long list of sundry articles which we have enumerated above; we find that § 509 of Art. 25 permits the Sunday operation of bathing beaches, amusement parks and similar facilities; we find that Art. 2B, § 28, permits the Sunday sale of alcoholic beverages, products strictly forbidden by predecessor statutes; we are told that Anne Arundel County allows Sunday bingo and the Sunday playing of pinball machines and slot machines, activities generally condemned by prior Maryland Sunday legislation. Certainly, these are not works of charity or necessity. Section 521's current stipulation that shops with only one employee may remain open on Sunday does not coincide with a religious purpose. These provisions, along with those which permit various sports and entertainments on Sunday, seem clearly to be fashioned for the purpose of providing a Sunday atmosphere of recreation, cheerfulness, repose and enjoyment. Coupled with the general proscription against other types of work, we believe that the air of the day is one of relaxation rather than one of religion.

The existing Maryland Sunday laws are not simply verbatim re-enactments of their religiously oriented antecedents. Only § 492 retains the appellation of "Lord's day" and even that section no longer makes recitation of religious purpose. It does talk in terms of "profan[ing] the Lord's day," but other sections permit the activities previously thought to be profane. Prior denunciation of Sunday drunkenness is now gone. Contemporary concern with these statutes is evidenced by the dozen changes made in 1959 and by the recent enactment of a majority of the exceptions.

Finally, the relevant pronouncements of the Maryland Court of Appeals dispel any argument that the statutes' announced purpose is religious. In *Hiller* v. *Maryland,* 124 Md. 385 (1914), the court had before it a Baltimore ordinance prohibiting Sunday baseball. The court said:

What the eminent chief judge said with respect to police enactments which deal with the protection of the public health, morals and safety apply with equal force to those which are concerned with the peace, order and quiet of the community on Sunday, for these social conditions are well recognized heads of the police power. Can the Court say that this ordinance has no real and substantial relation to the peace and order and quiet of Sunday, as a day of rest, in the City of Baltimore?

And, the Maryland court declared in its decision in the instant case: "The legislative plan is plain. It is to compel a day of rest from work, permitting only activities which are necessary or recreational." . . . After engaging in the close scrutiny demanded of us when First Amendment liberties are at issue, we accept the State Supreme Court's determination that the statutes' present purpose and effect is not to aid religion but to set aside a day of rest and recreation.

But, this does not answer all of appellants' contentions. We are told that the State has other means at its disposal to accomplish its secular purpose, other courses that would not even remotely or incidentally give state aid to religion. On this basis, we are asked to hold these statutes invalid on the ground that the State's power to regulate conduct in the public interest may only be executed in a way that does not unduly or unnecessarily infringe upon the religious provisions of the First Amendment. . . . However relevant this argument may be, we believe that the factual basis on which it rests is not supportable. It is true that if the State's interest were simply to provide for its citizens a periodic respite from work, a regulation demanding that everyone rest one day in seven, leaving the choice of the day to the individual, would suffice.

However, the State's purpose is not merely to provide a one-day-in-seven work's stoppage. In addition to this, the State seeks to set one day apart from all others as a day of rest, repose, recreation and tranquility—a day which all members of the family and community have the opportunity to spend and enjoy together, a day in which there exists relative quiet and disassociation from the everyday intensity of commercial activities, a day in which people may visit friends and relatives who are not available during working days.*

* This purpose has been articulated in various ways at different times. The parliamentary debates on the British Shops (Sunday Trading Restriction) Bill in 1936 are particularly instructive. The sponsor of the Bill stated:

"I realise also that the State to-day is interfering more and more with family life and more and more controlling the family liberty, and were this a Bill to restrict liberty, and above all to restrict the liberty of the family, I would not be responsible for introducing it. But I hope to show to the House that it is a Bill which is necessary to secure the family life and liberty of hundreds of thousands of our people. . . . They have the right to a holiday on Sunday, to be able to rest from work on that day and to go out into the parks or into the country on a summer day. That is the liberty for which they are asking, and that is the liberty which this Bill would give to them." 308 Parliamentary Debates, Commons 2157–2158.

Another member stated:

"As a family man let me say that my family life would be unduly disturbed if any member had his Sunday on a Tuesday. The value of a Sunday is that everybody in the family is at home on the same day. What is the use of talking about a six-day working week in which six members of a family would each have his day of rest on a different day of the week?" *Id.*, at 2198.

Reports of the International Labour Conferences are also revealing:

"Social custom requires that the same rest-day should as far as possible be accorded to the members of the same working family and to the working class community as a whole. It is a fact that originally religious motives determined the rest-day and that the tradition thus established has subsequently been maintained by law. It appears to be a universal rule that workers in the same area or in the same country have the same rest-day, and that the rest-day coincides with the day established by tradition or custom; and the International Labour Office proposes that this rule should be maintained." Rep. VII, International Labour Conference, 3d Sess. 1921, 127–128.

"A study of national standards shows that the most usual practice is to grant the weekly rest collectively on specified days of the week. This tendency to ensure that the weekly rest is taken at the same time by all workers on the day established by tradition or custom has an

Obviously, a state is empowered to determine that a rest-one-day-in-seven statute would not accomplish this purpose; that it would not provide a general cessation of activity, a special atmosphere of tranquility, a day which all members of the family or friends and relatives might spend together. Furthermore, it seems plain that the problems involved in enforcing such a provision would be exceedingly more difficult than those in enforcing a common-day-of-rest provision.

Moreover, it is common knowledge that the first day of the week has come to have special significance as a rest day in this country. People of all religions and people with no religion regard Sunday as a time for family activity, for visiting friends and relatives, for late-sleeping, for passive and active entertainments, for dining out and the like. "Vast masses of our people, in fact, literally millions, go out into the countryside on fine Sunday afternoons in the Summer. . . ." 308 Parliamentary Debates, Commons 2159. Sunday is a day apart from all others.* The cause is irrelevant; the fact exists. It would seem unrealistic for enforcement purposes and perhaps detrimental to the general welfare to require a state to choose a common-day-of-rest other than that which most persons would select of their own accord. For these reasons, we hold that the Maryland statutes are not laws respecting an establishment of religion.

The distinctions between the statutes in the case before us and the state action in *McCollum* v. *Board of Education,* the only case in this Court finding a violation of the "Establishment" Clause, lend further substantiation to our conclusion. In *McCollum,* state action permitted religious instruction in public school buildings during school hours and required students not attending the religious instructions to remain in their classrooms during that time. The Court found that this system had the effect of coercing the children to attend religious classes; no such coercion to attend church services is present in the situation at bar. In *McCollum,* the only alternative available to the nonattending students was to remain in their classrooms; the alternatives open to nonlaboring persons in the instant case are far more diverse. In *McCollum,* there was direct cooperation between state officials and religious ministers; no such direct participation exists under the Maryland laws. In *McCollum,* tax supported buildings were used to aid religion; in the case, no tax monies are being used in aid of religion.

Finally, we should make clear that this case deals only with the constitutionality of § 521 of the Maryland statute before us. We do not hold that Sunday legislation may not be a violation of the "Establishment" Clause if it can be demonstrated that its purpose—evidenced either on the face of the legislation, in conjunction with its legislative history, or in its operative effect—is to use the State's coercive power to aid religion.

Accordingly, the decision is affirmed.

---

obvious social purpose, namely to enable the workers to take part in the life of the community and in the special forms of recreation which are available on certain days." Rep. VII (1), International Labour Conference, 39th Sess. 1956, 24.

* The Constitution itself provides for a Sunday exception in the calculation of the ten days for presidential veto. U.S. Const., Art. I, § 7.

BRAUNFELD *v.* BROWN
366 US 599 (1961)

[Like the immediately preceding case, this case also involved the Sunday closing laws of Pennsylvania, but also was a companion case to *Gallagher* v. *Crown Kosher Super Market* in that it involved an attack on the statutes by merchants who adhered to the Orthodox Jewish faith and who contended that the compulsory Sunday closing violated their right to the free exercise of religion. The Court upheld the constitutionality of the laws. Justice Frankfurter wrote a concurring opinion, joined by Justice Harlan. Justices Douglas, Brennan, and Stewart dissented.]

Mr. Chief Justice Warren announced the judgment of the Court and an opinion in which Mr. Justice Black, Mr. Justice Clark, and Mr. Justice Whittaker concur:

This case concerns the constitutional validity of the application to appellants of the Pennsylvania criminal statute, enacted in 1959, which proscribes the Sunday retail sale of certain enumerated commodities. Among the questions presented are whether the statute is a law respecting an establishment of religion and whether the statute violates equal protection. Since both of these questions, in reference to this very statute, have already been answered in the negative, *Two Guys from Harrison–Allentown, Inc.,* v. *McGinley,* and since appellants present nothing new regarding them, they need not be considered here. Thus, the only question for consideration is whether the statute interferes with the free exercise of appellants' religion.

Appellants are merchants in Philadelphia who engage in the retail sale of clothing and home furnishings within the proscription of the statute in issue. Each of the appellants is a member of the Orthodox Jewish faith, which requires the closing of their places of business and a total abstention from all manner of work from nightfall each Friday until nightfall each Saturday. They instituted a suit in the court below seeking a permanent injunction against the enforcement of the 1959 statute. Their complaint, as amended, alleged that appellants had previously kept their places of business open on Sunday; that each of appellants had done a substantial amount of business on Sunday, compensating somewhat for their closing on Saturday; that Sunday closing will result in impairing the ability of all appellants to earn a livelihood and will render appellant Braunfeld unable to continue in his business, thereby losing his capital investment; that the statute is unconstitutional for the reasons stated above.

A three-judge court was properly convened and it dismissed the complaint on the authority of the *Two Guys from Harrison* case. . . . On appeal brought under 28 U.S.C. § 1253, we noted probable jurisdiction.

Appellants contend that the enforcement against them of the Pennsylvania statute will prohibit the free exercise of their religion because, due to the statute's compulsion to close on Sunday, appellants will suffer substantial economic loss, to the benefit of their non-Sabbatarian competitors, if appellants also continue their Sabbath observance by closing their businesses on Saturday; that this result will either compel appellants to give up their Sabbath observance, a basic tenet of the Orthodox Jewish faith, or will put appellants at a serious economic disadvantage if they continue to adhere to their Sabbath. Appellants also assert that the statute will operate so as to hinder the Orthodox Jewish faith in gaining new adherents. And the corollary to these arguments is that if the free exercise of appellants' religion is impeded, that religion is being subjected to discriminatory treatment by the State.

In *McGowan* v. *Maryland,* we noted the significance that this Court has attributed to the development of religious freedom in Virginia in determining the scope of the First Amendment's protection. We observed that when Virginia passed its Declaration of Rights in 1776, providing that "all men are equally entitled to the free exercise of religion," Virginia repealed its laws which in any way penalized "maintaining any opinions in matters of religion, forebearing to repair to church, or the exercising any mode of worship whatsoever." But, Virginia retained its laws prohibiting Sunday labor.

We also took cognizance, in *McGowan,* of the evolution of Sunday Closing Laws from wholly religious sanctions to legislation concerned with the establishment of a day of community tranquility, respite and recreation, a day when the atmosphere is one of calm and relaxation rather than one of commercialism, as it is during the other six days of the week. We reviewed the still growing state preoccupation with improving the health, safety, morals and general well-being of our citizens.

Concededly, appellants and all other persons who wish to work on Sunday will be burdened economically by the State's day of rest mandate; and appellants point out that their religion requires them to refrain from work on Saturday as well. Our inquiry then is whether, in these circumstances, the First and Fourteenth Amendments forbid application of the Sunday Closing Law to appellants.

Certain aspects of religious exercise cannot, in any way, be restricted or burdened by either federal or state legislation. Compulsion by law of the acceptance of any creed or the practice of any form of worship is strictly forbidden. The freedom to hold religious beliefs and opinions is absolute. *Cantwell* v. *Connecticut,* 310 US 296; *Reynolds* v. *United States,* 98 US 145. Thus, in *West Virginia State Board of Education* v. *Barnette,* 319 US 624, this Court held that state action compelling school children to salute the flag, on pain of expulsion from public school, was contrary to the First and Fourteenth Amendments when applied to those students whose religious beliefs forbade saluting a flag. But, this is not the case at bar; the statute before us does not make criminal the holding of any religious belief or opinion, nor does it force anyone to embrace any religious belief or to say or believe anything in conflict with his religious tenets.

However, the freedom to act, even when the action is in accord with one's religious convictions, is not totally free from legislative restrictions. . . . As pointed out in *Reynolds* v. *United States, supra,* . . . legislative power over mere opinion is forbidden but it may reach people's actions when they are found to be in violation of important social duties or subversive of good order, even when the actions are demanded by one's religion. This was articulated by Thomas Jefferson when he said:

Believing with you that religion is a matter which lies solely between man and his God, that he owes account to none other for his faith or his worship, that *the legislative powers of the government reach actions only, and not opinions,* I contemplate with sovereign reverence that act of the whole American people which declared that their legislature should "make no law respecting an establishment of religion, or prohibiting the free exercise thereof," thus building a wall of separation between church and State. Adhering to this expression of the supreme will of the nation in behalf of the rights of conscience, I shall see with sincere satisfaction the progress of those sentiments, which tend to restore to man all his natural rights, convinced *he has no natural right in opposition to his social duties.*" (Emphasis added.) 8 *Works of Thomas Jefferson* 113.*

And, in the *Barnette* case, the Court was careful to point out that "the freedom asserted by these appellees does not bring them into collision with rights asserted by any other individual. It is such conflicts which most frequently require intervention of the State to determine where the rights of one end and those of another begin. . . . It is . . . to be noted that the compulsory flag salute and pledge requires *affirmation of a belief* and an *attitude of mind.*" (Emphasis added.)

Thus, in *Reynolds* v. *United States,* this Court upheld the polygamy conviction of a member of the Mormon faith despite the fact that an accepted doctrine of his church then imposed upon its male members the *duty* to practice polygamy. And, in *Prince* v. *Massachusetts,* 321 US 158, this Court upheld a statute making it a crime for a girl under eighteen years of age to sell any newspapers, periodicals or merchandise in public places despite the fact that a child of the Jehovah's Witnesses faith believed that it was her religious *duty* to perform this work.

It is to be noted that, in the two cases just mentioned, the religious practices themselves conflicted with the public interest. In such cases, to make accommodation between the religious action and an exercise of state authority is a particularly delicate task, . . . because resolution in favor of the State results in the choice of the individual of either abandoning his religious principle or facing criminal prosecution.

But, again, this is not the case before us because the statute at bar does not make unlawful any religious practices of appellants; the Sunday law simply regulates a secular activity and, as applied to appellants, operates so as to make the practice of their religious beliefs more expensive. Furthermore, the law's effect does not inconvenience all members of the Orthodox Jewish faith but only those who believe it necessary to work on Sunday. And even these are not faced with as serious a choice as forsaking their religious practices or subjecting themselves to criminal prosecution. Fully recognizing that the alternatives open to appellants and others similarly situated—retaining their present occupations and incurring economic disadvantage or engaging in some other commercial activity which does not call for either Saturday or Sunday labor—may well result in some financial sacrifice in order to observe their religious beliefs, still the option is wholly different than when the legislation attempts to make a religious practice itself unlawful.

To strike down, without the most critical scrutiny, legislation which imposes only an indirect burden on the exercise of religion, i.e., legislation which does not make unlawful the religious practice itself, would radically restrict the operating latitude

---

* Oliver Ellsworth, a member of the Constitutional Convention and later Chief Justice, wrote:
"But while I assert the rights of religious liberty, I would not deny that the civil power has a right, in some cases, to interfere in matters of religion. It has a right to prohibit and punish gross immoralities and impieties; because the open *practice* of these is of evil example and detriment." (Emphasis added.) Written in the Connecticut *Courant,* Dec. 17, 1787, as quoted in 1 Stokes, *Church and State in the United States,* 535.

of the legislature. Statutes which tax income and limit the amount which may be deducted for religious contributions impose an indirect economic burden on the observance of the religion of the citizen whose religion requires him to donate a greater amount to his church; statutes which require the courts to be closed on Saturday and Sunday impose a similar indirect burden on the observance of the religion of the trial lawyer whose religion requires him to rest on a weekday. The list of legislation of this nature is nearly limitless.

Needless to say, when entering the area of religious freedom, we must be fully cognizant of the particular protection that the Constitution has accorded it. Abhorrence of religious persecution and intolerance is a basic part of our heritage. But we are a cosmopolitan nation made up of people of almost every conceivable religious preference. These denominations number almost three hundred. . . . Consequently, it cannot be expected, much less required, that legislators enact no law regulating conduct that may in some way result in an economic disadvantage to some religious sects and not to others because of the special practices of the various religions. We do not believe that such an effect is an absolute test for determining whether the legislation violates the freedom of religion protected by the First Amendment.

Of course, to hold unassailable all legislation regulating conduct which imposes solely an indirect burden on the observance of religion would be a gross oversimplification. If the purpose or effect of a law is to impede the observance of one or all religions or is to discriminate invidiously between religions, that law is constitutionally invalid even though the burden may be characterized as being only indirect. But if the State regulates conduct by enacting a general law within its power, the purpose and effect of which is to advance the State's secular goals, the statute is valid despite its indirect burden on religious observance unless the State may accomplish its purpose by means which do not impose such a burden. . . .

As we pointed out in *McGowan* v. *Maryland,* we cannot find a State without power to provide a weekly respite from all labor and, at the same time, to set one day of the week apart from the others as a day of rest, repose, recreation and tranquility—a day when the hectic tempo of everyday existence ceases and a more pleasant atmosphere is created, a day which all members of the family and community have the opportunity to spend and enjoy together, a day in which people may visit friends and relatives who are not available during working days, a day when the weekly laborer may best regenerate himself. This is particularly true in this day and age of increasing state concern with public welfare legislation.

Also, in *McGowan,* we examined several suggested alternative means by which it was argued that the State might accomplish its secular goals without even remotely or incidentally affecting religious freedom. We found there that a State might well find that those alternatives would not accomplish bringing about a general day of rest. We need not examine them again here.

However, appellants advance yet another means at the State's disposal which they would find unobjectionable. They contend that the State should cut an exception from the Sunday labor proscription for those people who, because of religious conviction, observe a day of rest other than Sunday. By such regulation, appellants contend, the economic disadvantages imposed by the present system would be removed and the State's interest in having all people rest one day would be satisfied.

A number of States provide such an exemption, and this may well be the wiser solution to the problem. But our concern is not with the wisdom of legislation but with its constitutional limitation. Thus, reason and experience teach that to permit the exemption might well undermine the State's goal of providing a day that, as best possible, eliminates the atmosphere of commercial noise and activity. Although not dispositive of the issue, enforcement problems would be more difficult since there would be two or more days to police rather than one and it would be more difficult to observe whether violations were occurring.

Additional problems might also be presented by a regulation of this sort. To allow only people who rest on a day other than Sunday to keep their businesses open on that day might well provide these people with an economic advantage over their competitors who must remain closed on that day;* this might cause the Sunday-observers to complain that their religions are being discriminated against. With this competitive advantage existing, there could well be the temptation for some, in order to keep their businesses open on Sunday, to assert that they have religious convictions which compel them to close their businesses on what had formerly been their least profitable day. This might make necessary a state-conducted inquiry into the sincerity of the individual's religious beliefs, a practice which a State might believe would itself run afoul of the spirit of constitutionally protected religious guarantees. Finally, in order to keep the disruption of the day at a minimum, exempted employers would probably have to hire employees who themselves qualified for the exemption because of their own religious beliefs, a practice which a State might feel to be opposed to its general policy prohibiting religious discrimination in hiring. For all of these reasons, we cannot say that the Pennsylvania statute before us is invalid, either on its face or as applied.

Accordingly, the decision is affirmed.

Mr. Justice Douglas, dissenting:

The question is not whether one day out of seven can be imposed by a State as a day of rest. The question is not whether Sunday can by force of custom and habit be retained as a day of rest. The question is whether a State can impose criminal sanctions on those who, unlike the Christian majority that makes up our society, worship on a different day or do not share the religious scruples of the majority.

If the "free exercise" of religion were subject to reasonable regulations, as it is under some constitutions, or if all laws "respecting the establishment of religion" were not proscribed, I could understand how rational men, representing a predominantly Christian civilization, might think these Sunday laws did not unreasonably interfer with any one's free exercise of religion and took no step toward a burdensome establishment of any religion.

---

* "If he [the Orthodox Jewish storekeeper] opens on Saturday, he is subjected to very fierce competition indeed from Christian shopkeepers, whereas on Sunday, supposing he closes on Saturday, he has an absolutely free run and no competition from Christian shopkeepers at all." 311 Parliamentary Debates, Commons, 492.

"It is true that the orthodox Jew will only be allowed to trade until two o'clock on Sunday, but during that time he will have a monopoly. That is a tremendous advantage. In many districts he will be the only trader with a shop open in that district." 101 Parliamentary Debates, Lords, 430.

But that is not the premise from which we start, as there is agreement that the fact that a State, and not the Federal Government, has promulgated these Sunday laws does not change the scope of the power asserted. For the classic view is that the First Amendment should be applied to the States with the same firmness as it is enforced against the Federal Government. . . . The most explicit statement perhaps was in *Board of Education* v. *Barnette* . . . [:]

> In weighing arguments of the parties it is important to distinguish between the due process clause of the Fourteenth Amendment as an instrument for transmitting the principles of the First Amendment and those cases in which it is applied for its own sake. The test of legislation which collides with the Fourteenth Amendment, because it also collides with the principles of the First, is much more definite than the test when only the Fourteenth is involved. Much of the vagueness of the due process clause disappears when the specific prohibitions of the First become its standard. The right of a State to regulate, for example, a public utility may well include, so far as the due process test is concerned, power to impose all of the restrictions which a legislature may have a "rational basis" for adopting. But freedoms of speech and of press, of assembly, and of worship may not be infringed on such slender grounds. They are susceptible of restriction only to prevent grave and immediate danger to interests which the State may lawfully protect. It is important to note that while it is the Fourteenth Amendment which bears directly upon the State it is the more specific limiting principles of the First Amendment that finally govern this case.

With that as my starting point I do not see how a State can make protesting citizens refrain from doing innocent acts on Sunday because the doing of those acts offends sentiments of their Christian neighbors.

The institutions of our society are founded on the belief that there is an authority higher than the authority of the State; that there is a moral law which the State is powerless to alter; that the individual possesses rights, conferred by the Creator, which government must respect. The Declaration of Independence stated the now familiar theme:

> We hold these truths to be self evident, that all men are created equal, that they are endowed by their Creator with certain inalienable rights, that among these are life, liberty, and the pursuit of happiness.

And the body of the Constitution as well as the Bill of Rights enshrined those principles.

The Puritan influence helped shape our constitutional law and our common law as Dean Pound has said: The Puritan "put individual conscience and individual judgment in the first place." *The Spirit of the Common Law* (1921), p. 42. For these reasons we stated in *Zorach* v. *Clauson*, 343 U.S. 306, "We are a religious people whose institutions presuppose a Supreme Being."

But those who fashioned the Constitution decided that if and when God is to be served, His service will not be motivated by coercive measures of government. "Congress shall make no law respecting an establishment of religion, or prohibiting the free exercise thereof"—such is the command of the First Amendment made applicable to the State by reason of the Due Process Clause of the Fourteenth. This means, as I understand it, that if a religious leaven is to be worked into the affairs of our people, it is to be done by individuals and groups, not by the government. This necessarily means, *first,* that the dogma, creed, scruples, or practices of no religious group or sect are to be preferred over those of any others; *second,* that no one shall be interfered with by government for practicing the religion of his choice; *third,* that the State may not require anyone to practice a religion or even any religion; and *fourth,* that the State cannot compel one so to conduct himself as not to offend the religious scruples of another. The idea, as I understand it, was to limit the power of government to act in religious matters . . . not to limit the freedom of religious men to act religiously nor to restrict the freedom of atheists or agnostics.

The First Amendment commands government to have no interest in theology or ritual; it admonishes government to be interested in allowing religious freedom to flourish—whether the result is to produce Catholics, Jews, or Protestants, or to turn the people toward the path of Buddha, or to end in a predominantly Moslem nation, or to produce in the long run atheists or agnostics. On matters of this kind government must be neutral. This freedom plainly includes freedom *from* religion with the right to believe, speak, write, publish and advocate antireligious programs. . . . Certainly the "free exercise" clause does not require that everyone embrace the theology of some church or of some faith, or observe the religious practices of any majority or minority sect. The First Amendment by its "establishment" clause prevents, of course, the selection of government of an "official" church. Yet the ban plainly extends farther than that. We said in *Everson* v. *Board of Education,* that it would be an "establishment" of a religion if the government financed one church or several churches. For what better way to "establish" an institution than to find the fund that will support it? The "establishment" clause protects citizens also against any law which selects any religious custom, practice, or ritual, puts the force of government behind it, and fines, imprisons, or otherwise penalizes a person for not observing it. The government plainly could not join forces with one religious group and decree a universal and symbolic circumcision. Nor could it require all children to be baptized or give tax exemptions only to those whose children were baptized.

Could it require a fast from sunrise to sunset throughout the Moslem month of Ramadan? I should think not. Yet why then can it make criminal the doing of other acts, as innocent as eating, during the day that Christians revere?

Sunday is a word heavily overlaid with connotations and traditions deriving from the Christian roots of our civilization that color all judgments concerning it. This is what the philosophers call "word magic."

> For most judges, for most lawyers, for most human beings, we are as unconscious of our value patterns as we are of the oxygen that we breathe. Cohen, *Legal Conscience* (1960), p. 169.

The issue of these cases would therefore be in better focus if we imagined that a state legislature, controlled by Orthodox Jews and Seventh Day Adventists, passed a law making it a crime to keep a shop open on Saturdays. Would a Baptist, Catholic, Methodist, or Presbyterian be compelled to obey that law or go to jail or pay a fine? Or suppose Moslems grew in political strength here and got a law through a state legislature making it a crime to keep a shop open on Fridays? Would the rest of us have to submit under the fear of criminal sanctions?

Dr. John Cogley recently summed up the dominance of the three-religion influence in our affairs:

> For the foreseeable future, it seems, the United States is going to be a three-religion nation. At the present time all three are characteristically "American," some think flavorlessly so. For religion in America is almost uniformly "respectable," bourgeois, and prosperous. In the Protestant world the "church" mentality has triumphed over

the more venturesome spirit of the "sect." In the Catholic world, the mystical is muted in favor of booming organization and efficiently administered good works. And in the Jewish world the prophet is too frequently without honor, while the synagogue emphasis is focused on suburban togetherness. There are exceptions to these rules, of course; each of the religious communities continues to cast up its prophets, its rebels and radicals. But a Jeremiah, one fears, would be positively embarrassing to the present position of the Jews; a Francis of Assisi upsetting the complacency of American Catholics would be rudely dismissed as a fanatic; and a Kierkegaard, speaking with an American accent, would be considerably less welcome than Norman Vincent Peale in most Protestant pulpits.

This religious influence has extended far, far back of the First and Fourteenth Amendments. Every Sunday school student knows the Fourth Commandment:

Remember the sabbath day, to keep it holy.
Six days shalt thou labour, and do thy work;
But the seventh day is the sabbath of the LORD thy God: in it thou shalt not do any work, thou, nor thy son, nor thy daughter, thy manservant, nor thy maidservant, nor thy cattle, nor thy stranger that is within thy gates:
For in six days the LORD made heaven and earth, the sea, and all that in them is, and rested the seventh day: wherefore the LORD blessed the sabbath day, and hallowed it. Exodus 20:8–11.

This religious mandate for observance of the Seventh Day became, under Emperor Constantine, a mandate for observance of the First Day "in conformity with the practice of the Christian Church." . . . This religious mandate has had a checkered history, but in general its command, enforced now by the ecclesiastical authorities, now by the civil authorities, and now by both, has held good down through the centuries. The general pattern of these laws in the United States was set in the eighteenth century and derives, most directly, from a seventeenth century English statute. . . . Judicial comment on the Sunday laws has always been a mixed bag. Some judges have asserted that the stautes have a "purely" civil aim, *i.e.,* limitation of work time and provision for a common and universal leisure. But other judges have recognized the religious significance of Sunday and that the laws existed to enforce the maintenance of that significance. In general, both threads of argument have continued to interweave in the case law on the subject. Prior to the time when the First Amendment was held applicable to the States by reason of the Due Process Clause of the Fourteenth, the Court at least by *obiter dictum* approved State Sunday laws on three occasions: *Soon Hing* v. *Crowley,* 113 US 703, in 1885; *Hennington* v. *Georgia,* 163 US 299, in 1896; *Petit* v. *Minnesota,* 117 US 164, in 1900. And in *Friedman* v. *New York,* 341 US 907, the Court, by a divided vote, dismissed "for want of a substantial federal question" an appeal from a New York decision upholding the validity of a Sunday law against an attack based on the First Amendement.

The *Soon Hing, Hennington,* and *Petit* cases all rested on the police power of the State—the right to safeguard the health of the people by requiring the cessation of normal activities one day of seven. The Court in the *Soon Hing* case rejected the idea that Sunday laws rested on the power of government "to legislate for the promotion of religious observances." The New York Court of Appeals in the *Friedman* case followed the reasoning of the earlier cases.

The Massachusetts Sunday law involved in one of these appeals was once characterized by the Massachusetts court as merely a civil regulation providing for a "fixed period of rest." *Commonwealth* v. *Has,* 122 Mass. 40. That decision was, according to the District Court in the *Gallagher* case, "an *ad hoc* improvisation" made "because of the realization that the Sunday law would be more vulnerable to constitutional attack under the State Constitution if the religious motivation of the statute were more explicitly avowed." Certainly prior to the *Has* case, the Massachusetts courts had indicated that the aim of the Sunday law was religious. . . . After the *Has* case the Massachusetts court construed the Sunday law as a religious measure. In *Davis* v. *Somerville,* 128 Mass. 594, it was said:

> Our Puritan ancestors intended that the day should be not merely a day of rest from labor, but also a day devoted to public and private worship and to religious meditation and repose, undisturbed by secular cares or amusements. They saw fit to enforce the observance of the day by penal legislation, and the statute regulations which they devised for that purpose have continued in force, without any substantial modification, to the present time. . . .

In *Commonwealth* v. *White,* 190 Mass. 578, 581, 177 N.E. 636, 637, the court refused to liberalize its construction of an exception in its Sunday law for works of "necessity." That word, it said, "was originally inserted to secure the observance of the Lord's day in accordance with the views of our ancestors, and it ever since has stood and still stands for the same purpose," In *Commonwealth* v. *McCarthy,* 244 Mass. 484, the court reiterated that the aim of the law was "to secure respect and reverence for the Lord's day."

The Pennsylvania Sunday laws before us . . . have received the same construction. "Rest and quiet, on the Sabbath day, with the right and privilege of public and private worship, undisturbed by any mere worldly employment, are exactly what the statute was passed to protect." *Sparhawk* v. *Union Passenger R. Co.,* 54 Pa. 401. . . . A recent pronouncement by the Pennsylvania Supreme Court is found in *Commonwealth* v. *American Baseball Club,* 290 Pa. 136: "Christianity is part of the common law of Pennsylvania . . . and its people are christian people. Sunday is the holy day among christians."

The Maryland court in sustaining the challenged law . . . relied on *Judefind* v. *State,* 78 Md. 510, and *Levering* v. *Park Commissioner,* 134 Md. 48. In the former the court said:

> It is undoubtedly true that rest from secular employment on Sunday does have a tendency to foster and encourage the Christian religion—of all sects and denominations that observe that day—as rest from work and ordinary occupation enables many to engage in public worship who probably would not otherwise do so. But it would scarcely be asked of a Court, in what professes to be a Christian land, to declare a law unconstitutional because it requires rest from bodily labor on Sunday (except works of necessity and charity), and *thereby* promotes the cause of Christianity. If the Christian religion is, incidentally or otherwise, benefited or fostered by having this day of rest, as it undoubtedly is, there is all the more reason for the enforcement of laws that help to preserve it. . . .

We have then in each of the four cases Sunday laws that find their source in Exodus, that were brought here by the Puritans, and that are today maintained, construed, and justified because they respect the views of our dominant religious groups and provide a needed day of rest.

The history was accurately summarized a century ago by Chief Justice Terry of the Supreme Court of California in *Ex parte Newman,* 9 Cal. 502.

The truth is, however much it may be disguised, that this one day of rest is a purely religious idea. Derived from the Sabbatical institutions of the ancient Hebrew, it has been adopted into all the creeds of succeeding religious sects throughout the civilized world; and whether it be the Friday of the Mohammedan, the Saturday of the Israelite, or the Sunday of the Christian, it is alike fixed in the affections of its followers, beyond the power of eradication, and in most of the States of our Confederacy, the aid of the law to enforce its observance has been given under the pretence of a civil, municipal, or police regulation.

That case involved the validity of a Sunday law under a provision of the California Constitution guaranteeing the "free exercise" of religion. . . . Justice Burnett stated why he concluded that the Sunday law, there sought to be enforced against a man selling clothing on Sunday, infringed California's constitution:

Had the act made Monday, instead of Sunday, a day of compulsory rest, the constitutional question would have been the same. The fact that the Christian *voluntarily* keeps holy the first day of the week, does not authorize the Legislature to make that observance *compulsory*. The Legislature can not compel the citizen to do that which the Constitution leaves him free to do or omit, at his election. The act violates as much the religious freedom of the Christian as of the Jew. Because the conscientious views of the Christian compel him to keep Sunday as a Sabbath, he has the right to object, when the Legislature invades his freedom of religious worship, and assumes the power to compel him to do that which he has the right to omit if he pleases. The principle is the same, whether the act of the Legislature *compels* us to do that which we wish to do, or not to do. . . .

Under the Constitution of this State, the Legislature can not pass any act, the legitimate effect of which is *forcibly* to establish any merely religious truth, or enforce any merely religious observances. The Legislature has no power over such a subject. When, therefore, the citizen is sought to be compelled by the Legislature to do any affirmative religious act, or to refrain from doing anything, because it violates simply a religious principle or observance, the act is unconstitutional.

The Court picks and chooses language from various decisions to bolster its conclusion that these Sunday laws in the modern setting are "civil regulations." No matter how much is written, no matter what is said, the parentage of these laws is the Fourth Commandment; and they serve and satisfy the religious predispositions of our Christian communities. After all, the labels a State places on its laws are not binding on us when we are confronted with a constitutional decision. We reach our own conclusion as to the character, effect, and practical operation of the regulation in determining its constitutionality. . . .

It seems to me plain that by these laws the State compel one, under sanction of law, to refrain from work or recreation on Sunday because of the majority's religious views about that day. The State by law makes Sunday a symbol of respect or adherence. Refraining from work or recreation in deference to the majority's religious feelings about Sunday is within every person's choice. By what authority can government compel it?

Cases are put where acts that are immoral by our standards but not by the standards of other religious groups are made criminal. That category of cases, until today, has been a very restricted one confined to polygamy (*Reynolds* v. *United States,* 98 US 145) and other extreme situations. The latest example is *Prince* v. *Massachusetts,* 321 US 158, which upheld a statute making it criminal for a child under twelve to sell papers, periodicals, or merchandise on a street or in any public place. It was sustained in spite of the finding that the child thought it was her religious duty to perform the act. But that was a narrow holding which turned on the effect which street solicitation might have on the child-solicitor. . . . None of the acts involved here implicates minors. None of the actions made constitutionally criminal today involves the doing of any act that any society has deemed to be immoral.

The conduct held constitutionally criminal today embraces the selling of pure, not impure, food; wholesome, not noxious, articles. Adults, not minors, are involved. The innocent acts, now constitutionally classified as criminal, emphasize the drastic break we make with tradition.

These laws are sustained because, it is said, the First Amendment is concerned with religious convictions or opinion, not with conduct. But it is a strange Bill of Rights that makes it possible for the dominant religious group to bring the minority to heel because the minority, in the doing of acts which intrinsically are wholesome and not antisocial, does not defer to the majority's religious beliefs. Some have religious scruples against eating pork. Those scruples, no matter how bizarre they might seem to some, are within the ambit of the First Amendment. . . . Is it possible that a majority of a state legislature having those religious scruples could make it criminal for the nonbeliever to sell pork? Some have religious scruples against slaughtering cattle. Could a state legislature, dominated by that group, make it criminal to run an abattoir?

The Court balances the need of the people for rest, recreation, late-sleeping, family visiting and the like against the command of the First Amendment that no one need bow to the religious beliefs of another. There is in this realm no room for balancing. I see no place for it in the constitutional scheme. A legislature of Christians can no more make minorities conform to their weekly regime than a legislature of Moslems, or a legislature of Hindus. The religious regime of every group must be respected—unless it crosses the line of criminal conduct. But no one can be forced to come to a halt before it, or refrain from doing things that would offend it. That is my reading of the Establishment Clause and the Free Exercise Clause. Any other reading imports, I fear, an element common in other societies but foreign to us. Thus Nigeria in Article 23 of her Constitution, after guaranteeing religious freedom, adds, "Nothing in this section shall invalidate any law that is reasonably justified in a democratic society in the interest of defense, public safety, public order, public morality, or public health." And see Article 25 of the Indian Constitution. That may be a desirable provision. But when the Court adds it to our First Amendment, as it does today, we make a sharp break with the American ideal of religious liberty as enshrined in the First Amendment.

The State can of course require one day of rest a week: one day when every shop or factory is closed. Quite a few States make that requirement. Then the "day of rest" becomes purely and simply a health measure. But the Sunday laws operate differently. They force minorities to obey the majority's religious feelings of what is due and proper for a Christian community; they provide a coercive spur to the "weaker brethern," to those who are indifferent to the claims of a Sabbath through apathy or scruple. Can there be any doubt that Christians, now aligned vigorously in favor of these laws, would be as strongly opposed, if they were prosecuted under a Moslem law that forbade them from engaging in secular activities on days that violated Moslem scruples?

There is an "establishment" of religion in the constitutional sense if any practice of any religious group has the sanction of law behind it. There is an interference with the "free exercise" of religion if what in conscience one can do or omit doing is required because of the religious scruples of the community. Hence I would declare each of those laws unconstitutional as applied to the complaining parties, whether or not they are members of a sect which observes as their Sabbath a day other than Sunday.

When these laws are applied to Orthodox Jews . . . or to Sabbatarians their vice is accentuated. If the Sunday laws are constitutional, Kosher markets are on a five-day week. Thus those laws put an economic penalty on those who observe Saturday rather than Sunday as the Sabbath. For the economic pressures on these minorities, created by the fact that our communities are predominantly Sunday-minded, there is no recourse. When, however, the State uses its coercive powers—here the criminal law—to compel minorities to observe a second Sabbath, not their own, the State undertakes to aid and "prefer one religion over another"—contrary to the command of the Constitution. . . .

In large measure the history of the religious clause of the First Amendment was a struggle to be free of economic sanctions for adherence to one's religion. . . . A small tax was imposed in Virginia for religious education. Jefferson and Madison led the fight against the tax, Madison writing his famous Memorial and Remonstrance against that law. As a result, the tax measure was defeated and instead Virginia's famous "Bill for Religious Liberty," written by Jefferson, was enacted. That Act provided:

> That no man shall be compelled to frequent or support any religious worship, place, or ministry whatsoever, nor shall be enforced, restrained, molested, or burthened in his body or goods, nor shall otherwise suffer on account of his religious opinions or belief. . . .

The reverse side of an "establishment" is a burden on the "free exercise" of religion. Receipt of funds from the state benefits the established church directly; laying an extra tax on nonmembers benefits the established church indirectly. Certainly the present Sunday laws place Orthdox Jews and Sabbatarians under extra burdens because of their religious opinions or beliefs. Requiring them to abstain from their trade or business on Sunday reduces their work-week to five days, unless they violate their religious scruples. This places them at a competitive disadvantage and penalizes them for adhering to their religious beliefs.

"The sanction imposed by the state for observing a day other than Sunday as holy time is certainly more serious economically than the imposition of a license tax for preaching," which we struck down in *Murdock* v. *Pennsylvania*, 319 US 105, and in *Follett* v. *McCormick*, 321 US 573. The special protection which Sunday laws give the dominant religious groups and the penalty they place on minorities whose holy day is Saturday constitute in my view state interference with the "free exercise" of religion.

I dissent from applying criminal sanctions against any of these complainants since to do so implicates the States in religious matters contrary to the constitutional mandate. Allan C. Parker, Jr., Pastor of the South Park Presbyterian Church, Seattle, Washington, has stated my views:

> We forget that, though Sunday-worshipping Christians are in the majority in this country among religious people, we do not have the right to force our practice upon the minority. Only a Church which deems itself without error and intolerant of error can justify its intolerance of the minority.
>
> A Jewish friend of mine runs a small business establishment. Because my friend is a Jew he closes his store voluntarily so that he will be able to worship his God in his fashion. Fine! But, as a Jew living under Christian inspired Sunday closing laws, he is required to close his store on Sunday so that I will be able to worship my God in my fashion.
>
> Around the corner from my church there is a small Seventh Day Baptist church. I disagree with the Seventh Day Baptists on many points of doctrine. Among the tenets of their faith with which I disagree is the "seventh day worship." But they

are good neighbors and fellow Christians, and while we disagree we respect one another. The good people of my congregation set aside their jobs on the first of the week and gather in God's house for worship. Of course, it is easy for them to set aside their jobs since Sunday closing laws—inspired by the Church—keep them from their work. At the Seventh Day Baptist church the people set aside their jobs on Saturday to worship God. This takes real sacrifice because Saturday is a good day for business. But that is not all—they are required by law to set aside their jobs on Sunday while more orthodox Christians worship. . . .

I do not believe that because I have set aside Sunday as a holy day I have the right to force all men to set aside that day also. Why should my faith be favored by the State over any other man's faith?

With all deference none of the opinions filed today in support of the Sunday laws have answered that question.

SHERBERT *v.* VERNER
374 US 398 (1963)

[A Seventh-Day Adventist was discharged by her employer for refusing to work on Saturday, and was then refused unemployment compensation by the state because she had refused to accept "available suitable work." The South Carolina state courts upheld the denial of unemployment compensation. The United States Supreme Court, by 7–2 vote, reversed, and held that the denial of unemployment compensation restricted her free exercise of religion. The Court distinguished this case from *Braunfeld* v. *Brown, supra*. The majority opinion was by Justice Brennan. Justices Douglas and Stewart wrote concurring opinions. Justice Harlan wrote a dissenting opinion, in which Justice White joined.]

Mr. Justice Brennan delivered the opinion of the Court:

Appellant, a member of the Seventh-day Adventist Church, was discharged by her South Carolina employer because she would not work on Saturday, the Sabbath Day of her faith.* When she was unable to obtain other employment because from conscientious scruples she would not take Saturday work,† she filed a claim for unemployment compensation benefits under the South Carolina Unemployment Compensation Act. That law provides that, to be eligible for benefits, a claimant must be "able to work and . . . available for work"; and, further, that a claimant is ineligible for benefits "[i]f . . . he has failed, without good cause . . . to accept available suitable work when offered him by the employment office or the

---

* Appellant became a member of the Seventh-day Adventist Church in 1957, at a time when her employer, a textile-mill operator, permitted her to work a five-day week. It was not until 1959 that the work week was changed to six days, including Saturday, for all three shifts in the employer's mill. No question has been raised in this case concerning the sincerity of appellant's religious beliefs. Nor is there any doubt that the prohibition against Saturday labor is a basic tenet of the Seventh-day Adventist creed, based upon that religion's interpretation of the Holy Bible.

† After her discharge, appellant sought employment with three other mills in the Spartanburg area, but found no suitable five-day work available at any of the mills. In filing her claim with the Commission, she expressed a willingness to accept employment at other mills, or even in another industry, so long as Saturday work was not required. The record indicates that of the 150 or more Seventh-day Adventists in the Spartanburg area, only appellant and one other have been unable to find suitable non-Saturday employment.

employer. . . ." The appellee Employment Security Commission, in administrative proceedings under the statute, found that appellant's restriction upon her availability for Saturday work brought her within the provision disqualifying for benefits insured workers who fail, without good cause, to accept "suitable work when offered . . . by the employment office or the employer. . . ." The Commission's finding was sustained by the Court of Common Pleas for Spartanburg County. That court's judgment was in turn affirmed by the South Carolina Supreme Court, which rejected appellant's contention that, as applied to her, the disqualifying provisions of the South Carolina statute abridged her right to the free exercise of her religion secured under the Free Exercise Clause of the First Amendment through the Fourteenth Amendment. The State Supreme Court held specifically that appellant's ineligibility infringed no constitutional liberties because such a construction of the statute "places no restriction upon the appellant's freedom of religion nor does it in any way prevent her in the exercise of her right and freedom to observe her religious beliefs in accordance with the dictates of her conscience." We noted probable jurisdiction of appellant's appeal. We reverse the judgment of the South Carolina Supreme Court and remand for further proceedings not inconsistent with this opinion. . . .

II

We turn first to the question whether the disqualification for benefits imposes any burden on the free exercise of appellant's religion. We think it is clear that it does. In a sense the consequences of such a disqualification to religious principles and practices may be only an indirect result of welfare legislation within the State's general competence to enact; it is true that no criminal sanctions directly compel appellant to work a six-day week. But this is only the beginning, not the end, of our inquiry. For "[i]f the purpose or effect of a law is to impede the observance of one or all religions or is to discriminate invidiously between religions, that law is constitutionally invalid even though the burden may be characterized as being only indirect." *Braunfeld* v. *Brown, supra.* Here not only is it apparent that appellant's declared ineligibility for benefits derives solely from the practice of her religion, but the pressure upon her to forgo that practice is unmistakable. The ruling forces her to choose between following the precepts of her religion and forfeiting benefits, on the one hand, and abandoning one of the precepts of her religion in order to accept work, on the other hand. Governmental imposition of such a choice puts the same kind of burden upon the free exercise of religion as would a fine imposed against appellant for her Saturday worship.

Nor may the South Carolina court's construction of the statute be saved from constitutional infirmity on the ground that unemployment compensation benefits are not appellant's "right" but merely a "privilege." It is too late in the day to doubt that the liberties of religion and expression may be infringed by the denial of or placing of conditions upon a benefit or privilege. . . . In *Speiser* v. *Randall,* 357 US 513, we emphasized that conditions upon public benefits cannot be sustained if they so operate, whatever their purpose, as to inhibit or deter the exercise of First Amendment freedoms. We there struck down a condition which limited the availability of a tax exemption to those members of the exempted class who affirmed their loyalty to the state government granting the exemption. While the State was surely under no obligation to afford such an exemption, we held that the imposition of such a condition upon even a gratuitous benefit inevitably deterred or discouraged the exercise of First Amendment rights of expression and thereby threatened to "produce a result which the State could not command directly. . . . To deny an exemption to claimants who engage in certain forms of speech is in effect to penalize them for such speech." Likewise, to condition the availability of benefits upon this appellant's willingness to violate a cardinal principle of her religious faith effectively penalizes the free exercise of her constitutional liberties.

Significantly, South Carolina expressly saves the Sunday worshipper from having to make the kind of choice which we here hold infringes the Sabbatarian's religious liberty. When in times of "national emergency" the textile plants are authorized by the State Commissioner of Labor to operate on Sunday, "no employee shall be required to work on Sunday . . . who is conscientiously opposed to Sunday work; and if any employee should refuse to work on Sunday on account of conscientious . . . objections he or she shall not jeopardize his or her seniority by such refusal or be discriminated against in any other manner." SC Code, § 64-4. No question of the disqualification of a Sunday worshipper for benefits is likely to arise, since we cannot suppose that an employer will discharge him in violation of this statute. The unconstitutionality of the disqualification of the Sabbatarian is thus compounded by the religious discrimination which South Carolina's general statutory scheme necessarily effects.

III

We must next consider whether some compelling state interest enforced in the eligibility provisions of the South Carolina statute justifies the substantial infringement of appellant's First Amendment right. It is basic that no showing merely of a rational relationship to some colorable state interest would suffice; in this highly sensitive constitutional area, "[o]nly the gravest abuses, endangering paramount interests, give occasion for permissible limitation," *Thomas* v. *Collins*, 323 US 516. No such abuse or danger has been advanced in the present case. The appellees suggest no more than a possibility that the filing of fraudulent claims by unscrupulous claimants feigning religious objections to Saturday work might not only dilute the unemployment compensation fund but also hinder the scheduling by employers of necessary Saturday work. But that possibility is not apposite here because no such objection appears to have been made before the South Carolina Supreme Court, and we are unwilling to assess the importance of an asserted state interest without the views of the state court. Nor, if the contention had been made below, would the record appear to sustain it; there is no proof whatever to warrant such fears of malingering or deceit as those which the respondents now advance. Even if consideration of such evidence is not foreclosed by the prohibition against judicial inquiry into the truth or falsity of religious beliefs, *United States* v. *Ballard*, 322 US 78—a question as to which we intimate no view since it is not before us—it is highly doubtful whether such evidence would be sufficient to warrant a substantial infringement of religious liberties. For even if the possibility of spurious claims did threaten to dilute the fund and disrupt the scheduling of work, it would plainly be incumbent upon the appellees to demonstrate that no alternative forms of regulation would combat such abuses without infringing First Amendment rights. . . .

In these respects, then, the state interest asserted in the present case is wholly dissimilar to the interests which were found to justify the less direct burden upon religious practices in *Braunfeld* v. *Brown, supra.* The Court recognized that the Sunday closing law which that decision sustained undoubtedly served "to make the practice of [the Orthodox Jewish merchants'] . . . religious beliefs more expensive." But the statute was nevertheless saved by a countervailing factor which finds no equivalent in the instant case—a strong state interest in providing one uniform day of rest for all workers. That secular objective could be achieved, the Court found, only by declaring Sunday to be that day of rest. Requiring exemptions for Sabbatarians, while theoretically possible, appeared to present an administrative problem of such magnitude, or to afford the exempted class so great a competitive advantage, that such a requirement would have rendered the entire statutory scheme unworkable. In the present case no such justifications underlie the determination of the state court that appellant's religion makes her ineligible to receive benefits.

IV

In holding as we do, plainly we are not fostering the "establishment" of the Seventh-day Adventist religion in South Carolina, for the extension of unemployment benefits to Sabbatarians in common with Sunday worshippers reflects nothing more than the governmental obligation of neutrality in the face of religious differences, and does not represent that involvement of religious with secular institutions which it is the object of the Establishment Clause to forestall. . . . Nor does the recognition of the appellant's right to unemployment benefits under the state statute serve to abridge any other person's religious liberties. Nor do we, by our decision today, declare the existence of a constitutional right to unemployment benefits on the part of all persons whose religious convictions are the cause of their unemployment. This is not a case in which an employee's religious convictions serve to make him a nonproductive member of society. Finally, nothing we say today constrains the States to adopt any particular form or scheme of unemployment compensation. Our holding today is only that South Carolina may not constitutionally apply the eligibility provisions so as to constrain a worker to abandon his religious convictions respecting the day of rest. This holding but reaffirms a principle that we announced a decade and a half ago, namely that no State may "exclude individual Catholics, Lutherans, Mohammedans, Baptists, Jews, Methodists, Nonbelievers, Presbyterians, or the members of any other faith, *because of their faith, or lack of it,* from receiving the benefits of public welfare legislation." *Everson* v. *Board of Education,* 330 US 1. . . .

The judgment of the South Carolina Supreme Court is reversed and the case is remanded for further proceedings not inconsistent with this opinion.

It is so ordered.

4. Religious Test Oaths

TORCASO v. WATKINS
367 US 488 (1961)

[The Maryland Constitution, as construed by the highest state court, required a declaration of belief in God as a qualification for public office. The Supreme Court unanimously held that this requirement invaded freedom of religion and was therefore in violation of the First and Fourteenth Amendments. Justices Frankfurter and Harlan concurred in the result without an opinion.]

Mr. Justice Black delivered the opinion of the Court:

Article 37 of the Declaration of Rights of the Maryland Constitution provides:

[N]o religious test ought ever to be required as a qualification for any office of profit or trust in this State, other than a declaration of belief in the existence of God. . . .

The appellant Torcaso was appointed to the office of Notary Public by the Governor of Maryland but was refused a commission to serve because he would not declare his belief in God. He then brought this action in a Maryland Circuit Court to compel issuance of his commission, charging that the State's requirement that he declare this belief violated "the First and Fourteenth Amendments to the Constitution of the United States. . . ." The Circuit Court rejected these federal constitutional contentions, and the highest court of the State, the Court of Appeals, affirmed, holding that the state constitutional provision is self-executing and requires declaration of belief in God as a qualification for office without need for implementing legislation. . . .

There is, and can be, no dispute about the purpose or effect of the Maryland Declaration of Rights requirement before us—it sets up a religious test which was designed to and, if valid, does bar every person who refuses to declare a belief in God from holding a public "office of profit or trust" in Maryland. The power and authority of the State of Maryland thus is put on the side of one particular sort of believers—those who are willing to say they believe in "the existence of God." It is true that there is much historical precedent for such laws. Indeed, it was largely to escape religious test oaths and declarations that a great many of the early colonists left Europe and came here hoping to worship in their own way. It soon developed, however, that many of those who had fled to escape religious test oaths turned out to be perfectly willing, when they had the power to do so, to force dissenters from their faith to take test oaths in conformity with that faith. This brought on a host of laws in the new Colonies imposing burdens and disabilities of various kinds upon varied beliefs depending largely upon what group happened to be politically strong enough to legislate in favor of its own beliefs. The effect of all this was the formal or practical "establishment" of particular religious faiths in most of the Colonies, with consequent burdens imposed on the free exercise of the faiths of nonfavored believers.

There were, however, wise and far-seeing men in the Colonies—too many to mention—who spoke out against test oaths and all the philosophy of intolerance behind them. One of these, it so happens, was George Calvert (the first Lord Baltimore), who took a most important part in the original establishment of the Colony of Maryland. He was a Catholic and had, for this reason, felt compelled by his conscience to refuse to take the Oath of Supremacy in England at the cost of resigning from high governmental office. He again refused to take that oath when it was demanded by the Council of the Colony of Virginia, and as a result he was denied settlement in that Colony. A recent historian of the early period of Maryland's life has said that it was Calvert's hope and purpose to establish in Maryland a colonial government free from the religious persecutions he had known—one "securely beyond the reach of oaths. . . ."

When our Constitution was adopted, the desire to put the people "securely beyond the reach" of religious test oaths brought about the inclusion in Article VI of that document of a provision that "no religious Test shall ever be required as a Qualification to any Office or public Trust under the United States." Article VI supports the accuracy of our observations in *Girouard* v. *United States,* 328 US 61, that "[t]he test oath is abhorrent to our tradition." Not satisfied, however, with Article VI and other guarantees in the original Constitution, the First Congress proposed and the states very shortly thereafter adopted our Bill of Rights, including the First Amendment. That Amendment broke new constitutional ground in the protection it sought to afford to freedom of religion, speech, press, petition and assembly. Since prior cases in this Court have thoroughly explored and documented the history behind the First Amendment, the reasons for it, and the scope of the religious freedom it protects, we need not cover that ground again. What was said in our prior cases we think controls our decision here.

In *Cantwell* v. *Connecticut,* 310 US 296, we said:

The First Amendment declares that Congress shall make no law respecting an establishment of religion or prohibiting the free exercise thereof. The Fourteenth Amendment has rendered the legislatures of the states as incompetent as Congress to enact such laws. . . . Thus the Amendment embraces two concepts,—freedom to believe and freedom to act. The first is absolute but, in the nature of things, the second cannot be.

Later we decided *Everson* v. *Board of Education,* 330 US 1, and said this at pages 15 and 16:

The "establishment of religion" clause of the First Amendment means at least this: Neither a state nor the Federal Government can set up a church. Neither can pass laws which aid one religion, aid all religions, or prefer one religion over another. Neither can force nor influence a person to go to or to remain away from church against his will or force him to profess a belief or disbelief in any religion. No person can be punished for entertaining or professing religious beliefs or disbeliefs, for church attendance or nonattendance. No tax in any amount, large or small, can be levied to support any religious activities or institutions, whatever they may be called, or whatever form they may adopt to teach or practice religion. Neither a state nor the Federal Government can, openly or secretly, participate in the affairs of any religious organizations or groups and *vice versa*. In the words of Jefferson, the clause against establishment of religion by law was intended to erect "a wall of separation between church and State."

While there were strong dissents in the *Everson* case, they did not challenge the Court's interpretation of the First Amendment's coverage as being too broad, but thought the Court was applying that interpretation too narrowly to the facts of that case. Not long afterward, in *Illinois ex rel. McCollum* v. *Board of Education,* 333 US 203, we were urged to repudiate as dicta the above-quoted *Everson* interpretation of the scope of the First Amendment's coverage. We declined to do this, but instead strongly reaffirmed what had been said in *Everson,* calling attention to the fact that both the majority and the minority in *Everson* had agreed on the principles declared in this part of the *Everson* opinion. And a concurring opinion in *McCollum,* written by Mr. Justice Frankfurter and joined by the other *Everson* dissenters, said this:

We are all agreed that the First and Fourteenth Amendments have a secular reach far more penetrating in the conduct of Government than merely to forbid an "established church." . . . We renew our conviction that "we have staked the very existence of our country on the faith that complete separation between the state and religion is best for the state and best for religion."

The Maryland Court of Appeals thought, and it is argued here, that this Court's later holding and opinion in *Zorach* v. *Clauson,* 343 US 306, had in part repudiated the statement in the *Everson* opinion quoted above and previously reaffirmed in *McCollum.* But the Court's opinion in *Zorach* specifically stated: "We follow the *McCollum* case." . . . Nothing decided or written in *Zorach* lends support to the idea that the Court there intended to open up the way for government, state or federal, to restore the historically and constitutionally discredited policy of probing religious beliefs by test oaths or limiting public offices to persons who have, or perhaps more properly, profess to have a belief in some particular kind of religious concept.

We repeat and again reaffirm that neither a State nor the Federal Government can constitutionally force a person "to profess a belief or disbelief in any religion." Neither can constitutionally pass laws nor impose requirements which aid all religions as against non-believers, and neither can aid those religions based on a belief in the existence of God as against those religions founded on different beliefs.*

In upholding the State's religious test for public office the highest court of Maryland said:

The petitioner is not compelled to believe or disbelieve, under threat of punishment or other compulsion. True, unless he makes the declaration of belief he cannot hold public office in Maryland, but he is not compelled to hold office.

The fact, however, that a person is not compelled to hold public office cannot possibly be an excuse for barring him from office by state-imposed criteria forbidden by the Constitution. This was settled by our holding in *Wieman* v. *Updegraff,* 344 US 183. We there pointed out that whether or not "an abstract right to public employment exists," Congress could not pass a law providing " '. . . that no federal employee shall attend Mass or take any active part in missionary work.' "

This Maryland religious test for public office unconstitutionally invades the ap-

---

* Among religions in this country which do not teach what would generally be considered a belief in the existence of God are Buddhism, Taoism, Ethical Culture, Secular Humanism, and others. . . .

pellant's freedom of belief and religion and therefore cannot be enforced against him.

The judgment of the Supreme Court of Maryland is accordingly reversed and the cause is remanded for further proceedings not inconsistent with this opinion.

5. *Ecclesiastical Self-Government: The Liberty of Churches*

WATSON *v.* JONES
13 WALL (US) 679 (1872)

[It is estimated that the number of churches in the United States is over 325,000, with a total membership of more than 80,000,000 persons, belonging to at least 230 denominations. Many of these churches and denominations had their origin in schisms. Factional disputes have often involved the question of the ultimate disposition or control of the church funds or property. American courts could have used property law issues in such a way as to make the courts arbiters of religious doctrines and practices. They have scrupulously avoided doing this. Rather they have held that when a church belongs to a denomination which is governed by a hierarchy, the members must abide by the decision of their own ecclesiastical authorities. This was the decision of the Supreme Court in *Watson* v. *Jones,* in which the factional dispute grew out of difference over slavery.

[This case was followed by the Court in 1952 when a similar issue was presented to it involving a split in the Russian Orthodox Church in North America. After the Bolshevik Revolution in 1917 a separatist movement developed within the Russian Orthodox Church in the United States. The schismatics declared themselves independent of the mother church and the Patriarch in Moscow, and they sought to win control of the church property and ecclesiastical positions. The New York Legislature passed statutes in 1945 and 1948 to aid the schismatics in their efforts to gain autonomy and thus free the church of atheistic and subversive influences. With this legislative aid separatists tried to eject from the Cathedral in New York those who occupied it by authority of the church authorities in Moscow. The Supreme Court, by an 8-to-1 vote, held that the New York legislation was unconstitutional as a violation of the guaranty of freedom of religion.

[Separatists, schismatics, dissenters may leave a church and organize their own congregation. They have a constitutional right to do this. But if the church was subject to an ecclesiastical authority—e.g., the Patriarch in Moscow—then the church property cannot be taken over by the separatists; it remains with those who are loyal to the church. *Kedroff* v. *Saint Nicholas Cathedral,* 344 US 94 (1952); *Kreshik* v. *Saint Nicholas Cathedral,* 363 US 190 (1960).

[This decision is in the interests of religious freedom. It reaffirms the decision of the *Watson Case:* the state is not to be an arbiter of religious beliefs and practices. If clergymen are guilty of subversive activities, they may be punished in the same way as the law may punish others; but neither the legislature nor the courts may take church property and positions away from one faction and turn them over to another faction on the ground that the action would free the church from subversive influences.]

Mr. Justice Miller delivered the opinion of the Court:

. . . This is a case of a division or schism in a church. It is a question as to which of two bodies shall be recognized as the Third or Walnut Street Presbyterian Church [Louisville, Ky.] . . . The issue here is no longer a mere question of eldership, but it is a separation of the original church members and officers into two distinct bodies, with distinct members and officers, each claiming to be the true Walnut Street Presbyterian Church, and denying the right of the other to any such claim. . . .

From the commencement of the late war of insurrection to its close, the General Assembly of the Presbyterian Church at its annual meetings expressed, in declaratory statements or resolutions, its sense of the obligation of all good citizens to support the Federal Government in that struggle; and when, by the Proclamation of President Lincoln, emancipation of the slaves of the States in insurrection was announced, that body also expressed views favorable to emancipation, and adverse to the institution of slavery. At its meeting in Pittsburgh, in May, 1865, instructions were given to the Presbyteries, the Board of Missions, and to the sessions of the Churches, that when any persons from the Southern States should make application for employment as missionaries, or for admission as members or ministers of churches, inquiry should be made as to their sentiments in regard to loyalty to the government, and on the subject of slavery; and if it was found that they had been guilty of voluntarily aiding the war of the rebellion, or held the doctrine announced by the large body of the churches in the insurrectionary States, which had organized a new General Assembly, that "the system of Negro slavery in the South is a divine institution, and that it is the peculiar mission of the Southern Church to conserve that institution" they should be required to repent and forsake these sins before they could be received.

In the month of September, thereafter, the Presbytery of Louisville, under whose immediate jurisdiction was the Walnut Street Church, adopted and published in pamphlet form, what is called "a declaration and testimony against the erroneous and heretical doctrines and practices which have obtained and been propagated in the Presbyterian Church of the United States during the last five years." This declaration denounced, in the severest terms, the action of the General Assembly in the matters we have just mentioned, declared their intention to refuse to be governed by that action, and invited the co-operation of all the members of the Presbyterian Church who shared these sentiments of the declaration, in a concerted resistance to what they called the usurpation of authority by the Assembly. . . .

The General Assembly of 1866 denounced the declaration and testimony, and declared that every Presbytery which refused to obey its order should be *ipso facto* dissolved and called to answer before the next General Assembly, giving the Louisville Presbytery an opportunity for repentance and conformity. The Louisville Presbytery divided, and the adherents of the declaration and testimony sought and obtained admission in 1868, into "The Presbyterian Church of the Confederate States." . . .

In January, 1866, the congregation of the Walnut Street Church became divided in the manner stated above, each claiming to constitute the Church. . . .

On the 19th June, 1866, the Synod of Kentucky became divided, the opposing parties in each claiming to constitute respectively the true Presbytery and the true Synod; each meanwhile recognizing and claiming to adhere to the same General Assembly. Of these contesting bodies, the appellants adhered to one; the appellees to another.

On the 1st of June, 1867, the Presbytery and Synod recognized by the appellants, were declared by the General Assembly to be "in no sense the true and lawful Synod and Presbytery in connection with and under the care and authority of the General Assembly of the Presbyterian Church in the United States of America"; and were permanently excluded from connection with or representation in the Assembly; by the same resolution the Synod and Presbytery adhered to by appellees were declared to be the true and lawful Presbytery of Louisville, and Synod of Kentucky.

The Synod of Kentucky thus excluded by a resolution adopted the 28th June, 1867, declared "That, in its future action, it will be governed by this recognized sundering of all its relation to the aforesaid revolutionary body (the General Assembly) by the acts of that body itself." The Presbytery took substantially the same action. . . .

The division and separation finally extended to the Presbytery of Louisville and the Synod of Kentucky. It is now complete and apparently irreconcilable, and we are called upon to declare the beneficial uses of the church property in this condition of total separation between the members of what was once a united and harmonious congregation of the Presbyterian Church.

The questions which have come before the civil courts concerning the rights to property held by ecclesiastical bodies, may, so far as we have been able to examine them, be profitably classified under three general heads, which of course do not include cases governed by considerations applicable to a church established and supported by law as the religion of the State.

1. The first of these is when the property which is the subject of controversy has been, by the deed or will of the donor, or other instrument by which the property is held, by the express terms of the instrument devoted to the teaching, support or spread of some specific form of religious doctrine or belief.

2. The second is when the property is held by a religious congregation which, by the nature of its organization, is strictly independent of other ecclesiastical associations, and so far as church government is concerned, owes no fealty or obligation to any higher authority.

3. The third is where the religious congregation of ecclesiastical body holding the property is but a subordinate member of some general church organization in which there are superior ecclesiastical tribunals with a general and ultimate power of control more or less complete in some supreme judicatory over the whole membership of that general organization.

In regard to the first of these classes it seems hardly to admit of a rational doubt that an individual or an association of individuals may dedicate property by way of trust to the purpose of sustaining, supporting and propagating definite religious doctrines or principles, providing that in doing so they violate no law of morality, and give to the instrument by which their purpose is evidenced, the formalities which the laws require. And it would seem also to be the obvious duty of the court, in a case properly made, to see that the property so dedicated is not diverted from the trust which is thus attached to its use. So long as there are persons qualified within the meaning of the original dedication, and who are also willing to teach the doctrines or principles prescribed in the act of dedication, and so long as there is any one so interested in the execution of the trust as to have a standing in court, it must be that they can prevent the diversion of the property or fund to other and different uses. This is the general doctrine of courts of equity as to charities, and it seems equally applicable to ecclesiastical matters.

In such case, if the trust is confided to a religious congregation of the independent or congregational form of church government, it is not in the power of the majority of that congregation, however preponderant, by reason of a change of views on religious subjects, to carry the property so confined to them to the support of new and conflicting doctrine. A pious man building and dedicating a house of worship to the sole and exclusive use of those who believe in the doctrine of the Holy Trinity, and placing it under the control of a congregation which at the time holds the same belief, has a right to expect that the law will prevent that property from being used as a means of support and dissemination of the Unitarian doctrine, and as a place of Unitarian worship. Nor is the principle varied when the organization to which the trust is confided is of the second or associated form of church government. The protection which the law throws around the trust is the same. And though the task may be a delicate one and a difficult one, it will be the duty of the court in such cases, when the doctrine to be taught or the form of worship to be used is definitely and clearly laid down, to inquire whether the party accused of violating the trust is holding or teaching a different doctrine, or using a form of worship which is so far variant as to defeat the declared objects of the trust. . . .

The second class of cases which we have described has reference to the case of a church of a strictly congregational or independent organization, governed solely within itself, either by a majority of its members or by such other local organism as it may have instituted for the purpose of ecclesiastical government; and to property held by such a church, either by way of purchase or donation, with no other specific trust attached to it in the hands of the church than that it is for the use of that congregation as a religious society.

In such cases, where there is a schism which leads to a separation into distinct and conflicting bodies, the rights of such bodies to the use of the property must be determined by the ordinary principles which govern voluntary associations. If the principle of government in such cases is that the majority rules, then the numerical majority of members must control the right to the use of the property. If there be within the congregation officers in whom are vested the powers of such control, then those who adhere to the acknowledged organism by which the body is governed are entitled to the use of the property. The minority in choosing to separate themselves into a distinct body, and refusing to recognize the authority of the governing body, can claim no rights in the property from the fact that they had once been members of the Church or congregation. This ruling admits of no inquiry into the existing religious opinions of those who comprise the legal or regular organizations; for, if such was permitted, a very small minority, without any officers of the church among them, might be found to be the only faithful supporters of the religious dogmas of the founders of the Church. There being no such trust imposed upon the property when purchased or given, the court will not imply one for the purpose of expelling from its use those who by regular succession and order constitute the Church, because they may have changed in some respect their views of religious truth. . . .

But the third of these classes of cases is the one which is oftenest found in the courts, and which, with reference to the number and difficulty of the questions involved, and to other considerations, is every way the most important.

It is the case of property acquired in any of the usual modes for the general use of a religious congregation which is itself part of a large and general organization of some religious denomination, with which it is more or less intimately connected by religious views and ecclesiastical government.

The case before us is one of this class, growing out of a schism which has divided the congregation and its officers, and the presbytery and synod, and which appeals to the courts to determine the right to the use of the property so acquired. Here is no case of property devoted forever by the instrument which conveyed it, or by any specific declaration of its owner, to the support of any special religious dogmas, or any peculiar form of worship, but of property purchased for the use of a religious congregation, and so long as any existing religious congregation can be ascertained to be that congregation, or its regular and legitimate successor, it is entitled to the use of the property. In the case of an independent congregation we have pointed out how this identity, or succession, is to be ascertained, but in cases of this character we are bound to look at the fact that the local congregation is itself but a member of a much larger and more important religious organization, and is under its government and control, and is bound by its orders and judgments. There are in the Presbyterian system of ecclesiastical government, in regular succession, the Presbytery over the session or local church, the Synod over the Presbytery, and the General Assembly over all. These are called, in the language of the church organs, "judicatories," and they entertain appeals from the decisions of those below, and prescribe corrective measures in other cases.

In this class of cases we think the rule of action which should govern the civil courts, founded in a broad and sound view of the relations of church and state under our system of laws, and supported by a preponderating weight of judicial authority is, that, whenever the questions of discipline or of faith, or ecclesiastical rule, custom or law have been decided by the highest of these church judicatories to which the matter has been carried, the legal tribunals must accept such decisions as final, and as binding on them, in their application to the case before them. . . .

In this country the full and free right to entertain any religious belief, to practice any religious principle, and to teach any religious doctrine which does not violate the laws of morality and property, and which does not infringe personal rights, is conceded to all. The law knows no heresy, and is committed to the support of no dogma, the establishment of no sect. The right to organize voluntary religious associations to assist in the expression and dissemination of any religious doctrine, and to create tribunals for the decision of controverted questions of faith within the association, and for the ecclesiastical government of all the individual members, congregations and officers within the general association, is unquestioned. All who unite themselves to such a body do so with an implied consent to this government, and are bound to submit to it. But it would be a vain consent and would lead to the total subversion of such religious bodies, if any one aggrieved by one of their decisions could appeal to the secular courts and have them reversed. It is of the essence of these religious unions, and of their right to establish tribunals for the decision of questions arising among themselves, that those decisions should be binding in all cases of ecclesiastical cognizance, subject only to such appeals as the organism itself provides for. . . .

But it is a very different thing where a subject matter of dispute, strictly and purely ecclesiastical in its character—a matter over which the civil courts exercise no jurisdiction—a matter which concerns theological controversy, church discipline, ecclesiastical government, or the conformity of the members of the church to the standard of morals required of them—becomes the subject of its action. It may be said here, also, that no jurisdiction has been conferred on the tribunal to try the particular case before it, or that, in its judgment, it exceeds the powers conferred upon it, or that the laws of the church do not authorize the particular form of proceeding adopted; and, in a sense often used in the courts, all of those may be said to be questions of jurisdiction. But it is easy to see that if the civil courts are to inquire into all these matters, the whole subject of the doctrinal theology, the usages and customs, the written laws, and fundamental organization of every religious denomination may, and must, be examined into with minuteness and care, for they would become, in almost every case, the *criteria* by which the validity of the ecclesiastical decree would be determined in the civil court. This principle would deprive these bodies of the right of construing their own church laws, would open the way to all the evils which we have depicted . . . and would in effect transfer to the civil courts where property rights were concerned the decision of all ecclesiastical questions. . . .

But we need pursue this subject no further. Whatever may have been the case before the Kentucky court, the appellants in the case presented to us have separated themselves wholly from the church organization to which they belonged when this controversy commenced. They now deny its authority, denounce its action and refuse to abide by its judgment. They have first erected themselves into a new organization, and have since joined themselves to another totally different, if not hostile, to the one to which they belonged when the difficulty first began. Under any of the decisions which we have examined, the appellants, in their present position, have no right to the property, or to the use of it, which is the subject of this suit. . . .

6. Conscription and Conscientious Objectors

UNITED STATES *v.* SEEGER
380 US 163 (1965)

[Just as *Toracso* v. *Watkins, supra,* held, *inter alia,* that the state may not constitutionally aid religions based on a belief in the existence of God as against religions founded on different beliefs, so, in the instant case, the Court defined "belief in a relation to a Supreme Being," as applied to conscientious objectors, to include more than a belief in "the orthodox God." The Court did not find it necessary, however, to pass on the claims of atheists under the Universal Military Training and Service Act. The Court's decision was unanimous. Justice Douglas wrote a concurring opinion.]

Mr. Justice Clark delivered the opinion of the Court:

These cases involve claims of conscientious objectors under § 6(j) of the Universal Military Training and Service Act, 50 U.S.C. App. § 456(j) (1958 ed.), which exempts from combatant training and service in the armed forces of the United States those persons who by reason of their religious training and belief are conscientiously opposed to participation in war in any form. The cases were consolidated for argument and we consider them together although each involves different facts and circumstances. The parties raise the basic question of the constitutionality of the section which defines the term "religious training and belief," as used in the Act, as "an individual's belief in a relation to a Supreme Being involving duties superior to those arising from any human relation, but [not including] essentially political, sociological, or philosophical views or a merely personal moral code." The constitutional attack is launched under the First Amendment's Establishment and Free Exercise Clauses and is twofold: (1) The section does not exempt nonreligious conscientious objectors; and (2) it discriminates between different forms of religious expression in violation of the Due Process Clause of the Fifth Amendment. Jakobson (No. 51) and Peter (No. 29) also claim that their beliefs come within the meaning of the section. Jakobson claims that he meets the standards of § 6(j) because his opposition to war is based on belief in a Supreme Reality and is therefore an obligation superior to those resulting from man's relationship to his fellow man. Peter contends that his opposition to war derives from his acceptance of the existence of a universal power beyond that of man and that this acceptance in fact constitutes belief in a Supreme Being, qualifying him for exemption. We granted certiorari in each of the cases because of their importance in the administration of the Act.

We have concluded that Congress, in using the expression "Supreme Being" rather than the designation "God," was merely clarifying the meaning of religious training and belief so as to embrace all religions and to exclude essentially political, sociological, or philosophical views. We believe that under this construction, the test of belief "in a relation to a Supreme Being" is whether a given belief that is sincere and meaningful occupies a place in the life of its possessor parallel to that filled by the orthodox belief in God of one who clearly qualifies for the exemption. Where such beliefs have parallel positions in the lives of their respective holders we cannot say that one is "in a relation to a Supreme Being" and the other is not. We have concluded that the beliefs of the objectors in these cases meet these criteria, and, accordingly, we affirm the judgments in Nos. 50 and 51 and reverse the judgment in No. 29.

The Facts in the Cases

No. 50: Seeger was convicted in the District Court for the Southern District of New York of having refused to submit to induction in the armed forces. He was originally classified 1–A in 1953 by his local board, but this classification was changed in 1955 to 2–S (student) and he remained in this status until 1958 when he was reclassified 1–A. He first claimed exemption as a conscientious objector in 1957 after successive annual renewals of his student classification. Although he did not adopt verbatim the printed Selective Service System form, he declared that he was conscientiously opposed to participation in war in any form by reason of his "religious" belief; that he preferred to leave the question as to his belief in a Supreme Being open, "rather than answer 'yes' or 'no' "; that his "skepticism or disbelief in the existence of God" did "not necessarily mean lack of faith in anything whatsoever"; that his was a "belief in and devotion to goodness and virtue for their own sakes, and a religious faith in a purely ethical creed." He cited such personages as Plato, Aristotle and Spinoza for support of his ethical belief in intellectual and moral integrity "without belief in God, except in the remotest sense." His belief was found to be sincere, honest, and made in good faith; and his conscientious objection to be based upon individual training and belief, both of which included research in religious and cultural fields. Seeger's claim, however, was denied solely because it was not based upon a "belief in a relation to a Supreme Being" as required by § 6(j) of the Act. At trial Seeger's counsel admitted that Seeger's belief was not in relation to a Supreme Being as commonly understood, but contended that he was entitled to the exemption because "under the present law Mr. Seeger's position would also include definitions of religion which have been stated more recently," and could be "accommodated" under the definition of religious training and belief in the 1948 Act. He was convicted and the Court of Appeals reversed, holding that the Supreme Being requirement of the section distinguished "between internally derived and externally compelled beliefs" and was, therefore, an "impermissible classification" under the Due Process Clause of the Fifth Amendment.

No. 51: Jakobson was also convicted in the Southern District of New York on a charge of refusing to submit to induction. On his appeal the Court of Appeals reversed on the ground that rejection of his claim may have rested on the factual finding, erroneously made, that he did not believe in a Supreme Being as required by § 6(j).

Jakobson was originally classified as 1–A in September 1953 and enjoyed a student classification until June 1956. It was not until April 1958 that he made claim to noncombatant classification (1–A–O) as a conscientious objector. He stated on the Selective Service System form that he believed in a "Supreme Being" who was "Creator of Man" in the sense of being "ultimately responsible for the existence of" man and who was "the Supreme Reality" of which "the existence of man is the *result*." (Emphasis in the original.) He explained that his religious and social thinking had developed after much meditation and thought. He had concluded that man must be "partly spiritual" and, therefore, "partly akin to the Supreme Reality"; and that his "most important religious law" was that "no man ought ever to wilfully sacrifice another man's life as a means to any other end. . . ." In December 1958 he requested a 1–O classification since he felt that participation in any form of military service would involve him in "too many situations and relationships that would be a strain on [his] conscience that [he felt he] must avoid." He submitted a long memorandum of "notes on religion" in which he defined religion as the *"sum and essence of one's basic attitudes to the fundamental problems of human existence"* (emphasis in the original); he said that he believed in "Godness" which was "the Ultimate Cause for the fact of the Being of the Universe"; that to deny its existence would but deny the existence of the universe because "anything that Is, has an Ultimate Cause for its Being." There was a relationship to Godness, he stated, in two directions, *i.e.,* "vertically, toward Godness directly," and "horizontally, towards Godness through Mankind and the World." He accepted the latter one. The Board classified him 1–A–O and Jakobson appealed. The hearing officer found that the claim was based upon a personal moral code and that he was not sincere in his claim. The Appeal Board classified him 1–A. It did not indicate upon what ground it based its decision, *i.e.,* insincerity or a conclusion that his belief was only a personal moral code. The Court of Appeals reversed, finding that his claim came within the requirements of § 6(j). Because it could not determine whether the Appeal Board had found that Jakobson's beliefs failed to come within the statutory definition, or whether it had concluded that he lacked sincerity, it directed dismissal of the indictment.

No. 29: Forest Britt Peter was convicted in the Northern District of California on a charge of refusing to submit to induction. In his Selective Service System form he stated that he was not a member of a religious sect or organization; he failed to execute section VII of the questionnaire but attached to it a quotation expressing opposition to war, in which he stated that he concurred. In a later form he hedged the question as to his belief in a Supreme Being by saying that it depended on the definition and he appended a statement that he felt it a violation of his moral code to take human life and that he considered this belief superior to his obligation to the state. As to whether his conviction was religious, he quoted with approval Reverend John Haynes Holmes' definition of religion as "the consciousness of some power manifest in nature which helps man in the ordering of his life in harmony with its demands . . . [it] is the supreme expression of human nature; it is man thinking his highest, feeling his deepest, and living his best." The source of his conviction he attributed to reading and meditation "in our democratic American culture, with its values derived from the western religious and philosophical tradition." As to his belief in a Supreme Being, Peter stated that he supposed "you could call that a belief in the Supreme Being or God. These just do not happen to be the words I use." In 1959 he was classified as 1–A, although there was no evidence in the record that he was not sincere in his beliefs. After his conviction for failure to report for induction the Court of Appeals, assuming *arguendo* that he was sincere, affirmed.

BACKGROUND OF § 6(j)

Chief Justice Hughes, in his opinion in *United States* v. *Macintosh,* 283 US 605 (1931), enunciated the rationale behind the long recognition of conscientious objection to participation in war accorded by Congress in our various conscription laws when he declared that "in the forum of conscience, duty to a moral power higher than the State has always been maintained." In a similar vein Harlan Fiske Stone, later Chief Justice, drew from the Nation's past when he declared that

both morals and sound policy require that the state should not violate the conscience of the individual. All our history gives confirmation to the view that liberty of conscience has a moral and social value which makes it worthy of preservation at the hands of the state. So deep in its significance and vital, indeed, is it to the integrity of man's moral and spiritual nature that nothing short of the self-preservation of the state should warrant its violation; and it may well be questioned whether the state which preserves its life by a settled policy of violation of the conscience of the individual will not in fact ultimately lose it by the process. Stone, "The Conscientious Objector," 21 *Col. Univ. Q.* 253, 269 (1919).

Governmental recognition of the moral dilemma posed for persons of certain religious faiths by the call to arms came early in the history of this country. Various methods of ameliorating their difficulty were adopted by the Colonies, and were later perpetuated in state statutes and constitutions. Thus by the time of the Civil War there existed a state pattern of exempting conscientious objectors on religious grounds. In the Federal Militia Law of 1862 control of conscription was left primarily in the States. However, General Order No. 99, issued pursuant to that Act, provided for striking from the conscription list those who were exempted by the States, it also established a commutation or substitution system fashioned from earlier state enactments. With the Federal Conscription Law of 1863, which enacted the commutation and substitution provisions of General Order No. 99, the Federal Government occupied the field entirely, and in the 1864 Draft Law it extended exemptions to those conscientious objectors who were members of religious denominations opposed to the bearing of arms and who were prohibited from doing so by the articles of faith of their denominations. . . . In that same year the Confederacy exempted certain pacifist sects from military duty.

The need for conscription did not again arise until World War I. The Draft Act of 1917, 40 Stat. 76, 78, afforded exemptions to conscientious objectors who were affiliated with a "well-recognized religious sect or organization [then] organized and existing and whose existing creed or principles [forbade] its members to participate in war in any form. . . ." The Act required that all persons be inducted into the armed service, but allowed the conscientious objectors to perform noncombatant service in capacities designated by the President of the United States. Although the 1917 Act excused religious objectors only, in January 1918, the Secretary of War instructed that "personal scruples against war" be considered as constituting "conscientious objection." This Act, including its conscientious objector provisions, was upheld against constitutional attack in the *Selective Draft Law Cases,* 245 US 366, 389–390 (1918).

In adopting the 1940 Selective Training and Service Act Congress broadened the exemption afforded in the 1917 Act by making it unnecessary to belong to a pacifist religious sect if the claimant's own opposition to war was based on "religious training and belief." 54 Stat. 889. Those found to be within the exemption were not inducted into the armed services but were assigned to noncombatant service under the supervision of the Selective Service System. The Congress recognized that one might be religious without belonging to an organized church just as surely as minority members of a faith not opposed to war might through religious reading reach a conviction against participation in war. . . . Indeed, the consensus of the witnesses appearing before the congressional committees was that individual belief—rather than membership in a church or sect—determined the duties that God imposed upon a person in his everyday conduct; and that "there is a higher loyalty than loyalty to this country, loyalty to God." . . . Thus, while shifting the test from membership in such a church to one's individual belief the Congress nevertheless continued its historic practice of excusing from armed service those who believed that they owed an obligation, superior to that due the state, of not participating in war in any form.

Between 1940 and 1948 two courts of appeals held that the phrase "religious training and belief" did not include philosophical, social or political policy. Then in 1948 the Congress amended the language of the statute and declared that "religious training and belief" was to be defined as "an individual's belief in a relation to a Supreme Being involving duties superior to those arising from any human relation but [not including] essentially political, sociological, or philosophical views or a merely personal moral code." The only significant mention of this change in the provision appears in the report of the Senate Committee recommending adoption. It said simply this: "This section reenacts substantially the same provisions as were found in subsection 5(g) of the 1940 act. Exemption extends to anyone who, because of religious training and belief in his relation to a Supreme Being, is conscientiously opposed to combatant military service or to both combatant and noncombatant military service. . . .

INTERPRETATION OF § 6(j)

1. The crux of the problem lies in the phrase "religious training and belief" which Congress has defined as "belief in a relation to a Supreme Being involving duties superior to those arising from any human relation." In assigning meaning to this statutory language we may narrow the inquiry by noting briefly those scruples expressly excepted from the definition. The section excludes those persons who, disavowing religious belief, decide on the basis of essentially political, sociological or economic considerations that war is wrong and that they will have no part of it. These judgments have historically been reserved for the Government, and in matters which can be said to fall within these areas the conviction of the individual has never been permitted to override that of the State. . . . The statute further excludes those whose opposition to war stems from a "merely personal moral code," a phrase to which we shall have occasion to turn later in discussing the application of § 6(j) to these cases. We also pause to take note of what is not involved in this litigation. No party claims to be an atheist or attacks the statute on this ground. The question is not, therefore, one between theistic and atheistic beliefs. We do not deal with or intimate any decision on that situation in this case. Nor do the parties claim the monotheistic belief that there is but one God; what they claim (with the possible exception of Seeger who bases his position here not on factual but on purely constitutional grounds) is that they adhere to theism, as opposed to atheism, which is "the belief in the existence of a god or gods; belief in superhuman

powers or spiritual agencies in one or many gods." Our question, therefore, is the narrow one: Does the term "Supreme Being" as used in § 6(j) mean the orthodox God or the broader concept of a power or being, or a faith, "to which all else is subordinate or upon which all else is ultimately dependent"? *Webster's New International Dictionary.* In considering this question we resolve it solely in relation to the language of § 6(j) and not otherwise.

2. Few would quarrel, we think, with the proposition that in no field of human endeavor has the tool of language proved so inadequate in the communication of ideas as it has in dealing with the fundamental questions of man's predicament in life, in death or in final judgment and retribution. This fact makes the task of discerning the intent of Congress in using the phrase "Supreme Being" a complex one. Nor is it made the easier by the richness and variety of spiritual life in our country. Over 250 sects inhabit our land. Some believe in a purely personal God, some in a supernatural deity; others think of religion as a way of life envisioning as its ultimate goal the day when all men can live together in perfect understanding and peace. There are those who think of God as the depth of our being; others, such as the Buddhists, strive for a state of lasting rest through self-denial and inner purification; in Hindu philosophy, the Supreme Being is the transcendental reality which is truth, knowledge and bliss. Even those religious groups who have traditionally opposed war in every form have splintered into various denominations: from 1940 to 1947 there were four denominations using the name "Friends" . . . ; the "Church of the Brethren" was the official name of the oldest and largest church body of four composed of those commonly called Brethren; and the "Mennonite Church was the largest of 17 denominations, including the Amish and Hutterites, grouped as "Mennonite bodies" in the 1936 report on the Census of Religious Bodies. This vast panoply of beliefs reveals the magnitude of the problem which faced the Congress when it set about providing an exemption from armed service. It also emphasizes the care that Congress realized was necessary in the fashioning of an exemption which would be in keeping with its long-established policy of not picking and choosing among religious beliefs.

In spite of the elusive nature of the inquiry, we are not without certain guidelines. In amending the 1940 Act, Congress adopted almost intact the language of Chief Justice Hughes in *United States* v. *Macintosh, supra:*

The essence of religion is belief in a relation to *God* involving duties superior to those arising from any human relation. (Emphasis supplied.)

By comparing the statutory definition with those words, however, it becomes readily apparent that the Congress deliberately broadened them by substituting the phrase "Supreme Being" for the appellation "God." And in so doing it is also significant that Congress did not elaborate on the form or nature of this higher authority which it chose to designate as "Supreme Being." By so refraining it must have had in mind the admonitions of the Chief Justice when he said in the same opinion that even the word "God" had myriad meanings for men of faith:

[P]utting aside dogmas with their particular conceptions of deity, freedom of conscience itself implies respect for an innate conviction of paramount duty. The battle for religious liberty has been fought and won with respect to religious beliefs and practices, which are not in conflict with good order, upon the very ground of the supremacy of conscience within its proper field.

Moreover, the Senate Report on the bill specifically states that § 6(j) was intended to re-enact "substantially the same provisions as were found" in the 1940 Act. That statute, of course, refers to "religious training and belief" without more. Admittedly, all of the parties here purport to base their objection on religious belief. It appears, therefore, that we need only look to this clear statement of congressional intent as set out in the report. Under the 1940 Act it was necessary only to have a conviction based upon religious training and belief; we believe that is all that is required here. Within that phrase would come all sincere religious beliefs which are based upon a power or being, or upon a faith, to which all else is subordinate or upon which all else is ultimately dependent. The test might be stated in these words: A sincere and meaningful belief which occupies in the life of its possessor a place paralled to that filled by the God of those admittedly qualifying for the exemption comes within the statutory definition. This construction avoids imputing to Congress an intent to classify different religious beliefs, exempting some and excluding others, and is in accord with the well-established congressional policy of equal treatment for those whose opposition to service is grounded in their religious tenets. . . .

4. Moreover, we believe this construction embraces the ever-broadening understanding of the modern religious community. The eminent Protestant theologian, Dr. Paul Tillich, whose views the Government concedes would come within the statute, identifies God not as a projection "out there" or beyond the skies but as the ground of our very being. The Court of Appeals stated in No. 51 that Jakobson's views "parallel [those of] this eminent theologian rather strikingly." In his book, *Systematic Theology,* Dr. Tillich says:

I have written of the God above the God of theism. . . . In such a state [of self-affirmation] the God of both religious and theological language disappears. But something remains, namely, the seriousness of that doubt in which meaning within meaninglessness is affirmed. The source of this affirmation of meaning within meaninglessness, of certitude within doubt, is not the God of traditional theism but the "God above God," the power of being, which works through those who have no name for it, not even the name of God. 2 *Systematic Theology* 12 (1957).

Another eminent cleric, the Bishop of Woolwich, John A. T. Robinson, in his book, *Honest To God* (1963), states:

The Bible speaks of a God "up there." No doubt its picture of a three decker universe, of "the heaven above, the earth beneath and the waters under the earth," was once taken quite literally. . . . [Later] in place of a God who is literally or physically "up there" we have accepted, as part of our mental furniture, a God who is spiritually or metaphysically "out there." But now it seems there is no room for him, not merely in the inn, but in the entire universe: for there are no vacant places left. In reality, of course, our new view of the universe has made not the slightest difference. . . .

But the idea of a God spiritually or metaphysically "out there" dies very much harder. Indeed most people would be seriously disturbed by the thought that it should need to die at all. For it *is* their God and they have nothing to put in its place. . . .

Everyone of us lives with some mental picture of a God "out there," a God who exists above and beyond the world he made, a God "to" whom we pray and to whom we "go" when we die. But the signs are that we are reaching the point at which the whole conception of God "out there," which has served us so well since the collapse of the three decker universe is becoming more a hindrance than a help.

The Schema of the recent Ecumenical Council included a most significant declaration on religion.

The community of all people is one. One is their origin, for God made the entire human race live on all the face of the earth. One, too, is their ultimate end, God. Men expect from the various religions answers to the riddles of the human condition: What is man? What is the meaning and purpose of our lives? What is the moral good and what is sin? What are death, judgment, and retribution after death? . . .

Ever since primordial days, numerous peoples have had a certain perception of that hidden power which hovers over the course of things and over the events that make up the lives of men; some have even come to know of a Supreme Being and Father. Religions in an advanced culture have been able to use more refined concepts and a more developed language in their struggle for an answer to man's religious questions. . . .

Nothing that is true and holy in these religions is scorned by the Catholic Church. Ceaselessly the Church proclaims Christ, "the Way, the Truth, and the Life," in whom God reconciled all things to Himself. The Church regards with sincere reverence those ways of action and of life, precepts and teachings which, although they differ from the ones she sets forth, reflect nonetheless a ray of that Truth which enlightens all men.

Dr. David Saville Muzzey, a leader in the Ethical Culture Movement, states in his book, *Ethics As a Religion* (1951), that "[e]verybody except the avowed atheists (and they are comparatively few) believes in some kind of God," and that "The proper question to ask, therefore, is not the futile one, Do you believe in God? but rather, What *kind* of a God do you believe in?" Dr. Muzzey attempts to answer that question:

Instead of positing a personal God, whose existence man can neither prove nor disprove, the ethical concept is founded on human experience. It is anthropocentric, not theocentric. Religion, for all the various definitions that have been given of it, must surely mean the devotion of man to the highest ideal that he can conceive. And that ideal is a community of spirits in which the latent moral potentialities of men shall have been elicited by their reciprocal endeavors to cultivate the best in their fellow men. What ultimate reality is we do not know; but we have the faith that expresses itself in the human world as the power which inspires in man moral purposes. . . .

Thus the "God" that we love is not the figure on the great white throne, but the perfect pattern, envisioned by faith, of humanity as it should be, purged of the evil elements which retard its progress toward "the knowledge, love and practice of the right."

These are but a few of the views that comprise the broad spectrum of religious beliefs found among us. But they demonstrate very clearly the diverse manners in which beliefs, equally paramount in the lives of their possessors, may be articulated. They further reveal the difficulties inherent in placing too narrow a construction on the provisions of § 6(j) and thereby lend conclusive support to the construction which we today find that Congress intended.

5. We recognize the difficulties that have always faced the trier of fact in these

cases. We hoped that the test that we lay down proves less onerous. The examiner is furnished a standard that permits consideration of criteria with which he has had considerable experience. While the applicant's words may differ, the test is simple of application. It is essentially an objective one, namely, does the claimed belief occupy the same place in the life of the objector as an orthodox belief in God holds in the life of one clearly qualified for exemption?

Moreover, it must be remembered that in resolving these exemption problems one deals with the beliefs of different individuals who will articulate them in a multitude of ways. In such an intensely personal area, of course, the claim of the registrant that his belief is an essential part of a religious faith must be given great weight. Recognition of this was implicit in this language, cited by the *Berman* court from *State* v. *Amana Society,* 132 Iowa 304, 109 N.W. 894 (1906):

Surely a scheme of life designed to obviate [man's inhumanity to man], and by removing temptations, and all the inducements of ambition and avarice, to nurture the virtues of unselfishness, patience, love, and service, ought not to be denounced as not pertaining to religion *when its devotee regards it as an essential tenet of their* [sic] *religious faith.* (Emphasis by the Court of Appeals.) 156 F. 2d 377.

The validity of what he believes cannot be questioned. Some theologians, and indeed some examiners, might be tempted to question the existence of the registrant's "Supreme Being" or the truth of his concepts. But these are inquiries foreclosed to Government. As Mr. Justice Douglas stated in *United States* v. *Ballard,* 322 US 78, 86 (1944): "Men may believe what they cannot prove. They may not be put to the proof of their religious doctrines or beliefs. Religious experiences which are real as life to some may be incomprehensible to others." Local boards and courts in this sense are not free to reject beliefs because they consider them "incomprehensible." Their task is to decide whether the beliefs professed by a registrant are sincerely held and whether they are, in his own scheme of things, religious.

But we hasten to emphasize that while the "truth" of a belief is not open to question, there remains the significant question whether it is "truly held." This is the threshold question of sincerity which must be resolved in every case. It is, of course, a question of fact—a prime consideration to the validity of every claim for exemption as a conscientious objector. The Act provides a comprehensive scheme for assisting the Appeals Board in making this determination, placing at their service the Federal Bureau of Investigation, hearing examiners and other facilities of the Department of Justice. . . .

APPLICATION OF § 6(j) TO THE INSTANT CASE

As we noted earlier, the statutory definition excepts those registrants whose beliefs are based on a "merely personal moral code." The records in these cases, however, show that at no time did any one of the applicants suggest that his objection was based on a "merely personal moral code." Indeed at the outset each of them claimed in his application that his objection was based on a religious belief. We have construed the statutory definition broadly and it follows that any exception to it must be interpreted narrowly. The use by Congress of the words "merely personal" seems to us to restrict the exception to a moral code which is not only personal but which is the sole basis for the registrant's belief and is in no way related to a Supreme Being. It follows, therefore, that if the claimed religious beliefs of the respective registrants in these cases meet the test that we lay down then their objections cannot be based on a "merely personal" moral code.

In *Seeger*, No. 50, the Court of Appeals failed to find sufficient "externally compelled beliefs." However, it did find that "it would seem impossible to say with assurance that [Seeger] is not bowing to 'external commands' in virtually the same sense as is the objector who defers to the will of a supernatural power." It found little distinction between Jakobson's devotion to a mystical force of "Godness" and Seeger's compulsion to "goodness." Of course, as we have said, the statute does not distinguish between externally and internally derived beliefs. Such a determination would, as the Court of Appeals observed, prove impossible as a practical matter, and we have found that Congress intended no such distinction.

The Court of Appeals also found that there was no question of the applicant's sincerity. He was a product of a devout Roman Catholic home; he was a close student of Quaker beliefs from which he said "much of [his] thought is derived"; he approved of their opposition to war in any form; he devoted his spare hours to the American Friends Service Committee and was assigned to hospital duty.

In summary, Seeger professed "religious belief" and "religious faith." He did not disavow any belief "in a relation to a Supreme Being"; indeed he stated that "the cosmic order does, perhaps, suggest a creative intelligence." He decried the tremendous "spiritual" price man must pay for his willingness to destroy human life. In light of his beliefs and the unquestioned sincerity with which he held them, we think the Board, had it applied the test we proposed today, would have granted him the exemption. We think it clear that the beliefs which prompted his objection occupy the same place in his life as the belief in a traditional deity holds in the lives of his friends, the Quakers. We are reminded once more of Dr. Tillich's thoughts:

And if that word [God] has not much meaning for you, translate it, and speak of your life, of the source of your being, of your ultimate concern, *of what you take seriously without any reservation*. Perhaps, in order to do so, you must forget everything traditional that you have learned about God. . . . Tillich, *The Shaking of the Foundations*, 56–57 (1948). (Emphasis supplied.)

It may be that Seeger did not clearly demonstrate what his beliefs were with regard to the usual understanding of the term "Supreme Being." But as we have said Congress did not intend that to be the test. We therefore affirm the judgment in No. 50.

In *Jakobson*, No. 51, the Court of Appeals found that the registrant demonstrated that his belief as to opposition to war was related to a Supreme Being. We agree and affirm that judgment.

We reach a like conclusion in No. 29. It will be remembered that Peter acknowledged "some power manifest in nature . . . the supreme expression" that helps man in ordering his life. As to whether he would call that belief in a Supreme Being, he replied, "You could call that a belief in the Supreme Being or God. Those just do not happen to be words I use." We think that under the test we establish here the

Board would grant the exemption to Peter and we therefore reverse the judgment in No. 29.

It is so ordered.

WELSH *v.* UNITED STATES
398 US 333 (1970)

[In this case the Court took a step beyond *Seeger*. It held that if the conscientious objector deeply and sincerely holds beliefs that are purely moral in source and substance but which nonetheless impose upon him the duty of conscience to refrain from participating in any war, he is entitled to conscientious objector exemption. The Court's opinion was by Justice Black. Justice Harlan wrote a concurring opinion. Justice White wrote a dissenting opinion in which he was joined by Chief Justice Burger and Justice Stewart. Justice Blackmun took no part in the case.]

Mr. Justice Black announced the judgment of the Court and delivered an opinion in which Mr. Justice Douglas, Mr. Justice Brennan, and Mr. Justice Marshall join:

The petitioner, Elliott Ashton Welsh, II, was convicted by a United States district judge of refusing to submit to induction into the Armed Forces in violation of 50 U.S.C. App. § 462(a), and was on June 1, 1966, sentenced to imprisonment for three years. One of petitioner's defenses to the prosecution was that § 6(j) of the Universal Military Training and Service Act exempted him from combat and non-combat service because he was "by reason of religious training and belief . . . conscientiously opposed to participation in war in any form." After finding that there was no religious basis for petitioner's conscientious objector claim, the Court of Appeals, Judge Hamley dissenting, affirmed the conviction. We granted certiorari. . . . For the reasons to be stated, and without passing upon the constitutional arguments which have been raised, we reverse the conviction because of its fundamental inconsistency with *United States* v. *Seeger*.

The controlling facts in this case are strikingly similar to those in *Seeger*. Both Seeger and Welsh were brought up in religious homes and attended church in their childhood, but in neither case was this church one which taught its members not to engage in war at any time for any reason. Neither Seeger nor Welsh continued his childhood religious ties into his young manhood, and neither belonged to any religious group or adhered to the teachings of any organized religion during the period of his involvement with the Selective Service System. At the time of their registration for the draft, neither had yet come to accept pacifist principles. Their views on war developed only in subsequent years, but when their ideas did fully mature both made application with their local draft boards for conscientious objector exemptions from military service under § 6(j) of the Universal Military Training and Service Act. That section then provided, in part:*

Nothing contained in this title shall be construed to require any person to be subject to

---

* 62 Stat. 612. An amendment to the Act in 1967, subsequent to the Court's decision in the *Seeger* case, deleted the reference to a "Supreme Being" but continued to provide that "religious training and belief" does not include "essentially political, sociological, or philosophical views, or a merely personal moral code." 81 Stat. 104, 50 U.S.C.App. § 456(j).

combatant training and service in the armed forces of the United States who, by reason of religious training and belief, is conscientiously opposed to participation in war in any form. Religious training and belief in this connection means an individual's belief in a relation to a Supreme Being involving duties superior to those arising from any human relation, but does not include essentially political, sociological, or philosophical views or a merely personal moral code.

In filling out their exemption applications both Seeger and Welsh were unable to sign the statement which, as printed in the Selective Service form, stated "I am, by reason of my religious training and belief, conscientiously opposed to participation in war of any form." Seeger could sign only after striking the words "training and" and putting quotation marks around the word "religious." Welsh could sign only after striking the words "religious training and." On those same applications, neither could definitely affirm or deny that he believed in a "Supreme Being," both stating that they preferred to leave the question open. But both Seeger and Welsh affirmed on those applications that they held deep conscientious scruples against taking part in wars where people were killed. Both strongly believed that killing in war was wrong, unethical, and immoral, and their consciences forbade them to take part in such an evil practice. Their objection to participating in war in any form could not be said to come from a "still, soft voice of conscience"; rather, for them that voice was so loud and insistent that both men preferred to go to jail rather than serve in the Armed Forces. There was never any question about the sincerity and depth of Seeger's convictions as a conscientious objector, and the same is true of Welsh. In this regard the Court of Appeals noted, "[t]he government concedes that (Welsh's) beliefs are held with the strength of more traditional religious convictions." But in both cases the Selective Service System concluded that the beliefs of these men were in some sense insufficiently "religious" to qualify them for conscientious objector exemptions under the terms of § 6(j). Seeger's conscientious objector claim was denied "solely because it was not based upon a 'belief in a relation to a Supreme Being' as required by § 6(j) of the Act," . . . while Welsh was denied the exemption because his Appeal Board and the Department of Justice hearing officer "could find no religious basis for the registrant's belief, opinions, and convictions." Both Seeger and Welsh subsequently refused to submit to induction into the military and both were convicted of that offense.

In *Seeger* the Court was confronted, first, with the problem that § 6(j) defined "religious training and belief" in terms of a "belief in a relation to a Supreme Being . . . ," a definition which arguably gave a preference to those who believed in a conventional God as opposed to those who did not. Noting the "vast panoply of beliefs" prevalent in our country, the Court construed the congressional intent as being in "keeping with its long-established policy of not picking and choosing among religious beliefs," and accordingly interpreted "the meaning of religious training and belief so as to embrace *all* religions. . . ." (Emphasis added.) But, having decided that all religious conscientious objectors were entitled to the exemption, we faced the more serious problem of determining which bliefs were "religious" within the meaning of the statute. This question was particularly difficult in the case of Seeger himself. Seeger stated that his was a "belief in and devotion to goodness and virtue for their own sakes, and a religious faith in a purely ethical creed." In a letter to his draft board, he wrote:

My decision arises from what I believe to be considerations of validity from the standpoint of the welfare of humanity and the preservation of the democratic values which we in the United States are struggling to maintain. I have concluded that war, from the practical standpoint, is futile and self-defeating, and that from the more important moral standpoint, it is unethical.

On the basis of these and similar assertions, the Government argued that Seeger's conscientious objection to war was not "religious" but stemmed from "essentially political, sociological, or philosophical views or a merely personal moral code."

In resolving the question whether Seeger and the other registrants in that case qualified for the exemption, the Court stated that "(the) task is to decide whether the beliefs professed by a registrant are sincerely held and whether they are, *in his own scheme of things,* religious." (Emphasis added.) The reference to the registrant's "own scheme of things" was intended to indicate that the central consideration in determining whether the registrant's beliefs are religious is whether these beliefs play the role of a religion and function as a religion in the registrant's life. The Court's principal statement of its test for determining whether a conscientious objector's beliefs are religious within the meaning of § 6(j) was as follows:

The test might be stated in these words: A sincere and meaningful belief which occupies in the life of its possessor a place parallel to that filled by the God of those admittedly qualifying for the exemption comes within the statutory definition.

The Court made it clear that these sincere and meaningful beliefs which prompt the registrant's objection to all wars need not be confined in either source or content to traditional or parochial concepts of religion. It held that § 6(j) "does not distinguish between externally and internally derived beliefs," and also held that "intensely personal" convictions which some might find "incomprehensible" or "incorrect" come within the meaning of "religious belief" in the Act. What is necessary under *Seeger* for a registrant's conscientious objection to all war to be "religious" within the meaning of § 6(j) is that this opposition to war stem from the registrant's moral, ethical, or religious beliefs about what is right and wrong and that these beliefs be held with the strength of traditional religious convictions. Most of the great religions of today and of the past have embodied the idea of a Supreme Being or a Supreme Reality—a God—who communicates to man in some way a consciousness of what is right and should be done, of what is wrong and therefore should be shunned. If an individual deeply and sincerely holds beliefs which are purely ethical or moral in source and content but which nevertheless impose upon him a duty of conscience to refrain from participating in any war at any time, those beliefs certainly occupy in the life of that individual "a place parallel to that filled by . . . God" in traditionally religious persons. Because his beliefs function as a religion in his life, such an individual is as much entitled to a "religious" conscientious objector exemption under § 6(j) as is someone who derives his conscientious opposition to war from traditional religious convictions.

Applying this standard to Seeger himself, the Court noted the "compulsion to 'goodness' " which informed his total opposition to war, the undisputed sincerity with which he held his views, and the fact that Seeger had "decried the tremendous 'spiritual' price man must pay for his willingness to destroy human life." The Court concluded:

We think it clear that the beliefs which prompted his objection occupy the same place in his life as the belief in a traditional deity holds in the lives of his friends, the Quakers.

Accordingly, the Court found that Seeger should be granted conscientious objector status.

In the case before us the Government seeks to distinguish our holding in *Seeger* on basically two grounds, both of which were relied upon by the Court of Appeals in affirming Welsh's conviction. First, it is stressed that Welsh was far more insistent and explicit than Seeger in denying that his views were religious. For example, in filling out their conscientious objector applications, Seeger put quotation marks around the word "religious," but Welsh struck the word "religious" entirely and later characterized his beliefs as having been formed "by reading in the fields of history and sociology." The Court of Appeals found that Welsh had "denied that his objection to war was premised on religious belief" and concluded that "the Appeal Board was entitled to take him at his word." We think this attempt to distinguish *Seeger* fails for the reason that it places undue emphasis on the registrant's interpretation of his own beliefs. The Court's statement in *Seeger* that a registrant's characterization of his own belief as "religious" should carry great weight, does not imply that his declaration that his views are nonreligious should be treated similarly. When a registrant states that his objections to war are "religious," that information is highly relevant to the question of the function his beliefs have in his life. But very few registrants are fully aware of the broad scope of the word "religious" as used in § 6(j), and accordingly a registrant's statement that his beliefs are nonreligious is a highly unreliable guide for those charged with administering the exemption. Welsh himself presents a case in point. Although he originally characterized his beliefs as nonreligious, he later upon reflection wrote a long and thoughtful letter to his Appeal Board in which he declared that his beliefs were "certainly religious in the ethical sense of that word." He explained:

I believe I mentioned taking of life as not being, for me, a religious wrong. Again, I assumed Mr. Bradley (the Department of Justice hearing officer) was using the word "religious" in the conventional sense, and, in order to be perfectly honest did not characterize my belief as "religious."

The Government also seeks to distinguish *Seeger* on the ground that Welsh's views, unlike Seeger's, were "essentially political, sociological, or philosophical or a merely personal moral code." As previously noted, the Government made the same argument about Seeger, and not without reason, for Seeger's views had a substantial political dimension. In this case, Welsh's conscientious objection to war was undeniably based in part on his perception of world politics. In a letter to his local board, he wrote:

I can only act according to what I am and what I see. And I see that the military complex wastes both human and material resources, that it fosters disregard for (what I consider a paramount concern) human needs and ends; I see that the means we employ to "defend" our "way of life" profoundly change that way of life. I see that in our failure to recognize the political, social, and economic realities of the world, we, *as a nation,* fail our responsibility *as a nation."*

We certainly do not think that § 6(j)'s exclusion of those persons with "essentially political, sociological, or philosophical views or a merely personal moral code" should be read to exclude those who hold strong beliefs about our domestic and foreign affairs or even those whose conscientious objection to participation in all wars is founded to a substantial extent upon considerations of public policy. The two groups of registrants which obviously do fall within these exclusions from the exemption are those whose beliefs are not deeply held and those whose objection to war does not rest at all upon moral, ethical, or religious principle but instead rests solely upon considerations of policy, pragmatism, or expediency. In applying § 6(j)'s exclusion of those whose views are "essentially political, etc.," it should be remembered that these exclusions are definitional and do not therefore restrict the category of persons who are conscientious objectors "by religious training and belief." Once the Selective Service System has taken the first step and determined under the standards set out here and in *Seeger* that the registrant is a "religious" conscientious objector, it follows that his views cannot be "essentially political, sociological or philosophical." Nor can they be a "merely personal moral code." . . .

Welsh stated that he "believe[d] the taking of life—anyone's life— to be morally wrong." In his original conscientious objector application he wrote the following:

I believe that human life is valuable in and of itself; in its living; therefore I will not injure or kill another human being. This belief (and the corresponding "duty" to abstain from violence toward another person) is not "superior to those arising from any human relation." On the contrary: *it is essential to every human relation.* I cannot, therefore, conscientiously comply with the Government's insistence that I assume duties which I feel are immoral and totally repugnant.

Welsh elaborated his beliefs in later communications with Selective Service officials. On the basis of these beliefs and the conclusion of the Court of Appeals that he held them "with the strength of more traditional religious convictions," we think Welsh was clearly entitled to a conscientious objector exemption. Section 6(j) requires no more. That section exempts from military service all those whose consciences, spurred by deeply held moral, ethical, or religious beliefs, would give them no rest or peace if they allowed themselves to become a part of an instrument of war.

The judgment is reversed.
Reversed.

GILLETTE *v.* UNITED STATES
NEGRE *v.* LARSEN
401 US 437 (1971)

[In these two cases the Court held that the Military Selective Service Act exempts one who is conscientiously opposed to participation in all war but does not exempt persons who object to participation only in a particular war. The Court held that the act as so construed does not violate either the Establishment Clause or the Free Exercise Clause of the First Amendment. The opinion for the Court was by Justice Marshall. Justice Black concurred in the judgment and in part I of the opinion. Justice Douglas wrote a dissenting opinion.]

Mr. Justice Marshall delivered the opinion of the Court:

These cases present the question whether conscientious objection to a particular war, rather than objection to war as such, relieves the objector from responsibilities of military training and service. Specifically, we are called upon to decide whether conscientious scruples relating to a particular conflict are within the purview of established provisions relieving conscientious objectors to war from military service. Both petitioners also invoke constitutional principles barring government interference with the exercise of religion and requiring governmental neutrality in matters of religion.

In No. 85, petitioner Gillette was convicted of willful failure to report for induction into the armed forces. Gillette defended on the ground that he should have been ruled exempt from induction as a conscientious objector to war. In support of his unsuccessful request for classification as a conscientious objector, this petitioner had stated his willingness to participate in a war of national defense or a war sponsored by the United Nations as a peace-keeping measure, but declared his opposition to American military operations in Vietnam, which he characterized as "unjust." Petitioner concluded that he could not in conscience enter and serve in the armed forces during the period of the Vietnam conflict. Gillette's view of his duty to abstain from any involvement in a war seen as unjust is, in his words, "based on a humanist approach to religion," and his personal decision concerning military service was guided by fundamental principles of conscience and deeply held views about the purpose and obligation of human existence.

The District Court determined that there was a basis in fact to support administrative denial of exemption in Gillette's case. The denial of exemption was upheld, and Gillette's defense to the criminal charge rejected, not because of doubt about the sincerity or the religious character of petitioner's objection to military service but because his objection ran to a particular war. In affirming the conviction, the Court of Appeals concluded that Gillette's conscientious beliefs "were specifically directed against the war in Vietnam," while the relevant exemption provision of the Military Selective Service Act of 1967, 50 U.S.C. App. § 456(j), "requires opposition 'to participation in war in any form.' "

In No. 325, petitioner Negre, after induction into the Army, completion of basic training, and receipt of orders for Vietnam duty commenced proceedings looking to his discharge as a conscientious objector to war. Application for discharge was denied, and Negre sought judicial relief by habeas corpus. The District Court found a basis in fact for the Army's rejection of petitioner's application for discharge. Habeas relief was denied, and the denial was affirmed on appeal, because, in the language of the Court of Appeals, Nerge "objects to the war in Vietnam, not to all wars," and therefore does "not qualify, for separation [from the Army], as a conscientious objector." Again, no question is raised as to the sincerity or the religious quality of this petitioner's views. In line with religious counseling and numerous religious texts, Negre, a devout Catholic, believes that it is his duty as a faithful Catholic to discriminate between "just" and "unjust" wars, and to foreswear participation in the latter. His assessment of the Vietnam conflict as an unjust war became clear in his mind after completion of infantry training, and Negre is now firmly of the view that any personal involvement in that war would contravene his conscience and "all that I had been taught in my religious training."

We granted certiorari in these cases, in order to resolve vital issues concerning the exercise of congressional power to raise and support armies, as affected by the religious guaranties of the First Amendment. We affirm the judgments below in both cases.

I

Each petitioner claims a nonconstitutional right to be relieved of the duty of military service in virtue of his conscientious scruples. Both claims turn on the proper construction of § 6(j) of the Military Selective Service Act of 1967, 50 U.S.C. App. § 456(j), which provides:

Nothing contained in this title . . . shall be construed to require any person to be subject to combatant training and service in the armed forces of the United States who, by reason of religious training and belief, is conscientiously opposed to participation in war in any form.*

This language controls Gillette's claim to exemption, which was asserted administratively prior to the point of induction. Department of Defense Directive No. 1300.6 (May 10, 1968), prescribes that post-induction claims to conscientious objector status shall be honored, if valid, by the various branches of the armed forces. Section 6(j) of the Act, as construed by the courts, is incorporated by the various service regulations issued pursuant to the Directive, and thus the standards for measuring claims of in-service objectors, such as Negre, are the same as the statutory tests applicable in a pre-induction situation.

For purposes of determining the statutory status of conscientious objection to a particular war, the focal language of § 6(j) is the phrase, "conscientiously opposed to participation in war in any form." This language, on a straightforward reading, can bear but one meaning; that conscientious scruples relating to war and military service must amount to conscientious opposition to participating personally in any war and all war. . . . It matters little for present purposes whether the words, "in any form," are read to modify "war" or "participation." On the first reading, conscientious scruples must implicate "war in any form," and an objection involving a particular war rather than all war would plainly not be covered by § 6(j). On the

---

* Section 6(j) provides further: "As used in this subsection, the term "religious training and belief" does not include essentially political, sociological, or philosophical views, or a merely personal moral code. Any person claiming exemption from combatant training and service because of such conscientious objections whose claim is sustained by the local board shall, if he is inducted into the armed forces . . . , be assigned to noncombatant service as defined by the President, or shall, if he is found to be conscientiously opposed to participation in such noncombatant service, in lieu of such induction, be ordered . . . to perform . . . civilian work contributing to the maintenance of the national health, safety, or interest. . . ."

other reading, an objector must oppose "participation in war." It would strain good sense to read this phrase otherwise than to mean, "participation in all war." For the word "war" would still be used in an unqualified, generic sense, meaning war as such. Thus, however the statutory clause be parsed, it remains that conscientious objection must run to war in any form.

A different result cannot be supported by reliance on the materials of legislative history. Petitioners and *amici* point to no episode or pronouncement in the legislative history of § 6(j), or of predecessor provisions, that tends to overthrow the obvious interpretation of the words themselves.*

It is true that the legislative materials reveal a deep concern for the situation of conscientious objectors to war, who absent special status would be put to a hard choice between contravening imperatives of religion and conscience or suffering penalties. Moreover, there are clear indications that congressional reluctance to impose such a choice stems from a recognition of the value of conscientious action to the democratic community at large, and from respect for the general proposition that fundamental principles of conscience and religious duty may sometimes override the demands of the secular state. . . . But there are countervailing considerations, which are also the concern of Congress, and the legislative materials simply do not support the view that Congress intended to recognize any conscientious claim whatever as a basis for relieving the claimant from the general responsibility or the various incidents of military service. The claim that is recognized by § 6(j) is a claim of conscience running against war as such. This claim, not one involving opposition to a particular war only, was plainly the focus of congressional concern.

Finding little comfort in the wording or the legislative history of § 6(j), petitioners rely heavily on dicta in the decisional law dealing with objectors whose conscientious scruples ran against war as such, but who indicated certain reservations of an abstract nature. It is instructive that none of the cases relied upon embraces an interpretation of § 6(j) at variance with the construction we adopt today.

Sicurella v. *United States*, 348 US 385 (1955), presented the only previous occasion for this Court to focus on the "participation in war in any form" language of § 6(j). In *Sicurella* a Jehovah's Witness who opposed participation in secular wars was held to possess the requisite conscientious scruples concerning war, al-

---

* Petitioners' sole argument having specific reference to the legislative materials is utterly flawed. It runs as follows: the 1948 revision of the exempting provision was inspired in part by the dissent of Chief Justice Hughes in *United States* v. *Macintosh*, 283 US 605, (1931); *Macintosh* involved a claimant whose conscientious scruples implicated only "unjust" wars, and the dissent remarked that "eminent statesmen here and abroad" have held such views, *id.*, at 635, 51 S.Ct. 579; thus Congress cannot fairly be deemed to have excluded objectors to particular wars from the 1948 exempting provision, predecessor to the present § 6(j). However, the very most that can be said about congressional reliance on the *Macintosh* dissent is that Congress used it in fashioning a definition of the words "religious training and belief." See *United States* v. *Seeger*. The language of the exempting provision that is relevant to the present dispute—"participation in war in any form"—was not altered in 1948 or thereafter. Moreover, the *Macintosh* dissent does not itself suggest that conscientious objection to a particular war is or has ever been a basis for relief from military service. The claimant in *Macintosh* did not seek relief from military service—his contention, and that of the dissent, was that conscientious unwillingness to bear arms is not a disqualifying factor, under the language of the applicable loyalty oath, in a naturalization proceeding. (The argument of the dissent was later adopted by the Court in *Girouard* v. *United States*, 328 US 61 (1946).)

though he was not opposed to participation in a "theocratic war" commanded by Jehovah. The Court noted that the "theocratic war" reservation was highly abstract —no such war had occurred since biblical times, and none was contemplated. Congress, on the other hand, had in mind "real shooting wars," and Sicurella's abstract reservations did not undercut his conscientious opposition to participating in such wars. Plainly *Sicurella* cannot be read to support the claims of those, like petitioners, who for a variety of reasons consider one particular "real shooting war" to be unjust, and therefore oppose participation in that war.

It should be emphasized that our cases explicating the "religious training and belief" clause of § 6(j), or cognate clauses of predecessor provisions, are not relevant to the present issue. The question here is not whether these petitioners' beliefs concerning war are "religious" in nature. Thus petitioners' reliance on *United States* v. *Seeger,* and *Welsh* v. *United States* is misplaced. Nor do we decide what conscientious objection to a particular war necessarily falls within § 6(j)'s expressly excluded class of "essentially political, sociological, or philosophical views, or a merely personal moral code." Rather we hold that Congress intended to exempt persons who oppose participating in all war—"participation in war in any form"— and that persons who object solely to participation in a particular war are not within the purview of the exempting section, even though the latter objection may have such roots in a claimant's conscience and personality that it is "religious" in character.

A further word may be said to clarify our statutory holding. Apart from abstract theological reservations, two other sorts of reservations concerning use of force have been thought by lower courts not to defeat a conscientious objector claim. Willingness to use force in self-defense, in defense of home and family, or in defense against immediate acts of aggressive violence toward other persons in the community, has not been regarded as inconsistent with a claim of conscientious objection to war as such. . . . But surely willingness to use force defensively in the personal situations mentioned is quite different from willingness to fight in some wars but not in others. . . . Somewhat more apposite to the instant situation are cases dealing with persons who oppose participating in all wars, but cannot say with complete certainty that their present convictions and existing state of mind are unalterable. . . . Unwillingness to deny the possibility of a change of mind, in some hypothetical future circumstances, may be no more than humble good sense, casting no doubt on the claimant's present sincerity of belief. At any rate there is an obvious difference between present sincere objection to all war, and present opposition to participation in a particular conflict only.

II

Both petitioners argue that § 6(j), construed to cover only objectors to all war, violates the religious clauses of the First Amendment. The First Amendment provides that "Congress shall make no law respecting an establishment of religion, or prohibiting the free exercise thereof. . . ." Petitioners contend that Congress interferes with free exercise of religion by failing to relieve objectors to a particular war from military service, when the objection is religious or conscientious in nature. While the two religious clauses—pertaining to "free exercise" and "establishment" of religion—overlap and interact in many ways it is best to focus first on petitioners' other contention, that § 6(j) is a law respecting the establishment of religion. For despite free exercise overtones, the gist of the constitutional complaint is that § 6(j) impermissibly discriminates among types of religious belief and affiliation.*

On the assumption that these petitioners' beliefs concerning war have roots that are "religious" in nature within the meaning of the Amendment as well as this Court's decisions construing § 6(j), petitioners ask how their claims to relief from military service can be permitted to fail, while other "religious" claims are upheld by the Act. It is a fact that § 6(j), properly construed, has this effect. Yet we cannot conclude in mechanical fashion, or at all, that the section works an establishment of religion.

An attack founded on disparate treatment of "religious" claims invokes what is perhaps the central purpose of the Establishment Clause—the purpose of ensuring governmental neutrality in matters of religion. . . . Here there is no claim that exempting conscientious objectors to war amounts to an over-reaching of secular purposes and an undue involvement of government in affairs of religion. . . . To the contrary, petitioners ask for greater "entanglement" by judicial expansion of the exemption to cover objectors to particular wars. Necessarily the constitutional value at issue is "neutrality." And as a general matter it is surely true that the Establishment Clause prohibits government from departing secular purposes in order to put an imprimatur on one religion, or on religion as such, or to favor the adherents of any sect or religious organization. . . . The metaphor of a "wall" or impassible barrier between Church and State, taken too literally, may mislead constitutional analysis, . . . but the Establishment Clause stands at least for the proposition that when government activities touch on the religious sphere, they must be secular in purpose, evenhanded in operation, and neutral in primary impact. . . .

A

The critical weakness of petitioners' establishment claim arises from the fact that § 6(j), on its face, simply does not discriminate on the basis of religious affiliation or religious belief, apart of course from beliefs concerning war. The section says that anyone who is conscientiously opposed to all war shall be relieved of military service. The specified objection must have a grounding in "religious training and belief," but no particular sectarian affiliation or theological position is required. The Draft Act of 1917 extended relief only to those conscientious objectors affiliated with some "well-recognized religious sect or organization" whose principles forbade members' participation in war, but the attempt to focus on particular sects apparently broke down in administrative practice, . . . and the 1940

---

* Petitioners also assert that the Fifth Amendment's Due Process Clause is violated, because the distinction embodied in § 6(j)—between objectors to all war and objectors to particular wars—is arbitrary and capricious and works an invidious discrimination in contravention of the "equal protection" principles encompassed by the Fifth Amendment. . . . This is not an independent argument in the context of these cases. . . . We hold that the section survives the Establishment Clause because there are neutral, secular reasons to justify the line that Congress has drawn, and it follows as a more general matter that the line is neither arbitrary nor invidious.

Selective Training and Service Act discarded all sectarian restriction. Thereafter Congress has framed the conscientious objector exemption in broad terms compatible with "its long-established policy of not picking and choosing among religious beliefs." . . .

Thus there is no occasion to consider the claim that when Congress grants a benefit expressly to adherents of one *religion,* courts must either nullify the grant or somehow extend the benefit to cover all religions. For § 6(j) does not single out any religious organization or religious creed for special treatment. Rather petitioners' contention is that since Congress has recognized one sort of conscientious objection concerning war, whatever its religious basis, the Establishment Clause commands that another, different objection be carved out and protected by the courts.

Properly phrased, petitioners' contention is that the special statutory status accorded conscientious objection to all war, but not objection to a particular war, works a de facto discrimination among religions. This happens, say petitioners, because some religious faiths themselves distinguish between personal participation in "just" and in "unjust" wars, commending the former and forbidding the latter, and therefore adherents of some religious faiths—and individuals whose personal beliefs of a religious nature include the distinction—cannot object to all wars consistently with what is regarded as the true imperative of conscience. Of course this contention of de facto religious discrimination, rendering § 6(j) fatally under-inclusive, cannot simply be brushed aside. The question of governmental neutrality is not concluded by the observation that § 6(j) on its face makes no discrimination between religions, for the Establishment Clause forbids subtle departures from neutrality, "religious gerrymanders," as well as obvious abuses. . . . Still a claimant alleging "gerrymander" must be able to show the absence of a neutral, secular basis for the lines government has drawn. . . . For the reasons that follow, we believe that petitioners have failed to make the requisite showing with respect to § 6(j).

Section 6(j) serves a number of valid purposes having nothing to do with a design to foster or favor any sect, religion, or cluster of religions. There are considerations of a pragmatic nature, such as the hopelessness of converting a sincere conscientious objector into an effective fighting man, . . . but no doubt the section reflects as well the view that "in the forum of conscience, duty to a moral power higher than the state has always been maintained." . . . We have noted that the legislative materials show congressional concern for the hard choice that conscription would impose on conscientious objectors to war, as well as respect for the value of conscientious action and for the principle of supremacy of conscience.

Naturally the considerations just mentionad are affirmative in character, going to support the existence of an exemption rather than its restriction specifically to persons who object to all war. The point is that these affirmative purposes are neutral in the sense of the Establishment Clause. Quite apart from the question whether the Free Exercise Clause might require some sort of exemption, it is hardly impermissible for Congress to attempt to accommodate free exercise values, in line with "our happy tradition" of "avoiding unnecessary clashes with the dictates of conscience." . . . "Neutrality" in matters of religion is not inconsistent with "benevolence" by way of exemptions from onerous duties, . . . so long as an exemption is tailored broadly enough that it reflects valid secular purposes. In the draft area for 30 years the exempting provision has focused on individual conscientious belief, not on sectarian affiliation. The relevant individual belief is simply objection to all war, not adherence to any extraneous theological viewpoint. And while the objection must have roots in conscience and personality that are "religious" in nature, this requirement has never been construed to elevate conventional piety or religiosity of any kind above the imperatives of a personal faith.

In this state of affairs it is impossible to say that § 6(j) intrudes upon "voluntarism" in religious life, . . . or that the congressional purpose in enacting § 6(j) is to promote or foster those religious organizations that traditionally have taught the duty to abstain from participation in any war. A claimant, seeking judicial protection for his own conscientious beliefs, would be hard put to argue that § 6(j) encourages membership in putatively "favored" religious organizations, for the painful dilemma of the sincere conscientious objector arises precisely because he feels himself bound in conscience not to compromise his beliefs or affiliations.

B

We conclude not only that the affirmative purposes underlying § 6(j) are neutral and secular, but also that valid neutral reasons exist for limiting the exemption to objectors to all war, and that the section therefore cannot be said to reflect a religious preference.

Apart from the Government's need for manpower, perhaps the central interest involved in the administration of conscription laws is the interest in maintaining a fair system for determining "who serves when not all serve." When the Government exacts so much, the importance of fair, evenhanded, and uniform decision-making is obviously intensified. The Government argues that the interest in fairness would be jeopardized by expansion of § 6(j) to include conscientious objection to a particular war. The contention is that the claim to relief on account of such objection is intrinsically a claim of uncertain dimensions, and that granting the claim in theory would involve a real danger of erratic or even discriminatory decision-making in administrative practice.

A virtually limitless variety of beliefs are subsumable under the rubric, "objection to a particular war."* All the factors that might go into nonconscientious dissent from policy, also might appear as the concrete basis of an objection that has roots as well in conscience and religion. Indeed, over the realm of possible situations, opposition to a particular war may more likely be political and nonconscientious, than otherwise. . . . The difficulties of sorting the two, with a sure hand, are considerable. Moreover, the belief that a particular war at a particular

---

* Matters relevant to such an objection, as the papers in these cases show, are whether the purposes of the war are thought ultimately defensive and pacific, or otherwise; whether the conflict is legal, or its prosecution decided upon by legal means; whether the implements of war are used humanely, or whether certain weapons should be used at all. A war may thought "just" or not depending on one's assessment of these factors and many more: the character of the foe, or of allies; the place the war is fought; the likelihood that a military clash will issue in benefits, of various kinds, enough to override the inevitable costs of the conflict. And so on.

time is unjust is by its nature changeable and subject to nullification by changing events. Since objection may fasten on any of an enormous number of variables, the claim is ultimately subjective, depending on the claimant's view of the facts in relation to his judgment that a given factor or congeries of factors colors the character of the war as a whole. In short, it is not at all obvious in theory what sorts of objections should be deemed sufficient to excuse an objector, and there is considerable force in the Government's contention that a program of excusing objectors to particular wars may be "impossible to conduct with any hope of reaching fair and consistent results. . . ."

For their part, petitioners make no attempt to provide a careful definition of the claim to exemption which they ask the courts to carve out and protect. They do not explain why objection to a particular conflict—much less an objection that focuses on a particular facet of a conflict—should excuse the objector from all military service whatever, even from military operations that are connected with the conflict at hand in remote or tenuous ways. They suggest no solution to the problems arising from the fact that altered circumstances may quickly render the objection to military service moot.

To view the problem of fairness and evenhanded decisionmaking, in the present context, as merely a commonplace chore of weeding out "spurious claims," is to minimize substantial difficulties of real concern to a responsible legislative body. For example, under the petitioners' unarticulated scheme for exemption, an objector's claim to exemption might be based on some feature of a current conflict which most would regard as incidental, or might be predicated on a view of the facts which most would regard as mistaken. The particular complaint about the war may itself be "sincere," but it is difficult to know how to judge the "sincerity" of the objector's conclusion that the war *in toto* is unjust and that any personal involvement would contravene conscience and religion. To be sure we have ruled, in connection with § 6(j), that "the 'truth' of a belief is not open to question"; rather, the question is whether the objector's beliefs are "truly held." . . . But we must also recognize that "sincerity" is a concept that can bear only so much adjudicative weight.

Ours is a Nation of enormous heterogeneity in respect of political views, moral codes, and religious persuasions. It does not bespeak an establishing of religion for Congress to forego the enterprise of distinguishing those whose dissent has some conscientious basis from those who simply dissent. There is a danger that as between two would-be objectors, both having the same complaint against a war, that objector would succeed who is more articulate, better educated, or better counseled. There is even a danger of unintended religious discrimination—a danger that a claim's chances of success would be greater the more familiar or salient the claim's connection with conventional religiosity could be made to appear. At any rate, it is true that "the more discriminating and complicated the basis of classification for an exemption—even a neutral one—the greater the potential for state involvement" in determining the character of persons' beliefs and affiliations, thus "entangl[ing] government in difficult classifications of what is or is not religious," or what is or is not conscientious. . . . While the danger of erratic decisionmaking unfortunately exists in any system of conscription that takes individual differences into account, no doubt the dangers would be enhanced if a conscientious objection of indeterminate scope were honored in theory.

In addition to the interest in fairness, the Government contends that neutral, secular reasons for the line drawn by § 6(j)—between objection to all war and objection to a particular war—may be found in the nature of the conscientious claim which these petitioners assert. Opposition to a particular war, states the Government's Brief, necessarily involves a judgment "that is political and particular," one "based on the same political, sociological and economic factors that the government necessarily considered" in deciding to engage in a particular conflict. Taken in a narrow sense, these considerations do not justify the distinction at issue, for however "political and particular" the judgment underlying objection to a particular war, the objection still might be rooted in religion and conscience, and although the factors underlying that objection were considered and rejected in the process of democratic decisionmaking, likewise the viewpoint of an objector to all war was no doubt considered and "necessarily" rejected as well. Nonetheless it can be seen on a closer view that this line of analysis, conjoined with concern for fairness, does support the statutory distinction.

Tacit at least in the Government's view of the instant cases is the contention that the limits of § 6(j) serve an overriding interest in protecting the integrity of democratic decisionmaking against claims to individual noncompliance. Despite emphasis on claims that have a "political and particular" component, the logic of the contention is sweeping. Thus the "interest" invoked is highly problematical, for it would seem to justify governmental refusal to accord any breathing space whatever to noncompliant conduct inspired by imperatives of religion and conscience.

On the other hand, some have perceived a danger that exempting persons who dissent from a particular war, albeit on grounds of conscience and religion in part, would "open the doors to a general theory of selective disobedience to law" and jeopardize the binding quality of democratic decisions. . . . Other fields of legal obligation aside, it is undoubted that the nature of conscription, much less war itself, requires the personal desires and perhaps the dissenting views of those who must serve to be subordinated in some degree to the pursuit of public purposes. It is also true that opposition to a particular war does depend *inter alia* upon particularistic factual beliefs and policy assessments, beliefs and assessments which presumably were overridden by the government that decides to commit lives and resources to a trial of arms. Further, it is not unreasonable to suppose that some persons who are *not* prepared to assert a conscientious objection, and instead accept the hardships and risks of military service, may well agree at all points with the objector, yet conclude, as a matter of conscience, that they are personally bound by the decision of the democratic process. The fear of the National Advisory Commission on Selective Service, apparently, is that exemption of objectors to particular wars would weaken the resolve of those who otherwise would feel themselves bound to serve despite personal cost, uneasiness at the prospect of violence, or even serious moral reservations or policy objections concerning the particular conflict.

We need not and do not adopt the view that a categorical, global "interest" in stifling individualistic claims to noncompliance, in respect of duties generally exacted, is the neutral and secular basis of § 6(j). As is shown by the long history of the very provision under discussion, it is not inconsistent with orderly democratic government for individuals to be exempted by law, on account of special character-istics, from general duties of a burdensome nature. But real dangers—dangers of the kind feared by the Commission—might arise if an exemption were made avail-able that in its nature could not be administered fairly and uniformly over the run of relevant fact situations. Should it be thought that those who go to war are chosen unfairly or capriciously, then a mood of bitterness and cynicism might corrode the spirit of public service and the values of willing performance of a citizen's duties that are the very heart of free government. In short, the considerations mentioned in the previous paragraph, when seen in conjunction with the central problem of fairness, are without question properly cognizable by Congress. In light of these valid concerns, we conclude that it is supportable for Congress to have decided that the objector to all war—to all killing in war—has a claim that is distinct enough and intense enough to justify special status, while the objector to a particular war does not.

Of course we do not suggest that Congress would have acted irrationally or un-reasonably had it decided to exempt those who object to particular wars. Our analysis of the policies of § 6(j) is undertaken in order to determine the existence *vel non* of a neutral, secular justification for the lines Congress has drawn. We find that justifying reasons exsit and therefore hold that the Establishment Clause is not violated.

III

Petitioners' remaining contention is that Congress interferes with the free exer-cise of religion by conscripting persons who oppose a particular war on grounds of conscience and religion. Strictly viewed, this complaint does not implicate problems of comparative treatment of different sorts of objectors, but rather may be examined in some isolation from the circumstance that Congress has chosen to exempt those who conscientiously object to all war.* And our holding that § 6(j) comports with the Establishment Clause does not automatically settle the present issue. For despite a general harmony of purpose between the two religious clauses of the First Amendment, the Free Exercise Clause no doubt has a reach of its own. . . .

Nonetheless, our analysis of § 6(j) for Establishment Clause purposes has re-vealed governmental interests of a kind and weight sufficient to justify under the Free Exercise Clause the impact of the conscription laws on those who object to particular wars.

Our cases do not at their farthest reach support the proposition that a stance of conscientious opposition relieves an objector from any colliding duty fixed by a democratic government. . . . To be sure, the Free Exercise Clause bars "govern-mental regulation of religious *beliefs* as such," . . . or interference with the dis-semination of religious ideas. . . . It prohibits misuse of secular governmental

---

* We are not faced with the question whether the Free Exercise Clause itself would require exemption of any class other than objectors to particular wars. A free exercise claim on behalf of such objectors collides with the distinct governmental interests already discussed, and at any rate, no other claim is presented. We note that the Court has previously suggested that relief for conscientious objectors is not mandated by the Constitution. . . .

programs "to impede the observance of one or all religions or . . . to discriminate invidiously between religions, . . . even though the burden may be characterized as being only indirect." . . . And even as to neutral prohibitory or regulatory laws having secular aims, the Free Exercise Clause may condemn certain applications clashing with imperatives of religion and conscience, when the burden on First Amendment values is not justifiable in terms of the Government's valid aims. . . . However, our analysis of § 6(j) shows that the impact of conscription on objectors to particular wars is far from unjustified. The conscription laws, applied to such persons as to others, are not designed to interfere with any religious ritual or practice, and do not work a penalty against any theological position. The incidental burdens felt by persons in petitioners' position are strictly justified by substantial governmental interests that relate directly to the very impacts questioned. And more broadly, of course, there is the Government's interest in procuring the manpower necessary for military purposes, pursuant to the constitutional grant of power to Congress to raise and support armies. Art. I, § 8.

IV

Since petitioners' statutory and constitutional claims to relief from military service are without merit, it follows that in Gillette's case (No. 85) there was a basis in fact to support administrative denial of exemption, and that in Negre's case (No. 325) there was a basis in fact to support the Army's denial of a discharge. Accordingly, the judgments below are affirmed.

Affirmed.

Mr. Justice Douglas, dissenting in No. 85:

Gillette's objection is to combat service in the Vietnam war, not to wars in general, and the basis of his objection is his conscience. His objection does not put him into the statutory exemption which extends to one "who, by reason of religious training and belief, is conscientiously opposed to participation in war in any form."

He stated his views as follows:

> I object to any assignment in the United States Armed Forces while this unnecessary and unjust was is being waged, on the grounds of religious belief specifically "Humanism." This essentially means respect and love for man, faith in his inherent goodness and perfectability, and confidence in his capability to improve some of the pains of the human condition.

This position is substantially the same as that of Sisson in *United States* v. *Sisson,* 297 F.Supp. 902, appeal dismissed, 399 US 267, where the District Court summarized the draftee's position as follows:

> Sisson's table of ultimate values is moral and ethical. It reflects quite as real, pervasive, durable, and commendable a marshalling of priorities as a formal religion. It is just as much a residue of culture, early training, and beliefs shared by companions and family. What another derives from the discipline of a church, Sisson derives from the discipline of conscience.

There is no doubt that the views of Gillette are sincere, genuine, and profound. The District Court in the present case faced squarely the issue presented in *Sisson* and being unable to distinguish the case on the facts, refused to follow *Sisson.*

The question, can a conscientious objector, whether his objection be rooted in "religion" or in moral values, be required to kill? has never been answered by the Court. . . .
Yet if *dicta* are to be our guide, my choice is the *dicta* of Chief Justice Hughes who, dissenting in *Macintosh,* spoke for Holmes, Brandeis, and Stone:

> Nor is there ground, in my opinion, for the exclusion of Professor Macintosh because his conscientious scruples have particular reference to wars believed to be unjust. There is nothing new in such an attitude. Among the most eminent statesmen here and abroad have been those who condemned the action of their country in entering into wars they thought to be unjustified. Agreements for the renunciation of war presuppose a preponderant public sentiment against wars of aggression. If, while recognizing the power of Congress, the mere holding of religious or conscientious scruples against all wars should not disqualify a citizen from holding office in this country, or an applicant otherwise qualified from being admitted to citizenship, there would seem to be no reason why a reservation of religious or conscientious objection to participation in wars believed to be unjust should constitute such a disqualification.

I think the Hughes' view is the constitutional view. It is true that the First Amendment speaks of the free exercise of religion not of the free exercise of conscience or belief. Yet conscience and belief are the main ingredients of First Amendment rights. They are the bedrock of free speech as well as religion. The implied First Amendment right of "conscience" is certainly as high as the "right of association" which we recognized in *Shelton* v. *Tucker,* 364 US 479, and *NAACP* v. *Alabama,* 357 US 449. Some indeed have thought it higher.*

Conscience is often the echo of religious faith. But, as this case illustrates, it may also be the product of travail, meditation, or sudden revelation related to a moral comprehension of the dimensions of a problem, not to a religion in the ordinary sense.

Tolstoy wrote of a man "who, as he himself says, is not a Christian, and who refuses military service, not from religious motives, but from motives of the simplest kind, motives intelligible and common to all men, of whatever religion or nation, whether Catholic, Mohammedan, Buddhist, Confucian, whether Spaniards or Japanese.

> Van de Veer refuses military service, not because he follows the commandment, "Thou shalt do no murder," not because he is a Christian but because he holds murder to be opposed to human nature. . . .

The "sphere of intellect and spirit," as we described the domain of the First Amendment in *West Virginia State Board of Education* v. *Barnette,* 319 US 624, was recognized in *United States* v. *Seeger,* 380 US 163, where we gave a broad construction to the statutory exemption of those who by their religious training or belief are conscientiously opposed to participation in war in any form. We said: "A sincere and meaningful belief which occupies in the life of its possessor a place parallel to that filled by the God of

---

* See Konvitz, *Religious Liberty and Conscience.* 106 (1968); Redlich and Feinberg, "Individual Conscience and the Selective Service Objector," 44 *N.Y.U.L.Rev.* 875, 891 (1969): "Free expression and the right of personal conscientious belief are closely intertwined. At the core of the first amendment's protection of individual expression, is the recognition that such expression represents the oral or written manifestation of conscience. The performance of certain acts, under certain circumstances, involves such a crisis of conscience as to invoke the protection which the first amendment provides for similar manifestations of conscience when expressed in verbal or written expressions of thought. The most awesome act which any society can demand of a citizen's conscience is the taking of a human life."

those admittedly qualifying for the exemption comes within the statutory definition."

Seeger does not answer the present question as Gillette is not "opposed to participation in war in any form."

But the constitutional infirmity in the present Act seems obvious once "conscience" is the guide. As Chief Justice Hughes said in the *Macintosh* case:

> But, in the forum of conscience, duty to a moral power higher than the state has always been maintained. The reservation of that supreme obligation, as a matter of principle, would unquestionably be made by many of our conscientious and law-abiding citizens. The essence of religion is belief in a relation to God involving duties superior to those arising from any human relation.

The law as written is a species of those which show an invidious discrimination in favor of religious persons and against others with like scruples. Mr. Justice Black once said: "The First Amendment has lost much if the religious follower and the atheist are no longer to be judicially regarded as entitled to equal justice under law." . . . We said as much in our recent decision in *Epperson* v. *Arkansas*, 393 US 97, where we struck down as unconstitutional a state law prohibiting the teaching of the doctrine of evolution in the public schools:

> Government in our democracy, state and national, must be neutral in matters of religious theory, doctrine, and practice. It may not be hostile to any religion or to the advocacy of no-religion; and it may not aid, foster, or promote one religion or religious theory against another or even against the militant opposite. The First Amendment mandates governmental neutrality between religion and religion, and between religion and nonreligion.

While there is no Equal Protection Clause in the Fifth Amendment, our decisions are clear that invidious classifications violate due process. *Bolling* v. *Sharpe*, 347 US 497, 500 held that segregation by race in the public schools was an invidious discrimination, and *Schneider* v. *Rusk*, 377 US 163, reached the same result based on penalties imposed on naturalized, not native-born citizens. A classification of "conscience" based on a "religion" and a "conscience" based on more generalized, philosophical grounds is equally invidious by reason of our First Amendment standards.

I had assumed that the welfare of the single human soul was the ultimate test of the vitality of the First Amendment.

This is an appropriate occasion to give content to our dictum in *West Virginia State Board of Education* v. *Barnette, supra:*

> . . . freedom to differ is not limited to things that do not matter much. . . . The test of its substance is the right to differ as to things that touch the heart of the existing order.

I would reverse this judgment.

Mr. Justice Douglas, dissenting in No. 325:

I approach the facts of this case with some diffidence, as they involve doctrines of the Catholic Church in which I was not raised. But we have on one of petititioner's briefs an authoritative lay Catholic scholar, Dr. John T. Noonan, Jr., and from that brief I deduce the following.

Under the doctrines of the Catholic Church a person has a moral duty to take part in wars declared by his government so long as they comply with the tests of his church for just wars. Conversely, a Catholic has a moral duty not to participate in unjust wars.

The Fifth Commandment, "Thou shall not kill," provides a basis for the distinction between just and unjust wars. In the 16th century Francisco Victoria, Dominican master of the University of Salamanca and pioneer in international law, elaborated on the distinction. "If a subject is convinced of the injustice of a war, he ought not to serve in it, even on the command of his prince. This is clear, for no one can authorize the killing of an innocent person." He realized not all men had the information of the prince and his counsellors on the causes of a war, but where "the proofs and tokens of the injustice of the war may be such that ignorance would be no excuse even to the subjects" who are not normally informed, that ignorance will not be an excuse if they participate. Well over 400 years later, today, the Baltimore Catechism makes an exception to the Fifth Commandment for a "soldier fighting in a just war."

No one can tell a Catholic that this or that war is either just or unjust. This is a personal decision that an individual must make on the basis of his own conscience after studying the facts.*

Like the distinction between just and unjust wars, the duty to obey conscience is not a new doctrine in the Catholic Church. When told to stop preaching to the Sanhedrin, to which he was subordinate by law, "Peter replied for himself and the apostles, 'We must obey God rather than men.'" That duty has not changed. Pope Paul VI has expressed it as follows: "On his part, man perceives and acknowledges the imperatives of the divine law through the mediation of the conscience. In all his activity a man is bound to follow his conscience faithfully, in order that he may come to God, for whom he was created."†

While the fact that the ultimate determination of whether a war is unjust rests on individual conscience, the Church has provided guides. Francisco Victoria referred to "killing of an innocent person." World War II had its impact on the doctrine. Writing shortly after the war Cardinal Ottaviani stated "modern wars can never fulfill those conditions which (as we stated earlier on in this essay) govern—theoretically—a just and lawful war. Moreover, no conceivable cause could ever be sufficient justification for the evils, the slaughter, the destruction, the moral and religious upheavals which war today entails. *In practice, then, a declaration of war will never be justifiable.*" The full impact of the horrors of modern war were emphasized in the Pastoral Constitution announced by Vatican II:

> The development of armaments by modern science has immeasurably magnified the horrors and wickedness of war. Warfare conducted with these weapons can inflict immense and indiscriminate havoc which goes far beyond the bounds of legitimate defense. Indeed, if the kind of weapons now stocked in the arsenals of the great powers were to be employed to the fullest, the result would be the almost

---

* Pope Paul VI in § 16 of the Pastoral Constitution states: "Deep within his conscience, man discovers a law which he has not laid upon himself but which he must obey. Its voice, ever calling him to love and to do what is good and avoid evil, tells him inwardly at the right moment to do this or to shun that. For man has in his heart a law written by God. His dignity lies in observing this law, and by it he will be judged." . . .

† Declaration on Religious Freedom I:3 in *Documents of Vatican* II 681 (1966). See also "Human Life in Our Day" issued by the National Conference of Catholic Bishops (Nov. 15, 1968): "Whether or not such modifications in our laws are in fact made, we continue to hope that, in the all-important issues of war and peace, all men will continue to follow their consciences. We can do no better than to recall, as did the Vatican Council, 'the permanent binding force of universal natural law and its all embracing principles, to which man's conscience itself gives ever more emphatic voice.'"

complete reciprocal slaughter of one side by the other, not to speak of the widespread devastation that would follow in the world and the deadly after-effects resulting from the use of such arms.

All of these factors force us to undertake a completely fresh reappraisal of war. . . .

It is one thing to wage a war of self-defense; it is quite another to seek to impose domination on another nation. . . .

The Pastoral Constitution announced that "every act of war directed to the indiscriminate destruction of whole cities or vast areas with their inhabitants is a crime against God and man which merits firm and unequivocal condemnation."

Louis Negre is a devout Catholic. In 1951 when he was four, his family immigrated to this country from France. He attended Catholic schools in Bakersfield, California, until graduation from high school. Then he attended Bakersfield Junior College for two years. Following that he was inducted into the Army.

At the time of his induction he had his own convictions about the Vietnam war and the Army's goals in the war. He wanted, however, to be sure of his convictions. "I agreed to myself that before making any decision or taking any type of stand on the issue, I would permit myself to see and understand the Army's explanation of its reasons for violence in Vietnam. For, without getting an insight on the subject, it would be unfair for me to say anything, without really knowing the answer."

On completion of his advanced infantry training, "I knew that if I would permit myself to go to Vietnam I would be violating my own concepts of natural law and would be going against all that I had been taught in my religious training." Negre applied for a discharge as a conscientious objector. His application was denied. He then refused to comply with an order to proceed for shipment to Vietnam. A general court martial followed, but he was acquitted. After that he filed this application for discharge as a conscientious objector.

Negre is opposed under his religious training and beliefs to participation in any form in the war in Vietnam. His sincerity is not questioned. His application for a discharge, however, was denied because his religious training and beliefs lead him to oppose only a particular war which according to his conscience was unjust.

For the reasons I have stated in my dissent in the *Gillette* case decided this day, I would reverse the judgment.

7. Tax-Exemption for Church Property

WALZ v. TAX COMMISSION OF CITY OF NEW YORK
397 US 664 (1970)

[An owner of property sought an injunction to prevent the local tax commission from granting tax exemption to religious societies for their properties used solely for religious worship. The New York State courts held against the complainant. The Supreme Court, with only Justice Douglas dissenting, upheld the State courts. The opinion for the Court was by Chief Justice Burger. Justices Brennan and Harlan each wrote a concurring opinion. Justice Douglas wrote a dissenting opinion.]

Mr. Chief Justice Burger delivered the opinion of the Court:

Appellant, owner of real estate in Richmond County, New York, sought an injunction in the New York courts to prevent the New York City Tax Commission from granting property tax exemptions to religious organizations for religious properties used solely for religious worship. The exemption from state taxes is authorized by Art. 16, § 1, of the New York Constitution, which provides:

Exemptions from taxation may be granted only by general laws. Exemptions may be altered or repealed except those exempting real or personal property used exclusively for religious, educational or charitable purposes as defined by law and owned by any corporation or association organized or conducted exclusively for one or more of such purposes and not operating for profit.*

The essence of appellant's contention was that the New York State Tax Commission's grant of an exemption to church property indirectly requires the appellant to make a contribution to religious bodies and thereby violates provisions prohibiting establishment of religion under the First Amendment which under the Fourteenth Amendment is binding on the States.

Appellee's motion for summary judgment was granted and the Appellate Division, New York Supreme Court, and the New York Court of Appeals affirmed. We noted jurisdiction, and affirm.

I

Prior opinions of this Court have discussed the development and historical background of the First Amendment in detail. See *Everson* v. *Board of Education,* 330 US 1 (1947); *Engel* v. *Vitale,* 370 US 421 (1962). It would therefore serve no useful purpose to review in detail the background of the Establishment and Free Exercise Clauses of the First Amendment or to restate what the Court's opinions have reflected over the years.

It is sufficient to note that for the men who wrote the Religious Clauses of the First Amendment the "establishment" of a religion connoted sponsorship, financial support, and active involvement of the sovereign in religious activity. In England, and in some Colonies at the time of the separation in 1776, the Church of England was sponsored and supported by the Crown as a state, or established, church; in other countries "establishment" meant sponsorship by the sovereign of the Lutheran or Catholic Church. . . . The exclusivity of established churches in the 17th and 18th centuries, of course, was often carried to prohibition of other forms of worship. . . .

The Establishment and Free Exercise Clauses of the First Amendment are not the most precisely drawn portions of the Constitution. The sweep of the absolute

* Art. 16, § 1, of the New York State Constitution is implemented by § 420, subd. 1, of the New York Real Property Tax Law, *McKinney's Consol.Laws,* c. 50-A which states in pertinent part: "Real property owned by a corporation or association organized exclusively for the moral or mental improvement of men and women, or for religious, bible, tract, charitable, benevolent, missionary, hospital, infirmary, educational, public playground, scientific, literary, bar association, medical society, library, patriotic, historical or cemetery purposes . . . and used exclusively for carrying out thereupon one or more of such purposes . . . shall be exempt from taxation as provided in this section."

prohibitions in the Religion Clauses may have been calculated; but the purpose was to state an objective, not to write a statute. In attempting to articulate the scope of the two Religious Clauses, the Court's opinions reflect the limitations inherent in formulating general principles on a case-by-case basis. The considerable internal inconsistency in the opinions of the Court derives from what, in retrospect, may have been too sweeping utterances on aspects of these clauses that seemed clear in relation to the particular cases but have limited meaning as general principles.

The Court has struggled to find a neutral course between the two Religion Clauses, both of which are cast in absolute terms, and either of which, if expanded to a logical extreme, would tend to clash with the other.

The course of constitutional neutrality in this area cannot be an absolutely straight line; rigidity could well defeat the basic purpose of these provisions, which is to insure that no religion be sponsored or favored, none commanded, and none inhibited. The general principle deducible from the First Amendment and all that has been said by the Court is this: that we will not tolerate either governmentally established religion or governmental interference with religion. Short of those expressly proscribed governmental acts there is room for play in the joints productive of a benevolent neutrality which will permit religious exercise to exist without sponsorship and without interference.

Each value judgment under the Religion Clauses must therefore turn on whether particular acts in question are intended to establish or interfere with religious beliefs and practices or have the effect of doing so. Adherence to the policy of neutrality that derives from an accommodation of the Establishment and Free Exercise Clauses has prevented the kind of involvement that would tip the balance toward government control of churches or governmental restraint on religious practice.

Adherents of particular faiths and individual churches frequently take strong positions on public issues including, as this case reveals in the several briefs *amici,* vigorous advocacy of legal or constitutional positions. Of course, churches as much as secular bodies and private citizens have that right. No perfect or absolute separation is really possible; the very existence of the Religion Clauses is an involvement of sorts—one which seeks to mark boundaries to avoid excessive entanglement.

The hazards of placing too much weight on a few words or phrases of the Court is abundantly illustrated within the pages of the Court's opinion in *Everson.* . . .

Mr. Justice Jackson, in perplexed dissent in *Everson,* noted that

the undertones of the opinion, advocating complete and uncompromising separation . . . seem utterly discordant with its conclusion. . . .

Perhaps so. One can sympathize with Mr. Justice Jackson's logical analysis but agree with the Court's eminently sensible and realistic application of the language of the Establishment Clause. In *Everson* the Court declined to construe the religion clauses with a literalness that would undermine the ultimate constitutional objective as illuminated by history. Surely, bus transportation and police protection to pupils who receive religious instruction "aid" that particular religion to maintain schools that plainly tend to assure future adherents to a particular faith by having control of their total education at an early age. No religious body that maintains schools would deny this as an affirmative if not dominant policy of church schools. But if as in *Everson* buses can be provided to carry and policemen to protect church school pupils, we fail to see how a broader range of police and fire protection given equally to all churches, along with nonprofit hospitals, art galleries, and libraries receiving the same tax exemption, is different for purposes of the religion clauses.

Similarly, making textbooks available to pupils in parochial schools in common with public schools was surely an "aid" to the sponsoring churches because it relieved those churches of an enormous aggregate cost for those books. Supplying of costly teaching materials was not seen either as manifesting a legislative purpose to aid or as having a primary effect of aid contravening the First Amendment. *Board of Education of Central School Dist. No. 1* v. *Allen,* 392 US 236 (1968). In so doing the Court was heeding both its own prior holdings and our religious tradition. Mr. Justice Douglas, in *Zorach* v. *Clauson, supra,* after recalling that we "are a religious people whose institutions presuppose a Supreme Being," went on to say:

We make room for as wide a variety of beliefs and creeds as the spiritual needs of man deem necessary. . . . *When the state encourages religious instruction . . . it follows the best of our traditions.* For it then respects the religious nature of our people and accommodates the public service to their spiritual needs. (Emphasis added.)

With all the risks inherent in programs that bring about administrative relationships between public education bodies and church-sponsored schools, we have been able to chart a course that preserved the autonomy and freedom of religious bodies while avoiding any semblance of established religion. This is a "tightrope" and one we have successfully traversed.

II

The legislative purpose of a property tax exemption is neither the advancement nor the inhibition of religion; it is neither sponsorship nor hostility. New York, in common with the other states, has determined that certain entities that exist in a harmonious relationship to the community at large, and that foster its "moral or mental improvement," should not be inhibited in their activities by property taxation or the hazard of loss of those properties for nonpayment of taxes. It has not singled out one particular church or religious group or even churches as such; rather, it has granted exemption to all houses of religious worship within a broad class of property owned by nonprofit, quasi-public corporations which include hospitals, libraries, playgrounds, scientific, professional, historical and patriotic groups. The State has an affirmative policy that considers these groups as beneficial and stabilizing influences in community life and finds this classification useful, desirable, and in the public interest. Qualification for tax exemption is not perpetual or immutable; some tax-exempt groups lose that status when their activities take them outside the classification and new entities can come into being and qualify for exemption.

Governments have not always been tolerant of religious activity, and hostility toward religion has taken many shapes and forms—economic, political, and sometimes harshly oppressive. Grants of exemption historically reflect the concern of authors of constitutions and statutes as to the latent dangers inherent in the imposition of property taxes; exemption constitutes a reasonable and balanced attempt to guard against those dangers. The limits of permissible state accommodation to religion are by no means coextensive with the noninterference mandated by the Free Exercise Clause. To equate the two would be to deny a national heritage with roots in the Revolution itself. . . . We cannot read New York's statute as attempting to establish religion; it is simply sparing the exercise of religion from the burden of property taxation levied on private profit institutions.

We find it unnecessary to justify the tax exemption on the social welfare services or "good works" that some churches perform for parishioners and others—family counselling, aid to the elderly and the infirm, and to children. Churches vary substantially in the scope of such services; programs expand or contract according to resources and need. As public-sponsored programs enlarge, private aid from the church sector may diminish. The exent of social services may vary, depending on whether the church serves an urban or rural, a rich or poor constituency. To give emphasis to so variable an aspect of the work of religious bodies would introduce an element of governmental evaluation and standards as to the worth of particular social welfare programs, thus producing a kind of continuing day-to-day relationship which the policy of neutrality seeks to minimize. Hence, the use of a social welfare yardstick as a significant element to qualify for tax exemption could conceivably give rise to confrontations that could escalate to constitutional dimensions.

Determining that the legislative purpose of tax exemption is not aimed at establishing, sponsoring, or supporting religion does not end the inquiry, however. We must also be sure that the end result—the effect—is not an excessive government entanglement with religion. The test is inescapably one of degree. Either course, taxation of churches or exemption, occasions some degree of involvement with religion. Elimination of exemption would tend to expand the involvement of government by giving rise to tax valuation of church property, tax liens, tax foreclosures, and the direct confrontations and conflicts that follow in the train of those legal processes.

Granting tax exemptions to churches necessarily operates to afford an indirect economic benefit and also gives rise to some, but yet a lesser, involvement than taxing them. In analyzing either alternative the questions are whether the involvement is excessive, and whether it is a continuing one calling for official and continuing surveillance leading to an impermissible degree of entanglement. Obviously a direct money subsidy would be a relationship pregnant with involvement and, as with most governmental grant programs, could encompass sustained and detailed administrative relationships for enforcement of statutory or administrative standards, but that is not this case. The hazards of churches supporting government are hardly less in their potential than the hazards of governments supporting churches; each relationship carries some involvement rather than the desired insulation and separation. We cannot ignore the instances in history when church support of government led to the kind of involvement we seek to avoid.

The grant of a tax exemption is not sponsorship since the government does not transfer part of its revenue to churches but simply abstains from demanding that the church support the state. No one has ever suggested that tax exemption has converted libraries, art galleries, or hospitals into arms of the state or employees "on the public payroll." There is no genuine nexus between tax exemption and establishment of religion. As Mr. Justice Holmes commented in a related context "a page of history is worth a volume of logic." . . . The exemption creates only a minimal and remote involvement between church and state and far less than taxation of churches. It restricts the fiscal relationship between church and state, and tends to complement and reinforce the desired separation insulating each from the other.

Separation in this context cannot mean absence of all contact; the complexities of modern life inevitably produce some contact, and the fire and police protection received by houses of religious worship are no more than incidental benefits accorded all persons or institutions within a State's boundaries, along with many other exempt organizations. The appellant has not established even an arguable quantitative correlation between the payment of an ad valorem property tax and the receipt of these municipal benefits.

All of the 50 States provide for tax exemption of places of worship, most of them doing so by constitutional guarantees. For so long as federal income taxes have had any potential impact on churches—over 75 years—religious organizations have been expressly exempt from the tax. Such treatment is an "aid" to churches no more and no less in principle than the real estate tax exemption granted by States. Few concepts are more deeply embedded in the fabric of our national life, beginning with pre-Revolutionary colonial times, than for the government to exercise at the very least this kind of benevolent neutrality toward churches and religious exercise generally so long as none was favored over others and none suffered interference.

It is significant that Congress, from its earliest days, has viewed the religion clauses of the Constitution as authorizing statutory real estate tax exemption to religious bodies. In 1802 the 7th Congress enacted a taxing statute for the County of Alexandria, adopting the 1800 Virginia statutory pattern which provided tax exemptions for churches. . . . As early as 1813 the 12th Congress refunded import duties paid by religious societies on the importation of religious articles. During this period the City Council of Washington, D.C., acting under congressional authority, Act of Incorporation, § 7, 2 Stat. 197 (May 3, 1802), enacted a series of real and personal property assessments which uniformly exempted church property. In 1870 the Congress specifically exempted all churches in the District of Columbia and appurtenant grounds and property "from any and all taxes or assessments, national, municipal, or county." . . .

It is obviously correct that no one acquires a vested or protected right in violation of the Constitution by long use, even when that span of time covers our entire national existence and indeed predates it. Yet an unbroken practice of according the exemption to churches, openly and by affirmative state action, not covertly or by state inaction, is not something to be lightly cast aside. Nearly 50 years ago Mr. Justice Holmes stated:

[I]f a thing has been practised for two hundred years by common consent, it will need a strong case for the Fourteenth Amendment to affect it. *Jackman* v. *Rosenbaum Co.,* 260 US (1922).

Nothing in this national attitude toward religious tolerance and two centuries of uninterrupted freedom from taxation has given the remotest sign of leading to an established church or religion, and on the contrary it has operated affirmatively to help guarantee the free exercise of all forms of religious beliefs. Thus, it is hardly useful to suggest that tax exemption is but the "foot in the door" or the "nose of the camel in the tent" leading to an established church. If tax exemption can be seen as this first step toward "establishment" of religion, as Mr. Justice Douglas fears, the second step has been long in coming. Any move which realistically "establishes" a church or tends to do so can be dealt with "while this Court sits."

Mr. Justice Cardozo commented in *The Nature of the Judicial Process* (1921) on the "tendency of a principle to expand itself to the limit of its logic"; such expansion must always be contained by the historical frame of reference of the principle's purpose and there is no lack of vigilance on this score by those who fear religious entanglement in government.

The argument that making "fine distinctions" between what is and what is not absolute under the Constitution is to render us a government of men, not laws, gives too little weight to the fact that it is an essential part of adjudication to draw distinctions, including fine ones, in the process of interpreting the Constitution. We must frequently decide, for example, what are "reasonable" searches and seizures under the Fourth Amendment. Determining what acts of government tend to establish or interfere with religion falls well within what courts have long been called upon to do in sensitive areas.

It is interesting to note that while the precise question we now decide has not been directly before the Court previously, the broad question was discussed by the Court in relation to real estate taxes assessed nearly a century ago on land owned by and adjacent to a church in Washington, D.C. At that time Congress granted real estate tax exemptions to buildings devoted to art, to institutions of public charity, libraries, cemeteries, and "church buildings, and grounds actually occupied by such buildings." In denying tax exemption as to land owned by but not used for the church, but rather to produce income, the Court concluded:

In the exercise of this [taxing] power, congress, like any state legislature unrestricted by constitutional provisions, may, at its discretion, wholly exempt certain classes of property from taxation, or may tax them at a lower rate than other property. *Gibbons* v. *District of Columbia,* 116 US 404 (1886).

It appears that at least up to 1885 this Court, reflecting more than a century of our history and uninterrupted practice, accepted without discussion the proposition that federal or state grants of tax exemption to churches were not a violation of the Religious Clauses of the First Amendment. As to the New York statute, we now confirm that view.

Affirmed.

IV. Freedom of Assembly, Petition, and Association

1. Freedom of Assembly and Freedom of Petition for Redress of Grievances

EDWARDS v. SOUTH CAROLINA
372 US 229 (1963)

[Occasionally, as part of the movement to end racial segregation, groups of Negro students marched peacefully to a state house or a city hall to publicize their discontent and their dissatisfaction with discriminatory practices. When 187 Negro high-school and college students participated in such a march in Columbia, South Carolina, they were arrested and convicted of the common-law crime of breach of the peace. With only Justice Clark dissenting, the Supreme Court reversed the convictions on the ground that the demonstrators' rights of free speech, free assembly, and freedom of petition for redress of grievances had been infringed.]

Mr. Justice Stewart delivered the opinion of the Court:

The petitioners, 187 in number, were convicted in a magistrate's court in Columbia, South Carolina, of the common-law crime of breach of the peace. Their convictions were ultimately affirmed by the South Carolina Supreme Court. We granted certiorari to consider the claim that these convictions cannot be squared with the Fourteenth Amendment of the United States Constitution.

There was no substantial conflict in the trial evidence. Late in the morning of March 2, 1961, the petitioners, high-school and college students of the Negro race, met at the Zion Baptist Church in Columbia. From there, at about noon, they walked in separate groups of about 15 to the South Carolina State House grounds, an area of two city blocks open to the general public. Their purpose was "to submit a protest to the citizens of South Carolina, along with the Legislative Bodies of South Carolina, our feelings and our dissatisfaction with the present condition of discriminatory actions against Negroes, in general, and to let them know that we were dissatisfied and that we would like for the laws which prohibited Negro privileges in this State to be removed."

Already on the State House grounds when the petitioners arrived were 30 or more law enforcement officers, who had advance knowledge that the petitioners were coming. Each group of petitioners entered the grounds through a driveway and parking area known in the record as the "horseshoe." As they entered, they were told by the law enforcement officials that "they had a right, as a citizen, to go through the State House grounds, as any other citizen has, as long as they were peaceful." During the next half hour or 45 minutes, the petitioners, in the same small groups, walked single file or two abreast in an orderly way though the grounds, each group carrying placards bearing such messages as "I am proud to be a Negro," and "Down with segregation."

During this time a crowd of some 200 to 300 onlookers had collected in the horseshoe area and on the adjacent sidewalks. There was no evidence to suggest that these onlookers were anything but curious, and no evidence at all of any threatening remarks, hostile gestures, or offensive language on the part of any member of the crowd. The City Manager testified that he recognized some of the onlookers, whom he did not identify, as "possible trouble makers," but his subsequent testimony made clear that nobody among the crowd actually caused or threatened any trouble. There was no obstruction of pedestrian or vehicular traffic within the State House grounds. No vehicle was prevented from entering or leaving the horseshoe area. Although vehicular traffic at a nearby street intersection was slowed down somewhat, an officer was dispatched to keep traffic moving. There were a number of bystanders on the public sidewalks adjacent to the State House grounds, but they all moved on when asked to do so, and there was no impediment of pedestrian traffic. Police protection at the scene was at all times sufficient to meet any foreseeable possibility of disorder.

In the situation and under the circumstances thus described, the police authorities advised the petitioners that they would be arrested if they did not disperse within 15 minutes. Instead of dispersing, the petitioners engaged in what the City Manager described as "boisterous," "loud," and "flamboyant" conduct, which, as his later testimony made clear, consisted of listening to a "religious harangue" by one of their leaders, and loudly singing "The Star Spangled Banner" and other patriotic and religious songs, while stamping their feet and clapping their hands. After 15 minutes had passed, the police arrested the petitioners and marched them off to jail.

Upon this evidence the state trial court convicted the petitioners of breach of the peace, and imposed sentences ranging from a $10 fine or five days in jail, to a $100 fine or 30 days in jail. In affirming the judgments, the Supreme Court of South Carolina said that under the law of that State the offense of breach of the peace "is not susceptible of exact definition," but that the "general definition of the offense" is as follows:

In general terms, a breach of the peace is a violation of public order, a disturbance of the public tranquility, by any act or conduct inciting to violence . . . , it includes any violation of any law enacted to preserve peace and good order. It may consist of an act of violence or an act likely to produce violence. It is not necessary that the peace be actually broken to lay the foundation for a prosecution for this offense. If what is done is unjustifiable and unlawful, tending with sufficient directness to break the peace, no more is required. Nor is actual personal violence an essential element in the offense. . . .

By "peace," as used in the law in this connection, is meant the tranquility enjoyed by citizens of a municipality or community where good order reigns among its members, which is the natural right of all persons in political society.

The petitioners contend that there was a complete absence of any evidence of the commission of this offense, and that they were thus denied one of the most basic elements of due process of law. *Thompson* v. *Louisville,* 362 US 199; see *Garner* v. *Louisiana,* 368 US 157; *Taylor* v. *Louisiana,* 370 US 154. Whatever the merits of this contention, we need not pass upon it in the present case. The state courts have held that the petitioners' conduct constituted breach of the peace under state law, and we may accept their decision as binding upon us to that extent. But it nevertheless remains our duty in a case such as this to make an independent examination of the whole record. . . . And it is clear to us that in arresting, convicting, and punishing the petitioners under the circumstances disclosed by this record, South Carolina infringed the petitioners' constitutionally protected rights of free speech, free assembly, and freedom to petition for redress of their grievances.

It has long been established that these First Amendment freedoms are protected by the Fourteenth Amendment from invasion by the States. . . . The circumstances in this case reflect an exercise of these basic constitutional rights in their most pristine and classic form. The petitioners felt aggrieved by laws of South Carolina which allegedly "prohibited Negro privileges in this State." They peaceably assembled at the site of the State Government and there peaceably expressed their grievances "to the citizens of South Carolina, along with the Legislative Bodies of South Carolina." Not until they were told by police officials that they must disperse on pain of arrest did they do more. Even then, they but sang patriotic and religious songs after one of their leaders had delivered a "religious harangue." There was no violence or threat of violence on their part, or on the part of any member of the crowd watching them. Police protection was "ample."

This, therefore, was a far cry from the situation in *Feiner* v. *New York,* 340 US 315, where two policemen were faced with a crowd which was "pushing, shoving, and milling around," where at least one member of the crowd "threatened violence if the police did not act," where "the crowd was pressing closer around petitioner and the officer," and where "the speaker passes the bounds of argument or persuasion and undertakes incitement to riot." And the record is barren of any evidence of "fighting words." See *Chaplinsky* v. *New Hampshire,* 315 US 568.

We do not review in this case criminal convictions resulting from the evenhanded application of a precise and narrowly drawn regulatory statute evincing a legislative judgment that certain specific conduct be limited or proscribed. If, for example, the petitioners had been convicted upon evidence that they had violated a law regulating traffic, or had disobeyed a law reasonably limiting the periods during which the State House grounds were open to the public, this would be a different case. . . . These petitioners were convicted of an offense so generalized as to be, in the words of the South Carolina Supreme Court, "not susceptible of exact definition." And they were convicted upon evidence which showed no more than that the opinions which they were peaceably expressing were sufficiently opposed to the views of the majority of the community to attract a crowd and necessitate police protection.

The Fourteenth Amendment does not permit a State to make criminal the peaceful expression of unpopular views. "[A] function of free speech under our system of government is to invite dispute. It may indeed best serve its high purpose when it induces a condition of unrest, creates dissatisfaction with conditions as they are, or even stirs people to anger. Speech is often provocative and challenging. It may strike at prejudices and preconceptions and have profound unsettling effects as it presses for acceptance of an idea. That is why freedom of speech, . . . is . . . protected against censorship or punishment, unless shown likely to produce a clear and present danger of a serious substantive evil that rises far above public inconvenience, annoyance, or unrest. . . . There is no room under our Constitution for a more restrictive view. For the alternative would lead to standardization of ideas either by legislatures, courts, or dominant political or community groups." . . . As in the *Terminiello* case, the courts of South Carolina have defined a criminal offense so as to permit conviction of the petitioners if their speech "stirred people to anger, invited public dispute, or brought about a condition of unrest. A conviction resting on any of those grounds may not stand."

As Chief Justice Hughes wrote in *Stromberg* v. *California,* "The maintenance of the opportunity for free political discussion to the end that government may be responsive to the will of the people and that changes may be obtained by lawful means, an opportunity essential to the security of the Republic, is a fundamental principle of our constitutional system. A statute which upon its face, and as authoritatively construed, is so vague and indefinite as to permit the punishment of the fair use of this opportunity is repugnant to the guaranty of liberty contained in the Fourteenth Amendment. . . ." 283 US 359.

For these reasons we conclude that these criminal convictions cannot stand. Reversed.

2. Freedom to Solicit Members for an Organization or a Cause

STAUB *v.* BAXLEY
355 US 313 (1958)

[Essential to the freedom of association is the right to solicit members for an organization. An ordinance of the city of Baxley, Georgia, made it a criminal offense to solicit members for any organization that requires the payment of dues, without first applying for and procuring a permit from the mayor and city council, who had the right to refuse a permit if they did not approve of the applicant or his organization or the organization's effect on the general welfare of the city. In a 7-to-2 decision the Court, in an opinion by Justice Whittaker, held that the ordinance violated the Fourteenth Amendment, which protects freedom of speech against invasion by a state (including a municipality acting under state authority). Cf. *Thomas* v. *Collins,* 323 US 516 (1945).

[Justice Frankfurter dissented (joined by Justice Clark) for the reason that, because of the procedure followed in the case, the decision of the Supreme Court of Georgia rested on an adequate nonfederal ground, which should not be reviewed by the United States Supreme Court.]

Mr. Justice Whittaker delivered the opinion of the Court:

Appellant, Rose Staub, was convicted in the Mayor's Court of the City of Baxley, Georgia, of violation of a city ordinance and was sentenced to imprisonment for 30 days or to pay a fine of $300. The Superior Court of the county affirmed the judgment of conviction; the Court of Appeals of the State affirmed the judgment of the Superior Court, . . . and the Supreme Court of the State denied an application for certiorari. The case comes here on appeal. . . .

Appellant was a salaried employee of The International Ladies' Garment Workers Union which was attempting to organize the employees of a manufacturing company located in the nearby town of Hazelhurst. A number of those employees lived in Baxley. On February 19, 1954, appellant and one Mamie Merritt, also a salaried employee of the union, went to Baxley and, without applying for permits required under the ordinance, talked with several of the employees at their homes about joining the union. While in a restaurant in Baxley on that day they were sought out and questioned by the Chief of Police concerning their activities in Baxley, and appellant told him that they were "going around talking to some of the women to organize the factory workers . . . and hold[ing] meetings with them for that purpose." Later that day a meeting was held at the home of one of the employees, attended by three other employees, at which, in the words of the hostess, appellant "just told us they wanted us to join the union, and said it would be a good thing for us to do . . . and went on to tell us how this union would help us." Appellant told those present that the membership dues would be 64 cents per week but would not be payable until the employees were organized. No money was asked or received from the persons at the meeting, but they were invited "to get other girls . . . there to join the union" and blank membership cards were offered for that use. Appellant further explained that the immediate objective was to "have enough cards signed to petition for an election . . . with the Labor Board."

On the same day a summons was issued and served by the Chief of Police commanding appellant to appear before the Mayor's Court three days later to answer "to the offense of soliciting members for an organization without a Permit & License." . . .

The First Amendment of the Constitution provides: "Congress shall make no law . . . abridging the freedom of speech. . . ." This freedom is among the fundamental personal rights and liberties which are protected by the Fourteenth Amendment from invasion by state action; and municipal ordinances adopted under state authority constitute state action. . . .

This ordinance in its broad sweep makes it an offense to "solicit" citizens of the City of Baxley to become members of any "organization, union or society" which requires "fees [or] dues" from its members without first applying for and receiving from the Mayor and Council of the City a "permit" . . . which they may grant or refuse to grant . . . after considering "the character of the applicant, the nature of the . . . organization for which members are desired to be solicited, and its effects upon the general welfare of [the] citizens of the City of Baxley." . . .

Appellant's first contention in this Court is that the ordinance is invalid on its face because it makes enjoyment of the constitutionally guaranteed freedom of speech contingent upon the will of the Mayor and Council of the City and thereby constitutes a prior restraint upon, and abridges, that freedom. Believing that appellant is right in that contention and that the judgment must be reversed for that reason, we confine our considerations to that particular question and do not reach other questions presented.

It will be noted that appellant was not accused of any act against the peace, good order or dignity of the community, nor for any particular thing she said in soliciting employees of the manufacturing company to join the union. She was simply charged and convicted for "soliciting members for an organization without a Permit." This solicitation, as shown by the evidence, consisted solely of speaking to those employees in their private homes about joining the union.

It will also be noted that the permit is not to be issued as a matter of course, but only upon the affirmative action of the Mayor and Council of the City. They are expressly authorized to refuse to grant the permit if they do not approve of the applicant or of the union or of the union's "effects upon the general welfare of the citizens of the City of Baxley." These criteria are without semblance of definitive standards or other controlling guides governing the action of the Mayor and Council in granting or withholding a permit. . . . It is thus plain that they act in this respect in their uncontrolled discretion.

It is settled by a long line of recent decisions of this Court that an ordinance which, like this one, makes the peaceful enjoyment of freedoms which the Constitution guarantees contingent upon the uncontrolled will of an official—as by requiring a permit or license which may be granted or withheld in the discretion of such official—is an unconstitutional censorship or prior restraint upon the enjoyment of those freedoms. . . .

It is undeniable that the ordinance authorized the Mayor and Council of the City of Baxley to grant "or refuse to grant" the required permit in their uncontrolled discretion. It thus makes enjoyment of speech contingent upon the will of the Mayor and Council of the City, although that fundamental right is made free from congressional abridgment by the First Amendment and is protected by the Fourteenth from invasion by state action. For these reasons, the ordinance, on its face, imposes an unconstitutional prior restraint upon the enjoyment of First Amendment freedoms and lays "a forbidden burden upon the exercise of liberty protected by the Constitution." . . . Therefore, the judgment of conviction must fall.

Reversed.

3. Freedom of Association

NATIONAL ASSN. FOR ADVANCEMENT OF COLORED PEOPLE *v.* ALABAMA
357 US 449 (1958)

[In the aftermath of the Court's decision in *Brown* v. *Topeka,* 347 US 483 (1954), prohibiting segregation in the schools, southern states attacked and tried to outlaw the NAACP. The Attorney General of Alabama sought an injunction to oust the Association from the state. In the course of proceedings in the state courts, the NAACP was ordered to produce records and papers, including names and addresses of all the Association's members and agents in the state. The Association produced all records except the membership lists. As to these lists, the NAACP contended that the state could not constitutionally compel disclosure.

[In a unanimous decision the Court upheld the claim of the Association. In his opinion for the Court, Justice Harlan said that the NAACP had the right to protect its membership lists on behalf of the right of the members to pursue their lawful private interests and to associate freely with others in the pursuit of their private interests. This right of the members, asserted for them by the Association, is protected by the Fourteenth Amendment against state action. The Due Process Clause of the Fourteenth Amendment protects the freedom to engage in association for the advancement of beliefs and ideas pertaining to political, economic, religious, or cultural matters.]

Mr. Justice Harlan delivered the opinion of the Court:

We review from the standpoint of its validity under the Federal Constitution a judgment of civil contempt entered against petitioner, the National Association for the Advancement of Colored People, in the courts of Alabama. The question presented is whether Alabama, consistently with the Due Process Clause of the Fourteenth Amendment, can compel petitioner to reveal to the State's Attorney General the names and addresses of all its Alabama members and agents, without regard to their positions or functions in the Association. The judgment of contempt was based upon petitioner's refusal to comply fully with a court order requiring in part the production of membership lists. Petitioner's claim is that the order, in the circumstances shown by this record, violated rights assured to petitioner and its members under the Constitution.

Alabama has a statute similar to those of many other States which requires foreign corporations, except as exempted, to qualify before doing business by filing the corporate charter with the Secretary of State and designating a place of business and an agent to receive service of process. The statute imposes a fine on a corporation transacting intrastate business before qualifying and provides for criminal prosecution of officers of such a corporation. . . . The National Association for the Advancement of Colored People is a nonprofit membership corporation organized under the laws of New York. Its purposes, fostered on a nationwide basis, are those indicated by its name, and it operates through chartered affiliates, which are independent unincorporated associations, with membership therein equivalent to membership in petitioner. The first Alabama affiliates were chartered in 1918. Since that time the aims of the Association have been advanced through activities of its affiliates, and in 1951 the Association itself opened a regional office in Alabama, at which it employed two supervisory persons and one clerical worker. The Association has never complied with the qualification statute, from which it considered itself exempt.

In 1956 the Attorney General of Alabama brought an equity suit in the State Circuit Court, Montgomery County, to enjoin the Association from conducting further activities within, and to oust it from, the State. Among other things the bill in equity alleged that the Association had opened a regional office and had organized various affiliates in Alabama; had recruited members and solicited contributions within the State; had given financial support and furnished legal assistance to Negro students seeking admission to the state university; and had supported a Negro boycott of the bus lines in Montgomery to compel the seating of passengers without regard to race. The bill recited that the Association, by continuing to do business in Alabama without complying with the qualification statute, was ". . . causing irreparable injury to the property and civil rights of the residents and citizens of the State of Alabama for which criminal prosecution and civil actions at law afford no adequate relief. . . ." On the day the complaint was filed, the Circuit Court issued *ex parte* an order restraining the Association, *pendente lite*, from engaging in further activities within the State and forbidding it ot take any steps to qualify itself to do business therein.

Petitioner demurred to the allegations of the bill and moved to dissolve the restraining order. It contended that its activities did not subject it to the qualification requirements of the statute and that in any event what the State sought to accomplish by its suit would violate rights to freedom of speech and assembly guaranteed under the Fourteenth Amendment to the Constitution of the United States. Before the date set for a hearing on this motion, the State moved for the production of a large number of the Association's records and papers, including bank statements, leases, deeds, and records containing the names and addresses of all Alabama "members" and "agents" of the Association. It alleged that all such documents were necessary for adequate preparation for the hearing, in view of petitioner's denial of the conduct of intrastate business within the meaning of the qualification statute. Over petitioner's objections, the court ordered the production of a substantial part of the requested records, including the membership lists, and postponed the hearing on the restraining order to a date later than the time ordered for production.

Thereafter petitioner filed its answer to the bill in equity. It admitted its Alabama activities substantially as alleged in the complaint and that it had not qualified to do business in the State. Although still disclaiming the state's application to it, petitioner offered to qualify if the bar from qualification made part of the restraining order were lifted, and it submitted with the answer an executed set of the forms required by the statute. However petitioner did not comply with the production order, and for this failure was adjudged in civil contempt and fined $10,000. The contempt judgment provided that the fine would be subject to reduction or remission if compliance were forthcoming within five days but otherwise would be increased to $100,000.

At the end of the five-day period petitioner produced substantially all the data called for by the production order except its membership lists, as to which it contended that Alabama could not constitutionally compel disclosure, and moved to modify or vacate the contempt judgment, or stay its execution pending appellate review. This motion was denied. While a similar stay application, which was later denied, was pending before the Supreme Court of Alabama, the Circuit Court made a further order adjudging petitioner in continuing contempt and increasing the fine already imposed to $100,000. Under Alabama law, . . . the effect of the contempt adjudication was to foreclose petitioner from obtaining a hearing on the merits of the underlying ouster action, or from taking any steps to dissolve the temporary restraining order which had been issued *ex parte*, until it purged itself of contempt. . . .

The State Supreme Court thereafter twice dismissed petitions for certiorari to review this final contempt judgment, the first time, . . . for insufficiency of the petition's allegations and the second time on procedural grounds. . . . We granted certiorari because of the importance of the constitutional questions presented. . . .

The Association both urges that it is constitutionally entitled to resist official inquiry into its membership lists, and that it may assert, on behalf of its members, a right personal to them to be protected from compelled disclosure by the State of their affiliation with the Association as revealed by the membership lists. We think that petitioner argues more appropriately the rights of its members, and that its nexus with them is sufficient to permit that it act as their representative before this Court. In so concluding, we reject respondent's argument that the Association lacks standing to assert here constitutional rights pertaining to the members, who are not of course parties to the litigation.

To limit the breadth of issues which must be dealt with in particular litigation, this Court has generally insisted that parties rely only on constitutional rights which are personal to themselves. . . . This rule is related to the broader doctrine that constitutional adjudication should where possible be avoided. . . . The principle is not disrespected where constitutional rights of persons who are not immediately before the Court could not be effectively vindicated except through an appropriate representative before the Court. . . .

If petitioner's rank-and-file members are constitutionally entitled to withhold their connection with the Association despite the production order, it is manifest that this right is properly assertable by the Association. To require that it be claimed by the members themselves would result in nullification of the right at the very moment of its assertion. Petitioner is the appropriate party to assert these rights, because it and its members are in every practical sense identical. The Association, which provides in its constitution that "[a]ny person who is in accordance with [its] principles and policies . . ." may become a member, is but the medium through which its individual members seek to make more effective the expression of their own views. The reasonable likelihood that the Assocaition itself through diminished financial support and membership may be adversely affected if production is compelled is a further factor pointing towards our holding that petitioner has standing to complain of the production order on behalf of its members. . . .

We thus reach petitioner's claim that the production order in the state litigation trespasses upon fundamental freedoms protected by the Due Process Clause of the Fourteenth Amendment. Petitioner argues that in view of the facts and circumstances shown in the record, the effect of compelled disclosure of the membership lists will be to abridge the rights of its rank-and-file members to engage in lawful association in support of their common beliefs. It contends that governmental action which, although not directly suppressing association, nevertheless carries this consequence, can be justified only upon some overriding valid interest of the State.

Effective advocacy of both public and private points of view, particularly controversial ones, is undeniably enhanced by group association, as this Court had more than once recognized by remarking upon the close nexus between the freedoms of speech and assembly. . . . It is beyond debate that freedom to engage in association for the advancement of beliefs and ideas is an inseparable aspect of the "liberty" assured by the Due Process Clause of the Fourteenth Amendment, which embraces freedom of speech. . . . Of course, it is immaterial whether the beliefs sought to be advanced by association pertain to political, economic, religious or cultural matters, and state action which may have the effect of curtailing the freedom to associate is subject to the closest scrutiny.

The fact that Alabama, so far as is relevant to the validity of the contempt judgment presently under review, has taken no direct action, . . . to restrict the right of petitioner's members to associate freely, does not end inquiry into the effect of the production order. See *American Communications Assn.* v. *Douds,* 339 US 382. In the domain of these indispensable liberties, whether of speech, press, or association, the decisions of this Court recognize that abridgment of such rights, even though unintended, may inevitably follow from varied forms of governmental action. Thus in *Douds,* the Court stressed that the legislation there challenged, which on its face sought to regulate labor unions and to secure stability in interstate commerce, would have the practical effect "of discouraging" the exercise of constitutionally protected political rights, . . . and it upheld the statute only after concluding that the reasons advanced for its enactment were constitutionally sufficient to justify its possible deterrent effect upon such freedoms. Similar recognition of possible unconstitutional intimidation of the free exercise of the right to advocate underlay this Court's narrow construction of the authority of a congressional committee investigating lobbying and of an Act regulating lobbying, although in neither case was there an effort to suppress speech. *United States* v. *Rumely,* 345 US 41; *United States* v. *Harriss,* 347 US 612. The governmental action challenged may appear to be totally unrelated to protected liberties. Statutes imposing taxes upon rather than prohibiting particular activity have been struck down when perceived to have the consequence of unduly curtailing the liberty of freedom of press assured under the Fourteenth Amendment. *Grosjean* v. *American Press Co.,* 297 US 233; *Murdock* v. *Pennsylvania,* 319 US 105.

It is hardly a novel perception that compelled disclosure of affiliation with groups engaged in advocacy may constitute as effective a restraint on freedom of association as the forms of governmental action in the cases above were thought likely to produce upon the particular constitutional rights there involved. This Court has recognized the vital relationship between freedom to associate and privacy in one's associations. When referring to the varied forms of governmental action which might interfere with freedom of assembly, it is said in *American Communications Assn.* v. *Douds,* . . . : "A requirement that adherents of particular religious faiths or political parties wear identifying armbands, for example, is obviously of this nature." Compelled disclosure of membership in an organization engaged in advocacy of particular beliefs is of the same order. Inviolability of privacy in group association may in many circumstances be indispensable to preservation of freedom of association, particularly where a group espouses dissident beliefs. . . .

We think that the production order, in the respects here drawn in question, must be regarded as entailing the likelihood of a substantial restraint upon the exercise by petitioner's members of their right to freedom of association. Petitioner has made an uncontroverted showing that on past occasions revelation of the identity of its rank-and-file members has exposed these members to economic reprisals, loss of employment, threat of physical coercion, and other manifestations of public hostility. Under these circumstances, we think it apparent that compelled disclosure of petitioner's Alabama membership is likely to affect adversely the ability of petitioner and its members to pursue their collective effort to foster beliefs which they admittedly have the right to advocate, in that it may induce members to withdraw from the Association and dissuade others from joining because of fear of exposure of their beliefs shown through their associations and of the consequences of this exposure.

It is not sufficient to answer, as the State does here, that whatever repressive effect compulsory disclosure of names of petitioner's members may have upon participation by Alabama citizens in petitioner's activities follows not from *state* action but from *private* community pressures. The crucial factor is the interplay of governmental and private action, for it is only after the initial exertion of state power represented by the production order that private action takes hold.

We turn to the final question whether Alabama has demonstrated an interest in obtaining the disclosures it seeks from petitioner which is sufficient to justify the deterrent effect which we have concluded these disclosures may well have on the free exercise by petitioner's members of their constitutionally protected right of association. . . . Such a ". . . subordinating interest of the State must be compelling," *Sweezy* v. *New Hampshire,* 354 US 234 (concurring opinion). It is not of moment that the State has here acted solely through its judicial branch, for whether legislative or judicial, it is still the application of state power which we are asked to scrutinize.

It is important to bear in mind that petitioner asserts no right to absolute immunity from state investigation, and no right to disregard Alabama's laws. As shown by its substantial compliance with the production order, petitioner does not deny Alabama's right to obtain from it such information as the State desires concerning the purposes of the Association and its activities within the State. Petitioner has not objected to divulging the identity of its members who are employed by or hold official positions with it. It has urged the rights solely of its ordinary rank-and-file members. This is therefore not analogous to a case involving the interest of a State in protecting its citizens in their dealings with paid solicitors or agents of foreign corporations by requiring identification. . . .

Whether there was "justification" in this instance turns solely on the substantiality of Alabama's interest in obtaining the membership lists. During the course of a hearing before the Alabama Circuit Court on a motion of petitioner to set aside the production order, the State Attorney General presented at length, under examination by petitioner, the State's reason for requesting the membership lists. The exclusive purpose was to determine whether petitioner was conducting intrastate business in violation of the Alabama foreign corporation registration statute, and the membership lists were expected to help resolve this question. The issues in the litigation commenced by Alabama by its bill in equity were whether the character of petitioner and its activities in Alabama had been such as to make petitioner subject to the registration statute, and whether the extent of petitioner's activities without qualifying suggested its permanent ouster from the State. Without intimating the slightest view upon the merits of these issues, we are unable to perceive that the disclosure of the names of petitioner's rank-and-file members has a substantial bearing on either of them. As matters stand in the state court, petitioner (1) has admitted its presence and conduct of activities in Alabama since 1918; (2) has offered to comply in all respects with the state qualification statute, although preserving its contention that the statute does not apply to it; and (3) has apparently complied satisfactorily with the production order, except for the membership lists, by furnishing the Attorney General with varied business records, its charter and statement of purposes, the names of all of its directors and officers, and with the total number of its Alabama members and the amount of their dues. These last items would not on this record appear subject to constitutional challenge and have been furnished, but whatever interest the State may have in obtaining names of ordinary members has not been shown to be sufficient to overcome petitioner's constitutional objections to the production order. . . .

We hold that the immunity from state scrutiny of membership lists which the Association claims on behalf of its members is here so related to the right of the members to pursue their lawful private interest privately and to associate freely with others in so doing as to come within the protection of the Fourteenth Amendment. And we conclude that Alabama has fallen short of showing a controlling justification for the deterrent effect on the free enjoyment of the right to associate which disclosure of membership lists is likely to have. Accordingly, the judgment of civil contempt and the $100,000 fine which resulted from petitioner's refusal to comply with the production order in this respect must fall. . . .

Reversed.

V. Freedom of Speech and Press

1. The Freedom Not to Speak

WEST VIRGINIA STATE BOARD OF EDUCATION v. BARNETTE
319 US 624 (1943)

[In 1940 there came before the Supreme Court *Minersville School District* v. *Gobitis,* 310 US 586, in which the Court upheld the requirement of participation by pupils in public schools in the ceremony of saluting the national flag. The Court held that a pupil belonging to Jehovah's Witnesses could not constitutionally claim exemption from this requirement on the ground that the flag salute would violate her religious beliefs and scruples. Justice Stone was the only dissenter.

[This decision was widely attacked. Three years later, in the *Barnette Case,* the Court dramatically reversed itself and expressly overruled the *Gobitis* decision. Justices Roberts, Reed, and Frankfurter dissented. In the *Barnette Case* the majority decision was put on the broad ground that the compulsory flag salute was an invasion of the sphere of intellect and spirit—a sphere protected from official control by the First and Fourteenth Amendments. National unity may be fostered by persuasion and example, but there may be no coerced uniformity. The Constitution guarantees the freedom to differ even "as to things that touch the heart of the existing order." Citizens may not be forced "to confess by word or act" their faith in any "orthodox" politics, nationalism, religion, or other matters of opinion.

[Justice Frankfurter, dissenting, said that the remedy for the unwise legislation involved in this case was to be found in the legislature and not in the courts. Much legislation affecting freedom of thought and speech, he said, "should offend a free-spirited society" and is yet constitutional. "Reliance for the most precious interests of civilization, therefore, must be found outside of their vindication in courts of law. Only a persistent positive translation of the faith of a free society into the convictions and habits of a community is the ultimate reliance against unabated temptations to fetter the human spirit."]

Mr. Justice Jackson delivered the opinion of the Court:

Following the decision by this Court on June 3, 1940, in *Minersville School Dist.* v. *Gobitis,* 310 US 586, the West Virginia legislature amended its statutes to require all schools therein to conduct courses of instruction in history, civics, and in the Constitutions of the United States and of the State "for the purpose of teaching, fostering and perpetuating the ideals, principles and spirit of Americanism, and increasing the knowledge of the organization and machinery of the government."

Appellant Board of Education was directed, with advice of the State Superintendent of Schools, to "prescribe the courses of study covering these subjects" for public schools. The Act made it the duty of private, parochial and denominational schools to prescribe courses of study "similar to those required for the public schools."

The Board of Education on January 9, 1942, adopted a resolution containing recitals taken largely from the Court's *Gobitis* opinion and ordering that the salute to the flag become "a regular part of the program of activities in the public schools," that all teachers and pupils "shall be required to participate in the salute honoring the Nation represented by the Flag; provided, however, that refusal to salute the Flag be regarded as an Act of insubordination, and shall be dealt wtih accordingly."

The resolution originally required the "commonly accepted salute to the Flag" which it defined. Objections to the salute as "being too much like Hitler's" were raised by the Parent and Teachers Association, the Boy and Girl Scouts, the Red Cross, and the Federation of Women's Clubs. Some modification appears to have been made in deference to these objections, but no concession was made to Jehovah's Witnesses. What is now required is the "stiff-arm" salute, the saluter to keep the right hand raised with palm turned up while the following is repeated: "I pledge allegiance to the Flag of the United States of America and to the Republic for which it stands; one Nation, indivisible, with liberty and justice for all."

Failure to conform is "insubordination" dealt with by expulsion. Readmission is denied by statute until compliance. Meanwhile the expelled child is "unlawfully absent" and may be proceeded against as a delinquent. His parents or guardians are liable to prosecution, and if convicted are subject to fine not exceeding $50 and jail term not exceeding thirty days.

Appellees, citizens of the United States and of West Virginia, brought suit in the United States District Court for themselves and others similarly situated asking its injunction to restrain enforcement of these laws and regulations against Jehovah's Witnesses. The Witnesses are an unincorporated body teaching that the obligation imposed by law of God is superior to that of laws enacted by temporal government. Their religious beliefs include a literal version of Exodus, Chapter 20, verses 4 and 5, which says: "Thou shalt not make unto thee any graven image, or any likeness of anything that is in heaven above, or that is in the earth beneath, or that is in the water under the earth; thou shalt not bow down thyself to them, nor serve them." They consider that the flag is an "image" within this command. For this reason they refuse to salute it.

Children of this faith have been expelled from school and are threatened with exclusion for no other cause. Officials threaten to send them to reformatories maintained for criminally inclined juveniles. Parents of such children have been prosecuted and are threatened with prosecutions for causing delinquency. . . .

This case calls upon us to reconsider a precedent decision, as the Court throughout its history often has been required to do. Before turning to the *Gobitis Case,* however, it is desirable to notice certain characteristics by which this controversy is distinguished.

The freedom asserted by these appellees does not bring them into collision with rights asserted by any other individuals. It is such conflicts which most frequently require intervention of the State to determine where the rights of one end and those of another begin. But the refusal of these persons to participate in the ceremony does not interfere with or deny rights of others to do so. Nor is there any question in this case that their behavior is peaceable and orderly. The sole conflict is between authority and rights of the individual. The State asserts power to condition access to public education on making a prescribed sign and profession and at the same time to coerce attendance by punishing both parent and child. The latter stand on a right of self-determination in matters that touch individual opinion and personal attitude.

As the present Chief Justice [Stone] said in dissent in the *Gobitis Case,* the State may "require teaching . . . in our history and in the structure and organization of our government, including the guaranties of civil liberty, which tend to inspire patriotism and love of country." Here, however, we are dealing with a compulsion of students to declare a belief. They are not merely made acquainted with the flag salute so that they may be informed as to what it is or even what it means. The issue here is whether this slow and easily neglected route to aroused loyalties constitutionally may be short-cut by substituting a compulsory salute and slogan. This issue is not prejudiced by the Court's previous holding that where a State, without compelling attendance, extends college facilities to pupils who voluntarily enroll, it may prescribe military training as part of the course without offense to the Constitution. It was held that those who take advantage of its opportunities may not on ground of conscience refuse compliance with such conditions. *Hamilton* v. *University of California,* 293 US 245. In the present case attendance is not optional. That case is also to be distinguished from the present one because, independently of college privileges or requirements, the State has power to raise militia and impose the duties of service therein upon its citizens.

There is no doubt that, in connection with the pledges, the flag salute is a form of utterance. Symbolism is a primitive but effective way of communicating ideas. The use of an emblem or flag to symbolize some system, idea, institution, or personality, is a short cut from mind to mind. Causes and nations, political parties, lodges, and ecclesiastical groups seek to knit the loyalty of their followings to a flag or banner, a color or design. The State announces rank, function, and authority through crowns and maces, uniforms and black robes; the church speaks through the Cross, the Crucifix, the altar and shrine, and clerical raiment. Symbols of State often convey political ideas just as religious symbols come to convey theological ones. Associated with many of these symbols are appropriate gestures of acceptance or respect: a salute, a bowed or bared head, a bended knee. A person gets from a symbol the meaning he puts into it, and what is one man's comfort and inspiration is another's jest and scorn.

Over a decade ago Chief Justice Hughes led this Court in holding that the display of a red flag as a symbol of opposition by peaceful and legal means to organized government was protected by the free speech guaranties of the Constitution. *Stromberg* v. *California,* 283 US 359. Here it is the State that employs a flag as a symbol of adherence to government as presently organized. It requires the individual to communicate by word and sign his acceptance of the political ideas it thus bespeaks.

Objection to this form of communication when coerced is an old one, well known to the framers of the Bill of Rights.

It is also to be noted that the compulsory flag salute and pledge requires affirmation of a belief and an attitude of mind. It is not clear whether the regulation contemplates that pupils forego any contrary convictions of their own and become unwilling converts to the prescribed ceremony or whether it will be acceptable if they simulate assent by words without belief and by a gesture barren of meaning. It is now a commonplace that censorship or suppression of expression of opinion is tolerated by our Constitution only when the expression presents a clear and present danger of action of a kind the State is empowered to prevent and punish. It would seem that involuntary affirmation could be commanded only on even more immediate and urgent grounds than silence. But here the power of compulsion is invoked without any allegation that remaining passive during a flag salute ritual creates a clear and present danger that would justify an effort even to muffle expression. To sustain the compulsory flag salute we are required to say that a Bill of Rights which guards the individual's right to speak his own mind, left it open to public authorities to compel him to utter what is not in his mind.

Whether the First Amendment to the Constitution will permit officials to order observance of ritual of this nature does not depend upon whether as a voluntary exercise we would think it to be good, bad or merely innocuous. Any credo of nationalism is likely to include what some disapprove or to omit what others think essential, and to give off different overtones as it takes on different accents or interpretations. If official power exists to coerce acceptance of any patriotic creed, what it shall contain cannot be decided by courts, but must be largely discretionary with the ordaining authority, whose power to prescribe would no doubt include power to amend. Hence validity of the asserted power to force an American citizen publicly to profess any statement of belief or to engage in any ceremony of assent to one, presents questions of power that must be considered independently of any idea we may have as to the utility of the ceremony in question.

Nor does the issue as we see it turn on one's possession of particular religious views or the sincerity with which they are held. While religion supplies appellees' motive for enduring the discomforts of making the issue in this case, many citizens who do not share these religious views hold such a compulsory rite to infringe constitutional liberty of the individual. It is not necessary to inquire whether nonconformist beliefs will exempt from the duty to salute unless we first find power to make the salute a legal duty.

The *Gobitis* decision, however, *assumed,* as did the argument in that case and in this, that power exists in the State to impose the flag salute discipline upon school children in general. The Court only examined and rejected a claim based on religious beliefs of immunity from an unquestioned general rule. The question which underlies the flag salute controversy is whether such a ceremony so touching matters of opinion and political attitude may be imposed upon the individual by official authority under powers committed to any political organization under our Constitution. We examine rather than assume existence of this power and, against this broader definition of issues in this case, reexamine specific grounds assigned for the *Gobitis* decision.

1. It was said that the flag-salute controversy confronted the Court with "the problem which Lincoln cast in memorable dilemma: 'Must a government of necessity be too *strong* for the liberties of its people, or too *weak* to maintain its own existence?' " and that the answer must be in favor of strength. *Minersville School Dist.* v. *Gobitis*.

We think these issues may be examined free of pressure or restraint growing out of such considerations.

It may be doubted whether Mr. Lincoln would have thought that the strength of government to maintain itself would be impressively vindicated by our confirming power of the state to expel a handful of children from school. Such oversimplification, so handy in political debate, often lacks the precision necessary to postulates of judicial reasoning. If validly applied to this problem, the utterance cited would resolve every issue of power in favor of those in authority and would require us to override every liberty thought to weaken or delay execution of their policies.

Government of limited power need not be anemic government. Assurance that rights are secure tends to diminish fear and jealousy of strong government, and by making us feel safe to live under it makes for its better support. Without promise of a limiting Bill of Rights it is doubtful if our Constitution could have mustered enough strength to enable its ratification. To enforce those rights today is not to choose weak government over strong government. It is only to adhere as a means of strength to individual freedom of mind in preference to officially disciplined uniformity for which history indicates a disappointing and disastrous end.

The subject now before us exemplifies this principle. Free public education, if faithful to the ideal of secular instruction and political neutrality, will not be partisan or enemy of any class, creed, party, or faction. If it is to impose any ideological discipline, however, each party or denomination must seek to control, or failing that, to weaken the influence of the educational system. Observance of the limitations of the Constitution will not weaken government in the field appropriate for its exercise.

2. It was also considered in the *Gobitis Case* that functions of educational officers in states, counties and school districts were such that to interfere with their authority "would in effect make us the school board for the country."

The Fourteenth Amendment, as now applied to the States, protects the citizen against the State itself and all of its creatures—Boards of Education not excepted. These have, of course, important, delicate, and highly discretionary functions, but none that they may not perform within the limits of the Bill of Rights. That they are educating the young for citizenship is reason for scrupulous protection of Constitutional freedoms of the individual, if we are not to strangle the free mind at its source and teach youth to discount important principles of our government as mere platitudes.

Such Boards are numerous and their territorial jurisdiction often small. But small and local authority may feel less sense of responsibility to the Constitution, and agencies of publicity may be less vigilant in calling it to account. The action of Congress in making flag observance voluntary and respecting the conscience of the objector in a matter so vital as raising the Army contrasts sharply with these local regulations in matters relatively trivial to the welfare of the nation. There are village tyrants as well as village Hampdens, but none who acts under color of law is beyond reach of the Constitution.

3. The *Gobitis* opinion reasoned that this is a field "where courts possess no marked and certainly no controlling competence," that it is committed to the legislatures as well as the courts to guard cherished liberties and that it is constitutionally appropriate to "fight out the wise use of legislative authority in the forum of public opinion and before legislative assemblies rather than to transfer such a contest to the judicial arena," since all the "effective means of inducing political changes are left free."

The very purpose of a Bill of Rights was to withdraw certain subjects from the vicissitudes of political controversy, to place them beyond the reach of majorities and officials and to establish them as legal principles to be applied by the courts. One's right to life, liberty, and property, to free speech, a free press, freedom of worship and assembly, and other fundamental rights may not be submitted to vote; they depend on the outcome of no elections.

In weighing arguments of the parties it is important to distinguish between the due process clause of the Fourteenth Amendment as an instrument for transmitting the principles of the First Amendment and those cases in which it is applied for its own sake. The test of legislation which collides with the Fourteenth Amendment, because it also collides wtih the principles of the First, is much more definite than the test when only the Fourteenth is involved. Much of the vagueness of the due process clause disappears when the specfic prohibitions of the First become its standard. The right of a State to regulate, for example, a public utility may well include, so far as the due process test is concerned, power to impose all of the restrictions which a legislature may have a "rational basis" for adopting. But freedoms of speech and of press, of assembly, and of worship may not be infringed on such slender grounds. They are susceptible of restriction only to prevent grave and immediate danger to interests which the state may lawfully protect. It is important to note that while it is the Fourteenth Amendment which bears directly upon the State it is the more specific limiting principles of the First Amendment that finally govern this case.

Nor does our duty to apply the Bill of Rights to assertions of official authority depend upon our possession of marked competence in the field where the invasion of rights occurs. True, the task of translating the majestic generalities of the Bill of Rights, conceived as part of the pattern of liberal government in the eighteenth century, into concrete restraints on officials dealing with the problems of the twentieth century, is one to disturb self-confidence. These principles grew in soil which also produced a philosophy that the individual was the center of society, that his liberty was attainable through mere absence of governmental restraints, and that government should be entrusted with few controls and only the mildest supervision over men's affairs. We must transplant these rights to a soil in which the laissez-faire concept or principle of non-interference has withered at least as to economic affairs, and social advancements are increasingly sought through closer integration of society and through expanded and strengthened governmental controls. These changed conditions often deprive precedents of reliability and cast us more than we would choose upon our judgment. But we act in these matters not by authority of our competence but by force of our commissions. We cannot, because of modest estimates of our competence in such specialties as public education, withhold the judgment that history authenticates as the function of this Court when liberty is infringed.

4. Lastly, and this is the very heart of the *Gobitis* opinion, it reasons that "national unity is the basis of national security," that the authorities have "the right to select appropriate means for its attainment," and hence reaches the conclusion that such compulsory measures toward "national unity" are constitutional. Upon the verity of this assumption depends our answer in this case.

National unity as an end which officials may foster by persuasion and example is not in question. The problem is whether under our Constitution compulsion as here employed is a permissible means for its achievement.

Struggles to coerce uniformity of sentiment in support of some end thought essential to their time and country have been waged by many good as well as by evil men. Nationalism is a relatively recent phenomenon but at other times and places the ends have been racial or territorial security, support of a dynasty or regime, and particular plans for saving souls. As first and moderate methods to attain unity have failed, those bent on its accomplishment must resort to an ever increasing severity. As governmental pressure toward unity becomes greater, so strife becomes more bitter as to whose unity it shall be. Probably no deeper division of our people could proceed from any provocation than from finding it necessary to choose what doctrine and whose program public educational officials shall compel youth to unite in embracing. Ultimate futility of such attempts to compel coherence is the lesson of every such effort from the Roman drive to stamp out Christianity as a disturber of its pagan unity, the Inquisition, as a means to religious and dynastic unity, the Siberian exiles as a means to Russian unity, down to the fast failing efforts of our present totalitarian enemies. Those who begin coercive elimination of dissent soon find themselves exterminating dissenters. Compulsory unification of opinion achieves only the unanimity of the graveyard.

It seems trite but necessary to say that the First Amendment to our Constitution was designed to avoid these ends by avoiding these beginnings. There is no mysticism in the American concept of the State or of the nature or origin of its authority. We set up government by consent of the governed, and the Bill of Rights denies those in power any legal opportunity to coerce that consent. Authority here is to be controlled by public opinion, not public opinion by authority.

The case is made difficult not because the principles of its decision are obscure but because the flag involved is our own. Nevertheless, we apply the limitations of the Constitution with no fear that freedom to be intellectually and spiritually diverse or even contrary will disintegrate the social organization. To believe that patriotism will not flourish if patriotic ceremonies are voluntary and spontaneous instead of a compulsory routine is to make an unflattering estimate of the appeal of our institutions to free minds. We can have intellectual individualism and the rich cultural diversities that we owe to exceptional minds only at the price of occasional eccentricity and abnormal attitudes. When they are so harmless to others or to the State as those we deal with here, the price is not too great. But freedom to differ is not limited to things that do not matter much. That would be a mere shadow of freedom. The test of its substance is the right to differ as to things that touch the heart of the existing order.

If there is any fixed star in our constitutional constellation, it is that no official, high or petty, can prescribe what shall be orthodox in politics, nationalism, religion, or other matters of opinion or force citizens to confess by word or act their faith therein. If there are any circumstances which permit an exception, they do not now occur to us.

We think the action of the local authorities in compelling the flag salute and pledge transcends constitutional limitations on their power and invades the sphere of intellect and spirit which it is the purpose of the First Amendment to our Constitution to reserve from all official control.

The decision of this Court in *Minersville School Dist.* v. *Gobitis* and the holdings of those few *per curiam* decisions which preceded and foreshadowed it are overruled, and the judgment enjoining enforcement of the West Virginia Regulation is affirmed.

Mr. Justice Frankfurter, dissenting:

One who belongs to the most vilified and persecuted minority in history is not likely to be insensible to the freedoms guaranteed by our Constitution. Were my purely personal attitude relevant I should wholeheartedly associate myself with the general libertarian views in the Court's opinion, representing as they do the thought and action of a lifetime. But as judges we are neither Jew or Gentile, neither Catholic nor agnostic. We owe equal attachment to the Constitution and are equally bound by our judicial obligations whether we derive our citizenship from the earliest or the latest immigrants to these shores. As a member of this Court I am not justified in writing my private notions of policy into the Constitution, no matter how deeply I may cherish them or how mischievous I may deem their disregard. The duty of a judge who must decide which of two claims before the Court shall prevail, that of a State to enact and enforce laws within its general competence or that of an individual to refuse obedience because of the demands of his conscience, is not that of the ordinary person. It can never be emphasized too much that one's own opinion about the wisdom or evil of a law should be excluded altogether when one is doing one's duty on the bench. The only opinion of our own even looking in that direction that is material is our opinion whether legislators could in reason have enacted such a law. In the light of all the circumstances, including the history of this question in this Court, it would require more daring than I possess to deny that reasonable legislators could have taken the action which is before us for review. Most unwillingly, therefore, I must differ from my brethren with regard to legislation like this. I cannot bring my mind to believe that the "liberty" secured by the Due Process Clause gives this Court authority to deny to the State of West Virginia the attainment of that which we all recognize as a legitimate legislative end, namely, the promotion of good citizenship, by employment of the means here chosen. . . .

The admonition that judicial self-restraint alone limits arbitrary exercise of our authority is relevant every time we are asked to nullify legislation. The Constitution does not give us greater veto power when dealing with one phase of "liberty" than with another, or when dealing with grade school regulations than with college regulations that offend conscience, as was the case in *Hamilton* v. *University of California*, 293 US 245. In neither situation is our function comparable to that of a legislature or are we free to act as though we were super-legislature. Judicial self-restraint is equally necessary whenever an exercise of political or legislative power is challenged. There is no warrant in the constitutional basis of this Court's authority for attributing different roles to it depending upon the nature of the challenge to the legislation. Our power does not vary according to the particular provision of the Bill of Rights which is invoked. The right not to have property taken without just compensation has, so far as the scope of judicial power is concerned, the same constitutional dignity as the right to be protected against unreasonable searches and seizures, and the latter has no less claim than freedom of the press or freedom of speech, or religious freedom. In no instance is this Court the primary protector of the particular liberty that is invoked. This Court has recognized what hardly could be denied, that all the provisions of the first ten Amendments are "specific" prohibitions, *United States* v. *Carolene Products Co.*, 304 US 144, 152, note 4. But each specific Amendment, insofar as embraced within the Fourteenth Amendment, must be equally respected, and the function of this Court does not differ in passing on the constitutionality of legislation challenged under different Amendments. . . .

The reason why from the beginning even the narrow judicial authority to nullify legislation has been viewed with a jealous eye is that it serves to prevent the full play of the democratic process. The fact that it may be an undemocratic aspect of our scheme of government does not call for its rejection or its disuse. But it is the best of reasons, as this Court has frequently recognized, for the greatest caution in its use. . . .

Under our constitutional system the legislature is charged solely with civil concerns of society. If the avowed or intrinsic legislative purpose is either to promote or to discourage some religious community or creed, it is clearly within the constitutional restrictions imposed on legislatures and cannot stand. But it by no means follows that legislative power is wanting whenever a general nondiscriminatory civil regulation in fact touches conscientious scruples or religious beliefs of an individual or a group. Regard for such scruples or beliefs undoubtedly presents one of the most reasonable claims for the exertion of legislative accommodation. It is, of course, beyond our power to rewrite the State's requirement, by providing exemptions for those who do not wish to participate in the flag salute or by making some other accommodations to meet their scruples. That wisdom might suggest the making of such accommodations and that school administration would not find it too difficult to make them and yet maintain the ceremony for those not refusing to conform, is outside our province to suggest. Tact, respect, and generosity toward variant views will always commend themselves to those charged with the duties of legislation so as to achieve a maximum of good will and to require a minimum of unwilling submission to a general law. But the real question is, who is to make such accommodations, the courts or the legislature? . . .

Conscientious scruples, all would admit, cannot stand against every legislative compulsion to do positive acts in conflict with such scruples. We have been told that such compulsions override religious scruples only as to major concerns of the state. But the determination of what is major and what is minor itself raises questions of policy. For the way in which men equally guided by reason appraise importance goes to the very heart of policy. Judges should be very diffident in setting their judgment against that of a state in determining what is and what is not a major concern, what means are appropriate to proper ends, and what is the total social cost in striking the balance of imponderables. . . .

The constitutional protection of religious freedom terminated disabilities, it did not create new privileges. It gave religious equality, not civil immunity. Its essence is freedom from conformity to religious dogma, not freedom from conformity to law because of religious dogma. Religious loyalties may be exercised without hindrance from the state, the state may not exercise that which except by leave of religious loyalties is within the domain of temporal power. Otherwise each individual could set up his own censor against obedience to laws conscientiously deemed for the public good by those whose business it is to make laws.

The prohibition against any religious establishment by the government placed denominations on an equal footing—it assured freedom from support by the government to any mode of worship and the freedom of individuals to support any mode of worship. Any person may therefore believe or disbelieve what he pleases. He may practice what he will in his own house of worship or publicly within the limits of public order. But the lawmaking authority is not circumscribed by the variety of religious beliefs, otherwise the constitutional guaranty would be not a protection of the free exercise of religion but a denial of the exercise of legislation.

The essence of the religious freedom guaranteed by our Constitution is therefore this: no religion shall either receive the state's support or incur its hostility. Religion is outside the sphere of political government. This does not mean that all matters on which religious organizations or beliefs may pronounce are outside the sphere of government. Were this so, instead of the separation of church and state, there would be the subordination of the state on any matter deemed within the sovereignty of the religious conscience. Much that is the concern of temporal authority affects the spiritual interests of men. But it is not enough to strike down a nondiscriminatory law that it may hurt or offend some dissident view. It would be too easy to cite numerous prohibitions and injunctions to which laws run counter if the variant interpretations of the Bible were made the tests of obedience to law. The validity of secular laws cannot be measured by their conformity to religious doctrines. It is only in a theocratic state that ecclesiastical doctrines measure legal right or wrong. . . .

When dealing with religious scruples we are dealing with an almost numberless variety of doctrines and beliefs entertained with equal sincerity by the particular groups for which they satisfy man's needs in his relation to the mysteries of the universe. There are in the United States more than 250 distinctive established religious denominations. In the state of Pennsylvania there are 120 of these, and in West Virginia as many as 65. But if religious scruples afford immunity from civic obedience to laws, they may be invoked by the religious beliefs of any individual even though he holds no membership in any sect or organized denomination. Certainly this Court cannot be called upon to determine what claims of conscience should be recognized and what should be rejected as satisfying the "religion" which the Constitution protects. That would indeed resurrect the very discriminatory treatment of religion which the Constitution sought forever to forbid.

Consider the controversial issue of compulsory Bible-reading in public schools. The educational policies of the states are in great conflict over this, and the state courts are divided in their decisions on the issue whether the requirement of Bible-reading offends constitutional provisions dealing with religious freedom. The requirement of Bible-reading has been justified by various state courts as an appropriate means of inculcating ethical precepts and familiarizing pupils with the most lasting expression of great English literature. Is this Court to overthrow such variant state educational policies by denying states the right to entertain such convictions in regard to their school systems, because of a belief that the King James version is in fact a sectarian text to which parents of the Catholic and Jewish faiths and of some Protestant persuasions may rightly object to having their children exposed? On the other hand the religious consciences of some parents may rebel at the absence of any Bible-reading in the schools. . . . Or is this

Court to enter the old controversy between science and religion by unduly defining the limits within which a state may experiment with its school curricula? The religious consciences of some parents may be offended by subjecting their children to the Biblical account of creation, while another state may offend parents by prohibiting a teaching of biology that contradicts such Biblical account. Compare *Scopes* v. *State,* 154 Tenn. 105. What of conscentious objections to what is devoutly felt by parents to be the poisoning of impressionable minds of children by chauvinistic teaching of history? This is very far from a fanciful suggestion, for in the belief of many thoughtful people nationalism is the seed-bed of war.

There are other issues in the offing which admonish us of the difficulties and complexities that confront states in the duty of administering their local school systems. All citizens are taxed for the support of public schools although this Court has denied the right of a state to compel all children to go to such schools and has recognized the right of parents to send children to privately maintained schools. Parents who are dissatisfied with the public schools thus carry a double educational burden. Children who go to public school enjoy in many states derivative advantages such as free textbooks, free lunch, and free transportation in going to and from school. What of the claims for equality of treatment of those parents who, because of religious scruples, cannot send their children to public schools? What of the claim that if the right to send children to privately maintained schools is partly an exercise of religious conviction, to render effective this right it should be accompanied by equality of treatment by the state in supplying free textbooks, free lunch, and free transportation to children who go to private schools? What of the claim that such grants are offensive to the cardinal constitutional doctrine of separation of church and state?

These questions assume increasing importance in view of the steady growth of parochial schools both in number and in population. I am not borrowing trouble by adumbrating these issues nor am I parading horrible examples of the consequences of today's decision. I am aware that we must decide the case before us and not some other case. But that does not mean that a case is dissociated from the past and unrelated to the future. We must decide this case with due regard for what went before and no less regard for what may come after. Is it really a fair construction of such a fundamental concept as the right freely to exercise one's religion that a state cannot choose to require all children who attend public school to make the same gesture of allegiance to the symbol of our national life because it may offend the conscience of some children, but that it may compel all children to attend public school to listen to the King James version although it may offend the consciences of their parents? And what of the larger issue of claiming immunity from obedience to a general civil regulation that has a reasonable relation to a public purpose within the general competence of the state? . . .

One's conception of the Constitution cannot be severed from one's conception of a judge's function in applying it. The Court has no reason for existence if it merely reflects the pressures of the day. Our system is built on the faith that men set apart for this special function, freed from the influences of immediacy and from the deflections of wordly ambition, will become able to take a view of longer range than the period of responsibility entrusted to Congress and legislatures. We are dealing with matters as to which legislators and voters have conflicting views. Are we as judges to impose our strong convictions on where wisdom lies? That which three years ago had seemed to five successive Courts to lie within permissible areas of legislation is now outlawed by the deciding shift of opinion of two Justices. What reason is there to believe that they or their successors may not have another view a few years hence? Is that which was deemed to be of so fundamental a nature as to be written into the Constitution to endure for all times to be the sport of shifting winds of doctrine? Of course, judicial opinions, even as to questions of constitutionality, are not immutable. As has been true in the past, the Court will from time to time reverse its position. But I believe that never before these Jehovah's Witnesses cases (except for minor deviations subsequently retraced) has this Court overruled decisions so as to restrict the powers of democratic government. Always heretofore, it has withdrawn narrow views of legislative authority so as to authorize what formerly it had denied.

In view of this history it must be plain that what thirteen Justices found to be within the constitutional authority of a state, legislators cannot be deemed unreasonable in enacting. Therefore, in denying to the states what heretofore has received such impressive judicial sanction, some other tests of unconstitutionality must surely be guiding the Court than the absence of a rational justification for the legislation. But I know of no other test which this Court is authorized to apply in nullifying legislation.

In the past this Court has from time to time set its views of policy against that embodied in legislation by finding laws in conflict with what was called the "spirit of the Constitution." Such undefined destructive power was not conferred on this Court by the Constitution. Before a duly enacted law can be judicially nullified, it must be forbidden by some explicit restriction upon political authority in the Constitution. Equally inadmissible is the claim to strike down legislation because to us as individuals it seems opposed to the "plan and purpose" of the Constitution. That is too tempting a basis for finding in one's personal views the purposes of the Founders.

The uncontrollable power wielded by this Court brings it very close to the most sensitive areas of public affairs. As appeal from legislation to adjudication becomes more frequent, and its consequences more far-reaching, judicial self-restraint becomes more and not less important, lest we unwarrantably enter social and political domains wholly outside our concern. I think I appreciate fully the objections to the law before us. But to deny that it presents a question upon which men might reasonably differ appears to me to be intolerance. And since men may so reasonably differ, I deem it beyond my constitutional power to assert my view of the wisdom of this law against the view of the State of West Virginia.

Jefferson's opposition to judicial review has not been accepted by history, but it still serves as an admonition against confusion between judicial and political functions. As a rule of judicial self-restraint, it is still valid as Lincoln's admonition. For those who pass laws not only are under duty to pass laws. They are also under duty to observe the Constitution. And even though legislation relates to civil liberties, our duty of deference to those who have the responsibility for making the laws is no less relevant or less exacting. And this is so especially when we consider the accidental contingencies by which one man may determine constitutionality and thereby confine the political power of the Congress of the United States and the legislatures of forty-eight states. The attitude of judicial humility which these considerations enjoin is not an abdication of the judicial function. It is a due observance of its limits. Moreover, it is to be borne in mind that in a question like this we are not passing on the proper distribution of political power as between the states and the central government. We are not discharging the basic function of this Court as the mediator of powers within the federal system. To strike down a law like this is to deny a power to all government. . . .

Of course patriotism cannot be enforced by the flag salute. But neither can the liberal spirit be enforced by judicial invalidation of illiberal legislation. Our constant preoccupation with the constitutionality of legislation rather than with its wisdom tends to preoccupation of the American mind with a false value. The tendency of focusing attention on constitutionality is to make constitutionality synonymous with wisdom, to regard a law as all right if it is constitutional. Such an attitude is a great enemy of liberalism. Particularly in legislation affecting freedom of thought and freedom of speech much which should offend a free-spirited society is constitutional. Reliance for the most precious interests of civilization, therefore, must be found outside of their vindication in courts of law. Only a persistent positive translation of the faith of a free society into the convictions and habits and actions of a community is the ultimate reliance against unabated temptations to fetter the human spirit.

2. *The Freedom* Not *to Listen*

PUBLIC UTILITIES COMMISSION *v.* POLLAK
343 US 451 (1952)

[In this "captive audience" case it appears that the Public Utilities Commission of the District of Columbia issued an order permitting the Capital Transit Company to broadcast on its buses and street cars radio programs consisting of 90 per cent music and 10 per cent announcements and commercial advertising.

[The Supreme Court held that these facts did not show a violation of any constitutional guaranty. Justice Black concurred, agreeing that the musical programs did not violate the First Amendment but making it clear that the broadcasting of news, speeches, commentators' views, or propaganda of any kind would, in his opinion, violate the Constitution. Justice Douglas dissented. He agreed with the views of Judge Edgerton of the United States Court of Appeals, who said that forcing a "captive audience" to listen is a violation of the "freedom of attention," which is destroyed by forced listening. "If Transit obliged its passengers to read what it liked," said Judge Edgerton, "or get off the car, invasion of their freedom would be obvious." Freedom of speech is guaranteed to every citizen so that he may reach the minds of willing, not coerced, listeners.

[Justice Frankfurter did not participate on the ground that, "as a victim of the practice," his feelings were "so strongly engaged" that he feared that his unconscious feelings may "operate in the ultimate judgment" or create the impression that they have so operated.]

Mr. Justice Burton delivered the opinion of the Court:

The principal question here is whether, in the District of Columbia, the Constitution of the United States precludes a street railway company from receiving and amplifying radio programs through loud speakers in its passenger vehicles under the circumstances of this case. The service and equipment of the company are subject to regulation by the Public Utilities Commission of the District of Columbia. The Commission, after an investigation and public hearings disclosing substantial grounds for doing so, has concluded that the radio service is not inconsistent with public convenience, comfort and safety and "tends to improve the conditions under which the public ride." The Commission, accordingly, has permitted the radio service to continue despite vigorous protests from some passengers that to do so violates their constitutional rights. For the reasons hereafter stated, we hold that neither the operation of the service nor the action of the Commission permitting its operation is precluded by the Constitution.

The Capital Transit Company, here called Capital Transit, is a privately owned public utility corporation, owning an extensive street railway and bus system which it operates in the District of Columbia under a franchise from Congress. Washington Transit Radio, Inc., here called Radio, also is a privately owned corporation doing business in the District of Columbia.

In March, 1948, Capital Transit experimented with "music as you ride" radio programs received and amplified through loudspeakers in a streetcar and in a bus. Those vehicles were operated on various lines at various hours. A poll of passengers who heard the programs showed that 92% favored their continuance. Experience in other cities was studied. Capital Transit granted Radio the exclusive right to install, maintain, repair and use radio reception equipment in Capital Transit's streetcars, buses, terminal facilities, waiting rooms and division headquarters. Radio, in return, agreed to contract with a broadcasting station for programs to be received during a minimum of eight hours every day, except Sundays. To that end Radio secured the services of Station WWDC-FM. Its programs were to meet the specifications stated in Capital Transit's contract. Radio agreed to pay Capital Transit, after a 90-day trial, $6 per month per radio installation, plus additional compensation dependent upon the station's receipts from sources such as commercial advertising on the programs. In February, 1949, when more than 20 installations had been made, the service went into regular operation. At the time of the Commission's hearings, October 27–November 1, 1949, there were 212. On that basis the minimum annual payment to Capital Transit came to $15,264. The potential minimum would be $108,000 based upon 1,500 installations. The contract covered five years, with an automatic five-year renewal in the absence of notice to the contrary from either party.

This proceeding began in July, 1949, when the Commission, on its own motion, ordered an investigation. . . .

The Commission concluded "that the installation and use of radios in streetcars and buses of the Capital Transit Company is not inconsistent with public convenience, comfort, and safety" and dismissed its investigation. . . .

In this proceeding the courts are expressly restricted to the facts found by the Commission, insofar as those findings do not appear to be unreasonable, arbitrary or capricious.

After reciting that it had given careful consideration to the testimony bearing on public convenience, comfort and safety, the Commission said that—

From the testimony of record, the conclusion is inescapable that radio reception in streetcars and buses is not an obstacle to safety of operation.

Further, it is evident that public comfort and convenience is not impaired and that, in fact, through the creation of better will among passengers, it tends to improve the conditions under which the public ride. . . .

In view of the findings and conclusions of the Commission, there can be little doubt that, apart from the constitutional questions here raised, there is no basis for setting aside the Commission's decision. It is within the statutory authority of the Commission to prohibit or to permit and regulate the receipt and amplification of radio programs under such conditions that the total utility service shall not be unsafe, uncomfortable or inconvenient. . . .

Applicability of the First and Fifth Amendments.—It was held by the court below that the action of Capital Transit in installing and operating the radio receivers, coupled with the action of the Public Utilities Commission in dismissing its own investigation of the practice, sufficiently involved the Federal Government in responsibility for the radio programs to make the First and Fifth Amendments to the Constitution of the United States applicable to this radio service. These Amendments concededly apply to and restrict only the Federal Government and not private persons. . . .

We find in the reasoning of the court below a sufficiently close relation between the Federal Government and the radio service to make it necessary for us to consider those Amendments. In finding this relation we do not rely on the mere fact that Capital Transit operates a public utility on the streets of the District of Columbia under authority of Congress. Nor do we rely upon the fact that, by reason of such federal authorization, Capital Transit now enjoys a substantial monopoly of street railway and bus transportation in the District of Columbia. We do, however, recognize that Capital Transit operates its service under the regulatory supervision of the Public Utilities Commission of the District of Columbia which is an agency authorized by Congress. We rely particularly upon the fact that that agency, pursuant to protests against the radio program, ordered an investigation of it and, after formal public hearings, ordered its investigation dismissed on the ground that the public safety, comfort and convenience were not impaired thereby. . . .

No violation of the First Amendment.—Pollak and Martin contend that the radio programs interfere with their freedom of conversation and that of other passengers by making it necessary for them to compete against the programs in order to be heard. The Commission, however, did not find, and the testimony does not compel a finding, that the programs interfered substantially with the conversation of passengers or with rights of communication constitutionally protected in public places. It is suggested also that the First Amendment guarantees a freedom to listen only to such points of view as the listener wishes to hear. There is no substantial claim that the programs have been used for objectionable propaganda. There is no issue of that kind before us. The inclusion in the program of a few announcements explanatory and commendatory of Capital Transit's own services does not sustain such an objection.

No violation of the Fifth Amendment.—The court below has emphasized the claim that the radio programs are an invasion of constitutional rights of privacy of the passengers. This claim is that no matter how much Capital Transit may wish to use radio in its vehicles as part of its service to its passengers and as a source of income, no matter how much the great majority of its passengers may desire radio in those vehicles, and however positively the Commission, on substantial evidence, may conclude that such use of radio does not interfere with the convenience, comfort and safety of the service but tends to improve it, yet if one passenger objects to the programs as an invasion of his constitutional right of privacy, the use of radio on the vehicles must be discontinued. This position wrongly assumes that the Fifth Amendment secures to each passenger on a public vehicle regulated by the Federal Government a right of privacy substantially equal to the privacy to which he is entitled in his own home. However complete his right of privacy may be at home, it is substantially limited by the rights of others when its possessor travels on a public thoroughfare or rides in a public conveyance. Streetcars and buses are subject to the immediate control of their owner and operator and, by virtue of their dedication to public service, they are for the common use of all of their passengers. The Federal Government in its regulation of them is not only entitled, but is required, to take into consideration the interests of all concerned.

In a public vehicle there are mutual limitations upon the conduct of everyone, including the vehicle owner. These conflicting demands limit policies on such matters as operating schedules and the location of car or bus stops, as well as policies relating to the desirability or nature of radio programs in the vehicles. Legislation prohibiting the making of artificially amplified raucous sounds in public places has been upheld. *Kovacs* v. *Cooper,* 336 US 77. . . . Conversely, where a regulatory body has jurisdiction, it will be sustained in its protection of activities in public places when those activities do not interfere with the general public convenience, comfort and safety. The supervision of such practices by a Public Utilities Commission in the manner prescribed in the District of Columbia meets the requirements both of substantive and procedural due process when it is not arbitrarily and capriciously exercised.

The contention of Pollak and Martin would permit an objector, with a status no different from that of other passengers, to override not only the preference of the majority of the passengers but also the considered judgment of the federally authorized Public Utilities Commission, after notice, investigation and public hearings, and upon a record reasonably justifying its conclusion that the policy of the owner and operator did not interfere with public convenience, comfort and safety but tended, in general, to improve the utility service.

We do not agree with that contention. The protection afforded to the liberty of the individual by the Fifth Amendment against the action of the Federal Government does not go that far. The liberty of each individual in a public vehicle or public place is subject to reasonable limitations in relation to the rights of others.

This Court expresses no opinion as to the desirability of radio programs in public vehicles. In this case that is a matter for decision between Capital Transit, the public and the Public Utilities Commission. The situation is not unlike that which arises when a utility makes a change in its running schedules or in the locations of its stops in the interest of the majority of the passengers but against the vigorous protests of the few who are inconvenienced by the change.

While the court below expressly refrained from stating its view of the constitutionality of the receipt and amplification in public vehicles of musical programs containing no commercial advertising and other announcements, it is clear that if programs containing commercial advertising and other announcements are permissible, then programs limited to the type of music here contracted for would not be less so. . . . . .

Reversed.

Separate opinion of Mr. Justice Black:

I concur in the Court's holding that this record shows no violation of the Due Process Clause of the Fifth Amendment. I also agree that Capital Transit's musical programs have not violated the First Amendment. I am of the opinion, however, that subjecting Capital Transit's passengers to the broadcasting of news, public speeches, views, or propaganda of any kind and by any means would violate the First Amendment. To the extent, if any, that the Court holds the contrary, I dissent.

3. Fighting Words

GOODING *v.* WILSON
405 US 518 (1972)

[In *Chaplinsky* v. *New Hampshire,* 315 US 568 (1942), the Supreme Court upheld as constitutional under the First Amendment a state statute which was interpreted by the highest state court as calling for punishment the utterance of "fighting words": words used face-to-face that are derisive and annoying and that plainly tend to excite the person addressed to a breach of the peace. Since *Chaplinsky,* the Court has recognized the constitutional power of a state to punish the utterance of "fighting words" under carefully-drawn statutes that were not broader than the confines imposed on the statute in *Chaplinsky.* In the instant case, by 5–2 vote, the Court held that the Georgia statute was unconstitutional for vagueness and overbreadth in that it was not limited to "fighting words" "which by their very utterance . . . tend to incite immediate breach of the peace." The Court's opinion was by Justice Brennan. Justice Blackmun wrote a dissenting opinion, in which Chief Justice Burger joined; the latter also wrote a separate dissenting opinion. Justices Powell and Rehnquist did not participate in the case.]

Mr. Justice Brennan delivered the opinion of the Court:

Appellee was convicted in Superior Court, Fulton County, Georgia, on two counts of using opprobrious words and abusive language in violation of Georgia Code § 26–6303, which provides: "Any person who shall, without provocation, use to or of another, and in his presence . . . opprobrious words or abusive language, tending to cause a breach of the peace . . . shall be guilty of a misdemeanor." Appellee appealed the conviction to the Supreme Court of Georgia on the ground, among others, that the statute violated the First and Fourteenth Amendments because vague and overbroad. The Georgia Supreme Court rejected that contention and sustained the conviction. . . . Appellee then sought federal habeas corpus relief in the District Court for the Northern District of Georgia. The District Court found that, because appellee had failed to exhaust his available state remedies as to the other grounds he relied upon in attacking his conviction, only the contention that § 26–6303 was facially unconstitutional was ripe for decision.* On the merits

---

* "Count 3 of the indictment alleged that the accused 'did without provocation use to and of M. G. Redding and in his presence, the following abusive language and opprobrious words, tending to cause a breach of the peace: "White son of a bitch, I'll kill you." "You son of a bitch, I'll choke you to death." ' Count 4 alleged that the defendant 'did without provocation

of that question, the District Court, in disagreement with the Georgia Supreme Court, held that § 26–6303, on its face, was unconstitutionally vague and broad and set aside appellee's conviction. The Court of Appeals for the Fifth Circuit affirmed. We noted probable jurisdiction of the State's appeal. We affirm.

Section 26–6303 punishes only spoken words. It can therefore withstand appellee's attack upon its facial constitutionality only if, as authoritatively construed by the Georgia courts, it is not susceptible of application to speech, although vulgar or offensive, that is protected by the First and Fourteenth Amendments, *Cohen* v. *California,* 403 US 15 (1971); *Terminiello* v. *Chicago,* 337 US 1 (1949). Only the Georgia courts can supply the requisite construction, since of course "we lack jurisdiction authoritatively to construe state legislation." . . . It matters not that the words appellee used might have been constitutionally prohibited under a narrowly and precisely drawn statute. At least when statutes regulate or proscribe speech and when "no readily apparent construction suggests itself as a vehicle for rehabilitating the statutes in a single prosecution," . . . the transcendent value to all society of constitutionally protected expression is deemed to justify allowing "attacks on overly broad statutes with no requirement that the person making the attack demonstrate that his own conduct could not be regulated by a statute drawn with the requisite narrow specificity." . . . This is deemed necessary because persons whose expression is constitutionally protected may well refrain from exercising their rights for fear of criminal sanctions provided by a statute susceptible of application to protected expression.

Although a statute may be neither vague, overbroad, nor otherwise invalid as applied to the conduct charged against a particular defendant, he is permitted to raise its vagueness or unconstitutional overbreadth as applied to others. And if the law is found deficient in one of these respects, it may not be applied to him either, until and unless a satisfactory limiting construction is placed on the statute. The statute, in effect, is stricken down on its face. This result is deemed justified since the otherwise continued existence of the statute in unnarrowed form would tend to suppress constitutionally protected rights.

The constitutional guarantees of freedom of speech forbid the States from punishing the use of words or language not within "narrowly limited classes of speech." . . . Even as to such a class, however, because "the line between speech unconditionally guaranteed and speech which may legitimately be regulated, suppressed, or punished is finely drawn," . . . "[i]n every case the power to regulate must be so exercised as not, in attaining a permissible end, unduly to infringe the protected freedom." . . . In other words, the statute must be carefully drawn or be authoritatively construed to punish only unprotected speech and not be susceptible of application to protected expression. "Because First Amendment freedoms need breathing space to survive, government may regulate in the area only with narrow specificity." . . .

Appellant does not challenge these principles but contends that the Georgia

---

use to and of T. L. Raborn, and in his presence, the following abusive language and opprobrious words, tending to cause a breach of the peace: "You son of a bitch, if you ever put your hands on me again, I'll cut you all to pieces." ' "

statute is narrowly drawn to apply only to a constitutionally unprotected class of words—"fighting" words—"those which by their very utterance inflict injury or tend to incite an immediate breach of the peace." *Chaplinsky* v. *New Hampshire,* 315 US 572. In *Chaplinsky,* we sustained a conviction under Chapter 378, § 2, of the Public Laws of New Hampshire, which provided: "No person shall address any offensive, derisive or annoying word to any other person who is lawfully in any street or other public place, nor call him by any offensive or derisive name. . . ." Chaplinsky was convicted for addressing to another on a public sidewalk the words, "You are a God damned racketeer," and "a damned Fascist and the whole government of Rochester are Fascists or agents of Fascists." Chaplinsky challenged the constitutionality of the statute as inhibiting freedom of expression because it was vague and indefinite. The Supreme Court of New Hampshire, however, "long before the words for which Chaplinsky was convicted," sharply limited the statutory language "offensive, derisive or annoying word" to "fighting" words:

no words were forbidden except such as have a direct tendency to cause acts of violence by the person to whom, individually, the remark is addressed. . . . The test is what men of common intelligence would understand would be words likely to cause an average addressee to fight. . . . Derisive and annoying words can be taken as coming within the purview of the statute . . . only when they have this characteristic of plainly tending to excite the addressee to a breach of the peace. . . . The statute, as construed, does no more than prohibit the face-to-face words plainly likely to cause a breach of the peace by the addressee. . . .

In view of that authoritative construction, this Court held: "We are unable to say that the limited scope of the statute as thus construed contravenes the constitutional right of free expression. It is a statute narrowly drawn and limited to define and punish specific conduct lying within the domain of state power, the use in a public place of words likely to cause a breach of the peace." Our decisions since *Chaplinsky* have continued to recognize state power constitutionally to punish "fighting" words under carefully drawn statutes not also susceptible of application to protected expression. . . .

Appellant argues that the Georgia appellate courts have by construction limited the proscription of § 26–6303 to "fighting" words, as the New Hampshire Supreme Court limited the New Hampshire statute. "A consideration of the [Georgia] cases construing the elements of the offense makes it clear that the opprobrious words and abusive language which are thereby prohibited are those which as a matter of common knowledge and under ordinary circumstances will, when used to or of another person, and in his presence, naturally tend to provoke violent resentment. The statute under attack simply states in statutory language what this Court has previously denominated 'fighting words.' " Brief for Appellant, p. 6. Neither the District Court nor the Court of Appeals so read the Georgia decisions. On the contrary, the District Court expressly stated, "Thus, in the decisions brought to this Court's attention, no meaningful attempt has been made to limit or properly define these terms." The District Judge and one member of the unanimous Court of Appeals panel were Georgia practitioners before they ascended the bench. Their views of Georgia law necessarily are persuasive with us. . . . We have, however, made our own examination of the Georgia cases, both those cited and others discovered in research. That examination brings us to the conclusion, in agreement with the courts below, that the Georgia appellate decisions have not construed § 26–6303 to be limited in application, as in *Chaplinsky,* to words that "have a direct tendency to cause acts of violence by the person to whom, individually, the remark is addressed."

The dictionary definitions of "opprobrious" and "abusive" give them greater reach than "fighting" words. Webster's Third New International Dictionary (1961) defined "opprobrious" as "conveying or intended to convey disgrace," and "abusive" as including "harsh insulting language." Georgia appellate decisions have construed § 26–6303 to apply to utterances that, although within these definitions, are not "fighting" words as *Chaplinsky* defines them. In *Lyons* v. *State,* 94 Ga.App. 570 (1956), a conviction under the statute was sustained for awakening 10 women scout leaders on a camp-out by shouting, "Boys, this is where we are going to spend the night." "Get the G—— d—— bed rolls out . . . let's see how close we can come to the G—— d—— tents." Again, in *Fish* v. *State,* 124 Ga. 416 (1905), the Georgia Supreme Court held that a jury question was presented by the remark, "You swore a lie." Again, *Jackson* v. *State,* 14 Ga.App. 19 (1913), held that a jury question was presented by the words addressed to another, "God damn you, why don't you get out of the road?" Plainly, although "conveying . . . disgrace" or "harsh insulting language," these were not words "which by their very utterance . . . tend to incite an immediate breach of the peace." . . .

Georgia appellate decisions construing the reach of "tendency to cause a breach of the peace" underscore that § 26–6303 is not limited, as appellant argues, to words that "naturally tend to provoke violent resentment." . . . Indeed, the Georgia Court of Appeals in *Elmore* v. *State,* 15 Ga.App. 461 (1914), construed "tending to cause a breach of the peace" as mere

words of description, indicating the kind of character of opprobrious words or abusive language that is penalized, and the use of words or language of this character is a violation of the statute, even though addressed to one who, on account of circumstances or by virtue of the obligations of office, cannot actually then and there resent the same by a breach of the peace. . . . Suppose that one at a safe distance and out of hearing of any other than the person to whom he spoke, addressed such language to one locked in a prison cell or on the opposite bank of an impassable torrent, and hence without power to respond immediately to such verbal insults by physical retaliation, could it be reasonably contended that, because no breach of the peace could then follow, the statute would not be violated? . . . [T]hough, on account of circumstances or obligations imposed by office, one may not be able at the time to assault and beat another on account of opprobrious words or abusive language, the words or language might still tend to cause a breach of the peace at some future time, when the person to whom they were addressed might be no longer hampered by physical inability, present conditions, or official position. . . .

Accordingly we agree with the District Court that our decisions . . . compel the conclusion that § 26–6303, as construed, does not define the standard of responsibility with requisite narrow specificity. . . .

We conclude that "[t]he separation of legitimate from illegitimate speech calls for more sensitive tools than [Georgia] has supplied." . . . The most recent decision of the Georgia Supreme Court, . . . in rejecting appellee's attack on the constitutionality of § 26–6303, stated that the statute "conveys a definite meaning as to the conduct forbidden, measured by common understanding and practice." Because earlier appellate decisions applied § 26–6303 to utterances where there was no likelihood that the person addressed would make an immediate violent response, it is clear that the standard allowing juries to determine guilt "measured by common understanding and practice" does not limit the application of § 26–6303 to "fighting" words defined by *Chaplinsky*. Rather, that broad standard effectively "licenses the jury to create its own standard in each case." . . . Accordingly, we agree with the conclusion of the District Court, "[t]he fault of the statute is that it leaves wide open the standard of responsibility, so that it is easily susceptible to improper application." . . .

Mr. Justice Blackmun, with whom the Chief Justice joins, dissenting:

It seems strange indeed that in this day a man may say to a police officer, who is attempting to restore access to a public building, "White son of a bitch, I'll kill you," and "You son of a bitch, I'll choke you to death," and say to an accompanying officer, "You son of a bitch, if you ever put your hands on me again, I'll cut you all to pieces," and yet constitutionally cannot be prosecuted and convicted under a state statute which makes it a misdemeanor to "use to or of another, and in his presence, opprobrious words or abusive language, tending to cause a breach of the peace. . . ." This, however, is precisely what the Court pronounces as the law today.

The Supreme Court of Georgia, when the conviction was appealed, unanimously held the other way. . . . Surely any adult who can read—and I do not exclude this appellee-defendant from that category—should reasonably expect no other conclusion. The words of Georgia Code § 26–6303 are clear. They are also concise. They are not, in my view, overbroad or incapable of being understood. Except perhaps for the "big" word "opprobrious—and no point is made of its bigness—any Georgia schoolboy would expect that this defendant's fighting and provocative words to the officers were covered by § 26–6303. Common sense permits no other conclusion. This is demonstrated by the fact that the appellee, and this Court, attacks the statute not as it applies to the appellee, but as it conceivably might apply to others who might utter other words.

The Court reaches its result by saying that the Georgia statute has been interpreted by the State's courts so as to be applicable in practice to otherwise constitutionally protected speech. It follows, says the Court, that the statute is overbroad and therefore is facially unconstitutional and to be struck down in its entirety. Thus Georgia apparently is to be left with no valid statute on its books to meet Wilson's bullying tactic. This result, achieved by what is indeed a very strict construction, will be totally incomprehensible to the State of Georgia, to its courts, and to its citizens. . . .

For me, *Chaplinsky* v. *New Hampshire,* was good law when it was decided and deserves to remain as good law now. A unanimous Court, including among its members Chief Justice Stone and Justices Black, Reed, Douglas, and Murphy, obviously thought it was good law. But I feel that by decisions such as this one and, indeed, *Cohen* v. *California* 403 US 15 (1971), the Court, despite its protestations to the contrary, is merely paying lip service to *Chaplinsky*. As the appellee states in a footnote to his brief, p. 14, "Although there is no doubt that the state can punish 'fighting words' this appears to be about all that is left of the decision in *Chaplinsky*." If this is what the overbreadth doctrine means, and if this is what it produces, it urgently needs re-examination. The Court has painted itself into a corner from which it, and the States, can extricate themselves only with difficulty.

4. Offensive Words

COHEN v. CALIFORNIA
403 US 15 (1971)

[California punished a person for wearing a jacket bearing an offensive word with respect to the military draft. The arrest was made in a courthouse corridor. The Supreme Court held that the state could not, under the First and Fourteenth Amendments, make the display of the four-letter word a criminal offense. Justice Harlan wrote the opinion for the Court. Justice Blackmun wrote a dissenting opinion in which he was joined by Chief Justice Burger and Justice Black, and in part by Justice White.]

Mr. Justice Harlan delivered the opinion of the Court:

This case may seem at first blush too inconsequential to find its way into our books, but the issue it presents is of no small constitutional significance.

Appellant Paul Robert Cohen was convicted in the Los Angeles Municipal Court of violating that part of California Penal Code § 415 which prohibits "maliciously and willfully disturb[ing] the peace or quiet of any neighborhood or person, . . . by . . . offensive conduct. . . . "* He was given 30 days' imprisonment. The facts upon which his conviction rests are detailed in the opinion of the Court of Appeal of California, Second Appellate District, as follows:

On April 26, 1968, the defendant was observed in the Los Angeles County Courthouse in the corridor outside of Division 20 of the Municipal Court wearing a jacket bearing the words "Fuck the Draft" which were plainly visible. There were women and children present in the corridor. The defendant was arrested. The defendant testified that he wore the jacket as a means of informing the public of the depth of his feelings against the Vietnam War and the draft.

The defendant did not engage in, nor threaten to engage in, nor did anyone as the result of his conduct in fact commit or threaten to commit any act of violence. The defendant did not make any loud or unusual noise, nor was there any evidence that he uttered any sound prior to his arrest.

In affirming the conviction the Court of Appeal held that "offensive conduct"

* The statute provides in full: "Every person who maliciously and willfully disturbs the peace or quiet of any neighborhood or person, by loud or unusual noise, or by tumultuous or offensive conduct, or threatening, traducing, quarreling, challenging to fight, or fighting, or who, on the public streets of any unincorporated town, or upon the public highways in such unincorporated town, run any horse-race, either for a wager or for amusement, or fire any gun or pistol in such unincorporated town, or use any vulgar, profane, or indecent language within the presence or hearing of women or children, in a loud and boisterous manner, is guilty of a misdemeanor, and upon conviction by any court of competent jurisdiction shall be punished by fine not exceeding two hundred dollars, or by imprisonment in the county jail for not more than ninety days, or by both fine and imprisonment, or either, at the discretion of the court."

means "behavior which has a tendency to provoke *others* to acts of violence or to in turn disturb the peace," and that the State had proved this element because, on the facts of this case, "[i]t was certainly reasonably foreseeable that such conduct might cause others to rise up to commit a violent act against the person of the defendant or attempt to forcibly remove his jacket." The California Supreme Court declined review by a divided vote. . . .

I

In order to lay hands on the precise issue which this case involves, it is useful first to canvass various matters which this record does *not* present.

The conviction quite clearly rests upon the asserted offensiveness of the *words* Cohen used to convey his message to the public. The only "conduct" which the State sought to punish is the fact of communication. Thus, we deal here with a conviction resting solely upon "speech," cf. *Stromberg* v. *California,* 283 US 359 (1931), not upon any separately identifiable conduct which allegedly was intended by Cohen to be perceived by others as expressive of particular views but which, on its face, does not necessarily convey any message and hence arguably could be regulated without effectively repressing Cohen's ability to express himself. Cf. *United States* v. *O'Brien,* 391 US 367 (1968). Further, the State certainly lacks power to punish Cohen for the underlying content of the message the inscription conveyed. At least so long as there is no showing of an intent to incite disobedience to or disruption of the draft, Cohen could not, consistently with the First and Four-teenth Amendments, be punished for asserting the evident position on the inutility or immorality of the draft his jacket reflected. *Yates* v. *United States,* 354 US 298 (1957).

Appellant's conviction, then, rests squarely upon his exercise of the "freedom of speech" protected from arbitrary governmental interference by the Constitution and can be justified, if at all, only as a valid regulation of the manner in which he exercised that freedom, not as a permissible prohibition on the substantive message it conveys. This does not end the inquiry, of course, for the First and Fourteenth Amendments have never been thought to give absolute protection to every individ-ual to speak whenever or wherever he pleases, or to use any form of address in any circumstances that he chooses. In this vein, too, however, we think it important to note that several issues typically associated with such problems are not presented here.

In the first place, Cohen was tried under a statute applicable throughout the en-tire State. Any attempt to support this conviction on the ground that the statute seeks to preserve an appropriately decorous atmosphere in the courthouse where Cohen was arrested must fail in the absence of any language in the statute that would have put appellant on notice that certain kinds of otherwise permissible speech or conduct would nevertheless, under California law, not be tolerated in certain places. See *Edwards* v. *South Carolina,* 372 US 229, 236–237, and n. 11 (1963). Cf. *Adderly* v. *Florida,* 385 US 39 (1966). No fair reading of the phrase "offensive conduct" can be said sufficiently to inform the ordinary person that dis-tinctions between certain locations are thereby created.*

---

* It is illuminating to note what transpired when Cohen entered a courtroom in the building.

In the second place, as it comes to us, this case cannot be said to fall within those relatively few categories of instances where prior decisions have established the power of government to deal more comprehensively with certain forms of individual expression simply upon a showing that such a form was employed. This is not, for example, an obscenity case. Whatever else may be necessary to give rise to the States' broader power to prohibit obscene expression, such expression must be, in some significant way, erotic. *Roth* v. *United States,* 354 US 476 (1957). It cannot plausibly be maintained that this vulgar allusion to the Selective Service System would conjure up such psychic stimulation in anyone likely to be confronted with Cohen's crudely defaced jacket.

This Court has also held that the States are free to ban the simple use, without a demonstration of additional justifying circumstances, of so-called "fighting words," those personally abusive epithets which, when addressed to the ordinary citizen, are, as a matter of common knowledge, inherently likely to provoke violent reaction. *Chaplinsky* v. *New Hampshire,* 315 US 568 (1942). While the four-letter word displayed by Cohen in relation to the draft is not uncommonly employed in a personally provocative fashion, in this instance it was clearly not "directed to the person of the hearer." *Cantwell* v. *Connecticut,* 310 US 296, 309 (1940). No individual actually or likely to be present could reasonably have regarded the words on appellant's jacket as a direct personal insult. Nor do we have here an instance of the exercise of the State's police power to prevent a speaker from intentionally provoking a given group to hostile reaction. Cf. *Feiner* v. *New York,* 340 US 315 (1951); *Terminiello* v. *Chicago,* 337 US 1 (1949). There is, as noted above, no showing that anyone who saw Cohen was in fact violently aroused or that appellant intended such a result.

Finally, in arguments before this Court much has been made of the claim that Cohen's distasteful mode of expression was thrust upon unwilling or unsuspecting viewers, and that the State might therefore legitimately act as it did in order to protect the sensitive from otherwise unavoidable exposure to appellant's crude form of protest. Of course, the mere presumed presence of unwitting listeners or viewers does not serve automatically to justify curtailing all speech capable of giving offense. . . . While this Court has recognized that government may properly act in many situations to prohibit intrusion into the privacy of the home of unwelcome views and ideas which cannot be totally banned from the public dialogue, . . . we have at the same time consistently stressed that "we are often 'captives' outside the sanctuary of the home and subject to objectionable speech." The ability of government, consonant with the Constitution, to shut off discourse solely to protect others from hearing it is, in other words, dependent upon a showing that substantial privacy interests are being invaded in an essentially intolerable manner. Any broader view of this authority would effectively empower a majority to silence dissidents simply as a matter of personal predilections.

In this regard, persons confronted with Cohen's jacket were in a quite different

---

He removed his jacket and stood with it folded over his arm. Meanwhile, a policeman sent the presiding judge a note suggesting that Cohen be held in contempt of court. The judge declined to do so and Cohen was arrested by the officer only after he emerged from the courtroom.

posture than, say, those subjected to the raucous emissions of sound trucks blaring outside their residences. Those in the Los Angeles courthouse could effectively avoid further bombardment of their sensibilities simply by averting their eyes. And, while it may be that one has a more substantial claim to a recognizable privacy interest when walking through a courthouse corridor than, for example, strolling through Central Park, surely it is nothing like the interest in being free from unwanted expression in the confines of one's own home. . . . Given the subtlety and complexity of the factors involved, if Cohen's "speech" was otherwise entitled to constitutional protection, we do not think the fact that some unwilling "listeners" in a public building may have been briefly exposed to it can serve to justify this breach of the peace conviction where, as here, there was no evidence that persons powerless to avoid appellant's conduct did in fact object to it, and where that portion of the statute upon which Cohen's conviction rests evinces no concern, either on its face or as construed by the California courts, with the special plight of the captive auditor, but, instead, indiscriminately sweeps within its prohibitions all "offensive conduct" that disturbs "any neighborhood or person." . . .*

II

Against this background, the issue flushed by this case stands out in bold relief. It is whether California can excise, as "offensive conduct," one particular scurrilous epithet from the public discourse, either upon the theory of the court below that its use is inherently likely to cause violent reaction or upon a more general assertion that the States, acting as guardians of public morality, may properly remove this offensive word from the public vocabulary.

The rationale of the California court is plainly untenable. At most it reflects an "undifferentiated fear or apprehension of disturbance [which] is not enough to overcome the right to freedom of expression." . . . We have been shown no evidence that substantial numbers of citizens are standing ready to strike out physically at whoever may assault their sensibilities with execrations like that uttered by Cohen. There may be some persons about with such lawless and violent proclivities, but that is an insufficient base upon which to erect, consistently with constitutional values, a governmental power to force persons who wish to ventilate their dissident views into avoiding particular forms of expression. The argument amounts to little more than the self-defeating proposition that to avoid physical censorship of one who has not sought to provoke such a response by a hypothetical coterie of the violent and lawless, the States may more appropriately effectuate that censorship themselves. . . .

Admittedly, it is not so obvious that the First and Fourteenth Amendments must be taken to disable the States from punishing public utterance of this unseemly

---

* In fact, other portions of the same statute do make some such distinctions. For example, the statute also prohibits disturbing "the peace or quiet . . . by loud or unusual noise" and using "vulgar, profane or indecent language within the presence or hearing of women or children, in a loud and boisterous manner." See n. *supra*. This second quoted provision in particular serves to put the actor on much fairer notice as to what is prohibited. It also buttresses our view that the "offensive conduct" portion, as construed and applied in this case, cannot legitimately be justified in this Court as designed or intended to make fine distinctions between differently situated recipients.

expletive in order to maintain what they regard as a suitable level of discourse within the body politic. We think, however, that examination and reflection will reveal the shortcomings of a contrary viewpoint.

At the outset, we cannot overemphasize that, in our judgment, most situations where the State has a justifiable interest in regulating speech will fall within one or more of the various established exceptions, discussed above but not applicable here, to the usual rule that governmental bodies may not prescribe the form or content of individual expression. Equally important to our conclusion is the constitutional backdrop against which our decision must be made. The constitutional right of free expression is powerful medicine in a society as diverse and populous as ours. It is designed and intended to remove governmental restraints from the arena of public discussion, putting the decision as to what views shall be voiced largely into the hands of each of us, in the hope that use of such freedom will ultimately produce a more capable citizenry and more perfect polity and in the belief that no other approach would comport with the premise of individual dignity and choice upon which our political system rests. . . .

To many, the immediate consequence of this freedom may often appear to be only verbal tumult, discord, and even offensive utterance. These are, however, within established limits, in truth necessary side effects of the broader enduring values which the process of open debate permits us to achieve. That the air may at times seem filled with verbal cacaphony is, in this sense not a sign of weakness but of strength. We cannot lose sight of the fact that, in what otherwise might seem a trifling and annoying instance of individual distasteful abuse of a privilege, these fundamental societal values are truly implicated. That is why "[w]holly neutral futilities . . . come under the protection of free speech as fully as do Keats' poems or Donne's sermons," . . . and why "so long as the means are peaceful, the communication need not meet standards of acceptability.". . .

Against this perception of the constitutional policies involved, we discern certain more particularized considerations that peculiarly call for reversal of this conviction. First, the principle contended for by the State seems inherently boundless. How is one to distinguish this from any other offensive word? Surely the State has no right to cleanse public debate to the point where it is grammatically palatable to the most squeamish among us. Yet no readily ascertainable general principle exists for stopping short of that result were we to affirm the judgment below. For, while the particular four-letter word being litigated here is perhaps more distasteful than most others of its genre, it is nevertheless often true that one man's vulgarity is another's lyric. Indeed, we think it is largely because governmental officials cannot make principled distinctions in this area that the Constitution leaves matters of taste and style so largely to the individual.

Additionally, we cannot overlook the fact, because it is well illustrated by the episode involved here, that much linguistic expression serves a dual communicative function: it conveys not only ideas capable of relatively precise, detached explication, but otherwise inexpressible emotions as well. In fact, words are often chosen as much for their emotive as their cognitive force. We cannot sanction the view that the Constitution, while solicitous of the cognitive content of individual speech, has little or no regard for that emotive function which, practically speaking, may often be the more important element of the overall message sought to be communicated. Indeed, as Mr. Justice Frankfurter has said, "[o]ne of the prerogatives of American citizenship is the right to criticize public men and measures—and that means not only informed and responsible criticism but the freedom to speak foolishly and without moderation." *Baumgartner* v. *United States,* 322 US 665, 675 (1944).

Finally, and in the same vein, we cannot indulge the facile assumption that one can forbid particular words without also running a substantial risk of suppressing ideas in the process. Indeed, governments might soon seize upon the censorship of particular words as a convenient guise for banning the expression of unpopular views. We have been able, as noted above, to discern little social benefit that might result from running the risk of opening the door to such grave results.

It is, in sum, our judgment that, absent a more particularized and compelling reason for its actions, the State may not, consistently with the First and Fourteenth Amendments, make the simple public display here involved of this single four-letter expletive a criminal offense. Because that is the only arguably sustainable rationale for the conviction here at issue, the judgment below must be reversed.

Mr. Justice Blackmun, with whom the Chief Justice and Mr. Justice Black join:

I dissent, and I do so for two reasons:

1. Cohen's absurd and immature antic, in my view, was mainly conduct and little speech. See *Street* v. *New York,* 394 US 576 (1969); *Cox* v. *Louisiana,* 379 US 536, 555 (1963); *Giboney* v. *Empire Storage Co.,* 336 US 490, 502 (1949). The California Court of Appeal appears so to have described it, and I cannot characterize it otherwise. Further, the case appears to me to be well within the sphere of *Chaplinsky* v. *New Hampshire,* where Mr. Justice Murphy, a known champion of First Amendment freedoms, wrote for a unanimous bench. As a consequence, this Court's agonizing over First Amendment values seems misplaced and unnecessary.

2. I am not at all certain that the California Court of Appeal's construction of § 415 is now the authoritative California construction. The Court of Appeal filed its opinion on October 22, 1969. The Supreme Court of California declined review by a four-to-three vote on December 17. A month later, on January 27, 1970, the State Supreme Court in another case construed § 415, evidently for the first time. *In re Bushman,* 1 Cal. 3d 767, 463 P. 2d 727. Chief Justice Traynor, who was among the dissenters to his court's refusal to take Cohen's case, wrote the majority opinion. He held that § 415 "is not unconstitutionally vague and overbroad" and further said:

> [T]hat part of Penal Code section 415 in question here makes punishable only wilful and malicious conduct that is violent and endangers public safety and order or that creates a clear and present danger that others will engage in violence of that nature. . . . [It] does not make criminal any nonviolent act unless the act incites or threatens to incite others to violence. . . .

Cohen was cited in *Bushman,* but I am not convinced that its description there and *Cohen* itself are completely consistent with the "clear and present danger" standard enunciated in *Bushman.* Inasmuch as this Court does not dismiss this case, it ought to be remanded to the California Court of Appeal for reconsideration in the light of the subsequently rendered decision by the State's highest tribunal in *Bushman.*

Mr. Justice White concurs in Paragraph 2 of Mr. Justice Blackmun's dissenting opinion.

5. Speech That May Be a Violation of Public Peace

FEINER *v.* NEW YORK
340 US 315 (1951)

[A university student, using a loud-speaker, addressed a crowd, which included some Negroes, from a box on the sidewalk in Syracuse, New York. He called then-President Truman "a bum" and said that Negroes "should rise up in arms and fight for their rights." Policemen asked him to stop speaking; since he ignored their requests, they arrested him. He was convicted for disorderly conduct. By a 6-to-3 decision the Supreme Court upheld the conviction on the ground that the speaker had created a clear danger of disorder on the public streets of the City. The dissenting Justices (Black, Douglas, and Minton) maintained that the speaker was punished for his unpopular views, expressed to an unsympathetic audience; that he was arrested before there was a present danger of a riot; that the police, rather than throwing their weight against him, should have protected him in the exercise of his constitutional rights against anyone in the crowd who may have threatened him with violence. The majority, however, were impressed with the fact that the state trial and appeals courts found that the speaker had created danger to public order.

[Justice Frankfurter's concurring opinion appears as part of another case decided the same day, *Niemotko* v. *Maryland,* 340 US 268.]

Mr. Chief Justice Vinson delivered the opinion of the Court:

Petitioner was convicted of the offense of disorderly conduct, a misdemeanor under the New York penal laws, in the Court of Special Sessions of the City of Syracuse and was sentenced to thirty days in the county penitentiary. . . .

On the evening of March 8, 1949, petitioner Irving Feiner was addressing an open-air meeting at the corner of South McBride and Harrison Streets in the City of Syracuse. At approximately 6:30 P.M., the police received a telephone complaint concerning the meeting, and two officers were detailed to investigate. One of these officers went to the scene immediately, the other arriving some twelve minutes later. They found a crowd of about seventy-five or eighty people, both Negro and white, filling the sidewalk and spreading out into the street. Petitioner, standing on a large wooden box on the sidewalk, was addressing the crowd through a loud-speaker system attached to an automobile. Although the purpose of his speech was to urge his listeners to attend a meeting to be held that night in the Syracuse Hotel, in its course he was making derogatory remarks concerning President Truman, the American Legion, the Mayor of Syracuse, and other local political officials.

The police officers made no effort to interfere with petitioner's speech, but were first concerned with the effect of the crowd on both pedestrian and vehicular traffic. They observed the situation from the opposite side of the street, noting that some pedestrians were forced to walk in the street to avoid the crowd. Since traffic was passing at the time, the officers attempted to get the people listening to petitioner back on the sidewalk. The crowd was restless and there was some pushing, shoving and milling around. One of the officers telephoned the police station from a nearby store, and then both policemen crossed the street and mingled with the crowd without any intention of arresting the speaker.

At this time, petitioner was speaking in a "loud, high-pitched voice." He gave the impression that he was endeavoring to arouse the Negro people against the whites, urging that they rise up in arms and fight for equal rights. The statements before such a mixed audience "stirred up a little excitement." Some of the onlookers made remarks to the police about their inability to handle the crowd and at least one threatened violence if the police did not act. There were others who appeared to be favoring petitioner's arguments. Because of the feeling that existed in the crowd both for and against the speaker, the officers finally "stepped in to prevent it from resulting in a fight." One of the officers approached the petitioner, not for the purpose of arresting him, but to get him to break up the crowd. He asked petitioner to get down off the box, but the latter refused to accede to his request and continued talking. The officer waited for a minute and then demanded that he cease talking. Although the officer had thus twice requested petitioner to stop over the course of several minutes, petitioner not only ignored him but continued talking. During all this time, the crowd was pressing closer around petitioner and the officer. Finally, the officer told petitioner he was under arrest and ordered him to get down from the box, reaching up to grab him. Petitioner stepped down, announcing over the microphone that "the law has arrived, and I suppose they will take over now." In all, the officer had asked petitioner to get down off the box three times over a space of four or five minutes. Petitioner had been speaking for over a half hour.

On these facts, petitioner was specifically charged with violation . . . of the Penal Law of New York. . . .

We are not faced here with blind condonation by a state court of arbitrary police action. Petitioner was accorded a full, fair trial. The trial judge heard testimony supporting and contradicting the judgment of the police officers that a clear danger of disorder was threatened. After weighing this contradictory evidence, the trial judge reached the conclusion that the police officers were justified in taking action to prevent a breach of the peace. The exercise of the police officers' proper discretionary power to prevent a breach of the peace was thus approved by the trial court and later by two courts on review. The courts below recognized petitioner's right to hold a street meeting at this locality, to make use of loud-speaking equipment in giving his speech, and to make derogatory remarks concerning public officials and the American Legion. They found that the officers in making the arrest were motivated solely by a proper concern for the preservation of order and protection of the general welfare, and that there was no evidence which could lend color to a claim that the acts of the police were a cover for suppression of petitioner's views and opinions. Petitioner was thus neither arrested nor convicted for the making or the content of his speech. Rather, it was the reaction which it actually engendered.

. . . The findings of the New York courts as to the condition of the crowd and the refusal of petitioner to obey the police requests, supported as they are by the record of this case, are persuasive that the conviction of petitioner for violation of public peace, order and authority does not exceed the bounds of proper state police action. This Court respects, as it must, the interest of the community in maintaining peace and order on its streets. . . . We cannot say that the preservation of that interest here encroaches on the constitutional rights of this petitioner.

We are well aware that the ordinary murmurings and objections of a hostile audience cannot be allowed to silence a speaker, and are also mindful of the possible danger of giving overzealous police officials complete discretion to break up otherwise lawful public meetings. "A State may not unduly suppress free communication of views, religious or other, under the guise of conserving desirable conditions." *Cantwell* v. *Connecticut.* . . . But we are not faced here with such a situation. It is one thing to say that the police cannot be used as an instrument for the suppression of unpopular views, and another to say that, when as here the speaker passes the bounds of argument or persuasion and undertakes incitement to riot, they are powerless to prevent a breach of the peace. Nor in this case can we condemn the considered judgment of three New York courts approving the means which the police, faced with a crisis, used in the exercise of their power and duty to preserve peace and order. The findings of the state courts as to the existing situation and the imminence of greater disorder coupled with petitioner's deliberate defiance of the police officers convince us that we should not reverse this conviction in the name of free speech.

Affirmed. . . .

Mr. Justice Black, dissenting:

The record before us convinces me that petitioner, a young college student, has been sentenced to the penitentiary for the unpopular views he expressed on matters of public interest while lawfully making a street-corner speech in Syracuse, New York. Today's decision, however, indicates that we must blind ourselves to this fact because the trial judge fully accepted the testimony of the prosecution witnesses on all important points. Many times in the past this Court has said that despite findings below, we will examine the evidence for ourselves to ascertain whether federally protected rights have been denied; otherwise review here would fail of its purpose in safeguarding constitutional guarantees. Even a partial abandonment of this rule marks a dark day for civil liberties in our Nation.

But still more has been lost today. Even accepting every "finding of fact" below, I think this conviction makes a mockery of the free speech guarantees of the First and Fourteenth Amendments. The end result of the affirmance here is to approve a simple and readily available technique by which cities and states can with impunity subject all speeches, political or otherwise, on streets or elsewhere, to the supervision and censorship of the local police. I will have no part or parcel in this holding which I view as a long step toward totalitarian authority.

Considering only the evidence which the state courts appear to have accepted, the pertinent "facts" are: Syracuse city authorities granted a permit for O. John Rogge, a former assistant attorney general, to speak in a public school building on March 8, 1948, on the subject of racial discrimination and civil liberties. On March 8th, however, the authorities canceled the permit. The Young Progressives under whose auspices the meeting was scheduled then arranged for Mr. Rogge to speak at the Hotel Syracuse. The gathering on the street where petitioner spoke was held to protest the cancellation and to publicize the meeting at the hotel. In this connection, petitioner used derogatory but not profane language with reference to the city authorities, President Truman and the American Legion. After hearing some of these remarks, a policeman, who had been sent to the meeting by his superiors, reported to Police Headquarters by telephone. To whom he reported or what was said does not appear in the record, but after returning from the call, he and another policeman started through the crowd toward petitioner. Both officers swore they did not intend to make an arrest when they started, and the trial court accepted their statements. They also said, and the court believed, that they heard and saw "angry mutterings, "pushing," "shoving and milling around" and "rest-lessness." Petitioner spoke in a "loud, high pitched voice." He said that "colored people don't have equal rights and they should rise up in arms and fight for them." One man who heard this told the officers that if they did not take that "S . . . O . . . B . . ." off the box, he would. The officers then approached petitioner for the first time. One of them first "asked" petitioner to get off the box, but petitioner continued urging his audience to attend Rogge's speech. The officer next "told" petitioner to get down, but he did not. The officer finally "demanded" that petitioner get down, telling him he was under arrest. Petitioner then told the crowd that "the law had arrived and would take over" and asked why he was arrested. The officer first replied that the charge was "un-lawful assembly" but later changed the ground to "disorderly conduct."

The Court's opinion apparently rests on this reasoning: The policeman, under the circumstances detailed, could reasonably conclude that serious fighting or even riot was imminent; therefore he could stop petitioner's speech to prevent a breach of peace; accordingly, it was "disorderly conduct" for petitioner to continue speaking in disobedi-ence of the officer's request. As to the existence of a dangerous situation on the street corner, it seems far-fetched to suggest that the "facts" show any imminent threat of riot or uncontrollable disorder. It is neither unusual nor unexpected that some people at public street meetings mutter, mill about, push, shove, or disagree, even violently, with the speaker. Indeed, it is rare where controversial topics are discussed that an outdoor crowd does not do some or all of these things. Nor does one isolated threat to assault the speaker forebode disorder. Especially should the danger be discounted where, as here, the person threatening was a man whose wife and two small children accompanied him and who, so far as the record shows, was never close enough to petitioner to carry out the threat.

Moreover, assuming that the "facts" did indicate a critical situation, I reject the implication of the Court's opinion that the police had no obligation to protect petitioner's constitutional right to talk. The police of course have power to prevent breaches of the peace. But if, in the name of preserving order, they ever can interfere with a lawful public speaker, they first must make all reasonable efforts to protect him. Here the policeman did not even pretend to try to protect petitioner. According to the officers' testimony, the crowd was restless but there is no showing of any attempt to quiet it; pedestrians were forced to walk into the street, but there was no effort to clear a path on the sidewalk; one person threatened to assault petitioner but the officers did nothing to discourage this when even a word might have sufficed. Their duty was to protect petitioner's right to talk, even to the extent of arresting the man who threatened to interfere. Instead, they shirked that duty and acted only to suppress the right to speak.

Finally, I cannot agree with the Court's statement that petitioner's disregard of the policeman's unexplained request amounted to such "deliberate defiance" as would justify an arrest or conviction for disorderly conduct. On the contrary, I think that the police-man's action was a "deliberate defiance" of ordinary official duty as well as of the constitutional right of free speech. For at least where time allows, courtesy and explana-tion of commands are basic elements of good official conduct in a democratic society.

Here petitioner was "asked" then "told" then "commanded" to stop speaking, but a man making a lawful address is certainly not required to be silent merely because an officer directs it. Petitioner was entitled to know why he should cease doing a lawful act. Not once was he told. I understand that people in authoritarian countries must obey arbitrary orders. I had hoped that there was no such duty in the United States.

In my judgment, today's holding means that as a practical matter, minority speakers can be silenced in any city. Hereafter, despite the First and Fourteenth Amendments, the policeman's club can take heavy toll of a current administration's public critics. Criticism of public officials will be too dangerous for all but the most courageous. . . .

In this case I would reverse the conviction, thereby adhering to the great principles of the First and Fourteenth Amendments as announced for this Court in 1940 by Mr. Justice Roberts:

> In the realm of religious faith and in that of political belief, sharp differences arise. In both fields, the tenets of one man may seem the rankest error to his neighbor. To persuade others to his own point of view, the pleader, as we know, at times resorts to exaggeration, to vilification of men who have been, or are, prominent in church or state, and even to false statement. But the people of this nation have ordained in the light of history, that, in spite of the probability of excesses and abuses, these liberties are, in the long view, essential to enlightened opinion and right conduct on the part of the citizens of a democracy. *Cantwell* v. *Connecticut,* 310 US 296. . . .

Mr. Justice Douglas, with whom Mr. Justice Minton concurs, dissenting:

Feiner, a university student, made a speech on a street corner in Syracuse, New York, on March 8, 1949. The purpose of the speech was to publicize a meeting of the Young Progressives of America to be held that evening. A permit authorizing the meeting to be held in a public school auditorium had been revoked and the meeting shifted to a local hotel.

Feiner delivered his speech in a small shopping area in a predominantly colored residential section of Syracuse. He stood on a large box and spoke over loudspeakers mounted on a car. His audience was composed of about 75 people, colored and white. A few minutes after he started two police officers arrived.

The speech was mainly devoted to publicizing the evening's meeting and protesting the revocation of the permit. It also touched on various public issues. The following are the only excerpts revealed by the record:

> Mayor Costello [of Syracuse] is a champagne-sipping bum; he does not speak for the Negro people.
> The 15th Ward is run by corrupt politicians, and there are horse rooms operating there.
> President Truman is a bum.
> Mayor O'Dwyer is a bum.
> The American Legion is a Nazi Gestapo.
> The Negroes don't have equal rights; they should rise up in arms and fight for their rights.

There was some pushing and shoving in the crowd and some angry muttering. That is the testimony of the police. But there were no fights and no "disorder" even by the standards of the police. There was not even any heckling of the speaker.

But after Feiner had been speaking about 20 minutes a man said to the police officers,

"If you don't get that son of a bitch off, I will go over and get him off there myself." It was then that the police ordered Feiner to stop speaking; when he refused, they arrested him.

Public assemblies and public speech occupy an important role in American life. One high function of the police is to protect these lawful gatherings so that the speakers may exercise their constitutional rights. When unpopular causes are sponsored from the public platform there will commonly be mutterings and unrest and heckling from the crowd. When a speaker mounts a platform it is not unusual to find him resorting to exaggeration, to vilification of ideas and men, to the making of false charges. But those extravagances . . . do not justify penalizing the speaker by depriving him of the platform or by punishing him for his conduct.

A speaker may not, of course, incite a riot any more than he may incite a breach of the peace by the use of "fighting words." . . . But this record shows no such extremes. It shows an unsympathetic audience and the threat of one man to haul the speaker from the stage. It is against that kind of threat that speakers need police protection. If they do not receive it and instead the police throw their weight on the side of those who would break up the meetings, the police become the new censors of speech. Police censorship has all the vices of the censorship from city halls which we have repeatedly struck down. . . .

TERMINIELLO v. CHICAGO
337 US 1 (1949)

[In the *Feiner Case,* it will be recalled, the Court found that the speaker had created a clear danger of public disorder; in the face of such danger, he should not have persisted in continuing his outdoor speech. In the *Terminiello Case* the speech was delivered in a hall hired for the occasion. This, it seems, is an important difference; for people who hear parts of a speech through an amplifying device as they walk on the street are members of a "captive audience," while people who attend a speech in a hall do so voluntarily. Another important difference is that Terminiello was convicted, not for creating a clear danger of public disorder, but for causing a breach of peace by delivering a speech which "stirs the public to anger, invites dispute, [or] brings about a condition of unrest." Terminiello, said the Court, could not, under these circumstances, be punished: "A function of free speech . . . is to invite dispute," induce a condition of unrest, create "dissatisfaction with conditions as they are," or even stir people to anger.

[The decision was 5 to 4, with Chief Justice Vinson and Justices Frankfurter, Jackson, and Burton dissenting. Three of these Justices dissented on what amounts to a procedural point, while Jackson dissented on this ground and also because he read the facts as showing that Terminiello had in fact incited the friendly audience in the hall and had provoked the hostile mob outside the hall, and that violence between the two crowds was threatened.]

Mr. Justice Douglas delivered the opinion of the Court:

Petitioner after jury trial was found guilty of disorderly conduct in violation of a city ordinance of Chicago and fined. The case grew out of an address he delivered in an auditorium in Chicago under the auspices of the Christian Veterans of America. The meeting commanded considerable public attention. The auditorium was filled to capacity with over eight hundred persons present. Others were turned away. Outside of the auditorium a crowd of about one thousand persons gathered to protest against the meeting. A cordon of policemen was assigned to the meeting to maintain order; but they were not able to prevent several disturbances. The crowd outside was angry and turbulent.

Petitioner in his speech condemned the conduct of the crowd outside and vigorously, if not viciously, criticized various political and racial groups whose activities he denounced as inimical to the nation's welfare.

The trial court charged that "breach of the peace" consists of any "misbehavior which violates the public peace and decorum"; and that the "misbehavior may constitute a breach of the peace if it stirs the public to anger, invites dispute, brings about a condition of unrest, or creates a disturbance, or if it molests the inhabitants in the enjoyment of peace and quiet by arousing alarm." Petitioner did not take exception to that instruction. But he maintained at all times that the ordinance as applied to his conduct violated his right of free speech under the Federal Constitution. . . .

The argument here has been focused on the issue of whether the content of petitioner's speech was composed of derisive, fighting words, which carried it outside the scope of the constitutional guarantees. See *Chaplinsky* v. *New Hampshire,* 315 US 568. . . . We do not reach that question, for there is a preliminary question that is dispositive of the case.

As we have noted, the statutory words "breach of the peace" were defined in instructions to the jury to include speech which "stirs the public to anger, invites dispute, brings about a condition of unrest, or creates a disturbance. . . ." That construction of the ordinance is a ruling on a question of state law that is as binding on us as though the precise words had been written into the ordinance. . . .

The vitality of civil and political institutions in our society depends on free discussion. As Chief Justice Hughes wrote in *De Jonge* v. *Oregon,* 299 US 353, . . . it is only through free debate and free exchange of ideas that government remains responsive to the will of the people and peaceful change is effected. The right to speak freely and to promote diversity of ideas and programs is therefore one of the chief distinctions that sets us apart from totalitarian regimes.

Accordingly a function of free speech under our system of government is to invite dispute. It may indeed best serve its high purpose when it induces a condition of unrest, creates dissatisfaction with conditions as they are, or even stirs people to anger. Speech is often provocative and challenging. It may strike at prejudices and preconceptions and have profound unsettling effects as it presses for acceptance of an idea. That is why freedom of speech, though not absolute, . . . is nevertheless protected against censorship or punishment, unless shown likely to produce a clear and present danger of a serious substantive evil that arises far above public inconvenience, annoyance, or unrest. . . . There is no room under our Constitution for a more restrictive view. For the alternative would lead to standardization of ideas either by legislatures, courts, or dominant political or community groups.

The ordinance as construed by the trial court seriously invaded this province. It permitted conviction of petitioner if his speech stirred people to anger, invited public dispute, or brought about a condition of unrest. A conviction resting on any of those grounds may not stand. . . .

But it is said that throughout the appellate proceedings the Illinois courts assumed that the only conduct punishable and punished under the ordinance was conduct constituting "fighting words." . . . Petitioner was not convicted under a statute so narrowly construed. For all anyone knows he was convicted under the parts of the ordinance (as construed) which, for example, make it an offense merely to invite dispute or to bring about a condition of unrest. We cannot avoid that issue by saying that all Illinois did was to measure petitioner's conduct, not the ordinance, against the Constitution. Petitioner raised both points—that his speech was protected by the Constitution; that the inclusion of his speech within the ordinance was a violation of the Constitution. . . .

Reversed.

Mr. Justice Jackson, dissenting:

The Court reverses this conviction by reiterating generalized approbations of freedom of speech with which, in the abstract, no one will disagree. Doubts as to their applicability are lulled by avoidance of more than passing reference to the circumstances of Terminiello's speech and judging it as if he had spoken to persons as dispassionate as empty benches, or like a modern Demosthenes practicing his Philippics on a lonely seashore.

But the local court that tried Terminiello was not indulging in theory. It was dealing with a riot and with a speech that provoked a hostile mob and incited a friendly one, and threatened violence between the two. When the trial judge instructed the jury that it might find Terminiello guilty of inducing a breach of the peace if his behavior stirred the public to anger, invited dispute, brought about unrest, created a disturbance or molested peace and quiet by arousing alarm, he was not speaking of these as harmless or abstract conditions. He was addressing his words to the concrete behavior and specific consequences disclosed by the evidence. He was saying to the jury, in effect, that if this particular speech added fuel to the situation already so inflamed as to threaten to get beyond police control, it could be punished as inducing a breach of peace. When the light of the evidence not recited by the Court is thrown upon the Court's opinion, it discloses that underneath a little issue of Terminiello and his hundred-dollar fine lurk some of the most far-reaching constitutional questions that can confront a people who value both liberty and order. This Court seems to regard these as enemies of each other and to be of the view that we must forego order to achieve liberty. So it fixes its eyes on a conception of freedom of speech so rigid as to tolerate no concession to society's need for public order.

An old proverb warns us to take heed lest we "walk into a well from looking at the stars." To show why I think the Court is in some danger of doing just that, I must bring these deliberations down to earth by a long recital of facts.

Terminiello, advertised as a Catholic Priest, but revealed at the trial to be under suspension by his Bishop, was brought to Chicago from Birmingham, Alabama, to address a gathering that assembled in response to a call signed by Gerald L. K. Smith, which, among other things, said:

> . . . The same people who hate Father Coughlin hate Father Terminiello. They have persecuted him, hounded him, threatened him, but he has remained unaffected

by their anti-Christian campaign against him. You will hear all sorts of reports concerning Father Terminiello. But remember that he is a Priest in good standing and a fearless lover of Christ and America.

The jury may have considered that this call attempted to capitalize the hatreds this man had stirred and foreshadowed, if it did not intend to invite the kind of demonstration that followed.

Terminiello's own testimony shows the conditions under which he spoke. So far as material it follows:

. . . We got there [the meeting place] approximately fifteen or twenty minutes past eight. The car stopped at the front entrance. There was a crowd of three or four hundred congregated there shouting and cursing and picketing. . . .

When we got there the pickets were not marching; they were body to body and covered the sidewalk completely, some on the steps so that we had to form a flying wedge to get through. Police escorted us to the building, and I noticed four or five others there.

They called us "God damned Fascists, Nazis, ought to hang the so and sos." When I entered the building I heard the howls of the people outside. . . . There were four or five plain clothes officers standing at the entrance to the stage and three or four at the entrance to the back door.

The officers threatened that if they broke the door again they would arrest them and every time they opened the door a little to look out something was thrown at the officers, including ice-picks and rocks.

A number of times the door was broken, was partly broken through. There were doors open this way and they partly opened and the officers looked out two or three times and each time ice-picks, stones and bottles were thrown at the police at the door. I took my place on the stage, before this I was about ten or fifteen minutes in the body of the hall.

I saw a number of windows broken by stones or missiles. I saw the back door being forced open, pushed open.

The front door was broken partly open after the doors were closed. There were about seven people seated on the stage. Smith opened the meeting with prayer, the Pledge of Allegiance to the Flag and singing of America. There were other speakers who spoke before me and before I spoke I heard things happening in the hall and coming from the outside.

I saw rocks being thrown through windows and that continued throughout at least the first half of the meeting, probably longer, and again attempts were made to force the front door, rather the front door was forced partly. The howling continued on the outside, cursing could be heard audibly in the hall at times. Police were rushing in and out of the front door protecting the front door, and there was a general commotion, all kinds of noises and violence—all from the outside.

Between the time the first speaker spoke and I spoke, stones and bricks were thrown in all the time. I started to speak about 35 or 40 minutes after the meeting started, a little later than nine o'clock. . . .

The Court below, in addition to this recital, heard other evidence, that the crowd reached an estimated number of 1,500. Picket lines obstructed and interfered with access to the building. The crowd constituted "a surging, howling mob hurling epithets at those who would enter and tried to tear their clothes off." One young woman's coat was torn off and she had to be assisted into the meeting by policemen. Those inside the hall could hear the loud noises and hear those on the outside yell, "Fascists, Hitlers!" and curse words like "damn Fascists." Bricks were thrown through the windowpanes before and during the speaking. About 28 windows were broken. The street was black with people on both sides for at least a block either way; bottles, stink bombs and brickbats were thrown. Police were unable to control the mob, which kept breaking the windows at the meeting hall, drowning out the speaker's voice at times and breaking in through the back door of the auditorium. About 17 of the group outside were arrested by the police.

Knowing of this environment, Terminiello made a long speech, from the stenographic record of which I omit relatively innocuous passages and add emphasis to what seems especially provocative:

Father Terminiello: Now, I am going to whisper my greetings to you, Fellow Christians. I will interpret it. I said, "Fellow *Christians,*" and I suppose there are *some of the scum got in by mistake,* so I want to tell a story about *the scum:*

. . . And nothing I could say tonight could begin to express the contempt I have for the *slimy scum* that got in by mistake.

. . . The subject I want to talk to you tonight about is the attempt *that is going on right outside this hall tonight,* the attempt that is going on to *destroy America by revolution.* . . .

I know I was told one time that my winter quarters were ready for me in Siberia. I was told that. Now, I am talking about the fifty-seven varieties that we have in America and we have fifty-seven varieties of pinks and reds and pastel shades in this country; and all of it can be traced back to the twelve years we spent under the New Deal, because that was the build-up for what is going on in the world today. . . .

Now, we are going to get the threats of the people of Argentine, the people of Spain. We have now declared, according to our officials, to have declared Franco to have taken the place of Hitler. *Franco was the savior of what was left of Europe.*

Now, let me say, I am going to talk about—I almost said, about the Jews. Of course, I would not want to say that. However, I am going to talk about some Jews, I hope that—I am a Christian minister. We must take a Christian attitude. I don't want you to go from this hall with hatred in your heart for any person, for no person. . . .

Now, this danger which we face—let us call them Zionist Jews if you will, let's call them atheistic, communistic Jewish or Zionist Jews, then let us not fear to condemn them. You remember the Apostles when they went into the upper room after the death of the Master, they went in there, after locking the doors; they closed the windows. (At this time there was a very loud noise as if something was being thrown into the building.)

Don't be disturbed. That happened by the way, while Mr. Gerald Smith was saying "Our Father who art in heaven" (just then a rock went through the window). *Do you wonder they were persecuted in other countries in the world?* . . .

That is why I say to you, men, don't you do it. Walk out of here dignified. The police will protect you. Put the women on the inside, where there will be no hurt to them. Just walk; don't stop and argue. . . . They want to picket our meetings. They don't want us to picket their meetings. It is the same kind of tolerance, if we said there was a bedbug in bed, "We don't care for you," or if we looked under the bed and found a snake and said, "I am going to be tolerant and leave the snake there." We will not be tolerant of that mob out there. We are not going to be tolerant any longer.

We are strong enough. We are not going to be tolerant of their smears any longer. We are going to *stand up and dare them to smear us.*

So, my friends, since we spent much time tonight trying to quiet the howling mob, I am going to bring my thoughts to a conclusion, and the conclusion is this. We must all be like the Apostles before the coming of the Holy Ghost. We must not lock ourselves in an upper room for fear of the Jews. I speak of the Communistic Zionistic Jew, and those are not American Jews. We don't want them here; we want them to go back where they came from. . . .

Such was the speech. Evidence showed that it stirred the audience not only to cheer and applaud but to expressions of immediate anger, unrest and alarm. One called the speaker a "God damned liar" and was taken out by the police. Another said that "Jews, niggers and Catholics would have to be gotten rid of." One response was, "Yes, the Jews are all killers, murderers. If we don't kill them first, they will kill us." The anti-Jewish stories elicited exclamations of "Oh!" and "Isn't that terrible!" and shouts of "Yes, send the Jews back to Russia," "Kill the Jews," "Dirty kikes," and much more of ugly tenor. This is the specific and concrete kind of anger, unrest and alarm, coupled with that of the mob outside, that the trial court charged the jury might find to be a breach of peace induced by Terminiello. It is difficult to believe that this Court is speaking of the same occasion, but it is the only one involved in this litigation.

Terminiello, of course, disclaims being a fascist. Doubtless many of the indoor audience were not consciously such. His speech, however, followed, with fidelity that is more than coincidental, the pattern of European fascist leaders.

The street mob, on the other hand, included some who deny being communists, but Terminiello testified and offered to prove that the demonstration was communist-organized and communist-led. He offered literature of left-wing organizations calling members to meet and "mobilize" for instruction as pickets and exhorting followers: "All out to fight Fascist Smith."

As this case declares a nation-wide rule that disables local and state authorities from punishing conduct which produces conflicts of this kind, it is unrealistic not to take account of the nature, methods and objectives of the forces involved. This was not an isolated, spontaneous and unintended collision of political, racial or ideological adversaries. It was a local manifestation of a world-wide and standing conflict between two organized groups of revolutionary fanatics, each of which has imported to this country the strong-arm technique developed in the struggle by which their kind has devastated Europe. Increasingly, American cities have to cope with it. One faction organizes a mass meeting, the other organizes pickets to harass it; each organizes squads to counteract the other's pickets; parade is met with counter-parade. Each of these mass demonstrations has the potentiality, and more than a few the purpose, of disorder and violence. This technique appeals not to reason but to fears and mob spirit; each is a show of force designed to bully adversaries and to overawe the indifferent. We need not resort to speculation as to the purposes for which these tactics are calculated nor as to their consequences. Recent European history demonstrates both.

Hitler summed up the strategy of the mass demonstration as used by both fascism and communism: "We should not work in secret conventicles but in mighty mass demonstrations, and it is not by dagger and poison or pistol that the road can be cleared for the movement but *by the conquest of the streets.* We must teach the Marxists that the future *master of the streets* is National Socialism, just as it will some day be the master of the state." . . .

The present obstacle to mastery of the streets by either radical or reactionary mob movements is not the opposing minority. It is the authority of local governments which represent the free choice of democratic and law-abiding elements, of all shades of opinion but who, whatever their differences, submit them to free elections which register the results of their free discussion. The fascist and communist groups, on the contrary, resort to these terror tactics to confuse, bully and discredit those freely chosen governments. Violent and noisy shows of strength discourage participation of moderates in discussions so fraught with violence and real discussion dries up and disappears. And people lose faith in the democratic process when they see public authority flouted and impotent and begin to think the time has come when they must choose sides in a false and terrible dilemma such as was posed as being at hand by the call for the Terminiello meeting: "Christian Nationalism or World Communism—Which?"

This drive by totalitarian groups to undermine the prestige and effectiveness of local democratic governments is advanced whenever either of them can win from this Court a ruling which paralyzes the power of these officials. This is such a case. The group of which Terminiello is a part claims that his behavior, because it involved a speech, is above the reach of local authorities. If the mild action those authorities have taken is forbidden, it is plain that hereafter there is nothing effective left that they can do. If they can do nothing as to him, they are equally powerless as to rival totalitarian groups. Terminiello's victory today certainly fulfills the most extravagant hopes of both right and left totalitarian groups, who want nothing so much as to paralyze and discredit the only democratic authority that can curb them in their battle for the streets.

I am unable to see that the local authorities have transgressed the Federal Constitution. Illinois imposed no prior censorship or suppression upon Terminiello. On the contrary, its sufferance and protection was all that enabled him to speak. It does not appear that the motive in punishing him is to silence the ideology he expressed as offensive to the State's policy or as untrue, or has any purpose of controlling his thought or its peaceful communication to others. There is no claim that the proceedings against Terminiello are designed to discriminate against him or the faction he represents or the ideas that he bespeaks. There is no indication that the charge against him is a mere pretext to give the semblance of legality to a covert effort to silence him or to prevent his followers or the public from hearing any truth that is in him.

A trial court and jury has found only that in the context of violence and disorder in which it was made, this speech was a provocation to immediate breach of the peace and therefore cannot claim constitutional immunity from punishment. Under the Constitution as it has been understood and applied, at least until most recently, the State was within its powers in taking this action.

Rioting is a substantive evil, which I take it no one will deny that the State and the City have the right and the duty to prevent and punish. Where an offense is induced by speech, the Court has laid down and often reiterated a test of the power of the authorities to deal with the speaking as also an offense. "The question in every case is whether the words *used are used in such circumstances* and are of *such a nature* as to create a *clear and present danger* that they will bring about the substantive evils that Congress [or the State or City] has a right to prevent." (Emphasis supplied.) Mr. Justice Holmes in *Schenck* v. *United States,* 249 US 47. No one ventures to contend that the State on the basis of this test, for whatever it may be worth, was not justified in punishing Terminiello. In this case the evidence proves beyond dispute that danger of rioting and violence in response to the speech was clear, present and immediate. If this Court has not silently abandoned this long standing test and substituted for the purposes of this case an unexpressed but more stringent test, the action of the State would have to be sustained.

Only recently this Court held that a state could punish as a breach of the peace use of epithets such as "damned racketeer" and "damned fascists," addressed to only one person, an official, because likely to provoke the average person to retaliation. But these are mild in comparison to the epithets "slimy scum," "snakes," "bedbugs," and the like, which Terminiello hurled at an already inflamed mob of his adversaries. Mr. Justice Murphy, writing for a unanimous Court in *Chaplinsky* v. *New Hampshire,* 315 US 568, said:

> There are certain well-defined and narrowly limited classes of speech, the prevention and punishment of which have never been thought to raise any Constitutional problem. These include the lewd and obscene, the profane, the libelous and the insulting or "fighting" words—those which by their very utterance inflict injury or tend to incite an immediate breach of the peace. It has been well observed that such utterances are no essential part of any exposition of ideas, and are of such slight social value as a step to truth that any benefit that may be derived from them is clearly outweighed by the social interest in order and morality. "Resort to epithets or personal abuse is not in any proper sense communication of information or opinion safeguarded by the Constitution, and its punishment as a criminal act would raise no question under that instrument." *Cantwell* v. *Connecticut,* 310 US 296.

. . . How this present decision, denying state power to punish civilly one who precipitated a public riot involving hundreds of fanatic fighters in a most violent melee, can be squared with those unanimous statements of law, is incomprehensible to me. . . .

However, these wholesome principles are abandoned today and in their place is substituted a dogma of absolute freedom for irresponsible and provocative utterance which almost completely sterilizes the power of local authorities to keep the peace as against this kind of tactics. . . .

This case demonstrates also that this Court's service to free speech is essentially negative and can consist only of reviewing actions by local magistrates. But if free speech is to be a practical reality, affirmative and immediate protection is required; and it can come only from nonjudicial sources. It depends on local police, maintained by law-abiding taxpayers, and who, regardless of their own feelings, risk themselves to maintain supremacy of law. Terminiello's theoretical right to speak free from interference would have no reality if Chicago should withdraw its officers to some other section of the city, or if the men assigned to the task should look the other way when the crowd threatens Terminiello. Can society be expected to keep these men at Terminiello's service if it has nothing to say of his behavior which may force them into dangerous action?

No one will disagree that the fundamental, permanent and overriding policy of police and courts should be to permit and encourage utmost freedom of utterance. It is the legal right of any American citizen to advocate peaceful adoption of fascism or communism, socialism or capitalism. He may go far in expressing sentiments whether pro-semitic or anti-semitic, pro-Negro or anti-Negro, pro-Catholic or anti-Catholic. He is legally free to argue for some anti-American system of government to supersede by constitutional methods the one we have. It is our philosophy that the course of government should be controlled by a consensus of the governed. This process of reaching intelligent popular decisions requires free discussion. Hence we should tolerate no law or custom of censorship or suppression.

But we must bear in mind also that no serious outbreak of mob violence, race rioting, lynching or public disorder is likely to get going without help of some speech-making to some mass of people. A street may be filled with men and women and the crowd still not be a mob. Unity of purpose, passion and hatred, which merges the many minds of a crowd into the mindlessness of a mob, almost invariably is supplied by speeches. It is naive, or worse, to teach that oratory with this object or effect is a service to liberty. No mob has ever protected any liberty, even its own, but if not put down it always winds up in an orgy of lawlessness which respects no liberties.

In considering abuse of freedom by provocative utterances it is necessary to observe that the law is more tolerant of discussion than are most individuals or communities. Law is so indifferent to subjects of talk that I think of none that is should close to discussion. Religious, social and political topics that in other times or countries have not been open to lawful debate may be freely discussed here.

Because a subject is legally arguable, however, does not mean that public sentiment will be patient of its advocacy at all times and in all manners. So it happens that, while peaceful advocacy of communism or fascism is tolerated by the law, both of these doctrines arouse passionate reactions. A great number of people do not agree that introduction to America of communism or fascism is even debatable. Hence many speeches, such as that of Terminiello, may be legally permissible but may nevertheless in some surroundings, be a menace to peace and order. When conditions show the speaker that this is the case, as it did here, there certainly comes a point beyond which he cannot indulge in provocations to violence without being answerable to society. . . .

The ways in which mob violence may be worked up are subtle and various. Barely will a speaker directly urge a crowd to lay hands on a victim or class of victims. An effective and safer way is to incite mob action while pretending to deplore it, after the classic example of Antony, and this was not lost on Terminiello. And whether one may be the cause of mob violence by his own personification or advocacy of ideas which a crowd already fears and hates, is not solved merely by going through a transcript of the speech to pick out "fighting words." The most insulting words can be neutralized if the speaker will smile when he says them, but a belligerent personality and an aggressive manner may kindle a fight without use of words that in cold type shock us. True judgment will be aided by observation of the individual defendant, as was possible for this jury and trial court but impossible for us. . . .

Invocation of constitutional liberties as part of the strategy for overthrowing them presents a dilemma to a free people which may not be soluble by constitutional logic alone.

But I would not be understood as suggesting that the United States can or should meet this dilemma by suppression of free, open and public speaking on the part of any group or ideology. Suppression has never been a successful permanent policy; any surface serenity that it creates is a false security, while conspirational forces go underground. My confidence in American institutions and in the sound sense of the American people is such that if with a stroke of the pen I could silence every fascist and communist speaker, I would not do it. . . .

This Court has gone far toward accepting the doctrine that civil liberty means the removal of all restraints from these crowds and that all local attempts to maintain order are impairments of the liberty of the citizen. The choice is not between order and liberty. It is between liberty with order and anarchy without either. There is danger that, if the Court does not temper its doctrinaire logic with a little practical wisdom it will convert the constitutional Bill of Rights into a suicide pact.

I would affirm the conviction.

6. Speech That Is a Threat

WATTS *v.* UNITED STATES
394 US 705 (1969)

[Watts was convicted for uttering words that threatened the life of the President. In a per curiam opinion, the Supreme Court upheld the constitutionality of the federal statute which made it a crime to threaten the life of the President, but said that the statute had to be interpreted in the light of the First Amendment, which allows uninhibited, vehement, caustic, and unpleasant attacks on public officials. The Court held that the words used by Watts did not constitute a "threat" in the criminal sense, and reversed the conviction. Justice Stewart would have denied certiorari (an action which would have allowed the judgment of conviction to stand). Justice Douglas wrote a concurring opinion, interesting for its historical content. Justice Fortas wrote a dissenting opinion, in which Justice Harlan joined.]

Per Curiam:

After a jury trial in the United States District Court for the District of Columbia, petitioner was convicted of violating a 1917 statute which prohibits any person from "knowingly and willfully . . . [making] any threat to take the life of or to inflict bodily harm upon the President of the United States. . . ."* The incident which led to petitioner's arrest occurred on August 27, 1966, during a public rally on the Washington Monument grounds. The crowd present broke up into small discussion groups and petitioner joined a gathering scheduled to discuss police brutality. Most of those in the group were quite young, either in their teens or early twenties. Petitioner, who himself was 18 years old, entered into the discussion after one member of the group suggested that the young people present should get more education before expressing their views. According to an investigator for the Army Counter Intelligence Corps who was present, petitioner responded: "They always holler at us to get an education. And now I have already received my draft classification as I–A and I have got to report for my physical this Monday coming. I am not going. If they ever make me carry a rifle the first man I want to get in my sights is L.B.J. They are not going to make me kill my black brothers." On the basis of this statement, the jury found that petitioner had committed a felony by knowingly and willfully threatening the President. The United States Court of Appeals for the District of Columbia Circuit affirmed by a two-to-one vote. We reverse.

At the close of the Government's case, petitioner's trial counsel moved for a judgment of acquittal. He contended that there was "absolutely no evidence on the basis of which the jury would be entitled to find that [petitioner] made

* 18 U.S.C. § 871(a) provides: "Whoever knowingly and willfully deposits for conveyance in the mail or for delivery from any post office or by any letter carrier any letter, paper, writing, print, missive, or document containing any threat to take the life of or to inflict bodily harm upon the President of the United States, the President-elect, the Vice President or other officer next in the order of succession to the office of President of the United States, or the Vice President-elect, or knowingly and willfully otherwise makes any such threat against the President, President-elect, Vice President or other officer next in the order of succession to the office of President, or Vice President-elect, shall be fined not more than $1,000 or imprisoned not more than five years, or both."

a threat against the life of the President." He stressed the fact that petitioner's statement was made during a political debate, that it was expressly made conditional upon an event—induction into the Armed Forces—which petitioner vowed would never occur, and that both petitioner and the crowd laughed after the statement was made. He concluded, "Now actually what happened here in all this was a kind of very crude offensive method of stating a political opposition to the President. What he was saying, he says, I don't want to shoot black people because I don't consider them my enemy, and if they put a rifle in my hand it is the people that put the rifle in my hand, as symbolized by the President, who are my real enemy." We hold that the trial judge erred in denying this motion.

Certainly the statute under which petitioner was convicted is constitutional on its face. The Nation undoubtedly has a valid, even an overwhelming, interest in protecting the safety of its Chief Executive and in allowing him to perform his duties without interference from threats of physical violence. . . . Nevertheless, a statute such as this one, which makes criminal a form of pure speech, must be interpreted with the commands of the First Amendment clearly in mind. What is a threat must be distinguished from what is constitutionally protected speech.

The judges in the Court of Appeals differed over whether or not the "willfullness" requirement of the statute implied that a defendant must have intended to carry out his "threat." Some early cases found the willfullness requirement met if the speaker voluntarily uttered the charged words with "an *apparent* determination to carry them into execution." . . . The majority below seemed to agree. Perhaps this interpretation is correct, although we have grave doubts about it. . . . But whatever the "willfullness" requirement implies, the statute initially requires the Government to prove a true "threat." We do not believe that the kind of political hyperbole indulged in by petitioner fits within that statutory term. For we must interpret the language Congress chose "against the background of a profound national commitment to the principle that debate on public issues should be uninhibited, robust, and wide-open, and that it may well include vehement, caustic, and sometimes unpleasantly sharp attacks on government and public officials." . . . The language of the political arena, like the language used in labor disputes, . . . is often vituperative, abusive, and inexact. We agree with petitioner that his only offense here was "a kind of very crude offensive method of stating a political opposition to the President." Taken in context, and regarding the expressly conditional nature of the statement and the reaction of the listeners, we do not see how it could be interpreted otherwise.

The motion for leave to proceed *in forma pauperis* and the petition for a writ of certiorari are granted and the judgment of the Court of Appeals is reversed. The case is remanded with instructions that it be returned to the District Court for entry of a judgment of acquittal.

It is so ordered.

Judgment for Court of Appeals reversed and case remanded with instructions.

Mr. Justice Douglas, concurring:

The charge in this case is of an ancient vintage.

The federal statute under which petitioner was convicted traces its ancestry to the

Statute of Treasons (25 Edw. III) which made it a crime "to compass and imagine the death of the King." . . . It is said that one Walter Walker, a 15th-century keeper of an inn known as the "Crown" was convicted under the Statute of Treasons for telling his son: "Tom, if thou behavest thyself well, I will make thee heir to the Crown." He was found guilty of compassing and imagining the death of the King, hanged, drawn, and quartered. . . .

In the time of Edward IV one Thomas Burdet who predicted that the king would "soon die with a view to alienate the affections" of the people was indicted for "compassing and imagining of the death of the King," . . . the crime of constructive treason with which the old reports are filled.

In the time of Charles II, one Edward Brownlow was indicted "for speaking these words, that he wished all the gentry in the land would kill one another, so that the communalty might live the better." . . . In the same year one Robert Thornell was indicted for saying "that if the Kinge did side with the Bishops, the divell take the Kinge and the Bishops too."

While our Alien and Sedition Laws were in force, John Adams, President of the United States, en route from Philadelphia, Pa., to Quincy, Massachusetts, stopped in Newark, New Jersey, where he was greeted by a crowd and by a committee that saluted him by firing a cannon.

A bystander said "There goes the President and they are firing at his ass." Luther Baldwin was indicted for replying that he did not care "if they fired through his ass." He was convicted in the federal court for speaking "seditious words tending to defame the President and Government of the United States" and fined, assessed court costs and expenses, and committed to jail until the fine and fees were paid. . . .

The Alien and Sedition Laws constituted one of our sorriest chapters; and I had thought we had done with them forever.

Yet the present statute has hardly fared better. "Like the Statute of Treasons, section 871 was passed in a 'relatively calm peacetime spring,' but has been construed under circumstances when intolerance for free speech was much greater than it normally might be." . . . Convictions under § 871 have been sustained for displaying posters urging passers-by to "hang [President] Roosevelt." . . . for declaring that "President Wilson ought to be killed. It is a wonder some one has not done it already. If I had an opportunity, I would do it myself." . . . for declaring that "Wilson is a wooden-headed son of a bitch. I wish Wilson was in hell, and if I had the power I would put him there." . . . In sustaining an indictment under the statute against a man who indicated that he would enjoy shooting President Wilson if he had the chance, the trial court explained the thrust of § 871:

> The purpose of the statute was undoubtedly not only the protection of the President, but also the prohibition of such statements as those alleged in this indictment. The expression of such direful intentions and desires, not only indicates a spirit of disloyalty to the nation bordering upon treason, but is, in a very real sense, a menace to the peace and safety of the country. . . . It arouses resentment and concern on the part of patriotic citizens. . . .

Suppression of speech as an effective police measure is an old, old device, outlawed by our Constitution.

Mr. Justice Fortas, with whom Mr. Justice Harlan joins, dissenting:

The Court holds, without hearing, that this statute is constitutional and that it is here wrongly applied. Neither of these rulings should be made without hearing, even if we assume that they are correct.

Perhaps this is a trivial case because of its peculiar facts and because the petitioner was merely given a suspended sentence. That does not justify the Court's action. It should induce us to deny certiorari, not to decide the case on its merits and to adjudicate the difficult questions that it presents.

7. *Symbolic Speech*

UNITED STATES *v.* O'BRIEN
391 US 367 (1968)

[The Supreme Court in this case upheld a conviction for burning a selective service registration certificate. The Court said that the punishment was directed at conduct and not at speech. The First Amendment, the Court held, guarantees freedom of expression but not all modes of communication of ideas by conduct. The Court's opinion was by Chief Justice Warren. Justice Harlan wrote a brief concurring opinion. Justice Marshall did not participate. Justice Douglas dissented, but only on the issue whether conscription is constitutional in the absence of a declaration of war by Congress; accordingly, he contended that the case should be set down for reargument on this question.]

Mr. Chief Justice Warren delivered the opinion of the Court:

On the morning of March 31, 1966, David Paul O'Brien and three companions burned their Selective Service registration certificates on the steps of the South Boston Courthouse. A sizable crowd, including several agents of the Federal Bureau of Investigation, witnessed the event. Immediately after the burning, members of the crowd began attacking O'Brien and his companions. An FBI agent ushered O'Brien to safety inside the courthouse. After he was advised of his right to counsel and to silence, O'Brien stated to FBI agents that he had burned his registration certificate because of his beliefs, knowing that he was violating federal law. He produced the charred remains of the certificate, which, with his consent, were photographed.

For this act, O'Brien was indicted, tried, convicted, and sentenced in the United States District Court for the District of Massachusetts. He did not contest the fact that he had burned the certificate. He stated in argument to the jury that he burned the certificate publicly to influence others to adopt his antiwar beliefs, as he put it, "so that other people would reevaluate their positions with Selective Service, with the armed forces, and reevaluate their place in the culture of today, to hopefully consider my position."

The indictment upon which he was tried charged that he "willfully and knowingly did mutilate, destroy, and change by burning . . . [his] Registration Certificate (Selective Service System Form No. 2); in violation of Title 50, App., United States Code, Section 462(b)." Section 462(b) is part of the Universal Military Training and Service Act of 1948. Section 462(b)(3), one of six numbered subdivisions of § 462(b), was amended by Congress in 1965, 79 Stat. 586 (adding the words italicized below), so that at the time O'Brien burned his certificate an offense was committed by any person,

who forges, alters, *knowingly destroys, knowingly mutilates,* or in any manner changes any such certificate . . . (Italics supplied.)

In the District Court, O'Brien argued that the 1965 Amendment prohibiting the knowing destruction or mutilation of certificates was unconstitutional because it was enacted to abridge free speech, and because it served no legitimate legislative purpose. The District Court rejected these arguments, holding that the statute on its face did not abridge First Amendment rights, that the court was not competent to inquire into the motives of Congress in enacting the 1965 Amendment, and that the Amendment was a reasonable exercise of the power of Congress to raise armies.

On appeal, the Court of Appeals for the First Circuit held the 1965 Amendment unconstitutional as a law abridging freedom of speech. At the time the Amendment was enacted, a regulation of the Selective Service System required registrants to keep their registration certificates in their "personal possession at all times." Willful violations of regulations promulgated pursuant to the Universal Military Training and Service Act were made criminal by statute. 50 U.S.C. App. § 462(b)(6). The Court of Appeals, therefore, was of the opinion that conduct punishable under the 1965 Amendment was already punishable under the nonpossession regulation, and consequently that the Amendment served no valid purpose; further, that in light of the prior regulation, the Amendment must have been "directed at public as distinguished from private destruction." On this basis, the Court concluded that the 1965 Amendment ran afoul of the First Amendment by singling out persons engaged in protests for special treatment. The Court ruled, however, that O'Brien's conviction should be affirmed under the statutory provision, 50 U.S.C. App. § 462(b)(6), which in its view made violation of the nonpossession regulation a crime, because it regarded such violation to be a lesser included offense of the crime defined by the 1965 Amendment.

The Government petitioned for certiorari, in No. 232, arguing that the Court of Appeals erred in holding the statute unconstitutional, and that its decision conflicted with decisions by the Court of Appeals for the Second and Eighth Circuits upholding the 1965 Amendment against identical constitutional challenges. O'Brien cross-petitioned for certiorari, in No. 233, arguing that the Court of Appeals erred in sustaining his conviction on the basis of a crime of which he was neither charged nor tried. We granted the Government's petition to resolve the conflict in the circuits, and we also granted O'Brien's cross-petition. We hold that the 1965 Amendment is constitutional both as enacted and as applied. We therefore vacate the judgment of the Court of Appeals and reinstate the judgment and sentence of the District Court without reaching the issue raised by O'Brien in No. 233.

I

When a male reaches the age of 18, he is required by the Universal Military Training and Service Act to register wtih a local draft board. He is assigned a Selective Service number, and within five days he is issued a registration certificate. Subsequently, and based on a questionnaire completed by the registrant, he is assigned a classification denoting his eligibility for induction, and "[a]s soon as practicable" thereafter he is issued a Notice of Classification. This initial classification is not necessarily permanent, and if in the interim before induction the registrant's status changes in some relevant way, he may be reclassified. After such a reclassification, the local board "as soon as practicable" issues to the registrant a new Notice of Classification.

Both the registration and classification certificates are small white cards, approximately 2 by 3 inches. The registration certificate specifies the name of the registrant, the date of registration, and the number and address of the local board with which he is registered. Also inscribed upon it are the date and place of the registrant's birth, his residence at registration, his physical description, his signature, and his Selective Service number. The Selective Service number itself indicates his State of registration, his local board, his year of birth, and his chronological position in the local board's classification record.

The classification certificate shows the registrant's name, Selective Service number, signature, and eligibility classification. It specifies whether he was so classified by his local board, an appeal board, or the President. It contains the address of his local board and the date the certificate was mailed.

Both the registration and classification certificates bear notices that the registrant must notify his local board in writing of every change in address, physical condition, and occupational, marital, family, dependency, and military status, and of any other fact which might change his classification. Both also contain a notice that the registrant's Selective Service number should appear on all communications to his local board.

Congress demonstrated its concern that certificates issued by the Selective Service System might be abused well before the 1965 Amendment here challenged. The 1948 Act, 62 Stat. 604, itself prohibited many different abuses involving "any registration certificate, . . . or any other certificate issued pursuant to or prescribed by the provisions of this title, or rules or regulations promulgated hereunder. . . ." Under § 12(b)(1)–(5) of the 1948 Act, it was unlawful (1) to transfer a certificate to aid a person in making false identification; (2) to possess a certificate not duly issued with the intent of using it for false identification; (3) to forge, alter, "or in any manner" change a certificate or any notation validly inscribed thereon; (4) to photograph or make an imitation of a certificate for the purpose of false identification; and (5) to possess a counterfeited or altered certificate. In addition, as previously mentioned, regulations of the Selective Service System required registrants to keep both their registration and classification certificates in their personal possession at all times. And § 12(b)(6) of the Act, made knowing violation of any provision of the Act or rules and regulations promulgated pursuant thereto a felony.

By the 1965 Amendment, Congress added to § 12(b)(3) of the 1948 Act the provision here at issue, subjecting to criminal liability not only one who "forges, alters, or in any manner changes" but also one who "knowingly destroys, [or] knowingly mutilates" a certificate. We note at the outset that the 1965 Amendment plainly does not abridge free speech on its face, and we do not understand O'Brien to argue otherwise. Amended § 12(b)(3) on its face deals with conduct having no connection with speech. It prohibits the knowing destruction of certificates issued by the Selective Service System, and there is nothing necessarily expressive about such conduct. The Amendment does not distinguish between public and private destruction, and it does not punish only destruction engaged in for the purpose of expressing views. Compare *Stromberg* v. *People of State of California,* 283 US 359 (1931). A law prohibiting destruction of Selective Service certificates no more abridges free speech on its face than a motor vehicle law prohibiting the destruction of drivers' licenses, or a tax law prohibiting the destruction of books and records.

O'Brien nonetheless argues that the 1965 Amendment is unconstitutional in its application to him, and is unconstitutional as enacted because what he calls the "purpose" of Congress was "to suppress freedom of speech." We consider these arguments separately.

II

O'Brien first argues that the 1965 Amendment is unconstitutional as applied to him because his act of burning his registration certificate was protected "symbolic speech" within the First Amendment. His argument is that the freedom of expression which the First Amendment guarantees includes all modes of "communication of ideas by conduct," and that his conduct is within this definition because he did it in "demonstration against the war and against the draft."

We cannot accept the view that an apparently limitless variety of conduct can be labeled "speech" whenever the person engaging in the conduct intends thereby to express an idea. However, even on the assumption that the alleged communicative element in O'Brien's conduct is sufficient to bring into play the First Amendment, it does not necessarily follow that the destruction of a registration certificate is constitutionally protected activity. This Court has held that when "speech" and "nonspeech" elements are combined in the same course of conduct, a sufficiently important governmental interest in regulating the nonspeech element can justify incidental limitations on First Amendment freedoms. To characterize the quality of the governmental interest which must appear, the Court has employed a variety of descriptive terms: compelling; substantial; subordinating; paramount; cogent; strong. Whatever imprecision inheres in these terms, we think it clear that a government regulation is sufficiently justified if it is within the constitutional power of the government; if it furthers an important or substantial governmental interest; if the governmental interest is unrelated to the suppression of free expression; and if the incidental restriction on alleged First Amendment freedom is no greater than is essential to the furtherance of that interest. We find that the 1965 Amendment to § 462(b)(3) of the Universal Military Training and Service Act meets all of these requirements, and consequently that O'Brien can be constitutionally convicted for violating it.

The constitutional power of Congress to raise and support armies and to make all laws necessary and proper to that end is broad and sweeping. . . . The power of Congress to classify and conscript manpower for military service is "beyond question." . . . Pursuant to this power, Congress may establish a system of registration for individuals liable for training and service, and may require such individuals within reason to cooperate in the registration system. The issuance of certificates indicating the registration and eligibility classification of individuals is a legitimate and substantial administrative aid in the functioning of this system. And legislation to insure the continuing availability of issued certificates serves a legitimate and substantial purpose in the system's administration.

O'Brien's argument to the contrary is necessarily premised upon his unrealistic characterization of Selective Service certificates. He essentially adopts the position that such certificates are so many pieces of paper designed to notify registrants of their registration or classification, to be retained or tossed in the wastebasket according to the convenience or taste of the registrant. Once the registrant has received notification, according to this view, there is no reason for him to retain the certificates. O'Brien notes that most of the information on a registration certificate serves no notification purpose at all; the registrant hardly needs to be told his address and physical characteristics. We agree that the registration certificate contains much information of which the registrant needs no notification. This circumstance, however, leads not to the conclusion that the certificate serves no purpose but that, like the classification certificate, it serves purposes in addition to initial notification. Many of these purposes would be defeated by the certificates' destruction or mutilation. Among these are:

1. The registration certificate serves as proof that the individual described thereon has registered for the draft. The classification certificate shows the eligibility classification of a named but undescribed individual. Voluntarily displaying the two certificates is an easy and painless way for a young man to dispel a question as to whether he might be delinquent in his Selective Service obligations. Correspondingly, the availability of the certificates for such display relieves the Selective Service System of the administrative burden it would otherwise have in verifying the registration and classification of all suspected delinquents. Further, since both certificates are in the nature of "receipts" attesting that the registrant has done what the law requires, it is in the interest of the just and efficient administration of the system that they be continually available, in the event, for example, of a mix-up in the registrant's file. Additionally, in a time of national crisis, reasonable availability to each registrant of the two small cards assures a rapid and uncomplicated means for determining his fitness for immediate induction, no matter how distant in our mobile society he may be from his local board.

2. The information supplied on the certificates facilitates communication between registrants and local boards, simplifying the system and benefiting all concerned. To begin with, each certificate bears the address of the registrant's local board, an item unlikely to be committed to memory. Further, each card bears the registrant's Selective Service number, and a registrant who has his number readily available so that he can communicate it to his local board when he supplies or requests information can make simpler the board's task in locating his file. Finally, a registrant's inquiry, particularly through a local board other than his own, concerning his eligibility status is frequently answerable simply on the basis of his classification certificate; whereas, if the certificate were not reasonably available and the registrant were uncertain of his classification, the task of answering his questions would be considerably complicated.

3. Both certificates carry continual reminders that the registrant must notify his

local board of any change of address, and other specified changes in his status. The smooth functioning of the system requires that local boards be continually aware of the status and whereabouts of registrants, and the destruction of certificates deprives the system of a potentially useful notice device.

4. The regulatory scheme involving Selective Service certificates includes clearly valid prohibitions against the alteration, forgery, or similar deceptive misuse of certificates. The destruction or mutilation of certificates obviously increases the difficulty of detecting and tracing abuses such as these. Further, a multilated certificate might itself be used for deceptive purposes.

The many functions performed by Selective Service certificates establish beyond doubt that Congress has a legitimate and substantial interest in preventing their wanton and unrestrained destruction and assuring their continuing availability by punishing people who knowingly and willfully destroy or mutilate them. And we are unpersuaded that the pre-existence of the nonpossession regulations in any way negates this interest.

In the absence of a question as to multiple punishment, it has never been suggested that there is anything improper in Congress providing alternative statutory avenues of prosecution to assure the effective protection of one and the same interest. . . . Here, the pre-existing avenue of prosecution was not even statutory. Regulations may be modified or revoked from time to time by administrative discretion. Certainly, the Congress may change or supplement a regulation.

Equally important, a comparison of the regulations with the 1965 Amendment indicates that they protect overlapping but not identical governmental interests, and that they reach somewhat different classes of wrongdoers. The gravamen of the offense defined by the statute is the deliberate rendering of certificates unavailable for the various purposes which they may serve. Whether registrants keep their certificates in their personal possession at all times, as required by the regulations, is of no particular concern under the 1965 Amendment, as long as they do not mutilate or destroy the certificates so as to render them unavailable. Although as we note below we are not concerned here with the nonpossession regulations, it is not inappropriate to observe that the essential elements of nonpossession are not identical with those of mutilation or destruction. Finally, the 1965 Amendment, like § 12(b) which it amended, is concerned with abuses involving *any* issued Selective Service certificates, not only with the registrant's own certificates. The knowing destruction or mutilation of someone else's certificates would therefore violate the statute but not the nonpossession regulations.

We think it apparent that the continuing availability to each registrant of his Selective Service certificates substantially furthers the smooth and proper functioning of the system that Congress has established to raise armies. We think it also apparent that the Nation has a vital interest in having a system for raising armies that functions with maximum efficiency and is capable of easily and quickly responding to continually changing circumstances. For these reasons, the Government has a substantial interest in assuring the continuing availability of issued Selective Service certificates.

It is equally clear that the 1965 Amendment specifically protects this substantial governmental interest. We perceive no alternative means that would more precisely

and narrowly assure the continuing availability of issued Selective Service certificates than a law which prohibits their willful mutilation or destruction. . . . The
1965 Amendment prohibits such conduct and does nothing more. In other words,
both the governmental interest and the operation of the 1965 Amendment are
limited to the noncommunicative aspect of O'Brien's conduct. The governmental
interest and the scope of the 1965 Amendment are limited to preventing a harm to
the smooth and efficient functioning of the Selective Service System. When O'Brien
deliberately rendered unavailable his registration certificate, he willfully frustrated
this governmental interest. For this noncommunicative impact of his conduct, and
for nothing else, he was convicted.

The case at bar is therefore unlike one where the alleged governmental interest
in regulating conduct arises in some measure because the communication allegedly
integral to the conduct is itself thought to be harmful. In *Stromberg* v. *People of
State of California,* for example, this Court struck down a statutory phrase which
punished people who expressed their "opposition to organized government" by displaying "any flag, badge, banner, or device." Since the statute there was aimed at
suppressing communication it could not be sustained as a regulation of noncommunicative conduct. . . .

In conclusion, we find that because of the Government's substantial interest in
assuring the continuing availability of issued Selective Service certificates, because
amended § 462(b) is an appropriately narrow means of protecting this interest
and condemns only the independent noncommunicative impact of conduct within
its reach, and because the noncommunicative impact of O'Brien's act of burning
his registration certificate frustrated the Government's interest, a sufficient governmental interest has been shown to justify O'Brien's conviction.

III

O'Brien finally argues that the 1965 Amendment is unconstitutional as enacted
because what he calls the "purpose" of Congress was "to suppress freedom of
speech." We reject this argument because under settled principles the purpose of
Congress, as O'Brien uses that term, is not a basis for declaring this legislation unconstitutional.

It is a familiar principle of constitutional law that this Court will not strike down
an otherwise constitutional statute on the basis of an alleged illicit legislative motive.
As the Court long ago stated:

The decisions of this court from the beginning lend no support whatever to the assumption that the judiciary may restrain the exercise of lawful power on the assumption that
a wrongful purpose or motive has caused the power to be exerted. *McCray* v. *United
States,* 195 US 27 (1904).

This fundamental principle of constitutional adjudication was reaffirmed and the
many cases were collected by Mr. Justice Brandeis for the Court in *State of Arizona* v. *State of California,* 283 US 423 (1931).

Inquiries into congressional motives or purposes are a hazardous matter. When
the issue is simply the interpretation of legislation, the Court will look to statements

by legislators for guidance as to the purpose of the legislature,* because the benefit to sound decision-making in this circumstance is thought sufficient to risk the possibility of misreading Congress' purpose. It is entirely a different matter when we are asked to void a statute that is, under well-settled criteria, constitutional on its face, on the basis of what fewer than a handful of Congressmen said about it. What motivates one legislator to make a speech about a statute is not necessarily what motivates scores of others to enact it, and the stakes are sufficiently high for us to eschew guesswork. We decline to void essentially on the ground that it is unwise legislation which Congress had the undoubted power to enact and which could be re-enacted in its exact form if the same or another legislator made a "wiser" speech about it. . . .

IV

Since the 1965 Amendment to § 12(b)(3) of the Universal Military Training and Service Act is constitutional as enacted and as applied, the Court of Appeals should have affirmed the judgment of conviction entered by the District Court. Accordingly, we vacate the judgment of the Court of Appeals, and reinstate the judgment and sentence of the District Court. This disposition makes unnecessary consideration of O'Brien's claim that the Court of Appeals erred in affirming his conviction on the basis of the nonpossession regulation.

It is so ordered.

TINKER *v.* DES MOINES INDEPENDENT COMMUNITY SCHOOL DISTRICT
393 US 503 (1969)

[A school regulation prohibited the wearing of black armbands by students while on school facilities. The Supreme Court held that the regulation was a violation of the students' right of expression of opinion. The Court's opinion was by Justice Fortas. Justices Stewart and White each wrote a brief concurring opinion. Justices Black and Harlan each wrote a dissenting opinion.]

* The Court may make the same assumption in a very limited and well-defined class of cases where the very nature of the constitutional question requires an inquiry into legislative purpose. The principal class of cases is readily apparent—those in which statutes have been challenged as bills of attainder. This Court's decisions have defined a bill of attainder as a legislative Act which inflicts punishment on named individuals or members of an easily ascertainable group without a judicial trial. In determining whether a particular statute is a bill of attainder, the analysis necessarily requires an inquiry into whether the three definitional elements—specificity in identification, punishment and lack of a judicial trial—are contained in the statute. The inquiry into whether the challenged statute contains the necessary element of punishment has on occasion led the Court to examine the legislative motive in enacting the statute. See, e. g., *United States* v. *Lovett*, 328 US 303 (1946). Two other decisions not involving a bill of attainder analysis contain an inquiry into legislative purpose or motive of the type that O'Brien suggests we engage in in this case. *Kennedy* v. *Mendoza-Martinez*, 372 US 144 (1963); *Trop* v. *Dulles*, 356 US 86 (1958). The inquiry into legislative purpose or motive in *Kennedy* and *Trop*, however, was for the same limited purpose as in the bill of attainder decisions—i. e., to determine whether the statutes under review were punitive in nature. We face no such inquiry in this case. The 1965 Amendment to § 462(b) was clearly penal in nature, designed to impose criminal punishment on designated acts.

Mr. Justice Fortas delivered the opinion of the Court:

Petitioner John F. Tinker, 15 years old, and petitioner Christopher Eckhardt, 16 years old, attended high schools in Des Moines. Petitioner Mary Beth Tinker, John's sister, was a 13-year-old student in junior high school.

In December 1965, a group of adults and students in Des Moines, Iowa, held a meeting at the Eckhardt home. The group determined to publicize their objections to the hostilities in Vietnam and their support for a truce by wearing black arm-bands during the holiday season and by fasting on December 16 and New Year's Eve. Petitioners and their parents had previously engaged in similar activities, and they decided to participate in the program.

The principals of the Des Moines schools became aware of the plan to wear armbands. On December 14, 1965, they met and adopted a policy that any student wearing an armband to school would be asked to remove it, and if he refused he would be suspended until he returned without the armband. Petitioners were aware of the regulation that the school authorities adopted.

On December 16, Mary Beth and Christopher wore black armbands to their schools. John Tinker wore his armband the next day. They were all sent home and suspended from school until they would come back without their armbands. They did not return to school until after the planned period for wearing armbands had expired—that is, until after New Year's Day.

This complaint was filed in the United States District Court by petitioners, through their fathers, under § 1983 of Title 42 of the United States Code. It prayed for an injunction restraining the defendant school officials and the defendant members of the board of directors of the school district from disciplining the petitioners, and it sought nominal damages. After an evidentiary hearing the District Court dismissed the complaint. It upheld the constitutionality of the school authorities' action on the ground that it was reasonable in order to prevent disturbance of school discipline. The court referred to but expressly declined to follow the Fifth Circuit's holding in a similar case that prohibition of the wearing of symbols like the armbands cannot be sustained unless it "materially and substantially interfere[s] with the requirements of appropriate discipline in the operation of the school." . . .

On appeal, the Court of Appeals for the Eighth Circuit considered the case *en banc.* The court was equally divided, and the District Court's decision was accordingly affirmed, without opinion. We granted certiorari.

I

The District Court recognized that the wearing of an armband for the purpose of expressing certain views is the type of symbolic act that is within the Free Speech Clause of the First Amendment. See *West Virginia State Board of Education* v. *Barnette,* 319 US 624 (1943); *Stromberg* v. *California,* 283 US 359 (1931). . . . As we shall discuss, the wearing of armbands in the circumstances of this case was entirely divorced from actually or potentially disruptive conduct by those participating in it. It was closely akin to "pure speech" which, we have repeatedly held, is entitled to comprehensive protection under the First Amendment. . . .

First Amendment rights, applied in light of the special characteristics of the school environment, are available to teachers and students. It can hardly be argued that either students or teachers shed their constitutional rights to freedom of speech or expression at the schoolhouse gate. This has been the unmistakable holding of this Court for almost 50 years. . . .

In *West Virginia State Board of Education* v. *Barnette, supra,* this Court held that under the First Amendment, the student in public school may not be compelled to salute the flag. Speaking through Mr. Justice Jackson, the Court said:

The Fourteenth Amendment, as now applied to the States, protects the citizen against the State itself and all of its creatures—Boards of Education not excepted. These have, of course, important, delicate, and highly discretionary functions, but none that they may not perform within the limits of the Bill of Rights. That they are educating the young for citizenship is reason for scrupulous protection of Constitutional freedoms of the individual, if we are not to strangle the free mind at its source and teach youth to discount important principles of our government as mere platitudes.

On the other hand, the Court has repeatedly emphasized the need for affirming the comprehensive authority of the States and of school authorities, consistent with fundamental constitutional safeguards, to prescribe and control conduct in the schools. . . . Our problem lies in the area where students in the exercise of First Amendment rights collide with the rules of the school authorities.

II

The problem presented by the present case does not relate to regulation of the length of skirts or the type of clothing, to hair style, or deportment. . . . It does not concern aggressive, disruptive action or even group demonstrations. Our problem involves direct, primary First Amendment rights akin to "pure speech."

The school officials banned and sought to punish petitioners for a silent, passive, expression of opinion, unaccompanied by any disorder or disturbance on the part of petitioners. There is here no evidence whatever of petitioners' interference, actual or nascent, with the school's work or of collision with the rights of other students to be secure and to be let alone. Accordingly, this case does not concern speech or action that intrudes upon the work of the school or the rights of other students.

Only a few of the 18,000 students in the school system wore the black armbands. Only five students were suspended for wearing them. There is no indication that the work of the school or any class was disrupted. Outside the classrooms, a few students made hostile remarks to the children wearing armbands, but there were no threats or acts of violence on school premises.

The District Court concluded that the action of the school authorities was reasonable because it was based upon their fear of a disturbance from the wearing of the armbands. But, in our system, undifferentiated fear or apprehension of disturbance is not enough to overcome the right to freedom of expression. Any departure from absolute regimentation may cause trouble. Any variation from the majority's opinion may inspire fear. Any word spoken, in class, in the lunchroom or on the campus, that deviates from the views of another person, may start an argument or cause a disturbance. But our Constitution says we must take this risk, *Terminiello* v. *Chicago,* 337 US 1 (1959); and our history says that it is this sort of hazardous freedom—this kind of openness—that is the basis of our national strength and of the independence and vigor of Americans who grow up and live in this relatively permissive, often disputatious society.

In order for the State in the person of school officials to justify prohibition of a particular expression of opinion, it must be able to show that its action was caused by something more than a mere desire to avoid the discomfort and unpleasantness that always accompany an unpopular viewpoint. Certainly where there is no finding and no showing that the exercise of the forbidden right would "materially and substantially interfere with the requirements of appropriate discipline in the operation of the school," the prohibition cannot be sustained. . . .

In the present case, the District Court made no such finding, and our independent examination of the record fails to yield evidence that the school authorities had reason to anticipate that the wearing of the armbands would substantially interfere with the work of the school or impinge upon the rights of other students. Even an official memorandum prepared after the suspension that listed the reasons for the ban on wearing the armbands made no reference to the anticipation of such disruption.

On the contrary, the action of the school authorities appears to have been based upon an urgent wish to avoid the controversy which might result from the expression, even by the silent symbol of armbands, of opposition to this Nation's part in the conflagration in Vietnam. It is revealing, in this respect, that the meeting at which the school principals decided to issue the contested regulation was called in response to a student's statement to the journalism teacher in one of the schools that he wanted to write an article on Vietnam and have it published in the school paper. (The student was dissuaded.)

It is also relevant that the school authorities did not purport to prohibit the wearing of all symbols of political or controversial significance. The record shows that students in some of the schools wore buttons relating to national political campaigns, and some even wore the Iron Cross, traditionally a symbol of nazism. The order prohibiting the wearing of armbands did not extend to these. Instead, a particular symbol—black armbands worn to exhibit opposition to this Nation's involvement in Vietnam—was singled out for prohibition. Clearly, the prohibition of expression of one particular opinion, at least without evidence that it is necessary to avoid material and substantial interference with school work or discipline, is not constitutionally permissible.

In our system, state-operated schools may not be enclaves of totalitarianism. School officials do not possess absolute authority over their students. Students in school as well as out of school are "persons" under our Constitution. They are possessed of fundamental rights which the State must respect, just as they themselves must respect their obligations to the State. In our system, students may not be regarded as closed-cricuit recipients of only that which the State chooses to communicate. They may not be confined to the expression of those sentiments that are officially approved. In the absence of a specific showing of constitutionally valid reasons to regulate their speech, students are entitled to freedom of expression of their views. As Judge Gewin, speaking for the Fifth Circuit said, school officials cannot suppress "expressions of feelings with which they do not wish to contend." . . .

In *Meyer* v. *Nebraska, supra,* Justice McReynolds expressed this Nation's repudiation of the principle that a State might so conduct its schools as to "foster a homogeneous people." He said:

In order to submerge the individual and develop ideal citizens, Sparta assembled the males at seven into barracks and intrusted their subsequent education and training to official guardians. Although such measures have been deliberately approved by men of great genius, their ideas touching the relation between individual and State were wholly different from those upon which our institutions rest; and it hardly will be affirmed that any Legislature could impose such restrictions upon the people of a state without doing violence to both letter and spirit of the Constitution.

This principle has been repeated by this Court on numerous occasions during the intervening years. In *Keyishian* v. *Board of Regents,* 385 US 589, Mr. Justice Brennan, speaking for the Court, said:

"The vigilant protection of constitutional freedom is nowhere more vital than in the community of American schools." *Shelton* v. *Tucker,* [364 US 479, 487, 81 S.Ct. 247, 5 L.Ed.2d 231]. The classroom is peculiarly the "marketplace of ideas." The Nation's future depends upon leaders trained through wide exposure to that robust exchange of ideas which discovers truth "out of a multitude of tongues, [rather] than through any kind of authoritative selection. . . ."

The principle of these cases is not confined to the supervised and ordained discussion which takes place in the classroom. The principal use to which the schools are dedicated is to accommodate students during prescribed hours for the purpose of certain types of activities. Among those activities is personal intercommunication among the students. This is not only an inevitable part of the process of attending school. It is also an important part of the educational process. A student's rights therefore, do not embrace merely the classroom hours. When he is in the cafeteria, or on the playing field, or on the campus during the authorized hours, he may express his opinions, even on controversial subjects like the conflict in Vietnam, if he does so "[without] materially and substantially interfering with . . . appropriate discipline in the operation of the school," and without colliding with the rights of others. *Burnside* v. *Byars, supra,* 363 F.2d 749. But conduct by the student, in class or out of it, which for any reason—whether it stems from time, place, or type of behavior—materially disrupts classwork or involves substantial disorder or invasion of the rights of others is, of course, not immunized by the constitutional guaranty of freedom of speech. . . .

Under our Constitution, free speech is not a right that is given only to be so circumscribed that it exists in principle but not in fact. Freedom of expression would not truly exist if the right could be exercised only in an area that a benevolent government has provided as a safe haven for crackpots. The Constitution says that Congress (and the States) may not abridge the right to free speech. This provision means what it says. We properly read it to permit reasonable regulation of speech-connected activities in carefully restricted circumstances. But we do not confine the permissible exercise of First Amendment rights to a telephone booth or the four corners of a pamphlet, or to supervised and ordained discussion in a school classroom.

If a regulation were adopted by school officials forbidding discussion of the Vietnam conflict, or the expression by any student of opposition to it anywhere on school property except as part of a prescribed classroom exercise, it would be obvious that the regulation would violate the constitutional rights of students, at least if it could not be justified by a showing that the students' activities would materially and substantially disrupt the work and discipline of the school. . . . In the circumstances of the present case, the prohibition of the silent, passive "witness of the armbands," as one of the children called it, is no less offensive to the constitution's guaranties.

As we have discussed, the record does not demonstrate any facts which might reasonably have led school authorities to forecast substantial disruption of or material interference with school activities, and no disturbances or disorders on the school premises in fact occurred. These petitioners merely went about their ordained rounds in school. Their deviation consisted only in wearing on their sleeve a band of black cloth, not more than two inches wide. They wore it to exhibit their disapproval of the Vietnam hostilities and their advocacy of a truce, to make their views known, and by their example, to influence others to adopt them. They neither interrupted school activities nor sought to intrude in the school affairs or the lives of others. They caused discussion outside of the classrooms, but no interference with work and no disorder. In the circumstances, our Constitution does not permit officials of the State to deny their form of expression.

We express no opinion as to the form of relief which should be granted, this being a matter for the lower courts to determine. We reverse and remand for further proceedings consistent with this opinion.

Reversed and remanded.

Mr. Justice Black, dissenting:

The Court's holding in this case ushers in what I deem to be an entirely new era in which the power to control pupils by the elected "officials of state-supported public schools . . ." in the United States is in ultimate effect transferred to the Supreme Court. The Court brought this particular case here on a petition for certiorari urging that the First and Fourteenth Amendments protect the right of school pupils to express their political views all the way "from kindergarten through high school." Here the constitutional right to "political expression" asserted was a right to wear black armbands during school hours and at classes in order to demonstrate to the other students that the petitioners were mourning because of the death of United States' soldiers in Vietnam and to protest that war which they were against. Ordered to refrain from wearing the armbands in school by the elected school officials and the teachers vested with state authority to do so, apparently only seven out of the school system's 18,000 pupils deliberately refused to obey the order. One defying pupil was Paul Tinker, 8 years old, who was in the second grade; another, Hope Tinker was 11 years old in the fifth grade; a third member of the Tinker family was 13, in the eighth grade; and a fourth member of the same family was John Tinker, 15 years old, an 11th grade high school pupil. Their father, a Methodist minister without a church, is paid a salary by the American Friends Service Committee. Another student who defied the school order and insisted on wearing an armband in school was Chris Eckhardt, an 11th grade pupil and a petitioner in this case. His mother is an official in the Women's International League for Peace and Freedom. . . ,

Assuming that the Court is correct in holding that the conduct of wearing armbands for the purpose of conveying political ideas is protected by the First Amendment, . . . the crucial remaining questions are whether students and teachers may use the schools at their whim as a platform for the exercise of free speech—"symbolic" or "pure"— and whether the Courts will allocate to themselves the function of deciding how the pupils' school day will be spent. While I have always believed that under the First and Fourteenth Amendments neither the State nor Federal Government has any authority to regulate or censor the content of speech, I have never believed that any person has a right to give speeches or engage in demonstrations where he pleases and when he pleases. This Court has already rejected such a notion. In *Cox* v. *Louisiana,* 379 US 536 (1964), for example, the Court clearly stated that the rights of free speech and assembly "do not mean than anyone with opinions or beliefs to express may address a group at any public place and at any time."

While the record does not show that any of these armband students shouted, used profane language or were violent in any manner, a detailed report by some of them shows their armbands caused comments, warnings by other students, the poking of fun at them, and a warning by an older football player that other, nonprotesting students had better let them alone. There is also evidence that the professor of mathematics had his lesson period practically "wrecked" chiefly by disputes with Beth Tinker, who wore her armband for her "demonstration." Even a casual reading of the record shows that this armband did divert students' minds from their regular lessons, and that talk, comments, etc., made John Tinker "self-conscious" in attending school with his armband. While the absence of obscene or boisterous and loud disorder perhaps justifies the Court's statement that the few armband students did not actually "disrupt" the classwork, I think the record overwhelmingly shows that the armbands did exactly what the elected school officials and principals foresaw it would, that is, took the students' minds off their classwork and diverted them to thoughts about the highly emotional subject of the Vietnam war. And I repeat that if the time has come when pupils of state-supported schools, kindergarten, grammar school or high school, can defy and flaunt orders of school officials to keep their minds on their own school work, it is the beginning of a new revolutionary era of permissiveness in this country fostered by the judiciary. The next logical step, it appears to me, would be to hold unconstitutional laws that bar pupils under 21 or 18 from voting, or from being elected members of the Boards of Education. . . .

I deny, therefore, that it has been the "unmistakable holding of this Court for almost 50 years" that "students" and "teachers" take with them into the "schoolhouse gate" constitutional rights to "freedom of speech or expression." Even *Meyer* did not hold that. It makes no reference to "symbolic speech" at all; what it did was to strike down as "unreasonable" and therefore unconstitutional a Nebraska law barring the teaching of the German language before the children reached their eighth grade. One can well agree with Justice Holmes and Mr. Justice Sutherland, as I do, that such a law was no more unreasonable than it would be to bar the teaching of Latin and Greek to pupils who have not reached the eighth grade. In fact, I think the majority's reason for invalidating the Nebraska law was that they did not like or in legal jargon that it "shocked the Court's conscience," "offended its sense of justice," was "contrary to fundamental concepts of the English-speaking world," as the Court has sometimes said. . . . The truth is that a teacher of kindergarten, grammar school, or high school pupils no more carries into a school with him a complete right to freedom of speech and expression than an anti-Catholic or anti-Semitic carries with him a complete freedom of speech and religion into a Catholic church or Jewish synagogue. Nor does a person carry with him into the United States Senate or House, or to the Supreme Court, or any other court, a complete constitutional right to go into those places contrary to their rules and speak his mind on any subject he pleases. It is a myth to say that any person has a constitutional right to say what he pleases, where he pleases, and when he pleases. Our Court has decided precisely the opposite. . . .

In my view, teachers in state-controlled public schools are hired to teach there. Although Mr. Justice McReynolds may have intimated to the contrary in *Meyer* v. *Nebraska, supra,* certainly a teacher is not paid to go into school and teach subjects the State does not hire him to teach as a part of its selected curriculum. Nor are public school students sent to the schools at public expense to broadcast political or any other views to educate and inform the public. The original idea of schools, which I do not believe is yet abandoned as worthless or out of date, was that children had not yet reached the point of experience and wisdom which enabled them to teach all of their elders. It may be that the Nation has outworn the old-fashioned slogan that "children are to be seen not heard," but one may, I hope, be permitted to harbor the thought that taxpayers send children to school on the premise that at their age they need to learn, not teach.

The true principles on this whole subject were in my judgment spoken by Mr. Justice McKenna for the Court in *Waugh* v. *Mississippi University,* 237 US 589. The State had there passed a law barring students from peaceably assembling in Greek letter fraternities and providing that students who joined them could be expelled from school. This law would appear on the surface to run afoul of the First Amendment's freedom of assembly clause. The law was attacked as violative of due process and as a deprivation of property, of liberty, and of the privileges and immunities clause of the Fourteenth Amendment. It was argued that the fraternity made its members more moral, taught discipline, and inspired its members to study harder and to obey better the rules of discipline and order. This Court rejected all the "fervid" pleas of the fraternities' advocates decided unanimously against these Fourteenth Amendment arguments. The Court in its closing paragraph made this statement which has complete relevance for us today:

> It is said that the fraternity to which complainant belongs is a moral and of itself a disciplinary force. This need not be denied. But whether such membership makes against discipline was for the State of Mississippi to determine. It is to be remembered that the University was established by the state and is under the control of the state, and the enactment of the statute may have been induced by the opinion that *membership in the prohibited societies divided the attention of the students and distracted from that singleness of purpose which the State desired to exist in its public educational institutions.* It is not for us to entertain conjectures in opposition to the views of the state and annul its regulations upon disputable considerations of their wisdom or necessity. (Emphasis supplied.)

It was on the foregoing argument that this Court sustained the power of Mississippi to curtail the First Amendment's right of peaceable assembly. And the same reasons are equally applicable to curtailing in the States' public schools the right to complete freedom of expression. Iowa's public schools, like Mississippi's university, are operated to give students an opportunity to learn, not to talk politics by actual speech, or by "symbolic" speech. And as I have pointed out before, the record amply shows that public protest in the school classes against the Vietnam war "distracted from that singleness of purpose which the state (here Iowa) desired to exist in its public educational institutions." Here the Court should accord Iowa educational institutions the same right to determine for itself what free expression and no more should be allowed in its schools that it accorded Mississippi with reference to freedom of assembly. But even if the record were silent as to protests against the Vietnam war distracting students from their assigned class work, members of this Court, like all other citizens, know, without being told, that the disputes over the wisdom of the Vietnam war have disrupted and divided this country as few other issues ever have. Of course students, like other people, cannot concentrate on lesser issues when black armbands are being ostentatiously displayed in their presence to call attention to the wounded and dead of the war, some of the wounded and the dead being their friends and neighbors. It was, of course, to distract the attention of other students that some students insisted up to the very point of their own suspension from school that they were determined to sit in school with their symbolic armbands.

Change has been said to be truly the law of life but sometimes the old and the tried and true are worth holding. The schools of this Nation have undoubtedly contributed to giving us tranquility and to making us a more law-abiding people. Uncontrolled and uncontrollable liberty is an enemy to domestic peace. We cannot close our eyes to the fact that some of the country's greatest problems are crimes committed by the youth, too many of school age. School discipline, like parental discipline, is an integral and important part of training our children to be good citizens—to be better citizens. Here a very small number of students have crisply and summarily refused to obey a school order designed to give pupils who want to learn the opportunity to do so. One does not need to be a prophet or the son of a prophet to know that after the Court's holding today that some students in Iowa schools and indeed in all schools will be ready, able, and willing to defy their teachers on practically all orders. This is the more unfortunate for the schools since groups of students all over the land are already running loose, conducting break-ins, sit-ins, lie-ins, and smash-ins. Many of these student groups, as is all too familiar to all who read the newspapers and watch the television news programs, have already engaged in rioting, property seizures, and destruction. They have picketed schools to force students not to cross their picket lines and have too often violently attacked earnest but frightened students who wanted an education that the picketers did not want them to get. Students engaged in such activities are apparently confident that they know far more about how to operate public school systems than do their parents, teachers, and elected school officials. It is no answer to say that the particular students here have not yet reached such high points in their demands to attend classes in order to exercise their political pressures. Turned loose with law suits for damages and injunctions against their teachers like they are here, it is nothing but wishful thinking to imagine that young, immature students will not soon believe it is their right to control the schools rather than the right of the States that collect the taxes to hire the teachers for the benefit of the pupils. This case, therefore, wholly without constitutional reasons in my judgment, subjects all the public schools in the country to the whims and caprices of their loudest-mouthed, but maybe not their brightest, students. I, for one, am not fully persuaded that school pupils are wise enough, even with this Court's expert help from Washington, to run the 23,390 public school systems' in our 50 States. I wish, therefore, wholly to disclaim any purpose on my part, to hold that the Federal Constitution compels the teachers, parents, and elected school officials to surrender control of the American public school system to public school students. I dissent.

Mr. Justice Harlan, dissenting:

I certainly agree that state public school authorities in the discharge of their responsibilities are not wholly exempt from the requirements of the Fourteenth Amendment respecting the freedoms of expression and association. At the same time I am reluctant to believe that there is any disagreement between the majority and myself on the proposition that school officials should be accorded the widest authority in maintaining discipline and good order in their institutions. To translate that proposition into a workable constitutional rule, I would, in cases like this, cast upon those complaining the burden of showing that a particular school measure was motivated by other than legitimate school concerns—for example, a desire to prohibit the expression of an unpopular point of view, while permitting expression of the dominant opinion.

Finding nothing in this record which impugns the good faith of respondents in promulgating the arm band regulation, I would affirm the judgment below.

STREET *v.* NEW YORK
394 US 576 (1969)

[Defendant was convicted of public desecration of the American flag. The conviction was reversed by 5–4 vote. Justice Harlan in his opinion for the majority took the position that the conviction may have been based on the words used by Street as well as on the fact that he publicly burned the flag. His words, however, were protected by the First Amendment, even though they may have been contemptuous of the flag. Chief Justice Warren, and Justices Black, White, and Fortas each wrote a dissenting opinion. They disagreed with the majority that the conviction was in part based on Street's spoken words and stated that they would have upheld the constitutionality of the flag desecration statute and the conviction thereunder.]

Mr. Justice Harlan delivered the opinion of the Court:

Appellant Street has been convicted in the New York courts of violating former § 1425(16)(d) of the New York Penal Law, McKinney's *Consol.Laws,* c. 40, which makes it a misdemeanor "publicly [to] mutilate, deface, defile, or defy, trample upon, or cast contempt upon either by words or act [any flag of the United States]."* He was given a suspended sentence. We must decide whether, in light of all the circumstances, that conviction denied to him rights of free expression protected by the First Amendment and assured against state infringement by the Fourteenth Amendment. . . .

According to evidence given at trial, the events which led to the conviction were these. Appellant testified that during the afternoon of June 6, 1966, he was listening to the radio in his Brooklyn apartment. He heard a news report that civil rights leader James Meredith had been shot by a sniper in Mississippi. Saying to himself, "They didn't protect him," appellant, himself a Negro, took from his drawer a neatly folded, 48-star American flag which he formerly had displayed on national holidays. Appellant left his apartment and carried the still-folded flag to the nearby intersection of St. James Place and Lafayette Avenue. Appellant stood on the northeast corner of the intersection, lit the flag with a match, and dropped the flag on the pavement when it began to burn.

---

* N.Y.Penal Law § 1425(16)(d) (1909). In 1967 § 1425(16)(d) was superseded by § 136 of the General Business Law, *McKinney's Consol.Laws,* c. 20, which defines the offense in identical language. See N.Y.Laws, c. 1031, § 52 (1965).

Soon thereafter, a police officer halted his patrol car and found the burning flag. The officer testified that he then crossed to the northwest corner of the intersection, where he found appellant "talking out loud" to a small group of persons. The officer estimated that there were some 30 persons on the corner near the flag and five to 10 on the corner with appellant. The officer testified that as he approached within 10 or 15 feet of appellant, he heard appellant say, "We don't need no damn flag," and that when he asked appellant whether he had burned the flag appellant replied: "Yes, that is my flag; I burned it. If they let that happen to Meredith, we don't need an American flag." Appellant admitted making the latter response, but he denied that he said anything else and asserted that he always had remained on the corner with the flag.

Later the same day, appellant was charged, by an information sworn to before a judge of the New York City Criminal Court, with having committed "the crime of Malicious Mischief in that [he] did willfully and unlawfully defile, cast contempt upon and burn an American Flag, in violation of 1425–16–D of the Penal Law, under the following circumstances: . . . [he] did willfully and unlawfully set fire to an American Flag and shout, 'If they did that to Meredith, we don't need an American Flag.' "

Appellant was tried before another Criminal Court judge, sitting without a jury, and was convicted of malicious mischief in violation of § 1425(16)(d). He was subsequently given a suspended sentence. The Appellate Division, Second Department, affirmed without opinion. Leave was granted to appeal to the New York Court of Appeals, and after plenary consideration that court unanimously affirmed. We noted probable jurisdiction.

Street argues that his conviction was unconstitutional for three different reasons. *First,* he claims that § 1425(16)(d) is overbroad, both on its face and as applied, because the section makes it a crime "publicly [to] defy . . . or cast contempt upon [an American flag] *by words.* . . ." (Emphasis added.) *Second,* he contends that § 1425(16)(d) is vague and imprecise because it does not clearly define the conduct which it forbids. *Third,* he asserts that New York may not constitutionally punish one who publicly destroys or damages an American flag as a means of protest, because such an act constitutes expression protected by the Fourteenth Amendment. We deem it unnecessary to consider the latter two arguments, for we hold that § 1425(16)(d) was unconstitutionally applied in appellant's case because it permitted him to be punished merely for speaking defiant or contemptuous words about the American flag. In taking this course, we resist the pulls to decide the constitutional issues involved in this case on a broader basis than the record before us imperatively requires.

Though our conclusion is a narrow one, it requires pursuit of four lines of inquiry: (1) whether the constitutionality of the "words" part of the statute was passed upon by the New York Court of Appeals; (2) whether, if appellant's conviction may have rested in whole or in part on his utterances and if the statute as thus applied is unconstitutional, these factors in themselves require reversal; (3) whether Street's words may in fact have counted independently in his conviction; and (4) whether the "words" provision of the statute, as presented by this case, is unconstitutional. . . .

III

We turn to considering whether appellant's words could have been the sole cause of his conviction, or whether the conviction could have been based on both his words and his burning of the flag. As *Stromberg* teaches, we cannot take the opinion of the New York Court of Appeals as obviating our duty to examine the record for ourselves in order to ascertain whether the conviction may have rested upon such grounds. The sworn information which charged appellant with the crime of malicious mischief, . . . recited not only that appellant had burned an American flag but also that he "[did] shout, 'If they did that to Meredith, we don't need an American flag.'" Section 1425(16)(d), the statute which appellant was charged with violating, made it a crime not only publicly to mutilate a flag but also "publicly [to] defy . . . or cast contempt upon [any American flag] by words."

The State argues that appellant's words were at most used to establish his unlawful intent in burning the flag. However, after a careful examination of the comparatively brief trial record, we find ourselves unable to say with certainty that appellant's words were not an independent cause of his conviction. While it is true that at trial greater emphasis was placed upon appellant's action in burning the flag than upon his words, a police officer did testify to the utterance of the words. The State never announced that it was relying exclusively upon the burning. The trial judge never indicated during the trial that he regarded appellant's words as relating solely to intent. The judge found appellant guilty immediately after the end of the trial, and he delivered no oral or written opinion.

In the face of an information explicitly setting forth appellant's words as an element of his alleged crime, and of appellant's subsequent conviction under a statute making it an offense to speak words of that sort, we find this record insufficient to eliminate the possibility either that appellant's words were the sole basis of his conviction or that appellant was convicted for both his words and his deed.

IV

We come finally to the question whether, in the circumstances of this case, New York may constitutionally inflict criminal punishment upon one who ventures "publicly [to] defy . . . or cast contempt upon [any American flag] by words. . . ."

The relevant evidence introduced at appellant's trial, considered in the light most favorable to the State, must be taken to establish the following. At the time of his arrest, appellant was standing on a street corner and speaking to a small crowd; on the opposite corner lay the burning flag. Appellant said to the crowd: "We don't need no damn flag"; and when questioned by a police officer appellant stated: "If they let that happen to Meredith, we don't need an American flag." According to the officer, the crowds which gathered around appellant and around the flag did not obstruct the street or sidewalk and were neither unruly nor threatening.

In these circumstances, we can think of four governmental interests which might conceivably have been furthered by punishing appellant for his words: (1) an interest in deterring appellant from vocally inciting others to commit unlawful acts; (2) an interest in preventing appellant from uttering words so inflammatory that they would provoke others to retaliate physically against him, thereby causing a breach of the peace; (3) an interest in protecting the sensibilities of passers-by who might be shocked by appellant's words about the American flag; and (4) an interest in assuring that appellant, regardless of the impact of his words upon others, showed proper respect for our national emblem.

In the circumstances of this case, we do not believe that any of these interests may constitutionally justify appellant's conviction under § 1425(16)(d) for speaking as he did. We begin with the interest in preventing incitement. Appellant's words, taken alone, did not urge anyone to do anything unlawful. They amounted only to somewhat excited public advocacy of the idea that the United States should abandon, at least temporarily, one of its national symbols. It is clear that the Fourteenth Amendment prohibits the States from imposing criminal punishment for public advocacy of peaceful change in our institutions. . . . Even assuming that appellant's words might be found incitive when considered together with his simultaneous burning of the flag, § 1425(16)(d) does not purport to punish only those defiant or contemptuous words which amount to incitement, and there is no evidence that the state courts regarded the statute as so limited. Hence, a conviction for words could not be upheld on this basis. . . .

Nor could such a conviction be justified on the second ground mentioned above: the possible tendency of appellant's words to provoke violent retaliation. Though it is conceivable that some listeners might have been moved to retaliate upon hearing appellant's disrespectful words, we cannot say that appellant's remarks were so inherently inflammatory as to come within that small class of "fighting words" which are "likely to provoke the average person to retaliation, and thereby cause a breach of the peace." *Chaplinsky* v. *New Hampshire,* 315 US 568, 574 (1942). And even if appellant's words might be found within that category, § 1425(16)(d) is not narrowly drawn to punish only words of that character, and there is no indication that it was so interpreted by the state courts. Hence, this case is again distinguishable from *Chaplinsky, supra,* in which the Court emphasized that the statute was "carefully drawn so as not unduly to impair liberty of expression. . . ."

Again, such a conviction could not be sustained on the ground that appellant's words were likely to shock passers-by. Except perhaps for appellant's incidental use of the word "damn," upon which no emphasis was placed at trial, any shock effect of appellant's speech must be attributed to the content of the ideas expressed. It is firmly settled that under our Constitution the public expression of ideas may not be prohibited merely because the ideas are themselves offensive to some of their hearers. And even if such a conviction might be upheld on the ground of "shock," there is again no indication that the state courts regarded the statute as limited to that purpose.

Finally, such a conviction could not be supported on the theory that by making the above-quoted remarks about the flag appellant failed to show the respect for our national symbol which may properly be demanded of every citizen. In *West Virginia State Board of Educ.* v. *Barnette,* 319 US 624 (1943), this Court held that to require unwilling schoolchildren to salute the flag would violate rights of free expression assured by the Fourteenth Amendment. In his opinion for the Court, Mr. Justice Jackson wrote words which are especially apposite here:

The case is made difficult not because the principles of its decision are obscure but because the flag involved is our own. Nevertheless, we apply the limitations of the Constitution with no fear that freedom to be intellectually and spiritually diverse or even contrary will disintegrate the social organization. . . . [F]reedom to differ is not limited to things that do not matter much. That would be a mere shadow of freedom. The test of its substance is the right to differ as to things that touch the heart of the existing order.

If there is any fixed star in our constitutional constellation, it is that no official, high or petty, can prescribe what shall be orthodox in politics, nationalism, religion, or other matters of opinion or force citizens to confess by word or act their faith therein. If there are any circumstances which permit an exception, they do not now occur to us.

We have no doubt that the constitutionally guaranteed "freedom to be intellectually . . . diverse and even contrary," and the "right to differ as to things that touch the heart of the existing order," encompass the freedom to express publicly one's opinions about our flag, including those opinions which are defiant or contemptuous.

Since appellant could not constitutionally be punished under § 1425(16)(d) for his speech, and since we have found that he may have been so punished, his conviction cannot be permitted to stand. In so holding, we reiterate that we have no occasion to pass upon the validity of this conviction insofar as it was sustained by the state courts on the basis that Street could be punished for his burning of the flag, even though the burning was an act of protest. Nor do we perceive any basis for our Brother White's fears that our decision today may be taken to require reversal whenever a defendant is convicted for burning a flag in protest, following a trial at which his words have been introduced to prove some element of that offense. Assuming that such a conviction would otherwise pass constitutional muster, a matter about which we express no view, nothing in this opinion would render the conviction impermissible merely because an element of the crime was proved by the defendant's words rather than in some other way. . . .

We add that disrespect for our flag is to be deplored no less in these vexed times than in calmer periods of our history. . . . Nevertheless, we are unable to sustain a conviction that may have rested on a form of expression, however distasteful, which the Constitution tolerates and protects.

For the reasons previously set forth, we reverse the judgment of the New York Court of Appeals and remand the case for further proceedings not inconsistent with this opinion.

It is so ordered.

Reversed and remanded.

Mr. Chief Justice Warren, dissenting:

I dissent from the reversal of this judgment, not only because the Court in my opinion has strained to bring this trial within *Stromberg* v. *California,* 283 US 359 (1931), but more particularly because it has declined to meet and resolve the basic question presented in the case. That question has been variously stated by the New York Court of Appeals and the parties. The court below employed the following statement of the question:

> We are called upon to decide whether the deliberate act of burning an American flag in public as a "protest" may be punished as a crime.

Appellant tells us that the issue presented is:

> May New York State constitutionally impose penal sanctions upon an individual charged with destroying or damaging an American flag in an attempt to dramatize his concern with social conditions existing in the country?

New York's statement of the issue is identical:

> May the State of New York constitutionally impose penal sanctions upon one who is charged with publicly and deliberately desecrating an American flag as a means of dramatizing his dissatisfaction with social conditions existing within our Country?

Any distinctions between the above questions are without a significant difference. The parties obviously believe that the constitutionality of flag desecration statutes is before the Court. The question posed by the Court of Appeals is the most succinct. Chief Judge Fuld, writing for a unanimous Court of Appeals, answered the question squarely; we should do likewise if we are to meet our responsibility. But the Court specifically refuses to decide this issue. Instead, it searches microscopically for the opportunity to decide the case on the peripheral *Stromberg* ground, holding that it is impossible to determine the basis for appellant's conviction. In my opinion a reading of the short trial record leaves no doubt that appellant was convicted solely for burning the American flag.

I

From the beginning to the end of the proceedings below the parties placed only two matters in issue: (1) is burning the flag protected symbolic speech, and (2) did appellant burn the flag for the purpose of casting contempt upon it or did he burn it in a dignified manner? The information alleged that "Sidney Street did commit the crime of Malicious Mischief in that the defendant did willfully and unlawfully defile, cast contempt upon and burn an American Flag, in violation of 1425–16–D of the Penal Law, under the following circumstances: On the aforesaid date, place and time, the defendant did willfully and unlawfully set fire to an American Flag and shout, 'If they did that to Meredith, we don't need an American Flag.'" Although the Court stresses the mention of appellant's words in the information as indicative that he was convicted for uttering these words, the trial proceedings demonstrate that the words were employed only to show appellant's purpose for burning the flag.

At the outset of the trial appellant's counsel moved to dismiss the indictment, clearly revealing the theory of appellant's defense that flag burning is constitutionally protected and that appellant burned the flag in a dignified manner.

> Mr. Goldstick [appellant's counsel]: "Before we plead to this case I would like to make a motion to dismiss the information upon the ground it does not state facts to constitute a crime on the following grounds: The defendant was engaged in a constitutionally protected activity, to wit, freedom of speech. The allegation simply says that the defendant did willfully and unlawfully set fire to an American flag and did say: 'If they did that to Meredith, we don't need an American flag.' Under the first amendment of the Constitution of the United States and under the New York State Constitution on freedom of speech they provide for protest in many forms, whether it be by *burning a flag*, demonstration or picketing. This is a form of demonstration and protest."
>
> Court: "You say *burning the flag* is a form of demonstration?"
>
> Mr. Goldstick: "Yes."
>
> Court: "Motion denied."

Mr. Goldstick: "Also, there is a Federal statute which provides for *burning the flag*. I refer Your Honor ——"

Court, interposing: "So does Section 1425 provide for the lawful disposition of a flag!"

Mr. Goldstick, continuing: "I refer Your Honor to page 6 of my brief, referring to the United States Code that a flag, when it is in such a condition that it is no longer a fitting emblem for display, should be destroyed in a dignified way, preferably by *burning*."

"Now, under the supremacy clause, if there is any conflict with any statute the Federal statute takes precedence; if a State law is in conflict with a Federal law the Federal law takes precedence. The Federal law provides you may *burn* an American flag; therefore, New York State is without power to make a complaint and convict a man for the *burning* of an American flag."

Court: "Motions denied. The question here would be whether he *burned* it because it was in such poor condition that it should be *burned*, or if it was an illegal demonstration." (Emphasis added).

Defense counsel insisted that burning the flag, an act he equated with a demonstration or picketing, was a form of speech for which his client could not be constitutionally punished. His colloquy with the trial judge does not give even the slightest suggestion that appellant was being prosecuted for words he might have spoken. The defense counsel belief that appellant's act, not his words, was at issue is further demonstrated by counsel's pre-emption argument. The federal statute to which counsel referred, 36 U.S.C. § 176(j), concerns the manner in which the flag is to be displayed and mandates that the flag, when no longer a fitting emblem for display, should be destroyed in a dignified way, preferably by burning. At the time of appellant's trial the federal prohibition of flag desecration, which in all material particulars was identical to New York's, applied only to the District of Columbia and could therefore not have pre-empted state legislation on the same subject.*

The trial testimony confirms my belief that appellant's act was the sole basis for the verdict as it contains nothing to suggest that either the parties or the trial judge believed that appellant was on trial for his words. The arresting officer testified that, as he was investigating the source of a fire, he heard appellant say, "We don't need no damn flag." The officer then asked appellant whether he was responsible for the burning of the flag; appellant replied that he was and that "If they let that happen to Meredith, we don't need an American flag." The officer's testimony concluded with a description of the number of people in the vicinity and the extinguishing of the fire. During cross-examination of the officer, defense counsel asked not one question concerning what, if anything, appellant said.

Appellant did not dispute the prosecution's version of the facts. He testified that, hearing the news report of Meredith's shooting, he removed a flag from his dresser drawer, walked to the corner of St. James Place and Lafayette Avenue and burned the flag. According to appellant, he made no remarks to the crowd that had gathered and his reference to Meredith was made to the police officer. Cross-examination by the prosecution explored appellant's motivation for burning the flag; no mention was made of words appellant might have spoken.

We are told by the Court that at least in part appellant's conviction rests on his words.

* See 4 U.S.C. § 3 (1964 ed.). Federal legislation enacting flag desecration prohibitions on a national scope was not passed until July 5, 1968, two years after appellant's trial. This legislation specifically does not pre-empt state flag-burning statutes. See 82 Stat. 291, 18 U.S.C. § 700(c).

If it does, the trial record is strangely silent, for the State made no attempt to prove that appellant's words were heard by the crowd. Appellant insisted that he spoke only to the officer, yet the New York statute requires that the accused's flag desecration be public. The State argues, without contradiction by appellant, that words spoken to a policeman would not be spoken publicly for purposes of the statute. I think it evident that appellant's words were mentioned in the indictment and introduced at trial only to show that he burned the flag with an intent to desecrate it, a necessary element of the State's case. In the absence of such evidence, the State would have proven that appellant burned a flag but have left open the possibility that the burning was designed to destroy it in a dignified manner. The fact that appellant's words supplied an element of the State's case does not mean that he was convicted for uttering these words. . . .

Neither the prosecution nor the defense nor the New York courts attached any independent significance to his words. To interpret this record in any other manner ignores the very basic fact that the trial judge and the parties thought that there was one issue in this trial—whether appellant could be criminally punished for burning the flag. This record is not sufficiently ambiguous to justify the Court's speculation that the verdict below might rest even in part upon a conviction for appellant's words.

II

I do not believe that the *Stromberg* line of cases allows us to avoid deciding whether flag burning is protected by the First Amendment. This case does not fit the *Stromberg* mold.

Miss Stromberg was one of the supervisors of a children's summer camp. She directed a daily ceremony during which the children raised the Soviet flag and recited a pledge of allegiance "to the worker's red flag." A California statute made it a criminal offense for any person to display a red flag (1) as a symbol of opposition to organized government or (2) as an invitation to anarchistic action or (3) as an aid to propaganda of a seditious character. The trial judge, following the express terms of the statute, charged that Miss Stromberg could be convicted if she displayed a red flag for any one of the three prohibited purposes. The Court first determined that a criminal conviction for display of a red flag as a symbol of opposition to organized government would impinge upon First Amendment freedoms. Since the jury charge was disjunctive, *i. e.*, Miss Stromberg could be convicted if the jury found that she conducted the ceremony for any of the three statutorily prohibited goals, it was possible that her conviction rested totally upon an act entitled to constitutional protection. Presumably, given the jury's general verdict, it could have convicted Miss Stromberg for raising a red flag solely as a symbol of opposition to organized government but not as either an invitation to anarchistic action or an aid to propaganda of a seditious character.

The teaching of *Stromberg* is that, if there is any possibility the general verdict below rests on speech or conduct entitled to constitutional protection, then the conviction must be reversed. The *Stromberg* analysis cannot be applied to appellant's conviction, as the factual patterns in the two cases are distinct. The record leaves no doubt that appellant did burn the flag. Nor can appellant argue that his act was not an act of desecration. The trial judge emphatically stated that the issue was whether appellant burned the flag to destroy it in a dignified manner or to cast contempt upon it. Appellant's conviction therefore must be based upon a finding that he desecrated the flag by burning and neither he nor the Court suggests otherwise. We are not confronted with a jury trial and the consequent inability to determine the basis for the verdict below. The trial judge at the very outset of the trial made known his view that appellant's motivation for burning the flag was the probative issue. Combining this act of burning with a verbalization of the reasons for it does not allow the Court to avoid determining the constitutionality of appellant's conduct. Since there can be no claim that appellant was convicted for his speech, *Stromberg* simply does not apply. . . .

I reiterate my belief that appellant was convicted for his act not his words. *Stromberg* and the cases based upon it do not allow us the luxury of refusing to treat appellant's claim that the burning of the flag as a protest is worthy of constitutional protection.

III

I am in complete agreement with the general rule that this Court should not treat broad constitutional questions when narrow ones will suffice to dispose of the litigation. However, where only the broad question is presented, it is our task and our responsibility to confront that question squarely and resolve it. In a time when the American flag has increasingly become an integral part of public protests, the constitutionality of the flag desecration statutes enacted by all of the States and Congress is a matter of the most widespread concern. Both those who seek constitutional shelter for acts of flag desecration perpetrated in the course of a political protest and those who must enforce the law are entitled to know the scope of constitutional protection. The Court's explicit reservation of the constitutionality of flag-burning prohibitions encourages others to test in the streets the power of our States and national government to impose criminal sanctions upon those who would desecrate the flag.

I believe that the States and the Federal Government do have the power to protect the flag from acts of desecration and disgrace. But because the Court has not met the issue, it would serve no purpose to delineate my reasons for this view. However, it is difficult for me to imagine that, had the Court faced this issue, it would have concluded otherwise. Since I am satisfied that the constitutionality of appellant's conduct should be resolved in this case and am convinced that this conduct can be criminally punished, I dissent.

Mr. Justice Black, dissenting:

I agree with the excellent opinion written by Chief Judge Fuld for a unanimous Court of Appeals, upholding the New York statute which this Court now holds unconstitutional as applied. The entire state court construed the statute as applied to this appellant as making it an offense publicly to burn an American flag in order to protest something that had occurred. In other words the offense which that court sustained was the burning of the flag and not the making of any statements about it. The Court seems to console itself for holding this New York flag-burning law unconstitutional as applied by saying that, as it reads the record, the conviction could have been based on the words spoken by the appellant as he was burning the flag. Those words indicated a desire on appellant's part to degrade and defame the flag. If I could agree with the Court's interpretation of the record as to the possibility of the conviction's resting on these spoken words, I would firmly and automatically agree that the law is unconstitutional. I would not feel constrained, as the Court seems to be, to search my imagination to see if I could think of interests the State may have in suppressing this freedom of speech. I would not balance away the First Amendment right that speech not be abridged in any fashion whatsoever. But I accept the unanimous opinion of the New York Court of Appeals that the conviction does not and could not have rested merely on the spoken words but that it rested entirely on the fact that the defendant had publicly burned the American flag—against the law of the State of New York.

It passes my belief that anything in the Federal Constitution bars a State from making the deliberate burning of the American flag an offense. It is immaterial to me that words are spoken in connection with the *burning*. It is the *burning* of the flag that the State has set its face against. "It rarely has been suggested that the constitutional freedom for speech and press extends its immunity to speech or writing used as an integral part of conduct in violation of a valid criminal statute." *Giboney* v. *Empire Storage Co.,* 336 US 490 (1949). In my view this quotation from the *Giboney* case precisely applies here. The talking that was done took place "as an integral part of conduct in violation of a valid criminal statute" against burning the American flag in public. I would therefore affirm this conviction.

Mr. Justice White, dissenting:

The Court has spun an intricate, technical web, but I fear it has ensnared itself in its own remorseless logic and arrived at a result having no support in the facts of the case or the governing law.

The Court's schema is this: the statute forbids insults to the flag either by act or words; the charge alleged both flag burning and speech; the Court rendered a general judgment; since the conviction might logically have been for speech alone or for both words and deeds and since in either event the conviction is invalid, the judgment of the New York courts must be set aside without passing upon the validity of a conviction for burning the flag. I reach precisely the opposite conclusion; before Street's conviction can either be reversed or affirmed, the Court *must* reach and decide the validity of a conviction for flag burning.

I reject first the Court's suggestion that we must assume from the trial court's judgment—which was that "on the charge of Malicious Mischief the defendant is convicted" —that Street might have been convicted for speech alone. True, the complaint referred to both burning and speaking, and the statute permits conviction for either insulting words or physical desecration. But surely the Court has its tongue in its cheek when it infers from this record the possibility that Street was not convicted for burning the flag but only for the words he uttered. It is a distortion of the record to read it in this manner, as The Chief Justice convincingly demonstrates. But even if it were fair to infer that he was convicted for speaking as well as burning, it is sheer fancy to conclude that the trial court convicted him for speech alone and acquitted him of flag burning. The appellant does not seriously argue such a claim; his major point is that he *was* convicted for burning as a protest and that such a conviction cannot stand. The Court of Appeals of New York characterized the issue before it as whether the defendant could be validly convicted for burning the flag as a protest. Moreover, without clear indication from the state courts, I would not assume that the particular words which Street spoke in this case would be deemed within the coverage of the statute. In any event, if Street was convicted for speaking, he most certainly was also convicted for flag burning. Hence, *Stromberg* v. *California,* and like cases to which I adhere, have no application by their own terms. . . .

Mr. Justice Fortas, dissenting:

I agree with the dissenting opinion filed by The Chief Justice, but I believe that it is necessary briefly to set forth the reasons why the States and the Federal Government have the power to protect the flag from acts of desecration committed in public.

If the national flag were nothing more than a chattel, subject only to the rules governing the use of private personality, its use would nevertheless be subject to certain types of state regulation. For example, regulations concerning the use of chattels which are reasonably designed to avoid danger to life or property, or impingement upon the rights of others to the quiet use of their property and of public facilities, would unquestionably be a valid exercise of police power. They would not necessarily be defeated by a claim that they conflicted with the rights of the owner of the regulated property. . . .

If a state statute provided that it is a misdemeanor to burn one's shirt or trousers or shoes on the public thoroughfare, it could hardly be asserted that the citizen's constitutional right is violated. If the arsonist asserted that he was burning his shirt or trousers or shoes as a protest against the Government's fiscal policies, for example, it is hardly possible that his claim to First Amendment shelter would prevail against the State's claim of a right to avert danger to the public and to avoid obstruction to traffic as a result of the fire. This is because action, even if clearly for serious protest purposes, is not entitled to the pervasive protection that is given to speech alone. . . . It may be subjected to reasonable regulation that appropriately takes into account the competing interests involved.

The test that is applicable in every case where conduct is restricted or prohibited is whether the regulation or prohibition is reasonable, due account being taken of the paramountcy of First Amendment values. If, as I submit, it is permissible to prohibit the burning of personal property on the public sidewalk, there is no basis for applying a different rule to flag burning. And the fact that the law is violated for purposes of protest does not immunize the violator. . . .

Beyond this, however, the flag is a special kind of personality. Its use is traditionally and universally subject to special rules and regulation. As early as 1907, this Court affirmed the constitutionality of a state statute making it a crime to use a representation of the United States flag for purposes of advertising. . . . Statutes prescribe how the flag may be displayed; how it may lawfully be disposed of; when, how, and for what purposes it may and may not be used. . . . A person may "own" a flag, but ownership is subject to special burdens and responsibilities. A flag may be property, in a sense; but it is property burdened with peculiar obligations and restrictions. Certainly, . . . these special conditions are not *per se* arbitrary or beyond governmental power under our Constitution.

One may not justify the burning of a house, even if it is his own, on the ground, however sincere, that he does so as a protest. One may not justify breaking the windows of a government building on that basis. Protest does not exonerate lawlessness. And the prohibition against flag burning on the public thoroughfare being valid, the misdemeanor is not excused merely because it is an act of flamboyant protest.

8. *Peaceful Picketing: The Speech-Action Complex*

GIBONEY v. EMPIRE STORAGE & ICE CO.
336 US 490 (1948)

[The right to strike has been given no constitutional foundation. The right to picket, however, has been afforded limited constitutional claims. In *Thornhill* v. *Alabama,* 310 US 88 (1940), the Supreme Court held that a state statute which prohibited all peaceful picketing was unconstitutional. But before long, decisions whittled down this broad holding. In the instant case, a union, seeking to organize peddlers, picketed a wholesale dealer in order to induce it to refrain from selling to nonunion peddlers. The state courts found that such an agreement between the union and the wholesale dealer would constitute a conspiracy in restraint of trade, in violation of the state's antitrust laws, and therefore enjoined the picketing. The

Supreme Court affirmed unanimously. The union, said the Court, was doing more than exercising a right of free speech. It was exercising its economic power to compel the wholesale dealer to abide by the union rather than by the state policy and law. The Court's opinion was by Justice Black. Cf. *International Brotherhood of Teamsters* v. *Vogt*, 354 US 284 (1957).]

Mr. Justice Black delivered the opinion of the Court:

This case here on appeal . . . raises questions concerning the constitutional power of a state to apply its antitrade restraint law to labor union activities, and to enjoin union members from peaceful picketing carried on as an essential and inseparable part of a course of conduct which is in violation of the state law. The picketing occurred in Kansas City, Missouri. The injunction was issued by a Missouri state court.

The appellants are members and officers of the Ice and Coal Drivers and Handlers Local Union No. 953, affiliated with the American Federation of Labor. Its membership includes about 160 of 200 retail ice peddlers who drive their own trucks in selling ice from door to door in Kansas City. The union began efforts to induce all the nonunion peddlers to join. One objective of the organizational drive was to better wage and working conditions of peddlers and their helpers. Most of the nonunion peddlers refused to join the union. To break down their resistance, the union adopted a plan which was designed to make it impossible for nonunion peddlers to buy ice to supply their retail customers in Kansas City. Pursuant to the plan the union set about to obtain from all Kansas City wholesale ice distributors agreements that they would not sell ice to nonunion peddlers. Agreements were obtained from all distributors except the appellee, Empire Storage and Ice Company. Empire refused to agree. The union thereupon informed Empire that it would use other means at its disposal to force Empire to come around to the union view. Empire still refused to agree. Its place of business was promptly picketed by union members although the only complaint registered against Empire, as indicated by placards carried by the pickets, was its continued sale of ice to nonunion peddlers.

Thus the avowed immediate purpose of the picketing was to compel Empire to agree to stop selling ice to nonunion peddlers. Missouri statutes, . . . make such an agreement a crime punishable by a fine of not more than $5,000 and by imprisonment in the penitentiary for not more than five years. Furthermore, had Empire made the agreement, the ice peddlers could have brought actions for triple damages for any injuries they sustained as a result of the agreement under Sec. 8308 of the Missouri Revised Statutes (1939).

About 85 percent of the truck drivers working for Empire's customers were members of labor unions. These union truck drivers refused to deliver goods to or from Empire's place of business. Had any one of them crossed the picket line he would have been subject to fine or suspension by the union of which he was a member. . . .

The trial court heard evidence, made findings and issued an injunction restraining the appellant from "placing pickets or picketing around or about the buildings" of Empire.

The State Supreme Court affirmed.

Attacking the Missouri statute as construed and applied, appellants broadly challenge the power of the state to issue any injunction against their conduct since, they assert, the primary objective of their combination and picketing was to improve wage and working conditions. On this premise they argue that their right to combine, to picket, and to publish must be determined by focusing attention exclusively upon their lawful purpose to improve labor conditions, and that their violation of the state antitrade restraint laws must be dismissed as merely incidental to this lawful purpose.

First. That states have constitutional power to prohibit competing dealers and their aiders and abettors from combining to restrain freedom of trade is beyond question. . . .

Second. It is contended that though the Missouri statute can be applied validly to combinations of businessmen who agree not to sell to certain persons, it cannot be applied constitutionally to combinations of union workers who agree in their self-interest to use their joint power to prevent sales to nonunion workers. This contention appears to be grounded on the guaranties of freedom of speech and press stemming from the Fourteenth and First Amendments. Aside from the element of disseminating information through peaceful picketers, later discussed, it is difficult to perceive how it could be thought that these constitutional guaranties afford labor union members a peculiar immunity from laws against trade restraint combinations; unless, as appellants contend, labor unions are given special constitutional protection denied all other people.

The objective of unions to improve wages and working conditions has sometimes commended itself to Congress and to state legislatures. To the extent that the state or Congress, for this or other reasons, have seen fit to exempt unions from antitrust laws, this Court has sustained legislative power to grant the exemptions. . . . On the other hand, where statutes have not granted exemptions, we have declared that violations of antitrust laws could not be defended on the ground that a particular accused combination would not injure but would actually help manufacturers, laborers, retailers, consumers, or the public in general. . . .

Third. It is contended that the injunction against picketing adjacent to Empire's place of business is an unconstitutional abridgment of free speech because the picketers were attempting peacefully to publicize truthful facts about a labor dispute. . . . But the record does not permit this publicizing to be treated in isolation. For according to the pleadings, the evidence, the findings, and the argument of the appellants, the sole immediate object of the publicizing adjacent to the premises of Empire, as well as the other activities of the appellants and their allies, was to compel Empire to agree to stop selling ice to nonunion peddlers. Thus all of appellants' activities—their powerful transportation combination, their patrolling, their formation of a picket line warning union men not to cross at peril of their union membership, their publicizing—constituted a single and integrated course of conduct, which was in violation of Missouri's valid law. In this situation, the injunction did no more than enjoin an offense against Missouri law, a felony. . . .

Neither *Thornhill* v. *Alabama,* 310 US 88, nor *Carlson* v. *California,* 310 US 106, both decided the same day, supports the contention that conduct otherwise unlawful is always immune from state regulation because an integral part of that conduct is carried on by display of placards by peaceful picketers. In both these cases this Court struck down statutes which banned all dissemination of information by people adjacent to certain premises, pointing out that the statutes were so broad that they could not only be utilized to punish conduct plainly illegal but could also be applied to ban all truthful publications of the facts of a labor controversy. . . .

We hold that the state's power to govern in this field is paramount, and that nothing in the constitutional guaranties of speech or press compels a state to apply or not to aply its antitrade restraint law to groups of workers, businessmen, or others. Of course this Court does not pass on the wisdom of the Missouri statute. We hold only that as here construed and applied it does not violate the Federal Constitution.

Affirmed.

9. Freedom of Anonymous Publication

TALLEY *v.* CALIFORNIA
362 US 60 (1960)

[A Los Angeles municipal ordinance made it a crime to distribute handbills that did not contain the names and addresses of the persons who prepared, distributed, or sponsored the handbills. By a 6-to-3 decision, the Supreme Court held this requirement unconstitutional. Justice Harlan wrote a concurring opinion. Justice Clark wrote a dissenting opinion, joined by Justices Frankfurter and Whittaker.]

Mr. Justice Black delivered the opinion of the Court:

The question presented here is whether the provisions of a Los Angeles City ordinance restricting the distribution of handbills "abridge the freedom of speech and of the press secured against state invasion by the Fourteenth Amendment of the Constitution." The ordinance, § 28.06 of the Municipal Code of the City of Los Angeles, provides:

No person shall distribute any hand-bill in any place under any circumstances, which does not have printed on the cover, or the face thereof, the name and address of the following:

(a) The person who printed, wrote, compiled or manufactured the same.

(b) The person who caused the same to be distributed; provided, however, that in the case of a fictitious person or club, in addition to such fictitious name, the true names and addresses of the owners, managers or agents of the person sponsoring said hand-bill shall also appear thereon.

The petitioner was arrested and tried in a Los Angeles Municipal Court for violating this ordinance. It was stipulated that the petitioner had distributed handbills in Los Angeles, and two of them were presented in evidence. Each had printed on it the following:

National Consumers Mobilization,
Box 6533,
Los Angeles 55, Calif.
PLeasant 9-1576.

The handbills urged readers to help the organization carry on a boycott against certain merchants and businessmen, whose names were given, on the ground that, as one set of handbills said, they carried products of "manufacturers who will not offer equal employment opportunities to Negroes, Mexicans, and Orientals." There also appeared a blank, which, if signed, would request enrollment of the signer as a "member of National Consumers Mobilization," and which was preceded by a statement that "I believe that every man should have an equal opportunity for employment no matter what his race, religion, or place of birth."

The Municipal Court held that the information printed on the handbills did not meet the requirements of the ordinance, found the petitioner guilty as charged, and fined him $10. The Appellate Department of the Superior Court of the County of Los Angeles affirmed the conviction, rejecting petitioner's contention, timely made in both state courts, that the ordinance invaded his freedom of speech and press in violation of the Fourteenth and First Amendments to the Federal Constitution. Since this was the highest state court available to petitioner, we granted certiorari to it to consider this constitutional contention.

In *Lovell* v. *Griffin,* 303 US 444, we held void on its face an ordinance that comprehensively forbade any distribution of literature at any time or place in Griffin, Georgia, without a license. Pamphlets and leaflets, it was pointed out, "have been historic weapons in the defense of liberty" and enforcement of the Griffin ordinance "would restore the system of license and censorship in its baldest form." A year later we had before us four ordinances each forbidding distribution of leaflets—one in Irving, New Jersey, one in Los Angeles, California, one in Milwaukee, Wisconsin, and one in Worcester, Massachusetts. *Schneider* v. *Irvington,* 308 US 147. Efforts were made to distinguish these four ordinances from the one held void in the *Griffin* case. The chief grounds urged for distinction were that the four ordinances had been passed to prevent either frauds, disorder, or littering, according to the records in these cases, and another ground urged was that two of the ordinances applied only to certain city areas. This Court refused to uphold the four ordinances on those grounds pointing out that there were other ways to accomplish these legitimate aims without abridging freedom of speech and press. Frauds, street littering and disorderly conduct could be denounced and punished as offenses, the Court said. Several years later we followed the *Griffin* and *Schneider* cases in striking down a Dallas, Texas, ordinance which was applied to prohibit the dissemination of information by the distribution of handbills. We said that although a city could punish any person for conduct on the streets if he violates a valid law, "one who is rightfully on a street . . . carries with him there as elsewhere the constitutional right to express his views in an orderly fashion . . . by handbills and literature as well as by the spoken words." *Jamison* v. *Texas,* 318 US 413.

The broad ordinance now before us, barring distribution of "any hand-bill in any place under any circumstances," falls precisely under the ban of our prior cases unless this ordinance is saved by the qualification that handbills can be distributed if they have printed on them the names and addresses of the persons who prepared, distributed or sponsored them. For, as in *Griffin,* the ordinance here is not limited to handbills whose content is "obscene or offensive to public morals or that advocates unlawful conduct." Counsel has urged that this ordinance is aimed at providing a way to identify those responsible for fraud, false advertising and libel. Yet the ordinance is in no manner so limited, nor have we been referred to any legislative history indicating such a purpose. Therefore we do not pass on the validity of an ordinance limited to prevent these or any other supposed evils. This ordinance simply bars all handbills under all circumstances anywhere that do not have the printed names and addresses on them in the place the ordinance requires.

There can be no doubt that such an identification requirement would tend to restrict freedom to distribute information and thereby freedom of expression. "Liberty of circulating is as essential to that freedom as liberty of publishing; indeed, without the circulation, the publication would be of little value." *Lovell* v. *Griffin,* 303 US 444.

Anonymous pamphlets, leaflets, brochures and even books have played an important role in the progress of mankind. Persecuted groups and sects from time to time throughout history have been able to criticize oppressive practices and laws either anonymously or not at all. The obnoxious press licensing law of England, which was also enforced on the Colonies, was due in part to the knowledge that exposure of the names of printers, writers and distributors would lessen the circulation of literature critical of the government. The old seditious libel cases in England show the length to which government had to go to find out who was responsible for books that were obnoxious to the rulers. John Lilburne was whipped, pilloried and fined for refusing to answer questions designed to get evidence to convict him or someone else for the secret distribution of books in England. Two Puritan ministers, John Penry and John Udall, were sentenced to death on charges that they were responsible for writing, printing or publishing books. Before the Revolutionary War colonial patriots frequently had to conceal their authorship or distribution of literature that easily could have brought down on them prosecutions by English controlled courts. Along about that time the Letters of Junius were written and the identity of their author is unknown to this day. Even the Federalist Papers, written in favor of the adoption of our Constitution, were published under fictitious names. It is plain that anonymity has sometimes been assumed for the most constructive purposes.

We have recently had occasion to hold in two cases that there are times and circumstances when States may not compel members of groups engaged in the dissemination of ideas to be publicly identified. *Bates* v. *Little Rock,* 361 US 516; *N.A.A.C.P.* v. *Alabama,* 357 US 449. The reason for those holdings was that identification and fear of reprisal might deter perfectly peaceful discussions of public matters of importance. This broad Los Angeles ordinance is subject to the same infirmity. We hold that it, like the Griffin, Georgia, ordinance, is void on its face.

The judgment of the Appellate Department of the Superior Court of the State of California is reversed and the cause is remanded to it for further proceedings not inconsistent with this opinion.

10. Taxes on Knowledge

GROSJEAN *v.* AMERICAN PRESS CO.
297 US 233 (1936)

[In 1712 Parliament imposed a tax on printed papers, pamphlets, and advertise-ments and required a stamp to be placed on every newspaper. Such taxes came to be known as "taxes on knowledge." The tax on pamphlets continued until 1833, on advertisements until 1852, and the stamp duty on newspapers until 1855. The effect of these duties was to restrict circulation of printed matter among the rela-tively poor.

[Pointing out that the American Revolution began in effect when England started to send stamps for newspaper duties to the American colonies, the Court in the present case unanimously condemned as unconstitutional any device that falls within the category of "taxes on knowledge." The decision has been followed in later cases; e.g., *Follett* v. *McCormick,* 321 US 573 (1944), in which the Court ex-tended the prohibition to a tax on the exercise of religion.]

Mr. Justice Sutherland delivered the opinion of the Court:

This suit was brought by appellees, nine publishers of newspapers in the State of Louisiana, to enjoin the enforcement against them of the provisions of § 1 of the act the legislature of Louisiana known as Act No. 23, passed and approved July 12, 1934, as follows:

That every person, firm, association or corporation, domestic or foreign, engaged in the business of selling, or making any charge for, advertising or for advertisements, whether printed or published, or to be printed or published, in any newspaper, magazine, periodical or publication whatever having a circulation of more than 20,000 copies per week, or displayed and exhibited, or to be displayed and exhibited by means of moving pictures, in the State of Louisiana, shall, in addition to all other taxes and licenses levied and assessed in this State, pay a license tax for the privilege of engaging in such business in this State of two per cent (2%) of the gross receipts of such business.

The nine publishers who brought the suit publish thirteen newspapers; and these thirteen publications are the only ones within the State of Louisiana having each a circulation of more than 20,000 copies per week, although the lower court finds there are four other daily newspapers each having a circulation of "slightly less than 20,000 copies per week" which are in competition with those published by appellees both as to circulation and as to advertising. In addition, there are 120 weekly newspapers published in the state, also in competition, to a greater or less degree, with the newspapers of appellees. The revenue derived from appellees' newspapers comes almost entirely from regular subscribers or purchasers thereof and from payments received for the insertion of advertisements therein.

The act requires everyone subject to the tax to file a sworn report every three months showing the amount and the gross receipts from the business described in § 1. The resulting tax must be paid when the report is filed. Failure to file the re-port or pay the tax as thus provided constitutes a misdemeanor and subjects the offender to a fine not exceeding $500, or imprisonment not exceeding six months, or both, for each violation. Any corporation violating the act subjects itself to the payment of $500 to be recovered by suit. . . .

The validity of the act is assailed as violating the federal Constitution in two particulars—(1) that it abridges the freedom of the press in contravention of the due process clause contained in § 1 of the Fourteenth Amendment; (2) that it denies appellees the equal protection of the laws in contravention of the same Amendment.

1. The first point presents a question of the utmost gravity and importance; for, if well made, it goes to the heart of the natural right of the members of an organized society, united for their common good, to impart and acquire information about their common interests. The First Amendment to the federal Constitution provides that "Congress shall make no law . . . abridging the freedom of speech, or of the press. . . ." While this provision is not a restraint upon the powers of the states, the states are precluded from abridging the freedom of speech or of the press by force of the due process clause of the Fourteenth Amendment. . . .

That freedom of speech and of the press are rights of the same fundamental character, safeguarded by the due process of law clause of the Fourteenth Amendment against abridgment by state legislation, has . . . been settled by a series of decisions of this court. . . . The word "liberty" contained in that amendment embraces not only the right of a person to be free from physical restraint, but the right to be free in the enjoyment of all his faculties as well. . . .

For more than a century prior to the adoption of the amendment—and, indeed, for many years thereafter—history discloses a persistent effort on the part of the British government to prevent or abridge the free expression of any opinion which seemed to criticize or exhibit in an unfavorable light, however truly, the agencies and operations of the government. The struggle between the proponents of measures to that end and those who asserted the right of free expression was continuous and unceasing. As early as 1644, John Milton, in [*Areopagitica*] an "Appeal for the Liberty of Unlicensed Printing," assailed an act of Parliament which had just been passed providing for censorship of the press previous to publication. He vigorously defended the right of every man to make public his honest views "without previous censure"; and declared the impossibility of finding any man base enough to accept the office of censor and at the same time good enough to be allowed to perform its duties. . . . The act expired by its own terms in 1695. It was never renewed; and the liberty of the press thus became . . . merely "a right or liberty to publish *without* a license what formerly could be published only *with* one." But mere exemption from previous censorship was soon recognized as too narrow a view of the liberty of the press.

In 1712, in response to a message from Queen Anne . . . , Parliament imposed a tax upon all newspapers and upon advertisements. . . . That the main purpose of these taxes was to suppress the publication of comments and criticisms objectionable to the Crown does not admit of doubt. . . . There followed more than a century of resistance to, and evasion of, the taxes, and of agitation for their repeal. . . . [It has been said that] these taxes constituted one of the factors that aroused the American colonists to protest against taxation for the purposes of the home government; and that the revolution really began when, in 1765, that government sent stamps for newspaper duties to the American colonies.

These duties were quite commonly characterized as "taxes on knowledge," a phrase used for the purpose of describing the effect of the exactions and at the same time condemning them. That the taxes had, and were intended to have, the effect of curtailing the circulation of newspapers, and particularly the cheaper ones whose readers were generally found among the masses of the people, went almost without question, even on the part of those who defended the act. May (*Constitutional History of England*, 7th ed., vol. 2, p. 245), after discussing the control by "previous censure," says ". . . a new restraint was devised in the form of a stamp duty on newspapers and advertisements,—avowedly for the purpose of repressing libels. This policy, being found effectual in limiting the circulation of cheap papers was improved upon in the two following reigns, and continued in high esteem until our own time." Collett ([*History of the Taxes on Knowledge,*] vol. 1, p. 14) says: "Any man who carried on printing or publishing for a livelihood was actually at the mercy of the Commissioners of Stamps, when they chose to exert their powers."

Citations of similar import might be multiplied many times; but the foregoing is enough to demonstrate beyond peradventure that in the adoption of the English newspaper stamp tax and the tax on advertisements, revenue was of subordinate concern; and that the dominant and controlling aim was to prevent, or curtail the opportunity for, the acquisition of knowledge by the people in respect of their governmental affairs. It is idle to suppose that so many of the best men of England would for a century of time have waged, as they did, stubborn and often precarious warfare against these taxes if a mere matter of taxation had been involved. The aim of the struggle was not to relieve taxpayers from a burden, but to establish and preserve the right of the English people to full information in respect of the doings or misdoings of their government. Upon the correctness of this conclusion the very characterization of the exactions as "taxes on knowledge" sheds a flood of corroborative light. In the ultimate, an informed and enlightened public opinion was the thing at stake; for, as Erskine, in his great speech in defense of Paine, has said: "The liberty of opinion keeps governments themselves in due subjection to their duties." . . .

In 1785, only four years before Congress had proposed the First Amendment, the Massachusetts legislature, following the English example, imposed a stamp tax on all newspapers and magazines. The following year an advertisement tax was imposed. Both taxes met with such violent opposition that the former was repealed in 1786, and the latter in 1788. Duniway, *Freedom of the Press in Massachusetts,* pp. 136, 137.

The framers of the First Amendment were familiar with the English struggle, which then had continued for nearly eighty years and was destined to go on for another sixty-five years, at the end of which time it culminated in a lasting abandonment of the obnoxious taxes. The framers were likewise familiar with the then recent Massachusetts episode; and while that occurrence did much to bring about the adoption of the amendment . . . , the predominant influence must have come from the English experience. It is impossible to concede that by the words "freedom of the press" the framers of the amendment intended to adopt merely the narrow view then reflected by the law of England that such freedom consisted only in immunity from previous censorship; for this abuse had then permanently disappeared from English practice. It is equally impossible to believe that it was not intended to bring within the reach of these words such modes of restraint as were embodied in the two forms of taxation already described. Such belief must be rejected in the face of the then well known purpose of the exactions and the general adverse sentiment of the colonies in respect to them. . . .

In the light of all that has now been said, it is evident that the restricted rules of the English law in respect of the freedom of the press in force when the Constitution was adopted were never accepted by the American colonists, and that by the First Amendment it was meant to preclude the national government, and by the Fourteenth Amendment to preclude the states, from adopting any form of previous restraint upon printed publications, or their circulation, including that which had theretofore been effected by these two well-known and odious methods. . . .

It is not intended by anything we have said to suggest that the owners of newspapers are immune from any of the ordinary forms of taxation for support of the government. But this is not an ordinary form of tax, but one single in kind, with a long history of hostile misuse against the freedom of the press.

The predominant purpose of the grant of immunity here invoked was to preserve an untrammeled press as a vital source of public information. The newspapers, magazines and other journals of the country, it is safe to say, have shed and continue to shed, more light on the public and business affairs of the nation than any other instrumentality of publicity; and since informed public opinion is the most potent of all restraints upon misgovernment, the suppression or abridgment of the publicity afforded by a free press cannot be regarded otherwise than with grave concern. The tax here involved is bad not because it takes money from the pockets of the appellees. If that were all, a wholly different question would be presented. It is bad because, in the light of its history and of its present setting, it is seen to be a deliberate and calculated device in the guise of a tax to limit the circulation of information to which the public is entitled in virtue of the constitutional guaranties. A free press stands as one of the great interpreters between the government and the people. To allow it to be fettered is to fetter ourselves.

In view of the persistent search for new subjects of taxation, it is not without significance that, with the single exception of the Louisiana statute, so far as we can discover, no state during the one hundred fifty years of our national existence has undertaken to impose a tax like that now in question.

The form in which the tax is imposed is in itself suspicious. It is not measured or limited by the volume of advertisements. It is measured alone by the extent of the circulation of the publication in which the advertisements are carried, with the plain purpose of penalizing the publishers and curtailing the circulation of a selected group of newspapers.

2. Having reached the conclusion that the act imposing the tax in question is unconstitutional under the due process of law clause because it abridges the freedom of the press, we deem it unnecessary to consider the further ground assigned that it also constitutes a denial of the equal protection of the laws.

Decree affirmed.

11. First Amendment Rights of Students

HEALY *v.* JAMES
408 US 169 (1972)

[Starting in the late 1960s, courts were frequently called upon to resolve conflicts between students and school authorities. There were cases involving regulations concerning length of hair, styles of dress, wearing antiwar armbands, the right to invite certain speakers, and similar problems, almost all implicating, directly or remotely, the First Amendment. *Cf.* the *Tinker* case (1969), *supra.* The instant case involved the right of students at a state college to win recognition for a local chapter of Students for a Democratic Society (SDS). The Supreme Court unanimously held in favor of the students, that is, that they have a right, under the First Amendment, to get recognition for their organization, provided that they agree to comply with a college rule requiring them to abide by reasonable campus regulations. The Court's opinion was by Justice Powell. Chief Justice Burger and Justices Douglas and Rehnquist wrote separate concurring opinions.]

Mr. Justice Powell delivered the opinion of the Court:

This case, arising out of a denial by a state college of official recognition to a group of students who desired to form a local chapter of Students for a Democratic Society (SDS), presents this Court with questions requiring the application of well-established First Amendment principles. While the factual background of this particular case raises these constitutional issues in a manner not heretofore passed on by the Court, and only infrequently presented to lower federal courts, our decision today is governed by existing precedent.

As the case involves delicate issues concerning the academic community, we approach our task with special caution, recognizing the mutual interest of students, faculty members, and administrators in an environment free from disruptive interference with the educational process.

We also are mindful of the equally significant interest in the widest latitude for free expression and debate consonant with the maintenance of order. Where these interests appear to compete, the First Amendment, made binding on the States by the Fourteenth Amendment, strikes the required balance.

I

We mention briefly at the outset the setting in 1969–1970. A climate of unrest prevailed on many college campuses in this country. There had been widespread civil disobedience on some campuses, accompanied by the seizure of buildings, vandalism, and arson. Some colleges had been shut down altogether, while at others files were looted and manuscripts destroyed. SDS chapters on some of those campuses had been a catalytic force during this period. Although the causes of campus disruption were many and complex, one of the prime consequences of such activities was the denial of the lawful exercise of First Amendment rights to the majority of students by the few. Indeed, many of the most cherished characteristics long associated with institutions of higher learning appeared to be endangered. Fortunately, with the passage of time, a calmer atmosphere and greater maturity now pervade our campuses. Yet, it was in this climate of earlier unrest that this case arose.

Petitioners are students attending Central Connecticut State College (CCSC), a state-supported institution of higher learning. In September 1969 they undertook to organize what they then referred to as a "local chapter" of Students for a Democratic Society (SDS). Pursuant to procedures established by the College, petitioners filed a request for official recognition as a campus organization with the Student Affairs Committee, a committee composed of four students, three faculty members and the Dean of Student Affairs. The request specified three purposes for the proposed organization's existence. It would provide "a forum of discussion and self-education for students developing an analysis of American society"; it would serve as "an agency for integrating thought with action so as to bring about constructive changes"; and it would endeavor to provide "a coordinating body for relating the problems of leftist students" with other interested groups on campus and in the community. The Committee, while satisfied that the statement of purposes was clear and unobjectionable on its face, exhibited concern over the relationship between the proposed local group and the National SDS organization. In response to inquiries, representatives of the proposed organization stated that they would not affiliate with any national organization and that their group would remain "completely independent."

In response to other questions asked by Committee members concerning SDS's reputation for campus disruption, the applicants made the following statements, which proved significant during the later stages of these proceedings:

Q. How would you respond to issues of violence as other SDS chapters have?
A. Our action would have to be dependent upon each issue.
Q. Would you use any means possible?
A. No I can't say that; would not know until we know what the issues are.

. . .

Q. Could you envision the SDS interrupting a class?
A. Impossible for me to say.

With this information before it, the Committee requested an additional filing by the applicants, including a formal statement regarding affiliations. The amended application filed in response stated flatly that "CCSC Students for a Democratic Society are not under the dictates of any National organization." At a second hearing before the Student Affairs Committee, the question of relationship with the National organization was raised again. One of the organizers explained that the National SDS was divided into several "factional groups," that the national-local relationship was a loose one, and that the local organization accepted only "certain ideas" but not all of the National organization's aims and philosophies.

By a vote of six to two the Committee ultimately approved the application and recommended to the President of the College, Dr. James, that the organization be accorded official recognition. In approving the application, the majority indicated that its decision was premised on the belief that varying viewpoints should be represented on campus and that since the Young Americans for Freedom, the Young Democrats, the Young Republicans, and the Liberal Party all enjoyed recognized status, a group should be available with which "left wing" students might identify. The majority also noted and relied on the organization's claim of independence. Finally, it admonished the organization that immediate suspension would be considered if the group's activities proved incompatible with the school's policies against interference with the privacy of other students or destruction of property. The two dissenting members based their reservation primarily on the lack of clarity regarding the organization's independence.

Several days later, the President rejected the Committee's recommendation, and issued a statement indicating that petitioners' organization was not to be accorded the benefits of official campus recognition. His accompanying remarks, which are set out in full in the margin,* indicate several reasons for his action. He found that the organization's philosophy was antithetical to the school's policies,† and that the

---

* The President stated:

"Though I have full appreciation for the action of the Student Affairs Committee and the reasons stated in their minutes for the majority vote recommending approval of a local chapter of Students for a Democratic Society, it is my judgment that the statement of purpose to form a local chapter of Students for a Democratic Society carries full and unmistakable adherence to at least some of the major tenets of the national organization, loose and divided though that organization may be. The published aims and philosophy of the Students for a Democratic Society, which include disruption and violence, are contrary to the approved policy (by faculty, students, and administration) of Central Connecticut State College which states:

" 'Students do not have the right to invade the privacy of others, to damage the property of others, to disrupt the regular and essential operation of the college, or to interfere with the rights of others.'

"The further statement on the request for recognition that 'CCSC Students for a Democratic Society are not under the dictates of any National organization' in no way clarifies why if a group intends to follow the established policy of the college, they wish to become a local chapter of an organization which openly repudiates such a policy.

"Freedom of speech, academic freedom on the campus, the freedom of establishing an open forum for the exchange of ideas, the freedoms outlined in the Statement on Rights, Freedoms, and Responsibilities of Students that 'college students and student organizations shall have the right to examine and discuss all questions of interest to them, to express opinion publicly and privately, and to support causes by orderly means. They may organize public demonstrations and protest gatherings and utilize the right of petition'—these are all precious freedoms that we cherish and are freedoms on which we stand. To approve any organization or individual who joins with an organization which openly repudiates those principles is contrary to those freedoms and to the approved 'Statement on the Rights, Freedoms, and Responsibilities of Students at Central.' "

† In 1969, CCSC adopted, as have many other colleges and universities, a Statement of Rights, Freedoms, and Responsibilities of Students. This statement, commonly referred to as the "Student Bill of Rights," is printed as an Appendix to the Second Circuit's majority opinion in this case, *Healy* v. *James*, 445 F.2d, at 1132–1136 (1971). Part V of that statement establishes the standards for approval of campus organizations and imposes several basic limitations on their campus activities:

"A. Care shall be taken in the establishment and organization of campus groups so that the basic rights, freedoms and responsibilities of students will be preserved.

"B. Student organizations shall submit a clear statement of purpose, criteria for membership, rules of procedures and a list of officers as a condition of institutional recognition. They shall not be required to submit a membership list as a condition of institutional recognition.

"C. Membership in campus organizations shall be limited to matriculated students (day or evening) at the college. Membership shall not be restricted by race, religion or nationality. The members shall have sole power to determine organization policy consistent with the regulations of the college.

"D. Each organization is free to choose its own adviser. Advisers to organizations shall advise but not control the organizations and their policies.

group's independence was doubtful. He concluded that approval should not be granted to any group that "openly repudiates" the College's dedication to academic freedom.

Denial of official recognition posed serious problems for the organization's existence and growth. Its members were deprived of the opportunity to place announcements regarding meetings, rallies or other activities in the student newspaper; they were precluded from using various campus bulletin boards; and—most importantly —nonrecognition barred them from using campus facilities for holding meetings. This latter disability was brought home to petitioners shortly after the President's announcement. Petitioners circulated a notice calling a meeting to discuss what further action should be taken in light of the group's official rejection. The members met at the coffee shop in the Student Center ("Devils' Den") but were disbanded on the President's order since nonrecognized groups were not entitled to use such facilities.

Their efforts to gain recognition having proved ultimately unsuccessful, and having been made to feel the burden of nonrecognition, petitioners resorted to the courts. They filed a suit in the United States District Court for Connecticut, seeking declaratory and injunctive relief against the President of the College, other administrators, and the State Board of Trustees. Petitioners' primary complaint centered on the denial of First Amendment rights of expression and association arising from denial of campus recognition. The cause was submitted initially on stipulated facts, and, after a short hearing, the judge ruled that petitioners had been denied procedural due process because the President had based his decision on conclusions regarding the applicant's affiliation which were outside the record before him. The court concluded that if the President wished to act on the basis of material outside the application he must at least provide petitioners a hearing and opportunity to introduce evidence as to their affiliations. While retaining jurisdiction over the case, the District Court ordered respondents to hold a hearing in order to clarify the several ambiguities surrounding the President's decision. One of the matters to be explored was whether the local organization, true to its repeated affirmations, was in fact independent of the National SDS. And if the hearing demonstrated that the two were not separable, the respondents were instructed that they might then review the "aims and philosophy" of the National organization.

Pursuant to the court's order, the President designated Dean Judd, the Dean of Student Affairs, to serve as hearing officer and a hearing was scheduled. The hearing, which spanned two dates and lasted approximately two hours, added little in terms of objective substantive evidence to the record in this case. Petitioners introduced a statement offering to change the organization's name from "CCSC local chapter of SDS" to "Students for a Democratic Society of Central Connecticut State College." They further reaffirmed that they would "have no connection whatsoever

---

"E. College students and student organizations shall have the right to examine and discuss all questions of interest to them, to express opinion publicly and privately, and to support causes by orderly means. They may organize public demonstrations and protest gatherings and utilize the right of petition. Students do not have the right to deprive others of the opportunity to speak or be heard, to invade the privacy of others, to damage the property of others, to disrupt the regular and essential operation of the college, or to interfere with the rights of others."

to the structure of an existing national organization." Petitioners also introduced the testimony of their faculty adviser to the effect that some local SDS organizations elsewhere were unaffiliated with any national organization. The hearing officer, in addition to introducing the minutes from the two pertinent Student Affairs Committee meetings, also introduced *sua sponte* portions of a transcript of hearings before the United States House of Representatives Internal Security Committee investigating the activities of SDS. Excerpts were offered both to prove that violent and disruptive activities had been attributed to SDS elsewhere and to demonstrate that there existed a national organization that recognized and cooperated with regional and local college campus affiliates. Petitioners did not challenge the asserted existence of a National SDS, nor did they question that it did have a system of affiliations of some sort. Their contention was simply that their organization would not associate with that network. Throughout the hearing the parties were acting at cross purposes. What seemed relevant to one appeared completely immaterial to the other. This failure of the hearing to advance the litigation was, at bottom, the consequence of a more basic failure to join issue on the considerations that should control the President's ultimate decision, a problem to which we will return in the ensuing section.

Upon reviewing the hearing transcript and exhibits, the President reaffirmed his prior decision to deny petitioners recognition as a campus organization. The reasons stated, closely paralleling his initial reasons, were that the group would be a "disruptive influence" as CCSC and that recognition would be "contrary to the orderly process of change" on the campus.

After the President's second statement issued, the case then returned to the District Court where it was ordered dismissed. The court concluded, first, that the formal requisites of procedural due process had been complied with, second, that petitioners had failed to meet their burden of showing that they could function free from the National organization, and third, that the College's refusal to place its stamp of approval on an organization whose conduct it found "likely to cause violent acts of disruption" did not violate petitioners' associational rights.

Petitioners appealed to the Second Circuit Court of Appeals where, by a two-to-one vote, the District Court's judgment was affirmed. The majority purported not to reach the substantive First Amendment issues on the theory that petitioners had failed to avail themselves of the due process accorded them and had failed to meet their burden of complying with the prevailing standards for recognition. Judge Smith dissented, disagreeing with the majority's refusal to address the merits and finding that petitioners had been deprived of basic First Amendment rights. This Court granted certiorari and, for the reasons that follow, we conclude that the judgment of the courts below must be reversed and the case remanded for reconsideration.

II

At the outset we note that state colleges and universities are not enclaves immune from the sweep of the First Amendment. "It can hardly be argued that either students or teachers shed their constitutional rights to freedom of speech or expression at the schoolhouse gate." *Tinker* v. *Des Moines Independent Community School District,* 393 US 503, 506 (1969). Of course, as Mr. Justice Fortas made clear in *Tinker,* First Amendment rights must always be applied "in light of the special characteristics of the . . . environment" in the particular case. And, where state-operated educational institutions are involved, this Court has long recognized "the need for affirming the comprehensive authority of the States and of school officials, consistent with fundamental constitutional safeguards, to prescribe and control conduct in the schools." Yet, the precedents of this Court leave no room for the view that, because of the acknowledged need for order, First Amendment protections should apply with less force on college campuses than in the community at large. Quite to the contrary, "[t]he vigilant protection of constitutional freedoms is nowhere more vital than in the community of American schools." *Shelton* v. *Tucker,* 364 US 479, 487 (1960). The college classroom with its surrounding environs is peculiarly the "market place of ideas" and we break no new constitutional ground in reaffirming this Nation's dedication to safeguarding academic freedom. *Keyishian* v. *Board of Regents,* 385 US 589, 603 (1967); *Sweezy* v. *New Hampshire,* 354 US 234, 249–250 (plurality opinion of Mr. Chief Justice Warren), 262 (1957) (Mr. Justice Frankfurter's concurring opinion).

Among the rights protected by the First Amendment is the right of individuals to associate to further their personal beliefs. While the freedom of association is not explicitly set out in the Amendment, it has long been held to be implicit in the freedoms of speech, assembly and petition. . . . There can be no doubt that denial of official recognition, without justification, to college organizations burdens or abridges that associational right. The primary impediment to free association flowing from nonrecognition is the denial of use of campus facilities for meetings and other appropriate purposes. The practical effect of nonrecognition was demonstrated in this case when, several days after the President's decision was announced, petitioners were not allowed to hold a meeting in the campus coffee shop because they were not an approved group.

Petitioners' associational interests also were circumscribed by the denial of the use of campus bulletin boards and the school newspaper. If an organization is to remain a viable entity in a campus community in which new students enter on a regular basis, it must possess the means of communicating with these students. Moreover, the organization's ability to participate in the intellectual give and take of campus debate, and to pursue its stated purposes, is limited by denial of access to the customary media for communicating with the administration, faculty members, and other students. Such impediments cannot be viewed as insubstantial.

Respondents and the courts below appear to have taken the view that denial of official recognition in this case abridged no constitutional rights. The District Court concluded that

President James' discretionary action in denying this application cannot be legitimately magnified and distorted into a constitutionally cognizable interference with the personal ideas or beliefs of any segment of the college students; neither does his action deter in any material way the individual advocacy of their personal beliefs; nor can his action be reasonably construed to be an invasion of, or having a chilling effect on academic freedom.

In that court's view all that was denied petitioners was the "administrative seal of official college respectability." A majority of the Court of Appeals agreed that petitioners had been denied only the "college's stamp of approval." Respondents take that same position here, arguing that petitioners still may meet as a group off campus, that they still may distribute written material off campus, and that they still may meet together informally on campus—as individuals but not as CCSC-SDS.

We do not agree with the characterization by the courts below of the consequences of nonrecognition. We may concede, as did Mr. Justice Harlan in his unanimous opinion for the Court in *NAACP* v. *Alabama ex rel. Patterson,* 357 US 449, 461 (1958), that the administration "has taken no direct action . . . to restrict the rights of petitioners' members to associate freely." But the Constitution's protection is not limited to direct interference with fundamental rights. The requirement in *Patterson* that the NAACP disclose its membership lists was found to be an impermissible, though indirect, infringement of the members' associational rights. Likewise, in this case, the group's possible ability to exist outside the campus community does not ameliorate significantly the disabilities imposed by the President's action. We are not free to disregard the practical realities. Mr. Justice Stewart has made the salient point: "Freedoms such as these are protected not only against heavy-handed frontal attack, but also from being stifled by more subtle governmental interference." *Bates* v. *City of Little Rock,* 361 US 516, 523 (1960). . . .

The opinions below also assumed that petitioners had the burden of showing entitlement to recognition by the College. While petitioners have not challenged the procedural requirement that they file an application in conformity with the rules of the College, they do question the view of the courts below that final rejection could rest on their failure to convince the administration that their organization was unaffiliated with the National SDS. For reasons to be stated later in this opinion, we do not consider the issue of affiliation to be a controlling one. But apart from any particular issue, once petitioners had filed an application in conformity with the requirements, the burden was upon the College administration to justify its decision of rejection. . . . It is to be remembered that the effect of the College's denial of recognition was a form of prior restraint, denying to petitioners' organization the range of associational activities described above. While a college has a legitimate interest in preventing disruption on the campus, which under circumstances requiring the safeguarding of that interest may justify such restraint, a "heavy burden" rests on the college to demonstrate the appropriateness of that action. . . .

III

These fundamental errors—discounting the existence of a cognizable First Amendment interest and misplacing the burden of proof—require that the judgments below be reversed. But we are unable to conclude that no basis exists upon which nonrecognition might be appropriate. Indeed, based on a reasonable reading of the ambiguous facts of this case, there appears to be at least one potentially acceptable ground for a denial of recognition. Because of this ambiguous state of the record we conclude that the case should be remanded, and, in an effort to provide guidance to the lower courts upon reconsideration, it is appropriate to discuss the several bases of President James' decision. Four possible justifications for non-recognition, all closely related, might be derived from the record and his statements. Three of those grounds are inadequate to substantiate his decision: a fourth, however, has merit.

A

From the outset the controversy in this case has centered in large measure around the relationship, if any, between petitioners' group and the National SDS. The Student Affairs Committee meetings, as reflected in its minutes, focused considerable attention on this issue; the court-ordered hearing also was directed primarily to this question. Despite assurances from petitioners and their counsel that the local group was in fact independent of the National organization, it is evident that President James was significantly influenced by his apprehension that there was a connection. Aware of the fact that some SDS chapters had been associated with disruptive and violent campus activity, he apparently considered that affiliation itself was sufficient justification for denying recognition.

Although this precise issue has not come before the Court heretofore, the Court has consistently disapproved governmental action imposing criminal sanctions or denying rights and privileges solely because of a citizen's association with an unpopular organization. . . . In these cases it has been established that "guilt by association alone, without [establishing] that an individual's association poses the threat feared by the Government," is an impermissible basis upon which to deny First Amendment rights. . . . The Government has the burden of establishing a knowing affiliation with an organization possessing unlawful aims and goals, and a specific intent to further those illegal aims.

Students for a Democratic Society, as conceded by the College and the lower courts, is loosely organized, having various factions and promoting a number of diverse social and political views, only some of which call for unlawful action. Not only did petitioners proclaim their complete independence from this organization, but they also indicated that they shared only some of the beliefs its leaders have expressed. On this record it is clear that the relationship was not an adequate ground for the denial of recognition.

B

Having concluded that petitioners were affiliated with, or at least retained an affinity for, National SDS, President James attributed what he believed to be the philosophy of that organization to the local group. He characterized the petitioning group as adhering to "some of the major tenets of the national organization," including a philosophy of violence and disruption. Understandably, he found that philosophy abhorrent. In an article signed by President James in an alumni periodical, and made a part of the record below, he announced his unwillingness to "sanction an organization that openly advocates the destruction of the very ideals and freedoms upon which the academic life is founded." He further emphasized that the petitioners' "philosophies" were "counter to the official policy of the college."

The mere disagreement of the President with the group's philosophy affords no reason to deny it recognition. As repugnant as these views may have been, especially to one with President James' responsibility, the mere expression of them would not justify the denial of First Amendment rights. Whether petitioners did in fact advocate a philosophy of "destruction" thus becomes immaterial. The College, acting here as the instrumentality of the State, may not restrict speech or association simply because it finds the views expressed by any group to be abhorrent. As Mr. Justice Black put it most simply and clearly:

"I do not believe that it can be too often repeated that the freedoms of speech, press, petition and assembly guaranteed by the First Amendment must be accorded to the ideas we hate or sooner or later they will be denied to the ideas we cherish." *Communist Party* v. *Subversive Activities Control Board,* 367 US 1, 137 (1961).

C

As the litigation progressed in the District Court, a third rationale for President James' decision—beyond the questions of affiliation and philosophy—began to emerge. His second statement, issued after the court-ordered hearing, indicates that he based rejection on a conclusion that this particular group would be a "disruptive influence at CCSC." This language was underscored in the second District Court opinion. In fact, the Court concluded that the President had determined that CCSC-SDS's "prospective campus activities were likely to cause a disruptive influence at CCSC."

If this reason, directed at the organization's activities rather than its philosophy, were factually supported by the record, this Court's prior decisions would provide a basis for considering the propriety of nonrecognition. The critical line heretofore drawn for determining the permissibility of regulation is the line between mere advocacy and advocacy "directed to inciting or producing imminent lawless action and . . . likely to incite or produce such action." *Brandenburg* v. *Ohio,* 395 US 444, 447, (1969) (unanimous *per curiam* opinion). . . . In the context of the "special characteristics of the school environment," the power of the government to prohibit "lawless action" is not limited to acts of a criminal nature. Also prohibitable are actions which "materially and substantially disrupt the work and discipline of the school." . . . Associational activities need not be tolerated where they infringe reasonable campus rules, interrupt classes, or substantially interfere with the opportunity of other students to obtain an education.

The "Student Bill of Rights" as CCSC, upon which great emphasis was placed by the President, draws precisely this distinction between advocacy and action. It purports to impose no limitations on the right of college student organizations "to examine and discuss *all* questions of interest to them." But it also states that students have no right (1) "to deprive others of the opportunity to speak or be heard," (2) "to invade the privacy of others," (3) "to damage the property of others," (4) "to disrupt the regular and essential operation of the college," or (5) "to interfere with the rights of others." The line between permissible speech and impermissible conduct tracks the constitutional requirement, and if there were an evidential basis to support the conclusion that CCSC-SDS posed a substantial threat of material disruption in violation of that command the President's decision should be affirmed.*

* It may not be sufficient merely to show the existence of a legitimate and substantial state

The record, however, offers no substantial basis for that conclusion. The only support for the view expressed by the President, other than the reputed affiliation with National SDS, is to be found in the ambivalent responses offered by the group's representatives at the Student Affairs Committee hearing, during which they stated that they did not know whether they might respond to "issues of violence" in the same manner that other SDS chapters had on other campuses. Nor would they state unequivocally that they could never "envision . . . interrupting a class." Whatever force these statements might be thought to have is largely dissipated by the following exchange between petitioners' counsel and the Dean of Student Affairs during the court-ordered hearing:

> Counsel: I just read the documents that you're offering [minutes from Student Affairs Committee meeting] and I can't see that there's anything in it that intimates that these students contemplate any illegal or disruptive practice.
>
> Dean: No. There's no question raised to that, counsel.

Dean Judd's remark reaffirms, in accord with the full record, that there was no substantial evidence that these particular individuals acting together would constitute a disruptive force on campus. Therefore, insofar as nonrecognition flowed from such fears, it constituted little more than the sort of "undifferentiated fear or apprehension of disturbance [which] is not enough to overcome the right to freedom of expression." . . .

D

These same references in the record to the group's equivocation regarding how it might respond to "issues of violence" and whether it could ever "envision . . . interrupting a class," suggest a fourth possible reason why recognition might have been denied to these petitioners. These remarks might well have been read as announcing petitioners' unwillingness to be bound by reasonable school rules governing conduct. The College's Statement of Rights, Freedoms and Responsibilities of Students, contains, as we have seen, an explicit statement with respect to campus disruption. The regulation, carefully differentiating between advocacy and action, is a reasonable one, and petitioners have not questioned it directly. Yet their statements raise considerable question whether they intend to abide by the prohibitions contained therein.*

---

interest. Where state action designed to regulate prohibitable action also restricts associational rights—as nonrecognition does—the State must demonstrate that the action taken is reasonably related to protection of the State's interest and that "the incidental restriction on alleged First Amendment freedoms is no greater than is essential to the furtherance of that interest. . . ."

* The Court of Appeals found that petitioners "failed candidly to respond to inquiries whether they would resort to violence and disruption on the CCSC campus, including interruption of classes." While petitioners' statements may be used as intimating a rejection of reasonable regulations in advance, there is in fact substantial ambiguity on this point. The questions asked by members of the Student Affairs Committee do not appear to have been propounded with any clear distinction in mind between that which the petitioners might advocate and the conduct in which they might engage. Nor did the Student Affairs Committee attempt to obtain a clarification of the petitioners' ambiguous answers by asking specifically whether the group was willing to abide by the Student Bill of Rights governing all campus organizations.

Moreover, this question was not among those referred by the District Court to the administrative hearing, and it was there addressed only tangentially. The group members who had

As we have already stated in Parts B and C, the critical line for First Amendment purposes must be drawn between advocacy, which is entitled to full protection, and action, which is not. Petitioners may, if they so choose, preach the propriety of amending or even doing away with any or all campus regulations. They may not, however, undertake to flout these rules. Mr. Justice Blackmun, at the time he was a circuit judge on the Eighth Circuit, stated:

"We . . . hold that a college has the inherent power to promulgate rules and regulations; that it has the inherent power properly to discipline; that it has power appropriately to protect itself and its property; that it may expect that its students adhere to generally accepted standards of conduct." . . .

Just as in the community at large, reasonable regulations with respect to the time, the place, and the manner in which student groups conduct their speech-related activities must be respected. A college administration may impose a requirement, such as may have been imposed in this case, that a group seeking official recognition affirm in advance its willingness to adhere to reasonable campus law. Such a requirement does not impose an impermissible condition on the students' associational rights. Their freedom to speak out, to assemble, or to petition for changes in school rules is in no sense infringed. It merely constitutes an agreement to conform with reasonable standards respecting conduct. This is a minimal requirement, in the interest of the entire academic community, of any group seeking the privilege of official recognition.

Petitioners have not challenged in this litigation the procedural or substantive aspects of the College's requirements governing applications for official recognition. Although the record is unclear on this point, CCSC may have, among its requirements for recognition, a rule that prospective groups affirm that they intend to comply with reasonable campus regulations. Upon remand it should first be determined whether the College recognition procedures contemplate any such requirement. If so, it should then be ascertained whether petitioners intend to comply. Since we do not have the terms of a specific prior affirmation rule before us, we are not called on to decide whether any particular formulation would or would not prove constitutionally acceptable. Assuming the existence of a valid rule, however, we do conclude that the benefits of participation in the internal life of the college community may be denied to any group that reserves the right to violate any valid campus rules with which they disagree.

IV

We think the above discussion establishes the appropriate framework for consideration of petitioners' request for campus recognition. Because respondents failed to accord due recognition to First Amendment principles, the judgment below approving respondents' denial of recognition must be reversed. Since we cannot con-

---

made statements before the Student Affairs Committee did not testify, and their position was not clarified. Their counsel, whose tactics were characterized as "disruptive" by the Court of Appeals, elected to make argumentative statements rather than elicit relevant testimony. Indeed, the District Court's failure to identify the question of willingness to abide by the College's rules and regulations as a significant subject of inquiry, coupled with the equivocation on the part of the group's representatives, lend support to our view that a remand is necesssary.

clude from this record that petitioners were willing to abide by reasonable campus rules and regulations, we order the case remanded for reconsideration. We note, in so holding, that the wide latitude accorded by the Constitution to the freedoms of expression and association is not without its costs in terms of the risk to the maintenance of civility and an ordered society. Indeed, this latitude often has resulted, on the campus and elsewhere, in the infringement of the rights of others. Though we deplore the tendency of some to abuse the very constitutional privileges they invoke, and although the infringement of rights of others certainly should not be tolerated, we reaffirm this Court's dedication to the principles of the Bill of Rights upon which our vigorous and free society is founded.

Reversed and remanded.

12. Demonstrations and the First Amendment

BROWN v. LOUISIANA
383 US 131 (1966)

[The case arose out of a peaceful demonstration by five Negroes in a public library. They were convicted for violation of a statute making it a criminal offense to congregate in a public building with intent to provoke, or under circumstances that may occasion, a breach of the peace, and to refuse to move on when so ordered by an authorized person. The Supreme Court reversed. Though the decision was 5–4, the majority could not agree on an opinion. Justice Fortas wrote an opinion in which Chief Justice Warren and Justice Douglas joined. Justices Brennan and White wrote concurring opinions. Justice Black wrote a dissenting opinion in which Justices Clark, Harlan, and Stewart joined.]

Mr. Justice Fortas announced the judgment of the Court and an opinion in which The Chief Justice and Mr. Justice Douglas join:

This is the fourth time in little more than four years that this Court has reviewed convictions by the Louisiana courts for alleged violations, in a civil rights context, of that State's breach of the peace statute. In the three preceding cases the convictions were reversed. *Garner* v. *State of Louisiana,* 368 US 157, decided in December 1961, involved sit-ins by Negroes at lunch counters catering only to whites. *Taylor* v. *State of Louisiana,* 370 US 154, decided in June 1962, concerned a sit-in by Negroes in a waiting room at a bus depot, reserved "for whites only." *Cox* v. *State of Louisiana,* 379 US 536, decided in January 1965, involved the leader of some 2,000 Negroes who demonstrated in the vicinity of a courthouse and jail to protest the arrest of fellow demonstrators. In each of these cases the demonstration was orderly. In each, the purpose of the participants was to protest the denial to Negroes of rights guaranteed them by State and Federal constitutions and to petition their governments for redress of grievances. In none was there evidence that the participants planned or intended disorder. In none were there circumstances which might have led to a breach of the peace chargeable to the protesting participants.*

In *Garner* the Court found the record utterly barren of evidence to support con-

* Participants in an orderly demonstration in a public place are not chargeable with the

victions under Title 14, Article 103(7) of the Louisiana Criminal Code, which then defined the crime of "disturbing the peace" in specific detail. The record contained no evidence of boisterous or disorderly actions or of "passive conduct likely to cause a public disturbance." In *Taylor,* which arose under the Louisiana statute as amended to read in its present form, the Court in a *per curiam* opinion set aside the convictions despite evidence of "restlessness" among the white onlookers. Finally, in *Cox,* the Court held that the facts would not permit application of Louisiana's breach of the peace statute, despite the large scale of the demonstrations and the fact that petitioner's speech occasioned "grumbling" on the part of white onlookers. Petitioner and the demonstrators as a group, though "well behaved," were far from silent. As an "additional reason" why the conviction could not be sustained, the Court . . . held that were the statute to be defined and applied as the Louisiana Supreme Court had done, it would be unconstitutional because the vagueness and breadth of the definition "would allow persons to be punished merely for peacefully expressing unpopular views. . . ."

Since the present case was decided under precisely the statute involved in *Cox* but before our decision in that case was announced, it might well be supposed that, without further ado, we would vacate and remand in light of *Cox.* But because the incident leading to the present convictions occurred in a public library and might be thought to raise materially different questions, we have heard argument and have considered the case *in extenso.*

The locus of the events was the Audubon Regional Library in the town of Clinton, Louisiana, Parish of East Feliciana. The front room of the building was used as a public library facility where patrons might obtain library services. It was a small room, containing two tables and one chair (apart from the Branch Assistant's desk and chairs), a stove, a card catalogue, and open book shelves. The room was referred to by the regional librarian, Mrs. Perkins, as "the adult reading-room, the adult service-room." The library permitted "registered borrowers" to "browse" among the books in the room or to borrow books. A "registered borrower" was one who could produce an identification card showing that he was registered by the Audubon Regional Library. Other space in the building included the headquarters of the regional library.

The Audubon Regional Library is operated jointly by the Parishes of East Feliciana, West Feliciana, and St. Helena. It has three branches and two bookmobiles. The bookmobiles served 33 schools, both white and Negro, as well as "individuals." One of the bookmobiles was red, the other blue. The red bookmobile served only white persons. The blue bookmobile served only Negroes. It is a permissible inference that no Negroes used the branch libraries.

The registration cards issued to Negroes were stamped with the word "Negro."

danger, unprovoked except by the fact of the constitutionally protected demonstration itself, that their critics might react with disorder or violence. See *Cox* v. *State of Louisiana, supra, Wright* v. *State of Georgia,* 373 US 284, cf. *Terminiello* v. *City of Chicago,* 337 US 1. Compare *Feiner* v. *People of State of New York,* 340 US 315, where one speaker was haranguing 75 or 80 "restless" listeners; *Chaplinsky* v. *State of New Hampshire,* 315 US 568, ("fighting words"); cf. *Niemotko* v. *State of Maryland,* 340 US 268 (concurring opinion of Frankfurter, J.). See generally on the problem of the "heckler's veto," Kalven, *The Negro and the First Amendment,* 140–160 (1965).

A Negro in possession of such a card was entitled to borrow books, but only from the blue bookmobile. A white person could not receive service from the blue bookmobile. He would have to wait until the red bookmobile came around, or would have to go to a branch library.

This tidy plan was challenged on Saturday, March 7, 1964, at about 11:30 A.M. Five young Negro males, all residents of East or West Feliciana Parishes, went into the adult reading or service room of the Audubon Regional Library at Clinton. The Branch Assistant, Mrs. Katie Reeves, was alone in the room. She met the men "between the tables" and asked if she "could help." Petitioner Brown requested a book, "The Story of the Negro" by Arna Bontemps. Mrs. Reeves checked the card catalogue, ascertained that the Branch did not have the book, so advised Mr. Brown, and told him that she would request the book from the State Library, that he would be notified upon its receipt and "he could either pick it up or it would be mailed to him." She told him that "his point of service was a bookmobile or it could be mailed to him." Mrs. Reeves testified that she expected that the men would then leave; they did not, and she asked them to leave. They did not. Petitioner Brown sat down and the others stood near him. They said nothing; there was no noise or boisterous talking. Mrs. Reeves called Mrs. Perkins, the regional librarian, who was in another room. Mrs. Perkins asked the men to leave. They remained.

Neither Mrs. Reeves nor Mrs. Perkins had called the sheriff, but in "10 to 15 minutes" from the time of the arrival of the men at the library, the sheriff and deputies arrived. The sheriff asked the Negroes to leave. They said they would not. The sheriff then arrested them. The sheriff had been notified that morning that members of the Congress of Racial Equality "were going to sit-in" at the library. Ordinarily, the sheriff testified, CORE tells him when they are going to demonstrate or picket. The sheriff was standing at his "place of business" when he saw "these 5 colored males coming down the street." He saw them enter the library. He called the jail to notify his deputies, and he reached the library immediately after the deputies got there. When the sheriff arrived, there was no noise, no disturbance. He testified that he arrested them "for not leaving a public building when asked to do so by an officer."

The library obtained the requested book and mailed it to Mr. Brown on March 29, 1964. The accompanying card said, "You may return the book either by mail or to the Blue Bookmobile." The reference to the color of the vehicle was obviously not designed to facilitate identification of the library vehicle. The blue bookmobile is for Negroes and for Negroes only.

In the course of argument before this Court, counsel for both the State and petitioners stated that the Clinton Branch was closed after the incident of March 7. Counsel for the State also advised the court that the use of cards stamped "Negro" continues to be the practice of the regional library.

On March 25, 1964, Mr. Brown and his four companions were tried and found guilty. Brown was sentenced to pay $150 and costs, and in default thereof to spend 90 days in the parish jail. His companions were sentenced to $35 and costs, or 15 days in jail. The charge was that they had congregated together in the public library of Clinton, Louisiana, "with the intent to provoke a breach of the peace and under circumstances such that a breach of the peace might be occasioned thereby" and failing and refusing "to leave said premises when ordered to do so" by the librarian and by the sheriff.

The Louisiana breach of peace statute under which they were accused reads as follows: "Whoever with intent to provoke a breach of the peace, or under circumstances such that a breach of the peace may be occasioned thereby: (1) crowds or congregates with others . . . in . . . a . . . public place or building . . . and who fails or refuses to disperse and move on, or disperse or move on, when ordered so to do by any law enforcement officer . . . or any other authorized person . . . shall be guilty of disturbing the peace."

Under Louisiana law, these convictions were not appealable. . . . Petitioners sought discretionary review by the Louisiana Supreme Court, which denied their application, finding no error. This Court granted certiorari and we reverse.

We may briefly dispose of certain threshold problems. Petitioners cannot constitutionally be convicted merely because they did not comply with an order to leave the library. . . . The statute itself reads in the conjunctive; it requires both the defined breach of peace *and* an order to move on. Without reference to the statute, it must be noted that petitioners' presence in the library was unquestionably lawful. It was a public facility, open to the public. Negroes could not be denied access since white persons were welcome. . . . Petitioners' deportment while in the library was unexceptionable. They were neither loud, boisterous, obstreperous, indecorous nor impolite. There is no claim that, apart from the continuation—for ten or fifteen minutes—of their presence itself, their conduct provided a basis for the order to leave, or for a charge of breach of the peace.

We come, then, to the barebones of the problem. Petitioners, five adult Negro men, remained in the library room for a total of ten or fifteen minutes. The first few moments were occupied by a ritualistic request for service and a response. We may assume that the response constituted service, and we need not consider whether it was merely a gambit in the ritual. This ceremony being out of the way, the Negroes proceeded to the business in hand. They sat and stood in the room, quietly, as monuments of protest against the segregation of the library. They were arrested and charged and convicted of breach of the peace under a specific statute.

If we compare this situation with that in *Garner,* we must inevitably conclude that here, too, there is not the slightest evidence which would or could sustain the application of the statute to petitioners. The statute requires a showing either of "intent to provoke a breach of the peace," or of "circumstances such that a breach of the peace may be occasioned" by the acts in question. There is not in this case the slightest hint of either. We need not be beguiled by the ritual of the request for a copy of "The Story of the Negro." We need not assume that petitioner Brown and his friends were in search of a book for night reading. We instead rest upon the manifest fact that they intended to and did stage a peaceful and orderly protest demonstration, with no "intent to provoke a breach of the peace. . . ."

Nor were the circumstances such that a breach of the peace might be "occasioned" by their actions, as the statute alternatively provides. The library room was empty, except for the librarians. There were no other patrons. There were no onlookers except for the vigilant and forewarned sheriff, and his deputies. Petitioners did nothing and said nothing even remotely provocative. The danger, if any existed, was surely less than in the course of the sit-in at the "white" lunch counters in *Garner*. And surely there was less danger that a breach of the peace might occur from Mrs. Katie Reeves and Mrs. Perkins in the adult reading room of the Clinton Branch Library than that disorder might result from the "restless" white people in the bus depot waiting room in *Taylor,* or from the 100 to 300 "grumbling" white onlookers in *Cox*. But in each of these cases, this Court refused to countenance convictions under Louisiana's breach of the peace statute.

The argument of the State of Louisiana, however, is that the issue presented by this case is much simpler than our statement would indicate. The issue, asserts the State, is simply that petitioners were using the library room "as a place in which to loaf or make a nuisance of themselves." The State argues that the "test"—the permissible civil rights demonstration—was concluded when petitioners entered the library, asked for service and were served. Having satisfied themselves, the argument runs, that they could get service, they should have departed. Instead, they simply sat there, "staring vacantly," and this was "enough to unnerve a woman in the situation Mrs. Reeves was in."

This is a piquant version of the affair, but the matter is hardly to be decided on points. It was not a game. It could not be won so handily by the gesture of service to this particular request. There is no dispute that the library system was segregated, and no possible doubt that these petitioners were there to protest this fact. But even if we were to agree with the State's ingenuous characterization of the events, we would have to reverse. There was no violation of the statute which petitioners are accused of breaching; no disorder, no intent to provoke a breach of the peace and no circumstances indicating that a breach might be occasioned by petitioners' actions. The sole statutory provision invoked by the State contains not a word about occupying the reading room of a public library for more than 15 minutes, any more than it purports to punish the bare refusal to obey an unexplained command to withdraw from a public street, . . . or public building. We can find nothing in the language of the statute, in fact, which would elevate the giving of cause for Mrs. Reeves' discomfort, however we may sympathize with her, to a crime against the State of Louisiana. . . .

But there is another and sharper answer which is called for. We are here dealing with an aspect of a basic constitutional right—the right under the First and Fourteenth Amendments guaranteeing freedom of speech and of assembly, and freedom to petition the Government for a redress of grievances. The Constitution of the State of Louisiana reiterates these guaranties. See Art. I, §§ 3, 5. As this Court has repeatedly stated, these rights are not confined to verbal expression. They embrace appropriate types of action which certainly include the right in a peaceable and orderly manner to protest by silent and reproachful presence, in a place where the protestant has every right to be, the unconstitutional segregation of public facilities. Accordingly, even if the accused action were within the scope of the statutory instrument, we would be required to assess the constitutional impact of its application, and we would have to hold that the statute cannot constitutionally be applied to punish petitioners' actions in the circumstances of this case. . . . The statute was deliberately and purposefully applied solely to terminate the reasonable, orderly, and limited exercise of the right to protest the unconstitutional segregation of a public facility. Interference with this right, so exercised, by state action is intolerable under our Constitution. . . .

It is an unhappy circumstance that the locus of these events was a public library —a place dedicated to quiet, to knowledge, and to beauty. It is a sad commentary that this hallowed place in the parishes of East and West Feliciana bore the ugly stamp of racism. It is sad, too, that it was a public library which, reasonably enough in the circumstances, was the stage for a confrontation between those discriminated against and the representatives of the offending parishes. Fortunately, the circumstances here were such that no claim can be made that use of the library by others was disturbed by the demonstration. Perhaps the time and method were carefully chosen with this in mind. Were it otherwise, a factor not present in this case would have to be considered. Here, there was no disturbance of others, no disruption of library activities, and no violation of any library regulations.

A State or its instrumentality may, of course, regulate the use of its libraries or other public facilities. But it must do so in a reasonable and nondiscriminatory manner, equally applicable to all and administered with equality to all. It may not do so as to some and not as to all. It may not provide certain facilities for whites and others for Negroes. And it may not invoke regulations as to use—whether they are *ad hoc* or general—as a pretext for pursuing those engaged in lawful, constitutionally protected exercise of their fundamental rights. . . .

The decision below is reversed.

Mr. Justice Black, with whom Mr. Justice Clark, Mr. Justice Harlan, and Mr. Justice Stewart join dissenting:

I do not believe that any provision of the United States Constitution forbids any one of the 50 States of the Union, including Louisiana, to make it unlawful to stage "sit-ins" or "stand-up" in their public libraries for the purpose of advertising objections to the State's public policies. That, however, is precisely what the Court or at least a majority of the Court majority here holds that all the States are forbidden to do by our Constitution. I dissent. The three opinions written for the majority of five who reverse these convictions make it necessary for me to state the relevant facts, circumstances, and issues in this case as I view them.

Representatives of the Congress of Racial Equality (CORE) claimed that Negroes had been "locked out" of libraries operated jointly by three Louisiana parishes. A "demonstration was planned" by the organization "to integrate the Library," and accordingly these five petitioners, all Negroes, went to the Audubon Regional Library located at Clinton, Lousiana on a Saturday morning about 11:30 A.M. "to sit-in at the Library." The county sheriff, whose office was in the courthouse within sight of the library building, had received information that "they [referring to CORE] were going to sit-in, or that something was going to take place at the Library that morning," and noticed the petitioners when they went by his office on their way to the library. Upon arrival at the library petitioners were met inside the building by Mrs. Reeves, who was the assistant librarian. She courteously asked them if she could help them in any way. One of the group, petitioner Brown, handed her a slip of paper on which was written the title of a book which he said he wanted. Mrs. Reeves went to her shelves and her catalogues, and after making a search, came back and told Mr. Brown that the library did not have the book, but that she could request it from the state library and probably get it for him. She told him she would do this. Mr. Brown then sat down in the only chair in the library room other than the chair at Mrs. Reeves' desk, and the other four petitioners stood around him. When petitioners did not leave, Mrs. Reeves told the group again that she would send for the book, and when Mr. Brown continued to sit and the others continued to stand, she asked them to leave. They did not leave, so Mrs. Reeves then called Mrs. Perkins, the regional librarian and told Mrs. Perkins about the situation. Mrs. Perkins went to Mr. Brown and told him she did not know whether he understood that a request for the book he had asked for would be sent to the state library. Along about that time Mr. Brown said to Mrs. Perkins, "what about the Constitution?" but did not request that any copy of the Constitution be given to him. Mrs. Perkins then repeated the request of Mrs. Reeves that petitioners leave the library telling them "that the one who seemed to want something had been served."About 10 or 15 minutes after the petitioners came to the library, when according to Mrs. Perkins' testimony she was just about to call the sheriff over the phone, the sheriff came into the library. Mrs. Perkins explained to him that Mrs. Reeves had taken petitioners' application for the book they wanted, that the book was not available, that she and Mrs. Reeves had both requested the petitioners to leave, and that they would not do so. After learning these facts, the sheriff also asked petitioners to leave the library building and stated that he would have to arrest them if they did not. The petitioners refused to leave, and speaking for the group, petitioner Brown told the sheriff "that he was not going to leave the Library." Thereupon the sheriff immediately arrested all of them. Petitioners, while in the library, never talked in unusually loud voices and used no bad language. Beyond Mr. Brown's request for the book which the library did not have, none of the petitioners at any time prior to his arrest requested any further service of either of the librarians nor did any petitioner in any other way seek to read in the library or otherwise use any of the library's facilities except for sitting and standing purposes.

The Clinton branch of the Audubon Regional Library is not a large one. It appears to be used almost entirely as a circulating and not a reading library. The duty of Mrs. Reeves, assistant librarian, according to her testimony which was not disputed, was "To assist people who came into the Library to select their books; check out the books to them; to keep the shelves in order, and to keep a record of the circulation of the day." In the library's "lobby," where the events of this case took place, there were book shelves and one table on each side; also in the room were a desk and chair for the librarian, and one other chair. The two tables were used mainly for book display and magazines. It was not against the policy of the library to allow citizens with library registration cards to read if they cared to. But according to Mrs. Reeves' testimony at trial, "very few people read; if a book is there and they want it, they take it and go." Mrs. Perkins testified that "We do not maintain a reading-room, as such, we do not have the space for it." Mrs. Perkins later referred to the "lobby" as the "adult reading-room, the adult service-room. . . ."

Because I think that the crucial issues to be decided here are much narrower and far less complicated than the prevailing opinion implies, I find it necessary first to point out that several matters discussed in that opinion are, in my judgment, either irrelevant, or that inferences drawn from them are not justified.

I

In concluding to reverse these convictions the prevailing opinion relies almost entirely on three prior breach of the peace cases which have come to this Court from the State of Louisiana, and *Edwards* v. *South Carolina,* 372 US 229. I think that none of these four cases has any appreciable bearing on what the Court should hold in this case.

(a) The first of these cases is *Garner* v. *State of Louisiana,* 368 US 157, decided in December 1961. That case, involving "sit-in" demonstrations at several lunch counters, was decided under an old Louisiana breach of the peace statute. The section involved here was added to the old law after the events described in that case took place, but before the Court's opinion. The old law considered in *Garner* did not contain any phrase similar to the one under consideration here which makes it an offense to disturb the peace by congregating in a public building over the protest of a person rightfully in charge of the building. Moreover, the majority of the Court in *Garner,* in construing the old law, noted the presence of the new section, and expressly contrasted its reach to that of the older statute. There are other significant differences between *Garner* and this case, but the fact that *Garner* involved an almost entirely different statute, which was expressly distinguished from the present one by the Court's opinion, makes it hard for me to see how the Court's *Garner* holding can provide any meaningful support for the reversal of these convictions.

(b) The second Louisiana breach of the peace case upon which the prevailing opinion relies for reversal is *Taylor* v. *State of Louisiana,* 370 US 154. That case as described today in the prevailing opinion "concerned a sit-in by Negroes in a waiting room at a bus depot, reserved 'for whites only.'" In *Taylor,* the Court in a short *per curiam* opinion held merely that the breach of the peace convictions could not be supported where "the only evidence to support the charge was that petitioners were violating a custom that segregated people in waiting rooms according to their race" contrary to federal law. There was no indication in that case that persons, having no business whatever in a bus depot except to stage a public protest against some state policy, have a constitutional right to occupy the depot's space after having been requested by competent authorities to leave.

(c) The case relied on most heavily by the prevailing opinion and my Brother Brennan is *Cox* v. *State of Louisiana,* 379 US 536. That case, unlike this one involved picketing and patrolling in the streets, and correspondingly that part of the Louisiana breach of the peace statute which prohibited certain kinds of street activity. The language of the phase of the statute under consideration here, relating to congregating in public buildings and refusing to move on when ordered to do so by an authorized person, was in no way involved or discussed in *Cox.* The problems of state regulation of the streets on the one hand, and public buildings on the other, are quite obviously separate and distinct. Public buildings such as libraries, school houses, fire departments, court houses, and executive mansions are maintained to perform certain specific and vital functions. Order and tranquility of a sort entirely unknown to the public streets are essential to their normal operation. Contrary to the implications in the prevailing opinion it is incomprehensible to me that a State must measure disturbances in its libraries and on the streets with identical standards. Furthermore, the vice of discriminatory enforcement, which contaminates the "public street" phase of this statute, does not beset the statute's application to activity in public buildings. In the public building, unlike the street, peace and quiet is a fast and necessary rule, and as a result there is much less room for peace officers to abuse their authority in enforcing the "public building" part of the statute. . . .

(d) The fourth case which the prevailing opinion cites as indicating that the "public building" phase of the Louisiana statute is unconstitutional is *Edwards* v. *South Carolina,* 372 US 229. This Court's holding in the *Edwards* case, however, was based on the fact that the statute construed there was not narrowly drawn to assure its nondiscriminatory application. Here the part of the Louisiana statute relating to public buildings, as construed and applied by the Louisiana courts, does clearly describe the offense. Nothing in *Edwards* as I read it, states any principle of constitutional law under which a State must permit its public libraries, dedicated to reading and learning and studying, to be used for the purpose of conducting protests against public or private policies. And that is the constitutional issue in the present case.

I find nothing in these four cases, nor in any other case decided by this Court that I can recall, which restricts Louisiana's power to enforce that part of its statute on which these convictions rest in order to maintain peace and order in its public libraries so as to further the extremely necessary purposes underlying their existence.

II

The prevailing opinion and to some extent the two separate concurring opinions treat this case as though Louisiana was here attempting to enforce a policy of denying Louisiana citizens the right to use the State's libraries on account of race. Whatever may have been the policy of the State of Louisiana in the past or may be the policy of that State at the present, at other places or in other circumstances, there simply was no racial discrimination practiced in this case. These petitioners were treated with every courtesy and granted every consideration to which they were entitled in the Audubon Library. They asked for a book, perhaps as the prevailing opinion suggests more as a ritualistic ceremonial than anything else. The lady in charge nevertheless hunted for the book, found she did not have it, sent for it, and later obtained it from the state library for petitioners' use. No petitioner asked for any other book, none indicated that he wanted to read any other book, and none attempted to read any other book or any other printed matter. As a matter of fact the record shows, and the prevailing opinion admits, that the five petitioners stayed in the library not to use it for learning but as "monuments of protest" to voice their disapproval of what they thought was a policy of the State. Although Mrs. Perkins, the branch's librarian, testified unambiguously that there was no racial discrimination practiced at her library, and although the record shows without the slightest dispute that there was no discrimination of any kind or character practiced against these petitioners, in at least the prevailing opinion and that of my Brother White it is nevertheless implied at several places that the equal treatment given these petitioners was some kind of subterfuge or sham. These aspersions are I think wholly without justification. The prevailing opinion refers to the "tidy plan" of the State; with reference to the service given petitioners it says that "We may assume that the response constituted service, and we need not consider whether it was merely a gambit in the ritual"; it insinuates that Louisiana was playing a "game" with petitioners' rights, and the courteous treatment given petitioners by the librarian is degraded by calling it a "gesture of service"; it, moreover, refers to the State's argument in this case as giving a "piquant version of the affair." I see no basis or reason for these innuendos against the State's defense or its convictions in this case. The State's District Attorney, who argued the case before us, stated frankly and forthrightly that there would be no defense had Louisiana denied these petitioners equal service at its public libraries on account of their race. There was no such denial. We must now consider the Court's reversal on it merits.

III

As best I can tell, one ground upon which both the prevailing opinion and that of my Brother White rely to reverse these convictions is that the State failed to prove its case. This conclusion appears to be based on the assumption that under the Louisiana statute properly construed, there can be no conviction unless persons who do not want library service stay there an unusually long time after being ordered to leave, make a big noise, use some bad language, engage in fighting, try to provoke a fight, or in some other way become boisterous. The argument seems to be that without a blatant, loud manifestation of aggressive hostility or an exceedingly long "sit-in" or "sojourn" in a public library, there are no circumstances which could foreseeably occasion a breach of the peace. Louisiana has not so construed its statute nor should we. Doing so goes against common sense and common understanding. While soft words can undoubtedly turn away wrath, they may also provoke it. Disturbers of the peace do not always rattle swords or shout invectives. It is high time to challenge the assumption in which too many people have too long acquiesced, that groups that think they have been mistreated or that have actually been mistreated have a constitutional right to use the public's streets, buildings, and property to protest whatever, wherever, whenever they want, without regard to whom it may disturb.

The phase of the Louisiana statute that we are considering here is for all intents and purposes aimed at trespassers on government property. In addition, subdivision (4) of the same Louisiana law makes it an offense for one to refuse to leave the premises of another when requested to do so by the owner. Both of these provisions of the state statute, however, provide that before an offense is committed, the conduct must be engaged in "with intent to provoke a breach of the peace, or under circumstances such that a breach of the peace may be occasioned thereby." There is a long history behind trespass laws in the United States. Invasion of another man's property over his protest is one of the surest ways any person can pick out to disturb the peace. Louisiana, just like any other State in this Union, has a right to pass and use laws based on knowledge of this fact, a knowledge so widespread and prevalent that it would probably be difficult to find a hermit ignorant of its existence.

I think that the evidence in this case established every element in the offense charged against petitioners. No one disputes the fact that petitioners congregated in a public building and refused to move on when ordered to do so by authorized persons. The only factual question which can possibly arise regarding the application of the statute here is whether under Louisiana law petitioners either intended to breach the peace or created circumstances under which a breach might have been occasioned. The record shows that petitioners, as part of a plan, entered the library and once there stayed despite the librarians' protests until its normal activity was completely disrupted. To be sure, there were not "100 to 300 'grumbling' white onlookers" as there were in *Cox* v. *State of Louisiana, supra,* but surely, in the prevailing opinion's futile effort to rely on *Cox,* it is not meant that 300 or 100 grumbling onlookers must be crowded into a library before Louisiana can maintain an action under this statute. A tiny, branch, parish library, staffed by two women, is not a department store as in *Garner* v. *State of Louisiana, supra,* nor a bus terminal as in *Taylor* v. *State of Lousiana, supra,* nor a public thoroughfare as in *Edwards* v. *South Carolina, supra,* and *Cox.* Short of physical violence, petitioners could not have more completely upset the normal, quiet functioning of the Clinton branch of Audubon Regional Library. The state courts below thought the disturbance created by petitioners constituted a violation of the statute. So far as the reversal here rests on a holding that the Louisiana statute was not violated, the Court simply substitutes its judgment for that of the Louisiana courts as to what conduct satisfies the requirements of that state statute. We are a long way off from what happened there to substitute our judgment for theirs. To do so not only upsets settled doctrine concerning the interpretation of state statutes by federal courts, ... but also is built on shifting sands that ignore the realities of life in our country.

IV

Having already attempted to hold, wrongfully I think, that these convictions should be set aside as unconstitutional because of a complete lack of evidence to prove the charge, the prevailing opinion ventures out in an attempt to decide other constitutional questions. It says:

> Accordingly, even if the accused action were within the scope of the statutory instrument, we would be required to assess the constitutional impact of its application, and we would have to hold that the statute cannot constitutionally be applied to punish petitioners' actions in the circumstances of this case.

I have sometimes thought that this Court has gone entirely too far in refusing to decide constitutional questions on the ground that they should be avoided where possible. The journey here, however, goes entirely too far in the opposite direction. Apparently unsatisfied with or unsure of the "no evidence" ground for reversing the convictions, the prevailing opinion goes on to state that the statute was used unconstitutionally in the circumstances of this case because it was "deliberately and purposefully applied solely to terminate the reasonable, orderly, and limited exercise of the right to protest the unconstitutional segregation of a public facility." First, I am constrained to say that this statement is wholly unsupported by the record in this case. There is simply no evidence in the record at all that petitioners were arrested because they were exercising the "right to protest." It is nevertheless said that this was the *sole* reason for the arrests. Moreover, the conclusion that the statute was unconstitutionally applied because it interfered with the petitioners' so-called protest establishes a completely new constitutional doctrine. In this case this new constitutional principle means that even though these petitioners did not want to use the Louisiana public library for library purposes, they had a constitutional right nevertheless to stay there over the protest of the librarian who had lawful authority to keep the library orderly for the use of people who wanted to use its books, its magazines, and its papers. But the principle espoused also a far broader meaning. It means that the Constitution, the First and the Fourteenth Amendments, requires the custodians and supervisors of the public libraries in this country to stand helplessly by while protesting groups advocating one cause or another, stage "sit-ins" or "stand-ups" to dramatize their particular views on particular issues. And it should be remembered that if one group can take over libraries for one cause, other groups will assert the right to do it for causes which, while wholly legal, may not be so appealing to this Court. The States are thus paralyzed with reference to control of their libraries for library purposes, and I suppose that inevitably the next step will be to paralyze the schools. Efforts to this effect have already been made all over the country. Furthermore, here it seems to have made no difference whatever that the Audubon Regional Library, at least in this instance, satisfied its constitutional duty by giving these petitioners its services in full measure without regard to their race.

The constitutional doctrine that actually prevails in this Court today for the first time in its history rests at least in great part on the Court's interpretation of the First Amendment as carried into the States by the Fourteenth. This is the First Amendment which, as I have said in the past, is to me the very heart of our free government without which liberty and equality cannot exist. But I have never thought and do not now think that the First Amendment can sustain the startling doctrine the prevailing opinion here creates. The First Amendment, I think, protects speech, writings, and expression of views in any manner in which they can be legitimately and validly communicated. But

I have never believed that it gives any person or group of persons the constitutional right to go wherever they want, whenever they please, without regard to the rights of private or public property or to state law. Indeed a majority of this Court said as much in *Cox* v. *State of Louisiana*. Though the First Amendment guarantees the right of assembly and the right of petition along with the rights of speech, press, and religion, it does not guarantee to any person the right to use someone else's property, even that owned by government and dedicated to other purposes, as a stage to express dissident ideas. The novel constitutional doctrine of the prevailing opinion nevertheless exalts the power of private nongovernmental groups to determine what use shall be made of governmental property over the power of the elected governmental officials of the States and the Nation.

The prevailing opinion seems to find some comfort in its very questionable assumption that in this case "no claim can be made that use of the library by others was disturbed by the demonstration. Perhaps the time and method were carefully chosen with this in mind." If this was the reason Saturday morning was selected, the only representative of CORE who testified was not aware of it. No one of the petitioners has suggested such a thing. The lawyers for the petitioners have not. In fact at the trial responses of the sheriff to questions asked him by petitioners' lawyer indicate that there was another patron in the library at the time the petitioners "sat-in" or "stood-up" there. But even if there were no other patrons there in this instance, with this new constitutional doctrine rather shakily established, it is pretty clear that organized protesters will not overlook the chance to go into the libraries and disturb those in there to learn at any time when their "demonstration" activities will obtain the most publicity.

The prevailing opinion laments the fact that the place where these events took place was "a public library—a place dedicated to quiet, to knowledge, and to beauty." I too lament this fact, and for this reason I am deeply troubled with the fear that powerful private groups throughout the Nation will read the Court's action, as I do—that is, as granting them a license to invade the tranquillity and beauty of our libraries whenever they have quarrel with some state policy which may or may not exist. It is an unhappy circumstance in my judgment that the group, which more than any other has needed a government of equal laws and equal justice, is now encouraged to believe that the best way for it to advance its cause, which is a worthy one, is by taking the law into its own hands from place to place and from time to time. Governments like ours were formed to substitute the rule of law for the rule of force. Illustrations may be given where crowds have gathered together peaceably by reason of extraordinarily good discipline reinforced by vigilant officers. "Demonstrations" have taken place without any manifestations of force at the time. But I say once more that the crowd moved by noble ideals today can become the mob ruled by hate and passion and greed and violence tomorrow. If we ever doubted that, we know it now. The peaceful songs of love can become as stirring and provocative as the Marseillaise did in the days when a noble revolution gave way to rule by successive mobs until chaos set in. The holding in this case today makes it more necessary than ever that we stop and look more closely at where we are going.

I would affirm.

ADDERLEY v. FLORIDA
385 US 39 (1966)

[Defendants, together with others, apparently all students at a Negro university in Florida, demonstrated outside the county jail against racial segregation and against the previous arrests of other demonstrators who were in the jail. They were asked to leave; when they refused, they were arrested and convicted on a charge of trespass. By 5–4 vote, the Supreme Court affirmed the convictions. Justice Douglas, joined by Chief Justice Warren and Justices Brennan and Fortas, dissented, contending that the trespass law was used to penalize defendants for exercising a constitutional right.]

Mr. Justice Black delivered the opinion of the Court:

Petitioners, Harriett Louise Adderley and 31 other persons, were convicted by a jury in a joint trial in the County Judge's Court of Leon County, Florida, on a charge of "trespass with a malicious and mischievous intent" upon the premises of the county jail contrary to § 821.18 of the Florida statutes set out below.* Petitioners, apparently all students of the Florida A. & M. University in Tallahassee, had gone from the school to the jail about a mile away, along with many other students, to "demonstrate" at the jail their protests because of arrests of other protesting students the day before, and perhaps to protest more generally against state and local policies and practices of racial segregation, including segregation of the jail. The county sheriff, legal custodian of the jail and jail grounds, tried to persuade the students to leave the jail grounds. When this did not work, he notified them that they must leave, notified them that they must leave or he would arrest them for trespassing, and notified them further that if they resisted arrest he would arrest them for resisting arrest as well. Some of the students left but others, including petitioners, remained and they were arrested. On appeal the convictions were affirmed by the Florida Circuit Court and then by the Florida District Court of Appeals. That being the highest state court to which they could appeal, petitioners applied to us for certiorari contending that, in view of petitioners' purpose to protest against jail and other segregation policies, their conviction denied them "rights of free speech, assembly, petition, due process of law and equal protection of the laws as guaranteed by the Fourteenth Amendment to the Constitution of the United States." On this "Question Presented" we granted certiorari. Petitioners present their argument on this question in four separate points, and for convenience we deal with each of their points in the order in which they present them.

I

Petitioners have insisted from the beginning of these cases that they are controlled and must be reversed because of our prior cases of *Edwards* v. *South Carolina,* 372 US 229, and *Cox* v. *Louisiana,* 379 US 536. We cannot agree.

The *Edwards* case, like this one, did come up when a number of persons demonstrated on public property against their State's segregation policies. They also sang hymns and danced, as did the demonstrators in this case. But here the analogies to this case end. In *Edwards,* the demonstrators went to the South Carolina State Capitol grounds to protest. In this case they went to the jail. Traditionally, state

* "Every trespass upon the property of another, committed with a malicious and mischievous intent, the punishment of which is not specially provided for, shall be punished by imprisonment not exceeding three months, or by fine not exceeding one hundred dollars." Fla. Stat. § 821.18 (1965).

capitol grounds are open to the public. Jails, built for security purposes, are not. The demonstrators at the South Carolina Capitol went in through a public driveway and as they entered they were told by state officials there that they had a right as citizens to go through the State House grounds as long as they were peaceful. Here the demonstrators entered the jail grounds through a driveway used only for jail purposes and without warning to or permission from the sheriff. More importantly, South Carolina sought to prosecute its State Capitol demonstrators by charging them with the common-law crime of breach of the peace. This Court in *Edwards* took pains to point out at length the indefinite, loose, and broad nature of this charge; indeed, this Court pointed out . . . that the South Carolina Supreme Court had itself declared that the "breach of the peace charge" is "not susceptible of exact definition." South Carolina's power to prosecute, it was emphasized . . . would have been different had it proceeded under a "precise and narrowly drawn regulatory statute evincing a legislative judgment that certain specific conduct be limited or proscribed" such as, for example, "limiting the periods during which the State House grounds were open to the public. . . ." The South Carolina breach-of-the-peace statute was thus struck down as being so broad and all-embracing as to jeopardize speech, press, assembly and petition, under the constitutional doctrine enunciated in *Cantwell* v. *Connecticut,* 310 US 296, and followed in many subsequent cases. And it was on this same ground of vagueness that in *Cox* v. *Louisiana,* the Louisiana breach-of-the-peace law used to prosecute Cox was invalidated.

The Florida trespass statute under which these petitioners were charged cannot be challenged on this ground. It is aimed at conduct of one limited kind, that is for one person or persons to trespass upon the property of another with a malicious and mischievous intent. There is no lack of notice in this law, nothing to entrap or fool the unwary.

Petitioners seem to argue that the Florida trespass law is void for vagueness because it requires a trespass to be "with a malicious and mischievous intent. . . ." But these words do not broaden the scope of trespass so as to make it cover a multitude of types of conduct as does the common-law breach-of-the-peace charge. On the contrary, these words narrow the scope of the offense. The trial court charged the jury as to their meaning and petitioners have not argued that this definition . . . is not a reasonable and clear definition of the terms. The use of these terms in the statute, instead of contributing to uncertainty and misunderstanding, actually makes its meaning more understandable and clear.

II

Petitioners in this Court invoke the doctrine of abatement announced by this Court in *Hamm* v. *City of Rock Hill,* 379 US 306. But that holding was that the Civil Rights Act of 1964, 78 Stat. 241, which made it unlawful for places of public accommodation to deny service to any person because of race, effected an abatement of prosecutions of persons for seeking such services that arose prior to the passage of the Act. But this case in no way involves prosecution of petitioners for seeking service in establishments covered by the Act. It involves only an alleged trespass on jail grounds—a trespass which can be prosecuted regardless of the fact that it is the means of protesting segregation of establishments covered by the Act.

III

Petitioners next argue that "petty criminal statutes may not be used to violate minorities' constitutional rights." This of course is true but this abstract proposition gets us nowhere in deciding this case.

IV

Petitioners here contend that "Petitioners' convictions are based on a total lack of relevant evidence." If true, this would be a denial of due process under *Garner* v. *Louisiana,* 368 US 157, and *Thompson* v. *City of Louisville,* 362 US 199. Both in the petition for certiorari and in the brief on the merits petitioners state that their summary of the evidence "does not conflict with the facts contained in the Circuit Court's opinion" which was in effect affirmed by the District Court of Appeals. That statement is correct and petitioners' summary of facts as well as that of the Circuit Court show an abundance of facts to support the jury's verdict of guilty in these cases.

In summary both these statements show testimony ample to prove this: Disturbed and upset by the arrest of their schoolmates the day before, a large number of Florida A. & M. students assembled on the school grounds and decided to march down to the county jail. Some apparently wanted to get themselves put in jail too, along with the students already there.* A group of around 200 marched from the school and arrived at the jail singing and clapping. They went directly to the jail door entrance where they were met by a deputy sheriff, evidently surprised by their arrival. He asked them to move back, claiming they were blocking the entrance to the jail and fearing that they might attempt to enter the jail. They moved back part of the way, where they stood or sat, singing, clapping and dancing, on the jail driveway and on an adjacent grassy area upon the jail premises. This particular jail entrance and driveway were not normally used by the public, but by the sheriff's department for transporting prisoners to and from the courts several blocks away and by commercial concerns for servicing the jail. Even after their partial retreat, the demonstrators continued to block vehicular passage over this driveway up to the entrance of the jail.† Someone called the sheriff who was at the moment apparently conferring with one of the state court judges about incidents connected with prior arrests for demonstrations. When the sheriff returned to the jail, he immedi-

---

* The three petitioners who testified insisted that they had not come to the jail for the purpose of being arrested. But both the sheriff and a deputy testified that they heard several of the demonstrators present at the jail loudly proclaim their desire to be arrested. Indeed, this latter version is borne out by the fact that, though assertedly protesting the prior arrests of their fellow students and the city's segregation policies, none of the demonstrators carried any signs and upon arriving at the jail, no speeches or other verbal protests were made.

† Although some of the petitioners testified that they had no intention of interfering with vehicular traffic to and from the jail entrance and that they noticed no vehicle trying to enter or leave the driveway, the deputy sheriff testified that it would have been impossible for automobiles to drive up to the jail entrance and that one serviceman, finished with his business in the jail, waited inside because the demonstrators were sitting around and leaning against his truck parked outside. The sheriff testified that the time the demonstrators were there, between 9:30 and 10 A.M. Monday morning, was generally a very busy time for using the jail entrance to transport weekend inmates to the courts and for tradesmen to make service calls on the jail.

ately inquired if all was safe inside the jail and was told it was. He then engaged in a conversation with two of the leaders. He told them that they were trespassing upon jail property and that he would give them 10 minutes to leave or he would arrest them. Neither of the leaders did anything to disperse the crowd, and one of them told the sheriff that they wanted to get arrested. A local minister talked with some of the demonstrators and told them not to enter the jail, because they could not arrest themselves, but just to remain where they were. After about 10 minutes, the sheriff, in a voice loud enough to be heard by all, told the demonstrators that he was the legal custodian of the jail and its premises, that they were trespassing on county property in violation of the law, that they should all leave forthwith or he would arrest them, and that if they attempted to resist arrest, he would charge them with that as a separate offense. Some of the group then left. Others, including all petitioners, did not leave. Some of them sat down. In a few minutes, realizing that the remaining demonstrators had no intention of leaving, the sheriff ordered his deputies to surround those remaining on jail premises and placed them, 107 demonstrators, under arrest. The sheriff unequivocally testified that he did not arrest any person other than those who were on the jail premises. Of the three petitioners testifying, two insisted that they were arrested before they had a chance to leave, had they wanted to, and one testified that she did not intend to leave. The sheriff again explicitly testified that he did not arrest any person who was attempting to leave.

Under the foregoing testimony the jury was authorized to find that the State had proven every essential element of the crime, as it was defined by the state court. That interpretation is, of course, binding on us, leaving only the question of whether conviction of the state offense, thus defined, unconstitutionally deprives petitioners of their rights to freedom of speech, press, assembly or petition. We hold it does not. The sheriff, as jail custodian, had power, as the state courts have here held, to direct that this large crowd of people get off the grounds. There is not a shred of evidence in this record that this power was exercised, or that its exercise was sanctioned by the lower courts, because the sheriff objected to what was being sung or said by the demonstrators or because he disagreed with the objectives of their protest. The record reveals that he objected only to their presence on that part of the jail grounds reserved for jail uses. There is no evidence at all that on any other occasion had similarly large groups of the public been permitted to gather on this portion of the jail grounds for any purpose. Nothing in the Constitution of the United States prevents Florida from even-handed enforcement of its general trespass statute against those refusing to obey the sheriff's order to remove themselves from what amounted to the curtilage of the jailhouse. The State, no less than a private owner of property, has power to preserve the property under its control for the use to which it is lawfully dedicated. For this reason there is no merit to the petitioners' argument that they had a constitutional right to stay on the property, over the jail custodian's objections, because this "area chosen for the peaceful civil rights demonstration was not only 'reasonable' but also particularly appropriate. . . ." Such an argument has as its major unarticulated premise the assumption that people who want to propagandize protests or views have a constitutional right to do so whenever and however and wherever they please. That concept of constitutional law was vigorously and forthrightfully rejected in two of the cases petitioners rely on. . . . We reject it again. The United States Constitution does not forbid a State to control the use of its own property for its own lawful nondiscriminatory purpose.

These judgments are affirmed.

SHUTTLESWORTH *v.* BIRMINGHAM
394 US 147 (1969)

[Defendant, a Negro minister, was convicted of violating the ordinance of Birmingham, Alabama, that made it an offense to participate in a public demonstration without first obtaining a permit. The Supreme Court reversed the judgment and held the ordinance unconstitutional as vesting too broad a discretion in city officials. Justice Stewart wrote the opinion of the Court. Justice Black concurred in the result. Justice Marshall did not participate in the case. Justice Harlan wrote a concurring opinion.]

Mr. Justice Stewart delivered the opinion of the Court:

The petitioner stands convicted for violating an ordinance of Birmingham, Alabama, making it an offense to participate in any "parade or procession or other public demonstration" without first obtaining a permit from the City Commission. The question before us is whether that conviction can be squared with the Constitution of the United States.

On the afternoon of April 12, Good Friday 1963, 52 people, all Negroes, were led out of a Birmingham church by three Negro ministers, one of whom was the petitioner, Fred L. Shuttlesworth. They walked in orderly fashion, two abreast for the most part, for four blocks. The purpose of their march was to protest the alleged denial of civil rights to Negroes in the city of Birmingham. The marchers stayed on the sidewalks except at street intersections, and they did not interfere with other pedestrians. No automobiles were obstructed, nor were traffic signals disobeyed. The petitioner was with the group for at least part of this time, walking alongside the others, and once moving from the front to the rear. As the marchers moved along, a crowd of spectators fell in behind them at a distance. The spectators at some points spilled out into the street, but the street was not blocked and vehicles were not obstructed.

At the end of four blocks the marchers were stopped by the Birmingham police, and were arrested for violating § 1159 of the General Code of Birmingham. That ordinance reads as follows:

It shall be unlawful to organize or hold, or to assist in organizing or holding, or to take part or participate in, any parade or procession or other public demonstration on the streets or other public ways of the city, unless a permit therefore has been secured from the commission.

To secure such permit, written application shall be made to the commission, setting forth the probable number of persons, vehicles and animals which will be engaged in such parade, procession or other public demonstration, the purpose for which it is to be held or had, and the streets or public ways over, along or in which it is desired to have or hold such parade, procession or other public demonstration. The commission shall grant a written permit for such parade, procession or other public demonstration, prescribing the streets or other public ways which may be used therefor, unless in its judgment the public welfare, peace, safety, health, decency, good order, morals or convenience require that it be refused. It shall be unlawful to use for such purposes any other streets or public ways than those set out in said permit.

The two preceding paragraphs, however, shall not apply to funeral processions.

The petitioner was convicted for violation of § 1159 and was sentenced to 90 days' imprisonment at hard labor and an additional 48 days at hard labor in default of payment of a $75 fine and $24 costs. The Alabama Court of Appeals reversed the judgment of conviction, holding the evidence was insufficient "to show a procession which would require, under the terms of § 1159, the getting of a permit," that the ordinance had been applied in a discriminatory fashion, and that it was unconstitutional in imposing an "invidious prior restraint" without ascertainable standards for the granting of permits. The Supreme Court of Alabama, however, giving the language of § 1159 an extraordinarily narrow construction, reversed the judgment of the Court of Appeals and reinstated the conviction. We granted certiorari to consider the petitioner's constitutional claims.

There can be no doubt that the Birmingham ordinance, as it was written, conferred upon the City Commission virtually unbridled and absolute power to prohibit any "parade," "procession," or "demonstration" on the city's streets or public ways. For in deciding whether or not to withhold a permit, the members of the Commission were to be guided only by their own ideas of "public welfare, peace, safety, health, decency, good order, morals or convenience." This ordinance as it was written, therefore, fell squarely within the ambit of the many decisions of this Court over the last 30 years, holding that a law subjecting the exercise of First Amendment freedoms to the prior restraint of a license, without narrow, objective, and definite standards to guide the licensing authority, is unconstitutional. "It is settled by a long line of recent decisions of this Court that an ordinance which, like this one, makes the peaceful enjoyment of freedoms which the Constitution guarantees contingent upon the uncontrolled will of an official—as by requiring a permit or license which may be granted or withheld in the discretion of such official— is an unconstitutional censorship or prior restraint upon the enjoyment of those freedoms." . . . And our decisions have made clear that a person faced with such an unconstitutional licensing law may ignore it, and engage with impunity in the exercise of the right of free expression for which the law purports to require a license. "The Constitution can hardly be thought to deny to one subjected to the restraints of such an ordinance the right to attack its constitutionality, because he has not yielded to its demands." . . .

It is argued, however, that what was involved here was not "pure speech," but the use of public streets and sidewalks, over which a municipality must rightfully exercise a great deal of control in the interest of traffic regulation and public safety. That, of course, is true. We have emphasized before this that "the First and Fourteenth Amendments [do not] afford the same kind of freedom to those who would communicate ideas by conduct such as patrolling, marching, and picketing on streets and highways, as these amendments afford to those who communicate ideas by pure speech." . . . "Governmental authorities have the duty and responsibility to keep their streets open and available for movement."

But our decisions have also made clear that picketing and parading may nonetheless constitute methods of expression, entitled to First Amendment protection. . . . "Whenever the title of streets and parks may rest, they have immemorially been held in trust for the use of the public and, time out of mind, have been used for purposes of assembly, communicating thoughts between citizens, and discussing public questions. Such use of the streets and public places has, from ancient times, been a part of the privileges, immunities, rights, and liberties of citizens. The privilege of a citizen of the United States to use the streets and parks for communication of views on national questions may be regulated in the interest of all; it is not absolute, but relative, and must be exercised in subordination to the general comfort and convenience, and in consonance with peace and good order; but it must not, in the guise of regulation, be abridged or denied." . . .

Accordingly, "although [a] this Court has recognized that a statute may be enacted which prevents serious interference with normal usage of streets and parks, . . . we have consistently condemned licensing systems which vest in an administrative official discretion to grant or withhold a permit upon broad criteria unrelated to proper regulation of public places." . . . Even when the use of its public streets and sidewalks is involved, therefore, a municipality may not empower its licensing officials to roam essentially at will, dispensing or withholding permission to speak, assemble, picket, or parade according to their own opinions regarding the potential effect of the activity in question on the "welfare," "decency," or "morals" of the community.

Understandably, under these settled principles, the Alabama Court of Appeals was unable to reach any conclusion other than that § 1159 was unconstitutional. The terms of the Birmingham ordinance clearly gave the City Commission extensive authority to issue or refuse to issue parade permits on the basis of broad criteria entirely unrelated to legitimate municipal regulation of the public streets and sidewalks.

It is said, however, that no matter how constitutionally invalid the Birmingham ordinance may have been as it was written, nonetheless the authoritative construction that has now been given it by the Supreme Court of Alabama has so modified and narrowed its terms as to render it constitutionally acceptable. It is true that in affirming the petitioner's conviction in the present case, the Supreme Court of Alabama performed a remarkable job of plastic surgery upon the face of the ordinance. The court stated that when § 1159 provided that the City Commission could withhold a permit whenever "in its judgment the public welfare, peace, safety, health, decency, good order, morals or convenience require," the ordinance really meant something quite different:

[We] do not construe this [language] as vesting in the Commission an unfettered discretion in granting or denying permits, but, in view of the purpose of the ordinance, one to be exercised in connection with the safety, comfort and convenience in the use of the streets by the general public. . . . The members of the Commission may not act as censors of what is to be said or displayed in any parade. . . .

[We] do not construe § 1159 as conferring upon the "commission" of the City of Birmingham the right to refuse an application for a permit to carry on a parade, procession or other public demonstration solely on the ground that such activities might tend to provoke disorderly conduct. . . .

We also hold that under § 1159 the Commission is without authority to act in an arbitrary manner or with unfettered discretion in regard to the issuance of permits. Its discretion must be exercised with uniformity of method of treatment upon the facts of each application, free from improper or inappropriate considerations and from unfair discrimination. A systematic, consistent and just order of treatment with reference to the convenience of public use of the streets and sidewalks must be followed. Applications for permits to parade must be granted if, after an investigation, it is found that the convenience of the public in the use of the streets or sidewalks would not thereby be unduly disturbed.

In transforming § 1159 into an ordinance authorizing no more than the objective and even-handed regulation of traffic on Birmingham's streets and public ways, the Supreme Court of Alabama made a commendable effort to give the legislation "a field of operation within constitutional limits." We may assume that this exercise was successful, and that the ordinance as now authoritatively construed would pass constitutional muster.* It does not follow, however, that the severely narrowing construction put upon the ordinance by the Alabama Supreme Court in November of 1967 necessarily serves to restore constitutional validity to a conviction that occurred in 1963 under the ordinance as it was written. . . .

In the present case we are confronted with quite a different situation. In April of 1963 the ordinance that was on the books in Birmingham contained language that affirmatively conferred upon the members of the Commission absolute power to refuse a parade permit whenever they thought "the public welfare, peace, safety, health, decency, good order, morals or convenience require that it be refused." It would have taken extraordinary clairvoyance for anyone to perceive that this language meant what the Supreme Court of Alabama was destined to find that it meant more than four years later; and, with First Amendment rights hanging in the balance, we would hesitate long before assuming that either the members of the Commission or the petitioner possessed any such clairvoyance at the time of the Good Friday march.

But we need not deal in assumptions. For, as the respondent in this case has reminded us, in assessing the constitutional claims of the petitioner, "[i]t is less than realistic to ignore the surrounding relevant circumstances. These include not only facts developed in the Record in this case, but also those shown in the opinions in the related case of *Walker* v. *City of Birmingham,* 388 US 307. . . ." The petitioner here was one of the petitioners in the *Walker* case, in which, just two Terms ago, we had before us a record showing many of the "surrounding relevant circumstances" of the Good Friday march. As the respondent suggests, we may properly take judicial notice of the record in that litigation between the same parties who are now before us.

Uncontradicted testimony was offered in *Walker* to show that over a week before the Good Friday march petitioner Shuttlesworth sent a representative to apply for a parade permit. She went to the City Hall and asked "to see the person or persons in charge to issue permits, permits for parading, picketing, and demonstrating."

* The validity of this assumption would depend upon, among other things, the availability of expeditious judicial review of the Commission's refusal of a permit. . . .

She was directed to Commissioner Connor, who denied her request in no uncertain terms. "He said, 'No, you will not get a permit in Birmingham, Alabama, to picket. I will picket you over to the City Jail,' and he repeated that twice."

Two days later petitioner Shuttlesworth himself sent a telegram to Commissioner Connor requesting, on behalf of his organization, a permit to picket "against the injustices of segregation and discrimination." His request specified the sidewalks where the picketing would take place, and stated that "the normal rules of picketing" would be obeyed. In reply, the Commissioner sent a wire stating that permits were the responsibility of the entire Commission rather than of a single Commissioner, and closing with the blunt admonition: "I insist that you and your people do not start any picketing on the streets in Birmingham, Alabama."*

These "surrounding relevant circumstances" make it indisputably clear, we think, that in April of 1963—at least with respect to this petitioner and his organization—the city authorities thought the ordinance meant exactly what it said. The petitioner was clearly given to understand that under no circumstances would he and his group be permitted to demonstrate in Birmingham, not that a demonstration would be approved if a time and place were selected that would minimize traffic problems. There is no indication whatever that the authorities considered themselves obligated —as the Alabama Supreme Court more than four years later said that they were— to issue a permit "if, after an investigation [they] found that the convenience of the public in the use of the streets or sidewalks would not thereby be unduly disturbed."

13. Oaths

CONNELL *v.* HIGGINBOTHAM
403 US 207 (1971)

[In this case the Supreme Court unanimously upheld as constitutional an oath required of state employees that they will support the Constitution of the United States and of the State. With respect to an oath that one does not believe in the overthrow of the government by force or violence, the Court held that it was unconstitutional; though with respect to such an oath there were some differences in the rationale. The opinion of the Court was a *per curiam;* Justice Marshall wrote a concurring opinion, in which he was joined by Justices Douglas and Brennan; Justice Stewart wrote an opinion in which he concurred in part and dissented in part.]

Per Curiam:

This is an appeal from an action commenced in the United States District Court for the Middle District of Florida challenging the constitutionality of §§ 876.05–

---

* The legal and constitutional issues involved in the *Walker* case were quite different from those involved here. The Court recently summarized the *Walker* decision as follows: "In that case, the Court held that demonstrators who had proceeded with their protest march in face of the prohibition of an injunctive order against such a march, could not defend contempt charges by asserting the unconstitutionality of the injunction. The proper procedure, it was held, was to seek judicial review of the injunction and not to disobey it, no matter how well-founded their doubts might be as to its validity." *Carroll* v. *President and Commissioners of Princess Anne,* 393 US 175.

876.10 of Fla. Stat. Ann., and the various loyalty oaths upon which appellant's employment as a schoolteacher was conditioned. The three-judge U.S. District Court declared three of the five clauses contained in the oaths to be unconstitutional,* and enjoined the State from conditioning employment on the taking of an oath including the language declared unconstitutional. The appeal is from that portion of the District Court decision which upheld the remaining two clauses in the oath: I do hereby solemnly swear or affirm (1) "that I will support the Constitution of the United States and of the State of Florida"; and (2) "that I do not believe in the overthrow of the government of the United States or of the State of Florida by force or violence."

On January 16, 1969, appellant made application for a teaching position with the Orange County school system. She was interviewed by the principal of Callahan Elementary School, and on January 27, 1969, appellant was employed as a substitute classroom teacher in the fourth grade of that school. Appellant was dismissed from her teaching position on March 19, 1969, for refusing to sign the loyalty oath required of all Florida public employees.

The first section of the oath upheld by the District Court, requiring all applicants to pledge to support the Constitution of the United States and of the State of Florida, demands no more of Florida public employees than is required of all state and federal officers. U.S. Const., Art. VI, § 3. The validity of this section of the oath would appear settled. . . .

The second portion of the oath, approved by the District Court, falls within the ambit of decisions of this Court proscribing summary dismissal from public employment without hearing or inquiry required by due process. *Slochower* v. *Board of Education,* 350 US 551 (1956). Cf. *Nostrand* v. *Little,* 362 US 474 (1960); *Speiser* v. *Randall,* 357 US 513 (1958). That portion of the oath, therefore, cannot stand.

Affirmed in part, and reversed in part.

Mr. Justice Marshall, with whom Mr. Justice Douglas, and Mr. Justice Brennan join, concurring in the result:

I agree that Florida may require state employees to affirm that they "will support the Constitution of the United States and of the State of Florida." Such a forward-looking, promissory oath of constitutional support does not in my view offend the First Amendment's command that the grant or denial of governmental benefits cannot be made to turn on the political viewpoints or affiliations of a would-be beneficiary. I also agree that Florida may not base its employment decisions, as to state teachers or any other hiring category, on an applicant's willingness *vel non* to affirm "that I do not believe in the overthrow of the government of the United States or of the State of Florida by force or violence."

However, in striking down the latter oath, the Court has left the clear implication

---

* The clauses declared unconstitutional by the court below required the employee to swear: (a) "that I am not a member of the Communist Party"; (b) "that I have not and will not lend my aid, support, advice, counsel or influence to the Communist Party"; and (c) "that I am not a member of any organization or party which believes in or teaches, directly or indirectly, the overthrow of the Government of the United States or of Florida by force or violence."

that its objection runs, not against Florida's determination to exclude those who "believe in the overthrow," but only against the State's decision to regard unwillingness to take the oath as conclusive, irrebuttable proof of the proscribed belief. Due process may rightly be invoked to condemn Florida's mechanistic approach to the question of proof. But in my view it simply does not matter what kind of evidence a State can muster to show that a job applicant "believes in the overthrow." For state action injurious to an individual cannot be justified on account of the nature of the individual's beliefs, whether he "believes in the overthrow" or has any other sort of belief. "If there is any fixed star in our constitutional constellation, it is that no official, high or petty, can prescribe what shall be orthodox in politics, nationalism, religion, or other matters of opinion. . . ." *Board of Education* v. *Barnette*, 319 US 624, 642 (1943).

I would strike down Florida's "overthrow" oath plainly and simply on the ground that belief as such cannot be the predicate of governmental action.

Mr. Justice Stewart, concurring in part and dissenting in part.

The Court upholds as clearly constitutional the first clause of the oath as it comes to us from the three-judge District Court: "I will support the Constitution of the United States and of the State of Florida. . . ." With this ruling I fully agree.

As to the second contested clause of the oath, "I do not believe in the overthrow of the government of the United States or of the State of Florida by force or violence," I would remand to the District Court to give the parties an opportunity to get from the state courts an authoritative construction of the meaning of the clause. If the clause embraces the teacher's philosophical or political beliefs, I think it is constitutionally infirm. *Baird* v. *State Bar of Arizona*, 401 US 1, 9–10 (concurring opinion); *West Virginia State Board of Education* v. *Barnette*, 319 US 624, 642; *Cantwell* v. *Connecticut*, 310 US 296. If, on the other hand, the clause does no more than test whether the first clause of the oath can be taken "without mental reservation or purpose of evasion," I think it is constitutionally valid. *Law Students Civil Rights Research Council, Inc.* v. *Wadmond*, 401 US 154. The Florida courts should, therefore, be given an opportunity to construe the clause before the federal courts pass on its constitutionality. . . .

COLE *v.* RICHARDSON
405 US 676 (1972)

[Loyalty oaths have long plagued the Supreme Court. Chief Justice Burger's opinion for the Court in this case provides a partial summary of precedents. The oath before the Court was in two parts: (1) to "uphold and defend" the United States Constitution and the state constitution, and (2) to oppose the overthrow of the governments of the United States and of the state by force, violence, or by any illegal or unconstitutional method. The Court unanimously upheld the constitutionality of the first part of the oath. The second part, however, was upheld by a 4–3 vote. Chief Justice Burger wrote the majority opinion. Justices Stewart and White wrote a concurring opinion. Justice Douglas wrote a dissenting opinion. Justice Marshall also wrote a dissenting opinion, in which Justice Brennan joined. Justices Powell and Rehnquist did not participate in the case.]

Mr. Chief Justice Burger delivered the opinion of the Court:

The appellee, Richardson, was hired as a research sociologist by the Boston State Hospital. The appellant is superintendent of the hospital. Soon after she entered on duty Mrs. Richardson was asked to subscribe to the oath required of all public employees in Massachusetts. The oath is as follows:

I do solemnly swear (or affirm) that I will uphold and defend the Constitution of the United States of America and the Constitution of the Commonwealth of Massachusetts and that I will oppose the overthrow of the government of the United States of America or of this Commonwealth by force, violence or by any illegal or unconstitutional method.

Mrs. Richardson informed the hospital's personnel department that she could not take the oath as ordered because of her belief that it was in violation of the United States Constitution. Approximately 10 days later appellant Cole personally informed Mrs. Richardson that under state law she could not continue as an employee of the Boston State Hospital unless she subscribed to the oath. Again she refused. On November 25, 1968, Mrs. Richardson's employment was terminated and she was paid through that date.

In March 1969 Mrs. Richardson filed a complaint in the United States District Court for Massachusetts. The complaint alleged the unconstitutionality of the statute, sought damages and an injunction against its continued enforcement, and prayed for the convocation of a three-judge court pursuant to 28 U.S. C. §§ 2281 and 2284.

A three-judge District Court held the oath statute unconstitutional and enjoined the appellant from applying the statute to prohibit Mrs. Richardson from working for Boston State Hospital. The District Court found the attack on the "uphold and defend" clause, the first part of the oath, foreclosed by *Knight* v. *Board of Regents,* 269 F.Supp. 339 (S.D. N.Y. 1967), affirmed, 390 US 36 (1968). But it found that the "oppose and overthrow" clause was "fatally vague and unspecific," and therefore a violation of First Amendment rights. The court granted the requested injunction but denied the claim for damages. . . .

We conclude that the Massachusetts oath is constitutionally permissible, and in light of the prolonged litigation of this case we set forth our reasoning at greater length than previously.

A review of the oath cases in this Court will put the instant oath into context. We have made clear that neither federal nor state governments may condition employment on taking oaths which impinge rights guaranteed by the First and Fourteenth Amendments respectively, as for example those relating to political beliefs. *Law Students Civil Rights Research Council* v. *Wadmond,* 401 US 154 (1971); *Baird* v. *State Bar of Arizona,* 401 US 1 (1971); *Connell* v. *Higgenbotham,* 403 US 207 (1971) (Marshall, J., concurring). Nor may employment be conditioned on an oath that one has not engaged, or will not engage, in protected speech activities such as the following: criticizing institutions of government; discussing political doctrine that approves the overthrow of certain forms of government; and supporting candidates for political office. *Keyishian* v. *Board of Regents,* 385 US 589 (1967); *Baggett* v. *Bullitt,* 377 US 360 (1964); *Cramp* v. *Board of Public Instruction,* 368 US 278, 285 (1961). Employment may not be conditioned on an oath denying past, or abjuring future, associational activities within constitutional protection; such protected activities include membership in organizations having illegal purposes unless one knows of the purpose and shares a specific intent to promote the illegal purpose. *Whitehill* v. *Elkins,* 389 US 54 (1967); *Keyishian* v. *Board of Regents, supra; Elfbrandt* v. *Russell,* 384 US 11 (1966); *Wieman* v. *Updegraff,* 344 US 183 (1952). Thus last Term in *Wadmond* the Court sustained inquiry into a bar applicant's associational activities only because it was narrowly confined to organizations which the individual had known to have the purpose of violent overthrow of the government and whose purpose the individual shared. And, finally, an oath may not be so vague that " 'men of common intelligence must necessarily guess at its meaning and differ as to its application, [because such an oath] violates the first essential of due process of law.' " *Cramp* v. *Board of Public Instruction,* 368 US at 287. Concern for vagueness in the oath cases has been especially great because uncertainty as to an oath's meaning may deter individuals from engaging in constitutionally protected activity conceivably within the scope of the oath.

An underlying, seldom articulated concern running throughout these cases is that the oaths under consideration often required individuals to reach back into their pasts to recall minor, sometimes innocent, activities. They put the government into "the censorial business of investigating, scrutinizing, interpreting, and then penalizing or approving the political viewpoint" and past activities of individuals. . . .

Several cases recently decided by the Court stand out among our oath cases because they have upheld the constitutionality of oaths, addressed to the future, promising constitutional support in broad terms. These cases have begun with a recognition that the Constitution itself prescribes comparable oaths in two articles. Article II, § 1, cl. 7, provides that the President shall swear that he will "faithfully execute the office . . . and will to the best of my ability preserve, protect and defend the Constitution of the United States." Article VI, cl. 3, provides that all state and federal officers shall be bound by an oath "to support this Constitution." The oath taken by attorneys as a condition of admission to the bar of this Court identically provides in part "that I will support the Constitution of the United States"; it also requires the attorney to state that he will "conduct himself uprightly and according to law."

Bond v. *Floyd,* 385 US 116 (1966), involved Georgia's statutory requirement that state legislators swear to "support the Constitution of this State and of the United States," a paraphrase of the constitutionally required oath. The Court there implicitly concluded that the First Amendment did not undercut the validity of the constitutional oath provisions. Although in theory the First Amendment might have invalidated those provisions, approval of the amendment by the same individuals who had included the oaths in the Constitution suggested strongly that they were consistent. The Court's recognition of this consistency did not involve a departure from its many decisions striking down oaths which infringed First and Fourteenth Amendment rights. The Court read the Georgia oath as calling simply for an acknowledgment of a willingness to abide by "constitutional processes of government." . . . Although disagreeing on other points, in *Wadmond, supra,* all members of the Court agreed on this point. Mr. Justice Marshall noted there, while dissenting as to other points,

The oath of constitutional support requires an individual assuming public responsibilities to affirm . . . that he will endeavor to perform his public duties lawfully.

The Court has further made clear that an oath need not parrot the exact language of the constitutional oaths to be constitutionally proper. Thus in *Ohlson* v. *Phillips,* 397 US 317 (1970), we sustained the constitutionality of a state requirement that teachers swear to "uphold" the Constitution. The District Court had concluded that the oath was simply a "recognition that ours is a government of laws and not of men," and that the oath involved an affirmation of "organic law" and rejection of "the use of force to overthrow the government." . . .

The District Court in the instant case properly recognized that the first clause of the Massachusetts oath, in which the individual swears to "uphold and defend" the constitutions of the United States and the Commonwealth, is indistinguishable from the oaths this Court has recently approved. Yet the District Court applied a highly literalistic approach to the second clause to strike it down. We view the second clause of the oath as essentially the same as the first.

The second clause of the oath contains a promise to "oppose the overthrow of the government of the United States of America or of this Commonwealth by force, violence or by any illegal or unconstitutional method." The District Court sought to give a dictionary meaning to this language and found "oppose" to raise the specter of vague, undefinable responsibilities actively to combat a potential overthrow of the government. That reading of the oath understandably troubled the court because of what it saw as vagueness in terms of what threats would constitute sufficient danger of overthrow to require the oathgiver to actively oppose overthrow, and exactly what actions he would have to take in that respect. . . .

But such a literal approach to the second clause is inconsistent with the Court's approach to the "support" oaths. One could make a literal argument that "support" involves nebulous, undefined responsibilities for action in some hypothetical situations. As Mr. Justice Harlan noted in his separate opinion on our earlier consideration of this case,

almost any word or phrase may be rendered vague and ambiguous by dissection with a semantic scalpel. [But such an approach] amounts to little more than verbal calisthenics, *Cole* v. *Richardson,* 397 US at 240.

We have rejected such rigidly literal notions and recognized that the purpose leading legislatures to enact such oaths, just as the purpose leading the Framers of our Constitution to include the two explicit constitutional oaths, was not to create specific responsibilities but to assure that those in positions of public trust were willing to commit themselves to live by the constitutional processes of our system as Mr. Justice Marshall suggested in *Wadmond,* 401 US at 192. Here the second clause does not require specific action in some hypothetical or actual situation. Plainly "force, violence or . . . any illegal or unconstitutional method" modifies "overthrow" and does not commit the oath taker to meet force with force. Just as the connotatively active word "support" has been interpreted to mean simply a commitment to abide by our constitutional system, the second clause of this oath is merely oriented to the negative implication of this notion; it is a commitment not to use illegal and constitutionally unprotected force to change the constitutional system. The second clause does not expand the obligation of the first; it simply makes clear the application of the first clause to a particular issue. Such repetition, whether for emphasis or cadence, seems to be wont with authors of oaths. That the second clause may be redundant is no ground to strike it down; we are not charged with correcting grammar but with enforcing a constitution.

The purpose of the oath is clear on its face. We cannot presume that the Massachusetts legislature intended by its use of such general terms as "uphold," "defend," and "oppose" to impose obligations of specific, positive action on oath takers. Any such construction would raise serious questions whether the oath was so vague as to amount to a denial of due process. . . .

Nor is the oath as interpreted void for vagueness. As Mr. Justice Harlan pointed out in his opinion on our earlier consideration of this case, the oath is "no more than an amenity." . . . It is punishable only by a prosecution for perjury and, since perjury is a knowing and willful falsehood, the constitutional vice of punishment without fair warning cannot occur here. . . . Nor here is there any problem of the punishment inflicted by mere prosecution. . . . There has been no prosecution under this statute since its 1948 enactment, and there is no indication that prosecutions have been planned or begun. The oath "triggered no serious possibility of prosecution" by the Commonwealth. . . . Were we confronted with a record of actual prosecutions or harassment through threatened prosecutions, we might be faced with a different question. Those who view the Massachusetts oath in terms of an endless "parade of horribles" would do well to bear in mind that many of the hazards of human existence that can be imagined are circumscribed by the classic observation of Mr. Justice Holmes, when confronted with the prophecy of dire consequences of certain judicial action, that it would not occur "while this Court sits." *Panhandle Oil Co.* v. *State of Miss. ex rel. Knox,* 277 US 218 (Holmes, J., dissenting).

Appellee mounts an additional attack on the Massachusetts oath program in that it does not provide for a hearing prior to the determination not to hire the individual based on the refusal to subscribe to the oath. All of the cases in this Court which require a hearing before discharge for failure to take an oath involved impermissible oaths. . . .

Since there is no constitutionally protected right to overthrow a government by force, violence, or illegal or unconstitutional means, no constitutional right is infringed by an oath to abide by the constitutional system in the future. Therefore there is no requirement that one who refuses to take the Massachusetts oath be granted a hearing for the determination of some other fact before being discharged.

The judgment of the District Court is reversed and the case is remanded for further proceedings consistent with this opinion.

14. Libel

NEW YORK TIMES COMPANY v. SULLIVAN
376 US 255 (1964)

[In a case decided in 1942, Justice Murphy stated for a unanimous Court that libelous words were among "certain well-defined . . . classes of speech, the prevention and punishment of which have never been thought to raise any Constitutional problem." *Chaplinsky* v. *New Hampshire,* 315 US 568. See also *Beauharnais* v. *Illinois,* 343 US 250 (1952). In the instant case, however, the Court, for the first time, subjected the law of libel to the limits of the First Amendment. The Court in this case dealt with the libel law only as it affected statements in a newspaper about public officials. The Court held that an aggrieved public official may recover damages only if he can prove that the statement was made with "actual malice"— "that is," said the Court, "with knowledge that it was false or with reckless disregard of whether it was false or not." The decision was unanimous. Justice Brennan wrote the opinion for the Court. Justice Goldberg, with Justice Douglas joining, wrote a concurring opinion.

[Subsequent cases have extended the holding of the Court. In *Time, Inc.* v. *Hill,* which appears in Ch. IX of this volume, the Court applied the *New York Times* standard of "knowing or reckless falsehood" to a statutory right of privacy action by a private individual against a publisher. In *Curtis Publishing Co.* v. *Butts* and *Associated Press* v. *Walker,* decided together, 388 US 130 (1967), the principle of the *New York Times* decision was applied in libel actions brought, not by public officials, but by persons who were "public figures" and involved in issues in which the public had a justified and important interest. In the *Butts* and *Walker* cases the Court was, however, divided. Justices Black and Douglas were for the complete and total immunity of the press under the First Amendment. Justices Harlan, Clark, Stewart, and Fortas were against the extension of the *New York Times* decision and against press immunity in these cases; Chief Justice Warren and Justices Brennan and White favored application of the *New York Times* rule.]

Mr. Justice Brennan delivered the opinion of the Court:

We are required for the first time in this case to determine the extent to which the constitutional protections for speech and press limit a State's power to award damages in a libel action brought by a public official against critics of his official conduct.

Respondent L. B. Sullivan is one of the three elected Commissioners of the City of Montgomery, Alabama. He testified that he was "Commissioner of Public Affairs and the duties are supervision of the Police Department, Fire Department, Department of Cemetery, and Department of Scales." He brought this civil libel action against the four individual petitioners, who are Negroes and Alabama clergymen, and against petitioner, the New York Times Company, a New York corporation which publishes the *New York Times,* a daily newspaper. A jury in the Circuit Court of Montgomery County awarded him damages of $500,000, the full amount claimed, against all the petitioners, and the Supreme Court of Alabama affirmed.

Respondent's complaint alleged that he had been libeled by statements in a full-page advertismeent that was carried in the *New York Times* on March 29, 1960. Entitled "Heed Their Rising Voices," the advertisement began by stating that "As the whole world knows by now, thousands of Southern Negro students are engaged in widespread nonviolent demonstrations in positive affirmation of the right to live in human dignity as guaranteed by the U.S. Constitution and the Bill of Rights." It went on to charge that "in their efforts to uphold these guarantees, they are being met by an unprecedented wave of terror by those who would deny and negate that document which the whole world looks upon as setting the pattern for modern freedom. . . ." Succeeding paragraphs purported to illustrate the "wave of terror" by describing certain alleged events. The text concluded with an appeal for funds for three purposes: support of the student movement, "the struggle for the right-to-vote," and the legal defense of Dr. Martin Luther King, Jr., leader of the movement, against a perjury indictment then pending in Montgomery.

The text appeared over the names of 64 persons, many widely known for their activities in public affairs, religion, trade unions, and the performing arts. Below these names, and under a line reading "We in the south who are struggling daily for dignity and freedom warmly endorse this appeal," appeared the names of the four individual petitioners and of 16 other persons, all but two of whom were identified as clergymen in various Southern cities. The advertisement was signed at the bottom of the page by the "Committee to Defend Martin Luther King and the Struggle for Freedom in the South," and the officers of the Committee were listed.

Of the 10 paragraphs of text in the advertisement, the third and a portion of the sixth were the basis of respondent's claim of libel. They read as follows:

Third paragraph:

In Montgomery, Alabama, after students sang "My Country, 'Tis of Thee" on the State Capitol steps, their leaders were expelled from school, and truckloads of police armed with shotguns and tear-gas ringed the Alabama State College Campus. When the entire student body protested to state authorities by refusing to re-register, their dining hall was padlocked in an attempt to starve them into submission.

Sixth paragraph:

Again and again the Southern violators have answered Dr. King's peaceful protests with intimidation and violence. They have bombed his home almost killing his wife and child. They have assaulted his person. They have arrested him seven times—for "speeding," "loitering" and similar "offenses." And now they have charged him with "perjury" —a *felony* under which they would imprison him for *ten years*. . . .

Although neither of these statements mentions respondent by name, he contended that the word "police" in the third paragraph referred to him as the Montgomery Commissioner who supervised the Police Department, so that he was being accused of "ringing" the campus with police. He further claimed that the paragraph would be read as imputing to the police, and hence to him, the padlocking of the dining hall in order to starve the students into submission. As to the sixth paragraph, he contended that since arrests are ordinarily made by the police, the statement "They have arrested [Dr. King] seven times" would be read as referring to him; he further contended that the "They" who did the arresting would be equated with the "They" who committed the other described acts and with the "Southern violators." Thus, he argued, the paragraph would be read as accusing the Montgomery police, and hence him, of answering Dr. King's protests with "intimidation and violence," bombing his home, assaulting his person, and charging him with perjury. Respondent and six other Montgomery residents testified that they read some or all of the statements as referring to him in his capacity as Commissioner.

It is uncontroverted that some of the statements contained in the two paragraphs were not accurate descriptions of events which occurred in Montgomery. Although

Negro students staged a demonstration on the State Capitol steps, they sang the National Anthem and not "My Country, 'Tis of Thee." Although nine students were expelled by the State Board of Education, this was not for leading the demonstration at the Capitol, but for demanding service at a lunch counter in the Montgomery County Courthouse on another day. Not the entire student body, but most of it, had protested the expulsion, not by refusing to register, but by boycotting classes on a single day; virtually all the students did register for the ensuing semester. The campus dining hall was not padlocked on any occasion, and the only students who may have been barred from eating there were the few who had neither signed a preregistration application nor requested temporary meal tickets. Although the police were deployed near the campus in large numbers on three occasions, they did not at any time "ring" the campus, and they were not called to the campus in connection with the demonstration on the State Capitol steps, as the third paragraph implied. Dr. King had not been arrested seven times, but only four; and although he claimed to have been assaulted some years earlier in connection with his arrest for loitering outside a courtroom, one of the officers who made the arrest denied that there was such an assault.

On the premise that the charges in the sixth paragraph could be read as referring to him, respondent was allowed to prove that he had not participated in the events described. Although Dr. King's home had in fact been bombed twice when his wife and child were there, both of these occasions antedated respondent's tenure as Commissioner, and the police were not only not implicated in the bombings, but had made every effort to apprehend those who were. Three of Dr. King's four arrests took place before respondent became Commissioner. Although Dr. King had in fact been indicted (he was subsequently acquitted) on two counts of perjury, each of which carried a possible five-year sentence, respondent had nothing to do with procuring the indictment.

Respondent made no effort to prove that he suffered actual pecuniary loss as a result of the alleged libel. One of his witnesses, a former employer, testified that if he had believed the statements, he doubted whether he "would want to be associated with anybody who would be a party to such things as are stated in that ad," and that he would not re-employ respondent if he believed "that he allowed the Police Department to do the things that the paper say he did." But neither this witness nor any of the others testified that he had actually believed the statements in their supposed reference to respondent.

The cost of the advertisement was approximately $4800, and it was published by the *Times* upon an order from a New York advertising agency acting for the signatory Committee. The agency submitted the advertisement with a letter from A. Philip Randolph, Chairman of the Committee, certifying that the persons whose names appeared on the advertisement had given their permission. Mr. Randolph was known to the *Times'* Advertising Acceptability Department as a responsible person, and in accepting the letter as sufficient proof of authorization it followed its established practice. There was testimony that the copy of the advertisement which accompanied the letter listed only the sixty-four names appearing under the text, and that the statement, "We in the south . . . warmly endorse this appeal" and the list of names thereunder, which included those of the individual petitioners, were subsequently added when the first proof of the advertisement was received. Each of the individual petitioners testified that he had not authorized the use of his name, and that he had been unaware of its use until receipt of respondent's demand for a retraction. The manager of the Advertising Acceptability Department testified that he had approved the advertisement for publication because he knew nothing to cause him to believe that anything in it was false, and because it bore the endorsement of "a number of people who are well known and whose reputation" he "had no reason to question." Neither he nor anyone else at the *Times* made an effort to confirm the accuracy of the advertisement, either by checking it against recent *Times* news stories relating to some of the described events or by some other means.

Alabama law denies a public officer recovery of punitive damages in a libel action brought on account of a publication concerning his official conduct unless he first makes a written demand for a public retraction and the defendant fails or refuses to comply. Alabama Code, Tit. 7, § 914. Respondent served such a demand upon each of the petitioners. None of the individual petitioners responded to the demand, primarily because each took the position that he had not authorized the use of his name on the advertisement and therefore had not published the statements that respondent alleged to have libeled him. The *Times* did not publish a retraction in response to the demand, but wrote respondent a letter stating, among other things, that "we . . . are somewhat puzzled as to how you think the statements in any way reflect on you," and "you might, if you desire, let us know in what respect you claim that the statements in the advertisement reflect on you." Respondent filed this suit a few days later without answering the letter. The *Times* did, however, subsequently publish a retraction of the advertisement upon the demand of Governor John Patterson of Alabama, who asserted that the publication charged him with "grave misconduct and . . . improper actions and omissions as Governor of Alabama and Ex-Officio Chairman of the State Board of Education of Alabama." When asked to explain why there had been a retraction for the Governor but not for respondent, the Secretary of the *Times* testified: "We did that because we didn't want anything that was published by The Times to be a reflection on the State of Alabama and the Governor was, as far as we could see, the embodiment of the State of Alabama and the proper representative of the State and, furthermore, we had by that time learned more of the actual facts which the ad purported to recite and, finally, the ad did refer to the action of the State authorities and the Board of Education presumably of which the Governor is ex-officio chairman. . . ." On the other hand, he testified that he did not think that "any of the language in there referred to Mr. Sullivan."

The trial judge submitted the case to the jury under instructions that the statements in the advertisement were "libelous per se" and were not privileged, so that petitioners might be held liable if the jury found that they had published the advertisement and that the statements were made "of and concerning" respondent. The jury was instructed that, because the statements were libelous *per se*, "the law . . . implies legal injury from the bare fact of publication itself," "falsity and malice are presumed," "general damages need not be alleged or proved but are presumed," and "punitive damages may be awarded by the jury even though the amount of actual damages is neither found nor shown." An award of punitive damages—as distinguished from "general" damages, which are compensatory in nature—apparently requires proof of actual malice under Alabama law, and the judge charged that "mere negligence or carelessness is not evidence of actual malice or malice in fact, and does not justify an award of exemplary or punitive damages." He refused to charge, however, that the jury must be "convinced" of malice, in the sense of "actual intent" to harm or "gross negligence and recklessness," to make such an award, and he also refused to require that a verdict for respondent differentiate between compensatory and punitive damages. The judge rejected petitioners' contention that his rulings abridged the freedoms of speech and of the press that are guaranteed by the First and Fourteenth Amendments.

In affirming the judgment, the Supreme Court of Alabama sustained the trial judge's rulings and instructions in all respects. It held that "where the words published tend to injure a person libeled by them in his reputation, profession, trade or business, or charge him with an indictable offense, or tend to bring the individual into public contempt," they are "libelous per se"; that "the matter complained of is, under the above doctrine, libelous per se, if it was published of and concerning the plaintiff"; and that it was actionable without "proof of pecuniary injury . . . , such injury being implied." It approved the trial court's ruling that the jury could find the statements to have been made "of and concerning" respondent, stating: "We think it common knowledge that the average person knows that municipal agents, such as police and firemen, and others, are under the control and direction of the city governing body, and more particularly under the direction and control of a single commissioner. In measuring the performance or deficiencies of such groups, praise or criticism is usually attached to the official in complete control of the body." In sustaining the trial court's determination that the verdict was not excessive, the court said that malice could be inferred from the *Times'* "irresponsibility" in printing the advertisement while "the *Times* in its own files had articles already published which would have demonstrated the falsity of the allegations in the advertisement"; from the *Times'* failure to retract for respondent while retracting for the Governor, whereas the falsity of some of the allegations was then known to the *Times* and "the matter contained in the advertisement was equally false as to both parties"; and from the testimony of the *Times'* Secretary that, apart from the statement that the dining hall was padlocked, he thought the two paragraphs were "substantially correct." The court reaffirmed a statement in an earlier opinion that "There is no legal measure of damages in cases of this character." It rejected petitioners' constitutional contentions with the brief statements that "The First Amendment of the U.S. Constitution does not protect libelous publications" and "The Fourteenth Amendment is directed against State action and not private action."

Because of the importance of the constitutional issues involved, we granted the separate petitions for certiorari of the individual petitioners and of the *Times*. We reverse the judgment. We hold that the rule of law applied by the Alabama courts is constitutionally deficient for failure to provide the safeguards for freedom of speech and of the press that are required by the First and Fourteenth Amendments in a libel action brought by a public official against critics of his official conduct.

We further hold that under the proper safeguards the evidence presented in this case is constitutionally insufficient to support the judgment for respondent.

I

We may dispose at the outset of two grounds asserted to insulate the judgment of the Alabama courts from constitutional scrutiny. The first is the proposition relied on by the State Supreme Court—that "The Fourteenth Amendment is directed against State action and not private action." That proposition has no application to this case. Although this is a civil lawsuit between private parties, the Alabama courts have applied a state rule of law which petitioners claim to impose invalid restrictions on their constitutional freedoms of speech and press. It matters not that that law has been applied in a civil action and that it is common law only, though supplemented by statute. The test is not the form in which state power has been applied but, whatever the form, whether such power has in fact been exercised.

The second contention is that the constitutional guarantees of freedom of speech and of the press are inapplicable here, at least so far as the *Times* is concerned, because the allegedly libelous statements were published as part of a paid, "commercial" advertisement. The argument relies on *Valentine* v. *Chrestensen,* 316 US 52, where the Court held that a city ordinance forbidding street distribution of commercial and business advertising matter did not abridge the First Amendment freedoms, even as applied to a handbill having a commercial message on one side but a protest against certain official action on the other. The reliance is wholly misplaced. The Court in *Chrestensen* reaffirmed the constitutional protection for "the freedom of communicating information and disseminating opinion"; its holding was based upon the factual conclusions that the handbill was "purely commercial advertising" and that the protest against official action had been added only to evade the ordinance.

The publication here was not a "commercial" advertisement in the sense in which the word was used in *Chrestensen*. It communicated information, expressed opinion, recited grievances, protested claimed abuses, and sought financial support on behalf of a movement whose existence and objectives are matters of the highest public interest and concern. . . . That the *Times* was paid for publishing the advertisement is as immaterial in this connection as is the fact that newspapers and books are sold. *Smith* v. *California,* 361 US 147; cf. *Bantam Books, Inc.* v. *Sullivan,* 372 US 58. Any other conclusion would discourage newspapers from carrying "editorial advertisements" of this type, and so might shut off an important outlet for the promulgation of information and ideas by persons who do not themselves have access to publishing facilities—who wish to exercise their freedom of speech even though they are not members of the press. Cf. *Lovell* v. *Griffin,* 303 US 444; *Schneider* v. *State,* 308 US 147. The effect would be to shackle the First Amendment in its attempt to secure "the widest possible dissemination of information from diverse and antagonistic sources." *Association Press* v. *United States,* 326 US 1. To avoid placing such a handicap upon the freedoms of expression, we hold that if the allegedly libelous statements would otherwise be constitutionally protected from the present judgment, they do not forfeit that protection because they were published in the form of a paid advertisement.

II

Under Alabama law as applied in this case, a publication is "libelous per se" if the words "tend to injure a person . . . in his reputation" or to "bring [him] into public contempt"; the trial court stated that the standard was met if the words are such as to "injure him in his public office, or impute misconduct to him in his office, or want of official integrity, or want of fidelity to a public trust. . . ." The jury must find that the words were published "of and concerning" the plaintiff, but where the plaintiff is a public official his place in the governmental hierarchy is sufficient evidence to support a finding that his reputation has been affected by statements that reflect upon the agency of which he is in charge. Once "libel per se" has been established, the defendant has no defense as to stated facts unless he can persuade the jury that they were true in all their particulars. . . . His privilege of "fair comment" for expressions of opinion depends on the truth of the facts upon which the comment is based. . . . Unless he can discharge the burden of proving truth, general damages are presumed, and may be awarded without proof of pecuniary injury. A showing of actual malice is apparently a prerequisite to recovery of punitive damages, and the defendant may in any event forestall these by a retraction meeting the statutory requirements. Good motives and belief in truth do not negate an inference of malice, but are relevant only in mitigation of punitive damages if the jury chooses to accord them weight. . . .

The question before us is whether this rule of liability, as applied to an action brought by a public official against critics of his official conduct, abridges the freedom of speech and of the press that is guaranteed by the First and Fourteenth Amendments.

Respondent relies heavily, as did the Alabama courts, on statements of this Court to the effect that the Constitution does not protect libelous publications. Those statements do not foreclose our inquiry here. None of the cases sustained the use of libel laws to impose sanctions upon expression critical of the official conduct of public officials. The dictum in *Pennekamp* v. *Florida,* 328 US 331, that "when the statements amount to defamation, a judge has such remedy in damages for libel as do other public servants," implied no view as to what remedy might constitutionally be afforded to public officials. In *Beauharnais* v. *Illinois,* 343 US 250, the Court sustained an Illinois criminal libel statute as applied to a publication held to be both defamatory of a racial group and "liable to cause violence and disorder." But the Court was careful to note that it "retains and exercises authority to nullify action which encroaches on freedom of utterance under the guise of punishing libel"; for "public men, are, as it were, public property," and "discussion cannot be denied and the right, as well as the duty, of criticism must not be stifled." In the only previous case that did present the question of constitutional limitations upon the power to award damages for libel of a public official, the Court was equally divided and the question was not decided. *Schenectady Union Pub. Co.* v. *Sweeney,* 316 US 642. In deciding the question now, we are compelled by neither precedent nor policy to give any more weight to the epithet "libel" than we have to other "mere labels" of state law. . . . Like "insurrection," contempt, advocacy of unlawful acts, breach of the peace, obscenity, solicitation of legal business, and the various other formulae for the repression of expression that have been challenged in this Court, libel can claim no talismanic immunity from constitutional limitations. It must be measured by standards that satisfy the First Amendment.

The general proposition that freedom of expression upon public questions is secured by the First Amendment has long been settled by our decisions. The constitutional safeguard, we have said, "was fashioned to assure the unfettered interchange of ideas for the bringing about of political and social changes desired by the people." . . . "The maintenance of the opportunity for free political discussion to the end that government may be responsive to the will of the people and that changes may be obtained by lawful means, an opportunity essential to the security of the Republic, is a fundamental principle of our constitutional system." . . . "[I]t is a prized American privilege to speak one's mind, although not always with perfect good taste, on all public institutions," . . . and this opportunity is to be afforded for "vigorous advocacy" no less than "abstract discussion." . . . The First Amendment, said Judge Learned Hand, "presupposes that right conclusions are more likely to be gathered out of a multitude of tongues, than through any kind of authoritative selection. To many this is, and always will be, folly; but we have staked upon it our all." . . . Mr. Justice Brandeis, in his concurring opinion in *Whitney* v. *California,* 274 US 357, gave the principle its classic formulation:

Those who won our independence believed . . . that public discussion is a political duty; and that this should be a fundamental principle of the American government. They recognized the risks to which all human institutions are subject. But they knew that order cannot be secured merely through fear of punishment for its infraction; that it is hazardous to discourage thought, hope and imagination; that fear breeds repression; that repression breeds hate; that hate menaces stable government; that the path of safety lies in the opportunity to discuss freely supposed grievances and proposed remedies; and that the fitting remedy for evil counsels is good ones. Believing in the power of reason as applied through public discussion, they eschewed silence coerced by law— the argument of force in its worst form. Recognizing the occasional tyrannies of governing majorities, they amended the Constitution so that free speech and assembly should be guaranteed.

Thus we consider this case against the background of a profound national commitment to the principle that debate on public issues should be uninhibited, robust, and wide-open, and that it may well include vehement, caustic, and sometimes unpleasantly sharp attacks on government and public officials. . . . The present advertisement, as an expression of grievance and protest on one of the major public issues of our time, would seem clearly to qualify for the constitutional protection. The question is whether it forfeits that protection by the falsity of some of its factual statements and by its alleged defamation of respondent.

Authoritative interpretations of the First Amendment guarantees have consistently refused to recognize an exception for any test of truth, whether administered by judges, juries, or administrative officials—and especially not one that puts the burden of proving truth on the speaker. . . . The constitutional protection does not turn upon "the truth, popularity, or social utility of the ideas and beliefs which are offered." . . . As Madison said, "Some degree of abuse is inseparable from the proper use of every thing; and in no instance is this more true than in that of the press." . . . In *Cantwell* v. *Connecticut,* 310 US 296, the Court declared:

In the realm of religious faith, and in that of political belief, sharp differences arise. In both fields the tenets of one man may seem the rankest error to his neighbor. To persuade others to his own point of view, the pleader, as we know, at times, resorts to exaggeration, to vilification of men who have been, or are, prominent in church or state, and even to false statement. But the people of this nation have ordained in the light of history, that, in spite of the probability of excesses and abuses, these liberties are, in the long view, essential to enlightened opinion and right conduct on the part of the citizens of a democracy.

That erroneous statement is inevitable in free debate, and that it must be protected if the freedoms of expression are to have the "breathing space" that they "need . . . to survive," . . . was also recognized by the Court of Appeals for the District of Columbia Circuit in *Sweeney* v. *Patterson,* 128 F.2d 457 (1942). Judge Edgerton spoke for a unanimous court which affirmed the dismissal of a Congressman's libel suit based upon a newspaper article charging him with anti-Semitism in opposing a judicial appointment. He said:

Cases which impose liability for erroneous reports of the political conduct of officials reflect the obsolete doctrine that the governed must not criticize their governors. . . . The interest of the public here outweighs the interest of appellant or any other individual. The protection of the public requires not merely discussion, but information. Political conduct and views which some respectable people approve, and others condemn, are constantly imputed to Congressmen. Errors of fact, particularly in regard to a man's mental states and processes, are inevitable. . . . Whatever is added to the field of libel is taken from the field of free debate.

Just as factual error affords no warrant for repressing speech that would otherwise be free, the same is true of injury to official reputation. Where judicial officers are involved, this Court has held that concern for the dignity and reputation of the courts does not justify the punishment as criminal contempt of criticism of the judge or his decision. . . . This is true even though the utterance contains "half-truths" and "misinformation." . . . Such repression can be justified, if at all, only by a clear and present danger of the obstruction of justice. . . . If judges are to be treated as "men of fortitude, able to thrive in a hardy climate," . . . surely the same must be true of other government officials, such as elected city commissioners. Criticism of their official conduct does not lose its constitutional protection merely because it is effective criticism and hence diminishes their official reputations.

If neither factual error nor defamatory content suffices to remove the constitutional shield from criticism of official conduct, the combination of the two elements is no less inadequate. This is the lesson to be drawn from the great controversy over the Sedition Act of 1798, 1 Stat. 596, which first crystallized a national awareness of the central meaning of the First Amendment. . . . That statute made it a crime, punishable by a $5,000 fine and five years in prison, "if any person shall write, print, utter or publish . . . any false, scandalous and malicious writing or writings against the government of the United States, or either house of the Congress . . . , or the President . . . , with the intent to defame . . . or to bring them or either of them, into contempt or disrepute; or to excite against them, or either or any of them, the hatred of the good people of the United States." The Act allowed the defendant the defense of truth, and provided that the jury were to be judges both of the law and the facts. Despite these qualifications, the Act was vigorously condemned as unconstitutional in an attack joined in by Jefferson and Madison. . . .

Although the Sedition Act was never tested in this Court, the attack upon its validity has carried the day in the court of history. Fines levied in its prosecution were repaid by Act of Congress on the ground that it was unconstitutional. . . . Jefferson, as President, pardoned those who had been convicted and sentenced under the Act and remitted their fines, stating: "I discharged every person under punishment or prosecution under the Sedition Law because I considered, and now consider, that law to be a nullity as absolute and palpable as if Congress had ordered us to fall down and worship a golden image." . . . The invalidity of the Act has also been assumed by Justices of this Court. These views reflect a broad consensus that the Act, because of the restraint it imposed upon criticism of government and public officials, was inconsistent with the First Amendment.

There is no force in respondent's argument that the constitutional limitations implicit in the history of the Sedition Act apply only to Congress and not to the States. It is true that the First Amendment was originally addressed only to action by the Federal Government, and that Jefferson, for one, while denying the power of Congress "to controul the freedom of the press," recognized such a power in the States. . . . But this distinction was eliminated with the adoption of the Fourteenth Amendment and the application to the States of the First Amendment's restrictions. . . .

What a State may not constitutionally bring about by means of a criminal statute is likewise beyond the reach of its civil law of libel. The fear of damage awards under a rule such as that invoked by the Alabama courts here may be markedly more inhibiting than the fear of prosecution under a criminal statute. Alabama, for example, has a criminal libel law which subjects to prosecution "any person who speaks, writes, or prints of and concerning another any accusation falsely and maliciously importing the commission by such person of a felony, or any other indictable offense involving moral turpitude," and which allows as punishment upon conviction a fine not exceeding $500 and a prison sentence of six months. . . . Presumably a person charged with violation of this statute enjoys ordinary criminal-law safeguards such as the requirements of an indictment and of proof beyond a reasonable doubt. These safeguards are not available to the defendant in a civil action. The judgment awarded in this case—without the need for any proof of actual pecuniary loss—was one thousand times greater than the maximum fine provided by the Alabama criminal statute, and one hundred times greater than that provided by the Sedition Act. And since there is no double-jeopardy limitation applicable to civil lawsuits, this is not the only judgment that may be awarded against petitioners for the same publication. Whether or not a newspaper can survive a succession of such judgments, the pall of fear and timidity imposed upon those who would give voice to public criticism is an atmosphere in which the First Amendment freedoms cannot survive. Plainly the Alabama law of civil libel is "a form of regulation that creates hazards to protected freedoms markedly greater than those that attend reliance upon the criminal law." . . .

The state rule of law is not saved by its allowance of the defense of truth. A defense for erroneous statements honestly made is no less essential here than was the requirement of proof of guilty knowledge which, in *Smith* v. *California,* 361 US 147, we held indispensable to a valid conviction of a bookseller for possessing obscene writings for sale. . . . A rule compelling the critic of official conduct to guarantee the truth of all his factual assertions—and to do so on pain of libel judgments virtually unlimited in amount—leads to a comparable "self-censorship." Allowance of the defense of truth, with the burden of proving it on the defendant, does not mean that only false speech will be deterred. Even courts accepting this defense as an adequate safeguard have recognized the difficulties of adducing legal proofs that the alleged libel was true in all its factual particulars. Under such a rule, would-be critics of official conduct may be deterred from voicing their criticism, even though it is believed to be true and even though it is in fact true, because of doubt whether it can be proved in court or fear of the expense of having to do so. They tend to make only statements which "steer far wider of the unlawful zone." . . . The rule thus dampens the vigor and limits the variety of public debate. It is inconsistent with the First and Fourteenth Amendments.

The constitutional guarantees require, we think, a federal rule that prohibits a public official from recovering damages for a defamatory falsehood relating to his official conduct unless he proves that the statement was made with "actual malice" —that is, with knowledge that it was false or with reckless disregard of whether it was false or not. . . .

Such a privilege for criticism of official conduct is appropriately analogous to the protection accorded a public official when *he* is sued for libel by a private citizen. In *Barr* v. *Matteo,* 360 US 564, this Court held the utterance of a federal official to be absolutely privileged if made "within the outer perimeter" of his duties. The States accord the same immunity to statements of their highest officers, although some differentiate their lesser officials and qualify the privilege they enjoy. But all hold that all officials are protected unless actual malice can be proved. The reason for the official privilege is said to be that the threat of damage suits would otherwise "inhibit the fearless, vigorous, and effective administration of policies of government" and "dampen the ardor of all but the most resolute, or the most irresponsible, in the unflinching discharge of their duties." . . . Analogous considerations support the privilege for the citizen-critic of government. It is as much his duty to criticize as it is the official's duty to administer. . . . As Madison said, "the censorial power is in the people over the Government, and not in the Government over the people." It would give public servants an unjustified preference over the public they serve, if critics of official conduct did not have a fair equivalent of the immunity granted to the officials themselves.

We conclude that such a privilege is required by the First and Fourteenth Amendments.

III

We hold today that the Constitution delimits a State's power to award damages for libel in actions brought by public officials against critics of their official conduct. Since this is such an action, the rule requiring proof of actual malice is applicable. While Alabama law apparently requires proof of actual malice for an award of punitive damages, where general damages are concerned malice is "presumed."

Such a presumption is inconsistent with the federal rule. "The power to create presumptions is not a means of escape from constitutional restrictions," . . . "the showing of malice required for the forfeiture of the privilege is not presumed but is a matter for proof by the plaintiff. . . ." Since the trial judge did not instruct the jury to differentiate between general and punitive damages, it may be that the verdict was wholly an award of one or the other. But it is impossible to know, in view of the general verdict returned. Because of this uncertainty, the judgment must be reversed and the case remanded. . . .

Since respondent may seek a new trial, we deem that considerations of effective judicial administration require us to review the evidence in the present record to determine whether it could constitutionally support a judgment for respondent. This Court's duty is not limited to the elaboration of constitutional principles; we must also in proper cases review the evidence to make certain that those principles have been constitutionally applied. This is such a case, particularly since the question is one of alleged trespass across "the line between speech unconditionally guaranteed and speech which may legitimately be regulated." . . . In cases where that line must be drawn, the rule is that we "examine for ourselves the statements in issue and the circumstances under which they were made to see . . . whether they are of a character which the principles of the First Amendment, as adopted by the Due Process Clause of the Fourteenth Amendment, protect." . . . We must "make an independent examination of the whole record," . . . so as to assure ourselves that the judgment does not constitute a forbidden intrusion on the field of free expression.

Applying these standards, we consider that the proof presented to show actual malice lacks the convincing clarity which the constitutional standard demands, and hence that it would not constitutionally sustain the judgment for respondent under the proper rule of law. The case of the individual petitioners requires little discussion. Even assuming that they could constitutionally be found to have authorized the use of their names on the advertisement, there was no evidence whatever that they were aware of any erroneous statements or were in any way reckless in that regard. The judgment against them is thus without constitutional support.

As to the *Times*, we similarly conclude that the facts do not support a finding of actual malice. The statement by the *Times*' Secretary that, apart from the padlocking allegation, he thought the advertisement was "substantially correct," affords no constitutional warrant for the Alabama Supreme Court's conclusion that it was a "cavalier ignoring of the falsity of the advertisement [from which] the jury could not have but been impressed with the bad faith of *The Times*, and its maliciousness inferable therefrom." The statement does not indicate malice at the time of the publication; even if the advertisement was not "substantially correct"—although respondent's own proofs tend to show that it was—that opinion was at least a reasonable one, and there was no evidence to impeach the witness' good faith in holding it. The *Times*' failure to retract upon respondent's demand, although it later retracted upon the demand of Governor Patterson, is likewise not adequate evidence of malice for constitutional purposes. Whether or not a failure to retract may ever constitute such evidence, there are two reasons why it does not here. *First,* the letter written by the *Times* reflected a reasonable doubt on its part as to whether the advertisement could reasonably be taken to refer to respondent at all. *Second,* it was not a final refusal, since it asked for an explanation on this point—a request that respondent chose to ignore. Nor does the retraction upon the demand of the Governor supply the necessary proof. It may be doubted that a failure to retract which is not itself evidence of malice can retroactively become such by virtue of a retraction subsequently made to another party. But in any event that did not happen here, since the explanation given by the *Times'* Secretary for the distinction drawn between respondent and the Governor was a reasonable one, the good faith of which was not impeached.

Finally, there is evidence that the *Times* published the advertisement without checking its accuracy against the news stories in the *Times'* own files. The mere presence of the stories in the files does not, of course, establish that the *Times* "knew" the advertisement was false, since the state of mind required for actual malice would have to be brought home to the persons in the *Times'* organization having responsibility for the publication of the advertisement. With respect to the failure of those persons to make the check, the record shows that they relied upon their knowledge of the good reputation of many of those whose names were listed as sponsors of the advertisement, and upon the letter from A. Philip Randolph, known to them as a responsible individual, certifying that the use of the names was authorized. There was testimony that the persons handling the advertisement saw nothing in it that would render it unacceptable under the *Times'* policy of rejecting advertisements containing "attacks of a personal character"; their failure to reject it on this ground was not unreasonable. We think the evidence against the *Times* supports at most a finding of negligence in failing to discover the misstatements, and is constitutionally insufficient to show the recklessness that is required for a finding of actual malice. . . .

The judgment of the Supreme Court of Alabama is reversed and the case is remanded to that court for further proceedings not inconsistent with this opinion.

Reversed and remanded.

VI. Prior Restraint or Censorship

NEAR v. MINNESOTA
283 US 697 (1931)

[Historically, censorship of publications was associated with licensing: a book or pamphlet could not be published unless it was first submitted to a censor or licensing official and his approval was procured. Publication without such a license from the censor was a criminal offense. It was against such censorship or previous restraint on publication that John Milton protested in his *Aeropagitica* in 1644. In the minds of Englishmen licensing by censors was associated with ecclesiastical supervision, the Inquisition, the Star Chamber, and monopolies. In 1695 the licensing system in England ended forever. Liberty of the press, wrote Blackstone in 1769, "consists in laying no previous restraints upon publication, and not in freedom from censure for criminal matters when published."

[This is still an essential aspect of liberty of the press under the Constitution: freedom from preliminary restraint, Justice Holmes has said, "extends as well to the false as to the true; . . ." *Patterson* v. *Colorado,* 205 US 454 (1907).

[Licensing requirements are frowned upon by the courts more than any other restrictive device. Even in the case of moving pictures, as we shall see, the Supreme Court has reached the point where it thinks that censorship is inconsistent with the demands of the Constitution. Licensing in radio broadcasting remains an exception to the rule. *Communications Commission* v. *N.B.C.,* 319 US 239 (1943). Injunctions against picketing in labor disputes are a form of previous restraint by judicial act and fall into a separate category.

[In *Near,* v. *Minnesota,* which condemns censorship as unconstitutional, the decision was 5 to 4, with Justices Butler, Van Devanter, McReynolds, and Sutherland dissenting. It is doubtful whether any Justice would dissent from the opinion of Chief Justice Hughes today.]

Mr. Chief Justice Hughes delivered the opinion of the Court:

Chapter 285 of the Session Laws of Minnesota for the year 1925 provides for the abatement, as a public nuisance, of a "malicious, scandalous and defamatory newspaper, magazine or other periodical." Section one of the act is as follows:

Section 1: Any person who, as an individual, or as a member or employee of a firm, or association or organization, or as an officer, director, member or employee of a corporation, shall be engaged in the business of regularly or customarily producing, publishing or circulating, having in possession, selling or giving away,

(a) an obscene, lewd, and lascivious newspaper, magazine, or other periodical, or

(b) a malicious, scandalous and defamatory newspaper, magazine or other periodical,

is guilty of a nuisance, and all persons guilty of such nuisance may be enjoined, as hereinafter provided.

Participation in such business shall constitute a commission of such nuisance and render the participant liable and subject to the proceedings, orders and judgments provided for in this act. Ownership, in whole or in part, directly or indirectly, of any such periodical, or of any stock or interest in any corporation or organization which owns the same in whole or in part, or which publishes the same, shall constitute such participation.

In actions brought under (b) above, there shall be available the defense that the truth was published with good motives and for justifiable ends and in such actions the plaintiff shall not have the right to report [*sic*] to issues or editions of periodicals taking place more than three months before the commencement of the action.

Section two provides that whenever any such nuisance is committed or exists, the county attorney of any county where any such periodical is published or circulated, or, in case of his failure or refusal to proceed upon written request in good faith of a reputable citizen, the attorney general, or upon like failure or refusal of the latter, any citizen of the county, may maintain an action in the district court of the county in the name of the state to enjoin perpetually the persons committing or maintaining any such nuisance from further committing or maintaining it. Upon such evidence as the court shall deem sufficient, a temporary injunction may be granted. The defendants have the right to plead by demurrer or answer, and the plaintiff may demur or reply as in other cases.

The action, by section three, is to be "governed by the practice and procedure applicable to civil actions for injunctions," and after trial the court may enter judgment permanently enjoining the defendants found guilty of violating the act from continuing the violation and, "in and by such judgment, such nuisance may be wholly abated." The court is empowered, as in other cases of contempt, to punish disobedience to a temporary or permanent injunction by fine of not more than $1,000 or by imprisonment in the county jail for not more than twelve months.

Under this statute, . . . the county attorney of Hennepin County brought this action to enjoin the publication of what was described as a "malicious, scandalous and defamatory newspaper, magazine and periodical," known as *The Saturday Press,* published by the defendants in the city of Minneapolis. The complaint alleged that the defendants, on September 24, 1927, and on eight subsequent dates in October and November, 1927, published and circulated editions of that periodical which were "largely devoted to malicious, scandalous and defamatory articles" concerning Charles G. Davis, Frank W. Brunskill, the *Minneapolis Tribune,* the *Minneapolis Journal,* Melvin C. Passolt, George E. Leach, the Jewish Race, the members of the grand jury of Hennepin County impaneled in November, 1927, and then holding office, and other persons, as more fully appeared in exhibits annexed to the complaint, consisting of copies of the articles described and constituting 327 pages of the record. While the complaint did not so allege, it appears from the briefs of both parties that Charles G. Davis was a special law enforcement officer employed by a civic organization, that George E. Leach was mayor of Minneapolis, that Frank

W. Brunskill was its chief of police, and that Floyd B. Olson (the relator in this action) was county attorney.

Without attempting to summarize the contents of the voluminous exhibits attached to the complaint, we deem it sufficient to say that the articles charged in substance that a Jewish gangster was in control of gambling, bootlegging and racketeering in Minneapolis, and that law enforcing officers and agencies were not energetically performing their duties. Most of the charges were directed against the chief of police; he was charged with gross neglect of duty, illicit relations with gangsters, and with participation in graft. The county attorney was charged with knowing the existing conditions and with failure to take adequate measures to remedy them. The mayor was accused of inefficiency and dereliction. One member of the grand jury was stated to be in sympathy with the gangsters. A special grand jury and a special prosecutor were demanded to deal with the situation in general, and, in particular, to investigate an attempt to assassinate one Guilford, one of the original defendants, who, it appears from the articles, was shot by gangsters after the first issue of the periodical had been published. There is no question but that the articles made serious accusations against the public officers named and others in connection with the prevalence of crimes and the failure to expose and punish them. . . .

This statute, for the suppression as a public nuisance of a newspaper or periodical, is unusual, if not unique, and raises questions of grave importance transcending the local interests involved in the particular action. It is no longer open to doubt that the liberty of the press and of speech is within the liberty safeguarded by the due process clause of the 14th Amendment from invasion by state action. It was found impossible to conclude that this essential personal liberty of the citizen was left unprotected by the general guaranty of fundamental rights of person and property. . . . Liberty of speech and of the press is . . . not an absolute right, and the state may punish its abuse. . . . Liberty, in each of its phases, has its history and connotation and, in the present instance, the inquiry is as to the historic conception of the liberty of the press and whether the statute under review violates the essential attributes of that liberty. . . .

The statute is not aimed at the redress of individual or private wrongs. Remedies for libel remain available and unaffected. The statute, said the state court, "is not directed at threatened libel but at an existing business which, generally speaking, involves more than libel." It is aimed at the distribution of scandalous matter as "detrimental to public morals and to the general welfare," tending "to disturb the peace of the community" and "to provoke assaults and the commission of crime." In order to obtain an injunction to suppress the future publication of the newspaper or periodical, it is not necessary to prove the falsity of the charges that have been made in the publication condemned. In the present action there was no allegation that the matter published was not true. It is alleged, and the statute requires the allegation, that the publication was "malicious." But, as in prosecutions for libel, there is no requirement of proof by the state of malice in fact as distinguished from malice inferred from the mere publication of the defamatory matter. The judgment in this case proceeded upon the mere proof of publication. The statute permits the defense, not of the truth alone, but only that the truth was published with good motives and for justifiable ends. It is apparent that under the statute the publication is to be regarded as defamatory if it injures reputation, and that it is scandalous if it circulates charges of reprehensible conduct, whether criminal or otherwise, and the publication is thus deemed to invite public reprobation and to constitute a public scandal. The court sharply defined the purpose of the statute, bringing out the precise point, in these words: "There is no constitutional right to publish a fact merely because it is true. It is a matter of common knowledge that prosecutions under the criminal libel statutes do not result in efficient repression or suppression of the evils of scandal. Men who are the victims of such assaults seldom resort to the courts. This is especially true if their sins are exposed and the only question relates to whether it was done with good motives and for justifiable ends. This law is not for the protection of the person attacked nor to punish the wrongdoer. It is for the protection of the public welfare." . . .

If we cut through mere details of procedure, the operation and effect of the statute in substance is that public authorities may bring the owner or publisher of a newspaper or periodical before a judge upon a charge of conducting a business of publishing scandalous and defamatory matter—in particular that the matter consists of charges against public officers of official dereliction—and unless the owner or publisher is able and disposed to bring competent evidence to satisfy the judge that the charges are true and are published with good motives and for justifiable ends, his newspaper or periodical is suppressed and further publication is made punishable as a contempt. This is of the essence of censorship.

The question is whether a statute authorizing such proceedings in restraint of publication is consistent with the conception of the liberty of the press as historically conceived and guaranteed. In determining the extent of the constitutional protection, it has been generally, if not universally, considered that it is the chief purpose of the guaranty to prevent previous restraints upon publication. The struggle in England, directed against the legislative power of the licenser, resulted in renunciation of the censorship of the press. The liberty deemed to be established was thus described by Blackstone: "The liberty of the press is indeed essential to the nature of a free state; but this consists in laying no *previous* restraints upon publications, and not in freedom from censure for criminal matter when published. Every freeman has an undoubted right to lay what sentiments he pleases before the public; to forbid this, is to destroy the freedom of the press; but if he publishes what is improper, mischievous or illegal, he must take the consequence of his own temerity." . . . The distinction was early pointed out between the extent of the freedom with respect to censorship under our constitutional system and that enjoyed in England. Here, as Madison said, "The great and essential rights of the people are secured against legislative as well as against executive ambition. They are secured, not by laws paramount to prerogative, but by constitutions paramount to laws. This security of the freedom of the press requires that it should be exempt not only from previous restraint by the executive, as in Great Britain, but from legislative restraint also." . . . This court said, in *Patterson* v. *Colorado,* 205 US 454: "In the first place, the main purpose of such constitutional provisions is 'to prevent all such *previous restraints* upon publications as had been practised by other governments,' and they do not prevent the subsequent punishment of such as may be deemed contrary to the public welfare. . . . The preliminary freedom extends as well to the false as to the true; the subsequent punishment may extend as well to the true as to the false. This was the law of criminal libel apart from statute in most cases, if not in all. . . ."

The criticism upon Blackstone's statement has not been because immunity from previous restraint upon publication has not been regarded as deserving of special emphasis, but chiefly because that immunity cannot be deemed to exhaust the conception of the liberty guaranteed by state and Federal constitutions. The point of criticism has been "that the mere exemption from previous restraints cannot be all that is secured by the constitutional provisions"; and that "the liberty of the press might be rendered a mockery and a delusion, and the phrase itself a by-word, if, while every man was at liberty to publish what he pleased, the public authorities might nevertheless punish him for harmless publications." 2 Cooley, *Constitutional Limitations*, 8th ed., p. 885. But it is recognized that punishment for the abuse of the liberty accorded to the press is essential to the protection of the public, and that the common law rules that subject the libeler to responsibility for the public offense, as well as for the private injury, are not abolished by the protection extended in our constitutions. . . . The law of criminal libel rests upon that secure foundation. There is also the conceded authority of courts to punish for contempt when publications directly tend to prevent the proper discharge of judicial functions. . . . In the present case, we have no occasion to inquire as to the permissible scope of subsequent punishment. For whatever wrong the appellant has committed or may commit, by his publications, the state appropriately affords both public and private redress by its libel laws. As has been noted, the statute in question does not deal with punishments; it provides for no punishment, except in case of contempt for voilation of the court's order, but for suppression and injunction, that is, for restraint upon publication.

The objection has also been made that the principle as to immunity from previous restraint is stated too broadly, if every such restraint is deemed to be prohibited. That is undoubtedly true; the protection even as to previous restraint is not absolutely unlimited. But the limitation has been recognized only in exceptional cases. "When a nation is at war many things that might be said in time of peace are such a hindrance to its effort that their utterance will not be endured so long as men fight and that no court could regard them as protected by any constitutional right." *Schenck* v. *United States*, 249 US 47. No one would question but that a government might prevent actual obstruction to its recruiting service or the publication of the sailing dates of transports or the number and location of troops. On similar grounds, the primary requirements of decency may be enforced against obscene publications. The security of the community life may be protected against incitements to acts of violence and the overthrow by force of orderly government. The constitutional guaranty of free speech does not "protect a man from an injunction against uttering words that may have all the effect of force. . . ." *Schenck* v. *United States*. These limitations are not applicable here. Nor are we now concerned with questions as to the extent of authority to prevent publications in order to protect private rights according to the principles governing the exercise of the jurisdiction of courts of equity.

The exceptional nature of its limitations places in a strong light the general conception that liberty of the press, historically considered and taken up by the Federal Constitution, has meant, principally, although not exclusively, immunity from previous restraints or censorship. The conception of the liberty of the press in this country had broadened with the exigencies of the colonial period and with the efforts to secure freedom from oppressive administration. That liberty was especially cherished for the immunity it afforded from previous restraint of the publication of censure of public officers and charges of official misconduct. . . .

The fact that for approximately one hundred and fifty years there has been almost an entire absence of attempts to impose previous restraints upon publications relating to the malfeasance of public officers is significant of the deep-seated conviction that such restraints would violate constitutional right. Public officers, whose character and conduct remain open to debate and free discussion in the press, find their remedies for false accusations in actions under libel laws providing for redress and punishment, and not in proceedings to restrain the publication of newspapers and periodicals. The general principle that the constitutional guaranty of the liberty of the press gives immunity from previous restraints has been approved in many decisions under the provision of state constitutions.

The importance of this immunity has not lessened. While reckless assaults upon public men, and efforts to bring obloquy upon those who are endeavoring faithfully to discharge official duties, exert a baleful influence and deserve the severest condemnation in public opinion, it cannot be said that this abuse is greater, and it is believed to be less, than that which characterized the period in which our institutions took shape. Meanwhile, the administration of government has become more complex, the opportunities for malfeasance and corruption have multiplied, crime has grown to most serious proportions, and the danger of its protection by unfaithful officials and of the impairment of the fundamental security of life and property by criminal alliances and official neglect, emphasizes the primary need of a vigilant and courageous press, especially in great cities. The fact that the liberty of the press may be abused by miscreant purveyors of scandal does not make any the less necessary the immunity of the press from previous restraint in dealing with official misconduct. Subsequent punishment for such abuses as may exist is the appropriate remedy, consistent with constitutional privilege. . . .

Judgment reversed.

ORGANIZATION FOR A BETTER AUSTIN *v.* KEEFE
402 US 415 (1971)

[A real estate broker procured from the Illinois courts an injunction enjoining an interracial community organization from distributing leaflets critical of his alleged activities in blockbusting in the Austin area of Chicago. The injunction was issued, according to the state courts, to protect his right of privacy. The Supreme Court, by 8–1 vote, reversed, holding that Keefe had not met the heavy burden of justifying the prior restraint on the peaceful distribution of informational leaflets. Chief Justice Burger wrote the opinion for the Court. Justice Harlan wrote a dissenting opinion.]

Mr. Chief Justice Burger delivered the opinion of the Court:

We granted the writ in this case to consider the claim that an order of the Circuit Court of Cook County, Illinois, enjoining petitioners from distributing leaflets anywhere in the town of Westchester, Illinois, violates petitioners' rights under the Federal Constitution.

Petitioner Organization for a Better Austin (OBA) is a racially integrated community organization in the Austin neighborhood of Chicago. Respondent is a real estate broker whose office and business activities are in the Austin neighborhood. He resides in Westchester, Illinois, a suburb of Chicago some seven miles from the Austin area.

OBA is an organization whose stated purpose is to "stabilize" the racial ratio in the Austin area. For a number of years the boundary of the Negro segregated area of Chicago has moved progressively west to Austin. OBA, in its efforts to "stabilize" the area—so it describes its program—has opposed and protested various real estate tactics and activities generally known as "blockbusting" or "panic peddling."

It was the contention of OBA that respondent had been one of those who engaged in such tactics, specifically that he aroused the fears of the local white residents that Negroes were coming into the area and then, exploiting the reactions and emotions so aroused, was able to secure listings and sell homes to Negroes. OBA alleged that since 1961 respondent had from time to time actively promoted sales in this manner by means of flyers, phone calls, and personal visits to residents of the area in which his office is located, without regard to whether the persons solicited had expressed any desire to sell their homes. As the "boundary" marking the furthest westward advance of Negroes moved into the Austin area, respondent is alleged to have moved his office along with it.

Community meetings were arranged with respondent to try to persuade him to change his real estate practices. Several other real estate agents were prevailed on to sign an agreement whereby they would not solicit property, by phone, flyer or visit, in the Austin community. Respondent who has consistently denied that he is engaging in "panic peddling" or "blockbusting" refused to sign, contending that it was his right under Illinois law to solicit real estate business as he saw fit.

Thereafter, during September and October of 1967, members of petitioner organization distributed leaflets in Westchester describing respondent's activities. There was no evidence of picketing in Westchester. The challenged publications, now enjoined, were critical of respondent's real estate practices in the Austin neighborhood; one of the leaflets set out the business card respondent used to solicit listings, quoted him as saying "I only sell to Negroes," cited a Chicago Daily News article describing his real estate activities and accused him of being a "panic peddler." Another leaflet, of the same general order, stated that "When he signs the agreement, we stop coming to Westchester." Two of the leaflets requested recipients to call respondent at his home phone number and urge him to sign the "no solicitation" agreement. On several days leaflets were given to persons in a Westchester shopping center. On two other occasions leaflets were passed out to some parishioners on their way to or from respondent's church in Westchester. Leaflets were also left at the doors of his neighbors. The trial court found that petitioners' "distribution of leaflets was on all occasions conducted in a peaceful and orderly manner, did not cause any disruption of pedestrian or vehicular traffic, and did not precipitate any fights, disturbances or other breaches of the peace." One of the officers of OBA testified at trial that he hoped that respondent would be induced to sign the no-solicitation agreement by letting "his neighbors know what he was doing to us."

Respondent sought an injunction in the Circuit Court of Cook County, Illinois, on December 20, 1967. After an adversary hearing the trial court entered a temporary injunction enjoining petitioners "from passing out pamphlets, leaflets or literature of any kind, and from picketing, anywhere in the City of Westchester, Illinois."

On appeal to the Appellate Court of Illinois, First District, that court affirmed. It sustained the finding of fact that petitioners' activities in Westchester had invaded respondent's right of privacy, had caused irreparable harm, and were without adequate remedy at law. The Appellate Court appears to have viewed the alleged activities as coercive and intimidating, rather than informative and therefore as not entitled to First Amendment protection. The Appellate Court rested its holding on its belief that the public policy of the State of Illinois strongly favored protection of the privacy of home and family from encroachment of the nature of petitioners' activities.

It is elementary, of course, that in a case of this kind the court do not concern themselves with the truth or validity of the publication. Under *Near* v. *Minnesota*, 283 US 697 (1931), the injunction, so far as it imposes prior restraint on speech and publication, constitutes an impermissible restraint on First Amendment rights. Here, as in that case, the injunction operates not to redress alleged private wrongs, but to suppress, on the basis of previous publications, distribution of literature "of any kind" in a city of 18,000.

This Court has often recognized that the activity of peaceful pamphleteering is a form of communication protected by the First Amendment. *E.g., Martin* v. *City of Struthers*, 319 US 141 (1943); *Schneider* v. *State*, 308 US 147 (1939); *Lovell* v. *Griffin*, 303 US 444 (1938). In sustaining the injunction, however, the Appellate Court was apparently of the view that petitioners' purpose in distributing their literature was not to inform the public, but to "force" respondent to sign a no-solicitation agreement. The claim that the expressions were intended to exercise a coercive impact on respondent does not remove them from the reach of the First Amendment. Petitioners plainly intended to influence respondent's conduct by their activities; this is not fundamentally different from the function of a newspaper. . . . Petitioners were engaged openly and vigorously in making the public aware of respondent's real estate practices. Those practices were offensive to them, as the views and practices of petitioners are no doubt offensive to others. But so long as the means are peaceful, the communication need not meet standards of acceptability.

Any prior restraint on expression comes to this Court with a "heavy presumption" against its constitutional validity. . . . Respondent thus carries a heavy burden of showing justification for the imposition of such a restraint. He has not met that burden. No prior decisions support the claim that the interest of an individual in being free from public criticism of his business practices in pamphlets or leaflets warrants use of the injunctive power of a court. Designating the conduct as an invasion of privacy, the apparent basis for the injunction here, is not sufficient to support an injunction against peaceful distribution of informational literature of the nature revealed by this record. *Rowan* v. *United States Post Office Dept.*, 397 US 728 (1970), relied on by respondent, is not in point; the right of privacy involved in that case is not shown here. Among other important distinctions, respondent is not attempting to stop the flow of information into his own household, but to the public. Accordingly, the injunction issued by the Illinois court must be vacated.

Reversed.

KUNZ *v.* NEW YORK
340 US 290 (1951)

[An ordinance of the City of New York required a permit for public meetings on streets. It failed to define the circumstances under which officials might refuse to issue permits. The officials construed the ordinance as authorizing them to refuse a permit, in their discretion, if the appellant *in the past* had ridiculed or denounced some religious belief. Kunz had engaged in attacks on Catholics and Jews; when he applied for a permit to speak, he was denied one for this reason; he spoke at Columbus Circle without a permit and was arrested. The Court held that the ordinance was unconstitutional as a previous restraint on rights guaranteed by the First Amendment. Only Justice Jackson dissented.]

Mr. Chief Justice Vinson delivered the opinion of the Court:

New York City has adopted an ordinance which makes it unlawful to hold public worship meetings on the streets without first obtaining a permit from the city police commissioner. Appellant, Carl Jacob Kunz, was convicted and fined $10 for violating this ordinance by holding a religious meeting without a permit. . . .

Appellant is an ordained Baptist minister who speaks under the auspices of the "Outdoor Gospel Work," of which he is the director. He has been preaching for about six years, and states that it is his conviction and duty to "go out on the highways and byways and preach the word of God." In 1946, he applied for and received a permit under the ordinance in question, there being no question that appellant comes within the classes of persons entitled to receive permits under the ordinance. This permit, like all others, was good only for the calendar year in which issued. In November, 1946, his permit was revoked after a hearing by the police commissioner. The revocation was based on evidence that he had ridiculed and denounced other religious beliefs in his meetings.

Although the penalties of the ordinance apply to anyone who "ridicules and denounces other religious beliefs," the ordinance does not specify this as a ground for permit revocation. Indeed, there is no mention in the ordinance of any power or revocation. However, appellant did not seek judicial or administrative review of the revocation proceedings, and any question as to the propriety of the revocation is not before us in this case. In any event, the revocation affected appellant's rights to speak in 1946 only. Appellant applied for another permit in 1947, and again in

1948, but was notified each time that his application was "disapproved," with no reason for the disapproval being given. On September 11, 1948, appellant was arrested for speaking at Columbus Circle in New York City without a permit. It is from the conviction which resulted that this appeal has been taken.

Appellant's conviction was thus based upon his failure to possess a permit for 1948. We are here concerned only with the propriety of the action of the police commissioner in refusing to issue that permit. Disapproval of the 1948 permit application by the police commissioner was justified by the New York courts on the ground that a permit had previously been revoked "for good reasons." It is noteworthy that there is no mention in the ordinance of reasons for which such a permit application can be refused. This interpretation allows the police commissioner, an administrative official, to exercise discretion in denying subsequent permit applications on the basis of his interpretation, at that time, of what is deemed to be conduct condemned by the ordinance. We have here, then, an ordinance which gives an administrative official discretionary power to control in advance the right of citizens to speak on religious matters on the streets of New York. As such, the ordinance is clearly invalid as a prior restraint on the exercise of First Amendment rights.

In considering the right of a municipality to control the use of public streets for the expression of religious views, we start with the words of Mr. Justice Roberts that "Wherever the title of streets and parks may rest, they have immemorially been held in trust for the use of the public and, time out of mind, have been used for purposes of assembly, communicating thoughts between citizens, and discussing public questions." *Hague* v. *C.I.O.*, 307 US 496. . . .

The court below has mistakenly derived support for its conclusion from the evidence produced at the trial that appellant's religious meetings had, in the past, caused some disorder. There are appropriate public remedies to protect the peace and order of the community if appellant's speeches should result in disorder or violence. "In the present case, we have no occasion to inquire as to the permissible scope of subsequent punishment." *Near* v. *Minnesota*, 283 US 697. We do not express any opinion on the propriety of punitive remedies which the New York authorities may utilize. We are here concerned with suppression—not punishment. It is sufficient to say that New York cannot vest restraining control over the right to speak on religious subjects in an administrative official where there are no appropriate standards to guide his action.

Reversed. . . .

The Pentagon Papers
NEW YORK TIMES COMPANY *v.* UNITED STATES
UNITED STATES *v.* WASHINGTON POST COMPANY
403 US 713 (1971)

[In American constitutional history, this case will be considered one of the most important precedents on freedom of the press. It was the hardest test of the principle that the First Amendment will not tolerate any prior restraint on publication. After the *New York Times* had published three installments of articles based on the secret Pentagon papers, the United States Government went before the U.S. District

Court in New York and asked for an injunction to bar further publication. This was the first time in American history that the Federal Government had sought an injunction against publication. Judge Gurfein issued a temporary restraining order to have an opportunity to hear the matter but then denied the motion for a temporary injunction. The Court of Appeals for the Second Circuit, on June 23, 1971, reversed Judge Gurfein's order and remanded the case to the District Court for *in camera* proceedings to determine, on or before July 3, whether disclosure of any papers, particularly specified by the Government, "pose such grave and immediate danger to the security of the United States as to warrant their publication being enjoined." Meantime the *Washington Post* had begun publication of the papers, and the Government asked the District Court in the District of Columbia for similar relief, and that court denied a preliminary injunction, and that decision was affirmed, on June 23, by the Court of Appeals for the District of Columbia. On the following day the *New York Times* applied to the Supreme Court for certiorari, and on the same day the Government asked the Court to review the decision of the Circuit Court in the *Washington Post* case. Each party asked for interim relief and accelerated consideration. By 5–4, the Supreme Court stayed both newspapers from further publication of the Pentagon papers but set a hearing before the Court on June 26. On June 30 the Court announced its decision.

[In a brief *per curiam,* the Supreme Court affirmed the judgment of the Court of Appeals in the *Washington Post* case and reversed the judgment of the Court of Appeals in the *New York Times* case. It lifted the restraints on publication it had imposed on June 24. Each of the nine Justices wrote an opinion. Three of the opinions are identified by their authors as dissents: those of Chief Justice Burger and of Justices Harlan and Blackmun. The point emphasized by the dissenters seems to be that these Justices wanted the cases sent back to the District Courts for consideration of the Government's claim that publication of certain of the papers would cause national harm. The rationale of the *per curiam,* in light of the dissents, seems to be that if there was to be no further exploration of this question —in view of the vote of six of the Justices—then there should be no restraint on publication.]

Per Curiam:

We granted certiorari in these cases in which the United States seeks to enjoin the New York Times and the Washington Post from publishing the contents of a classified study entitled "History of U.S. Decision-Making Process on Viet Nam Policy."

"Any system of prior restraints of expression comes to this Court bearing a heavy presumption against its constitutional validity." *Bantam Books, Inc.* v. *Sullivan,* 372 US 58, 70 (1963); see also *Near* v. *Minnesota,* 283 US 697 (1931). The Government "thus carries a heavy burden of showing justification for the enforcement of such a restraint." *Organization for a Better Austin* v. *Keefe* (1971). The District Court for the Southern District of New York in the *New York Times* case and the District Court for the District of Columbia and the Court of Appeals for the District of Columbia Circuit in the *Washington Post* case held that the Government had not met that burden. We agree.

The judgment of the Court of Appeals for the District of Columbia Circuit is therefore affirmed. The order of the Court of Appeals for the Second Circuit is reversed, and the case is remanded with directions to enter a judgment affirming the judgment of the District Court for the Southern District of New York. The stays entered June 25, 1971, by the Court are vacated. The mandates shall issue forthwith.

So ordered.

Mr. Justice Brennan, concurring:

I

I write separately in these cases only to emphasize what should be apparent: that our judgment in the present cases may not be taken to indicate the propriety, in the future, of issuing temporary stays and restraining orders to block the publication of material sought to be suppressed by the Government. So far as I can determine, never before has the United States sought to enjoin a newspaper from publishing information in its possession. The relative novelty of the questions presented, the necessary haste with which decisions were reached, the magnitude of the interests asserted, and the fact that all the parties have concentrated their arguments upon the question whether permanent restraints were proper may have justified at least some of the restraints heretofore imposed in these cases. Certainly it is difficult to fault the several courts below for seeking to assure that the issues here involved were preserved for ultimate review by this Court. But even if it be assumed that some of the interim restraints were proper in the two cases before us, that assumption has no bearing upon the propriety of similar judicial action in the future. To begin with, there has now been ample time for reflection and judgment; whatever values there may be in the preservation of novel questions for appellate review may not support any restraints in the future. More important, the First Amendment stands as an absolute bar to the imposition of judicial restraints in circumstances of the kind presented by these cases.

II

The error which has pervaded these cases from the outset was the granting of any injunctive relief whatsoever, interim or otherwise. The entire thrust of the Government's claim throughout these cases has been that publication of the material sought to be enjoined "could," or "might," or "may" prejudice the national interest in various ways. But the First Amendment tolerates absolutely no prior judicial restraints of the press predicated upon surmise or conjecture that untoward consequences may result.* Our cases, it is true, have indicated that there is a single, extremely narrow class of cases in which the First Amendment's ban on prior judicial restraint may be overriden. Our cases have thus far indicated that such cases may arise only when the Nation "is at

---

* *Freedman* v. *Maryland,* 380 US 51 (1965), and similar cases regarding temporary restraints of allegedly obscene materials are not in point. For those cases rest upon the proposition that "obscenity is not protected by the freedoms of speech and press." *Roth* v. *United States,* 354 US 476 (1957). Here there is no question but that the material sought to be suppressed is within the protection of the First Amendment; the only question is whether, notwithstanding that fact, its publication may be enjoined for a time because of the presence of an overwhelming national interest. Similarly, copyright cases have no pertinence here: the Government is not asserting an interest in the particular form of words chosen in the documents, but is seeking to suppress the ideas expressed therein. And the copyright laws, of course, protect only the form of expression and not the ideas expressed.

war," *Schenck* v. *United States,* 249 US 47, 52 (1919), during which times "no one would question but that a Government might prevent actual obstruction to its recruiting service or the publication of the sailing dates of transports or the number and location of troops." *Near* v. *Minnesota,* 283 US 697, 716 (1931). Even if the present world situation were assumed to be tantamount to a time of war, or if the power of presently available armaments would justify even in peacetime the suppression of information that would set in motion a nuclear holocaust, in neither of these actions has the Government presented or even alleged that publication of items from or based upon the material at issue would cause the happening of an event of that nature. "The chief purpose of [the First Amendment's] guarantee [is] to prevent previous restraints upon publication." *Near* v. *Minnesota, supra,* at 713. Thus, only governmental allegation and proof that publication must inevitably, directly, and immediately cause the occurrence of an event kindred to imperiling the safety of a transport already at sea can support even the issuance of an interim restraining order. In no event may mere conclusions be sufficient: for if the Executive Branch seeks judicial aid in preventing publication, it must inevitably submit the basis upon which that aid is sought to scrutiny by the judiciary. And therefore, every restraint issued in this case, whatever its form, has violated the First Amendment—and none the less so because that restraint was justified as necessary to afford the court an opportunity to examine the claim more thoroughly. Unless and until the Government has clearly made out its case, the First Amendment commands that no injunction may issue.

Mr. Chief Justice Burger, dissenting:

So clear are the constitutional limitations on prior restraint against expression, that from the time of *Near* v. *Minnesota,* 283 US 697 (1931), until recently in *Organization for a Better Austin* v. *Keefe* (1971), we have had little occasion to be concerned with cases involving prior restraints against news reporting on matters of public interest. There is, therefore, little variation among the members of the Court in terms of resistance to prior restraints against publication. Adherence to this basic constitutional principle, however, does not make this case a simple one. In this case, the imperative of a free and unfettered press comes into collision with another imperative, the effective functioning of a complex modern government and specifically the effective exercise of certain constitutional powers of the Executive. Only those who view the First Amendment as an absolute in all circumstances—a view I respect, but reject—can find such a case as this to be simple or easy.

This case is not simple for another and more immediate reason. We do not know the facts of the case. No District Judge knew all the facts. No Court of Appeals judge knew all the facts. No member of this Court knows all the facts.

Why are we in this posture, in which only those judges to whom the First Amendment is absolute and permits of no restraint in any circumstances or for any reason, are really in a position to act?

I suggest we are in this posture because these cases have been conducted in unseemly haste. Mr. Justice Harlan covers the chronology of events demonstrating the hectic pressures under which these cases have been processed and I need not restate them. The prompt setting of these cases reflects our universal abhorrence of prior restraint. But prompt judicial action does not mean unjudicial haste.

Here, moreover, the frenetic haste is due in large part to the manner in which the *Times* proceeded from the date it obtained the purloined documents. It seems reasonably clear now that the haste precluded reasonable and deliberate judicial treatment of these cases and was not warranted. The precipitous action of this Court aborting a trial not yet completed is not the kind of judicial conduct which ought to attend the disposition of a great issue.

The newspapers make a derivative claim under the First Amendment; they denominate this right as the public right-to-know; by implication, the *Times* asserts a sole trusteeship of that right by virtue of its journalist "scoop." The right is asserted as an absolute. Of course, the First Amendment right itself is not an absolute, as Justice Holmes so long ago pointed out in his aphorism concerning the right to shout of fire in a crowded theater. There are other exceptions, some of which Chief Justice Hughes mentioned by way of example in *Near* v. *Minnesota*. There are no doubt other exceptions no one has had occasion to describe or discuss. Conceivably such exceptions may be lurking in these cases and would have been flushed had they been properly considered in the trial courts, free from unwarranted deadlines and frenetic pressures. A great issue of this kind should be tried in a judicial atmosphere conducive to thoughtful, reflective deliberation, especially when haste, in terms of hours, is unwarranted in light of the long period the *Times*, by its own choice, deferred publication.

It is not disputed that the *Times* has had unauthorized possession of the documents for three to four months, during which it has had its expert analysts studying them, presumably digesting them and preparing the material for publication. During all of this time, the *Times*, presumably in its capacity as trustee of the public's "right-to-know," has held up publication for purposes it considered proper and thus public knowledge was delayed. No doubt this was for a good reason; the analysis of 7,000 pages of complex material drawn from a vastly greater volume of material would inevitably take time, and the writing of good news stories takes time. But why should the United States Government, from whom this information was illegally acquired by someone, along with all the counsel, trial judges, and appellate judges be placed under needless pressure? After these months of deferral, the alleged right-to-know has somehow and suddenly become a right that must be vindicated instanter.

Would it have been unreasonable, since the newspaper could anticipate the government's objections to release of secret material, to give the government an opportunity to review the entire collection and determine whether agreement could be reached on publication? Stolen or not, if security was not in fact jeopardized, much of the material could no doubt have been declassified, since it spans a period ending in 1968. With such an approach—one that great newpapers have in the past practiced and stated editorially to be the duty of an honorable press—the newspapers and government might well have narrowed the area of disagreement as to what was and was not publishable, leaving the remainder to be resolved in orderly litigation if necessary. To me it is hardly believable that a newspaper long regarded as a great institution in American life would fail to perform one of the basic and simple duties of every citizen with respect to the discovery or possession of stolen property or secret government documents. That duty, I had thought—perhaps naively—was to report forthwith, to responsible public officers. This duty rests on taxi drivers, Justices, and the *New York Times*. The course followed by the *Times*, whether so calculated or not, removed any possibility of orderly litigation of the issues. If the action of the judges up to now has been correct, that result is sheer happenstance.

Our grant of the writ before final judgment in the *Times* case aborted the trial in the District Court before it had made a complete record pursuant to the mandate of the Court of Appeals, Second Circuit.

The consequence of all this melancholy series of events is that we literally do not know what we are acting on. As I see it we have been forced to deal with litigation concerning rights of great magnitude without an adequate record, and surely without time for adequate treatment either in the prior proceedings or in this Court. It is interesting to note that counsel in oral argument before this Court were frequently unable to respond to questions on factual points. Not surprisingly they pointed out that they had been working literally "around the clock" and simply were unable to review the documents that give rise to these cases and were not familiar with them. This Court is in no better posture. I agree with Mr. Justice Harlan and Mr. Justice Blackmun but I am not prepared to reach the merits.*

I would affirm the Court of Appeals for the Second Circuit and allow the District Court to complete the trial aborted by our grant of certiorari meanwhile preserving the *status quo* in the *Post* case. I would direct that the District Court on remand give priority to the *Times* case to the exclusion of all other business of that court but I would not set arbitrary deadlines.

I should add that I am in general agreement with much of what Mr. Justice White has expressed with respect to penal sanctions concerning communication or retention of documents or information relating to the national defense.

We all crave speedier judicial processes but when judges are pressured as in these cases the result is a parody of the judicial process.

---

* With respect to the question of inherent power of the Executive to classify papers, records and documents as secret, or otherwise unavailable for public exposure, and to secure aid of the courts for enforcement, there may be an analogy with respect to this Court. No statute gives this Court express power to establish and enforce the utmost security measures for the secrecy of our deliberations and records. Yet I have little doubt as to the inherent power of the Court to protect the confidentiality of its internal operations by whatever judicial measures may be required.

VII. The Clear and Present Danger Doctrine: Teaching, Advocacy, and Incitement

DE JONGE v. OREGON
299 US 353 (1937)

[The First Amendment provides that Congress shall make no law "abridging . . . the right of the people peaceably to assemble, and to petition the Government for a redress of grievances." Not until 1876 was the Supreme Court called upon to construe this provision. In *United States* v. *Cruikshank,* 92 US 542 (1876) the Court gave this provision a restricted meaning, holding that the First Amendment guarantees to citizens the freedom to assemble in order that they may petition Congress for a redress of grievances. Apparently, only a peaceful assembly called for this purpose was constitutionally protected. Freedom of assembly was thus dependent upon the right of petition, which had its origin in Magna Carta, reaffirmed in the Bill of Rights of 1689.

[In the *De Jonge Case,* however, freedom of assembly was liberated from dependence upon the right of petition and was held to be as fundamental as are freedom of speech and freedom of the press. In this case the meeting was called under the auspices of the Communist Party, but the Court held that it is a matter of constitutional indifference under whose auspices a meeting is called, or who the speakers are; the only question is whether "their utterances transcend the bounds of the freedom of speech which the Constitution protects."

[In this significant unanimous decision the Court also held that freedom of speech and of the press and the right of peaceable assembly are safeguarded against infringement by state action: these freedoms are assimilated into the Due Process Clause of the Fourteenth Amendment.]

Mr. Chief Justice Hughes delivered the opinion of the Court:

Appellant, Dirk De Jonge, was indicted in Multnomah County, Oregon for violation of the Criminal Syndicalism Law of that State. The act . . . defines "criminal syndicalism" as "the doctrine which advocates crime, physical violence, sabotage, or any unlawful acts or methods as a means of accomplishing or effecting industrial or political change or revolution." With this preliminary definition the Act proceeds to describe a number of offenses, embracing the teaching of criminal syndicalism, the printing or distribution of books, pamphlets, etc., advocating that doctrine, the organization of a society or assemblage which advocates it, and presiding at or assisting in conducting a meeting of such an organization, society or group. The prohibited acts are made felonies, punishable by imprisonment for not less than one year nor more than ten years, or by a fine of not more than $1,000, or by both.

We are concerned with but one of the described offenses and with the validity of the statute in this particular application. The charge is that appellant assisted in the conduct of a meeting which was called under the auspices of the Communist Party, an organization advocating criminal syndicalism. The defense was that the meeting was public and orderly and was held for a lawful purpose; that, while it was held under the auspices of the Communist Party, neither criminal syndicalism nor any unlawful conduct was taught or advocated at the meeting either by appellant or by others. Appellant moved for a direction of acquittal, contending that the statute as applied to him, for merely assisting at a meeting called by the Communist Party at which nothing unlawful was done or advocated, violated the due process clause of the Fourteenth Amendment of the Constitution of the United States.

This contention was overruled. Appellant was found guilty as charged and was sentenced to imprisonment for seven years. The judgment was affirmed by the Supreme Court of the State. . . . The case comes here on appeal.

The record does not present the evidence adduced at the trial. The parties have substituted a stipulation of facts. . . .

The stipulation, after setting forth the charging part of the indictment, recites in substance the following: That on July 27, 1934, there was held in Portland a meeting which had been advertised by handbills issued by the Portland section of the Communist Party; that the number of persons in attendance was variously estimated at from 150 to 300; that some of those present, who were members of the Communist Party, estimated that not to exceed 10 to 15 per cent of those in attendance were such members; that the meeting was open to the public without charge and no questions were asked of those entering, with respect to their relation to the Communist Party; that the notice of the meeting advertised it as a protest against illegal raids on workers' halls and homes and against the shooting of striking longshoremen by Portland police; that the chairman stated that it was a meeting held by the Communist Party; that the first speaker dwelt on the activities of the Young Communist League; that the defendant De Jonge, the second speaker, was a member of the Communist Party and went to the meeting to speak in its name; that in his talk he protested against conditions in the county jail, the action of city police in relation to the maritime strike then in progress in Portland and numerous other matters; that he discussed the reason for the raids on the Communist headquarters and workers' halls and offices; that he told the workers that these attacks were due to efforts on the part of the steamship companies and stevedoring companies to break the maritime longshoreman's and seamen's strike; that they hoped to break the strike by pitting the longshoremen and seamen against the Communist movement; that there was also testimony to the effect that defendant asked those present to do more work in obtaining members for the Communist Party and requested all to be at the meeting of the party to be held in Portland on the following evening and to bring their friends to show their defiance to local police authority and to assist them in their revolutionary tactics; that there was also testimony that defendant urged the purchase of certain communist literature which was sold at the meeting; that while the meeting was still in progress it was raided by the police; that the meeting was conducted in an orderly manner; that defendant and several others who were actively conducting the meeting were arrested by the police; and that on searching the hall the police found a quantity of communist literature.

The stipulation then set forth various extracts from the literature of the Communist Party to show its advocacy of criminal syndicalism. The stipulation does not disclose any activity by the defendant as a basis for his prosecution other than his participation in the meeting in question. Nor does the stipulation show that the communist literature distributed at the meeting contained any advocacy of criminal syndicalism or of any lawful conduct. It was admitted by the Attorney General of the State in his argument at the bar of this Court that the literature distributed in the meeting was not of that sort and that the extracts contained in the stipulation were taken from communist literature found elsewhere. Its introduction in evidence was for the purpose of showing that the Communist Party as such did advocate the doctrine of criminal syndicalism, a fact which is not disputed on this appeal.

The indictment charged as follows:

The said Dirk De Jonge, Don Cluster, Edward R. Denny and Earl Stewart on the 27th day of July, A.D. 1934, in the county of Multnomah and state of Oregon, then and there being, did then and there unlawfully and feloniously preside at, conduct and assist in conducting an assemblage of persons, organization, society and group, to wit: The Communist Party, a more particular description of which said assemblage of persons, organization, society and group is to this grand jury unknown, which said assemblage of persons, organization, society and group did then and there unlawfully and feloniously teach and advocate the doctrine of criminal syndicalism and sabotage, contrary to the statutes in such cases made and provided, and against the peace and dignity of the state of Oregon.

On the theory that this was a charge that criminal syndicalism and sabotage were advocated at the meeting in question, defendant moved for acquittal, insisting that the evidence was insufficient to warrant his conviction. The trial court denied his motion, and error in this respect was assigned on appeal. The Supreme Court of the State put aside that contention by ruling that the indictment did not charge that criminal syndicalism or sabotage was advocated at the meeting described in the evidence, either by defendant or by anyone else. The words of the indictment that "said assemblage of persons, organization, society, and group did then and there unlawfully and feloniously teach and advocate the doctrine of criminal syndicalism and sabotage," referred not to the meeting in question, or to anything then and there said or done by defendant or others, but to the advocacy of criminal syndicalism and sabotage by the Communist Party in Multnomah County. The ruling of the State court upon this point was precise. . . .

In this view, lack of sufficient evidence as to illegal advocacy or action at the meeting became immaterial. Having limited the charge to defendant's participation in a meeting called by the Communist Party, the state court sustained the conviction upon that basis regardless of what was said or done at the meeting.

We must take the indictment as thus construed. Conviction upon a charge not made would be sheer denial of due process. It thus appears that, while defendant was a member of the Communist Party, he was not indicted for participating in its organization, or for joining it, or for soliciting members or for distributing its literature. He was not charged with teaching or advocating criminal syndicalism or sabotage or any unlawful acts, either at the meeting or elsewhere. He was accordingly deprived of the benefit of evidence as to the orderly and unlawful conduct of the meeting and that it was not called or used for the advocacy of criminal syndicalism or sabotage or any unlawful action. His sole offense as charged, and for which he was convicted and sentenced to imprisonment for seven years, was that he had assisted in the conduct of a public meeting, albeit otherwise lawful, which was held under the auspices of the Communist Party.

The broad reach of the statute as thus applied is plain. While defendant was a member of the Communist Party, that membership was not necessary to conviction on such a charge. A like fate might have attended any speaker, although not a member, who "assisted in the conduct" of the meeting. However innocuous the object of the meeting, however lawful the subjects and tenor of the addresses, however reasonable and timely the discussion, all those assisting in the conduct of the meeting would be subject to imprisonment as felons if the meeting were held by the Communist Party. . . . Thus, if the Communist Party had called a public meeting in Portland to discuss the tariff, or the foreign policy of the Government, or taxation, or relief, or candidacies for the offices of President, members of Congress, Governor, or state legislators, every speaker who assisted in the conduct of the meeting would be equally guilty with the defendant in this case, upon the charge as here defined and sustained. The list of illustrations might be indefinitely extended to every variety of meetings under the auspices of the Communist Party although held for the discussion of political issues or to adopt protests and pass resolutions of an entirely innocent and proper character.

While the States are entitled to protect themselves from the abuse of the privileges of our institutions through an attempted substitution of force and violence in the place of peaceful political action in order to effect revolutionary changes in government, none of our decisions go to the length of sustaining such a curtailment of the right of free speech and assembly as the Oregon statute demands in its present application. . . . The right of peaceable assembly is a right cognate to those of free speech and free press and is equally fundamental. As this Court said in *United States* v. *Cruikshank,* 92 US 542: "The very idea of a government, republican in form, implies a right on the part of its citizens to meet peaceably for consultation in respect to public affairs and to petition for a redress of grievances." The First Amendment of the Federal Constitution expressly guarantees that right against abridgment by Congress. But explicit mention there does not argue exclusion elsewhere. For the right is one that cannot be denied without violating those fundamental principles of liberty and justice which lie at the base of all civil and political institutions—principles which the Fourteenth Amendment embodies in the general terms of its due process clause. . . .

These rights may be abused by using speech or press or assembly in order to incite to violence and crime. The people through their legislatures may protect themselves against that abuse. But the legislative intervention can find constitutional justification only by dealing with the abuse. The rights themselves must not be curtailed. The greater the importance of safeguarding the community from incitements to the overthrow of our institutions by force and violence, the more imperative is the need to preserve inviolate the constitutional rights of free speech, free press and free assembly in order to maintain the opportunity for free political discussion, to the end that government may be responsive to the will of the people and that changes, if desired, may be obtained by peaceful means. Therein lies the security of the Republic, the very foundation of constitutional government.

It follows from these considerations that, consistently with the Federal Constitution, peaceable assembly for lawful discussion cannot be made a crime. The holding of meetings for peaceable political action cannot be proscribed. Those who assist in the conduct of such meetings cannot be branded as criminals on that score. The question, if the rights of free speech and peaceable assembly are to be preserved, is not as to the auspices under which the meeting is held but as to its purpose; not as to the relations of the speakers, but whether their utterances transcend the bounds of the freedom of speech which the Constitution protects. If the persons assembling have committed crimes elsewhere, if they have formed or are engaged in a conspiracy against the public peace and order, they may be prosecuted for their conspiracy or other violation of valid laws. But it is a different matter when the State, instead of prosecuting them for such offenses, seizes upon mere participation in a peaceable assembly and a lawful public discussion as the basis for a criminal charge.

We are not called upon to review the findings of the state court as to the objectives of the Communist Party. Notwithstanding those objectives, the defendant still enjoyed his personal right of free speech and to take part in a peaceable assembly having a lawful purpose, although called by that party. The defendant was none the less entitled to discuss the public issues of the day and thus in a lawful manner, without incitement to violence or crime, to seek redress of alleged grievances. That was of the essence of his guaranteed personal liberty.

We hold that the Oregon statute as applied to the particular charge as defined by the state court is repugnant to the due process clause of the Fourteenth Amendment. The judgment of conviction is reversed. . . .

DENNIS *v.* UNITED STATES
341 US 494 (1951)

[Speech and publications are protected by the First Amendment unless "the expression presents a clear and present danger of action of a kind the State is empowered to prevent and punish." This proposition was stated for the Court in the second flag-salute case, *West Virginia State Board of Education* v. *Barnette, supra.* While the rights of free speech and press are fundamental, "their exercise is subject to restriction, if the particular restriction proposed is required in order to protect the state from destruction or from serious injury, political, economic or moral." The necessity for restriction does not exist "unless speech would produce, or is intended to produce, a clear and imminent danger of some substantive evil which the State constitutionally may seek to prevent." Justice Brandeis in *Whitney* v. *California,* 274 US 357 (1927). To justify suppression of free speech, Brandeis added, there must be "reasonable ground to fear that serious evil will result if free speech is practiced . . . ; that the danger apprehended is imminent . . . ; that the evil to be prevented is a serious one." He distinguished advocacy from incitement, preparation from attempt, assembly from conspiracy. To some authorities these are still the essential elements of the clear and present danger doctrine.

[The doctrine was first stated in the Supreme Court by Justice Holmes in *Schenck* v. *United States,* 249 US 47 (1919). His opinion was that of a unanimous Court. In some later cases, however, the Court failed effectively to use the clear and present danger test, and accordingly Holmes and Brandeis dissented, as in *Abrams* v. *United States,* 250 US 616 (1919). In *Gitlow* v. *New York,* 268 US 652 (1925), a majority of the Court declined to follow the test. Holmes and Brandeis dissented. While the *Gitlow Case* has not been expressly overruled, later cases have used the clear and present danger test as formulated by Holmes and Brandeis—e.g., *Herndon* v. *Lowry,* 301 US 242 (1937).

[But the force and reach of the clear and present danger doctrine are matters concerning which members of the Court have differing views. Courts differ as to how it can be determined when a danger is "clear," or when it is "present," or when the evil sought to be prevented by a restriction on free speech is "substantial." Justice Frankfurter even doubted if Holmes meant the clear and present danger doctrine to be "a technical legal doctrine" or to "convey a formula for adjudicating cases." *Pennekamp* v. *Florida,* 328 US 331 (1946).

[The *Dennis Case,* involving the conviction of eleven Communist Party leaders, reflects the diversity of views and the strains and stresses to which the Holmes-Brandeis doctrine has been subjected. In a 6-to-2 decision (Justice Clark not participating and Justices Black and Douglas dissenting) the Court upheld the conviction for conspiracy under the Smith Act of 1940. Seven of the Justices agreed that the standard to be used is that of the clear and present danger; only Justice Jackson maintained that in a conspiracy case such as this one the conspirators could be convicted even if there was no clear and present danger of overthrow of the Government. The dissenting Justices, on the other hand, ignored the conspiracy element and put all their weight on the clear and present danger test.

[It should be borne in mind that the Court had before it a conviction for *criminal conspiracy;* for the law has always considered conspiracy a much graver threat to the state than the acts of a solitary criminal. Following the *Dennis Case,* other Communists have been convicted—state and local as well as national leaders of the party. But in *Yates* v. *United States,* 354 US 298 (1957), the Supreme Court held that the term "organize" in the Smith Act refers only to acts involving the creation of a new organization. Since the party was organized in 1945, indictments for conspiracy to organize had to be brought within three years from 1945, as provided by the statute of limitations. The decision on this point was 5 to 2. After *Yates,* the Government moved to discontinue pending prosecutions for conspiracy. In all, twenty-nine persons served prison terms for convictions under the conspiracy provision of the Smith Act.

[In *Scales* v. *United States,* 367 US 203 (1961), the Court upheld the constitutionality of the membership provision of the Smith Act, which the Court interpreted as requiring proof of "active" as distinguished from merely nominal or passive membership in the Communist Party. But in a companion case, *Noto* v. *United States,* the Court unanimously reversed the conviction under the membership clause. Following this reversal, the Government moved to discontinue pending prosecutions under the membership clause. Scales was, therefore, the only person to serve a prison sentence under the membership provision of the Smith Act.]

Mr. Chief Justice Vinson:

Petitioners were indicted in July, 1948, for violation of the conspiracy provisions of the Smith Act, 54 Stat. 671, 18 U.S.C. (1946 ed.) § 11, during the period of April, 1945, to July, 1948. . . . A verdict of guilty as to all the petitioners was returned by the jury on October 14, 1949. The Court of Appeals affirmed the convictions. . . . We granted certiorari, . . . limited to the following two questions: (1) Whether either § 2 or § 3 of the Smith Act, inherently or as construed and applied in the instant case, violates the First Amendment and other provisions of the Bill of Rights; (2) whether either § 2 or § 3 of the Act, inherently or as construed and applied in the instant case, violates the First and Fifth Amendments because of indefiniteness.

Sections 2 and 3 of the Smith Act provide as follows:

Sec. 2.
(a) It shall be unlawful for any person—
(1) to knowingly or willfully advocate, abet, advise, or teach the duty, necessity, desirability, or propriety of overthrowing or destroying any government in the United States by force or violence, or by the assassination of any officer of any such government;
(2) with the intent to cause the overthrow or destruction of any government in the United States, to print, publish, edit, issue, circulate, sell, distribute, or publicly display any written or printed matter advocating, advising, or teaching the duty, necessity, desirability, or propriety of overthrowing or destroying any government in the United States by force or violence;
(3) to organize or help to organize any society, group, or assembly of persons who teach, advocate, or encourage the overthrow or destruction of any government in the United States by force or violence; or to be or become a member of, or affiliate with, any such society, group, or assembly of persons, knowing the purposes thereof.
(b) For the purposes of this section, the term "government in the United States" means the Government of the United States, the government of any State, Territory, or possession of the United States, the government of the District of Columbia, or the government of any political sub-division of any of them.
Sec. 3. It shall be unlawful for any person to attempt to commit, or to conspire to commit, any of the acts prohibited by the provisions of . . . this title.

The indictment charged the petitioners with wilfully and knowingly conspiring (1) to organize as the Communist Party of the United States of America a society, group and assembly of persons who teach and advocate the overthrow and destruction of the Government of the United States by force and violence, and (2) knowingly and wilfully to advocate and teach the duty and necessity of overthrowing and destroying the Government of the United States by force and violence. The indictment further alleged that § 2 of the Smith Act proscribes these acts and that any conspiracy to take such action is a violation of § 3 of the Act.

The trial of the case extended over nine months, six of which were devoted to the taking of evidence, resulting in a record of 16,000 pages. Our limited grant of the writ of certiorari has removed from our consideration any question as to the sufficiency of the evidence to support the jury's determination that petitioners are guilty of the offense charged. Whether on this record petitioners did in fact advocate the overthrow of the Government by force and violence is not before us, and we must base any discussion of this point upon the conclusions stated in the opinion of the Court of Appeals, which treated the issue in great detail. That court held that the record in this case amply supports the necessary finding of the jury that petitioners, the leaders of the Communist Party in this country, were unwilling to work within our framework of democracy, but intended to initiate a violent revolution whenever the propitious occasion appeared. Petitioners dispute the meaning to be drawn from the evidence, contending that the Marxist-Leninist doctrine they advocated taught that force and violence to achieve a Communist form of government in an existing democratic state would be necessary only because the ruling classes of that state would never permit the transformation to be accomplished peacefully, but would use force and violence to defeat any peaceful political and economic gain the Communists could achieve. But the Court of Appeals held that the record supports the following broad conclusions: By virtue of their control over the political apparatus of the Communist Political Association, petitioners were able to transform that organization into the Communist Party; that the policies of the Association were changed from peaceful cooperation with the United States and its economic and political structure to a policy which had existed before the United States and the Soviet Union were fighting a common enemy, namely, a policy which worked for the overthrow of the Government by force and violence; that the Communist Party is a highly disciplined organization adept at infiltration into strategic positions, use of aliases, and double-meaning language; that the Party is rigidly controlled; that Communists, unlike other political parties, tolerate no dissension from the policy laid down by the guiding forces, but that the approved program is slavishly followed by the members of the Party; that the literature of the Party and the statements and activities of its leaders . . . advocate, and the general goal of the Party was, during the period in question, to achieve a successful overthrow of the existing order by force and violence.

. . . The structure and purpose of the statute demand the inclusion of intent as an element of the crime. Congress was concerned with those who advocate and organize for the overthrow of the Government. Certainly those who recruit and combine for the purpose of advocating overthrow intend to bring about that overthrow. We hold that the statute requires as an essential element of the crime proof of the intent of those who are charged with its violation to overthrow the Government by force and violence. . . .

Nor does the fact that there must be an investigation of a state of mind under this interpretation afford any basis for rejection of that meaning. A survey of Title 18 of the U.S. Code indicates that the vast majority of the crimes designated by that Title require, by express language, proof of the existence of a certain mental state in words such as "knowingly," "maliciously," "wilfully," "with the purpose of," "with intent to," or combinations or permutations of these and synonymous terms. The existence of a *mens rea* is the rule of, rather than the exception to, the principles of Anglo-American criminal jurisprudence. . . .

The obvious purpose of the statute is to protect existing Government, not from change by peaceable, lawful and constitutional means, but from change by violence, revolution and terrorism. That it is within the *power* of the Congress to protect the Government of the United States from armed rebellion is a proposition which requires little discussion. Whatever theoretical merit there may be to the argument that there is a "right" to rebellion against dictatorial governments is without force where the existing structure of the government provides for peaceful and orderly change. We reject any principle of governmental helplessness in the face of preparation for revolution, which principle, carried to its logical conclusion, must lead to anarchy. No one could conceive that it is not within the power of Congress to prohibit acts intended to overthrow the Government by force and violence. The question with which we are concerned here is not whether Congress has such *power*, but whether the *means* which it has employed conflict with the First and Fifth Amendments to the Constitution.

One of the bases for the contention that the means which Congress has employed are invalid takes the form of an attack on the face of the statute on the grounds that by its terms it prohibits academic discussion of the merits of Marxism-Leninism, that it stifles ideas and is contrary to all concepts of a free speech and a free press. . . .

The very language of the Smith Act negates the interpretation which petitioners would have us impose on that Act. It is directed at advocacy, not discussion. Thus, the trial judge properly charged the jury that they could not convict if they found that petitioners did "no more than pursue peaceful studies and discussions or teaching and advocacy in the realm of ideas." He further charged that it was not unlawful "to conduct in an American college and university a course explaining the philosophical theories set forth in the books which have been placed in evidence." Such a charge is in strict accord with the statutory language, and illustrates the meaning to be placed on those words. Congress did not intend to eradicate the free discussion of political theories, to destroy the traditional rights of Americans to discuss and evaluate ideas without fear of governmental sanction. Rather Congress was concerned with the very kind of activity in which the evidence showed these petitioners engaged.

. . . The basis of the First Amendment is the hypothesis that speech can rebut speech, propaganda will answer propaganda, free debate of ideas will result in the wisest governmental policies. It is for this reason that this Court has recognized the inherent value of free discourse. An analysis of the leading cases in this Court which have involved direct limitations on speech, however, will demonstrate that both the majority of the Court and the dissenters in particular cases have recognized that this is not an unlimited, unqualified right, but that the societal value of speech must, on occasion, be subordinated to other values and considerations. . . .

The rule we deduce from these cases is that where an offense is specified by a statute in nonspeech or nonpress terms, a conviction relying upon speech or press as evidence of violation may be sustained only when the speech or publication created a "clear and present danger" of attempting or accomplishing the prohibited crime, e.g., interference with enlistment. . . .

. . . Neither Justice Holmes nor Justice Brandeis ever envisioned that a shorthand phrase should be crystallized into a rigid rule to be applied inflexibly without regard to the circumstances of each case. Speech is not an absolute, above and beyond control by the legislature when its judgment, subject to review here, is that certain kinds of speech are so undesirable as to warrant criminal sanction. Nothing is more certain in modern society than the principle that there are no absolutes, that a name, a phrase, a standard has meaning only when associated with the considerations which gave birth to the nomenclature. . . . To those who would paralyze our Government in the face of impending threat by encasing it in a semantic straitjacket we must reply that all concepts are relative.

. . . In this case we are squarely presented with the application of the "clear and present danger" test, and must decide what that phrase imports. We first note that many of the cases in which this Court has reversed convictions by use of this or similar tests have been based on the fact that the interest which the State was attempting to protect was itself too insubstantial to warrant restriction of speech. . . . Overthrow of the Government by force and violence is certainly a substantial enough interest for the Government to limit speech. Indeed, this is the ultimate value of any society, for if a society cannot protect its very structure from armed internal attack, it must follow that no subordinate value can be protected. If, then, this interest may be protected, the literal problem which is presented is what has been meant by the use of the phrase "clear and present danger" of the utterances bringing about the evil within the power of Congress to punish.

. . . Obviously, the words cannot mean that before the Government may act, it must wait until the *putsch* is about to be executed, the plans have been laid and the signal is awaited. If Government is aware that a group aiming at its overthrow is attempting to indoctrinate its members and to commit them to a course whereby they will strike when the leaders feel the circumstances permit, action by the Government is required. The argument that there is no need for Government to concern itself, for Government is strong, it possesses ample powers to put down a rebellion, it may defeat the revolution with ease needs no answer. For that is not the question. Certainly an attempt to overthrow the Government by force, even though doomed from the outset because of inadequate numbers or power of the revolutionists, is a sufficient evil for Congress to prevent. The damage which such attempts create both physically and politically to a nation makes it impossible to measure the validity in terms of the probability of success, or the immediacy of a successful attempt. In the instant case the trial judge charged the jury that they could not convict unless they found that petitioners intended to overthrow the Government "as speedily as circumstances would permit." This does not mean, and could not properly mean, that they would not strike until there was certainty of success. What was meant was that the revolutionists would strike when they thought the time was ripe. We must therefore reject the contention that success or probability of success is the criterion.

. . . Chief Judge Learned Hand, writing for the majority below, interpreted the phrase as follows: "In each case [courts] must ask whether the gravity of the 'evil,' discounted by its improbability, justifies such invasion of free speech as is necessary to avoid the danger." . . . We adopt this statement of the rule. As articulated by

Chief Judge Hand, it is an succinct and inclusive as any other we might devise at this time. It takes into consideration those factors which we deem relevant, and relates their significances. More we cannot expect from words.

. . . Likewise, we are in accord with the court below, which affirmed the trial court's finding that the requisite danger existed. The mere fact that from the period 1945 to 1948 petitioners' activities did not result in an attempt to overthrow the Government by force and violence is of course no answer to the fact that there was a group that was ready to make the attempt. The formation by petitioners of such a highly organized conspiracy, with rigidly disciplined members subject to call when the leaders, these petitioners, felt that the time had come for action, coupled with the inflammable nature of world conditions, similar uprisings in other countries, and the touch-and-go nature of our relations with countries with whom petitioners were in the very least ideologically attuned, convince us that their convictions were justified on this score. And this analysis disposes of the contention that a conspiracy to advocate, as distinguished from the advocacy itself, cannot be constitutionally restrained, because it comprises only the preparation. It is the existence of the conspiracy which creates the danger. . . . If the ingredients of the reaction are present, we cannot bind the Government to wait until the catalyst is added.

. . . Although we have concluded that the finding that there was a sufficient danger to warrant the application of the statute was justified on the merits, there remains the problem of whether the trial judge's treatment of the issue was correct. He charged the jury, in relevant part, as follows: . . .

If you are satisfied that the evidence establishes beyond a reasonable doubt that the defendants, or any of them, are guilty of a violation of the statute as I have interpreted it to you, I find as a matter of law that there is sufficient danger of a substantive evil that the Congress has a right to prevent to justify the application of the statute under the First Amendment of the Constitution.

This is matter of law about which you have no concern. It is a finding on a matter of law which I deem essential to support my ruling that the case should be submitted to you to pass upon the guilt or innocence of the defendants. . . .

It is thus clear that he reserved the question of the existence of the danger for his own determination, and the question becomes whether the issue is of such a nature that it should have been submitted to the jury.

. . . The argument that the action of the trial court is erroneous, in declaring as a matter of law that such violation shows sufficient danger to justify the punishment despite the First Amendment, rests on the theory that a jury must decide a question of the application of the First Amendment. We do not agree. . . .

The question in this case is whether the statute which the legislature has enacted may be constitutionally applied. In other words, the Court must examine judicially the application of the statute to the particular situation, to ascertain if the Constitution prohibits the conviction. We hold that the statute may be applied where there is a "clear and present danger" of the substantive evil which the legislature had the right to prevent. Bearing, as it does, the marks of a "question of law," the issue is properly one for the judge to decide.

There remains to be discussed the question of vagueness—whether the statute as we have interpreted it is too vague, not sufficiently advising those who would speak of the limitations upon their activity. It is urged that such vagueness contravenes the First and Fifth Amendments. . . .

We agree that the standard as defined is not a neat, mathematical formulary. Like all verbalizations it is subject to criticism on the score of indefiniteness. But petitioners themselves contend that the verbalization, "clear and present danger," is the proper standard. We see no difference from the standpoint of vagueness, whether the standard of "clear and present danger" is one contained in *haec verba* within the statute, or whether it is the judicial measure of constitutional applicability. We have shown the indeterminate standard the phrase necessarily connotes. We do not think we have rendered that standard any more indefinite by our attempt to sum up the factors which are included within its scope. We think it well serves to indicate to those who would advocate constitutionally prohibited conduct that there is a line beyond which they may not go—a line, which they, in full knowledge of what they intend and the circumstances in which their activity takes place, will well appreciate and understand. . . .

We hold that §§ 2(a) (1), 2(a) (3) and 3 of the Smith Act, do not inherently, or as construed or applied in the instant case, violate the First Amendment and other provisions of the Bill of Rights, or the First and Fifth Amendments because of indefiniteness. Petitioners intended to overthrow the Government of the United States as speedily as the circumstances would permit. Their conspiracy to organize the Communist Party and to teach and advocate the overthrow of the Government of the United States by force and violence created a "clear and present danger" of an attempt to overthrow the Government by force and violence. They were properly and constitutionally convicted for violation of the Smith Act. The judgments of conviction are affirmed.

Mr. Justice Frankfurter, concurring in affirmance of the judgment:

. . . Few questions of comparable import have come before this Court in recent years. The appellants maintain that they have a right to advocate a political theory, so long, at least, as their advocacy does not create an immediate danger of obvious magnitude to the very existence of our present scheme of society. On the other hand, the Government asserts the right to safeguard the security of the Nation by such a measure as the Smith Act. Our judgment is thus solicited on a conflict of interests of the utmost concern to the well-being of the country. This conflict of interests cannot be resolved by a dogmatic preference for one or the other, nor by a sonorous formula which is in fact only a euphemistic disguise for an unresolved conflict. If adjudication is to be a rational process we cannot escape a candid examination of the conflicting claims with full recognition that both are supported by weighty title-deeds.

I

. . . Our whole history proves even more decisively than the course of decisions in this Court that the United States has the powers inseparable from a sovereign nation. "America has chosen to be, in many respects, and to many purposes, a nation; and for all these purposes, her government is complete; to all these objects, it is competent." Chief Justice Marshall in *Cohens* v. *Virginia*, 6 Wheat. 264. The right of a government to maintain its existence—self-preservation—is the most pervasive aspect of sovereignty. "Security against foreign danger," wrote Madison, "is one of the primitive objects of civil society." *The Federalist,* No. 41. The constitutional power to act upon this basic principle has been recognized by this Court at different periods and under diverse circumstances. . . . The most tragic experience in our history is a poignant reminder that the Nation's continued existence may be threatened from within. To protect itself from such threats, the Federal Government "is invested with all those inherent and implied powers which, at the time of adopting the Constitution, were generally considered to belong to every government as such, and as being essential to the exercise of its functions." Mr. Justice Bradley, concurring in *Legal Tender Cases,* 12 Wall. 457. . . .

But even the all-embracing power and duty of self-preservation is not absolute. Like the war power, which is indeed an aspect of the power of self-preservation, it is subject to applicable constitutional limitations. . . . Our Constitution has no provision lifting restrictions upon governmental authority during periods of emergency, although the scope of a restriction may depend on the circumstances in which it is invoked.

The First Amendment is such a restriction. It exacts obedience even during periods of war; it is applicable when war clouds are not figments of the imagination no less than when they are. The First Amendment categorically demands that "Congress shall make no law respecting an establishment of religion, or prohibiting the free exercise thereof; or abridging the freedom of speech, or of the press; or the right of the people peaceably to assemble, and to petition the Government for a redress of grievances." The right of a man to think what he pleases, to write what he thinks, and to have his thoughts made available for others to hear or read has an engaging ring of universality. The Smith Act and this conviction under it no doubt restrict the exercise of free speech and assembly. Does that, without more, dispose of the matter?

Just as there are those who regard as invulnerable every measure for which the claim of national survival is invoked, there are those who find in the Constitution a wholly unfettered right of expression. Such literalness treats the words of the Constitution as though they were found on a piece of out-worn parchment instead of being words that have called into being a nation with a past to be preserved for the future. The soil in which the Bill of Rights grew was not a soil of arid pedantry. The historic antecedents of the First Amendment preclude the notion that its purpose was to give unqualified immunity to every expression that touched on matters within the range of political interest. . . .

The language of the First Amendment is to be read not as barren words found in a dictionary but as symbols of historic experience illumined by the presuppositions of those who employed them. Not what words did Madison and Hamilton use, but what was it in their minds which they conveyed? Free speech is subject to prohibition of those abuses of expression which a civilized society may forbid. As in the case of every other provision of the Constitution that is not crystallized by the nature of its technical concepts, the fact that the First Amendment is not self-defining and self-enforcing neither impairs its usefulness nor compels its paralysis as a living instrument.

"The law is perfectly well settled," this Court said over fifty years ago, "that the first 10 amendments to the constitution, commonly known as the 'Bill of Rights,' were not intended to lay down any novel principles of government, but simply to embody certain guaranties and immunities which we had inherited from our English ancestors, and which had, from time immemorial, been subject to certain well-recognized exceptions, arising from the necessities of the case. In incorporating these principles into the fundamental law, there was no intention of disregarding the exceptions, which continued to be recognized as if they had been formally expressed." *Robertson* v. *Baldwin,* 165 US 275. That this represents the authentic view of the Bill of Rights and the spirit in which it must be construed has been recognized again and again in cases that have come here within the last fifty years. . . . Absolute rules would inevitably lead to absolute exceptions, and such exceptions would eventually corrode the rules. The demands of free speech in a democratic society as well as the interest in national security are better served by candid and informed weighing of the competing interests, within the confines of the judicial process, than by announcing dogmas too inflexible for the non-Euclidian problems to be solved.

But how are competing interests to be assessed? Since they are not subject to quantitative ascertainment, the issue necessarily resolves itself into asking, who is to make the adjustment?—who is to balance the relevant factors and ascertain which interest is in the circumstances to prevail? Full responsibility for the choice cannot be given to the courts. Courts are not representative bodies. They are not designed to be a good reflex of a democratic society. Their judgment is best informed, and therefore most dependable, within narrow limits. Their essential quality is detachment, founded on independence. History teaches that the independence of the judiciary is jeopardized when courts become embroiled in the passions of the day and assume primary responsibility in choosing between competing political, economic and social pressures.

Primary responsibility for adjusting the interests which compete in the situation before us of necessity belongs to the Congress. The nature of the power to be exercised by this Court has been delineated in decisions not charged with the emotional appeal of situations such as that now before us. We are to set aside the judgment of those whose duty it is to legislate only if there is no reasonable basis for it. . . . We must scrupulously observe the narrow limits of judicial authority even though self-restraint is alone set over us. Above all we must remember that this Court's power of judicial review is not "an exercise of the powers of a super-Legislature." Mr. Justice Brandeis and Mr. Justice Holmes, dissenting in *Jay Burns Baking Co.* v. *Bryan,* 264 US 504. . . .

In reviewing statutes which restrict freedoms protected by the First Amendment, we have emphasized the close relation which those freedoms bear to maintenance of a free society. . . . Some members of the Court—and at times a majority—have done more. They have suggested that our function in reviewing statutes restricting freedom of expression differs sharply from our normal duty in sitting in judgment on legislation. It has been said that such statutes "must be justified by clear public interest, threatened not doubtedly or remotely, but by clear and present danger. The rational connection between the remedy provided and the evil to be curbed, which in other contexts might support legislation against attack on due process grounds, will not suffice." *Thomas* v. *Collins,* 323 US 516. It has been suggested, with the casualness of a footnote, that such legislation is not presumptively valid, see *United States* v. *Carolene Products Co.,* 304 US 144, and it has been weightily reiterated that freedom of speech has a "preferred position" among constitutional safeguards. *Kovacs* v. *Cooper,* 336 US 77.

The precise meaning intended to be conveyed by these phrases need not now be pursued. It is enough to note that they have recurred in the Court's opinions, and their cumulative force has, not without justification, engendered belief that there is a constitutional principle, expressed by those attractive but imprecise words, prohibiting restriction upon utterance unless it creates a situation of "imminent" peril against which legislation may guard. It is on this body of the Court's pronouncements that the defendants' argument here is based. . . .

II

We have recognized and resolved conflicts between speech and competing interests in six different types of cases. . . .

6. Statutes prohibiting speech because of its tendency to lead to crime present a conflict of interests which bears directly on the problem now before us. The first case in which we considered this conflict was *Fox* v. *Washington,* 236 US 273. The statute there challenged had been interpreted to prohibit publication of matter "encouraging an actual breach of law." We held that the Fourteenth Amendment did not prohibit application of the statute to an article which we concluded incited a breach of laws against indecent exposure. We said that the statute "lays hold of encouragements that, apart from statute, if directed to a particular person's conduct, generally would make him who uttered them guilty of a misdemeanor if not an accomplice or a principal in the crime encouraged, and deals with the publication of them to a wider and less selected audience." To be sure, the *Fox Case* preceded the explicit absorption of the substance of the First Amendment in the Fourteenth. But subsequent decisions extended the *Fox* principle to free-speech situations. They are so important to the problem before us that we must consider them in detail.

(a) The first important application of the principle was made in six cases arising under the Espionage Act of 1917. That Act prohibits conspiracies and attempts to "obstruct the recruiting or enlistment service." In each of the first three cases Mr. Justice Holmes wrote for a unanimous Court, affirming the convictions. The evidence in *Schenck* v. *United States,* 249 US 47, showed that the defendant had conspired to circulate among men called for the draft 15,000 copies of a circular which asserted a "right" to oppose the draft. The defendant in *Frohwerk* v. *United States,* 249 US 204, was shown to have conspired to publish in a newspaper twelve articles describing the sufferings of American troops and the futility of our war aims. The record was inadequate, and we said that it was therefore "impossible to say that it might not have been found that the circulation of the paper was in quarters where a little breath would be enough to kindle a flame and that the fact was known and relied upon by those who sent the paper out." In *Debs* v. *United States,* 249 US 211, the indictment charged that the defendant had delivered a public speech expounding socialism and praising Socialists who had been convicted of abetting violation of the draft laws.

The ground of decision in each case was the same. The First Amendment "cannot have been, and obviously was not, intended to give immunity for every possible use of language. . . ." *Frohwerk* v. *United States.* . . . "The question in every case is whether the words used in such circumstances and are of such a nature as to create a clear and present danger that they will bring about the substantive evils that Congress has a right to prevent. It is a question of proximity and degree." *Schenck* v. *United States.* . . . When "the words used had as their natural tendency and reasonably probable effect to obstruct the recruiting service," and "the defendant had the specific intent to do so in his mind," conviction in wartime is not prohibited by the Constitution. *Debs* v. *United States.*

In the three succeeding cases Holmes and Brandeis, JJ., dissented from judgments of the Court affirming convictions. The indictment in *Abrams* v. *United States,* 250 US 616, was laid under an amendment to the Espionage Act which prohibited conspiracies to advocate curtailment of production of material necessary to prosecution of the war, with the intent thereby to hinder the United States in the prosecution of the war. It appeared that the defendants were anarchists who had printed circulars and distributed them in New York City. The leaflets repeated standard Marxist slogans, condemned

American intervention in Russia, and called for a general strike in protest. In *Schaefer* v. *United States*, 251 US 466, the editors of a German language newspaper in Philadelphia were charged with obstructing the recruiting service and with wilfully publishing false reports with the intent to promote the success of the enemies of the United States. The evidence showed publication of articles which accused American troops of weakness and mendacity and in one instance misquoted or mistranslated two words of a Senator's speech. The indictment in *Pierce* v. *United States*, 252 US 239, charged that the defendants had attempted to cause insubordination in the armed forces and had conveyed false reports with intent to interfere with military operations. Conviction was based on circulation of a pamphlet which belittled Allied war aims and criticized conscription in strong terms.

In each case both the majority and the dissenting opinions relied on *Schenck* v. *United States*. The Court divided on its view of the evidence. The majority held that the jury could infer the required intent and the probable effect of the articles from their content. Holmes and Brandeis, JJ., thought that only "expressions of opinion and exhortations," were involved, that they were "puny anonymities," "impotent to produce the evil against which the statute aimed," and that from them the specific intent required by the statute could not reasonably be inferred. The Court agreed that an incitement to disobey the draft statute could constitutionally be punished. It disagreed over the proof required to show such an incitement.

(b) In the eyes of a majority of the Court, *Gitlow* v. *New York*, 268 US 652, presented a very different problem. There the defendant had been convicted under a New York statute nearly identical to the Smith Act now before us. The evidence showed that the defendant was an official of the Left Wing Section of the Socialist Party, and that he was responsible for publication of a Left Wing Manifesto. This document repudiated "moderate Socialism," and urged the necessity of a militant "revolutionary Socialism," based on class struggle and revolutionary mass action. No evidence of the effect of the Manifesto was introduced; but the jury was instructed that they could not convict unless they found that the document advocated employing unlawful acts for the purpose of overthrowing organized government.

The conviction was affirmed. The question, the Court held, was entirely different from that involved in *Schenck* v. *United States*, where the statute prohibited acts without reference to language. Here, where "the legislative body has determined generally, in the constitutional exercise of its discretion, that utterances of a certain kind involve such danger of substantive evil that they may be punished, the question whether any specific utterance coming within the prohibited class is likely, in and of itself, to bring about the substantive evil, is not open to consideration." It is sufficient that the defendant's conduct falls within the statute, and that the statute is a reasonable exercise of legislative judgment.

This principle was also applied in *Whitney* v. *California*, 274 US 357, to sustain a conviction under a State criminal syndicalism statute. That statute made it a felony to assist in organizing a group assembled to advocate the commission of crime, sabotage, or unlawful acts of violence as a means of effecting political or industrial change. The defendant was found to have assisted in organizing the Communist Labor Party of California, an organization found to have the specified character. It was held that the legislature was not unreasonable in believing organization of such a party "involves such danger to the public peace and the security of the State, that these acts should be penalized in the exercise of its police power."

In neither of these cases did Mr. Justice Holmes and Mr. Justice Brandeis accept the reasoning of the Court. " 'The question,' " they said, quoting from *Schenck* v. *United States,* " 'in every case is whether the words used are used in such circumstances and are of such a nature as to create a clear and present danger that they will bring about the substantive evils that [the State] has a right to prevent.' " Since the manifesto circulated by Gitlow "had no chance of starting a present conflagration," they dissented from the affirmance of his conviction. In *Whitney* v. *California,* they concurred in the result reached by the Court, but only because the record contained some evidence that organization of the Communist Labor Party might further a conspiracy to commit immediate serious crimes, and the credibility of the evidence was not put in issue by the defendant.

(c) Subsequent decisions have added little to the principles established in these two groups of cases. In the only case arising under the Espionage Act decided by this Court during the last war, the substantiality of the evidence was the crucial issue. The defendant in *Hartzel* v. *United States,* 322 US 680, was an educated man and a citizen, not actively affiliated with any political group. In 1942 he wrote three articles condemning our wartime allies and urging that the war be converted into a racial conflict. He mailed the tracts to 600 people, including high-ranking military officers. According to his testimony his intention was to "create sentiment against war amongst the white races." The majority of this Court held that a jury could not reasonably infer from these facts that the defendant had acted with a specific intent to cause insubordination or disloyalty in the armed forces.

Of greater importance is the fact that the issue of law which divided the Court in the *Gitlow* and *Whitney Cases* has not again been clearly raised, although in four additional instances we have reviewed convictions under comparable statutes. *Fiske* v. *Kansas,* 274 US 380, involved a criminal syndicalism statute similar to that before us in *Whitney* v. *California.* We reversed a conviction based on evidence that the defendant exhibited an innocuous preamble to the constitution of the Industrial Workers of the World in soliciting members for that organization. In *Herndon* v. *Lowry,* 301 US 242, the defendant had solicited members for the Communist Party, but there was no proof that he had urged or even approved those of the Party's aims which were unlawful. We reversed a conviction obtained under a statute prohibiting an attempt to incite to insurrection by violence, on the ground that the Fourteenth Amendment prohibited conviction where on the evidence a jury could not reasonably infer that the defendant had violated the statute the State sought to apply.

The other two decisions go no further than to hold that the statute as construed by the State courts exceeded the bounds of a legislative judgment founded in reason. The statute presented in *De Jonge* v. *Oregon,* 299 US 353, had been construed to apply to anyone who merely assisted in the conduct of a meeting held under the auspices of the Communist Party. In *Taylor* v. *Mississippi,* 319 US 583, the statute prohibited dissemination of printed matter "designed and calculated to encourage violence, sabotage, or disloyalty to the government of the United States, or the state of Mississippi." We reversed a conviction for what we concluded was mere criticism and prophecy, without indicating whether we thought the statute could in any circumstances validly be applied. What the defendants communicated, we said, "is not claimed or shown to have been done with an evil or sinister purpose, to have advocated or incited subversive action against the nation or state, or to have threatened any clear and present danger to our institutions or our government."

I must leave to others the ungrateful task of trying to reconcile all these decisions. In some instances we have too readily permitted juries to infer deception from error, or intention from argumentative or critical statements. . . . In other instances we weighted the interest in free speech so heavily that we permitted essential conflicting values to be destroyed. . . . Viewed as a whole, however, the decisions express an attitude toward the judicial function and a standard of values which for me are decisive of the case before us.

First.—Free-speech cases are not an exception to the principle that we are not legislators, that direct policy-making is not our province. How best to reconcile competing interests is the business of legislatures, and the balance they strike is a judgment not to be displaced by ours, but to be respected unless outside the pale of fair judgment.

On occasion we have strained to interpret legislation in order to limit its effect on interests protected by the First Amendment. . . . In some instances we have denied to States the deference to which I think they are entitled. . . . Once in this recent course of decisions the Court refused to permit a jury to draw inferences which seemed to me to be obviously reasonable. . . .

But in no case has a majority of this Court held that a legislative judgment, even as to freedom of utterance, may be overturned merely because the Court would have made a different choice between the competing interests had the initial legislative judgment been for it to make. In the cases in which the opinions go farthest towards indicating a total rejection of respect for legislative determinations, the interests between which choice was actually made were such that decision might well have been expressed in the familiar terms of want of reason in the legislative judgment. . . .

In other cases, moreover, we have given clear indication that even when free speech is involved we attach great significance to the determination of the legislature. . . .

In *Gitlow* v. *New York*, we put our respect for the legislative judgment in terms which, if they were accepted here, would make decision easy. For that case held that when the legislature has determined that advocacy of forceful overthrow should be forbidden, a conviction may be sustained without a finding that in the particular case the advocacy had a close relation to a serious attempt at overthrow. We held that it was enough that the statute be a reasonable exercise of the legislative judgment, and that the defendant's conduct fall within the statute.

One of the judges below rested his affirmance on the *Gitlow* decision, and the defendants do not attempt to distinguish the case. They place their argument squarely on the ground that the case has been overruled by subsequent decisions. It has not been explicitly overruled. But it would be disingenuous to deny that the dissent in *Gitlow* has been treated with the respect usually accorded to a decision.

The result of the *Gitlow* decision was to send a left-wing Socialist to jail for publishing a Manifesto expressing Marxist exhortations. It requires excessive tolerance of the legislative judgment to suppose that the *Gitlow* publication in the circumstances could justify serious concern.

In contrast, there is ample justification for a legislative judgment that the conspiracy now before us is a substantial threat to national order and security. If the Smith Act is justified at all, it is justified precisely because it may serve to prohibit the type of conspiracy for which these defendants were convicted. The court below properly held that as a matter of separability the Smith Act may be limited to those situations to which it can constitutionally be applied. . . . Our decision today certainly does not mean that the Smith Act can constitutionally be applied to facts like those in *Gitlow* v. *New York*. While reliance may properly be placed on the attitude of judicial self-restraint which the *Gitlow* decision reflects, it is not necessary to depend on the facts or the full extent of the theory of the case in order to find that the judgment of Congress, as applied to the facts of the case now before us, is not in conflict with the First Amendment.

Second.—A survey of the relevant decisions indicates that the results which we have reached are on the whole those that would ensue from careful weighing of conflicting interests. The complex issues presented by regulation of speech in public places, by picketing, and by legislation prohibiting advocacy of crime have been resolved by scrutiny of many factors besides the imminence and gravity of the evil threatened. The matter has been well summarized by a reflective student of the Court's work. "The truth is that the clear-and-present-danger test is an over-simplified judgment unless it takes account also of a number of other factors: the relative seriousness of the danger in comparison with the value of the occasion for speech or political activity; the availability of more moderate controls than those which the state has imposed; and perhaps the specific intent with which the speech or activity is launched. No matter how rapidly we utter the phrase 'clear and present danger,' or how closely we hyphenate the words, they are not a substitute for the weighing of values. They tend to convey a delusion of certitude when what is most certain is the complexity of the strands in the web of freedoms which the judge must disentangle." Freund, *On Understanding the Supreme Court*, 27–28.

It is a familiar experience in the law that new situations do not fit neatly into legal conceptions that arose under different circumstances to satisfy different needs. So it was when the injunction was tortured into an instrument of expression against labor in industrial conflicts. So it is with the attempt to use the direction of thought lying behind the criterion of "clear and present danger" wholly out of the context in which it originated, and to make of it an absolute dogma and definitive measuring rod for the power of Congress to deal with assaults against security through devices other than overt physical attempts.

Bearing in mind that Mr. Justice Holmes regarded questions under the First Amendment as questions of "proximity and degree," *Schenck* v. *United States,* it would be a distortion, indeed a mockery, of his reasoning to compare the "puny anonymities," to which he was addressing himself in the *Abrams Case* in 1919 or the publication that was "futile and too remote from possible consequences" in the *Gitlow Case* in 1925 with the setting of events in this case in 1950.

"It does an ill-service to the author of the most quoted judicial phrases regarding freedom of speech, to make him the victim of a tendency which he fought all his life, whereby phrases are made to do service for critical analysis by being turned into dogma. 'It is one of the misfortunes of the law that ideas become encysted in phrases and thereafter for a long time cease to provoke further analysis.' " Holmes, J., dissenting, in *Hyde* v. *United States,* 225 US 347. The phrase "clear and present danger," in its origin, "served to indicate the importance of freedom of speech to a free society but also to emphasize that its exercise must be compatible with the preservation of other freedoms essential to a democracy and guaranteed by our Constitution." *Pennekamp* v. *Florida* (concurring). It were far better that the phrase be abandoned than that it be sounded once more to hide from the believers in an absolute right of free speech the plain fact that the interest in speech, profoundly important as it is, is no more conclusive in judicial review than other attributes of democracy or than a determination of the people's representatives that a measure is necessary to assure the safety of government itself.

Third.—Not every type of speech occupies the same position on the scale of values. There is no substantial public interest in permitting certain kinds of utterances: "the lewd and obscene, the profane, the libelous, and the insulting or 'fighting' words—those which by their very utterance inflict injury or tend to incite an immediate breach of the peace." *Chaplinsky* v. *New Hampshire,* 315 US 568. We have frequently indicated that the interest in protecting speech depends on the circumstances of the occasion.

. . . It is pertinent to the decision before us to consider where on the scale of values we have in the past placed the type of speech now claiming constitutional immunity.

The defendants have been convicted of conspiring to organize a party of persons who advocate the overthrow of the Government by force and violence. The jury has found that the object of the conspiracy is advocacy as "a rule or principle of action," "by language reasonably and ordinarily calculated to incite persons to such action," and with the intent to cause the overthrow "as speedily as circumstances would permit."

On any scale of values which we have hitherto recognized, speech of this sort ranks low.

Throughout our decisions there has recurred a distinction between the statement of an idea which may prompt its hearers to take unlawful action, and advocacy that such action be taken. The distinction has its root in the conception of the common law that a person who procures another to do an act is responsible for that act as though he had done it himself. This principle was extended in *Fox* v. *Washington, supra,* to words directed to the public generally which would constitute an incitement were they directed to an individual. It was adopted in *Schenck* v. *United States, supra,* into a rule of evidence designed to restrict application of the Espionage Act. It was relied on by the Court in *Gitlow* v. *New York, supra.* The distinction has been repeated in many of the decisions in which we have upheld the claims of speech. We frequently have distinguished protected forms of expression from statements which "incite to violence and crime and threaten the overthrow of organized government by unlawful means." . . .

It is true that there is no divining rod by which we may locate "advocacy." Exposition of ideas readily merges into advocacy. The same Justice who gave currency to application of the incitement doctrine in this field dissented four times from what he thought was its misapplication. As he said in the *Gitlow* dissent, "Every idea is an incitement." Even though advocacy of overthrow deserves little protection, we should hesitate to prohibit it if we thereby inhibit the interchange of rational ideas so essential to representative government and free society.

But there is underlying validity in the distinction between advocacy and the interchange of ideas, and we do not discard a useful tool because it may be misused. That such a distinction could be used unreasonably by those in power against hostile or unorthodox views does not negate the fact that it may be used reasonably against an organization wielding the power of the centrally controlled international Communist movement. The object of the conspiracy before us is clear enough that the chance of error in saying that the defendants conspired to advocate rather than to express ideas is slight. Mr. Justice Douglas quite properly points out that the conspiracy before us is not a conspiracy to overthrow the Government. But it would be equally wrong to treat it as a seminar in political theory. . . .

Civil liberties draw at best only limited strength from legal guaranties. Preoccupation by our people with the constitutionality, instead of with the wisdom of legislation or of executive action, is preoccupation with a false value. Even those who would most freely use the judicial brake on the democratic process by invalidating legislation that goes deeply against their grain, acknowledge, at least by paying lip service, that constitutionality does not exact a sense of proportion or the sanity of humor or an absence of fear. Focusing attention on constitutionality tends to make constitutionality synonymous with wisdom. When legislation touches freedom of thought and freedom of speech, such a tendency is a formidable enemy of the free spirit. Much that should be rejected as illiberal, because repressive and envenoming, may well be not unconstitutional. The ultimate reliance for the deepest needs of civilization must be found outside their vindication in courts of law; apart from all else, judges, howsoever they may conscientiously seek to discipline themselves against it, unconsciously are too apt to be moved by the deep undercurrents of public feeling. A persistent, positive translation of the liberating faith into the feelings and thoughts and actions of men and women is the real protection against attempts to strait-jacket the human mind. Such temptations will have their way, if fear and hatred are not exorcised. The mark of a truly civilized man is confidence in the strength and security derived from the inquiring mind. We may be grateful for such honest comforts as it supports, but we must be unafraid of its uncertitudes. Without open minds there can be no open society. And if society be not open the spirit of man is mutilated and becomes enslaved. . . .

BRANDENBURG *v.* OHIO
395 US 444 (1969)

[The Supreme Court unanimously, and in a per curiam opinion, held that the Ohio Criminal Syndicalism Act was unconstitutional for punishing mere advocacy and for failing to distinguish advocacy from incitement to imminent lawless action. Justices Black and Douglas wrote concurring opinions.]

Per Curiam:

The appellant, a leader of a Ku Klux Klan group, was convicted under the Ohio Criminal Syndicalism Statute of "advocat[ing] . . . the duty, necessity, or propriety of crime, sabotage, violence, or unlawful methods of terrorism as a means of accomplishing industrial or political reform" and of "voluntarily assembl[ing] with any society, group or assemblage of persons formed to teach or advocate the doctrines of criminal syndicalism." Ohio Rev. Code ¶ 2923.13. He was fined $1,000 and sentenced to one to 10 years' imprisonment. The appellant challenged the constitutionality of the Criminal Syndicalism Statute under the First and Fourteenth Amendments to the United States Constitution, but the intermediate appellate court of Ohio affirmed his conviction without opinion. The Supreme Court of Ohio dismissed his appeal, *sua sponte,* "for the reason that no substantial constitutional question exists herein." It did not file an opinion or explain its conclusions. Appeal was taken to this Court, and we noted probable jurisdiction. We reverse.

The record shows that a man, identified at trial as the appellant, telephoned an announcer-reporter on the staff of a Cincinnati television station and invited him to come to a Ku Klux Klan "rally" to be held at a farm in Hamilton County. With the cooperation of the organizers, the reporter and a cameraman attended the meeting and filmed the events. Portions of the films were later broadcast on the local station and on a national network.

The prosecution's case rested on the films and on testimony identifying the appellant as the person who communicated with the reporter and who spoke at the rally. The State also introduced into evidence several articles appearing in the film, incliuding a pistol, a rifle, a shotgun, ammunition, a Bible, and a red hood worn by the speaker in the films.

One film showed 12 hooded figures, some of whom carried firearms. They were gathered around a large wooden cross, which they burned. No one was present other than the participants and the newsmen who made the film. Most of the words uttered during the scene were incomprehensible when the film was projected, but scattered phrases could be understood that were derogatory of Negroes and, in one instance, of Jews.* Another scene on the same film showed the appellant, in Klan regalia, making a speech. The speech, in full, was as follows:

This is an organizers' meeting. We have had quite a few members here today which are—we have hundreds, hundreds of members throughout the State of Ohio. I can quote from a newspaper clipping from the Columbus Ohio Dispatch, five weeks ago Sunday morning. The Klan has more members in the State of Ohio than does any other organization. We're not a revengent organization, but if our President, our Congress, our Supreme Court, continues to suppress the white, Caucasian race, it's possible that there might have to be some revengence taken.

We are marching on Congress July the Fourth, four hundred thousand strong. From there we are dividing into two groups, one group to march on St. Augustine, Florida, the other group to march into Mississippi. Thank you.

The second film showed six hooded figures one of whom, later identified as the appellant, repeated a speech very similar to that recorded on the first film. The reference to the possibility of "revengence" was ommitted, and one sentence was added: "Personally, I believe the nigger should be returned to Africa, the Jew returned to Israel." Though some of the figures in the films carried weapons, the speaker did not.

The Ohio Criminal Syndicalism Statute was enacted in 1919. From 1917 to 1920, identical or quite similar laws were adopted by 20 States and two territories. . . . In 1927, this Court sustained the constitutionality of California's Criminal Syndicalism Act, Cal. Penal Code §§ 11400–11402, the text of which is quite similar to that of the laws of Ohio. *Whitney* v. *California,* 274 US 357 (1927). The Court upheld the statute on the ground that, without more, "Advocating" violent means to effect political and economic change involves such danger to the security of the State that the State may outlaw it. *Cf. Fiske* v. *Kansas,* 274 US 380 (1927). But *Whitney* has been thoroughly discredited by later decisions. See *Dennis* v. *United States,* 341 US 494, at 507 (1951). These later decisions have fashioned the principle that the constitutional guarantees of free speech and free press do not permit a State to forbid or proscribe advocacy of the use of force or of law violation except where such advocacy is directed to inciting or producing imminent lawless action and is likely to incite or produce such action.† As we said in *Noto* v. *United States,* 367 US 290 (1961), "the mere abstract teaching . . . of the moral propriety or even moral necessity for a resort to force and violence, is not the same

* The significant phrases that could be understood were: "How far is the nigger going to— yeah"; "This is what we are going to do to the niggers"; "A dirty nigger"; "Send the Jews back to Israel"; "Let's give them back to the dark garden"; "Save America"; "Let's go back to constitutional betterment"; "Bury the niggers"; "We intend to do our part"; "Give us our state rights"; "Freedom for the whites"; "Nigger will have to fight for every inch he gets from now on."

† It was on the theory that the Smith Act, 54 Stat. 670, 18 U.S.C. § 2385, embodied such a principle and that it had been applied only in conformity with it that this Court sustained the Act's constitutionality. *Dennis* v. *United States,* 341 US (1951). That this was the basis for *Dennis* was emphasized in *Yates* v. *United States,* 354 US 298 (1957), in which the Court overturned convictions for advocacy of the forcible overthrow of the Government under the Smith Act, because the trial judge's instructions had allowed conviction for mere advocacy, unrelated to its tendency to produce forcible action.

as preparing a group for violent action and steeling it to such action." See also *Herndon* v. *Lowry,* 301 US 242 (1937); *Bond* v. *Floyd,* 385 US 116 (1966). A statute which fails to draw this distinction impermissibly intrudes upon the freedoms guaranteed by the First and Fourteenth Amendments. It sweeps within its condemnation speech which our Constitution has immunized from governmental control. . . .

Measured by this test, Ohio's Criminal Syndicalism Act cannot be sustained. The Act punishes persons who "advocate or teach the duty, necessity, or propriety" of violence "as a means of accomplishing industrial or political reform"; or who publish or circulate or display any book or paper containing such advocacy; or who "justify" the commission of violent acts "with intent to exemplify, spread or advocate the propriety of the doctrines of criminal syndicalism"; or who ". . . voluntarily assemble" with a group formed "to teach or advocate the doctrines of criminal syndicalism." Neither the indictment nor the trial judge's instructions to the jury in any way refined the statute's bald definition of the crime in terms of mere advocacy not distinguished from incitement to imminent lawless action.

Accordingly, we are here confronted with a statute which, by its own words and as applied, purports to punish mere advocacy and to forbid, on pain of criminal punishment, assembly with others merely to advocate the described type of action.* Such a statute falls within the condemnation of the First and Fourteenth Amendments. The contrary teaching of *Whitney* v. *California, supra,* cannot be supported, and that decision is therefore overruled.

Reversed.

Mr. Justice Black, concurring:

I agree with the views expressed by Mr. Justice Douglas in his concurring opinion in this case that the "clear and present danger" doctrine should have no place in the interpretation of the First Amendment. I join the Court's opinion, which, as I understand it, simply cites *Dennis* v. *United States,* 341 US 494, (1951), but does not indicate any agreement on the Court's part with the "clear and present danger" doctrine on which *Dennis* purported to rely.

Mr. Justice Douglas, concurring:

While I join the opinion of the Court, I desire to enter a *caveat.*

The "clear and present danger" test was adumbrated by Mr. Justice Holmes in a case arising during World War I—a war "declared" by the Congress not by the Chief Executive. The case was *Schenck* v. *United States,* 249 US 47, where the defendant was charged with attempts to cause insubordination in the military and obstruction of enlistment. The pamphlets that were distributed urged resistance to the draft, denounced conscription, and impugned the motives of those backing the war effort. The First Amendment was tendered as a defense. Mr. Justice Holmes in rejecting that defense said:

> The question in every case is whether the words used are used in such circumstances and are of such a nature as to create a clear and present danger that they will

---

* Statutes affecting the right of assembly, like those touching on freedom of speech, must observe the established distinctions between mere advocacy and incitement to imminent lawless action. . . .

bring about the substantive evils that Congress has a right to prevent. It is a question of proximity and degree.

Frohwerk v. *United States,* 249 US 204, also authored by Mr. Justice Holmes, involved prosecution and punishment for publication of articles very critical of the war effort in World War I. *Schenck* was referred to as a conviction for obstructing security "by words of persuasion." And the conviction in *Frohwerk* was sustained because "the circulation of the paper was in quarters where a little breath would be enough to kindle a flame."

Debs v. *United States,* 249 US 211, was the third of the trilogy of the 1918 Term. Debs was convicted of speaking in opposition to the war where his "opposition was so expressed that its natural and intended effect would be to obstruct recruiting."

> If that was intended and if, in all the circumstances, that would be its probable effect, it would not be protected by reason of its being part of a general program in expression of a general and conscientious belief. *Ibid.*

In the 1919 Term, the Court applied the *Schenck* doctrine to affirm the convictions of other dissidents in World War I. *Abrams* v. *United States,* 250 US 616, was one instance. Mr. Justice Holmes, with whom Mr. Justice Brandeis concurred, dissented. While adhering to *Schenck,* he did not think on the facts that a case for overriding the First Amendment had been made out:

> It is only the present danger of immediate evil or an intent to bring it about that warrants Congress in setting a limit to the expression of opinion where private rights are not concerned. Congress certainly cannot forbid all effort to change the mind of the country.

Another instance was *Schaefer* v. *United States,* 251 US 466, in which Mr. Justice Brandeis, joined by Mr. Justice Holmes, dissented. A third was *Pierce* v. *United States,* 252 US 239, in which Mr. Justice Brandeis, joined by Mr. Justice Holmes, dissented.

Those then were the *World War I* cases that put the gloss of "clear and present danger" on the First Amendment. Whether the war power—the greatest leveler of them all—is adequate to sustain that doctrine is debatable. The dissents in *Abrams, Schaefer,* and *Pierce* show how easily "clear and present danger" is manipulated to crush what Brandeis called "the fundamental right of free men to strive for better conditions through new legislation and new institutions" by argument and discourse (*Pierce* v. *United States, supra,* at 273) even in time of war. Though I doubt if the "clear and present danger" test is congenial to the First Amendment in time of a declared war, I am certain it is not reconcilable with the First Amendment in days of peace.

The Court quite properly overrules *Whitney* v. *California,* which involved advocacy for ideas which the majority of the Court deemed unsound and dangerous.

Mr. Justice Holmes, though never formally abandoning the "clear and present danger" test, moved closer to the First Amendment ideal when he said in dissent in *Gitlow* (*Gitlow* v. *People of State of New York,* 268 US 652):

> Every idea is an incitement. It offers itself for belief and if believed it is acted on unless some other belief outweighs it or some failure of energy stifles the movement at its birth. The only difference between the expression of an opinion and an incitement in the narrower sense is the speaker's enthusiasm for the result. Eloquence may set fire to reason. But whatever may be thought of the redundant discourse before us it had no chance of starting a present conflagration. If in the

long run the beliefs expressed in proletarian dictatorship are destined to be accepted by the dominant forces of the community, the only meaning of free speech is that they should be given their chance and have their way.

We have never been faithful to the philosophy of that dissent.

The Court in *Herndon* v. *Lowry,* 301 US 242, overturned a conviction for exercising First Amendment rights to incite insurrection because of lack of evidence of incitement. And see *Hartzel* v. *United States,* 322 US 680. In *Bridges* v. *California,* 314 US 252, we approved the "clear and present danger" test in an elaborate dictum that tightened it and confined it to a narrow category. But in *Dennis* v. *United States,* 341 US 494, we opened wide the door, distorting the "clear and present danger" test beyond recognition.

In that case the prosecution dubbed an agreement to teach the Marxist creed—a "conspiracy." The case was submitted to a jury on a charge that the jury could not convict unless they found the defendants "intended to overthrow the government 'as speedily as circumstances would permit.'" The Court sustained convictions under that charge, construing it to mean a determination of "whether the gravity of the 'evil, discounted by its improbability, justifies such invasion of free speech as is necessary to avoid the danger.'"

Out of the "clear and present danger" test came other offspring. Advocacy and teaching of forcible overthrow of government as an abstract principle is immune from prosecution. *Yates* v. *United States,* 354 US 298. But an "active" member, who has a guilty knowledge and intent of the aim to overthrow the Government by violence, *Noto* v. *United States,* 367 US 290, may be prosecuted. *Scales* v. *United States,* 367 US 203. And the power to investigate, backed by the powerful sanction of contempt, includes the power to determine which of the two categories fits the particular witness. *Barenblatt* v. *United States,* 360 US 109. And so the investigator roams at will through all of the beliefs of the witness, ransacking his conscience and his innermost thoughts.

Judge Learned Hand who wrote for the Court of Appeals in affirming the judgment in *Dennis,* coined the "not improbable" test, . . . which this Court adopted and which Judge Hand preferred over the "clear and present danger" test. Indeed, in his book, *The Bill of Rights,* p. 59 (1958), in referring to Holmes' creation of the "clear and present danger" test, he said, "I cannot help thinking that for once Homer nodded."

My own view is quite different. I see no place in the regime of the First Amendment for any "clear and present danger" test whether strict and tight as some would make it or free-wheeling as the Court in *Dennis* rephrased it.

When one reads the opinions closely and sees when and how the "clear and present danger" test has been applied, great misgivings are aroused. First, the threats were often loud but always puny and made serious only by judges so wedded to the *status quo* that critical analysis made them nervous. Second the test was so twisted and perverted in *Dennis* as to make the trial of those teachers of Marxism an all-out political trial which was part and parcel of the Cold War that has eroded substantial parts of the First Amendment.

Action is often a method of expression and within the protection of the First Amendment.

Suppose one tears up his own copy of the Constitution in eloquent protest to a decision of this Court. May he be indicted?

Suppose one rips his own Bible to shreds to celebrate his departure from one "faith" and his embrace of atheism. May he be indicted?

Last Term the Court held in *United States* v. *O'Brien,* 391 US 367, that a registrant under Selective Service who burned his draft card in protest to the war in Vietnam could be prosecuted. The First Amendment was tendered as a defense and rejected, the Court saying:

> The issuance of certificates indicating the registration and eligibility classification of individuals is a legitimate and substantial administrative aid in the functioning of this system. And legislation to insure the continuing availability of issued certificates serves a legitimate and substantial purpose in the system's administration.

But O'Brien was not prosecuted for not having his draft card available when asked for by a federal agent. He was indicted, tried, and convicted for burning the card. And this Court's affirmance of that conviction was not, with all respect, consistent with the First Amendment.

The act of praying often involves body posture and movement as well as utterances. It is nonetheless protected by the Free Exercise Clause. Picketing, as we have said on numerous occasions, is "free speech plus." . . . That means that it can be regulated when it comes to the "plus" or "action" side of the protest. It can be regulated as to the number of pickets and the place and hours . . . because traffic and other community problems would otherwise suffer.

But none of these considerations are implicated in the symbolic protest to the Vietnam war in the burning of a draft card.

One's beliefs have long been thought to be sanctuaries which government could not invade. *Barenblatt* is one example of the ease with which that sanctuary can be violated. The lines drawn by the Court between the criminal act of being an "active" Communist and the innocent act of being a nominal or inactive Communist mark the difference only between deep and abiding belief and casual or uncertain belief. But I think that all matters of belief are beyond the reach of subpoenas or the probings of investigators. That is why the invasions of privacy made by investigating committees was notoriously unconstitutional. That is the deep-seated fault in the infamous loyalty-security hearings which, since 1947 when Truman launched them, have processed 20,000,000 men and women. Those hearings were primarily concerned with one's thoughts, ideas, beliefs, and convictions. They were the most blatant violations of the First Amendment we have ever known.

The line between what is permissible and not subject to control and what may be made impermissible and subject to regulation is the line between ideas and overt acts.

The example usually given by those who would punish speech is the case of one who falsely shouts fire in a crowded theatre.

This is, however, a classic case where speech is brigaded with action. See *Speiser* v. *Randall*, 357 US 513, 536–537. They are indeed inseparable and a prosecution can be launched for the overt acts actually caused. Apart from rare instances of that kind, speech is, I think, immune from prosecution. Certainly there is no constitutional line between advocacy of abstract ideas as in *Yates* and advocacy of political action as in *Scales*. The quality of advocacy turns on the depth of the conviction; and government has no power to invade that sanctuary of belief and conscience.

VIII. Obscenity and Censorship of Literature and the Arts

1. Post Office Control

HANNEGAN v. ESQUIRE, INC.
327 US 146 (1946)

[The second-class-mail privilege is a valuable asset to a periodical; for, if this privilege were denied, a periodical would have to pay substantially higher postage rates, which would subject it to a serious competitive disadvantage. If the Postmaster General were given wide discretionary powers in awarding or denying the second-class-mail privilege, he could "make" or "break" a publication; the privilege could be used to impose political, economic, religious, literary, or aesthetic orthodoxy on the press.

[The Court has held that Congress need not open second-class-mail "to publications of all types." The furthest the Court ever went in sustaining a revocation of the privilege was in the *Milwaukee Leader Case,* 255 US 407 (1921). The Court (Justices Holmes and Brandeis dissented) upheld the order of the Postmaster General revoking the privilege on the ground that the newspaper had systematically published matter that was banned by the Espionage Act of 1917. The newspaper was thus not merely punished for its *past* misdeeds but was subjected to penalties as to the *future.*

[In the present case the Postmaster General attempted to accomplish the same result with respect to *Esquire,* a monthly magazine, because its contents seemed to him, by reason of vulgarity or poor taste, not to "contribute to the public good and the public welfare." The Court unanimously decided in favor of the publication. The ends of the legislation that provides for the second-class privilege, said the Court, "can be served only by uncensored distribution of literature." A requirement "that literature or art conform to some norm prescribed by an official smacks of an ideology foreign to our system." If the Postmaster General could withdraw the privilege from *Esquire,* he might try to do the same thing tomorrow respecting a periodical "whose social or economic views seemed harmful." It is doubtful, in the light of this decision and opinion, whether the *Milwaukee Leader Case* is still good law; in the *Esquire Case,* it should be noted, the Court cited only the dissents of Holmes and Brandeis in the earlier case.]

Mr. Justice Douglas delivered the opinion of the Court:

Congress has made obscene material nonmailable (18 USCA § 334), and has applied criminal sanctions for the enforcement of that policy. It has divided mailable matter into four classes, periodical publications constituting the second-class. . . . And it has specified four conditions upon which a publication shall be admitted to the second-class. . . . The Fourth condition, which is the only one relevant here, provides:

Except as otherwise provided by law, the conditions upon which a publication shall be admitted to the second class are as follows . . . Fourth. It must be originated and published for the dissemination of information of a public character, or devoted to literature, the sciences, arts, or some special industry, and having a legitimate list of subscribers. Nothing herein contained shall be so construed as to admit to the second-class rate regular publications designed primarily for advertising purposes, or for free circulation, or for circulation at nominal rates.

Respondent is the publisher of *Esquire Magazine,* a monthly periodical which was granted a second-class permit in 1933. In 1943, pursuant to 39 USCA § 232, a citation was issued to respondent by the then Postmaster General (for whom the present Postmaster General has now been substituted as petitioner) to show cause why that permit should not be suspended or revoked. A hearing was held before a board designated by the then Postmaster General. The board recommended that the permit not be revoked. Petitioner's predecessor took a different view. He did not find that *Esquire Magazine* contained obscene material and therefore was non-mailable. He revoked its second-class permit because he found that it did not comply with the Fourth condition. The gist of his holding is contained in the following excerpt from his opinion:

The plain language of this statute does not assume that a publication must in fact be "obscene" within the intendment of the postal obscenity statutes before it can be found not to be "originated and published for the dissemination of information of a public character, or devoted to literature, the sciences, arts, or some special industry."

Writings and pictures may be indecent, vulgar, and risque and still not be obscene in a technical sense. Such writings and pictures may be in that obscure and treacherous borderland zone where the average person hesitates to find them technically obscene, but still may see ample proof that they are morally improper and not for the public welfare and the public good. When such writings or pictures occur in isolated instances their dangerous tendencies and malignant qualities may be considered of lesser importance.

When, however, they become a dominant and systematic feature they most certainly cannot be said to be for the public good, and a publication which uses them in that manner is not making the "special contribution to the public welfare" which Congress intended by the Fourth condition.

A publication to enjoy these unique mail privileges and special preferences is bound to do more than refrain from disseminating material which is obscene or bordering on the obscene. It is under a positive duty to contribute to the public good and the public welfare. . . .

The issues of *Esquire Magazine* under attack are those for January to November inclusive of 1943. The material complained of embraces in bulk only a small percentage of those issues. Regular features of the magazine (called "The Magazine for Men") include articles on topics of current interest, short stories, sports articles or stories, short articles by men prominent in various fields of activities, articles about men prominent in the news, a book review department headed by the late William Lyon Phelps, a theatrical department headed by George Jean Nathan, . . . [a department on] lively arts by Gilbert Seldes, . . . pictorial features, including war action paintings, color photographs of game birds and reproductions of famous paintings, prints and drawings. There was very little in the features which was challenged. But petitioner's predecessor found that the objectionable items, though a small percentage of the total bulk, were regular recurrent features which gave the magazine its dominant tone or characteristic. These include jokes, cartoons, pictures, articles, and poems. They were said to reflect the smoking-room type of humor, featuring, in the main, sex. Some witnesses found the challenged items highly objectionable, calling them salacious and indecent. Others thought they were only racy and risque. Some condemned them as being merely in poor taste. Other witnesses could find no objection to them.

An examination of the items makes plain, we think, that the controversy is not whether the magazine publishes "information of a public character" or is devoted to "literature" or to the "arts." It is whether the contents are "good" or "bad." To uphold the order of revocation would, therefore, grant the Postmaster General a power of censorship. Such a power is so abhorrent to our traditions that a purpose to grant it should not be easily inferred. . . .

If the Fourth condition is read in that way, it is plain that Congress made no radical or basic change in the type of regulation which it adopted for second-class mail in 1879. The inauguration of even a limited type of censorship would have been such a startling change as to have left some traces in the legislative history. But we find none. . . .

We may assume that Congress has a broad power of classification and need not open second-class mail to publications of all types. The categories of publications entitled to that classification have indeed varied through the years. And the Court held in *Ex parte Jackson,* 96 US 727, that Congress could constitutionally make it a crime to send fraudulent or obscene material through the mails. But grave constitutional questions are immediately raised once it is said that the use of the mails is a privilege which may be extended or withheld on any grounds whatsoever. . . . Under that view the second-class rate could be granted on condition that certain economic or political ideas not be disseminated. The provisions of the Fourth condition would have to be far more explicit for us to assume that Congress made such a radical departure from our traditions and undertook to clothe the Postmaster General with the power to supervise the tastes of the reading public of the country.

. . . Under our system of government there is an accommodation for the widest varieties of tastes and ideas. What is good literature, what has educational value, what is refined public information, what is good art, varies with individuals as it does from one generation to another. There doubtless would be a contrariety of views concerning Cervantes' *Don Quixote,* Shakespeare's *Venus and Adonis,* or Zola's *Nana.* But a requirement that literature or art conform to some norm prescribed by an official smacks of an ideology foreign to our system. The basic values implicit in the requirements of the Fourth condition can be served only by uncensored distribution of literature. From the multitude of competing offerings the public will pick and choose. What seems to one to be trash may have for others fleeting or even enduring values. But to withdraw the second-class rate from this publication today because its contents seemed to one official not good for the public would sanction withdrawal of the second-class rate tomorrow from another periodical whose social or economic views seemed harmful to another official. The validity of the obscenity laws is recognition that the mails may not be used to satisfy all tastes, no matter how perverted. But Congress has left the Postmaster General with no power to prescribe standards for the literature or the art which a mailable periodical disseminates. . . .

Affirmed. [The order of the Postmaster General may be enjoined.]

GROVE PRESS *v.* CHRISTENBERRY
276 F. 2d 433 (1960)

[Soon after Grove Press announced that it would publish the unexpurgated *Lady Chatterley's Lover* by D. H. Lawrence, the Postmaster General formally barred the book from the mails. Judge Bryan, of the Federal District Court, issued an order permanently restraining the Post Office, and this judgment was affirmed by the Court of Appeals, Second Circuit. The opinion of Judge Clark for the latter court is published below. The Post Office, on the advice of the Solicitor General of the United States, did not appeal to the United States Supreme Court.]

Clark, Circuit Judge:

D. H. Lawrence completed the third manuscript version of his novel "Lady Chatterley's Lover" in Italy in 1928, and it was then published in Florence for private distribution. It is this version which has now been published by the plaintiff Grove Press, Inc., in a sumptuous edition selling for $6.00, with a prefatory letter of commendation by Archibald MacLeish, poet, playwright, and Boylston Professor of Rhetoric and Oratory at Harvard University, and with an extensive Introduction and a concluding Bibliographical Note by Mark Schorer, Professor of English Literature at the University of California and a Lawrence scholar.* The book (together with circulars showing its availability by Readers' Subscription, Inc., the second plaintiff) has been detained as unmailable by the New York Postmaster and, after a hearing before the Judicial Officer of the Post Office Department and reference to the Postmaster General for final departmental decision, was held by the latter to be "obscene and non-mailable pursuant to 18 U.S. Code § 1461." The Postmaster General wrote a substantial decision, of which these are salient paragraphs:

The contemporary community standards are not such that this book should be allowed to be transmitted in the mails.

The book is replete with descriptions in minute detail of sexual acts engaged in or discussed by the book's principal characters. These descriptions utilize filthy, offensive and degrading words and terms. Any literary merit the book may have is far outweighed

---

* This edition has never before been legally published in this country or in England, although it has been frequently pirated here; and an abridged edition was published by Knopf in 1930. The complete version, however, has been published in some continental countries in English and in most in translation. It is not protected here by copyright, and various paperback editions—we are told—are now appearing. . . .

by the pornographic and smutty passages and words, so that the book, taken as a whole, is an obscene and filthy work.

The plaintiffs then sought a declaratory judgment and an injunction from the court below to reverse this decision. On cross motions for summary judgment, Judge Bryan gave a declaration that the Grove Edition here involved "is neither obscene, lewd, lascivious, indecent nor filthy in content or character, and is not nonmailable matter within the meaning of Title 18, Section 1461 of the United States Code." He also held that the bar order of the Postmaster General "is illegal and void and violates plaintiffs' rights in contravention of the Constitution," and entered an order permanently enjoining its enforcement. His complete and reasoned opinion, with which we are in accord, gives further background, and reference is therefore made to it.

The important question on the merits is whether this now famous book is obscene within the meaning of 18 U.S.C. § 1461. This is a lengthy statute going back to 1876 and 1873 and amended as recently as 1958, which in portions here pertinent provides: "Every obscene, lewd, lascivious, indecent, filthy or vile article . . . is declared to be nonmailable matter and shall not be conveyed in the mails or delivered from any post office or by any letter carrier. Whoever knowingly uses the mails for the mailing, carriage in the mails, or delivery of anything declared by this section to be nonmailable . . . shall be fined not more than $5,000 or imprisoned not more than five years, or both, for the first such offense, and shall be fined not more than $10,000 or imprisoned not more than ten years, or both, for each such offense thereafter."

But before we reach the merits, we must consider the procedural aspects of the issue involved, since the government on this appeal has directed much the greater force of its argument to a reliance upon the principle of administrative law that an agency action supported by substantial evidence is beyond judicial review. Its major contention is that the statute obligates the Post Office Department to prevent the conveyance of obscene matter through the mails and that, since the Postmaster General has made a finding of obscenity based upon substantial evidence, the district court erred in reviewing it. The district court rejected this contention of agency finality, and so do we.

Preliminarily we should note the query whether the statute, being one defining a crime with criminal penalties, may afford justification for the acts of seizure by the Postmaster General in any event, or whether its sanction is not limited to criminal prosecution for crimes already committed. This is an issue which divided the court in *Sunshine Book Co.* v. *Summerfield*, F. 2d 114, summarily reversed in 355 US 372. It is one of serious difficulty; but we shall not attempt to resolve it here, since we think the result is clear on other grounds.

Judge Bryan ruled that the issue was one of law fully reviewable by a court of law, since there was no dispute in matters of evidence and hence there was no occasion for the application of the substantial evidence rule. Although this conclusion is vigorously attacked by the government, it is difficult to see why it is not sound, particularly as reinforced by the constitutional overtones implicit in the issue. There can be no doubt that in large areas of postal activity involving the delivery of the mail the Post Office Department exercises discretion not to be controlled by courts. But to determine whether a work of art or literature is obscene has little, if anything, to do with the expedition or efficiency with which the mails are dispatched. And here it is clear that no question of evidence was involved. In fact the Departmental officials considered only the novel itself against the background of the statute and declined to consider the expert opinion proffered by the plaintiffs. The question was thus one starkly of law. Moreover, the plaintiffs raised the constitutional issue of freedom of expression, Judge Bryan ruled upon it below, and it can hardly be escaped in this class of cases. . . . Even factual matters must be reviewed on appeal against a claim of denial of a constitutional right. . . . Both legally and practically the claim of final censorship powers here made for the Postmaster General is extreme. Indeed it has received an incisive answer in the public press thus: "And courts, not post offices, are the proper places for a determination of what is and is not protected by the Constitution."

Passing then to the merits we must of course be cognizant of the risk run by judges in enforcing obscenity statutes such as this and thus perchance condemning what become classics of our intellectual heritage. Some of the present Justices of the Supreme Court revolt against all this supervision as violative of constitutional precepts. But since the statute has been upheld by majority vote, . . . it remains the duty of those of us who sit in inferior courts to enforce it as best we may. And we need have no illusions but that a large business is done in exploiting "hard core pornography" for money's sake. In general this trash is easily recognized, with its repetitive emphasis (usually illustrated) upon purely physical action without character or plot development; and even if its direct connection with crime or incitement to juvenile or other delinquency is not proven—as many now assert—it cannot arouse sympathy because of its essentially repulsive, as well as fraudulent, character. It is when we come to more genuine works of literature that troublesome issues arise.

At the outset we may well recall the classic warning by a great American judge in probably the leading case on the subject prior to the recent utterances of the Supreme Court, Judge Augustus N. Hand in *United States* v. *One Book Entitled Ulysses by James Joyce:* "The foolish judgments of Lord Eldon about one hundred years ago, proscribing the works of Byron and Southey, and the finding by the jury under a charge by Lord Denman that the publication of Shelley's 'Queen Mab' was an indictable offense are a warning to all who have to determine the limits of the field within which authors may exercise themselves." And he went on to this judgment upon a then disputed book now recognized as classic: "We think that *Ulysses* is a book of originality and sincerity of treatment and that it has not the effect of promoting lust." Here we have one advantage over our predecessors in that the time which has elapsed since the writing and original publication of this book has been sufficient for the crystallization of at least a literary judgment upon it. And it seems clear without dissent from the expert evaluations presented both in the record and in the introductory material to this edition, as well as in the contemporary literature, that this is a major and a distinguished novel, and Lawrence one of the great writers of the era.*

* This judgment of Messrs. MacLeish, Schorer, Malcolm Cowley, Alfred Kazin, and other

For present purposes our test must be based upon that prescribed by the majority in *Roth* v. *United States,* 354 US 476. Justice Brennan said:

However, sex and obscenity are not synonymous. Obscene material is material which deals with sex in a manner appealing to prurient interest. The portrayal of sex, e.g., in art, literature and scientific works, is not itself sufficient reason to deny material the constitutional protection of freedom of speech and press. Sex, a great and mysterious motive force in human life, has indisputably been a subject of absorbing interest to mankind through the ages; it is one of the vital problems of human interest and public concern.

And he gave support to the definition in the A.L.I. Model Penal Code thus:

We perceive no significant difference between the meaning of obscenity developed in the case law and the definition of the A.L.I., Model Penal Code, § 207.10 (2) (Tent. Draft No. 6, 1957), viz.:
". . . A thing is obscene if, considered as a whole, its predominant appeal is to prurient interest, i.e., a shameful or morbid interest in nudity, sex, or excretion, and if it goes substantially beyond customary limits of candor in description or representation of such matters. . . ."

Examined with care and "considered as a whole," the predominant appeal of "Lady Chatterley's Lover" in our judgment is demonstrably not to "prurient interest," as thus defined. By now the story of the novel is well known. It is thus succinctly summarized in Professor Schorer's Introduction: "Constance Chatterley, the frustrated wife of an aristocratic mine owner who has been wounded in the war and left paralyzed and impotent, is drawn to his game-keeper, the misanthropic son of a miner, becomes pregnant by him, and hopes at the end of the book to be able to divorce her husband and leave her class for a life with the other man." But of course the story is a small part of the work. Actually the book is a polemic against three things which Lawrence hated: the crass industrialization of the English Midlands, the British caste system, and inhibited sex relations between man and woman. We may not see the close relation he did between the three as instruments of repression of the natural man, but we can understand his plea for greater freedom and naturalness even if we may not share his conviction of the all-inclusive nature of his remedy. Lawrence grew up in the English coal regions as the son of a miner who had married a teacher, and the theme of a relationship between a man of a low social status with a woman of a higher level is one he has used in previous works. The rationale he seeks to establish is thus one surely arguable and open to a writer. And if the aristocratic, but frustrated, heroine is to be taught naturalness in self-expression by her husband's servant, the plot line is rather clearly indicated. It is hardly surprising, therefore, that we find descriptions of increasingly more inti-

competent critics appearing in the record or offered at the departmental hearing seems to be rather regularly and continuously confirmed in literary journals. For example, the reviewer for the *Saturday Review,* Granville Hicks, in an article entitled, "D. H. Lawrence Reconsidered," *Saturday Review,* Dec. 19, 1959, p. 31, quotes the distinguished English scholar John Middleton Murray as saying shortly before his death in 1957 that "since the end of the Second World War, there has emerged a growing consensus of opinion that he [Lawrence] is the most significant writer of his time." So Professor Harry T. Moore, Lawrence's biographer, reviewing this book for the *N.Y. Times* Book Review Section, May 3, 1959, terms it "our time's most significant romance."

mate scenes between the two protagonists and an increasingly greater use of "nat- ural" language as the man's demonstration of naturalness to his feminine partner is stepped up to the author's climax.

What has apparently given surprise over the years—probably less so now than formerly in view of the changing climate of opinion—is the degree or extent to which the author has carried his plan. Undoubtedly to these critics of morals a little description of sex goes a long way; and judging by other examples, classical and modern, less directness would have left the work unchallenged. Obviously a writer can employ various means to achieve the effect he has in mind, and so probably Lawrence could have omitted some of the passages found "smutty" by the Postmaster General and yet have produced an effective work of literature. But clearly it would not have been the book he planned, because for what he had in mind his selection was most effective, as the agitation and success of the book over the years have proven.* In these sex descriptions showing how his aristocratic, but frustrated, lady achieved fulfillment and naturalness in her life, he also writes with power and indeed with a moving tenderness which is compelling, once our age- long inhibitions against sex revelations in print have been passed. In actuality his thesis here is only that pressed continuously in the modern marriage-counseling and doctors' books written with apparently quite worthy objectives and advertised stead- ily in our most sober journals and magazines. Of course it is old in literature; one may recall, for instance, the passionate love scenes between the young tutor and his employer's wife in Stendhal's classic, *Le Rouge et le Noir* (The Red and the Black), published in 1830. Actually in present-day literature such descriptions of physical relations appear as regular staples of literary diet and quiet without Law- rence's straightforward and somewhat refreshing candor.†

The same is true of the so-called four-letter words found particularly objection- able by the Postmaster General. These appear in the latter portion of the book in the mouth of the game-keeper in his tutelage of the lady in naturalness and are accepted by her as such. Again this could be taken as an object lesson at least in directness as compared to the smirk of much contemporary usage, which (perhaps strangely) does not seem to have offended our mailmen. In short, all these passages to which the Postmaster General takes exception—in bulk only a portion of the book—are subordinate, but highly useful, elements to the development of the author's central purpose. And that is not prurient. Should a court in reading mean- ing into the word "obscene"—which proves far from self-defining—make it so all-

---

* The defense complains that Lawrence need not "so vividly" have portrayed his scenes of sex and objects to the "Constant repetition of such intimate scenes." But that was at least one way of arousing reader interest, as the careful textual examination by the distinguished govern- ment counsel and associate counsel demonstrates. Compare the comment in a somewhat analogous situation of the New York Times Scandinavian reporter Werner Wiskari upon the presently popular Swedish motion picture director Ingmar Bergman, in the *Sunday Times Magazine,* Dec. 20, 1959, § 6, p. 20: "Why does Bergman insist on such brutality? Because he cannot abide the merely indifferent presence of a popcorn-chewing audience. In creating scenes that are almost physically felt in the midsection, he aims to involve the onlooker in the action so as to win active understanding of the motivations of his characters."

† As in a recent book of wide popularity in respected book circles, said to have had a sale of nearly three million copies, a tale of continuous seduction of or by a twelve-year-old girl by or with a middle-aged lover; or another, locally nominated for the Nobel prize, depicting in detail the sexual activities, marital and extra-marital, of a middle-aged Pennsylvania lawyer.

inclusive as to prohibit a writer from making use of normal and no longer unusual descriptions and parts of English speech to accomplish a worthy objective? And should a mature and sophisticated reading public be kept in blinders because a government official thinks reading certain works of power and literary value is not good for it? We agree with the court below in believing and holding that definitions of obscenity consistent with modern intellectual standards and morals neither require nor permit such a restriction.

Judgment affirmed.

MANUAL ENTERPRISES *v.* DAY
370 US 478 (1962)

[The Post Office barred from the mails certain magazines published primarily for homosexuals. The Supreme Court held that the magazines were not subject to repression as legally obscene. Justices Frankfurter and White did not participate in the case. Justice Black concurred in the result. Justice Brennan wrote a concurring opinion, in which Chief Justice Warren and Justice Douglas joined. Justice Clark dissented.]

Mr. Justice Harlan announced the judgment of the Court and an opinion in which Mr. Justice Stewart joins:

This case draws in question a ruling of the Post Office Department, sustained both by the District Court and the Court of Appeals, . . . barring from the mails a shipment of petitioners' magazines. That ruling was based on alternative determinations that the magazines were (1) themselves "obscene," and (2) gave information where obscene matter could be obtained, thus rendering them nonmailable under two separate provisions of 18 U.S.C. § 1461, known as the Comstock Act.* Certiorari was granted to consider the claim that this ruling was inconsistent with the proper interpretation and application of § 1461, and with principles established in two of this Court's prior decisions, *Roth* v. *United States,* 354 US 476; *Smith* v. *California,* 361 US 147.

Petitioners are three corporations respectively engaged in publishing magazines titled *MANual, Trim,* and *Grecian Guild Pictorial.* They have offices at the same address in Washington, D.C., and a common president, one Herman L. Womack. The magazines consist largely of photographs of nude, or near-nude, male models

---

* Section 1461 of 18 U.S.C. provides in part:

"Every obscene, lewd, lascivious, indecent, filthy or vile article, matter, thing, device, or substance; and— . . .

"Every written or printed card, letter, circular, book, pamphlet, advertisement, or notice of any kind giving information, directly, or indirectly, where, or how, or from whom, or by what means any of such mentioned matters, articles, or things may be obtained or made. . . .

"Is declared to be nonmailable matter and shall not be conveyed in the mails or delivered from any post office or by any letter carrier.

"Whoever knowingly uses the mails for the mailing, carriage in the mails, or delivery of anything declared by this section to be nonmailable, or knowingly causes to be delivered by mail according to the direction thereon, or at the place at which it is directed to be delivered by the person to whom it is addressed, or knowingly takes any such thing from the mails for the purpose of circulating or disposing thereof, or of aiding in the circulation or disposition thereof, shall be fined not more than $5,000 or imprisoned not more than five years. . . ."

and give the names of each model and the photographer, together with the address of the latter. They also contain a number of advertisements by independent photographers offering nudist photographs for sale.

On March 25, 1960, six parcels containing an aggregate of 405 copies of the three magazines, destined from Alexandria, Virginia, to Chicago, Illinois, were detained by the Alexandria postmaster, pending a ruling by his superiors at Washington as to whether the magazines were "nonmailable." Following an evidentiary hearing before the Judicial Officer of the Post Office Department there ensued the administrative and court decisions now under review.

I

On the issue of obscenity, as distinguished from unlawful advertising, the case comes to us with the following administrative findings, which are supported by substantial evidence and which we, and indeed the parties, for the most part, themselves, accept: (1) the magazines are not, as initially asserted by petitioners, physical culture or "bodybuilding" publications, but are composed primarily, if not exclusively, for homosexuals, and have no literary, scientific or other merit; (2) they would appeal to the "prurient interest" of such sexual deviates, but would not have any interest for sexually normal individuals; and (3) the magazines are read almost entirely by homosexuals, and possibly a few adolescent males; the ordinary male adult would not normally buy them.

On these premises, the question whether these magazines are "obscene," as it was decided below and argued before us, was thought to depend solely on a determination as to the relevant "audience" in terms of which their "prurient interest" appeal should be judged. This view of the obscenity issue evidently stemmed from the belief that in *Roth* v. *United States,* this Court established the following *single* test for determining whether challenged material is obscene: "whether to the average person, applying contemporary community standards, the dominant theme of the material taken as a whole appeals to prurient interest." . . . On this basis the Court of Appeals, rejecting the petitioners' contention that the "prurient interest" appeal of the magazines should be judged in terms of their likely impact on the "average person," even though not a likely recipient of the magazines, held that the administrative finding respecting their impact on the "average homosexual" sufficed to establish the Government's case as to their obscenity.

We do not reach the question thus thought below to be dispositive on this aspect of the case. For we find lacking in these magazines an element which, no less than "prurient interest," is essential to a valid determination of obscenity under § 1461, and to which neither the Post Office Department nor the Court of Appeals addressed itself at all: These magazines cannot be deemed so offensive on their face as to affront current community standards of decency—a quality that we shall hereafter refer to as "patent offensivenss" or "indecency." Lacking that quality, the magazines cannot be deemed legally "obscene," and we need not consider the question of the proper "audience" by which their "prurient interest" appeal should be judged.

The words of § 1461, "obscene, lewd, lascivious, indecent, filthy or vile" connote something that is portrayed in a manner so offensive as to make it unacceptable under current community *mores.* While in common usage the words have different shades of meaning, the statute since its inception has always been taken as aimed at obnoxiously debasing portrayals of sex. Although the statute condemns such material irrespective of the *effect* it may have upon those into whose hands it falls, the early case of *United States* v. *Bennett*, 24 Fed. Cas. 1093 (No. 14571), put a limiting gloss upon the statutory language: the statute reaches only indecent material which, as now expressed in *Roth* v. *United States, supra,* "taken as a whole appeals to prurient interest." This "effect" element, originally cast in somewhat different language from that of *Roth* . . . , was taken into federal obscenity law from the leading English case of *Regina* v. *Hicklin* [1868] L.R. 3 Q.B. 360, of which a distinguished Australian judge has given the following illuminating analysis:

As soon as one reflects that the word "obscene," as an ordinary English word, has nothing to do with corrupting or depraving susceptible people, and that it is used to describe things which are offensive to current standards of decency and not things which may induce to sinful thoughts, it becomes plain, I think, that Cockburn, C. J., in . . . *R.* v. *Hicklin* . . . was not propounding a logical definition of the word "obscene," but was merely explaining that particular characteristic which was necessary to bring an obscene publication within the law relating to obscene libel. . . . The tendency to deprave is not the characteristic which makes a publication obscene but is the characteristic which makes an obscene publication criminal. It is at once an essential element in the crime and the justification for the intervention of the common law. But it is not the whole and sole test of what constitutes an obscene libel. There is not obscene libel unless what is published is *both* offensive according to current standards of decency *and* calculated or likely to have the effect described in *R.* v. *Hicklin.* . . .

The thoughtful studies of the American Law Institute reflect the same twofold concept of obscenity. Its earlier draft of a Model Penal Code contains the following definition of "obscene": "A thing is obscene if, considered as a whole, its predominant appeal is to prurient interest . . . *and* if it goes substantially beyond customary limits of candor in description or representation of such matters." A.L.I., Model Penal Code, Tent. Draft No. 6 (1957), § 207.10 (2). (Emphasis added.) The same organization's currently proposed definition reads: "Material is obscene if, considered as a whole, its predominant appeal is to prurient interest . . . and if *in addition* it goes substantially beyond customary limits of candor in describing or representing such matters." A.L.I., Model Penal Code, Proposed Official Draft (May 4, 1962), § 251.4 (1). (Emphasis added.)*

Obscenity under the federal statute thus requires proof of two distinct elements: (1) patent offensiveness; and (2) "prurient interest" appeal. Both must conjoin before challenged material can be found "obscene" under § 1461. In most obscenity cases, to be sure, the two elements tend to coalesce, for that which is patently offensive will also usually carry the requisite "prurient interest" appeal. It is only in the unusual instance where, as here, the "prurient interest" appeal of the material is found limited to a particular class of persons that occasion arises for a truly independent inquiry into the question whether or not the material is patently offensive.

The Court of Appeals was mistaken in considering that *Roth* made "prurient in-

---

* This definition was approved by the Institute, as part of the "Proposed Official Draft," at its annual meeting in Washington, D.C., in May 1962.

terest" appeal the sole test of obscenity. Reading that case as dispensing with the requisite of patently offensive portrayal would be not only inconsistent with § 1461 and its common-law background, but out of keeping with *Roth's* evident purpose to tighten obscenity standards. The Court there both rejected the "isolated excerpt" and "particularly susceptible persons" tests of the *Hicklin* case, . . . and was at pains to point out that not all portrayals of sex could be reached by obscenity laws but only those treating that subject "in a manner appealing to prurient interest." . . . That, of course, was but a compendious way of embracing in the obscenity standard *both* the concept of patent offensiveness, manifested by the terms of § 1461 itself, and the element of the likely corruptive effect of the challenged material, brought into federal law via *Regina* v. *Hicklin*.

To consider that the "obscenity" exception in "the area of constitutionally protected speech or press," *Roth,* . . . does not require any determination as to the patent offensiveness *vel non* of the material itself might well put the American public in jeopardy of being denied access to many worthwhile works in literature, science, or art. For one would not have to travel far even among the acknowledged masterpieces in any of these fields to find works whose "dominant theme" might, not beyond reason, be claimed to appeal to the "prurient interest" of the reader or observer. We decline to attribute to Congress any such quixotic and deadening purpose as would bar from the mails all material, not patently offensive, which stimulates impure desires relating to sex. Indeed such a construction of § 1461 would doubtless encounter constitutional barriers. *Roth.* . . . Consequently we consider the power exercised by Congress in enacting § 1461 as no more embracing than the interdiction of "obscenity" as it had theretofore been understood. It is only material whose indecency is self-demonstrating *and* which, from the standpoint of its effect, may be said predominantly to appeal to the prurient interest that Congress has chosen to bar from the mails by the force of § 1461.

We come then to what we consider the dispositive question on this phase of the case. Are these magazines offensive on their face? Whether this question be deemed one of fact or of mixed fact and law, . . . we see no need of remanding the case for initial consideration by the Post Office Department or the Court of Appeals of this missing factor in their determinations. That issue, involving factual matters entangled in a constitutional claim, see *Grove Press, Inc.,* v. *Christenberry,* 276 F. 2d 433, is ultimately one for this Court. The relevant materials being before us, we determine the issue for ourselves.

There must first be decided the relevant "community" in terms of whose standards of decency the issue must be judged. We think that the proper test under this federal statute, reaching as it does to all parts of the United States whose population reflects many different ethnic and cultural backgrounds, is a national standard of decency. We need not decide whether Congress could constitutionally prescribe a lesser geographical framework for judging this issue which would not have the intolerable consequence of denying some sections of the country access to material, there deemed acceptable, which in others might be considered offensive to prevailing community standards of decency. . . .

As regards the standard for judging the element of "indecency," the *Roth* case gives little guidance beyond indicating that the standard is a constitutional one which, as with "prurient interest," requires taking the challenged material "as a whole." . . . Being ultimately concerned only with the question whether the First and Fourteenth Amendments protect material that is admittedly obscene, the Court there had no occasion to explore the application of a particular obscenity standard. At least one important state court and some authoritative commentators have considered *Roth* and subsequent cases to indicate that only "hard-core" pornography can constitutionally be reached under this or similar state obscenity statutes. . . . Whether "hard-core" pornography, or something less, be the proper test, we need go no further in the present case than to hold that the magazines in question, taken as a whole, cannot, under any permissible constitutional standard, be deemed to be beyond the pale of contemporary notions of rudimentary decency.

We cannot accept in full the Government's description of these magazines which, contrary to *Roth*, tends to emphasize and in some respects overdraw certain features in several of the photographs, at the expense of what the magazines fairly taken as a whole depict. Our own independent examination of the magazines leads us to conclude that the most that can be said of them is that they are dismally unpleasant, uncouth, and tawdry. But this is not enough to make them "obscene." Divorced from their "prurient interest" appeal to the unfortunate persons whose patronage they were aimed at capturing (a separate issue), these portrayals of the male nude cannot fairly be regarded as more objectionable than many portrayals of the female nude that society tolerates. Of course not every portrayal of male or female nudity is obscene. . . . Were we to hold that these magazines, although they do not transcend the prevailing bounds of decency, may be denied access to the mails by such undifferentiated legislation as that before us, we would be ignoring the admonition that "the door . . . into this area [the First Amendment] cannot be left ajar; it must be kept tightly closed and opened only the slightest crack necessary to prevent encroachment upon more important interests." . . . *Roth*. . . .*

II

There remains the question of the advertising. It is not contended that the petitioners held themselves out as purveyors of obscene material, or that the advertisements, as distinguished from the other contents of the magazines, were obscene on their own account. The advertisements were all by independent third-party photographers. And, neither with respect to the advertisements nor the magazines themselves, do we understand the Government to suggest that the "advertising" provisions of § 1461 are violated if the mailed material merely "gives the leer that promises the customer some obscene pictures." . . . Such an approach to the statute could not withstand the underlying precepts of *Roth*. . . . The claim on this branch of the case rests, then, on the fact that some of the third-party advertisers were found in possession of what undoubtedly may be regarded as "hard-core" photographs, and that postal officials, although not obtaining the names of

* Since Congress has sought to bar from the mails only material that is "obscene, lewd, lascivious, indecent, filthy, or vile," and it is within this statutory framework that we must judge the materials before us, we need not consider whether these magazines could constitutionally be reached under "a statute narrowly drawn to define and punish specific conduct as constituting a clear and present danger." *Cantwell* v. *Connecticut,* 310 US 296.

the advertisers from the lists in petitioners' magazines, received somewhat less offensive material through the mails from certain studios which were advertising in petitioner's magazines.

A question of law must first be dealt with. Should the "obscene-advertising" proscription of § 1461 be construed as not requiring proof that the publisher *knew* that at least some of his advertisers were offering to sell obscene material? In other words, although the criminal provisions of § 1461 do require *scienter* . . . can the Post Office Department in civil proceedings under that section escape with a lesser burden of proof? We are constrained to a negative answer. *First,* Congress has required *scienter* in respect of one indicted for mailing material proscribed by the statute. In the constitutional climate in which this statute finds itself, we should hesitate to attribute to Congress a purpose to render a publisher civilly responsible for the innocuous advertisements of the materials of others, in the absence of any showing that he knew that the character of such materials was offensive. And with no express grant of authority to the Post Office Department to keep obscene matter from the mail . . . we should be slow to accept the suggestion that an element of proof expressly required in a criminal proceeding may be omitted in an altogether parallel civil proceeding. *Second,* this Court's ground of decision in *Smith* v. *California,* 361 US 147, indicates that a substantial constitutional question would arise were we to construe § 1461 as not requiring proof of *scienter* in civil proceedings. For the power of the Post Office to bar a magazine from the mails, if exercised without proof of the publisher's knowledge of the character of the advertisements included in the magazine, would as effectively "impose a severe limitation on the public's access to constitutionally protected matter," . . . as would a state obscenity statute which makes criminal the possession of obscene material without proof of *scienter*. Since publishers cannot practically be expected to investigate each of their advertisers, and since the economic consequences of an order barring even a single issue of a periodical from the mails might entail heavy financial sacrifice, a magazine publisher might refrain from accepting advertisements from those whose own materials could conceivably be deemed objectionable by the Post Office Department. This would deprive such materials, which might otherwise be entitled to constitutional protection, of a legitimate and recognized avenue of access to the public. To be sure, the Court found it unnecessary in *Smith* to delineate the scope of *scienter* which would satisfy the Fourteenth Amendment. Yet it may safely be said that a federal statute which, as we construe it, requires the presence of that element is not satisfied, as the Government suggests it might be, merely by showing that a defendant did not make a "good faith effort" to ascertain the character of his advertiser's materials.

On these premises we turn to the record in this case. Although postal officials had informed petitioners' president, Womack, that their Department was *prosecuting* several of his advertisers for sending obscene matter through the mails, there is no evidence that any of this material was shown to him. He thus was afforded no opportunity to judge for himself as to its alleged obscenity. Contrariwise, one of the government witnesses at the administrative hearing admitted that the petitioners had deleted the advertisements of several photographic studios after being informed by the Post Office that the proprietors had been *convicted* of mailing obscene material. The record reveals that none of the postal officials who received allegedly obscene matter from some of the advertisers obtained their names from petitioners' magazines; this material was received as a result of independent test checks. Nor on the record before us can petitioners be linked with the material seized by the police. . . . The only such asserted connection—that "hard-core" matter was seized at the studio of one of petitioners' advertisers—falls short of an adequate showing that petitioners knew that the advertiser was offering for sale obscene matter. Womack's own conviction for sending obscene material through the mails, *Womack* v. *United States,* 294 F. 2d 204, is remote from proof of like conduct on the part of the advertisers. At that time he was acting as president of another studio; the vendee of the material, while an advertiser in petitioners' magazines, had closed his own studio before the present issues were published. Finally, the general testimony by one postal inspector to the effect that in his experience advertisers of this character, after first leading their customers on with borderline material, usually followed up with "hard-core" matter, can hardly be deemed of probative significance on the issue at hand.

At best the Government's proof showed no more than that petitioners were chargeable with knowledge that these advertisers were offering photographs of the same character, and with the same purposes, as those reflected in their own magazines. This is not enough to satisfy the Government's burden of proof on this score.

In conclusion, nothing in this opinion of course remotely implies approval of the type of magazines published by these petitioners, still less of the sordid motives which prompted their publication. All we decide is that on this record these particular magazines are not subject to repression under § 1461.

Reversed.

ROWAN *v.* U.S. POST OFFICE DEPARTMENT
397 US 728 (1970)

[An act of Congress provides that the recipient of pandering advertisements may request the Postmaster General to issue an order to the sender prohibiting further mailing to the addressee. The Supreme Court in this case upheld the act as constitutional, saying that "a mailer's right to communicate must stop at the mailbox of an unreceptive addressee." The Court's opinion was by Chief Justice Burger. Justice Brennan wrote a short concurring opinion in which Justice Douglas joined.]

Mr. Chief Justice Burger delivered the opinion of the Court:

Appellants challenge the constitutionality of Title III of the Postal Revenue and Federal Salary Act of 1967, 81 Stat. 645, 39 U.S.C. § 4009 (Supp. IV, 1969), under which a householder may require that a mailer remove his name from its mailing lists and stop all future mailings to the householder. The appellants are publishers, distributors, owners, and operators of mail order houses, mailing list brokers, and owners and operators of mail service organizations whose business activities are affected by the challenged statute.

A brief description of the statutory framework will facilitate our analysis of the questions raised in this appeal. Title III of the Act is entitled "Prohibition of pandering advertisements in the mails." It provides a procedure whereby any householder may insulate himself from advertisements that offer for sale "matter which the addressee in his sole discretion believes to be erotically arousing or sexually provocative." 39 U.S.C. § 4009(a).*

Subsection (b) mandates the Postmaster, upon receipt of a notice from the addressee specifying that he has received advertisements found by him to be within the statutory category, to issue on the addressee's request an order directing the sender and his agents or assigns to refrain from further mailings of such materials to the named addressees. Additionally, subsection (c) requires the Postmaster to order the affected sender to delete the name of the designated addressee from all mailing lists owned or controlled by the sender and prohibits the sale, rental, exchange, or other transactions involving mailing lists bearing the name of the designated addressee.

If the Postmaster has reason to believe that an order issued under this section has been violated, subsection (d) authorizes him to notify the sender by registered or certified mail of his belief and the reasons therefor, and grant him an opportunity to respond and have a hearing on whether a violation has occurred.

If the Postmaster thereafter determines that the order has been or is being violated, he is authorized to request the Attorney General to seek an order from a United States District Court directing compliance with the prohibitory order. Subsection (e) grants to the District Court jurisdiction to issue a compliance order upon application of the Attorney General.

Appellants initiated an action in the United States District Court for the Central District of California upon a complaint and petition for declaratory relief on the ground that 39 U.S.C. § 4009 is unconstitutional. They alleged that they have received numerous prohibitory orders pursuant to the provisions of the statute. Appellants contended that the section violates their rights of free speech and due process guaranteed by the First and Fifth Amendments to the United States Constitution. Additionally, appellants argued that the section is unconstitutionally vague, without standards and ambiguous.

A three-judge court was convened pursuant to 28 U.S.C. § 2284 (1964) and determined that the section was constitutional when interpreted to prohibit advertisements similar to those initially mailed to the addressee.

The District Court construed subsections (b) and (c) to prohibit "advertisements similar" to those initially mailed to the addressee; future mailings, in the view of the District Court, "are to be measured by the objectionable materials of such first mailing." In our view Congress did not intend so restrictive a scope to those provisions.

(1) Background and Congressional Objectives

Section 4009 was a response to public and congressional concern with use of mail facilities to distribute unsolicited advertisements that recipients found to be offensive because of their lewd and salacious character. Such mail was found to be pressed upon minors as well as adults who did not seek and did not want it. Use

---

* Subsection (g) provides that upon the addressee's request the order shall include names of the addressee's minor children who reside with him and who have not attained their nineteenth birthday.

of mailing lists of youth organizations was part of the mode of doing business. At the congressional hearings it developed that complaints to the Postmaster General increased from 50,000 to 250,000 annually. The legislative history, including testimony of child psychology specialists and psychiatrists, reflected concern over the impact of the materials before the Committee on the development of children. A declared objective of Congress was to protect minors and the privacy of homes from such material and to place the judgment of what constitutes an offensive invasion of those interests in the hands of the addressee.

To accomplish these objectives Congress provided in subsection (a) that the mailer is subject to an order "to refrain from further mailings of such materials to designated addressees." Subsection (b) states that the Postmaster General shall direct the sender to refrain from "further mailings to the named addressees." Subsection (c) in describing the Postmaster's order states that it shall "expressly prohibit the sender . . . from making any further mailings to the designated addressees. . . ." Subsection (c) also requires the sender to delete the addressee's name "from all mailing lists" and prohibits the sale, transfer, and exchange of lists bearing the addressee's name.

There are three plausible constructions of the statute, with respect to the scope of the prohibitory order. The order could prohibit all future mailings to the addressees, all future mailings of advertising material to the addressees, or all future mailings of similar materials.

The seeming internal statutory inconsistency is undoubtedly a residue of the language of the section as it was initially proposed. The section as originally reported by the House Committee on the Post Office and the Civil Service prohibited "further mailings of such pandering advertisements." § 4009(a), "further mailings of such matter," § 4009(b), and "any further mailings of pandering advertisements," § 4009(c). . . . The section required the Postmaster General to make a determination whether the particular piece of mail came within the proscribed class of pandering advertisements, "as that term is used in the *Ginzburg* case (*Ginzburg* v. *United States,* 383 US 463."

The section was subsequently amended by the House of Representatives to eliminate from the Post Office any censorship function. Congressman Waldie, who proposed the amendment, envisioned a minimal role for the Post Office. The amendment was intended to remove "the right of the Government to involve itself in any determination of the content and nature of these objectionable materials. . . ." The only determination left for the Postmaster General is whether or not the mailer has removed the addressee's name from the mailing list. Statements by the proponents of the legislation in both the House and Senate manifested an intent to prohibit all further mailings from the sender. In describing the effect of his proposed amendment Congressman Waldie stated:

So I have said in my amendment that if you receive literature in your household that you consider objectionable . . . you can inform the Postmaster General to have your name stricken from that mailer's mailing list.

The Senate Committee Report on the bill contained similar language:

If a person receives an advertisement which . . . he . . . believes to be erotically arousing . . . he may notify the Postmaster General of his determination. The Postmaster General is then required to issue an order directing him to refrain from sending any further mailings of any kind to such person.

Senator Monroney, a major proponent of the legislation in the Senate, described the bill as follows:

With respect to the test contained in the bill, if the addressee declared it to be erotically arousing or sexually provocative the Postmaster General would have to notify the sender to send no more mail to that address. . . .

The legislative history of subsection (a) thus supports an interpretation that prohibits all future mailings independent of any objective test. This reading is consistent with the provisions of related subsections in the section. Subsection (c) provides that the Postmaster General "shall also direct the sender and his agents or assigns to delete immediately the names of the designated addressees from all mailing lists owned or controlled by the sender or his agents or assigns and, further, shall prohibit the sender and his agents or assigns from the sale, rental, exchange, or other transaction involving mailing lists bearing the names of the designated addressees."

It would be anomalous to read the statute to affect only similar material or advertisements and yet require the Postmaster General to order the sender to remove the addressee's name from all mailing lists in his actual or constructive possession. The section was intended to allow the addressee complete and unfettered discretion in electing whether or not he desired to receive further material from a particular sender. The impact of this aspect of the statute is on the mailer, not the mail. The interpretation of the statute that most completely effectuates that intent is one which prohibits any further mailings. Limiting the prohibitory order to similar materials or advertisements is open to at least two criticisms: (a) it would expose the householder to further burdens of scrutinizing the mail for objectionable material and possible harassment, and (b) it would interpose the Postmaster General between the sender and the addressee and, at the least, create the appearance if not the substance of governmental censorship. It is difficult to see how the Postmaster General could decide whether the materials were "similar" or possessing touting or pandering characteristics without an evaluation suspiciously like censorship. Additionally, such an interpretation would be incompatible with the unequivocal language in subsection (c).

(2) First Amendment Contentions

The essence of appellants' argument is that the statute violates their constitutional right to communicate. One sentence in appellants' brief perhaps characterizes their entire position:

The freedom to communicate orally and by the written word and, indeed, in every manner whatsoever is imperative to a free and sane society.

Without doubt the public postal system is an indispensable adjunct of every civilized society, and communication is imperative to a healthy social order. But the right of every person "to be let alone" must be placed in the scales with the right of others to communicate.

In today's complex society we are inescapably captive audiences for many purposes, but a sufficient measure of individual autonomy must survive to permit every householder to exercise control over unwanted mail. To make the householder the exclusive and final judge of what will cross his threshold undoubtedly has the effect of impeding the flow of ideas, information and arguments which, ideally, he should receive and consider. Today's merchandising methods, the plethora of mass mailings subsidized by low postal rates, and the growth of the sale of large mailing lists as an industry in itself have changed the mailman from a carrier of primarily private communications, as he was in a more leisurely day, and has made him an adjunct of the mass mailer who sends unsolicited and often unwanted mail into every home. It places no strain on the doctrine of judicial notice to observe that whether measured by pieces or pounds, Everyman's mail today is made up overwhelmingly of material he did not seek from persons he does not know. And all too often it is matter he finds offensive.

In *Martin* v. *City of Struthers,* 319 US 141 (1943), Mr. Justice Black, for the Court, while supporting the "[f]reedom to distribute information to every citizen," acknowledged a limitation in terms of leaving "with the homeowner himself" the power to decide "whether distributors of literature may lawfully call at a home." Weighing the highly important right to communicate, but without trying to determine where it fits into constitutional imperatives, against the very basic right to be free from sights, sounds and tangible matter we do not want, it seems to us that a mailer's right to communicate must stop at the mailbox of an unreceptive addressee.

The Court has traditionally respected the right of a householder to bar, by order or notice, solicitors, hawkers, and peddlers from his property. See *Martin* v. *City of Struthers, supra; . . .* In this case the mailer's right to communicate is circumscribed only by an affirmative act of the addressee giving notice that he wishes no further mailings from that mailer.

To hold less would tend to license a form of trespass and would make hardly more sense than to say that a radio or television viewer may not twist the dial to cut off an offensive or boring communication and thus bar its entering his home. Nothing in the Constitution compels us to listen to or view any unwanted communication, whatever its merit; we see no basis for according the printed word or pictures a different or more preferred status because they are sent by mail. The ancient concept that "a man's home is his castle" into which "not even the king may enter" has lost none of its vitality, and none of the recognized exceptions includes any right to communicate offensively with another. . . .

Both the absoluteness of the citizen's right under § 4009 and its finality are essential; what may not be provocative to one person may well be to another. In operative effect the power of the householder under the statute is unlimited; he or she may prohibit the mailing of a dry-goods catalog because he objects to the contents—or indeed the text of the language touting the merchandise. Congress provided this sweeping power not only to protect privacy but to avoid possible constitutional questions that might arise from vesting the power to make any discretionary evaluation of the material in a governmental official.

In effect, Congress has erected a wall—or more accurately permits a citizen to erect a wall—that no advertiser may penetrate without his acquiescence. The continuing operative effect of a mailing ban once imposed presents no constitutional obstacles; the citizen cannot be put to the burden of determining on repeated occasions whether the offending mailer has altered his material so as to make it acceptable. Nor should the householder be at risk that offensive material come into the hands of his children before it can be stopped.

We therefore categorically reject the argument that a vendor has a right under the Constitution or otherwise to send unwanted material into the home of another. If this prohibition operates to impede the flow of even valid ideas, the answer is that no one has a right to press even "good" ideas on an unwilling recipient. That we are often "captives" outside the sanctuary of the home and subject to objectionable speech and other sound does not mean we must be captives everywhere. . . . The asserted right of a mailer, we repeat, stops at the outer boundary of every person's domain.

The statutory scheme at issue accords to the sender an "opportunity to be heard upon such notice and proceedings as are adequate to safeguard the right for which the constitutional protection is invoked." . . . It thus comports with the Due Process Clause of the Fifth Amendment. The statutory scheme accomplishes this by providing that the Postmaster General shall issue a prohibitory order to the sender on the request of the complaining addressee. Only if the sender violates the terms of the order is the Postmaster General authorized to serve a complaint on the sender, who is then allowed 15 days to respond. The sender can then secure an administrative hearing. The sender may question whether the initial material mailed to the addressee was an advertisement and whether he sent any subsequent mailings. If the Postmaster General thereafter determines that the prohibitory order has been violated, he is authorized to make application in a United States District Court for a compliance order; a second hearing is required if an order is to be entered.

The only administrative action not preceded by a full hearing is the initial issuance of the prohibitory order. Since the sender risks no immediate sanction by failing to comply with that order—it is only a predicate for later steps—it cannot be said that this aspect of the procedure denies due process. It is sufficient that all available defenses, such as proof that no mail was sent, may be presented to a competent tribunal before a contempt finding can be made. . . .

The appellants also contend that the requirement that the sender remove the addressee's name from all mailing lists in his possession violates the Fifth Amendment because it constitutes a taking without due process of law. The appellants are not prohibited from using, selling, or exchanging their mailing lists; they are simply required to delete the names of the complaining addressees from the lists and cease all mailings to those persons. Appellants next contend that compliance with the statute is confiscatory because the costs attending removal of the names are prohibitive. We agree with the conclusion of the District Court that the "burden does not amount to a violation of due process guaranteed by the Fifth Amendment. Particularly when in the context before the Court it is being applied to commercial enterprises." . . .

There is no merit to the appellants' allegations that the statute is unconstitutionally vague. A statute is fatally vague only when it exposes a potential actor to some risk or detriment without giving him fair warning of the nature of the proscribed conduct. . . . Here the appellants know precisely what they must do on receipt of a prohibitory order. The complainants' names must be removed from the sender's mailing lists and he must refrain from future mailings to the named addressees. The sender is exposed to a contempt sanction only if he continues to mail to a particular addressee after administrative and judicial proceedings. Appellants run no substantial risk of miscalculation.

For the reasons stated, the judgment appealed from is affirmed.

It is so ordered.

Judgment affirmed.

BLOUNT *v.* RIZZI
400 US 410 (1971)

[The Postal Reorganization Act created on administrative censorship system under which, following hearings, the Postmaster General may halt use of the mails for commerce in allegedly obscene materials; under the statutory scheme, the Postmaster General may also obtain a court order permitting him to detain defendant's incoming mail pending the outcome of proceedings. The Supreme Court unanimously held that the system violated First Amendment rights. The Court's opinion was by Justice Brennan. Justice Black concurred in the result.]

Mr. Justice Brennan delivered the opinion of the Court:

Mail Box, No. 55, draws into question the constitutionality of 39 U.S.C. § 4006 (1964) (now 39 U.S.C. § 3006, Postal Reorganization Act, 84 Stat. 719, 747–748), under which the Postmaster General, following administrative hearings, may halt use of the mails and of postal money orders for commerce in allegedly obscene materials. *Book Bin,* No. 58, also draws into question the constitutionality of § 4006, and, in addition, the constitutionality of 39 U.S.C. § 4007 (1964) (now 39 U.S.C. § 3007), under which the Postmaster General may obtain a court order permitting him to detain the defendant's incoming mail pending the outcome of § 4006 proceedings against him.

39 U.S.C. § 4006 provides in pertinent part:

Upon evidence satisfactory to the Postmaster General that a person is obtaining or attempting to obtain remittances of money or property of any kind through the mail for an obscene . . . matter . . . or is depositing or causing to be deposited in the United States mail information as to where, how, or from whom the same may be obtained, the Postmaster General may—

(1) direct postmasters at the office at which registered letters or other letters or mail arrive, addressed to such a person or his representative, to return the registered letters or other letters or mail to the sender marked "Unlawful"; and

(2) forbid the payment by a postmaster to such a person or his representative of any money order or postal note drawn to the order of either and provide for the return to the remitters of the sums named in the money orders or postal notes.

Proceedings under § 4006 are conducted according to departmental regulations. A proceeding is begun by the General Counsel of the Post Office Department by written complaint and notice of hearing. The Judicial Officer of the Department holds a trial-type hearing at which a full record is transcribed. He renders an opinion which includes findings of fact and a statement of reasons. The decision is to "be rendered with all due speed," and there is an administrative appeal. No § 4006 order may issue against the defendant until completion of the administrative proceedings. If, however, the Postmaster General wishes to detain the defendant's incoming mail before the termination of the § 4006 proceedings, he may apply to the United States District Court for the district in which the defendant resides under 39 U.S.C. § 4007, which in pertinent part provides:

In preparation for or during the pendency of proceedings under [§ 4006] of this title, the United States district court in the district in which the defendant receives his mail shall, upon application therefor by the Postmaster General and upon a showing of probable cause to believe the statute is being violated, enter a temporary restraining order and preliminary injunction pursuant to rule 65 of the Federal Rules of Civil Procedure directing the detention of the defendant's incoming mail by the postmaster pending the conclusion of the statutory proceedings and any appeal therefrom. The district court may provide in the order that the detained mail be open to examination by the defendant and such mail be delivered as is clearly not connected with alleged unlawful activity. An action taken by a court hereunder does not affect or determine any fact at issue in the statutory proceedings.

In *Mail Box,* the Postmaster General began administrative proceedings under § 4006 November 1, 1968. The administrative hearing was concluded December 5, 1968. The Judicial Officer filed his decision December 31, 1968, finding that the specified magazines were obscene and, therefore, entered a § 4006 order—61 days after the complaint was filed. Mail Box filed a complaint in the United States District Court for the Central District of California seeking a declaratory judgment that § 4006 was unconstitutional and an injunction against enforcement of the administrative order. A three-judge court was convened and held that 39 U.S.C. § 4006 "is unconstitutional on its face, because it fails to meet the requirements of *Freedman* v. *Maryland* (1965) 380 US 51." The court, therefore, vacated the administrative order, directed the delivery "forthwith" of all mail addressed to Mail Box, and enjoined any proceedings to enforce § 4006.

In *Book Bin,* the Postmaster General applied to the District Court for the Northern District of Georgia for a § 4007 order pending the completion of § 4006 proceedings against Book Bin. Book Bin counterclaimed, asserting that both §§ 4006 and 4007 were unconstitutional and that their enforcement should be enjoined. A three-judge court was convened and held both sections unconstitutional. It agreed with the three-judge court in *Mail Box* that the procedures of § 4006 were fatally deficient under *Freedman* v. *Maryland, supra,* and also held that the finding under § 4007 merely of "probable cause" to believe material was obscene was not a constitutionally sufficient standard to support a temporary mail detention order.

We noted probable jurisdiction of the Government's appeals. We affirm the judgment in each case.

Our discussion appropriately begins with Mr. Justice Holmes' frequently quoted admonition that, "The United States may give up the Post Office when it sees fit, but while it carries it on the use of the mails is almost as much a part of free speech as the right to use our tongues. . . ." *United States ex rel. Milwaukee Social Demo-cratic Pub. Co.* v. *Burleson,* 255 US 407, 437 (1921) (dissenting opinion); see also *Lamont* v. *Postmaster General,* 381 US 301 (1965). Since § 4006 on its face, and § 4007 as applied, are procedures designed to deny use of the mails to commercial distributors of obscene literature, those procedures violate the First Amendment unless they include built-in safeguards against curtailment of constitutionally protected expression, for Government "is not free to adopt whatever procedures it pleases for dealing with obscenity . . . without regard to the possible consequences for constitutionally protected speech." . . . Rather, the First Amendment requires that procedures be incorporated which "ensure against the curtailment of constitutionally protected expression, which is often separated from obscenity only by a dim and uncertain line. . . . Our insistence that regulations of obscenity scrupulously embody the most rigorous procedural safeguards . . . is . . . but a special instance of the larger principle that the freedoms of expression must be ringed about with adequate bulwarks. . . ." *Bantam Books, Inc.* v. *Sullivan,* 372 US 58 (1963). Since we have recognized that "the line between speech unconditionally guaranteed and speech which may legitimately be regulated . . . is finely drawn. . . . [t]he separation of legitimate from illegitimate speech calls for . . . sensitive tools. . . ." *Speiser* v. *Randall,* 357 US 513 (1958).

The procedure established by § 4006 and the implementing regulations omit those "sensitive tools" essential to satisfy the requirements of the First Amendment. The three-judge courts correctly held in these cases that our decision in *Freedman* v. *Maryland, supra.* compels this conclusion. We there considered the constitutionality of a motion picture censorship procedure administered by a State Board of Censors. We held that to avoid constitutional infirmity a scheme of administrative censorship must: place the burdens of initiating judicial review and of proving that the material is unprotected expression on the censor; require "prompt judicial review"—a final judicial determination on the merits within a specified, brief period —to prevent the administrative decision of the censor from achieving an effect of finality; and limit to preservation of the status quo for the shortest, fixed period compatible with sound judicial resolution, any restraint imposed in advance of the final judicial determination.

These safeguards are lacking in the administrative censorship scheme created by §§ 4006, 4007, and the regulations.*

The scheme has no statutory provision requiring governmentally initiated judicial participation in the procedure which bars the magazines from the mails, or even any provision assuring prompt judicial review. The scheme does differ from the Maryland scheme involved in *Freedman* in that under the Maryland scheme the motion picture could not be exhibited pending conclusion of the administrative hearing, whereas under § 4006 the order to return mail or to refuse to pay money orders is not imposed until there has been an administrative determination that the magazines are obscene. This, however, does not redress the fatal flaw of the procedure in failing to require that the Postmaster General seek to obtain a prompt

---

* We therefore have no occasion to consider the argument of appellees that *Stanley* v. *Georgia,* 394 US 557 (1969) presupposes that an individual has a constitutional right to obtain possession of the challenged materials by delivery through the mail.

judicial determination of the obscenity of the material; rather, once the administrative proceedings disapprove the magazines the distributor "must assume the burden of instituting judicial proceedings and of persuading the courts that the . . . [magazines are] . . . protected expression." The First Amendment demands that the Government must assume this burden. "The teaching of our cases is that, because only a judicial determination in an adversary proceeding ensures the necessary sensitivity to freedom of expression, only a procedure requiring a judicial determination suffices to impose a valid final restraint."

Moreover, once a § 4006 administrative order has been entered against the distributor, there being no provision for judicial review, the Postmaster may stamp as "unlawful" and immediately return to the sender orders for purchase of the magazines addressed to the distributor, and prohibit the payment of postal money orders to him. Such a scheme "presents peculiar dangers to constitutionally protected speech. . . . Because the censor's business is to censor, there inheres the danger that he may well be less responsive than a court—part of an independent branch of government—to the constitutionally protected interests in free expression. And if it is made unduly onerous, by reason of delay or otherwise, to seek judicial review, the censor's determination may in practice be final." The Government suggests that we avoid the constitutional question raised by the failure of § 4006 to provide that the Government seek a prompt judicial determination by construing that section to deny the administrative order any effect whatever, if judicial review is sought by the distributor, until the completion of that review. Apart from the fact that this suggestion neither requires that the Government initiate judicial proceedings, nor provides for a prompt judicial determination, it is for Congress, not this Court, to rewrite the statute.

The authority of the Postmaster General under § 4007 to apply to a district court for an order directing the detention of the distributor's incoming mail pending the conclusion of the § 4006 administrative proceedings and any appeal therefrom plainly does not remedy the defects in § 4006. That section does not provide a prompt proceeding for a judicial adjudication of the challenged obscenity of the magazine. First, it is entirely discretionary with the Attorney General whether to institute a § 4007 action and, therefore, the section does not satisfy the requirement that the Government assume the burden of seeking a judicial determination of the alleged obscenity of the magazines. Second, the district court is required to grant the relief sought by the Postmaster upon a showing merely of "probable cause" to believe § 4006 is being violated. We agree with the three-judge court in *Book Bin* that to satisfy the demand of the First Amendment "it is vital that prompt judicial review on the issue of obscenity—rather than merely probable cause—be assured on the Government's initiative before the severe restrictions in §§ 4006, 4007 are invoked." Indeed, the statute expressly provides that, "An action taken by a court hereunder does not affect or determine any fact at issue in the statutory proceedings."

Moreover, § 4007 does not in any event itself meet the requisites of the First Amendment. Any order issued by the district court remains in effect "pending the conclusion of the statutory proceedings and any appeal therefrom." Thus, the statute not only fails to provide that the district court should make a final judicial determination of the question of obscenity, expressly giving that authority to the judicial officer, but it fails to provide that "[a]ny restraint imposed in advance of a final judicial determination on the merits must . . . be limited to preservation of the status quo for the shortest fixed period compatible with sound judicial resolution."

The appellees here not only were not afforded "prompt judicial review" but they "can only get full judicial review on the question of obscenity—by which the Postmaster would be actually bound—after lengthy administrative proceedings, and then only by [their] own initiative. During the interim, the prolonged threat of an adverse administrat[ive] decision in § 4006 or the reality of a sweeping § 4007 order, will have a severe restriction on the exercise of [appellees'] First Amendment rights —all without a *final* judicial determination of obscenity."

The judgments of the three-judge courts in Nos. 55 and 58 are affirmed. Affirmed.

2. Customs Control

UNITED STATES *v.* ONE BOOK CALLED "ULYSSES"
5 F. Supp. 182 (1933)

[A form of censorship that might have a serious effect on American culture could be achieved by customs officials if they stopped at the border books that they considered objectionable. Literary, aesthetic or political isolationism could be strengthened in this way.

[Until the law was changed by Congress in 1930 customs officials prevented the entry of such classics as Rousseau's *Confessions,* Casanova's *Memoirs,* the *Golden Ass* of Apuleius, all of Rabelais, Boccaccio's *Decameron, The Arabian Nights,* Voltaire's *Candide,* and modern books like *The Enormous Room* by E. E. Cummings and *Psychopathia Sexualis* by Krafft-Ebing. Many of these books had already been published in the United States, but this fact did not impress the customs officials; they seized and confiscated the books, and the citizen was quite helpless. Congress in 1930 amended the Tariff Act to authorize the Secretary of the Treasury to admit classics and books of recognized scientific or literary merit when imported for noncommercial purposes. The act provided also that, when a book was seized, the collector was to notify the federal district attorney, who was to institute proceedings in the Federal District Court for the forfeiture of the book. Any party in interest could demand a trial by jury.

[In 1933 an attempt was made to keep out a copy of *Ulysses* by James Joyce. In a notable decision, Judge Woolsey of the Federal District Court ruled that the book was not "obscene" within the meaning of the act and so was not subject to seizure and confiscation. His decision was affirmed by the Court of Appeals. 72 F. 2d 705 (1934). The 1930 statute and Judge Woolsey's decision have, on the whole, emancipated books from customs censorship.]

On cross motions for a decree in a libel of confiscation, supplemented by a stipulation—hereinafter described—brought by the United States against the book *Ulysses* by James Joyce, under Section 305 of the Tariff Act of 1930, Title 19 United States Code, Section 1305, on the ground that the book is obscene within the meaning of that Section, and, hence, is not importable into the United States, but is subject to seizure, forfeiture and confiscation and destruction.

Judge Woolsey:

The motion for a decree dismissing the libel herein is granted, and, consequently, of course, the Government's motion for a decree of forfeiture and destruction is denied.

Accordingly a decree dismissing the libel without costs may be entered herein.

I. The practice followed in this case is in accordance with the suggestion made by me in the case of *United States* v. *One Book Entitled "Contraception,"* 51 F. 2d 525, and is as follows:

After issue was joined by the filing of the claimant's answer to the libel for forfeiture against *Ulysses,* a stipulation was made between the United States Attorney's office and the attorneys for the claimant providing:

1. That the book *Ulysses* should be deemed to have been annexed to and to have become part of the libel just as if it had been incorporated in its entirety therein.

2. That the parties waived their right to a trial by jury.

3. That each party agreed to move for decree in its favor.

4. That on such cross motions the Court might decide all the questions of law and fact involved and render a general finding thereon.

5. That on the decision of such motions the decree of the Court might be entered as if it were a decree after trial.

It seems to me that a procedure of this kind is highly appropriate in libels for the confiscation of books such as this. It is an especially advantageous procedure in the instant case because on account of the length of *Ulysses* and the difficulty of reading it, a jury trial would have been an extremely unsatisfactory, if not an almost impossible, method of dealing with it.

II. I have read *Ulysses* once in its entirety and I have read those passages of which the Government particularly complains several times. In fact, for many weeks, my spare time has been devoted to the consideration of the decision which my duty would require me to make in this matter.

Ulysses is not an easy book to read or to understand. But there has been much written about it, and in order properly to approach the consideration of it, it is advisable to read a number of other books which have now become its satellites. The study of *Ulysses* is, therefore, a heavy task.

III. The reputation of *Ulysses* in the literary world, however, warranted my taking such time as was necessary to enable me to satisfy myself as to the intent with which the book was written, for, of course, in any case where a book is claimed to be obscene it must first be determined, whether the intent with which it was written was what is called, according to the usual phrase, pornographic,—that is, written for the purpose of exploiting obscenity.

If the conclusion is that the book is pornographic that is the end of the inquiry and forfeiture must follow.

But in *Ulysses,* in spite of its unusual frankness, I do not detect anywhere the leer of the sensualist. I hold, therefore, that it is not pornographic.

IV. In writing *Ulysses,* Joyce sought to make a serious experiment in a new, if not wholly novel, literary genre. He takes persons of the lower middle class living in Dublin in 1904 and seeks not only to describe what they did on a certain day early in June of that year as they went about the City bent on their usual occupations, but also to tell what many of them thought about the while.

Joyce has attempted—it seems to me, with astonishing success—to show how the screen of consciousness with its ever-shifting kaleidoscopic impressions carries, as it were on a plastic palimpsest, not only what is the focus of each man's observation of the actual things about him, but also in a penumbral zone residua of past impressions, some recent and some drawn up by association from the domain of the subconscious. He shows how each of these impressions affects the life and behavior of the character which he is describing.

What he seeks to get is not unlike the result of a double or, if that is possible, a multiple exposure on a cinema film which would give a clear foreground with a background visible but somewhat blurred and out of focus in varying degrees.

To convey by words an effect which obviously lends itself more appropriately to a graphic technique, accounts, it seems to me, for much of the obscurity which meets a reader of *Ulysses.* And it also explains another aspect of the book, which I have further to consider, namely, Joyce's sincerity and his honest effort to show exactly how the minds of his character operate.

If Joyce did not attempt to be honest in developing the technique which he has adopted in *Ulysses* the result would be psychologically misleading and thus unfaithful to his chosen technique. Such an attitude would be artistically inexcusable.

It is because Joyce has been loyal to his technique and has not funked its necessary implications, but has honestly attempted to tell fully what his characters think about, that he has been the subject of so many attacks and that his purpose has been so often misundertsood and misrepresented. For his attempt sincerely and honestly to realize his objective has required him incidentally to use certain words which are generally considered dirty words and has led at times to what many think is a too poignant preoccupation with sex in the thoughts of his characters.

The words which are criticized as dirty are old Saxon words known to almost all men and, I venture, to many women, and are such words as would be naturally and habitually used, I believe, by the types of folk whose life, physical and mental, Joyce is seeking to describe. In respect of the recurrent emergence of the theme of sex in the minds of his characters, it must always be remembered that his locale was Celtic and his season Spring.

Whether or not one enjoys such a technique as Joyce uses is a matter of taste on which disagreement or argument is futile, but to subject that technique to the standards of some other technique seems to me to be little short of absurd.

Accordingly, I hold that *Ulysses* is a sincere and honest book and I think that the criticisms of it are entirely disposed of by its rationale.

V. Furthermore, *Ulysses* is an amazing *tour de force* when one considers the success which has been in the main achieved with such a difficult objective as Joyce set for himself. As I have stated, *Ulysses* is not an easy book to read. It is brilliant and dull, intelligible and obscure by turns. In many places it seems to me to be disgusting, but although it contains, as I have mentioned above, many words usually considered dirty, I have not found anything that I consider to be dirt for dirt's sake. Each word of the book contributes like a bit of mosaic to the detail of the picture which Joyce is seeking to construct for his readers.

If one does not wish to associate with such folk as Joyce describes, that is one's own choice. In order to avoid indirect contact with them one may not wish to read *Ulysses;* that is quite understandable. But when such a real artist in words, as Joyce undoubtedly is, seeks to draw a true picture of the lower middle class in a European city, ought it to be impossible for the American public legally to see that picture?

To answer this question it is not sufficient merely to find, as I have found above, that Joyce did not write *Ulysses* with what is commonly called pornographic intent, I must endeavor to apply a more objective standard to his book in order to determine its effect in the result, irrespective of the intent with which it was written.

VI. The statute under which the libel is filed only denounces, in so far as we are here concerned, the importation into the United States from any foreign country of "any obscene book." Section 305 of the Tariff Act of 1930, Title 19 United States Code, Section 1305. It does not marshal against books the spectrum of condemnatory adjectives found, commonly, in laws dealing with matters of this kind. I am, therefore, only required to determine whether *Ulysses* is obscene within the legal definition of that word.

The meaning of the word "obscene" as legally defined by the Courts is: tending to stir the sex impulses or to lead to sexually impure and lustful thoughts. . . .

Whether a particular book would tend to excite such impulses and thoughts must be tested by the Court's opinion as to its effect on a person with average sex instincts—what the French would call *l'homme moyen sensuel*—who plays, in this branch of legal inquiry, the same role of hypothetical reagent as does the "reasonable man" in the law of torts and "the man learned in the art" on questions of invention in patent law.

The risk involved in the use of such a reagent arises from the inherent tendency of the trier of facts, however fair he may intend to be, to make his reagent too much subservient to his own idiosyncrasies. Here, I have attempted to avoid this, if possible, and to make my reagent herein more objective than he might otherwise be, by adopting the following course:

After I had made my decision in regard to the aspect of *Ulysses,* now under consideration, I checked my impressions with two friends of mine who in my opinion answered to the above stated requirement for my reagent.

These literary assessors—as I might properly describe them—were called on separately, and neither knew that I was consulting the other. They are men whose opinion on literature and on life I value most highly. They had both read *Ulysses,* and, of course, were wholly unconnected with this cause.

Without letting either of my assessors know what my decision was, I gave to each of them the legal definition of obscene and asked each whether in his opinion *Ulysses* was obscene within that definition.

I was interested to find that they both agreed with my opinion: that reading *Ulysses* in its entirety, as a book must be read on such a test as this, did not tend to excite sexual impulses or lustful thoughts but that its net effect on them was only that of a somewhat tragic and very powerful commentary on the inner lives of men and women.

It is only with the normal person that the law is concerned. Such a test as I have described, therefore, is the only proper test of obscenity in the case of a book like *Ulysses* which is a sincere and serious attempt to devise a new literary method for the observation and description of mankind.

I am quite aware that owing to some of its scenes *Ulysses* is a rather strong draught to ask some sensitive, though normal, persons to take. But my considered opinion, after long reflection, is that whilst in many places the effect of *Ulysses* on the reader undoubtedly is somewhat emetic, nowhere does it tend to be an aphrodisiac.

Ulysses may, therefore, be admitted into the United States.

3. Obscenity and the First Amendment

ROTH v. UNITED STATES
ALBERTS v. CALIFORNIA
354 US 476 (1957)

[In these cases, decided together, the Court held broadly that state and federal obscenity statutes may be enforced without a showing that the obscene material mailed or produced will create a clear and present danger of antisocial conduct, for obscene matter is not constitutionally protected. In one case the Court upheld a conviction for mailing obscene literature, in the other case for keeping for sale obscene books and publishing an obscene advertisement of them.

[In the majority opinion, however, Justice Brennan stated that, while obscenity is not within the area of constitutionally protected speech or press, it is vital that the standards for judging obscenity shall "safeguard the protection of freedom of speech and press for material which does not treat sex in a manner appealing to prurient interests." Accordingly, he rejected the *Hicklin* test as unconstitutionally restrictive of speech and press insofar as it permits judgment on the basis of the effect of isolated passages on the most susceptible persons. The publication must be judged as a whole, and only the effect on the average or normal person should be considered.

[Chief Justice Warren wrote a short concurring opinion; Justice Harlan concurred in the state case but dissented in the federal case; Justices Douglas and Black dissented in both cases.]

Mr. Justice Brennan delivered the opinion of the Court:

The constitutionality of a criminal obscenity statute is the question in each of these cases. In *Roth,* the primary constitutional question is whether the federal obscenity statute violates the provision of the First Amendment that "Congress shall make no law . . . abridging the freedom of speech, or of the press. . . ." In *Alberts,* the primary constitutional question is whether the obscenity provisions of the California Penal Code invade the freedoms of speech and press as they may be incorporated in the liberty protected from state action by the Due Process Clause of the Fourteenth Amendment.

Other constitutional questions are: whether these statutes violate due process, because too vague to support conviction for crime; whether power to punish speech and press offensive to decency and morality is in the states alone, so that the federal obscenity statute violates the Ninth and Tenth Amendments (raised in *Roth*); and whether Congress, by enacting the federal obscenity statute, under the power delegated by Art. I, § 8, cl. 7, to establish post offices and post roads, pre-empted the regulation of the subject matter (raised in *Alberts*).

Roth conducted a business in New York in the publication and sale of books, photographs and magazines. He used circulars and advertising matter to solicit sales. He was convicted by a jury in the District Court for the Southern District of New York upon 4 counts of a 26-count indictment charging him with mailing obscene circulars and advertising, and an obscene book, in violation of the federal obscenity statute. His conviction was affirmed by the Court of Appeals for the Second Circuit. We granted certiorari.

Alberts conducted a mail-order business from Los Angeles. He was convicted by the Judge of the Municipal Court of the Beverly Hills Judicial District (having waived a jury trial) under a misdemeanor complaint which charged him with lewdly keeping for sale obscene and indecent books, and with writing, composing and publishing an obscene advertisement of them, in violation of the California Penal Code. The conviction was affirmed by the Appellate Department of the Superior Court of the State of California in and for the County of Los Angeles. We noted probable jurisdiction.

The dispositive question is whether obscenity is utterance within the area of protected speech and press. Although this is the first time the question has been squarely presented to this Court, either under the First Amendment or under the Fourteenth Amendment, expressions found in numerous opinions indicate that this Court has always assumed that obscenity is not protected by the freedoms of speech and press. . . .

The guaranties of freedom of expression in effect in 10 of the 14 States which by 1792 had ratified the Constitution, gave no absolute protection for every utterance. Thirteen of the 14 States provided for the prosecution of libel, and all of those states made either blasphemy or profanity, or both, statutory crimes. As early as 1712, Massachusetts made it criminal to publish "any filthy, obscene, or profane song, pamphlet, libel or mock sermon" in imitation or mimicking of religious services. . . . Thus, profanity and obscenity were related offenses.

In light of this history, it is apparent that the unconditional phrasing of the First Amendment was not intended to protect every utterance. This phrasing did not prevent this Court from concluding that libelous utterances are not within the area of constitutionally protected speech. *Beauharnais* v. *Illinois,* 343 US 250. At the time of the adoption of the First Amendment, obscenity law was not as fully developed as libel law, but there is sufficiently contemporaneous evidence to show that obscenity, too, was outside the protection intended for speech and press.

The protection given speech and press was fashioned to assure unfettered interchange of ideas for the bringing about of political and social changes desired by the people. This objective was made explicit as early as 1774 in a letter of the Continental Congress to the inhabitants of Quebec:

> The last right we shall mention, regards the freedom of the press. The importance of this consists, besides the advancement of truth, science, morality, and arts in general, in its diffusion of liberal sentiments on the administration of Government, its ready communication of thoughts between subjects, and its consequential promotion of union among them, whereby oppressive officers are shamed or intimidated, into more honourable and just modes of conducting affairs. 1 *Journals of the Continental Congress* 108 (1774).

All ideas having even the slightest redeeming social importance—unorthodox ideas, controversial ideas, even ideas hateful to the prevailing climate of opinion—have the full protection of the guaranties, unless excludable because they encroach upon the limited area of more important interests. But implicit in the history of the First Amendment is the rejection of obscenity as utterly without redeeming social importance. This rejection for that reason is mirrored in the universal judgment that obscenity should be restrained, reflected in the international agreement of over 50 nations, in the obscenity laws of all of the 48 States, and in the 20 obscenity laws enacted by the Congress from 1842 to 1956. . . . We hold that obscenity is not within the area of constitutionally protected speech or press.

It is strenuously urged that these obscenity statutes offend the constitutional guaranties because they punish incitation to impure sexual *thoughts*, not shown to be related to any overt antisocial conduct which is or may be incited in the persons stimulated to such *thoughts*. In *Roth*, the trial judge instructed the jury: "The words 'obscene, lewd and lascivious' as used in the law, signify that form of immorality which has relation to sexual impurity and has a tendency to excite lustful *thoughts*." (Emphasis added.) In *Alberts*, the trial judge applied the test . . . namely, whether the material has "a substantial tendency to deprave or corrupt its readers by inciting lascivious *thoughts* or arousing lustful desires." (Emphasis added.) It is insisted that the constitutional guaranties are violated because convictions may be had without proof either that obscene material will perceptibly create a clear and present danger of antisocial conduct, or will probably induce its recipients to such conduct. But, in light of our holding that obscenity is not protected speech, the complete answer to this argument is in the holding of this Court in *Beauharnais* v. *Illinois, supra*. . . .

> Libelous utterances not being within the area of constitutionally protected speech, it is unnecessary, either for us or for the State courts, to consider the issues behind the phrase "clear and present danger." Certainly no one would contend that obscene speech, for example, may be punished only upon a showing of such circumstances. Libel, as we have seen, is in the same class.

However, sex and obscenity are not synonymous. Obscene material is material which deals with sex in a manner appealing to prurient interest. The portrayal of sex, e.g., in art, literature and scientific works, is not itself sufficient reason to deny material the constitutional protection of freedom of speech and press. Sex, a great and mysterious motive force in human life, has indisputably been a subject of absorbing interest to mankind through the ages; it is one of the vital problems of human interest and public concern. As to all such problems, this Court said in *Thornhill* v. *Alabama,* 310 US 88:

The freedom of speech and of the press guaranteed by the Constitution embraces at the least the liberty to discuss publicly and truthfully *all matters of public concern* without previous restraint or fear of subsequent punishment. The exigencies of the colonial period and the efforts to secure freedom from oppressive administration developed a broadened conception of these liberties as adequate to supply the public need for *information and education with respect to the significant issues of the times.* . . . Freedom of discussion, if it would fulfill its historic function in this nation, must embrace *all issues about which information is needed or appropriate to enable the members of society to cope with the exigencies of their period.* (Emphasis added.)

The fundamental freedoms of speech and press have contributed greatly to the development and well-being of our free society and are indispensable to its continued growth. Ceaseless vigilance is the watchword to prevent their erosion by Congress or by the states. The door barring federal and state intrusion into this area cannot be left ajar; it must be kept tightly closed and opened only the slightest crack necessary to prevent encroachment upon more important interests. It is therefore vital that the standards for judging obscenity safeguard the protection of freedom of speech and press for material which does not treat sex in a manner appealing to prurient interest.

The early leading standard of obscenity allowed material to be judged merely by the effect of an isolated excerpt upon particularly susceptible persons. *Regina* v. *Hicklin* [1868] L.R. 3 Q.B. 360. Some American courts adopted this standard but later decisions have rejected it and substituted this test: whether to the average person, applying contemporary community standards, the dominant theme of the material taken as a whole appeals to prurient interest. The *Hicklin* test, judging obscenity by the effect of isolated passages upon the most susceptible persons, might well encompass material legitimately treating with sex, and so it must be rejected as unconstitutionally restrictive of the freedoms of speech and press. On the other hand, the substituted standard provides safeguards adequate to withstand the charge of constitutional infirmity.

Both trial courts below sufficiently followed the proper standard. Both courts used the proper definition of obscenity. In addition, in the *Alberts* case, in ruling on a motion to dismiss, the trial judge indicated that, as the trier of facts, he was judging each item as a whole as it would affect the normal person, and in *Roth,* the trial judge instructed the jury as follows:

. . . The test is not whether it would arouse sexual desires or sexual impure thoughts in those comprising a particular segment of the community, the young, the immature or the highly prudish or would leave another segment, the scientific or highly educated or the so-called worldly-wise and sophisticated indifferent and unmoved. . . .

The test in each case is the effect of the book, picture or publication considered as a whole, not upon any particular class, but upon all those whom it is likely to reach. In other words, you determine its impact upon the average person in the community. The books, pictures and circulars must be judged as a whole, in their entire context, and you are not to consider detached or separate portions in reaching a conclusion. You judge the circulars, pictures and publications which have been put in evidence by present-day standards of the community. You may ask yourselves does it offend the common conscience of the community by present-day standards. . . .

In this case, ladies and gentlemen of the jury, you and you alone are the exclusive judges of what the common conscience of the community is, and in determining that conscience you are to consider the community as a whole, young and old, educated and uneducated, the religious and the irreligious—men, women and children.

It is argued that the statutes do not provide reasonably ascertainable standards of guilt and therefore violate the constitutional requirements of due process. *Winters* v. *New York,* 333 US 507. The federal obscenity statute makes punishable the mailing of material that is "obscene, lewd, lascivious, or filthy . . . or other publication of an indecent character." The California statute makes punishable, *inter alia,* the keeping for sale or advertising material that is "obscene or indecent." The thrust of the argument is that these words are not sufficiently precise because they do not mean the same thing to all people, all the time, everywhere.

Many decisions have recognized that these terms of obscenity statutes are not precise. This Court, however, has consistently held that lack of precision is not itself offensive to the requirements of due process. ". . . [T]he Constitution does not require impossible standards"; all that is required is that the language "conveys sufficiently definite warning as to the proscribed conduct when measured by common understanding and practices. . . . " . . . These words, applied according to the proper standard for judging obscenity, already discussed, give adequate warning of the conduct proscribed and mark ". . . boundaries sufficiently distinct for judges and juries fairly to administer the law." . . .

In summary, then, we hold that these statutes, applied according to the proper standard for judging obscenity, do not offend constitutional safeguards against convictions based upon protected material, or fail to give men in acting adequate notice of what is prohibited.

Roth's argument that the federal obscenity statute unconstitutionally encroaches upon the powers reserved by the Ninth and Tenth Amendments to the states and to the people to punish speech and press where offensive to decency and morality is hinged upon his contention that obscenity is expression not excepted from the sweep of the provision of the First Amendment that *"Congress* shall make *no law* . . . abridging the freedom of speech, or of the press. . . ." (Emphasis added.) That argument falls in light of our holding that obscenity is not expression protected by the First Amendment. We therefore hold that the federal obscenity statute punishing the use of the mails for obscene material is a proper exercise of the postal power delegated to Congress by Art. I, § 8, cl. 7. . . .

Alberts argues that because his was a mail-order business, the California statute is repugnant to Art. I, § 8, cl. 7, under which the Congress allegedly pre-empted the regulatory field by enacting the federal obscenity statute punishing the mailing or advertising by mail of obscene material. The federal statute deals only with actual mailing; it does not eliminate the power of the state to punish "keeping for sale" or "advertising" obscene material. The state statute in no way imposes a burden or interferes with the federal postal functions. . . .

The judgments are affirmed.

Mr. Justice Harlan, concurring in the result in Alberts *v.* California, *and dissenting in* Roth *v.* United States:

I regret not to be able to join the Court's opinion. I cannot do so because I find lurking beneath its disarming generalizations a number of problems which not only leave me with serious misgivings as to the future effect of today's decisions, but which also, in my view, call for different results in these two cases.

I

My basic difficulties with the Court's opinion are three-fold. First, the opinion paints with such a broad brush that I fear it may result in a loosening of the tight reins which state and federal courts should hold upon the enforcement of obscenity statutes. Second, the Court fails to discriminate between the different factors which, in my opinion, are involved in the constitutional adjudication of state and federal obscenity cases. Third, relevant distinctions between the two obscenity statutes here involved, and the Court's own definition of "obscenity," are ignored.

In final analysis, the problem presented by these cases is how far, and on what terms, the state and federal governments have power to punish individuals for disseminating books considered to be undesirable because of their nature or supposed deleterious effect upon human conduct. Proceeding from the premise that "no issue is presented in either case, concerning the obscenity of the material involved," the Court finds the "dispositive question" to be "whether obscenity is utterance within the area of protected speech and press," and then holds that "obscenity" is not so protected because it is "utterly without redeeming social importance." This sweeping formula appears to me to beg the very question before us. The Court seems to assume that "obscenity" is a peculiar *genus* of "speech and press," which is as distinct, recognizable, and classifiable as poison ivy is among other plants. On this basis the *constitutional* question before us simply becomes, as the Court says, whether "obscenity," as an abstraction, is protected by the First and Fourteenth Amendments, and the question whether a *particular* book may be suppressed becomes a mere matter of classification, of "fact," to be entrusted to a fact-finder and insulated from independent constitutional judgment. But surely the problem cannot be solved in such a generalized fashion. Every communication has an individuality and "value" of its own. The suppression of a particular writing or other tangible form of expression is, therefore, an *individual* matter, and in the nature of things every such suppression raises an individual constitutional problem in which a reviewing court must determine for *itself* whether the attacked expression is suppressible within constitutional standards. Since those standards do not readily lend themselves to generalized definitions, the constitutional problem in the last analysis becomes one of particularized judgments which appellate courts must make for themselves.

I do not think that reviewing courts can escape this responsibility by saying that the trier of the facts, be it a jury or a judge, has labeled the questioned matter as "obscene," for, if "obscenity" is to be suppressed, the question whether a particular work is of that character involves not really an issue of fact but a question of constitutional *judgment* of the most sensitive and delicate kind. Many juries might find that Joyce's *Ulysses* or Boccaccio's *Decameron* was obscene, and yet the conviction of a defendant for selling either book would raise, for me, the gravest constitutional problems, for no such verdict could convince me, without more, that these books are "utterly without redeeming social importance." In short, I do not understand how the Court can resolve the constitutional problems now before it without making its own independent judgment upon the character of the material upon which these convictions were based. I am very much afraid that the broad manner in which the Court has decided these cases will tend to obscure the peculiar responsibilities resting on state and federal courts in this field and encourage them to rely on easy labeling and jury verdicts as a substitute for facing up to the tough individual problems of constitutional judgment involved in every obscenity case.

My second reason for dissatisfaction with the Court's opinion is that the broad strides with which the Court has proceeded has led it to brush aside with perfunctory ease the vital constitutional considerations which, in my opinion, differentiate these two cases. It does not seem to matter to the Court that in one case we balance the power of a State in this field against the restrictions of the Fourteenth Amendment, and in the other the power of the Federal Government against the limitations of the First Amendment. I deal with this subject more particularly later.

Thirdly, the Court has not been bothered by the fact that the two cases involve different statutes. In California the book must have a "tendency to deprave or corrupt readers"; under the federal statute it must tend "to stir sexual impulses and lead to sexually impure thoughts." The two statutes do not seem to me to present the same problems. Yet the Court compounds confusion when it superimposes on these two statutory definitions a third, drawn from the American Law Institute's Model Penal Code, Tentative Draft No. 6: "A thing is obscene if, considered as a whole, its predominant appeal is to prurient interest." The bland assurance that this definition is the same as the ones with which we deal flies in the face of the authors' express rejection of the "deprave and corrupt" and "sexual thoughts" test:

> Obscenity [in the Tentative Draft] is defined in terms of material which appeals predominantly to prurient interest in sexual matters and which goes beyond customary freedom of expression in these matters. We reject the prevailing test of tendency to arouse lustful thoughts or desires because it is unrealistically broad for a society that plainly tolerates a great deal of erotic interest in literature, advertising, and art, and because regulation of thought or desire, unconnected with overt misbehavior, raises the most acute constitutional as well as practical difficulties. We likewise reject the common definition of obscene as that which "tends to corrupt or debase." If this means anything different from tendency to arouse lustful thought and desire, it suggests that change of character or actual misbehavior follows from contact with obscenity. Evidence of such consequences is lacking. . . . On the other hand, "appeal to prurient interest" refers to qualities of the material itself: the capacity to attract individuals eager for a forbidden look. . . .

As this passage makes clear, there is a significant distinction between the definitions used in the prosecutions before us, and the American Law Institute formula. If, therefore, the latter is the correct standard, as my Brother Brennan elsewhere intimates, then these convictions should surely be reversed. Instead, the Court merely assimilates the various tests into one indiscriminate potpourri.

I now pass to the consideration of the two cases before us.

II

I concur in the judgment of the Court in . . . *Alberts* v. *California.*

The question in this case is whether the defendant was deprived of liberty without due process of law when he was convicted for selling certain materials found by the judge to be obscene because they would have a "tendency to deprave or corrupt readers by exciting lascivious thoughts or arousing lustful desire."

In judging the constitutionality of this conviction, we should remember that our function in reviewing state judgments under the Fourteenth Amendment is a narrow one. We do not decide whether the policy of the State is wise, or whether it is based on assumptions scientifically substantiated. We can inquire only whether the state action so subverts the fundamental liberties implicit in the Due Process Clause that it cannot be sustained as a rational exercise of power. . . . The States' power to make printed words criminal is, of course, confined by the Fourteenth Amendment, but only insofar as such power is inconsistent with our concepts of "ordered liberty." *Palko* v. *Connecticut*, 302 US 319.

What, then, is the purpose of this California statute? Clearly the state legislature has made the judgment that printed words *can* "deprave or corrupt" the reader—that words can incite to anti-social or immoral action. The assumption seems to be that the distribution of certain types of literature will induce criminal or immoral sexual conduct. It is well known, of course, that the validity of this assumption is a matter of dispute among critics, sociologists, psychiatrists, and penologists. There is a large school of thought, particularly in the scientific community, which denies any causal connection between the reading of pornography and immorality, crime, or delinquency. Others disagree. Clearly it is not our function to decide this question. That function belongs to the state legislature. Nothing in the Constitution requires California to accept as truth the most advanced and sophisticated psychiatric opinion. It seems to me clear that it is not irrational, in our present state of knowledge, to consider that pornography can induce to a type of sexual conduct which a State may deem obnoxious to the moral fabric of society. In fact the very division of opinion on the subject counsels us to respect the choice made by the State.

Furthermore, even assuming that pornography cannot be deemed ever to cause, in an immediate sense, criminal sexual conduct, other interests within the proper cognizance of the States may be protected by the prohibition placed on such materials. The State can reasonably draw the inference that over a long period of time the indiscriminate dissemination of materials, the essential character of which is to degrade sex, will have an eroding effect on moral standards. And the State has a legitimate interest in protecting the privacy of the home against invasion of unsolicited obscenity.

Above all stands the realization that we deal here with an area where knowledge is small, data is insufficient, and experts are divided. Since the domain of sexual morality is pre-eminently a matter of state concern, this Court should be slow to interfere with state legislation calculated to protect that morality. It seems to me that nothing in the broad and flexible command of the Due Process Clause forbids California to prosecute one who sells books whose dominant tendency might be to "deprave or corrupt a reader." I agree with the Court, of course, that the books must be judged as a whole and in relation to the normal adult reader.

What has been said, however, does not dispose of the case. It still remains for us to decide whether the state court's determination that this material should be suppressed is consistent with the Fourteenth Amendment; and that, of course, presents a federal question as to which we, and not the state court, have the ultimate responsibility. And so, in the final analysis, I concur in the judgment because, upon an independent perusal of the material involved, and in light of the considerations discussed above, I cannot say that its suppression would so interfere with the communication of "ideas" in any proper sense of that term that it would offend the Due Process Clause. I therefore agree with the Court that appellant's conviction must be affirmed.

III

I dissent in . . . *Roth* v. *United States*.

We are faced here with the question whether the federal obscenity statute, as construed and applied in this case, violates the First Amendment to the Constitution. To me, this question is of quite a different order than one where we are dealing with state legislation under the Fourteenth Amendment. I do not think it follows that state and federal powers in this area are the same, and that just because the State may suppress a particular utterance, it is automatically permissible for the Federal Government to do the same. I agree with Mr. Justice Jackson that the historical evidence does not bear out the claim that the Fourteenth Amendment "incorporates" the First in any literal sense. . . . But laying aside any consequences which might flow from that conclusion, . . . I prefer to rest my views about this case on broader and less abstract grounds.

The Constitution differentiates between those areas of human conduct subject to the regulation of the States and those subject to the powers of the Federal Government. The substantive powers of the two governments, in many instances, are distinct. And in every case where we are called upon to balance the interest in free expression against other interests, it seems to me important that we should keep in the forefront the question of whether those other interests are state or federal. Since under our constitutional scheme the two are not necessarily equivalent, the balancing process must needs often produce different results. Whether a particular limitation on speech or press is to be upheld because it subserves a paramount governmental interest must, to a large extent, I think, depend on whether that government has, under the Constitution, a direct substantive interest, that is, the power to act, in the particular area involved.

The Federal Government has, for example, power to restrict seditious speech directed against it, because that Government certainly has the substantive authority to protect itself against revolution. . . . But in dealing with obscenity we are faced with the converse situation, for the interests which obscenity statutes purportedly protect are primarily entrusted to the care, not of the Federal Government, but of the States. Congress has no substantive power over sexual morality. Such powers as the Federal Government has in this field are but incidental to its other powers, here the postal power, and are not of the same nature as those possessed by the States, which bear direct responsibility for the protection of the local moral fabric. What Mr. Justice Jackson said in *Beauharnais* about criminal libel is equallly true of obscenity:

> The inappropriateness of a single standard for restricting State and Nation is indicated by the disparity between their functions and duties in relation to those freedoms. Criminality of defamation is predicated upon power either to protect the private right to enjoy integrity of reputation or the public right to tranquility. Neither of these are objects of federal cognizance except when necessary to the accomplishment of some delegated power. . . . When the Federal Government puts liberty of press in one scale, it has a very limited duty to personal reputation or local tranquility to weigh against it in the other. But state action affecting speech or press can and should be weighed against and reconciled with these conflicting social interests.

Not only is the federal interest in protecting the Nation against pornography attenuated, but the dangers of federal censorship in this field are far greater than anything the States may do. It has often been said that one of the great strengths of our federal system is that we have, in the forty-eight States, forty-eight experimental social laboratories. "State statutory law reflects predominantly this capacity of a legislature to introduce novel techniques of social control. The federal system has the immense advantage of providing forty-eight separate centers for such experimentation." Different States will have different attitudes toward the same work of literature. The same book which is freely read in one State might be classed as obscene in another. And it seems to me that no overwhelming danger to our freedom to experiment and to gratify our tastes in literature is likely to result from the suppression of a borderline book in one of the States, so long as there is no uniform nation-wide suppression of the book, and so long as other States are free to experiment with the same or bolder books.

Quite a different situation is presented, however, where the Federal Government imposes the ban. The danger is perhaps not great if the people of one State, through their legislature, decide that *Lady Chatterley's Lover* goes so far beyond the acceptable standards of candor that it will be deemed offensive and nonsellable, for the State next door is still free to make its own choice. At least we do not have one uniform standard. But the dangers to free thought and expression are truly great if the Federal Government imposes a blanket ban over the Nation on such a book. The prerogative of the States to differ on their ideas of morality will be destroyed, the ability of States to experiment will be stunted. The fact that the people of one State cannot read some of the works of D. H. Lawrence seems to me, if not wise or desirable, at least acceptable. But that no person in the United States should be allowed to do so seems to me to be intolerable, and violative of both the letter and spirit of the First Amendment.

I judge this case, then, in view of what I think is the attenuated federal interest in this field, in view of the very real danger of a deadening uniformity which can result from nation-wide federal censorship, and in view of the fact that the constitutionality of this conviction must be weighed against the First and not the Fourteenth Amendment. So viewed, I do not think that this conviction can be upheld. The petitioner was convicted under a statute which, under the judge's charge, makes it criminal to sell any book which "tends to stir sexual impulses and lead to sexually impure thoughts." I cannot agree that any book which "tends to stir sexual impulses and lead to sexually impure thoughts" necessarily is "utterly without redeeming social importance." Not only did this charge fail to measure up to the standards which I understand the Court to approve, but as far as I can see, much of the great literature of the world could lead to conviction under such a view of the statute. Moreover, in no event do I think that the limited federal interest in this area can extend to mere "thoughts." The Federal Government has no business, whether under the postal or commerce power, to bar the sale of books because they might lead to any kind of "thoughts."

It is no answer to say, as the Court does, that obscenity is not protected speech. The point is that this statute, as here construed, defines obscenity so widely that it encompasses matters which might very well be protected speech. I do not think that the federal statute can be constitutionally construed to reach other than what the Government has termed as "hard-core" pornography. Nor do I think the statute can fairly be read as directed only at *persons* who are engaged in the business of catering to the prurient minded, even though their wares fall short of hard-core pornography. Such a statute would raise constitutional questions of a different order. That being so, and since in my opinion the material here involved cannot be said to be hard-core pornography, I would reverse this case with instructions to dismiss the indictment.

Mr. Justice Douglas, with whom Mr. Justice Black concurs, dissenting:

When we sustain these convictions, we make the legality of a publication turn on the purity of thought which a book or tract instills in the mind of the reader. I do not think we can approve that standard and be faithful to the command of the First Amendment which by its terms is a restraint on Congress and which by the Fourteenth is a restraint on the states.

In the *Roth* case the trial judge charged the jury that the statutory words "obscene, lewd, and lascivious" describe "that form of immorality which has relation to sexual impurity and has a tendency to excite lustful thoughts." He stated that the term "filthy" in the statute pertains "to that sort of treatment of sexual matters in such a vulgar and indecent way, so that it tends to arouse a feeling of disgust and revulsion." He went on to say that the material "must be calculated to corrupt and debauch the minds and morals" of "the average person in the community," not those of any particular class. "You judge the circulars, pictures and publications which have been put in evidence by present-day standards of the community. You may ask yourselves does it offend the common conscience of the community by present-day standards."

The trial judge who, sitting without a jury, heard the *Alberts* case and the appellate court that sustained the judgment of conviction, took California's definition of "obscenity" from *People* v. *Wepplo,* 78 Cal. App. 2d Supp. 959. That case held that a book is obscene "if it has a substantial tendency to deprave or corrupt its readers by inciting lascivious thoughts or arousing lustful desire."

By these standards punishment is inflicted for thoughts provoked, not for overt acts nor anti-social conduct. This test cannot be squared with our decisions under the First Amendment. Even the ill-starred *Dennis* case conceded that speech to be punishable must have some relation to action which could be penalized by government. *Dennis* v. *United States,* 341 US 494. . . . This issue cannot be avoided by saying that obscenity is not protected by the First Amendment. The question remains, what is the constitutional test of obscenity?

The tests by which these convictions were obtained require only the arousing of sexual thoughts. Yet the arousing of sexual thoughts and desires happens every day in normal life in dozens of ways. Nearly 30 years ago a questionnaire sent to college and normal school women graduates asked what things were most stimulating sexually. Of 409 replies, 9 said "music"; 18 said "pictures"; 29 said "dancing"; 40 said "drama"; 95 said "books"; and 218 said "man." . . .

The test of obscenity the Court endorses today gives the censor free range over a vast domain. To allow the state to step in and punish mere speech or publication that the judge or the jury thinks has an *undesirable* impact on thoughts but that is not shown to be a part of unlawful action is drastically to curtail the First Amendment. . . .

If we were certain that impurity of sexual thoughts impelled to action, we would be on less dangerous ground in punishing the distributors of this sex literature. But it is by no means clear that obscene literature, as so defined, is a significant factor in influencing substantial deviations from the community standards.

There are a number of reasons for real and substantial doubts as to the soundness of that hypothesis. (1) Scientific studies of juvenile delinquency demonstrate that those who get into trouble, and are the greatest concern of the advocates of censorship, are far less inclined to read than those who do not become delinquent. The delinquents are generally the adventurous type, who have little use for reading and other non-active entertainment. Thus, even assuming that reading sometimes has an adverse effect upon moral conduct, the effect is not likely to be substantial, for those who are susceptible seldom read. (2) Sheldon and Eleanor Glueck, who are among the country's leading authorities on the treatment and causes of juvenile delinquency, have recently published the results of a ten-year study of its causes.

They exhaustively studied approximately 90 factors and influences that might lead to or explain juvenile delinquency, but the Gluecks gave no consideration to the type of reading material, if any, read by the delinquents. This is, of course, consistent with their finding that delinquents read very little. When those who know so much about the problem of deliquency among youth—the very group about whom the advocates of censorship are most concerned—conclude that what delinquents read has so little effect upon their conduct that it is not worth investigating in an exhaustive study of causes, there is good reason for serious doubt concerning the basis hypothesis on which obscenity censorship is defended. (3) The many other influences in society that stimulate sexual desire are so much more frequent in their influence, and so much more potent in their effect, that the influence of reading is likely, at most, to be relatively insignificant in the composite of forces that lead an individual into conduct deviating from the community sex standards. The Kinsey studies show the minor degree to which literature serves as a potent sexual stimulant. And the studies demonstrating that sex knowledge seldom results from reading indicates the relative unimportance of literature in sex thoughts as compared with other factors in society. Lockhart and McClure, 38 *Minn. L. Rev.* 295.

The absence of dependable information on the effect of obscene literature on human conduct should make us wary. It should put us on the side of protecting society's interest in literature, except and unless it can be said that the particular publication has an impact on action that the government can control.

As noted, the trial judge in the *Roth* case charged the jury in the alternative that the federal obscenity statute outlaws literature dealing with sex which offends "the common conscience of the community." That standard is, in my view, more inimical still to freedom of expression.

The standard of what offends "the common conscience of the community" conflicts, in my judgment, with the command of the First Amendment that "Congress shall make no law . . . abridging the freedom of speech, or of the press." Certainly that standard would not be an acceptable one if religion, economics, politics or philosophy were involved. How does it become a constitutional standard when literature treating with sex is concerned?

Any test that turns on what is offensive to the community's standards is too loose, too capricious, too destructive of freedom of expression to be squared with the First Amendment. Under that test, juries can censor, suppress, and punish what they don't like, provided the matter relates to "sexual impurity" or has a tendency "to excite lustful thoughts." This is community censorship in one of its worst forms. It creates a regime where in the battle between the literati and the Philistines, the Philistines are certain to win. If experience in this field teaches anything, it is that "censorship of obscenity has almost always been both irrational and indiscriminate." . . . The test adopted here accentuates that trend.

I assume there is nothing in the Constitution which forbids Congress from using its power over the mails to proscribe *conduct* on the grounds of good morals. No one would suggest that the First Amendment permits nudity in public places, adultery, and other phases of sexual misconduct.

I can understand (and at times even sympathize) with programs of civic groups and church groups to protect and defend the existing moral standards of the community. I can understand the motives of the Anthony Comstocks who would impose Victorian standards on the community. When speech alone is involved, I do not think that government, consistently with the First Amendment, can become the sponsor of any of these movements. I do not think that government, consistently with the First Amendment, can throw its weight behind one school or another. Government should be concerned with anti-social conduct, not with utterances. Thus if the First Amendment guarantee of freedom of speech and press is to mean anything in this field, it must allow protests even against the moral code that the standard of the day sets for the community. In other words, literature should not be suppressed merely because it offends the moral code of the censor.

The legality of a publication in this country should never be allowed to turn either on the purity of thought which it instills in the mind of the reader or on the degree to which it offends the community conscience. By either test the role of the censor is exalted, and society's values in literary freedom are sacrificed.

The Court today suggests a third standard. It defines obscene material as that "which deals with sex in a manner appealing to prurient interest." Like the standards applied by the trial judges below, that standard does not require any nexus between the literature which is prohibited and action which the legislature can regulate or prohibit. Under the First Amendment, that standard is no more valid than those which the courts below adopted.

I do not think that the problem can be resolved by the Court's statement that "obscenity is not expression protected by the First Amendment." With the exception of *Beauharnais* v. *Illinois,* none of our cases have resolved problems of free speech and free press by placing any form of expression beyond the pale of the absolute prohibition of the First Amendment. Unlike the law of libel, wrongfully relied on in *Beauharnais,* there is no special historical evidence that literature dealing with sex was intended to be treated in a special manner by those who drafted the First Amendment. In fact, the first reported court decision in this country involving obscene literature was in 1821. . . . I reject too the implication that problems of freedom of speech and of the press are to be resolved by weighing against the values of free expression, the judgment of the Court that a particular form of that expression has "no redeeming social importance." The First Amendment, its prohibition in terms absolute, was designed to preclude courts as well as legislatures from weighing the values of speech against silence. The First Amendment puts free speech in the preferred position.

Freedom of expression can be suppressed if, and to the extent that, it is so closely brigaded with illegal action as to be an inseparable part of it. . . . As a people, we cannot afford to relax that standard. For the test that suppresses a cheap tract today can suppress a literary gem tomorrow. All it need do is to incite a lascivious thought or arouse a lustful desire. The list of books that judges or juries can place in that category is endless.

I would give the broad sweep of the First Amendment full support. I have the same confidence in the ability of our people to reject noxious literature as I have in their capacity to sort out the true from the false in theology, economics, politics, or any other field.

BUTLER v. MICHIGAN
352 US 380 (1957)

[A Michigan statute made it a crime to make available for the general reading public a book "tending to incite minors to violent or depraved or immoral acts, manifestly tending to the corruption of the morals of youth." The Court unanimously held that the statute was unconstitutional. In his opinion for the Court, Justice Frankfurter pointed out that the effect of the statute was to set for the general, adult reading public a standard that reduced the adult to the level of the immature. The decision is significant for emancipating adult literature from police tests that might be appropriate for children's books. Justice Black concurred in the result.]

Mr. Justice Frankfurter delivered the opinion of the Court:

This appeal from a judgment of conviction entered by the Recorder's Court of the City of Detroit, Michigan, challenges the constitutionality of the following provision, § 343, of the Michigan Penal Code:

Any person who shall import, print, publish, sell, possess with the intent to sell, design, prepare, loan, give away, distribute or offer for sale, any book, magazine, newspaper, writing, pamphlet, ballad, printed paper, print, picture, drawing, photograph, publication or other thing, including any recordings, containing obscene, immoral, lewd or lascivious language, or obscene, immoral, lewd or lascivious prints, pictures, figures or descriptions, tending to incite minors to violent or depraved or immoral acts, manifestly tending to corruption of the morals of youth, or shall introduce into any family, school or place of education or shall buy, procure, receive or have in his possession, any such book, pamphlet, magazine, newspaper, writing, ballad, printed paper, print, picture, drawing, photograph, publication or other thing, either for the purpose of sale, exhibition, loan or circulation, or with intent to introduce the same into any family, school or place of education, shall be guilty of a misdemeanor.

Appellant was charged with its violation for selling to a police officer what the trial judge characterized as "a book containing obscene, immoral, lewd, lascivious language, or descriptions, tending to incite minors to violent or depraved or immoral acts, manifestly tending to the corruption of the morals of youth." Appellant moved to dismiss the proceeding on the claim that application of § 343 unduly restricted freedom of speech as protected by the Due Process Clause of the Fourteenth Amendment in that the statute (1) prohibited distribution of a book to the general public on the basis of the undesirable influence it may have upon youth; (2) damned a book and proscribed its sale merely because of some isolated passages that appeared objectionable when divorced from the book as a whole; and (3) failed to provide a sufficiently definite standard of guilt. After hearing the evidence, the trial judge denied the motion, and, in an oral opinion, held that ". . . the defendant is guilty because he sold a book in the City of Detroit containing this language [the passages deemed offensive], and also because the Court feels that even viewing the book as a whole, it [the objectionable language] was not necessary to the proper development of the theme of the book nor of the conflict expressed therein." Appellant was fined $100.

Pressing his federal claims, appellant applied for leave to appeal to the Supreme Court of Michigan. Although the State consented to the granting of the application "because the issues involved in this case are of great public interest, and because it appears that further clarification of the language of . . . [the statute] is necessary," leave to appeal was denied. In view of this denial, the appeal is here from the Recorder's Court of Detroit. . . .

Appellant's argument here took a wide sweep. We need not follow him. Thus, it is unnecessary to dissect the remarks of the trial judge in order to determine whether he construed § 343 to ban the distribution of books merely because certain of their passages, when viewed in isolation, were deemed objectionable. Likewise, we are free to put aside the claim that the Michigan law falls within the doctrine whereby a New York obscenity statute was found invalid in *Winters* v. *New York,* 333 US 507.

It is clear on the record that appellant was convicted because Michigan, by § 343, made it an offense for him to make available for the general reading public (and he in fact sold to a police officer) a book that the trial judge found to have a potentially deleterious influence upon youth. The State insists that, by thus quarantining the general reading public against books not too rugged for grown men and women in order to shield juvenile innocence, it is exercising its power to promote the general welfare. Surely, this is to burn the house to roast the pig. Indeed, the Solicitor General of Michigan has, with characteristic candor, advised the Court that Michigan has a statute specifically designed to protect its children against obscene matter "tending to the corruption of the morals of youth." But the appellant was not convicted for violating this statute.

We have before us legislation not reasonably restricted to the evil with which it is said to deal. The incidence of this enactment is to reduce the adult population of Michigan to reading only what is fit for children. It thereby arbitrarily curtails one of those liberties of the individual, now enshrined in the Due Process Clause of the Fourteenth Amendment, that history has attested as the indispensable conditions for the maintenance and progress of a free society. We are constrained to reverse this conviction.

Reversed.

ATTORNEY GENERAL *v.* THE BOOK NAMED "TROPIC OF CANCER"
184 N.E. 2d 328 (Mass., 1962)

[Soon after Grove Press published *Tropic of Cancer* by Henry Miller, the Attorney General of Massachusetts started a proceeding against the book. The Supreme Judicial Court of Massachusetts, in a 4-to-3 decision, held that the book was not obscene and was entitled to protection under the First Amendment.]

Cutter, Justice:

The Attorney General proceeds under G.L. c. 272, §§ 28C–28G (inserted by St. 1945, c. 278, § 1*), against a book by Henry Miller, *Tropic of Cancer* (Tropic), published by Grove Press, Inc. (Grove). Answers were filed by Grove, Miller, and

---

* Section 28C reads in part, "Whenever there is reasonable cause to believe that a book which is being . . . distributed . . . is obscene, indecent or impure, the attorney general . . . shall bring an information . . . in equity in the superior court directed against said book by name." Then follow provisions for issuing an order of notice to interested persons and for interlocutory action. Section 28E provides for an adjudication against the book, in the event of default, "if the court finds that the book is obscene, indecent or impure. . . ." Section 28F provides for a similar adjudication in the event of a contested hearing, at which "the court may receive the testimony of experts and may receive evidence as to the literary, cultural or educational character of said book and as to the manner and form of its publication, advertisement, and distribution."

other interveners, alleging that c. 272, §§ 28C through 28H, "as applied herein
. . . violate rights of the intervenor[s] guaranteed . . . by the . . . Constitution
of the United States," under the First Amendment, "as embraced in the Fourteenth
Amendment," and under the Constitution of the Commonwealth, Part I, arts. 10,
12, and 16. The case was heard by a judge of the Superior Court, who made a
report of material facts. A final decree was entered adjudging Tropic to be "obscene." The interveners appealed. The evidence is reported. The trial judge made
the findings summarized below.

"The book was first published in Paris in 1934. The first publication in the
United States was on June 24, 1961." Its distribution in Massachusetts was enjoined on July 24, 1961. "There is no connected plot. . . . It is largely a tale of
the sex experiences of an American . . . [who went to] Paris . . . in the hope of
becoming a writer, and who, except on a few occasions, lived the life of a down-
and-outer, sponging on friends. . . . It graphically describes sex episodes with
almost minute detail. It is in many respects filthy, disgusting, nauseating and offensive to good taste. As one favorable review, which was introduced in evidence, put
it, 'Now it must be granted that parts of *Tropic of Cancer* will hammer away at
some of the strongest of stomachs.' "* The book, several book reviews, and some
advertising were in evidence. "Persons who qualified as literary experts testified."
The trial judge stated that he was "irresistibly led to the conclusion that the book
is obscene, indecent and impure."

1. The opinion testimony is significant principally in that it discloses that competent critics entertain (and, in some cases, have entertained since 1934) the view that
Tropic has great literary merit despite its repulsive features. Because the only important evidence is documentary, we are in essentially the same position as the trial judge,
and "may draw our own inferences . . . from the basic facts . . . without deference to any inferences . . . drawn by the trial judge." . . .

2. The issue "is whether the" material can "reasonably and constitutionally be
found to be obscene." . . . The interveners "concede that the statute covers all
material that is obscene in the constitutional sense."

In *Roth* v. *United States,* 354 US 476, the majority rejected the test of obscenity
in *Regina* v. *Hicklin,* L.R. 3 Q.B. 360 (1868), and pointed out that later decisions
have sought to determine "whether to the average person, applying contemporary
community standards, the dominant theme of the material taken as a whole appeals
to prurient interest." Material "appealing to prurient interest" was defined as "material having a tendency to excite lustful thoughts" and was equated by him to the
definition of obscenity in A.L.I., Model Penal Code, § 207.10(2) (Tent. Draft No.
6, 1957). The *Roth* case recognized that there is constitutional protection for works
containing "ideas having even the slightest redeeming social importance—unorthodox ideas, controversial ideas, even ideas hateful to the prevailing climate of opin-

---

* The findings also state, "Of the 318 pages of the book, there are sex episodes on 85 pages,
some of which are described on two or more pages, and all of which are described with precise
physical detail and four-letter words. The author's descriptive powers are truly impressive
and he rises to great literary heights when he describes Paris. And suddenly he descends into
the filthy gutter. The literary experts testified that the book depicts a type of life in the thirties
in a portion of Paris and that it has great literary merit."

ion—[which] have the full protection of the [First Amendment] guaranties, unless excludable because they encroach upon the limited area of more important interests." The court, however, stated that "implicit in the history of the First Amendment is the rejection of obscenity as utterly without redeeming social importance" and that "obscenity is not within the area of constitutionally protected speech or press."

The *Roth* opinions discuss "obscenity" on a highly theoretical basis. Indeed the court said, "No issue is presented . . . concerning the obscenity of the material." . . . At least the Chief Justice thought that he was dealing with "the commercial exploitation of the morbid and shameful craving for materials with prurient effect."

Some principles have been established by the *Roth* case, as applied in the *Moniz* case, 338 Mass. 442. (1) Hard core, commercial pornography, "utterly without redeeming social importance" (see 354 US 476, 484–485, 77 S. Ct. 1304, 1309), is not within the protection of the First Amendment. (2) "The portrayal of sex, e.g., in art, literature and scientific works, is not itself sufficient reason to deny material the constitutional protection of freedom of speech and press." (3) "[W]hether a particular work is . . . [obscene] involves not . . . an issue of fact but a question of constitutional *judgment* of the most sensitive . . . kind." . . . (4) Material must be judged by its effect upon the *"average* person" (not susceptible persons or youths) and by whether the *"dominant theme* of the material *taken as a whole* appeals to prurient interest" (emphasis supplied). (5) "[A] work may not be adjudged obscene only because" objectionable "to many citizens as violative of accepted standards of propriety." Apart from these principles, what the Supreme Court means by "obscenity" must be determined by what it has done in other cases.

(a) In *Kingsley Books, Inc.* v. *Brown,* 354 US 436, the New York courts were sustained in enjoining distribution of fourteen booklets, "Nights of Horror," clearly hard core pornography. The Supreme Court assumed that the books were obscene and that only the issue of the constitutionality of the testing statute was before it.

(b) In four per curiam decisions (October term, 1957) the Supreme Court reversed decisions of Federal courts of appeal which had treated several different types of material as obscene. See *Times Film Corp.* v. *Chicago,* 355 US 35 (on a film dealing with the seduction of a sixteen-year-old boy by an older woman, and other "illicit sexual intimacies and acts"); *Mounce* v. *United States,* 355 US 180 (nudist publications; see *United States* v. *4200 Copies International Journal,* 134 F. Supp. 490 [E.D., Wash.]); *One, Inc.* v. *Olesen,* 355 US 371 (dealing with a post office order in respect of "One—The Homosexual Magazine"); *Sunshine Book Co.* v. *Summerfield,* 355 US 372 (nudist material). . . .

(c) In *Kingsley International Pictures Corp.* v. *Regents of Univ. of N.Y.,* 360 US 684, a New York decision was reversed which has sustained the denial of a license to show the film *Lady Chatterley's Lover.* The majority did not consider whether the film was obscene, but said, "What New York has done . . . is to prevent the exhibition of a motion picture because that picture advocates an idea— that adultery under certain circumstances may be proper behavior. . . . [The First Amendment's] guarantee is not confined to the expression of ideas that are conventional or shared by a majority. It protects advocacy of the opinion that adultery may sometimes be proper, no less than advocacy of socialism or the single tax."

(d) *Manual Enterprises, Inc.* v. *Day,* 370 US 478, dealt with a ruling of the Post Office Department barring from the mails magazines ("titled MANual, Trim, and Grecian Guild Pictorial") consisting "largely of photographs of nude, or near-nude, male models"; and containing "advertisements . . . offering nudist photographs for sale." Mr. Justice Harlan's opinion accepts findings that "(1) the magazines . . . are composed primarily, if not exclusively, for homosexuals, and have no literary, scientific or other merit; [and] (2) they would appeal to the 'prurient interest" of such sexual deviates, but would not have any interest for sexually normal individuals." The Supreme Court on a diversity of grounds reversed the Court of Appeals decision which had sustained the post office order. . . .

The New York Court of Appeals has interpreted § 1141 of the New York Penal Law dealing with obscenity, as applying "only to . . . 'hard-core pornography.' " . . .

The issue is where to draw the line between what the First Amendment protects and what is obscene in the constitutional sense. . . . The Supreme Court of the United States thus far, as Mr. Justice Harlan's opinion in the *Manual Enterprises* case indicates, has not drawn that line with precision. We, however, are confronted with litigation which should be decided under the law as it now stands, and it is our duty to draw that line as well as we can according to our best judgment of the dictates of the authoritative decisions. A majority of the court feels that we cannot properly evade that duty, even though (as the dissenting opinion points out) the *Roth* case in some respects is a "dim . . . beacon."

Referring to the three general categories of allegedly obscene material, it appears that the Supreme Court already has treated some "borderline entertainment" material and works "of serious . . . intent" as not obscene. Hard core pornography (which involves a "kind of 'pandering' " or "commerce in the obscene," see Model Penal Code, Tent. Draft No. 6, pp. 13–17) is clearly obscene. The most difficult area is that of works which some persons reasonably believe to have literary merit but which, equally reasonably, may be even more objectional to others than *Lady Chatterley's Lover.*

We think, in the light of the decisions reviewed above, that the First Amendment protects material which has value because of ideas, news, or artistic, literary, or scientific attributes. If the appeal of material (taken as a whole) to adults is not predominantly prurient, adults cannot be denied the material. When the public risks of suppressing ideas are weighed against the risks of permitting their circulation, the guaranties of the First Amendment must be given controlling effect. The dangers of subjective judgments in the matter of censorship lead to a strong presupposition against suppression. We conclude, therefore, as in effect the New York court did in the Richmond County News case, that, with respect to material designed for general circulation, only predominantly "hard core" pornography, without redeeming social significance, is obscene in the constitutional sense.

The Attorney General relies largely on earlier Massachusetts decisions. *Commonwealth* v. *Isenstadt,* 318 Mass. 543 (conviction for the sale of a book called *Strange Fruit,* under G.L. c. 272, § 28, prior to its amendment by St. 1945, c. 278, § 1). *Attorney General* v. *"God's Little Acre,"* 326 Mass. 281. These cases were decided, respectively, in 1945 and 1950, each several years before the decision in the *Roth* case. Compare *Attorney General* v. *"Forever Amber,"* 323 Mass. 302; *Attorney*

General v. *"Serenade,"* 326 Mass. 324, also decided in 1950. The later Supreme Court cases, to the extent inconsistent with our earlier decisions, are controlling, of course, on constitutional issues.

3. Whether Tropic is "obscene" in the constitutional sense thus depends upon whether the appeal (if any) of Tropic (taken as a whole) to the normal adult is predominantly prurient. It is not relevant that we think that the book at many places is repulsive, vulgar, and grossly offensive in the use of four letter words, and in the detailed and coarse statement of sexual episodes. That a serious work uses four letter words and has a grossly offensive tone does not mean that the work is not entitled to constitutional protection. Much in modern art, literature, and music is likely to seem ugly and thoroughly objectionable to those who have different standards of taste. It is not the function of judges to serve as arbiters of taste or to say that an author must regard vulgarity as unnecessary to his portrayal of particular scenes or characters or to establish particular ideas. Within broad limits each writer, attempting to be a literary artist, is entitled to determine such matters for himself, even if the result is as dull, dreary, and offensive as the writer of this opinion finds almost all of Tropic.

Competent critics assert, and we conclude, that Tropic has serious purpose* even if many will find that purpose obscure. There can be no doubt that a significant segment of the literary world has long regarded the book as of literary importance. A majority of the court are of opinion that the predominant effect and purpose of the book as a whole is not prurient. If under the *Roth* case it be a relevant consideration, a majority of the court are of opinion that Tropic is more likely to discourage than "to excite lustful thoughts." We think that the book must be accepted as a conscious effort to create a work of literary art and as having significance, which prevents treating it as hard core pornography. In reaching this conclusion, we have carefully considered all the aspects of the book upon which the dissenting justices and the trial judge have commented.

This is not the first time that Tropic has run into censorship. In *Besig* v. *United States,* 208 F.2d 142, the court sustained a customs prohibition of its importation, relying, however, upon something very close to the discredited *Hicklin* test of obscenity. A customs libel of the book by the United States, however, was recently withdrawn. See order of the United States District Court, Eastern District, New

---

* Professor Levin of Harvard testified that he thought the author's attitude was "one of disgust with sex" and "the mood . . . one of sexual revulsion. Although a good deal of sex is presented, the author, as it were, is backing away from it and even admonishing against it. It doesn't seem . . . [that] it would be a book to incite lustful thoughts. . . . [I]t . . . [seems] designed to show up western culture at a late stage by dealing with the most ignoble sides of it. . . . [I]t also has passages of some critical and philosophic purport in which the author endeavors to take a more positive view. . . . [S]ome interpreters . . . end by thinking . . . that it is a very healthy book. In my opinion, it is a somewhat morbid book, but a serious one. . . . I think the author is saying, in effect, 'All this is morbid. I am fed up with it.'" More favorable appraisals of the merits of the book were given by other qualified expert witnesses, who expressed, or referred to, opinions that the book contains substantial areas showing literary power. These witnesses included Research Professor Harry T. Moore, Southern Illinois University; Professor Mark Schorer, Chairman of the Department of English, University of California (Berkeley); Professor Morton Bloomfield, English Department, Harvard.

York, dated August 15, 1961, in evidence. Compare the discussion by Judge Murphy in *Upham* v. *Dill,* 195 F. Supp. 5, decided June 27, 1961. An unreported case (*Haiman* v. *Morris,* Illinois Superior Court, Cook County, February 21, 1962) has held the book not to be obscene. The Pennsylvania Court of Common Pleas reached a contrary conclusion in *Commonwealth* v. *Robin,* 30 US L. Week 2551 (dec. April 17, 1962).

We hold that Tropic is not "obscene" in the constitutional sense. It cannot constitutionally be held to be obscene under G.L. c. 272, §§ 28C, 28E, and 28F. We rest our decision squarely on the First Amendment, so that, if review of our decision is sought, there may be no doubt that this case has been decided solely upon the Federal issue.

4. We are not confronted with any question arising under G.L. c. 272, § 28, as amended through St. 1948, c. 328, providing for prosecution for a sale to "a person under the age of eighteen years [of] a book . . . which is obscene . . . *or manifestly tends to corrupt* the morals of youth" (emphasis supplied). See *Butler* v. *Michigan,* 352 US 380. . . .

5. The final decree is reversed. A new decree is to be entered that the book *Tropic of Cancer* is entitled to the protection of the First Amendment and cannot be held to be obscene under G.L. c. 272, §§ 28C, 28E, and 28F.

So ordered.

A BOOK NAMED "JOHN CLELAND'S MEMOIRS OF A WOMAN OF PLEASURE" *v.* ATTORNEY GENERAL OF MASSACHUSETTS 383 US 413 (1966)

[The courts of Massachusetts declared the book commonly known as *Fanny Hill* to be obscene and not entitled to constitutional protection. The Supreme Court, by 6–3 vote, reversed. But a majority could not agree on an opinion. Justice Brennan —joined by Chief Justice Warren and Justice Fortas—held that the Massachusetts court misinterpreted the social value test of *Roth* v. *United States,* 354 US 476 (1957). Justices Black and Douglas, in concurring opinions, argued that there is no constitutional power to censor speech or press. Justice Stewart concurred on the ground that *Fanny Hill* was not "hard-core pornography." Justices Clark, Harlan, and White wrote separate dissenting opinions.]

Mr. Justice Brennan announced the judgment of the Court and delivered an opinion in which The Chief Justice and Mr. Justice Fortas join:

This is an obscenity case in which *Memoirs of a Woman of Pleasure* (commonly known as *Fanny Hill*), written by John Cleland in about 1750, was adjudged obscene in a proceeding that put on trial the book itself, and not its publisher or distributor. The proceeding was a civil equity suit brought by the Attorney General of Massachusetts, pursuant to General Laws of Massachusetts, Chapter 272, §§ 28C–28H, to have the book declared obscene. Section 28C requires that the petition commencing the suit be "directed against [the] book by name" and that an order to show cause "why said book should not be judicially determined to be obscene" be published in a daily newspaper and sent by registered mail "to all persons interested in the publication." Publication of the order in this case occurred in a Boston daily newspaper, and a copy of the order was sent by registered mail to G. P. Putnam's Sons, alleged to be the publisher and copyright holder of the book.

As authorized by § 28D, G. P. Putnam's Sons intervened in the proceedings in behalf of the book, but it did not claim the right provided by that section to have the issue of obscenity tried by a jury. At the hearing before a justice of the Superior Court, which was conducted, under § 28F, "in accordance with the usual course of proceedings in equity," the court received the book in evidence and also, as allowed by the section, heard the testimony of experts and accepted other evidence, such as book reviews, in order to assess the literary, cultural, or educational character of the book. This constituted the entire evidence, as neither side availed itself of the opportunity provided by the section to introduce evidence "as to the manner and form of its publication, advertisement, and distribution." The trial justice entered a final decree, which adjudged *Memoirs* obscene and declared that the book "is not entitled to the protection of the First and Fourteenth amendments to the Constitution of the United States against action by the Attorney General or other law enforcement officers pursuant to the provisions of . . . § 28B, or otherwise."

The Massachusetts Supreme Judicial Court affirmed the decree. We noted probable jurisdiction. We reverse.

I

The term "obscene" appearing in the Massachusetts statute has been interpreted by the Supreme Judicial Court to be as expansive as the Constitution permits: the "statute covers all material that is obscene in the constitutional sense." *Attorney General* v. *A Book Named "Tropic of Cancer,"* 345 Mass. 11. Indeed, the final decree before us equates the finding that *Memoirs* is obscene within the meaning of the statute with the declaration that the book is not entitled to the protection of the First Amendment. Thus the sole question before the state courts was whether *Memoirs* satisfies the test of obscenity established in *Roth* v. *United States,* 354 US 476.

We defined obscenity in *Roth* in the following terms: "Whether to the average persons, applying contemporary community standards, the dominant theme of the material taken as a whole appeals to prurient interest." Under this definition, as elaborated in subsequent cases, three elements must coalesce: it must be established that (a) the dominant theme of the material taken as a whole appeals to a prurient interest in sex; (b) the material is patently offensive because it affronts contemporary community standards relating to the description or representation of sexual matters; and (c) the material is utterly without redeeming social value.

The Supreme Judicial Court purported to apply the *Roth* definition of obscenity and held all three criteria satisfied. We need not consider the claim that the court erred in concluding that *Memoirs* satisfied the prurient appeal and patent offensiveness criteria; for reversal is required because the court misinterpreted the social value criterion. The court applied the criterion in this passage:

It remains to consider whether the book can be said to be "utterly without social importance." We are mindful that there was expert testimony, much of which was strained, to the effect that *Memoirs* is a structural novel with literary merit; that the book displays a skill in characterization and a gift for comedy; that it plays a part in the history of the development of the English novel; and that it contains a moral, namely, that sex with love is superior to sex in a brothel. But the fact that the testimony may indicate this book has some minimal literary value does not mean it is of any social importance. We do not interpret the "social importance" test as requiring that a book which appeals to prurient interest and is patently offensive must be unqualifiedly worthless before it can be deemed obscene.

The Supreme Judicial Court erred in holding that a book need not be "unqualifiedly worthless before it can be deemed obscene." A book can not be proscribed unless it is found to be *utterly* without redeeming social value. This is so even though the book is found to possess the requisite prurient appeal and to be patently offensive. Each of the three federal constitutional criteria is to be applied independently; the social value of the book can neither be weighed against nor canceled by its prurient appeal or patent offensiveness. Hence, even on the view of the court below that *Memoirs* possessed only a modicum of social value, its judgment must be reversed as being founded on an erroneous interpretation of a federal constitutional standard.

II

It does not necessarily follow from this reversal that a determination that *Memoirs* is obscene in the constitutional sense would be improper under all circumstances. On the premise, which we have no occasion to assess, that *Memoirs* has the requisite prurient appeal and is patently offensive, but has only a minimum of social value, the circumstances of production, sale, and publicity are relevant in determining whether or not the publication and distribution of the book is constitutionally protected. Evidence that the book was commercially exploited for the sake of prurient appeal, to the exclusion of all other values, might justify the conclusion that the book was utterly without redeeming social importance. It is not that in such a setting the social value test is relaxed so as to dispense with the requirement that a book be *utterly* devoid of social value, but rather that, as we elaborate in *Ginzburg* v. *United States,* where the purveyor's sole emphasis is on the sexually provocative aspects of his publications, a court could accept his evaluation at its face value. In this proceeding, however, the courts were asked to judge the obscenity of *Memoirs* in the abstract, and the declaration of obscenity was neither aided nor limited by a specific set of circumstances of production, sale, and publicity. All possible uses of the book must therefore be considered, and the mere risk that the book might be exploited by panderers because it so pervasively treats sexual matters cannot alter the fact—given the view of the Massachusetts court attributing to *Memoirs* a modicum of literary and historical value—that the book will have redeeming social importance in the hands of those who publish or distribute it on the basis of that value.

Reversed.

Mr. Justice Clark, dissenting:

It is with regret that I write this dissenting opinion. However, the public should know of the continuous flow of pornographic material reaching this Court and the increasing problem States have in controlling it. *Memoirs of a Woman of Pleasure,* the book involved here, is typical. I have "stomached" past cases for almost ten years without much outcry. Though I am not known to be a purist—or a shrinking violet—this book is too much even for me. It is important that the Court has refused to declare it obscene and thus gives it further circulation. In order to give my remarks the proper setting I have been obliged to portray the book's contents, which gives me embarrassment. However, quotations from typical episodes would so debase our reports that I will not follow that course. . . .

III

Memoirs is nothing more than a series of minutely and vividly described sexual episodes. The book starts with Fanny Hill, a young 15-year-old girl, arriving in London to seek household work. She goes to an employment office where through happenstance she meets the mistress of a bawdy house. This takes 10 pages. The remaining 200 pages of the book detail her initiation to various sexual experiences, from a lesbian encounter with a sister prostitute to all sorts and types of sexual debauchery in bawdy houses and as the mistress of a variety of men. This is presented to the reader through an uninterrupted succession of descriptions by Fanny, either as an observer or participant, of sexual adventures so vile that one of the male expert witnesses in the case was hesitant to repeat any one of them in the courtroom. These scenes run the gamut of possible sexual experience such as lesbianism, female masturbation, homosexuality between young boys, the destruction of a maidenhead with consequent gory descriptions, the seduction of a young virgin boy, the flagellation of male by female, and vice versa, followed by fervid sexual engagement, and other abhorrent acts, including over two dozen separate bizarre descriptions of different sexual intercourses between male and female characters. In one sequence four girls in a bawdy house are required in the presence of one another to relate the lurid details of their loss of virginity and their glorification of it. This is followed the same evening by "publick trials" in which each of the four girls engages in sexual intercourse with a different man while the others witness, with Fanny giving a detailed description of the movement and reaction of each couple.

In each of the sexual scenes the exposed bodies of the participants are described in minute and individual detail. The pubic hair is often used for a background to the most vivid and precise descriptions of the response, condition, size, shape, and color of the sexual organs before, during and after orgasms. There are some short transitory passages between the various sexual episodes, but for the most part they only set the scene and identify the participants for the next orgy, or make smutty reference and comparison to past episodes.

There can be no doubt that the whole purpose of the book is to arouse the prurient interest. Likewise the repetition of sexual episode after episode and the candor with which they are described renders the book "patently offensive." These facts weigh heavily in any appraisal of the book's claims to "redeeming social importance."

Let us now turn to evidence of the book's alleged social value. While unfortunately the state offered little testimony, the defense called several experts to attest that the book has literary merit and historical value. A careful reading of testimony, however, reveals that it has no substance. For example, the first witness testified:

I think it is a work of art . . . it asks for and receives a literary response . . . presented in an orderly and organized fashion, with a fictional central character, and with a literary style. . . . I think the central character is . . . what I call an intellectual . . . someone who is exceedingly curious about life and who seeks . . . to record with accuracy the details of the external world, physical sensations, psychological responses . . . an empiricist. . . . I find that this tells me things . . . about the 18th Century that I might not otherwise know.

If a book of art is one that asks for and receives a literary response, *Memoirs* is no work of art. The sole response evoked by the book is sensual. Nor does the orderly presentation of *Memoirs* make a difference; it presents nothing but lascivious scenes organized solely to arouse prurient interest and produce sustained erotic tension. Certainly the book's baroque style cannot vitiate the determination of obscenity. From a legal standpoint, we must remember that obscenity is no less obscene though it be expressed in "elaborate language." Indeed, the more meticulous its presentation, the more it appeals to the prurient interest. To say that Fanny is an "intellectual" is an insult to those who travel under that tag. She was nothing but a harlot—a sensualist—exploiting her sexual attractions which she sold for fun, for money, for lodging and keep, for an inheritance, and finally for a husband. If she was curious about life, her curiosity extended only to the pursuit of sexual delight wherever she found it. The book describes nothing in the "external world" except bawdy houses and debaucheries. As an empiricist, Fanny confines her observations and "experiments" to sex, with primary attention to depraved, lewd, and deviant practices.

Other experts produced by the defense testified that the book emphasizes the profound "idea that a sensual passion is only truly experienced when it is associated with the emotion of love" and that the sexual relationship "can be wholesome, healthy, experience itself," whereas in certain modern novels "the relationship between the sexes is seen as another manifestation of modern decadence, insterility or perversion." In my view this proves nothing as to social value. The state court properly gave such testimony no probative weight. A review offered by the defense noted that "where 'pornography' does not brutalize, it idealizes. The book is, in this sense, an erotic fantasy—and a male fantasy, at that, put into the mind of a woman. The male organ is phenomenal to the point of absurdity." Finally, it saw the book as "a minor fantasy, deluding as a guide to conduct, but respectful of our delight in the body . . . an interesting footnote in the history of the English novel." These unrelated assertions reveal to me nothing whatever of literary, historical, or social value. Another review called the book "a great novel . . . one which turns its conventions upside down. . . ." Admittedly Cleland did not attempt "high art" because he was writing "an erotic novel. He can skip the elevation and get on with the erections." Fanny's "downfall" is seen as "one long delightful swoon into the depths of pleasurable sensation." Rather than indicating social value in the book, this evidence reveals just the contrary. Another item offered by the defense described *Memoirs* as being "widely accredited as the first deliberately dirty novel in English." However, the reviewer found Fanny to be "no common harlot. Her 'Memoirs' combine literary grace with a disarming enthusiasm for an activity which is, after all, only human. What is more, she never uses a dirty word." The short answer to such "expertise" is that none of these so-called attributes have any value to society. On the contrary, they accentuate the prurient appeal.

Another expert described the book as having "detectable literary merit" since it reflects "an effort to interpret a rather complex character . . . going through a number of very different adventures." To illustrate his assertion that the "writing is very skillfully done" this expert pointed to the description of a whore, "Phoebe, who is 'red faced, fat and in her early 50's, who waddles into a room.' She doesn't walk in, she waddles in." Given this standard for "skillful writing," it is not surprising that he found the book to have merit.

The remaining experts testified in the same manner, claiming the book to be a "record of the historical, psychological, and social events of the period." One has but to read the history of the 18th century to disprove this assertion. The story depicts nothing besides the brothels that are present in metropolitan cities in every period of history. One expert noticed "in this book a tendency away from nakedness during the sexual act which I find an interesting sort of sociological observation" on tastes different from contemporary ones. As additional proof, he marvels that Fanny "refers constantly to the male sexual organ as an engine . . . which is pulling you away from the way these events would be described in the 19th or 20th century." How this adds social value to the book is beyond my comprehension. It only indicates the lengths to which these experts go in their effort to give the book some semblance of value. For example, the ubiquitous descriptions of sexual acts are excused as being necessary in tracing the "moral progress" of the heroine, and the giving of a silver watch to a servant is found to be "an odd and interesting custom that I would like to know more about." This only points up the bankruptcy of *Memoirs* in both purpose and content, adequately justifying the trial court's finding that it had absolutely no social value.

It is, of course, the duty of the judge or the jury to determine the question of obscenity, viewing the book by contemporary community standards. It can accept the appraisal of experts or discount their testimony in the light of the material itself or other relevant testimony. So-called "literary obscenity," *i. e.*, the use of erotic fantasies of the hard-core type clothed in an engaging literary style has no constitutional protection. If a book deals solely with erotic material in a manner calculated to appeal to the prurient interest, it matters not that it may be expressed in beautiful prose. There are obviously dynamic connections between art and sex—the emotional, intellectual, and physical— but where the former is used solely to promote prurient appeal, it cannot claim constitutional immunity. Cleland uses this technique to promote the prurient appeal of *Memoirs*. It is true that Fanny's perverse experiences finally bring from her the observation that "the height of [sexual] enjoyment cannot be achieved until true affection prepares the bed of passion." But this merely emphasizes that sex, wherever and however found, remains the sole theme of *Memoirs*. In my view, the book's repeated and unrelieved appeals to the prurient interest of the average person leave it utterly without redeeming social importance.

IV

In his separate concurrence, my Brother Douglas asserts there is no proof that obscenity produces antisocial conduct. I had thought that this question was foreclosed by the determination in *Roth* that obscenity was not protected by the First Amendment. I find it necessary to comment upon Brother Douglas' views, however, because of the new requirement engrafted upon *Roth* by Brother Brennan, *i. e.*, that material which "appeals to the prurient interest" and which is "patently offensive" may still not be suppressed unless it is "utterly without redeeming social value." The question of antisocial effect thus becomes relevant to the more limited question of social value. Brother Brennan indicates that the social importance criteria encompasses only such things as the artistic, literary, and historical qualities of the material. But the phrasing of the "utterly without redeeming social value" test suggests that other evidence must be considered. To say that social value may "redeem" implies that courts must balance alleged esthetic merit against the harmful consequences that may flow from pornography. Whatever the scope of the social value criterion—which need not be defined with precision here—it at least anticipates that the trier of fact weigh evidence of the material's influence in causing deviant or criminal conduct, particularly sex crimes, as well as its effect upon the mental, moral, and physical health of the average person. Brother Douglas' view as to the lack of proof in this area is not so firmly held among behavioral scientists as he would lead us to believe. For this reason, I should mention that there is a division of thought on the correlation between obscenity and socially deleterious behavior.

Psychological and physiological studies clearly indicate that many persons become sexually aroused from reading obscene material. While erotic stimulation caused by pornography may be legally insignificant in itself, there are medical experts who believe that such stimulation frequently manifests itself in criminal sexual behavior or other anti-social conduct. For example, Dr. George W. Henry of Cornell University has expressed the opinion that obscenity, with its exaggerated and morbid emphasis on sex, particularly abnormal and perverted practices, and its unrealistic presentation of sexual behavior and attitudes, may induce anti-social conduct by the average person. A number of sociologists think that this material may have adverse effects upon individual mental health, with potentially disruptive consequences for the community.

In addition, there is persuasive evidence from criminologists and police officials. Inspector Herbert Case of the Detroit Police Department contends that sex murder cases are invariably tied to some form of obscene literature. And the Director of the Federal Bureau of Investigation, J. Edgar Hoover, has repeatedly emphasized that pornography is associated with an overwhelmingly large number of sex crimes. Again, while the correlation between possession of obscenity and deviant behavior has not been conclusively established, the files of our law enforcement agencies contain many reports of persons who patterned their criminal conduct after behavior depicted in obscene material.

The clergy are also outspoken in their belief that pornography encourages violence, degeneracy and sexual misconduct. In a speech reported by the *New York Journal-American*, August 7, 1964, Cardinal Spellman particularly stressed the direct influence obscenity has on immature persons. These and related views have been confirmed by practical experience. After years of service with the West London Mission, Rev. Donald Soper found that pornography was a primary cause of prostitution. . . .

Congress and the legislatures of every State have enacted measures to restrict the distribution of erotic and pornographic material, justifying these controls by reference to evidence that anti-social behavior may result in part from reading obscenity. Likewise, upon another trial, the parties may offer this sort of evidence along with other "social value" characteristics that they attribute to the book.

But this is not all that Massachusetts courts might consider. I believe it can be established that the book "was commercially exploited for the sake of prurient appeal, to the exclusion of all other values" and should therefore be declared obscene under the test of commercial exploitation announced today in *Ginzburg* and *Mishkin*.

As I have stated, my study of *Memoirs* leads me to think that it has no conceivable "social importance." The author's obsession with sex, his minute description of phalli, and his repetitive accounts of bawdy sexual experiences and deviant sexual behavior indicate the book was designed solely to appeal to prurient interests. In addition, the record before the Court contains extrinsic evidence tending to show that the publisher was fully aware that the book attracted readers desirous of vicarious sexual pleasure, and sought to profit solely from its prurient appeal. The publisher's "Introduction" recites that Cleland, a "never-do-well bohemian," wrote the book in 1794 to make a quick 20 guineas. Thereafter, various publications of the book, often "embellished with fresh inflammatory details" and "highly exaggerated illustrations," appeared in "surreptitious circulation." Indeed, the cover of *Memoirs* tempts the reader with the announcement that the sale of the book has finally been permitted "after 214 years of suppression." Although written in a sophisticated tone, the "Introduction" repeatedly informs the reader that he may expect graphic descriptions of genitals and sexual exploits. For instance, it states:

> Here and there, Cleland's descriptions of lovemaking are marred by what perhaps could be best described as his adherence to the "longitudinal fallacy"—the formidable bodily equipment of his most accomplished lovers is apt to be described with quite unnecessary relish. . . .

Many other passages in the "Introduction" similarly reflect the publisher's "own evaluation" of the book's nature. The excerpt printed on the jacket of the hardcover edition is typical:

> *Memoirs of a Woman of Pleasure* is the product of a luxurious and licentious, but not a commercially degraded, era. . . . For all its abounding improprieties, his priapic novel is not a vulgar book. It treats of pleasure as the aim and end of existence, and of sexual satisfaction as the epitome of pleasure, but does so in a style that despite its inflammatory subject, never stoops to a gross or unbecoming word.

Cleland apparently wrote only one other book, a sequel called *Memoirs of a Coxcomb,* published by Lancer Books, Inc. The "Introduction" to that book labels *Memoirs of a Woman of Pleasure* as "the most sensational piece of erotica in English literature." I dare say that this fact alone explains why G. P. Putnam's Sons published this obscenity —preying upon prurient and carnal proclivities for its own pecuniary advantage. I would affirm the judgment.

Mr. Justice Harlan, dissenting:

The central development that emerges from the aftermath of *Roth* v. *United States,* 354 US 476, is that no stable approach to the obscenity problem has yet been devised by this Court. Two Justices believe that the First and Fourteenth Amendments absolutely protect obscene and nonobscene material alike. Another Justice believes that neither the States nor the Federal Government may suppress any material save for "hard-core pornography." *Roth* in 1957 stressed prurience and utter lack of redeeming social importance; as *Roth* has been expounded in this case, in *Ginzburg* v. *United States,* and in *Mishkin* v. *New York,* it has undergone significant transformation. The concept of "pandering," emphasized by the separate opinion of The Chief Justice in *Roth,* now emerges as an uncertain gloss or interpretive aid, and the further requisite of "patent offensiveness" has been made explicit as a result of intervening decisions. Given this tangled state of affairs. I feel free to adhere to the principles first set forth in my separate opinion in *Roth,* which I continue to believe represent the soundest constitutional solution to this intractable problem.

My premise is that in the area of obscenity the Constitution does not bind the States and the Federal Government in precisely the same fashion. This approach is plainly consistent with the language of the First and Fourteenth Amendments and, in my opinion, more responsive to the proper functioning of a federal system of government in this area. . . . I believe it is also consistent with past decisions of this Court. Although some 40 years have passed since the Court first indicated that the Fourteenth Amendment protects "free speech," see *Gitlow* v. *New York,* 268 US 652; *Fiske* v. *Kansas,* 274 US 380, the decisions have never declared that every utterance the Federal Government may not reach or every regulatory scheme it may not enact is also beyond the power of the State. The very criteria used in opinions to delimit the protection of free speech—the gravity of the evil being regulated, see *Schnieder* v. *State,* 308 US 147; how "clear and present" is the danger, *Schenck* v. *United States,* 249 US 47, (Holmes, J.); the magnitude of "such invasion of free speech as is necessary to avoid the danger," *United States* v. *Dennis,* 183 F.2d 201 (L. Hand, J.)—may and do depend on the particular context in which power is exercised. When, for example, the Court in *Beauharnais* v. *Illinois,* 343 US 250, upheld a criminal group-libel law because of the "social interest in order and morality," it was acknowledging the responsibility and capacity of the States in such public-welfare matters and not committing itself to uphold any similar federal statute applying to such communications as Congress might otherwise regulate under the commerce power. See also *Kovacs* v. *Cooper,* 336 US 77.

Federal suppression of allegedly obscene matter should, in my view, be constitutionally limited to that often described as "hard-core pornography." To be sure, that rubric is not a self-executing standard, but it does describe something that most judges and others will "know . . . when [they] see it" (Stewart, J., in *Jacobellis* v. *Ohio,* 378 US 184) and that leaves the smallest room for disagreement between those of varying tastes. To me it is plain, for instance, that *Fanny Hill* does not fall within this class and could not be barred from the federal mails. If further articulation is meaningful, I would characterize as "hard-core" that prurient material that is patently offensive or whose indecency is self-demonstrating and I would describe it substantially as does Mr. Justice Stewart's opinion in *Ginzburg.* The Federal Government may be conceded a limited interest in excluding from the mails such gross pornography, almost universally condemned in this country. But I believe the dangers of national censorship and the existence of primary responsibility at the state level amply justify drawing the line at this point.

State obscenity laws present problems of quite a different order. The varying conditions across the country, the range of views on the need and reasons for curbing obscenity, and the traditions of local self-government in matters of public welfare all favor a far more flexible attitude in defining the bounds for the States. From my standpoint, the Fourteenth Amendment requires of a State only that it apply criteria rationally related to the accepted notion of obscenity and that it reach results not wholly out of step with current American standards. As to criteria, it should be adequate if the court or jury considers such elements as offensiveness, pruriency, social value, and the like. The latitude which I believe the States deserve cautions against any federally imposed formula listing the exclusive ingredients of obscenity and fixing their proportions. This approach concededly lacks precision, but imprecision is characteristic of mediating constitutional standards; voluntariness of a confession, clear and present danger, and probable cause are only the most ready illustrations. In time and with more litigated examples, predictability increases, but there is no shortcut to satisfactory solutions in this field, and there is no advantage in supposing otherwise.

I believe the tests set out in the prevailing opinion, judged by their application in this case, offer only an illusion of certainty and risk confusion and prejudice. The opinion declares that a book cannot be banned unless it is "utterly without redeeming social value." To establish social value in the present case, a number of acknowledged experts in the field of literature testified that *Fanny Hill* held a respectable place in serious writing, and unless such largely uncontradicted testimony is accepted as decisive it is very hard to see that the "utterly without redeeming social value" test has any meaning at all. Yet the prevailing opinion, while denying that social value may be "weighed against" or "canceled by" prurience or offensiveness, terminates this case unwilling to give a conclusive decision on the status of *Fanny Hill* under the Constitution. Apparently, the Court believes that the social value of the book may be negated if proof of pandering is present. Using this inherently vague "pandering" notion to offset "social value" wipes out any certainty the latter term might be given by reliance on experts, and admits into the case highly prejudicial evidence without appropriate restrictions. . . . I think it more satisfactory to acknowledge that on this record the book has been shown to have some quantum of social value, that it may at the same time be deemed offensive and salacious, and that the State's decision to weigh these elements and to ban this particular work does not exceed constitutional limits.

A final aspect of the obscenity problem is the role this Court is to play in administering its standards, a matter that engendered justified concern at the oral argument of the cases now decided. Short of saying that no material relating to sex may be banned, or that all of it may be, I do not see how this Court can escape the task of reviewing obscenity decisions on a case-by-case basis. The views of literary or other experts could be made controlling, but those experts had their say in *Fanny Hill* and apparently the majority is no more willing than I to say that Massachusetts must abide by their verdict. Yet I venture to say that the Court's burden of decision would be ameliorated under the constitutional principles that I have advocated. "Hard-core pornography" for judging federal cases is one of the more tangible concepts in the field. As to the States, the due latitude my approach would leave them ensures that only the unusual case would require plenary review and correction by this Court.

There is plenty of room, I know, for disagreement in this area of constitutional law. Some will think that what I propose may encourage States to go too far in this field. Others will consider that the Court's present course unduly restricts state experimentation with the still elusive problem of obscenity. For myself, I believe it is the part of wisdom for those of us who happen currently to possess the "final word" to leave room for such experimentation, which indeed is the underlying genius of our federal system.

On the premises set forth in this opinion, supplementing what I have earlier said in my opinions in *Roth, Manual Enterprises, Inc.* v. *Day,* 370 US 478, and *Jacobellis* v. *Ohio,* 378 US 203, I would affirm the judgment of the Massachusetts Supreme Judicial Court.

GINZBURG *v.* UNITED STATES
383 US 463 (1966)

[Ralph Ginzburg and several corporations which he controlled used the mail to distribute a magazine called *Eros,* of which only four quarterly issues were published, a bi-weekly newsletter, and *The Housewife's Handbook on Promiscuity.* A federal district court judge sitting without a jury convicted defendants on charges of having violated the federal obscenity statute. By 5–4 vote, the Supreme Court affirmed.

[In his opinion for the majority, Justice Brennan held that even if the publications were not obscene in the abstract, the circumstances showing the way in which the publications were advertised and otherwise exploited made it appear that the defendants engaged in the sordid business of pandering, i.e., the business of purveying publications openly advertised to appeal to the erotic interest of customers. Justices Black, Douglas, Harlan, and Stewart each wrote a dissenting opinion.

[The Case was decided on the same day with the *Fanny Hill* case.]

Mr. Justice Brennan delivered the opinion of the Court:

A judge sitting without a jury in the District Court for the Eastern District of Pennsylvania convicted petitioner Ginzburg and three corporations controlled by him upon all 28 counts of an indictment charging violation of the federal obscenity statute, 18 U.S.C. § 1461.* Each count alleged that a resident of the Eastern District received mailed matter, either one of three publications challenged as obscene, or advertising telling how and where the publications might be obtained. The Court of Appeals for the Third Circuit affirmed. We granted certiorari. We affirm. Since petitioners do not argue that the trial judge misconceived or failed to apply the standards we first enunciated in *Roth* v. *United States,* 354 US 476, the only serious question is whether those standards were correctly applied.

In the cases in which this Court has decided obscenity questions since *Roth,* it has regarded the materials as sufficient in themselves for the determination of the question. In the present case, however, the prosecution charged the offense in the context of the circumstances of production, sale, and publicity and assumed that, standing alone, the publications themselves might not be obscene. We agree that the question of obscenity may include consideration of the setting in which the publications were presented as an aid to determining the question of obscenity, and assume without deciding that the prosecution could not have succeeded otherwise. As in *Mishkin* v. *New York, post,* and as did the courts below, we view the publications against a background of commercial exploitation of erotica solely for the sake of their prurient appeal. The record in that regard amply supports the decision of the trial judge that the mailing of all three publications offended the statute.

The three publications were *Eros,* a hard-cover magazine of expensive format; *Liaison,* a bi-weekly newsletter; and *The Housewife's Handbook on Selective Promiscuity* (hereinafter the *Handbook*), a short book. The issue of *Eros* specified in the indictment, Vol. 1, No. 4, contains 15 articles and photo-essays on the subject of love, sex, and sexual relations. The specified issue of *Liaison,* Vol. 1, No. 1, contains a prefatory "Letter from the Editors" announcing its dedication to "keeping sex an art and preventing it from becoming a science." The remainder of the issue consists of digests of two articles concerning sex and sexual relations which had earlier appeared in professional journals and a report of an interview with a psycho-

---

* The federal obscenity statute, 18 U.S.C. § 1461, provides in pertinent part:

"Every obscene, lewd, lascivious, indecent, filthy or vile article, matter, thing, device, or substance; and. . . .

"Every written or printed card, letter, circular, book, pamphlet, advertisement, or notice of any kind giving information, directly or indirectly, where, or how, or from whom, or by what means of such mentioned mattters . . . may be obtained. . . .

"Is declared to be nonmailable matter and shall not be conveyed in the mails or delivered from any post office or by any letter carrier.

"Whoever knowingly uses the mails for the mailing, carriage in the mails, or delivery of anything declared by this section to be nonmailable . . . shall be fined not more than $5000 or imprisoned not more than five years, or both, for the first such offense. . . ."

therapist who favors the broadest license in sexual relationships. As the trial judge noted, "[w]hile the treatment is largely superficial, it is presented entirely without restraint of any kind. According to defendants' own expert, it is entirely without literary merit." The *Handbook* purports to be a sexual autobiography detailing with complete candor the author's sexual experiences from age 3 to age 36. The text includes, and prefatory and concluding sections of the book elaborate, her views on such subjects as sex education of children, laws regulating private consensual adult sexual practices, and the equality of women in sexual relationships. It was claimed at trial that women would find the book valuable, for example as a marriage manual or as an aid to the sex education of their children.

Besides testimony as to the merit of the material, there was abundant evidence to show that each of the accused publications was originated or sold as stock in trade of the sordid business of pandering—"the business of purveying textual or graphic matter openly advertised to appeal to the erotic interest of their customers." *Eros* early sought mailing privilege from the postmasters of Intercourse and Blue Ball, Pennsylvania. The trial court found the obvious, that these hamlets were chosen only for the value their names would have in furthering petitioners' efforts to sell their publications on the basis of salacious appeal; the facilities of the post offices were inadequate to handle the anticipated volume of mail, and the privileges were denied. Mailing privileges were then obtained from the postmaster of Middlesex, New Jersey. *Eros* and *Liaison* thereafter mailed several million circulars soliciting subscriptions from that post office; over 5,500 copies of the *Handbook* were mailed.

The "leer of the sensualist" also permeates the advertising for the three publications. The circulars sent for *Eros* and *Liaison* stressed the sexual candor of the respective publications, and openly boasted that the publishers would take full advantage of what they regarded an unrestricted license allowed by law in the expression of sex and sexual matters. The advertising for the *Handbook,* apparently mailed from New York, consisted almost entirely of a reproduction of the introduction of the book, written by one Dr. Albert Ellis. Although he alludes to the book's informational value and its putative therapeutic usefulness, his remarks are preoccupied with the book's sexual imagery. The solicitation was indiscriminate, not limited to those, such as physicians or psychiatrists, who might independently discern the book's therapeutic worth. Inserted in each advertisement was a slip labeled "GUARANTEE" and reading, "Documentary Books, Inc. unconditionally guarantees full refund of the price of THE HOUSEWIFE'S HANDBOOK ON SELECTIVE PROMISCUITY if the book fails to reach you because of U.S. Post Office censorship interference." Similar slips appeared in the advertising for *Eros* and *Liaison;* they highlighted the gloss petitioners put on the publications, eliminating any doubt what the purchaser was being asked to buy.

This evidence, in our view, was relevant in determining the ultimate question of "obscenity" and, in the context of this record, serves to resolve all ambiguity and doubt. The deliberate representation of petitioners' publications as erotically arousing, for example, stimulated the reader to accept them as prurient; he looks for titillation, not for saving intellectual content. Similarly, such representation would tend to force public confrontation with the potentially offensive aspects of the work; the brazenness of such an appeal heightens the offensiveness of the publications to those who are offended by such material. And the circumstances of presentation and dissemination of material are equally relevant to determining whether social importance claimed for material in the courtroom was, in the circumstances, pretense or reality—whether it was the basis upon which it was traded in the marketplace or a spurious claim for litigation purposes. Where the purveyor's sole emphasis is on the sexually provocative aspects of his publications, that fact may be decisive in the determination of obscenity. Certainly in a prosecution which, as here, does not necessarily imply suppression of the materials involved, the fact that they originate or are used as a subject of pandering is relevant to the application of the *Roth* test.

A proposition argued as to *Eros,* for example, is that the trial judge improperly found the magazine to be obscene as a whole, since he concluded that only four of the 15 articles predominantly appealed to prurient interest and substantially exceeded community standards of candor, while the other articles were admittedly nonoffensive. But the trial judge found that "[t]he deliberate and studied arrangement of *Eros* is editorialized for the purpose of appealing predominantly to prurient interest and to insulate through the inclusion of nonoffensive material." However erroneous such a conclusion might be if unsupported by the evidence of pandering, the record here supports it. *Eros* was created, represented and sold solely as a claimed instrument of the sexual stimulation it would bring. Like the other publications, its pervasive treatment of sex and sexual matters rendered it available to exploitation by those who would make a business of pandering to "the widespread weakness for titillation by pornography." Petitioners' own expert agreed, correctly we think, that "[i]f the object [of a work] is material gain for the creator through an appeal to the sexual curiosity and appetite," the work is pornographic. In other words, by animating sensual detail to give the publication a salacious cast, petitioners reinforced what is conceded by the Government to be an otherwise debatable conclusion.

A similar analysis applies to the judgment regarding the *Handbook.* The bulk of the proofs directed to social importance concerned this publication. Before selling publication rights to petitioners, its author had printed it privately; she sent circulars to persons whose names appeared on membership lists of medical and psychiatric associations, asserting its value as an adjunct in therapy. Over 12,000 sales resulted from this solicitation, and a number of witnesses testified that they found the work useful in their professional practice. The Government does not seriously contest the claim that the book has worth in such a controlled, or even neutral, environment. Petitioners, however, did not sell the book to such a limited audience, or focus their claims for it on its supposed therapeutic or educational value; rather, they deliberately emphasized the sexually provocative aspects of the work, in order to catch the salaciously disposed. They proclaimed its obscenity; and we cannot conclude that the court below erred in taking their own evaluation at its face value and declaring the book as a whole obscene despite the other evidence.

The decision in *Rebhuhn* v. *United States,* 109 F.2d 512, is persuasive authority for our conclusion. That was a prosecution under the predecessor to § 1461, brought in the context of pandering of publications assumed useful to scholars and members of learned professions. The books involved were written by authors proved in many instances to have been men of scientific standing, as anthropologists or psychiatrists. The Court of Appeals for the Second Circuit therefore assumed that many of the books were entitled to the protection of the First Amendment, and "could lawfully have passed through the mails, if directed to those who would be likely to use them for the purposes for which they were written. . . ." But the evidence, as here, was that the defendants had not disseminated them for their "proper use, but . . . woefully misused them, and it was that misuse which constituted the gravamen of the crime." Speaking for the Court in affirming the conviction, Judge Learned Hand said:

. . . [T]he works themselves had a place, though a limited one, in anthropology and in psychotherapy. They might also have been lawfully sold to laymen who wished seriously to study the sexual practices of savage or barbarous peoples, or sexual aberrations; in other words most of them were not obscene per se. In several decisions we have held that the statute does not in all circumstances forbid the dissemination of such publications. . . . However, in the case at bar, the prosecution succeeded . . . when it showed that the defendants had indiscriminately flooded the mails with advertisements, plainly designed merely to catch the prurient, though under the guise of distributing works of scientific or literary merit. We do not mean that the distributor of such works is charged with a duty to insure that they shall reach only proper hands, nor need we say what care he must use, for these defendants exceeded any possible limit; the circulars were no more than appeals to the salaciously disposed, and no [fact finder] could have failed to pierce the fragile screen, set up to cover that purpose.

We perceive no threat to First Amendment guarantees in thus holding that in close cases evidence of pandering may be probative with respect to the nature of the material in question and thus satisfy the *Roth* test. No weight is ascribed to the fact that petitioners have profited from the sale of publications which we have assumed but do not hold cannot themselves be adjudged obscene in the abstract; to sanction consideration of this fact might indeed induce self-censorship, and offend the frequently stated principle that commercial activity, in itself, is no justification for narrowing the protection of expression secured by the First Amendment. Rather, the fact that each of these publications was created or exploited entirely on the basis of its appeal to prurient interests strengthens the conclusion that the transactions here were sales of illicit merchandise, not sales of constitutionally protected matter. A conviction for mailing obscene publications, but explained in part by the presence of this element, does not necessarily suppress the materials in question, nor chill their proper distribution for a proper use. Nor should it inhibit the enterprise of others seeking through serious endeavor to advance human knowledge or understanding in science, literature, or art. All that will have been determined is that questionable publications are obscene in a context which brands them as obscene as that term is defined in *Roth*—a use inconsistent with any claim to the shelter of the First Amendment. "The nature of the materials is, of course, relevant as an attribute of the defendant's conduct, but the materials are thus placed in context from which they draw color and character. A wholly different result might be reached in a different setting," *Roth* v. *United States,* 354 US, at 495 (Warren, C. J., concurring).

It is important to stress that this analysis simply elaborate the test by which the obscenity vel non of the material must be judged. Where an exploitation of interests in titillation by pornography is shown with respect to material lending itself to such exploitation through pervasive treatment or description of sexual matters, such evidence may support the determination that the material is obscene even though in other contexts the material would escape such condemnation. . . .

Mr. Justice Stewart, dissenting:

The petitioner has been sentenced to five years in prison for sending through the mail copies of a magazine, a pamphlet, and a book. There was testimony at his trial that these publications possess artistic and social merit. Personally, I have a hard time discerning any. Most of the material strikes me as both vulgar and unedifying. But if the First Amendment means anything, it means that a man cannot be sent to prison merely for distributing publications which offend a judge's esthetic sensibilities, mine or any other's.

Censorship reflects a society's lack of confidence in itself. It is a hallmark of an authoritarian regime. Long ago those who wrote our First Amendment charted a different course. They believed a society can be truly strong only when it is truly free. In the realm of expression they put their faith, for better or for worse, in the enlightened choice of the people, free from the interference of a policeman's intrusive thumb or a judge's heavy hand. So it is that the Constitution protects coarse expression as well as refined, and vulgarity no less than elegance. A book worthless to me may convey something of value to my neighbor. In the free society to which our Constitution has committed us, it is for each to choose for himself.

Because such is the mandate of our Constitution, there is room for only the most restricted view of this Court's decision in *Roth* v. *United States*. In that case the Court held that "obscenity is not within the area of constitutionally protected speech or press." The Court there characterized obscenity as that which is "utterly without redeeming social importance," "deals with sex in a manner appealing to prurient interest," and "goes substantially beyond customary limits of candor in description or representation of such matters." In *Manual Enterprises* v. *Day,* 370 US 478, I joined Mr. Justice Harlan's opinion adding "patent indecency" as a further essential element of that which is not constitutionally protected.

There does exist a distinct and easily identifiable class of material in which all of these elements coalesce. It is that, and that alone, which I think government may constitutionally suppress, whether by criminal or civil sanctions. I have referred to such material before as hard-core pornography, without trying further to define it. *Jacobellis* v. *Ohio,* 378 US 184, at 197 (concurring opinion). In order to prevent any possible misunderstanding, I have set out in the margin a description, borrowed from the Solicitor General's brief, of the kind of thing to which I have reference. . . .*

Although arguments can be made to the contrary, I accept the proposition that the general dissemination of matter of this description may be suppressed under valid laws.

---

* ". . . Such materials include photographs, both still and motion picture, with no pretense of artistic value, graphically depicting acts of sexual intercourse, including various acts of sodomy and sadism, and sometimes involving several participants in scenes of orgy-like character. They also include strips of drawings in comic-book format grossly depicting similar activities in an exaggerated fashion. There are, in addition, pamphlets and booklets, sometimes with photographic illustrations, verbally describing such activities in a bizarre manner with no attempt whatsoever to afford portrayals of character or situation and with no pretense to literary value. All of this material . . . cannot conceivably be characterized as embodying communication of ideas or artistic values inviolate under the First Amendment. . . ."

That has long been the almost universal judgment of our society. . . . But material of this sort is wholly different from the publications mailed by the petitioner in the present case, and different not in degree but in kind.

The Court today appears to concede that the materials Ginzburg mailed were themselves protected by the First Amendment. But, the Court says, Ginzburg can still be sentenced to five years in prison for mailing them. Why? Because, says the Court, he was guilty of "commercial exploitation," of "pandering," and of "titillation." But Ginzburg was not charged with "commercial exploitation"; he was not charged with "pandering"; he was not charged with "titillation." Therefore, to affirm his conviction now on any of those grounds, even if otherwise valid, is to deny him due process of law. . . . But those grounds are *not,* of course, otherwise valid. Neither the statute under which Ginzburg was convicted nor any other federal statute I know of makes "commercial exploitation" or "pandering" or "titillation" a criminal offense. And any criminal law that sought to do so in the terms so elusively defined by the Court would, of course, be unconstitutionally vague and therefore void. All of these matters are developed in the dissenting opinions of my Brethren, and I simply note here that I fully agree with them.

For me, however, there is another aspect of the Court's opinion in this case that is even more regrettable. Today the Court assumes the power to deny Ralph Ginzburg the protection of the First Amendment because it disapproves of his "sordid business." That is a power the Court does not possess. For the First Amendment protects us all with an even hand. It applies to Ralph Ginzburg with no less completeness and force than to G. P. Putnam Sons. In upholding and enforcing the Bill of Rights, this Court has no power to pick or to choose. When we lose sight of that fixed star of constitutional adjudication, we lose our way. For then we forsake a government of law and are left with government by Big Brother.

I dissent.

4. Obscenity and Minors

GINSBERG *v.* NEW YORK
390 US 629 (1968)

[A New York statute prohibited the sale of obscene materials to minors under 17 years of age. Defendant was convicted of selling some "girlie" magazines to a 16-year-old boy—publications which would not have been obscene for adults. The Supreme Court upheld the conviction. It held that the statute did not invade the constitutional liberties of minors. Justice Brennan wrote the opinion of the Court. Justice Stewart wrote a concurring opinion. Justice Douglas wrote a dissenting opinion, in which Justice Black joined. Justice Fortas wrote a dissenting opinion.]

Mr. Justice Brennan delivered the opinion of the Court:

This case presents the question of the constitutionality on its face of a New York criminal obscenity statute which prohibits the sale to minors under 17 years of age of material defined to be obscene on the basis of its appeal to them whether or not it would be obscene to adults.

Appellant and his wife operate "Sam's Stationery and Luncheonette" in Bellmore, Long Island. They have a lunch counter, and, among other things, also sell magazines including some so-called "girlie" magazines. Appellant was prosecuted under two informations, each in two counts, which charged that he personally sold a 16-year-old boy two "girlie" magazines on each of two dates in October 1965, in violation of § 484–h of the New York Penal Law, *McKinney's Consol.Laws,* c. 40. He was tried before a judge without a jury in Nassau County District Court and was found guilty on both counts. The judge found (1) that the magazines contained pictures which depicted female "nudity" in a manner defined in subsection 1(b), that is "the showing of . . . female . . . buttocks with less than a full opaque covering, or the showing of the female breast with less than a fully opaque covering of any portion thereof below the top of the nipple . . . ," and (2) that the pictures were "harmful to minors" in that they had, within the meaning of subsection 1(f) ". . . that quality of . . . representation . . . of nudity . . . [which] . . . (i) predominantly appeals to the prurient, shameful or morbid interest of minors, and (ii) is patently offensive to prevailing standards in the adult community as a whole with respect to what is suitable material for minors, and (iii) is utterly without redeeming social importance for minors." He held that both sales to the 16-year-old boy therefore constituted the violation under § 484–h of "knowingly to sell . . . to a minor" under 17 of "(a) any picture . . . which depicts nudity . . . and which is harmful to minors," and "(b) any . . . magazine . . . which contains . . . [such pictures] . . . and which, taken as a whole, is harmful to minors." The conviction was affirmed without opinion by the Appellate Term, Second Department, of the Supreme Court. Appellant was denied leave to appeal to the New York Court of Appeals and then appealed to this Court. We noted probable jurisdiction.

I

The "girlie" picture magazines involved in the sales here are not obscene for adults, *Redrup* v. *State of New York,* 386 US 767. But § 484–h does not bar the appellant from stocking the magazines and selling them to persons 17 years of age or older, and therefore the conviction is not invalid under our decision in *Butler* v. *State of Michigan,* 352 US 380.

Obscenity is not within the area of protected speech or press. *Roth* v. *United States,* 354 US 476. The three-pronged test of subsection 1(f) for judging the obscenity of material sold to minors under 17 is a variable from the formulation for determining obscenity under *Roth* stated in the plurality opinion in *A Book Named "John Cleland's Memoirs of a Woman of Pleasure"* v. *Attorney General of Com. of Massachusetts,* 383 US 413. Appellant's primary attack upon § 484–h is leveled at the power of the State to adapt this *Memoirs* formulation to define the material's obscenity on the basis of its appeal to minors, and thus exclude material so defined from the area of protected expression. He makes no argument that the magazines are not "harmful to minors" within the definition in subsection 1(f). Thus "[n]o issue is presented . . . concerning the obscenity of the material involved." . . .

The New York Court of Appeals "upheld the Legislature's power to employ variable concepts of obscenity" in a case in which the same challenge to state power to enact such a law was also addressed to § 484–h. . . .

Appellant's attack is not that New York was without power to draw the line at age 17. Rather, his contention is the broad proposition that the scope of the constitutional freedom of expression secured to a citizen to read or see material concerned with sex cannot be made to depend upon whether the citizen is an adult or a minor. He accordingly insists that the denial to minors under 17 of access to material condemned by § 484–h, insofar as that material is not obscene for persons 17 years of age or older, constitutes an unconstitutional deprivation of protected liberty.

We have no occasion in this case to consider the impact of the guarantees of freedom of expression upon the totality of the relationship of the minor and the State. . . . It is enough for the purposes of this case that we inquire whether it was constitutionally impermissible for New York, insofar as § 484–h does so, to accord minors under 17 a more restricted right than that assured to adults to judge and determine for themselves what sex material they may read or see. We conclude that we cannot say that the statute invades the area of freedom of expression constitutionally secured to minors.

Appellant argues that there is an invasion of protected rights under § 484–h constitutionally indistinguishable from the invasions under the Nebraska statute forbidding children to study German, which was struck down in *Meyer* v. *State of Nebraska,* the Oregon statute interfering with children's attendance at private and parochial schools, which was struck down in *Pierce* v. *Society of Sisters of the Holy Names of Jesus and Mary,* and the statute compelling children against their religious scruples to give the flag salute, which was struck down in *West Virginia State Board of Education* v. *Barnette.* We reject that argument. We do not regard New York's regulation in defining obscenity on the basis of its appeal to minors under 17 as involving an invasion of such minors' constitutionally protected freedoms. Rather § 484–h simply adjusts the definition of obscenity ". . . to social realities by permitting the appeal of this type of material to be assessed in terms of the sexual interests . . ." of such minors. . . . That the State has power to make that adjustment seems clear, for we have recognized that even where there is an invasion of protected freedoms ". . . the power of the state to control the conduct of children reaches beyond the scope of its authority over adults. . . ." *Prince* v. *Commonwealth of Massachusetts,* 321 US 158. In *Prince* we sustained the conviction of the guardian of a nine-year-old girl, both members of the sect of Jehovah's Witnesses, for violating the Massachusetts Child Labor Law by permitting the girl to sell the sect's religious tracts on the streets of Boston.

The well-being of its children is of course a subject within the State's constitutional power to regulate, and, in our view, two interests justify the limitations in § 484–h upon the availability of sex material to minors under 17, at least if it was rational for the legislature to find that the minors' exposure to such material might be harmful. First of all, constitutional interpretation has consistently recognized that parents' claims to authority in their own households to direct the rearing of their children is basic in the structure of our society. "It is cardinal with us that the custody, care and nurture of the child reside first in the parents, whose primary function and freedom include preparation for obligations the state can neither supply nor hinder." . . . The legislature could properly conclude that parents and others, teachers for example, who have this primary responsibility for children's well-being are entitled to the support of laws designed to aid discharge of that responsibility. Indeed, subsection 1(f)(ii) of § 484–h expressly recognizes the parental role in assessing sex-related material harmful to minors according "to prevailing standards in the adult community as a whole with respect to what is suitable material for minors." Moreover, the prohibition against sales to minors does not bar parents who so desire from purchasing the magazines for their children.

The State also has an independent interest in the well-being of its youth. The New York Court of Appeals squarely bottomed its decision on that interest in *Bookcase, Inc.* v. *Broderick*, 18 N.Y.2d, at 75. Judge Fuld, now Chief Judge Fuld, also emphasized its significance in the earlier case of *People* v. *Kahan*, 15 N.Y.2d 311, which had struck down the first version of § 484–h on grounds of vagueness. In his concurring opinion, he said:

"While the supervision of children's reading may best be left to their parents, the knowledge that parental control or guidance cannot always be provided and society's transcendent interest in protecting the welfare of children justify reasonable regulation of the sale of material to them. It is, therefore, altogether fitting and proper for a state to include in a statute designed to regulate the sale of pornography to children special standards, broader than those embodied in legislation aimed at controlling dissemination of such material to adults."

In *Prince* v. *Commonwealth of Massachusetts,* this Court, too, recognized that the State has an interest "to protect the welfare of children" and to see that they are "safeguarded from abuses" which might prevent their "growth into free and independent well-developed men and citizens." The only question remaining, therefore, is whether the New York Legislature might rationally conclude, as it has, that exposure to the materials proscribed by § 484–h constitutes such an "abuse."

Section 484–e of the law states a legislative finding that the material condemned by § 484–h is "a basic factor in impairing the ethical and moral development of our youth and a clear and present danger to the people of the state." It is very doubtful that this finding expresses an accepted scientific fact. But obscenity is not protected expression and may be suppressed without a showing of the circumstances which lie behind the phrase "clear and present danger" in its application to protected speech. *Roth* v. *United States.** To sustain state power to exclude material defined as obscenity by § 484–h requires only that we be able to say that it was not irrational for the legislature to find that exposure to material condemned by the statute is harmful to minors. In *Meyer* v. *State of Nebraska,* we were able to say that children's knowledge of the German language "cannot reasonably be regarded as harmful." That cannot be said by us of minors' reading and seeing of sex material. To be sure, there is no lack of "studies" which purport to demonstrate that obscenity is or is not "a basic factor in impairing the ethical and moral de-

---

* Our conclusion in Roth, 354 US, at 486–487, 77 S.Ct., that the clear and present danger test was irrelevant to the determination of obscenity made it unnecessary in that case to consider the debate among the authorities whether exposure to pornography caused antisocial consequences. . . .

velopment of . . . youth and a clear and present danger to the people of the state." But the growing consensus of commentators is that "[w]hile these studies all agree that a causal link has not been demonstrated, they are equally agreed that a causal link has not been disproved either." We do not demand of legislatures a "scientifically certain criteria of legislation." . . . We therefore cannot say that § 484–h, in defining the obscenity of material on the basis of its appeal to minors under 17, has no rational relation to the objective of safeguarding such minors from harm. . . .

The attack on subsection (f) is that the definition of obscenity "harmful to minors" is so vague that an honest distributor of publications cannot know when he might be held to have violated § 484–h. But the New York Court of Appeals construed this definition to be "virtually identical to the Supreme Court's most recent statement of the elements of obscenity. . . .

As is required by *Smith* v. *People of State of California,* 361 US 147, § 484–h prohibits only those sales made "knowingly." The challenge to the *scienter* requirement of subsection (g) centers on the definition of "knowingly" insofar as it includes "reason to know" or "a belief or ground for belief which warrants further inspection or inquiry of both: (i) the character and content of any material described herein which is reasonably susceptible of examination by the defendant, and (ii) the age of the minor, provided however, that an honest mistake shall constitute an excuse from liability hereunder if the defendant made a reasonable bona fide attempt to ascertain the true age of such minor."

As to (i), § 484–h was passed after the New York Court of Appeals decided *People* v. *Finkelstein,* 9 N.Y.2d 342, which read the requirement of *scienter* into New York's general obscenity statute, § 1141 of the Penal Law. The constitutional requirement of *scienter,* in the sense of knowledge of the contents of material, rests on the necessity "to avoid the hazard of self-censorship of constitutionally protected material and to compensate for the ambiguities inherent in the definition of obscenity." . . . The Court of Appeals in *Finkelstein* interpreted § 1141 to require "the vital element of scienter" and defined that requirement in these terms: "A reading of the statute [§ 1141] as a whole clearly indicates that only those who are *in some manner aware of the character of the material* they attempt to distribute should be punished. It is not innocent but *calculated* purveyance of filth which is exorcised. . . ."

Appellant also attacks provision (ii) as impermissibly vague. This attack however is leveled only at the provision's proviso according the defendant a defense of "honest mistake" as to the age of the minor. Appellant argues that "the statute does not tell the bookseller what effort he must make before he can be excused." The argument is wholly without merit. The proviso states expressly that the defendant must be acquitted on the ground of "honest mistake" if the defendant proves that he made "a reasonable bona fide attempt to ascertain the true age of such minor." . . .

Affirmed.

5. *Obscenity and the Right of Privacy*

STANLEY *v.* GEORGIA
394 US 557 (1969)

[The Supreme Court in this case held that the mere possession of obscene material cannot be made a criminal offense. The Court's opinion was by Justice Marshall. Justice Black wrote a brief concurring opinion; Justice Stewart wrote a concurring opinion, in which Justices Brennan and White joined.]

Mr. Justice Marshall delivered the opinion of the Court:

An investigation of appellant's alleged bookmaking activities led to the issuance of a search warrant for appellant's home. Under authority of this warrant, federal and state agents secured entrance. They found very little evidence of bookmaking activity, but while looking through a desk drawer in an upstairs bedroom, one of the federal agents, accompanied by a state officer, found three reels of eight-millimeter film. Using a projector and screen found in an upstairs living room, they viewed the films. The state officer concluded that they were obscene and seized them. Since a further examination of the bedroom indicated that appellant occupied it, he was charged with possession of obscene matter and placed under arrest. He was later indicted for "knowingly hav[ing] possession of obscene matter" in violation of Georgia law. Appellant was tried before a jury and convicted. The Supreme Court of Georgia affirmed. . . . We noted probable jurisdiction of an appeal brought under 28 U.S.C. § 1257(2). . . .

Appellant raises several challenges to the validity of his conviction. We find it necessary to consider only one. Appellant argues here, and argued below, that the Georgia obscenity statute, insofar as it punishes mere private possession of obscene matter, violates the First Amendment, as made applicable to the States by the Fourteenth Amendment. For reasons set forth below, we agree that the mere private possession of obscene matter cannot constitutionally be made a crime. . . .

The State and appellant both agree that the question here before us is whether "a statute imposing criminal sanctions upon the mere [knowing] possession of obscene matter" is constitutional. In this context, Georgia concedes that the present case appears to be one of "first impression . . . on this exact point," but contends that since "obscenity is not within the area of constitutionally protected speech or press," . . . the States are free, subject to the limits of other provisions of the Constitution, . . . to deal with it any way deemed necessary, jus as they may deal with possession of other things thought to be detrimental to the welfare of their citizens. If the State can protect the body of a citizen, may it not, argues Georgia, protect his mind?

It is true that *Roth* does declare, seemingly without qualification, that obscenity is not protected by the First Amendment. That statement has been repeated in various forms in subsequent cases. . . . None of the statements cited by the Court in *Roth* for the proposition that "this Court has always assumed that obscenity is not protected by the freedoms of speech and press" were made in the context of a statute punishing mere private possession of obscene material; the cases cited deal for the most part with use of the mails to distribute objectionable material or with some form of public distribution or dissemination. Moreover, none of this Court's decisions subsequent to *Roth* involved prosecution for private possession of obscene materials. Those cases dealt with the power of the State and Federal Governments to prohibit or regulate certain public actions taken or intended to be taken with respect to obscene matter. Indeed, with one exception, we have been unable to discover any case in which the issue in the present case has been fully considered.

In this context, we do not believe that this case can be decided simply by citing *Roth*. *Roth* and its progeny certainly do mean that the First and Fourteenth Amendments recognize a valid governmental interest in dealing with the problem of obscenity. . . . *Roth* and the cases following it discerned such an "important interest" in the regulation of commercial distribution of obscene material. That holding cannot foreclose an examination of the constitutional implications of a statute forbidding mere private possession of such material.

It is now well established that the Constitution protects the right to receive information and ideas. "This freedom [of speech and press] . . . necessarily protects the right to receive. . . ." This right to receive information and ideas, regardless of their social worth, . . . is fundamental to our free society. Moreover, in the context of this case—a prosecution for mere possession of printed or filmed matter in the privacy of a person's own home—that right takes on an added dimension. For also fundamental is the right to be free, except in very limited circumstances, from unwanted governmental intrusions into one's privacy. . . .

These are the rights that appellant is asserting in the case before us. He is asserting the right to read or observe what he pleases—the right to satisfy his intellectual and emotional needs in the privacy of his own home. He is asserting the right to be free from state inquiry into the contents of his library. Georgia contends that appellant does not have these rights, that there are certain types of materials that the individual may not read or even possess. Georgia justifies this assertion by arguing that the films in the present case are obscene. But we think that mere categorization of these films as "obscene" is insufficient justification for such a drastic invasion of personal liberties guaranteed by the First and Fourteenth Amendments. Whatever may be the justifications for other statutes regulating obscenity, we do not think they reach into the privacy of one's own home. If the First Amendment means anything, it means that a State has no business telling a man, sitting alone in his own house, what books he may read or what films he may watch. Our whole constitutional heritage rebels at the thought of giving government the power to control men's minds.

And yet, in the face of these traditional notions of individual liberty, Georgia asserts the right to protect the individual's mind from the effects of obscenity. We are not certain that this argument amounts to anything more than the assertion that the State has the right to control the moral content of a a person's thoughts. To some, this may be a noble purpose, but it is wholly inconsistent with the philosophy of the First Amendment. . . . Nor is it relevant that obscenity in general, or the particular films before the Court, are arguably devoid of any ideological content. The line between the transmission of ideas and mere entertainment is much too elusive for this Court to draw, if indeed such a line can be drawn at all. . . .

Whatever the power of the state to control public dissemination of ideas inimical to the public morality, it cannot constitutionally premise legislation on the desirability of controlling a person's private thoughts.

Perhaps recognizing this, Georgia asserts that exposure to obscenity may lead to deviant sexual behavior or crimes of sexual violence. There appears to be little empirical basis for that assertion. But more importantly, if the State is only concerned about literature inducing antisocial conduct, we believe that in the context of private consumption of ideas and information we should adhere to the view that "[a]mong free men, the deterrents ordinarily to be applied to prevent crime are education and punishment for violations of the law. . . ." Given the present state of knowledge, the State may no more prohibit mere possession of obscenity on the ground that it may lead to antisocial conduct than it may prohibit possession of chemistry books on the ground that they may lead to the manufacture of homemade spirits.

It is true that in *Roth* this Court rejected the necessity of proving that exposure to obscene material would create a clear and present danger of antisocial conduct or would probably induce its recipients to such conduct. But that case dealt with public distribution of obscene materials and such distribution is subject to different objections. For example, there is always the danger that obscene material might fall into the hands of children, . . . or that it might intrude upon the sensibilities or privacy of the general public. . . . No such dangers are present in this case.

Finally, we are faced with the argument that prohibition of possession of obscenity is a necessary incident to statutory schemes prohibiting distribution. That argument is based on alleged difficulties of proving an intent to distribute or in producing evidence of actual distribution. We are not convinced that such difficulties exist, but even if they did we do not think that they would justify infringement of the individual's right to read or observe what he pleases. Because that right is so fundamental to our scheme of individual liberty, its restriction may not be justified by the need to ease the administration of otherwise valid criminal laws. . . .

We hold that the First and Fourteenth Amendments prohibit making mere private possession of obscene material a crime. . . .

UNITED STATES *v.* THIRTY-SEVEN (37) PHOTOGRAPHS
402 US 363 (1971)

[As Milton Luros arrived in the United States, customs inspectors found in his luggage photographs which were allegedly obscene, and accordingly they were seized. In a counterclaim action brought by Luros, a three-judge District Court declared the customs statute under which the seizure was effected unconstitutional. The Supreme Court, avoiding the issue of constitutionality, construed the statute in such a way as to read into it procedural requirements held necessary by the Court's precedents. This part of the Court's judgment had six votes in its support: Justice White, Chief Justice Burger, Justices Brennan, Blackmun, Harlan, and Stewart. Justice White wrote the opinion for the first four; Justices Harlan and Stewart each wrote a concurring opinion.

[Luros also contended that the seizure was invalid under *Stanley* v. *Georgia, supra,* as violative of his right of privacy. The Court held that the right of privacy does not include the right to use foreign commerce to bring obscene materials into one's home—"a port of entry is not a traveler's home." The same six members of the Court named above, while concurring in the Court's judgment, did not all concur in this part (Part II) of Justice White's opinion. Justices Harlan and Stewart did not concur in Part II of the plurality opinion: the former stated that since Luros imported the photographs with the intention to use them commercially, he lacked standing to raise the issue of privacy; the latter, while agreeing that the seizure in this case was valid, said that a book imported for one's private use could not be seized.

[Justices Marshall, Black, and Douglas dissented. Their dissenting opinions are to be found at the end of the next case, *United States* v. *Reidel,* decided the same day as the Luros case.]

Mr. Justice White announced the judgment of the Court, an opinion in which the Chief Justice, Mr. Justice Brennan, and Mr. Justice Blackmun join:

When Milton Luros returned to the United States from Europe on October 24, 1969, he brought with him in his luggage the 37 photographs here involved. United States customs agents, acting pursuant to 19 U.S.C. § 1305(a),* seized the photographs as obscene. They referred the matter to the United States Attorney, who on November 6 instituted proceedings in the United States District Court for forfeiture of the material. Luros, as claimant, answered, denying the photographs were obscene and setting up a counterclaim alleging the unconstitutionality of § 1305(a)

---

* 19 U.S.C. § 1305(a) provides in pertinent part:

"All persons are prohibited from importing into the United States from any foreign country . . . any obscene book, pamphlet, paper, writing, advertisement, circular, print, picture, drawing, or other representation, figure, or image on or of paper or other material, or any cast, instrument, or other article which is obscene or immoral. . . . No such articles whether imported separately or contained in packages with other goods entitled to entry, shall be admitted to entry; and all such articles and, unless it appears to the satisfaction of the collector that the obscene or other prohibited articles contained in the package were inclosed therein without the knowledge or consent of the importer, owner, agent, or consignee, the entire contents of the package in which such articles are contained, shall be subject to seizure and forfeiture as hereinafter provided: . . . *Provided, further,* That the Secretary of the Treasury may, in his discretion, admit the so-called classics or books of recognized and established literary or scientific merit, but may, in his discretion, admit such classics or books only when imported for noncommercial purposes.

"Upon the appearance of any such book or matter at any customs office, the same shall be seized and held by the collector to await the judgment of the district court as hereinafter provided; and no protest shall be taken to the United States Customs Court from the decision of the collector. Upon the seizure of such book or matter the collector shall transmit information thereof to the district attorney of the district in which is situated the office at which such seizure has taken place, who shall institute proceedings in the district court for the forfeiture, confiscation, and destruction of the book or matter seized. Upon the adjudication that such book or matter thus seized is of the character the entry of which is by this section prohibited, it shall be ordered destroyed and shall be destroyed. Upon adjudication that such book or matter thus seized is not of the character the entry of which is by this section prohibited, it shall not be excluded from entry under the provisions of this section.

"In any such proceeding any party in interest may upon demand have the facts at issue determined by a jury and any party may have an appeal or the right of review as in the case of ordinary actions or suits."

on its face and as applied to him. He demanded that a three-judge court be convened to issue an injunction prayed for in the counterclaim. The parties stipulated a time for hearing the three-judge court motion. Formal order convening the court was entered on November 20. The parties then stipulated a briefing schedule expiring on December 16. The court ordered a hearing for January 9, also suggesting the parties stipulate facts, which they did. The stipulation revealed, among other things, that some or all of the 37 photographs were intended to be incorporated in a hard cover edition of The Kama Sutra of Vatsyayana, a widely distributed book candidly describing a large number of sexual positions. Hearing was held as scheduled on January 9, and on January 27 the three-judge court filed its judgment and opinion declaring § 1305(a) unconstitutional and enjoining its enforcement against the 37 photographs, which were ordered returned to Luros. The judgment of invalidity rested on two grounds: first, that the section failed to comply with the procedural requirements of *Freedman* v. *Maryland,* 380 US 51 (1965), and second, that under *Stanley* v. *Georgia,* 394 US 557 (1969), § 1305(a) could not validly be applied to the seized material. We shall deal with each of these grounds separately.

I

In *Freedman* v. *Maryland, supra,* we struck down a state scheme for administrative licensing of motion pictures, holding "that, because only a judicial determination in an adversary proceeding ensures the necessary sensitivity to freedom of expression, only a procedure requiring a judicial determination suffices to impose a valid final restraint." To insure that a judicial determination occurs promptly so that administrative delay does not in itself become a form of censorship, we further held (1) there must be assurance, "by statute or authoritative judicial construction, that the censor will, within the specified brief period, either issue a license or go to court to restrain showing the film"; (2) "[a]ny restraint imposed in advance of a final judicial determination on the merits must similarly be limited to preservation of the status quo for the shortest fixed period compatible with sound judicial resolution"; and (3) ". . . the procedure must also assure a prompt final judicial decision" to minimize the impact of possibly erroneous administrative action.

Subsequently, we invalidated Chicago's motion picture censorship ordinance because it permitted an unduly long administrative procedure before the invocation of judicial action and also because the ordinance, although requiring prompt resort to the courts after administrative decision and an early hearing, did not assure "a prompt judicial decision of the question of the alleged obscenity of the film." *Teitel Film Corp.* v. *Cusack,* 390 US 139 (1968). So too in *Blount* v. *Rizzi,* 400 US 410 (1971), we held unconstitutional certain provisions of the postal laws designed to control use of the mails for commerce in obscene materials. Under those laws an administrative order restricting use of the mails could become effective without judicial approval, the burden of obtaining prompt judicial review was placed upon the user of the mails rather than the Government, and the interim judicial order, which the Government was permitted, though not required to obtain pending completion of administrative action, was not limited to preserving the status quo for the shortest fixed period compatible with sound judicial administration.

As enacted by Congress, § 1305(a) does not contain explicit time limits of the sort required by *Freedman, Teitel,* and *Blount.* These cases do not, however, require that we pass upon the constitutionality of § 1305(a), for it is possible to construe the section to bring it in harmony with constitutional requirements. It is true that we noted in *Blount* that "it is for Congress, not this Court, to rewrite the statute," and that we similarly refused to rewrite Maryland's statute and Chicago's ordinance in *Freedman* and *Teitel.* On the other hand, we must remember that, "[w]hen the validity of an act of Congress is drawn in question, and . . . a serious doubt of constitutionality is raised, it is a cardinal principle that this Court will first ascertain whether a construction of the statute is fairly possible by which the question may be avoided." . . . This cardinal principle did not govern *Freedman, Teitel,* and *Blount* only because the statutes there involved could not be construed so as to avoid all constitutional difficulties.

The obstacle in *Freedman* and *Teitel* was that the statutes were enacted pursuant to state rather than federal authority; while *Freedman* recognized that a statute which failed to specify time limits could be saved by judicial construction, it held that such construction had to be "authoritative," and we lack jurisdiction authoritatively to construe state legislation. . . . In *Blount,* we were dealing with a federal statute and thus had power to give it an authoritative construction; salvation of that statute, however, would have required its complete rewriting in a manner inconsistent with the expressed intentions of some of its authors. For the statute at issue in *Blount* not only failed to specify time limits within which judicial proceedings must be instituted and completed; it also failed to give any authorization at all to the administrative agency, upon a determination that material was obscene, to seek judicial review. To have saved the statute we would thus have been required to give such authorization and to create mechanisms for carrying it into effect, and we would have had to do this in the face of legislative history indicating that the Postmaster General, when he had testified before Congress, had expressly sought to forestall judicial review pending completion of administrative proceedings.

No such obstacles confront us in construing § 1305(a). In fact, the reading into the section of the time limits required by *Freedman* is fully consistent with its legislative purpose. When the statute, which in its present form dates back to 1930, was first presented to the Senate, concern immediately arose that it did not provide for determinations of obscenity to be made by courts rather than administrative officers and that it did not require that judicial rulings be obtained promptly. In language strikingly parallel to that of the Court in *Freedman,* Senator Walsh protested against the "attempt to enact a law that would vest an administrative officer with power to take books and confiscate them and destroy them, because, in his judgment, they were obscene or indecent," and urged that the law "oblige him to go into court and file his information there, . . . and have it determined in the usual way, the same as every other crime is determined." . . . Senator Wheeler likewise could not "conceive how any man" could "possibly object" to an amendment to the proposed legislation that required a customs officer, if he concluded material was obscene, to "turn . . . it over to the district attorney, and the district attorney prosecutes the man, and he has a right of trial by jury in that case." Other Senators similarly indicated their aversion to censorship "by customs clerks and bureaucratic officials," . . . preferring that determinations of obscenity should be left to courts and juries. Senators also expressed the concern later expressed in *Freedman* that judicial proceedings be commenced and concluded promptly. Speaking in favor of another amendment, Senator Pittman noted that a customs officer seizing obscene matter "should *immediately* report to the nearest United States district attorney having authority under the law to proceed to confiscate. . . ." Commenting on an early draft of another amendment that was ultimately adopted, Senator Swanson noted that officers would be required to go to court "immediately." Then he added:

The *minute* there is a suspicion on the part of a revenue or customs officer that a certain book is improper to be admitted into this country, he presents the matter to the district court, and there will be a *prompt* determination of the matter by a decision of that court. (Emphasis added.)

Before it finally emerged from Congress, § 1305(a) was amended in response to objections of the sort voiced above: it thus reflects the same policy considerations that induced this Court to hold in *Freedman* that censors must resort to the courts "within a specified brief period" and that such resort must be followed by "a prompt final judicial decision. . . ." Congress' sole omission was its failure to specify exact time limits within which resort to the courts must be had and judicial proceedings be completed. No one during the congressional debates ever suggested inclusion of such limits, perhaps because experience had not yet demonstrated a need for them. Since 1930, however, the need has become clear. Our researches have disclosed cases sanctioning delays of as long as 40 days and even six months between seizure of obscene goods and commencement of judicial proceedings. . . . Similarly, we have found cases in which completion of judicial proceedings has taken as long as three, four, and even seven months. . . . We conclude that to sanction such delays would be clearly inconsistent with the concern for promptness that was so frequently articulated during the course of the Senate's debates, and that fidelity to Congress' purpose dictates that we read explicit time limits into the section. The only alternative would be to hold § 1305(a) unconstitutional in its entirety, but Congress has explicitly directed that the section not be invalidated in its entirety merely because its application to some persons be adjudged unlawful. Nor does the construction of § 1305(a) to include specific time limits require us to decide issues of policy appropriately left to the Congress or raise other questions upon which Congress possesses special legislative expertise, for Congress has already set its course in favor of promptness and we possess as much expertise as Congress in determining the sole remaining question—that of the speed with which prosecutorial and judicial institutions can, as a practical matter, be expected to function in adjudicating § 1305(a) matters. We accordingly see no reason for declining to specify the time limits which must be incorporated into § 1305(a)—a specification that is fully consistent with congressional purpose and that will obviate the constitutional objections raised by appellee. Indeed, we conclude that the legislative history of the section and the policy of giving legislation a saving construction in order to avoid decision of constitutional questions requires that we undertake this task of statutory construction.

We begin by examining cases in the lower federal courts in which proceedings have been brought under § 1305(a). That examination indicates that in many of the cases which have come to our attention the Government in fact instituted forfeiture proceedings within 14 days of the date of seizure of the allegedly obscene goods, . . . and judicial proceedings were completed within 60 days of their commencement. . . . Given this record, it seems clear that no undue hardship will be imposed upon the Government and the lower federal courts by requiring that forfeiture proceedings be commenced within 14 days and completed within 60 days of their commencement, nor does a delay of as much as 74 days seem undue for importers engaged in the lengthy process of bringing goods into this country from abroad. Accordingly, we construe § 1305(a) to require intervals of no more than 14 days from seizure of the goods to the institution of judicial proceedings for their forfeiture and no longer than 60 days from the filing of the action to final decision in the District Court. No seizure or forfeiture will be invalidated for delay, however, where the claimant is responsible for extending either administrative action or judicial determination beyond the allowable time limits or where administrative or judicial proceedings are postponed pending the consideration of constitutional issues appropriate only for a three-judge court.

Of course, we do not now decide that these are the only constitutionally permissible time limits. We note, furthermore, that constitutionally permissible limits may vary in different contexts; in other contexts, such as a claim by a state censor that a movie is obscene, the Constitution may impose different requirements with respect to the time between the making of the claim and the institution of judicial proceedings or between their commencement and completion than in the context of a claim of obscenity made by customs officials at the border. We decide none of these questions today. We do nothing in this case but construe § 1305(a) in its present form, fully cognizant that Congress may re-enact it in a new form specifying new time limits, upon whose constitutionality we will then be required to pass.

So construed, § 1305(a) may constitutionally be applied to the case before us. Seizure in the present case took place on October 24 and forfeiture proceedings were instituted on November 6—a mere 13 days after seizure. Moreover, decision on the obscenity of Luros' materials might well have been forthcoming within 60 days had petitioner not challenged the validity of the statute and caused a three-judge court to be convened. We hold that proceedings of such brevity fully meet the constitutional standards set out in *Freedman, Teitel,* and *Blount.* Section 1305(a) accordingly may be applied to the 37 photographs, providing that on remand the obscenity issue is resolved in the District Court within 60 days, excluding any delays caused by Luros.

II

We next consider Luros' second claim, which is based upon *Stanley* v. *Georgia, supra.* On the authority of *Stanley,* Luros urged the trial court to construe the First Amendment as forbidding any restraints on obscenity except where necessary to protect children or where it intruded itself upon the sensitivity or privacy of an unwilling adult. Without rejecting this position, the trial court read *Stanley* as protecting, at the very least, the right to read obscene material in the privacy of one's own home and to receive it for that purpose. It therefore held that § 1305(a), which bars the importation of obscenity for private use as well as for commercial distribution, is overbroad and hence unconstitutional.

The trial court erred in reading *Stanley* as immunizing from seizure obscene materials possessed at a port of entry for the purpose of importation for private use. In *United States* v. *Reidel*, we have today held that Congress may constitutionally prevent the mails from being used for distributing pornography. In this case, neither Luros nor his putative buyers have rights which are infringed by the exclusion of obscenity from incoming foreign commerce. By the same token, obscene materials may be removed from the channels of commerce when discovered in the luggage of a returning foreign traveler even though intended solely for his private use. That the private user under *Stanley* may not be prosecuted for possession of obscenity in his home does not mean that he is entitled to import it from abroad free from the power of Congress to exclude noxious articles from commerce. *Stanley's* emphasis was on the freedom of thought and mind in the privacy of the home. But a port of entry is not a traveler's home. His right to be let alone neither prevents the search of his luggage nor the seizure of unprotected, but illegal, materials when his possession of them is discovered during such a search. Customs officers characteristically inspect luggage and their power to do so is not questioned in this case; it is an old practice and is intimately associated with excluding illegal articles from the country. Whatever the scope of the right to receive obscenity adumbrated in *Stanley*, that right, as we said in *Reidel*, does not extend to one who is seeking, as was Luros here to distribute obscene materials to the public, nor does it extend to one seeking to import obscene materials from abroad, whether for private use or public distribution. As we held in *Roth* v. *United States*, 354 US 476 (1957), and reiterated today in *Reidel*, obscenity is not within the scope of firstamendment protection. Hence Congress may declare it contraband and prohibit its importation, as it has elected in § 1305(a) to do.

The judgment of the District Court is reversed and the case is remanded for further proceedings consistent with this opinion.

It is so ordered.

Judgment reversed and case remanded.

UNITED STATES *v.* REIDEL
402 US 351 (1971)

[Reidel had advertised in a newspaper the sale, to persons over 21 years of age, of a booklet. He was indicted for use of the mails to send three copies of the booklet, which the Government alleged to be obscene, in violation of the federal obscenity statute. The Court held that the statute was constitutional as applied to the distribution of obscene materials even to recipients who are adults and who indicate a willingness to receive such materials. The Court's opinion was by Justice White. The Court stated that the right of privacy as conceived of in the *Stanley* case, *supra*, does not include the right to receive, despite precautions to prevent dissemination among children or unconsenting adults. Justice Harlan wrote a concurring opinion. Justice Marshall concurred in the judgment. Justice Black, joined by Justice Douglas, wrote a dissenting opinion covering both *Reidel* and the preceding case involving Luros.]

Mr. Justice White delivered the opinion of the Court:

Section 1461 of Title 18, U.S.C., prohibits the knowing use of the mails for the delivery of obscene matter.* The issue presented by the jurisdictional statement in this case is whether § 1461 is constitutional as applied to the distribution of obscene materials to willing recipients who state that they are adults. The District Court held that it was not. We disagree and reverse the judgment.

I

On April 15, 1970, the appellee, Norman Reidel, was indicted on three counts, each count charging him with having mailed a single copy of an illustrated booklet entitled, "The True Facts about Imported Pornography." One of the copies had been mailed to a postal inspector stipulated to be over the age of 21, who had responded to a newspaper advertisement.† The other two copies had been seized during a search of appellee's business premises; both of them had been deposited in the mail by Reidel but had been returned to him in their original mailing envelopes bearing the mark "undelivered." As to these two booklets, the Government conceded that it had no evidence as to the identity or age of the addressees or as to their willingness to receive the booklets. Nor does the record indicate why the booklets were returned undelivered.

Reidel moved in the District Court before trial to dismiss the indictment, contending, among other things, that § 1461 was unconstitutional. Assuming for the purpose of the motion that the booklets were obscene, the trial judge granted the motion to dismiss on the ground that Reidel had made a constitutionally protected delivery and hence that § 1461 was unconstitutional as applied to him. The Government's direct appeal is here under 18 U.S.C. § 3731.

II

In *Roth* v. *United States,* 354 US 476 (1957), Roth was convicted under § 1461

---

* The statute in pertinent part provides:

"Every obscene, lewd, lascivious, indecent, filthy or vile article, matter, thing, device, or substance; and . . .

"Every written or printed card, letter, circular, book, pamphlet, advertisement, or notice of any kind giving information, directly or indirectly, where, or how, or from whom, or by what means any of such mentioned matters, articles, or things may be obtained or made, or where or by whom any act or operation of any kind for the procuring or producing of abortion will be done or performed, or how or by what means conception may be prevented or abortion produced, whether sealed or unsealed; . . .

"Is declared to be nonmailable matter and shall not be conveyed in the mails or delivered from any post office or by any letter carrier.

"Whoever knowingly uses the mails for the mailing, carriage in the mails, or delivery of anything declared by this section to be nonmailable, or knowingly causes to be delivered by mail according to the direction thereon, or at the place at which it is directed to be delivered by the person to whom it is addressed, or knowingly takes any such thing from the mails for the purpose of circulating or disposing thereof, or of aiding in the circulation or disposition thereof, shall be fined not more than $5,000 or imprisoned not more than five years, or both, for the first such offense, and shall be fined not more than $10,000 or imprisoned not more than ten years, or both, for each such offense thereafter."

† The advertisement was as follows:

"IMPORTED PORNOGRAPHY—Learn the true facts before sending money abroad. Send $1.00 for our fully illustrated booklet. You must be 21 years of age and so state. Normax Press, P.O. Box 989, Fontana, California, 92335."

for mailing obscene circulars and advertising. The Court affirmed the conviction, holding that "obscenity is not within the area of constitutionally protected speech or press," and that § 1461, "applied according to the proper standard for judging obscenity, do[es] not offend constitutional safeguards against convictions based upon protected material, or fail to give men in acting adequate notice of what is prohibited." *Roth* has not been overruled. It remains the law in this Court and governs this case. Reidel, like Roth, was charged with using the mails for the distribution of obscene material. His conviction, if it occurs and the materials are found in fact to be obscene, would be no more vulnerable than was Roth's.

Stanley v. *Georgia,* 394 US 557 (1969), compels no different result. There, pornographic films were found in Stanley's home and he was convicted under Georgia statutes for possessing obscene material. This Court reversed the conviction, holding that the mere private possession of obscene matter cannot constitutionally be made a crime. But it neither overruled nor disturbed the holding in *Roth.* Indeed, in the Court's view, the constitutionality of proscribing private possession of obscenity was a matter of first impression in this Court, a question neither involved nor decided in *Roth.* The Court made its point expressly: *"Roth* and the cases following that decision are not impaired by today's holding. As we have said, the States retain broad power to regulate obscenity; that power simply does not extend to mere possession by the individual in the privacy of his own home." Nothing in *Stanley* questioned the validity of *Roth* insofar as the distribution of obscene material was concerned. Clearly the Court had no thought of questioning the validity of § 1461 as applied to those who, like Reidel, are routinely disseminating obscenity through the mails and who have no claim, and could make none, about unwanted governmental intrusions into the privacy of their home. The Court considered this sufficiently clear to warrant summary affirmance of the judgment of the United States District Court for the Northern District of Georgia rejecting claims that under *Stanley* v. *Georgia,* Georgia's obscenity statute could not be applied to book sellers. *Gable* v. *Jenkins,* 397 US 592 (1970).

The District Court ignored both *Roth* and the express limitations on the reach of the *Stanley* decision. Relying on the statement in *Stanley* that "the Constitution protects the right to receive information and ideas . . . regardless of their social worth," the trial judge reasoned that "if a person has the right to receive and possess this material, then someone must have the right to deliver it to him." He concluded that § 1461 could not be validly applied "where obscene material is not directed at children, or it is not directed at an unwilling public, where the material such as in this case is solicited by adults. . . ."

The District Court gave *Stanley* too wide a sweep. To extrapolate from Stanley's right to have and peruse obscene material in the privacy of his own home a First Amendment right in Reidel to sell it to him would effectively scuttle *Roth,* the precise result that the *Stanley* opinion abjured. Whatever the scope of the "right to receive" referred to in *Stanley,* it is not so broad as to immunize the dealings in obscenity in which Reidel engaged here—dealings which *Roth* held unprotected by the First Amendment.

The right Stanley asserted was "the right to read or observe what he pleases —the rigth to satisfy his intellectual and emotional needs in the privacy of his own home." The Court's response was that "a State has no business telling a man, sitting alone in his own house, what books he may read or what films he may watch. Our whole constitutional heritage rebels at the thoughts of giving government the power to control men's minds." The focus of this language was on freedom of mind and thought and on the privacy of one's home. It does not require that we fashion or recognize a constitutional right in people like Reidel to distribute or sell obscene materials. The personal constitutional rights of those like Stanley to possess and read obscenity in their homes and their freedom of mind and thought do not depend on whether the materials are obscene or whether obscenity is constitutionally protected. Their rights to have and view that material in private are independently saved by the Constitution.

Reidel is in a wholly different position. He has no complaints about governmental violations of his private thoughts or fantasies, but stands squarely on a claimed First Amendment right to do business in obscenity and use the mails in the process. But *Roth* has squarely placed obscenity and its distribution outside the reach of the First Amendment and they remain there today. *Stanley* did not overrule *Roth* and we decline to do so now.

III

A postscript is appropriate. *Roth* and like cases have interpreted the First Amendment not to insulate obscenity from statutory regulation. But the Amendment itself neither proscribes dealings in obscenity nor directs or suggests legislative oversight in this area. The relevant constitutional issues have arisen in the courts only because lawmakers having the exclusive legislative power have consistently insisted on making the distribution of obscenity a crime or otherwise regulating such materials and because the laws they pass are challenged as unconstitutional invasions of free speech and press.

It is urged that there is developing sentiment that adults should have complete freedom to produce, deal in, possess, and consume whatever communicative materials may appeal to them and that the law's involvement with obscenity should be limited to those situations where children are involved or where it is necessary to prevent imposition on unwilling recipients of whatever age. The concepts involved are said to be so elusive and the laws so inherently unenforceable without extravagant expenditures of time and effort by enforcement officers and the courts that basic reassessment is not only wise but essential. This may prove to be the desirable and eventual legislative course. But if it is, the task of restructuring the obscenity laws lies with those who pass, repeal, and amend statutes and ordinances. *Roth* and like cases pose no obstacle to such developments.

The judgment of the District Court is reversed.

So ordered.

Reversed.

Mr. Justice Marshall, dissenting in No. 133 and concurring in No. 534:

Only two years ago in *Stanley* v. *Georgia,* the Court fully canvassed the range of state interests which might possibly justify regulation of obscenity. That decision refused to legitimize the argument that obscene materials could be outlawed because the materials might somehow encourage antisocial conduct, and unequivocally rejected the out-landish notion that the State may police the thoughts of its citizenry. The Court did, however, approve the validity of regulatory action taken to protect children and unwill-ing adults from exposure to materials deemed to be obscene. The need for such protec-tion of course arises when obscenity is distributed or displayed publicly; and the Court reaffirmed the principles of *Roth* v. *United States, Redrup* v. *New York,* and other decisions which involved the commercial distribution of obscene materials. Thus, *Stanley* turned on an assessment of which state interests may legitimately underpin governmen-tal action, and it is disingenuous to contend that Stanley's conviction was reversed because his home, rather than his person or luggage, was the locus of a search.

I would employ a similar adjudicative approach in deciding the cases presently before the Court. In No. 133 the material in question was seized from appellee's luggage upon his return to the United States from a European trip. Although appellee stipulated that he intended to use some of the photographs to illustrate a book which would be later distributed commercially, the seized items were then in his purely private possession and threatened neither children nor anyone else. In my view, the Government has ample opportunity to protect its valid interests if and when commercial distribution should take place. Since threats to these interests arise in the context of public or commercial distribution, the magnitude of the threats can best be assessed when distribution actually occurs; and it is always possible that petitioner might include only some of the photo-graphs in the final commercial product or might later abandon his intention to use any of them. I find particularly troubling the Court's suggestion that there is no need to scrutinize the Government's behavior because a "border search" is involved. While necessity may dictate some diminution of traditional constitutional safeguards at our Nation's borders, I should have thought that any such reduction would heighten the need jealously to protect those liberties which remain rather than justify the suspension of any and all safeguards.

No. 534 presents a different situation in which allegedly obscene materials were dis-tributed through the mails. Plainly, any such mail-order distribution poses the danger that obscenity will be sent to children, and although the appellee in No. 534 indicated his intent to sell only to adults who requested his wares, the sole safeguard designed to prevent the receipt of his merchandise by minors was his requirement that buyers declare their age. While the record does not reveal that any children actually received appellee's materials, I believe that distributors of purportedly obscene merchandise may be required to take more stringent steps to guard against possible receipt by minors. This case comes to us without the benefit of a full trial, and, on this sparse record, I am not prepared to find that appellee's conduct was not within a constitutionally valid construction of the federal statute.

Accordingly, I dissent in No. 133 and concur in the judgment in No. 534.

Mr. Justice Black, with whom Mr. Justice Douglas joins, dissenting:

I

I dissent from the judgments of the Court for the reasons stated in many of my prior opinions. . . . In my view the First Amendment denies Congress the power to act as censor and determine what books our citizens may read and what pictures they may watch.

I particularly regret to see the Court revive the doctrine of *Roth* v. *United States,* that "obscenity" is speech for some reason unprotected by the First Amendment. As the Court's many decisions in this area demonstrate, it is extremely difficult for judges or any other citizens to agree on what is "obscene." Since the distinctions between protected speech and "obscenity" are so elusive and obscure, almost every "obscenity" case involves difficult constitutional issues. After *Roth* our docket and those of other courts have constantly been crowded with cases where judges are called upon to decide whether a particular book, magazine, or movie may be banned. I have expressed before my view that I can imagine no task for which this Court of lifetime judges is less equipped to deal. . . .

In view of the difficulties with the *Roth* approach, it is not surprising that many recent decisions have at least implicitly suggested that it should be abandoned. . . . Despite the proven shortcomings of *Roth,* the majority today reaffirms the validity of that dubious decision. Thus, for the foreseeable future this Court must sit as a Board of Supreme Censors, sifting through books and magazines and watching movies because some official fears they deal too explicitly with sex. I can imagine no more distasteful, useless, and time-consuming task for the members of this Court than perusing this material to determine whether it has "redeeming social value." This absurd spectacle could be avoided if we would adhere to the literal command of the First Amendment that "Congress shall make no law . . . abridging the freedom of speech, or of the press. . . ."

II

Wholly aside from my own views of what the First Amendment demands, I do not see how the reasoning of Mr. Justice White's opinion today in *United States* v. *Thirty-Seven Photographs* can be reconciled with the holdings of earlier cases. That opinion insists that the trial court erred in reading *Stanley* v. *Georgia, supra,* "as immunizing from seizure obscene materials possessed at a port of entry for the purpose of importation for private use." But it is never satisfactorily explained just why the trial court's reading of *Stanley* was erroneous. It would seem to me that if a citizen had a right to possess "obscene" material in the privacy of his home he should have the right to receive it voluntarily through the mail. Certainly when a man legally purchases such material abroad he should be able to bring it with him through customs to read later in his home. The mere act of importation for private use can hardly be more offensive to others than is private perusal in one's home. The right to read and view any literature and pictures at home is hollow indeed if it does not include a right to carry that material privately in one's luggage when entering the country.

The plurality opinion seems to suggest that *Thirty-Seven Photographs* differs from *Stanley* because "Customs officials characteristically inspect luggage and their power to do so is not questioned in this case. . . ." But surely this observation does not distinguish *Stanley,* because police frequently search private homes as well, and their power to do so is unquestioned so long as the search is reasonable within the meaning of the Fourth Amendment.

Perhaps, however, the plurality reasons silently that a prohibition against importation of obscene materials for private use is constitutionally permissible because it is necessary to prevent ultimate commercial distribution of obscenity. It may feel that an importer's intent to distribute obscene materials commercially is so difficult to prove that all such importation may be outlawed without offending the First Amendment. A very similar argument was made by the State in *Stanley* when it urged that enforcement of a possession law was necessary because of the difficulties of proving intent to distribute or actual distribution. However, the Court unequivocally rejected that argument because an individual's right to "read or observe what he pleases" is so "fundamental to our scheme of individual liberty."

Furthermore, any argument that all importation may be banned to stop possible commercial distribution simply ignores numerous holdings of this Court that legislation touching on First Amendment freedoms must be precisely and narrowly drawn to avoid stifling the expression the Amendment was designed to protect. Certainly the Court has repeatedly applied the rule against overbreadth in past censorship cases, . . .

Since the plurality opinion offers no plausible reason to distinguish private possession of "obscenity" from importation for private use, I can only conclude that at least four members of the Court would overrule *Stanley.* Or perhaps in the future that case will be recognized as good law only when a man writes salacious books in his attic, prints them in his basement, and reads them in his living room. . . .

6. Movie Censorship

BURSTYN, INC. *v.* WILSON
343 US 495 (1952)

[The Supreme Court in 1915 excluded the movies from the protection of the First Amendment. It held that movies are purely business undertakings, conducted for profit, and in no sense part of the press of the country. *Mutual Film Corp.* v. *Ohio Industrial Comm.,* 236 US 230 (1915). This meant that movies were subject to state and local licensing or censorship.

[In the present case, commonly referred to as the *Miracle Case,* the Court overruled the principle of the *Mutual Film Case.* Six members of the Court, in an opinion by Justice Clark, held that the basic principles of freedom of speech and press applied to motion pictures. The Court did not, however, outlaw movie censorship if exercised within narrowly defined rules; it left this question open. The decision was limited to the holding that the guaranty of free speech and press prevents a state from banning a film on a finding by a censor that it is "sacrilegious." Justice Frankfurter, with the concurrence of Justices Jackson and Burton, held that the term "sacrilegious" as used in the New York statute was unconstitutionally vague.

[Early in 1953 the Court unanimously held that New York could not ban the French film "La Ronde" on the ground that it was "immoral" and that Ohio could not ban the American picture "M" as "tending to promote crime." The Court cited their decision in the *Miracle Case* as the basis for their decision regarding these two films. The decision with respect to these films has not completely outlawed all movie censorship.

[Preceding Justice Clark's opinion for the Court, we present the following statement of facts from Justice Frankfurter's concurring opinion:

[A practiced hand has thus summarized the story of "The Miracle":

[A poor, simple-minded girl is tending a herd of goats on a mountainside one day, when a bearded stranger passes. Suddenly it strikes her fancy that he is St. Joseph, her favorite saint, and that he has come to take her to heaven, where she will be happy and free. While she pleads with him to transport her, the stranger gently plies the girl with wine, and when she is in a state of tumult, he apparently ravishes her. (This incident in the story is only briefly and discreetly implied.)

[The girl awakens later, finds the stranger gone, and climbs down the mountain not knowing whether he was real or a dream. She meets an old priest who tells her that it is quite possible that she did see a saint, but a younger priest scoffs at the notion. "Materialist!" the old priest says.

[There follows now a brief sequence—intended to be symbolic, obviously—in which the girl is reverently sitting with other villagers in church. Moved by a whim of appetite, she snitches an apple from the basket of a woman next to her. When she leaves the church, a cackling beggar tries to make her share the apple with him, but she chases him away as by habit and munches the fruit contentedly.

[Then, one day, while tending the village youngsters as their mothers work at the vines, the girl faints and the women discover that she is going to have a child. Frightened and bewildered, she suddenly murmurs, "It is the grace of God!" and she runs to the church in great excitement, looks for the statute of St. Joseph, and then prostrates herself on the floor.

[Thereafter she meekly refuses to do any menial work and the housewives humor her greatly but the young people are not so kind. In a scene of brutal torment, they first flatter and laughingly mock her, then they cruelly shove and hit her and clamp a basin as a halo on her head. Even abused by the beggars, the poor girl gathers together her pitiful rags and sadly departs from the village to live alone in a cave.

[When she feels her time coming upon her, she starts towards the village. But then she sees the crowds in the streets; dark memories haunt her; so she turns towards a church on a high hill and instinctively struggles towards it, crying desperately to God. A goat is her sole companion. She drinks water dripping from a rock. And when she comes to the church and finds the door locked, the goat attracts her to a small side door. Inside the church, the poor girl braces herself for her labor pains. There is a dissolve, and when we next see her sad face, in closeup, it is full of a tender light. There is the cry of an unseen baby. The girl reaches towards it and murmurs, "My son! My love! My flesh!"]

["The Miracle"—a film lasting forty minutes—was produced in Italy by Roberto Rossellini. Anna Magnani played the lead as the demented goat-tender. It was first shown at the Venice Film Festival in August, 1948, combined with another moving picture, "L'Umano Voce," into a diptych called "Amore." According to an affidavit from the Director of that Festival, if the motion picture had been "blasphemous" it would have been barred by the Festival Committee. In a review of the film in *L'Osservatore Romano*, the organ of the Vatican, its film critic, Piero Regnoli, wrote: "Opinions may vary and questions may arise—even serious ones—of a religious nature (not to be diminished by the fact that the woman portrayed is mad [because] the author who attributed madness to her is not mad). . . . While acknowledging that there were "passages of undoubted cinematic distinction," Regnoli criticized the film as being "on such a pretentiously cerebral plane that it reminds one of the early d'Annunzio." The Vatican newspaper's critic concluded: "We continue to believe in Rossellini's art and we look forward to his next achievement." In October, 1948, a month after the Rome premiere of "The Miracle," the Vatican's censorship agency, the Catholic Cinematographic Centre, declared that the picture "constitutes in effect an abominable profanation from religious and moral viewpoints." By the Lateran agreements and the Italian Constitution the Italian Government is bound to bar whatever may offend the Catholic religion. However, the Catholic Cinematographic Centre did not invoke any governmental sanction thereby afforded. The Italian Government's censorship agency gave "The Miracle" the regular *nulla osta* clearance. The film was freely shown throughout Italy, but was not a great success. Italian movie critics divided in opinion. The critic for *Il Popolo*, speaking for the Christian Democratic Party, the Catholic party, profusely praised the picture as "a beautiful thing, humanly felt, alive, true and without religious profanation as someone has said, because in our opinion the meaning of the characters is clear and there is no possibility of misunderstanding." Regnoli again reviewed "The Miracle" for *L'Osservatore Romano*. After criticizing the film for technical faults, he found "the most courageous and interesting passage of Rossellini's work" in contrasting portrayals in the film; he added: "Unfortunately, concerning morals, it is necessary to note some slight defects." He objected to its "carnality" and to the representation of illegitimate motherhood. But he did not suggest that the picture was "sacrilegious." The tone of Regnoli's critique was one of respect for Rossellini, "the illustrious Italian producer."

[On March 2, 1949, "The Miracle" was licensed in New York State for showing without English titles. However, it was never exhibited until after a second license was issued on November 30, 1950, for the trilogy, "Ways of Love," combining "The Miracle" with two French films, Jean Renoir's "A Day in the Country" and Marcel Pagnol's "Jofroi." All had English subtitles. Both licenses were issued in the usual course after viewings of the picture by the Motion Picture Division of the New York State Education Department. . . . The trilogy opened on December 12, 1950, at the Paris Theatre on 58th Street in Manhattan. It was promptly attacked as "a sacrilegious and blasphemous mockery of Christian religious truth" by the National Legion of Decency, a private Catholic organization for film censorship, whose objectives have intermittently been approved by various non-Catholic church and social groups since its formation in 1933. However, the National Board of Review (a non-industry lay organization devoted to raising the level of motion pictures by mobilizing public opinion, under the slogan "Selection Not Censorship") recommended the picture as "especially worth seeing." New York critics on the whole praised "The Miracle"; those who dispraised did not suggest sacrilege. On December 27 the critics selected the "Ways of Love" as the best foreign language film in 1950. Meanwhile on December 23, Edward T. McCaffrey, Commissioner of Licenses for New York City, declared the film "officially and personally blasphemous" and ordered it withdrawn at the risk of suspension of the license to operate the Paris Theatre. A week later the program was restored at the theatre upon the decision by the New York Supreme Court that the City License Commissioner had exceeded his authority in that he was without powers of movie censorship.

[Upon the failure of the License Commissioner's effort to cut off showings of "The Miracle," the controversy took a new turn. On Sunday, January 7, 1951, a statement of His Eminence, Francis Cardinal Spellman, condemning the picture and calling on "all right thinking citizens" to unite to tighten censorship laws, was read at all masses in St. Patrick's Cathedral.

[The views of Cardinal Spellman aroused dissent among other devout Christians, Protestant clergymen, representing various denominations, after seeing the picture, found in it nothing "sacrilegious or immoral to the views held by Christian men and women," and with a few exceptions agreed that the film was "unquestionably one of unusual artistic merit."

[In this estimate some Catholic laymen concurred. Their opinion is represented by the comment by Otto L. Spaeth, Director of the American Federation of Arts and prominent in Catholic lay activities:

> [At the outbreak of the controversy, I immediately arranged for a private showing of the film. I invited a group of Catholics, competent and respected for their writings on both religious and cultural subjects. The essential approval of the film was unanimous.
>
> [There was indeed "blasphemy" in the picture—but it was the blasphemy of the villagers, who stopped at nothing, not even the mock singing of a hymn to the Virgin, in their brutal badgering of the tragic woman. The scathing indictment of their evil behaviour, implicit in the film, was seemingly overlooked by its critics.

[William C. Clancy, a teacher at the University of Notre Dame, wrote in *The Commonweal,* the well-known Catholic weekly, that "the film is not *obviously* blasphemous or obscene, either in its intention or execution." *The Commonweal* itself questioned the wisdom of tranforming Church dogma which Catholics may obey as "a free act" into state-enforced censorship for all. Allen Tate, the well-known Catholic poet and critic, wrote: "The picture seems to me to be superior in acting and photography but inferior dramatically. . . . In the long run what Cardinal Spellman will have succeeded in doing is insulting the intelligence and faith of American Catholics with the assumption that a second-rate motion picture could in any way undermine their morals or shake their faith."

[At the time "The Miracle" was filmed, all the persons having significant positions in the production—producer, director, and cast—were Catholics. Roberto Rossellini, who had Vatican approval in 1949 for filming a life of St. Francis, using in the cast members of the Franciscan Order, cabled Cardinal Spellman protesting against boycott of "The Miracle":

> [In "The Miracle" men are still without pity because they still have not come back to God, but God is already in the faith, however confused, of that poor, persecuted woman; and since God is wherever a human being suffers and is misunderstood, "The Miracle" occurs when at the birth of the child the poor, demented woman regains sanity in her eternal love.

[In view of the controversy thus aroused by the picture, the Chairman of the Board of Regents appointed a committee of three Board members to review the action of the Motion Picture Division in granting the two licenses. After viewing the picture on Jan. 15, 1951, the committee declared it "sacrilegious." The Board four days later issued an order to the licensees to show cause why the licenses should not be canceled in that the picture was "sacrilegious." The Board of Regents rescinded the licenses on Feb. 16, 1951, saying that the "mockery or profaning of these beliefs that are sacred to any portion of our citizenship is abhorrent to the laws of this great State." On review the Appellate Division upheld the Board of Regents, holding that the banning of any motion picture "that may fairly be deemed sacrilegious to the adherents of any religious group . . . is directly related to public peace and order" and is not a denial of religious freedom, and that there was "substantial evidence upon which the Regents could act."

[The New York Court of Appeals, with one judge concurring in a separate opinion and two others dissenting, affirmed the order of the Appellate Division. . . .]

Mr. Justice Clark delivered the opinion of the Court:

The issue here is the constitutionality, under the First and Fourteenth Amendments, of a New York statute which permits the banning of motion picture films on the ground that they are sacrilegious." That statute makes it unlawful "to exhibit, or to sell, lease or lend for exhibition at any place of amusement for pay or in connection with any business in the state of New York, any motion picture film or reel [with specified exceptions not relevant here], unless there is at the time in full force and effect a valid license or permit therefor of the education department. . . . " The statute further provides:

The director of the [motion picture] division [of the education department] or, when authorized by the regents, the officers of a local office or bureau shall cause to be promptly examined every motion picture film submitted to them as herein required, and unless such film or a part thereof is obscene, indecent, immoral, inhuman, sacrilegious, or is of such a character that its exhibition would tend to corrupt morals or incite to crime, shall issue a license therefor. If such director or, when so authorized, such officer shall not license any film submitted, he shall furnish to the applicant therefor a written report of the reasons for his refusal and a description of each rejected part of a film not rejected in toto. . . .

Appellant brought the present action in the New York courts to review the determination of the Regents. Among the claims advanced by appellant were (1) that the statute violates the Fourteenth Amendment as a prior restraint upon freedom of speech and of the press; (2) that it is invalid under the same Amendment as a violation of the guaranty of separate church and state and as a prohibition of the free exercise of religion; and, (3) that the term "sacrilegious" is so vague and indefinite as to offend due process. . . . The case is here on appeal. . . .

As we view the case, we need consider only appellant's contention that the New York statute is an unconstitutional abridgment of free speech and a free press. In *Mutual Film Corp.* v. *Industrial Comm. of Ohio,* 236 US 230 (1915), . . . this Court stated:

It cannot be put out of view that the exhibition of motion pictures is a business, pure and simple, originated and conducted for profit, like other spectacles, not to be regarded, nor intended to be regarded by the Ohio Constitution, we think, as part of the press of the country, or as organs of public opinion.

In a series of decisions beginning with *Gitlow* v. *People of State of New York,* 268 US 652 (1925), this Court held that the liberty of speech and of the press which the First Amendment guarantees against abridgment by the federal government is within the liberty safeguarded by the Due Process Clause of the Fourteenth Amendment from invasion by state action. That principle has been followed and reaffirmed to the present day. Since this series of decisions came after the *Mutual* decision, the present case is the first to present squarely to us the question whether motion pictures are within the ambit of protection which the First Amendment, through the Fourteenth, secures to any form of "speech" or "the press."

It cannot be doubted that motion pictures are a significant medium for the communication of ideas. They may affect public attitudes and behaviors in a variety of ways, ranging from direct espousal of a political or social doctrine to the subtle shaping of thought which characterizes all artistic expression. The importance of motion pictures as an organ of public opinion is not lessened by the fact that they are designed to entertain as well as to inform. As was said in *Winters* v. *People of State of New York,* 333 US 507 (1948), "The line between the informing and the entertaining is too elusive for the protection of that basic right [a free press]. Everyone is familiar with instances of propaganda through fiction. What is one man's amusement, teaches another's doctrine."

It is urged that motion pictures do not fall within the First Amendment's aegis because their production, distribution, and exhibition is a large-scale business conducted for private profit. We cannot agree. That books, newspapers, and magazines are published and sold for profit does not prevent them from being a form of expression whose liberty is safeguarded by the First Amendment. We fail to see why operation for profit should have any different effect in the case of motion pictures.

It is further urged that motion pictures possess a greater capacity for evil, particularly among the youth of a community, than other modes of expression. Even if one were to accept this hypothesis, it does not follow that motion pictures should be disqualified from First Amendment protection. If there be capacity for evil it may be relevant in determining the permissible scope of community control, but it does not authorize substantially unbridled censorship such as we have here.

For the foregoing reasons, we conclude that expression by means of motion pictures is included within the free speech and free press guaranty of the First and Fourteenth Amendments. To the extent that language in the opinion in *Mutual Film Corp.* v. *Industrial Comm., supra,* is out of harmony with the views here set forth, we no longer adhere to it.

To hold that liberty of expression by means of motion pictures is guaranteed by the First and Fourteenth Amendments, however, is not the end of our problem. It does not follow that the Constitution requires absolute freedom to exhibit every motion picture of every kind at all times and all places. That much is evident from the series of decisions of this Court with respect to other media of communication of ideas. Nor does it follow that motion pictures are necessarily subject to the precise rules governing any other particular method of expression. Each method tends to present its own peculiar problems. But the basic principles of freedom of speech and the press, like the First Amendment's command, do not vary. Those principles, as they have frequently been enunciated by this Court, make freedom of expression the rule. There is no justification in this case for making an exception to that rule.

The statute involved here does not seek to punish, as a past offense, speech or writing falling within the permissible scope of subsequent punishment. On the contrary, New York requires that permission to communicate ideas be obtained in advance from state officials who judge the content of the words and pictures sought to be communicated. This Court recognized many years ago that such a previous restraint is a form of infringement upon freedom of expression to be especially condemned. *Near* v. *State of Minnesota* ex rel. *Olson,* 283 US 697 (1931). . . .

New York's highest court says there is "nothing mysterious" about the statutory provision applied in this case: "It is simply this: that no religion, as that word is understood by the ordinary, reasonable person, shall be treated with contempt, mockery, scorn and ridicule. . . ." This is far from the kind of narrow exception to freedom of expression which a state may carve out to satisfy the adverse demands of other interests of society. In seeking to apply the broad and all-inclusive definition of "sacrilegious" given by the New York courts, the censor is set adrift upon a boundless sea amid a myriad of conflicting currents of religious views, with no charts but those provided by the most vocal and powerful orthodoxies. New York cannot vest such unlimited restraining control over motion pictures in a censor. . . . Under such a standard the most careful and tolerant censor would find it virtually impossible to avoid favoring one religion over another, and he would be subject to an inevitable tendency to ban the expression of unpopular sentiments sacred to a religious minority. Application of the "sacrilegious" test, in these or other respects, might raise substantial questions under the First Amendment's guaranty of separate church and state with freedom of worship for all. However, from the standpoint of freedom of speech and the press, it is enough to point out that the state has no legitimate interest in protecting any or all religions from views distasteful to them which is sufficient to justify prior restraints upon the expression of those views. It is not the business of government in our nation to suppress real or imagined attacks upon a particular religious doctrine, whether they appear in publications, the State has no legitimate interest in protecting any or all religious speeches, or motion pictures.

Since the term "sacrilegious" is the sole standard under attack here, it is not necessary for us to decide, for example, whether a state may censor motion pictures under a clearly-drawn statute designed and applied to prevent the showing of obscene films. That is a very different question from the one now before us. We hold only that under the First and Fourteenth Amendments a state may not ban a film on the basis of a censor's conclusion that it is "sacrilegious."

Reversed.

KINGSLEY INTERNATIONAL PICTURES CORP. *v.* REGENTS OF UNIVERSITY OF STATE OF NEW YORK 360 US 684 (1959)

[The film "Lady Chatterley's Lover," based on the novel by D. H. Lawrence, was banned in the State of New York. The ban was unanimously upset by the United States Supreme Court. The New York statute required the denial of a license to motion pictures "which are immoral in that they portray 'acts of sexual immorality . . . as desirable, acceptable, or proper patterns of behavior.'" The New York authorities held that this language required the denial of a license to the film "because its subject matter is adultery presented as being right and desirable for certain people under certain circumstances." The United States Supreme Court held that the ban on the film violated the First Amendment guarantee of the freedom to advocate ideas. The Constitution "protects advocacy of the opinion that adultery may sometimes be proper, no less than advocacy of socialism or the single tax."]

Mr. Justice Stewart delivered the opinion of the Court:

Once again the Court is required to consider the impact of New York's motion picture licensing law upon First Amendment liberties, protected by the Fourteenth Amendment from infringement by the States. . . .

The New York statute makes it unlawful "to exhibit, or to sell, lease or lend for exhibition at any place of amusement for pay or in connection with any business in the state of New York, any motion picture film or reel [with certain exceptions not relevant here], unless there is at the time in full force and effect a valid license or permit therefor of the education department. . . ." The law provides that a license shall issue "unless such film or a part thereof is obscene, indecent, immoral, inhuman, sacrilegious, or is of such a character that its exhibition would tend to corrupt morals or incite to crime. . . ." A recent statutory amendment provides that, "the term 'immoral' and the phrase 'of such a character that its exhibition would tend to corrupt morals' shall denote a motion picture film or part thereof, the dominant purpose or effect of which is erotic or pornographic; or which portrays acts of sexual immorality, perversion, or lewdness, or which expressly or impliedly presents such acts as desirable, acceptable or proper patterns of behavior."

As the distributor of a motion picture entitled "Lady Chatterley's Lover," the appellant Kingsley submitted that film to the Motion Picture Division of the New York Education Department for a license. Finding three isolated scenes in the film " 'immoral' within the intent of our Law," the Division refused to issue a license until the scenes in question were deleted. The distributor petitioned the Regents of the State of New York for a review of that ruling. The Regents upheld the denial of a license, but on the broader ground that "the whole theme of this motion picture is immoral under said law, for that theme is the presentation of adultery as a desirable, acceptable and proper pattern of behavior."

Kingsley sought judicial review of the Regents' determination. The Appellate Division unanimously annulled the action of the Regents and directed that a license be issued. . . . A sharply divided Court of Appeals, however, reversed the Appellate Division and upheld the Regents' refusal to license the film for exhibition. . . .

The Court of Appeals unanimously and explicitly rejected any notion that the film is obscene. . . . Rather, the court found that the picture as a whole "alluringly portrays adultery as proper behavior." As Chief Judge Conway's prevailing opinion emphasized, therefore, the only portion of the statute involved in this case is that part of §§ 122 and 122(a) of the Education Law requiring the denial of a license to motion pictures "which are immoral in that they portray 'acts of sexual immorality . . . as desirable, acceptable, or proper patterns of behavior.' " A majority of the Court of Appeals ascribed to that language a precise purpose of the New York Legislature to require the denial of a license to a motion picture "because its subject matter is adultery presented as being right and desirable for certain people under certain circumstances."

We accept the premise that the motion picture here in question can be so characterized. We accept too, as we must, the construction of the New York Legislature's language which the Court of Appeals has put upon it. . . . That construction, we emphasize, gives to the term "sexual immorality" a concept entirely different from the concept embraced in words like "obscenity" or "pornography." Moreover, it is not suggested that the film would itself operate as an incitement to illegal action. Rather, the New York Court of Appeals tells us that the relevant portion of the New York Education Law requires the denial of a license to any motion picture which approvingly portrays an adulterous relationship, quite without reference to the manner of its portrayal.

What New York has done, therefore, is to prevent the exhibition of a motion pictures because that picture advocates an idea—that adultery under certain circumstances may be proper behavior. Yet the First Amendment's basic guarantee is of freedom to advocate ideas. The State, quite simply, has thus struck at the very heart of constitutionally protected liberty.

It is contended that the State's action was justified because the motion picture attractively portrays a relationship which is contrary to the moral sandards, the religious precepts, and the legal code of its citizenry. This argument misconceives what it is that the Constitution protects. Its guarantee is not confined to the expression of ideas that are conventional or shared by a majority. It protects advocacy of the opinion that adultery may sometimes be proper, no less than advocacy of socialism or the single tax. And in the realm of ideas it protects expression which is eloquent no less than that which is unconvincing.

Advocacy of conduct proscribed by law is not, as Mr. Justice Brandeis long ago pointed out, "a justification for denying free speech where the advocacy falls short of incitement and there is nothing to indicate that the advocacy would be immediately acted on." *Whitney* v. *California,* 274 US 357, at 376 (concurring opinion). "Among free men, the deterrents ordinarily to be applied to prevent crime are education and punishment for violations of the law, not abridgment of the rights of free speech. . . ." *Id.,* at 378.*

The inflexible command which the New York Court of Appeals has attributed to the State Legislature thus cuts so close to the core of constitutional freedom as to make it quite needless in this case to examine the periphery. Specifically, there is no occasion to consider the appellant's contention that the State is entirely without power to require films of any kind to be licensed prior to their exhibition. Nor need we here determine whether, despite problems peculiar to motion pictures, the controls which a State may impose upon this medium of expression are precisely coextensive with those allowable for newspapers, books, or individual speech. It is enough for the present case to reaffirm that motion pictures are within the First and Fourteenth Amendments' basic protection. *Joseph Burstyn, Inc.,* v. *Wilson,* 343 US 495.

Reversed.

TIMES FILM CORPORATION v. CHICAGO
365 US 43 (1961)

[An ordinance of the city of Chicago required the submission of moving pictures to a censor as a prerequisite to a public showing. Petitioner applied for a permit to

---

* Thomas Jefferson wrote more than a hundred and fifty years ago, "But we have nothing to fear from the demoralizing reasonings of some, if others are left free to demonstrate their errors. And especially when the law stands ready to punish the first criminal *act* produced by the false reasoning. These are safer correctives than the conscience of a judge." Letter of Thomas Jefferson to Elijah Boardman, July 3, 1801, Jefferson Papers, Library of Congress, Vol. 115, folio 19761.

show "Don Juan" but refused to submit the film for examination. The permit was refused. Petitioner applied for an injunction ordering the issuance of the permit without prior submission of the film, on the ground that the ordinance on its face was unconstitutional as a prior restraint. The injunction was denied. The Supreme Court affirmed the judgments below, holding that the ordinance was not void on its face. Chief Justice Warren dissented, joined by Justices Black, Douglas, and Brennan. Justice Douglas also wrote a dissenting opinion, in which he was joined by Chief Justice Warren and Justice Black.]

Mr. Justice Clark delivered the opinion of the Court:

Petitioner challenges on constitutional grounds the validity on its face of that portion of § 155-4 of the Municipal Code of the City of Chicago which requires submission of all motion pictures for examination prior to their public exhibition. Petitioner is a New York corporation owning the exclusive right to publicly exhibit in Chicago the film known as "Don Juan." It applied for a permit as Chicago's ordinance required, and tendered the license fee but refused to submit the film for examination. The appropriate city official refused to issue the permit and his order was made final on appeal to the Mayor. The sole ground for denial was petitioner's refusal to submit the film for examination as required. Petitioner then brought this suit seeking injunctive relief ordering the issuance of the permit without submission of the film and restraining the city officials from interfering with the exhibition of the picture. Its sole ground is that the provision of the ordinance requiring submission of the film constitutes, on its face, a prior restraint within the prohibition of the First and Fourteenth Amendments. The District Court dismissed the complaint on the grounds, *inter alia,* that neither a substantial federal question nor even a justiciable controversy was presented. The Court of Appeals affirmed, finding that the case presented merely an abstract question of law since neither the film nor evidence of its content was submitted. The precise question at issue here never having been specially decided by this Court, we granted certiorari.

We are satisfied that a justiciable controversy exists. The section of Chicago's ordinance in controversy specifically provides that a permit for the public exhibition of a motion picture must be obtained; that such "permit shall be granted only after the motion picture film for which said permit is requested has been produced at the office of the commissioner of police for examination"; that the Commissioner shall refuse the permit if the picture does not meet certain standards; and that in the event of such refusal the applicant may appeal to the Mayor for a *de novo* hearing and his action shall be final. Violation of the ordinance carries certain punishments. The petitioner complied with the requirements of the ordinance, save for the production of the film for examination. The claim is that this concrete and specific statutory requirement, the production of the film at the office of the Commissioner for examination, is invalid as a previous restraint on freedom of speech. In *Joseph Burstyn, Inc.,* v. *Wilson,* 343 US 495 (1952), we held that motion pictures are included "within the free speech and free press guaranty of the First and Fourteenth Amendments." Admittedly, the challenged section of the ordinance imposes a previous restraint, and the broad justiciable issue is therefore present as to whether the ambit of constitutional protection includes complete and absolute freedom to exhibit, at least once, any and every kind of motion picture. It is that question alone which we decide. We have concluded that § 155-4 of Chicago's ordinance requiring the submission of films prior to their public exhibition is not, on the grounds set forth, void on its face.

Petitioner's narrow attack upon the ordinance does not require that any consideration be given to the validity of the standards set out therein. They are not challenged and are not before us. Prior motion picture censorship cases which reached this Court involved questions of standards. The films had all been submitted to the authorities and permits for their exhibition were refused because of their content. Obviously, whether a particular statute is "clearly drawn," or "vague," or "indefinite," or whether a clear standard is in fact met by a film are different questions involving other constitutional challenges to be tested by considerations not here involved.

Moreover, there is not a word in the record as to the nature and content of "Don Juan." We are left entirely in the dark in this regard, as were the city officials and the other reviewing courts. Petitioner claims that the nature of the film is irrelevant, and that even if this film contains the basest type of pornography, or incitement to riot, or forceful overthrow of orderly government, it may nonetheless be shown without prior submission for examination. The challenge here is to the censor's basic authority; it does not go to any statutory standards employed by the censor or procedural requirements as to the submission of the film.

In this perspective we consider the prior decisions of this Court touching on the problem. Beginning over a third of a century ago in *Gitlow* v. *New York,* 268 US 652 (1925), they have consistently reserved for future decision possible situations in which the claimed First Amendment privilege might have to give way to the necessities of the public welfare. It has never been held that liberty of speech is absolute. Nor has it been suggested that all previous restraints on speech are invalid. On the contrary, in *Near* v. *Minnesota,* 283 US 697 (1931), Chief Justice Hughes, in discussing the classic legal statements concerning the immunity of the press from censorship, observed that the principle forbidding previous restraint "is stated too broadly, if every such restraint is deemed to be prohibited. . . . [T]he protection even as to previous restraint is not absolutely unlimited. But the limitation has been recognized only in exceptional cases." These included, the Chief Justice found, utterances creating "a hindrance" to the Government's war effort, and "actual obstruction to its recruiting service or the publication of the sailing dates of transports or the number and location of troops." In addition, the Court said that "the primary requirements of decency may be enforced against obscene publications" and the "security of the community life may be protected against incitements to acts of violence and the overthrow by force of orderly government." Some years later a unanimous Court, speaking through Mr. Justice Murphy, in *Chaplinsky* v. *New Hampshire,* 315 US 568 (1942), held that there were "certain well-defined and narrowly limited classes of speech, the prevention and punishment of which have never been thought to raise any Constitutional problem. These include the lewd and obscene, the profane, the libelous, and the insulting or 'fighting' words— those which by their very utterance inflict injury or tend to incite an immediate breach of the peace." Thereafter, as we have mentioned, in *Joseph Burstyn, Inc.,* v.

Wilson, supra, we found motion pictures to be within the guarantees of the First and Fourteenth Amendments, but we added that this was "not the end of our problem. It does not follow that the Constitution requires absolute freedom to exhibit every motion picture of every kind at all times and all places." Five years later, in *Roth* v. *United States,* 354 US 476 (1957), we held that "in light of . . . history it is apparent that the unconditional phrasing of the first amendment was not intended to protect every utterance." Even those in dissent found that "freedom of expression can be suppressed if, and to the extent that, it is so closely brigaded with illegal action as to be an inseparable part of it." And, during the same Term, in *Kingsley Books, Inc.,* v. *Brown,* 354 US 436 (1957), after characterizing *Near* v. *Minnesota, supra,* as "one of the landmark opinions" in its area, we took notice that *Near* "left no doubts that 'Liberty of speech, and of the press, is also not an absolute right . . . the protection even as to previous restraint is not absolutely unlimited.' . . . The judicial angle of vision," we said there, "in testing the validity of a statute like § 22-a [New York's injunctive remedy against certain forms of obscenity] is 'the operation and effect of the statute in substance.' " And as if to emphasize the point involved here, we added that "The phrase 'prior restraint' is not a self-wielding sword. Nor can it serve as a talismanic test." Even as recently as our last Term we again observed the principle, albeit in an allied area, that the State possesses some measure of power "to prevent the distribution of obscene matter." *Smith* v. *California,* 361 US 147 (1959).

Petitioner would have us hold that the public exhibition of motion pictures must be allowed under any circumstances. The State's sole remedy, it says, is the invocation of criminal process under the Illinois pornography statute, . . . and then only after a transgression. But this position, as we have seen, is founded upon the claim of absolute privilege against prior restraint under the First Amendment—a claim without sanction in our cases. To illustrate its fallacy we need only point to one of the "exceptional cases" which Chief Justice Hughes enumerated in *Near* v. *Minnesota, supra,* namely, "the primary requirements of decency [that] may be enforced against obscene publications." Moreover, we later held specifically "that obscenity is not within the area of constitutionally protected speech or press." *Roth* v. *United States. . . .* Chicago emphasizes here its duty to protect its people against the dangers of obscenity in the public exhibition of motion pictures. To this argument petitioner's only answer is that regardless of the capacity for, or extent of such an evil, previous restraint cannot be justified. With this we cannot agree. We recognized in *Burstyn, supra,* that "capacity for evil . . . may be relevant in determining the permissible scope of community control," and that motion pictures were not "necessarily subject to the precise rules governing any other particular method of expression. Each method," we said, "tends to present its own peculiar problems." Certainly petitioner's broadside attack does not warrant, nor could it justify on the record here, our saying that—aside from any consideration of the other "exceptional cases" mentioned in our decisions—the State is stripped of all constitutional power to prevent, in the most effective fashion, the utterance of this class of speech. It is not for this Court to limit the State in its selection of the remedy it deems most effective to cope with such a problem, absent, of course, a showing of unreasonable strictures on individual liberty resulting from its application in particular circumstances. . . . We, of course, are not holding that city officials may be granted the power to prevent the showing of any motion picture they deem unworthy of a license. . . .

As to what may be decided when a concrete case involving a specific standard provided by this ordinance is present, we intimate no opinion. The petitioner has not challenged all—or for that matter any—of the ordinance's standards. Naturally we could not say that every one of the standards, including those which Illinois' highest court has found sufficient, is so vague on its face that the entire ordinance is void. At this time we say no more than this—that we are dealing only with motion pictures and, even as to them, only in the context of the broadside attack presented on this record.

Affirmed.

JACOBELLIS v. OHIO
378 US 184 (1964)

[A theater in Cleveland Heights, Ohio, showed the French film *Les Amants* (The Lovers). The manager of the theater was convicted for possessing and exhibiting the film, which the state authorities found to be obscene. By 6 to 3, the U.S. Supreme Court reversed the judgment of conviction. There were four opinions favoring reversal of the judgment, and two dissenting opinions. Dissenting were Chief Justice Warren, and Justices Clark and Harlan. The case is especially important for the discussion of national *contra* local standards of propriety.]

Mr. Justice Brennan announced the judgment of the Court and delivered an opinion in which Mr. Justice Goldberg joins:

Appellant, Nico Jacobellis, manager of a motion picture theater in Cleveland Heights, Ohio, was convicted on two counts for possessing and exhibiting an obscene film in violation of Ohio Revised Code § 2905.34.* He was fined $500 on the first count and $2,000 on the second, and was sentenced to the workhouse if the fines were not paid. His conviction, by a court of three judges upon waiver of trial by jury, was affirmed by an intermediate appellate court, and by the Supreme

---

* *"Selling, exhibiting, and possessing obscene literature or drugs, for criminal purposes*:
"No person shall knowingly sell, lend, give away, exhibit, or offer to sell, lend, give away, or exhibit, or publish or offer to publish or have in his possession or under his control an obscene, lewd, or lascivious book, magazine, pamphlet, paper, writing, advertisement, circular, print, picture, photograph, motion picture film, or book, pamphlet, paper, magazine not wholly obscene but containing lewd or lascivious articles, advertisements, photographs, or drawing, representation, figure, image, cast, instrument, or article of an indecent or immoral nature, or a drug, medicine, article, or thing intended for the prevention of conception or for causing an abortion, or advertise any of them for sale, or write, print, or cause to be written or printed a card, book, pamphlet, advertisement, or notice giving information when, where, how, of whom, or by what means any of such articles or things can be purchased or obtained, or manufacture, draw, print, or make such articles or things, or sell, give away, or show to a minor, a book, pamphlet, magazine, newspaper, story paper, or other paper devoted to the publication, or principally made up, of criminal news, police reports, or accounts of criminal deeds, or pictures and stories of immoral deeds, lust, or crime, or exhibit upon a street or highway or in a place which may be within the view of a minor, any of such books, papers, magazines, or pictures.
"Whoever violates this section shall be fined not less than two hundred nor more than two thousand dollars or imprisoned not less than one nor more than seven years, or both."

Court of Ohio. We noted probable jurisdiction of the appeal, and subsequently restored the case to the calendar for reargument. The dispositive question is whether the state courts properly found that the motion picture involved, a French film called *"Les Amants"* ("The Lovers"), was obscene and hence not entitled to the protection for free expression that is guaranteed by the First and Fourteenth Amendments. We conclude that the film is not obscene and that the judgment must accordingly be reversed.

Motion pictures are within the ambit of the constitutional guarantees of freedom of speech and of the press. *Joseph Burstyn, Inc., v. Wilson,* 343 US 495. But in *Roth* v. *United States* and *Alberts* v. *California,* 354 US 476, we held that obscenity is not subject to those guarantees. Application of an obscenity law to suppress a motion picture thus requires ascertainment of the "dim and uncertain line" that often separates obscenity from constitutionally protected expression. . . . It has been suggested that this is a task in which our Court need not involve itself. We are told that the determination whether a particular motion picture, book, or other work of expression is obscene can be treated as a purely factual judgment on which a jury's verdict is all but conclusive, or that in any event the decision can be left essentially to state and lower federal courts, with this Court exercising only a limited review such as that needed to determine whether the ruling below is supported by "sufficient evidence." The suggestion is appealing, since it would lift from our shoulders a difficult, recurring, and unpleasant task. But we cannot accept it. Such an abnegation of judicial supervision in this field would be inconsistent with our duty to uphold the constitutional guarantees. Since it is only "obscenity" that is excluded from the constitutional protection, the question whether a particular work is obscene necessarily implicates an issue of constitutional law. . . . Such an issue, we think, must ultimately be decided by this Court. Our duty admits of no "substitute for facing up to the tough individual problems of constitutional judgment involved in every obscenity case." . . .

In other areas involving constitutional rights under the Due Process Clause, the Court has consistently recognized its duty to apply the applicable rules of law upon the basis of an independent review of the facts of each case. . . . And this has been particularly true where rights have been asserted under the First Amendment guarantees of free expression. . . . We cannot understand why the Court's duty should be any different in the present case, where Jacobellis has been subjected to a criminal conviction for disseminating a work of expression and is challenging that conviction as a deprivation of rights guaranteed by the First and Fourteenth Amendments. Nor can we understand why the Court's performance of its constitutional and judicial function in this sort of case should be denigrated by such epithets as "censor" or "super-censor." In judging alleged obscenity the Court is no more "censoring" expression than it has in other cases "censored" criticism of judges and public officials, advocacy of governmental overthrow, or speech alleged to constitute a breach of the peace. Use of an opprobrious label can neither obscure nor impugn the Court's performance of its obligation to test challenged judgments against the guarantees of the First and Fourteenth Amendments and, in doing so, to delineate the scope of constitutionally protected speech. Hence we reaffirm the principle that, in "obscenity" cases as in all others involving rights derived from the

First Amendment guarantees of free expression, this Court cannot avoid making an independent constitutional judgment on the facts of the case as to whether the material involved is constitutionally protected.

The question of the proper standard for making this determination has been the subject of much discussion and controversy since our decision in *Roth-Alberts* seven years ago. Recognizing that the test for obscenity enunciated there— "whether to the average person, applying contemporary community standards, the dominant theme of the material taken as a whole appeals to prurient interest," is not perfect, we think any substitute would raise equally difficult problems, and we therefore adhere to that standard. We would reiterate, however, our recognition in *Roth* that obscenity is excluded from the constitutional protection only because it is "utterly without redeeming social importance," and that "the portrayal of sex, e.g., in art, literature, and scientific works, is not itself sufficient reason to deny material the constitutional protection of freedom of speech and press." It follows that material dealing with sex in a manner that advocates ideas, . . . or that has literary or scientific or artistic value or any other form of social importance, may not be branded as obscenity and denied the constitutional protection. Nor may the constitutional status of the material be made to turn on a "weighing" of its social importance against its prurient appeal, for a work cannot be proscribed unless it is "utterly" without social importance. . . . It should also be recognized that the *Roth* standard requires in the first instance a finding that the material "goes substantially beyond customary limits of candor in description or representation of such matters." This was a requirement of the Model Penal Code test that we approved in *Roth,* and it is explicitly reaffirmed in the more recent "Proposed Official Draft" of the Code. In the absence of such a deviation from society's standards of decency, we do not see how any official inquiry into the allegedly prurient appeal of a work of expression can be squared with the guarantees of the First and Fourteenth Amendments. . . .

It has been suggested that the "contemporary community standards" aspect of the *Roth* test implies a determination of the constitutional question of obscenity in each case by the standards of the particular local community from which the case arises. This is an incorrect reading of *Roth.* The concept of "contemporary community standards" was first expressed by Judge Learned Hand in *United States* v. *Kennerley,* 209 F.2d 119 D.S.C.D. N.Y. 1913), where he said:

Yet, if the time is not yet when men think innocent all that which is honestly germane to a pure subject, however little it may mince its words, still I scarcely think that they would forbid all which might corrupt the most corruptible, or that society is prepared to accept for its own limitations those which may perhaps be necessary to the weakest of its members. If there be no abstract definition, such as I have suggested, should not the word "obscene" be allowed to indicate the present critical point in the compromise between candor and shame at which *the community may have arrived here and now?* . . . To put thought in leash to the *average conscience of the time* is perhaps tolerable, but to fetter it by the necessities of the lowest and least capable seems a fatal policy. . . .

Nor is it an objection, I think, that such an interpretation gives to the words of the statute a varying meaning from time to time. Such words as these do not embalm the precise morals of an age or place; while they presuppose that some things will always be shocking to the public taste, the vague subject-matter is left to the gradual development of general notions about what is decent. . . . (Italics added.)

It seems clear that in this passage Judge Hand was referring not to state and local "communities," but rather to "the community" in the sense of "society at large; . . . the public, or people in general." Thus, he recognized that under his standard the concept of obscenity would have "a varying meaning from time to time"—not from county to county, or town to town.

We do not see how any "local" definition of the "community" could properly be employed in delineating the area of expression that is protected by the Federal Constitution. Mr. Justice Harlan pointed out in *Manual Enterprises, Inc.,* v. *Day,* that a standard based on a particular local community would have "the intolerable consequence of denying some sections of the country access to material, there deemed acceptable, which in others might be considered offensive to prevailing community standards of decency. . . . It is true that *Manual Enterprises* dealt with the federal statute banning obscenity from the mails. But the mails are not the only means by which works of expression cross local-community lines in this country. It can hardly be assumed that all the patrons of a particular library, bookstand, or motion picture theater are residents of the smallest local "community" that can be drawn around that establishment. Furthermore, to sustain the suppression of a particular book or film in one locality would deter its dissemination in other localities where it might be held not obscene, since sellers and exhibitors would be reluctant to risk criminal conviction in testing the variation between the two places. It would be a hardy person who would sell a book or exhibit a film anywhere in the land after this Court had sustained the judgment of one "community" holding it to be outside the constitutional protection. The result would thus be "to restrict the public's access to forms of the printed word which the State could not constitutionally suppress directly." . . .

It is true that local communities throughout the land are in fact diverse, and that in cases such as this one the Court is confronted with the task of reconciling the rights of such communities with the rights of individuals. Communities vary, however, in many respects other than their toleration of alleged obscenity, and such variances have never been considered to require or justify a varying standard for application of the Federal Constitution. The Court has regularly been compelled, in reviewing criminal convictions challenged under the Due Process Clause of the Fourteenth Amendment, to reconcile the conflicting rights of the local community which brought the prosecution and of the individual defendant. Such a task is admittedly difficult and delicate, but it is inherent in the Court's duty of determining whether a particular conviction worked a deprivation of rights guaranteed by the Federal Constitution. The Court has not shrunk from discharging that duty in other areas, and we see no reason why it should do so here. The Court has explicitly refused to tolerate a result whereby "the constitutional limits of free expression in the Nation would vary with state lines," . . . we see even less justification for allowing such limits to vary with town or county lines. We thus reaffirm the position taken in *Roth* to the effect that the constitutional status of an allegedly obscene work must be determined on the basis of a national standard. It is, after all, a national Constitution we are expounding.

We recognize the legitimate and indeed exigent interest of States and localities throughout the Nation in preventing the dissemination of material deemed harmful to children. But that interest does not justify a total suppression of such material, the effect of which would be to "reduce the adult population . . . to reading only what is fit for children." . . . State and local authorities might well consider whether their objectives in this area would be better served by laws aimed specifically at preventing distribution of objectionable material to children, rather than at totally prohibiting its dissemination. Since the present conviction is based upon exhibition of the film to the public at large and not upon its exhibition to children, the judgment must be reviewed under the strict standard applicable in determining the scope of the expression that is protected by the Constitution.

We have applied that standard to the motion picture in question. "The Lovers" involves a woman bored with her life and marriage who abandons her husband and family for a young archaeologist with whom she has suddenly fallen in love. There is an explicit love scene in the last reel of the film, and the State's objections are based almost entirely upon that scene. The film was favorably reviewed in a number of national publications, although disparaged in others, and was rated by at least two critics of national stature among the best films of the year in which it was produced. It was shown in approximately 100 of the larger cities in the United States, including Columbus and Toledo, Ohio. We have viewed the film, in the light of the record made in the trial court, and we conclude that it is not obscene within the standards enunciated in *Alberts* v. *California* and *Roth* v. *United States,* which we reaffirm here.

Reversed.

Opinion of Mr. Justice Black, with whom Mr. Justice Douglas joins:

I concur in the reversal of this judgment. My belief, as stated in *Kingsley International Pictures Corp.* v. *Regents,* 360 US 684, is that "If despite the Constitution . . . this Nation is to embark on the dangerous road of censorship, my belief is that this Court is about the most inappropriate Supreme Board of Censors that could be found." My reason for reversing is that I think the conviction of appellant or anyone else for exhibiting a motion picture abridges freedom of the press as safeguarded by the First Amendment, which is made obligatory on the States by the Fourteenth. . . .

Mr. Justice Stewart, concurring:

It is possible to read the Court's opinion in *Alberts* v. *California* and *Roth* v. *United States* in a variety of ways. In saying this, I imply no criticism of the Court, which in those cases was faced with the task of trying to define what may be indefinable. I have reached the conclusion, which I think is confirmed at least by negative implication in the Court's decisions since *Roth* and *Alberts,* that under the First and Fourteenth Amendments criminal laws in this area are constitutionally limited to hard-core pornography. I shall not today attempt further to define the kinds of material I understand to be embraced within that short-hand description; and perhaps I could never succeed in intelligibly doing so. But I know it when I see it, and the motion picture involved in this case is not that.

Mr. Justice Goldberg, concurring:

The question presented is whether the First and Fourteenth Amendments permit the imposition of criminal punishment for exhibiting the motion picture entitled "The Lovers." I have viewed the film and I wish merely to add to my Brother Brennan's description that the love scene deemed objectionable is so fragmentary and fleeting that only a censor's alert would make an audience conscious that something "questionable" is being portrayed. Except for this rapid sequence, the film concerns itself with the history of an ill-matched and unhappy marriage—a familiar subject in old and new novels and in current television soap operas.

Although I fully agree with what my Brother Brennan has written, I am also of the view that adherence to the principles stated in *Joseph Burstyn, Inc.*, v. *Wilson*, 343 US 495, requires reversal. In *Burstyn* Mr. Justice Clark, delivering the unanimous judgment of the Court, said:

> [E]xpression by means of motion pictures is included within the free speech and free press guaranty of the First and Fourteenth Amendments. . . .
>
> To hold that liberty of expression by means of motion pictures is guaranteed by the First and Fourteenth Amendments, however, is not the end of our problem. It does not follow that the Constitution requires absolute freedom to exhibit every motion picture of every kind at all times and all places. . . . Nor does it follow that motion pictures are necessarily subject to the precise rules governing any other particular method of expression. Each method tends to present its own peculiar problems. But the basic principles of freedom of speech and the press, like the First Amendment's command, do not vary. Those principles, as they have frequently been enunciated by this Court, make freedom of expression the rule.

As in *Burstyn* "[t]here is no justification in this case for making an exception to that rule," *id.*, at 503, for by any arguable standard and criteria the exhibitors of this motion picture may not be criminally prosecuted unless the exaggerated character of the advertising rather than the obscenity of the film is to be the constitutional criterion.

The Chief Justice, with whom Mr. Justice Clark joins, dissenting:

In this and other cases in this area of the law, which are coming to us in ever-increasing numbers, we are faced with the resolution of rights basic both to individuals and to society as a whole. Specifically, we are called upon to reconcile the right of the Nation and of the States to maintain a decent society and, on the other hand, the right of individuals to express themselves freely in accordance with the guarantees of the First and Fourteenth Amendments. Although the Federal Government and virtually every State has had laws proscribing obscenity since the Union was formed, and although this Court has recently decided that obscenity is not within the protection of the First Amendment, neither courts nor legislatures have been able to evolve a truly satisfactory definition of obscenity. In other areas of the law, terms like "negligence," although in common use for centuries, have been difficult to define except in the most general manner. Yet the courts have been able to function in such areas with a reasonable degree of efficiency. The obscenity problem, however, is aggravated by the fact that it involves the area of public expression, an area in which a broad range of freedom is vital to our society and is constitutionally protected.

Recently this Court put its hand to the task of defining the term "obscenity" in *Roth* v. *United States*, 354 US 476. The definition enunciated in that case has generated much legal speculation, as well as further judicial interpretation by state and federal courts.

It has also been relied upon by legislatures. Yet obscenity cases continue to come to this Court, and it becomes increasingly apparent that we must settle as well as we can the question of what constitutes "obscenity" and the question of what standards are permissible in enforcing proscriptions against obscene matter. This Court hears cases such as the instant one not merely to rule upon the alleged obscenity of a specific film or book but to establish principles for the guidance of lower courts and legislatures. Yet most of our decisions since *Roth* have been given without opinion and have thus failed to furnish such guidance. Nor does the Court in the instant case—which has now been twice argued before us—shed any greater light on the problem. Therefore, I consider it appropriate to state my views at this time.

For all the sound and fury that the *Roth* test has generated, it has not been proved unsound, and I believe that we should try to live with it—at least until a more satisfactory definition is evolved. No government—be it federal, state, or local—should be forced to choose between repressing all material, including that within the realm of decency, and allowing unrestrained license to publish any material, no matter how vile. There must be a rule of reason in this as in other areas of the law, and we have attempted in the *Roth* case to provide such a rule.

It is my belief that when the Court said in *Roth* that obscenity is to be defined by reference to "community standards," it meant community standards—not a national standard, as is sometimes argued. I believe that there is no provable "national standard," and perhaps there should be none. At all events, this Court has not been able to enunciate one, and it would be unreasonable to expect local courts to divine one. It is said that such a "community" approach may well result in material being proscribed as obscene in one community but not in another, and, in all probability, that is true. But communities throughout the Nation are in fact diverse, and it must be remembered that, in cases such as this one, the Court is confronted with the task of reconciling conflicting rights of the diverse communities within our society and of individuals.

We are told that only "hard core pornography" should be denied the protection of the First Amendment. But who can define "hard core pornography" with any greater clarity than "obscenity"? And even if we were to retreat to that position, we would soon be faced with the need to define that term just as we now are faced with the need to define "obscenity." Meanwhile, those who profit from the commercial exploitation of obscenity would continue to ply their trade unmolested.

In my opinion, the use to which various materials are put—not just the words and pictures themselves—must be considered in determining whether or not the materials are obscene. A technical or legal treatise on pornography may well be inoffensive under most circumstances but, at the same time, "obscene" in the extreme when sold or displayed to children.

Finally, material which is in fact obscene under the *Roth* test may be proscribed in a number of ways—for instance, by confiscation of the material or by prosecution of those who disseminate it—provided always that the proscription, whatever it may be, is imposed in accordance with constitutional standards. If the proceeding involved is criminal, there must be a right to a jury trial, a right to counsel, and all the other safeguards necessary to assure due process of law. If the proceeding is civil in nature, the constitutional requirements applicable in such a case must also be observed. There has been some tendency in dealing with this area of the law for enforcement agencies to do only that which is easy to do—for instance, to seize and destroy books with only a minimum of protection. As a result, courts are often presented with procedurely bad cases and, in dealing with them, appear to be acquiescing in the dissemination of obscenity. But if cases were well prepared and were conducted with the appropriate concern for constitutional safeguards, courts would not hesitate to enforce the laws against obscenity. Thus, enforcement agencies must realize that there is no royal road to enforcement; hard and conscientious work is required.

In light of the foregoing, I would reiterate my acceptance of the rule of the *Roth* case: Material is obscene and not constitutionally protected against regulation and proscription if "to the average person, applying contemporary community standards, the dominant theme of the material taken as a whole appeals to prurient interest." I would commit the enforcement of this rule to the appropriate state and federal courts, and I would accept their judgments made pursuant to the *Roth* rule, limiting myself to a consideration only of whether there is sufficient evidence in the record upon which a finding of obscenity could be made. If there is no evidence in the record upon which such a finding could be made, obviously the material involved cannot be held obscene. . . . But since a mere modicum of evidence may satisfy a "no evidence" standard, I am unwilling to give the important constitutional right of free expression such limited protection. However, protection of society's right to maintain its moral fiber and the effective administration of justice require that this Court not establish itself as an ulti- mate censor, in each case reading the entire record, viewing the accused material, and making an independent *de novo* judgment on the question of obscenity. Therefore, once a finding of obscenity has been made below under a proper application of the *Roth* test, I would apply a "sufficient evidence" standard of review—requiring something more than merely any evidence but something less than "substantial evidence on the record [including the allegedly obscene material] as a whole." . . . This is the only reasonable way I can see to obviate the necessity of this Court's sitting as the Super Censor of all the obscenity purveyed throughout the Nation.

While in this case, I do not subscribe to some of the State's extravagant contentions, neither can I say that the courts below acted with intemperance or without sufficient evidence in finding the moving picture obscene within the meaning of the *Roth* test. Therefore, I would affirm the judgment.

Mr. Justice Harlan, dissenting:

While agreeing with my Brother Brennan's opinion that the responsibilities of the Court in this area are no different than those which attend the adjudication of kindred constitutional questions, I have heretofore expressed the view that the States are con- stitutionally permitted greater latitude in determining what is bannable on the score of obscenity than is so with the Federal Government. . . . While, as correctly said in Mr. Justice Brennan's opinion, the Court has not accepted that view, I nonetheless feel free to adhere to it in this still developing aspect of constitutional law.

The more I see of these obscenity cases the more convinced I become that in per- mitting the States wide, but not federally unrestricted, scope in this field, while holding the Federal Government with a tight rein, lies the best promise for achieving a sensible accommodation between the public interest sought to be served by obscenity laws . . . and protection of genuine rights of free expression.

I experience no greater ease than do other members of the Court in attempting to verbalize generally the respective constitutional tests, for in truth the matter in the last analysis depends on how particular challenged material happens to strike the minds of jurors or judges and ultimately those of a majority of the members of this Court. The application of any general constitutional tests must thus necessarily be pricked out on a case-by-case basis, but as a point of departure I would apply to the Federal Gov- ernment the *Roth* standards as amplified in my opinion in *Manual Enterprises, supra.*

As to the States, I would make the federal test one of rationality. I would not prohibit them from banning any material which, taken as a whole, has been reasonably found in state judicial proceedings to treat with sex in a fundamentally offensive manner, under rationally established criteria for judging such material.

On this basis, having viewed the motion picture in question, I think the State acted within permissible limits in condemning the film and would affirm the judgment of the Ohio Supreme Court.

FREEDMAN v. MARYLAND
380 US 51 (1965)

[The Court in the instant case held that movie censorship, to meet the constitutional test, must contain certain procedural safeguards: (1) the censoring agency, rather than the exhibitor, must have the burden of instituting judicial proceeding; (2) any restraint prior to judicial review can only be for a brief period to preserve the status quo; and (3) there must be assurance of a prompt judicial review. The decision was unanimous; Justice Douglas, however, wrote a brief concurring opinion, in which he was joined by Justice Black, in which he stated that he would put an end to all types of censorship "and give full literal meaning to the command of the First Amendment."]

Mr. Justice Brennan delivered the opinion of the Court:

Appellant sought to challenge the constitutionality of the Maryland motion picture censorship statute, and exhibited the film "Revenge at Daybreak" at his Baltimore theatre without first submitting the picture to the State Board of Censors as required by § 2 of the statute. The State concedes that the picture does not violate the statutory standards and would have received a license if properly submitted, but the appellant was convicted of a § 2 violation despite his contention that the statute in its entirety unconstitutionally impaired freedom of expression. The Court of Appeals of Maryland affirmed, and we noted probable jurisdiction. We reverse.

I

In *Times Film Corp.* v. *City of Chicago,* 365 US 43, we considered and upheld a requirement of submission of motion pictures in advance of exhibition. The Court of Appeals held, on the authority of that decision, that "the Maryland censorship law must be held to be not void on its face as violative of the freedoms protected against State action by the First and Fourteenth Amendments." This reliance on *Times Film* was misplaced. The only question tendered for decision in that case was "whether a prior restraint was necessarily unconstitutional *under all circumstances.*" *Bantam Books, Inc.* v. *Sullivan,* 372 US 58, 70, n. 10 (emphasis in original). The exhibitor's argument that the requirement of submission without more amounted to a constitutionally prohibited prior restraint was interpreted by the Court in *Times Film* as a contention that the "constitutional protection includes complete and absolute freedom to exhibit, at least once, any and every kind of motion picture . . . even if this film contains the basest type of pornography, or incitement to riot, or forceful overthrow of orderly government. . . ." The Court held that on this "narrow" question, the argument stated the principle against prior restraints too broadly; citing a number of our decisions, the Court quoted the statement from *Near* v. *Minnesota,* 283 US 697, 716, that "the protection even as to previous restraint is not absolutely unlimited." In rejecting the proffered proposition in *Times Film* the Court emphasized, however, that "[i]t is that question alone which we decide," and it would therefore be inaccurate to say that *Times Film* upheld the specific features of the Chicago censorship ordinance.

Unlike the petitioner in *Times Film,* appellant does not argue that § 2 is unconstitutional simply because it may prevent even the first showing of a film whose exhibition may legitimately be the subject of an obscenity prosecution. He presents a question quite distinct from that passed on in *Times Film;* accepting the rule in *Times Film,* he argues that § 2 constitutes an invalid prior restraint because, in the context of the remainder of the statute, it presents a danger of unduly suppressing protected expression. He focuses particularly on the procedure for an initial decision by the censorship board, which, without any judicial participation, effectively bars exhibition of any disapproved film, unless and until the exhibitor undertakes a time-consuming appeal to the Maryland courts and succeeds in having the Board's decision reversed. Under the statute, the exhibitor is required to submit the film to the Board for examination, but no time limit is imposed for completion of Board action. If the film is disapproved, or any elimination ordered, § 19 provides that

the person submitting such film or view for examination will receive immediate notice of such elimination or disapproval, and if appealed from, such film or view will be promptly re-examined, in the presence of such person, by two or more members of the Board, and the same finally approved or disapproved promptly after such re-examination, with the right of appeal from the decision of the Board to the Baltimore City Court of Baltimore City. There shall be a further right of appeal from the decision of the Baltimore City Court to the Court of Appeals of Maryland, subject generally to the time and manner provided for taking appeal to the Court of Appeals.

Thus there is no statutory provision for judicial participation in the procedure which bars a film, nor even assurance of prompt judicial review. Risk of delay is built into the Maryland procedure, as is borne out by experience; in the only reported case indicating the length of time required to complete an appeal, the initial judicial determination has taken four months and final vindication of the film on appellate review, six months. . . .

In the area of freedom of expression it is well established that one has standing to challenge a statute on the ground that it delegates overly broad licensing discretion to an administrative office, whether or not his conduct could be proscribed by a properly drawn statute, and whether or not he applied for a license. "One who might have had a license for the asking may . . . call into question the whole scheme of licensing when he is prosecuted for failure to procure it." . . . In substance his argument is that, because the apparatus operates in a statutory context in which judicial review may be too little and too late, the Maryland statute lacks sufficient safeguards for confining the censor's action to judicially determined constitutional limits, and therefore contains the same vice as a statute delegating excessive administrative discretion.

II

Although the Court has said that motion pictures are not "necessarily subject to the precise rules governing any other particular method of expression," *Joseph Burstyn, Inc.* v. *Wilson,* 343 US 495, 503, it is as true here as of other forms of expression that "[a]ny system of prior restraints of expression comes to this Court bearing a heavy presumption against its constitutional validity." . . . "[U]nder the Fourteenth Amendment, a State is not free to adopt whatever procedures it pleases for dealing with obscenity . . . without regard to the possible consequences for constitutionally protected speech." *Marcus* v. *Search Warrant,* 367 US 717, 731. The administration of a censorship system for motion pictures presents peculiar dangers to constitutionally protected speech. Unlike a prosecution for obscenity, a censorship proceeding puts the initial burden on the exhibitor or distributor. Because the censor's business is to censor, there inheres the danger that he may well be less responsive than a court—part of an independent branch of government—to the constitutionally protected interests in free expression. And if it is made unduly onerous, by reason of delay or otherwise, to seek judicial review, the censor's determination may in practice be final.

Applying the settled rule of our cases, we hold that a noncriminal process which requires the prior submission of a film to a censor avoids constitutional infirmity only if it takes place under procedural safeguards designed to obviate the dangers of a censorship system. First, the burden of proving that the film is unprotected expression must rest on the censor. As we said in *Speiser* v. *Randall,* 357 US 513, 526, "Where the transcendent value of speech is involved, due process certainly requires . . . that the State bear the burden of persuasion to show that the appellants engaged in criminal speech." Second, while the State may require advance submission of all films, in order to proceed effectively to bar all showings of unprotected films, the requirement cannot be administered in a manner which would lend an effect of finality to the censor's determination whether a film constitutes protected expression. The teaching of our cases is that, because only a judicial determination in an adversary proceeding ensures the necessary sensitivity to freedom of expression, only a procedure requiring a judicial determination suffices to impose a valid final restraint. . . . To this end, the exhibitor must be assured, by statute or authoritative judicial construction, that the censor will, within a specified brief period, either issue a license or go to court to restrain showing the film. Any restraint imposed in advance of a final judicial determination on the merits must similarly be limited to preservation of the status quo for the shortest fixed period compatible with sound judicial resolution. Moreover, we are well aware that, even after expiration of a temporary restraint, an administrative refusal to license, signifying the censor's view that the film is unprotected, may have a discouraging effect on the exhibitor. . . . Therefore, the procedure must also assure a prompt final judicial decision, to minimize the deterrent effect of an interim and possibly erroneous denial of a license.

Without these safeguards, it may prove too burdensome to seek review of the censor's determination. Particularly in the case of motion pictures, it may take very little to deter exhibition in a given locality. The exhibitor's stake in any one picture may be insufficient to warrant a protracted and onerous course of litigation. The distributor, on the other hand, may be equally unwilling to accept the burdens and delays of litigation in a particular area when, without such difficulties, he can freely exhibit his film in most of the rest of the country; for we are told that only four States and a handful of municipalities have active censorship laws.*

It is readily apparent that the Maryland procedural scheme does not satisfy these criteria. First, once the censor disapproves the film, the exhibitor must assume the burden of instituting judicial proceedings and of persuading the courts that the film is protected expression. Second, once the Board has acted against a film, exhibition is prohibited pending judicial review, however protracted. Under the statute, appellant could have been convicted if he had shown the film after unsuccessfully seeking a license, even though no court had ever ruled on the obscenity of the film. Third, it is abundantly clear that the Maryland statute provides no assurance of prompt judicial determination. We hold, therefore, that appellant's conviction must be reversed. The Maryland scheme fails to provide adequate safeguards against undue inhibition of protected expression, and this renders the § 2 requirement of prior submission of films to the Board an invalid previous restraint.

III

How or whether Maryland is to incorporate the required procedural safeguards in the statutory scheme is, of course, for the State to decide. But a model is not lacking: In *Kingsley Books, Inc.* v. *Brown,* 354 US 436, we upheld a New York injunctive procedure designed to prevent the sale of obscene books. That procedure postpones any restraint against sale until a judicial determination of obscenity following notice and an adversary hearing. The statute provides for a hearing one day after joinder of issue; the judge must hand down his decision within two days after termination of the hearing. The New York procedure operates without prior submission to a censor, but the chilling effect of a censorship order, even one which requires judicial action for its enforcement, suggests all the more reason for expeditious determination of the question whether a particular film is constitutionally protected. . . .

The requirement of prior submission to a censor sustained in *Times Film* is consistent with our recognition that films differ from other forms of expression. Similarly, we think that the nature of the motion picture industry may suggest different time limits for a judicial determination. It is common knowledge that films are scheduled well before actual exhibition, and the requirement of advance submission in § 2 recognizes this. One possible scheme would be to allow the exhibitor or distributor to submit his film early enough to ensure an orderly final disposition of the case before the scheduled exhibition date—far enough in advance so that the exhibitor could safely advertise the opening on a normal basis. Failing such a scheme or sufficiently early submission under such a scheme, the statute would have to require adjudication

---

* An appendix to the brief *amici curiae* of the American Civil Liberties Union and its Maryland Branch lists New York, Virginia and Kansas as the three States having statutes similar to the Maryland statute, and the cities of Chicago, Detroit, Fort Worth and Providence as having similar ordinances. Twenty-eight of the remaining 39 municipal ordinances and codes are listed as "inactive."

considerably more prompt than has been the case under the Maryland statute. Otherwise litigation might be unduly expensive and protracted, or the victorious exhibitor might find the most propitious opportunity for exhibition past. We do not mean to lay down rigid time limits or procedures, but to suggest considerations in drafting legislation to accord with local exhibition practices, and in doing so to avoid the potentially chilling effect of the Maryland statute on protected expression.

Reversed.

7. Sexual Entertainment and the Sale of Liquor Drinks

CALIFORNIA v. LA RUE
93 S.Ct. 390 (1972)

[The California Department of Alcoholic Beverage Control, following hearings, issued regulations prohibiting sexual live entertainment and films at bars and other establishments licensed to dispense liquor by the drink. A three-judge District Court held the regulations unconstitutional on their face under the First and Fourteenth Amendments. The Supreme Court reversed and held that in the context, not of censoring dramatic performances in a theater, but of a state licensing bars and nightclubs to sell liquor by the drink, the states have broad latitude to control the manner and circumstances under which liquor may be dispensed. The exercise of the state's power here was not irrational or unreasonable. The Court's opinion was by Justice Rehnquist. Justice Stewart wrote a brief concurring opinion. Dissenting opinions were written by Justices Douglas, Brennan, and Marshall. Justice Douglas argued that the case should not have been decided on the text of the regulations; there should have been no constitutional decision "until and unless the generalized provisions of the Rules were given particularized meaning." Justice Brennan objected that the regulations were overbroad: while they prohibit some speech and conduct which are unprotected, they apply to some speech that is clearly protected by the Constitution; the state may not impose an unconstitutional condition on the grant of a license as a means "for the deliberate inhibition of protected, even if distasteful, forms of expression." Justice Marshall objected that the regulations, reviewed on their face, are overbroad, so that they stifle First Amendment freedoms.]

Mr. Justice Rehnquist delivered the opinion of the Court:

Appellant Kirby is the director of the Department of Alcoholic Beverage Control, an administrative agency vested by the California Constitution with primary authority for the licensing of the sale of alcoholic beverages in that State, and with the authority to suspend or revoke any such license if it determines that its continuation would be contrary to public welfare or morals. Appellees include holders of various liquor licenses issued by appellant, and dancers at premises operated by such licensees. In 1970 the Department promulgated rules regulating the type of entertainment which might be presented in bars and nightclubs which it licensed. Appellees then brought this action in the United States District Court for the Central District of California. . . . A three-judge court was convened . . . and the majority of that Court held that substantial portions of the regulations conflicted with the First and Fourteenth Amendments to the United States Constitution.

Concerned with the progression in a few years' time from "topless" dancers to "bottomless" dancers and other forms of "live entertainment" in bars and nightclubs which it licensed, the Commission heard a number of witnesses on this subject at public hearings held prior to the promulgation of the rules. The majority opinion of the District Court described the testimony in these words:

Law enforcement agencies, counsel and owners of licensed premises and investigators for the Department testified. The story that unfolded was a sordid one, primarily relating to sexual conduct between dancers and customers. . . .

References to the transcript of the hearings submitted by the Department to the District Court indicated that in licensed establishments where "topless" and "bottomless" dancers, nude entertainers, and films displaying sexual acts were shown, numerous incidents of legitimate concern to the Department had occurred. . . .

At the conclusion of the evidence, the Department promulgated the regulations here challenged, imposing standards as to the type of entertainment which could be presented in bars and nightclubs which it licensed. Those portions of the regulations found to be unconstitutional by the majority of the District Court prohibited the following kinds of conduct on licensed premises:

(a) The performance of acts, or simulated acts, of "sexual intercourse, masturbation, sodomy, bestiality, oral copulation, flagellation or any sexual acts which are prohibited by law";

(b) The actual or simulated "touching, caressing or fondling on the breast, buttocks, anus, or genitals";

(c) The actual or simulated "displaying of the pubic hair, anus, vulva, or genitals";

(d) The permitting by a licensee of "any person to remain in or upon the licensed premises who exposes to public view any portion of his or her genitals or anus"; and, by a companion section,

(e) The displaying of films or pictures depicting acts a live performance of which was prohibited by the regulations quoted above. . . .

Shortly before the effective date of the Department's regulations, appellees unsuccessfully sought discretionary review of them in both the State Court of Appeals and in the Supreme Court of California. The Department then joined with appellees in requesting the three-judge District Court to decide the merits of appellees' claims that the regulations were invalid under the Federal Constitution.

The District Court majority upheld the appellees' claim that the regulations in question unconstitutionally abridged their freedom of expression guaranteed to them by the First and Fourteenth Amendments to the United States Constitution. It reasoned that the state regulations had to be justified either as a prohibition of obscenity in accordance with the *Roth* line of decisions in this Court, or else as a regulation of "conduct" having a communicative element in it under the standards laid down by this Court in *United States* v. *O'Brien,* 391 US 367 (1968). Concluding that the regulations would bar some entertainment which could not be called obscene under the *Roth* line of cases, and that the governmental interest being furthered by the regulations did not meet the tests laid down in *O'Brien,* the Court enjoined the enforcement of the regulations. We noted probable jurisdiction.

The state regulations here challenged come to us not in the context of censoring a dramatic performance in a theater, but rather in a context of licensing bars and nightclubs to sell liquor by the drink. In *Seagram and Sons* v. *Hostetter,* 384 US 35, 41 (1966), this Court said:

Consideration of any State law regulating intoxicating beverages must begin with the Twenty-first Amendment, the second section of which provides that: "the transportation or importation to any State, territory or possession of the United States for delivery or use therein of intoxicating liquors, in violation of the laws thereof, is hereby prohibited."

While the States, vested as they are with general police power, require no specific grant of authority in the Federal Constitution to legislate with respect to matters traditionally within the scope of the police power, the broad sweep of the Twenty-first Amendment has been recognized as conferring something more than the normal state authority over public health, welfare, and morals. In *Hostetter* v. *Idlewild Liquor Corp.,* 377 US 324, 330 (1964), the Court reaffirmed that by reason of the Twenty-first Amendment "a State is totally unconfined by traditional Commerce Clause limitations when it restricts the importation of intoxicants destined for use, distribution, or consumption within its borders." Still earlier, the Court stated in *State Board* v. *Young's Market Co.,* 299 US 59, 64 (1936):

A classification recognized by the Twenty-first Amendment cannot be deemed forbidden by the Fourteenth.

These decisions did not go so far as to hold or say that the Twenty-first Amendment supersedes all other provisions of the United States Constitution in the area of liquor regulations. In *Wisconsin* v. *Constantineau,* 400 US 433 (1971), the fundamental notice and hearing requirement of the Due Process Clause of the Fourteenth Amendment was held applicable to Wisconsin's statute providing for the public posting of names of persons who had engaged in excessive drinking. But the case for upholding state regulation in the area covered by the Twenty-first Amendment is undoubtedly strengthened by that enactment:

Both the Twenty-first Amendment and the Commerce Clause are parts of the same Constitution. Like other provisions of the Constitution, each must be considered in the light of the other, and in the context of the issues and interests at stake in any concrete case. *Hostetter* v. *Idlewild Liquor Corp.,* 377 US 324, 332 (1964).

A common element in the regulations struck down by the District Court appears to be the Department's conclusion that the sale of liquor by the drink and lewd or naked dancing and entertainment should not take place simultaneously in bars and cocktail lounges for which it has licensing responsibility. Based on the evidence from the hearings which it cited to the District Court, and mindful of the principle that in legislative rulemaking the agency may reason from the particular to the general. . . . We do not think it can be said that the Department's conclusion in this respect was an irrational one.

Appellees insist that the same results could have been accomplished by requiring that patrons already well on the way to intoxication be excluded from the licensed premises. But wide latitude as to choice of means to accomplish a permissible end must be accorded to the state agency which is itself the repository of the State's power under the Twenty-first Amendment. . . . Nothing in the record before us nor in common experience compels the conclusion that either self-discipline on the part of the customer or self-regulation on the part of the bartender could have been relied upon by the Department to secure compliance with such an alternate plan of regulation. The Department's choice of a prophylactic solution instead of one which would have required its own personnel to judge individual instances of inebriation cannot, therefore, be deemed an unreasonable one under the holdings of our prior cases. . . .

We do not disagree with the District Court's determination that these regulations on their face would proscribe some forms of visual presentation which would not be found obscene under *Roth* and subsequent decision of this Court. . . . But we do not believe that the state regulatory authority in this case was limited to either dealing with the problem it confronted within the limits of our decisions as to obscenity, or in accordance with the limits prescribed for dealing with some forms of communicative conduct in *O'Brien, supra*.

Our prior cases have held that both motion pictures and theatrical productions are within the protection of the First and Fourteenth Amendments. In *Joseph Burstyn, Inc.* v. *Wilson,* 343 US 495 (1952), it was held that motion pictures are "included within the free speech and free press guarantees of the First and Fourteenth Amendments" though not "necessarily subject to the precise rules governing any other particular method of expression." In *Schacht* v. *United States,* 398 US 58, 63 (1970), the Court said with respect to theatrical productions:

An actor, like everyone else in our country, enjoys a constitutional right to freedom of speech, including the right openly to criticize the government during a dramatic performance.

But as the mode of expression moves from the printed page to the commission of public acts which may themselves violate valid penal statutes, the scope of permissible state regulations significantly increases. States may sometimes proscribe expression which is directed to the accomplishment of an end which the State has declared to be illegal when such expression consists, in part, of "conduct" or "action," *Hughes* v. *Superior Court,* 339 US 460 (1950); *Giboney* v. *Empire Storage & Ice Co.,* 336 US 490 (1949).* In *O'Brien, supra,* the Court suggested that the extent to which "conduct" was protected by the First Amendment depended on the presence of a "communicative element," and stated:

We cannot accept the view that an apparently limitless variety of conduct can be labeled "speech" whenever the person engaging in the conduct intends thereby to express an idea.

---

* Similarly, States may validly limit the manner in which the First Amendment freedoms are exercised by forbidding sound trucks in residential neighborhoods, *Kovacs* v. *Cooper,* 336 US 77 (1949), and may enforce a nondiscriminatory requirement that those who would parade on a public thoroughfare first obtain a permit. *Cox* v. *New Hampshire,* 312 US 569 (1941). Other state limitations on the "time, manner and place" of the exercise of First Amendment rights have been sustained. See, *e. g., Cameron* v. *Johnson,* 390 US 611 (1968), and *Cox* v. *Louisiana,* 379 US 559 (1965).

The substance of the regulations struck down prohibit licensed bars or nightclubs from displaying, either in the form of movies or live entertainment, "performances" which partake more of gross sexuality than of communication. While we agree that at least some of the performances to which these regulations address themselves are within the limits of the constitutional protection of freedom of expression, the critical fact is that California has not forbidden these performances across the board. It has merely proscribed such performances in establishments which it licenses to sell liquor by the drink.

Viewed in this light, we conceive the State's authority in this area to be somewhat broader than did the District Court. This is not to say that all such conduct and performance is without the protection of the First and Fourteenth Amendments. But we would poorly serve both the interests for which the State may validly seek vindication and the interests protected by the First and Fourteenth Amendments were we to insist that the sort of Bacchanalian revelries which the Department sought to prevent by these liquor regulations were the constitutional equivalent of a performance by a scantily clad ballet troupe in a theater.

The Department's conclusion, embodied in these regulations, that certain sexual performances and the dispensation of liquor by the drink ought not to occur simultaneously at premises which have licenses was not an irrational one. Given the added presumption in favor of the validity of the state regulation in this area which the Twenty-first Amendment requires, we cannot hold that the regulations on their face violate the Federal Constitution.*

The contrary holding of the District Court is therefore reversed.

---

* Because of the posture of this case, we have necessarily dealt with the regulations on their face, and have found them to be valid. The admonition contained in the Court's opinion in *Seagram and Sons* v. *Hostetter, supra,* is equally in point here: "Although is it possible that specific future applications of [the statute] may engender concrete problems of constitutional dimension, it will be time enough to consider any such problems when they arise. We deal here only with the statute on its face. And we hold that, so considered, the legislation is constitutionally valid." *Seagram and Sons* v. *Hostetter, supra,* at 52.

IX. Personal Rights and Equal Rights

1. Privacy

GRISWOLD v. CONNECTICUT
381 US 479 (1965)

[In this case the Supreme Court for the first time elaborated on and rationalized the constitutional right of privacy. A Connecticut statute made the use of contraceptives a criminal offense (even when used by a married couple). Certain officers of the Planned Parenthood League were convicted as accessories for giving information, instruction and advice to married persons as to the use of contraceptives. The Supreme Court, by 7–2 vote, reversed the convictions. In his opinion for the Court, Justice Douglas held the statute invalid as an unconstitutional invasion of the right of privacy of married persons. In a concurring opinion, Justice Goldberg (joined by Chief Justice Warren and Justice Brennan) declared that the Fourteenth Amendment concept of liberty protects fundamental personal rights whether or not specifically mentioned in the Bill of Rights. There were concurring opinions also by Justices Harlan and White. Justices Black and Stewart wrote dissenting opinions.

[In *Eisenstadt* v. *Baird,* 92 S.Ct. 1029 (1972), the Supreme Court held that a Massachusetts statute that permitted married persons to obtain contraceptives but prohibited distribution to single persons violated the Equal Protection Clause of the Fourteenth Amendment.]

Mr. Justice Douglas delivered the opinion of the Court:

Appellant Griswold is Executive Director of the Planned Parenthood League of Connecticut. Appellant Buxton is a licensed physician and a professor at the Yale Medical School who served as Medical Director for the League at its Center in New Haven—a center open and operating from November 1 to November 10, 1961, when appellants were arrested.

They gave information, instruction, and medical advice to *married persons* as to the means of preventing conception. They examined the wife and prescribed the best contraceptive device or material for her use. Fees were usually charged, although some couples were serviced free.

The statutes whose constitutionality is involved in this appeal are §§ 53–32 and 54–196 of the General Statutes of Connecticut (1938). The former provides:

Any person who uses any drug, medicinal article or instrument for the purpose of preventing conception shall be fined not less than fifty dollars or imprisoned not less than sixty days nor more than one year or be both fined and imprisoned.

Section 54–196 provides:

Any person who assists, abets, counsels, causes, hires, or commands another to commit any offense may be prosecuted and punished as if he were the principal offender.

The appellants were found guilty as accessories and fined $100 each, against the claim that the accessory statute as so applied violated the Fourteenth Amendment. The Appellate Division of the Circuit Court affirmed. The Court of Errors affirmed that judgment. We noted probable jurisdiction. . . .

Coming to the merits, we are met with a wide range of questions that implicate the Due Process Clause of the Fourteenth Amendment. Overtones of some arguments suggest that *Lochner* v. *New York,* 198 US 45, should be our guide. But we decline that invitation as we did in *West Coast Hotel Co.* v. *Parish,* 300 US 379. . . . We do not sit as a super-legislature to determine the wisdom, need, and propriety of laws that touch economic problems, business affairs, or social conditions. This law, however, operates directly on an intimate relation of husband and wife and their physician's role in one aspect of that relation.

The association of people is not mentioned in the Constitution nor in the Bill of Rights. The right to educate a child in a school of the parents' choice—whether public or private or parochial—is also not mentioned. Nor is the right to study any particular subject or any foreign language. Yet the First Amendment has been construed to include certain of those rights.

By *Pierce* v. *Society of Sisters,* the right to educate one's children as one chooses is made applicable to the States by the force of the First and Fourteenth Amendments. By *Meyer* v. *Nebraska,* the same dignity is given the right to study the German language in a private school. In other words, the State may not, consistently with the spirit of the First Amendment, contract the spectrum of available knowledge. The right of freedom of speech and press includes not only the right to utter or to print, but the right to distribute, the right to receive, the right to read (*Martin* v. *Struthers,* 319 US 141) and freedom of inquiry, freedom of thought, and freedom to teach (see *Wieman* v. *Updegraff,* 344 US 183)—indeed the freedom of the entire university community. *Sweezy* v. *New Hampshire,* 354 US 234; *Barenblatt* v. *United States,* 360 US 109; *Baggett* v. *Bullitt,* 377 US 360. Without those peripheral rights the specific rights would be less secure. And so we reaffirm the principle of the *Pierce* and the *Meyer* cases.

In *NAACP* v. *Alabama* 357 US 449, we protected the "freedom to associate and privacy in one's association," noting that freedom of association was a peripheral First Amendment right. Disclosure of membership lists of a constitutionally valid association, we held, was invalid "as entailing the likelihood of a substantial restraint upon the exercise by petitioner's members of their right to freedom of association." Ibid. In other words, the First Amendment has a penumbra where privacy is protected from governmental intrusion. In like context, we have protected forms of "association" that are not political in the customary sense but pertain to the social, legal, and economic benefit of the members. *NAACP* v. *Button,* 371 US 415. In *Schware* v. *Board of Bar Examiners,* 353 US 232, we held it not permissible to bar a lawyer from practice, because he had once been a member of the Communist Party. The man's "association with that Party" was not shown to be "anything more than a political faith in a political party" and not action of a kind proving bad moral character.

Those cases involved more than the "right of assembly"—a right that extends to all irrespective of their race or ideology. *DeJonge* v. *Oregon, 299* US 353. The right of "association," like the right of belief (*Board of Education* v. *Barnette,* 319 US 624), is more than the right to attend a meeting; it includes the right to express one's attitudes or philosophies by membership in a group or by affiliation with it or by other lawful means. Association in that context is a form of expression of opinion; and while it is not expressly included in the First Amendment its existence is necessary in making the express guarantees fully meaningful.

The foregoing cases suggest that specific guarantees in the Bill of Rights have penumbras, formed by emanations from those guarantees that help give them life and substance. . . . Various guarantees create zones of privacy. The right of association contained in the penumbra of the First Amendment is one, as we have seen. The Third Amendment in its prohibition against the quartering of soldiers "in any house" in time of peace without the consent of the owner is another facet of that privacy. The Fourth Amendment explicitly affirms the "right of the people to be secure in their persons, houses, papers, and effects against unreasonable searches and seizures." The Fifth Amendment in its Self-Incrimination Clause enables the citizen to create a zone of privacy which government may not force him to surrender to his detriment. The Ninth Amendment provides: "The enumeration in the Constitution, of certain rights, shall not be construed to deny or disparage others retained by the people."

The Fourth and Fifth Amendments were described in *Boyd* v. *United States,* 116 US 616, as protection against all governmental invasions "of the sanctity of a man's home and the privacies of life." We recently referred in *Mapp* v. *Ohio,* 367 US 643, to the Fourth Amendment as creating a "right of privacy, no less important than any other right carefully and particularly reserved to the people. . . ."

We have had many controversies over these penumbral rights of "privacy and repose." See, e.g. *Breard* v. *Alexandria,* 341 US 622; *Public Utilities Comm'n* v. *Pollak,* 343 US 451; *Monroe* v. *Pape,* 365 US 167; *Lanza* v. *New York,* 370 US 139; *Frank* v. *Maryland,* 359 US 360; *Skinner* v. *Oklahoma,* 316 US 535. These cases bear witness that the right of privacy which presses for recognition here is a legitimate one.

The present case, then, concerns a relationship lying within the zone of privacy created by several fundamental constitutional guarantees. And it concerns a law which, in forbidding the *use* of contraceptives rather than regulating their manufacture or sale, seeks to achieve its goals by means having a maximum destructive impact upon that relationship. Such a law cannot stand in light of the familiar principle, so often applied by this Court, that a "governmental purpose to control or prevent activities constitutionally subject to state regulation may not be achieved by means which sweep unnecessarily broadly and thereby invade the area of protected freedom." *NAACP* v. *Alabama,* 377 US 288. Would we allow the police to search the sacred precincts of marital bedrooms for telltale signs of the use of contraceptives? The very idea is repulsive to the notions of privacy surrounding the marriage relationship.

We deal with a right of privacy older than the Bill of Rights—older than our political parties, older than our school system. Marriage is a coming together for better or for worse, hopefully enduring, and intimate to the degree of being sacred. It is an association that promotes a way of life, not causes; a harmony in living, not political faiths; a bilateral loyalty, not commercial or social projects. Yet it is an association for as noble a purpose as any involved in our prior decisions.

Reversed.

Mr. Justice Goldberg, whom The Chief Justice and Mr. Justice Brennan join, concurring:

I agree with the Court that Connecticut's birth control law unconstitutionally intrudes upon the right of marital privacy, and I join in its opinion and judgment. Although I have not accepted the view that " 'due process' as used in the Fourteenth Amendment incorporates all of the first eight Amendments," . . . I do agree that the concept of liberty protects those personal rights that are fundamental, and is not confined to the specific terms of the Bill of Rights. My conclusion that the concept of liberty is not so restricted and that it embraces the right of marital privacy though that right is not mentioned explicitly in the Constitution is supported both by numerous decisions of this Court, referred to in the Court's opinion, and by the language and history of the Ninth Amendment. In reaching the conclusion that the right of marital privacy is protected, as being within the protected penumbra of specific guarantees of the Bill of Rights, the Court refers to the Ninth Amendment. . . . I add these words to emphasize the relevance of that Amendment to the Court's holding.

The Court stated many years ago that Due Process Clause protects those liberties that are "so rooted in the traditions and conscience of our people as to be ranked as fundamental." *Snyder* v. *Massachusetts,* 291 US 97. In *Gitlow* v. *New York,* 268 US 652, the Court said:

> For present purposes we may and do assume that freedom of speech and of the press—which are protected by the First Amendment from abridgment by Congress —are among the *fundamental* personal rights and "liberties" protected by the due process clause of the Fourteenth Amendment from impairment by the States. (Emphasis added.)

And, in *Meyer* v. *Nebraska,* 262 US 390, 399, the Court, referring to the Fourteenth Amendment, stated:

> While this Court has not attempted to define with exactness the liberty thus guaranteed, the term has received much consideration and some of the included things have been definitely stated. Without doubt, it denotes not merely freedom from bodily restraint, but also [for example] the right . . . to marry, establish a home and bring up children. . . .

This Court, in a series of decisions, has held that the Fourteenth Amendment absorbs and applies to the States those specifics of the first eight amendments which express fundamental personal rights. The language and history of the Ninth Amendment reveal that the Framers of the Constitution believed that there are additional fundamental rights, protected from governmental infringement, which exist alongside those fundamental rights specifically mentioned in the first eight constitutional amendments.

The Ninth Amendment reads, "The enumeration in the Constitution, of certain rights, shall not be construed to deny or disparage others retained by the people." The Amendment is almost entirely the work of James Madison. It was introduced in Congress by him and passed the House and Senate with little or no debate and virtually no change in language. It was proffered to quiet expressed fears that a bill of specifically enumerated rights could not be sufficiently broad to cover all essential rights and that the specific mention of certain rights would be interpreted as a denial that others were protected.

In presenting the proposed Amendment, Madison said:

> It has been objected also against a bill of rights, that, by enumerating particular exceptions to the grant of power, it would disparage those rights which were not placed in that enumeration; and it might follow by implication, that those rights which were not signaled out, were intended to be assigned into the hands of the General Government, and were consequently insecure. This is one of the most plausible arguments I have ever heard urged against the admission of a bill of rights into this system; but, I conceive, that it may be guarded against. I have attempted it, as gentlemen may see by turning to the last clause of the fourth resolution [the Ninth Amendment]. I Annals of Congress 440 (Gales and Seaton ed 1834).

Mr. Justice Story wrote of this argument against a bill of rights and the meaning of the Ninth Amendment:

> In regard to . . . [a] suggestion, that the affirmance of certain rights might disparage others, or might lead to argumentative implications in favor of other powers, it might be sufficient to say that such a course of reasoning could never be sustained upon any solid basis. . . . But a conclusive answer is, that such an attempt may be interdicted (as it has been) by a positive declaration in such a bill of rights that the enumeration of certain rights shall not be construed to deny or disparage other rights retained by the people. II Story on the Constitution 626–627 (5th ed 1891).

He further stated, referring to the Ninth Amendment:

> This clause was manifestly introduced to prevent any perverse or ingenious misapplication of the well-known maxim, that an affirmation in particular cases implies a negation in all others; and, e converso, that a negation in particular cases implies an affirmation in all others. Id., at 651.

These statements of Madison and Storey make clear that the Framers did not intend that the first eight amendments be construed to exhaust the basic and fundamental rights which the Constitution guaranteed to the people.

While this Court has had little occasion to interpret the Ninth Amendment, "[i]t cannot be presumed that any clause in the constitution is intended to be without effect." *Marbury* v. *Madison,* 1 Cranch 137, 174, 2 L Ed. 60, 72. In interpreting the Constitution, "real effect should be given to all the words it uses." *Myers* v. *United States,* 272 US 52. The Ninth Amendment to the Constitution may be regarded by some as a recent discovery and may be forgotten by others, but since 1791 it has been a basic part of the Constitution which we are sworn to uphold. To hold that a right so basic and fundamental and so deep-rooted in our society as the right of privacy in marriage may be infringed because that right is not guaranteed in so many words by the first eight amendments to the Constitution is to ignore the Ninth Amendment and to give it no effect whatsoever. Moreover, a judicial construction that this fundamental right is not protected by the Constitution because it is not mentioned in explicit terms by one of the first eight amendments or elsewhere in the Constitution would violate the Ninth Amendment, which specifically states that "[t]he enumeration in the Constitution, of certain rights, shall not be *construed* to deny or disparage others retained by the people." (Emphasis added.)

A dissenting opinion suggests that my interpretation of the Ninth Amendment somehow "broaden[s] the powers of this Court." With all due respect, I believe that it misses the import of what I am saying. I do not take the position of my Brother Black in his dissent in *Adamson* v. *California,* 332 US 46, that the entire Bill of Rights is incorporated in the Fourteenth Amendment, and I do not mean to imply that the Ninth Amendment is applied against the States by the Fourteenth. Nor do I mean to state that the Ninth Amendment constitutes an independent source of righs protected from infringement by either the States or Federal Government. Rather, the Ninth Amendment shows a belief of the Constitution's authors that fundamental rights exist that are not expressly enumerated in the first eight amendments and an intent that the list of rights included there not be exhaustive. As any student of this Court's opinions knows, this Court has held, often unanimously, that the Fifth and Fourteenth Amendments protect certain fundamental personal liberties from abridgment by the Federal Government or the States. . . . The Ninth Amendment simply shows the intent of the Constitution's authors that other fundamental personal rights should not be denied such protection or disparaged in any other way simply because they are not specifically listed in the first eight constitutional amendments. I do not see how this broadens the authority of the court; rather it serves to support what this Court has been doing in protecting fundamental rights.

Nor am I turning somersaults with history in arguing that the Ninth Amendment is relevant in a case dealing with a *State's* infringement of a fundamental right. While the Ninth Amendment—and indeed the entire Bill of Rights—originally concerned restrictions upon *federal* power, the subsequently enacted Fourteenth Amendment prohibits the States as well from abridging fundamental personal liberties. And, the Ninth Amendment, in indicating that not all such liberties are specifically mentioned in the first eight amendments, is surely relevant in showing the existence of other fundamental personal rights, now protected from state, as well as federal, infringement. In sum, the Ninth Amendment simply lends strong support to the view that the "liberty" protected by the Fifth and Fourteenth Amendments from infringement by the Federal Government or the States is not restricted to rights specifically mentioned in the first eight amendments. . . .

In determining which rights are fundamental, judges are not left at large to decide cases in light of their personal and private notions. Rather, they must look to the "traditions and [collective] conscience of our people" to determine whether a principle is "so rooted [there] . . . as to be ranked as fundamental." *Snyder* v. *Massachusetts,* 291 US 97. The inquiry is whether a right involved "is of such a character that it cannot be denied without violating those 'fundamental principles of liberty and justice which lie at the base of all our civil and political institutions.' . . . ." *Powell* v. *Alabama,* 287 US 45. "Liberty" also "gains content from the emanations of . . . specific [constitutional] guarantees" and "from experience with the requirements of a free society." *Poe* v. *Ullman,* 367 US 497.

I agree fully with the Court that, applying these tests, the right of privacy is a fundamental personal right, "emanating from the totality of the constitutional scheme under which we live." Mr. Justice Brandeis, dissenting in *Olmstead* v. *United States,* 277 US 438, comprehensively summarized the principles underlying the Constitution's guarantees of privacy:

> The protection guaranteed by the [Fourth and Fifth] Amendments is much broader in scope. The makers of our Constitution undertook to secure conditions favorable to the pursuit of happiness. They recognized the significance of man's spiritual nature, of his feelings and of his intellect. They knew that only part of the pain, pleasure, and satisfactions of life are to be found in material things. They sought to protect Americans in their beliefs, their thoughts, their emotions and their sensations. They conferred as against the Government, the right to be let alone—the most comprehensive of rights and the right most valued by civilized men.

The Connecticut statutes here involved deal with a particularly important and sensitive area of privacy—that of the marital relation and the marital home. This Court recognized in *Meyer* v. *Nebraska,* that the right "to marry, establish a home and bring up children" was an essential part of the liberty guaranteed by the Fourteenth Amendment. In *Pierce* v. *Society of Sisters,* the Court held unconstitutional an Oregon Act which forbid parents from sending their children to private schools because such an act "unreasonably interferes with the liberty of parents and guardians to direct the upbringing and education of children under their control." As this Court said in *Prince* v. *Massachusetts,* 321 US 158, the *Meyer* and *Pierce* decisions "have respected the private realm of family life which the state cannot enter."

I agree with Mr. Justice Harlan's statement in his dissenting opinion in *Poe* v. *Ullman,* 367 US 497: "Certainly the safeguarding of the home does not follow merely from the sanctity of property rights. The home derives its pre-eminence as the seat of family life. And the integrity of that life is something so fundamental that it has been found to draw to its protection the principles of more than one explicitly granted Constitutional right. . . . Of this whole 'private realm of family life' it is difficult to imagine what is more private or more intimate than a husband and wife's marital relations."

The entire fabric of the Constitution and the purposes that clearly underlie its specific guarantees demonstrate that the rights to marital privacy and to marry and raise a family are of similar order and magnitude as the fundamental rights specifically protected.

Although the Constitution does not speak in so many words of the right of privacy in marriage I cannot believe that it offers these fundamental rights no protection. The fact that no particular provision of the Constitution explicitly forbids the State from disrupting the traditional relation of the family—a relation as old and as fundamental as our entire civilization—surely does not show that the Government was meant to have the power to do so. Rather, as the Ninth Amendment expressly recognizes, there are fundamental personal rights such as this one, which are protected from abridgment by the Government though not specifically mentioned in the Constitution.

My Brother Stewart, while characterizing the Connecticut birth control law as "an uncommonly silly law," would nevertheless let it stand on the ground that it is not for the courts to " 'substitute their social and economic beliefs for the judgment of legislative bodies who are elected to pass laws.' " Elsewhere, I have stated that "[w]hile I quite agree with Mr. Justice Brandeis that . . . 'a . . . state may . . . serve as a laboratory; and try novel social and economic experiments,' *New State Ice Co.* v. *Liebmann,* 285 US 262, I do not believe that this includes the power to experiment with the fundamental liberties of citizens. . . ." The vice of the dissenters' views is that it would permit such experimentation by the States in the area of the fundamental personal rights of its citizens. I cannot agree that the Constitution grants such power either to the States or to the Federal Government.

The logic of the dissents would sanction federal or state legislation that seems to me even more plainly unconstitutional than the statute before us. Surely the Government, absent a showing of a compelling subordinate state interest, could not decree that all husbands and wives must be sterilized after two children have been born to them. Yet by their reasoning such an invasion of marital privacy would not be subject to constitutional challenge because, while it might be "silly," no provision of the Constitution specifically prevents the Government from curtailing the marital right to bear children and raise a family. While it may shock some of my Brethren that the Court today holds that the Constitution protects the right of marital privacy, in my view it is far more shocking to believe that the personal liberty guaranteed by the Constitution does not include protection against such totalitarian limitation of family size, which is at complete variance with our constitutional concepts. Yet, if upon a showing of a slender basis of rationality, a law outlawing voluntary birth control by married persons is valid, then, by the same reasoning, a law requiring compulsory birth control also would seem to be valid. In my view, however, both types of law would unjustifiably intrude upon rights of marital privacy which are constitutionally protected.

In a long series of cases this Court has held that where fundamental personal liberties are involved, they may not be abridged by the States simply on a showing that a regulatory statute has some rational relationship to the effectuation of a proper state purpose. "Where there is a significant encroachment upon personal liberty, the State may prevail only upon showing a subordinating interest which is compelling," *Bates* v. *Little Rock*, 361 US 516. The law must be shown "necessary, and not merely rationally related, to the accomplishment of a permissible state policy." *McLaughlin* v. *Florida*, 379 US 184. . . .

Although the Connecticut birth control law obviously encroaches upon a fundamental personal liberty, the State does not show that the law serves any "subordinating state interest which is compelling" or that it is "necessary . . . to the accomplishment of a permissible state policy." The State, at most, argues that there is some rational relation between this statute and what is admittedly a legitimate subject of state concern—the discouraging of extra-marital relations. It says that preventing the use of birth control devices by married persons helps prevent the indulgence by some in such extra-marital relations. The rationality of this justification is dubious, particularly in light of the admitted widespread availability to all persons in the State of Connecticut, unmarried as well as married, of birth control devices for the prevention of disease, as distinguished from the prevention of conception, see *Tileston* v. *Ullman*, 129 Conn. 84, 26 A2d 582. But, in any event, it is clear that the State interest in safeguarding marital fidelity can be served by a more discriminately tailored statute, which does not, like the present one, sweep unnecessarily broadly, reaching far beyond the evil sought to be dealt with and intruding upon the privacy of all married couples. . . . Here, as elsewhere, "[p]recision of regulation must be the touchstone in an area so closely touching our most precious freedoms." *NAACP* v. *Button*. The State of Connecticut does have statutes, the constitutionality of which is beyond doubt, which prohibit adultery and fornication. See Conn Gen Stat §§ 53–218, 53–219 et seq. These statutes demonstrate that means for achieving the same basic purpose of protecting marital fidelity are available to Connecticut without the need to "invade the area of protected freedoms. . . ."

Finally, it should be said of the Court's holding today that it in no way interferes with a State's proper regulation of sexual promiscuity or misconduct. As my Brother Harlan so well stated in his dissenting opinion in *Poe* v. *Ullman:*

> Adultery, homosexuality and the like are sexual intimacies which the State forbids . . . but the intimacy of husband and wife is necessarily an essential and accepted feature of the institution of marriage, an institution which the State not only must allow, but which always and in every age it has fostered and protected. It is one thing when the State exerts its power either to forbid extra-marital sexuality . . . or to say who may marry, but it is quite another when, having acknowledged a marriage and the intimacies inherent in it, it undertakes to regulate by means of the criminal law the details of that intimacy.

In sum, I believe that the right of privacy in the marital relation is fundamental and basic—a personal right "retained by the people" within the meaning of the Ninth Amendment. Connecticut cannot constitutionally abridge this fundamental right, which is protected by the Fourteenth Amendment from infringement by the States. I agree with the Court that petitioners' convictions must therefore be reversed.

TIME, INC. *v.* HILL
385 US 374 (1967)

[In *Griswold* v. *Connecticut,* the immediately preceding case, the Court had before it the constitutional right of privacy; in the instant case, the Court had to consider the right of privacy as provided for by a New York statute and balance it against the constitutionally guaranteed freedom of the press.

[Hill brought an action under the New York privacy act claiming damages for an article in *Life* magazine which falsely reported that a play portrayed an experience suffered by Hill and his family when they were held as hostages in the Hill home by escaped convicts. The jury awarded Hill compensatory and punitive damages. The Appellate Division of the New York Supreme Court sustained the jury verdict of liability but ordered a new trial as to damages. At the new trial, a jury was waived, and the trial court awarded only compensatory damages. The New York Court of Appeals affirmed.

[The Supreme Court set aside the judgment and remanded the case. This decision was by 6–3 vote. In his opinion for the Court, Justice Brennan held that constitutional protection for speech and press precluded the application of the privacy statute to redress false reports of matters of public interest in the absence of proof that *Life* had published the report with knowledge of its falsity or in reckless disregard of the truth. In its instructions to the jury, on the question of liability, the trial court had used an incorrect standard of liability—a standard which curtailed freedom of the press.

[Justices Black and Douglas wrote concurring opinions. Justice Harlan concurred in the result but dissented as to the proper standard of liability required by the Constitution. Justice Fortas dissented, joined by Chief Justice Warren and Justice Clark, on the ground that there was no reason for a new trial, since the trial court's instructions were acceptable.

[Cf. *New York Times Company* v. *Sullivan, supra.*]

Mr. Justice Brennan delivered the opinion of the Court:

The question in this case is whether appellant, publisher of *Life* magazine, was denied constitutional protections for speech and press by the application by the New York courts of §§ 50–51 of the New York Civil Rights Law, McKinney's Consol. Laws, c. 6* to award appellee damages on allegations that *Life* falsely reported that a new play portrayed an experience suffered by appellee and his family.

The article appeared in *Life* in February 1955. It was entitled "True Crime Inspires Tense Play," with the subtitle, "The ordeal of a family trapped by convicts gives Broadway a new thriller, 'The Desperate Hours.'" The text of the article reads as follows:

Three years ago Americans all over the country read about the desperate ordeal of the James Hill family, who were held prisoners in their homes outside Philadelphia by three escaped convicts. Later they read about it in Joseph Hayes' novel, *The Desperate Hours*, inspired by the family's experience. Now they can see the story re-enacted in Hayes' Broadway play based on the book, and the next year will see it in his movie, which has been filmed but is being held up until the play has had a chance to pay off.

The play, directed by Robert Montgomery and expertly acted, is a heart-stopping account of how a family rose to heroism in a crisis. *Life* photographed the play during its Philadelphia tryout, transported some of the actors to the actual house where the Hills were beseiged. On the next page scenes from the play are re-enacted on the site of the crime.

The pictures on the ensuing two pages included an enactment of the son being "roughed up" by one of the convicts, entitled "brutish convict," a picture of the daughter biting the hand of a convict to make him drop a gun, entitled "daring

---

* The complete text of New York Civil Rights Law §§ 50–51 is as follows:

"§ 50. *Right of privacy*

"A person, firm or corporation that uses for advertising purposes, or for the purposes of trade, the name, portrait or picture of any living person without having first obtained the written consent of such person, or if a minor of his or her parent or guardian, is guilty of a misdemeanor."

"§51. *Action for injunction and for damages*

"Any person whose name, portrait or picture is used within this state for advertising purposes or for the purposes of trade without the written consent first obtained as above provided may maintain an equitable action in the supreme court of this state against the person, firm or corporation so using his name, portrait or picture, to prevent and restrain the use thereof; and may also sue and recover damages for any injuries sustained by reason of such use and if the defendant shall have knowingly used such person's name, portrait or picture in such manner as is forbidden or declared to be unlawful by the last section, the jury, in its discretion, may award exemplary damages. But nothing contained in this act shall be so construed as to prevent any person, firm or corporation, practicing the profession of photography, from exhibiting in or about his or its establishment specimens of the work of such establishment, unless the same is continued by such person, firm or corporation after written notice objecting thereto has been given by the person portrayed; and nothing contained in this act shall be so construed as to prevent any person, firm or corporation from using the name, portrait or picture of any manufacturer or dealer in connection with the goods, wares and merchandise manufactured, produced or dealt in by him which he has sold or disposed of with such name, portrait or picture used in connection therewith; or from using the name, portrait or picture of any author, composer or artist in connection with his literary, musical or artistic productions which he has sold or disposed of with such name, portrait or picture used in connection therewith."

daughter," and one of the father throwing his gun through the door after a "brave try" to save his family is foiled.

The James Hill referred to in the article is the appellee. He and his wife and five children involuntarily became a front-page news story after being held hostage by three escaped convicts in their suburban, Whitemarsh, Pennsylvania, home for 19 hours on September 11–12, 1952. The family was released unharmed. In an interview with newsmen after the convicts departed, appellee stressed that the convicts had treated the family courteously, had not molested them, and had not been at all violent. The convicts were thereafter apprehended in a widely publicized encounter with the police which resulted in the killing of two of the convicts. Shortly thereafter the family moved to Connecticut. The appellee discouraged all efforts to keep them in the public spotlight through magazine articles or appearances on television.

In the spring of 1953, James Hayes' novel, *The Desperate Hours* was published. The story depicted the experience of a family of four held hostage by three escaped convicts in the family's suburban home. But unlike Hill's experience, the family of the story suffer violence at the hands of the convicts; the father and son are beaten and the daughter subjected to a verbal sexual insult.

The book was made into a play, also entitled *The Desperate Hours,* and it is *Life's* article about the play which is the subject of appellee's action. The complaint sought damages under §§ 50–51 on allegations that the *Life* article was intended to, and did, give the impression that the play mirrored the Hill family's experience, which, to the knowledge of defendant ". . . was false and untrue." Appellant's defense was that the subject of the article was "a subject of legitimate news interest," "a subject of general interest and of value and concern to the public" at the time of publication, and that it was "published in good faith without any malice whatsoever. . . ." A motion to dismiss the complaint for substantially these reasons was made at the close of the case and was denied by the trial judge on the ground that the proofs presented a jury question as to the truth of the article.

The jury awarded appellee $50,000 compensatory and $25,000 punitive damages. On appeal the Appellate Division of the Supreme Court ordered a new trial as to damages but sustained the jury verdict of liability. The court said as to liability:

Although the play was fictionalized, *Life's* article portrayed it as a reenactment of the Hills' experience. It is an inescapable conclusion that this was done to advertise and attract further attention to the play, and to increase present and future magazine circulations as well. It is evident that the article cannot be characterized as a mere dissemination of news, nor even an effort to supply legitimate newsworthy information in which the public had, or might have a proper interest.

At the new trial on damages, a jury was waived and the court awarded $30,000 compensatory damages without punitive damages.

The New York Court of Appeals affirmed the Appellate Division "on the majority and concurring opinions at the Appellate Division," two judges dissenting. We noted probable jurisdiction of the appellant's appeal to consider the important constitutional questions of freedom of speech and press involved. After argument last Term, the case was restored to the docket for reargument. We reverse and remand the case to the Court of Appeals for further proceedings not inconsistent with this opinion.

I

Since the reargument, we have had the advantage of an opinion of the Court of Appeals of New York which has materially aided us in our understanding of that court's construction of the statute. It is the opinion of Judge Keating for the court in *Spahn v. Julian Messner, Inc.,* 18 NY 2d 324, 274 NYS 2d 877, 221 N.E. 2d 543 (1966). The statute was enacted in 1903 following the decision of the Court of Appeals in 1902 in *Roberson v. Rochester Folding Box Co.,* 171 NY 538, 64 N.E. 442. *Roberson* was an action against defendants for adorning their flour bags with plaintiff's picture without her consent. It was grounded upon an alleged invasion of a "right of privacy," defined by the Court of Appeals to be "the claim that a man has the right to pass through this world, if he wills, without having his picture published . . . or his eccentricities commented upon either in handbills, circulars, catalogues, periodicals or newspapers. . . ." The Court of Appeals traced the theory to the celebrated article of Warren and Brandeis entitled "The Right to Privacy" published in 1890. 4 Harv.L.Rev. 193. The Court of Appeals however denied the existence of such a right at common law but observed that "[t]he legislative body could very well interfere and arbitrarily provide that no one should be permitted for his own selfish purpose to use the picture or the name of another for advertising purposes without his consent." The legislature enacted §§ 50–51 in response to that observation.

Although "Right to Privacy" is the caption of § 51, the term nowhere appears in the text of the statute itself. The text of the statute appears to proscribe only conduct of the kind involved in *Roberson,* that is, the appropriation and use in advertising or to promote the sale of goods, of anothers' name, portrait or picture without his consent. An application of that limited scope would present different questions of violation of the constitutional protections for speech and press.

The New York courts have, however, construed the statute to operate much more broadly. In *Spahn* the Court of Appeals stated that "Over the years since the statute's enactment in 1903, its social desirability and remedial nature have led to its being given a liberal construction consonant with its over-all purpose. . . ." Specifically, it has been held in some circumstances to authorize a remedy against the press and other communications media which publish the names, pictures, or portraits of people without their consent. Reflecting the fact, however, that such applications may raise serious questions of conflict with the constitutional protections for speech and press, decisions under the statute have tended to limit the statute's application. "[E]ver mindful that the written word or picture is involved, courts have engrafted exceptions and restrictions onto the statute to avoid any conflict with the free dissemination of thoughts, ideas, newsworthy events, and matters of public interest."

In the light of questions that counsel were asked to argue on reargument, it is particularly relevant that the Court of Appeals made crystal clear in the *Spahn* opinion that truth is a complete defense in actions under the statute based upon reports of newsworthy people or events. The opinion states: "The factual reporting of newsworthy persons and events is in the public interest and is protected." Constitutional questions which might arise if truth were not a defense are therefore no concern.

But although the New York statute affords "little protection" to the "privacy" of a newsworthy person, "whether he be such by choice or involuntarily" the statute gives him a right of action when his name, picture, or portrait is the subject of a "fictitious" report or article. *Spahn* points up the distinction. *Spahn* was an action under the statute brought by the well-known professional baseball pitcher, Warren Spahn. He sought an injunction and damages against the unauthorized publication of what purported to be a biography of his life. The trial judge had found that "[t]he record unequivocally establishes that the book publicizes areas of Warren Spahn's personal and private life, albeit inaccurate and distorted, and consists of a host, a preponderant percentage, of factual errors, distortions and fanciful passages. . . ." The Court of Appeals sustained the holding that in these circumstances the publication was proscribed by § 51 of the Civil Rights Law and was not within the exceptions and restrictions for newsworthy events engrafted on the statute. The Court of Appeals said:

> But it is erroneous to confuse privacy with "personality" or to assume that privacy, though lost for a certain time or in a certain context, goes forever unprotected. . . . Thus it may be appropriate to say that the plaintiff here, Warren Spahn, is a public personality and that, insofar as his professional career is involved, he is substantially without a right to privacy. That is not to say, however, that his "personality" may be fictionalized and that, as fictionalized, it may be exploited for the defendants' commercial benefit through the medium of an unauthorized biography.

As the instant case went to the jury, appellee too was regarded to be a newsworthy person "substantially without a right to privacy" insofar as his hostage experience was involved, but to be entitled to his action insofar as that experience was "fictionalized" and "exploited for the defendant's commercial benefit." "Fictionalization," the *Spahn* opinion states, "is the heart of the cases in point."

The opinion goes on to say that the "establishment of minor errors in an otherwise accurate" report does not prove "fictionalization." Material and substantial falsification is the test. However, it is not clear whether proof of knowledge of the falsity or that the article was prepared with reckless disregard for the truth is also required. In *New York Times Co.* v. *Sullivan,* 376 US 254, we held that the Constitution delimits a State's power to award damages for libel in actions brought by public officials against critics of their official conduct. Factual error, content defamatory of official reputation, or both, are insufficient to an award of damages for false statements unless actual malice—knowledge that the statements are false or in reckless disregard of the truth—is alleged and proved. The *Spahn* opinion reveals that the defendant in that case relied on *New York Times* as the basis of an argument that application of the statute to the publication of a substantially fictitious biography would run afoul of the constitutional guarantees. The Court of Appeals held that *New York Times* had no application. The court, after distinguishing the cases on the ground that *Spahn* did not deal with public officials or official conduct, then says, "The free speech which is encouraged and essential to the operation of a healthy government is something quite different from an individual's attempt to enjoin the publication of a fictitious biography of him. No public interest is served by protecting the dissemination of the latter. We perceive no constitutional infirmities in this respect."

If this is meant to imply that proof of knowing or reckless falsity is not essential to a constitutional application of the statute in these cases, we disagree with the Court of Appeals. We hold that the constitutional protections for speech and press preclude the application of the New York statute to redress false reports of matters of public interest in the abscence of proof that the defendant published the report with knowledge of its falsity or in reckless disregard of the truth.

The guarantees for speech and press are not the preserve of political expression or comment upon public affairs, essential as those are to healthy government. One need only pick up any newspaper or magazine to comprehend the vast range of published matter which exposes persons to public view, both priviate citizens and public officials. Exposure of the self to others in varying degrees is a concomitant of life in a civilized community. The risk of this exposure is an essential incident of life in a society which places a primary value on freedom of speech and of press. "Freedom of discussion, if it would fulfill its historic function in this nation, must embrace all issues about which information is needed or appropriate to enable the members of society to cope with the exigencies of their period. . . ." "No suggestion can be found in the Constitution that the freedom there guaranteed for speech and the press bears an inverse ratio to the timeliness and importance of the ideas seeking expression. . . ." We have no doubt that the subject of the *Life* article, the opening of a new play linked to an actual incident, is a matter of public interest. "The line between the informing and the entertaining is too elusive for the protection of . . . [freedom of the press]. . . ." Erroneous statement is no less inevitable in such case than in the case of comment upon public affairs, and in both, if innocent or merely negligent, ". . . it must be protected if the freedoms of expression are to have the 'breathing space' that they 'need . . . to survive.' . . ." As James Madison said, "Some degree of abuse is inseparable from the proper use of everything and in no instance is this more true than of the press." 4 Elliots Debates on the Federal Constitution (1876), p. 571. We create grave risk of serious impairment of the indispensable service of a free press in a free society if we saddle the press with the impossible burden of verifying to a certainty the facts associated in news articles with a person's name, picture or portrait, particularly as related to nondefamatory matter. Even negligence would be a most elusive standard, especially when the content of the speech itself affords no warning of prospective harm to another through falsity. A negligence test would place on the press the intolerable burden of guessing how a jury might assess the reasonableness of steps taken by it to verify the accuracy of every reference to a name, picture or portrait.

In this context, sanctions against either innocent or negligent misstatement would present a grave hazard of discouraging the press from exercising the constitutional guarantees. Those guarantees are not for the benefit of the press so much as for the benefit of all of us. A broadly defined freedom of the press assures the maintenance of our political system and an open society. Fear of large verdicts in damage suits for innocent or mere negligent misstatement, even fear of the expense involved in their defense, must inevitably cause publishers to "steer far wider of the unlawful zone. . . ." and thus "create the danger that the legitimate utterance will be penalized."

But the constitutional guarantees can tolerate sanctions against *calculated* falsehood without significant impairment of their essential function. We held in *New York Times* that calculated falsehood enjoyed no immunity in the case of alleged defamation of a public official's official conduct. Similarly calculated falsehood should enjoy no immunity in the situation here presented us. What we said in *Garrison* v. *State of Louisiana,* 379 US, at 75, is equally applicable:

The use of the calculated falsehood . . . would put a different cast on the constitutional question. Although honest utterance, even if inaccurate, may further the fruitful exercise of the right of free speech, it does not follow that the lie, knowingly and deliberately published . . . should enjoy a like immunity. . . . For the use of the known lie as a tool is at once at odds with the premises of democratic government and with the orderly manner in which economic, social, or political change is to be effected. Calculated falsehood falls into that class of utterances which "are no essential part of any exposition of ideas, and are of such slight social value as a step to truth that any benefit that may be derived from them is clearly outweighed by the social interest in order and morality. . . ." *Chaplinsky* v. *New Hampshire,* 315 US 568. Hence the knowingly false statement and the false statement made with reckless disregard of the truth, do not enjoy constitutional protection.

We find applicable here the standard of knowing or reckless falsehood not through blind application of *New York Times Co.* v. *Sullivan,* relating solely to libel actions by public officials, but only upon consideration of the factors which arise in the particular context of the application of the New York statute in cases involving private individuals. This is neither a libel action by a private individual nor a statutory action by a public official. Therefore, although the First Amendment principles pronounced in *New York Times* guide our conclusion, we reach that conclusion only by applying these principles in this discrete context. It therefore serves no purpose to distinguish the facts here from those in *New York Times.* Were this a libel action, the distinction which has been suggested between the relative opportunities of the public official and private individual to rebut defamatory charges might be germane. And the additional state interest in the protection of the individual against damage to his reputation would be involved. . . . Moreover, a different test might be required in a statutory action by a public official, as opposed to a libel action by a public official or a statutory action by a private individual. Different considerations might arise concerning the degree of "waiver" of the protection the State might afford. But the question whether the same standard should be applicable both to persons voluntarily and involuntarily thrust into the public limelight is not here before us.

II

Turning to the facts of the present case, the proofs reasonably would support either a jury finding of innocent or mere negligent misstatement by *Life,* or a finding that *Life* portrayed the play as a reenactment of the Hill family's experience reckless of the truth or with actual knowledge that the portrayal was false. The relevant testimony is as follows.

Joseph Hayes, author of the book, also wrote the play. The story theme was inspired by the desire to write about "true crime" and for years before writing the book, he collected newspaper clippings of stories of hostage incidents. His story was not shaped by any single incident, but by several, including incidents which occurred in California, New York, and Detroit. He said that he did not consciously portray any member of the Hill family, or the Hill family's experience, although admitting that "in a very direct way" the Hill experience "triggered" the writing of the book and the play.

The *Life* article was prepared at the direction and under the supervision of its entertainment editor, Prideaux. He learned of the production of the play from a news story. The play's director, Robert Montgomery, later suggested to him that its interesting stage setting would make the play a worthwhile subject for an article in *Life*. At about the same time, Prideaux ran into a friend of author Hayes, a free-lance photographer, who told Prideaux in casual conversation that the play had a "substantial connection with a true-life incident of a family being held by escaped convicts near Philadelphia." As the play was trying out in Philadelphia, Prideaux decided to contact the author. Hayes confirmed that an incident somewhat similar to the play had occurred in Philadelphia, and agreed with Prideaux to find out whether the former Hill residence would be available to shoot pictures for a *Life* article. Prideaux then met with Hayes in Philadelphia where he saw the play and drove with Hayes to the former Hill residence to test its suitability for a picture story. Neither then nor thereafter did Prideaux question Hayes about the extent to which the play was based on the Hill incident. "A specific question of that nature was never asked, but a discussion of the play itself, what the play was about, in light of my own knowledge of what the true incident was about, confirmed in my mind beyond any doubt that there was a relationship, and Mr. Hayes' presence at this whole negotiation was tacit proof of that."

Prideaux sent photographers to the Hill residence for location photographs of scenes of the play enacted in the home, and proceeded to construct the text of the article. In his "story file" were several news clippings about the Hill incident which revealed its nonviolent character, and a *New York Times* article by Hayes in which he stated that the play "was based on various news stories," mentioning incidents in New York, California, Detroit and Philadelphia.

Prideaux's first draft made no mention of the Hill name except for the caption of one of the photographs. The text related that a true story of a suburban Philadelphia family had "sparked off" Hayes to write the novel, that the play was a "somewhat fictionalized" account of the family's heroism in time of crisis. Prideaux's research assistant, whose task it was to check the draft for accuracy, put a question mark over the words "somewhat fictionalized." Prideaux testified that the question mark "must have been" brought to his attention, although he did not recollect having seen it. The draft was also brought before the copy editor, who, in the presence of Prideaux, made several changes in emphasis and substance. The first sentence was changed to focus on the Hill incident, using the family's name; the novel was said to have been "inspired" by that incident, and the play was referred to as a "reenactment." The words "somewhat fictionalized" were deleted.

Prideaux labeled as "emphatically untrue" defense counsel's suggestion during redirect examination that from the beginning he knew that the play had no relationship to the Hill incident apart from being a hostage incident. Prideaux admitted that he knew the play was "between a little bit and moderately fictionalized," but stated that he thought beyond doubt that the important quality, the "heart and soul" of the play, was the Hill incident.

The jury might reasonably conclude from this evidence—particularly that the *New York Times'* article was in the story file, that the copy editor deleted "somewhat fictionalized" after the research assistant questioned its accuracy, and that Prideaux admitted that he knew the play was "between a little bit and moderately fictionalized"—that *Life* knew or was reckless of the truth in stating in the article that "the story re-enacted" the Hill family's experience. On the other hand, the jury might reasonably predicate a finding of innocent or only negligent misstatement on the testimony that a statement was made to Prideaux by the free lance photographer that linked the play to an incident in Philadelphia, that the author Hayes cooperated in arranging for the availability of the former Hill home, and that Prideaux thought beyond doubt that the "heart and soul" of the play was the Hill incident.

III

We do not think however that the instructions confined the jury to a verdict of liability based on a finding that the statements in the article were made with knowledge of their falsity or in reckless disregard of the truth. The jury was instructed that liability could not be found under §§ 50–51 "merely because of some incidental mistake of fact, or some incidental incorrect statement," and that a verdict of liability could rest only on findings that (1) *Life* published the article "not to disseminate news, but was using plaintiffs' name in connection with a fictionalized episode as to plaintiffs' relationship to *The Desperate Hours*"; the Court variously restated this "fictionalization" requirement in terms such as whether appellant "altered or changed the true facts concerning plaintiffs' relationship to *The Desperate Hours,* so that the article, as published, constituted substantially fiction or a fictionalized version . . . ," whether the article constituted "fiction," or was "fictionalized"; and (2) that the article was published to advertise the play or "for trade purposes"; this latter purpose was variously defined as one "to amuse, thrill, astonish or move the reading public so as to increase the circulation of the magazine or for some other material benefit," "to increase circulation or enhance the standing of the magazine with its readers," and "for the publisher's profits through increased circulation induced by exploitation of the plaintiffs."

The court also instructed the jury that an award of punitive damages was justified if the jury found that the appellant falsely connected appellee to the play "knowingly or through failure to make a reasonable investigation," adding "You do not need to find that there was any actual ill will or personal malice toward the plaintiffs if you find a reckless or wanton disregard of the plaintiffs' rights."

Appellee argues that the instructions to determine whether *Life* "altered or changed" the true facts, and whether apart from incidental errors, the article was a "substantial fiction" or a "fictionalized version" were tantamount to instructions that the jury must find that *Life* knowingly falsified the facts. We do not think that the instructions bear that interpretation, particularly in light of the marked contrast in the instructions on compensatory and punitive damages. The element of "knowingly" is mentioned only in the instruction that punitive damages must be supported by a finding that *Life* falsely connected the Hill family with the play "knowingly or through failure to make a reasonable investigation." Moreover, even as to punitive damages, the instruction that such damages were justified on the basis of "failure to make a reasonable investigation" is an instruction that proof of negligent misstatement is enough, and we have rejected the test of negligent misstatement as inadequate. Next, the trial court plainly did not regard his instructions as limiting the jury to a verdict of liability based on a finding of knowing or reckless falsity, he denied appellant's motion to dismiss after the close of the evidence because he perceived that it was for the jury to find "whether the *Life* article was true or whether an inference could be obtained from reading it that it was not true." This implies a view that "fictionalization" was synonymous with "falsity" without regard to knowledge or even negligence, except for the purposes of an award of punitive damages. Finally, nothing in the New York cases decided at the time of trial limited liability to cases of knowing or reckless falsity and *Spahn,* decided since, has left the question in doubt.

The requirement that the jury also find that the article was published "for trade purposes," as defined in the charge, cannot save the charge from constitutional infirmity. "That books, newspapers, and magazines are published and sold for profit does not prevent them from being a form of expression whose liberty is safeguarded by the First Amendment. . . ."

IV

The appellant argues that the statute should be declared unconstitutional on its face if construed by the New York courts to impose liability without proof of knowing or reckless falsity. Such a declaration would not be warranted even if it were entirely clear that this is the view of the New York courts. The New York Court of Appeals, as the *Spahn* opinion demonstrates, has been assiduous to construe the statute to avoid invasion of the constitutional protections for speech and press. We therefore confidently expect that the New York courts will apply the statute consistently with the constitutional command. Any possible difference with us as to the thrust of the constitutional command is narrowly limited in this case to the failure of the trial judge to instruct the jury that a verdict of liability could be predicated only on a finding of knowing or reckless falsity in the publication of the *Life* article.

The judgment of the Court of Appeals is set aside and the case is remanded for further proceedings not inconsistent with this opinion.

It is so ordered.

2. Rights of Women

REED *v.* REED
404 US 71 (1971)

[The Equal Rights Amendment, passed by Congress and pending before the states for ratification, provides that "equality of rights under the law shall not be denied or abridged by the United States or by any state on account of sex." Apart from what this constitutional amendment may accomplish, there are other constitutional provisions and principles which offer women constitutional protection against discrimination. The instant case can stand as paradigmatic. The Probate Code of Idaho provided that where persons seek appointment as administrators of estates of deceased relatives, males must be preferred to females when they are persons of equal entitlement to appointment, e.g., as between parents, the father is to be preferred to the mother. The Supreme Court unanimously held that this law violated the Equal Protection Clause of the Fourteenth Amendment. Chief Justice Burger wrote the opinion.

[Some leading opponents of the Equal Rights Amendment have argued that the Equal Protection Clause offers sufficient protection against arbitrary sexual discrimination, especially when enforced under legislative provisions, such as those of Title VII of the Civil Rights Act of 1964, which prohibits such discrimination in employment.]

Mr. Chief Justice Burger delivered the opinion of the Court:

Richard Lynn Reed, a minor, died intestate in Ada County, Idaho, on March 29, 1967. His adoptive parents, who had separated sometime prior to his death, are the parties to this appeal. Approximately seven months after Richard's death, his mother, appellant Sally Reed, filed a petition in the Probate Court of Ada County, seeking appointment as administratrix of her son's estate. Prior to the date set for a hearing on the mother's petition, appellee Cecil Reed, the father of the decedent, filed a competing petition seeking to have himself appointed administrator of the son's estate. The probate court held a joint hearing on the two petitions and thereafter ordered that letters of administration be issued to appellee Cecil Reed upon his taking the oath and filing the bond required by law. The court treated §§ 15–312 and 15–314 of the Idaho Code as the controlling statutes and read those sections as compelling a preference for Cecil Reed because he was a male.

Section 15–312* designates the persons who are entitled to administer the estate

---

* Section 15–312 provides as follows:

"Administration of the estate of a person dying intestate must be granted to some one or more of the persons hereinafter metioned, and they are respectively entitled thereto in the following order:

"1. The surviving husband or wife or some competent person whom he or she may request to have appointed.

"2. The children.

"3. The father or mother.

"4. The brothers.

"5. The sisters.

"6. The grandchildren.

of one who dies intestate. In making these designations, that section lists 11 classes of persons who are so entitled and provides, in substance, that the order in which those classes are listed in the section shall be determinative of the relative rights of competing applicants for letters of administration. One of the 11 classes so enumerated is "[t]he father or mother" of the person dying intestate. Under this section, then, appellant and appellee, being members of the same entitlement class, would seem to have been equally entitled to administer their son's estate. Section 15–314 provides, however, that "[o]f several persons claiming and equally entitled [under § 15–312] to administer, males must be preferred to females, and relatives of the whole to those of the half blood."

In issuing its order, the probate court implicitly recognized the equality of entitlement of the two applicants under § 15–312 and noted that neither of the applicants was under any legal disability; the court ruled, however, that appellee, being a male, was to be preferred to the female appellant "by reason of Section 15–314 of the Idaho Code." In stating this conclusion, the probate judge gave no indication that he had attempted to determine the relative capabilities of the competing applicants to perform the functions incident to the administration of an estate. It seems clear the probate judge considered himself bound by statute to give preference to the male candidate over the female, each being otherwise "equally entitled."

Sally Reed appealed from the probate court order, and her appeal was treated by the District Court of the Fourth Judicial District of Idaho as a constitutional attack on § 15–314. In dealing with the attack, that court held that the challenged section violated the Equal Protection Clause of the Fourteenth Amendment and was, therefore, void; the matter was ordered "returned to the Probate Court for its determination of which of the two parties" was better qualified to administer the estate.

This order was never carried out, however, for Cecil Reed took a further appeal to the Idaho Supreme Court, which reversed the District Court and reinstated the original order naming the father administrator of the estate. In reaching this result, the Idaho Supreme Court first dealt with the governing statutory law and held that under § 15–312 "a father and mother are 'equally entitled' to letters of administration," but the preference given to males by § 15–314 is "mandatory" and leaves no room for the exercise of a probate court's discretion in the appointment of administrators. Having thus definitively and authoritatively interpreted the statutory provisions involved, the Idaho Supreme Court then proceeded to examine, and reject, Sally Reed's contention that § 15–314 violates the Equal Protection Clause by giving a mandatory preference to males over females, without regard to their individual qualifications as potential estate administrators.

Sally Reed thereupon appealed for review by this Court pursuant to 28 U.S.C. § 1257(2), and we noted probable jurisdiction. Having examined the record and considered the briefs and oral arguments of the parties, we have concluded that the

---

"7. The next of kin entitled to share in the distribution of the estate.
"8. Any of the kindred.
"9. The public administrator.
"10. The creditors of such person at the time of death.
"11. Any person legally competent.
"If the decedent was a member of a partnership at the time of his decease, the surviving partner must in no case be appointed administrator of his estate."

arbitrary preference established in favor of males by § 15–314 of the Idaho Code cannot stand in the face of the Fourteenth Amendment's command that no State deny the equal protection of the laws to any person within its jurisdiction.

Idaho does not, of course, deny letters of administration to women altogether. Indeed, under § 15–312, a woman whose spouse dies intestate has a preference over a son, father, brother, or any other male relative of the decedent. Moreover, we can judicially notice that in this country, presumably due to the greater longevity of women, a large proportion of estates, both intestate and under wills of decedents, are administered by surviving widows.

Section 15–314 is restricted in its operation to those situations where competing applications for letters of administration have been filed by both male and female members of the same entitlement class established by § 15–312. In such situations, § 15–314 provides that different treatment be accorded to the applicants on the basis of their sex; it thus establishes a classification subject to scrutiny under the Equal Protection Clause.

In applying that clause, this Court has consistently recognized that the Fourteenth Amendment does not deny to States the power to treat different classes of persons in different ways. . . . The Equal Protection Clause of that Amendment does, however, deny to States the power to legislate that different treatment be accorded to persons placed by a statute into different classes on the basis of criteria wholly unrelated to the objective of that statute. A classification "must be reasonable, not arbitrary, and must rest upon some ground of difference having a fair and substantial relation to the object of the legislation, so that all persons similarly circumstanced shall be treated alike." . . . The question presented by this case, then, is whether a difference in the sex of competing applicants for letters of administration bears a rational relationship to a state objective that is sought to be advanced by the operation of §§ 15–312 and 15–314.

In upholding the latter section, the Idaho Supreme Court concluded that its objective was to eliminate one area of controversy when two or more persons, equally entitled under § 15–312, seek letters of administration and thereby present the probate court "with the issue of which one should be named." The court also concluded that where such persons are not of the same sex, the elimination of females from consideration "is neither an illogical nor arbitrary method devised by the legislature to resolve an issue that would otherwise require a hearing as to the relative merits . . . of the two or more petitioning relatives. . . ."

Clearly the objective of reducing the workload on probate courts by eliminating one class of contests is not without some legitimacy. The crucial question, however, is whether § 15–314 advances that objective in a manner consistent with the command of the Equal Protection Clause. We hold that it does not. To give a mandatory preference to members of either sex over members of the other, merely to accomplish the elimination of hearings on the merits, is to make the very kind of arbitrary legislative choice forbidden by the Equal Protection Clause of the Fourteenth Amendment; and whatever may be said as to the positive values of avoiding intrafamily controversy, the choice in this context may not lawfully be mandated solely on the basis of sex.

We note finally that if § 15–314 is viewed merely as a modifying appendage to

§ 15–312 and as aimed at the same objective, its constitutionality is not thereby saved. The objective of § 15–312 clearly is to establish degrees of entitlement of various classes of persons in accordance with their varying degrees and kinds of relationship to the intestate. Regardless of their sex, persons within any one of the enumerated classes of that section are similarly situated with respect to that objective. By providing dissimilar treatment for men and women who are thus similarly situated, the challenged section violates the Equal Protection Clause. *Royster Guano Co.* v. *Virginia, supra.*

The judgment of the Idaho Supreme Court is reversed and the case remanded for further proceedings not inconsistent with this opinion.

Reversed and remanded.

3. Rights of the Poor

SHAPIRO v. THOMPSON
394 US 618 (1969)

[Until the late 1960s one hardly ever heard of the *rights* of the poor or of those who are on relief or welfare. But since then "poverty law" has developed into a separate branch of constitutional, statutory, and administrative law. Many aspects of personal and social relations affecting the poor have been successfully litigated, including rights of tenants in public housing, eligibility for welfare, personal rights and liberties of those who are on welfare, adequacy of welfare payments, consumer credit problems, and rights of children, including illegitimate children. In the instant case (which consolidated appeals involving statutes of Connecticut and Pennsylvania, and an act of Congress with respect to the District of Columbia) the Supreme Court declared unconstitutional state or federal statutory provisions which denied welfare assistance to persons who have not resided within their jurisdictions for at least one year. Absent a "compelling" governmental or state interest, such a requirement violates the Equal Protection Clause of the Fourteenth Amendment or the Due Process Clause of the Fifth Amendment, and impinges upon the constitutional right to travel freely within the United States. The decision was 6–3. Justice Brennan wrote the Court's opinion. Justice Stewart wrote a concurring opinion. Chief Justice Warren wrote a dissenting opinion in which Justice Black joined; Justice Harlan wrote a dissenting opinion.]

Mr. Justice Brennan delivered the opinion of the Court:

These three appeals were restored to the calendar for reargument. Each is an appeal from a decision of a three-judge District Court holding unconstitutional a State or District of Columbia statutory provision which denies welfare assistance to residents of the State or District who have not resided within their jurisdictions for at least one year immediately preceding their applications for such assistance. We affirm the judgments of the District Courts in the three cases.

I

In No. 9, the Connecticut Welfare Department invoked § 17–2d of the Connecticut General Statutes to deny the application of appellee Vivian Marie Thompson for assistance under the program for Aid to Families with Dependent Children (AFDC). She was a 19-year-old unwed mother of one child and pregnant with her second child when she changed her residence in June 1966 from Dorchester, Massachusetts, to Hartford, Connecticut, to live with her mother, a Hartford resident. She moved to her own apartment in Hartford in August 1966, when her mother was no longer able to support her and her infant son. Because of her pregnancy, she was unable to work or enter a work-training program. Her application for AFDC assistance, filed in August, was denied in November solely on the ground that, as required by § 17–2d, she had not lived in the State for a year before her application was filed. She brought this action in the District Court for the District of Connecticut where a three-judge court, one judge dissenting, declared § 17–2d unconstitutional. The majority held that the waiting-period requirement is unconstitutional because it "has a chilling effect on the right to travel." The majority also held that the provision was a violation of the Equal Protection Clause of the Fourteenth Amendment because the denial of relief to those resident in the State for less than a year is not based on any permissible purpose but is solely designed, as "Connecticut states quite frankly," "to protect its fisc by discouraging entry of those who come needing relief." We noted probable jurisdiction.

In No. 33, there are four appellees. Three of them—appellees Harrell, Brown, and Legrant—applied for and were denied AFDC aid. The fourth, appellee Barley, applied for and was denied benefits under the program for Aid to the Permanently and Totally Disabled. The denial in each case was on the ground that the applicant had not resided in the District of Columbia for one year immediately preceding the filing of her application, as required by § 3–203 of the District of Columbia Code.

Appellee Minnie Harrell, now deceased, had moved with her three children from New York to Washington in September 1966. She suffered from cancer and moved to be near members of her family who lived in Washington.

Appellee Barley, a former resident of the District of Columbia, returned to the District in March 1941 and was committed a month later to St. Elizabeths Hospital as mentally ill. She has remained in that hospital ever since. She was deemed eligible for release in 1965, and a plan was made to transfer her from the hospital to a foster home. The plan depended, however, upon Mrs. Barley's obtaining welfare assistance for her support. Her application for assistance under the program for Aid to the Permanently and Totally Disabled was denied because her time spent in the hospital did not count in determining compliance with the one-year requirement.

Appellee Brown lived with her mother and two of her three children in Fort Smith, Arkansas. Her third child was living with appellee Brown's father in the District of Columbia. When her mother moved from Fort Smith to Oklahoma, appellee Brown, in February 1966, returned to the District of Columbia where she had lived as a child. Her application for AFDC assistance was approved insofar as it sought assistance for the child who had lived in the District with her father but was denied to the extent it sought assistance for the two other children.

Appellee Legrant moved with her two children from South Carolina to the District of Columbia in March 1967 after the death of her mother. She planned to live with a sister and brother in Washington. She was pregnant and in ill health when she applied for and was denied AFDC assistance in July 1967.

The several cases were consolidated for trial, and a three-judge District Court was convened. The court, one judge dissenting, held § 3–203 unconstitutional. The majority rested its decision on the ground that the one-year requirement was unconstitutional as a denial of the right to equal protection secured by the Due Process Clause of the Fifth Amendment. We noted probable jurisdiction.

In No. 34, there are two appellees, Smith and Foster, who were denied AFDC aid on the sole ground that they had not been residents of Pennsylvania for a year prior to their applications as required by § 432(6) of the Pennsylvania Welfare Code. Appellee Smith and her five minor children moved in December 1966 from Delaware to Philadelphia, Pennsylvania, where her father lived. Her father supported her and her children for several months until he lost his job. Appellee then applied for AFDC assistance and had received two checks when the aid was terminated. Appellee Foster, after living in Pennsylvania from 1953 to 1965, had moved with her four children to South Carolina to care for her grandfather and invalid grandmother and had returned to Pennsylvania in 1967. A three-judge District Court for the Eastern District of Pennsylvania, one judge dissenting, declared § 432(6) unconstitutional. The majority held that the classification established by the waiting-period requirement is "without rational basis and without legitimate purpose or function" and therefore a violation of the Equal Protection Clause. The majority noted further that if the purpose of the statute was "to erect a barrier against the movement of indigent persons into the State or to effect their prompt departure after they have gotten there," it would be "patently improper and its implementation plainly impermissible." We noted probable jurisdiction.

II

There is no dispute that the effect of the waiting-period requirement in each case is to create two classes of needy resident families indistinguishable from each other except that one is composed of residents who have resided a year or more, and the second of residents who have resided less than a year, in the jurisdiction. On the basis of this sole difference the first class is granted and the second class is denied welfare aid upon which may depend the ability of the families to obtain the very means to subsist—food, shelter, and other necessities of life. In each case, the District Court found that appellees met the test for residence in their jurisdictions, as well as all other eligibility requirements except the requirement of residence for a full year prior to their applications. On reargument, appellees' central contention is that the statutory prohibition of benefits to residents of less than a year creates a classification which constitutes an invidious discrimination denying them equal protection of the laws. We agree. The interests which appellants assert are promoted by the classification either may not constitutionally be promoted by government or are not compelling governmental interests.

III

Primarily, appellants justify the waiting-period requirement as a protective device to preserve the fiscal integrity of state public assistance programs. It is asserted that people who require welfare assistance during their first year of residence in a State are likely to become continuing burdens on state welfare programs. Therefore, the argument runs, if such people can be deterred from entering the jurisdiction by denying them welfare benefits during the first year, state programs to assist long-time residents will not be impaired by a substantial influx of indigent newcomers.

There is weighty evidence that exclusion from the jurisdiction of the poor who need or may need relief was the specific objective of these provisions. In the Congress, sponsors of federal legislation to eliminate all residence requirements have been consistently opposed by representatives of state and local welfare agencies who have stressed the fears of the States that elimination of the requirements would result in a heavy influx of individuals into States providing the most generous benefits. . . .

We do not doubt that the one-year waiting-period device is well suited to discourage the influx of poor families in need of assistance. An indigent who desires to migrate, resettle, find a new job, and start a new life will doubtless hesitate if he knows that he must risk making the move without the possibility of falling back on state welfare assistance during his first year of residence when his need may be most acute. But the purpose of inhibiting migration by needy persons into the State is constitutionally impermissible.

This Court long ago recognized that the nature of our Federal Union and our constitutional concepts of personal liberty unite to require that all citizens be free to travel throughout the length and breadth of our land uninhibited by statutes, rules, or regulations which unreasonably burden or restrict this movement. . . .

We have no occasion to ascribe the source of this right to travel interstate to a particular constitutional provision. It suffices that, as Mr. Justice Stewart said for the Court in *United States* v. *Guest,* 383 US 745:

The constitutional right to travel from one State to another . . . occupies a position fundamental to the concept of our Federal Union. It is a right that has been firmly established and repeatedly recognized.

. . . [The] right finds no explicit mention in the Constitution. The reason, it has been suggested, is that a right so elementary was conceived from the beginning to be a necessary concomitant of the stronger Union the Constitution created. In any event, freedom to travel throughout the United States has long been recognized as a basic right under the Constitution.

Thus, the purpose of deterring the in-migration of indigents cannot serve as justification for the classification created by the one-year waiting period, since that purpose is constitutionally impermissible. If a law has "no other purpose . . . than to chill the assertion of constitutional rights by penalizing those who choose to exercise them, then it [is] patently unconstitutional." . . .

Alternatively, appellants argue that even if it is impermissible for a State to attempt to deter the entry of all indigents, the challenged classification may be justified as a permissible state attempt to discourage those indigents who would enter the State solely to obtain larger benefits. We observe first that none of the statutes before us is tailored to serve that objective. Rather, the class of barred newcomers is all-inclusive, lumping the great majority who come to the State for other purposes with those who come for the sole purpose of collecting higher benefits. In actual operation, therefore, the three statutes enact what in effect are nonrebuttable presumptions that every applicant for assistance in his first year of residence came to the jurisdiction solely to obtain higher benefits. Nothing whatever in any of these records supplies any basis in fact for such a presumption.

More fundamentally, a State may no more try to fence out those indigents who seek higher welfare benefits than it may try to fence out indigents generally. Implicit in any such distinction is the notion that indigents who enter a State with the hope of securing higher welfare benefits are somehow less deserving than indigents who do not take this consideration into account. But we do not perceive why a mother who is seeking to make a new life for herself and her children should be regarded as less deserving because she considers, among other factors, the level of a State's public assistance. Surely such a mother is no less deserving than a mother who moves into a particular State in order to take advantage of its better educational facilities.

Appellants argue further that the challenged classification may be sustained as an attempt to distinguish between new and old residents on the basis of the contribution they have made to the community through the payment of taxes. We have difficulty seeing how long-term residents who qualify for welfare are making a greater present contribution to the State in taxes than indigent residents who have recently arrived. If the argument is based on contributions made in the past by the long-term residents, there is some question, as a factual matter, whether this argument is applicable in Pennsylvania where the record suggests that some 40% of those denied public assistance because of the waiting period had lengthy prior residence in the State. But we need not rest on the particular facts of these cases. Appellants' reasoning would logically permit the State to bar new residents from schools, parks, and libraries or deprive them of police and fire protection. Indeed it would permit the State to apportion all benefits and services according to the past tax contributions of its citizens. The Equal Protection Clause prohibits such an apportionment of state services.

We recognize that a State has a valid interest in preserving the fiscal integrity of its programs. It may legitimately attempt to limit its expenditures, whether for public assistance, public education, or any other program. But a State may not accomplish such a purpose by invidious distinctions between classes of its citizens. It could not, for example, reduce expenditures for education by barring indigent children from its schools. Similarly, in the cases before us, appellants must do more than show that denying welfare benefits to new residents saves money. The saving of welfare costs cannot justify an otherwise invidious classification.

In sum, neither deterrence of indigents from migrating to the State nor limitation of welfare benefits to those regarded as contributing to the State is a constitutionally permissible state objective.

IV

Appellants next advance as justification certain administrative and related governmental objectives allegedly served by the waiting-period requirement. They argue that the requirement (1) facilitates the planning of the welfare budget; (2)

provides an objective test of residency; (3) minimizes the opportunity for recipients fraudulently to receive payments from more than one jurisdiction; and (4) encourages early entry of new residents into the labor force.

At the outset, we reject appellants' argument that a mere showing of a rational relationship between the waiting period and these four admittedly permissible state objectives will suffice to justify the classification. . . . The waiting-period provision denies welfare benefits to otherwise eligible applicants solely because they have recently moved into the jurisdiction. But in moving from State to State or to the District of Columbia, appellees were exercising a constitutional right, and any classification which serves to penalize the exercise of that right, unless shown to be necessary to promote a *compelling* governmental interest, is unconstitutional. . . .

The argument that the waiting-period requirement facilitates budget predictability is wholly unfounded. The records in all three cases are utterly devoid of evidence that either State or the District of Columbia in fact uses the one-year requirement as a means to predict the number of people who will require assistance in the budget year. None of the appellants takes a census of new residents or collects any other data that would reveal the number of newcomers in the State less than a year. Nor are new residents required to give advance notice of their need for welfare assistance. Thus, the welfare authorities cannot know how many new residents come into the jurisdiction in any year, much less how many of them will require public assistance. In these circumstances, there is simply no basis for the claim that the one-year waiting requirement serves the purpose of making the welfare budget more predictable. In Connecticut and Pennsylvania the irrelevance of the one-year requirement to budgetary planning is further underscored by the fact that temporary, partial assistance is given to some new residents and full assistance is given to other new residents under reciprocal agreements. Finally, the claim that a one-year waiting requirement is used for planning purposes is plainly belied by the fact that the requirement is not also imposed on applicants who are long-term residents, the group that receives the bulk of welfare payments. In short, the States rely on methods other than the one-year requirement to make budget estimates. In No. 34, the Director of the Pennsylvania Bureau of Assistance Policies and Standards testified that, based on experience in Pennsylvania and elsewhere, her office had already estimated how much the elimination of the one-year requirement would cost and that the estimates of costs of other changes in regulations have proven exceptionally accurate.

The argument that the waiting period serves as an administratively efficient rule of thumb for determining residency similarly will not withstand scrutiny. The residence requirement and the one-year waiting-period requirement are distinct and independent prerequisites for assistance under these three statutes, and the facts relevant to the determination of each are directly examined by the welfare authorities. Before granting an application, the welfare authorities investigate the applicant's employment, housing, and family situation and in the course of the inquiry necessarily learn the facts upon which to determine whether the applicant is a resident.

Similarly, there is no need for a State to use the one-year waiting period as a safeguard against fraudulent receipt of benefits, for less drastic means are available, and are employed, to minimize that hazard. Of course, a State has a valid interest in preventing fraud by any applicant, whether a newcomer or a long-time resident. It is not denied, however, that the investigations now conducted entail inquiries into facts relevant to that subject. In addition, cooperation among state welfare departments is common. The District of Columbia, for example, provides interim assistance to its former residents who have moved to a State which has a waiting period. As a matter of course, District officials send a letter to the welfare authorities in the recipient's new community "to request the information needed to continue assistance." A like procedure would be an effective safeguard against the hazard of double payments. Since double payments can be prevented by a letter or a telephone call, it is unreasonable to accomplish this objective by the blunderbuss method of denying assistance to all indigent newcomers for an entire year.

Pennsylvania suggests that the one-year waiting period is justified as a means of encouraging new residents to join the labor force promptly. But this logic would also require a similar waiting period for long-term residents of the State. A state purpose to encourage employment provides no rational basis for imposing a one-year waiting-period restriction on new residents only.

We conclude therefore that appellants in these cases do not use and have no need to use the one-year requirement for the governmental purposes suggested. Thus, even under traditional equal protection tests a classification of welfare applicants according to whether they have lived in the State for one year would seem irrational and unconstitutional. But, of course, the traditional criteria do not apply in these cases. Since the classification here touches on the fundamental right of interstate movement, its constitutionality must be judged by the stricter standard of whether it promotes a *compelling* state interest. Under this standard, the waiting-period requirement clearly violates the Equal Protection Clause. . . .

VI

The waiting-period requirement in the District of Columbia Code involved in No. 33 is also unconstitutional even though it was adopted by Congress as an exercise of federal power. In terms of federal power, the discrimination created by the one-year requirement violates the Due Process Clause of the Fifth Amendment. "[W]hile the Fifth Amendment contains no equal protection clause, it does forbid discrimination that is 'so unjustifiable as to be violative of due process.' " . . . For the reasons we have stated in invalidating the Pennsylvania and Connecticut provisions, the District of Columbia provision is also invalid—the Due Process Clause of the Fifth Amendment prohibits Congress from denying public assistance to poor persons otherwise eligible solely on the ground that they have not been residents of the District of Columbia for one year at the time their applications are filed.

Accordingly, the judgments in Nos. 9, 33, and 34 are affirmed.

4. Rights of Prisoners

CRUZ *v.* BETO
405 US 319 (1972)

[Traditionally it was assumed that inmates of jails and prisons had no constitutional rights; that, as they entered the penitentiary, they left outside all the rights that they might have been able to enjoy as free men. One of the essential components of this assumption was the proposition that prison officials have full authority to administer prison affairs, and that the courts would not, and ought not, to presume any competence to enter that domain. For various reasons, these positions are no longer maintained by the courts; many cases decided in the late 1960's and in the 1970's have radically altered the legal picture—the courts have passed on the constitutional questions raised in cases that have challenged prison administrations with respect to harsh disciplinary measures, the rights of prisoners with respect to mailing privileges and reading matter, with respect to the preparation of petitions for writs of habeas corpus, law libraries, legal assistance, and other claims and questions. In the instant case, the Supreme Court passed on the right of prisoners under the Free Exercise Clause of the First Amendment. The Court, in a Per Curiam opinion, upheld the claim of a Buddhist prisoner to this right. Chief Justice Burger and Justice Blackmun concurred in the result. Justice Rehnquist dissented.]

Per Curiam:

The complaint, alleging a cause of action under 42 U.S.C. § 1983, states that Cruz is a Buddhist, who is in a Texas prison. While prisoners who are members of other religious sects are allowed to use the prison chapel, Cruz is not. He shared his Buddhist religious material with other prisoners and, according to the allegations, in retaliation was placed in solitary confinement on a diet of bread and water for two weeks, without access to newspapers, magazines, and all other sources of news. He also alleged that he was prohibited from corresponding with his religious advisor in the Buddhist sect. Those in the isolation unit spend 22 hours a day in total idleness.

Again, according to the allegations, Texas encourages inmates to participate in other religious programs; providing at state expense chaplains of the Catholic, Jewish, and Protestant faiths, providing also at state expense copies of the Jewish and Christian Bibles, conducting weekly Sunday school classes and religious services. According to the allegations, points of good merit are given prisoners as a reward for attending orthodox religious services, those points enhancing a prisoner's eligibility for desirable job assignments and early parole consideration. Respondent answered, denying the allegations and moving to dismiss.

The Federal District Court denied relief without a hearing or without any findings, saying the complaint was in an area that should be left "to the sound discretion of prison administrators." It went on to say, "Valid disciplinary and security reasons not known to this court may prevent the 'equality' of exercise of religious practices in prison." The Court of Appeals affirmed.

Federal courts sit not to supervise prisons but to enforce the constitutional rights of all "persons" which include prisoners. We are not unmindful that prison officials must be accorded latitude in the administration of prison affairs, and that prisoners necessarily are subject to appropriate rules and regulations. But persons in prison, like other individuals, have the right to petition the Government for redress of grievances which, of course, includes "access of prisoners to the courts for the purpose of presenting their complaints." . . . Moreover, racial segregation, which is unconstitutional outside prisons, is unconstitutional within prisons, save for "the necessities of prison security and discipline." *Lee* v. *Washington,* 390 US 333. Even more closely in point is *Cooper* v. *Pate,* 378 US 546, where we reversed a dismissal of a complaint brought under 42 U.S.C. § 1983. We said "Taking as true the allegations of the complaint, as they must be on a motion to dismiss, the complaint stated a cause of action." *Ibid.* The allegation made by that petitioner was that solely because of his religious beliefs he was denied permission to purchase certain religious publications and denied other privileges enjoyed by other prisoners. . . .

If Cruz was a Buddhist and if he was denied a reasonable opportunity of pursuing his faith comparable to the opportunity afforded fellow prisoners who adhere to conventional religious precepts, then there was palpably discrimination by the State against the Buddhist religion, established 600 B.C., long before the Christian era.* The First Amendment applicable to the States by reason of the Fourteenth Amendment, . . . prohibits government from making a law "prohibiting the free exercise [of religion]." If the allegations of this complaint are assumed to be true, as they must be on the motion to dismiss, Texas has violated the First and Fourteenth Amendments.

The motion in forma pauperis and petition for certiorari is granted, the judgment is vacated, and the cause remanded for a hearing and appropriate findings.

Vacated and remanded.

Mr. Chief Justice Burger, joining in the result:

I join in the result reached even though the allegations of the complaint are on the borderline necessary to compel an evidentiary hearing. Some of the claims alleged are frivolous; others do not present justiciable issues. There cannot possibly be any constitutional or legal requirement that the government provide materials for every religion and sect practiced in this diverse country. At most, Buddhist materials cannot be denied to prisoners if someone offers to supply them.

Mr. Justice Rehnquist, dissenting:

Unlike the Court, I am not persuaded that petitioner's complaint states a claim under the First Amendment, nor that if the opinion of the Court of Appeals is vacated the trial court must necessarily conduct a trial upon the complaint.

Under the First Amendment, of course, Texas may neither "establish a religion" nor may it "impair the free exercise" thereof. Petitioner alleges that voluntary services are made available at prison facilities so that Protestants, Catholics, and Jews may attend church services of their choice. None of our prior holdings indicates that such a program on the part of prison officials amounts to the establishment of a religion.

Petitioner is a prisoner, serving 15 years for robbery in a Texas penitentiary. He is understandably not as free to practice his religion as if he were outside the prison walls. But there is no intimation in his pleadings that he is being punished for his religious

---

* We do not suggest, of course, that every religious sect or group within a prison—however few in numbers—must have identical facilities or personnel. A special chapel or place of worship need not be provided for every faith regardless of size; nor must a chaplain, priest, or minister be provided without regard for the extent of the demand. But reasonable opportunities must be afforded to all prisoners to exercise the religious freedom guaranteed by the First and Fourteenth Amendments without fear of penalty.

views, as was the case in *Cooper* v. *Pate,* 378 US 546 (1964), where a prisoner was denied the receipt of mail about his religion. *Cooper* presented no question of interference with prison administration of the type which would be involved here in retaining chaplains, scheduling the use of prison facilities, and timing the activities of various prisoners.

None of our holdings under the First Amendment requires that, in addition to being allowed freedom of religious belief, prisoners be allowed freely to evangelize their views among other prisoners. There is no indication in petitioner's complaint that the prison officials have dealt more strictly with his efforts to convert other convicts to Buddhism than with efforts of communicants of other faiths to make similar conversions.

By reason of his status petitioner is obviously limited in the extent to which he may *practice* his religion. He is assuredly not free to attend the church of his choice outside the prison walls. But the fact that the Texas prison system offers no Buddhist services at this particular prison does not, under the circumstances pleaded in his complaint, demonstrate that his religious freedom is being impaired. Presumably prison officials are not obligated to provide facilities for any particular denominational services within a prison, although once they undertake to provide them for some they must make only such reasonable distinctions as may survive analysis under the Fourteenth Amendment Equal Protection Clause.

What petitioner's basic claim amounts to is that because prison facilities are provided for denominational services for religions with more numerous followers, the failure to provide prison facilities for Buddhist services amounts to a denial of the equal protection of the laws. There is no indication from petitioner's complaint how many practicing Buddhists there are in the particular prison facility in which he is incarcerated, nor is there any indication of the demand upon available facilities for other prisoner activities. Neither the decisions of this Court after full argument, nor those summarily reversing the dismissal of a prisoner's civil rights complaint have ever given full consideration to the proper balance to be struck between prisoners' rights and the extensive administrative discretion which must rest with correction officials. I would apply the rule of deference to administrative discretion which has been overwhelmingly accepted in the courts of appeals. Failing that, I would at least hear argument as to what rule should govern.

A long line of decisions by this Court has recognized that the "equal protection of the laws" guaranteed by the Fourteenth Amendment is not to be applied in a precisely equivalent way in the multitudinous fact situations which may confront the courts. On the one hand, we have held that racial classifications are "invidious" and "suspect." I think it quite consistent with the intent of the framers of the Fourteenth Amendment, many of whom would doubtless be surprised to know that convicts came within its ambit, to treat prisoner claims at the other end of the spectrum from claims of racial discrimination. Absent a complaint alleging facts showing that the difference in treatment between petitioner and his fellow Buddhists and practitioners of more numerous denominations could not reasonably be justified under any rational hypothesis, I would leave the matter in the hands of the prison officials. . . .

5. *Rights of Illegitimate Children*

WEBER v. AETNA CASUALTY & SURETY CO.
406 US 164 (1972)

[Traditionally, illegitimate children have suffered disabilities imposed by common law or statutes. Beginning, however, in the late 1960's, a more liberal attitude began to be expressed by the courts. In *Levy* v. *Louisiana,* 391 US 68 (1968), the Supreme Court held that a statute which permitted only a legitimate child to sue for the wrongful death of his mother denied illegitimate children their rights under the Equal Protection Clause of the Fourteenth Amendment. In a companion case, *Glona* v. *American Guarantee and Liability Insurance Company,* 391 US 73 (1968), the Court held that it was unconstitutional to preclude a wrongful death action recovery by a mother for the death of her illegitimate child. Some state courts, relying on these precedents, have gone even further in declaring unconstitutional legal disabilities to which illegitimate children have been subjected.

[Illegitimate children have received varied treatment under workmen's compensation laws. Where statutes based eligibility for recovery on relationship to the workman, and included "children," many courts have construed the term to exclude illegitimate children.

[In the instant case, the deceased workman was married and had four children by his wife. She was committed to a mental hospital; at the time of his death, another woman was living with him. There were also living with him his four legitimate children and one illegitimate child. A second illegitimate child was born posthumously. Under the Louisiana workmen's compensation law, the illegitimate children, unless "acknowledged" through a legal, formal instrument, were relegated to an inferior status and received no compensation. The Supreme Court held that the Louisiana law, which placed the unacknowledged illegitimate children in an inferior class for purposes of recovery under workmen's compensation law violated the Equal Protection Clause of the Fourteenth Amendment. Justice Powell wrote the Court's opinion. Justice Blackmun wrote a concurring opinion. Justice Rehnquist wrote a dissenting opinion.]

Mr. Justice Powell delivered the opinion of the Court:

The question before us, on writ of certiorari to the Supreme Court of Louisiana, concerns the right of dependent unacknowledged, illegitimate children to recover under Louisiana workmen's compensation laws benefits for the death of their natural father on an equal footing with his dependent legitimate children. We hold that Louisiana's denial of the equal recovery rights to dependent unacknowledged illegitimates violates the Equal Protection Clause of the Fourteenth Amendment. *Levy* v. *Louisiana,* 391 US 68 (1968). *Glona* v. *American Guarantee and Liability Insurance Company,* 391 US 73 (1968).

On June 22, 1967, Henry Clyde Stokes died in Louisiana of injuries received during the course of his employment the previous day. At the time of his death Stokes resided and maintained a household with one Willie Mae Weber, to whom he was not married. Living in the household were four legitimate minor children, born of the marriage between Stokes and Adlay Jones Stokes who was at the time committed to a mental hospital. Also living in the home was one unacknowledged illegitimate child born of the relationship between Stokes and Willie Mae Weber. A second illegitimate child of Stokes and Weber was born posthumously.

On June 29, 1967, Stokes' four legitimate children, through their maternal grandmother as guardian, filed a claim for their father's death under Louisiana's workmen's compensation law. The defendant employer and its insurer, impleaded

Willie Mae Weber who appeared and claimed compensation benefits for the two illegitimate children.

Meanwhile, the four legitimate children had brought another suit for their father's death against a third-party tortfeasor which was settled for an amount in excess of the maximum benefits allowable under workmen's compensation. The illegitimate children did not share in this settlement. Subsequently, the employer in the initial action requested the extinguishment of all parties' workmen's compensation claims by reason of the tort settlement.

The trial judge awarded the four legitimate children the maximum allowable amount of compensation and declared their entitlement had been satisfied from the tort suit settlement. Consequently, the four legitimate children dismissed their workmen's compensation claim. Judgment was also awarded to Stokes' two illegitimate offspring to the extent that maximum compensation benefits were not exhausted by the four legitimate children. Since such benefits had been entirely exhausted by the amount of the tort settlement, in which only the four dependent legitimate offspring participated, the two dependent illegitimate children received nothing.

I

For purposes of recovery under workmen's compensation, Louisiana law defines children to include "only legitimate children, step-children, posthumous children, and illegitimate children acknowledged under the provisions of Civil Code Articles 203, 204, and 205."* Thus legitimate children and acknowledged illegitimates may recover on an equal basis. Unacknowledged illegitimate children, however, are relegated to the lesser status of "other dependents" under § 1232(8) of the workmen's compensation statute and may recover *only* if there are not enough surviving dependents in the preceding classifications to exhaust the maximum allowable benefits. Both the Louisiana Court of Appeal and a divided Louisiana Supreme Court sustained these statutes over appellants' constitutional objections, holding that our decision in *Levy, supra,* was not controlling.

We disagree. In *Levy,* the Court held invalid as denying equal protection of law, a Louisiana statute which barred an illegitimate child from recovering for the wrongful death of its mother when such recoveries by legitimate children were authorized. The Court there decided that the fact of a child's birth out of wedlock

---

* La. Rev. Stat. § 23:1021(3). The relevant provisions for acknowledgment of an illegitimate child are as follows:

Louisiana Civil Code, Art 202: "Illegitimate children who have been acknowledged by their father, are called natural children; those who have not been acknowledged by their father, or whose father and mother were incapable of contracting marriage at the time of conception, or whose father is unknown, are contradistinguished by the appellation of bastards."

Louisiana Civil Code, Art 203: "The acknowledgment of an illegitimate child shall be made by a declaration executed before a notary public, in presence of two witnesses, by the father and mother of either of them, whenever it shall not have been made in the registering of the birth or baptism of such child."

Louisiana Civil Code, Art 204: "Such acknowledgment shall not be made in favor of children whose parents were incapable of contracting marriage at the time of conception; however, such acknowledgment may be made if the parents should contract a legal marriage with each other."

bore no reasonable relation to the purpose of wrongful death statutes which compensate children for the death of a mother. As the Court said in *Levy:*

> Legitimacy or illegitimacy of birth has no relation to the nature of the wrong allegedly inflicted on the mother. These children, though illegitimate, were dependent on her; she cared for them and nurtured them; they were indeed hers in the biological and in the spiritual sense; in her death they suffered wrong in the sense that any dependent would. . . .

The court below sought to distinguish *Levy* as involving a statute which absolutely excluded *all* illegitimates from recovery, whereas in the compensation statute in the instant case acknowledged illegitimates may recover equally with legitimate children and ". . . the unacknowledged illegitimate child is not *denied* a right to recover compensation, he being merely relegated to a less favorable position as are other dependent relatives such as parents; . . ." The Louisiana Supreme Court likewise characterized *Levy* as a tort action where the tortfeasor escaped liability on the fortuity of the potential claimant's illegitimacy, whereas in the present action full compensation was rendered, and "no tortfeasor goes free because of the law." . . .

We do not think *Levy* can be disposed of by such finely carved distinctions. The Court in *Levy* was not so much concerned with the tortfeasor going free as with the equality of treatment under the statutory recovery scheme. Here, as in *Levy,* there is impermissible discrimination. An unacknowledged illegitimate child may suffer as much from the loss of a parent as a child born within wedlock or an illegitimate later acknowledged. So far as this record shows, the dependency and natural affinity of the unacknowledged illegitimate child for her father were as great as those of the four legitimate children whom Louisiana law has allowed to recover.* The legitimate children and the illegitimate child all lived in the home of the deceased and were equally dependent upon him for maintenance and support. It is inappropriate, therefore, for the court below to talk of relegating the unacknowledged illegitimate "to a less favorable position as are other dependent relatives such as parents." The unacknowledged illegitimate is *not* a parent or some "other dependent relative"; in this case she is a *dependent child,* and as such is entitled to rights granted other *dependent children.*

Respondent contends that our recent ruling in *Labine v. Vincent,* 401 US 532 (1971), controls this case. In *Labine,* the Court upheld, against constitutional objections, Louisiana intestacy laws which had barred an acknowledged illegitimate child from sharing equally with legitimate children in her father's estate. That decision reflected, in major part, the traditional deference to a State's prerogative to regulate the disposition at death of property within its borders. . . . The Court has long afforded broad scope to state discretion in this area. Yet the substantial state interest in providing for "the stability of . . . land titles and the prompt and

---

* The affinity and dependency on the father of the posthumously born illegitimate child is, of course, not comparable to that of offspring living at the time of their father's death. This fact, however, does not alter our view of the case. We think a posthumously born illegitimate child should be treated the same as a posthumously born legitimate child, which the Louisiana statutes fail to do.

definitive determination of the valid ownership of property left by decedents," . . . is absent in the case at hand.

Moreover, in *Labine* the intestate, unlike deceased in the present action, might easily have modified his daughter's disfavored position. As the Court there remarked:

Ezra Vincent could have left one-third of his property to his illegitimate daughter had he bothered to follow the simple formalities of executing a will. He could, of course, have legitimatized the child by marrying her mother in which case the child could have inherited his property either by intestate succession or by will as any other legitimate child.

Such options, however, were not realistically open to Henry Stokes. Under Louisiana law he could not have acknowledged his illegitimate children even had he desired to do so.* The burdens of illegitimacy, already weighty, become doubly so when neither parent nor child can legally lighten them.

Both the statute in *Levy* and the statute in the present case involve state-created compensation schemes, designed to provide close relatives and dependents of a deceased a means of recovery for his often abrupt and accidental death. Both wrongful death statutes and workmen's compensation codes represent outgrowths and modifications of our basic tort law. The former alleviated the harsh common-law rule under which "no person could inherit the personal right of another for tortious injuries to his body"; the latter removed difficult obstacles to recovery in work-related injuries by offering a more certain, though generally less remunerative compensation. In the instant case, the recovery sought under the workmen's compensation statute was in lieu of an action under the identical death statute which was at issue in *Levy*. Given the similarities in the origins and purposes of these two statutes, and the similarity of Louisiana's pattern of discrimination in recovery rights, it would require a disregard of precedent and the principles of stare decisis to hold that *Levy* did not control the facts of the case before us. It makes no difference that illegitimates are not so absolutely or broadly barred here as in *Levy;* the discrimination remains apparent.

II

Having determined that *Levy* is the applicable precedent, we briefly reaffirm here the reasoning which produced that result. The tests to determine the validity of state statutes under the Equal Protection Clause have been variously expressed, but this Court requires, at a minimum, that a statutory classification bear some rational relationship to a legitimate state purpose. . . . Though the latitude given state economic and social regulation is necessarily broad, when state statutory classifications approach sensitive and fundamental personal rights, this Court exercises a

---

* La. Civ. Code, Art 204, *supra,* prohibits acknowledgment of children whose parents were incapable of contracting marriage at the time of conception. Acknowledgment may only be made if the parents could contract a legal marriage with each other. Decedent in the instant case remained married to his first wife—the mother of his four legitimate children—until his death. Thus, at all times he was legally barred from marrying Willie Mae Weber, the mother of the two illegitimate children. It therefore was impossible for him to acknowledge legally his illegitimate children and thereby qualify them for protection under the Louisiana Workmen's Compensation Act. . . .

stricter scrutiny. . . . The essential inquiry in all the foregoing cases is, however, inevitably a dual one: What legitimate state interest does the classification promote? What fundamental personal rights might the classification endanger?

The Louisiana Supreme Court emphasized strongly the State's interest in protecting "legitimate family relationships," and the regulation and protection of the family unit has indeed been a venerable state concern. We do not question the importance of that interest; what we do question is how the challenged statute will promote it. As was said in *Glona:* ". . . we see no possible rational basis . . . for assuming that if the natural mother is allowed recovery for the wrongful death of her illegitimate child, the cause of illegitimacy will be served. It would, indeed, be farfetched to assume that women have illegitimate children so that they can be compensated in damages for their death." . . . Nor can it be thought here that persons will shun illicit relations because the offspring may not one day reap the benefits of workmen's compensation.

It may perhaps be said that statutory distinctions between the legitimate and illegitimate reflect closer family relationships in that the illegitimate is more often not under care in the home of the father nor even supported by him. The illegitimate, so this argument runs, may thus be made less eligible for the statutory recoveries and inheritances reserved for those more likely to be within the ambit of familial care and affection. Whatever the merits elsewhere of this contention, it is not compelling in a statutory compensation scheme where dependency on the deceased is a prerequisite to anyone's recovery, and where the acknowledgment so necessary to equal recovery rights may be unlikely to occur or legally impossible to effectuate even where the illegitimate child may be nourished and loved.

Finally, we are mindful that States have frequently drawn arbitrary lines in workmen's compensation and wrongful death statutes to facilitate potentially difficult problems of proof. Nothing in our decision would impose on state court systems a greater burden in this regard. By limiting recovery to dependents of the deceased, Louisiana substantially lessens the possible problems of locating illegitimate children and of determining uncertain claims of parenthood. Our decision fully respects Louisiana's choice on this matter. It will not expand claimants for workmen's compensation beyond those in a direct blood and dependency relationship with the deceased and avoids altogether diffuse questions of affection and affinity which pose difficult probative problems. Our ruling requires equality of treatment between two classes of persons, the genuineness of whose claims the State might in any event be required to determine.

The state interest in legitimate family relationships is not served by the statute; the state interest in minimizing problems of proof is not significantly disturbed by our decision. The inferior classification of dependent unacknowledged illegitimates bears, in this instance, no significant relationship to those recognized purposes of recovery which workmen's compensation statutes commendably serve.

The status of illegitimacy has expressed through the ages society's condemnation of irresponsible liaisons beyond the bonds of marriage. But visiting this condemnation on the head of an infant is illogical and unjust. Moreover, imposing disabilities on the illegitimate child is contrary to the basic concept of our system that legal burdens should bear some relationship to individual responsibility or wrongdoing.

Obviously, no child is responsible for his birth, and penalizing the illegitimate child is an ineffectual—as well as an unjust—way of deterring the parent. Courts are powerless to prevent the social opprobrium suffered by these hapless children, but the Equal Protection Clause does enable us to strike down discriminatory laws relating to status of birth where—as in this case—the classification is justified by no legitimate state interest, compelling or otherwise.

Reversed and remanded.

6. Right to a Passport and Right to Travel

APTHEKER v. SECRETARY OF STATE
378 US 500 (1964)

[In *Shapiro* v. *Thompson, supra,* the Supreme Court gave constitutional dignity to the right to move freely from state to state. In the instant case the Court had before it the question of the constitutional right to a passport, to enable a citizen to travel freely out of the United States. The Secretary of State claimed that Congress had given him the power to refuse issuance of a passport to members of the Communist Party. By 6–3 vote, the Court held the statute to be unconstitutional on its face, as an invasion of liberty guaranteed by the Fifth Amendment. The Court also linked the freedom to travel with free speech and association. Justice Goldberg wrote the opinion for the Court. Justices Black and Douglas wrote separate concurring opinions. Justice Clark wrote a dissenting opinion, in which he was joined by Justices Harlan and White.]

Mr. Justice Goldberg delivered the opinion of the Court:

This appeal involves a single question: the constitutionality of § 6 of the Subversive Activities Control Act of 1950, 64 Stat. 993, 50 U.S.C. § 785. Section 6 provides in pertinent part that:

(a) When a Communist organization . . . is registered, or there is in effect a final order of the Board requiring such organization to register, it shall be unlawful for any member of such organization, with knowledge or notice that such organization is so registered or that such order has become final—(1) to make application for a passport, or the renewal of a passport, to be issued or renewed by or under the authority of the United States; or (2) to use or attempt to use any such passport.

Section 6 became effective, with respect to appellants, on October 20, 1961, when a final order of the Subversive Activities Control Board issued directing the Communist Party of the United States to register under § 7 of the Subversive Activities Control Act. The registration order had been upheld earlier in 1961 by this Court's decision in *Communist Party of the United States* v. *Subversive Activities Control Board,* 367 US 1. Prior to issuance of the final registration order both appellants, who are native-born citizens and residents of the United States, had held valid passports. Subsequently, on January 22, 1962, the Acting Director of the Passport Office notified appellants that their passports were revoked because the Department of State believed that their use of the passports would violate § 6.

Appellants were also notified of their right to seek administrative review of the revocations under Department of State regulations.

Appellants requested and received hearings to review the revocations of their passports. The respective hearing examiners concluded that "the Department of State had reason to believe that [appellants are] within the purview of Sec. 6(a)(2) of the Subversive Activities Control Act, and as a result thereof . . . use of a passport would be in violation of the law." On the basis of this conclusion the examiners recommended that the passport revocations be sustained. Both appellants appealed to the Board of Passport Appeals which recommended affirmance of the revocations. The Secretary of State subsequently approved the recommendations of the Board. The Secretary stated that he "relied solely on the evidence in the record" and that, as the basis of his decision, he:

specifically adopted as his own the [Board's] finding of fact that at all material times [appellants were members] of the Communist Party of the United States with knowledge or notice that such organization had been required to register as a Communist organization under the Subversive Activities Control Act.

Appellants thereupon filed separate complaints seeking declaratory and injunctive relief in the United States District Court for the District of Columbia. The complaints, which have been considered together, asked that judgments be entered declaring § 6 of the Subversive Activities Control Act unconstitutional and ordering the Secretary of State to issue passports to appellants. Each appellant-plaintiff alleged that § 6 was unconstitutional as, *inter alia,* "a deprivation without due process of law of plaintiff's constitutional liberty to travel abroad, in violation of the Fifth Amendment to the Constitution of the United States." Appellants conceded that the Secretary of State had an adequate basis for finding that they were members of the Communist Party of the United States and that the action revoking their passports was proper if § 6 was constitutional. The parties agreed that all administrative remedies had been exhausted and that it would be futile, and indeed a criminal offense, for either appellant to apply for a passport while remaining a member of the Communist Party.

The three-judge District Court, which was convened to review the constitutional question, rejected appellants' contentions, sustained the constitutionality of § 6 of the Control Act, and granted the Secretary's motion for summary judgment. The court concluded that:

the enactment by Congress of section 6, which prohibits these plaintiffs from obtaining passports so long as they are members of an organization—in this case the Communist Party—under a final order to register with the Attorney General . . . is a valid exercise of the power of Congress to protect and preserve our Government against the threat posed by the world Communist movement and that the regulatory scheme bears a reasonable relation thereto.

This Court noted probable jurisdiction.

Appellants attack § 6, both on its face and as applied, as an unconstitutional deprivation of the liberty guaranteed in the Bill of Rights. The Government, while conceding that the right to travel is protected by the Fifth Amendment, contends that the Due Process Clause does not prevent the reasonable regulation of liberty and that § 6 is a reasonable regulation because of its relation to the danger the world Communist movement presents for our national security. Alternatively, the Government argues that "whether or not denial of passports to some members of the Communist Party might be deemed not reasonably related to national security, surely Section 6 was reasonable as applied to the top-ranking Party leaders involved here."

We hold, for the reasons stated below, that § 6 of the Control Act too broadly and indiscriminately restricts the right to travel and thereby abridges the liberty guaranteed by the Fifth Amendment.

I

In 1958 in *Kent* v. *Dulles,* 357 US 116, this Court declared that the right to travel abroad is "an important aspect of the citizen's 'liberty' " guaranteed in the Due Process Clause of the Fifth Amendment. The Court stated that:

> The right to travel is a part of the "liberty" of which the citizen cannot be deprived without due process of law under the Fifth Amendment. . . . Freedom of movement across frontiers in either direction, and inside frontiers as well, was a part of our heritage. Travel abroad, like travel within the country, may be as close to the heart of the individual as the choice of what he eats, or wears, or reads. Freedom of movement is basic in our scheme of values.

In *Kent,* however, the Court concluded that Congress had not conferred authority upon the Secretary of State to deny passports because of alleged Communist beliefs and associations. Therefore, although the decision protected the constitutional right to travel, the Court did not examine "the extent to which it can be curtailed." The Court, referring to § 6 of the Subversive Activities Control Act, noted that "the only law which Congress has passed expressly curtailing the movement of Communists across our borders has not yet become effective." Two years later in *Communist Party of the United States* v. *Subversive Activities Control Board, supra,* this Court reviewed and upheld the registration requirement of § 7 of the Control Act. The Court, however, did not pass upon the "various consequences of the Party's registration for its individual members," because:

> It is wholly speculative now to foreshadow whether, or under what conditions, a member of the Party may in the future *apply for a passport,* or seek government or defense-facility or labor-union employment, or, being an alien, become a party to a naturalization or denaturalization proceeding. None of these things may happen. If they do, appropriate administrative and judicial procedures will be available to test the constitutionality of applications of particular sections of the Act to particular persons in particular situations. Nothing justifies previsioning those issues now. (Emphasis added.)

The present case, therefore, is the first in which this Court has been called upon to consider the constitutionality of the restrictions which § 6 imposes on the right to travel.

The substantiality of the restrictions cannot be doubted. The denial of a passport, given existing domestic and foreign laws, is a severe restriction upon, and in effect a prohibition against, world-wide foreign travel. Present laws and regulations make it a crime for a United States citizen to travel outside the Western Hemisphere or to Cuba without a passport. By its plain import § 6 of the Control Act effectively prohibits travel anywhere in the world outside the Western Hemisphere by members of any "Communist organization"—including "Communist-action" and "Communist-front" organizations. The restrictive effect of the legislation cannot be gainsaid by emphasizing, as the Government seems to do, that a member of a registering organization could recapture his freedom to travel by simply in good faith abandoning his membership in the organization. Since freedom of association is itself guaranteed in the First Amendment, restrictions imposed upon the right to travel cannot be dismissed by asserting that the right to travel could be fully exercised if the individual would first yield up his membership in a given association.

Although previous cases have not involved the constitutionality of statutory restrictions upon the right to travel abroad, there are well-established principles by which to test whether the restrictions here imposed are consistent with the liberty guaranteed in the Fifth Amendment. It is a familiar and basic principle, recently reaffirmed in *NAACP* v. *Alabama,* 84 S. Ct. 1302, that "a governmental purpose to control or prevent activities constitutionally subject to state regulation may not be achieved by means which sweep unnecessarily broadly and thereby invade the area of protected freedoms." . . . In applying this principle the Court in *NAACP* v. *Alabama, supra,* referred to the criteria enunciated in *Shelton* v. *Tucker:*

[E]ven though the governmental purpose be legitimate and substantial, that purpose cannot be pursued by means that broadly stifle fundamental personal liberties when the end can be more narrowly achieved. The breadth of legislative abridgment must be viewed in the light of less drastic means for achieving the same basic purpose.

This principle requires that we consider the congressional purpose underlying § 6 of the Control Act. The Government emphasizes that the legislation in question flows, as the statute itself declares, from the congressional desire to protect our national security. That Congress under the Constitution has power to safeguard our Nation's security is obvious and unarguable. Cf. *Kennedy* v. *Mendoza-Martinez,* 372 US 144. As we said in *Mendoza-Martinez,* "while the Constitution protects against invasions of individual rights, it is not a suicide pact." At the same time the Constitution requires that the powers of government "must be so exercised as not, in attaining a permissible end, unduly to infringe" a constitutionally protected freedom. . . .

Section 6 provides that any member of a Communist organization which has registered or has been ordered to register commits a crime if he attempts to use or obtain a United States passport. The section applies to members who act "with knowledge or notice" that the organization is under a final registration order. "Notice" is specifically defined in § 13(k). That section provides that publication in the *Federal Register* of the fact of registration or of issuance of a final registration order "shall constitute notice to all members of such organization that such order has become final." Thus the terms of § 6 apply whether or not the member actually knows or believes that he is associated with what is deemed to be a "Communist-action" or a "Communist-front" organization. The section also applies whether or not one knows or believes that he is associated with an organization operating to further aims of the world Communist movement and "to establish a Communist totalitarian dictatorship in the countries throughout the world. . . ." 64 Stat. 987, 50 U.S.C. § 781(1). The provision therefore sweeps within its prohibition both knowing and unknowing members. In related contexts this Court has had occasion to consider substantiality of the relationship between an individual and a group where, as here, the fact of membership in that group has been made the sole criterion for limiting the individual's freedom. In *Wieman* v. *Updegraff,* 344 US 183, the Court held that due process guarantee of the Constitution was violated when a State, in an attempt to bar disloyal individuals from its employ, excluded persons solely on the basis of organizational memberships without regard to their knowledge concerning the organizations to which they had belonged. The Court concluded that: "Indiscriminate classification of innocent with knowing activity must fall as an assertion or arbitrary power."

Section 6 also renders irrelevant the member's degree of activity in the organization and his commitment to its purpose. These factors, like knowledge, would bear on the likelihood that travel by such a person would be attended by the type of activity which Congress sought to control. As the Court has elsewhere noted, "men in adhering to a political party or other organization notoriously do not subscribe unqualifiedly to all of its platforms or asserted principles." Cf. *Schneiderman* v. *United States,* 320 US 118. It was in this vein that the Court in *Schware* v. *Board of Bar Examiners,* 353 US, at 246, stated that even "[a]ssuming that some members of the Communist Party . . . had illegal aims and engaged in illegal activities, it cannot automatically be inferred that all members shared their evil purposes or participated in their illegal conduct." Section 6, however, establishes an irrebuttable presumption that individuals who are members of the specified organizations will, if given passports, engage in activities inimical to the security of the United States.

In addition to the absence of criteria linking the bare fact of membership to the individual's knowledge, activity or commitment, § 6 also excludes other considerations which might more closely relate the denial of passports to the stated purpose of the legislation. The prohibition of § 6 applies regardless of the purposes for which an individual wishes to travel. Under the statute it is a crime for a notified member of a registered organization to apply for a passport to travel abroad to visit a sick relative, to receive medical treatment, or for any other wholly innocent purpose. In determining whether there has been an abridgment of the Fifth Amendment's guarantee of liberty, this Court must recognize the danger of punishing a member of a Communist organization "for his adherence to lawful and constitutionally protected purposes, because of other and unprotected purposes which he does not necessarily share." *Noto* v. *United States,* 367 US 290; *Scales* v. *United States,* 367 US 203. In addition it must be noted that § 6 applies to a member regardless of the security-sensitivity of the areas in which he wishes to travel. As a result, if a notified member of a registered organization were to apply for a passport to visit a relative in Ireland, or to read rare manuscripts in the Bodleian Library of Oxford University, the applicant would be guilty of a crime; whereas, if he were to travel to Canada or Latin America to carry on criminal activities directed against the United States, he could do so free from the prohibitive reach of § 6.

In determining the constitutionality of § 6, it is also important to consider that Congress has within its power "less drastic" means of achieving the congressional objective of safeguarding our national security. *Shelton* v. *Tucker,* 364 US, at 488. The Federal Employee Loyalty Program, which was before this Court in *Joint Anti-Fascist Refuge Comm.* v. *McGrath,* 341 US 123, provides an example. Under Executive Order No. 9835, membership in a Communist organization is not considered conclusive but only as one factor to be weighed in determining the loyalty of an applicant or employee. It is relevant to note that less than a month after the decision in *Kent* v. *Dulles, supra,* President Eisenhower sent a message to Congress stating that: "Any limitations on the right to travel can only be tolerated in terms of overriding requirements of our national security, and must be subject to substantive and procedural guaranties." . . . The legislation which the President proposed did not make membership in a Communist organization, without more, a disqualification for obtaining a passport. . . . Irrespective of views as to the validity of this or other such proposals, they demonstrate the conviction of the Executive Branch that our national security can be adequately protected by means which, when compared with § 6, are more discriminately tailored to the constitutional liberties of individuals.

In our view the foregoing considerations compel the conclusion that § 6 of the Control Act is unconstitutional on its face. The section, judged by its plain import and by the substantive evil which Congress sought to control, sweeps too widely and too indiscriminately across the liberty guaranteed in the Fifth Amendment. The prohibition against travel is supported only by a tenuous relationship between the bare fact of organizational membership and the activity Congress sought to proscribe. The broad and enveloping prohibition indiscriminately excludes plainly relevant considerations such as the individual's knowledge, activity, commitment, and purposes in and places for travel. The section therefore is patently not a regulation "narrowly drawn to prevent the supposed evil," cf. *Cantwell* v. *Connecticut,* 310 US, at 307, yet here, as elsewhere, precision must be the touchstone of legislation so affecting basic freedoms, *NAACP* v. *Button,* 371 US, at 438.

II

The Government alternatively urges that, if § 6 cannot be sustained on its face, the prohibition should nevertheless be held constitutional as applied to these particular appellants. The Government argues that "surely Section 6 was reasonable as applied to the top-ranking Party leaders involved here." It is not disputed that appellants are top-ranking leaders: Appellant Aptheker is editor of *Political Affairs,* the "theoretical organ" of the Party in this country and appellant Flynn is chairman of the Party.

It must be remembered that "[a]lthough this Court will often strain to construe legislation so as to save it against constitutional attack. it must not and will not carry this to the point of perverting the purpose of a statute . . ." or judicially rewriting it. *Scales* v. *United States, supra.* To put the matter another way, this Court will not consider the abstract question of whether Congress might have enacted a valid statute but instead must ask whether the statute that Congress did enact will permissibly bear a construction rendering it free from constitutional defect.

The clarity and preciseness of the provision in question make it impossible to narrow its indiscriminately cast and overly broad scope without substantial rewriting. The situation here is different from that in cases such as *United States* v. *National Dairy Products Corp.*, 372 US 29, where the Court is called upon to consider the content of allegedly vague statutory language. Here, in contrast, an attempt to "construe" the statute and to probe its recesses for some core of constitutionality would inject an element of vagueness into the statute's scope and application; the plain words would thus become uncertain in meaning only if courts proceeded on a case-by-case basis to separate out constitutional from unconstitutional areas of coverage. This course would not be proper, or desirable, in dealing with a section which so severely curtails personal liberty.

Since this case involves a personal liberty protected by the Bill of Rights, we believe that the proper approach to legislation curtailing that liberty must be that adopted by this Court in *NAACP* v. *Button*, 371 US 415, and *Thornhill* v. *Alabama*, 310 US 88. In *NAACP* v. *Button* the Court stated that:

[I]n appraising a statute's inhibitory effect upon such rights, this Court has not hesitated to take into account possible applications of the statute in other factual contexts besides that at bar. *Thornhill* v. *Alabama*, 310 US 88; *Winters* v. *New York*, [333 US 507]. Cf. *Staub* v. *City of Baxley*, 355 US 313. . . . The objectionable quality of vagueness and overbreadth does not depend upon absence of fair notice to a criminally accused or upon unchanneled delegation of legislative powers, but upon the danger of tolerating, in the area of First Amendment freedoms, the existence of a penal statute susceptible of sweeping and improper application. Cf. *Marcus* v. *Search Warrant*, 367 US 717. These freedoms are delicate and vulnerable, as well as supremely precious in our society. The threat of sanctions may deter their exercise almost as potently as the actual application of sanctions.

For essentially the same reasons this Court had concluded that the constitutionality of the statute in *Thornhill* v. *Alabama* should be judged on its face:

An accused, after arrest and conviction under such a statute [on its face unconstitutionally abridging freedom of speech], does not have to sustain the burden of demonstrating that the State could not constitutionally have written a different and specific statute covering his activities as disclosed by the charge and the evidence introduced against him. 310 US, at 98.

Similarly, since freedom of travel is a constitutional liberty closely related to rights of free speech and association, we believe that appellants in this case should not be required to assume the burden of demonstrating that Congress could have written a statute which might constitutionally have prohibited their travel.

Accordingly the judgment of the three-judge District Court is reversed and the cause remanded for proceedings in conformity with this opinion.

Reversed and remanded.

X. Freedom from Race Discrimination

1. No Segregation by Zoning

BUCHANAN v. WARLEY
245 US 60 (1917)

[As a consequence of the Civil War the Thirteenth Amendment was adopted in 1865, the Fourteenth in 1868, and the Fifteenth in 1870. Congress passed enforcement and federal election acts. These were all efforts by the Federal Government to remove from the Negro the badge of slavery as well as to end slavery itself. Reconstruction ended, however, in 1877, when federal troops were removed from the states that had seceded; the Negro was then left to the mercy of the South. In 1894 Congress was controlled by the Democratic Party, for the first time since the Civil War, and it proceeded to repeal many of the civil rights provisions in federal law. In 1883 the Supreme Court declared the Civil Rights Act of 1875 unconstitutional. This decision made it possible for the states to enact laws that would segregate Negroes in many ways: in transportation facilities, schools, hospitals, jails and prisons, places of amusement, sport, and recreation, and elsewhere. In *Plessy* v. *Ferguson*, 163 US 537 (1896), the Court upheld a Louisiana statute that provided for "separate but equal" accommodations on railroads for white and Negro passengers. Segregation, operating under the sanction of the "separate but equal" formula, became the pattern in Southern states.

[The Supreme Court did not, however, uniformly uphold segregation laws as constitutional. A law that attempted to segregate Negroes in the location of their homes in the city of Louisville, Kentucky, was unanimously declared unconstitutional in the present case.]

Mr. Justice Day delivered the opinion of the Court:

Buchanan . . . brought an action in the chancery branch of Jefferson circuit court of Kentucky for the specific performance of a contract for the sale of certain real estate situated in the city of Louisville. . . . The offer in writing to purchase the property contained a proviso:

It is understood that I am purchasing the above property for the purpose of having erected thereon a house which I propose to make my residence, and it is a distinct part of this agreement that I shall not be required to accept a deed to the above property or to pay for said property unless I have the right, under the laws of the state of Kentucky and the city of Louisville, to occupy said property as a residence.

This offer was accepted by the plaintiff.

To the action for specific performance the defendant, by way of answer, set up the condition above set forth, that he is a colored person, and that on the block of which the lot in controversy is a part, there are ten residences, eight of which, at the time of the making of the contract, were occupied by white people, and only two (those nearest the lot in question) were occupied by colored people, and that, under and by virtue of the ordinance of the city of Louisville, approved May 11, 1914, he would not be allowed to occupy the lot as a place of residence.

In reply to this answer the plaintiff set up, among other things, that the ordinance was in conflict with the 14th Amendment to the Constitution of the United States, and hence no defense to the action for specific performance of the contract. . . .

The title of the ordinance is:

An ordinance to prevent conflict and ill-feeling between the white and colored races in the city of Louisville, and preserve the public peace and promote the general welfare by making reasonable provisions requiring as far as practicable, the use of separate blocks for residences, places of abode, and places of assembly by white and colored people respectively. . . .

We pass . . . to a consideration of the case upon its merits. This ordinance prevents the occupancy of a lot in the city of Louisville by a person of color in a block where the greater number of residences are occupied by white persons; where such a majority exists, colored persons are excluded. This interdiction is based wholly upon color; simply that, and nothing more. In effect, premises situated as are those in question in the so-called white block are effectively debarred from sale to persons of color, because, if sold, they cannot be occupied by the purchaser nor by him sold to another of the same color.

This drastic measure is sought to be justified under the authority of the state in the exercise of the police power. It is said such legislation tends to promote the public peace by preventing racial conflicts; that it tends to maintain racial purity; that it prevents the deterioration of property owned and occupied by white people, which deterioration, it is contended, is sure to follow the occupancy of adjacent premises by persons of color.

The authority of the state to pass laws in the exercise of the police power, having for their object the promotion of the public health, safety, and welfare, is very broad, as has been affirmed in numerous and recent decisions of this court. Furthermore, the exercise of this power, embracing nearly all legislation of a local character, is not to be interfered with by the courts where it is within the scope of legislative authority and the means adopted reasonably tend to accomplish a lawful purpose. But it is equally well established that the police power, broad as it is, cannot justify the passage of a law or ordinance which runs counter to the limitations of the Federal Constitution; that principle has been so frequently affirmed in this court that we need not stop to cite the cases.

The Federal Constitution and laws passed within its authority are, by the express terms of that instrument, made the supreme law of the land. The 14th Amendment protects life, liberty, and property from invasion by the states without due process of law. Property is more than the mere thing which a person owns. It is elementary that it includes the right to acquire, use, and dispose of it. The Constitution protects these essential attributes of property. . . .

True it is that dominion over property springing from ownership is not absolute and unqualified. The disposition and use of property may be controlled, in the exercise of the police power, in the interest of public health, convenience, or welfare. Harmful occupations may be controlled and regulated. Legitimate business may also be regulated in the interest of the public. Certain uses of property may be confined to portions of the municipality other than the residence district, such as livery stables, brickyards, and the like, because of the impairment of the health and comfort of the occupants of neighboring property. Many illustrations might be given from the decisions of this court and other courts, of this principle, but these cases do not touch the one at bar.

The concrete question here is: May the occupancy, and, necessarily, the purchase and sale of property of which occupancy is an incident, be inhibited by the states, or by one of its municipalities, solely because of the color of the proposed occupant of the premises? That one may dispose of his property, subject only to the control of lawful enactments curtailing that right in the public interest, must be conceded. The question now presented makes it pertinent to inquire into the constitutional right of the white man to sell his property to a colored man, having in view the legal status of the purchaser and occupant.

Following the Civil War certain amendments to the Federal Constitution were adopted, which have become an integral part of that instrument, equally binding upon all the states and fixing certain fundamental rights which all are bound to respect. The 13th Amendment abolished slavery in the United States and in all places subject to their jurisdiction, and gave Congress power to enforce the Amendment by appropriate legislation. The 14th Amendment made all persons born or naturalized in the United States, citizens of the United States and of the states in which they reside, and provided that no state shall make or enforce any law which shall abridge the privileges or immunities of citizens of the United States, and that no state shall deprive any person of life, liberty, or property without due process of law, nor deny to any person the equal protection of the laws. . . .

That there exists a serious and difficult problem arising from a feeling of race hostility which the law is powerless to control, and to which it must give a measure of consideration, may be freely admitted. But its solution cannot be promoted by depriving citizens of their constitutional rights and privileges.

As we have seen, this court has held laws valid which separated the races on the basis of equal accommodations in public conveyances, and courts of high authority have held enactments lawful which provide for separation in the public schools of white and colored pupils where equal privileges are given. But, in view of the rights secured by the 14th Amendment to the Federal Constitution, such legislation must have its limitations, and cannot be sustained where the exercise of authority exceeds the restraints of the Constitution. We think these limitations are exceeded in laws and ordinances of the character now before us.

It is the purpose of such enactments, and it is frankly avowed it will be their ultimate effect, to require by law, at least in residential districts, the compulsory separation of the races on account of color. Such action is said to be essential to the maintenance of the purity of the races, although it is to be noted in the ordinance under consideration that the employment of colored servants in white families is permitted, and nearby residences of colored persons not coming within the blocks, as defined in the ordinance, are not prohibited.

The case presented does not deal with an attempt to prohibit the amalgamation of the races. The right which the ordinance annulled was the civil right of a white man to dispose of his property if he saw fit to do so to a person of color, and of a colored person to make such disposition to a white person.

It is urged that this proposed segregation will promote the public peace by preventing race conflicts. Desirable as this is, and important as is the preservation of the public peace, this aim cannot be accomplished by laws or ordinances which deny rights created or protected by the Federal Constitution.

It is said that such acquisitions by colored persons depreciate property owned in the neighborhood by white persons. But property may be acquired by undesirable white neighbors, or put to disagreeable though lawful uses with like results.

We think this attempt to prevent the alienation of the property in question to a person of color was not a legitimate exercise of the police interference with property rights except by due process of law. That power of the state, and is in direct violation of the fundamental law enacted in the 14th Amendment of the Constitution preventing state being the case, the ordinance cannot stand. . . .

Reversed.

2. Restrictive Covenants Unenforceable

SHELLEY v. KRAEMER
334 US 1 (1948)

[Segregation by zoning, as we have seen, was held invalid by the Court in 1917. Efforts were then concentrated on achieving racial segregation through the device known as the restrictive covenant, an undertaking in a deed or other formal instrument that the property described therein will not be sold or rented to Negroes. It was thought that such arrangements would be upheld as legal because they were private undertakings. In *Corrigan* v. *Buckley,* 271 US 323 (1926), the Court upheld such private covenants. But in *Shelley* v. *Kraemer,* the present case, the Court unanimously held that while such covenants are private, their *enforcement* by state courts is *state action* and is, therefore, unconstitutional as a denial of equal protection of the laws. (Justices Reed, Rutledge, and Jackson did not participate in the case.) The restrictive covenant in the District of Columbia was also barred by the Court in *Hurd* v. *Hodge,* 334 US 24 (1948). The last loophole was closed when the Court, with one Justice dissenting, held in *Barrows* v. *Jackson,* 346 US 249 (1953), that one party to a restrictive covenant may not recover damages from another party who broke the covenant. In brief, racial restrictive covenants are not enforceable either in equity or by an action for damages, in either state or federal courts. Parties may voluntarily observe the terms of their covenants, but no court may aid them.]

Mr. Chief Justice Vinson delivered the opinion of the Court:

. . . It is well, at the outset, to scrutinize the terms of the restrictive agreements involved in these cases. In the Missouri case, the covenant declares that no part of the affected property shall be "occupied by any person not of the Caucasion race, it being intended hereby to restrict the use of said property . . . against the occupancy as owners or tenants of any portion of said property for resident or other purposed by people of the Negro or Mongolian Race." Not only does the restriction seek to proscribe use and occupancy of the affected properties by members of the excluded class, but as construed by the Missouri courts, the agreement requires that title of any person who uses his property in violation of the restriction shall be divested. The restriction of the covenant in the Michigan case seeks to bar occupancy by persons of the excluded class. It provides that "This property shall not be used or occupied by any person or persons except those of the Caucasian race."

It should be observed that these covenants do not seek to proscribe any particular use of the affected properties. Use of the properties for residential occupancy, as such, is not forbidden. The restrictions of these agreements, rather, are directed toward a designated class of persons and seek to determine who may and who may not own or make use of the properties for residential purposes. The excluded class is defined wholly in terms of race or color; "simply that and nothing more."

In cannot be doubted that among the civil rights intended to be protected from discriminatory state action by the Fourteenth Amendment are the rights to acquire, enjoy, own and dispose of property. Equality in the enjoyment of property rights was regarded by the framers of that Amendment as an essential pre-condition to the realization of other basic civil rights and liberties which the Amendment was intended to guarantee. Thus, . . . 8 USCA § 42, . . . derived from § 1 of the Civil Rights Act of 1866 which was enacted by Congress while the Fourteenth Amendment was also under consideration, provides: "All citizens of the United States shall have the same right, in every State and Territory, as is enjoyed by white citizens thereof to inherit, purchase, lease, sell, hold, and convey real and personal property." This Court has given specific recognition to the same principle. . . .

We conclude, therefore, that the restrictive agreements standing alone cannot be regarded as violative of any rights guaranteed to petitioners by the Fourteenth Amendment. So long as the purposes of those agreements are effectuated by voluntary adherence to their terms, it would appear clear that there has been no action by the State and the provisions of the Amendment have not been violated. . . .

But here there was more. These are cases in which the purposes of the agreements were secured only by judicial enforcement by state courts of the restrictive terms of the agreements. The respondents urge that judicial enforcement of private agreement does not amount to state action; or, in any event, the participation of the States is so attenuated in character as not to amount to state action within the meaning of the Fourteenth Amendment. Finally, it is suggested, even if the States in these cases may be deemed to have acted in the constitutional sense, their action did not deprive petitioners of rights guaranteed by the Fourteenth Amendment. We move to a consideration of these matters. . . .

The short of the matter is that from the time of the adoption of the Fourteenth

Amendment until the present, it has been the consistent ruling of this Court that the action of the States to which the Amendment has reference, includes action of state courts and state judicial officials. Although, in construing the terms of the Fourteenth Amendment, differences have from time to time been expressed as to whether particular types of state action may be said to offend the Amendment's prohibitory provisions, it has never been suggested that state court action is immunized from the operation of those provisions simply because the act is that of the judicial branch of the state government.

Against this background of judicial construction, extending over a period of some three-quarters of a century, we are called upon to consider whether enforcement by state courts of the restrictive agreements in these cases may be deemed to be the acts of those States; and, if so, whether that action has denied these petitioners the equal protection of the laws which the Amendment was intended to insure.

We have no doubt that there has been state action in these cases in the full and complete sense of the phrase. The undisputed facts disclose that petitioners were willing purchasers of properties upon which they desired to establish homes. The owners of the properties were willing sellers; and contracts of sale were accordingly consummated. It is clear that but for the active intervention of the state courts, supported by the full panoply of state power, petitioners would have been free to occupy the properties in question without restraint.

These are not cases, as has been suggested, in which the States have merely abstained from action, leaving private individuals free to impose such discriminations as they see fit. Rather, these are cases in which the States have made available to such individuals the full coercive power of government to deny to petitioners, on the grounds of race or color, the enjoyment of property rights in premises which petitioners are willing and financially able to acquire and which the grantors are willing to sell. The difference between judicial enforcement and nonenforcement of the restrictive covenants is the difference to petitioners between being denied rights of property available to other members of the community and being accorded full enjoyment of those rights on an equal footing.

The enforcement of the restrictive agreements by the state courts in these cases was directed pursuant to the common-law policy of the States as formulated by those courts in earlier decisions. In the Missouri case, enforcement of the covenant was directed in the first instance by the highest court of the State after the trial court had determined the agreement to be invalid for want of the requisite number of signatures. In the Michigan case, the order of enforcement by the trial court was affirmed by the highest state court. The judicial action in each case bears the clear and unmistakable imprimatur of the State. We have noted that previous decisions of this Court have established the proposition that judicial action is not immunized from the operation of the Fourteenth Amendment simply because it is taken pursuant to the state's common-law policy. Nor is the Amendment ineffective simply because the particular pattern of discrimination, which the State has enforced, was defined initially by the terms of a private agreement. State action, as that phrase is understood for the purposes of the Fourteenth Amendment, refers to exertions of state power in all forms. And when the effect of that action is to deny rights subject to the protection of the Fourteenth Amendment, it is the obligation of this Court to enforce the constitutional commands.

We hold that in granting judicial enforcement of the restrictive agreements in these cases, the States have denied petitioners the equal protection of the laws and that, therefore, the action of the state courts cannot stand. We have noted that freedom from discrimination by the States in the enjoyment of property rights was among the basic objectives sought to be effectuated by the framers of the Fourteenth Amendment. That such discrimination has occurred in these cases is clear. Because of the race or color of these petitioners they have been denied rights of ownership or occupancy enjoyed as a matter of course by other citizens of different race or color. The Fourteenth Amendment declares "that all persons whether colored or white, shall stand equal before the laws of the States, and, in regard to the colored race, for whose protection the amendment was primarily designed, that no discrimination shall be made against them by law because of their color." . . . Only recently this Court has had occasion to declare that a state law which denied equal enjoyment of property rights to a designated class of citizens of specified race and ancestry, was not a legitimate exercise of the state's police power but violated the guaranty of the equal protection of the laws. *Oyama* v. *California,* 332 US 633 (1948). Nor may the discriminations imposed by the state courts in these cases be justified as proper exertions of state police power. . . .

The historical context in which the Fourteenth Amendment became a part of the Constitution should not be forgotten. Whatever else the framers sought to achieve, it is clear that the matter of primary concern was the establishment of equality in the enjoyment of basic civil and political rights and the preservation of those rights from discriminatory action on the part of the States based on considerations of race or color. Seventy-five years ago this Court announced that the provisions of the Amendment are to be construed with this fundamental purpose in mind. Upon full consideration, we have concluded that in these cases the States have acted to deny petitioners the equal protection of the laws guaranteed by the Fourteenth Amendment. Having so decided, we find it unnecessary to consider whether petitioners have also been deprived of property without due process of law or denied privileges and immunities of citizens of the United States.

For the reasons stated, the judgment of the Supreme Court of Missouri and the judgment of the Supreme Court of Michigan must be reversed.

3. Right to Purchase and Lease Property

JONES v. ALFRED H. MAYER CO.
392 US 409 (1968)

[In this case the Supreme Court upheld as constitutional under the Thirteenth Amendment the Civil Rights Act of 1866, which provides that the right to purchase and lease property was to be enjoyed equally throughout the United States by Negro and white citizens alike. The Court held that this right is secure against interference from any source, governmental or private. The Court also held that Secs. 803–813 of the Civil Rights Act of 1968 had no effect upon the statute of 1866. The opinion for the Court was by Justice Stewart. The opinion is important not only for its holding but also for the historical review of the Reconstruction legislation in the area of civil rights. Justice Douglas wrote a concurring opinion. Justice Harlan wrote a dissenting opinion in which Justice White joined.]

Mr. Justice Stewart delivered the opinion of the Court:

In this case we are called upon to determine the scope and constitutionality of an Act of Congress, 42 U.S.C. § 1982, which provides that:

All citizens of the United States shall have the same right, in every State and Territory, as is enjoyed by white citizens thereof to inherit, purchase, lease, sell, hold, and convey real and personal property.

On September 2, 1965, the petitioners filed a complaint in the District Court for the Eastern District of Missouri, alleging that the respondents had refused to sell them a home in the Paddock Woods community of St. Louis County for the sole reason that petitioner Joseph Lee Jones is a Negro. Relying in part upon § 1982, the petitioners sought injunctive and other relief. The District Court sustained the respondents' motion to dismiss the complaint, and the Court of Appeals for the Eighth Circuit affirmed, concluding that § 1982 applies only to state action and does not reach private refusals to sell. We granted certiorari to consider the questions thus presented. For the reasons that follow, we reverse the judgment of the Court of Appeals. We hold that § 1982 bars *all* racial discrimination, private as well as public, in the sale or rental of property, and that the statute, thus construed, is a valid exercise of the power of Congress to enforce the Thirteenth Amendment.*

I

At the outset, it is important to make clear precisely what this case does *not* involve. Whatever else it may be, 42 U.S.C. § 1982 is not a comprehensive open housing law. In sharp contrast to the Fair Housing Title (Title VIII) of the Civil Rights Act of 1968, Pub.L. 90–284, 82 Stat. 73, the statute in this case deals only with racial discrimination and does not address itself to discrimination on grounds of religion or national origin. It does not deal specifically with discrimination in the provision of services or facilities in connection with the sale or rental of a dwelling. It does not prohibit advertising or other representations that indicate discriminatory preferences. It does not refer explicitly to discrimination in financing arrangements or in the provision of brokerage services. It does not empower a federal administrative agency to assist aggrieved parties. It makes no provision for intervention by the Attorney General. And, although it can be enforced by injunction, it contains no provision expressly authorizing a federal court to order the payment of damages.

Thus, although § 1982 contains none of the exemptions that Congress included in the Civil Rights Act of 1968, it would be a serious mistake to suppose that § 1982 in any way diminishes the significance of the law recently enacted by Con-

---

* Because we have concluded that the discrimination alleged in the petitioners' complaint violated a federal statute that Congress had the power to enact under the Thirteenth Amendment, we find it unnecessary to decide whether that discrimination also violated the Equal Protection Clause of the Fourteenth Amendment.

gress. Indeed, the Senate Subcommittee on Housing and Urban Affairs was informed in hearings held after the Court of Appeals had rendered its decision in this case that § 1982 might well be "a presently valid federal statutory ban against discrimination by private persons in the sale or lease of real property." The Subcommittee was told, however, that even if this Court should so construe § 1982, the existence of that statute would not "eliminate the need for congressional action" to spell out "responsibility on the part of the federal government to enforce the rights it protects." The point was made that, in light of the many difficulties confronted by private litigants seeking to enforce such rights on their own, "legislation is needed to establish federal machinery for enforcement of the rights guaranteed under Section 1982 of Title 42 even if the plaintiffs in *Jones* v. *Alfred H. Mayer Company* should prevail in the United States Supreme Court."

On April 10, 1968, Representative Kelly of New York focused the attention of the House upon the present case and its possible significance. She described the background of this litigation, recited the text of § 1982, and then added:

> When the Attorney General was asked in court about the effect of the old law [§ 1982] as compared with the pending legislation which is being considered on the House floor today, he said that the scope was somewhat different, the remedies and procedures were different, and that the new law was still quite necessary.

Later the same day, the House passed the Civil Rights Act of 1968. Its enactment had no effect upon § 1982 and no effect upon this litigation, but it underscored the vast differences between, on the one hand, a general statute applicable only to racial discrimination in the rental and sale of property and enforceable only by private parties acting on their own initiative, and, on the other hand, a detailed housing law, applicable to a broad range of discriminatory practices and enforceable by a complete arsenal of federal authority. Having noted these differences, we turn to a consideration of § 1982 itself.

II

This Court last had occasion to consider the scope of 42 U.S.C. § 1982 in 1948, in *Hurd* v. *Hodge,* 334 US 24. That case arose when property owners in the District of Columbia sought to enforce racially restrictive covenants against the Negro purchasers of several homes on their block. A federal district court enforced the restrictive agreements by declaring void the deeds of the Negro purchasers. It enjoined further attempts to sell or lease them the properties in question and directed them to "remove themselves and all of their personal belongings" from the premises within 60 days. The Court of Appeals for the District of Columbia affirmed, and this Court granted certiorari to decide whether § 1982, then § 1978 of the Revised Statutes of 1874, barred enforcement of the racially restrictive agreements in that case.

The agreements in *Hurd* covered only two-thirds of the lots of a single city block, and preventing Negroes from buying or renting homes in that specific area would not have rendered them ineligible to do so elsewhere in the city. Thus, if § 1982 had been thought to do no more than grant Negro citizens the legal capacity to buy and rent property free of prohibitions that wholly disabled them because of their race, judicial enforcement of the restrictive covenants at issue would not have violated § 1982. But this Court took a broader view of the statute. Although the covenants could have been enforced without denying the general right of Negroes to purchase or lease real estate, the enforcement of those covenants would nonetheless have denied the Negro purchasers "the same right 'as is enjoyed by white citizens . . . to inherit, purchase, lease, sell, hold, and convey real and personal property.' " That result, this Court concluded, was prohibited by § 1982. To suggest otherwise, the Court said, "is to reject the plain meaning of language."

Hurd v. *Hodge, supra,* squarely held, therefore, that a Negro citizen who is denied the opportunity to purchase the home he wants "[s]olely because of [his] race and color," has suffered the kind of injury that § 1982 was designed to prevent. . . . The basic source of the injury in *Hurd* was, of course, the action of private individuals—white citizens who had agreed to exclude Negroes from a residential area. But an arm of the Government—in that case, a federal court— had assisted in the enforcement of that agreement. Thus *Hurd* v. *Hodge, supra,* did not present the question whether *purely* private discrimination, unaided by any action on the part of government, would violate § 1982 if its effect were to deny a citizen the right to rent or buy property solely because of his race or color.

The only federal court (other than the Court of Appeals in this case) that has ever squarely confronted that question held that a wholly private conspiracy among white citizens to prevent a Negro from leasing a farm violated § 1982. *United States* v. *Morris, D.C.,* 125 F. 322. It is true that a dictum in *Hurd* said that § 1982 was directed only toward "governmental action," but neither *Hurd* nor any other case before or since has presented that precise issue for adjudication in this Court. Today we face that issue for the first time.

III

We begin with the language of the statute itself. In plain and unambiguous terms, § 1982 grants to all citizens, without regard to race or color, "the same right" to purchase and lease property "as is enjoyed by white citizens." As the Court of Appeals in this case evidently recognized, that right can be impaired as effectively by "those who place property on the market" as by the State itself. For, even if the State and its agents lend no support to those who wish to exclude persons from their communities on racial grounds, the fact remains that, whenever property "is placed on the market for whites only, whites have a right denied to Negroes." So long as a Negro citizen who wants to buy or rent a home can be turned away simply because he is not white, he cannot be said to enjoy "the *same* right . . . as is enjoyed by white citizens . . . to . . . purchase [and] lease . . . real and personal property." 42 U.S.C. § 1982. (Emphasis added.)

On its face, therefore, § 1982 appears to prohibit *all* discrimination against Negroes in the sale or rental of property—discrimination by private owners as well as discrimination by public authorities. Indeed, even the respondents seem to concede that, if § 1982 "means what it says"—to use the words of the respondents' brief—then it must encompass every racially motivated refusal to sell or rent and cannot be confined to officially sanctioned segregation in housing. Stressing what they consider to be the revolutionary implications of so literal a reading of § 1982, the respondents argue that Congress cannot possibly have intended any such result. Our examination of the relevant history, however, persuades us that Congress meant exactly what it said.

IV

In its original form, 42 U.S.C. § 1982 was part of § 1 of the Civil Rights Act of 1866. That section was cast in sweeping terms:

Be it enacted by the Senate and House of Representatives of the United States of America in Congress assembled, That all persons born in the United States and not subject to any foreign power, . . . are hereby declared to be citizens of the United States; and such citizens, of every race and color, without regard to any previous condition of slavery or involuntary servitude . . . shall have the same right, in every State and Territory in the United States, to make and enforce contracts, to sue, be parties, and give evidence, to inherit, purchase, lease, sell, hold, and convey real and personal property, and to full and equal benefit of all laws and proceedings for the security of person and property, as is enjoyed by white citizens, and shall be subject to like punishment, pains, and penalties, and to none other, any law, statute, ordinance, regulation, or custom, to the contrary notwithstanding.

The crucial language for our purposes was that which guaranteed all citizens "the same right, in every State and Territory in the United States . . . to inherit, purchase, lease, sell, hold, and convey real and personal property . . . as is enjoyed by white citizens. . . ." To the Congress that passed the Civil Rights Act of 1866, it was clear that the right to do these things might be infringed not only by "State or local law" but also by "custom, or prejudice." Thus, when Congress provided in § 1 of the Civil Rights Act that the right to purchase and lease property was to be enjoyed equally throughout the United States by Negro and white citizens alike, it plainly meant to secure that right against interference from any source whatever, whether governmental or private.

Indeed, if § 1 had been intended to grant nothing more than an immunity from *governmental* interference, then much of § 2 would have made no sense at all. For that section, which provided fines and prison terms for certain individuals who deprived others of rights "secured or protected" by § 1, was carefully drafted to exempt private violations of § 1 from the criminal sanctions it imposed. There would, of course, have been no private violations to exempt if the only "right" granted by § 1 had been a right to be free of discrimination by public officials. Hence the structure of the 1866 Act, as well as its language, points to the conclusion urged by the petitioners in this case—that § 1 was meant to prohibit *all* racially motivated deprivations of the rights enumerated in the statute, although only those deprivations perpetrated "under color of law" were to be criminally punishable under § 2.

In attempting to demonstrate the contrary, the respondents rely heavily upon the fact that the Congress which approved the 1866 statute wished to eradicate the recently enacted Black Codes—laws which had saddled Negroes with "onerous disabilities and burdens, and curtailed their rights . . . to such an extent that their freedom was of little value. . . ." *Slaughter-House Cases,* 16 Wall. 36. The respondents suggest that the only evil Congress sought to eliminate was that of racially discriminatory laws in the former Confederate States. But the Civil Rights Act was drafted to apply throughout the country, and its language was far broader than would have been necessary to strike down discriminatory statutes.

That broad language, we are asked to believe, was a mere slip of the legislative pen. We disagree. For the same Congress that wanted to do away with the Black Codes *also* had before it an imposing body of evidence pointing to the mistreatment of Negroes by private individuals and unofficial groups, mistreatment unrelated to any hostile state legislation. "Accounts in newspapers North and South, Freedmen's Bureau and other official documents, private reports and correspondence were all adduced" to show that "private outrage and atrocity" was "daily inflicted on freedmen. . . ." The congressional debates are replete with references to private injustices against Negroes—references to white employers who refused to pay their Negro workers, white planters who agreed among themselves not to hire freed slaves without the permission of their former masters, white citizens who assaulted Negroes or who combined to drive them out of their communities.

Indeed, one of the most comprehensive studies then before Congress stressed the prevalence of private hostility toward Negroes and the need to protect them from the resulting persecution and discrimination. The report noted the existence of laws virtually prohibiting Negroes from owning or renting property in certain towns, but described such laws as "mere isolated cases," representing "the local outcroppings of a spirit . . . found to prevail everywhere"—a spirit expressed, for example, by lawless acts of brutality directed against Negroes who traveled to areas where they were not wanted. The report concluded that, even if anti-Negro legislation were "repealed in all the States lately in rebellion," equal treatment for the Negro would not yet be secured.

In this setting, it would have been strange indeed if Congress had viewed its task as encompassing merely the nullification of racist laws in the former rebel States. That the Congress which assembled in the Nation's capital in December 1865 in fact had a broader vision of the task before it became clear early in the session, when three proposals to invalidate discriminatory state statutes were rejected as "too narrowly conceived." From the outset it seemed clear, at least to Senator Trumbull of Illinois, Chairman of the Judiciary Committee, that stronger legislation might prove necessary. After Senator Wilson of Massachusetts had introduced his bill to strike down all racially discriminatory laws in the South, . . . on January 5, 1866, Senator Trumbull introduced the bill he had in mind—the bill which later became the Civil Rights Act of 1866. He described its objectives in terms that belie any attempt to read it narrowly:

Mr. President, I regard the bill to which the attention of the Senate is now called as the most important measure that has been under its consideration since the adoption of the constitutional amendment abolishing slavery. That amendment declared that all persons in the United States should be free. This measure is intended to give effect to that declaration and secure to all persons within the United States practical freedom. There is very little importance in the general declaration of abstract truths and principles unless they can be carried into effect, unless the persons who are to be affected by them have some means of availing themselves of their benefits.

Of course, Senator Trumbull's bill would, as he pointed out, "destroy all [the] discriminations" embodied in the Black Codes, but it would do more: It would affirmatively secure for all men, whatever their race or color, what the Senator called the "great fundamental rights":

. . . the right to acquire property, the right to go and come at pleasure, the right to enforce rights in the courts, to make contracts, and to inherit and dispose of property.

As to those basic civil rights, the Senator said, the bill would "break down *all* discrimination between black men and white men."

That the bill would indeed have so sweeping an effect was seen as its great virtue by its friends and as its great danger by its enemies but was disputed by none. Opponents of the bill charged that it would not only regulate state laws but would directly "determine the persons who [would] enjoy . . . property within the States," threatening the ability of white citizens "to determine who [would] be members of [their] communit[ies]. . . ." The bill's advocates did not deny the accuracy of those characterizations. Instead, they defended the propriety of employing federal authority to deal with "the white man . . . [who] would invoke the power of local prejudice" against the Negro. Thus, when the Senate passed the Civil Rights Act on February 2, 1866, it did so fully aware of the breadth of the measure it had approved.

In the House, as in the Senate, much was said about eliminating the infamous Black Codes. But, like the Senate, the House was moved by a larger objective—that of giving real content to the freedom guaranteed by the Thirteenth Amendment. . . . it did so on the same assumption that had prevailed in the Senate: It too believed that it was approving a comprehensive statute forbidding *all* racial discrimination affecting the basic civil rights enumerated in the Act.

President Andrew Johnson vetoed the Act on March 27, and in the brief congressional debate that followed, his supporters characterized its reach in all-embracing terms. One stressed the fact that § 1 would confer "the right . . . to purchase . . . real estate . . . without any qualification and without any restriction whatever. . . ." Another predicted, as a corollary, that the Act would preclude preferential treatment for white persons in the rental of hotel rooms and in the sale of church pews. Those observations elicited no reply. On April 6 the Senate, and on April 9 the House, overrode the President's veto by the requisite majorities, and the Civil Rights Act of 1866 became law.

In light of the concerns that led Congress to adopt it and the contents of the debates that preceded its passage, it is clear that the Act was designed to do just what its terms suggest: to prohibit all racial discrimination, whether or not under color of law, with respect to the rights enumerated therein—including the right to purchase or lease property.

Nor was the scope of the 1866 Act altered when it was re-enacted in 1870, some two years after the ratification of the Fourteenth Amendment. It is quite true that some members of Congress supported the Fourteenth Amendment "in order to eliminate doubt as to the constitutional validity of the Civil Rights Act as applied to the States." . . . But it certainly does not follow that the adoption of the Fourteenth Amendment or the subsequent readoption of the Civil Rights Act were meant somehow to *limit* its application to state action. The legislative history furnishes not the slightest factual basis for any such speculation, and the conditions prevailing in 1870 make it highly implausible. For by that time most, if not all, of the former Confederate States, then under the control of "reconstructed" legislatures, had formally repudiated racial discrimination, and the focus of congressional concern had clearly shifted from hostile statutes to the activities of groups like the Ku Klux Klan, operating wholly outside the law.

Against this background, it would obviously make no sense to assume, without any historical support whatever, that Congress made a silent decision in 1870 to exempt private discrimination from the operation of the Civil Rights Act of 1866. "The cardinal rule is that repeals by implication are not favored." . . . All Congress said in 1870 was that the 1866 law "is hereby re-enacted." That is all Congress meant.

As we said in a somewhat different setting two Terms ago, "We think that history leaves no doubt that, if we are to give [the law] the scope that its origins dictate, we must accord it a sweep as broad as its language." . . . "We are not at liberty to seek ingenious analytical instruments," to carve from § 1982 an exception for private conduct—even though its application to such conduct in the present context is without established precedent. And, as the Attorney General of the United States said at the oral argument of this case, "The fact that the statute lay partially dormant for many years cannot be held to diminish its force today."

V

The remaining question is whether Congress has power under the Constitution to do what § 1982 purports to do: to prohibit all racial discrimination, private and public, in the sale and rental of property. Our starting point is the Thirteenth Amendment, for it was pursuant to that constitutional provision that Congress originally enacted what is now § 1982. The Amendment consists of two parts. Section 1 states:

Neither slavery nor involuntary servitude, except as a punishment for a crime whereby the party shall have been duly convicted, shall exist within the United States, or any place subject to their jurisdiction.

Section 2 provides:

Congress shall have power to enforce this article by appropriate legislation.

As its text reveals, the Thirteenth Amendment "is not a mere prohibition of state laws establishing or upholding slavery, but an absolute declaration that slavery or involuntary servitude shall not exist in any part of the United States." . . . It has never been doubted, therefore, "that the power vested in Congress to enforce the article by appropriate legislation," includes the power to enact laws "direct and primary, operating upon the acts of individuals, whether sanctioned by state legislation or not."

Thus, the fact that § 1982 operates upon the unofficial acts of private individuals, whether or not sanctioned by state law, presents no constitutional problem. If Congress has power under the Thirteenth Amendment to eradicate conditions that prevent Negroes from buying and renting property because of their race or color, then no federal statute calculated to achieve that objective can be thought to exceed the constitutional power of Congress simply because it reaches beyond state action to regulate the conduct of private individuals. The constitutional question in this case, therefore, comes to this: Does the authority of Congress to enforce the Thirteenth Amendment "by appropriate legislation" include the power to eliminate all racial barriers to the acquisition of real and personal property? We think the answer to that question is plainly yes.

"By its own unaided force and effect," the Thirteenth Amendment "abolished slavery, and established universal freedom." . . . Whether or not the Amendment *itself* did any more than that—a question not involved in this case—it is at least clear that the Enabling Clause of that Amendment empowered Congress to do much more. For that clause clothed "Congress with power to pass *all laws necessary and proper for abolishing all badges and incidents of slavery in the United States."* (Emphasis added.)

Those who opposed passage of the Civil Rights Act of 1866 argued in effect that the Thirteenth Amendment merely authorized Congress to dissolve the legal bond by which the Negro slave was held to his master. Yet many had earlier opposed the Thirteenth Amendment on the very ground that it would give Congress virtually unlimited power to enact laws for the protection of Negroes in every State. And the majority leaders in Congress—who were, after all, the authors of the Thirteenth Amendment—had no doubt that its Enabling Clause contemplated the sort of positive legislation that was embodied in the 1866 Civil Rights Act. Their chief spokesman, Senator Trumbull of Illinois, the Chairman of the Judiciary Committee, had brought the Thirteenth Amendment to the floor of the Senate in 1864. In defending the constitutionality of the 1866 Act, he argued that, if the narrower construction of the Enabling Clause were correct, then

the trumpet of freedom that we have been blowing throughout the land has given an "uncertain sound," and the promised freedom is a delusion. Such was not the intention of Congress, which proposed the constitutional amendment, nor is such the fair meaning of the amendment itself. . . . I have no doubt that under this provision . . . we may destroy all these discriminations in civil rights against the black man; and if we cannot, our constitutional amendment amounts to nothing. It was for that purpose that the second clause of that amendment was adopted, which says that Congress shall have authority, by appropriate legislation, to carry into effect the article prohibiting slavery. Who is to decide what that appropriate legislation is to be? The Congress of the United States; and it is for Congress to adopt such appropriate legislation as it may think proper, so that it be a means to accomplish the end.

Surely Senator Trumbull was right. Surely Congress has the power under the Thirteenth Amendment rationally to determine what are the badges and the incidents of slavery, and the authority to translate that determination into effective legislation. Nor can we say that the determination Congress has made is an irrational one. For this Court recognized long ago that, whatever else they may have encompassed, the badges and incidents of slavery—its "burdens and disabilities" —included restraints upon "those fundamental rights which are the essence of civil freedom, namely, the same right . . . to inherit, purchase, lease, sell, and convey property, as is enjoyed by white citizens." . . . Just as the Black Codes, enacted after the Civil War to restrict the free exercise of those rights, were substitutes for the slave system, so the exclusion of Negroes from white communities became a substitute for the Black Codes. And when racial discrimination herds men into ghettos and makes their ability to buy property turn on the color of their skin, then it too is a relic of slavery.

Negro citizens North and South, who saw in the Thirteenth Amendment a promise of freedom—freedom to "go and come at pleasure" and to "buy and sell when they please"—would be left with "a mere paper guarantee" if Congress were powerless to assure that a dollar in the hands of a Negro will purchase the same thing as a dollar in the hands of a white man. At the very least, the freedom that Congress is empowered to secure under the Thirteenth Amendment includes the freedom to buy whatever a white man can buy, the right to live wherever a white man can live. If Congress cannot say that being a free man means at least this much, then the Thirteenth Amendment made a promise the Nation cannot keep.

Representative Wilson of Iowa was the floor manager in the House for the Civil Rights Act of 1866. In urging that Congress had ample authority to pass the pending bill, he recalled the celebrated words of Chief Justice Marshall in *McCulloch* v. *State of Maryland,* 4 Wheat. 316:

Let the end be legitimate, let it be within the scope of the constitution, and all means which are appropriate, which are plainly adapted to that end, which are not prohibited, but consist with the letter and spirit of the constitution, are constitutional.

"The end is legitimate," the Congressman said, "because it is defined by the Constitution itself. The end is the maintenance of freedom. . . . A man who enjoys the civil rights mentioned in this bill cannot be reduced to slavery. . . . This settles the appropriateness of this measure, and that settles its constitutionality."

We agree. The judgment is reversed.

4. Interracial Marriages

LOVING *v.* VIRGINIA
388 US 1 (1967)

[Statutes in sixteen states outlawed interracial marriages (popularly known as the crime of miscegenation). The Supreme Court, in an opinion by Chief Justice Warren, unanimously held the Virginia statute to be a violation of the Equal Protection Clause and the Due Process Clause of the Fourteenth Amendment. Justice Stewart concurred in a brief opinion.]

Mr. Chief Justice Warren delivered the opinion of the Court:

This case presents a constitutional question never addressed by this Court: whether a statutory scheme adopted by the State of Virginia to prevent marriages between persons solely on the basis of racial classifications violates the Equal Protection and Due Process Clauses of the Fourteenth Amendment. For reasons which seem to us to reflect the central meaning of those constitutional commands, we conclude that these statutes cannot stand consistently with the Fourteenth Amendment.

In June 1958, two residents of Virginia, Mildred Jeter, a Negro woman, and Richard Loving, a white man, were married in the District of Columbia pursuant to its laws. Shortly after their marriage, the Lovings returned to Virginia and established their marital abode in Caroline County. At the October Term, 1958, of the Circuit Court of Caroline County, a grand jury issued an indictment charging the Lovings with violating Virginia's ban on interracial marriages. On January 6, 1959, the Lovings pleaded guilty to the charge and were sentenced to one year in jail; however, the trial judge suspended the sentence for a period of 25 years on the condition that the Lovings leave the State and not return to Virginia together for 25 years, stating that:

Almighty God created the races white, black, yellow, malay, and red, and he placed them on separate continents. And but for the interference with his arrangement there would be no cause for such marriages. The fact that he separated the races shows that he did not intend for the races to mix.

After their convictions, the Lovings took up residence in the District of Columbia. On November 6, 1963, they filed a motion in the state trial court to vacate the judgment and set aside the sentence on the ground that the statutes which they had violated were repugnant to the Fourteenth Amendment. The motion not having been decided by October 28, 1964, the Lovings instituted a class action in the United States District Court for the Eastern District of Virginia requesting that a three-judge court be convened to declare the Virginia antimiscegenation statutes unconstitutional and to enjoin state officials from enforcing their convictions. On January 22, 1965, the state trial judge denied the motion to vacate the sentences, and the Lovings perfected an appeal to the Supreme Court of Appeals of Virginia. On February 11, 1965, the three-judge District Court continued the case to allow the Lovings to present their constitutional claims to the highest state court.

The Supreme Court of Appeals upheld the constitutionality of the antimiscegenation statutes and, after modifying the sentence, affirmed the convictions. The Lovings appealed this decision, and we noted probable jurisdiction on December 12, 1966.

The two statutes under which appellants were convicted and sentenced are part of a comprehensive statutory scheme aimed at prohibiting and punishing interracial marriages. The Lovings were convicted of violating § 20–58 of the Virginia Code:

Leaving State to evade law.—If any white person and colored person shall go out of this State, for the purpose of being married, and with the intention of returning, and be married out of it, and afterwards return to and reside in it, cohabiting as man and wife, they shall be punished as provided in § 20–59, and the marriage shall be governed by the same law as if it had been solemnized in this State. The fact of their cohabitation here as man and wife shall be evidence of their marriage.

Section 20–59, which defines the penalty for miscegenation, provides:

Punishment for marriage.—If any white person intermarry with a colored person, or any colored person intermarry with a white person, he shall be guilty of a felony and shall be punished by confinement in the penitentiary for not less than one nor more than five years.

Other central provisions in the Virginia statutory scheme are § 20–57, which automatically voids all marriages between "a white person and a colored person" without any judicial proceeding,* and §§ 20–54 and 1–14 which, respectively, define "white persons" and "colored persons and Indians" for purposes of the statutory prohibitions.† The Lovings have never disputed in the course of this litigation that Mrs. Loving is a "colored person" or that Mr. Loving is a "white person" within the meanings given those terms by the Virginia statutes.

Virginia is now one of 16 States which prohibit and punish marriages on the basis of racial classifications.‡ Penalties for miscegenation arose as an incident to slavery and have been common in Virginia since the colonial period. The present statutory scheme dates from the adoption of the Racial Integrity Act of 1924, passed during the period of extreme nativism which followed the end of the First World War. The central features of this Act, and current Virginia law, are the absolute prohibition of a "white person" marrying other than another "white person," a prohibition against issuing marriage licenses until the issuing official is satisfied that the applicants' statements as to their race are correct, certificates of "racial composition" to be kept by both local and state registrars, and the carrying forward of earlier prohibitions against racial intermarriage.

* Section 20–57 of the Virginia Code provides:
"Marriages void without decree.—All marriages between a white person and a colored person shall be absolutely void without any decree of divorce or other legal process." Va.Code Ann. § 20–57 (1966).

† Section 20–54 of the Virginia Code provides:
"Intermarriage prohibited; meaning of term 'white persons.'—It shall hereafter be unlawful for any white person in this State to marry any save a white person, or a person with no other admixture of blood than white and American Indian. For the purpose of this chapter, the term 'white person' shall apply only to such person as has no trace whatever of any blood other than Caucasian; but persons who have one-sixteenth or less of the blood of the American Indian and have no other non-Caucasic blood shall be deemed to be white persons. All laws heretofore passed and now in effect regarding the intermarriage of white and colored persons shall apply to marriages prohibited by this chapter," Av.Code Ann. § 20–54 (1966).

The exception for persons with less than one-sixteenth "of the blood of the American Indian" is apparently accounted for, in the words of a tract issued by the Registrar of the State Bureau of Vital Statistics, "by the desire of all to recognize as an integral and honored part of the white race the descendants of John Rolfe and Pocahontas. . . ."

Section 1–14 of the Virginia Code provides:
Colored persons and Indians defined.—Every person in whom there is ascertainable any Negro blood shall be deemed and taken to be a colored person, and every person not a colored person having one fourth or more of American Indian blood shall be deemed an American Indian; except that members of Indian tribes existing in this Commonwealth having one fourth or more of Indian blood and less than one sixteenth of Negro blood shall be deemed tribal Indians." Va.Code Ann. § 1–14 (1966).

‡ After the initiation of this litigation, Maryland repealed its prohibitions against interracial marriage, Md.Laws 1967, c. 6, leaving 16 States with statutes outlawing interracial marriage: . . .

Over the past 15 years, 14 States have repealed laws outlawing interracial marriages: Arizona, California, Colorado, Idaho, Indiana, Maryland, Montana, Nebraska, Nevada, North Dakota, Oregon, South Dakota, Utah, and Wyoming.

The first state court to recognize that miscegenation statutes violate the Equal Protection Clause was the Supreme Court of California. *Perez* v. *Lippold,* 32 Cal.2d 711, 198 P.2d 17 (1948).

I

In upholding the constitutionality of these provisions in the decision below, the Supreme Court of Appeals of Virginia referred to its 1955 decision in *Naim* v. *Naim,* 197 Va. 80, 87 S.E.2d 749, as stating the reasons supporting the validity of these laws. In *Naim,* the state court concluded that the State's legitimate purposes were "to preserve the racial integrity of its citizens," and to prevent "the corruption of blood," "a mongrel breed of citizens," and "the obliteration of racial pride," obviously an endorsement of the doctrine of White Supremacy. The court also reasoned that marriage has traditionally been subject to state regulation without federal intervention, and, consequently, the regulation of marriage should be left to exclusive state control by the Tenth Amendment.

While the state court is no doubt correct in asserting that marriage is a social relation subject to the State's police power, . . . the state does not contend in its argument before this Court that its powers to regulate marriage are unlimited notwithstanding the commands of the Fourteenth Amendment. Nor could it do so in light of *Meyer* v. *State of Nebraska,* 262 US 390, and *Skinner* v. *State of Oklahoma,* 316 US 535. Instead, the State argues that the meaning of the Equal Protection Clause, as illuminated by the statements of the Framers, is only that state penal laws containing an interracial element as part of the definition of the offense must apply equally to whites and Negroes in the sense that members of each race are punished to the same degree. Thus, the State contends that, because its miscegenation statutes punish equally both the white and the Negro participants in an interracial marriage, these statutes, despite their reliance on racial classifications do not constitute an invidious discrimination based upon race. The second argument advanced by the State assumes the validity of its equal application theory. The argument is that, if the Equal Protection clause does not outlaw miscegenation statutes because of their reliance on racial classifications, the question of constitutionality would thus become whether there was any rational basis for a State to treat interracial marriages differently from other marriages. On this question, the State argues, the scientific evidence is substantially in doubt and, consequently, this Court should defer to the wisdom of the state legislature in adopting its policy of discouraging interracial marriages.

Because we reject the notion that the mere "equal application" of a statute containing racial classifications is enough to remove the classifications from the Fourteenth Amendment's proscription of all invidious racial discriminations, we do not accept the State's contention that these statutes should be upheld if there is any possible basis for concluding that they serve a rational purpose. The mere fact of equal application does not mean that our analysis of this statute should follow the approach we have taken in cases involving no racial discrimination where the Equal Protection Clause has been arrayed against a statute discriminating between the kinds of advertising which may be displayed on trucks in New York City, *Railway Express Agency, Inc.* v. *People of State of New York,* 336 US 106, or an exemption in Ohio's ad valorem tax for merchandise owned by a non-resident in a storage warehouse, *Allied Stores of Ohio, Inc.* v. *Bowers,* 358 US 522. In these cases, involving distinctions not drawn according to race, the Court has merely asked whether there is any rational foundation for the discriminations, and has deferred to the wisdom of the state legislatures. In the case at bar, however, we deal with statutes containing racial classifications, and the fact of equal application does not immunize the statutes from the very heavy burden of justification which the Fourteenth Amendment has traditionally required of state statutes drawn according to race.

The State argues that statements in the Thirty-ninth Congress about the time of the passage of the Fourteenth Amendment indicate that the Framers did not intend the Amendment to make unconstitutional state miscegenation laws. Many of the statements alluded to by the State concern the debates over the Freemen's Bureau Bill, which President Johnson vetoed, and the Civil Rights Act of 1866, enacted over his veto. While these statements have some relevance to the intention of Congress in submitting the Fourteenth Amendment, it must be understood that they pertained to the passage of specific statutes and not to the broader, organic purpose of a constitutional amendment. As for the various statements directly concerning the Fourteenth Amendment, we have said in connection with a related problem, that although these historical sources "cast some light" they are not sufficient to resolve the problem; "[a]t best, they are inconclusive. The most avid proponents of the post-War Amendments undoubtedly intended them to remove all legal distinctions among 'all persons born or naturalized in the United States.' Their opponents, just as certainly, were antagonistic to both the letter and the spirit of the Amendments and wished them to have the most limited effect." *Brown et al.* v. *Board of Education of Topeka et al.,* 347 US 483. . . . We have rejected the proposition that the debates in the Thirty-ninth Congress or in the state legislatures which ratified the Fourteenth Amendment supported the theory advanced by the State, that the requirement of equal protection of the laws is satisfied by penal laws defining offenses based on racial classifications so long as white and Negro participants in the offense were similarly punished. *McLaughlin et al.* v. *State of Florida,* 379 US 184.

The State finds support for its "equal application" theory in the decision of the Court in *Pace* v. *State of Alabama,* 106 US 583. In that case, the Court upheld a conviction under an Alabama statute forbidding adultery or fornication between a white person and a Negro which imposed a greater penalty than that of a statute proscribing similar conduct by members of the same race. The Court reasoned that the statute could not be said to discriminate against Negroes because the punishment for each participant in the offense was the same. However, as recently as the 1964 Term, in rejecting the reasoning of that case, we stated *"Pace* represents a limited view of the Equal Protection Clause which has not withstood analysis in the subsequent decisions of this Court." *McLaughlin et al.* v. *Florida, supra.* As we there demonstrated, the Equal Protection Clause requires the consideration of whether the classifications drawn by any statute constitute an arbitrary and invidious discrimination. The clear and central purpose of the Fourteenth Amendment was to eliminate all official state sources of invidious racial discrimination in the States. . . .

There can be no question but that Virginia's miscegenation statutes rest solely upon distinctions drawn according to race. The statutes proscribe generally accepted conduct if engaged in by members of different races. Over the years, this Court has consistently repudiated "[d]istinctions between citizens solely because of their ancestry" as being "odious to a free people whose institutions are founded upon the doctrine of equality." *Hirabayashi* v. *United States,* 320 US 81. At the very least, the Equal Protection Clause demands that racial classifications, especially suspect in criminal statutes, be subjected to the "most rigid scrutiny," *Korematsu* v. *United States,* 323 US 214, and, if they are ever to be upheld, they must be shown to be necessary to the accomplishment of some permissible state objective, independent of the racial discrimination which it was the object of the Fourteenth Amendment to eliminate. Indeed, two members of this Court have already stated that they "cannot conceive of a valid legislative purpose . . . which makes the color of a person's skin the test of whether his conduct is a criminal offense." *McLaughlin* v. *Florida, supra* (Stewart, J., joined by Douglas, J., concurring).

There is patently no legitimate overriding purpose independent of invidious racial discrimination which justifies this classification. The fact that Virginia only prohibits interracial marriages involving white persons demonstrates that the racial classifications must stand on their own justification, as measures designed to maintain White Supremacy.* We have consistently denied the constitutionality of measures which restrict the rights of citizens on account of race. There can be no doubt that restricting the freedom to marry solely because of racial classifications violates the central meaning of the Equal Protection Clause.

II

These statutes also deprive the Lovings of liberty without due process of law in violation of the Due Process Clause of the Fourteenth Amendment. The freedom to marry has long been recognized as one of the vital personal rights essential to the orderly pursuit of happiness by free men.

Marriage is one of the "basic civil rights of man," fundamental to our very existence and survival. . . . To deny this fundamental freedom on so unsupportable a basis as the racial classifications embodied in these statutes, classifications so directly subversive of the principle of equality at the heart of the Fourteenth Amendment, is surely to deprive all the State's citizens of liberty without due process of law. The Fourteenth Amendment requires that the freedom of choice to marry not be restricted by invidious racial discriminations. Under our Constitution, the freedom to marry or not marry, a person of another race resides with the individual and cannot be infringed by the State.

These convictions must be reversed. It is so ordered.

Reversed.

---

* Appellants point out that the State's concern in these statutes, as expressed in the words of the 1924 Act's title, "An Act to Preserve Racial Integrity," extends only to the integrity of the white race. While Virginia prohibits whites from marrying any nonwhite (subject to the exception for the descendants of Pocahontas), Negroes, Orientals, and any other racial class may intermarry without statutory interference. Appellants contend that this distinction renders Virginia's miscegenation statutes arbitrary and unreasonable even assuming the constitutional validity of an official purpose to preserve "racial integrity." We need not reach this contention because we find the racial classifications in these statutes repugnant to the Fourteenth Amendment, even assuming an even-handed state purpose to protect the "integrity" of all races.

5. *Equality of Job Opportunities*

GRIGGS *v.* DUKE POWER CO.
401 US 424 (1971)

[An obstacle to the employment of Negroes has been the imposition of tests or other requirements that may be fair in form but that work discriminatorily. The Supreme Court in this case unanimously held that such practices are outlawed by the Civil Rights Act of 1964, Title VII. The Court's opinion was by Chief Justice Burger. Justice Brennan took no part in the case.]

Mr. Chief Justice Burger delivered the opinion of the Court:

We granted the writ in this case to resolve the question whether an employer is prohibited by the Civil Rights Act of 1964, Title VII, from requiring a high school education or passing of a standardized general intelligence test as a condition of employment in or transfer to jobs when (a) neither standard is shown to be significantly related to successful job performance, (b) both requirements operate to disqualify Negroes at a substantially higher rate than white applicants, and (c) the jobs in question formerly had been filled only by white employees as part of a longstanding practice of giving preference to whites.*

Congress provided, in Title VII of the Civil Rights Act of 1964, for class actions for enforcement of provisions of the Act and this proceeding was brought by a group of incumbent Negro employees against Duke Power Company. All the petitioners are employed at the Company's Dan River Steam Station, a power generating facility located at Draper, North Carolina. At the time this action was instituted, the Company had 95 employees at the Dan River Station, 14 of whom were Negroes; 13 of these are petitioners here.

The District Court found that prior to July 2, 1965, the effective date of the Civil Rights Act of 1964, the Company openly discriminated on the basis of race in the hiring and assigning of employees at its Dan River plant. The plant was organized into five operating departments: (1) Labor, (2) Coal Handling, (3) Operations, (4) Maintenance, and (5) Laboratory and Test. Negroes were employed only in the Labor Department where the highest paying jobs paid less than the lowest paying jobs in the other four "operating" departments in which only whites were employed. Promotions were normally made within each department on the basis of job seniority. Transferees into a department usually began in the lowest position.

In 1955 the Company instituted a policy of requiring a high school education for

---

* The Act provides:

"Sec. 703(a). It shall be an unlawful employment practice for an employer . . .

"(2) to limit, segregate, or classify his employees in any way which would deprive or tend to deprive any individual of employment opportunities or otherwise adversely affect his status as an employee, because of such individual's race, color, religion, sex, or national origin. . . .

"(h) Notwithstanding any other provision of this title, it shall not be an unlawful employment practice for an employer . . . to give and to act upon the results of any professionally developed ability test provided that such test, its administration or action upon the results is not designed, intended, or used to discriminate because of race, color, religion, sex or national origin. . . ."

initial assignment to any department except Labor, and for transfer from the Coal Handling to any "inside" department (Operations, Maintenance, or Laboratory). When the Company abandoned its policy of restricting Negroes to the Labor Department in 1965, completion of high school also was made a prerequisite to transfer from Labor to any other department. From the time the high school requirement was instituted to the time of trial, however, white employees hired before the time of the high school education requirement continued to perform satisfactorily and achieve promotions in the "operating" departments. Findings on this score are not challenged.

The Company added a further requirement for new employees on July 2, 1965, the date on which Title VII became effective. To qualify for placement in any but the Labor Department it became necessary to register satisfactory scores on two professionally prepared aptitude tests, as well as to have a high school education. Completion of high school alone continued to render employees eligible for transfer to the four desirable departments from which Negroes had been excluded if the incumbent had been employed prior to the time of the new requirement. In September 1965 the Company began to permit incumbent employees who lacked a high school education to qualify for transfer from Labor or Coal Handling to an "inside" job by passing two tests—the Wonderlic Personnel Test, which purports to measure general intelligence, and the Bennett Mechanical Aptitude Test. Neither was directed or intended to measure the ability to learn to perform a particular job or category of jobs. The requisite scores used for both initial hiring and transfer approximated the national median for high school graduates.

The District Court had found that while the Company previously followed a policy of overt racial discrimination in a period prior to the Act, such conduct had ceased. The District Court also concluded that Title VII was intended to be prospective only and, consequently, the impact of prior inequities was beyond the reach of corrective action authorized by the Act.

The Court of Appeals was confronted with a question of first impression, as are we, concerning the meaning of Title VII. After careful analysis a majority of that court concluded that a subjective test of the employer's intent should govern, particularly in a close case, and that in this case there was no showing of a discriminatory purpose in the adoption of the diploma and test requirements. On this basis, the Court of Appeals concluded there was no violation of the Act.

The Court of Appeals reversed the District Court in part, rejecting the holding that residual discrimination arising from prior employment practices was insulated from remedial action. The Court of Appeals noted, however, that the District Court was correct in its conclusion that there was no finding of a racial purpose of invidious intent in the adoption of the high school diploma requirement or general intelligence test and that these standards had been applied fairly to whites and Negroes alike. It held that, in the absence of a discriminatory purpose, use of such requirements was permitted by the Act. In so doing, the Court of Appeals rejected the claim that because these two requirements operated to render ineligible a markedly disproportionate number of Negroes, they were unlawful under Title VII unless shown to be job-related. We granted the writ on these claims.

The objective of Congress in the enactment of Title VII is plain from the language of the statute. It was to achieve equality of employment opportunities and remove barriers that have operated in the past to favor an identifiable group of white employees over other employees. Under the Act, practices, procedures, or tests neutral on their face, and even neutral in terms of intent, cannot be maintained if they operate to "freeze" the status quo of prior discriminatory employment practices.

The Court of Appeals' opinion, and the partial dissent, agreed that, on the record in the present case, "whites fare far better on the Company's alternative requirements" than Negroes.* This consequence would appear to be directly traceable to race. Basic intelligence must have the means of articulation to manifest itself fairly in a testing process. Because they are Negroes, petitioners have long received inferior education in segregated schools and this Court expressly recognized these differences in *Gaston County* v. *United States,* 395 US 285 (1969). There, because of the inferior education received by Negroes in North Carolina, this Court barred the institution of a literacy test for voter registration on the ground that the test would abridge the right to vote indirectly on account of race. Congress did not intend by Title VII, however, to guarantee a job to every person regardless of qualifications. In short, the Act does not command that any person be hired simply because he was formerly the subject of discrimination, or because he is a member of a minority group. Discrimination preference for any group, minority or majority, is precisely and only what Congress has proscribed. What is required by Congress is the removal of artificial, arbitrary, and unnecessary barriers to employment when the barriers operate invidiously to discriminate on the basis of racial or other impermissible classification.

Congress has now provided that tests or criteria for employment or promotion may not provide equality of opportunity only in the sense of the fabled offer of milk to the stork and the fox. On the contrary, Congress has now required that the posture and condition of the job seeker be taken into account. It has—to resort again to the fable—provided that the vessel in which the milk is proffered be one all seekers can use. The Act proscribes not only overt discrimination but also practices that are fair in form, but discriminatory in operation. The touchstone is business necessity. If an employment practice which operates to exclude Negroes cannot be shown to be related to job performance, the practice is prohibited.

On the record before us, neither the high school completion requirement nor the general intelligence test is shown to bear a demonstrable relationship to successful performance of the jobs for which it was used. Both were adopted, as the Court of Appeals noted, without meaningful study of their relationship to job-performance ability. Rather, a vice president of the Company testified, the requirements were instituted on the Company's judgment that they generally would improve the overall quality of the work force.

The evidence, however, shows that employees who have not completed high school or taken the tests have continued to perform satisfactorily and make pro-

* In North Carolina, 1960 census statistics show that, while 34% of white males had completed high school, only 12% of Negro males had done so. . . .
Similarly, with respect to standardized tests, the EEOC in one case found that use of a battery of tests, including the Wonderlic and Bennett tests used by the Company in the instant case, resulted in 58% of whites passing the tests, as compared with only 6% of the blacks. . . .

gress in departments for which the high school and test criteria are now used. The promotion record of present employees who would not be able to meet the new criteria thus suggests the possibility that the requirements may not be needed even for the limited purpose of preserving the avowed policy of advancement within the Company. In the context of this case, it is unnecessary to reach the question whether testing requirements that take into account capability for the next succeeding position or related future promotion might be utilized upon a showing that such long range requirements fulfill a genuine business need. In the present case the Company has made no such showing.

The Court of Appeals held that the Company had adopted the diploma and test requirements without any "intention to discriminate against Negro employees." We do not suggest that either the District Court or the Court of Appeals erred in examining the employer's intent; but good intent or absence of discriminatory intent does not redeem employment procedures or testing mechanisms that operate as "built-in headwinds" for minority groups and are unrelated to measuring job capability.

The Company's lack of discriminatory intent is suggested by special efforts to help the undereducated employees through Company financing of two-thirds the cost of tuition for high school training. But Congress directed the thrust of the Act to the *consequences* of employment practices, not simply the motivation. More than that, Congress has placed on the employer the burden of showing that any given requirement must have a manifest relationship to the employment in question.

The facts of this case demonstrate the inadequacy of broad and general testing devices as well as the infirmity of using diplomas or degrees as fixed measures of capability. History is filled with examples of men and women who rendered highly effective performance without the conventional badges of accomplishment in terms of certificates, diplomas, or degrees. Diplomas and tests are useful servants, but Congress had mandated the common-sense proposition that they are not to become masters of reality.

The Company contends that its general intelligence tests are specifically permitted by § 703(h) of the Act. That section authorizes the use of "any professionally developed ability test" that is not "designed, intended, or *used* to discriminate because of race. . . ." (Emphasis added.)

The Equal Employment Opportunity Commission, having enforcement responsibility, has issued guidelines interpreting § 703(h) to permit only the use of job-related tests. The administrative interpretation of the Act by the enforcing agency is entitled to great deference. . . . Since the Act and its legislative history support the Commission's construction, this affords good reason to treat the Guidelines as expressing the will of Congress.

Section 703(h) was not contained in the House version of the Civil Rights Act but was added in the Senate during extended debate. For a period, debate revolved around claims that the bill as proposed would prohibit all testing and force employers to hire unqualified persons simply because they were part of a group formerly subject to job discrimination. Proponents of Title VII sought throughout the debate to assure the critics that the Act would have no effect on job-related tests. Senators Case of New Jersey and Clark of Pennsylvania, comanagers of the bill on the Senate floor, issued a memorandum explaining that the proposed Title VII "expressly protects the employer's right to insist that any prospective applicant, Negro or white, *must meet the applicable job qualifications.* Indeed, the very purpose of Title VII is to promote hiring on the basis of job qualifications, rather than on the basis of race or color." (Emphasis added.) Despite these assurances, Senator Tower of Texas introduced an amendment authorizing "professionally developed ability tests." Proponents of Title VII opposed the amendment because, as written, it would permit an employer to give any test, "whether it was a good test or not, so long as it was professionally designed. Discrimination could actually exist under the guise of compliance with the statute." . . .

The amendment was defeated and two days later Senator Tower offered a substitute amendment which was adopted verbatim and is now the testing provision of § 703(h). Speaking for the supporters of Title VII, Senator Humphrey, who had vigorously opposed the first amendment, endorsed the substitute amendment, stating: "Senators on both sides of the aisle who were deeply interested in Title VII have examined the text of this amendment and have found it to be in accord with the intent and purpose of that title." . . . The amendment was then adopted. From the sum of the legislative history relevant in this case, the conclusion is inescapable that the EEOC's construction of § 703(h) to require that employment tests be job-related comports with congressional intent.

Nothing in the Act precludes the use of testing or measuring procedures; obviously they are useful. What Congress has forbidden is giving these devices and mechanisms controlling force unless they are demonstrably a reasonable measure of job performance. Congress has not commanded that the less qualified be preferred over the better qualified simply because of minority origins. Far from disparaging job qualifications as such, Congress has made such qualifications the controlling factor, so that race, religion, nationality, and sex become irrelevant. What Congress has commanded is that any tests used must measure the person for the job and not the person in the abstract.

The judgment of the Court of Appeals is, as to that portion of the judgment appealed from, reversed.

6. Fair and Impartial Juries

CASSELL v. TEXAS
339 US 282 (1950)

[In the present case a Negro was convicted of murder. The jury that convicted him had been chosen admittedly without racial discrimination, but it was argued that there had been discrimination in the selection of the grand jury that indicted him.

[All the Justices agreed (Justice Douglas did not participate) that the Equal Protection Clause of the Fourteenth Amendment prohibits racial discrimination in the selection of grand juries, and seven of the Justices agreed that discrimination was shown in this case. The conviction was reversed. Justices Frankfurter and Clark wrote concurring opinions; Justice Jackson dissented.

["It has been settled law since 1880," said Justice Frankfurter in his concurring opinion, "that the Civil War Amendments barred the States from discriminating because of race in the selection of juries, whether grand or petty." At least a score of Supreme Court decisions can be cited for this proposition.

[The principle is not that a Negro is entitled to have members of his race on the jury that indicts or convicts him; what the Constitution guarantees is that members of his race may not be intentionally excluded.]

Mr. Justice Reed announced the judgment of the Court and an opinion in which Chief Justice Vinson, Mr. Justice Black and Mr. Justice Clark concurred:

Review was sought in this case to determine whether there has been a violation by Texas of petitioner's federal constitutional right to a fair and impartial grand jury. The federal question was raised by a motion to quash the indictment on the ground that petitioner, a Negro, suffered unconstitutional discrimination through the selection of white men only for the grand jury that indicted him. . . .

The [Texas] Court of Criminal Appeals accepted the federal rule that a Negro is denied the equal protection of the laws when he is indicted by a grand jury from which Negroes as a race have been intentionally excluded. . . . It was from an examination of facts that the court deduced its conclusion that racial discrimination had not been practiced. Since the result reached may deny a federal right, we may reexamine the facts to determine whether petitioner has sustained by proof his allegation of discrimination. . . .

Acting under the Texas statutes, the Dallas County grand-jury commissioners chose a list of sixteen males for this September 1947 grand jury from citizens eligible under the statute. The judge chose twelve of these for the panel. No challenge is now made to the fairness of this statutory system. We have approved it.

Petitioner's attack is upon the way the statutory method of grand-jury selection has been administered by the jury commissioners. One charge is that discrimination must have been practiced because the Negro proportion of grand jurors is less than the Negro population of the county's population. Under the 1940 census the total population of Dallas County was 398,564, of whom 61,605 were Negroes. This is about 15.5%. In weighing this matter of custom, we limit ourselves, as do the parties, to the period between June 1, 1942, . . . and November 1947, when petitioner was indicted. There were 21 grand juries in this period; of the 252 members of the panels, 17, or 6.7% were Negroes. But this apparent discrepancy may be explained by the fact that Texas grand jurors must possess certain statutory qualifications. Grand jurors must ordinarily be eligible to vote; eligibility requires payment of a poll tax; and the validity of a poll-tax requirement is not challenged. The record shows 5,500 current Negro poll-tax payers in Dallas County in 1947, and nothing indicates that this number varied substantially from year to year. The corresponding figure for all poll-tax payers, male and female, is 83,667. These figures would indicate that as a proportional matter 6.5% of grand jurors would be Negroes, a percentage approximating the ratio of Negroes actually sitting on the 21 grand jury panels. Without more it cannot be said that Negroes had been left off grand-jury panels to such a degree as to establish a prima facie case of discrimination.

A different question is presented by petitioner's next charge that . . . the Dallas County grand jury commissioners for 21 consecutive lists had consistently limited Negroes selected for grand-jury service to not more than one on each grand jury. . . . Since the *Hill Case,* 316 US 400, the judges of the trial court have been careful to instruct their jury commissioners that discrimination on grounds of race or color is forbidden. The judge did so here. If, notwithstanding this caution by the trial court judges, commissioners should limit proportionally the number of Negroes elected for grand-jury service, such limitations would violate our Constitution. Jurymen should be selected as individuals, on the basis of individual qualifications, and not as members of a race.

We have recently written why proportional representation of races on a jury is not a constitutional requisite. Succinctly stated, our reason was that the Constitution requires only a fair jury selected without regard to race. Obviously the number of races and nationalities appearing in the ancestry of our citizens would make it impossible to meet a requirement of proportional representation. Similarly, since there can be no exclusion of Negroes as a race and no discrimination because of color, proportional limitation is not permissible. That conclusion is compelled by the United States Code, 18 USCA 243, based on § 4 of the Civil Rights Act of 1875. While the language of the section directs attention to the right to serve as a juror, its command has long been recognized also to assure rights to an accused. Prohibiting racial disqualification of Negroes for jury service, this congressional enactment under the Fourteenth Amendment, § 5, has been consistently sustained and its violation held to deny a proper trial to a Negro accused. Proportional racial limitation is therefore forbidden. An accused is entitled to have charges against him considered by a jury in the selection of which there has been neither inclusion nor exclusion because of race.

Our holding that there was discrimination in the selection of grand jurors in this case, however, is based on another ground. In explaining the fact that no Negroes appeared on this grand jury list, the commissioners said that they knew none available who qualified; at the same time they said they chose jurymen only from those people with whom they were personally acquainted. It may be assumed that in ordinary activities in Dallas County, acquaintanceship between the races is not on a sufficiently familiar basis to give citizens eligible for appointment as jury commissioners an opportunity to know the qualifications for grand-jury service of many members of another race. An individual's qualifications for grand-jury service, however, are not hard to ascertain, and with no evidence to the contrary, we must assume that a large proportion of the Negroes of Dallas County met the statutory requirements for jury service. When the commissioners were appointed as judicial administrative officials, it was their duty to familiarize themselves fairly with the qualifications of the eligible jurors of the county without regard to race and color. They did not do so here, and the result has been racial discrimination. . . .

The existence of the kind of discrimination described in the *Hill* case does not depend upon systematic exclusion continuing over a long period and practiced by a succession of jury commissioners. Since the issue must be whether there has been discrimination in the selection of the jury that has indicted petitioner, it is enough to have direct evidence based on the statements of the jury commissioners in the very case. Discrimination may be proved in other ways than by evidence of long continued unexplained absence of Negroes from many panels. The statements of the jury commissioners that they chose only whom they knew, and that they knew no eligible Negroes in an area where Negroes made up so large a proportion of the population, prove the intentional exclusion that is discrimination in violation of petitioner's constitutional rights.

The judgment of the Court of Criminal Appeals of Texas is reversed.

7. Equality in Public Education

BROWN v. BOARD OF EDUCATION OF TOPEKA
347 US 483 (1954)

[In 1896, in *Plessy* v. *Ferguson,* 163 US 537, a case involving transportation, the Supreme Court approved segregation of the races as constitutional and formulated the doctrine of "separate but equal" facilities. Under the protection of this doctrine 17 states maintained segregated schools under the compulsion of state legislation; Congress enacted a school segregation act for the District of Columbia; in addition, 4 states adopted laws that permitted segregation on a local option basis. In the remaining states, 16 prohibited segregation, and in 11 there was no specific legislation. In 1954 there were over eight million white and two and a half million Negro pupils who attended segregated elementary and high schools.

[The "separate but equal" doctrine was under attack for many years. The Court in 1950 interpreted and applied the doctrine in such a way as to make segregation in professional and graduate study impossible. *Sweatt* v. *Painter,* 339 US 629, and *McLaurin* v. *Oklahoma State Regents,* 339 US 637. These were unanimous decisions. It became apparent that it was only a matter of time before the Court would feel itself compelled to extend the logic of these decisions to grade and high schools, for the doctrine had been drained of moral force.

[In the present case, decided by a unanimous Supreme Court in 1954, the "separate but equal" doctrine was rejected. The Court held that "separate educational facilities are inherently unequal," and hence the segregation statutes violate the Equal Protection Clause of the Fourteenth Amendment.

[A notable feature of the opinion by Chief Justice Warren is his use of psychological and sociological data to show the harmful effects of segregation.

[In a companion case, *Bolling* v. *Sharpe,* decided at the same time, the Supreme Court held that the federal act which compelled segregated schools in the District of Columbia was a violation of the Due Process Clause of the Fifth Amendment.]

Mr. Chief Justice Warren delivered the opinion of the Court:

These cases come to us from the States of Kansas, South Carolina, Virginia, and Delaware. They are premised on different facts and different local conditions, but a common legal question justifies their consideration together in this consolidated opinion.

In each of the cases, minors of the Negro race, through their legal representatives, seek the aid of the courts in obtaining admission to the public schools of their community on a nonsegregated basis. In each instance, they had been denied admission to schools attended by white children under laws requiring or permitting segregation according to race. This segregation was alleged to deprive the plaintiffs of the equal protection of the laws under the Fourteenth Amendment. In each of the cases other than the Delaware case, a three-judge federal district court denied relief to the plaintiffs on the so-called "separate but equal" doctrine announced by this Court in *Plessy* v. *Ferguson,* 163 US 537. Under that doctrine, equality of treatment is accorded when the races are provided substantially equal facilities, even though these facilities be separate. In the Delaware case, the Supreme Court of Delaware adhered to that doctrine, but ordered that the plaintiffs be admitted to the white schools because of their superiority to the Negro schools.

The plaintiffs contend that segregated public schools are not "equal" and cannot be made "equal," and that hence they are deprived of the equal protection of the laws. Because of the obvious importance of the question presented, the Court took jurisdiction. Argument was heard in the 1952 Term, and reargument was heard this Term on certain questions propounded by the Court.

Reargument was largely devoted to the circumstances surrounding the adoption of the Fourteenth Amendment in 1868. It covered exhaustively consideration of the Amendment in Congress, ratification by the states, then existing practices in racial segregation, and the views of proponents and opponents of the Amendment. This discussion and our own investigation convince us that, although these sources cast some light, it is not enough to resolve the problem with which we are faced. At best, they are inconclusive. The most avid proponents of the post-War Amendments undoubtedly intended them to remove all legal distinctions among "all persons born or naturalized in the United States." Their opponents, just as certainly, were antagonistic to both the letter and the spirit of the Amendments and wished them to have the most limited effect. What others in Congress and the state legislature had in mind cannot be determined with any degree of certainty.

An additional reason for the inconclusive nature of the Amendment's history, with respect to segregated schools, is the status of public education at that time. In the South, the movement toward free common schools, supported by general taxation, had not yet taken hold. Education of white children was largely in the hands of private groups. Education of Negroes was almost nonexistent, and practically all of the race were illiterate. In fact, any education of Negroes was forbidden by law in some states. Today, in contrast, many Negroes have achieved outstanding success in the arts and sciences as well as in the business and professional world. It is true that public education had already advanced further in the North, but the effect of the Amendment on Northern States was generally ignored in the congressional debates. Even in the North, the conditions of public education did not approximate those existing today. The curriculum was usually rudimentary; ungraded schools were common in rural areas; the school term was but three months a year in many states; and compulsory school attendance was virtually unknown. As a consequence, it is not suprising that there should be so little in the history of the Fourteenth Amendment relating to its intended effect on public education.

In the first cases in this Court construing the Fourteenth Amendment, decided shortly after its adoption, the Court interpreted it as proscribing all state-imposed discriminations against the Negro race. The doctrine of "separate but equal" did not make its appearance in this Court until 1896 in the case of *Plessy* v. *Ferguson, supra,* involving not education but transportation. American courts have since labored with the doctrine for over half a century. In this Court, there have been six cases involving the "separate but equal" doctrine in the field of public education.

In *Cumming* v. *County Board of Education,* 175 US 528, and *Gong Lum* v. *Rice,* 275 US 78, the validity of the doctrine itself was not challenged. In more recent cases, all on the graduate school level, inequality was found in that specific benefits enjoyed by white students were denied to Negro students of the same educational qualifications. *Missouri* ex rel. *Gaines* v. *Canada,* 305 US 337; *Sipuel* v. *Oklahoma,* 332 US 631; *Sweatt* v. *Painter,* 339 US 629; *McLaurin* v. *Oklahoma State Regents,* 339 US 637. In none of these cases was it necessary to reexamine the doctrine to grant relief to the Negro plaintiff. And in *Sweatt* v. *Painter, supra,* the Court expressly reserved decision on the question whether *Plessy* v. *Ferguson* should be held inapplicable to public education.

In the instant cases, that question is directly presented. Here, unlike *Sweatt* v. *Painter,* there are findings below that the Negro and white schools involved have been equalized, or are being equalized, with respect to buildings, curricula, qualifications and salaries of teachers, and other "tangible" factors. Our decisions, therefore, cannot turn on merely a comparison of these tangible factors in the Negro and white schools involved in each of the cases. We must look instead to the effect of segregation itself on public education.

In approaching this problem, we cannot turn the clock back to 1868 when the Amendment was adopted, or even to 1896 when *Plessy* v. *Ferguson* was written. We must consider public education in the light of its full development and its present place in American life throughout the Nation. Only in this way can it be determined if segregation in public schools deprives these plaintiffs of the equal protection of the laws.

Today, education is perhaps the most important function of state and local governments. Compulsory school attendance laws and the great expenditures for education both demonstrate our recognition of the importance of education to our democratic society. It is required in the performance of our most basic public responsibilities, even service in the armed forces. It is the very foundation of good citizenship. Today it is a principal instrument in awakening the child to cultural values, in preparing him for later professional training, and in helping him to adjust normally to his environment. In these days, it is doubtful that any child may reasonably be expected to succeed in life if he is denied the opportunity of an education. Such an opportunity, where the state has undertaken to provide it, is a right which must be made available to all on equal terms.

We come then to the question presented: Does segregation of children in public schools solely on the basis of race, even though the physical facilities and other "tangible" factors may be equal, deprive the children of the minority group of equal educational opportunities? We believe that it does.

In *Sweatt* v. *Painter, supra,* in finding that a segregated law school for Negroes could not provide them equal educational opportunities, this Court relied in large part on "those qualities which are incapable of objective measurement but which make for greatness in a law school." In *McLaurin* v. *Oklahoma State Regents, supra,* the Court, in requiring that a Negro admitted to a white graduate school be treated like all other students, again resorted to intangible considerations: ". . . his ability to study, to engage in discussions and exchange views with other students, and, in general, to learn his profession." Such considerations apply with added force to children in grade and high schools. To separate them from others of similar age and qualifications solely because of their race generates a feeling of inferiority as to their status in the community that may affect their hearts and minds in a way unlikely ever to be undone. The effect of this separation on their educational opportunities was well stated by a finding in the Kansas case by a court which nevertheless felt compelled to rule against the Negro plaintiffs:

Segregation of white and colored children in public schools has a detrimental effect upon the colored children. The impact is greater when it has the sanction of the law; for the policy of separating the races is usually interpreted as denoting the inferiority of the Negro group. A sense of inferiority affects the motivation of a child to learn. Segregation with the sanction of law, therefore, has a tendency to retard the educational and mental development of Negro children and to deprive them of some of the benefits they would receive in a racially integrated school system.

Whatever may have been the extent of psychological knowledge at the time of *Plessy* v. *Ferguson,* this finding is amply supported by modern authority.* Any language in *Plessy* v. *Ferguson* contrary to this finding is rejected.

We conclude that in the field of public education the doctrine of "separate but equal" has no place. Separate educational facilities are inherently unequal. Therefore, we hold that the plaintiffs and others similarly situated for whom the actions have been brought are, by reason of the segregation complained of, deprived of the equal protection of the laws guaranteed by the Fourteenth Amendment. This disposition makes unnecessary any discussion whether such segregation also violates the Due Process Clause of the Fourteenth Amendment.

Because these are class actions, because of the wide applicability of this decision, and because of the great variety of local conditions, the formulation of decrees in these cases presents problems of considerable complexity. On reargument, the consideration of appropriate relief was necessarily subordinated to the primary question—the constitutionality of segregation in public education. We have now announced that such segregation is a denial of the equal protection of the laws. In order that we may have the full assistance of the parties in formulating decrees, the cases will be restored to the docket, and the parties are requested to present further argument on Questions 4 and 5 previously propounded by the Court for the reargument this Term. The Attorney General of the United States is again invited

* K. B. Clark, "Effect of Prejudice and Discrimination on Personality Development" (Midcentury White House Conference on Children and Youth, 1950); Witmer and Kotinsky, *Personality in the Making* (1952), ch. VI; Deutscher and Chein, "The Psychological Effects of Enforced Segregation: A Survey of Social Science Opinion," 26 *J. Psychol.* 259 (1948); Chein, "What Are the Psychological Effects of Segregation under Conditions of Equal Facilities?" 3 *Int. J. Opinion and Attitude Res.* 229 (1949); Brameld, "Educational Costs," in *Discrimination and National Welfare* (MacIver, ed., 1949), 44–48; Frazier, *The Negro in the United States* (1949), 674–681. And see generally Myrdal, *An American Dilemma* (1944).

to participate. The Attorneys General of the states requiring or permitting segregation in public education will also be permitted to appear as *amici curiae* upon request to do so by September 15, 1954, and submission of briefs by October 1, 1954.

It is so ordered.

GOSS *v*. BOARD OF EDUCATION OF KNOXVILLE
373 US 683 (1963)

[The school desegregation plan involved in this case made it possible for a pupil to transfer back to a school that was racially segregated, but made it much more difficult for him to transfer to a school in which members of his race were in a minority. The U.S. Supreme Court, in an opinion by Justice Clark for a unanimous Court, held the plan unconstitutional as a violation of the Equal Protection Clause of the Fourteenth Amendment.]

Mr. Justice Clark delivered the opinion of the Court:

We granted certiorari limited to the question whether petitioners, Negro school children seeking desegregation of the public school systems of Knoxville, Tennessee (the Goss case), and Davidson County, Tennessee, an area adjacent to Nashville (the Maxwell case), are deprived of rights under the Fourteenth Amendment. The question centers around substantially similar transfer provisions incorporated in formal desegregation plans adopted by the respective local school boards pursuant to court orders. The claim is that the transfer programs are invalid because they are based solely on race and tend to perpetuate the pre-existing racially segregated school system. Under the overall desegregation plans presented to the trial courts, school districts would be rezoned without reference to race. However, by the terms of the transfer provisions, a student, upon request, would be permitted, solely on the basis of his own race and the racial composition of the school to which he has been assigned by virtue of rezoning, to transfer from such school where he would be in the racial minority, back to his former segregated school where his race would be in the majority. The appropriate District Courts and the Court of Appeals approved the transfer plans. The transfer plans being based solely on racial factors which, under their terms, inevitably lead toward segregation of the students by race, we conclude that they run counter to the admonition of *Brown* v. *Board of Education of Topeka,* 349 US 294 (1955), wherein the District Courts were directed to "consider the adequacy of any plans" proposed by school authorities "to effectuate a . . . racially nondiscriminatory school system." Our conclusion here leads to a reversal of the judgments of the Court of Appeals to the extent they approve the transfer provisions of respondent boards in each of the cases. The only question with which we are here concerned relates solely to the transfer provisions, and we are not called upon either to discuss or pass on the other provisions of the desegregation plans.

I

These cases were brought by Negro public school pupils and their parents as class actions against the respective school authorities. They challenged, among other points in the desegregation plans not here relevant, the transfer provisions which permitted a pupil to transfer, upon request, from the zone of his residence to another school. The transfer plans are essentially the same, each containing, in addition to the provisions at issue here, general provisions providing for transfers on a showing of "good cause." The crucial provision, however, present in somewhat the same form in each plan, is exemplified by § 6 of the Knoxville plan:

> 6. The following will be regarded as some of the valid conditions to support requests for transfer:
>
> a. When a white student would otherwise be required to attend a school previously serving colored students only:
>
> b. When a colored student would otherwise be required to attend a school previously serving white students only:
>
> c. When a student would otherwise be required to attend a school where the majority of students of that school or in his or her grade are of a different race.

This provision is attacked as providing racial factors as valid conditions to support transfers which by design and operation would perpetuate racial segregation. It is also said that no showing is made that the transfer provisions are essential to effectuation of desegregation and that other procedures are available.

II

It is readily apparent that the transfer system proposed lends itself to perpetuation of segregation. Indeed, the provisions can work only toward that end. While transfers are available to those who choose to attend school where their race is in the majority, there is no provision whereby a student might transfer upon request to a school in which his race is in a minority, unless he qualifies for a "good cause" transfer. As the Superintendent of Davidson County's schools put it, the effect of the racial transfer plan was "to permit a child [or his parents] to choose segregation outside of his zone but not to choose integration outside of his zone." Here the right of transfer, which operates solely on the basis of a racial classification, is a one-way ticket leading to but one destination, i.e., the majority race of the transferee and continued segregation. This Court has decided that state-imposed separation in public schools is inherently unequal and results in discrimination in violation of the Fourteenth Amendment. *Brown* v. *Board of Education of Topeka,* 347 US 483 (1954). Our task then is to decide whether these transfer provisions are likewise unconstitutional. In doing so, we note that if the transfer provisions were made available to all students regardless of their race and regardless as well of the racial composition of the school to which he requested transfer we would have an entirely different case. Pupils could then at their option (or that of their parents) choose, entirely free of any imposed racial considerations, to remain in the school of their zone or transfer to another.

III

Classifications based on race for purposes of transfers between public schools, as here, violate the Equal Protection Clause of the Fourteenth Amendment. As the Court said in *Steele* v. *Louisville & Nashville R. Co.,* 323 US 192 (1944), racial classifications are "obviously irrelevant and invidious." The cases of this Court reflect a variety of instances in which racial classifications have been held to be invalid, i.e., public parks and playgrounds, *Watson* v. *City of Memphis,* 83 S. Ct. 1314 (1963); trespass convictions, where local segregation ordinances preempt private choice, *Peterson* v. *City of Greenville,* 83 S. Ct. 1119 (1963); seating in courtrooms, *Johnson* v. *Virginia,* 373 US 61 (1963); restaurants in public buildings, *Burton* v. *Wilmington Parking Authority,* 365 US 715 (1961); bus terminals, *Boyington* v. *Com. of Virginia,* 364 US 454 (1960); public schools, *Brown* v. *Board of Education, supra;* railroad dining-car facilities, *Henderson* v. *United States,* 339 US 816 (1950); state enforcement of restrictive covenants based on race, *Shelley* v. *Kraemer,* 334 US 1 (1948); labor unions acting as statutory representatives of a craft, *Steele* v. *Louisville & Nashville R. Co., supra;* voting, *Smith* v. *Allwright,* 321 US 649 (1944); and juries, *Strauder* v. *West Virginia,* 100 US 303 (1879). The recognition of race as an absolute criterion for granting transfers which operate only in the direction of schools in which the transferee's race is in the majority is no less unconstitutional than its use for original admission or subsequent assignment to public schools. . . .

The alleged equality—which we view as only superficial—of enabling each race to transfer from a desegregated to a segregated school does not save the plans. Like arguments were made without success in *Brown, supra,* in support of the separate but equal educational program. Not only is race the factor upon which the transfer plans operate, but also the plans lack a provision whereby a student might with equal facility transfer from a segregated to a desegregated school. The obvious one-way operation of these two factors in combination underscores the purely racial character and purpose of the transfer provisions. We hold that the transfer plans promote discrimination and are therefore invalid.

This is not to say that appropriate transfer provisions, upon the parents' request, consistent with sound school administration and not based upon any state-imposed racial conditions, would fall. Likewise, we would have a different case here if the transfer provisions were unrestricted, allowing transfers to or from any school regardless of the race of the majority therein. But no official transfer plan or provision of which racial segregation is the inevitable consequence may stand under the Fourteenth Amendment.

In reaching this result we are not unmindful of the deep-rooted problems involved. Indeed, it was consideration for the multifarious local difficulties and "variety of obstacles" which might arise in this transition that led this Court eight years age to frame its mandate in *Brown* in such language as "good faith compliance at the earliest practicable date" and "all deliberate speed." . . . Now, however, eight years after this decree was rendered and over nine years after the first *Brown* decision, the context in which we must interpret and apply this language to plans for desegregation has been significantly altered. . . . The transfer provisions here cannot be deemed to be reasonably designed to meet legitimate local problems, and therefore do not meet the requirements of *Brown.* Accordingly, the decisions of the Court of Appeals, insofar as they approve the transfer provisions submitted by the boards of education of Knoxville, Tennessee, and Davidson County, Tennessee, are reversed and the cases are remanded to the Court of Appeals with directions to remand to the District Court for further proceedings in accordance with this opinion.

Reversed and remanded.

GRIFFIN *v.* COUNTY SCHOOL BOARD OF PRINCE EDWARD COUNTY
377 US 218 (1964)

[Prince Edward County, Virginia, closed its public schools in order to avoid desegregation, and paid public funds to help support private schools which excluded Negro children because of their race. The U.S. Supreme Court declared this action unconstitutional as a denial of equal protection. The opinion for the Court was by Justice Black. In a brief note, Justices Clark and Harlan joined in the Court's opinion except that they disagreed that the federal courts are empowered to order the reopening of the public schools in the county.]

Mr. Justice Black delivered the opinion of the Court:

This litigation began in 1951 when a group of Negro school children living in Prince Edward County, Virginia, filed a complaint in the United States District Court for the Eastern District of Virginia alleging that they had been denied admission to public schools attended by white children and charging that Virginia laws requiring such school segregation denied complainants equal protection of the laws in violation of the Fourteenth Amendment. On May 17, 1954, ten years ago, we held that the Virginia segregation laws did deny equal protection. *Brown* v. *Board of Education,* 347 US 483 (1954). On May 31, 1955, after reargument on the nature of relief, we remanded this case, along with others heard with it, to the District Courts to enter such orders as "necessary and proper to admit [complainants] to public schools on a racially nondiscriminatory basis with all deliberate speed. . . ." *Brown* v. *Board of Education,* 349 US 294 (1955).

Efforts to desegregate Prince Edward County's schools met with resistance. In 1956 Section 141 of the Virginia Constitution was amended to authorize the General Assembly and local governing bodies to appropriate funds to assist students to go to public or to nonsectarian private schools, in addition to those owned by the State or the locality. The General Assembly met in special session and enacted legislation to close any public schools where white and colored children were enrolled together, to cut off state funds to such schools, to pay tuition grants to children in nonsectarian private schools, and to extend state retirement benefits to teachers in newly created private schools. The legislation closing mixed schools and cutting off state funds was later invalidated by the Supreme Court of Appeals of Virginia, which held that these laws violated the Virginia Constitution. . . . In April 1959 the General Assembly abandoned "massive resistance" to desegregation and turned instead to what was called a "freedom of choice" program. The Assembly repealed the rest of the 1956 legislation, as well as a tuition grant law of January 1959, and enacted a new tuition grant program. At the same time the Assembly repealed Virginia's compulsory attendance laws and instead made school attendance a matter of local option.

In June 1959, the United States Court of Appeals for the Fourth Circuit directed the Federal District Court (1) to enjoin discriminatory practices in Prince Edward County schools, (2) to require the County School Board to take "immediate steps" toward admitting students without regard to race to the white high school "in the school term beginning September 1959," and (3) to require the Board to make plans for admissions to elementary schools without regard to race. . . . Having as early as 1956 resolved that they would not operate public schools "wherein white and colored children are taught together," the Supervisors of Prince Edward County refused to levy any school taxes for the 1959–1960 school year, explaining that they were "confronted with a Court decree which requires the admission of white and colored children to all the schools of the county without regard to race or color." As a result, the county's public schools did not reopen in the fall of 1959 and have remained closed ever since, although the public schools of every other county in Virginia have continued to operate under laws governing the State's public school system and to draw funds provided by the State for that purpose. A private group, the Prince Edward School Foundation, was formed to operate private schools for white children in Prince Edward County and, having built its own school plant, has been in operation ever since the closing of the public schools. An offer to set up private schools for colored children in the county was rejected, the Negroes of Prince Edward preferring to continue the legal battle for desegregated public schools, and colored children were without formal education from 1959 to 1963, when federal, state, and county authorities cooperated to have classes conducted for Negroes and whites in school buildings owned by the county. During the 1959–1960 school year the Foundation's schools for white children were supported entirely by private contributions, but in 1960 the General Assembly adopted a new tuition grant program making every child, regardless of race, eligible for tuition grants of $125, or $150 to attend a nonsectarian private school or a public school outside his locality, and also authorizing localities to provide their own grants. The Prince Edward Board of Supervisors then passed an ordinance providing tuition grants of $100, so that each child attending the Prince Edward School Foundation's schools received a total of $225 if in elementary school or $250 if in high school. In the 1960–1961 session the major source of financial support for the Foundation was in the indirect form of these state and county tuition grants, paid to children attending Foundation schools. At the same time, the County Board of Supervisors passed an ordinance allowing property tax credits up to 25% for contributions to any "nonprofit, nonsectarian private school" in the county.

In 1961 petitioners here filed a supplemental complaint, adding new parties and seeking to enjoin the respondents from refusing to operate an efficient system of public free schools in Prince Edward County and to enjoin payment of public funds to help support private schools which excluded students on account of race. The District Court, finding that "the end result of every action taken by that body [Board of Supervisors] was designed to preserve separation of the races in the schools of Prince Edward County," enjoined the county from paying tuition grants or giving tax credits so long as public schools remained closed. At this time the District Court did not pass on whether the public schools of the county could be closed but abstained pending determination by the Virginia courts of whether the constitution and laws of Virginia required the public schools to be kept open. Later, however, without waiting for the Virginia courts to decide the question, the District Court held that "the public schools of Prince Edward County may not be closed to avoid the effect of the law of the land as interpreted by the Supreme Court, while the Commonwealth of Virginia permits other public schools to remain open at the expense of the taxpayers." . . . Soon thereafter, a declaratory judgment suit was brought by the County Board of Supervisors and the County School Board in a Virginia Circuit Court. Having done this, these parties asked the Federal District Court to abstain from further proceedings until the suit in the state courts had run its course, but the District Court declined; it repeated its order that Prince Edward's public schools might not be closed to avoid desegregation while the other public schools in Virginia remained open. The Court of Appeals reversed, Judge Bell dissenting, holding that the District Court should have abstained to await state court determination of the validity of the tuition grants and the tax credits, as well as the validity of the closing of the public schools. . . . We granted certiorari, stating:

In view of the long delay in the case since our decision in the *Brown* case and the importance of the questions presented, we grant certiorari and put the case down for argument March 30, 1964 on the merits, as we have done in other comparable situations without waiting for final action by the Court of Appeals.

For reasons to be stated, we agree with the District Court that, under the circumstances here, closing the Prince Edward County Schools while public schools in all the other counties of Virginia were being maintained, denied the petitioners and the class of Negro students they represent, the equal protection of the laws guaranteed by the Fourteenth Amendment.

II

In *County School Board of Prince Edward County* v. *Griffin*, 204 V. 650, 133 S.E. 2d 565 (1963), the Supreme Court of Appeals of Virginia upheld as valid under state law the closing of the Prince Edward County public schools, the state and county tuition grants for children who attend private schools, and the county's tax concessions for those who make contributions to private schools. The same opinion also held that each county had an "option to operate or not to operate public schools." We accept this case as a definitive and authoritative holding of Virginia law, binding on us, but we cannot accept the Virginia court's further holding, based largely on the Court of Appeals' opinion in this case, that closing the county's public schools under the circumstances of the case did not deny the colored school children of Prince Edward County equal protection of the laws guaranteed by the Federal Constitution.

Since 1959, all Virginia counties have had the benefits of public schools but one: Prince Edward. However, there is no rule that counties, as counties, must be treated alike; the Equal Protection Clause relates to equal protection of the laws "between persons as such rather than between areas." Indeed, showing that different persons are treated differently is not enough, without more, to show a denial of equal protection. It is the circumstances of each case which govern.

Virginia law, as here applied, unquestionably treats the school children of Prince

Edward differently from the way it treats the school children of all other Virginia counties. Prince Edward children must go to a private school or none at all; all other Virginia children can go to public schools. Closing Prince Edward's schools bears more heavily on Negro children in Prince Edward County since white children there have accredited private schools which they can attend, while colored children until very recently have had no available private schools, and even the school they now attend is a temporary expedient. Apart from this expedient, the result is that Prince Edward County school children, if they go to school in their own county, must go to racially segregated schools which, although designated as private, are beneficiaries of county and state support.

A State, of course, has a wide discretion in deciding whether laws shall operate statewide or shall operate only in certain counties, the legislature "having in mind the needs and desires of each." A State may wish to suggest, . . . that there are reasons why one county ought not to be treated like another. But the record in the present case could not be clearer that Prince Edward's public schools were closed and private schools operated in their place with state and county assistance, for one reason, and one reason only: to ensure, through measures taken by the county and the State, that white and colored children in Prince Edward County would not, under any circumstances, go to the same school. Whatever nonracial grounds might support a State's allowing a county to abandon public schools, the object must be a constitutional one, and grounds of race and opposition to desegregation do not qualify as constitutional.

In *Hall* v. *St. Helena Parish School Board,* 197 F. Supp. 649 (D.C.E.D. La. 1961), a three-judge District Court invalidated a Louisiana statute which provided "a means by which public schools under desegregation orders may be changed to 'private' schools operated in the same way, in the same buildings, with the same furnishings, with the same money, and under the same supervision as the public schools." In addition, that statute also provided that where the public schools were "closed," the school board was "charged with responsibility for furnishing free lunches, transportation, and grants-in-aid to the children attending the 'private' schools." We affirmed the District Court's judgment invalidating the Louisiana statute as a denial of equal protection. 368 US 515 (1962). While the Louisiana plan and the Virginia plan worked in different ways, it is plain that both were created to accomplish the same thing: the perpetuation of racial segregation by closing public schools and operating only segregated schools supported directly or indirectly by state or county funds. . . . Either plan works to deny colored students equal protection of the laws. Accordingly, we agree with the District Court that closing the Prince Edward schools and meanwhile contributing to the support of the private segregated white schools that took their place denied petitioners the equal protection of the laws. . . .

III

The District Court held that "the public schools of Prince Edward County may not be closed to avoid the effect of the law of the land as interpreted by the Supreme Court, while the Commonwealth of Virginia permits other public schools to remain open at the expense of the taxpayers." . . . At the same time the court gave notice that it would later consider an order to accomplish this purpose if the public schools were not reopened by September 7, 1962. That day has long passed, and the schools are still closed. On remand, therefore, the court may find it necessary to consider further such an order. An order of this kind is within the court's power if required to assure these petitioners that their constitutional rights will no longer be denied them. The time for mere "deliberate speed" has run out, and that phrase can no longer justify denying these Prince Edward County school children their constitutional rights to an education equal to that afforded by the public schools in the other parts of Virginia.

The judgment of the Court of Appeals is reversed, the judgment of the District Court is affirmed, and the cause is remanded to the District Court with directions to enter a decree which will guarantee that these petitioners will get the kind of education that is given in the State's public schools. And, if it becomes necessary to add new parties to accomplish this end, the District Court is free to do so. It is so ordered.

Judgment of Court of Appeals reversed, judgment of the District Court affirmed and cause remanded with directions.

GREEN *v.* COUNTY SCHOOL BOARD OF NEW KENT COUNTY, VA.
391 US 430 (1968)

[In New Kent County in rural Virginia, the school board set up a "freedom-of-choice" plan allowing each pupil to choose the public school he wished to attend. After three years, not a single white child had chosen to attend a former Negro school, which was still attended by 85% of all Negro children in the system. The Supreme Court held that the plan failed to meet the constitutional requirements for a realistic plan to desegregate the school system. Justice Brennan wrote the opinion for the unanimous Court.]

Mr. Justice Brennan delivered the opinion of the Court:

The question for decision is whether, under all the circumstances here, respondent School Board's adoption of a "freedom-of-choice" plan which allows a pupil to choose his own public school constitutes adequate compliance with the Board's responsibility "to achieve a system of determining admission to the public schools on a nonracial basis. . . ." *Brown* v. *Board of Education of Topeka,* 349 US 294 (*Brown II*).

Petitioners brought this action in March 1965 seeking injunctive relief against respondent's continued maintenance of an alleged racially segregated school system. New Kent County is a rural county in Eastern Virginia. About one-half of its population of some 4,500 are Negroes. There is no residential segregation in the county; persons of both races reside throughout. The school system has only two schools, the New Kent school on the east side of the county and the George W. Watkins school on the west side. In a memorandum filed May 17, 1966, the District Court found that the "school system serves approximately 1,300 pupils, of which 740 are Negro and 550 are white. The School Board operates one white combined elementary and high school [New Kent], and one Negro combined elementary and high school [George W. Watkins]. There are no attendance zones. Each school serves the entire county." The record indicates that 21 school buses—11 serving the Watkins school and 10 serving the New Kent school—travel overlapping routes throughout the county to transport pupils to and from the two schools.

The segregated system was initially established and maintained under the compulsion of Virginia constitutional and statutory provisions mandating racial segregation in public education, . . . These provisions were held to violate the Federal Constitution in *Davis* v. *County School Board of Prince Edward County,* decided with *Brown* v. *Board of Education of Topeka,* 347 US 483 (*Brown I*). The respondent School Board continued the segregated operation of the system after the *Brown* decisions, presumably on the authority of several statutes enacted by Virginia in resistance to those decisions. Some of these statutes were held to be unconstitutional on their face or as applied. One statute, the Pupil Placement Act, Va. Code, § 22–232.1 et seq. (1964), not repealed until 1966, divested local boards of authority to assign children to particular schools and placed that authority in a State Pupil Placement Board. Under that Act children were each year automatically reassigned to the school previously attended unless upon their application the State Board assigned them to another school; students seeking enrollment for the first time were also assigned at the discretion of the State Board. To September 1964, no Negro pupil had applied for admission to the New Kent school under this statute and no white pupil had applied for admission to the Watkins school.

The School Board initially sought dismissal of this suit on the ground that petitioners had failed to apply to the State Board for assignment to New Kent school. However on August 2, 1965, five months after the suit was brought, respondent School Board, in order to remain eligible for federal financial aid, adopted a "freedom-of-choice" plan for desegregating the schools.* Under that plan, each pupil may annually choose between the New Kent and Watkins schools and, except for the first and eighth grades, pupils not making a choice are assigned to the school previously attended; first and eighth grade pupils must affirmatively choose a school. After the plan was filed the District Court denied petitioner's prayer for an injunction and granted respondent leave to submit an amendment to the plan with respect to employment and assignment of teachers and staff on a racially nondiscriminatory basis. The amendment was duly filed and on June 28, 1966, the District Court approved the "freedom-of-choice" plan as so amended. The Court of Appeals for

---

* Congress, concerned with the lack of progress in school desegregation, included provisions in the Civil Rights Act of 1964 to deal with the problem through various agencies of the Federal Government. 42 U.S.C. §§ 2000c et seq., 2000d et seq., 2000h-2. In Title VI Congress declared that

"No person in the United States shall, on the ground of race, color, or national origin, be excluded from participation in, be denied the benefits of, or be subjected to discrimination under any program or activity receiving Federal financial assistance." 42 U.S.C. § 2000d.

The Department of Health, Education, and Welfare issued regulations covering racial discrimination in federally aided school systems, as directed by 42 U.S.C. § 2000d-1, and in a statement of policies, or "guidelines," the Department's Office of Education established standards according to which school systems in the process of desegregation can remain qualified for federal funds. 45 CFR §§ 80.1–80.13, 181.1–181.76 (1967). "Freedom-of-choice" plans are among those considered acceptable, so long as in operation such a plan proves effective. The regulations provide that a school system "subject to a final order of a court of the United States for the desegregation of such school . . . system" with which the system agrees to comply is deemed to be in compliance with the statute and regulations. . . .

the Fourth Circuit, en banc, affirmed the District Court's approval of the "freedom-of-choice" provisions of the plan but remanded the case to the District Court for entry of an order regarding faculty "which is much more specific and more comprehensive" and which would incorporate in addition to a "minimal, objective time table" some of the faculty provisions of the decree entered by the Court of Appeals for the Fifth Circuit in *United States* v. *Jefferson County Board of Education,* 372 F.2d 836, aff'd en banc, 380 F.2d 385 (1967). Judges Soboloff and Winter concurred with the remand on the teacher issue but otherwise disagreed, expressing the view "that the District Court should be directed . . . also to set up procedures for periodically evaluating the effectiveness of the [Board's] 'freedom of choice' [plan] in the elimination of other features of a segregated school system." We granted certiorari.

The pattern of separate "white" and "Negro" schools in the New Kent County school system established under compulsion of state laws is precisely the pattern of segregation to which *Brown I* and *Brown II* were particularly addressed, and which *Brown I* declared unconstitutionally denied Negro school children equal protection of the laws. Racial identification of the system's schools was complete, extending not just to the composition of student bodies at the two schools but to every facet of school operations—faculty, staff, transportation, extracurricular activities and facilities. In short, the State, acting through the local school board and school officials, organized and operated a dual system, part "white" and part "Negro."

It was such dual systems that 14 years ago *Brown I* held unconstitutional and a year later *Brown II* held must be abolished; school boards operating such school systems were *required* by *Brown II* "to effectuate a transition to a racially nondiscriminatory school system." It is of course true that for the time immediately after *Brown II* the concern was with making an initial break in a long-established pattern of excluding Negro children from schools attended by white children. The principal focus was on obtaining for those Negro children courageous enough to break with tradition a place in the "white" schools. . . . Under *Brown II* that immedaite goal was only the first step, however. The transition to a unitary, nonracial system of public education was and is the ultimate end to be brought about; it was because of the "complexities arising from the transition to a system of public education freed of racial discrimination" that we provided for "all deliberate speed" in the implementation of the principles of *Brown I.* Thus we recognized the task would necessarily involve solution of "varied local school problems." In referring to the "personal interest of the plaintiffs in admission to public schools as soon as practicable on a nondiscriminatory basis," we also noted that "[t]o effectuate this interest may call for elimination of a variety of obstacles in making the transition. . . ." Yet we emphasized that the constitutional rights of Negro children required school officials to bear the burden of establishing that additional time to carry out the ruling in an effective manner "is necessary in the public interest and is consistent with good faith compliance at the earliest practicable date." We charged the district courts in their review of particular situations to

consider problems related to administration, arising from the physical condition of the school plant, the school transportation system, personnel, revision of school districts and attendance areas into compact units to achieve a system of determining admission to the public schools on a nonracial basis, and revision of local laws and regulations which may be necessary in solving the foregoing problems. They will also consider the adequacy of any plans the defendants may propose to meet these problems and to effectuate a transition to a racially nondiscriminatory school system.

It is against this background that 13 years after *Brown II* commanded the abolition of dual systems we must measure the effectiveness of respondent School Board's "freedom-of-choice" plan to achieve that end. The School Board contends that it has fully discharged its obligation by adopting a plan by which every student, regardless of race, may "freely" choose the school he will attend. The Board attempts to cast the issue in its broadest form by arguing that its "freedom-of-choice" plan may be faulted only by reading the Fourteenth Amendment as universally requiring "compulsory integration," a reading it insists the wording of the Amendment will not support. But that argument ignores the thrust of *Brown II*. In the light of the command of that case, what is involved here is the question whether the Board has achieved the "racially nondiscriminatory school system" *Brown II* held must be effectuated in order to remedy the established unconstitutional deficiencies of its segregated system. In the context of the state-imposed segregated pattern of long standing, the fact that in 1965 the Board opened the doors of the former "white" school to Negro children and of the "Negro" school to white children merely begins, not ends, our inquiry whether the Board has taken steps adequate to abolish its dual, segregated system. *Brown II* was a call for the dismantling of well-entrenched dual systems tempered by an awareness that complex and multifaceted problems would arise which would require time and flexibility for a successful resolution. School boards such as the respondent then operating state-compelled dual systems were nevertheless clearly charged with the affirmative duty to take whatever steps might be necessary to convert to a unitary system in which racial discrimination would be eliminated root and branch. . . . The constitutional rights of Negro school children articulated in *Brown I* permit no less than this; and it was to this end that *Brown II* commanded school boards to bend their efforts.

In determining whether respondent School Board met that command by adopting its "freedom-of-choice" plan, it is relevant that this first step did not come until some 11 years after *Brown I* was decided and 10 years after *Brown II* directed the making of a "prompt and reasonable start." This deliberate perpetuation of the unconstitutional dual system can only have compounded the harm of such a system. Such delays are no longer tolerable, for "the governing constitutional principles no longer bear the imprint of newly enunciated doctrine." . . . Moreover, a plan that at this late date fails to provide meaningful assurance of prompt and effective disestablishment of a dual system is also intolerable. "The time for mere 'deliberate speed' has run out," . . . "the context in which we must interpret and apply this language [of *Brown II*] to plans for desegregation has been significantly altered." . . . The burden on a school board today is to come forward with a plan that promises realistically to work, and promises realistically to work *now*.

The obligation of the district courts, as it always has been, is to assess the effectiveness of a proposed plan in achieving desegregation. There is no universal answer to complex problems of desegregation; there is obviously no one plan that will do the job in every case. The matter must be assessed in light of the circumstances present and the options available in each instance. It is incumbent upon the school board to establish that its proposed plan promises meaningful and immediate progress toward disestablishing state-imposed segregation. It is incumbent upon the district court to weigh that claim in light of the facts at hand and in light of any alternatives which may be shown as feasible and more promising in their effectiveness. Where the court finds the board to be acting in good faith and the proposed plan to have real prospects for dismantling the state-imposed dual system "at the earliest practicable date," then the plan may be said to provide effective relief. Of course, where other, more promising courses of action are open to the board, that may indicate a lack of good faith; and at the least it places a heavy burden upon the board to explain its preference for an apparently less effective method. Moreover, whatever plan is adopted will require evaluation in practice, and the court should retain jurisdiction until it is clear that state-imposed segregation has been completely removed. . . .

We do not hold that "freedom of choice" can have no place in such a plan. We do not hold that a "freedom-of-choice" plan might of itself be unconstitutional, although that argument has been urged upon us. Rather, all we decide today is that in desegregating a dual system a plan utilizing "freedom of choice" is not an end in itself. As Judge Soboloff has put it,

"Freedom of choice" is not a sacred talisman; it is only a means to a constitutionally required end—the abolition of the system of segregation and its effects. If the means prove effective, it is acceptable, but if it fails to undo segregation, other means must be used to achieve this end. The school officials have the continuing duty to take whatever action may be necessary to create a "unitary, nonracial system." . . .

Although the general experience under "freedom of choice" to date has been such as to indicate its ineffectiveness as a tool of desegregation, there may well be instances in which it can serve as an effective device. Where it offers real promise of aiding a desegregation program to effectuate conversion of a state-imposed dual system to a unitary, nonracial system there might be no objection to allowing such a device to prove itself in operation. On the other hand, if there are reasonably available other ways, such for illustration as zoning, promising speedier and more effective conversion to a unitary, nonracial school system, "freedom of choice" must be held unacceptable.

The New Kent School Board's "freedom-of-choice" plan cannot be accepted as a sufficient step to "effectuate a transition" to a unitary system. In three years of operation not a single white child has chosen to attend Watkins school, and although 115 Negro children enrolled in New Kent school in 1967 (up from 35 in 1965 and 111 in 1966) 85% of the Negro children in the system still attend the all-Negro Watkins school. In other words, the school system remains a dual system. Rather than further the dismantling of the dual system, the plan has operated simply to burden children and their parents with a responsibility which *Brown II* placed squarely on the School Board. The Board must be required to formulate a new plan and, in light of other courses which appear open to the Board, such as zoning, fashion steps which promise realistically to convert promptly to a system without a "white" school and a "Negro" school, but just schools.

The judgment of the Court of Appeals is vacated insofar as it affirmed the District Court and the case is remanded to the District Court for further proceedings consistent with this opinion. It is so ordered.

SWANN *v.* CHARLOTTE-MECKLENBURG BOARD OF EDUCATION
402 US 1 (1971)

[In a series of cases involving school desegregation in the South, all decided on April 20, 1971, the Supreme Court removed what it unanimously found to be obstacles, interposed by laws or regulations, standing in the way of ending racial segregation that was rooted in a racially-oriented system imposed by state laws and customs. In this case the Court, in an opinion by Chief Justice Burger, held that in order to desegregate schools, a racial ratio may have a proper but very limited use as a starting point toward a remedy; that the Court must scrutinize one-race schools to assure that they are not the result of present or past discrimination; that transfer provisions must include free transportation; that the principle of neighborhood schools must not be used to sustain a discriminatory system; that the pairing of noncontiguous school zones is a permissible tool.]

Mr. Chief Justice Burger delivered the opinion of the Court:

We granted certiorari in this case to review important issues as to the duties of school authorities and the scope of powers of federal courts under this Court's mandates to eliminate racially separate public schools established and maintained by state action. *Brown* v. *Board of Education.*

This case and those argued with it arose in states having a long history of maintaining two sets of schools in a single school system deliberately operated to carry out a governmental policy to separate pupils in schools solely on the basis of race. That was what *Brown* v. *Board of Education* was all about. These cases present us with the problem of defining in more precise terms than heretofore the scope of the duty of school authorities and district courts in implementing *Brown I* and the mandate to eliminate dual systems and establish unitary systems at once. Meanwhile district courts and courts of appeals have struggled in hundreds of cases with a multitude and variety of problems under this Court's general directive. Understandably, in an area of evolving remedies, those courts had to improvise and experiment without detailed or specific guidelines. This Court, in *Brown I,* appropriately dealt with the large constitutional principles; other federal courts had to grapple with the flinty, intractable realities of day-to-day implementation of those constitutional commands. Their efforts, of necessity, embraced a process of "trial and error," and our effort to formulate guidelines must take into account their experience.

I

The Charlotte-Mecklenburg school system, the 43rd largest in the Nation, encompasses the city of Charlotte and surrounding Mecklenburg County, North Carolina. The area is large—550 square miles—spanning roughly 22 miles east-west and 36 miles north-south. During the 1968–1969 school year the system served more than 84,000 pupils in 107 schools. Approximately 71% of the pupils were found to be white and 29% Negro. As of June 1969 there were approximately 24,000 Negro students in the system, of whom 21,000 attended schools within the city of Charlotte. Two-thirds of those 21,000—approximately 14,000 Negro students—attended 21 schools which were either totally Negro or more than 99% Negro.

This situation came about under a desegregation plan approved by the District Court at the commencement of the present litigation in 1965, based upon geographic zoning with a free transfer provision. The present proceedings were initiated in September 1968 by Petitioner Swann's motion for further relief based on *Green* v. *County School Board,* 391 US 430 (1968), and its companion cases. All parties now agree that in 1969 the system fell short of achieving the unitary school system that those cases require.

The District Court held numerous hearings and received voluminous evidence. In addition to finding certain actions of the school board to be discriminatory, the court also found that residential patterns in the city and county resulted in part from federal, state, and local government action other than school board decisions. School board action based on these patterns, for example, by locating schools in Negro residential areas and fixing the size of the schools to accommodate the needs of immediate neighborhoods, resulted in segregated education. These findings were subsequently accepted by the Court of Appeals.

In April 1969 the District Court ordered the school board to come forward with a plan for both faculty and student desegregation. Proposed plans were accepted by the court in June and August 1969 on an interim basis only, and the board was ordered to file a third plan by November 1969. In November the board moved for an extension of time until February 1970, but when that was denied the board submitted a partially completed plan. In December 1969 the District Court held that the board's submission was unacceptable and appointed an expert in education administration, Dr. John Finger, to prepare a desegregation plan. Thereafter in February 1970, the District Court was presented with two alternative pupil assignment plans—the finalized "board plan" and the "Finger plan."

The Board Plan. As finally submitted, the school board plan closed seven schools and reassigned their pupils. It restructured school attendance zones to achieve greater racial balance but maintained existing grade structures and rejected techniques such as pairing and clustering as part of a desegregation effort. The plan created a single athletic league, eliminated the previously racial basis of the school bus system, provided racially mixed faculties and administrative staffs, and modified its free transfer plan into an optional majority-to-minority transfer system.

The board plan proposed substantial assignment of Negroes to nine of the system's 10 high schools, producing 17% to 36% Negro population in each. The projected Negro attendance at the 10th school, Independence, was 2%. The proposed attendance zones for the high schools were typically shaped like wedges of a pie, extending outward from the center of the city to the suburban and rural areas of the county in order to afford residents of the center city area access to outlying schools.

As for junior high schools, the board plan rezoned the 21 school areas so that in 20 the Negro attendance would range from 0% to 38%. The other school, located in the heart of the Negro residential area, was left with an enrollment of 90% Negro.

The board plan with respect to elementary schools relied entirely upon gerrymandering of geographic zones. More than half of the Negro elementary pupils were left in nine schools that were 86% to 100% Negro; approximately half of the white elementary pupils were assigned to schools 86% and 100% white.

The Finger Plan. The plan submitted by the court-appointed expert, Dr. Finger, adopted the school board zoning plan for senior high schools with one modification: it required that an additional 300 Negro students be transported from the Negro residential area of the city to the nearly all-white Independence High School.

The Finger plan for the junior high schools employed much of the rezoning plan of the board, combined with the creation of nine "satellite" zones. Under the satellite plan, inner-city Negro students were assigned by attendance zones to nine outlying predominately white junior high schools, thereby substantially desegregating every junior high school in the system.

The Finger plan departed from the board plan chiefly in its handling of the system's 76 elementary schools. Rather than relying solely upon geographic zoning, Dr. Finger proposed use of zoning, pairing, and grouping techniques, with the result that student bodies throughout the system would range from 9% to 38% Negro.

The District Court described the plan thus:

Like the Board plan, the Finger plan does as much by rezoning school attendance lines as can reasonably be accomplished. However, unlike the board plan, it does not stop there. It goes further and desegregates all the rest of the elementary schools by the technique of grouping two or three outlying schools with one black inner city school; by transporting black students from grades one through four to the outlying white schools; and by transporting white students from the fifth and sixth grades from the outlying white schools to the inner city black school.

Under the Finger plan, nine inner-city Negro schools were grouped in this manner with 24 suburban white schools.

On February 5, 1970, the District Court adopted the board plan, as modified by Dr. Finger, for the junior and senior high schools. The court rejected the board elementary school plan and adopted the Finger plan as presented. . . .

On appeal the Court of Appeals affirmed the District Court's order as to faculty desegregation and the secondary school plans, but vacated the order respecting elementary schools. While agreeing that the District Court properly disapproved the board plan concerning these schools, the Court of Appeals feared that the pairing and grouping of elementary schools would place an unreasonable burden on the board and the system's pupils. The case was remanded to the District Court for reconsideration and submission of further plans. This Court granted certiorari and directed reinstatement of the District Court's order pending further proceedings in that court.

On remand the District Court received two new plans for the elementary schools: a plan prepared by the United States Department of Health, Education, and Welfare (the HEW plan) based on contiguous grouping and zoning of schools, and a plan prepared by four members of the nine-member school board (the minority plan) achieving substantially the same results as the Finger plan but apparently with slightly less transportation. A majority of the school board declined to amend its proposal. After a lengthy evidentiary hearing the District Court concluded that its own plan (the Finger plan), the minority plan, and an earlier draft of the Finger plan were all reasonable and acceptable. It directed the board to adopt one of the three or in the alternative to come forward with a new, equally effective plan of its own; the court ordered that the Finger plan would remain in effect in the event the school board declined to adopt a new plan. On August 7, the board indicated it would "acquiesce" in the Finger plan, reiterating its view that the plan was unreasonable. The District Court, by order dated August 7, 1970, directed that the Finger plan remain in effect.

II

Nearly 17 years ago this Court held, in explicit terms, that state-imposed segregation by race in public schools denies equal protection of the laws. At no time has the Court deviated in the slightest degree from that holding or its constitutional underpinnings. None of the parties before us challenges the Court's decision of May 17, 1954, that

in the field of public education the doctrine of "separate but equal" has no place. Separate educational facilities are inherently unequal. Therefore, we hold that the plaintiffs and others similarly situated . . . are, by reason of the segregation complained of, deprived of the equal protection of the laws guaranteed by the Fourteenth Amendment. . . .

Because these are class actions, because of the wide applicability of this decision, and because of the great variety of local conditions, the formulation of decrees in these cases presents problems of considerable complexity. *Brown* v. *Board of Education.*

None of the parties before us questions the Court's 1955 holding in *Brown II,* that

[s]chool authorities have the primary responsibility for elucidating, assessing, and solving these problems; courts will have to consider whether the action of school authorities constitutes good faith implementation of the governing constitutional principles. Because of their proximity to local conditions and the possible need for further hearings, the courts which originally heard these cases can best perform this judicial appraisal. Accordingly, we believe it appropriate to remand the cases to those courts.

In fashioning and effectuating the decrees, the courts will be guided by equitable principles. Traditionally, equity has been characterized by a practical flexibility in shaping its remedies and by a facility for adjusting and reconciling public and private needs. These cases call for the exercise of these traditional attributes of equity power. At stake is the personal interest of the plaintiffs in admission to public schools as soon as practicable on a nondiscriminatory basis. To effectuate this interest may call for elimination of a variety of obstacles in making the transition to school systems operated in accordance with the constitutional principles set forth in our May 17, 1954, decision. Courts of equity may properly take into account the public interest in the elimination of such obstacles in a systematic and effective manner. But it should go without saying that the vitality of these constitutional principles cannot be allowed to yield simply because of disagreement with them. *Brown* v. *Board of Education,* 349 US 294.

Over the 15 years since *Brown II,* many difficulties were encountered in implementation of the basic constitutional requirement that the State not discriminate between public school children on the basis of their race. Nothing in our national experience prior to 1955 prepared anyone for dealing with changes and adjustments of the magnitude and complexity encountered since then. Deliberate resistance of some to the Court's mandates has impeded the good-faith efforts of others to bring school systems into compliance. The detail and nature of these dilatory tactics have been noted frequently by this Court and other courts.

By the time the Court considered *Green* v. *County School Board,* 391 US 430, in 1968, very little progress had been made in many areas where dual school systems had historically been maintained by operation of state laws. In *Green,* the Court was confronted with a record of a freedom-of-choice program that the District Court had found to operate in fact to preserve a dual system more than a decade after *Brown II.* While acknowledging that a freedom-of-choice concept could be a valid remedial measure in some circumstances, its failure to be effective in *Green* required that

The burden on a school board today is to come forward with a plan that promises realistically to work . . . *now* . . . until it is clear that state-imposed segregation has been completely removed.

This was plain language, yet the 1969 Term of Court brought fresh evidence of the dilatory tactics of many school authorities. *Alexander* v. *Holmes County Board of Education,* 396 US 19, restated the basic obligation asserted in *Griffin* v. *School Board,* 377 US 218 (1964), and *Green, supra,* that the remedy must be implemented *forthwith.*

The problems encountered by the district courts and courts of appeals make plain that we should now try to amplify guidelines, however incomplete and imperfect, for the assistance of school authorities and courts.* The failure of local authorities to meet their constitutional obligations aggravated the massive problem of converting from the state-enforced discrimination of racially separate school systems. This process has been rendered more difficult by changes since 1954 in the structure and patterns of communities, the growth of student population,† movement of families, and other changes, some of which had marked impact on school planning, sometimes neutralizing or negating remedial action before it was fully implemented. Rural areas accustomed for half a century to the consolidated school systems implemented by bus transportation could make adjustments more readily than metropolitan areas with dense and shifting population, numerous schools, congested and complex traffic patterns.

---

* The necessity for this is suggested by the situation in the Fifth Circuit where 166 appeals in school desegregation cases were heard between December 2, 1969, and September 24, 1970.

† Elementary public school population (grades 1–6) grew from 17,447,000 in 1954 to 23,103,000 in 1969; secondary school population grew from 11,183,000 in 1954 to 20,775,000 in 1969. . . .

III

The objective today remains to eliminate from the public schools all vestiges of state-imposed segregation. Segregation was the evil struck down by *Brown I* as contrary to the equal protection guarantees of the Constitution. That was the violation sought to be corrected by the remedial measures of *Brown II*. That was the basis for the holding in *Green* that school authorities are "clearly charged with the affirmative duty to take whatever steps might be necessary to convert to a unitary system in which racial discrimination would be eliminated root and branch."

If school authorities fail in their affirmative obligations under these holdings, judicial authority may be invoked. Once a right and a violation have been shown, the scope of a district court's equitable powers to remedy past wrongs is broad, for breadth and flexibility are inherent in equitable remedies. . . .

In seeking to define even in broad and general terms how far this remedial power extends it is important to remember that judicial powers may be exercised only on the basis of a constitutional violation. Remedial judicial authority does not put judges automatically in the shoes of school authorities whose powers are plenary. Judicial authority enters only when local authority defaults.

School authorities are traditionally charged with broad power to formulate and implement educational policy and might well conclude, for example, that in order to prepare students to live in a pluralistic society each school should have a prescribed ratio of Negro to white students reflecting the proportion for the district as a whole. To do this as an educational policy is within the broad discretionary powers of school authorities; absent a finding of a constitutional violation, however, that would not be within the authority of a federal court. As with any equity case, the nature of the violation determines the scope of the remedy. In default by the school authorities of their obligation to proffer acceptable remedies, a district court has broad power to fashion a remedy that will assure a unitary school system.

The school authorities argue that the equity powers of federal district courts have been limited by Title IV of the Civil Rights Act of 1964, 42 U.S.C. § 2000c. The language and the history of Title IV shows that it was not enacted to limit but to define the role of the Federal Government in the implimentation of the *Brown I* decision. It authorizes the Commissioner of Education to provide technical assistance to local boards in the preparation of desegregation plans, to arrange "training institutes" for school personnel involved in desegregation efforts, and to make grants directly to schools to ease the transition to unitary systems. It also authorizes the Attorney General, in specified circumstances, to initiate federal desegregation suits, Section 2000c(b) defines "desegregation" as it is used in Title IV:

"Desegregation" means the assignment of students to public schools and within such schools without regard to their race, color, religion, or national origin, but "desegregation" shall not mean the assignment of students to public schools in order to overcome racial imbalance.

Section 2000c–6, authorizing the Attorney General to institute federal suits, contains the following proviso:

nothing herein shall empower any official or court of the United States to issue any order seeking to achieve a racial balance in any school by requiring the transportation of pupils or students from one school to another or one school district to another in order to achieve such racial balance, or otherwise enlarge the existing power of the court to insure compliance with constitutional standards.

On their face, the sections quoted purport only to insure that the provisions of Title IV of the Civil Rights Act of 1964 will not be read as granting new powers. The proviso in § 2000c–6 is in terms designed to foreclose any interpretation of the Act as expanding the *existing* powers of federal courts to enforce the Equal Protection Clause. There is no suggestion of an intention to restrict those powers or withdraw from courts their historic equitable remedial powers. The legislative history of Title IV indicates that Congress was concerned that the Act might be read as creating a right of action under the Fourteenth Amendment in the situation of so-called "de facto segregation," where racial imbalance exists in the schools but with no showing that this was brought about by discriminatory action of state authorities. In short, there is nothing in the Act which provides us material assistance in answering the question of remedy for state-imposed segregation in violation of *Brown I.* The basis of our decision must be the prohibition of the Fourteenth Amendment that no State shall "deny to any person within its jurisdiction the equal protection of the laws."

IV

We turn now to the problem of defining with more particularity the responsibilities of school authorities in desegregating a state-enforced dual school system in light of the Equal Protection Clause. Although the several related cases before us are primarily concerned with problems of student assignment, it may be helpful to begin with a brief discussion of other aspects of the process.

In *Green,* we pointed out that existing policy and practice with regard to faculty, staff, transportation, extracurricular activities, and facilities were among the most important indicia of a segregated system. Independent of student assignment, where it is possible to identify a "white school" or a "Negro school" simply by reference to the racial composition of teachers and staff, the quality of school buildings and equipment, or the organization of sports activities, a *prima facie* case of violation of substantive constitutional rights under the Equal Protection Clause is shown.

When a system has been dual in these respects, the first remedial responsibility of school authorities is to eliminate invidious racial distinctions. With respect to such matters as transportation, supporting personnel, and extracurricular activities, no more than this may be necessary. Similar corrective action must be taken with regard to the maintenance of buildings and the distribution of equipment. In these areas, normal administrative practice should produce schools of like quality, facilities, and staffs. Something more must be said, however, as to faculty assignment and new school construction.

In the companion *Davis* case, the Mobile school board has argued that the Constitution requires that teachers be assigned on a "color blind" basis. It also argues that the Constitution prohibits district courts from using their equity power to order assignment of teachers to achieve a particular degree of faculty desegregation. We reject that contention.

In *United States* v. *Montgomery County Board of Education,* 395 US 225 (1969), the District Court set as a goal a plan of faculty assignment in each school with a ratio of white to Negro faculty members substantially the same throughout the system. This order was predicated on the District Court finding that

The evidence does not reflect any real administrative problems involved in immediately desegregating the substitute teachers, the student teachers, the night school faculties, and in the evolvement of a really legally adequate program for the substantial desegregation of the faculties of all schools in the system commencing with the school year 1968–69.

The District Court in *Montgomery* then proceeded to set an initial ratio for the whole system of at least two Negro teachers out of each 12 in any given school. The Court of Appeals modified the order by eliminating what it regarded as "fixed mathematical ratios" of faculty and substituted an initial requirement of "substantially or approximately" a five-to-one ratio. With respect to the future, the Court of Appeals held that the numerical ratio should be eliminated and that compliance should not be tested solely by the achievement of specified proportions.

We reversed the Court of Appeals and restored the District Court's order in its entirety, holding that the order of the District Judge

was adopted in the spirit of this Court's opinion in *Green* . . . in that his plan "promises realistically to work, and promises realistically to work *now.*" The modifications ordered by the panel of the Court of Appeals, while of course not intended to do so, would, we think, take from the order some of its capacity to expedite, by means of specific commands, the day when a completely unified, unitary, nondiscriminatory school system becomes a reality instead of a hope. . . . We also believe that under all the circumstances of this case we follow the original plan outlined in *Brown II* . . . by accepting the more specific and expeditious order of [District] Judge Johnson. . . .

The principles of *Montgomery* have been properly followed by the District Court and the Court of Appeals in this case.

The construction of new schools and the closing of old ones is one of the most important functions of local school authorities and also one of the most complex. They must decide questions of location and capacity in light of population growth, finances, land values, site availability, through an almost endless list of factors to be considered. The result of this will be a decision which, when combined with one technique or another of student assignment, will determine the racial composition of the student body in each school in the system. Over the long run, the consequences of the choices will be far reaching. People gravitate toward school facilities, just as schools are located in response to the needs of people. The location of schools may thus influence the patterns of residential development of a metropolitan area and have important impact on composition of inner city neighborhoods.

In the past, choices in this respect have been used as a potent weapon for creating or maintaining a state-segregated school system. In addition to the classic pattern of building schools specifically intended for Negro or white students, school authorities have sometimes, since *Brown,* closed schools which appeared likely to become racially mixed through changes in neighborhood residential patterns. This was sometimes accompanied by building new schools in the areas of white suburban expansion farthest from Negro population centers in order to maintain the separation of the races with a minimum departure from the formal principles of "neighborhood zoning." Such a policy does more than simply influence the short-run composition of the student body of a new school. It may well promote segregated residential patterns which, when combined with "neighborhood zoning," further lock the school system into the mold of separation of the races. Upon a proper showing a district court may consider this in fashioning a remedy.

In ascertaining the existence of legally imposed school segregation, the existence of a pattern of school construction and abandonment is thus a factor of great weight. In devising remedies where legally imposed segregation has been established, it is the responsibility of local authorities and district courts to see to it that future school construction and abandonment is not used and does not serve to perpetuate or re-establish the dual system. When necessary, district courts should retain jurisdiction to assure that these responsibilities are carried out. . . .

V

The central issue in this case is that of student assignment, and there are essentially four problem areas:

(1) to what extent racial balance or racial quotas may be used as an implement in a remedial order to correct a previously segregated system;

(2) whether every all-Negro and all-white school must be eliminated as an indispensable part of a remedial process of desegregation;

(3) what are the limits, if any, on the rearrangement of school districts and attendance zones, as a remedial measure; and

(4) what are the limits, if any, on the use of transportation facilities to correct state-enforced racial school segregation.

(1) *Racial Balances or Racial Quotas*

The constant theme and thrust of every holding from *Brown I* to date is that state-enforced separation of races in public schools is discrimination that violates the Equal Protection Clause. The remedy commanded was to dismantle dual school systems.

We are concerned in these cases with the elimination of the discrimination inherent in the dual school systems, not with myriad factors of human existence which can cause discrimination in a multitude of ways on racial, religious, or ethnic grounds. The target of the cases from *Brown I* to the present was the dual school system. The elimination of racial discrimination in public schools is a large task and one that should not be retarded by efforts to achieve broader purposes lying beyond the jurisdiction of school authorities. One vehicle can carry only a limited amount of baggage. It would not serve the important objective of *Brown I* to seek to use school desegregation cases for purposes beyond their scope, although desegregation of schools ultimately will have impact on other forms of discrimination. We do not reach in this case the question whether a showing that school segregation is a consequence of other types of state action, without any discriminatory action by the school authorities, is a constitutional violation requiring remedial action by a school desegregation decree. This case does not present that question and we therefore do not decide it.

Our objective in dealing with the issues presented by these cases is to see that school authorities exclude no pupil of a racial minority from any school, directly or indirectly, on account of race; it does not and cannot embrace all the problems of racial prejudice, even when those problems contribute to disproportionate racial concentrations in some schools.

In this case it is urged that the District Court has imposed a racial balance requirement of 71%–29% on individual schools. The fact that no such objective was actually achieved—and would appear to be impossible—tends to blunt that claim, yet in the opinion and order of the District Court of December 1, 1969, we find that court directing:

> that efforts should be made to reach a 71–29 ratio in the various schools so that there will be no basis for contending that one school is racially different from the others . . . , that no school [should] be operated with an all-black or predominantly black student body, [and] that pupils of all grades [should] be assigned in such a way that as nearly as practicable the various schools at various grade levels have about the same proportion of black and white students.

The District Judge went on to acknowledge that variation "from that norm may be unavoidable." This contains intimations that the "norm" is a fixed mathematical racial balance reflecting the pupil constituency of the system. If we were to read the holding of the District Court to require, as a matter of substantive constitutional right, any particular degree of racial balance or mixing, that approach would be disapproved and we would be obliged to reverse. The constitutional command to desegregate schools does not mean that every school in every community must always reflect the racial composition of the school system as a whole.

As the voluminous record in this case shows, the predicate for the District Court's use of the 71%–29% ratio was twofold: first, its express finding, approved by the Court of Appeals and not challenged here, that a dual school system had been maintained by the school authorities at least until 1969; second, its finding, also approved by the Court of Appeals, that the school board had totally defaulted in its acknowledged duty to come forward with an acceptable plan of its own, notwithstanding the patient efforts of the District Judge who, on at least three occasions, urged the board to submit plans. As the statement of facts shows, these findings are abundantly supported by the record. It was because of this total failure of the school board that the District Court was obliged to turn to other qualified sources, and Dr. Finger was designated to assist the District Court to do what the board should have done.

We see therefore that the use made of mathematical ratios was no more than a starting point in the process of shaping a remedy, rather than an inflexible requirement. From that starting point the District Court proceeded to frame a decree that was within its discretionary powers, an equitable remedy for the particular circumstances. As we said in *Green,* a school authority's remedial plan or a district court's remedial decree is to be judged by its effectiveness. Awareness of the racial composition of the whole school system is likely to be a useful starting point in shaping a remedy to correct past constitutional violations. In sum, the very limited use made of mathematical ratios was within the equitable remedial discretion of the District Court.

(2) *One-Race Schools*

The record in this case reveals the familiar phenomenon that in metropolitan areas minority groups are often found concentrated in one part of the city. In some circumstances certain schools may remain all or largely of one race until new schools can be provided or neighborhood patterns change. Schools all or predominately of one race in a district of mixed population will require close scrutiny to determine that school assignments are not part of state-enforced segregation.

In light of the above, it should be clear that the existence of some small number of one-race, or virtually one-race, schools within a district is not in and of itself the mark of a system which still practices segregation by law. The district judge or school authorities should make every effort to achieve the greatest possible degree of actual desegregation and will thus necessarily be concerned with the elimination of one-race schools. No *per se* rule can adequately embrace all of the difficulties of reconciling the competing interests involved; but in a system with a history of segregation the need for remedial criteria of sufficient specificity to assure a school authority's compliance with its constitutional duty warrants a presumption against schools that are substantially disproportionate in their racial composition. Where the school authority's proposed plan for conversion from a dual to a unitary system contemplates the continued existence of some schools that are all or predominately of one race, they have the burden of showing that such school assignments are genuinely nondiscriminatory. The court should scrutinize such schools, and the burden upon the school authorities will be to satisfy the court that their racial composition is not the result of present or past discriminatory action on their part.

An optional majority-to-minority transfer provision has long been recognized as a useful part of every desegregation plan. Provision for optional transfer of those in the majority racial group of a particular school to other schools where they will be in the minority is an indispensable remedy for those students willing to transfer to other schools in order to lessen the impact on them of the state-imposed stigma of segregation. In order to be effective, such a transfer arrangement must grant the transferring student free transportation and space must be made available in the school to which he desires to move. . . .

(3) *Remedial Altering of Attendance Zones*

The maps submitted in these cases graphically demonstrate that one of the principal tools employed by school planners and by courts to break up the dual school system has been a frank—and sometimes drastic—gerrymandering of school districts and attendance zones. An additional step was pairing, "clustering," or "grouping" of schools with attendance assignments made deliberately to accomplish the transfer of Negro students out of formerly segregated Negro schools and transfer of white students to formerly all-Negro schools. More often than not, these zones are neither compact nor contiguous; indeed they may be on opposite ends of the city. As an interim corrective measure, this cannot be said to be beyond the broad remedial powers of a court.

Absent a constitutional violation there would be no basis for judicially ordering assignment of students on a racial basis. All things being equal, with no history of discrimination, it might well be desirable to assign pupils to schools nearest their homes. But all things are not equal in a system that has been deliberately constructed and maintained to enforce racial segregation. The remedy for such segregation may be administratively awkward, inconvenient, and even bizarre in some situations and may impose burdens on some; but all awkwardness and inconvenience cannot be avoided in the interim period when remedial adjustments are being made to eliminate the dual school systems.

No fixed or even substantially fixed guidelines can be established as to how far a court can go, but it must be recognized that there are limits. The objective is to dismantle the dual school system. "Racially neutral" assignment plans proposed by school authorities to a district court may be inadequate; such plans may fail to counteract the continuing effects of past school segregation resulting from discriminatory location of school sites or distortion of school size in order to achieve or maintain an artificial racial separation. When school authorities present a district court with a "loaded game board," affirmative action in the form of remedial altering of attendance zones is proper to achieve truly nondiscriminatory assignments. In short, an assignment plan is not acceptable simply because it appears to be neutral.

In this area, we must of necessity rely to a large extent, as this Court has for more than 16 years, on the informed judgment of the district courts in the first instance and on courts of appeals.

We hold that the pairing and grouping of noncontiguous school zones is a permissible tool and such action is to be considered in light of the objectives sought. Judicial steps in shaping such zones going beyond combinations of contiguous areas should be examined in light of what is said in subdivisions (1), (2), and (3) of this opinion concerning the objectives to be sought. Maps do not tell the whole story since noncontiguous school zones may be more accessible to each other in terms of the critical travel time, because of traffic patterns and good highways, than schools geographically closer together. Conditions in different localities will vary so widely that no rigid rules can be laid down to govern all situations.

(4) *Transportation of Students*

The scope of permissible transportation of students as an implement of a remedial decree has never been defined by this Court and by the very nature of the problem it cannot be defined with precision. No rigid guidelines as to student transportation can be given for application to the infinite variety of problems presented in thousands of situations. Bus transportation has been an integral part of the public education system for years, and was perhaps the single most important factor in the transition from the one-room schoolhouse to the consolidated school. Eighteen million of the nation's public school children, approximately 39%, were transported to their schools by bus in 1969–1970 in all parts of the country.

The importance of bus transportation as a normal and accepted tool of educational policy is readily discernible in this and the companion case.* The Charlotte school authorities did not purport to assign students on the basis of geographically drawn zones until 1965 and then they allowed almost unlimited transfer privileges. The District Court's conclusion that assignment of children to the school nearest their home serving their grade would not produce an effective dismantling of the dual system is supported by the record.

Thus the remedial techniques used in the District Court's order were within that court's power to provide equitable relief; implementation of the decree is well within the capacity of the school authority.

The decree provided that the buses used to implement the plan would operate on direct routes. Students would be picked up at schools near their homes and transported to the schools they were to attend. The trips for elementary school pupils average about seven miles and the District Court found that they would take "not over 35 minutes at the most." This system compares favorably with the transportation plan previously operated in Charlotte under which each day 23,600 students on all grade levels were transported an average of 15 miles one way for an average trip requiring over an hour. In these circumstances, we find no basis for holding that the local school authorities may not be required to employ bus transportation as one tool of school desegregation. Desegregation plans cannot be limited to the walk-in school.

An objection to transportation of students may have validity when the time or distance of travel is so great as to risk either the health of the children or significantly impinge on the educational process. District courts must weigh the soundness of any transportation plan in light of what is said in subdivisions (1), (2), and (3) above. It hardly needs stating that the limits on time of travel will vary with many factors, but probably with none more than the age of the students. The reconcilation of competing values in a desegregation case is, of course, a difficult task with many sensitive facets but fundamentally no more so than remedial measures courts of equity have traditionally employed.

VI

The Court of Appeals, searching for a term to define the equitable remedial power of the district courts, used the term "reasonableness." In *Green, supra,* this Court used the term "feasible" and by implication, "workable," "effective," and "realistic" in the mandate to develop "a plan that promises realistically to work, and . . . to work *now.*" On the facts of this case, we are unable to conclude that the order of the District Court is not reasonable, feasible, and workable. However, in seeking to define the scope of remedial power or the limits on remedial power of courts in an area as sensitive as we deal with here, words are poor instruments to

* During 1967–1968, for example, the Mobile board used 207 buses to transport 22,094 students daily for an average round trip of 31 miles. During 1966–1967, 7,116 students in the metropolitan area were bussed daily. In Charlotte-Mecklenburg, the system as a whole, without regard to desegregation plans, planned to bus approximately 23,000 students this year, for an average daily round trip of 15 miles. More elementary school children than high school children were to be bussed, and four- and five-year-olds travel the longest routes in the system.

convey the sense of basic fairness inherent in equity. Substance, not semantics, must govern, and we have sought to suggest the nature of limitations without frustrating the appropriate scope of equity.

At some point, these school authorities and others like them should have achieved full compliance with this Court's decision in *Brown I*. The systems will then be "unitary" in the sense required by our decisions in *Green* and *Alexander*.

It does not follow that the communities served by such systems will remain demographically stable, for in a growing, mobile society, few will do so. Neither school authorities nor district courts are constitutionally required to make year-by-year adjustments of the racial composition of student bodies once the affirmative duty to desegregate has been accomplished and racial discrimination through official action is eliminated from the system. This does not mean that federal courts are without power to deal with future problems; but in the absence of a showing that either the school authorities or some other agency of the State has deliberately attempted to fix or alter demographic patterns to affect the racial composition of the schools, further intervention by a district court should not be necessary.

For reasons herein set forth, the judgment of the Court of Appeals is affirmed as to those parts in which it affirmed the judgment of the District Court. The order of the District Court dated August 7, 1970, is also affirmed.

DAVIS *v.* BOARD OF SCHOOL COMMISSIONERS OF MOBILE COUNTY
402 US 33 (1971)

[This case was decided on the same day as the *Swann* case, *supra*. In the instant case the Supreme Court disapproved a school desegregation plan that gave inadequate consideration to busing and the restructuring of school zones. Chief Justice Burger's opinion was for a unanimous Court.]

Mr. Chief Justice Burger delivered the opinion of the Court:

Petitioners in this case challenge as inadequate a school desegregation plan for Mobile County, Alabama. The county is large and populous, embracing 1,248 square miles and the City of Mobile. The school system had 73,500 pupils in 91 schools at the beginning of the 1969 academic year; approximately 58% of the pupils were white and 42% Negro. During the 1967–1968 school year, the system transported 22,000 pupils daily in over 200 school buses, both in the rural areas of the county and in the outlying areas of metropolitan Mobile.

The present desegregation plan evolved from one developed by the District Court in response to the decision of the Court of Appeals for the Fifth Circuit . . . that an earlier desegregation plan formulated by the District Court on the basis of unified geographic zones was "constitutionally insufficient and unacceptable, and such zones must be redrawn." The Court of Appeals held that that earlier plan had "ignored the unequivocal directive to make a conscious effort in locating attendance zones to desegregate and eliminate past segregation."

The District Court responded with a new zoning plan which left 18,623, or 60%, of the system's 30,800 Negro children in 19 all-Negro or nearly all-Negro schools. On appeal, the Court of Appeals reviewed all aspects of desegregation in Mobile County. Additional information was requested regarding earlier desegregation plans for the rural parts of the county, and those plans were approved. They are not before us now. The Court of Appeals concluded that with respect to faculty and staff desegregation the board had "almost totally failed to comply" with earlier orders, and directed the District Court to require the board to establish a faculty and staff ratio in each school "substantially the same" as that for the entire district. We affirm that part of the Court of Appeals' opinion for the reasons given in *Swann* v. *Charlotte-Mecklenburg Board of Education.*

Regarding junior and senior high schools, the Court of Appeals reversed the District Court and directed implementation of a plan which was intended to eliminate the seven all-Negro schools remaining under the District Court's scheme. This was to be achieved through pairing and adjusting grade structures within metropolitan Mobile, without bus transportation or split zoning. The Court of Appeals then turned to the difficult problem of desegregating the elementary schools of metropolitan Mobile. The metropolitan area is divided by a major north-south highway. About 94% of the Negro students in the metropolitan area live on the east side of the highway between it and the Mobile River. The schools on that side of the highway are 65% Negro and 35% white. On the west side of the highway, however, the schools are 12% Negro and 88% white. Under the District Court's elementary school plan for the metropolitan area, the eastern and western sections were treated as distinct, without either interlocking zones or transportation across the highway. Not surprisingly, it was easy to desegregate the western section, but in the east the District Court left 12 all-Negro or nearly all-Negro elementary schools, serving over 90% of all the Negro elementary students in the metropolitan area.

The Court of Appeals rejected this solution in favor of a modified version of a plan submitted by the Department of Justice. As further modified after a second appeal, this plan reduced the number of all-Negro or nearly all-Negro elementary schools from 12 to six schools, projected to serve 5,310 students, or about 50% of the Negro elementary students in the metropolitan area. Like the District Court's plan, the Court of Appeals' plan was based on treating the western section in isolation from the eastern. There were unified geographic zones, and no transportation of students for purposes of desegregation. The reduction in the number of all-Negro schools was achieved through pairing, rezoning, and adjusting grade structures within the eastern section. With yet further modifications not material here, this plan went into effect at the beginning of the 1970–1971 school year.

The enrollment figures for the 1970–1971 school year show that the projections on which the Court of Appeals based its plan for metropolitan Mobile were inaccurate. Under the Court of Appeals' plan as actually implemented, nine elementary schools in the eastern section of metropolitan Mobile were over 90% Negro as of September 21, 1970 (instead of six as projected), and they housed 7,651 students, or 64% of all the Negro elementary school pupils in the metropolitan area. Moreover, the enrollment figures indicate that 6,746 Negro junior and senior high school students in metropolitan Mobile, or over half, were then attending all-Negro or nearly all-Negro schools, rather than none as projected by the Court of Appeals. These figures are derived from a report of the school board to the District Court; they were brought to our attention in a supplemental brief for petitioners filed on October 10, 1970, and have not been challenged by respondents.

As we have held, "neighborhood school zoning," whether based strictly on home-to-school distance or on "unified geographic zones" is not the only constitutionally permissible remedy; nor is it *per se* adequate to meet the remedial responsibilities of local boards. Having once found a violation, the district judge or school authorities should make every effort to achieve the greatest possible degree of actual desegregation, taking into account the practicalities of the situation. A district court may and should consider the use of all available techniques including restructuring of attendance zones and both contiguous and noncontiguous attendance zones. . . . The measure of any desegregation plan is its effectiveness.

On the record before us, it is clear that the Court of Appeals felt constrained to treat the eastern part of metropolitan Mobile in isolation from the rest of the school system, and that inadequate consideration was given to the possible use of bus transportation and split zoning. For these reasons, we reverse the judgment of the Court of Appeals as to the parts dealing with student assignment, and remand the case for the development of a decree "that promises realistically to work, and promises realistically to work *now.*" *Green* v. *County School Board,* 391 US 430 (1968).

NORTH CAROLINA STATE BOARD OF EDUCATION *v.* SWANN
402 US 43 (1971)

[This is the third school desegregation case decided by the Supreme Court on April 20, 1971, and is to be considered together with *Swann* v. *Charlotte-Mecklenburg Board of Education* and *Davis* v. *Board of School Commissioners, supra.* In the instant case the Court declared unconstitutional the North Carolina Anti-Busing Law. Chief Justice Burger's opinion was for a unanimous Court.]

Mr. Chief Justice Burger delivered the opinion of the Court:

This case is here on direct appeal pursuant to 28 U.S.C. § 1253 from the judgment of a three-judge court in the United States District Court for the Western District of North Carolina. The District Court declared unconstitutional a portion of the North Carolina General Statutes known as the Anti-Busing Law,* and granted an injunction against its enforcement. The proceeding before the three-judge court was an ancillary proceeding connected with the school desegregation case heretofore discussed, *Swann* v. *Charlotte-Mecklenburg, supra.* The instant appeal was taken by the North Carolina State Board of Education and four state officials. We granted the Charlotte-Mecklenburg School Board's motion to join in the appeal, 400 US 804 (1970).

When the litigation in the *Swann* case recommenced in the spring of 1969, the District Court specifically directed that the school board consider altering attendance areas, pairing or consolidation of schools, bus transportation of students, and any other method which would effectuate a racially unitary system. That litigation was actively prosecuted. The board submitted a series of proposals, all rejected by

* So far as here relevant, North Carolina General Statute § 115–176.1 reads as follows: "No student shall be assigned or compelled to attend any school on account of race, creed, color or national origin, or for the purpose of creating a balance or ratio of race, religion or national origins. Involuntary bussing of students in contravention of this article is prohibited and public funds shall not be used for any such bussing."

the District Court as inadequate. In the midst of this litigation over the remedy to implement the District Court's order, the North Carolina Legislature enacted the anti-busing bill, set forth in relevant part in footnote 1.

Following enactment of the anti-busing statute the plaintiffs in the *Swann* case obtained leave to file a supplemental complaint which sought injunctive and declaratory relief against the statute. They sought to convene a three-judge court, but no action was taken on the requests at that time because the school board thought that the anti-busing law did not interfere with the school board's proposed plan to transport about 4,000 Negro children to white suburban schools. 306 F.Supp 1291 (WDNC 1969). Other parties were added as defendants by order of the District Court dated February 25. In addition certain persons who had brought a suit in state court to enjoin or impede the order of the federal court, the attorneys for those litigants, and state judges who at various times entered injunctions against the school authorities and blocked compliance with orders of the District Court were also joined; a three-judge court was then convened.

We observed in *Swann*, that school authorities have wide discretion in formulating school policy, and that as a matter of educational policy school authorities may well conclude that some kind of racial balance in the schools is desirable quite apart from any constitutional requirements. However, if a state-imposed limitation on a school authority's discretion operates to inhibit or obstruct the operation of a unitary school system or impede the disestablishing of a dual school system, it must fall; state policy must give way when it operates to hinder vindication of federal constitutional guarantees.

The legislation before us flatly forbids assignment of any student on account of race or for the purpose of creating a racial balance or ratio in the schools. The prohibition is absolute, and it would inescapably operate to obstruct the remedies granted by the District Court in the *Swann* case. But more important the statute exploits an apparently neutral form to control school assignment plans by directing that they be "color blind"; that requirement, against the background of segregation, would render illusory the promise of *Brown* v. *Board of Education,* 347 US 483 (1954). Just as the race of students must be considered in determining whether a constitutional violation has occurred, so also must race be considered in formulating a remedy. To forbid, at this stage, all assignments made on the basis of race would deprive school authorities of the one tool absolutely essential to fulfillment of their constitutional obligation to eliminate existing dual school systems.

Similarly the flat prohibition against assignment of students for the purpose of creating a racial balance must inevitably conflict with the duty of school authorities to disestablish dual school systems. As we have held in *Swann*, the Constitution does not compel any particular degree of racial balance or mixing, but when past and continuing constitutional violations are found, some ratios are likely to be useful starting points in shaping a remedy. An absolute prohibition against use of such a device—even as a starting point—contravenes the implicit command of *Green* v. *County School Board,* 391 US 430 (1968), that all reasonable methods be available to formulate an effective remedy.

We likewise conclude that an absolute prohibition against transportation of students assigned on the basis of race, "or for the purpose of creating a balance or ratio," will similarly hamper the ability of local authorities to effectively remedy constitutional violations. As noted in *Swann,* bus transportation has long been an integral part of all public educational systems, and it is unlikely that a truly effective remedy could be devised without continued reliance upon it. . . .

Affirmed.

8. *Equality in Use of Public Facilities*

WRIGHT *v.* GEORGIA
373 US 284 (1963)

[Six Negroes were convicted in Savannah, Georgia, of a violation of the breach-of-the-peace statute by playing basketball in a public park after the police ordered them to leave the park. The U.S. Supreme Court unanimously reversed the convictions. The opinion for the Court was by Chief Justice Warren.]

Mr. Chief Justice Warren delivered the opinion of the Court:

Petitioners, six young Negroes, were convicted of breach of the peace for peacefully playing basketball in a public park in Savannah, Georgia, on the early afternoon of Monday, January 23, 1961. The record is devoid of evidence of any activity which a breach of the peace statute might be thought to punish. Finding that there is no adequate state ground to bar review by this Court and that the convictions are violative of due process of law secured by the Fourteenth Amendment, we hold that the judgments below must be reversed.

Only four witnesses testified at petitioners' trial: the two arresting officers, the city recreational superintendent, and a sergeant of police. All were prosecution witnesses. No witness contradicted any testimony given by any other witnesses. On the day in question the petitioners were playing in a basketball court at Daffin Park, Savannah, Georgia. The park is owned and operated by the city for recreational purposes, is about 50 acres in area, and is customarily used only by whites. A white woman notified the two police officer witnesses of the presence of petitioners in the park. They investigated, according to one officer, "because some colored people were playing in the park. I did not ask this white lady how old these people were. As soon as I found out these were colored people I immediately went there." The officer also conceded that "I have never made previous arrests in Daffin Park because people played basketball there. . . . I arrested these people for playing basketball in Daffin Park. One reason was because they were negroes. I observed the conduct of these people, when they were on the basketball court and they were doing nothing besides playing basketball, they were just normally playing basketball, and none of the children from the schools were there at that particular time." The other officer admitted that petitioners "were not necessarily creating any disorder, they were just 'shooting at the goal,' that's all they were doing, they wasn't disturbing anything." Petitioners were neat and well dressed. Nevertheless, the officers ordered the petitioners to leave the park. One petitioner asked one of the officers "by what authority" he asked them to leave; the officer responded that he "didn't need any orders to come out there. . . ." But he admitted that "it is [not] unusual for one to inquire 'why' they are being arrested." When arrested the petitioners obeyed the police orders and without disturbance entered the cruiser to be transported to police headquarters. No crowd assembled.

The recreational superintendent's testimony was confused and contradictory. In essence he testified that school children had preference in the use of the park's playground facilities but that there was no objection to use by older persons if children were not there at the time. No children were present at this time. The arrests were made at about 2 P.M. The schools released their students at 2:30 and, according to one officer, it would have been at least 30 minutes before any children could have reached the playground. The officer also stated that he did not know whether the basketball court was reserved for a particular age group and did not know the rules of the City Recreational Department. It was conceded at the trial that no signs were posted in the park indicating what areas, if any, were reserved for younger children at particular hours. In oral argument before this Court it was conceded that the regulations of the park were not printed.

The accusation charged petitioners with assembling "for the purpose of disturbing the public peace . . ." and not dispersing at the command of the officers. The jury was charged, with respect to the offense itself, only in terms of the accusation and the statute. Upon conviction five petitioners were sentenced to pay a fine of $100 or to serve five months in prison. Petitioner Wright was sentenced to pay a fine of $125 or to serve six months in prison.

Petitioners' principal contention in this Court is that the breach of the peace statute did not give adequate warning that their conduct violated that enactment in derogation of their rights under the Due Process Clause of the Fourteenth Amendment of the Constitution of the United States. This contention was plainly raised at the trial, both in a demurrer to the accusation and in motions for a new trial, and was pressed on appeal to the Georgia Supreme Court. Both the demurrer and new trial motions raised a number of other issues. The Georgia Supreme Court held that error in the denial of the motions for a new trial could not be considered because it was not properly briefed on the appeal. But the court nevertheless seemed to pass upon the claim because it had been raised in the demurrer, and affirmed the convictions. Certiorari was granted.

Since there is some question as to whether the Georgia Supreme Court considered petitioners' claim of vagueness to have been properly raised in the demurrer, we prefer to rest our jurisdiction upon a firmer foundation. We hold, for the reasons set forth hereinafter, that there was no adequate state ground for the Georgia court's refusal to consider error in the denial of petitioners' motions for a new trial. . . .

II

Three possible bases for petitioners' convictions are suggested. First, it is said that failure to obey the command of a police officer constitutes a traditional form of breach of the peace. Obviously, however, one cannot be punished for failing to obey the command of an officer if that command is itself violative of the Constitution. The command of the officers in this case was doubly a violation of petitioners' constitutional rights. It was obviously based, according to the testimony of the arresting officers themselves, upon their intention to enforce racial discrimination in the park. For this reason the order violated the Equal Protection Clause of the Fourteenth Amendment. . . . The command was also violative of petitioners' rights because, as will be seen, the other asserted basis for the order—the possibility of disorder by others—could not justify exclusion of the petitioners from the park. Thus petitioners could not constitutionally be convicted for refusing to obey the officers. If petitioners were held guilty of violating the Georgia statute because they disobeyed the officers, this case falls within the rule that a generally worded statute which is construed to punish conduct which cannot constitutionally be punished is unconstitutionally vague to the extent that it fails to give adequate warning of the boundary between the constitutionally permissible and constitutionally impermissible applications of the statute. . . .

Second, it is argued that petitioners were guilty of a breach of the peace because their activity was likely to cause a breach of the peace by others. The only evidence to support this contention is testimony of one of the police officers that "The purpose of asking them to leave was to keep down trouble, which looked like to me might start—there were five or six cars driving around the park at the time, white people." But that officer also stated that this "was [not] unusual traffic for that time of day." And the park was 50 acres in area. Respondent contends the petitioners were forewarned that their conduct would be held to violate the statute. . . . But it is sufficient to say again that a generally worded statute, when construed to punish conduct which cannot be constitutionally punished, is unconstitutionally vague. And the possibility of disorder by others cannot justify exclusion of persons from a place if they otherwise have a constitutional right (founded upon the Equal Protection Clause) to be present. *Taylor* v. *Louisiana,* 370 US 154; *Garner* v. *Louisiana,* 368 US 157; see also *Buchanan* v. *Warley,* 245 US 60.

Third, it is said that the petitioners were guilty of a breach of the peace because a park rule reserved the playground for the use of younger people at the time. However, neither the existence nor the posting of any such rule has been proved. . . . The police officers did not inform them of it because they had no knowledge of any such rule themselves. Furthermore, it is conceded that there was no sign or printed regulation which would give notice of any such rule.

Under any view of the facts alleged to constitute the violation it cannot be maintained that petitioners had adequate notice that their conduct was prohibited by the breach of the peace statute. It is well established that a conviction under a criminal enactment which does not give adequate notice that the conduct charged is prohibited is violative of due process. . . .

Reversed.

WATSON *v.* MEMPHIS
373 US 526 (1963)

[Negro citizens of Memphis, Tennessee, sought to have the city parks and other publicly owned or operated recreational facilities immediately desegregated. The city, pointing to partial desegregation already achieved, sought delay by urging the need and wisdom of moving slowly and gradually. The U.S. Supreme Court unanimously denied delay and explicated the meaning of "all deliberate speed," the phrase used by the Court in *Brown* v. *Topeka,* 349 US 294 (the second *Brown* case). Justice Goldberg wrote the opinion for the Court.]

Mr. Justice Goldberg delivered the opinion of the Court:

The issue in this case, simply stated, is whether the City of Memphis may further delay in meeting fully its constitutional obligation under the Fourteenth Amendment to desegregate its public parks and other municipal recreational facilities.

The petitioners, adult Negro residents of Memphis, commenced this action against the city in May 1960 in the United States District Court for the Western District of Tennessee, seeking declaratory and injunctive relief directing immediate desegregation of municipal parks and other city-owned or operated recreational facilities from which Negroes were then still excluded. The city denied neither the fact that the majority of the relevant facilities were operated on a segregated basis nor its duty under the Fourteenth Amendment to terminate its policy of conditioning use of such facilities on race. Instead, it pointed to the partial desegregation already effected and attempted to justify its further delay in conforming fully and at once to constitutional mandates by urging the need and wisdom of proceeding slowly and gradually in its desegregation efforts.

The District Court denied the relief sought by the petitioners and ordered the city to submit, within six months, a plan providing additional time for desegregation of the relevant facilities. The Court of Appeals for the Sixth Circuit affirmed. We granted certiorari to consider the important question presented and the applicability here of the principles enunciated by this Court in the second *Brown* decision, *Brown* v. *Board of Education,* 349 US 294, upon which the courts below relied in further delaying complete vindication of the petitioners' constitutional rights.

We find the second *Brown* decision to be inapplicable here and accordingly reverse the judgment below.

I

It is important at the outset to note the chronological context in which the city makes its claim to entitlement to additional time within which to work out complete elimination of racial barriers to use of the public facilities here involved. It is now more than nine years since this Court held in the first *Brown* decision, *Brown* v. *Board of Education,* 347 US 483, that racial segregation in state public schools violates the Equal Protection Clause of the Fourteenth Amendment. And it was almost eight years ago—in 1955, the year after the decision on the merits in *Brown* —that the constitutional proscription of state enforced racial segregation was found to apply to public recreational facilities. See *Dawson* v. *Mayor and City Council of Baltimore,* 4 Cir., 220 F. 2d 386, aff'd, 350 US 877; see also *Muir* v. *Louisville Park Theatrical Assn.,* 347 US 971.

Thus, the applicability here of the factors and reasoning relied on in framing the 1955 decree in the second *Brown* decision, *supra,* which contemplated the possible need of some limited delay in effecting total desegregation of public schools, must be considered not only in the context of factual similarities, if any, between that case and this one, but also in light of the significant fact that the governing constitutional principles no longer bear the imprint of newly enunciated doctrine. In considering the appropriateness of the equitable decree entered below inviting a plan calling for an even longer delay in effecting desegregation, we cannot ignore the passage of a substantial period of time since the original declaration of the manifest unconstitutionality of racial practices such as are here challenged, the repeated and numerous decisions giving notice of such illegality, and the many intervening opportunities heretofore available to attain the equality of treatment which the Fourteenth Amendment commands the States to achieve. These factors must inevitably and substantially temper the present import of such broad policy considerations as may have underlain, even in part, the form of decree ultimately framed in the *Brown* case. Given the extended time which has elapsed, it is far from clear that the mandate of the second *Brown* decision requiring that desegregation proceed with "all deliberate speed" would today be fully satisfied by types of plans or programs for desegregation of public educational facilities which eight years ago might have been deemed sufficient. *Brown* never contemplated that the concept of "deliberate speed" would countenance indefinite delay in elimination of racial barriers in schools, let alone other public facilities not involving the same physical problems or comparable conditions.

II

When, in 1954, in the first *Brown* decision, this Court declared the constitutional impermissibility of racial segregation in public schools, it did not immediately frame a decree, but instead invited and heard further argument on the question of relief. In its subsequent opinion, the Court noted that "[f]ull implementation of these [applicable] constitutional principles may require solution of varied and local school problems" and indicated an appropriate scope for the application of equitable principles consistent with both public and private need and for "exercise of [the] . . . traditional attributes of equity power." The District Courts to which the cases there under consideration were remanded were invested with a discretion appropriate to ultimate fashioning of detailed relief consonant with properly cognizable local conditions. This did not mean, however, that the discretion was even then unfettered or exercisable without restraint. Basic to the remand was the concept that desegregation must proceed with "all deliberate speed," and the problems which might be considered and which might justify a decree requiring something less than immediate and total desegregation were severely delimited. Hostility to the constitutional precepts underlying the original decision was expressly and firmly pretermitted as such an operative factor.

The nature of the ultimate resolution effected in the second *Brown* decision largely reflected no more than a recognition of the unusual and particular problems inhering in desegregating large numbers of schools throughout the country. The careful specification of factors relevant to a determination whether any delay in complying fully and completely with the constitutional mandate would be warranted demonstrated a concern that delay not be conditioned upon insufficient reasons or, in any event, tolerated unless it imperatively and compellingly appeared unavoidable.

This case presents no obvious occasion for the application of *Brown*. We are not here confronted with attempted desegregation of a local school system with any or all of the perhaps uniquely attendant problems, administrative and other, specified in the second *Brown* decision as proper considerations in weighing the need for further delay in vindicating the Fourteenth Amendment rights of petitioners. Desegregation of parks and other recreational facilities does not present the same kinds of cognizable difficulties inhering in elimination of racial classification in schools, at which attendance is compulsory, the adequacy of teachers and facilities crucial, and questions of geographic assignment often of major significance.

Most importantly, of course, it must be recognized that even the delay countenanced by *Brown* was a necessary, albeit significant, adaptation of the usual principle that any deprivation of constitutional rights calls for prompt rectification. The rights here asserted are, like all such rights, *present* rights; they are not merely hopes to some *future* enjoyment of some formalistic constitutional promise. The basic guarantees of our Constitution are warrants for the here and now and, unless there is an overwhelmingly compelling reason, they are to be promptly fulfilled. The second *Brown* decision is but a narrowly drawn, and carefully limited, qualification upon usual precepts of constitutional adjudication and is not to be unnecessarily expanded in application.

Solely because of their race, the petitioners here have been refused the use of city-owned or operated parks and other recreational facilities which the Constitution mandates be open to their enjoyment on equal terms with white persons. The city has effected, continues to effect, and claims the right or need to prolong patently unconstitutional racial discriminations violative of now long-declared and well-established individual rights. The claims of the city to further delay in affording the petitioners that to which they are clearly and unquestionably entitled cannot be upheld except upon the most convincing and impressive demonstration by the city that such delay is manifestly compelled by constitutionally cognizable circumstances warranting the exercise of an appropriate equitable discretion by a court. In short, the city must sustain an extremely heavy burden of proof.

Examination of the facts of this case in light of the foregoing discussion discloses with singular clarity that this burden has not been sustained; indeed, it is patent from the record that the principles enunciated in the second *Brown* decision have absolutely no application here.

III

The findings of the District Court disclose an unmistakable and pervasive pattern of local segregation, which, in fact, the city makes no attempt to deny, but merely to justify as necessary for the time being. Memphis owns 131 parks, all of which are operated by the Memphis Park Commission. Of these, only 25 were at the time of trial open to use without regard to race; 58 were restricted to use by whites and 25 to use by Negroes; the remaining 23 parks were undeveloped raw land. Subject to exceptions, neighborhood parks were generally segregated according to the racial character of the area in which located. The City Park Commission also operates a number of additional recreational facilities, by far the largest share of which were found to be racially segregated. Though a zoo, an art gallery and certain boating and other facilities are now desegregated, about two-thirds (40) of the 61 city-owned playgrounds were at the time of trial reserved for whites only, and the remainder were set aside for Negro use. Thirty of the 56 playgrounds and other facilities operated by the municipal Park Commission on property owned by churches, private groups, or the School Board were set aside for the exclusive use of whites, while 26 were reserved for Negroes. All 12 of the municipal community centers were segregated, eight being available only to whites and four to Negroes. Only two of the seven city golf courses were open to Negroes; play on the remaining five was limited to whites. While several of these properties have been desegregated since the filing of suit, the general pattern of racial segregation in such public recreational facilities persists.

The city asserted in the court below, and states here, that its good faith in attempting to comply with the requirements of the Constitution is not in issue, and contends that gradual desegregation on a facility-by-facility basis is necessary to prevent interracial disturbances, violence, riots, and community confusion and turmoil. The compelling answer to this contention is that constitutional rights may not be denied simply because of hostility to their assertion or exercise. . . . As declared in *Cooper* v. *Aaron,* 358 US 1, "law and order are not . . . to be preserved by depriving the Negro children of their constitutional rights." This is really no more than an application of a principle enunciated much earlier in *Buchanan* v. *Warley,* 245 US 60, a case dealing with a somewhat different form of state-ordained segregation—enforced separation of Negroes and whites by neighborhood. An unanimous Court, in striking down the officially imposed pattern of racial segregation there in question, declared almost a half-century ago:

It is urged that this proposed segregation will promote the public peace by preventing race conflicts. Desirable as this is, and important as is the preservation of the public peace, this aim cannot be accomplished by laws or ordinances which deny rights created or protected by the federal Constitution.

Beyond this, however, neither the asserted fears of violence and tumult nor the asserted inability to preserve the peace were demonstrated at trial to be anything more than personal speculations or vague disquietudes of city officials. There is no indication that there had been any violence or meaningful disturbances when other recreational facilities had been desegregated. In fact, the only evidence in the record was that such prior transitions had been peaceful. The Chairman of the Memphis Park Commission indicated that the city had "been singularly blessed by the absence of turmoil up to this time on this race question"; notwithstanding the prior desegregation of numerous recreational facilities, the same witness could point as evidence of the unrest or turmoil which would assertedly occur upon complete desegregation of such facilities only to a number of anonymous letters and phone calls which he had received. The Memphis Chief of Police mentioned without further description some "troubles" at the time bus service was desegregated and referred to threatened violence in connection with a "sit-in" demonstration at a local store, but, beyond making general predictions, gave no concrete indication of any inability of authorities to maintain the peace. The only violence referred to at any park or recreational facility occurred in segregated parks and was not the product of attempts at desegregation. Moreover, there was no factual evidence to support the bare testimonial speculations that authorities would be unable to cope successfully with any problems which in fact might arise or to meet the need for additional protection should the occasion demand.

The existing and commendable goodwill between the races in Memphis, to which both the District Court and some of the witnesses at trial made express and emphatic reference as in some inexplicable fashion supporting the need for further delay, can best be preserved and extended by the observance and protection, not the denial, of the basic constitutional rights here asserted. The best guarantee of civil peace is adherence to, and respect for, the law.

The other justifications for delay urged by the city or relied upon by the courts below are no more substantial, either legally or practically. It was, for example, asserted that immediate desegregation of playgrounds and parks would deprive a number of children—both Negro and white—of recreational facilities; this contention was apparently based on the premise that a number of such facilities would have to be closed because of the inadequacy of the "present" park budget to provide additional "supervision" assumed to be necessary to operate unsegregated playgrounds. As already noted, however, there is no warrant in this record for assuming that such added supervision would, in fact, be required, much less that police and recreation personnel would be unavailable to meet such needs if they should arise. More significantly, however, it is obvious that vindication of conceded constitutional rights cannot be made dependent upon any theory that it is less expensive to deny than to afford them. We will not assume that the citizens of Memphis accept the questionable premise implicit in this argument or that either the resources of the city are inadequate, or its government unresponsive, to the needs of all of its citizens.

In support of its judgment, the District Court also pointed out that the recreational facilities available for Negroes were roughly proportional to their number and therefore presumably adequate to meet their needs. While the record does not clearly support this, no more need be said than that, even if true, it reflects an impermissible obeisance to the now thoroughly discredited doctrine of "separate but equal." The sufficiency of Negro facilities is beside the point; it is the segregation by race that is unconstitutional.

Finally, the District Court deferred ruling as to the propriety of ordering elimination of racial barriers at one facility, an art museum, pending initiation of, and decision in, a state court action to construe a racially restrictive covenant contained in the deed of the property to the city. Of course, the outcome of the state suit is irrelevant to whether the city may constitutionally enforce the segregation, regardless of the effect which desegregation may have on its title. . . . In any event, there is no reason to believe that the restrictive provision will be invoked. The museum has already been opened to Negroes one day a week without complaint.

Since the city has completely failed to demonstrate any compelling or convincing reason requiring further delay in implementing the constitutional proscription of segregation of publicly owned or operated recreational facilities there is no cause whatsoever to depart from the generally operative and here clearly controlling principle that constitutional rights are to be promptly vindicated. The continued denial to petitioners of the use of city facilities solely because of their race is without warrant. Under the facts in this case, the District Court's undoubted discretion in the fashioning and timing of equitable relief was not called into play; rather, affirmative judicial action was required to vindicate plain and present constitutional rights. Today, no less than 50 years ago, the solution to the problems growing out of race relations "cannot be promoted by depriving citizens of their constitutional rights and privileges," . . .

The judgment below must be and is reversed and the cause is remanded for further proceedings consistent herewith.

Reversed.

PALMER *v.* THOMPSON
403 US 217 (1971)

[The city of Jackson, Mississippi (population 100,000 whites and 50,000 Negroes) operated four swimming pools for whites and one for Negroes. The city closed all pools. The lower federal courts upheld the closing. The Supreme Court affirmed. The Court's opinion was by Justice Black. Chief Justice Burger and Justice Blackmun each wrote a concurring opinion. Justice Douglas wrote a dissenting opinion. Justice Marshall wrote a dissenting opinion in which Justices Brennan and White joined. Justice White wrote a dissenting opinion in which Justices Brennan and Marshall joined.]

Mr. Justice Black delivered the opinion of the Court:

In 1962 the city of Jackson, Mississippi, was maintaining five public parks along with swimming pools, golf links, and other facilities for use by the public on a racially segregated basis. Four of the swimming pools were used by whites only and one by Negroes only. Plaintiffs brought an action in the United States District Court seeking a declaratory judgment that this state-enforced segregation of the races was a violation of the Thirteenth and Fourteenth Amendments, and asking an injunction to forbid such practices. After hearings the district court entered a judgment declaring that enforced segregation denied equal protection of the laws but it declined to issue an injunction. The Court of Appeals affirmed, and we denied certiorari. The city proceeded to desegregate its public parks, auditoriums, golf course, and the city zoo. However, the city council decided not to try to operate the public swimming pools on a desegregated basis. Acting in its legislative capacity, the council surrendered its lease on one pool and closed four which it owned. A number of Negro citizens of Jackson then filed this suit to force the city to reopen the pools and operate them on a desegregated basis. The District Court found that the closing was justified to preserve peace and order and because the pools could not be operated economically on an integrated basis. It held the city's action did not deny black citizens equal protection of the laws. The Court of Appeals sitting *en banc* affirmed, six out of 13 judges dissenting. That court rejected the contention that since the pools had been closed either in whole or in part to avoid desegregation the city council's action was a denial of equal protection of the laws. We granted certiorari to decide that question. We affirm.

I

Petitioners rely chiefly on the first section of the Fourteenth Amendment which forbids any State to "deny to any person within its jurisdiction the equal protection of the laws." There can be no doubt that a major purpose of this Amendment was to safeguard Negroes against discriminatory state laws—state laws that fail to give Negroes protection equal to that afforded white people. History shows that the achievement of equality for Negroes was the urgent purpose not only for passage of the Fourteenth Amendment but for the Thirteenth and Fifteenth Amendments as well. . . . Thus the Equal Protection Clause was principally designed to protect Negroes against discriminatory action by the States. Here there has unquestionably been "state action" because the official local government legislature, the city council, has closed the public swimming pools of Jackson. The question, however, is whether this closing of the pools is state action that denies "the equal protection of the laws" to Negroes. It should be noted first that neither the Fourteenth Amendment nor any act of Congress purports to impose an affirmative duty on a State to begin to operate or to continue to operate swimming pools. Furthermore, this is not a case where whites are permitted to use public facilities while blacks are denied access. It is not a case where a city is maintaining different sets of facilities for blacks and whites and forcing the races to remain separate in recreational or educational activities. . . .

Unless, therefore, as petitioners urge, certain past cases require us to hold that closing the pools to all denied equal protection to Negroes, we must agree with the courts below and affirm.

II

Although petitioners cite a number of our previous cases, the only two which even plausibly support their argument are *Griffin* v. *County School Board of Prince Edward County,* 377 US 218 (1964), and *Reitman* v. *Mulkey,* 387 US 369 (1967). For the reasons that follow, however, neither case leads us to reverse the judgment here.

A. In *Griffin* the public schools of Prince Edward County, Virginia, were closed under authority of state and county law, and so-called "private schools" were set up in their place to avoid a court desegregation order. At the same time, public schools in other counties in Virginia remained open. In Prince Edward County the "private schools" were open to whites only and these schools were in fact run by a practical partnership between state and county, designed to preserve segregated education. We pointed out in *Griffin* the many facets of state involvement in the running of the "private schools." The State General Assembly had made available grants of $150 per child to make the program possible. This was supplemented by a county grant program of $100 per child and county property tax credits for citizens contributing to the "private schools." Under those circumstances we held that the closing of public schools in just one county while the State helped finance "private schools" was a scheme to perpetuate segregation in education which constituted a denial of equal protection of the laws. Thus the *Griffin* case simply treated the school program for what it was—an operation of Prince Edward County schools under a thinly disguised "private" school system actually planned and carried out by the State and the county to maintain segregated education with public funds. That case can give no comfort to petitioners here. This record supports no intimation that Jackson has not completely and finally ceased running swimming pools for all time. Unlike Prince Edward County, Jackson has not pretended to close public pools only to run them under a "private" label. It is true that the Leavell Woods pool, previously leased by the city from the YMCA, is now run by that organization and appears to be open only to whites. And according to oral argument, another pool owned by the city before 1963 is now owned and operated by Jackson State College, a predominantly black institution, for college students and their guests. But unlike the "private schools" in Prince Edward County there is nothing here to show the city is directly or indirectly involved in the funding or operation of either pool. If the time ever comes when Jackson attempts to run segregated public pools either directly or indirectly, or participates in a subterfuge whereby pools are nominally run by "private parties" but actually by the city, relief will be available in the federal courts.

B. Petitioners also claim that Jackson's closing of the public pools authorizes or encourages private pool owners to discriminate on account of race and that such "encouragement" is prohibited by *Reitman* v. *Mulkey, supra.*

In *Reitman,* California had repealed two laws relating to racial discrimination in the sale of housing by passing a constitutional amendment establishing the right of private persons to discriminate on racial grounds in real estate transactions. This Court there accepted what it designated as the holding of the Supreme Court of California, namely that the constitutional amendment was an official authorization of racial discrimination which significantly involved the State in the discriminatory acts of private parties. . . .

In the first place there are no findings here about any state "encouragement" of discrimination, and it is not clear that any such theory was ever considered by the District Court. The implication of petitioner's argument appears to be that the fact the city turned over to the YMCA a pool it had previously leased is sufficient to show automatically that the city has conspired with the YMCA to deprive Negroes of the opportunity to swim in integrated pools. Possibly in a case where the city and the YMCA were both parties, a court could find that the city engaged in a subterfuge, and that liability could be fastened on it as an active participant in a conspiracy with the YMCA. We need not speculate upon such a possibility, for there is no such finding here, and it does not appear from this record that there was evidence to support such a finding. *Reitman* v. *Mulkey* was based on a theory that the evidence was sufficient to show the State was abetting a refusal to rent an apartment on racial grounds. On this record, *Reitman* offers no more support to petitioners than does *Griffin.*

III

Petitioners have also argued that respondents' action violates the Equal Protection Clause because the decision to close the pools was motivated by a desire to avoid integration of the races. But no case in this Court has held that a legislative act may violate equal protection solely because of the motivations of the men who voted for it. The pitfalls of such analysis were set forth clearly in the landmark opinion of Mr. Justice Marshall in *Fletcher* v. *Peck,* 6 Cranch 87, 130 (1810), where the Court declined to set aside the Georgia Legislature's sale of lands on the theory that its members were corruptly motivated in passing the bill.

A similar contention that illicit motivation should lead to a finding of unconstitutionality was advanced in *United States* v. *O'Brien,* 391 US 367, 383 (1968), where this Court rejected the argument that a defendant could not be punished for burning his draft card because Congress had allegedly passed the statute to stifle dissent. That opinion explained well the hazards of declaring a law unconstitutional because of the motivations of its sponsors. First, it is extremely difficult for a court to ascertain the motivation, or collection of different motivations, that lie behind a legislative enactment. Here, for example, petitioners have argued that the Jackson pools were closed because of ideological opposition to racial integration in swimming pools. Some evidence in the record appears to support this argument. On the other hand the courts below found that the pools were closed because the city counsel felt they could not be operated safely and economically on an integrated basis. There is substantial evidence in the record to support this conclusion. It is difficult or impossible for any court to determine the "sole" or "dominant" motivation behind the choices of a group of legislators. Furthermore, there is an element of futility in a judicial attempt to invalidate a law because of the bad motives of its supporters. If the law is struck down for this reason, rather than because of its facial content or effect, it would presumably be valid as soon as the legislature or relevant governing body repassed it for different reasons.

It is true there is language in some of our cases interpreting the Fourteenth and Fifteenth Amendments which may suggest that the motive or purpose behind a law is relevant to its constitutionality. *Griffin* v. *Prince Edward County, supra; Gomillion* v. *Lightfoot,* 364 US 339, 347 (1960). But the focus in those cases was on the actual effect of the enactments, not upon the motivation which led the States to behave as they did. In *Griffin,* as discussed *supra,* the State was in fact perpetuating a segregated public school system by financing segregated "private" academies. And in *Gomillion* the Alabama Legislature's gerrymander of the boundaries of Tuskeegee excluded virtually all Negroes from voting in town elections. Here the record indicates only that Jackson once ran segregated public swimming pools and that no public pools are now maintained by the city. Moreover, there is no evidence in this record to show that the city is now covertly aiding the maintenance and operation of pools which are private in name only. It shows no state action affecting blacks differently from whites.

Petitioners have argued strenuously that a city's possible motivations to ensure safety and save money cannot validate an otherwise impermissible state action. This proposition is of course true. Citizens may not be compelled to forgo their constitutional rights because officials fear public hostility or desire to save money. *Buchanan* v. *Warley,* 245 US 60 (1917); *Cooper* v. *Aaron,* 358 US 1 (1958); *Watson* v. *City of Memphis,* 373 US 526 (1963). But the issue here is whether black citizens in Jackson *are* being denied their constitutional rights when the city has closed the public pools to black and white alike. Nothing in the history or the language of the Fourteenth Amendment nor in any of our prior cases persuades us that the closing of the Jackson swimming pools to all its citizens constitutes a denial of "the equal protection of the laws."

IV

Finally, some faint and unpersuasive argument has been made by petitioners that the closing of the pools violated the Thirteenth Amendment which freed the Negroes from slavery. The argument runs this way: The first Mr. Justice Harlan's dissent in *Plessy* v. *Ferguson,* 163 US 537, 552 (1896), argued strongly that the purpose of the Thirteenth Amendment was not only to outlaw slavery but all of its "badges and incidents." This broad reading of the Amendment was affirmed in *Jones* v. *Alfred Mayer Co.,* 392 US 409 (1968). The denial of the right of Negroes to swim in pools with white people is said to be a "badge or incident" of slavery. Consequently, the argument seems to run, this Court should declare that the city's closing of the pools to keep the two races from swimming together violates the Thirteenth Amendment. To reach that result from the Thirteenth Amendment would severely stretch its short simple words and do violence to its history. Establishing this Court's authority under the Thirteenth Amendment to declare new laws to govern the thousands of towns and cities of the country would grant it a lawmaking power far beyond the imaginations of the Amendment's authors. Finally, although the Thirteenth Amendment is a skimpy collection of words to allow this Court to legislate new laws to control the operation of swimming pools throughout the length and breadth of this Nation, the Amendment does contain other words that we held in *Jones* v. *Alfred Mayer Co.* could empower Congress to outlaw "badges of slavery." The last sentence of the Amendment reads: ". . . Congress shall have power to enforce this Article by appropriate legislation." But Congress has passed no law under this power to regulate a city's opening or closing of swimming pools or other recreational facilities.

It has not been so many years since it was first deemed proper and lawful for cities to tax their citizens to build and operate swimming pools for the public. Probably few persons, prior to this case, would have imagined that cities could be forced by five lifetime judges to construct or refurbish swimming pools which they choose not to operate for any reason, sound or unsound. Should citizens of Jackson or any other city be able to establish in court that public, tax-supported swimming pools are being denied to one group because of color and supplied to another, they will be entitled to relief. But that is not the case here.

The judgment is affirmed.

Mr. Justice Marshall, with whom Mr. Justice Brennan and Mr. Justice White join, dissenting:

While I am in complete agreement with the opinions of Justices Douglas and White, I am obliged to add a few words of my own.

First, the majority and concurring opinions' reliance on the "racially equal effect upon all citizens" of the decision to discontinue all public pools is misplaced. As long ago as 1948 in *Skelley* v. *Kraemer,* 344 US 1, 22 (1948), this Court held:

> The rights created by the first section of the Fourteenth Amendment are, by its terms, guaranteed to the individual. The rights established are personal rights. It is, therefore, no answer to these petitioners to say that the courts may also be induced to deny white persons rights of ownership and occupancy on grounds of race or

color. Equal protection of the laws is not achieved through indiscriminate imposition of inequalities.

In short, when the officials of Jackson, Mississippi, in the circumstances of this case, detailed by Mr. Justice White, denied a single Negro child the opportunity to go swimming simply because he is a Negro, rights guaranteed to that child by the Fourteenth Amendments were lost. The fact that the color of his skin is used to prevent others from swimming in public pools is irrelevant.

Second, since *Brown* v. *Board of Education,* 347 US 483 (1954), public schools and public recreational facilities such as swimming pools have received identical Fourteenth Amendment protection. Indeed, exactly one week after *Brown I* this Court remanded three cases in the *same* Per Curiam: *Florida ex rel. Hawkins* v. *Board of Control of Florida et al; Tureand* v. *Board of Supervisors;* and *Muir* v. *Louisville Theatrical Association,* 347 US 970. The first two involved university *education* and the latter involved *recreational facilities.*

Even before *Brown II* it was recognized as obvious that "racial segregation in recreational activities can no longer be sustained as a proper exercise of the police power of the State; for if that power cannot be invoked to sustain racial segregation in the schools, where attendance is compulsory and racial friction may be apprehended from the enforced commingling of the races, it cannot be sustained with respect to public beach and bathhouse facilities, the use of which is entirely optional." *Dawson* v. *Mayor and City Council of Baltimore,* 220 F.2d 386, 387 (1955), aff'd *per curiam,* 350 US 877. . . .

By effectively removing publicly owned swimming pools from the protection of the Fourteenth Amendment—at least if the pools are ouside school buildings—the majority and concurring opinions turn the clock back 17 years. After losing a hard fought legal battle to maintain segregation in public facilities, the Jackson, Mississippi, authorities now seek to pick and choose* which of the existing facilities will be kept open. Their choice is rationalized on the basis of economic need and is even more transparent than putting the matter to a referendum vote.

Finally, I cannot conceive why the writers of the concurring opinions believe that the city is "locked in" and must operate the pools no matter what the economic consequences. Certainly, I am not bound by any admission of an attorney at oral argument as to his version of the law. Equity courts have always had continuing supervisory powers over their decrees; and if a proper basis for closing the facilities—other than a conclusory statement about the projected human and thus economic consequences of desegregation—could be shown, swimming pools, as I imagine schools or even golf courses, could be closed.

I dissent.

9. Equality in Places of Public Accommodation: Civil Rights Act of 1964

HEART OF ATLANTA MOTEL *v.* UNITED STATES
379 US 241 (1964)

[Early in 1960, Negro students started the sit-in demonstrations at lunch counters. Convictions arising out of these demonstrations were reversed by the Supreme

---

* The economic loss incident to the operation of public swimming pools could not be much more than that incident to maintaining public golf courses that charge green fees of $.75 to $1.25, admittedly the lowest in the country.

Court but on grounds that avoided decision on the constitutional merits. *Garner* v. *Louisiana,* 368 US 157 (1961); *Taylor* v. *Louisiana,* 370 US 154 (1962); *Peterson* v. *Greenville* 373 US 244 (1963); *Lombard* v. *Louisiana,* 373 US 267 (1963); *Robinson* v. *Florida,* 378 US 153 (1964); *Bouie* v. *Columbia,* 378 US 347 (1964); *Barr* v. *Columbia,* 378 US 146 (1964); *Bell* v. *Maryland,* 378 US 226 (1964). *Cf. Griffin* v. *Maryland,* 378 US 130 (1964). On July 2, 1964, the Civil Rights Act of 1964 was approved. In *Hamm* v. *City of Rock Hill,* 379 US 306 (1964), the Supreme Court held that the act abated trespass convictions of sit-in demonstrators in South Carolina and Arkansas. This decision was 5-to-4, with Justices Black, Harlan, Stewart, and White dissenting. These decisions had the effect of reversing thousands of convictions arising out of the demonstrations.

[The instant case tested the constitutionality of the provisions of the Civil Rights Act of 1964 that prohibits racial discrimination in places of public accommodation if their operations "affect commerce." The Court unanimously upheld the constitutionality of these provisions. The Court's opinion was by Justice Clark. Concurring opinions were written by Justices Black, Douglas, and Goldberg.]

Mr. Justice Clark delivered the opinion of the Court:

This is a declaratory judgment action, 28 U.S.C. § 2201 and § 2202, attacking the constitutionality of Title II of the Civil Rights Act of 1964, 78 Stat. 241. In addition to declaratory relief the complaint sought an injunction restraining the enforcement of the Act and damages against respondents based on allegedly resulting injury in the event compliance was required. Appellees counterclaimed for enforcement under § 206(a) of the Act and asked for a three-judge district court under § 206(b). A three-judge court, empaneled under § 206(b) as well as 28 U.S.C. § 2282, sustained the validity of the Act and issued a permanent injunction on appellee's counterclaim restraining appellants from continuing to violate the Act which remains in effect on order of Mr. Justice Black, 85 S. Ct. 1. We affirm the judgment.

(1) The Factual Background and Contentions of the Parties

The case comes here on admissions and stipulated facts. Appellant owns and operates the Heart of Atlanta Motel which has 216 rooms available to transient guests. The motel is located on Courtland Street, two blocks from downtown Peachtree Street. It is readily accessible to interstate highways 75 and 85 and state highways 23 and 41. Appellant solicits patronage from outside the State of Georgia through various national advertising media, including magazines of national circulation; it maintains over 50 billboards and highway signs within the State, soliciting patronage for the motel; it accepts convention trade from outside Georgia and approximately 75% of its registered guests are from out of State. Prior to passage of the Act the motel had followed a practice of refusing to rent rooms to Negroes, and it alleged that it intended to continue to do so. In an effort to perpetuate that policy this suit was filed.

The appellant contends that Congress in passing this Act exceeded its power to regulate commerce under Art. I, § 8, cl. 3, of the Constitution of the United States; that the Act violates the Fifth Amendment because appellant is deprived of the right to choose its customers and operate its business as it wishes, resulting in a taking of its liberty and property without due process of law and a taking of its property without just compensation; and, finally, that by requiring appellant to rent available rooms to Negroes against its will, Congress is subjecting it to involuntary servitude in contravention of the Thirteenth Amendment.

The appellees counter that the unavailability to Negroes of adequate accommodations interferes significantly with interstate travel, and that Congress, under the Commerce Clause, has power to remove such obstructions and restraints; that the Fifth Amendment does not forbid reasonable regulation and that consequential damage doth not constitute a "taking" within the meaning of that amendment; that the Thirteenth Amendment claim fails because it is entirely frivolous to say that an amendment directed to the abolition of human bondage and the removal of widespread disabilities associated with slavery places discrimination in public accommodations beyond the reach of both federal and state law.

At the trial the appellant offered no evidence, submitting the case on the pleadings, admissions and stipulation of facts; however, appellees proved the refusal of the motel to accept Negro transients after the passage of the Act. The District Court sustained the constitutionality of the sections of the Act under attack (§§ 201(a), (b) (1) and (c) (1)) and issued a permanent injunction on the counterclaim of the appellees. It restrained the appellant from "refusing to accept Negroes as guests in the motel by reason of their race or color" and from "making any distinction whatever upon the basis of race or color in the availability of the goods, services, facilities, privileges, advantages or accommodations offered or made available to guests of the motel, or to the general public, within or upon any of the premises of the Heart of Atlanta Motel, Inc."

(2) *The History of the Act*

Congress first evidenced its interest in civil rights legislation in the Civil Rights or Enforcement Act of April 9, 1866. There followed a series of six Acts, culminating in the Civil Rights Act of March 1, 1875. In 1883 this Court struck down the public accommodations sections of the 1875 Act in *The Civil Rights Cases,* 109 US 3. No major legislation in this field had been enacted by Congress for 82 years when the Civil Rights Act of 1957 became law. It was followed by the Civil Rights Act of 1960. Three years later, on June 19, 1963, the late President Kennedy called for civil rights legislation in a message to Congress to which he attached a proposed bill. Its stated purpose was

to promote the general welfare, by eliminating discrimination based on race, color, religion, or national origin in . . . public accommodations through the exercise by Congress of the powers conferred upon it . . . to enforce the provisions of the Fourteenth and Fifteenth Amendments, to regulate commerce among the several states, and to make laws necessary and proper to execute the powers conferred upon it by the Constitution.

Bills were introduced in each House of the Congress, embodying the President's suggestion, the one in the Senate being S. 1732 and that in the House, H.R. 7152. However, it was not until July 2, 1964 that the Civil Rights Bill of 1964, here under attack, was finally passed.

After extended hearings each of these bills was favorably reported to its respective house, H.R. 7152 on November 20, 1963, H.R. Rep. No. 914, 88th Cong., 1st Sess., and S. 1732 on February 10, 1964, S. Rep. No. 872, 88th Cong., 2d Sess. Although each bill originally incorporated extensive findings of fact these were eliminated from the bills as they were reported. The House passed its bill in January 1964, and sent it to the Senate. Through a bipartisan coalition of Senators Humphrey and Dirksen, together with other Senators, a substitute was worked out in informal conferences. This substitute was adopted by the Senate and sent to the House where it was adopted without change. This expedited procedure prevented the usual report on the substitute bill in the Senate as well as a Conference Committee report ordinarily filed in such matters. Our only frame of reference as to the legislative history of the Act is, therefore, the hearings, reports and debates on the respective bills in each house.

The Act as finally adopted was most comprehensive, undertaking to prevent through peaceful and voluntary settlement discrimination in voting, as well as in places of accommodation and public facilities, federally secured programs and in employment. Since Title II is the only portion under attack here, we confine our consideration to those public accommodation provisions.

(3) *Title II of the Act*

This Title is divided into seven sections beginning with § 201(a) which provides that:

All persons shall be entitled to the full and equal enjoyment of the goods, services, facilities, privileges, advantages, and accommodations of any place of public accommodations, as defined in this section, without discrimination or segregation on the ground of race, color, religion, or national origin.

There are listed in § 201(b) four classes of business establishments, each of which "serves the public" and "is a place of public accommodation" within the meaning of § 201(a) "if its operations affect commerce, or if discrimination or segregation by it is supported by State action." The covered establishments are:

(1) any inn, hotel, motel, or other establishment which provides lodging to transient guests, other than an establishment located within a building which contains not more than five rooms for rent or hire and which is actually occupied by the proprietor of such establishment as his residence;

(2) any restaurant, cafeteria . . . [not here involved];

(3) any motion picture house . . . [not here involved];

(4) any establishment . . . which is physically located within the premises of any establishment otherwise covered by this subsection, or . . . within the premises of which is physically located any such covered establishment . . . [not here involved].

Section 201(c) defines the phrase "affect commerce" as applied to the above establishments. It first declares that "any inn, hotel, motel, or other establishment which provides lodging to transient guests" affects commerce *per se*. Restaurants, cafeterias, etc., in the second class affect commerce only if they serve or offer to serve interstate travelers or if a substantial portion of the food which they serve or products which they sell have "moved in commerce." Motion picture houses and other places listed in class three affect commerce if they customarily present films, performances, etc., "which move in commerce." And the establishments listed in class four affect commerce if they are within, or include within their own premises, an establishment "the operations of which affect commerce." Private clubs are excepted under certain conditions. See § 201(e).

Section 201(d) declares that "discrimination or segregation" is supported by state action when carried on under color of any law, statute, ordinance, regulation or any custom or usage required or enforced by officials of the State or any of its subdivisions.

In addition, § 202 affirmatively declares that all persons "shall be entitled to be free, at any establishment or place, from discrimination or segregation of any kind on the ground of race, color, religion, or national origin, if such discrimination or segregation is or purports to be required by any law, statute, ordinance, regulation, rule, or order of a State or any agency or political subdivision thereof."

Finally § 203 prohibits the withholding or denial, etc., of any right or privilege secured by § 201 and § 202 or the intimidation, threatening or coercion of any person with the purpose of interfering with any such right or the punishing etc., of any person for exercising or attempting to exercise any such right.

The remaining sections of the Title are remedial ones for violations of any of the previous sections. Remedies are limited to civil actions for preventive relief. The Attorney General may bring suit where he has "reasonable cause to believe that any person or group of persons is engaged in a pattern or practice of resistance to the full enjoyment of any of the rights secured by this title, and that the pattern or practice is of such a nature and is intended to deny the full exercise of the rights herein described. . . . § 206(a)." Thirty days written notice before filing any such action must be given to the appropriate authorities of a State or subdivision the law of which prohibits the act complained of and which has established an authority which may grant relief therefrom. § 204(c). In States where such condition does not exist the court after a case is filed may refer it to the Community Relations Service which is established under Title X of the Act. § 204(d). This Title establishes such services in the Department of Commerce, provides for a Director to be appointed by the President with the advice and consent of the Senate and grants it certain powers, including the power to hold hearings, with reference to matters coming to its attention by reference from the court or between communities and persons involved in disputes arising under the Act.

(4) *Application of Title II to Heart of Atlanta Motel*

It is admitted that the operation of the motel brings it within the provisions of § 201(a) of the Act and that appellant refused to provide lodging for transient Negroes because of their race or color and that it intends to continue that policy unless restrained.

The sole question posed is, therefore, the constitutionality of the Civil Rights Act of 1964 as applied to these facts. The legislative history of the Act indicates that Congress based the Act on § 5 and the Equal Protection Clause of the Fourteenth Amendment as well as its power to regulate interstate commerce under Art. I, § 8, cl. 3 of the Constitution.

The Senate Commerce Committee made it quite clear that the fundamental object of Title II was to vindicate "the deprivation of personal dignity that surely accompanies denials of equal access to public establishments." At the same time, however, it noted that such an objective has been and could be readily achieved "by congressional action based on the commerce power of the Constitution." S. Rep. No. 872, at 16–17. Our study of the legislative record, made in the light of prior cases, has brought us to the conclusion that Congress possessed ample power in this regard, and we have therefore not considered the other grounds relied upon. This is not to say that the remaining authority upon which it acted was not adequate, a question upon which we do not pass, but merely that since the commerce power is sufficient for our decision here we have considered it alone. Nor is § 201(d) or § 202, having to do with state action, involved here and we do not pass upon those sections.

(5) *The Civil Rights Cases, 109 US 3 (1883), and their Application*

In light of our ground for decision, it might be well at the outset to discuss the *Civil Rights Cases, supra,* which declared provisions of the Civil Rights Act of 1875 unconstitutional. . . . We think that decision inapposite, and without precedential value in determining the constitutionality of the present Act. Unlike Title II of the present legislation, the 1875 Act broadly proscribed discrimination in "inns, public conveyances on land or water, theaters, and other public places of amusement," without limiting the categories of affected businesses to those impinging upon interstate commerce. In contrast, the applicability of Title II is carefully limited to enterprises having a direct and substantial relation to the interstate flow of goods and people, except where state action is involved. Further, the fact that certain kinds of businesses may not in 1875 have been sufficiently involved in interstate commerce to warrant bringing them within the ambit of the commerce power is not necessarily dispositive of the same question today. Our populace had not reached its present mobility, nor were facilities, goods and services circulating as readily in interstate commerce as they are today. Although the principles which we apply today are those first formulated by Chief Justice Marshall in *Gibbons* v. *Ogden,* 9 Wheat. 1 (1824), the conditions of transportation and commerce have changed dramatically, and we must apply those principles to the present state of commerce. The sheer increase in volume of interstate traffic alone would give discriminatory practices which inhibit travel a far larger impact upon the nation's commerce than such practices had in the economy of another day. Finally, there is language in the *Civil Rights Cases* which indicates that the Court did not fully consider whether the 1875 Act could be sustained as an exercise of the commerce power. Though the Court observed that "no one will contend that the power to pass it was contained in the Constitution before adoption of the last three amendments (Thirteenth, Fourteenth, and Fifteenth)," the Court went on specifically to note that the Act was not "conceived" in terms of the commerce power and expressly pointed out:

Of course, these remarks [as to lack of congressional power] do not apply to those cases in which Congress is clothed with direct and plenary powers of legislation over the whole subject, accompanied with an express or implied denial of such power to the States, as in the regulation of commerce with foreign nations, among the several States, and with the Indian tribes. . . . In these cases Congress has power to pass laws for regulating the subjects specified in every detail, and the conduct and transactions of individuals in respect thereof.

Since the commerce power was not relied on by the Government and was without support in the record it is understandable that the Court narrowed its inquiry and excluded the Commerce Clause as a possible source of power. In any event, it is clear that such a limitation renders the opinion devoid of authority for the proposition that the Commerce Clause gives no power to Congress to regulate discriminatory practices now found substantially to affect interstate commerce. We, therefore, conclude that the *Civil Rights Cases* have no relevance to the basis of decision here where the Act not only explicitly relies upon the commerce power, but the record is filled with testimony of obstructions and restraints resulting from the discriminations found to be existing. We now pass to that phase of the case.

(6) *The Basis of Congressional Action*

While the Act as adopted carried no congressional findings the record of its passage through each house is replete with evidence of the burdens that discrimination by race or color places upon interstate commerce. . . . This testimony included the fact that our people have become increasingly mobile with millions of all races traveling from State to State; that Negroes in particular have been the subject of discrimination in transient accommodations, having to travel great distances to secure the same; that often they have been unable to obtain accommodations and have had to call upon friends to put them up overnight, . . .; and that these conditions had become so acute as to require the listing of available lodging for Negroes in a special guidebook which was itself "dramatic testimony of the difficulties" Negroes encounter in travel. . . . These exclusionary practices were found to be nationwide, the Under Secretary of Commerce testifying that there is "no question that this discrimination in the North still exists to a large degree" and in the West and Midwest as well. . . . This testimony indicated a qualitative as well as quantitative effect on interstate travel by Negroes. The former was the obvious impairment of the Negro traveler's pleasure and convenience that resulted when he continually was uncertain of finding lodging. As for the latter, there was evidence that this uncertainty stemming from racial discrimination had the effect of discouraging travel on the part of a substantial portion of the Negro community. . . . This was the conclusion not only of the Under Secretary of Commerce but also of the Administrator of the Federal Aviation Agency who wrote the Chairman of the Senate Commerce Committee that it was his "belief that air commerce is adversely affected by the denial to a substantial segment of the traveling public of adequate and desegregated public accommodations." . . . We shall not burden this opinion with further details since the voluminous testimony presents overwhelming evidence that discrimination by hotels and motels impedes interstate travel.

(7) *The Power of Congress over Interstate Travel*

The power of Congress to deal with these obstructions depends on the meaning of the Commerce Clause. Its meaning was first enunciated 140 years ago by the great Chief Justice John Marshall in *Gibbons* v. *Ogden,* 9 Wheat. 1 (1824), in these words:

The subject to be regulated is commerce; and . . . to ascertain the extent of the power, it becomes necessary to settle the meaning of the word. The counsel for the appellee would limit it to traffic, to buying and selling, or the interchange of commodities . . . but it is something more: it is intercourse . . . between nations, and parts of nations, in all its branches, and is regulated by prescribing rules for carrying on that intercourse. . . .

To what commerce does this power extend? The constitution informs us, to commerce "with foreign nations, and among the several States, and with the Indian tribes."

It has, we believe, been universally admitted, that these words comprehend every species of commercial intercourse. . . . No sort of trade can be carried on . . . to which this power does not extend. . . .

The subject to which the power is next applied, is to commerce "among the several States." The word "among" means intermingled. . . .

[I]t may very properly be restricted to that commerce which concerns more States than one. . . . The genius and character of the whole government seems to be, that its action is to be applied to all the . . . internal concerns [of the nation] which affect the States generally; but not to those which are completely within a particular State, which do not affect other States, and with which it is not necessary to interfere, for the purpose of executing some of the general powers of the government. . . .

We are now arrived at the inquiry—What is this power?

It is the power to regulate; that is, to proscribe the rule by which commerce is to be governed. This power, like all others vested in Congress, is complete in itself, may be exercised to its utmost extent, and acknowledges no limitations, other than are prescribed in the constitution. . . . If, as has always been understood, the sovereignty of Congress . . . is plenary as to those objects [specified in the Constitution], the power over commerce . . . is vested in Congress as absolutely as it would be in a single government, having in its constitution the same restrictions on the exercise of the power as are found in the Constitution of the United States. The wisdom and the discretion of Congress, their identity with the people, and the influence which their constituents possess at elections, are, in this, as in many other instances, as that, for example, of declaring war, the sole restraints on which they have relied, to secure them from its abuse. They are the restraints on which the people must often rely solely, in all representative governments.

In short, the determinative test of the exercise of power by the Congress under the Commerce Clause is simply whether the activity sought to be regulated is "commerce which concerns more than one state" and has a real and substantial relation to the national interest. Let us now turn to this facet of the problem.

That the "intercourse" of which the Chief Justice spoke included the movement of persons through more States than one was settled as early as 1849, in the *Passenger Cases,* 7 How. 283, where Mr. Justice McLean stated: "That the transportation of passengers is a part of commerce is not now an open question." Again in 1913 Mr. Justice McKenna, speaking for the Court, said: "Commerce among the States, as we have said, consists of intercourse and traffic between their citizens, and includes the transportation of persons and property." *Hoke* v. *United States,* 227 US 308, 320. And only four years later in 1916 in *Caminetti* v. *United States,* 242 US 470, Mr. Justice Day held for the Court:

The transportation of passengers in interstate commerce, it has long been settled, is within the regulatory power of Congress, under the commerce clause of the Constitution, and the authority of Congress to keep the channels of interstate commerce free from immoral and injurious uses has been frequently sustained, and is no longer open to question.

Nor does it make any difference whether the transportation is commercial in character. In *Morgan* v. *Virginia,* 328 US 373 (1946), Mr. Justice Reed observed as to the modern movement of persons among the States:

The recent changes in transportation brought about by the coming of automobiles does not seem of great significance in the problem. People of all races travel today more extensively than in 1878 when this Court first passed upon state regulation of racial segregation in commerce. [It but] emphasizes the soundness of this Court's early conclusion in *Hall* v. *DeCuir,* 95 US 485.

The same interest in protecting interstate commerce which led Congress to deal with segregation in interstate carriers and the white slave traffic has prompted it to extend the exercise of its power to gambling. *Lottery Case,* 188 US 321 (1903); to criminal enterprises, *Brooks* v. *United States,* 267 US 432 (1925); to deceptive practices in the sale of products, *Federal Trade Comm'n* v. *Mandel Bros., Inc.,* 359 US 385 (1959); to fraudulent security transactions, *Securities & Exchange Comm'n* v. *Ralston Purina Co.,* 346 US 119 (1953); to misbranding of drugs, *Weeks* v. *United States,* 245 US 618 (1918); to wages and hours, *United States* v. *Darby,* 312 US 100 (1941); to members of labor unions, *Labor Board* v. *Jones & Laughlin Steel Corp.,* 301 US 1 (1937); to crop control, *Wickard* v. *Filburn,* 317 US 111 (1942); to discrimination against shippers, *United States* v. *Baltimore & Ohio R. Co.,* 333 US 169 (1948); to the protection of small business from injurious price cutting, *Moore* v. *Mead's Fine Bread Co.,* 348 US 115 (1954); to resale price maintenance, *Hudson Distributors, Inc.,* v. *Eli Lilly & Co.,* 377 US 386 (1964); *Schwegmann* v. *Calvert Distillers Corp.,* 341 US 384 (1951); to professional football, *Radovich* v. *National Football League,* 352 US 445 (1957); and to racial discrimination by owners and managers of terminal restaurants, *Boynton* v. *Virginia,* 364 US 454 (1960).

That Congress was legislating against moral wrongs in many of these areas rendered its enactments no less valid. In framing Title II of this Act Congress was also dealing with what it considered a moral problem. But that fact does not detract from the overwhelming evidence of the disruptive effect that racial discrimination has had on commercial intercourse. It was this burden which empowered Congress to enact appropriate legislation, and, given this basis for the exercise of its power, Congress was not restricted by the fact that the particular obstruction to interstate commerce with which it was dealing was also deemed a moral and social wrong.

It is said that the operation of the motel here is of a purely local character. But, assuming this to be true, "if it is interstate commerce that feels the pinch, it does not matter how local the operation that applies the squeeze." *United States* v.

Women's Sportswear Mfrs. Assn., 336 US 460, 464 (1949). See *Labor Board* v. *Jones & Laughlin Steel Corp., supra.* As Chief Justice Stone put it in *United States* v. *Darby, supra:*

The power of Congress over interstate commerce is not confined to the regulation of commerce among the states. It extends to those activities intrastate which so affect interstate commerce or the exercise of the power of Congress over it as to make regulation of them appropriate means to the attainment of a legitimate end, the exercise of the granted power of Congress to regulate interstate commerce. See *McCulloch* v. *Maryland,* 4 Wheat. 316, 421.

Thus the power of Congress to promote interstate commerce also includes the power to regulate the local incidents thereof, including local activities in both the States of origin and destination, which might have a substantial and harmful effect upon that commerce. One need only examine the evidence which we have discussed above to see that Congress may—as it has—prohibit racial discrimination by motels serving travelers, however "local" their operations may appear.

Nor does the Act deprive appellant of liberty or property under the Fifth Amendment. The commerce power invoked here by the Congress is a specific and plenary one authorized by the Constitution itself. The only questions are: (1) whether Congress had a rational basis for finding that racial discrimination by motels affected commerce, and (2) if it had such a basis, whether the means it selected to eliminate that evil are reasonable and appropriate. If they are, appellant has no "right" to select its guests as it sees fit, free from governmental regulation.

There is nothing novel about such legislation. Thirty-two States now have it on their books either by statute or executive order and many cities provide such regulation. Some of these Acts go back four-score years. It has been repeatedly held by this Court that such laws do not violate the Due Process Clause of the Fourteenth Amendment. Perhaps the first such holding was in the *Civil Rights Cases,* themselves, where Mr. Justice Bradley for the Court inferentially found that innkeepers, "by the laws of all of the States, so far as we are aware, are bound, to the extent of their facilities, to furnish proper accommodation to all unobjectionable persons who in good faith apply for them."

As we have pointed out, 32 States now have such statutes and no case has been cited to us where the attack on a state statute has been successful, either in federal or state courts. Indeed, in some cases the Due Process and Equal Protection Clause objections have been specifically discarded in this Court. *Bob-Lo Excursion Co.* v. *Michigan,* 333 US 28, 34, n. 12 (1948). As a result the constitutionality of such state statutes stands unquestioned. "The authority of the Federal Government over interstate commerce does not differ," it was held in *United States* v. *Rock Royal Co-op., Inc.,* 307 US 533 (1939), "in extent or character from that retained by the states over intrastate commerce." . . .

It is doubtful if in the long run appellant will suffer economic loss as a result of the Act. Experience is to the contrary where discrimination is completely obliterated as to all public accommodations. But whether this be true or not is of no consequence since this Court has specifically held that the fact that a "member of the class which is regulated may suffer economic losses not shared by others . . . has never been a barrier" to such legislation. . . . Likewise in a long line of cases this Court has rejected the claim that the prohibition of racial discrimination in public accommodations interferes with personal liberty. See *District of Columbia* v. *John R. Thompson Co.,* 346 US 100 (1953), and cases there cited, where we concluded that Congress had delegated law-making power to the District of Columbia "as broad as the police power of a state" which included the power to adopt "a law prohibiting discriminations against Negroes by the owners and managers of restaurants in the District of Columbia." Neither do we find any merit in the claim that the Act is a taking of property without just compensation. The cases are to the contrary. . . .

We find no merit in the remainder of appellant's contentions, including that of "involuntary servitude." As we have seen, 32 States prohibit racial discrimination in public accommodations. These laws but codify the common-law innkeeper rule which long predated the Thirteenth Amendment. It is difficult to believe that the Amendment was intended to abrogate this principle. Indeed, the opinion of the Court in *The Civil Rights Cases* is to the contrary as we have seen, it having noted with approval the laws of "all of the states" prohibiting discrimination. We could not say that the requirements of the Act in this regard are in any way "akin to African slavery." . . .

We, therefore, conclude that the action of the Congress in the adoption of the Act as applied here to a motel which concededly serves interstate travelers is within the power granted it by the Commerce Clause of the Constitution, as interpreted by this Court for 140 years. It may be argued that Congress could have pursued other methods to eliminate the obstructions it found in interstate commerce caused by racial discrimination. But this is a matter of policy that rests entirely with the Congress not with the courts. How obstructions in commerce may be removed—what means are to be employed—is within the sound and exclusive discretion of the Congress. It is subject only to one *caveat*—that the means chosen by it must be reasonably adapted to the end permitted by the Constitution. We cannot say that its choice here was not so adapted. The Constitution requires no more.

Affirmed.

DANIEL *v.* PAUL
395 US 298 (1969)

[The Supreme Court in this case held that a snack bar at a privately operated recreational facility met the tests of a public accommodation as intended by the Civil Rights Act of 1964, and that this finding automatically brought the entire recreational facility for swimming, dancing, boating, and miniature golf within prohibition against discrimination as provided by the act. Justice Brennan delivered the Court's opinion. Justice Douglas, concurring, would have rested the decision on the Fourteenth Amendment. Justice Black wrote a dissenting opinion.]

Mr. Justice Brennan delivered the opinion of the Court:

Petitioners, Negro residents of Little Rock, Arkansas, brought this class action in the District Court for the Eastern District of Arkansas to enjoin respondent from denying them admission to a recreational facility called Lake Nixon Club owned and operated by respondent, Euell Paul, and his wife. The complaint alleged that Lake Nixon Club was a "public accommodation" subject to the provisions of Title II of the Civil Rights Act of 1964, 42 U.S.C. § 2000a et seq., and that respondent violated the Act in refusing petitioners admission solely on racial grounds. After trial, the District Court, although finding that respondent had refused petitioners admission solely because they were Negroes, dismissed the complaint on the ground that Lake Nixon Club was not within any of the categories of "public accommodations" covered by the 1964 Act. . . . The Court of Appeals for the Eighth Circuit affirmed, one judge dissenting. We granted certiorari. We reverse.

Lake Nixon Club, located 12 miles west of Little Rock, is a 232-acre amusement area with swimming, boating, sun bathing, picnicking, miniature golf, and dancing facilities and a snack bar. The Pauls purchased the Lake Nixon site in 1962 and subsequently operated this amusement business there in a racially segregated manner.

Title II of the Civil Rights Act of 1964 enacted a sweeping prohibition of discrimination or segregation on the ground of race, color, religion, or national origin at places of public accommodation whose operations affect commerce. This prohibition does not extend to discrimination or segregation at private clubs. But, as both courts below properly found, Lake Nixon is not a private club. It is simply a business operated for a profit with none of the attributes of self-government and member-ownership traditionally associated with private clubs. It is true that following enactment of the Civil Rights Act of 1964, the Pauls began to refer to the establishment as a private club. They even began to require patrons to pay a 25-cent "membership" fee, which gains a purchaser a "membership" card entitling him to enter the Club's premises for an entire season and, on payment of specified additional fees, to use the swimming, boating, and miniature golf facilities. But this "membership" device seems no more than a subterfuge designed to avoid coverage of the 1964 Act. White persons are routinely provided "membership" cards, and some 100,000 whites visit the establishment each season. As the District Court found, Lake Nixon is "open in general to all of the public who are members of the white race." Negroes, on the other hand, are uniformly denied "membership" cards, and thus admission, because of the Pauls' fear that integration would "ruin" the "business." The conclusion of the courts below that Lake Nixon is not a private club is plainly correct—indeed, respondent does not challenge that conclusion here.

We therefore turn to the question whether Lake Nixon Club is "a place of public accommodation" as defined by § 201(b) of the 1964 Act, and, if so, whether its operations "affect commerce" within the meaning of § 201(c) of that Act.

Section 201(b) defines four categories of establishments as covered public accommodations. Three of these categories are relevant here:

Each of the following establishments which serves the public is a place of public accommodation within the meaning of this title if its operations affect commerce. . . .

(2) any restaurant, cafeteria, lunchroom, lunch counter, soda fountain, or other facility principally engaged in selling food for consumption on the premises, including, but not limited to, any such facility located on the premises of any retail establishment; or any gasoline station;

(3) any motion picture house, theater, concert hall, sports arena, stadium or other place of exhibition or entertainment; and

(4) any establishment (A) . . . (ii) within the premises of which is physically located any such covered establishment, and (B) which holds itself out as serving patrons of such covered establishment.

Section 201(c) sets forth standards for determining whether the operations of an establishment in any of these categories affect commerce within the meaning of Title II:

The operations of an establishment affect commerce within the meaning of this subchapter if . . . (2) in the case of an establishment described in paragraph (2) [set out *supra*] . . . it serves or offers to serve interstate travelers or a substantial portion of the food which it serves, or gasoline or other products which it sells, has moved in commerce; (3) in the case of an establishment described in paragraph (3) [set out *supra*] . . . it customarily presents films, performances, athletic teams, exhibitions, or other sources of entertainment which move in commerce; and (4) in the case of an establishment described in paragraph (4) [set out *supra*] . . . there is physically located within its premises, an establishment the operations of which affect commerce within the meaning of this subsection. For purposes of this section, "commerce" means travel, trade, traffic, commerce, transportation, or communication among the several States. . . .

Petitioners argue first that Lake Nixon's snack bar is a covered public accommodation under §§ 201(a)(2) and 201(c)(2), and that as such it brings the entire establishment within the coverage of Title II under §§ 201(b)(4) and 201(c)(4). Clearly, the snack bar is "principally engaged in selling food for consumption on the premises." Thus, it is a covered public accommodation if "it serves or offers to serve interstate travelers or a substantial portion of the food which it serves . . . has moved in commerce." We find that the snack bar is a covered public accommodation under either of these standards.

The Pauls advertise the Lake Nixon Club in a monthly magazine called "Little Rock Today," which is distributed to guests at Little Rock hotels, motels, and restaurants, to acquaint them with available tourist attractions in the area. Regular advertisements for Lake Nixon were also broadcast over two area radio stations. In addition, Lake Nixon has advertised in the "Little Rock Air Force Base," a monthly newspaper published at the Little Rock Air Force Base in Jacksonville, Arkansas. This choice of advertising media leaves no doubt that the Pauls were seeking broad-based patronage from an audience which they knew to include interstate travelers. Thus, the Lake Nixon Club unquestionably offered to serve out-of-state visitors to the Little Rock area. And it would be unrealistic to assume that none of the 100,000 patrons actually served by the Club each season was an interstate traveler. Since the Lake Nixon Club offered to serve and served out-of-state persons, and since the Club's snack bar was established to serve all patrons of the entire facility, we must conclude that the snack bar offered to serve and served out-of-state persons. . . .

The record, although not as complete on this point as might be desired, also demonstrates that a "substantial portion of the food" served by the Lake Nixon Club snack bar has moved in interstate commerce. The snack bar serves a limited fare—hot dogs and hamburgers on buns, soft drinks, and milk. The District Court took judicial notice of the fact that the "principal ingredients going into the bread were produced and processed in other States" and that "certain ingredients [of the soft drinks] were probably obtained . . . from out-of-State sources." Thus, at the very least, three of the four food items sold at the snack bar contain ingredients originating outside of the State. There can be no serious doubt that a "substantial portion of the food" served at the snack bar has moved in interstate commerce. . . .

The snack bar's status as a covered establishment automatically brings the entire Lake Nixon facility within the ambit of Title II. Civil Rights Act of 1964, §§ 201(b)(4) and 201(c)(4), set out *supra*. . . .

Petitioners also argue that the Lake Nixon Club is a covered public accommodation under §§ 201(b)(3) and 201(c)(3) of the 1964 Act. These sections proscribe discrimination by "any motion picture house, theater, concert hall, sports arena, stadium, or other place of exhibition or entertainment" which "customarily presents films, performances, athletic teams, exhibitions, or other sources of entertainment which move in commerce." Under any accepted definition of "entertainment," the Lake Nixon Club would surely qualify as a "place of entertainment." And indeed it advertises itself as such. Respondent argues, however, that in the context of § 201(b)(3) "place of entertainment" refers only to establishments where patrons are entertained as spectators or listeners rather than those where entertainment takes the form of direct participation in some sport or activity. We find no support in the legislative history for respondent's reading of the statute. The few indications of legislative intent are to the contrary.

President Kennedy, in submitting to Congress the public accommodations provisions of the proposed Civil Rights Act, emphasized that "no action is more contrary to the spirit of our democracy and Constitution—or more rightfully resented by a Negro citizen who seeks only equal treatment—than the barring of that citizen from restaurants, hotels, theatres, *recreational areas* and other public accommodations and facilities." (Emphasis added.) While Title II was being considered by the Senate, a civil rights demonstration occurred at a Maryland amusement park. The then Assistant Majority Leader of the Senate, Hubert Humphrey, took note of the demonstration and opined that such an amusement park would be covered by the provisions which were eventually enacted as Title II:

In this particular instance, I am confident that merchandise and facilities used in the park were transported across State lines. . . .

The spectacle of national church leaders being hauled off to jail in a paddy wagon demonstrates the absurdity of the present situation regarding equal access to public facilities in Maryland and the absurdity of the arguments of those who oppose Title II of the President's omnibus civil rights bill. 109 Cong.Rec. 12276 (1963).

Senator Magnuson, floor manager of Title II, spoke in a similar vein.

Admittedly, most of the discussion in Congress regarding the coverage of Title II focused on places of spectator entertainment rather than recreational areas. But it does not follow that the scope of § 201(b)(3) should be restricted to the primary objects of Congress' concern when a natural reading of its language would call for broader coverage. In light of the overriding purpose of Title II "to move the daily affront and humiliation involved in discriminatory denials of access to facilities ostensibly open to the general public," . . . we agree with the en banc decision of the Court of Appeals for the Fifth Circuit in *Miller* v. *Amusement Enterprises, Inc.,* 394 F.2d 342 (1968), that the statutory language "place of entertainment" should be given full effect according to its generally accepted meaning and applied to recreational areas.

The remaining question is whether the operations of the Lake Nixon Club "affect commerce" within the meaning of § 201(c)(3). We conclude that they do. Lake Nixon's customary "sources of entertainment . . . move in commerce." The Club leases 15 paddle boats on a royalty basis from an Oklahoma company. Another boat was purchased from the same company. The Club's juke box was manufactured outside Arkansas and plays records manufactured outside the State. The legislative history indicates that mechanical sources of entertainment such as these were considered by Congress to be "sources of entertainment" within the meaning of § 201(c)(3).

Reversed.

XI. The Electoral Process

1. Legislative Apportionment

BAKER v. CARR
369 US 186 (1962)

[Plaintiffs, qualified to vote for members of the Tennessee legislature representing their counties, brought a class action for a declaration that the state act of 1901, under which the apportionment was made, was unconstitutional, and for an injunction restraining the conduct of further elections under that act. They alleged a gross disproportion of representation to voting population, which placed them in a position of inequality. The federal district court dismissed the action on the ground that it lacked jurisdiction of the subject matter and could not grant relief. By 6 to 2, the U.S. Supreme Court reversed the judgment.

[Justice Brennan, in his opinion for the Court, held that the lower court had jurisdiction of the subject matter, that a justiciable cause of action was stated upon which plaintiffs were entitled to relief. Concurring opinions were written by Justices Douglas, Clark, and Stewart. Justice Frankfurter wrote a dissenting opinion, in which Justice Harlan concurred; and Justice Harlan wrote a dissenting opinion, in which Justice Frankfurter concurred. Justice Whittaker did not participate.

[With the decision in this case, the Court opened the doors of the courts for judicial review of legislative apportionment, and made possible relief where it is shown that the state irrationally disregards its own apportionment standards, or any rational standards, and thus effects a gross disproportion of representation to voting population, and disfavors the voters in some counties—e.g., urban counties—in relation to others. Such action violates the Equal Protection Clause of the Fourteenth Amendment. If discrimination is shown, the right to relief under the Equal Protection Clause is not negated or diminished by the fact that the discrimination relates to political rights. The "political question" doctrine has no relevance to the relationship between the federal courts and the states.]

Mr. Justice Brennan delivered the opinion of the Court:

This civil action was brought under 42 U.S.C. §§ 1983 and 1988, 42 U.S.C.A. §§ 1983, 1988 to redress the alleged deprivation of federal constitutional rights. The complaint, alleging that by means of a 1901 statute of Tennessee apportioning the members of the General Assembly among the State's 95 counties, "these plaintiffs and others similarly situated, are denied the equal protection of the laws accorded them by the Fourteenth Amendment to the Constitution of the United

States by virtue of the debasement of their votes," was dismissed by a three-judge court convened under 28 U.S.C. § 2281, 28 U.S.C.A. § 2281 in the Middle District of Tennessee. The court held that it lacked jurisdiction of the subject matter and also that no claim was stated upon which relief could be granted. We noted probable jurisdiction of the appeal. We hold that the dismissal was error, and remand the cause to the District Court for trial and further proceedings consistent with this opinion.

The General Assembly of Tennessee consists of the Senate with 33 members and the House of Representatives with 99 members. The Tennessee Constitution provides in Art. II as follows:

Sec. 3. Legislative authority—Term of office.—The Legislative authority of this State shall be vested in a General Assembly, which shall consist of a Senate and House of Representatives, both dependent on the people; who shall hold their offices for two years from the day of the general election.

Sec. 4. Census.—An enumeration of the qualified voters, and an apportionment of the Representatives in the General Assembly, shall be made in the year one thousand eight hundred and seventy-one, and within every subsequent term of ten years.

Sec. 5. Apportionment of representatives.—The number of Representatives shall, at the several periods of making the enumeration, be apportioned among the several counties or districts, according to the number of qualified voters in each; and shall not exceed seventy-five, until the population of the State shall be one million and a half, and shall never exceed ninety-nine; Provided, that any county having two-thirds of the ratio shall be entitled to one member.

Sec. 6. Apportionment of senators.—The number of Senators shall, at the several periods of making the enumeration, be apportioned among the several counties or districts according to the number of qualified electors in each, and shall not exceed one-third the number of representatives. In apportioning the Senators among the different counties, the fraction that may be lost by any county or counties, in the apportionment of members to the House of Representatives, shall be made up to such county or counties in the Senate, as near as may be practicable. When a district is composed of two or more counties, they shall be adjoining; and no county shall be divided in forming a district.

Thus, Tennessee's standard for allocating legislative representation among her counties is the total number of qualified voters resident in the respective counties, subject only to minor qualifications. Decennial reapportionment in compliance with the constitutional scheme was effected by the General Assembly each decade from 1871 to 1901. The 1871 apportionment was preceded by an 1870 statute requiring an enumeration. The 1881 apportionment involved three statutes, the first authorizing an enumeration, the second enlarging the Senate from 25 to 33 members and the House from 75 to 99 members, and the third apportioning the membership of both Houses. In 1891 there was both an enumeration and an apportionment. In 1901 the General Assembly abandoned separate enumeration in favor of reliance upon the Federal Census and passed the Apportionment Act here in controversy. In the more than 60 years since that action, all proposals in both Houses of the General Assembly for reapportionment have failed to pass.

Between 1901 and 1961, Tennessee has experienced substantial growth and redistribution of her population. In 1901 the population was 2,020,616, of whom

487,380 were eligible to vote. The 1960 Federal Census reports the State's population at 3,567,089, of whom 2,092,891 are eligible to vote. The relative standings of the counties in terms of qualified voters have changed significantly. It is primarily the continued application of the 1901 Apportionment Act to this shifted and enlarged voting population which gives rise to the present controversy.

Indeed, the complaint alleges that the 1901 statute, even as of the time of its passage, "made no apportionment of Representatives and Senators in accordance with the constitutional formula . . . , but instead arbitrarily and capriciously apportioned representatives in the Senate and House without reference . . . to any logical or reasonable formula whatever." It is further alleged that "because of the population changes since 1900, and the failure of the legislature to reapportion itself since 1901," the 1901 statute became "unconstitutional and obsolete." Appellants also argue that, because of the composition of the legislature effected by the 1901 Apportionment Act, redress in the form of a state constitutional amendment to change the entire mechanism for reapportioning, or any other change short of that, is difficult or impossible. The complaint concludes that "these plaintiffs and others similarly situated, are denied the equal protection of the laws accorded them by the Fourteenth Amendment to the Constitution of the United States by virtue of the debasement of their votes." They seek a declaration that the 1901 statute is unconstitutional and an injunction restraining the appellees from acting to conduct any further elections under it. They also pray that unless and until the General Assembly enacts a valid reapportionment, the District Court should either decree a reapportionment by mathematical application of the Tennessee constitutional formulae to the most recent Federal Census figures, or direct the appellees to conduct legislative elections, primary and general, at large. They also pray for such other and further relief as may be appropriate. . . .

II
JURISDICTION OF THE SUBJECT MATTER

The District Court was uncertain whether our cases withholding federal judicial relief rested upon a lack of federal jurisdiction or upon the inappropriateness of the subject matter for judicial consideration—what we have designated "nonjusticiability." The distinction between the two grounds is significant. In the instance of nonjusticiability, consideration of the cause is not wholly and immediately foreclosed; rather, the Court's inquiry necessarily proceeds to the point of deciding whether the duty asserted can be judicially identified and its breach judicially determined, and whether protection for the right asserted can be judicially molded. In the instance of lack of jurisdiction the cause either does not "arise under" the Federal Constitution, laws or treaties (or fall within one of the other enumerated categories of Art. III, § 2), or is not a "case or controversy" within the meaning of that section; or the cause is not one described by any jurisdictional statute. Our conclusion, . . . that this cause presents no nonjusticiable "political question" settles the only possible doubt that it is a case or controversy. Under the present heading of "Jurisdiction of the Subject Matter" we hold only that the matter set forth in the complaint does arise under the Constitution and is within 28 U.S.C. § 1343, 28, U.S.C.A. § 1343.

Article III, § 2, of the Federal Constitution provides that "the judicial Power shall extend to all Cases, in Law and Equity, arising under this Constitution, the Laws of the United States, and Treaties made, or which shall be made, under their Authority. . . ." It is clear that the cause of action is one which "arises under" the Federal Constitution. The complaint alleges that the 1901 statute effects an apportionment that deprives the appellants of the equal protection of the laws in violation of the Fourteenth Amendment. Dismissal of the complaint upon the ground of lack of jurisdiction of the subject matter would, therefore, be justified only if that claim were "so attenuated and unsubstantial as to be absolutely devoid of merit," . . . or "frivolous." . . . Since the District Court obviously and correctly did not deem the asserted federal constitutional claim unsubstantial and frivolous, it should not have dismissed the complaint for want of jurisdiction of the subject matter. And of course no further consideration of the merits of the claim is relevant to a determination of the court's jurisdiction of the subject matter. . . .

Since the complaint plainly sets forth a case arising under the Constitution, the subject matter is within the federal judicial power defined in Art. III, § 2, and so within the power of Congress to assign to the jurisdiction of the District Courts. Congress has exercised that power in 28 U.S.C. § 1343(3), 28 U.S.C.A. § 1343(3):

> The district courts shall have original jurisdiction of any civil action authorized by law to be commenced by any person . . . to redress the deprivation, under color of any State law, statute, ordinance, regulation, custom or usage, of any right, privilege or immunity secured by the Constitution of the United States. . . .

An unbroken line of our precedents sustains the federal courts' jurisdiction of the subject matter of federal constitutional claims of this nature. . . .

The appellees refer to *Colegrove* v. *Green,* 328 US 549, as authority that the District Court lacked jurisdiction of the subject matter. Appellees misconceive the holding of that case. The holding was precisely contrary to their reading of it. Seven members of the Court participated in the decision. Unlike many other cases in this field which have assumed without discussion that there was jurisdiction, all three opinions filed in *Colegrove* discussed the question. Two of the opinions expressing the views of four of the Justices, a majority, flatly held that there was jurisdiction of that subject matter. . . .

Several subsequent cases similar to *Colegrove* have been decided by the Court in summary *per curiam* statements. None was dismissed for want of jurisdiction of the subject matter.

Two cases decided with opinions after *Colegrove* likewise plainly imply that the subject matter of this suit is within District Court jurisdiction. . . .

We hold that the District Court has jurisdiction of the subject matter of the federal constitutional claim asserted in the complaint.

III
STANDING

A federal court cannot "pronounce any statute, either of a state or of the United States, void, because irreconcilable with the constitution, except as it is called upon to adjudge the legal rights of litigants in actual controversies." . . . Have the appellants alleged such a personal stake in the outcome of the controversy as to assure that concrete adverseness which sharpens the presentation of issues upon which the court so largely depends for illumination of difficult constitutional questions? This is the gist of the question of standing. It is, of course, a question of federal law.

The complaint was filed by residents of Davidson, Hamilton, Knox, Montgomery, and Shelby Counties. Each is a person allegedly qualified to vote for members of the General Assembly representing his county. These appellants sued "on their own behalf and on behalf of all qualified voters of their respective counties, and further, on behalf of all voters of the State of Tennessee who are similarly situated. . . ." The appellees are the Tennessee Secretary of State, Attorney General, Coordinator of Elections, and members of the State Board of Elections; the members of the State Board are sued in their own right and also as representatives of the County Election Commissioners whom they appoint.

We hold that the appellants do have standing to maintain this suit. Our decisions plainly support this conclusion. Many of the cases have assumed rather than articulated the premise in deciding the merits of similar claims. And *Colegrove* v. *Green, supra,* squarely held that voters who allege facts showing disadvantage to themselves as individuals have standing to sue. A number of cases decided after *Colegrove* recognized the standing of the voters there involved to bring those actions. . . .

It would not be necessary to decide whether appellants' allegations of impairment of their votes by the 1901 apportionment will, ultimately, entitle them to any relief, in order to hold that they have standing to seek it. If such impairment does produce a legally cognizable injury, they are among those who have sustained it. They are asserting "a plain, direct and adequate interest in maintaining the effectiveness of their votes." . . . They are entitled to a hearing and to the District Court's decision on their claims. "The very essence of civil liberty certainly consists in the right of every individual to claim the protection of the laws, whenever he receives an injury." . . .

IV
JUSTICIABILITY

In holding that the subject matter of this suit was not justiciable, the District Court relied on *Colegrove* v. *Green, supra,* and subsequent *per curiam* cases. The court stated: "From a review of these decisions there can be no doubt that the federal rule . . . is that the federal courts . . . will not intervene in cases of this type to compel legislative reapportionment." We understand the District Court to have read the cited cases as compelling the conclusion that since the appellants sought to have a legislative apportionment held unconstitutional their suit presented a "political question" and was therefore nonjusticiable. We hold that this challenge to an apportionment presents no nonjusticiable "political question." The cited cases do not hold the contrary.

Of course the mere fact that the suit seeks protection of a political right does not mean it presents a political question. Such an objection "is little more than a play upon words." . . . Rather, it is argued that apportionment cases, whatever the actual wording of the complaint, can involve no federal constitutional right except one resting on the guaranty of a republican form of government, and that complaints based on that clause have been held to present political questions which are nonjusticiable.

We hold that the claim pleaded here neither rests upon nor implicates the Guaranty Clause and that its justiciability is therefore not foreclosed by our decisions of cases involving that clause. The District Court misinterpreted *Colegrove v. Green* and other decisions of this Court on which it relied. Appellants' claim that they are being denied equal protection is justiciable, and if "discrimination is sufficiently shown, the right to relief under the equal protection clause is not diminished by the fact that the discrimination relates to political rights." . . . To show why we reject the argument based on the Guaranty Clause, we must examine the authorities under it. But because there appears to be some uncertainty as to why those cases did present political questions, and specifically as to whether this apportionment case is like those cases, we deem it necessary first to consider the contours of the "political question" doctrine.

Our discussion, even at the price of extending this opinion, requires review of a number of political question cases, in order to expose the attributes of the doctrine —attributes which, in various settings, diverge, combine, appear, and disappear in seeming disorderliness. Since that review is undertaken solely to demonstrate that neither singly nor collectively do these cases support a conclusion that this apportionment case is nonjusticiable, we of course do not explore their implications in other contexts. That review reveals that in the Guaranty Clause cases and in the other "political question" cases, it is the relationship between the judiciary and the coordinate branches of the Federal Government, and not the federal judiciary's relationship to the States, which gives rise to the "political question."

We have said that "in determining whether a question falls within [the political question] category, the appropriateness under our system of government of attributing finality to the action of the political departments and also the lack of satisfactory criteria for a judicial determination are dominant considerations." . . . The nonjusticiability of a political question is primarily a function of the separation of powers. Much confusion results from the capacity of the "political question" label to obscure the need for case-by-case inquiry. Deciding whether a matter has in any measure been committed by the Constitution to another branch of government, or whether the action of that branch exceeds whatever authority has been committed, is itself a delicate exercise in constitutional interpretation, and is a responsibility of this Court as ultimate interpreter of the Constitution. To demonstrate this requires no less than to analyze representative cases and to infer from them the analytical threads that make up the political question doctrine. We shall then show that none of those threads catches this case.

Foreign relations: There are sweeping statements to the effect that all questions touching foreign relations are political questions. Not only does resolution of such issues frequently turn on standards that defy judicial application, or involve the exercise of a discretion demonstrably committed to the executive or legislature; but many such questions uniquely demand single-voiced statement of the Government's views. Yet it is error to suppose that every case or controversy which touches foreign relations lies beyond judicial cognizance. Our cases in this field seem invariably to show a discriminating analysis of the particular question posed, in terms of the history of its management by the political branches, of its susceptibility to judicial handling in the light of its nature and posture in the specific case, and of the possible consequences of judicial action. For example, though a court will not ordinarily inquire whether a treaty has been terminated, since on that question "governmental action . . . must be regarded as of controlling importance," if there has been no conclusive "governmental action" then a court can construe a treaty and may find it provides the answer. . . . Though a court will not undertake to construe a treaty in a manner inconsistent with a subsequent federal statute, no similar hesitancy obtains if the asserted clash is with state laws. . . .

While recognition of foreign governments so strongly defies judicial treatment that without executive recognition a foreign state has been called "a republic of whose existence we know nothing," and the judiciary ordinarily follows the executive as to which nation has sovereignty over disputed territory, once sovereignty over an area is politically determined and declared, courts may examine the resulting status and decide independently whether a statute applies to that area. Similarly, recognition of belligerency abroad is an executive responsibilty, but if the executive proclamations fall short of an explicit answer, a court may construe them seeking, for example, to determine whether the situation is such that statutes designed to assure American neutrality have become operative. . . .

Dates of duration of hostilities: Though it has been stated broadly that "the power which declared the necessity is the power to declare its cessation, and what the cessation requires," . . . here too analysis reveals isolable reasons for the presence of political questions, underlying this Court's refusal to review the political departments' determination of when or whether a war has ended. Dominant is the need for finality in the political determination, for emergency's nature demands "a prompt and unhesitating obedience." . . . Moreover, "the cessation of hostilities does not necessarily end the war power.

Validity of enactments: In *Coleman* v. *Miller, supra,* this Court held that the questions of how long a proposed amendment to the Federal Constitution remained open to ratification, and what effect a prior rejection had on a subsequent ratification, were committed to congressional resolution and involved criteria of decision that necessarily escaped the judicial grasp. Similar considerations apply to the enacting process: "the respect due to coequal and independent departments," and the need for finality and certainty about the status of a statute contribute to judicial reluctance to inquire whether, as passed, it complied with all requisite formalities. . . . But it is not true that courts will never delve into a legislature's records upon such a quest: If the enrolled statute lacks an effective date, a court will not hesitate to seek it in the legislative journals in order to preserve the enactment. . . . The political question doctrine, a tool for maintenance of governmental order, will not be so applied as to promote only disorder.

The status of Indian tribes: This Court's deference to the political departments in determining whether Indians are recognized as a tribe, while it reflects familiar attributes of political questions, . . . also has a unique element in that "the relation of the Indians to the United States is marked by peculiar and cardinal distinctions which exist no where else. . . . [The Indians are] domestic dependent nations . . . in a state of pupilage. Their relation to the United States resembles that of a ward to his guardian." . . . Yet, here too, there is no blanket rule. While " 'It is for [Congress] . . . , and not for the courts, to determine when the true interests of the Indian require his release from [the] condition of tutelage.' . . . it is not meant by this that Congress may bring a community or body of people within the range of this power by arbitrarily calling them an Indian tribe. . . .'" Able to discern what is "distinctly Indian," the courts will strike down any heedless extension of that label. They will not stand impotent before an obvious instance of a manifestly unauthorized exercise of power.

It is apparent that several formulations which vary slightly according to the settings in which the questions arise may describe a political question, although each has one or more elements which identifies it as essentially a function of the separation of powers. Prominent on the surface of any case held to involve a political question is found a textually demonstrable constitutional commitment of the issue to a coordinate political department; or a lack of judicially discoverable and manageable standards for resolving it; or the impossibility of deciding without an initial policy determination of a kind clearly for nonjudicial discretion; or the impossibility of a court's undertaking independent resolution without expressing lack of the respect due coordinate branches of government; or an unusual need for unquestioning adherence to a political decision already made; or the potentiality of embarrassment from multifarious pronouncements by various departments on one question.

Unless one of these formulations is inextricable from the case at bar, there should be no dismissal for nonjusticiability on the ground of a political question's presence. The doctrine of which we treat is one of "political questions," not one of "political cases." The courts cannot reject as "no law suit" a bona fide controversy as to whether some action denominated "political" exceeds constitutional authority. The cases we have reviewed show the necessity for discriminating inquiry into the precise facts and posture of the particular case, and the impossibility of resolution by any semantic cataloguing.

But it is argued that this case shares the characteristics of decisions that constitute a category not yet considered, cases concerning the Constitution's guaranty, in Art. IV, § 4, of a republican form of government. A conclusion as to whether the case at bar does present a political question cannot be confidently reached until we have considered those cases with special care. We shall discover that Guaranty Clause claims involve those elements which define a "political question," and for that reason and no other, they are nonjusticiable. In particular, we shall discover that the nonjusticiability of such claims has nothing to do with their touching upon matters of state governmental organization.

Republican form of government: Luther v. Borden, 7 How. 1, 48 US 1, 12 L. Ed. 581, though in form simply an action for damages for trespass was, as Daniel Webster said in opening the argument for the defense, "an unusual case." The defendants, admitting an otherwise tortious breaking and entering, sought to justify their action on the ground that they were agents of the established lawful government of Rhode Island, which State was then under martial law to defend itself from active insurrection; that the plaintiff was engaged in that insurrection; and that they entered under orders to arrest the plaintiff. The case arose "out of the unfortunate political differences which agitated the people of Rhode Island in 1841 and 1842," which had resulted in a situation wherein two groups laid competing claims to recognition as the lawful government. The plaintiff's right to recover depended upon which of the two groups was entitled to such recognition; but the lower court's refusal to receive evidence or hear argument on that issue, its charge to the jury that the earlier established or "charter" government was lawful, and the verdict for the defendants, were affirmed upon appeal to this Court.

Chief Justice Taney's opinion for the Court reasoned as follows: (1) If a court were to hold the defendants' acts unjustified because the charter government had no legal existence during the period in question, it would follow that all of that government's actions—laws enacted, taxes collected, salaries paid, accounts settled, sentences passed—were of no effect; and that "the officers who carried their decisions into operation [were] answerable as trespassers, if not in some cases as criminals." There was, of course, no room for application of any doctrine of *de facto* status to uphold prior acts of an officer not authorized *de jure,* for such would have defeated the plaintiff's very action. A decision for the plaintiff would inevitably have produced some significant measure of chaos, a consequence to be avoided if it could be done without abnegation of the judicial duty to uphold the Constitution.

(2) No state court had recognized as a judicial responsibility settlement of the issue of the locus of state governmental authority. Indeed, the courts of Rhode Island had in several cases held that "it rested with the political power to decide whether the charter government had been displaced or not," and that that department had acknowledged no change.

(3) Since "the question relates, altogether, to the constitution and laws of [the] . . . State," the courts of the United States had to follow the state courts' decisions unless there was a federal constitutional ground for overturning them.

(4) No provision of the Constitution could be or had been invoked for this purpose except Art. IV, § 4, the Guaranty Clause. Having already noted the absence of standards whereby the choice between governments could be made by a court acting independently, Chief Justice Taney now found further textual and practical reasons for concluding that, if any department of the United States was empowered by the Guaranty Clause to resolve the issue, it was not the Judiciary. . . .

Clearly, several factors were thought by the Court in *Luther* to make the question there "political": the commitment to the other branches of the decision as to which is the lawful state government; the unambiguous action by the President, in recognizing the charter government as the lawful authority; the need for finality in the executive's decision; and the lack of criteria by which a court could determine which form of government was republican.

But the only significance that *Luther* could have for our immediate purposes is in its holding that the Guaranty Clause is not a repository of judicially manageable standards which a court could utilize independently in order to identify a State's lawful government. The Court has since refused to resort to the Guaranty Clause— which alone had been invoked for the purpose—as the source of a constitutional standard for invalidating state action. . . .

Just as the Court has consistently held that a challenge to state action based on the Guaranty Clause presents no justiciable question so has it held, and for the same reasons, that challenges to congressional action on the ground of inconsistency with that clause present no justiciable question. In *Georgia* v. *Stanton,* 6 Wall. 50, 73 US 50, the State sought by an original bill to enjoin execution of the Reconstruction Acts, claiming that it already possessed "a republican State, in every political, legal, constitutional, and juridical sense," and that enforcement of the new Acts "instead of keeping the guaranty against a forcible overthrow of its government by foreign invaders or domestic insurgents, . . . is destroying that very government by force." Congress had clearly refused to recognize the republican character of the government of the suing State. It seemed to the Court that the only constitutional claim that could be presented was under the Guaranty Clause, and Congress having determined that the effects of the recent hostilities required extraordinary measures to restore governments of a republican form, this Court refused to interfere with Congress' action at the behest of a claimant relying on that very guaranty. . . .

We come, finally to the ultimate inquiry whether our precedents as to what constitutes a nonjusticiable "political question" bring the case before us under the umbrella of that doctrine. A natural beginning is to note whether any of the common characteristics which we have been able to identify and label descriptively are present. We find none: The question here is the consistency of state action with the Federal Constitution. We have no question decided, or to be decided, by a political branch of government coequal with this Court. Nor do we risk embarrassment of our government abroad, or grave disturbance at home if we take issue with Tennessee as to the constitutionality of her action here challenged. Nor need the appellants, in order to succeed in this action, ask the Court to enter upon policy determinations for which judicially manageable standards are lacking. Judicial standards under the Equal Protection Clause are well developed and familiar, and it has been open to courts since the enactment of the Fourteenth Amendment to determine, if on the particular facts they must, that a discrimination reflects *no* policy, but simply arbitrary and capricious action.

This case does, in one sense, involve the allocation of political power within a State, and the appellants might conceivably have added a claim under the Guaranty Clause. Of course, as we have seen, any reliance on that clause would be futile. But because any reliance on the Guaranty Clause could not have succeeded it does not follow that appellants may not be heard on the equal protection claim which in fact they tender. True, it must be clear that the Fourteenth Amendment claim is not so enmeshed with those political question elements which render Guaranty Clause claims nonjusticiable as actually to present a political question itself. But we have found that not to be the case here. . . .

We conclude then that the nonjusticiability of claims resting on the Guaranty Clause which arises from their embodiment of questions that were thought "political," can have no bearing upon the justiciability of the equal protection claim presented in this case. Finally, we emphasize that it is the involvement in Guaranty Clause claims of the elements thought to define "political questions," and no other feature, which could render them nonjusticiable. Specifically, we have said that such claims are not held nonjusticiable because they touch matters of state governmental organization. . . .

We conclude that the complaint's allegations of a denial of equal protection present a justiciable constitutional cause of action upon which appellants are entitled to a trial and a decision. The right asserted is within the reach of judicial protection under the Fourteenth Amendment.

The judgment of the District Court is reversed and the cause is remanded for further proceedings consistent with this opinion.

Reversed and remanded.

2. *Equality in Suffrage: Voting Rights Act of 1965*

SOUTH CAROLINA *v.* KATZENBACH
383 US 301 (1966)

[South Carolina, with the support of five other states, filed a bill of complaint in the Supreme Court seeking a declaration that certain provisions of the Voting Rights Act of 1965 violated the Constitution. The Court upheld the constitutionality of provisions for suspension of literacy and other voting tests in states to which the act applied, for the appointment of federal examiners to list qualified voters, and certain other provisions. The Court, in an opinion by Chief Justice Warren, upheld the validity of the provisions under the powers of Congress to enforce the Fifteenth Amendment. Justice Black concurred with substantially all of the Court's opinion but dissented from the holding that the provisions in Section 5 were valid.]

Mr. Chief Justice Warren delivered the opinion of the Court:

By leave of the Court, South Carolina has filed a bill of complaint, seeking a declaration that selected provisions of the Voting Rights Act of 1965 violate the Federal Constitution, and asking for an injunction against enforcement of these provisions by the Attorney General. Original jurisdiction is founded on the presence of a controversy between a State and a citizen of another State under Art. III, § 2, of the Constitution. . . . Because no issues of fact were raised in the complaint, and because of South Carolina's desire to obtain a ruling prior to its primary elections in June 1966, we dispensed with appointment of a trial master and expedited our hearing of the case.

Recognizing that the questions presented were of urgent concern to the entire country, we invited all of the States to participate in this proceeding as friends of the Court. A majority responded by submitting or joining in briefs on the merits, some supporting South Carolina and others the Attorney General.* Seven of these States also requested and received permission to argue the case orally at our hearing. Without exception, despite the emotional overtones of the proceednig, the briefs

---

* States supporting South Carolina: Alabama, Georgia, Louisiana, Mississippi, and Virginia. States supporting the Attorney General: California, Illinois, and Massachusetts, joined by Hawaii, Indiana, Iowa, Kansas, Maine, Maryland, Michigan, Montana, New Jersey, New York, Oklahoma, Oregon, Pennsylvania, Rhode Island, Vermont, West Virginia, and Wisconsin.

and oral arguments were temperate, lawyerlike and constructive. All viewpoints on the issues have been fully developed, and this additional assistance has been most helpful to the Court.

The Voting Rights Act was designed by Congress to banish the blight of racial discrimination in voting, which has infected the electoral process in parts of our country for nearly a century. The Act creates stringent new remedies for voting discrimination where it persists on a pervasive scale, and in addition the statute strengthens existing remedies for pockets of voting discrimination elsewhere in the country. Congress assumed the power to prescribe these remedies from § 2 of the Fifteenth Amendment, which authorizes the national legislature to effectuate by "appropriate" measures the constitutional prohibition against racial discrimination in voting. We hold that the sections of the Act which are properly before us are an appropriate means for carrying out Congress' constitutional responsibilities and are consonant with all other provisions of the Constitution. We therefore deny South Carolina's request that enforcement of these sections of the Act be enjoined.

The Constitutional propriety of the Voting Rights Act of 1965 must be judged with reference to the historical experience which it reflects. Before enacting the measure, Congress explored with great care the problem of racial discrimination in voting. The House and Senate Committees on the Judiciary each held hearings for nine days and received testimony from a total of 67 witnesses. More than three full days were consumed discussing the bill on the floor of the House, while the debate in the Senate covered 26 days in all. At the close of these deliberations, the verdict of both chambers was overwhelming. The House approved the Act by a vote of 328–74, and the measure passed the Senate by a margin of 79–18.

Two points emerge vividly from the voluminous legislative history of the Act contained in the committee hearings and floor debates. First: Congress felt itself confronted by an insidious and pervasive evil which had been perpetuated in certain parts of our country through unremitting and ingenious defiance of the Constitution. Second: Congress concluded that the unsuccessful remedies which it had prescribed in the past would have to be replaced by sterner and more elaborate measures in order to satisfy the clear commands of the Fifteenth Amendment. We pause here to summarize the majority reports of the House and Senate Committees, which document in considerable detail the factual basis for these reactions by Congress.

The Fifteenth Amendment to the Constitution was ratified in 1870. Promptly therafter Congress passed the first Enforcement Act, which made it a crime for public officers and private persons to obstruct exercise of the right to vote. The statute was amended in the following year, to provide for detailed federal supervision of the electoral process, from registration to the certification of returns. As the years passed and fervor for racial equality waned, enforcement of the laws became spotty and ineffective, and most of their provisions were repealed in 1894. The remnants have had little significance in the recently renewed battle against voting discrimination.

Meanwhile, beginning in 1890, the States of Alabama, Georgia, Louisiana, Mississippi, North Carolina, South Carolina, and Virginia enacted tests still in use which were specifically designed to prevent Negroes from voting. Typically, they made the ability to read and write a registration qualification and also required completion of a registration form. These laws were based on the fact that as of 1890 in each of the named States, more than two-thirds of the adult Negroes were illiterate while less than one-quarter of the adult whites were unable to read or write.* At the same time, alternate tests were prescribed in all of the named States to assure that white illiterates would not be deprived of the franchise. These included grandfather clauses, property qualifications, "good character" tests, and the requirement that registrants "understand" or "interpret" certain matter.

The course of subsequent Fifteenth Amendment litigation in this Court demonstrates the variety and persistence of these and similar institutions designed to deprive Negores of the right to vote. Grandfather clauses were invalidated in *Guinn* v. *United States,* 238 US 347, and *Myers* v. *Anderson,* 238 US 368. Procedural hurdles were struck down in *Lane* v. *Wilson,* 307 US 268. The white primary was outlawed in *Smith* v. *Allwright,* 321 US 649, and *Terry* v. *Adams,* 345 US 461. Improper challenges were nullified in *United States* v. *Thomas,* 362 US 58. Racial gerrymandering was forbidden by *Gomillion* v. *Lightfoot,* 364 US 339. Finally, discriminatory application of voting tests was condemned in *Schnell* v. *Davis,* 336 US 933, *Alabama* v. *United States,* 371 US 37, and *Louisiana* v. *United States,* 380 US 145.

According to the results of recent Justice Department voting suits, the latter stratagem is now the principal method used to bar Negroes from the polls. Discriminatory administration of voting qualifications has been found in all eight Alabama cases, in all nine Louisiana cases, and in all nine Mississippi cases which have gone to final judgment. Moreover, in almost all of these cases, the courts have held that the discrimination was pursuant to a widespread "pattern or practice." White applicants for registration have often been excused altogether from the literacy and understanding tests or have been given easy versions, have received extensive help from voting officials, and have been registered despite serious errors in their answers.† Negroes, on the other hand, have typically been required to pass difficult versions of all the tests, without any outside assistance and without the slightest error.‡ The good morals requirement is so vague and subjective that it has constituted an open invitation to abuse at the hands of voting officials. Negroes obliged to obtain vouchers from registered voters have found it virtually impossible to comply in areas where almost no Negroes are on the rolls.

In recent years, Congress has repeatedly tried to cope with the problem by facili-

---

* Prior to the Civil War, most of the slave States made it a crime to teach Negroes how to read or write. Following the war, these States rapidly instituted racial segregation in their public schools. Throughout the period, free public education in the South had barely begun to develop. See *Brown* v. *Board of Education,* 347 US 483, 489–490, n. 4, 74 S.Ct. 686, 688–689, 98 L.Ed. 873; 1959 Comm'n on Civil Rights Rep. 147–151.

† A white applicant in Louisiana satisfied the registrar of his ability to interpret the state constitution by writing, "FRDUM FOOF SPETGH." *United States* v. *State of Louisiana,* D.C., 225 F.Supp. 353, 384. A white applicant in Alabama who had never completed the first grade of school was enrolled after the registrar filled out the entire form for him. *United States* v. *Penton,* D.C., 212 F.Supp. 193, 210–211.

‡ In Panola County, Mississippi, the registrar required Negroes to interpret the provision of the state constitution concerning "the rate of interest on the fund known as the 'Chickasaw School Fund.'" *United States* v. *Duke,* 5 Cir., 332 F.2d 759, 764, 765. In Forrest County, Mississippi, the registrar rejected six Negroes with baccalaureate degrees, three of whom were also Masters of Arts. *United States* v. *Lynd,* 5 Cir., 301 F.2d 818, 821.

tating case-by-case litigation against voting discrimination. The Civil Rights Act of 1957 authorized the Attorney General to seek injunctions against public and private interference with the right to vote on racial grounds. Perfecting amendments in the Civil Rights Act of 1960 permitted the joinder of States as party defendants, gave the Attorney General access to local voting records, and authorized courts to register voters in areas of systematic discrimination. Title I of the Civil Rights Act of 1964 expedited the hearing of voting cases before three-judge courts and outlawed some of the tactics used to disqualify Negroes from voting in federal elections.

Despite the earnest efforts of the Justice Department and of many federal judges, these new laws have done little to cure the problem of voting discrimination. According to estimates by the Attorney General during hearings on the Act, registration of voting age Negroes in Alabama rose only from 10.2% to 19.4% between 1958 and 1964; in Louisiana it barely inched ahead from 31.7% to 31.8% between 1956 and 1965; and in Mississippi it increased only from 4.4% to 6.4% between 1954 and 1964. In each instance, registration of voting age whites ran roughly 50 percentage points or more ahead of Negro registration.

The previous legislation has proved ineffective for a number of reasons. Voting suits are unusually onerous to prepare, sometimes requiring as many as 6,000 man-hours spent combing through registration records in preparation for trial. Litigation has been exceedingly slow, in part because of the ample opportunities for delay afforded voting officials and others involved in the proceedings. Even when favorable decisions have finally been obtained, some of the States affected have merely switched to discriminatory devices not covered by the federal decrees or have enacted difficult new tests designed to prolong the existing disparity between white and Negro registration. Alternatively, certain local officials have defied and evaded court orders or have simply closed their registration offices to freeze the voting rolls. The provision of the 1960 law authorizing registration by federal officers has had little impact on local maladministration because of its procedural complexities.

During the hearings and debates on the Act, Selma, Alabama, was repeatedly referred to as the pre-eminent example of the ineffectiveness of existing legislation. In Dallas County, of which Selma is the seat, there were four years of litigation by the Justice Department and two findings by the federal courts of widespread voting discrimination. Yet in those four years, Negro registration rose only from 156 to 383, although there are approximately 15,000 Negroes of voting age in the county. Any possibility that these figures were attributable to political apathy was dispelled by the protest demonstrations in Selma in the early months of 1965. The House Committee on the Judiciary summed up the reaction of Congress to these developments in the following words:

"The litigation in Dallas County took more than four years to open the door to the exercise of constitutional rights conferred almost a century ago. The problem on a national scale is that the difficulties experienced in suits in Dallas County have been encountered over and over again under existing voting laws. Four years is too long. The burden is too heavy—the wrong to our citizens is too serious—the damage to our national conscience is too great not to adopt more effective measures than exist today. Such is the essential justification for the pending bill." House Report 11.

II

The Voting Rights Act of 1965 reflects Congress' firm intention to rid the country of racial discrimination in voting. The heart of the Act is a complex scheme of stringent remedies aimed at areas where voting discrimination has been most flagrant. Section 4(a)–(d) lays down a formula defining the States and political subdivisions to which these new remedies apply. The first of the remedies, contained in § 4(a), is the suspension of literacy tests and similar voting qualifications for a period of five years from the last occurrence of substantial voting discrimination. Section 5 prescribes a second remedy, the suspension of all new voting regulations pending review by federal authorities to determine whether their use would perpetuate voting discrimination. The third remedy, covered in §§ 6(b), 7, 9, and 13(a), is the assignment of federal examiners by the Attorney General to list qualified applicants who are thereafter entitled to vote in all elections.

Other provisions of the Act prescribe subsidiary cures for persistent voting discrimination. Section 8 authorizes the appointment of federal poll-watchers in places to which federal examiners have already been assigned. Section 10(d) excuses those made eligible to vote in sections of the country covered by § 4(b) of the Act from paying accumulated past poll taxes for state and local elections. Section 12(e) provides for balloting by persons denied access to the polls in areas where federal examiners have been appointed.

The remaining remedial portions of the Act are aimed at voting discrimination in any area of the country where it may occur. Section 2 broadly prohibits the use of voting rules to abridge exercise of the franchise on racial grounds. Sections 3, 6(a), and 13(b) strengthen existing procedures for attacking voting discrimination by means of litigation. Section 4(e) excuses citizens educated in American schools conducted in a foreign language from passing English-language literacy tests. Section 10(a)–(c) facilitates constitutional litigation challenging the imposition of all poll taxes for state and local elections. Sections 11 and 12(a)–(d) authorize civil and criminal sanctions against interference with the exercise of rights guaranteed by the Act.

At the outset, we emphasize that only some of the many portions of the Act are properly before us. South Carolina has not challenged §§ 2, 3, 4(e), 6(a), 8, 10, 12(d) and (e), 13(b), and other miscellaneous provisions having nothing to do with this lawsuit. Judicial review of these sections must await subsequent litigation. In addition, we find that South Carolina's attack on §§ 11 and 12(a)–(c) is premature. No person has yet been subjected to, or even threatened with, the criminal sanctions which these sections of the Act authorize. . . . Consequently, the only sections of the Act to be reviewed at this time are §§ 4(a)–(d), 5, 6(b), 7, 9, 13(a), and certain procedural portions of § 14, all of which are presently in actual operation in South Carolina. We turn now to a detailed description of these provisions and their present status.

Coverage formula

The remedial sections of the Act assailed by South Carolina automatically apply to any State, or to any separate political subdivision such as a county or parish, for which two findings have been made: (1) the Attorney General has determined that on November 1, 1964, it maintained a "test or device," and (2) the Director of the Census has determined that less than 50% of its voting age residents were registered on November 1, 1964, or voted in the presidential election of November 1964. These findings are not reviewable in any court and are final upon publication in the Federal Register. § 4(b). As used throughout the Act, the phrase "test or device" means any requirement that a registrant or voter must "(1) demonstrate the ability to read, write, understand, or interpret any matter, (2) demonstrate any educational achievement or his knowledge of any particular subject, (3) possess good moral character, or (4) prove his qualifications by the voucher of registered voters or members of any other class." § 4(c).

Statutory coverage of a State or political subdivision under § 4(b) is terminated if the area obtains a declaratory judgment from the District Court for the District of Columbia, determining that tests and devices have not been used during the preceding five years to abridge the franchise on racial grounds. The Attorney General shall consent to entry of the judgment if he has no reason to believe that the facts are otherwise. § 4(a). For the purposes of this section, tests and devices are not deemed to have been used in a forbidden manner if the incidents of discrimination are few in number and have been promptly corrected, if their continuing effects have been abated, and if they are unlikely to recur in the future. § 4(d). On the other hand, no area may obtain a declaratory judgment for five years after the final decision of a federal court (other than the denial of a judgment under this section of the Act), determining that discrimination through the use of tests or devices has occurred anywhere in the State or political subdivision. These declaratory judgment actions are to be heard by a three-judge panel, with direct appeal to this Court. § 4(a).

South Carolina was brought within the coverage formula of the Act on August 7, 1965, pursuant to appropriate administrative determinations which have not been challenged in this proceeding. On the same day, coverage was also extended to Alabama, Alaska, Georgia, Louisiana, Mississippi, Virginia, 26 counties in North Carolina, and one county in Arizona. Two more counties in Arizona, one county in Hawaii, and one county in Idaho were added to the list on November 19, 1965. Thus far Alaska, the three Arizona counties, and the single county in Idaho have asked the District Court for the District of Columbia to grant a declaratory judgment terminating statutory coverage.

Suspension of tests

In a State or political subdivision covered by § 4(b) of the Act, no person may be denied the right to vote in any election because of his failure to comply with a "test or device." § 4(a).

On account of this provision, South Carolina is temporarily barred from enforcing the portion of its voting laws which requires every applicant for registration to show that he:

Can both read and write any section of [the State] Constitution submitted to [him] by the registration officer or can show that he owns, and has paid all taxes collectible during the previous year on, property in this State assessed at three hundred dollars or more. 23 S.C.Code 62(4) (1965 Supp.).

The Attorney General has determined that the property qualification is inseparable from the literacy test, and South Carolina makes no objection to this finding. Similar tests and devices have been temporarily suspended in the other sections of the country listed above.

Review of new rules

In a State or political subdivision covered by § 4(b) of the Act, no person may be denied the right to vote in any election because of his failure to comply with a voting qualification or procedure different from those in force on November 1, 1964. This suspension of new rules is terminated, however, under either of the following circumstances: (1) if the area has submitted the rules to the Attorney General, and he has not interposed an objection within 60 days, or (2) if the area has obtained a declaratory judgment from the District Court for the District of Columbia, determining that the rules will not abridge the franchise on racial grounds. These declaratory judgment actions are to be heard by a three-judge panel, with direct appeal to this Court. § 5.

South Carolina altered its voting laws in 1965 to extend the closing hour at polling places from 6 P.M. to 7 P.M. The State has not sought judicial review of this change in the District Court for the District of Columbia, nor has it submitted the new rule to the Attorney General for his scrutiny, although at our hearing the Attorney General announced that he does not challenge the amendment. There are indications in the record that other sections of the country listed above have also altered their voting laws since November 1, 1964.

Federal examiners

In any political subdivision covered by § 4(b) of the Act, the Civil Service Commission shall appoint voting examiners whenever the Attorney General certifies either of the following facts: (1) that he has received meritorious written complaints from at least 20 residents alleging that they have been disenfranchised under color of law because of their race, or (2) that the appointment of examiners is otherwise necessary to effectuate the guarantees of the Fifteenth Amendment. In making the latter determination, the Attorney General must consider, among other factors, whether the registration ratio of non-whites to whites seems reasonably attributable to racial discrimination, or whether there is substantial evidence of good-faith efforts to comply with the Fifteenth Amendment. § 6(b). These certifications are not reviewable in any court and are effective upon publication in the Federal Register. § 4(b).

The examiners who have been appointed are to test the voting qualifications of applicants according to regulations of the Civil Service Commission prescribing times, places, procedures, and forms. §§ 7(a) and 9(b). Any person who meets the voting requirements of state law, insofar as these have not been suspended by the Act, must promptly be placed on a list of eligible voters. Examiners are to transmit their lists at least once a month to the appropriate state or local officials, who in turn are required to place the listed names on the official voting rolls. Any person listed by an examiner is entitled to vote in all elections held more than 45 days after his name has been transmitted. § 7(b).

A person shall be removed from the voting list by an examiner if he has lost his eligibility under valid state law, or if he has been successfully challenged through the procedure prescribed in § 9(a) of the Act. § 7(d). The challenge must be filed at the office within the State designated by the Civil Service Commission; must be submitted within 10 days after the listing is made available for public inspection; must be supported by the affidavits of at least two people having personal knowledge of the relevant facts; and must be served on the person challenged by mail or at his residence. A hearing officer appointed by the Civil Service Commission shall hear the challenge and render a decision within 15 days after the challenge is filed. A petition for review of the hearing officer's decision must be submitted within an additional 15 days after service of the decision on the person seeking review. The court of appeals for the circuit in which the person challenged resides is to hear the petition and affirm the hearing officer's decision unless it is clearly erroneous. Any person listed by an examiner is entitled to vote pending a final decision of the hearing officer or the court. § 9(a).

The listing procedures in a political subdivision are terminated under either of the following circumstances: (1) if the Attorney General informs the Civil Service Commission that all persons listed by examiners have been placed on the official voting rolls, and that there is no longer reasonable cause to fear abridgement of the franchise on racial grounds, or (2) if the political subdivision has obtained a declaratory judgment from the District Court for the District of Columbia, ascertaining the same facts which govern termination by the Attorney General, and the Director of the Census has determined that more than 50% of the non-white residents of voting age are registered to vote. A political subdivision may petition the Attorney General to terminate listing procedures or to authorize the necessary census, and the District Court itself shall request the census if the Attorney General's refusal to do so is arbitrary or unreasonable. § 13(a). The determinations by the Director of the Census are not reviewable in any court and are final upon publication in the Federal Register. § 4(b).

On October 30, 1965, the Attorney General certified the need for federal examiners in two South Carolina counties, and examiners appointed by the Civil Service Commission have been serving there since November 8, 1965. Examiners have also been assigned to 11 counties in Alabama, five parishes in Louisiana, and 19 counties in Mississippi. The examiners are listing people found eligible to vote, and the challenge procedure has been employed extensively. No political subdivision has yet sought to have federal examiners withdrawn through the Attorney General or the District Court for the District of Columbia.

III

These provisions of the Voting Rights Act of 1965 are challenged on the fundamental ground that they exceed the powers of Congress and encroach on an area reserved to the States by the Constitution. South Carolina and certain of the *amici curiae* also attack specific sections of the Act for more particular reasons. They argue that the coverage formula prescribed in § 4(a)–(d) violates the principle of the equality of States, denies due process by employing an invalid presumption and by barring judicial review of administrative findings, constitutes a forbidden bill of attainder, and impairs the separation of powers by adjudicating guilt through legislation. They claim that the review of new voting rules required in § 5 infringes Article III by directing the District Court to issue advisory opinions. They contend that the review of new voting rules required in § 5 infringes Article III by directing the District Court to issue advisory opinions. They contend that the assignment of federal examiners authorized in § 6(b) abridges due process by precluding judicial review of administrative findings and impairs the separation of powers by giving the Attorney General judicial functions; also that the challenge procedure prescribed in § 9 denies due process on account of its speed. Finally, South Carolina and certain of the *amici curiae* maintain that §§ 4(a) and 5, buttressed by § 14(b) of the Act, abridge due process by limiting litigation to a distant forum.

Some of these contentions may be dismissed at the outset. The word "person" in the context of the Due Process Clause of the Fifth Amendment cannot, by any reasonable mode of interpretation, be expanded to encompass the States of the Union, and to our knowledge no court has ever done so. . . . Likewise, courts have consistently regarded the Bill of Attainder Clause of Article I and the principle of the separation of powers only as protections for individual persons and private groups, those who are peculiarly vulnerable to nonjudicial determinations of guilt. . . . Nor does a State have standing as the parent of its citizens to invoke these constitutional provisions against the Federal Government, the ultimate *parens patriae* of every American citizen. . . . The objections to the Act which are raised under these provisions may therefore be considered only as additional aspects of the basic question presented by the case: Has Congress exercised its powers under the Fifteenth Amendment in an appropriate manner with relation to the States?

The ground rules for resolving this question are clear. The language and purpose of the Fifteenth Amendment, the prior decision construing its several provisions, and the general doctrines of constitutional interpretation, all point to one fundamental principle. As against the reserved powers of the States, Congress may use any rational means to effectuate the constitutional prohibition of racial discrimination in voting. . . . We turn now to a more detailed description of the standards which govern our review of the Act.

Section 1 of the Fifteenth Amendment declares that "the right of citizens of the United States to vote shall not be denied or abridged by the United States or by any State on account of race, color, or previous condition of servitude." This declaration has always been treated as self-executing and has repeatedly been construed, without further legislative specification, to invalidate state voting qualifications or procedures which are discriminatory on their face or in practice. . . . These decisions have been rendered with full respect for the general rule, . . . that States "have broad powers to determine the conditions under which the right of suffrage may be exercised." The gist of the matter is that the Fifteenth Amendment supersedes contrary exertions of state power. "When a State exercises power wholly within the domain of state interest, it is insulated from federal judicial review. But such insulation is not carried over when state power is used as an instrument for circumventing a federally protected right." . . .

South Carolina contends that the cases . . . are precedents only for the authority of the judiciary to strike down state statutes and procedures—that to allow an exercise of this authority by Congress would be to rob the courts of their rightful constitutional role. On the contrary, § 2 of the Fifteenth Amendment expressly declares that "Congress shall have the power to enforce this article by appropriate legislation." By adding this authorization, the Framers indicated that Congress was to be chiefly responsible for implementing the rights created in § 1. "It is the power of Congress which has been enlarged. Congress is authorized to *enforce* the prohibitions by appropriate legislation. Some legislation is contemplated to make the [Civil War] amendments fully effective." . . . Accordingly, in addition to the courts, Congress has full remedial powers to effectuate the constitutional prohibition against racial discrimination in voting.

Congress has repeatedly exercised these powers in the past, and its enactments have repeatedly been upheld. . . .

The basic test to be applied in a case involving § 2 of the Fifteenth Amendment is the same as in all cases concerning the express powers of Congress with relation to the reserved powers of the States. Chief Justice Marshall laid down the classic formulation, 50 years before the Fifteenth Amendment was ratified:

Let the end be legitimate, let it be within the scope of the constitution, and all means which are appropriate, which are plainly adapted to that end, which are not prohibited, but consist with the letter and spirit of the constitution, are constitutional. *McCulloch* v. *Maryland*, 4 Wheat. 316, 421, 4 L.Ed. 579.

The Court has subsequently echoed his language in describing each of the Civil War Amendments:

Whatever legislation is appropriate, that is, adapted to carry out the objects the amendments have in view, whatever tends to enforce submission to the prohibitions they contain, and to secure to all persons the enjoyment of perfect equality of civil rights and the equal protection of the laws against State denial or invasion, if not prohibited, is brought within the domain of congressional power. *Ex parte Virginia*, 100 US, at 345–346, 25 L.Ed. 676.

This language was again employed, nearly 50 years later, with reference to Congress' related authority under § 2 of the Eighteenth Amendment. . . .

We therefore reject South Carolina's argument that Congress may appropriately do no more than to forbid violations of the Fifteenth Amendment in general terms —that the task of fashioning specific remedies or of applying them to particular localities must necessarily be left entirely to the courts. Congress is not circumscribed by any such artificial rules under § 2 of the Fifteenth Amendment. In the oft-repeated words of Chief Justice Marshall, referring to another specific legislative authorization in the Constitution. "This power, like all others vested in Congress, is complete in itself, may be exercised to its utmost extent, and acknowledges no limitations, other than are prescribed in the constitution." *Gibbons* v. *Ogden*, 9 Wheat. 1, 196, 6 L.Ed. 23.

IV

Congress exercised its authority under the Fifteenth Amendment in an inventive manner when it enacted the Voting Rights Act of 1965. First: The measure prescribes remedies for voting discrimination which go into effect without any need for prior adjudication. This was clearly a legitimate response to the problem, for which there is ample precedent under other constitutional provisions. . . . Congress had found that case-by-case litigation was inadequate to combat widespread and persistent discrimination in voting, because of the inordinate amount of time and energy required to overcome the obstructionist tactics invariably encountered in these lawsuits. After enduring nearly a century of systematic resistance to the Fifteenth Amendment, Congress might well decide to shift the advantage of time and inertia from the perpetrators of the evil to its victims. The question remains, of course, whether the specific remedies prescribed in the Act were an appropriate means of combatting the evil, and to this question we shall presently address ourselves.

Second: The Act intentionally confines these remedies to a small number of States and political subdivisions which in most instances were familiar to Congress by name. This, too, was a permissible method of dealing with the problem. Congress had learned that substantial voting discrimination presently occurs in certain sections of the country, and it knew no way of accurately forecasting whether the evil might spread elsewhere in the future. In acceptable legislative fashion, Congress chose to limit its attention to the geographic areas where immediate action seemed necessary. . . . The doctrine of the equality of States, invoked by South Carolina, does not bar this approach, for that doctrine applies only to the terms upon which States are admitted to the Union, and not to the remedies for local evils which have subsequently appeared. . . .

Coverage formula

We now consider the related question of whether the specific States and political subdivisions within § 4(b) of the Act were an appropriate target for the new remedies. South Carolina contends that the coverage formula is awkwardly designed in a number of respects and that it disregards various local conditions which have nothing to do with racial discrimination. These arguments, however, are largely beside the point. Congress began work with reliable evidence of actual voting discrimination in a great majority of the States and political subdivisions affected by the new remedies of the Act. The formula eventually evolved to describe these areas was relevant to the problem of voting discrimination, and Congress was therefore entitled to infer a significant danger of the evil in the few remaining States and political subdivisions covered by § 4(b) of the Act. No more was required to justify the application to these areas of Congress' express powers under the Fifteenth Amendment. . . .

To be specific, the new remedies of the Act are imposed on three States—Alabama, Louisiana, and Mississippi—in which federal courts have repeatedly found substantial voting discrimination. Section 4(b) of the Act also embraces two other States—Georgia and South Carolina—plus large portions of a third State—North Carolina—for which there was more fragmentary evidence of recent voting discrimination mainly adduced by the Justice Department and the Civil Rights Commission. All of these areas were appropriately subjected to the new remedies. In identifying past evils, Congress obviously may avail itself of information from any probative source. . . .

The areas listed above, for which there was evidence of actual voting discrimination, share two characteristics incorporated by Congress into the coverage formula: the use of tests and devices for voter registration, and a voting rate in the 1964 presidential election at least 12 points below the national average. Tests and devices are relevant to voting discrimination because of their long history as a tool for perpetrating the evil; a low voting rate is pertinent for the obvious reason that widespread disenfranchisement must inevitably affect the number of actual voters. Accordingly, the coverage formula is rational in both practice and theory. It was therefore permissible to impose the new remedies on the few remaining States and political subdivisions covered by the formula, at least in the absence of proof that they have been free of substantial voting discrimination in recent years. Congress is clearly not bound by the rules relating to statutory presumptions in criminal cases when it prescribes civil remedies against other organs of government under § 2 of the Fifteenth Amendment. . . .

It is irrelevant that the coverage formula excludes certain localities which do not employ voting tests and devices but for which there is evidence of voting discrimination by other means. Congress had learned that widespread and persistent discrimination in voting during recent years has typically entailed the misuse of tests and devices, and this was the evil for which the new remedies were specifically designed. At the same time, through §§ 3, 6(a), and 13(b) of the Act, Congress strengthened existing remedies for voting discrimination in other areas of the country. Legislation need not deal with all phases of a problem in the same way, so long as the distinctions drawn have some basis in practical experience. . . . There are no States or political subdivisions exempted from coverage under § 4(b) in which the record reveals recent racial discrimination involving tests and devices. This fact confirms the rationality of the formula.

Acknowledging the possibility of overbreadth, the Act provides for termination of special statutory coverage at the behest of States and political subdivisions in which the danger of substantial voting discrimination has not materialized during the preceding five years. Despite South Carolina's argument to the contrary, Congress might appropriately limit litigation under this provision to a single court in the District of Columbia, pursuant to its constitutional power under Art. III, § 1, to "ordain and establish" inferior federal tribunals. . . . At the present time, contractual claims against the United States for more than $10,000 must be brought in the Court of Claims, and until 1962, the District of Columbia was the sole venue of suits against federal officers officially residing in the Nation's capital. We have discovered no suggestion that Congress exceeded constitutional bounds in imposing these limitations on litigation against the Federal Government, and the Act is no less reasonable in this respect.

South Carolina contends that these termination procedures are a nullity because they impose an impossible burden of proof upon States and political subdivisions entitled to relief. As the Attorney General pointed out during hearings on the Act, however, an area need do no more than to submit affidavits from voting officials, asserting that they have not been guilty of racial discrimination through the use of tests and devices during the past five years, and then to refute whatever evidence to the contrary may be adduced by the Federal Government. Section 4(d) further assures that an area need not disprove each isolated instance of voting discrimination in order to obtain relief in the termination proceedings. The burden of proof is therefore quite bearable, particularly since the relevant facts relating to the conduct of voting officials are peculiarly within the knowledge of the States and political subdivisions themselves. . . .

The Act bars direct judicial review of the findings by the Attorney General and the Director of the Census which trigger application of the coverage formula. We reject the claim by Alabama as *amicus curiae* that this provision is invalid because it allows the new remedies of the Act to be imposed in an arbitrary way. The Court has already permitted Congress to withdraw judicial review of administrative determinations in numerous cases involving the statutory rights of private parties. . . . In this instance, the findings not subject to review consist of objective statistical determinations by the Census Bureau and a routine analysis of state statutes by the Justice Department. These functions are unlikely to arouse any plausible dispute, as South Carolina apparently concedes. In the event that the formula is improperly applied, the area affected can always go into court and obtain termination of coverage under § 4(b), provided of course that it has not been guilty of voting discrimination in recent years. This procedure serves as a partial substitute for direct judicial review.

Suspension of tests

We now arrive at consideration of the specific remedies prescribed by the Act for areas included within the coverage formula. South Carolina assails the temporary suspension of existing voting qualifications, reciting the rule laid down by *Lassiter* v. *Northampton County Bd. of Elections,* 360 US 45, that literacy tests and related devices are not in themselves contrary to the Fifteenth Amendment. In that very case, however, the Court went on to say, "Of course a literacy test, fair on its face, may be employed to perpetuate that discrimination which the Fifteenth Amendment was designed to uproot." The record shows that in most of the States covered by the Act, including South Carolina, various tests and devices have been instituted with the purpose of disenfranchising Negroes, have been framed in such a way as to facilitate this aim, and have been administered in a discriminatory fashion for many years. Under these circumstances, the Fifteenth Amendment has clearly been violated. . . .

The Act suspends literacy tests and similar devices for a period of five years from the last occurrence of substantial voting discrimination. This was a legitimate response to the problem, for which there is ample precedent in Fifteenth Amendment cases. Underlying the response was the feeling that States and political subdivisions which had been allowing white illiterates to vote for years could not sincerely complain about "dilution" of their electorates through the registration of Negro illiterates. Congress knew that continuance of the tests and devices in use at the present time, no matter how fairly administered in the future, would freeze the effect of past discrimination in favor of unqualified white registrants. Congress permissibly rejected the alternative of requiring a complete re-registration of all voters, believing that this would be too harsh on many whites who had enjoyed the franchise for their entire adult lives.

Review of new rules

The Act suspends new voting regulations pending scrutiny by federal authorities to determine whether their use would violate the Fifteenth Amendment. This may have been an uncommon exercise of congressional power, as South Carolina contends, but the Court has recognized that exceptional conditions can justify legislative measures not otherwise appropriate. . . . Congress knew that some of the States covered by § 4(b) of the Act had resorted to the extraordinary stratagem of contriving new rules of various kinds for the sole purpose of perpetuating voting discrimination in the face of adverse federal decrees. Congress had reason to suppose that these States might try similar maneuvers in the future, in order to evade the remedies for voting discrimination contained in the Act itself. Under the compulsion of these unique circumstances, Congress responded in a permissibly decisive manner.

For reasons already stated, there was nothing inappropriate about limiting litigation under this provision to the District Court for the District of Columbia, and in putting the burden of proof on the areas seeking relief. Nor has Congress authorized the District Court to issue advisory opinions, in violation of the principles of Article III invoked by Georgia as *amicus curiae*. The Act automatically suspends the operation of voting regulations enacted after November 1, 1964, and furnishes mechanisms for enforcing the suspension. A State or political subdivision wishing to make use of a recent amendment to its voting laws therefore has a concrete and immediate "controversy" with the Federal Government. . . . An appropriate remedy is a judicial determination that continued suspension of the new rule is unnecessary to vindicate rights guaranteed by the Fifteenth Amendment.

Federal examiners

The Act authorizes the appointment of federal examiners to list qualified applicants who are thereafter entitled to vote, subject to an expeditious challenge procedure. This was clearly an appropriate response to the problem, closely related to remedies authorized in prior cases. . . . In many of the political subdivisions covered by § 4(b) of the Act, voting officials have persistently employed a variety of procedural tactics to deny Negroes the franchise, often in direct defiance or evasion of federal decrees. Congress realized that merely to suspend voting rules which have been misused or are subject to misuse might leave this localized evil undisturbed. As for the briskness of the challenge procedure, Congress knew that in some of the areas affected, challenges had been persistently employed to harass registered Negroes. It chose to forestall this abuse, at the same time providing alternative ways for removing persons listed through error or fraud. In addition to the judicial challenge procedure, § 7(d) allows for the removal of names by the examiner himself, and § 11(c) makes it a crime to obtain a listing through fraud.

In recognition of the fact that there were political subdivisions covered by § 4(b) of the Act in which the appointment of federal examiners might be unnecessary,

Congress assigned the Attorney General the task of determining the localities to which examiners should be sent. There is no warrant for the claim, asserted by Georgia as *amicus curiae,* that the Attorney General is free to use this power in an arbitrary fashion, without regard for the purposes of the Act. Section 6(b) sets adequate standards to guide the exercise of his discretion, by directing him to calculate the registration ratio of non-whites to whites, and to weigh evidence of good-faith efforts to avoid possible voting discrimination. At the same time, the special termination procedures of § 13(a) provide indirect judicial review for the political subdivisions affected, assuring the withdrawal of federal examiners from areas where they are clearly not needed. . . .

After enduring nearly a century of widespread resistance to the Fifteenth Amendment, Congress has marshalled an array of potent weapons against the evil, with authority in the Attorney General to employ them effectively. Many of the areas directly affected by this development have indicated their willingness to abide by any restraints legitimately imposed upon them. We here hold that the portions of the Voting Rights Act properly before us are a valid means for carrying out the commands of the Fifteenth Amendment. Hopefully, millions of non-white Americans will now be able to participate for the first time on an equal basis in the government under which they live. We may finally look forward to the day when truly "the right of citizens of the United States to vote shall not be denied or abridged by the United States or by any State on account of race, color, or previous condition of servitude."

The bill of complaint is dismissed.

Bill dismissed.

XII. Personal Security: Procedural Rights

1. Bills of Attainder

UNITED STATES v. LOVETT
328 US 303 (1946)

[In 1943 Congressman Martin Dies read to the House of Representatives the names of thirty-eight employees of the Federal Government who, he said, had "subversive affiliations." The House directed a subcommittee of the Appropriations Committee to determine the subversive nature of each of the accused employees. The subcommittee conducted secret hearings and found that in its opinion three of the thirty-eight persons deserved dismissal. The House then attached a rider to the Urgent Deficiency Appropriation Act forbidding the payment of compensation to the three employees. These employees attacked the rider as a bill of attainder, and their contentions were sustained by a unanimous Supreme Court in the present case.

[In the fourteenth century Parliament began to enact bills of attainder, acts punishing named persons by death or exile. Acts that provided milder penalties were also passed and were known as bills of pains and penalties. Both types of acts were criticized severely. Parliament has not passed a bill of attainder since 1696, and the last time it tried, without success, to pass a bill of pains and penalties was in 1821. The American colonies during the Revolution and until the adoption of the Constitution passed bills of attainder against Loyalists.

[The Constitution, Art. I, Sec. 9, Cl. 3, provides that Congress shall not pass a bill of attainder. As interpreted by the Court, the prohibition on bills of attainder comprehends also bills of pains and penalties: the Constitution prohibits all legislative acts, regardless of their form, if they inflict punishment without a judicial trial on named persons or on the easily ascertainable members of a group.

[The Constitution also prohibits states from passing bills of attainder. Art. I, Sec. 10.]

Mr. Justice Black delivered the opinion of the Court:

In 1943 the respondents, Lovett, Watson, and Dodd, were and had been for several years working for the Government. The Government agencies which had lawfully employed them were fully satisfied with the quality of their work and wished to keep them employed on their jobs. Over the protest of those employing agencies, Congress provided in Section 304 of the Urgent Deficiency Appropriation Act of 1943, by way of an amendment attached to the House bill, that after November 15, 1943, no salary or compensation should be paid respondents out of any monies then or thereafter appropriated except for services as jurors or members of the armed forces, unless they were prior to November 15, 1943, again appointed to jobs by the President with the advice and consent of the Senate. Notwithstanding the Congressional enactment, and the failure of the President to reappoint respondents, the agencies kept all the respondents at work on their jobs for varying periods after November 15, 1943; but their compensation was discontinued after that date. To secure compensation for this post-November 15 work, respondents brought these actions in the Court of Claims. They urged that Section 304 is unconstitutional and void on the grounds that: (1) The Section, properly interpreted, shows a Congressional purpose to exercise the power to remove executive employees, a power not entrusted to Congress but to the Excutive Branch of Government under Article II, Sections 1, 2, 3, and 4 of the Constitution; (2) the Section violates Article I, Section 9, Clause 3, of the Constitution which provides that "no bill of attainder or ex post facto law shall be passed"; (3) the Section violates the Fifth Amendment, in that it singles out these three respondents and deprives them of their liberty and property without due process of law. The Solicitor General, appearing for the Government, joined in the first two of respondents' contentions but took no position on the third. [A] House Resolution . . . authorized a special counsel to appear on behalf of the Congress. This counsel denied all three of respondents' contentions. . . . The Court of Claims entered judgments in favor of respondents. . . .

I

In view of the facts just set out we cannot agree with the two judges of the Court of Claims who held that Section 304 required "a mere stoppage of disbursing routine, nothing more," and left the employer governmental agencies free to continue employing respondents and to incur contractual obligations by virtue of such continued work which respondents could enforce in the Court of Claims. Nor can we agree with counsel for Congress that the Section did not provide for the dismissal of respondents but merely forbade governmental agencies to compensate respondents for their work or to incur obligations for such compensation at any and all times. We therefore cannot conclude, as he urges, that Section 304 is a mere appropriation measure, and that since Congress under the Constitution has complete control over appropriations, a challenge to the measure's constitutionality does not present a justiciable question in the courts, but is merely a political issue over which Congress has final say.

We hold that the purpose of Section 304 was not merely to cut off respondents' compensation through regular disbursing channels but permanently to bar them from government service, and that the issue of whether it is constitutional is justiciable. The Section's language as well as the circumstances of its passage which we have just described show that no mere question of compensation procedure or of appropriations was involved, but that it was designed to force the employing agencies to discharge respondents and to bar their being hired by any other governmental agency. . . . Any other interpretation of the Section would completely frustrate the purpose of all who sponsored Section 304, which clearly was to "purge" the then existing and all future lists of Government employees of those whom Congress deemed guilty of "subversive activities" and therefore "unfit" to hold a federal job. What was challenged therefore is a statute which, because of what Congress thought to be their political beliefs, prohibited respondents from ever engaging in any government work, except as jurors or soldiers. Respondents claimed that their discharge was unconstitutional; that they consequently rightfully continued to work for the Government and that the Government owes them compensation for services performed under contracts of employment. Congress has established the Court of Claims to try just such controversies. What is involved here is a Congressional proscription of Lovett, Watson, and Dodd, prohibiting their ever holding a Government job. Were this case to be not justiciable, Congressional action, aimed at three named individuals, which stigmatized their reputation and seriously impaired their chance to earn a living, could never be challenged in any court. Our Constitution did not contemplate such a result. To quote Alexander Hamilton

. . . a limited constitution . . . [is] one which contains certain specified exceptions to the legislative authority; such, for instance, as that it shall pass no bills of attainder, no ex post facto laws, and the like. Limitations of this kind can be preserved in practice no other way than through the medium of the courts of justice; whose duty it must be to declare all acts contrary to the manifest tenor of the Constitution void. Without this, all the reservations of particular rights or privileges would amount to nothing. Federalist Paper No. 78.

II

We hold that Section 304 falls precisely within the category of Congressional actions which the Constitution barred by providing that "No Bill of Attainder or ex post facto Law shall be passed." In *Cummings* v. *State of Missouri,* 4 Wall. 277, this Court said, "A bill of attainder is a legislative act which inflicts punishment without a judicial trial. If the punishment be less than death, the act is termed a bill of pains and penalties. Within the meaning of the Constitution, bills of attainder include bills of pains and penalties." The *Cummings* decision involved a provision of the Missouri Reconstruction Constitution which required persons to take an Oath of Loyalty as a prerequisite to practicing a profession. Cummings, a Catholic Priest, was convicted for teaching and preaching as a minister without taking the oath. The oath required an applicant to affirm that he had never given aid or comfort to persons engaged in hostility to the United States and had never "been a member of, or connected with, any order, society, or organization, inimical to the government of the United States. . . ." In an illuminating opinion which gave the historical background of the Constitutional prohibition against bills of attainder, this Court invalidated the Missouri Constitutional provision both because it constituted a bill of attainder and because it had an ex post facto operation. On the same day the *Cummings Case* was decided, the Court, in *Ex parte Garland,* 4 Wall. 333, also held invalid on the same grounds an Act of Congress which required attorneys practicing before this Court to take a similar oath. Neither of these cases has ever been overruled. They stand for the proposition that legislative acts, no matter what their form, that apply either to named individuals or to easily ascertainable members of a group in such a way as to inflict punishment on them without a judicial trial are bills of attainder prohibited by the Constitution. Adherence to this principle requires invalidation of Section 304. We do adhere to it.

Section 304 was designed to apply to particular individuals. Just as the statute in the two cases mentioned it "operates as a legislative decree of perpetual exclusion" from a chosen vocation. This permanent proscription from any opportunity to serve the Government is punishment, and of a most severe type. It is a type of punishment which Congress has only invoked for special types of odious and dangerous crimes, such as treason, . . . acceptance of bribes by members of Congress, . . . or by other government officials, . . . and interference with elections by Army and Navy officers. . . .

Section 304, thus, clearly accomplishes the punishment of named individuals without a judicial trial. The fact that the punishment is inflicted through the instrumentality of an Act specifically cutting off the pay of certain named individuals found guilty of disloyalty, makes it no less galling or effective than if it had been done by an Act which designated the conduct as criminal. No one would think that Congress could have passed a valid law, stating that after investigation it had found Lovett, Dodd, and Watson "guilty" of the crime of engaging in "subversive activities," defined that term for the first time, and sentenced them to perpetual exclusion from any government employment. Section 304, while it does not use that language, accomplishes that result. The effect was to inflict punishment without the safeguards of a judicial trial and "determined by no previous law or fixed rule." The Constitution declares that that cannot be done either by a state or by the United States.

Those who wrote our Constitution well knew the danger inherent in special legislative acts which take away the life, liberty, or property of particular named persons, because the legislature thinks them guilty of conduct which deserves punishment. They intended to safeguard the people of this country from punishment without trial by duly constituted courts. . . . And even the courts to which this important function was entrusted, were commanded to stay their hands until and unless certain tested safeguards were observed. An accused in court must be tried by an impartial jury, has a right to be represented by counsel, he must be clearly informed of the charge against him, the law which he is charged with violating must have been passed before he committed the act charged, he must be confronted by the witnesses against him, he must not be compelled to incriminate himself, he cannot twice be put in jeopardy for the same offense, and even after conviction no cruel and unusual punishment can be inflicted upon him. . . . When our Constitution and Bill of Rights were written, our ancestors had ample reason to know that legislative trials and punishments were too dangerous to liberty to exist in the nation of free men they envisioned. And so they proscribed bills of attainder. Section 304 is one. Much as we regret to declare that an Act of Congress violates the Constitution, we have no alternative here.

Section 304 therefore does not stand as an obstacle to payment of compensation to Lovett, Watson, and Dodd. The judgment in their favor is affirmed.

2. *Unreasonable Searches and Seizures*

MAPP *v.* OHIO
367 US 643 (1961)

[The Fourth Amendment prohibits unreasonable searches and seizures. It does not expressly, however, make inadmissible the evidence that has been obtained in violation of this constitutional prohibition. In *Wolf* v. *Colorado,* 338 US 25 (1949), a majority of the Court seemed to be of the opinion that the exclusion of such evidence in a federal court is not a command of the Fourth Amendment but is a judicially created rule. A minority of Justices maintained that the exclusion of such evidence was required by the Constitution. Whether constitutional or judicially created, the rule was settled that in a federal court evidence obtained by means of an illegal search and seizure by public officers is not admissible against a defendant in a criminal prosecution if he makes timely objection.

[In the *Wolf* case the Court unanimously held that security of a person's privacy against arbitrary intrusion by the police is a basic requirement in a free society and is, therefore, enforceable against the states through the Due Process Clause of the Fourteenth Amendment. But though the state violates the Constitution by procuring evidence by an unreasonable search and seizure, the courts of the state may nonetheless admit the evidence—the admissibility or inadmissibility of such evidence is a matter for the state to decide. Justices Murphy, Rutledge, and Douglas, dissenting, said that the Constitution prohibits the use of such evidence in both federal and state courts.

[In *Mapp*, the Court, by 6 to 3, overruled *Wolf*. In the opinion of Justice Clark, the Court held that, as a matter of due process under the Fourteenth Amendment, evidence obtained by a search and seizure in violation of the Fourth Amendment is inadmissible in a state court, as it is in a federal court.

[Justice Black, in a concurring opinion, expressed the view that the Fourth Amendment, standing alone, would not be sufficient to bar the introduction into evidence of papers and effects seized in violation of its commands. But taking the Fourth Amendment together with the Fifth Amendment's ban against compelled self-incrimination, a constitutional basis emerges for the exclusionary rule as a constitutional requirement. Justice Douglas also wrote a concurring opinion, in which he attacked the "double standard" that resulted from the *Wolf* decision. Justice Harlan wrote a dissenting opinion, in which Justices Frankfurter and Whittaker joined, wherein he contended that *Wolf* was a sound decision and should not be overruled.

[The decision in *Mapp* is one of the most important decisions in federal-state relations and has aroused much controversy.]

Mr. Justice Clark delivered the opinion of the Court:

Appellant stands convicted of knowingly having had in her possession and under her control certain lewd and lascivious books, pictures, and photographs in violation of § 2905.34 of Ohio's Revised Code. As officially stated in the syllabus to its opinion, the Supreme Court of Ohio found that her conviction was valid though "based primarily upon the introduction in evidence of lewd and lascivious books and pictures unlawfully seized during an unlawful search of defendant's home. . . ."

On May 23, 1957, three Cleveland police officers arrived at appellant's residence in that city pursuant to information "a person [was] hiding out in the home who was wanted for questioning in connection with a recent bombing, and that there was a large amount of policy paraphernalia being hidden in the home." Miss Mapp and her daughter by a former marriage lived on the top floor of the two-family dwelling. Upon their arrival at that house, the officers knocked on the door and demanded entrance, but appellant, after telephoning her attorney, refused to admit them without a search warrant. They advised their headquarters of the situation and undertook a surveillance of the house.

The officers again sought entrance some three hours later when four or more additional officers arrived on the scene. When Miss Mapp did not come to the door immediately, at least one of the several doors to the house was forcibly opened and the policemen gained admittance. Meanwhile Miss Mapp's attorney arrived, but the officers, having secured their own entry, and continuing in their defiance of the law, would permit him neither to see Miss Mapp nor to enter the house. It appears that Miss Mapp was halfway down the stairs from the upper floor to the front door when the officers, in this highhanded manner, broke into the hall. She demanded to see the search warrant. A paper, claimed to be a warrant, was held up by one of the officers. She grabbed the "warrant" and placed it in her bosom. A struggle ensued in which the officers recovered the piece of paper and as a result of which they handcuffed appellant because she had been "belligerent" in resisting their official rescue of the "warrant" from her person. Running roughshod over appellant, a policeman "grabbed" her, "twisted [her] hand," and she "yelled [and] pleaded with him" because "it was hurting." Appellant, in handcuffs, was then forcibly taken upstairs to her bedroom, where the officers searched a dresser, a chest of drawers, a closet and some suitcases. They also looked into a photo album and through personal papers belonging to the appellant. The search spread to the rest of the second floor including the child's bedroom, the living room, the kitchen and a dinette. The basement of the building and a trunk found therein were also searched. The obscene materials for possession of which she was ultimately convicted were discovered in the course of that widespread search.

At the trial no search warrant was produced by the prosecution, nor was the failure to produce one explained or accounted for. At best, "there is, in the record, considerable doubt as to whether there ever was any warrant for the search of defendant's home." The Ohio Supreme Court believed a "reasonable argument" could be made that the conviction should be reversed "because the 'methods' employed to obtain the [evidence] . . . were such as to offend 'a sense of justice,'" but the court found determinative the fact that the evidence had not been taken "from defendant's person by the use of brutal or offensive physical force against defendant."

The State says that even if the search were made without authority, or otherwise unreasonably, it is not prevented from using the unconstitutionality seized evidence at trial, citing *Wolf* v. *Colorado,* 338 US 25 (1949), in which this Court did indeed hold "that in a prosecution in a State court for a State crime the Fourteenth Amendment does not forbid the admission of evidence obtained by an unreasonable search and seizure." On this appeal, of which we have noted probable jurisdiction, it is urged once again that we review that holding.

I

Seventy-five years ago, in *Boyd* v. *United States,* 116 US 616 (1886), considering the Fourth and Fifth Amendments as running "almost into each other" on the facts before it, this Court held that the doctrines of those Amendments

. . . apply to all invasions on the part of the government and its employees of the sanctity of a man's home and the privacies of life. It is not the breaking of his doors, and the rummaging of his drawers, that constitutes the essence of the offense; but it is the invasion of his indefeasible right of personal security, personal liberty and private property. . . . Breaking into a house and opening boxes and drawers are circumstances of aggravation; but any forcible and compulsory extortion of a man's own testimony or of his private papers to be used as evidence to convict him of crime or to forfeit his goods, is within the condemnation . . . [of those Amendments].

The Court noted that

constitutional provisions for the security of person and property should be liberally construed. . . . It is the duty of courts to be watchful for the constitutional rights of the citizen, and against any stealthy encroachments thereon.

In this jealous regard for maintaining the integrity of individual rights the Court gave life to Madison's prediction that "independent tribunals of justice . . . will be naturally led to resist every encroachment upon rights expressly stipulated for in the Constitution by the declaration of rights." I *Annals of Cong.* 439 (1789). Concluding, the Court specifically referred to the use of the evidence there seized as "unconstitutional."

Less than 30 years after *Boyd,* this Court, in *Weeks* v. *United States,* 232 US 383 (1914), stated that

the Fourth Amendment . . . put the courts of the United States and Federal officials, in the exercise of their power and authority, under limitations and restraints [and] . . . forever secure[d] the people, their persons, houses, papers and effects against all unreasonable searches and seizures under the guise of law . . . and the duty of giving to it force and effect is obligatory upon all entrusted under our Federal system with the enforcement of the laws.

Specifically dealing with the use of the evidence unconstitutionally seized, the Court concluded:

If letters and private documents can thus be seized and held and used in evidence against a citizen accused of an offense, the protection of the Fourth Amendment declaring his right to be secure against such searches and seizures is of no value, and, so far as those thus placed are concerned, might as well be stricken from the Constitution. The efforts of the courts and their officials to bring the guilty to punishment, praiseworthy as they are, are not to be aided by the sacrifice of those great principles established by years of endeavor and suffering which have resulted in their embodiment in the fundamental law of the land.

Finally, the Court in that case clearly stated that use of the seized evidence involved "a denial of the constitutional rights of the accused." Thus, in the year 1914, in the *Weeks* case, this Court "for the first time" held that "in a federal prosecution the Fourth Amendment barred the use of evidence secured through an illegal search and seizure." This Court has ever since required of federal law officers a strict adherence to that command which this Court has held to be a clear, specific, and constitutionally required—even if judicially implied—deterrent safeguard without insistence upon which the Fourth Amendment would have been reduced to "a form of words." . . . It meant, quite simply, that "conviction by means of unlawful seizures and enforced confessions . . . should find no sanction in the judgments of the courts . . ." and that such evidence "shall not be used at all." . . .

There are in the cases of this Court some passing references to the *Weeks* rule as being one of evidence. But the plain and unequivocal language of *Weeks*—and its later paraphrase in *Wolf*—to the effect that the *Weeks* rule is of constitutional origin, remains entirely undisturbed. . . .

II

In 1949, 35 years after *Weeks* was announced, this Court, in *Wolf* v. *Colorado,* again for the first time, discussed the effect of the Fourth Amendment upon the States through the operation of the Due Process Clause of the Fourteenth Amendment. It said:

[W]e have no hesitation in saying that were a State affirmatively to sanction such police incursion into privacy it would run counter to the guaranty of the Fourteenth Amendment.

Nevertheless, after declaring that the "security of one's privacy against arbitrary intrusion by the police" is "implicit in the 'concept of ordered liberty' and as such enforceable against the States through the Due Process Clause," cf. *Palko* v. *Connecticut,* 320 US 319 (1937), and announcing that it "stoutly adhere[d]" to the *Weeks* decision, the Court decided that the *Weeks* exclusionary rule would not then be imposed upon the States as "an essential ingredient of the right." The Court's reasons for not considering essential to the right of privacy, as a curb imposed upon the States by the Due Process Clause, that which decades before had been posited as part and parcel of the Fourth Amendment's limitation upon federal encroachment of individual privacy, were bottomed on factual considerations.

While they are not basically relevant to a decision that the exclusionary rule is an essential ingredient of the Fourth Amendment as the right it embodies is vouchsafed against the States by the Due Process Clause, we will consider the current validity of the factual grounds upon which *Wolf* was based.

The Court in *Wolf* first stated that "[t]he contrariety of views of the States" on the adoption of the exclusionary rule of *Weeks* was "particularly impressive" and, in this connection, that it could not "brush aside the experience of States which deem the incidence of such conduct by the police too slight to call for a deterrent remedy . . . by overriding the [States'] relevant rules of evidence." While in 1949, prior to the *Wolf* case, almost two-thirds of the States were opposed to the use of the exclusionary rule, now, despite the *Wolf* case, more than half of those since passing upon it, by their own legislative or judicial decision, have wholly or partly adopted or adhered to the *Weeks* rule. See *Elkins* v. *United States,* 364 US 206, Appendix, pp. 224–232 (1960). Significantly, among those now following the rule is California which, according to its highest court, was "compelled to reach that conclusion because other remedies have completely failed to secure compliance with the constitutional provisions. . . ." In connection with this California case, we note that the second basis elaborated in *Wolf* in support of its failure to enforce the exclusionary doctrine against the States was that "other means of protection" have been afforded "the right to privacy." The experience of California that such other remedies have been worthless and futile is buttressed by the experience of other States. The obvious futility of relegating the Fourth Amendment to the protection of other remedies has, moreover, been recognized by this Court since *Wolf*. See *Irvine* v. *California,* 347 US 128, 137 (1954).

Likewise, time has set its face against what *Wolf* called the "weighty testimony of *People* v. *Defore,* 242 N.Y. 13 (1926). There Justice (then Judge) Cardozo, rejecting adoption of the *Weeks* exclusionary rule in New York, had said that "[t]he Federal rule as it stands is either too strict or too lax." However, the force of that reasoning has been largely vitiated by later decisions of this Court. These include the recent discarding of the "silver platter" doctrine which allowed federal judicial use of evidence seized in violation of the Constitution by state agents, *Elkins* v. *United States;* the relaxation of the formerly strict requirements as to standing to challenge the use of evidence thus seized, so that now the procedure of exclusion, "ultimately referable to constitutional safeguards," is available to anyone even "legitimately on [the] premises" unlawfully searched, *Jones* v. *United States,* 362 US 257 (1960); and, finally, the formulation of a method to prevent state use of evidence unconstitutionally seized by federal agents, *Rea* v. *United States,* 350 US 214 (1956). Because there can be no fixed formula, we are admittedly met with "recurring questions of the reasonableness of searches," but less is not to be expected when dealing with a Constitution, and, at any rate, "[r]easonableness is in the first instance for the [trial court] . . . to determine." . . .

It, therefore, plainly appears that the factual considerations supporting the failure of the *Wolf* Court to include the *Weeks* exclusionary rule when it recognized the enforceability of the right to privacy against the States in 1949, while not basically relevant to the constitutional consideration, could not, in any analysis, now be deemed controlling.

III

Some five years after *Wolf*, in answer to a plea made here Term after Term that we overturn its doctrine on applicability of the *Weeks* exclusionary rule, this Court indicated that such should not be done until the States had "adequate opportunity to adopt or reject the [*Weeks*] rule." *Irvine* v. *California.* There again it was said:

Never until June of 1949 did this Court hold the basic search-and-seizure prohibition in any way applicable to the states under the Fourteenth Amendment.

And only last Term, after again carefully re-examining the *Wolf* doctrine in *Elkins*

v. *United States,* the Court pointed out that "the controlling principles" as to search and seizure and the problem of admissibility "seemed clear" until the announcement in *Wolf* "that the Due Process Clause of the Fourteenth Amendment does not itself require state courts to adopt the exclusionary rule" of the *Weeks* case. At the same time the Court pointed out, "the underlying constitutional doctrine which *Wolf* established . . . that the Federal Constitution . . . prohibits unreasonable searches and seizures by state officers" had undermined the "foundation upon which the admissibility of state-seized evidence in a federal trial originally rested. . . ." The Court concluded that it was therefore obliged to hold, although it chose the narrower ground on which to do so, that all evidence obtained by an unconstitutional search and seizure was inadmissible in a federal court regardless of its source. Today we once again examine *Wolf's* constitutional documentation of the right to privacy free from unreasonable state intrusion, and, after its dozen years on our books, are led by it to close the only courtroom door remaining open to evidence secured by official lawlessness in flagrant abuse of that basic right, reserved to all persons as a specific guarantee against that very same unlawful conduct. We hold that all evidence obtained by searches and seizures in violation of the Constitution is, by that same authority, inadmissible in a state court.

IV

Since the Fourth Amendment's right of privacy has been declared enforceable against the States through the Due Process Clause of the Fourteenth, it is enforceable against them by the same sanction of exclusion as is used against the Federal Government. Were it otherwise, then just as without the *Weeks* rule the assurance against unreasonable federal searches and seizures would be "a form of words," valueless and undeserving of mention in a perpetual charter of inestimable human liberties, so too, without that rule the freedom from state invasions of privacy would be so ephemeral and so neatly severed from its conceptual nexus with the freedom from all brutish means of coercing evidence as not to merit this Court's high regard as a freedom "implicit in the concept of ordered liberty." As the time that the Court held in *Wolf* that the Amendment was applicable to the States through the Due Process Clause, the cases of this Court, as we have seen, had steadfastly held that as to federal officers the Fourth Amendment included the exclusion of the evidence seized in violation of its provisions. Even *Wolf* "stoutly adhered" to that proposition. The right to privacy, when conceded operatively enforceable against the States, was not susceptible of destruction by avulsion of the sanction upon which its protection and enjoyment had always been deemed dependent under the *Boyd, Weeks* and *Silverthorne* [251 US 385 (1920)] cases. Therefore, in extending the substantive protections of due process to all constitutionally unreasonable searches—state or federal—it was logically and constitutionally necessary that the exclusion doctrine —an essential part of the right to privacy—be also insisted upon as an essential ingredient of the right newly recognized by the *Wolf* case. In short, the admission of the new constitutional right by *Wolf* could not consistently tolerate denial of its most important constitutional privilege; namely, the exclusion of the evidence which an accused had been forced to give by reason of the unlawful seizure. To hold otherwise is to grant the right but in reality to withhold its privilege and enjoyment. Only last year the Court itself recognized that the purpose of the exclusionary rule "is to deter—to compel respect for the constitutional guaranty in the only effectively available way—by removing the incentive to disregard it." *Elkins* v. *United States.*

Indeed, we are aware of no restraint, similar to that rejected today, conditioning the enforcement of any other basic constitutional right. The right to privacy, no less important than any other right carefully and particularly reserved to the people, would stand in marked contrast to all other rights declared as "basic to a free society." *Wolf* v. *Colorado.* This Court has not hesitated to enforce as strictly against the States as it does against the Federal Government the rights of free speech and of a free press, the rights to notice and to a fair, public trial, including, as it does, the right not to be convicted by use of a coerced confession, however logically relevant it be, and without regard to its reliability. *Rogers* v. *Richmond,* 365 US 534 (1961). And nothing could be more certain than that when a coerced confession is involved, "the relevant rules of evidence" are overridden without regard to "the incidence of such conduct by the police," slight or frequent. Why should not the same rule apply to what is tantamount to coerced testimony by way of unconstitutional seizure of goods, papers, effects, documents, etc.? We find that, as to the Federal Government, the Fourth and Fifth Amendments and, as to the States, the freedom from unconscionable invasions of privacy and the freedom from convictions based upon coerced confessions do enjoy an "intimate relation" in their perpetuation of "principles of humanity and civil liberty [secured] . . . only after years of struggle." . . . They express "supplementing phases of the same constitutional purpose—to maintain inviolate large areas of personal privacy." . . . The philosophy of each Amendment and of each freedom is complementary to, although not dependent upon, that of the other in its sphere of influence—the very least that together they assure in either sphere is that no man is to be convicted on unconstitutional evidence. . . .

V

Moreover, our holding that the exclusionary rule is an essential part of both the Fourth and Fourteenth Amendments is not only the logical dictate of prior cases, but it also makes very good sense. There is no war between the Constitution and common sense. Presently, a federal prosecutor may make no use of evidence illegally seized, but a State's attorney across the street may, although he supposedly is operating under the enforceable prohibitions of the same Amendment. Thus the State, by admitting evidence unlawfully seized, serves to encourage disobedience to the Federal Constitution which it is bound to uphold. Moreover, as was said in *Elkins,* "[t]he very essence of a healthy federalism depends upon the avoidance of needless conflict between state and federal courts."

Federal-state cooperation in the solution of crime under constitutional standards will be promoted, if only by recognition of their now mutual obligation to respect the same fundamental criteria in their approaches. "However much in a particular case insistence upon such rules may appear as a technicality that inures to the benefit of a guilty person, the history of the criminal law proves that tolerance of short-cut methods in law enforcement impairs its enduring effectiveness." . . . Denying shortcuts to only one of two cooperating law enforcement agencies tends naturally to breed legitimate suspicion of "working arrangements" whose results are equally tainted. . . .

There are those who say, as did Justice (then Judge) Cardozo, that under our constitutional exclusionary doctrine "[t]he criminal is to go free because the constable has blundered." . . . In some cases this will undoubtedly be the result. But, as was said in *Elkins,* "there is another consideration—the imperative of judicial integrity." The criminal goes free, if he must, but it is the law that sets him free. Nothing can destroy a government more quickly than its failure to observe its own laws, or worse, its disregard of the charter of its own existence. As Mr. Justice Brandeis, dissenting, said in *Olmstead* v. *United States,* 277 US 438 (1928): "Our Government is the potent, the omnipresent teacher. For good or for ill, it teaches the whole people by its example. . . . If the Government becomes a lawbreaker, it breeds contempt for law; it invites every man to become a law unto himself; it invites anarchy." Nor can it lightly be assumed that, as a practical matter, adoption of the exclusionary rule fetters law enforcement. Only last year this Court expressly considered that contention and found that "pragmatic evidence of a sort" to the contrary was not wanting. *Elkins* v. *United States.* The Court noted that

The federal courts themselves have operated under the exclusionary rule of *Weeks* for almost half a century; yet it has not been suggested either that the Federal Bureau of Investigation has thereby been rendered ineffective, or that the administration of criminal justice in the federal courts has thereby been disrupted. Moreover, the experience of the states is impressive. . . . The movement toward the rule of exclusion has been halting but seemingly inexorable.

The ignoble shortcut to conviction left open to the State tends to destroy the entire system of constitutional restraints on which the liberties of the people rest. Having once recognized that the right to privacy embodied in the Fourth Amendment is enforceable against the States, and that the right to be secure against rude invasions of privacy by state officers is, therefore, constitutional in origin, we can no longer permit that right to remain an empty promise. Because it is enforceable in the same manner and to like effect as other basic rights secured by the Due Process Clause, we can no longer permit it to be revocable at the whim of any police officer who, in the name of law enforcement itself, chooses to suspend its enjoyment. Our decision, founded on reason and truth, gives to the individual no more than that which the Constitution guarantees him, to the police officer no less than that to which honest law enforcement is entitled, and, to the courts, that judicial integrity so necessary in the true administration of justice.

The judgment of the Supreme Court of Ohio is reversed and the cause remanded for further proceedings not inconsistent with this opinion.

Reversed and remanded.

3. *Self-Incrimination: The Right to be Silent*

MIRANDA *v.* ARIZONA
384 US 436 (1966)

[One federal and three consolidated state cases dealt with the admissibility of statements obtained from a person subjected to custodial police interrogation, and the necessity of procedures to assure that he is accorded the privilege against self-incrimination. A majority of five, in an opinion by Chief Justice Warren, formulated the guiding principles, required by the Constitution for the admissibility of such statements, the most important of which is that—in the absence of a clear, intelligent waiver—the suspect must be warned, prior to questioning, that he has a right to remain silent, that any statement he makes may be used as evidence against him, and that he has a right to the presence of an attorney, retained by him or appointed by the court. Justice Clark concurred in part and dissented in part. Justice Harlan wrote a dissenting opinion in which Justices Stewart and White joined. Justice White wrote a separate dissenting opinion.]

Mr. Chief Justice Warren delivered the opinion of the Court:

The cases before us raise questions which go to the roots of our concepts of American criminal jurisprudence: the restraints society must observe consistent with the Federal Constitution in prosecuting individuals for crime. More specifically, we deal with the admissibility of statements obtained from an individual who is subjected to custodial police interrogation and the necessity for procedures which assure that the individual is accorded his privilege under the Fifth Amendment to the Constitution not to be compelled to incriminate himself.

We dealt with certain phases of this problem recently in *Escobedo v. State of Illinois,* 378 US 478. There, as in the four cases before us, law enforcement officials took the defendant into custody and interrogated him in a police station for the purpose of obtaining a confession. The police did not effectively advise him of his right to remain silent or of his right to consult with his attorney. Rather, they confronted him with an alleged accomplice who accused him of having perpetrated a murder. When the defendant denied the accusation and said "I didn't shoot Manuel, you did it," they handcuffed him and took him to an interrogation room. There, while handcuffed and standing, he was questioned for four hours until he confessed. During this interrogation, the police denied his request to speak to his attorney, and they prevented his retained attorney, who had come to the police station, from consulting with him. At his trial, the State, over his objection, introduced the confession against him. We held that the statements thus made were constitutionally inadmissible.

This case has been the subject of judicial interpretation and spirited legal debate since it was decided two years ago. Both state and federal courts, in assessing its implications, have arrived at varying conclusions. A wealth of scholarly material has been written tracing its ramifications and underpinnings. Police and prosecutor have speculated on its range and desirability. We granted certiorari in this case in order further to explore some facets of the problems, thus exposed, of applying the privilege against self-incrimination to in-custody interrogation, and to give concrete constitutional guidelines for law enforcement agencies and courts to follow.

We start here, as we did in *Escobedo*, with the premise that our holding is not an innovation in our jurisprudence, but is an application of principles long recognized and applied in other settings. We have undertaken a thorough re-examination of the *Escobedo* decision and the principles it announced, and we reaffirm it. That case was but an explication of basic rights that are enshrined in our Constitution—that "No person . . . shall be compelled in any criminal case to be a witness against himself," and that "the accused shall . . . have the Assistance of Counsel"—rights which were put in jeopardy in that case through official overbearing. These precious rights were fixed in our Constitution only after centuries of persecution and struggle. And in the words of Chief Justice Marshall, they were secured "for ages to come and . . . designed to approach immortality as nearly as human institutions can approach it," *Cohens* v. *Commonwealth of Virginia*, 6 Wheat. 264, 387, 5 L.Ed. 27 (1821).

Over 70 years ago, our predecessors on this Court eloquently stated:

> The maxim *'Nemo tenetur seipsum accusare,'* had its origin in a protest against the inquisitorial and manifestly unjust methods of interrogating accused persons, which has long obtained in the continental system, and, until the expulsion of the Stuarts from the British throne in 1688, and the erection of additional barriers for the protection of the people against the exercise of arbitrary power, was not uncommon even in England. While the admissions or confessions of the prisoner, when voluntarily and freely made, have always ranked high in the scale of incriminating evidence, if an accused person be asked to explain his apparent connection with a crime under investigation, the ease with which the questions put to him may assume an inquistorial character, the temptation to press the witness unduly, to browbeat him if he be timid or reluctant, to push him into a corner, and to entrap him into fatal contradictions, which is so painfully evidenced in many of these earlier state trials, notably in those of Sir Nicholas Throckmorton, and Udal, the Puritan minister, made the system so odious as to give rise to a demand for its total abolition. The change in the English criminal procedure in that particular seems to be founded upon no statute and no judicial opinion, but upon a general and silent acquiescence of the courts in a popular demand. But, however adopted, it has become firmly embedded in English, as well as in American jurisprudence. So deeply did the inequities of the ancient system impress themselves upon the minds of the American colonists that the states, with one accord, made a denial of the right to question an accused person a part of their fundamental law, so that a maxim, which in England was a mere rule of evidence, became clothed in this country with the impregnability of a constitutional enactment. *Brown* v. *Walker*, 161 US 591.

In stating the obligation of the judiciary to apply these constitutional rights, this Court declared in *Weems* v. *United States*, 217 US 349:

> . . . our contemplation cannot be only what has been, but of what may be. Under any other rule a constitution would indeed be as easy of application as it would be deficient in efficacy and power. Its general principles would have little value, and be converted by precedent into impotent and lifeless formulas. Rights declared in words might be lost in reality. And this has been recognized. The meaning and vitality of the Constitution have developed against narrow and restrictive construction.

This was the spirit in which we delineated, in meaningful laguage, the manner in which the constitutional rights of the individual could be enforced against over-zealous police practices. It was necessary in *Escobedo*, as here, to insure that what was proclaimed in the Constitution had not become but a "form of words," . . . in the hands of government officials. And it is in this spirit, consistent with our role as judges, that we adhere to the principles of *Escobedo* today.

Our holding will be spelled out with some specificity in the pages which follow but briefly stated it is this: the prosecution may not use statements, whether ex-culpatory or inculpatory, stemming from custodial interrogation of the defendant unless it demonstrates the use of procedural safeguards effective to secure the privilege against self-incrimination. By custodial interrogation, we mean questioning initiated by law enforcement officers after a person has been taken into custody or otherwise deprived of his freedom of action in any significant way. As for the pro-cedural safeguards to be employed, unless other fully effective means are devised to inform accused persons of their right of silence and to assure a continuous oppor-tunity to exercise it, the following measures are required. Prior to any questioning, the person must be warned that he has a right to remain silent, that any statement he does make may be used as evidence against him, and that he has a right to the presence of an attorney, either retained or appointed. The defendant may waive effectuation of these rights, provided the waiver is made voluntarily, knowingly and intelligently. If, however, he indicates in any manner and at any stage of the process that he wishes to consult with an attorney before speaking there can be no ques-tioning. Likewise, if the individual is alone and indicates in any manner that he does not wish to be interrogated, the police may not question him. The mere fact that he may have answered some questions or volunteered some statements on his own does not deprive him of the right to refrain from answering any further inquiries until he has consulted with an attorney and thereafter consents to be questioned.

I

The constitutional issue we decide in each of these cases is the admissibility of statements obtained from a defendant questioned while in custody and deprived of his freedom of action. In each, the defendant was questioned by police officers, detectives, or a prosecuting attorney in a room in which he was cut off from the outside world. In none of these cases was the defendant given a full and effective warning of his rights at the outset of the interrogation process. In all the cases, the questioning elicited oral admissions, and in three of them, signed statements as well which were admitted at their trials. They all thus share salient features—incom-municado interrogation of individuals in a police-dominated atmosphere, resulting in self-incriminating statements without full warnings of constitutional rights.

An understanding of the nature and setting of this in-custody interrogation is essential to our decisions today. The difficulty in depicting what transpires at such interrogations stems from the fact that in this country they have largely taken place incommunicado. From extensive factual studies undertaken in the early 1930's, including the famous Wickersham Report to Congress by a Presidential Commis-sion, it is clear that police violence and the "third degree" flourished at that time.

In a series of cases decided by this Court long after these studies, the police resorted to physical brutality—beatings, hanging, whipping—and to sustained and protracted questioning incommunicado in order to extort confessions. The 1961 Commission on Civil Rights found much evidence to indicate that "some policemen still resort to physical force to obtain confessions." . . . The use of physical brutality and violence is not, unfortunately, relegated to the past or to any part of the country. Only recently in Kings County, New York, the police brutally beat, kicked and placed lighted cigarette butts on the back of a potential witness under interrogation for the purpose of securing a statement incriminating a third party. . . .

The examples given above are undoubtedly the exception now, but they are sufficiently widespread to be the object of concern. Unless a proper limitation upon custodial interrogation is achieved—such as these decisions will advance—there can be no assurance that practices of this nature will be eradicated in the foreseeable future. The conclusion of the Wickersham Commission Report, made over 30 years ago, is still pertinent:

To the contention that the third degree is necessary to get the facts, the reporters aptly reply in the language of the present Lord Chancellor of England (Lord Sankey): "It is not admissible to do a great right by doing a little wrong. . . . It is not sufficient to do justice by obtaining a proper result by irregular or improper means." Not only does the use of the third degree involve a flagrant violation of law by the officers of the law, but it involves also the dangers of false confessions, and it tends to make police and prosecutors less zealous in the search for objective evidence. As the New York prosecutor quoted in the report said, "It it a short cut and makes the police lazy and unenterprising." Or, as another official quoted remarked: "If you use your fists, you are not so likely to use your wits." We agree with the conclusion expressed in the report, that "The third degree brutalizes the police, hardens the prisoner against society, and lowers the esteem in which the administration of justice is held by the public." IV National Commission on Law Observance and Enforcement, Report on Lawlessness in Law Enforcement (1931), 5.

Again we stress that the modern practice of in-custody interrogation is psychologically rather than physically oriented. As we have stated before, "Since *Chambers* v. *State of Florida,* 309 US 227, this Court has recognized that coercion can be mental as well as physical, and that the blood of the accused is not the only hallmark of an unconstitutional inquisition." *Blackburn* v. *State of Alabama,* 361 US 199. Interrogation still takes place in privacy. Privacy results in secrecy and this in turn results in a gap in our knowledge as to what in fact goes on in the interrogation rooms. A valuable source of information about present police practices, however, may be found in various police manuals and texts which document procedures employed with success in the past, and which recommend various other effective tactics. These texts are used by law enforcement agencies themselves as guides. It should be noted that these texts professedly present the most enlightened and effective means presently used to obtain statements through custodial interrogation. By considering these texts and other data, it is possible to describe procedures observed and noted around the country.

The officers are told by the manuals that the "principal psychological factor contributing to a successful interrogation is privacy—being alone with the person under interrogation." The efficacy of this tactic has been explained as follows:

If at all practicable, the interrogation should take place in the investigator's office or at least in a room of his own choice. The subject should be deprived of every psychological advantage. In his own home he may be confident, indignant, or recalcitrant. He is more keenly aware of his rights and more reluctant to tell of his indiscretions of criminal behavior within the walls of his own home. Moreover his family and other friends are nearby, their presence lending moral support. In his office, the investigator possesses all the advantages. The atmosphere suggests the invincibility of the forces of the law.

To highlight the isolation and unfamiliar surroundings, the manuals instruct the police to display an air of confidence in the suspect's guilt and from outward appearance to maintain only an interest in confirming certain details. The guilt of the subject is to be posited as a fact. The interrogator should direct his comments toward the reasons why the subject committed the act, rather than to court failure by asking the subject whether he did it. Like other men, perhaps the subject has had a bad family life, had an unhappy childhood, had too much to drink, had an unrequited attraction to women. The officers are instructed to minimize the moral seriousness of the offense, to cast blame on the victim or on society. These tactics are designed to put the subject in a psychological state where his story is but an elaboration of what the police purport to know already—that he is guilty. Explanations to the contrary are dismissed and discouraged.

The texts thus stress that the major qualities an interrogator should possess are patience and perseverance. One writer describes the efficacy of these characteristics in this manner:

In the preceding paragraphs emphasis has been placed on kindness and stratagems. The investigator will, however, encounter many situations where the sheer weight of his personality will be the deciding factor. Where emotional appeals and tricks are employed to no avail, he must rely on an oppressive atmosphere of dogged persistence. He must interrogate steadily and without relent, leaving the subject no prospect of surcease. He must dominate his subject and overwhelm him with his inexorable will to obtain the truth. He should interrogate for a spell of several hours pausing only for the subject's necessities in acknowledgement of the need to avoid a charge of duress that can be technically substantiated. In a serious case, the interrogation may continue for days, with the required intervals for food and sleep, but with no respite from the atmosphere of domination. It is possible in this way to induce the subject to talk without resorting to duress or coercion. This method should be used only when the guilt of the subject appears highly probable.

The manuals suggest that the suspect be offered legal excuses for his actions in order to obtain an initial admission of guilt. Where there is a suspected revenge-killing, for example, the interrogator may say:

Joe, you probably didn't go out looking for this fellow with the purpose of shooting him. My guess is, however, that you expected something from him and that's why you carried a gun—for your own protection. You knew him for what he was, no good. Then when you met him he probably started using foul, abusive language and he gave some indication that he was about to pull a gun on you, and that's when you had to act to save your own life. That's about it, isn't it, Joe?

Having then obtained the admission of shooting, the interrogator is advised to refer to circumstantial evidence which negates the self-defense explanation. This should enable him to secure the entire story. One text notes that "Even if he fails to do so, the inconsistency between the subject's original denial of the shooting and his present admission of at least doing the shooting will serve to deprive him of a self-defense 'out' at the time of trial."

When the techniques described above prove unavailing, the texts recommend they be alternated with a show of some hostility. One ploy often used has been termed the "friendly-unfriendly" or the "Mutt and Jeff" act:

. . . In this technique, two agents are employed, Mutt, the relentless investigator, who knows the subject is guilty and is not going to waste any time. He's sent a dozen men away for this crime and he's going to send the subject away for the full term. Jeff, on the other hand, is obviously a kind-hearted man. He has a family himself. He has a brother who was involved in a little scrape like this. He disapproves of Mutt and his tactics and will arrange to get him off the case if the subject will cooperate. He can't hold Mutt off for very long. The subject would be wise to make a quick decision. The technique is applied by having both investigators present while Mutt acts out his role. Jeff may stand by quietly and demur at some of Mutt's tactics. When Jeff makes his plea for cooperation, Mutt is not present in the room.

The interrogators sometimes are instructed to induce a confession out of trickery. The technique here is quite effective in crimes which require identification or which run in series. In the identification situation, the interrogator may take a break in his questioning to place the subject among a group of men in a line-up. "The witness or complainant (previously coached, if necessary) studies the line-up and confidently points out the subject as the guilty party." Then the questioning resumes "as though there were now no doubt about the guilt of the subject." A variation on this technique is called the "reverse line-up":

The accused is placed in a line-up, but this time he is identified by several fictitious witnesses or victims who associated him with different offenses. It is expected that the subject will become desperate and confess to the offense under investigation in order to escape from the false accusations.

The manuals also contain instructions for police on how to handle the individual who refuses to discuss the matter entirely, or who asks for an attorney or relatives. The examiner is to concede him the right to remain silent. "This usually has a very undermining effect. First of all, he is disappointed in his expectation of an unfavorable reaction on the part of the interrogator. Secondly, a concession of this right to remain silent impresses the subject with the apparent fairness of his interrogator." After this psychological conditioning, however, the officer is told to point out the incriminating significance of the suspect's refusal to talk:

Joe, you have a right to remain silent. That's your privilege and I'm the last person in the world who'll try to take it away from you. If that's the way you want to leave this, O. K. But let me ask you this. Suppose you were in my shoes and I were in yours and you called me in to ask me about this and I told you, "I don't want to answer any of your questions." You'd think I had something to hide, and you'd probably be right in thinking that. That's exactly what I'll have to think about you, and so will everybody else. So let's sit here and talk this whole thing over.

Few will persist in their initial refusals to talk, it is said, if this monologue is employed correctly.

In the event that the subject wishes to speak to a relative or an attorney, the following advice is tendered:

[T]he interrogator should respond by suggesting the subject first tell the truth to the interrogator himself rather than get anyone else involved in the matter. If the request is for an attorney, the interrogator may suggest that the subject save himself or his family the expense of any such professional service, particularly if he is innocent of the offense under investigation. The interrogator may also add, "Joe, I'm only looking for the truth, and if you're telling the truth, that's it. You can handle this by yourself."

From these representative samples of interrogation techniques, the setting prescribed by the manuals and observed in practice becomes clear. In essence, it is this: To be alone with the subject is essential to prevent distraction and to deprive him of any outside support. The aura of confidence in his guilt undermines his will to resist. He merely confirms the preconceived story the police seek to have him describe. Patience and persistence, at times relentless questioning, are employed. To obtain a confession, the interrogator must "patiently maneuver himself or his quarry into a position from which the desired object may be obtained." When normal procedures fail to produce the needed result, the police may resort to deceptive stratagems such as giving false legal advice. It is important to keep the subject off balance, for example, by trading on his insecurity about himself or his surroundings. The police then persuade, trick, or cajole him out of exercising his constitutional rights.

Even without employing brutality, the "third degree" or the specific stratagems described above, the very fact of custodial interrogation exacts a heavy toll on individual liberty and trades on the weakness of individuals. . . .

In the cases before us today, given this background, we concern ourselves primarily with this interrogation atmosphere and the evils it can bring. In No. 759, *Miranda* v. *Arizona,* the police arrested the defendant and took him to a special interrogation room where they secured a confession. In No. 760, *Vignera* v. *New York,* the defendant made oral admissions to the police after interrogation in the afternoon, and then signed an inculpatory statement upon being questioned by an assistant district attorney later the same evening. In No. 761, *Westover* v. *United States,* the defendant was handed over to the Federal Bureau of Investigation by local authorities after they had detained and interrogated him for a lengthy period, both at night and the following morning. After some two hours of questioning, the federal officers had obtained signed statements from the defendant. Lastly, in No. 584, *California* v. *Stewart,* the local police held the defendant five days in the station and interrogated him on nine separate occasions before they secured his inculpatory statement.

In these cases, we might not find the defendants' statements to have been involuntary in traditional terms. Our concern for adequate safeguards to protect precious Fifth Amendment rights is, of course, not lessened in the slightest. In each of the cases, the defendant was thrust into an unfamiliar atmosphere and run through menacing police interrogation procedures. The potentiality for compulsion is forcefully apparent, for example, in *Miranda,* where the indigent Mexican defendant was a seriously disturbed individual with pronounced sexual fantasies, and in *Stewart,* in which the defendant was an indigent Los Angeles Negro who had dropped out of school in the sixth grade. To be sure, the records do not evince overt physical coercion or patented psychological ploys. The fact remains that in none of these cases did the officers undertake to afford appropriate safeguards at the outset of the interrogation to insure that the statements were truly the product of free choice.

It is obvious that such an interrogation environment is created for no purpose other than to subjugate the individual to the will of his examiner. This atmosphere carries its own badge of intimidation. To be sure, this is not physical intimidation, but it is equally destructive of human dignity. The current practice of incommunicado interrogation is at odds with one of our Nation's most cherished principles— that the individual may not be compelled to incriminate himself. Unless adequate protective devices are employed to dispel the compulsion inherent in custodial surroundings, no statement obtained from the defendant can truly be the product of his free choice.

From the foregoing, we can readily perceive an intimate connection between the privilege against self-incrimination and police custodial questioning. It is fitting to turn to history and precedent underlying the Self-Incrimination Clause to determine its applicability in this situation.

II

We sometimes forget how long it has taken to establish the privilege against self-incrimination, the sources from which it came and the fervor with which it was defended. Its roots go back into ancient times.* Perhaps the critical historical event shedding light on its origins and evolution was the trial of one John Lilburn, a vocal anti-Stuart Leveller, who was made to take the Star Chamber Oath in 1637. The oath would have bound him to answer to all questions posed to him on any subject. The Trial of John Lilburn and John Wharton, 3 How.St.Tr. 1315 (1637–1645). He resisted the oath and declaimed the proceedings, stating:

Another fundamental right I then contended for, was, that no man's conscience ought to be racked by oaths imposed, to answer to questions concerning himself in matters criminal, or pretended to be so. Heller and Davies, *The Leveller Tracts* 1647–1653 (1944), 454.

On account of the Lilburn Trial, Parliament abolished the inquisitorial Court of Star Chamber and went further in giving him generous reparation. The lofty

---

* Thirteenth century commentators found an analogue to the privilege grounded in the Bible. "To sum up the matter, the principle that no man is to be declared guilty on his own admission is a divine decree." Maimonides, Mishneh Torah (Code of Jewish Law), Book of Judges, Laws of the Sanhedrin, c. 18, ¶ 6, 3 Yale Judaica Series 52–53. See also Lamm, "The Fifth Amendment and Its Equivalent in the Halakha," 5 Judaism 53 (Winter, 1956).

principles to which Lilburn had appealed during his trial gained popular acceptance in England. These sentiments worked their way over to the Colonies and were implanted after great struggle into the Bill of Rights. Those who framed our Constitution and the Bill of Rights were ever aware of subtle encroachments on individual liberty. They knew that "illegitimate and unconstitutional practices get their first footing . . . by silent approaches and slight deviations from legal modes of procedure." . . . The privilege was elevated to constitutional status and has always been "as broad as the mischief against which it seeks to guard." . . . We cannot depart from this noble heritage.

Thus we may view the historical development of the privilege as one which groped for the proper scope of governmental power over the citizen. As a "noble principle often transcends its origins," the privilege has come rightfully to be recognized in part as an individual's substantive right, a "right to a private enclave where he may lead a private life. That right is the hallmark of our democracy." . . . We have recently noted that the privilege against self-incrimination—the essential mainstay of our adversary system—is founded on a complex of values. . . . All these policies point to one overriding thought: the constitutional foundation underlying the privilege is the respect a government—state or federal—must accord to the dignity and integrity of its citizens. To maintain a "fair state-individual balance," to require the government "to shoulder the entire load," . . . to respect the inviolability of the human personality, our accusatory system of criminal justice demands that the government seeking to punish an individual produce the evidence against him by its own independent labors, rather than by the cruel, simple expedient of compelling it from his own mouth. . . . In sum, the privilege is fulfilled only when the person is guaranteed the right "to remain silent unless he chooses to speak in the unfettered exercise of his own will." . . .

The question in these cases is whether the privilege is fully applicable during a period of custodial interrogation. In this Court, the privilege has consistently been accorded a liberal construction. . . . We are satisfied that all the principles embodied in the privilege apply to informal compulsion exerted by law-enforcement officers during in-custody questioning. An individual swept from familiar surroundings into police custody, surrounded by antagonistic forces, and subjected to the techniques of persuasion described above cannot be otherwise than under compulsion to speak. As a practical matter, the compulsion to speak in the isolated setting of the police station may well be greater than in courts or other official investigations, where there are often impartial observers to guard against intimidation or trickery. . . .

Because of the adoption by Congress of Rule 5(a) of the Federal Rules of Criminal Procedure, and the Court's effectuation of that Rule in *McNabb* v. *United States,* 318 US 332, and *Mallory* v. *United States,* 354 US 449, we have had little occasion in the past quarter century to reach the constitutional issues in dealing with federal interrogations. These supervisory rules, requiring production of an arrested person before a commissioner "without unnecessary delay" and excluding evidence obtained in default of that statutory obligation, were nonetheless responsive to the same considerations of Fifth Amendment policy that unavoidably face us now as to the States. In *McNabb,* and in *Mallory* we recognized both the dangers of interrogation and the appropriateness of prophylaxis stemming from the very fact of interrogation itself.

Our decision in *Malloy* v. *Hogan*, 378 US 1, necessitates an examination of the scope of the privilege in state cases as well. In *Malloy*, we squarely held the privilege applicable to the States, and held that the substantive standards underlying the privilege applied with full force to state court proceedings. There . . . we applied the existing Fifth Amendment standards to the case before us. Aside from the holding itself, the reasoning in *Malloy* made clear what had already become apparent—that the substantive and procedural safeguards surrounding admissibility of confessions in state cases had become exceedingly exacting, reflecting all the policies embedded in the privilege. The voluntariness doctrine in the state cases, as *Malloy* indicates, encompasses all interrogation practices which are likely to exert such pressure upon an individual as to disable him from making a free and rational choice. The implications of this proposition were elaborated in our decision in *Escobedo* v. *State of Illinois*, decided one week after *Malloy* applied the privilege to the States.

Our holding there stressed the fact that the police had not advised the defendant of his constitutional privilege to remain silent at the outset of the interrogation, and we drew attention to that fact at several points in the decision. This was no isolated factor, but an essential ingredient in our decision. The entire thrust of police interrogation there, as in all the cases today, was to put the defendant in such an emotional state as to impair his capacity for rational judgment. The abdication of the constitutional privilege—the choice on his part to speak to the police—was not made knowingly or competently because of the failure to apprise him of his rights; the compelling atmosphere of the in-custody interrogation, and not an independent decision on his part, caused the defendant to speak.

A different phase of the *Escobedo* decision was significant in its attention to the absence of counsel during the questioning. There, as in the cases today, we sought a protective device to dispel the compelling atmosphere of the interrogation. In *Escobedo*, however, the police did not relieve the defendant of the anxieties which they had created in the interrogation rooms. Rather, they denied his request for the assistance of counsel. This heightened his dilemma, and made his later statements the product of this compulsion. . . . The denial of the defendant's request for his attorney thus undermined his ability to exercise the privilege—to remain silent if he chose or to speak without any intimidation, blatant or subtle. The presence of counsel, in all the cases before us today, would be the adequate protective device necessary to make the process of police interrogation conform to the dictates of the privilege. His presence would insure that statements made in the government-established atmosphere are not the product of compulsion.

It was in this manner that *Escobedo* explicated another facet of the pre-trial privilege, noted in many of the Court's prior decisions: the protection of rights at trial. That counsel is present when statements are taken from an individual during interrogation obviously enhances the integrity of the fact-finding processes in court. The presence of an attorney, and the warnings delivered to the individual, enable the defendant under otherwise compelling circumstances to tell his story without fear, effectively, and in a way that eliminates the evils in the interrogation process. Without the protections flowing from adequate warning and the rights of counsel, "all the careful safeguards erected around the giving of testimony, whether by an accused or any other witness, would become empty formalities in a procedure where the most compelling possible evidence of guilt, a confession, would have already been obtained at the unsupervised pleasure of the police." . . .

III

Today, then, there can be no doubt that the Fifth Amendment privilege is available outside of criminal court proceedings and serves to protect persons in all settings in which their freedom of action is curtailed from being compelled to incriminate themselves. We have concluded that without proper safeguards the process of in-custody interrogation of persons suspected or accused of crime contains inherently compelling pressures which work to undermine the individual's will to resist and to compel him to speak where he would not otherwise do so freely. In order to combat these pressures and to permit a full opportunity to exercise the privilege against self-incrimination, the accused must be adequately and effectively apprised of his rights and the exercise of those rights must be fully honored.

It is impossible for us to foresee the potential alternatives for protecting the privilege which might be devised by Congress or the States in the exercise of their creative rule-making capacities. Therefore we cannot say that the Constitution necessarily requires adherence to any particular solution for the inherent compulsions of the interrogation process as it is presently conducted. Our decision in no way creates a constitutional strait-jacket which will handicap sound efforts at reform, nor is it intended to have this effect. We encourage Congress and the States to continue their laudable search for increasingly effective ways of protecting the rights of the individual while promoting efficient enforcement of our criminal laws. However, unless we are shown other procedures which are at least as effective in apprising accused persons of their right of silence and in assuring a continuous opportunity to exercise it, the following safeguards must be observed.

At the outset, if a person in custody is to be subjected to interrogation, he must first be informed in clear and unequivocal terms that he has the right to remain silent. For those unaware of the privilege, the warning is needed simply to make them aware of it—the threshold requirement for an intelligent decision as to its exercise. More important, such a warning is an absolute prerequisite in overcoming the inherent pressures of the interrogation atmosphere. It is not just the subnormal or woefully ignorant who succumb to an interrogator's imprecations, whether implied or expressly stated, that the interrogation will continue until a confession is obtained or that silence in the face of accusation is itself damning and will bode ill when presented to a jury. Further, the warning will show the individual that his interrogators are prepared to recognize his privilege should he choose to exercise it.

The Fifth Amendment privilege is so fundamental to our system of constitutional rule and the expedient of giving an adequate warning as to the availability of the privilege so simple, we will not pause to inquire in individual cases whether the defendant was aware of his rights without a warning being given. Assessments of the knowledge the defendant possessed, based on information as to his age, education, intelligence, or prior contact with authorities, can never be more than speculation; a warning is a clearcut fact. More important, whatever the background of the person interrogated, a warning at the time of the interrogation is indispensable to overcome its pressures and to insure that the individual knows he is free to exercise the privilege at that point in time.

The warning of the right to remain silent must be accompanied by the explanation that anything said can and will be used against the individual in court. This warning is needed in order to make him aware not only of the privilege, but also of the consequences of forgoing it. It is only through an awareness of these consequences that there can be any assurance of real understanding and intelligent exercise of the privilege. Moreover, this warning may serve to make the individual more acutely aware that he is faced with a phase of the adversary system—that he is not in the presence of persons acting solely in his interest.

The circumstances surrounding in-custody interrogation can operate very quickly to overbear the will of one merely made aware of his privilege by his interrogators. Therefore, the right to have counsel present at the interrogation is indispensable to the protection of the Fifth Amendment privilege under the system we delineate today. Our aim is to assure that the individual's right to choose between silence and speech remains unfettered throughout the interrogation process. A once-stated warning, delivered by those who will conduct the interrogation, cannot itself suffice to that end among those who most require knowledge of their rights. A mere warning given by the interrogators is not alone sufficient to accomplish that end. Prosecutors themselves claim that the admonishment of the right to remain silent without more "will benefit only the recidivist and the professional." Brief for the National District Attorneys Association as *amicus curiae*, p. 14. Even preliminary advice given to the accused by his own attorney can be swiftly overcome by the secret interrogation process. . . . Thus, the need for counsel to protect the Fifth Amendment privilege comprehends not merely a right to consult with counsel prior to questioning, but also to have counsel present during any questioning if the defendant so desires.

The presence of counsel at the interrogation may serve several significant subsidiary functions as well. If the accused decides to talk to his interrogators, the assistance of counsel can mitigate the dangers of untrustworthiness. With a lawyer present the likelihood that the police will practice coercion is reduced, and if coercion is nevertheless exercised the lawyer can testify to it in court. The presence of a lawyer can also help to guarantee that the accused gives a fully accurate statement to the police and that the statement is rightly reported by the prosecution at trial. . . .

An individual need not make a pre-interrogation request for a lawyer. While such request affirmatively secures his right to have one, his failure to ask for a lawyer does not constitute a waiver. No effective waiver of the right to counsel during interrogation can be recognized unless specifically made after the warnings we here delineate have been given. The accused who does not know his right and therefore does not make a request may be the person who most needs counsel. As the California Supreme Court has aptly put it:

Finally, we must recognize that the imposition of the requirement for the request would discriminate against the defendant who does not know his rights. The defendant who does not ask for counsel is the very defendant who most needs counsel. We cannot penalize a defendant who, not understanding his constitutional rights, does not make the formal request and by such failure demonstrates his helplessness. To require the request would be to favor the defendant whose sophistication or status has fortuitously prompted him to make it. *People* v. *Dorado,* 62 Cal.2d 338, 351.

In *Carnley* v. *Cochran,* 369 US 506, we stated: "[I]t is settled that where the assistance of counsel is a constitutional requisite, the right to be furnished counsel does not depend on a request." This proposition applies with equal force in the context of providing counsel to protect an accused's Fifth Amendment privilege in the face of interrogation. Although the role of counsel at trial differs from the role during interrogation, the differences are not relevant to the question whether a request is a prerequisite.

Accordingly we hold that an individual held for interrogation must be clearly informed that he has the right to consult with a lawyer and to have the lawyer with him during interrogation under the system for protecting the privilege we delineate today. As with the warnings of the right to remain silent and that anything stated can be used in evidence against him, this warning is an absolute prerequisite to interrogation. No amount of circumstantial evidence that the person may have been aware of this right will suffice to stand in its stead. Only through such a warning is there ascertainable assurance that the accused was aware of this right.

If an individual indicates that he wishes the assistance of counsel before any interrogation occurs, the authorities cannot rationally ignore or deny his request on the basis that the individual does not have or cannot afford a retained attorney. The financial ability of the individual has no relationship to the scope of the rights involved here. The privilege against self-incrimination secured by the Constitution applies to all individuals. The need for counsel in order to protect the privilege exists for the indigent as well as the affluent. In fact, were we to limit these constitutional rights to those who can retain an attorney, our decisions today would be of little significance. The cases before us as well as the vast majority of confession cases with which we have dealt in the past involve those unable to retain counsel. While authorities are not required to relieve the accused of his poverty, they have the obligation not to take advantage of indigence in the administration of justice. Denial of counsel to the indigent at the time of interrogation while allowing an attorney to those who can afford one would be no more supportable by reason or logic than the similar situation at trial and on appeal struck down in *Gideon* v. *Wainwright,* 372 US 335, and *Douglas* v. *People of State of California,* 372 US 353.

In order fully to apprise a person interrogated of the extent of his rights under this system then, it is necessary to warn him not only that he has the right to consult with an attorney, but also that if he is indigent a lawyer will be appointed to represent him. Without this additional warning, the admonition of the right to consult with counsel would often be understood as meaning only that he can consult with a lawyer if he has one or has the funds to obtain one. The warning of a right to counsel would be hollow if not couched in terms that would convey to the indigent—the person most often subjected to interrogation—the knowledge that he too has a right to have counsel present. As with the warnings of the right to remain silent and of the general right to counsel, only by effective and express explanation to the indigent of this right can there be assurance that he was truly in a position to exercise it.

Once warnings have been given, the subsequent procedure is clear. If the individual indicates in any manner, at any time prior to or during questioning, that he wishes to remain silent, the interrogation must cease. At this point he has shown that he intends to exercise his Fifth Amendment privilege; any statement taken after the person invokes his privilege cannot be other than the product of compulsion, subtle or otherwise. Without the right to cut off questioning, the setting of in-custody interrogation operates on the individual to overcome free choice in producing a statement after the privilege has been once invoked. If the individual states that he wants an attorney, the interrogation must cease until an attorney is present. At that time, the individual must have an opporunity to confer with the attorney and to have him present during any subsequent questioning. If the individual cannot obtain an attorney and he indicates that he wants one before speaking to police, they must respect his decision to remain silent.

This does not mean, as some have suggested, that each police station must have a "station house lawyer" present at all times to advise prisoners. It does mean, however, that if police propose to interrogate a person they must make known to him that he is entitled to a lawyer and that if he cannot afford one, a lawyer will be provided for him prior to any interrogation. If authorities conclude that they will not provide counsel during a reasonable period of time in which investigation in the field is carried out, they may do so without violating the person's Fifth Amendment privilege so long as they do not question him during that time.

If the interrogation continues without the presence of an attorney and a statement is taken, a heavy burden rests on the Government to demonstrate that the defendant knowingly and intelligently waived his privilege against self-incrimination and his right to retained or appointed counsel. . . . This Court has always set high standards of proof for the waiver of constitutional rights and we reassert these standards as applied to in-custody interrogation. Since the State is responsible for establishing the isolated circumstances under which the interrogation takes place and has the only means of making available corroborated evidence of warnings given during incommunicado interrogation, the burden is rightly on its shoulders.

An express statement that the individual is willing to make a statement and does not want an attorney followed closely by a statement could constitute a waiver. But a valid waiver will not be presumed simply from the silence of the accused after warnings are given or simply from the fact that a confession was in fact eventually obtained. A statement we made in *Carnley* v. *Cochran,* 369 US 506 is applicable here:

Presuming waiver from a silent record is impermissible. The record must show, or there must be an allegation and evidence which show, that an accused was offered counsel but intelligently and understandingly rejected the offer. Anything less is not waiver.

See also *Glasser* v. *United States,* 315 US 60. Moreover, where in-custody interrogation is involved, there is no room for the contention that the privilege is waived if the individual answers some questions or gives some information on his own prior to invoking his right to remain silent when interrogated.

Whatever the testimony of the authorities as to waiver of rights by an accused, the fact of lengthy interrogation or incommunicado incarceration before a statement is made is strong evidence that the accused did not validly waive his rights. In these circumstances the fact that the individual eventually made a statement is consistent with the conclusion that the compelling influence of the interrogation finally forced him to do so. It is inconsistent with any notion of a voluntary relinquishment of the privilege. Moreover, any evidence that the accused was threatened, tricked, or cajoled into a waiver will, of course, show that the defendant did not voluntarily waive his privilege. The requirement of warnings and waiver of rights is a fundamental with respect to the Fifth Amendment privilege and not simply a preliminary ritual to existing methods of interrogation.

The warnings required and the waiver necessary in accordance with our opinion today are, in the absence of a fully effective equivalent, prerequisites to the admissibility of any statement made by a defendant. No distinction can be drawn between statements which are direct confessions and statements which amount to "admissions" of part or all of an offense. The privilege against self-incrimination protects the individual from being compelled to incriminate himself in any manner; it does not distinguish degrees of incrimination. Similarly, for precisely the same reason, no distinction may be drawn between inculpatory statements and statements alleged to be merely "exculpatory." If a statement made were in fact truly exculpatory it would, of course, never be used by the prosecution. In fact, statements merely intended to be exculpatory by the defendant are often used to impeach his testimony at trial or to demonstrate untruths in the statement given under interrogation and thus to prove guilt by implication. These statements are incriminating in any meaningful sense of the word and may not be used without the full warnings and effective waiver required for any other statement. In *Escobedo* itself, the defendant fully intended his accusation of another as the slayer to be exculpatory as to himself.

The principles announced today deal with the protection which must be given to the privilege against self-incrimination when the individual is first subjected to police interrogation while in custody at the station or otherwise deprived of his freedom of action in any way. It is at this point that our adversary system of criminal proceedings commences, distinguishing itself at the outset from the inquisitorial system recognized in some countries. Under the system of warnings we delineate today or under any other system which may be devised and found effective, the safeguards to be erected about the privilege must come into play at this point.

Our decision is not intended to hamper the traditional function of police officers in investigating crime. . . . When an individual is in custody on probable cause, the police may, of course, seek out evidence in the field to be used at trial against him. Such investigation may include inquiry of persons not under restraint. General on-the-scene questioning as to facts surrounding a crime or other general questioning of citizens in the fact-finding process is not affected by our holding. It is an act of responsible citizenship for individuals to give whatever information they may have to aid in law enforcement. In such situations the compelling atmosphere inherent in the process of in-custody interrogation is not necessarily present.

In dealing with statements obtained through interrogation, we do not purport to find all confessions inadmissible. Confessions remain a proper element in law enforcement. Any statement given freely and voluntarily without any compelling influences is, of course, admissible in evidence. The fundamental import of the privilege while an individual is in custody is not whether he is allowed to talk to the police without the benefit of warnings and counsel, but whether he can be interrogated. There is no requirement that police stop a person who enters a police station and states that he wishes to confess to a crime, or a person who calls the police to offer a confession or any other statement he desires to make. Volunteered statements of any kind are not barred by the Fifth Amendment and their admissibility is not affected by our holding today.

To summarize, we hold that when an individual is taken into custody or otherwise deprived of his freedom by the authorities and is subjected to questioning, the privilege against self-incrimination is jeopardized. Procedural safeguards must be employed to protect the privilege, and unless other fully effective means are adopted to notify the person of his right of silence and to assure that the exercise of the right will be scrupulously honored, the following measures are required. He must be warned prior to any questioning that he has the right to remain silent, that anything he says can be used against him in a court of law, that he has the right to the presence of an attorney, and that if he cannot afford an attorney one will be appointed for him prior to any questioning if he so desires. Opportunity to exercise these rights must be afforded to him throughout the interrogation. After such warnings have been given, and such opportunity afforded him, the individual may knowingly and intelligently waive these rights and agree to answer questions or make a statement. But unless and until such warnings and waiver are demonstrated by the prosecution at trial, no evidence obtained as a result of interrogation can be used against him.

IV

A recurrent argument made in these cases is that society's need for interrogation outweighs the privilege. This argument is not unfamiliar to this Court. . . . The whole thrust of our foregoing discussion demonstrates that the Constitution has prescribed the rights of the individual when confronted with the power of government when it provided in the Fifth Amendment that an individual cannot be compelled to be a witness against himself. That right cannot be abridged. As Mr. Justice Brandeis once observed:

Decency, security, and liberty alike demand that government officials shall be subjected to the same rules of conduct that are commands to the citizen. In a government of laws, existence of the government will be imperilled if it fails to observe the law scrupulously. Our government is the potent, the omnipresent teacher. For good or for ill, it teaches the whole people by its example. Crime is contagious. If the government becomes a lawbreaker, it breeds contempt for law; it invites every man to become a law unto himself; it invites anarchy. To declare that in the administration of the criminal law the end justifies the means . . . would bring terrible retribution. Against that pernicious doctrine this court should resolutely set its face. *Olmstead* v. *United States,* 277 US 438.

In this connection, one of our country's distinguished jurists has pointed out: "The quality of a nation's civilization can be largely measured by the methods it uses in the enforcement of its criminal law."

If the individual desires to exercise his privilege, he has the right to do so. This is not for the authorities to decide. An attorney may advise his client not to talk to police until he has had an opportunity to investigate the case, or he may wish to be present with his client during any police questioning. In doing so an attorney is merely exercising the good professional judgment he has been taught. This is not cause for considering the attorney a menace to law enforcement. He is merely carrying out what he is sworn to do under his oath—to protect to the extent of his ability the rights of his client. In fulfilling this responsibility the attorney plays a vital role in the administration of criminal justice under our Constitution.

In announcing these principles, we are not unmindful of the burdens which law enforcement officials must bear, often under trying circumstances. We also fully recognize the obligation of all citizens to aid in enforcing the criminal laws. This Court, while protecting individual rights, has always given ample latitude to law enforcement agencies in the legitimate exercise of their duties. The limits we have placed on the interrogation process should not constitute an undue interference with a proper system of law enforcement. As we have noted, our decision does not in any way preclude police from carrying out their traditional investigatory functions. Although confessions may play an important role in some convictions, the cases before us present graphic examples of the overstatement of the "need" for confessions. In each case authorities conducted interrogations ranging up to five days in duration despite the presence, through standard investigating practices, of considerable evidence against each defendant. Further examples are chronicled in our prior cases. . . .

It is also urged that an unfettered right to detention for interrogation should be allowed because it will often redound to the benefit of the person questioned. When police inquiry determines that there is no reason to believe that the person has committed any crime, it is said, he will be released without need for further formal procedures. The person who has committed no offense, however, will be better able to clear himself after warnings, with counsel present than without. It can be assumed that in such circumstances a lawyer would advise his client to talk freely to police in order to clear himself.

Custodial interrogation, by contrast, does not necessarily afford the innocent an opportunity to clear themselves. A serious consequence of the present practice of the interrogation alleged to be beneficial for the innocent is that many arrests "for investigation" subject large numbers of innocent persons to detention and interrogation. In one of the cases before us, No. 584, *California* v. *Stewart,* police held four persons, who were in the defendant's house at the time of the arrest, in jail for five days until defendant confessed. At that time they were finally released. Police stated that there was "no evidence to connect them with any crime."

Available statistics on the extent of this practice where it is condoned indicate that these four are far from alone in being subjected to arrest, prolonged detention, and interrogation without the requisite probable cause.

Over the years the Federal Bureau of Investigation has compiled an exemplary record of effective law enforcement while advising any suspect or arrested person, at the outset of an interview, that he is not required to make a statement, that any statement may be used against him in court, that the individual may obtain the services of an attorney of his own choice and, more recently, that he has a right to free counsel if he is unable to pay. A letter received from the Solicitor General in response to a question from the Bench makes it clear that the present pattern of warnings and respect for the rights of the individual followed as a practice by the FBI is consistent with the procedure which we delineate today. It states:

At the oral argument of the above cause, Mr. Justice Fortas asked whether I could provide certain information as to the practices followed by the Federal Bureau of Investigation. I have directed these questions to the attention of the Director of the Federal Bureau of Investigation and am submitting herewith a statement of the questions and of the answers which we have received.

"(1) When an individual is interviewed by agents of the Bureau, what warning is given to him?

"The standard warning long given by Special Agents of the FBI to both suspects and persons under arrest is that the person has a right to say nothing and a right to counsel, and that any statement he does make may be used against him in court.

"After passage of the Criminal Justice Act of 1964, which provides free counsel for Federal defendants unable to pay, we added to our instructions to Special Agents the requirement that any person who is under arrest for an offense under FBI jurisdiction, or whose arrest is contemplated following the interview, must also be advised of his right to free counsel if he is unable to pay, and the fact that such counsel will be assigned by the Judge. At the same time, we broadened the right to counsel warning to read counsel of his own choice, or anyone else with whom he might wish to speak.

"(2) When is the warning given?

"The FBI warning is given to a suspect at the very outset of the interview, . . . The warning may be given to a person arrested as soon as practicable after the arrest, . . . but in any event it must precede the interview with the person for a confession or admission of his own guilt.

"(3) What is the Bureau's practice in the event that (a) the individual requests counsel and (b) counsel appears?

"When the person who has been warned of his right to counsel decides that he wishes to consult with counsel before making a statement, the interview is terminated at that point. . . . It may be continued, however, as to all matters *other* than the person's own guilt or innocence. If he is indecisive in his request for counsel, there may be some question on whether he did or did not waive counsel. Situations of this kind must necessarily be left to the judgment of the interviewing Agent. . . .

"A person being interviewed and desiring to consult counsel by telephone must be permitted to do so. . . . When counsel appears in person, he is permitted to confer with his client in private.

"(4) What is the Bureau's practice if the individual requests counsel, but cannot afford to retain an attorney?

"If any person being interviewed after warning of counsel decides that he wishes to consult with counsel before proceeding further the interview is terminated, as shown above. FBI Agents do not pass judgment on the ability of the person to pay for counsel. They do, however, advise those who have been arrested for an offense under FBI jurisdiction, or whose arrest is contemplated following the interview, of a right to free counsel *if* they are unable to pay, and the availability of such counsel from the Judge."

The practice of the FBI can readily be emulated by state and local enforcement agencies. The argument that the FBI deals with different crimes than are dealt with by state authorities does not mitigate the significance of the FBI experience.

The experience in some other countries also suggests that the danger to law enforcement in curbs on interrogation is overplayed. The English procedure since 1912 under the Judge's Rules is significant. As recently strengthened, the Rules require that a cautionary warning be given an accused by a police officer as soon as he has evidence that affords reasonable grounds for suspicion; they also require that any statement made be given by the accused without questioning by police. The right of the individual to consult with an attorney during this period is expressly recognized.

The safeguards present under Scottish law may be even greater than in England. Scottish judicial decisions bar use in evidence of most confessions obtained through police interrogation. In India, confessions made to police not in the presence of a magistrate have been excluded by rule of evidence since 1872, at a time when it operated under British law. Identical provisions appear in the Evidence Ordinance of Ceylon, enacted in 1895. Similarly, in our country the Uniform Code of Military Justice has long provided that no suspect may be interrogated without first being warned of his right not to make a statement and that any statement he makes may be used against him. Denial of the right to consult counsel during interrogation has also been proscribed by military tribunals. There appears to have been no marked detrimental effect on criminal law enforcement in these jurisdictions as a result of these rules. Conditions of law enforcement in our country are sufficiently similar to permit reference to this experience as assurance that lawlessness will not result from warning an individual of his rights or allowing him to exercise them. Moreover, it is consistent with our legal system that we give at least as much protection to these rights as is given in the jurisdictions described. We deal in our country with rights grounded in a specific requirement of the Fifth Amendment of the Constitution, whereas other jurisdictions arrived at their conclusions on the basis of principles of justice not so specifically defined. . . .

V

Because of the nature of the problem and because of its recurrent significance in numerous cases, we have to this point discussed the relationship of the Fifth Amendment privilege to police interrogation without specific concentration on the facts of the cases before us. We turn now to these facts to consider the application to these cases of the constitutional principles discussed above. In each instance, we have concluded that statements were obtained from the defendant under circumstances that did not meet constitutional standards for protection of the privilege. . . .

4. *Assistance of Counsel*

GIDEON *v.* WAINWRIGHT
372 US 335 (1963)

[English common law denied the aid of counsel to a defendant charged with treason or a felony on the theory that the judge would be counsel for him; but persons accused of misdemeanors were entitled to the assistance of counsel. After the English Revolution of 1688–1689 the rule was dropped as to treason but was otherwise maintained until, in 1836, Parliament granted the right of counsel in all felony cases. The rule excluding counsel was constantly attacked as a barbarous perversion of justice.

[The American colonies departed from English practice. A Pennsylvania statute of 1718, for example, provided for the assignment of counsel in capital cases. Before the adoption of the Constitution, twelve colonies provided for the assistance of counsel in a substantial measure. *Powell* v. *Alabama,* 287 US 45 (1932).

[The Sixth Amendment provides that in all criminal prosecutions the accused shall enjoy the right "to have the assistance of counsel for his defense." This Amendment has been implemented, in trials in the federal courts, by the Federal Rules of Criminal Procedure, which provided that if the defendant appears in court without counsel, the court is required to advise him of his right to counsel, and to assign counsel to represent him at every stage of the proceeding, unless he elects to proceed without counsel or is able to obtain counsel.

[But the constitutional guarantee was interpreted restrictively insofar as it concerned state prosecutions. The Court held that the Sixth Amendment requirement was not part of the Due Process Clause of the Fourteenth Amendment. Justices Murphy, Rutledge, Black, and Douglas protested against a different rule for state cases than that which obtained for federal cases.

[There was, however, agreement in the Court that the Due Process Clause of the Fourteenth Amendment required states to afford the assistance of counsel to defendants who could not obtain their own counsel, in all capital cases. In noncapital cases the states were held to be required to afford the assistance of counsel when there are special circumstances, such as extreme youth, ignorance, imbecility, or the complicated nature of the offense. Cases were to be decided on their facts. *Rice* v. *Olson,* 324 US 786 (1945); *Palmer* v. *Ashe,* 342 US 134 (1951). The leading case was *Betts* v. *Brady,* 316 US 455 (1942), which held that the Due Process Clause does not require that in every case, regardless of circumstances, an indigent defendant must be furnished counsel by the state.

[In the instant case *Betts* v. *Brady* was overruled. Justice Black, in an opinion for seven Justices, held that the Sixth Amendment was made obligatory upon the states by the Fourteenth Amendment. Justice Douglas wrote a concurring opinion. Justice Clark wrote a concurring opinion, in which he based his decision entirely on the Fourteenth Amendment. Justice Harlan also wrote a concurring opinion, in which he argued that the Court's decision should not be interpreted as carrying over the entire body of federal law on the point and applying it to the states in full constitutional sweep.]

Mr. Justice Black delivered the opinion of the Court:

Petitioner was charged in a Florida state court with having broken and entered a poolroom with intent to commit a misdemeanor. This offense is a felony under Florida law. Appearing in court without funds and without a lawyer, petitioner asked the court to appoint counsel for him, whereupon the following colloquy took place:

The COURT: Mr. Gideon, I am sorry, but I cannot appoint Counsel to represent you in this case. Under the laws of the State of Florida, the only time the Court can appoint Counsel to represent a Defendant is when that person is charged with a capital offense. I am sorry, but I will have to deny your request to appoint Counsel to defend you in this case.

The DEFENDANT: The United States Supreme Court says I am entitled to be represented by Counsel.

Put to trial before a jury, Gideon conducted his defense about as well as could be expected from a layman. He made an opening statement to the jury, cross-examined the State's witnesses, presented witnesses in his own defense, declined to testify himself, and made a short argument "emphasizing his innocence to the charge contained in the Information filed in this case." The jury returned a verdict of guilty, and petitioner was sentenced to serve five years in the state prison. Later, petitioner filed in the Florida Supreme Court this habeas corpus petition attacking his conviction and sentence on the ground that the trial court's refusal to appoint counsel for him denied him rights "guaranteed by the Constitution and the Bill of Rights by the United States Government." Treating the petition for habeas corpus as properly before it, the State Supreme Court, "upon consideration thereof" but without an opinion, denied all relief. Since 1942, when *Betts* v. *Brady,* 316 US 455, was decided by a divided Court, the problem of a defendant's federal constitutional right to counsel in a state court has been a continuing source of controversy and litigation in both state and federal courts. To give this problem another review here, we granted certiorari. Since Gideon was proceeding *in forma pauperis,* we appointed counsel to represent him and requested both sides to discuss in their briefs and oral arguments the following: "Should this Court's holding in *Betts* v. *Brady,* 316 US 455, be reconsidered?"

I

The facts upon which Betts claimed that he had been unconstitutionally denied the right to have counsel appointed to assist him are strikingly like the facts upon which Gideon here bases his federal constitutional claim. Betts was indicted for robbery in a Maryland state court. On arraignment, he told the trial judge of his lack of funds to hire a lawyer and asked the court to appoint one for him. Betts was advised that it was not the practice in that county to appoint counsel for indigent defendants except in murder and rape cases. He then pleaded not guilty, had witnesses summoned, cross-examined the State's witnesses, examined his own and chose not to testify himself. He was found guilty by the judge, sitting without a jury, and sentenced to eight years in prison. Like Gideon, Betts sought release by habeas corpus, alleging that he had been denied the right to assistance of counsel in violation of the Fourteenth Amendment. Betts was denied any relief, and on review this Court affirmed. It was held that a refusal to appoint counsel for an indigent defendant charged with a felony did not necessarily violate the Due Process Clause of the Fourteenth Amendment, which for reasons given the Court deemed to be the only applicable federal constitutional provision. The Court said:

Asserted denial [of due process] is to be tested by an appraisal of the totality of facts in a given case. That which may, in one setting, constitute a denial of fundamental fairness, shocking to the universal sense of justice, may, in other circumstances, and in the light of other considerations, fall short of such denial.

Treating due process as "a concept less rigid and more fluid than those envisaged in other specific and particular provisions of the Bill of Rights," the Court held that refusal to appoint counsel under the particular facts and circumstances in the *Betts* case was not so "offensive to the common and fundamental ideas of fairness" as to amount to a denial of due process. Since the facts and circumstances of the two cases are so nearly indistinguishable, we think the *Betts* v. *Brady* holding if left standing would require us to reject Gideon's claim that the Constitution guarantees him the assistance of counsel. Upon full reconsideration we conclude that *Betts* v. *Brady* should be overruled.

II

The Sixth Amendment provides, "In all criminal prosecutions, the accused shall enjoy the right . . . to have the Assistance of Counsel for his defence." We have construed this to mean that in federal courts counsel must be provided for defendants unable to employ counsel unless the right is competently and intelligently waived. Betts argued that this right is extended to indigent defendants in state courts by the Fourteenth Amendment. In response the Court stated that, while the Sixth Amendment laid down "no rule for the conduct of the states, the question recurs whether the constraint laid by the amendment upon the national courts expresses a rule so fundamental and essential to a fair trial, and so, to due process of law, that it is made obligatory upon the states by the Fourteenth Amendment." In order to decide whether the Sixth Amendment's guarantee of counsel is of this fundamental nature, the Court in *Betts* set out and considered "[r]elevant data on the subject . . . afforded by constitutional and statutory provisions subsisting in the colonies and the states prior to the inclusion of the Bill of Rights in the national Constitution, and in the constitutional, legislative, and judicial history of the states to the present date." On the basis of this historical data the Court concluded that "appointment of counsel is not a fundamental right, essential to a fair trial." It was for this reason the *Betts* Court refused to accept the contention that the Sixth Amendment's guarantee of counsel for indigent federal defendants was extended to or, in the words of that Court, "made obligatory upon the states by the Fourteenth Amendment." Plainly, had the Court concluded that appointment of counsel for an indigent criminal defendant was "a fundamental right, essential to a fair trial," it would have held that the Fourteenth Amendment requires appointment of counsel in a state court, just as the Sixth Amendment requires in a federal court.

We think the Court in *Betts* had ample precedent for acknowledging that those guarantees of the Bill of Rights which are fundamental safeguards of liberty immune from federal abridgment are equally protected against state invasion by the Due Process Clause of the Fourteenth Amendment. This same principle was recognized, explained, and applied in *Powell* v. *Alabama,* 287 US 45 (1932), a case upholding the right of counsel, where the Court held that despite sweeping language to the contrary in *Hurtado* v. *California,* 110 US 516 (1884), the Fourteenth Amendment "embraced" those " 'fundamental principles of liberty and justice which lie at the base of all our civil and political institutions,' " even though they had been "specifically dealt with in another part of the Federal Constitution." In many cases other than *Powell* and *Betts,* this Court has looked to the fundamental nature of original Bill of Rights guarantees to decide whether the Fourteenth Amendment makes them obligatory on the States. Explicitly recognized to be of this "fundamental nature" and therefore made immune from state invasion by the Fourteenth, or some part of it, are the First Amendment's freedoms of speech, press, religion, assembly, association, and petition for redress of grievances. For the same reason, though not always in precisely the same terminology, the Court has made obligatory on the States the Fifth Amendment's command that private property shall not be taken for public use without just compensation, the Fourth Amendment's prohibition of unreasonable searches and seizures, and the Eight's ban on cruel and unusual punishment. On the other hand, this Court in *Palko* v. *Connecticut,* 302 US 319 (1937), refused to hold that the Fourteenth Amendment made the double jeopardy provision of the Fifth Amendment obligatory on the States. In so refusing, however, the Court, speaking through Mr. Justice Cardozo, was careful to emphasize that "immunities that are valid as against the federal government by force of the specific pledges of particular amendments have been found to be implicit in the concept of ordered liberty, and thus, through the Fourteenth Amendment, become valid as against the states" and that guarantees "in their origin . . . effective against the federal government alone" had by prior cases "been taken over from the earlier articles of the Federal Bill of Rights and brought within the Fourteenth Amendment by a process of absorption."

We accept *Betts* v. *Brady's* assumption, based as it was on our prior cases, that a provision of the Bill of Rights which is "fundamental and essential to a fair trial" is made obligatory upon the State by the Fourteenth Amendment. We think the Court in *Betts* was wrong, however, in concluding that the Sixth Amendment's guarantee of counsel is not one of these fundamental rights. Ten years before *Betts* v. *Brady,* this Court, after full consideration of all the historical data examined in *Betts,* had unequivocally declared that "the right to the aid of counsel is of this fundamental character." . . . While the Court at the close of its *Powell* opinion did by its language, as this Court frequently does, limit its holding to the particular facts and circumstances of that case, its conclusions about the fundamental nature of the right to counsel are unmistakable. Several years later, in 1936, the Court re-emphasized what it had said about the fundamental nature of the right to counsel. . . .

In light of these and many other prior decisions of this Court, it is not surprising that the *Betts* Court, when faced with the contention that "one charged with crime, who is unable to obtain counsel, must be furnished counsel by the state," conceded that "[e]xpressions in the opinions of this court lend color to the argument." . . . The fact is that in deciding as it did—that "appointment of counsel is not a fundamental right, essential to a fair trial"—the Court in *Betts* v. *Brady* made an abrupt break with its own well-considered precedents. In returning to these old precedents, sounder we believe than the new, we but restore constitutional principles established to achieve a fair system of justice. Not only these precedents but also reason and reflection require us to recognize that in our adversary system of criminal justice, any person haled into court, who is too poor to hire a lawyer, cannot be assured a fair trial unless counsel is provided for him. This seems to us to be an obvious truth. Governments, both state and federal, quite properly spend vast sums of money to establish machinery to try defendants accused of crime. Lawyers to prosecute are everywhere deemed essential to protect the public's interest in an orderly society. Similarly, there are few defendants charged with crime, few indeed, who fail to hire the best lawyers they can get to prepare and present their defenses. That government hires lawyers to prosecute and defendants who have the money hire lawyers to defend are the strongest indications of the widespread belief that lawyers in criminal courts are necessities, not luxuries. The right of one charged with crime to counsel may not be deemed fundamental and essential to fair trials in some countries, but it is in ours. From the very beginning, our state and national constitutions and laws have laid great emphasis on procedural and substantive safeguards designed to assure fair trials before impartial tribunals in which every defendant stands equal before the law. This noble ideal cannot be realized if the poor man charged with crime has to face his accusers without a lawyer to assist him. A defendant's need for a lawyer is nowhere better stated than in the moving words of Mr. Justice Sutherland in *Powell* v. *Alabama:*

The right to be heard would be, in many cases, of little avail if it did not comprehend the right to be heard by counsel. Even the intelligent and educated layman has small and sometimes no skill in the science of law. If charged with crime, he is incapable, generally, of determining for himself whether the indictment is good or bad. He is unfamiliar with the rules of evidence. Left without the aid of counsel he may be put on trial without a proper charge, and convicted upon incompetent evidence, or evidence irrelevant to the issue or otherwise inadmissible. He lacks both the skill and knowledge adequately to prepare his defense, even though he have a perfect one. He requires the guiding hand of counsel at every step in the proceedings against him. Without it, though he be not guilty, he faces the danger of conviction because he does not know how to establish his innocence.

The Court in *Betts* v. *Brady* departed from the sound wisdom upon which the Court's holding in *Powell* v. *Alabama* rested. Florida, supported by two other States, has asked that *Betts* v. *Brady* be left intact. Twenty-two States, as friends of the Court, argue that *Betts* was "an anachronism when handed down" and that it should now be overruled. We agree.

The judgment is reversed and the cause is remanded to the Supreme Court of Florida for further action not inconsistent with this opinion.

Reversed.

ARGERSINGER *v.* HAMLIN
407 US 25 (1972)

[The Sixth Amendment provides that in "all criminal prosecutions" the accused shall enjoy the right "to have the assistance of counsel for his defense." In *Gideon, supra,* the Court made this Sixth Amendment guarantee applicable to the states under the Fourteenth Amendment. The Court there held that the state had the obligation to assign counsel to an indigent defendant charged with a felony. In the instant case, the Court held that no accused may be deprived of his liberty as the result of any criminal prosecution, *whether felony or misdemeanor,* if he was denied the assistance of counsel. The opinion for the Court was by Justice Douglas. Chief Justice Burger wrote an opinion concurring in the result. Justice Brennan wrote a concurring opinion in which he was joined by Justices Douglas and Stewart. Justice Powell, joined by Justice Rehnquist, wrote an opinion concurring in the result.]

Mr. Justice Douglas delivered the opinion of the Court:

Petitioner, an indigent, was charged in Florida with carrying a concealed weapon, an offense punishable by imprisonment up to six months and a $1,000 fine. The trial was to a judge, and petitioner was unrepresented by counsel. He was sentenced to serve 90 days in jail and brought this habeas corpus action in the Florida Supreme Court, alleging that, being deprived of his right to counsel, he was unable as an indigent layman properly to raise and present to the trial court good and sufficient defenses to the charges for which he stands convicted. The Florida Supreme Court by a four-to-three decision, in ruling on the right to counsel, followed the line we marked out in *Duncan* v. *Louisiana,* 391 US 145, 159, as respects the right to trial by jury and held that the right to court-appointed counsel extends only to trials "for nonpetty offenses punishable by more than six months imprisonment."

The case is here on a petition for certiorari which we granted. We reverse.

The Sixth Amendment, which in enumerated situations has been made applicable to the States by reason of the Fourteenth Amendment . . . provides specified standards for "all criminal prosecutions." . . .

In *Washington* v. *Texas, supra,* we said, "We have held that due process requires that the accused have the assistance of counsel for his defense, that he be confronted with the witnesses against him, and that he have the right to a speedy and public trial." Respecting the right to a speedy and public trial, the right to be informed of the nature and cause of the accusation, the right to confront and cross-examine witnesses, the right to compulsory process for obtaining witnesses, it was recently stated, "It is simply not arguable nor has any court ever held, that the trial of a petty offense may be held in secret, or without notice to the accused of the charges, or that in such cases the defendant has no right to confront his accusers or to compel the attendance of witnesses in his own behalf." . . .

District of Columbia v. *Clawans,* 300 US 617, illustrates the point. There, the offense was engaging without a license in the business of dealing in secondhand property, an offense punishable by a fine of $300 or imprisonment for not more than 90 days. The Court held that the offense was a "petty" one and could be tried without a jury. But the conviction was reversed and a new trial ordered, because the trial court had prejudicially restricted the right of cross-examination, a right guaranteed by the Sixth Amendment.

The right to trial by jury, also guaranteed by the Sixth Amendment by reason of the Fourteenth, was limited by *Duncan* v. *Louisiana* to trials where the potential punishment was imprisonment of six months or more. But as the various opinions in *Baldwin* v. *New York,* 399 US 66, make plain, the right to trial by jury has a different genealogy and is brigaded with a system of trial to a judge alone. As stated in *Duncan:*

Providing an accused with the right to be tried by a jury of his peers gave him an inestimable safeguard against the corrupt or overzealous prosecutor and against the complaint, biased, or eccentric judge. If the defendant preferred the common-sense judgment of a jury to the more tutored but perhaps less sympathetic reaction of the single judge, he was to have it. Beyond this, the jury trial provisions in the Federal and State Constitutions reflect a fundamental decision about the exercise of official power—a reluctance to entrust plenary powers over the life and liberty of the citizen to one judge or to a group of judges. Fear of unchecked power, so typical of our State and Federal Governments in other respects, found expression in the criminal law in this insistence upon community participation in the determination of guilt or innocence. The deep commitment of the Nation to the right of jury trial in serious criminal cases as a defense against arbitrary law enforcement qualifies for protection under the Due Process Clause of the Fourteenth Amendment, and must therefore be respected by the States.

While there is historical support for limiting the "deep commitment" to trial by jury to "serious criminal cases," there is no such support for a similar limitation on the right to assistance of counsel:

Originally, in England, a person charged with treason or felony was denied the aid of counsel, except in respect of legal questions which the accused himself might suggest. At the same time parties in civil cases and persons accused of misdemeanors were entitled to the full assistance of counsel. . . . [It] appears that in at least twelve of the thirteen colonies the rule of the English common law, in the respect now under consideration, had been definitively rejected and the right to counsel fully recognized in all criminal prosecutions, save that in one or two instances the right was limited to capital offenses or to the more serious crimes. . . . *Powell* v. *Alabama,* 287 US 60 and 64–65.

The Sixth Amendment thus extended the right to counsel beyond its common-law dimensions. But there is nothing in the language of the Amendment, its history, or in the decisions of this Court, to indicate that it was intended to embody a retraction of the right in petty offenses wherein the common law previously did require that counsel be provided. . . .

We reject, therefore, the premise that since prosecutions for crimes punishable by imprisonment for less than six months may be tried without a jury, they may always be tried without a lawyer.

The assistance of counsel is often a requisite to the very existence of a fair trial. The Court in *Powell* v. *Alabama*—a capital case—said:

The right to be heard would be, in many cases, of little avail if it did not comprehend the right to be heard by counsel. Even the intelligent and educated layman has small and sometimes no skill in the science of law. If charged with crime, he is incapable, generally, of determining for himself whether the indictment is good or bad. He is unfamiliar with the rules of evidence. Left without the aid of counsel he may be put on trial without a proper charge, and convicted upon incompetent evidence, or evidence irrelevant to the issue or otherwise inadmissible. He lacks both the skill and knowledge adequately to prepare his defense, even though he have a perfect one. He requires the guiding hand of counsel at every step in the proceedings against him. Without it, though he be not guilty, he faces the danger of conviction because he does not know how to establish his innocence. If that be true of men of intelligence, how much more true is it of the ignorant and illiterate, or those of feeble intellect.

In *Gideon* v. *Wainwright,* . . . we dealt with a felony trial. But we did not so limit the need of the accused for a lawyer. We said:

in our adversary system of criminal justice, any person haled into court, who is too poor to hire a lawyer, cannot be assured a fair trial unless counsel is provided for him. This seems to us to be an obvious truth. Governments, both state and federal, quite properly spend vast sums of money to establish machinery to try defendants accused of crime. Lawyers to prosecute are everywhere deemed essential to protect the public's interest in an orderly society. Similarly, there are few defendants charged with crime, few indeed, who fail to hire the best lawyers they can get to prepare and present their defenses. That government hires lawyers to prosecute and defendants who have the money hire lawyers to defend are the strongest indications of the widespread belief that lawyers in criminal courts are necessities, not luxuries. The right of one charged with crime to counsel may not be deemed fundamental and essential to fair trials in some countries, but it is in ours. From the very beginning, our state and national constitutions and laws have laid great emphasis on procedural and substantive safeguards designed to assure fair trials before impartial tribunals in which every defendant stands equal before the law. This noble ideal cannot be realized if the poor man charged with crime has to face his accusers without a lawyer to assist him.

Both *Powell* and *Gideon* involved felonies. But their rationale has relevance to any criminal trial, where an accused is deprived of his liberty. *Powell* and *Gideon* suggest that there are certain fundamental rights applicable to all such criminal prosecutions, even those, such as *In re Oliver* where the penalty is 60 days' imprisonment:

A person's right to reasonable notice of a charge against him, and an opportunity to be heard in his defense—a right to his day in court—are basic in our system of jurisprudence; and these rights included, as a minimum, a right to examine the witnesses against him, to offer testimony, *and to be represented by counsel.* 333 US, at 273 (emphasis supplied).

The requirement of counsel may well be necessary for a fair trial even in a petty offense prosecution. We are by no means convinced that legal and constitutional questions involved in a case that actually leads to imprisonment even for a brief period are any less complex than when a person can be sent off for six months or more. . . .

Beyond the problem of trials and appeals is that of the guilty plea, a problem which looms large in misdemeanor as well as in felony cases. Counsel is needed so that the accused may know precisely what he is doing, so that he is fully aware of the prospect of going to jail or prison, and so that he is treated fairly by the prosecution.

In addition, the volume of misdemeanor cases,* far greater in number than felony prosecutions, may create an obsession for speedy dispositions, regardless of the fairness of the result. The Report by the President's Commission on Law Enforcement and Administration of Justice, The Challenge of Crime in a Free Society, p. 128 (1967), states:

For example, until legislation last year increased the number of judges, the District of Columbia Court of General Sessions had four judges to process the preliminary stages of more than 1,500 felony cases, 7,500 serious misdemeanor cases, and 38,000 petty offenses and an equal number of traffic offenses per year. An inevitable consequence of volume that large is the almost total preoccupation in such a court with the movement of cases. The calendar is long, speed often is substituted for care, and casually arranged out-of-court compromise too often is substituted for adjudication. Inadequate attention tends to be given to the individual defendant, whether in protecting his rights, sifting the facts at trial, deciding the social risk he presents, or determining how to deal with him after conviction. The frequent result is futility and failure. As Dean Edward Barrett recently observed:

"Wherever the visitor looks at the system, he finds great numbers of defendants being processed by harassed and overworked officials. Police have more cases than they can investigate. Prosecutors walk into courtrooms to try simple cases as they take their initial looks at the files. Defense lawyers appear having had no more than time for hasty conversations with their clients. Judges face long calendars with the certain knowledge that their calendars tomorrow and the next day will be, if anything, longer, and so there is no choice but to dispose of the cases.

"Suddenly it becomes clear that for most defendants in the criminal process, there is scant regard for them as individuals. They are numbers on dockets, faceless ones to be processed and sent on their way. The gap between the theory and the reality is enormous.

"Very little such observation of the administration of criminal justice in operation is required to reach the conclusion that it suffers from basic ills."

That picture is seen in almost every report. "The misdemeanor trial is characterized by insufficient and frequently irresponsible preparation on the part of the defense, the prosecution, and the court. Everything is rush, rush." . . .

There is evidence of the prejudice which results to misdemeanor defendants from this "assembly-line justice." One study concluded that "Misdemeanants represented by attorneys are five times as likely to emerge from police court with all charges dismissed as are defendants who face similar charges without counsel." ACLU, Legal Counsel for Misdemeanants, Preliminary Report, 1 (1970).

We must conclude, therefore, that the problems associated with misdemeanor

---

* In 1965, 314,000 defendants were charged with felonies in state courts, and 24,000 were charged with felonies in federal courts. President's Commission on Law Enforcement and Administration of Justice, Task Force Report: The Courts 55 (1967). Exclusive of traffic offenses, however, it is estimated that there are annually between four and five million court cases involving misdemeanors, *Ibid.* And, while there are no authoritative figures, extrapolations indicate that there are probably between 40.8 and 50 million traffic offenses each year. . . .

and petty offenses often require the presence of counsel to insure the accused a fair trial. Mr. Justice Powell suggests that these problems are raised even in situations where there is no prospect of imprisonment. We need not consider the requirements of the Sixth Amendment as regards the right to counsel where loss of liberty is not involved, however, for here, petitioner was in fact sentenced to jail. And, as we said in *Baldwin* v. *New York,* 399 US, at 73: "[T]he prospect of imprisonment for however short a time will seldom be viewed by the accused as a trivial or 'petty' matter and may well result in quite serious repercussions affecting his career and his reputation."

We hold, therefore, that absent a knowing and intelligent waiver, no person may be imprisoned for any offense, whether classified as petty, misdemeanor, or felony, unless he was represented by counsel at his trial.* . . .

Under the rule we announce today, every judge will know when the trial of a misdemeanor starts that no imprisonment may be imposed, even though local law permits it, unless the accused is represented by counsel. He will have a measure of the seriousness and gravity of the offense and therefore know when to name a lawyer to represent the accused before the trial starts.

The run of misdemeanors will not be affected by today's ruling. But in those that end up in the actual deprivation of a person's liberty, the accused will receive the benefit of "the guiding hand of counsel" so necessary when one's liberty is in jeopardy.

Reversed.

5. Speedy Trial

BARKER v. WINGO
407 US 514 (1972)

[The Sixth Amendment provides that in all criminal prosecutions, the accused shall, *inter alia,* "enjoy the right to a speedy and public trial." The Supreme Court has held that the right to a speedy trial is "as fundamental as any of the rights secured by the Sixth Amendment." *Klopfer* v. *North Carolina,* 386 US 213 (1967). In the instant case, in his opinion for a unanimous Court, Justice Powell analyzes the complex of factors that must enter into any consideration of the question whether or not the right to a speedy trial has been observed. In this case, even though there was a delay of over five years between arrest and trial, the Court, after applying the balancing tests, concluded that the right had not been denied. Justice White, with Justice Brennan joining, wrote a brief concurring opinion.]

Mr. Justice Powell delivered the opinion of the Court:

Although a speedy trial is guaranteed the accused by the Sixth Amendment to the Constitution, this Court has dealt with that right on infrequent occasions. . . .

---

* We do not share Mr. Justice Powell's doubt that the Nation's legal resources are insufficient to implement the rule we announce today. It has been estimated that between 1,575 and 2,300 full-time counsel would be required to represent *all* indigent misdemeanants, excluding traffic offenders. . . .

The Court's opinion in *Klopfer* v. *North Carolina,* 386 US 213 (1967), established that the right to speedy trial is "fundamental" and is imposed by the Due Process Clause of the Fourteenth Amendment on the States. See *Smith* v. *Hooey,* 393 US 374 (1969); *Dickey* v. *Florida,* 398 US 30 (1970). As Mr. Justice Brennan pointed out in his concurring opinion in *Dickey,* in none of these cases have we attempted to set out the criteria by which the speedy trial right is to be judged. This case compels us to make such an attempt.

I

On July 20, 1958, in Christian County, Kentucky, an elderly couple was beaten to death by intruders wielding an iron tire tool. Two suspects, Silas Manning and Willie Barker, the petitioner, were arrested shortly thereafter. The grand jury indicted them on September 15. Counsel was appointed on September 17, and Barker's trial was set for October 21. The Commonwealth had a stronger case against Manning, and it believed that Barker could not be convicted unless Manning testified against him. Manning was naturally unwilling to incriminate himself. Accordingly, on October 23, the day Silas Manning was brought to trial, the Commonwealth sought and obtained the first of what was to be a series of 16 continuances of Barker's trial. Barker made no objection. By first convicting Manning, the Commonwealth would remove possible problems of self-incrimination and would be able to assure his testimony against Barker.

The Commonwealth encountered more than a few difficulties in its prosecution of Manning. The first trial ended in a hung jury. A second trial resulted in a conviction, but the Kentucky Court of Appeals reversed because of the admission of evidence obtained by an illegal search. . . . At his third trial, Manning was again convicted, and the Court of Appeals again reversed because the trial court had not granted a change of venue. . . . A fourth trial resulted in a hung jury. Finally, after five trials, Manning was convicted, in March 1962, of murdering one victim, and after a sixth trial, in December 1962, he was convicted of murdering the other.

The Christian County Circuit Court holds three terms each year—in February, June, and September. Barker's initial trial was to take place in the September term of 1958. The first continuance postponed it until the February 1959 term. The second continuance was granted for one month only. Every term thereafter for as long as the Manning prosecutions were in process, the Commonwealth routinely moved to continue Barker's case to the next term. When the case was continued from the June 1959 term until the following September, Barker, having spent 10 months in jail, obtained his release by posting a $5,000 bond. He thereafter remained free in the community until his trial. Barker made no objection, through his counsel, to the first 11 continuances.

When on February 12, 1962, the Commonwealth moved for the twelfth time to continue the case until the following term, Barker's counsel filed a motion to dismiss the indictment. The motion to dismiss was denied two weeks later, and the State's motion for a continuance was granted. The State was granted further continuances in June 1962 and September 1962, to which Barker did not object.

In February 1963, the first term of court following Manning's final conviction, the Commonwealth moved to set Barker's trial for March 19. But on the day scheduled for trial, it again moved for a continuance until the June term. It gave as its reason the illness of the ex-sheriff who was the chief investigating officer in the case. To this continuance, Barker objected unsuccessfully.

The witness was still unable to testify in June, and the trial, which had been set for June 19, was continued again until the September term over Barker's objection. This time the court announced that the case would be dismissed for lack of prosecution if it were not tried during the next term. The final trial date was set for October 9, 1963. On that date, Barker again moved to dismiss the indictment, and this time specified that his right to a speedy trial had been violated. The motion was denied; the trial commenced with Manning as the chief prosecution witness; Barker was convicted and given a life sentence.

Barker appealed his conviction to the Kentucky Court of Appeals, relying in part on his speedy trial claim. The court affirmed. . . . In February 1970 Barker petitioned for habeas corpus in the United States District Court for the Western District of Kentucky. Although the District Court rejected the petition without holding a hearing, the Court granted petitioner leave to appeal *in forma pauperis* and a certificate of probable cause to appeal. On appeal, the Court of Appeals for the Sixth Circuit affirmed the District Court. It ruled that Barker had waived his speedy trial claim for the entire period before February 1963, the date on which the court believed he had first objected to the delay by filing a motion to dismiss. In this belief the Court was mistaken, for the record reveals that the motion was filed in February 1962. The Commonwealth so conceded at oral argument before this Court. The court held further that the remaining period after the date on which Barker first raised his claim and before his trial—which it thought was only eight months but which was actually 20 months—was not unduly long. In addition, the Court held that Barker had shown no resulting prejudice, and that the illness of the ex-sheriff was a valid justification for the delay: We granted Barker's petition for certiorari.

II

The right to a speedy trial is generically different from any of the other rights enshrined in the Constitution for the protection of the accused. In addition to the general concern that all accused persons be treated according to decent and fair procedures, there is a societal interest in providing a speedy trial which exists separate from and at times in opposition to the interests of the accused. The inability of courts to provide a prompt trial has contributed to a large backlog of cases in urban courts which, among other things, enables defendants to negotiate more effectively for pleas of guilty to lesser offenses and otherwise manipulate the system. In addition, persons released on bond for lengthy periods awaiting trial have an opportunity to commit other crimes. It must be of little comfort to the residents of Christian County, Kentucky, to know that Barker was at large on bail for over four years while accused of a vicious and brutal murder of which he was ultimately convicted. Moreover, the longer an accused is free awaiting trial, the more tempting becomes his opportunity to jump bail and escape. Finally, delay between arrest and punishment may have a detrimental effect on rehabilitation.

If an accused cannot make bail, he is generally confined, as was Barker for 10 months, in a local jail. This contributes to the overcrowding and generally deplorable state of those institutions. Lengthy exposure to these conditions "has a destructive effect on human character and makes the rehabilitation of the individual offender much more difficult." At times the result may even be violent rioting. Finally, lengthy pretrial detention is costly. The cost of maintaining a prisoner in jail varies from $3 to $9 per day, and this amounts to millions across the Nation. In addition, society loses wages which might have been earned, and it must often support families of incarcerated breadwinners.

A second difference between the right to speedy trial and the accused's other constitutional rights is that deprivation of the right may work to the accused's advantage. Delay is not an uncommon defense tactic. As the time between the commission of the crime and trial lengthens, witnesses may become unavailable or their memories may fade. If the witnesses support the prosecution, its case will be weakened, sometimes seriously so. And it is the prosecution which carries the burden of proof. Thus, unlike the right to counsel or the right to be free from compelled self-incrimination, deprivation of the right to speedy trial does not *per se* prejudice the accused's ability to defend himself.

Finally, and perhaps most importantly, the right to speedy trial is a more vague concept than other procedural rights. It is, for example, impossible to determine with precision when the right has been denied. We cannot definitely say how long is too long in a system where justice is supposed to be swift but deliberate. As a consequence, there is no fixed point in the criminal process when the State can put the defendant to the choice of either exercising or waiving the right to a speedy trial. If, for example, the State moves for a 60-day continuance, granting that continuance is not a violation of the right to speedy trial unless the circumstances of the case are such that further delay would endanger the values the right protects. It is impossible to do more than generalize about when those circumstances exist. There is nothing comparable to the point in the process when a defendant exercises or waives his right to counsel or his right to a jury trial. Thus, . . . any inquiry into a speedy trial claim necessitates a functional analysis of the right in the particular context of the case:

The right of speedy trial is necessarily relative. It is consistent with delays and depends upon circumstances. It secures rights to a defendant. It does not preclude the rights of public justice.

The amorphous quality of the right also leads to the unsatisfactorily severe remedy of dismissal of the indictment when the right has been deprived. This is indeed a serious consequence because it means that a defendant who may be guilty of a serious crime will go free, without having been tried. Such a remedy is more serious than an exclusionary rule or a reversal for a new trial, but it is the only possible remedy.

III

Perhaps because the speedy trial right is so slippery, two rigid approaches are urged upon us as ways of eliminating some of the uncertainty which courts experience in protecting the right. The first suggestion is that we hold that the Constitution requires a criminal defendant to be offered a trial within a specified time period. The result of such a ruling would have the virtue of clarifying when the right is infringed and of simplifying courts' application of it. Recognizing this, some legislatures have enacted laws, and some courts have adopted procedural rules which more narrowly define the right. The United States Court of Appeals for the Second Circuit has promulgated rules for the District Courts in that Circuit establishing that the government must be ready for trial within six months of the date of arrest, except in unusual circumstances, or the charge will be dismissed. This type of rule is also recommended by the American Bar Association.

But such a result would require this Court to engage in legislative or rulemaking activity, rather than in the adjudicative process to which we should confine our efforts. We do not establish procedural rules for the States, except when mandated by the Constitution. We find no constitutional basis for holding that the speedy trial right can be quantified into a specified number of days or months. The States, of course, are free to prescribe a reasonable period consistent with constitutional standards, but our approach must be less precise.

The second suggested alternative would restrict consideration of the right to those cases in which the accused has demanded a speedy trial. Most States have recognized what is loosely referred to as the "demand rule," although eight States reject it. It is not clear, however, precisely what is meant by that term. Although every Federal Court of Appeals that has considered the question has endorsed some kind of demand rule, some have regarded the rule within the concept of waiver, whereas others have viewed it as a factor to be weighed in assessing whether there has been a deprivation of the speedy trial right. We shall refer to the former approach as the demand-waiver doctrine. The demand-waiver doctrine provides that a defendant waives any consideration of his right to speedy trial for any period prior to which he has not demanded a trial. Under this rigid approach, a prior demand is a necessary condition to the consideration of the speedy trial right. This essentially was the approach the Sixth Circuit took below.

Such an approach, by presuming waiver of a fundamental right from inaction, is inconsistent with this Court's pronouncements on waiver of constitutional rights. The Court has defined waiver as "an intentional relinquishment or abandonment of a known right or privilege." *Johnson* v. *Zerbst,* 304 US 458, 464 (1938). Courts should "indulge every reasonable presumption against waiver," . . . and they should "not presume acquiescence in the loss of fundamental rights." . . . In *Carnley* v. *Cochran,* 369 US 506 (1962), we held:

Presuming waiver from a silent record is impermissible. The record must show, or there must be an allegation and evidence which show, that an accused was offered counsel, but intelligently and understandably rejected the offer. Anything less is not waiver.

The Court has ruled similarly with respect to waiver of other rights designed to protect the accused. . . .

In excepting the right to speedy trial from the rule of waiver we have applied to other fundamental rights, courts that have applied the demand-waiver rule have relied on the assumption that delay usually works for the benefit of the accused and on the absence of any readily ascertainable time in the criminal process for a defendant to be given the choice of exercising or waiving his right. But it is not necessarily true that delay benefits the defendant. There are cases in which delay appreciably harms the defendant's ability to defend himself. Moreover, a defendant confined to jail prior to trial is obviously disadvantaged by delay as is a defendant released on bail but unable to lead a normal life because of community suspicion and his own anxiety.

The nature of the speedy-trial right does make it impossible to pinpoint a precise time in the process when the right must be asserted or waived, but that fact does not argue for placing the burden of protecting the right solely on defendants. A defendant has no duty to bring himself to trial; the State has that duty as well as the duty of insuring that the trial is consistent with due process. Moreover, for the reasons earlier expressed, society has a particular interest in bringing swift prosecutions, and society's representatives are the ones who should protect that interest.

It is also noteworthy that such a rigid view of the demand rule places defense counsel in an awkward position. Unless he demands a trial early and often, he is in danger of frustrating his client's right. If counsel is willing to tolerate some delay because he finds it reasonable and helpful in preparing his own case, he may be unable to obtain a speedy trial for his client at the end of that time. Since under the demand-waiver rule no time runs until the demand is made, the government will have whatever time is otherwise reasonable to bring the defendant to trial after a demand has been made. Thus, if the first demand is made three months after arrest in a jurisdiction which prescribes a six months rule, the prosecution will have a total of nine months—which may be wholly unreasonable under the circumstances. The result in practice is likely to be either an automatic, *pro forma* demand made immediately after appointment of counsel or delays which, but for the demand-waiver rule, would not be tolerated. Such a result is not consistent with the interests of defendants, society, or the Constitution.

We reject, therefore, the rule that a defendant who fails to demand a speedy trial forever waives his right. This does not mean, however, that the defendant has no responsibility to assert his right. We think the better rule is that the defendant's assertion of or failure to assert his right to a speedy trial is one of the factors to be considered in an inquiry into the deprivation of the right. Such a formulation avoids the rigidities of the demand-waiver rule and the resulting possible unfairness in its application. It allows the trial court to exercise a judicial discretion based on the circumstances, including due consideration of any applicable formal procedural rule. It would permit, for example, a court to attach a different weight to a situation in which the defendant knowingly fails to object from a situation in which his attorney acquiesces in long delay without adequately informing his client or from a situation in which no counsel is appointed. It would also allow a court to weigh the frequency and force of the objections as opposed to attaching significant weight to a purely *pro forma* objection.

In ruling that a defendant has some responsibility to assert a speedy-trial claim, we do not depart from our holdings in other cases concerning the waiver of fundamental rights, in which we have placed the entire responsibility on the prosecution to show that the claimed waiver was knowingly and voluntarily made. Such cases have involved rights which must be exercised or waived at a specific time or under clearly identifiable circumstances, such as the rights to plead not guilty, to demand a jury trial, to exercise the privilege against self-incrimination, and to have the assistance of counsel. We have shown above that the right to a speedy trial is unique in its uncertainty as to when and under what circumstances it must be asserted or may be deemed waived. But the rule we announce today, which comports with constitutional principles, places the primary burden on the courts and the prosecutors to assure that cases are brought to trial. We hardly need add that if delay is attributable to the defendant, then his waiver may be given effect under standard waiver doctrine, the demand rule aside.

We, therefore, reject both of the inflexible approaches—the fixed time period because it goes further than the Constitution requires; the demand-waiver rule because it is insensitive to a right which we have deemed fundamental. The approach we accept is a balancing test, in which the conduct of both the prosecution and the defendant are weighed.

IV

A balancing test necessarily compels courts to approach speedy-trial cases on an *ad hoc* basis. We can do little more than identify some of the factors which courts should assess in determining whether a particular defendant has been deprived of his right. Though some might express them in different ways, we identify four such factors: Length of delay, the reason for the delay, the defendant's assertion of his right, and prejudice to the defendant.

The length of the delay is to some extent a triggering mechanism. Until there is some delay which is presumptively prejudicial, there is no necessity for inquiry into the other factors that go into the balance. Nevertheless, because of the imprecision of the right to speedy trial, the length of delay that will provoke such an inquiry is necessarily dependant upon the peculiar circumstances of the case. To take but one example, the delay that can be tolerated for an ordinary street crime is considerably less than for a serious, complex conspiracy charge.

Closely related to length of delay is the reason the government assigns to justify the delay. Here, too, different weights should be assigned to different reasons. A deliberate attempt to delay the trial in order to hamper the defense should be weighed heavily against the government. A more neutral reason such as negligence or overcrowded courts should be weighed less heavily but nevertheless should be considered since the ultimate responsibility for such circumstances must rest with the government rather than with the defendant. Finally, a valid reason, such as a missing witness, should serve to justify appropriate delay.

We have already discussed the third factor, the defendant's responsibility to assert his right. Whether and how a defendant asserts his right is closely related to the other factors we have mentioned. The strength of his efforts will be affected by the length of the delay, to some extent by the reason for the delay, and most particularly by the personal prejudice, which is not always readily identifiable, that he experiences. The more serious the deprivation, the more likely a defendant is to complain. The defendant's assertion of his speedy trial right, then, is entitled to strong evidentiary weight in determining whether the right is being deprived. We emphasize that failure to assert the right will make it difficult for a defendant to prove that he was denied a speedy trial.

A fourth factor is prejudice to the defendant. Prejudice, of course, should be assessed in the light of the interests of defendants which the speedy trial right has designed to protect. This Court has identified three such interests: (i) to prevent oppressive pretrial incarceration; (ii) to minimize anxiety and concern of the accused; and (iii) to limit the possibility that the defense will be impaired. Of these, the most serious is the last, because the inability of a defendant adequately to prepare his case skews the fairness of the entire system. If witnesses die or disappear during a delay, the prejudice is obvious. There is also prejudice if defense witnesses are unable to recall accurately events of the distant past. Loss of memory, however, is not always reflected in the record because what has been forgotten can rarely be shown.

We have discussed previously the societal disadvantages of lengthy pretrial incarceration, but obviously the disadvantages for the accused who cannot obtain his release are even more serious. The time spent in jail awaiting trial has a detrimental impact on the individual. It often means loss of a job; it disrupts family life; and it enforces idleness. Most jails offer little or no recreational or rehabilitative programs. The time spent in jail is simply dead time. Moreover, if a defendant is locked up, he is hindered in his ability to gather evidence, contact witnesses, or otherwise prepare his defense. Imposing those consequences on anyone who has not yet been convicted is serious. It is especially unfortunate to impose them on those persons who are ultimately found to be innocent. Finally, even if an accused is not incarcerated prior to trial, he is still disadvantaged by restraints on his liberty and by living under a cloud of anxiety, suspicion, and often hostility. . . .

We regard none of the four factors identified above as either a necessary or sufficient condition to the finding of a deprivation of the right of speedy trial. Rather, they are related factors and must be considered together with such other circumstances as may be relevant. In sum, these factors have no talismanic qualities; courts must still engage in a difficult and sensitive balancing process. But, because we are dealing with a fundamental right of the accused, this process must be carried out with full recognition that the accused's interest in a speedy trial is specifically affirmed in the Constitution.

V

The difficulty of the task of balancing these factors is illustrated by this case, which we consider to be close. It is clear that the length of delay between arrest and trial—well over five years—was extraordinary. Only seven months of that period can be attributed to a strong excuse, the illness of the ex-sheriff who was in charge of the investigation. Perhaps some delay would have been permissible under ordinary circumstances, so that Manning could be utilized as a witness in Barker's trial, but more than four years was too long a period, particularly since a good part of that period was attributable to the Commonwealth's failure or inability to try Manning under circumstances that comported with due process.

Two counterbalancing factors, however, outweigh these deficiencies. The first is that prejudice was minimal. Of course, Barker was prejudiced to some extent by living for over four years under a cloud of suspicion and anxiety. Moreover, although he was released on bond for most of the period, he did spend 10 months in jail before trial. But there is no claim that any of Barker's witnesses died or otherwise became unavailable owing to the delay. The trial transcript indicates only two very minor lapses of memory—one on the part of a prosecution witness—which were in no way significant to the outcome.

More important than the absence of serious prejudice, is the fact that Barker did not want a speedy trial. Counsel was appointed for Barker immediately after his indictment and represented him throughout the period. No question is raised as to the competency of such counsel. Despite the fact that counsel had notice of the motions for continuances, the record shows no action whatever taken between October 21, 1958, and February 12, 1962, that could be construed as the assertion of the speedy-trial right. On the latter date, in response to another motion for continuance, Barker moved to dismiss the indictment. The record does not show on what ground this motion was based, although it is clear that no alternative motion was made for an immediate trial. Instead the record strongly suggests that while he hoped to take advantage of the delay in which he had acquiesced, and thereby obtain a dismissal of the charges, he definitely did not want to be tried. Counsel conceded as much at oral argument:

> Your honor, I would concede that Willie Mae Barker—probably—I don't know this for a fact—probably did not want to be tried. I don't think any man wants to be tried. And I don't consider this a liability on his behalf. I don't blame him.

The probable reason for Barker's attitude was that he was gambling on Manning's acquittal. The evidence was not terribly strong against Manning, as the reversals and hung juries suggest, and Barker undoubtedly thought that if Manning were acquitted, he would never be tried. Counsel also conceded this:

> Now, it's true that the reason for this delay was the Commonwealth of Kentucky's desire to secure the testimony of the accomplice, Silas Manning. And it's true that if Silas Manning were never convicted, Willie Mae Barker would never have been convicted. We conclude this.

That Barker was gambling on Manning's acquittal is also suggested by his failure, following the *pro forma* motion to dismiss filed in February 1962, to object to the Commonwealth's next two motions for continuances. Indeed, it was not until March 1963, after Manning's convictions were final, that Barker, having lost his gamble, began to object to further continuances. At that time, the Commonwealth's excuse was the illness of the ex-sheriff, which Barker has conceded justified the further delay.

We do not hold that there may never be a situation in which an indictment may be dismissed on speedy-trial grounds where the defendant has failed to object to continuances. There may be a situation in which the defendant was represented by incompetent counsel, was severely prejudiced, or even cases in which the continuances were granted *ex parte*. But barring extraordinary circumstances, we would be reluctant indeed to rule that a defendant was denied this constitutional right on a record that strongly indicates, as does this one, that the defendant did not want a speedy trial. We hold, therefore, that Barker was not deprived of his due process right to a speedy trial.

The judgment of the Court of Appeals is affirmed.

6. *Cruel and Unusual Punishment: The Death Penalty Cases*

FURMAN *v.* GEORGIA
408 US 238 (1972)

[In June 1972 the Supreme Court decided three cases, two from Georgia and one from Texas, in which the death penalty had been imposed—one for murder, and two for rape. But more than the three prisoners were involved; for at the time of the decision, the death penalty was authorized in 41 states and in the District of Columbia, and some 600 persons were under death sentences in federal and state prisons. Now, for the first time in its history, the Supreme Court passed on the constitutionality of capital punishment. Very few cases in the history of the Court could be said to have had the transcendent importance that one can find in *Furman v. Georgia.*

[The Court's decision, in a one-paragraph Per Curiam, was that the death penalty in these cases constituted cruel and unusual punishment in violation of the Eighth Amendment and the Fourteenth Amendment. But following this Per Curiam, there were nine individual opinions. Only two of the members of the Court, Justices Brennan and Marshall, held that the death penalty is now *per se* a violation of the Eighth Amendment—i.e., that it is unconstitutional in *all* cases, regardless of the nature of the crime. Justices Stewart and White held that the penalty was unconstitutional as it is presently administered. Along the same line, Justice Douglas held that the death penalty, being discretionary with the trial judge, where there is no jury, or with the jury, has been used discriminatorily; the statutes which provide for the penalty are, therefore, unconstitutional in their operation. Justice Douglas expressly stated that he did not reach the question whether the mandatory death penalty would be constitutional. These five Justices comprised the Court's majority; but, as noted, they did not agree on a rationale for their decision invalidating the death penalty. Each wrote a concurring opinion in which no member of the Court joined.

[Chief Justice Burger wrote a dissenting opinion, in which Justices Blackmun, Powell, and Rehnquist joined. Justices Powell and Rehnquist each wrote a dissenting opinion in which the other three dissenting Justices joined, and Justice Blackmun, while he joined the opinions of his three colleagues, wrote a separate dissenting opinion in which no member of the Court joined.

[Quite apart from the merits of the debate over capital punishment, on which some of the opinions throw much light, the debate in the Court is also important for the contribution it makes to some perplexing problems of judicial method and judicial administration, including the relation between moral judgment and law; the role of history in attempting to arrive at the meaning of constitutional provisions; the question how the Court is to discover the level of public morality and the content and mandate of public opinion; the role of precedent and *stare decisis* in constitutional adjudication; the double-edged use of logical analysis; and the accommodation between the power of judicial review and the imperative of judicial self-restraint.]

Per Curiam:

Petitioner in No. 69–5003 was convicted of murder in Georgia and was sentenced to death pursuant to Ga. Code Ann. § 26–1005 (Supp. 1971) (effective prior to July 1, 1969). Petitioner in No. 69–5030 was convicted of rape in Georgia and was sentenced to death pursuant to Ga. Code Ann. § 26–1302 (Supp. 1971) (effective prior to July 1, 1969). Petitioner in No. 69–5031 was convicted of rape in Texas and was sentenced to death pursuant to Tex. Penal Code Ann., Art. 1189 (1961). Certiorari was granted limited to the following question: "Does the imposition and carrying out of the death penalty in [these cases] constitute cruel and unusual punishment in violation of the Eighth and Fourteenth Amendments?" The Court holds that the imposition and carrying out of the death penalty in these cases constitutes cruel and unusual punishment in violation of the Eighth and Fourteenth Amendments. The judgment in each case is therefore reversed insofar as it leaves undisturbed the death sentence imposed, and the cases are remanded for further proceedings.

So ordered.

Mr. Justice Brennan, concurring:

The question presented in these cases is whether death is today a punishment for crime that is "cruel and unusual" and consequently, by virtue of the Eighth and Fourteenth Amendments, beyond the power of the State to inflict.*

Almost a century ago, this Court observed that "[d]ifficulty would attend the effort to define with exactness the extent of the constitutional provision which provides that cruel and unusual punishments shall not be inflicted." . . . Less than 15 years ago, it was again noted that "[t]he exact scope of the constitutional phrase 'cruel and unusual' has not been detailed by this Court." . . . Those statements remain true today. The Cruel and Unusual Punishments Clause, like the other great clauses of the Constitution, is not susceptible to precise definition. Yet we know that the values and ideals it embodies are basic to our scheme of government. And we know also that the Clause imposes upon this Court the duty, when the issue is properly presented, to determine the constitutional validity of a challenged punishment, whatever that punishment may be. In these cases, "[t]hat issue confronts us, and the task of resolving it is inescapably ours." . . .

III

The punishment challenged in these cases is death. Death, of course, is a "traditional" punishment, . . . one that "has been employed throughout our history," and its constitutional background is accordingly an appropriate subject of inquiry.

There is, first, a textual consideration raised by the Bill of Rights itself. The Fifth Amendment declares that if a particular crime is punishable by death, a person charged with that crime is entitled to certain procedural protections. We can thus infer that the

---

* The Eighth Amendment provides: "Excessive bail shall not be required, nor excessive fines imposed, *nor cruel and unusual punishments inflicted.*" (Emphasis added.) The Cruel and Unusual Punishments Clause is fully applicable to the States through the Due Process Clause of the Fourteenth Amendment. *Robinson* v. *California*, 370 US 660 (1962); *Gideon* v. *Wainwright*, 372 US 335, (1963); *Malloy* v. *Hogan*, 378 US 1, 6, n. 6 (1964); *Powell* v. *Texas*, 392 US 514 (1968).

Framers recognized the existence of what was then a common punishment. We cannot, however, make the further inference that they intended to exempt this particular punishment from the express prohibition of the Cruel and Unusual Punishments Clause. Nor is there any indication in the debates on the Clause that a special exception was to be made for death. If anything, the indication is to the contrary, for Livermore specifically mentioned death as a candidate for future proscription under the Clause. Finally, it does not advance analysis to insist that the Framers did not believe that adoption of the Bill of Rights would immediately prevent the infliction of the punishment of death; neither did they believe that it would immediately prevent the infliction of other corporal punishments that, although common at the time, are now acknowledged to be impermissible. . . .*

There is also the consideration that this Court has decided three cases involving constitutional challenges to particular methods of inflicting this punishment. . . . Past assumptions, however, are not sufficient to limit the scope of our examination of this punishment today. The constitutionality of death itself under the Cruel and Unusual Punishments Clause is before this Court for the first time; we cannot avoid the question by recalling past cases that never directly considered it.

The question, then, is whether the deliberate infliction of death is today consistent with the command of the Clause that the State may not inflict punishments that do not comport with human dignity. I will analyze the punishment of death in terms of the principles set out above and the cumulative test to which they lead: It is a denial of human dignity for the State arbitrarily to subject a person to an unusually severe punishment that society has indicated it does not regard as acceptable and that cannot be shown to serve any penal purpose more effectively than a significantly less drastic punishment. Under these principles and this test, death is today a "cruel and unusual" punishment.

Death is a unique punishment in the United States. In a society that so strongly affirms the sanctity of life, not surprisingly the common view is that death is the ultimate sanction. This natural human feeling appears all about us. There has been no national debate about punishment, in general or by imprisonment, comparable to the debate about the punishment of death. No other punishment has been so continuously restricted, nor has any State yet abolished prisons, as some have abolished this punishment. And those States that still inflict death reserve it for the most heinous crimes. Juries, of course, have always treated death cases differently, as have governors exercising their commutation powers. Criminal defendants are of the same view. "As all practicing lawyers know, who have defended persons charged with capital offenses, often the only goal possible is to avoid the death penalty." . . . Some legislatures have required particular procedures, such as two-stage trials and automatic appeals, applicable only in death cases. "It is the universal experience in the administration of criminal justice that those charged with capital offenses are granted special considerations." . . . This Court, too, almost always treats death cases as a class apart. And the unfortunate effect of this punishment upon the functioning of the judicial process is well known; no other punishment has a similar effect.

The only explanation for the uniqueness of death is its extreme severity. Death is

* Cf. *McGautha* v. *California*, 402 US 183, 226 (1971) (separate opinion of Black, J.): "The [Clause] forbids 'cruel and unusual punishments.' In my view, these words cannot be read to outlaw capital punishment because that penalty was in common use and authorized by law here and in the countries from which our ancestors came at the time the [Clause] was adopted. It is inconceivable to me that the framers intended to end capital punishment by the [Clause]." Under this view, of course, any punishment that was in common use in 1791 is forever exempt from the Clause.

today an unusually severe punishment, unusual in its pain, in its finality, and in its enormity. No other existing punishment is comparable to death in terms of physical and mental suffering. Although our information is not conclusive, it appears that there is no method available that guarantees an immediate and painless death. Since the discontinuance of flogging as a constitutionally permissible punishment, *Jackson* v. *Bishop,* 404 F.2d 571 (CA8 1968), death remains as the only punishment that may involve the conscious infliction of physical pain. In addition, we know that mental pain is an inseparable part of our practice of punishing criminals by death, for the prospect of pending execution exacts a frightful toll during the inevitable long wait between the imposition of sentence and the actual infliction of death. . . . As the California Supreme Court pointed out, "the process of carrying out a verdict of death is often so degrading and brutalizing to the human spirit as to constitute psychological torture." . . . Indeed, as Mr. Justice Frankfurter noted, "the onset of insanity while awaiting execution of a death sentence is not a rare phenomenon." . . . The "fate of ever-increasing fear and distress" to which the expatriate is subjected, *Trop* v. *Dulles,* 356 US, at 102, can only exist to a greater degree for a person confined in prison awaiting death.

The unusual severity of death is manifested most clearly in its finality and enormity. Death, in these respects, is in a class by itself. Expatriation, for example, is a punishment that "destroys for the individual the political existence that was centuries in the development," that "strips the citizen of his status in the national and international political community," and that puts "[h]is very existence" in jeopardy. Expatriation thus inherently entails "the total destruction of the individual's status in organized society." "In short, the expatriate has lost the right to have rights." Yet, demonstrably, expatriation is not "a fate worse than death." Although death, like expatriation, destroys the individual's "political existence" and his "status in organized society," it does more, for, unlike expatriation, death also destroys "[h]is very existence." There is, too, at least the possibility that the expatriate will in the future regain "the right to have rights." Death forecloses even that possibility.

Death is truly an awesome punishment. The calculated killing of a human being by the State involves, by its very nature, a denial of the executed person's humanity. The contrast with the plight of a person punished by imprisonment is evident. An individual in prison does not lose "the right to have rights." A prisoner retains, for example, the constitutional rights to the free exercise of religion, to be free of cruel and unusual punishments, and to treatment as a "person" for purposes of due process of law and the equal protection of the laws. A prisoner remains a member of the human family. Moreover, he retains the right of access to the courts. His punishment is not irrevocable. Apart from the common charge, grounded upon the recognition of human fallibility, that the punishment of death must inevitably be inflicted upon innocent men, we know that death has been the lot of men whose convictions were unconstitutionally secured in view of later, retroactively applied, holdings of this Court. The punishment itself may have been unconstitutionally inflicted, . . . yet the finality of death precludes relief. An executed person has indeed "lost the right to have rights." As one 19th century proponent of punishing criminals by death declared. "When a man is hung, there is an end of our relations with him. His execution is a way of saying, 'You are not fit for this world. Take your chance elsewhere.'"

In comparison to all other punishments today, then, the deliberate extinguishment of human life by the State is uniquely degrading to human dignity. I would not hesitate to hold, on that ground alone, that death is today a "cruel and unusual" punishment, were it not that death is a punishment of longstanding usage and acceptance in this country. I therefore turn to the second principle—that the State may not arbitrarily inflict an unusually severe punishment.

The outstanding characteristic of our present practice of punishing criminals by death is the infrequency with which we resort to it. The evidence is conclusive that death is not the ordinary punishment for any crime.

There has been a steady decline in the infliction of this punishment in every decade since the 1930's, the earliest period for which accurate statistics are available. In the 1930's, executions averaged 167 per year; in the 1940's, the average was 128; in the 1950's, it was 72; and in the years 1960–1962, it was 48. There have been a total of 46 executions since then, 36 of them in 1963–1964.* Yet our population and the numbers of capital crimes committed have increased greatly over the past four decades. The contemporary rarity of the infliction of this punishment is thus the end result of a long-continued decline. That rarity is plainly revealed by an examination of the years 1961–1970, the last 10-year period for which statistics are available. During that time, an average of 106 death sentences were imposed each year. Not nearly that number, however, could be carried out, for many were precluded by commutations to life or a term of years, transfers to mental institutions because of insanity, resentences to life or a term of years, grants of new trials and orders for resentencing, dismissals of indictments and reversals of convictions, and deaths by suicide and natural causes. On January 1, 1961, the death row population was 219; on December 31, 1970, it was 608; during that span, there were 135 executions. Consequently, had the 389 additions to death row also been executed, the annual average would have been 52. In short, the country might, at most, have executed one criminal each week. In fact, of course, far fewer were executed. Even before the moratorium on executions began in 1967, executions totaled only 42 in 1961 and 47 in 1962, an average of less than one per week; the number dwindled to 21 in 1963, to 15 in 1964, and to seven in 1965; in 1966, there was one execution, and in 1967, there were two.

When a country of over 200 million people inflicts an unusually severe punishment no more than 50 times a year, the inference is strong that the punishment is not being regularly and fairly applied. To dispel it would indeed require a clear showing of non-arbitrary infliction.

Although there are no exact figures available, we know that thousands of murders and rapes are committed annually in States where death is an authorized punishment for those crimes. However the rate of infliction is characterized—as "freakishly" or "spectacularly" rare, or simply as rare—it would take the purest sophistry to deny that death is inflicted in only a minute fraction of these cases. How much rarer, after all, could the infliction of death be?

When the punishment of death is inflicted in a trivial number of the cases in which it is legally available, the conclusion is virtually inescapable that it is being inflicted arbitrarily. Indeed, it smacks of little more than a lottery system. The States claim, however, that this rarity is evidence not of arbitrariness, but of informed selectivity: Death is inflicted, they say, only in "extreme" cases.

Informed selectivity, of course, is a value not to be denigrated. Yet presumably the States could make precisely the same claim if there were 10 executions per year, or five,

---

* From 1930 to 1939: 155, 153, 140, 160, 168, 199, 195, 147, 190, 160. From 1940 to 1949: 124, 123, 147, 131, 120, 117, 131, 153, 119, 119. From 1950 to 1959: 82, 105, 83, 62, 81, 76, 65, 65, 49, 49. From 1960 to 1967: 56, 42, 47, 21, 15, 7, 1, 2. National Prisoner Statistics No. 46, Capital Punishment 1930–1970, at 8 (August 1971). The last execution in the United States took place on June 2, 1967.

or even if there were but one. That there may be as many as 50 per year does not strengthen the claim. When the rate of infliction is at this low level, it is highly implausible that only the worst criminals or the criminals who commit the worst crimes are selected for this punishment. No one has yet suggested a rational basis that could differentiate in those terms the few who die from the many who go to prison. Crimes and criminals simply do not admit of a distinction that can be drawn so finely as to explain, on that ground, the execution of such a tiny sample of those eligible. Certainly the laws that provide for this punishment do not attempt to draw that distinction; all cases to which the laws apply are necessarily "extreme." Nor is the distinction credible in fact. If, for example, petitioner Furman or his crime illustrate the "extreme," then nearly all murderers and their murders are also "extreme."* Furthermore, our procedures in death cases, rather than resulting in the selection of "extreme" cases for this punishment, actually sanction an arbitrary selection. For this Court has held that juries may, as they do, make the decision whether to impose a death sentence wholly unguided by standards governing that decision. . . . In other words, our procedures are not constructed to guard against the totally capricious selection of criminals for the punishment of death.

Although it is difficult to imagine what further facts would be necessary in order to prove that death is, as my Brother Stewart puts it, "wantonly and freakishly" inflicted, I need not conclude that arbitrary infliction is patently obvious. I am not considering this punishment by the isolated light of one principle. The probability of arbitrariness is sufficiently substantial that it can be relied upon, in combination with the other principles, in reaching a judgment on the constitutionality of this punishment.

When there is a strong probability that an unusually severe and degrading punishment is being inflicted arbitrarily, we may well expect that society will disapprove of its infliction. I turn, therefore, to the third principle. An examination of the history and present operation of the American practice of punishing criminals by death reveals that this punishment has been almost totally rejected by contemporary society.

I cannot add to my Brother Marshall's comprehensive treatment of the English and American history of this punishment. I emphasize, however, one significant conclusion that emerges from that history. From the beginning of our Nation, the punishment of death has stirred acute public controversy. Although pragmatic arguments for and against the punishment have been frequently advanced, this longstanding and heated controversy cannot be explained solely as the result of differences over the practical

* The victim surprised Furman in the act of burglarizing the victim's home in the middle of the night. While escaping, Furman killed the victim with one pistol shot fired through the closed kitchen door from the outside. At the trial, Furman gave his version of the killing: "They got me charged with murder and I admit, I admit going to these folks' home and they did caught me in there and I was coming back out, backing up and there was a wire down there on the floor. I was coming out backwards and fell back and I didn't intend to kill nobody. I didn't know they was behind the door. The gun went off and I didn't know nothing about no murder until they arrested me, and when the gun went off I was down on the floor and I got up and ran. That's all to it."

The Georgia Supreme Court accepted that version: "The admission in open court by the accused . . . that during the period in which he was involved in the commission of a criminal act at the home of the deceased, he accidentally tripped over a wire in leaving the premises causing the gun to go off, together with other facts and circumstances surrounding the death of the deceased by violent means, was sufficient to support the verdict of guilty of murder. . . ."

About Furman himself, the jury knew only that he was black and that, according to his statement at trial, he was 26 years old and worked at "Superior Upholstery." It took the jury one hour and 35 minutes to return a verdict of guilt and a sentence of death.

wisdom of a particular government policy. At bottom, the battle has been waged on moral grounds. The country has debated whether a society for which the dignity of the individual is the supreme value can without a fundamental inconsistency follow the practice of deliberately putting some of its members to death. In the United States as in other nations of the western world, "the struggle about this punishment has been one between ancient and deeply rooted beliefs in retribution, atonement or vengeance on the one hand, and, on the other, beliefs in the personal value and dignity of the common man that were born of the democratic movement of the eighteenth century, as well as beliefs in the scientific approach to an understanding of the motive forces of human conduct, which are the result of the growth of the sciences of behavior during the nineteenth and twentieth centuries." It is this essentially moral conflict that forms the backdrop for the past changes in and the present operation of our system of imposing death as a punishment for crime.

Our practice of punishing criminals by death has changed greatly over the years. One significant change has been in our methods of inflicting death. Although this country never embraced the more violent and repulsive methods employed in England, we did for a long time rely almost exclusively upon the gallows and the firing squad. Since the development of the supposedly more humane methods of electrocution late in the 19th century and lethal gas in the 20th, however, hanging and shooting have virtually ceased.* Our concern for decency and human dignity, moreover, has compelled changes in the circumstances surrounding the execution itself. No longer does our society countenance the spectacle of public executions, once thought desirable as a deterrent to criminal behavior by others. Today we reject public executions as debasing and brutalizing to us all.

Also significant is the drastic decrease in the crimes for which the punishment of death is actually inflicted. While esoteric capital crimes remain on the books, since 1930 murder and rape have accounted for nearly 99% of the total executions, and murder alone for about 87%. In addition, the crime of capital murder has itself been limited. As the Court noted in *McGautha* v. *California,* 402 US, at 198, there was in this country a "rebellion against the common-law rule imposing a mandatory death sentence on all convicted murderers." Initially that rebellion resulted in legislative definitions that distinguished between degrees of murder, retaining the mandatory death sentence only for murder in the first degree. Yet "[t]his new legislative criterion for isolating crimes appropriately punishable by death soon proved as unsuccessful as the concept of 'malice aforethought,' " the common-law means of separating murder from manslaughter. Not only was the distinction between degrees of murder confusing and uncertain in practice, but even in clear cases of first-degree murder juries continued to take the law into their own hands: if they felt that death was an inappropriate punishment, "they simply refused to convict of the capital offense." The phenomenon of jury nullification thus remained to counteract the rigors of mandatory death sentences. Bowing to reality, "legislatures did not try, as before, to refine further the definition of capital homicides. Instead they adopted the method of forthrightly granting juries the discretion which they had been exercising in fact." In consequence, virtually all death sentences today are discretionarily imposed. Finally, it is significant that nine States no longer inflict the

---

* Eight States still employ hanging as the method of execution, and one, Utah, also employs shooting. These nine States have accounted for less than 3% of the executions in the United States since 1930. . . .

punishment of death under any circumstances,* and five others have restricted it to extremely rare crimes.†

Thus, although "the death penalty has been employed throughout our history," . . . in fact the history of this punishment is one of successive restriction. What was once a common punishment has become, in the context of a continuing moral debate, increasingly rare. The evolution of this punishment evidences not that it is an inevitable part of the American scene, but that it has proved progressively more troublesome to the national conscience. The result of this movement is our current system of administering the punishment, under which death sentences are rarely imposed and death is even more rarely inflicted. It is, of course, "We, the People" who are responsible for the rarity both of the imposition and the carrying out of this punishment. Juries, "express[ing] the conscience of the community on the ultimate question of life or death," . . . have been able to bring themselves to vote for death in a mere 100 or so cases among the thousands tried each year where the punishment is available. Governors, elected by and acting for us, have regularly commuted a substantial number of those sentences. And it is our society that insists upon due process of law to the end that no person will be unjustly put to death, thus ensuring that many more of those sentences will not be carried out. In sum, we have made death a rare punishment today.

The progressive decline in and the current rarity of the infliction of death demonstrate that our society seriously questions the appropriateness of this punishment today. The States point out that many legislatures authorize death as the punishment for certain crimes and that substantial segments of the public, as reflected in opinion polls and referendum votes, continue to support it. Yet the availability of this punishment through statutory authorization, as well as the polls and referenda, which amount simply to approval of that authorization, simply underscores the extent to which our society has in fact rejected this punishment. When an unusually severe punishment is authorized for wide-scale application but not, because of society's refusal, inflicted save in a few instances, the inference is compelling that there is a deep-seated reluctance to inflict it. Indeed, the likelihood is great that the punishment is tolerated only because of its disuse. The objective indicator of society's view of an unusually severe punishment is what society does with it. And today society will inflict death upon only a small sample of the eligible criminals. Rejection could hardly be more complete without becoming absolute. At the very least, I must conclude that contemporary society views this punishment with substantial doubt.

The final principle to be considered is that an unusually severe and degrading punish-

---

* Alaska, Hawaii, Iowa, Maine, Michigan, Minnesota, Oregon, West Virginia, and Wisconsin have abolished death as a punishment for crimes. . . . In addition, the California Supreme Court held the punishment unconstitutional under the state counterpart of the Cruel and Unusual Punishments Clause. . . .

† New Mexico, New York, North Dakota, Rhode Island, and Vermont have almost totally abolished death as a punishment for crimes. . . . Indeed, these five States might well be considered *de facto* abolition States. North Dakota and Rhode Island, which restricted the punishment in 1915 and 1852 respectively, have not carried out an execution since at least 1930; nor have there been any executions in New York, Vermont, or New Mexico since they restricted the punishment in 1965, 1965, and 1969 respectively. As of January 1, 1971, none of the five States had even a single prisoner under sentence of death.

In addition, six States, while retaining the punishment on the books in generally applicable form, have made virtually no use of it. Since 1930, Idaho, Montana, Nebraska, New Hampshire, South Dakota, and Wyoming have carried out a total of 22 executions. As of January 1, 1971, these six States had a total of three prisoners under sentences of death. Hence, assuming 25 executions in 42 years, each State averaged about one execution every 10 years.

ment may not be excessive in view of the purposes for which it is inflicted. This principle, too, is related to the others. When there is a strong probability that the State is arbitrarily inflicting an unusually severe punishment that is subject to grave societal doubts, it is likely also that the punishment cannot be shown to be serving any penal purpose that could not be served equally well by some less severe punishment.

The States' primary claim is that death is a necessary punishment because it prevents the commission of capital crimes more effectively than any less severe punishment. The first part of this claim is that the infliction of death is necessary to stop the individuals executed from committing further crimes. The sufficient answer to this is that if a criminal convicted of a capital crime poses a danger to society, effective administration of the State's pardon and parole laws can delay or deny his release from prison, and techniques of isolation can eliminate or minimize the danger while he remains confined.

The more significant argument is that the threat of death prevents the commission of capital crimes because it deters potential criminals who would not be deterred by the threat of imprisonment. The argument is not based upon evidence that the threat of death is a superior deterrent. Indeed, as my Brother Marshall establishes, the available evidence uniformly indicates, although it does not conclusively prove, that the threat of death has no greater deterrent effect than the threat of imprisonment. The States argue, however, that they are entitled to rely upon common human experience, and that experience, they say, supports the conclusion that death must be a more effective deterrent than any less severe punishment. Because people fear death the most, the argument runs, the threat of death must be the greatest deterrent.

It is important to focus upon the precise import of this argument. It is not denied that many, and probably most, capital crimes cannot be deterred by the threat of punishment. Thus the argument can apply only to those who think rationally about the commission of capital crimes. Particularly is that true when the potential criminal, under this argument, must not only consider the risk of punishment, but also distinguish between two possible punishments. The concern, then, is with a particular type of potential criminal, the rational person who will commit a capital crime knowing that the punishment is long-term imprisonment, which may well be for the rest of his life, but will not commit the crime knowing that the punishment is death. On the face of it, the assumption that such persons exist is implausible.

In any event, this argument cannot be appraised in the abstract. We are not presented with the theoretical question whether under any imaginable circumstances the threat of death might be a greater deterrent to the commission of capital crimes than the threat of imprisonment. We are concerned with the practice of punishing criminals by death as it exists in the United States today. Proponents of this argument necessarily admit that its validity depends upon the existence of a system in which the punishment of death is invariably and swiftly imposed. Our system, of course, satisfies neither condition. A rational person contemplating a murder or rape is confronted not with the certainty of a speedy death, but with the slightest possibility that he will be executed in the distant future. The risk of death is remote and improbable; in contrast, the risk of long-term imprisonment is near and great. In short, whatever the speculative validity of the assumption that the threat of death is a superior deterrent, there is no reason to believe that as currently administered the punishment of death is necessary to deter the commission of capital crimes. Whatever might be the case were all or substantially all eligible criminals quickly put to death, unverifiable possibilities are an insufficient basis upon which to conclude that the threat of death today has any greater deterrent efficacy than the threat of imprisonment.*

* There is also the more limited argument that death is a necessary punishment when

There is, however, another aspect to the argument that the punishment of death is necessary for the protection of society. The infliction of death, the States urge, serves to manifest the community's outrage at the commission of the crime. It is, they say, a concrete public expression of moral indignation that inculcates respect for the law and helps assure a more peaceful community. Moreover, we are told, not only does the punishment of death exert this widespread moralizing influence upon community values, it also satisfies the popular demand for grievous condemnation of abhorrent crimes and thus prevents disorder, lynching, and attempts by private citizens to take the law into their own hands.

The question, however, is not whether death serves these supposed purposes of punishment, but whether death serves them more effectively than imprisonment. There is no evidence whatever that utilization of imprisonment rather than death encourages private blood feuds and other disorders. Surely if there were such a danger, the execution of a handful of criminals each year would not prevent it. The assertion that death alone is a sufficiently emphatic denunciation for capital crimes suffers from the same defect. If capital crimes require the punishment of death in order to provide moral reinforcement for the basic values of the community, those values can only be undermined when death is so rarely inflicted upon the criminals who commit the crimes. Furthermore, it is certainly doubtful that the infliction of death by the State does in fact strengthen the community's moral code; if the deliberate extinguishment of human life has any effect at all, it more likely tends to lower our respect for life and brutalize our values. That, after all, is why we no longer carry out public executions. In any event, this claim simply means that one purpose of punishment is to indicate social disapproval of crime. To serve that purpose our laws distribute punishments according to the gravity of crimes and punish more severely the crimes society regards as more serious. That purpose cannot justify any particular punishment as the upper limit of severity.

There is, then, no substantial reason to believe that the punishment of death, as currently administered, is necessary for the protection of society. The only other purpose suggested, one that is independent of protection for society, is retribution. Shortly stated, retribution in this context means that criminals are put to death because they deserve it.

Although it is difficult to believe that any State today wishes to proclaim adherence to "naked vengeance," . . . the States claim, in reliance upon its statutory authorization, that death is the only fit punishment for capital crimes and that this retributive purpose justifies its infliction. In the past, judged by its statutory authorization, death was considered the only fit punishment for the crime of forgery, for the first federal criminal statute provided a mandatory death penalty for that crime. . . . Obviously, concepts of justice change; no immutable moral order requires death for murderers and rapists. The claim that death is a just punishment necessarily refers to the existence of certain public beliefs. The claim must be that for capital crimes death alone comports with society's

---

criminals are already serving or subject to a sentence of life imprisonment. If the only punishment available is further imprisonment, it is said, those criminals will have nothing to lose by committing further crimes, and accordingly the threat of death is the sole deterrent. But "life" imprisonment is a misnomer today. Rarely, if ever, do crimes carry a mandatory life sentence without possibility of parole. That possibility ensures that criminals do not reach the point where further crimes are free of consequences. Moreover, if this argument is simply an assertion that the threat of death is a more effective deterrent than the threat of increased imprisonment by denial of release on parole, then, as noted above, there is simply no evidence to support it.

notion of proper punishment. As administered today, however, the punishment of death cannot be concluded that death serves the purpose of retribution more effectively than the overwhelming number of criminals who commit capital crimes go to prison, it cannot be concluded that death serves the purpose of retribution more effectively than imprisonment. The asserted public belief that murderers and rapists deserve to die is flatly inconsistent with the execution of a random few. As the history of the punishment of death in this country shows, our society wishes to prevent crime; we have no desire to kill criminals simply to get even with them.

In sum, the punishment of death is inconsistent with all four principles: Death is an unusually severe and degrading punishment; there is a strong probability that it is inflicted arbitrarily; its rejection by contemporary society is virtually total; and there is no reason to believe that it serves any penal purpose more effectively than the less severe punishment of imprisonment. The function of these principles is to enable a court to determine whether a punishment comports with human dignity. Death, quite simply, does not.

IV

When this country was founded, memories of the Stuart horrors were fresh, and severe corporal punishments were common. Death was not then a unique punishment. The practice of punishing criminals by death, moreover, was widespread and by and large acceptable to society. Indeed, without developed prison systems, there was frequently no workable alternative. Since that time, successive restrictions, imposed against the background of a continuing moral controversy, have drastically curtailed the use of this punishment. Today death is a uniquely and unusually severe punishment. When examined by the principles applicable under the Cruel and Unusual Punishments Clause, death stands condemned as fatally offensive to human dignity. The punishment of death is therefore "cruel and unusual," and the States may no longer inflict it as a punishment for crimes. Rather than kill an arbitrary handful of criminals each year, the States will confine them in prison. "The State thereby suffers nothing and loses no power. The purpose of punishment is fulfilled, crime is repressed by penalties of just, not tormenting, severity, its repetition is prevented, and hope is given for the reformation of the criminal." . . .

I concur in the judgments of the Court.

7. Right to a Public Trial

Re OLIVER
333 US 257 (1948)

[The Sixth Amendment provides that in all criminal prosecutions the accused shall enjoy the right to a "public trial." The constitutions of forty-one states have similar provisions; two states provide for public trial by statute; and one state has achieved the same end by a decision of its highest court. In this case the Court held that the Due Process Clause of the Fourteenth Amendment makes it improper for a state court to sentence a defendant without a public trial.

[The Court also held that an accused must be advised of the charges against him and must be afforded a reasonable opportunity to prepare a defense. These rights are part of "the law of the land." Justice Rutledge, in a concurring opinion, would put the demands of the Sixth Amendment into the Fourteenth Amendment as restrictions upon the states. He thus would declare the entire one-man grand jury system of Michigan unconstitutional.

[Justices Frankfurter and Jackson dissented on procedural grounds.]

Mr. Justice Black delivered the opinion of the Court:

A Michigan circuit judge summarily sent the petitioner to jail for contempt of court. We must determine whether he was denied the procedural due process guaranteed by the Fourteenth Amendment.

In obedience to a subpoena the petitioner appeared as a witness before a Michigan circuit judge who was then conducting, in accordance with Michigan law, a "one-man grand jury" investigation into alleged gambling and official corruption. The investigation presumably took place in the judge's chambers, though that is not certain. Two other circuit judges were present in an advisory capacity. A prosecutor may have been present. A stenographer was most likely there. The record does not show what other members, if any, of the judge's investigatorial staff participated in the proceedings. It is certain, however, that the public was excluded—the questioning was secret in accordance with the traditional grand jury method.

After petitioner had given certain testimony, the judge–grand jury, still in secret session, told petitioner that neither he nor his advisors believed petitioner's story—that it did not "jell." This belief of the judge–grand jury was not based entirely on what the petitioner had testified. As will later be seen, it rested in part on beliefs or suspicions of the judge-jury derived from the testimony of at least one other witness who had previously given evidence in secret. Petitioner had not been present when the witness testified and so far as appears was not even aware that he had testified. Based on its beliefs thus formed—that petitioner's story did not "jell"—the judge–grand jury immediately charged him with contempt, immediately convicted him, and immediately sentenced him to sixty days in jail. Under these circumstances of haste and secrecy, petitioner, of course, had no chance to enjoy the benefits of counsel, no chance to prepare his defense, and no opportunity either to cross examine the other grand jury witness or to summon witnesses to refute the charge against him.

Three days later a lawyer filed on petitioner's behalf in the Michigan Supreme Court the petition for habeas corpus now under consideration. It alleged among other things that the petitioner's attorney had not been allowed to confer with him and that, to the best of the attorney's knowledge, the petitioner was not held in jail under any judgment, decree or execution, and was "not confined by virtue of any legal commitment directed to the sheriff as required by law." An order was then entered signed by the circuit judge that he had while "sitting as a One-Man Grand Jury" convicted the petitioner of contempt of court because petitioner had testified "evasively" and had given "contradictory answers" to questions. The order directed that petitioner "be confined in the county jail . . . for a period of sixty days . . . or until such time as he . . . shall appear and answer the questions heretofore propounded to him by this Court. . . ."

The case requires a brief explanation of Michigan's unique one-man grand jury system. That state's first constitution (1835), like the Fifth Amendment to the Federal Constitution, required that most criminal prosecutions be begun by presentment or indictment of a grand jury. . . . This compulsory provision was left out of the 1850 constitution and from the present constitution (1908). However, Michigan judges may still in their discretion summon grand juries, but we are told by the attorney general that this discretion is rarely exercised and that the "One-Man Grand Jury" has taken the place of the old Michigan 16-to-23-member grand jury, particularly in probes of alleged misconduct of public officials.

The one-man grand jury law was passed in 1917 following a recommendation of the State Bar Association that, in the interest of more rigorous law enforcement, greater emphasis should be put upon the "investigative procedure" for "probing" and for "detecting" crime. With this need uppermost in its thinking the Bar Association recommended a bill which provided that justices of the peace be vested with the inquisitorial powers traditionally conferred only on coroners and grand juries. The bill as passed imposed the recommended investigatory powers not only on justices of the peace, but on police judges and judges of courts of record as well. . . .

Whenever this judge–grand jury may summon a witness to appear, it is his duty to go and to answer all material questions that do not incriminate him. Should he fail to appear, fail to answer material questions, or should the judge–grand jury believe his evidence false and evasive, or deliberately contradictory, he may be found guilty of contempt. This offense may be punishable by a fine or not more than one hundred dollars, or imprisonment in the county jail not exceeding sixty days, or both, at the discretion of the judge–grand jury. If after having been so sentenced he appears and satisfactorily answers the questions propounded by the judge-jury, his sentence may, within the judge-jury's discretion, be commuted or suspended. At the end of his first sentence he can be resummoned and subjected to the same inquiries. Should the judge-jury again believe his answers false and evasive, or contradictory, he can be sentenced to serve sixty days more unless he reappears before the judge-jury during the second 60-day period and satisfactorily answers the questions, and the judge-jury within its discretion then decides to commute or suspend his sentence.

In carrying out this authority a judge–grand jury is authorized to appoint its own prosecutors, detectives and aides at public expense, all or any of whom may, at the discretion of the justice of the peace or judge, be admitted to the inquiry. . . . A witness may be asked questions on all subjects and need not be advised of his privilege against self-incrimination, even though the questioning is in secret. And these secret interrogations can be carried on day or night, in a public place or a "hideout," a courthouse, an office building, a hotel room, a home, or a place of business; so well is this ambulatory power understood in Michigan that the one-man grand jury is also popularly referred to as the "portable grand jury."

It was a circuit court judge–grand jury before which petitioner testified. That judge-jury filed in the State Supreme Court an answer to this petition for habeas corpus. The answer contained fragments of what was apparently a stenographic transcript of petitioner's testimony given before the grand jury. It was these fragments of testimony, so the answer stated, that the "Grand Jury" had concluded to be "false and evasive." The petitioner then filed a verified motion with the State

Supreme Court seeking to have the complete transcript of his testimony before the judge-jury produced for the habeas corpus hearing. He alleged that a full report of his testimony would disclose that he had freely, promptly, and to the best of his ability, answered all questions asked, and that the full transcript would refute the charge that he had testified evasively or falsely. In his answer to the motion the circuit judge did not deny these allegations. However, he asserted that the fragments contained in the original answer showed "all of the Grand Jury testimony necessary to the present proceeding" and that "the full disclosure of petitioner's testimony would seriously retard Grand Jury activities." The State Supreme Court then denied the petitioner's motion. Thus when that Court later dismissed the petition for habeas corpus it had seen only a copy of a portion of the record of the testimony given by the petitioner.

The petitioner does not here challenge the constitutional power of Michigan to grant traditional inquisitorial grand jury power to a single judge, and therefore we do not concern ourselves with that question. It has long been recognized in this country however that the traditional 12-to-23-member grand juries may examine witnesses in secret sessions. Oaths of secrecy are ordinarily taken both by the members of such grand juries and by witnesses before them. Many reasons have been advanced to support grand jury secrecy. . . . But those reasons have never been thought to justify secrecy in the trial of an accused charged with violations of law for which he may be fined or sent to jail. Grand juries investigate, and the usual end of their investigation is either a report, a "no-bill" or an indictment. They do not try and they do not convict. They render no judgment. When their work is finished by the return of an indictment, it cannot be used as evidence against the person indicted. Nor may he be fined or sentenced to jail until he has been tried and convicted after having been afforded the procedural safeguards required by due process of law. Even when witnesses before grand juries refuse to answer proper questions, the grand juries do not adjudge the witnesses guilty of contempt of court in secret or in public or at all. Witnesses who refuse to testify before grand juries are tried on contempt charges before judges sitting in open court. And though the powers of a judge even when acting as a one-man grand jury may be, as Michigan holds, judicial in their nature, the due process clause may apply with one effect on the judge's grand jury investigation, but with quite a different effect when the judge–grand jury suddenly makes a witness before it a defendant in a contempt case.

Here we are concerned, not with petitioner's rights as a witness in a secret grand jury session, but with his rights as a defendant in a contempt proceeding. The powers of the judge–grand jury who tried and convicted him in secret and sentenced him to jail on a charge of false and evasive swearing must likewise be measured, not by the limitations applicable to grand jury proceedings, but by the constitutional standards applicable to court proceedings in which an accused may be sentenced to fine or imprisonment or both. Thus our first question is this: Can an accused be tried and convicted for contempt of court in grand jury secrecy?

First. Counsel have not cited and we have been unable to find a single instance of a criminal trial conducted in camera in any federal, state, or municipal court during the history of this country. Nor have we found any record of even one such secret criminal trial in England since abolition of the Court of Star Chamber in

1641, and whether that court ever convicted people secretly is in dispute. Summary trials for alleged misconduct called contempt of court have not been regarded as an exception to this universal rule against secret trials, unless some other Michigan one-man grand jury case may represent such an exception.

This nation's accepted practice of guaranteeing a public trial to an accused has its roots in our English common law heritage. The exact date of its origin is obscure, but it likely evolved long before the settlement of our land as an accompaniment of the ancient institution of jury trial. In this country the guarantee to an accused of the right to a public trial first appeared in a state constitution in 1776. Following the ratification in 1791 of the Federal Constitution's Sixth Amendment, which commands that "In all criminal prosecutions, the accused shall enjoy the right to a speedy and public trial . . ." most of the original states and those subsequently admitted to the Union adopted similar constitutional provisions. Today almost without exception every state by constitution, statute, or judicial decision, requires that all criminal trials be open to the public.

The traditional Anglo-American distrust for secret trials has been variously ascribed to the notorious use of this practice by the Spanish Inquisition, to the excesses of the English Court of Star Chamber, and to the French monarchy's abuse of the lettre de cachet. All of these institutions obviously symbolized a menace to liberty. In the hands of despotic groups each of them had become an instrument for the suppression of political and religious heresies in ruthless disregard of the right of an accused to a fair trial. Whatever other benefits the guarantee to an accused that his trial be conducted in public may confer upon our society, the guarantee has always been recognized as a safeguard against any attempt to employ our courts as instruments of persecution. The knowledge that every criminal trial is subject to contemporaneous review in the forum of public opinion is an effective restraint on possible abuse of judicial power. One need not wholly agree with a statement made on the subject by Jeremy Bentham over 120 years ago to appreciate the fear of secret trials felt by him, his predecessors and contemporaries. Bentham said:

. . . suppose the proceedings to be completely secret, and the court, on the occasion, to consist of no more than a single judge,—that judge will be at once indolent and arbitrary: how corrupt soever his inclination may be, it will find no check, at any rate no tolerably efficient check, to oppose it. Without publicity, all other checks are insufficient: in comparison of publicity, all other checks are of small account. Recordation, appeal, whatever other institutions might present themselves in the character of checks, would be found to operate rather as cloaks than checks; as cloaks in reality, as checks only in appearance.

In giving content to the constitutional and statutory commands that an accused be given a public trial, the state and federal courts have differed over what groups of spectators, if any, could properly be excluded from a criminal trial. But, unless in Michigan and in one-man grand jury contempt cases, no court in this country has ever before held, so far as we can find, that an accused can be tried, convicted, and sent to jail, when everybody else is denied entrance to the court, except the judge and his attaches. And without exception all courts have held that an accused is at the very least entitled to have his friends, relatives and counsel present, no matter with what offense he may be charged. In *Gaines* v. *Washington*, 277 US 81, . . . this Court assumed that a criminal trial conducted in secret would violate the procedural requirements of the Fourteenth Amendment's due process clause, although its actual holding there was that no violation had in fact occurred, since the trial court's order barring the general public had not been enforced. Certain proceedings in a judge's chambers, including convictions for contempt of court, have occasionally been countenanced by state courts, but there has never been any intimation that all of the public, including the accused's relatives, friends, and counsel, were barred from the trial chamber.

In the case before us, the petitioner was called as a witness to testify in secret before a one-man grand jury conducting a grand jury investigation. In the midst of petitioner's testimony the proceedings abruptly changed. The investigation became a "trial," the grand jury became a judge, and the witness became an accused charged with contempt of court—all in secret. Following a charge, conviction and sentence, the petitioner was led away to prison—still without any break in the secrecy. Even in jail, according to undenied allegations, his lawyer was denied an opportunity to see and confer with him. And that was not the end of secrecy. His lawyer filed in the State Supreme Court this habeas corpus proceeding. Even there, the mantle of secrecy enveloped the transaction and the State Supreme Court ordered him sent back to jail without ever having seen a record of his testimony, and without knowing all that took place in the secrecy of the judge's chambers. In view of this nation's historic distrust of secret proceedings, their inherent dangers to freedom, and the universal requirement of our federal and state governments that criminal trials be public, the Fourteenth Amendment's guarantee that no one shall be deprived of his liberty without due process of law means at least that an accused cannot be thus

Second. We further hold that failure to afford the petitioner a reasonable oppor-
sentenced to prison.
tunity to defend himself against the charge of false and evasive swearing was a denial of due process of law. A person's right to reasonable notice of a charge against him, and an opportunity to be heard in his defense—a right to his day in court—are basic in our system of jurisprudence; and these rights include, as a minimum, a right to examine the witnesses against him, to offer testimony, and to be represented by counsel. Michigan, not denying the existence of these rights in criminal cases generally, apparently concedes that the summary conviction here would have been a denial of procedural due process but for the nature of the charge, namely, a contempt of court, committed, the State urges, in the court's actual presence.

It is true that courts have long exercised a power summarily to punish certain conduct committed in open court without notice, testimony or hearing. *Ex parte Terry*, 128 US 289, . . . was such a case. There Terry committed assault on the marshal who was at the moment removing a heckler from the courtroom. The "violence and misconduct" of both the heckler and the marshal's assailant occurred within the "personal view" of the judge, "under his own eye," and actually interrupted the trial of a cause then under way. This Court held that under such circumstances a judge has power to punish an offender at once, without notice and without hearing, although his conduct may also be punishable as a criminal offense. This Court reached its conclusion because it believed that a court's business could not be conducted unless it could suppress disturbances within the courtroom by immediate punishment. However, this Court recognized that such a departure from the accepted standards of due process was capable of grave abuses, and for that reason gave no encouragement to its expansion beyond the suppression and punishment of the court-disrupting misconduct which alone justified its exercise. . . .

That the holding in the *Terry Case* is not to be considered as an unlimited abandonment of the basic due process procedural safeguards, even in contempt cases, was spelled out with emphatic language in *Cooke* v. *United States,* 267 US 517. . . .

Except for a narrowly limited category of contempts, due process of law as explained in the *Cooke Case* requires that one charged with contempt of court be advised of the charges against him, have a reasonable opportunity to meet them by way of defense or explanation, have the right to be represented by counsel, and have a chance to testify and call other witnesses in his behalf, either by way of defense or explanation. The narrow exception to these due process requirements includes only charges of misconduct, in open court, in the presence of the judge, which disturbs the court's business, where all of the essential elements of the misconduct are under the eye of the court, are actually observed by the court, and where immediate punishment is essential to prevent "demoralization of the court's authority" before the public. If some essential elements of the offense are not personally observed by the judge, so that he must depend upon statements made by others for his knowledge about these essential elements, due process requires, according to the *Cooke Case,* that the accused be accorded notice and a fair hearing as above set out.

The facts shown by this record put this case outside the narrow category of cases that can be punished as contempt without notice, hearing and counsel. Since the petitioner's alleged misconduct all occurred in secret, there could be no possibility of a demoralization of the court's authority before the public. . . .

Nor is there any reason suggested why "demoralization of the court's authority" would have resulted from giving the petitioner a reasonable opportunity to appear and offer a defense in open court to a charge of perjury or to the charge of contempt. The traditional grand juries have never punished contempts. The practice that has always been followed with recalcitrant grand jury witnesses is to take them into open court, and that practice, consistent with due process, has not demoralized the authority of courts. Reported cases reveal no instances in which witnesses believed by grand juries on the basis of other testimony to be perjurers, have been convicted for contempt, or for perjury, without notice of the specific charges against them, and opportunity to prepare a defense, to obtain counsel, to cross-examine the witnesses against them and to offer evidence in their own defense. The right to be heard in open court before one is condemned is too valuable to be whittled away under the guise of "demoralization of the court's authority."

It is "the law of the land" that no man's life, liberty or property be forfeited as a punishment until there has been a charge fairly made and fairly tried in a public tribunal. . . . The petitioner was convicted without that kind of trial. . . .

Reversed and remanded.

8. *Arraignment without Unnecessary Delay*

MALLORY *v.* UNITED STATES
354 US 449 (1957)

[A nineteen-year-old boy of limited intelligence was arrested on suspicion of rape. Police questioned him for about a half-hour, then asked him to submit to a lie-detector test, and four hours later to another such test. He was not advised of his right to counsel, his right to a preliminary examination before a magistrate, his right to keep silent, nor was he warned that any statement might be used against him. Not until after he had confessed did the police arraign him before a magistrate, although arraignment easily could have been made.

[The Court unanimously reversed the conviction, holding, in an opinion by Justice Frankfurter, that the confession was inadmissible. Although reliance is placed on the fact that the confession was obtained while defendant was detained in violation of Rule 5(a) of the Federal Rules of Criminal Procedure, requiring arraignment without unnecessary delay, the opinion may be read as intimating a constitutional necessity for Rule 5(a).]

Mr. Justice Frankfurter delivered the opinion of the Court:

Petitioner was convicted of rape in the United States District Court for the District of Columbia, and, as authorized by the District Code, the jury imposed a death sentence. The Court of Appeals affirmed, one judge dissenting. Since an important question involving the interpretation of the Federal Rules of Criminal Procedure, 18 U.S.C.A., was involved in this capital case, we granted the petition for certiorari.

The rape occurred at 6 P.M. on April 7, 1954, in the basement of the apartment house inhabited by the victim. She had descended to the basement a few minutes previous to wash some laundry. Experiencing some difficulty in detaching a hose in the sink, she sought help from the janitor, who lived in a basement apartment with his wife, two grown sons, a younger son and the petitioner, his nineteen-year-old half-brother. Petitioner was alone in the apartment at the time. He detached the hose and returned to his quarters. Very shortly thereafter, a masked man, whose general features were identified to resemble those of both petitioners and his two grown nephews, attacked the woman. She had heard no one descend the wooden steps that furnished the only means of entering the basement from above.

Petitioner and one of his grown nephews disappeared from the apartment house shortly after the crime was committed. The former was apprehended the following afternoon between 2 and 2:30 P.M. and was taken, along with his older nephews, also suspects, to police headquarters. At least four officers questioned him there in the presence of other officers for thirty to forty-five minutes, beginning the examination by telling him, according to his testimony, that his brother had said that he was the assailant. Petitioner strenuously denied his guilt. He spent the rest of the afternoon at headquarters, in the company of the other two suspects and his brother a good part of the time. About 4 P.M. the three suspects were asked to submit to "lie detector" tests, and they agreed. The officer in charge of the polygraph machine was not located for almost two hours, during which time the suspects received food and drink. The nephews were then examined first. Questioning of petitioner began just after 8 P.M. Only he and the polygraph operator were present in a small room, the door to which was closed.

Following almost an hour and one-half of steady interrogation, he "first stated that he could have done this crime, or that he might have done it. He finally stated that he was responsible. . . ." Not until 10:00 P.M., after petitioner had repeated his confession to other officers, did the police attempt to reach a United States Commissioner for the purpose of arraignment. Failing in this, they obtained petitioner's consent to examination by the deputy coroner, who noted no indicia of physical or psychological coercion. Petitioner was then confronted by the complaining witness and "[p]ractically every man in the Sex Squad," and in response to questioning by three officers, he repeated the confession. Between 11:30 P.M. and 12:30 A.M. he dictated the confession to a typist. The next morning he was brought before a Commissioner. At the trial, which was delayed for a year because of doubt about petitioner's capacity to understand the proceedings against him, the signed confession was introduced in evidence.

The case calls for the proper application of Rule 5(a) of the Federal Rules of Criminal Procedure, promulgated in 1946, 327 US 821. That Rule provides:

(a) Appearance before the Commissioner. An officer making an arrest under a warrant issued upon a complaint or any person making an arrest without a warrant shall take the arrested person without unnecessary delay before the nearest available commissioner or before any other nearby officer empowered to commit persons charged with offenses against the laws of the United States. When a person arrested without a warrant is brought before a commissioner or other officer, a complaint shall be filed forthwith.

This provision has both statutory and judicial antecedents for guidance in applying it. The requirement that arraignment be "without unnecessary delay" is a compendious restatement, without substantive change, of several prior specific federal statutory provisions. . . . Nearly all the States have similar enactments.

In *McNabb* v. *United States,* 318 US 332, we spelled out the important reasons of policy behind this body of legislation:

The purpose of this impressively pervasive requirement of criminal procedure is plain. . . . The awful instruments of the criminal law cannot be entrusted to a single functionary. The complicated process of criminal justice is therefore divided into different parts, responsibility for which is separately vested in the various participants upon whom the criminal law relies for its vindication. Legislation such as this, requiring that the police must with reasonable promptness show legal cause for detaining arrested persons, constitutes an important safeguard—not only in assuring protection for the innocent but also in securing conviction of the guilty by methods that commend themselves to a progressive and self-confident society. For this procedural requirement checks resort to those reprehensible practices known as the "third degree" which, though universally rejected as indefensible, still find their way into use. It aims to avoid all the evil implications of secret interrogation of persons accused of crime.

Since such unwarranted detention led to tempting utilization of intensive interrogation, easily gliding into the evils of "the third degree," the Court held that police detention of defendants beyond the time when a committing magistrate was readily accessible constituted "wilful disobedience of law." In order adequately to enforce the congressional requirement of prompt arraignment, it was deemed necessary to render inadmissible incriminating statements elicited from defendants during a period of unlawful detention.

In *Upshaw* v. *United States*, 335 US 410, which came here after the Federal Rules of Criminal Procedure had been in operation, the Court made it clear that Rule 5(a)'s standard of "without unnecessary delay" implied no relaxation of the *McNabb* doctrine.

The requirement of Rule 5(a) is part of the procedure devised by Congress for safeguarding individual rights without hampering effective and intelligent law enforcement. Provisions related to Rule 5(a) contemplate a procedure that allows arresting officers little more leeway than the interval between arrest and the ordinary administrative steps required to bring a suspect before the nearest available magistrate. Rule 4(a) provides: "If it appears from the complaint that there is probable cause to believe that an offense has been committed and that the defendant has committed it, a warrant for the arrest of the defendant shall issue. . . ." Rule 4(b) requires that the warrant "shall command that the defendant be arrested and brought before the nearest available commissioner." And Rules 5(b) and (c) reveal the function of the requirement of prompt arraignment:

(b) Statement by the Commissioner. The commissioner shall inform the defendant of the complaint against him, of his right to retain counsel and of his right to have a preliminary examination. He shall also inform the defendant that he is not required to make at statement and that any statement made by him may be used against him. The commissioner shall allow the defendant reasonable time and opportunity to consult counsel and shall admit the defendant to bail as provided in these rules.

(c) Preliminary Examination. The defendant shall not be called upon to plead. If the defendant waives preliminary examination, the commissioner shall forthwith hold him to answer in the district court. If the defendant does not waive examination, the commissioner shall hear the evidence within a reasonable time. The defendant may cross-examine witnesses against him and may introduce evidence in his own behalf. If from the evidence it appears to the commissioner that there is probable cause to believe that an offense has been committed and that the defendant has committed it, the commissioner shall forthwith hold him to answer in the district court; otherwise the commissioner shall discharge him. The commissioner shall admit the defendant to bail as provided in these rules.

The scheme for initiating a federal prosecution is plainly defined. The police may not arrest upon mere suspicion but only on "probable cause." The next step in the proceeding is to arraign the arrested person before a judicial officer as quickly as possible so that he may be advised of his rights and so that the issue of probable cause may be promptly determined. The arrested person may, of course, be "booked" by the police. But he is not to be taken to police headquarters in order to carry out a process of inquiry that lends itself, even if not so designed, to eliciting damaging statements to support the arrest and ultimately his guilt.

The duty enjoined upon arresting officers to arraign "without unnecessary delay" indicates that the command does not call for mechanical or automatic obedience.

Circumstances may justify a brief delay between arrest and arraignment, as for instance, where the story volunteered by the accused is susceptible of quick verification through third parties. But the delay must not be of a nature to give opportunity for the extraction of a confession.

The circumstances of this case preclude a holding that arraignment was "without unnecessary delay." Petitioner was arrested in the early afternoon and was detained at headquarters within the vicinity of numerous committing magistrates. Even though the police had ample evidence from other sources than the petitioner for regarding the petitioner as the chief suspect, they first questioned him for approximately a half hour. When this inquiry of a nineteen-year-old lad of limited intelligence produced no confession, the police asked him to submit to a lie-detector test. He was not told of his rights to counsel or to a preliminary examination before a magistrate, nor was he warned that he might keep silent and "that any statement made by him may be used against him." After four hours of further detention at headquarters, during which arraignment could easily have been made in the same building in which the police headquarters were housed, petitioner was examined by the lie-detector operator for another hour and a half before his story began to waver. Not until he had confessed, when any judicial caution had lost its purpose, did the police arraign him.

We cannot sanction this extended delay, resulting in confession, without subordinating the general rule of prompt arraignment to the discretion of arresting officers in finding exceptional circumstances for its disregard. In every case where the police resort to interrogation of an arrested person and secure a confession, they may well claim, and quite sincerely, that they were merely trying to check on the information given by him. Against such a claim and the evil potentialities of the practice for which it is urged stands Rule 5(a) as a barrier. Nor is there an escape from the constraint laid upon the police by that Rule in that two other suspects were involved for the same crime. Presumably, whomever the police arrest they must arrest on "probable cause." It is not the function of the police to arrest, as it were, at large and to use an interrogating process at police headquarters in order to determine whom they should charge before a committing magistrate on "probable cause."

Reversed and remanded.

9. Conviction without Proof of Crime

THOMPSON v. LOUISVILLE
362 US 199 (1960)

[The defendant was convicted in the Louisville police court of two offenses, loitering and disorderly conduct. The U.S. Supreme Court, on reviewing the trial record, found no evidence to sustain the conviction and unanimously reversed. Loitering and disorderly conduct are made criminal offenses under countless statutes and ordinances throughout the country, and are very frequently resorted to by police officers as bases for arrests when other charges do not seem applicable. In an opinion by Justice Black for the Court, it was held a denial of due process to convict a person of these crimes without proof of his guilt. It is not a crime to argue with a policeman, said the Court. The case was later used as a precedent in some of the civil rights sit-in demonstration cases.]

Mr. Justice Black delivered the opinion of the Court:

Petitioner was found guilty in the Police Court of Louisville, Kentucky, of two offenses—loitering and disorderly conduct. The ultimate question presented to us is whether the charges against petitioner were so totally devoid of evidentiary support as to render his conviction unconstitutional under the Due Process Clause of the Fourteenth Amendment. Decision of this question turns not on the sufficiency of the evidence, but on whether this conviction rests upon any evidence at all.

The facts as shown by the record are short and simple. Petitioner, a long-time resident of the Louisville area, went into the Liberty End Cafe about 6:20 on a Saturday evening, January 24, 1959. In addition to selling food, the cafe was licensed to sell beer to the public, and some 12 to 30 patrons were present during the time petitioner was there. When petitioner had been in the cafe about half an hour, two Louisville police officers came in on a "routine check." Upon seeing petitioner "out there on the floor dancing by himself," one of the officers, according to his testimony, went up to the manager who was sitting on a stool nearby and asked him how long petitioner had been in there and if he had bought anything. The officer testified that upon being told by the manager that petitioner had been there "a little over a half-hour and that he had not bought anything," he accosted Thompson and "asked him what was his reason for being in there and he said he was waiting on a bus." The officer then informed petitioner that he was under arrest and took him outside. This was the arrest for loitering. After going outside, the officer testified, petitioner "was very argumentative—he argued with us back and forth and so then we placed a disorderly conduct charge on him." Admittedly the disorderly conduct conviction rests solely on this one sentence description of petitioner's conduct after he left the cafe.

The foregoing evidence includes all that the city offered against him, except a record purportedly showing a total of 54 previous arrests of petitioner. Before putting on his defense, petitioner moved for a dismissal of the charges against him on the ground that a judgment of conviction on this record would deprive him of property and liberty without due process of law under the Fourteenth Amendment in that (1) there was no evidence to support findings of guilt and (2) the two arrests and prosecutions were reprisals against him because petitioner had employed counsel and demanded a judicial hearing to defend himself against prior and allegedly baseless charges by the police. This motion was denied.

Petitioner then put in evidence on his own behalf, none of which in any way strengthened the city's case. He testified that he bought, and one of the cafe employees served him, a dish of macaroni and a glass of beer and that he remained in the cafe waiting for a bus to go home. Further evidence showed without dispute that at the time of his arrest petitioner gave the officers his home address; that he had money with him, and a bus schedule showing that a bus to his home would stop within half a block of the cafe at about 7:30; that he owned two unimproved lots of land; that in addition to work he had done for others, he had regularly worked one day or more a week for the same family for 30 years; that he paid no rent in the home where he lived and that his meager income was sufficient to meet his needs. The cafe manager testified that petitioner had frequently patronized the cafe, and that he had never told petitioner that he was unwelcome there. The manager further testified that on this very occasion he saw petitioner "standing there in the middle of the floor and patting his foot," and that he did not at any time during petitioner's stay there object to anything he was doing. There is no evidence that anyone else in the cafe objected to petitioner's shuffling his feet in rhythm with the music of the juke box or that his conduct was boisterous or offensive to anyone present. At the close of his evidence, petitioner repeated his motion for dismissal of the charges on the ground that a conviction on the foregoing evidence would deprive him of liberty and property without due process under the Fourteenth Amendment. The court denied the motion, convicted him of both offenses, and fined him $10 on each charge. A motion for new trial, on the same grounds, also was denied, which exhausted petitioner's remedies in the police court. . . .

Our examination of the record presented in the petition for certiorari convinced us that although the fines here are small, the due process questions presented are substantial and we therefore granted certiorari to review the police court's judgments. . . .

The city correctly assumes here that if there is no support for these convictions in the record they are void as denials of due process. The pertinent portion of the city ordinance under which petitioner was convicted of loitering reads as follows:

It shall be unlawful for any person . . . , without visible means of support, or who cannot give a satisfactory account of himself, . . . to sleep, lie, loaf, or trespass in or about any premises, building, or other structure in the City of Louisville, without first having obtained the consent of the owner or controller of said premises, structure, or building. . . .

In addition to the fact that petitioner proved he had "visible means of support," the prosecutor at trial said "This is a loitering charge here. There is no charge of no visible means of support." Moreover, there is no suggestion that petitioner was sleeping, lying or trespassing in or about this cafe. Accordingly he could only have been convicted for being unable to give a satisfactory account of himself while loitering in the cafe, without the consent of the manager. Under the words of the ordinance itself, if the evidence fails to prove all three elements of this loitering charge, the conviction is not supported by evidence, in which event it does not comport with due process of law. The record is entirely lacking in evidence to support any of the charges.

Here, petitioner spent about half an hour on a Saturday evening in January in a public cafe which sold food and beer to the public. When asked to account for his presence there, he said he was waiting for a bus. The city concedes that there is no law making it an offense for a person in such a cafe to "dance," "shuffle" or "pat" his feet in time to music. The undisputed testimony of the manager, who did not know whether petitioner had bought macaroni and beer or not but who did see the patting, shuffling or dancing, was that petitioner was welcome there. The manager testified that he did not, at any time during petitioner's stay in the cafe, object to anything petitioner was doing and that he never saw petitioner do anything that would cause any objection. Surely this is implied consent, which the city admitted in oral argument satisfies the ordinance. The arresting officer admitted that there was nothing in any way "vulgar" about what he called petitioner's "ordinary dance," whatever relevance, if any, vulgarity might have to a charge of loitering. There simply is no semblance of evidence from which any person could reasonably infer that petitioner could not give a satisfactory account of himself or that he was loitering or loafing there (in the ordinary sense of the words) without "the consent of the owner or controller" of the cafe.

Petitioner's conviction for disorderly conduct was under § 85–8 of the city ordinance which, without definition, provides that "whoever shall be found guilty of disorderly conduct in the City of Louisville shall be fined. . . ." The only evidence of "disorderly conduct" was the single statement of the policeman that after petitioner was arrested and taken out of the cafe he was very argumentative. There is no testimony that petitioner raised his voice, used offensive language, resisted the officers or engaged in any conduct of any kind likely in any way to adversely affect the good order and tranquility of the City of Louisville. The only information the record contains on what the petitioner was "argumentative" about is his statement that he asked the officers "what they arrested me for." We assume, for we are justified in assuming, that merely "arguing" with a policeman is not, because it could not be, "disorderly conduct" as a matter of the substantive law of Kentucky. . . . Moreover, Kentucky law itself seems to provide that if a man wrongfully arrested fails to object to the arresting officer, he waives any right to complain later that the arrest was unlawful. *Nickell* v. *Commonwealth*, 285 S.W. 2d 495, 496.

Thus we find no evidence whatever in the record to support these convictions. Just as "Conviction upon a charge not made would be sheer denial of due process," so is it a violation of due process to convict and punish a man without evidence of his guilt.

The judgments are reversed and the cause is remanded to the Police Court of the City of Louisville for proceedings not inconsistent with this opinion.

Reversed and remanded.

10. Trial by News Media

SHEPPARD *v.* MAXWELL
384 US 333 (1966)

[Dr. Samuel H. Sheppard, accused of murdering his wife, was tried before a jury in Ohio. Both before and during the trial, which began two weeks before an election in which the trial judge and the prosecutor were candidates for judgeships, the defendant was the subject of extensive newspaper, radio, and television publicity. The trial lasted nine weeks. The trial judge made no effort to control releases to the press by witnesses, prosecuting attorneys, and others. Sheppard was convicted of second degree murder, and the judgment was affirmed by the state's appellate courts. The U.S. Supreme Court denied certiorari. Several years later, however, Sheppard instituted habeas corpus proceedings in the U.S. district court, which held that he had been denied a fair trial and was entitled to be released. The court of appeals reversed. On certiorari, the Supreme Court agreed with the district court that Sheppard had been denied a fair trial and ordered that he be released unless the state tries him again within a reasonable time. The decision was 8–1, with Justice Black dissenting without opinion. The Court's opinion was by Justice Clark.]

Mr. Justice Clark delivered the opinion of the Court:

This federal habeas corpus application involves the question whether Sheppard was deprived of a fair trial in his state conviction for the second-degree murder of his wife because of the trial judge's failure to protect Sheppard sufficiently from the massive, pervasive and prejudicial publicity that attended his prosecution. The United States District Court held that he was not afforded a fair trial and granted the writ subject to the State's right to put Sheppard to trial again. The Court of Appeals for the Sixth Circuit reversed by a divided vote. We granted certiorari. We have concluded that Sheppard did not receive a fair trial consistent with the Due Process Clause of the Fourteenth Amendment and, therefore, reverse the judgment.

I

Marilyn Sheppard, petitioner's pregnant wife, was bludgeoned to death in the upstairs bedroom of their lakeshore home in Bay Village, Ohio, a suburb of Cleveland. On the day of the tragedy, July 4, 1954, Sheppard pieced together for several local officials the following story: He and his wife had entertained neighborhood friends, the Aherns, on the previous evening at their home. After dinner they watched television in the living room. Sheppard became drowsy and dozed off to sleep on a couch. Later, Marilyn partially awoke him saying that she was going to bed. The next thing he remembered was hearing his wife cry out in the early morning hours. He hurried upstairs and in the dim light from the hall saw a "form" standing next to his wife's bed. As he struggled with the "form" he was struck on the back of the neck and rendered unconscious. On regaining his senses he found himself on the floor next to his wife's bed. He raised up, looked at her, took her pulse and "felt that she was gone." He then went to his son's room and found him unmolested. Hearing a noise he hurried downstairs. He saw a "form" running out the door and pursued it to the lake shore. He grappled with it on the beach and again lost consciousness. Upon his recovery he was laying face down with the lower portion of his body in the water. He returned to his home, checked the pulse on his wife's neck, and "determined or thought that she was gone." He then went downstairs and called a neighbor, Mayor Houk of Bay Village. The Mayor and his wife came over at once, found Sheppard slumped in an easy chair downstairs and asked, "What happened?" Sheppard replied: "I don't know but somebody ought to try to do something for Marilyn." Mrs. Houk immediately went up to the bedroom. The Mayor told Sheppard, "Get hold of yourself. Can you tell me what happened?" Sheppard then related the above-outlined events. After Mrs. Houk discovered the body, the Mayor called the local police, Dr. Richard Sheppard, petitioner's brother, and Aherns. The local police were the first to arrive. They in turn notified the Coroner and Cleveland police. Richard Sheppard then arrived, determined that

Marilyn was dead, examined his brother's injuries, and removed him to the nearby clinic operated by the Sheppard family. When the Coroner, the Cleveland police and other officials arrived, the house and surrounding area were thoroughly searched, the rooms of the house were photographed, and many persons, including the Houks and the Aherns, were interrogated. The Sheppard home and premises were taken into "protective custody" and remained so until after the trial.

From the outset officials focused suspicion on Sheppard. After a search of the house and premises on the morning of the tragedy, Dr. Gerber, the Coroner, is reported—and it is undenied—to have told his men, "Well, it is evident the doctor did this, so let's go get the confession out of him." He proceeded to interrogate and examine Sheppard while the latter was under sedation in his hospital room. On the same occasion, the Coroner was given the clothes Sheppard wore at the time of the tragedy together with the personal items in them. Later that afternoon Chief Eaton and two Cleveland police officers interrogated Sheppard at some length, confronting him with evidence and demanding explanations. Asked by Officer Shotke to take a lie detector test, Sheppard said he would if it were reliable. Shotke replied that it was "infallible" and "you might as well tell us all about it now." At the end of the interrogation Shotke told Sheppard: "I think you killed your wife." Still later in the same afternoon a physician sent by the Coroner was permitted to make a detailed examination of Sheppard. Until the Coroner's inquest on July 22, at which time he was subpoenaed, Sheppard made himself available for frequent and extended questioning without the presence of an attorney.

On July 7, the day of Marilyn Sheppard's funeral, a newspaper story appeared in which Assistant County Attorney Mahon—later the chief prosecutor of Sheppard—sharply criticized the refusal of the Sheppard family to permit his immediate questioning. From there on headline stories repeatedly stressed Sheppard's lack of cooperation with the police and other officials. Under the headline "Testify Now In Death, Bay Doctor Is Ordered," one story described a visit by Coroner Gerber and four police officers to the hospital on July 8. When Sheppard insisted that his lawyer be present, the Coroner wrote out a subpoena and served it on him. Sheppard then agreed to submit to questioning without counsel and the subpoena was torn up. The officers questioned him for several hours. On July 9, Sheppard, at the request of the Coroner, re-enacted the tragedy at his home before the Coroner, police officers, and a group of newsmen, who apparently were invited by the Coroner. The home was locked so that Sheppard was obliged to wait outside until the Coroner arrived. Sheppard's performance was reported in detail by the news media along with photographs. The newspapers also played up Sheppard's refusal to take a lie detector test and "the protective ring" thrown up by his family. Front-page newspaper headlines announced on the same day that "Doctor Balks At Lie Test; Retells Story." A column opposite that story contained an "exclusive" interview with Sheppard headlined: " 'Loved My Wife, She Loved Me,' Sheppard Tells News Reporters." The next day, another headline story disclosed that Sheppard had "again late yesterday refused to take a lie detector test" and quoted an Assistant County Attorney as saying that "at the end of a nine-hour questioning of Dr. Sheppard, I felt he was now ruling [a test] out completely." But subsequent newspaper articles reported that the Coroner was still pushing Sheppard for a lie detector test. More stories appeared when Sheppard would not allow authorities to inject him with "truth serum."

On the 20th, the "editorial artillery" opened fire with a front-page charge that somebody is "getting away with murder." The editorial attributed the ineptness of the investigation to "friendships, relationships, hired lawyers, a husband who ought to have been subjected instantly to the same third degree to which any person under similar circumstances is subjected. . . ." The following day, July 21, another page-one editorial was headed: "Why No Inquest? Do It Now, Dr. Gerber." The Coroner called an inquest the same day and subpoenaed Sheppard. It was staged the next day in a school gymnasium; the Coroner presided with the County Prosecutor as his advisor and two detectives as bailiffs. In the front of the room was a long table occupied by reporters, television and radio personnel, and broadcasting equipment. The hearing was broadcast with live microphones placed at the Coroner's seat and the witness stand. A swarm of reporters and photographers attended. Sheppard was brought into the room by police who searched him in full view of several hundred spectators. Sheppard's counsel were present during the three-day inquest but were not permitted to participate. When Sheppard's chief counsel attempted to place some documents in the record, he was forcibly ejected from the room by the Coroner, who received cheers, hugs, and kisses from ladies in the audience. Sheppard was questioned for five and one-half hours about his actions on the night of the murder, his married life, and a love affair with Susan Hayes. At the end of the hearing the Coroner announced that he "could" order Sheppard held for the grand jury, but did not do so.

Throughout this period the newspapers emphasized evidence that tended to incriminate Sheppard and pointed out discrepancies in his statements to authorities. At the same time, Sheppard made many public statements to the press and wrote feature articles asserting his innocence. During the inquest on July 26, a headline in large type stated "Kerr [Captain of the Cleveland Police] Urges Sheppard's Arrest." In the story, Detective McArthur "disclosed that scientific tests at the Sheppard home have definitely established that the killer washed off a trail of blood from the murder bedroom to the downstairs section," a circumstance casting doubt on Sheppard's accounts of the murder. No such evidence was produced at trial. The newspapers also delved into Sheppard's personal life. Articles stressed his extramarital love affairs as a motive for the crime. The newspapers portrayed Sheppard as a Lothario, fully explored his relationship with Susan Hayes, and named a number of other women who were allegedly involved with him. The testimony at trial never showed that Sheppard had any illicit relationships besides the one with Susan Hayes.

On July 28, an editorial entitled "Why Don't Police Quiz Top Suspect" demanded that Sheppard be taken to police headquarters. It described him in the following language:

Now proved under oath to be a liar, still free to go about his business, shielded by his family, protected by a smart lawyer who has made monkeys of the police and authorities, carrying a gun part of the time, left free to do whatever he pleases. . . .

A front-page editorial on July 30 asked: "Why Isn't Sam Sheppard in Jail?" It was later titled "Quit Stalling—Bring Him In." After calling Sheppard "the most unusual murder suspect ever seen around these parts" the article said that "[e]xcept for some superficial questioning during Coroner Sam Gerber's inquest he has been scot-free of any official grilling. . . ." It asserted that he was "surrounded by an iron curtain of protection [and] concealment."

That night at 10 o'clock Sheppard was arrested at his father's home on a charge of murder. He was taken to the Bay Village City Hall where hundreds of people, newscasters, photographers and reporters were awaiting his arrival. He was immediately arraigned—having been denied a temporary delay to secure the presence of counsel—and bound over to the grand jury.

The publicity then grew in intensity until his indictment on August 17. Typical of the coverage during this period is a front-page interview entitled: "DR. SAM: 'I Wish There Was Something I Could Get Off My Chest—but There Isn't.'" Unfavorable publicity included items such as a cartoon of the body of a sphinx with Sheppard's head and the legend below: "'I Will Do Everything In My Power to Help Solve This Terrible Murder.'—Dr. Sam Sheppard." Headlines announced, *inter alia,* that: "Doctor Evidence is Ready for Jury," "Corrigan Tactics Stall Quizzing." "Sheppard 'Gay Set' Is Revealed By Houk," "Blood Is Found In Garage," "New Murder Evidence Is Found, Police Claim," "Dr. Sam Faces Quiz At Jail On Marilyn's Fear Of Him." On August 18, an article appeared under the headline "Dr. Sam Writes His Own Story." And reproduced across the entire front page was a portion of the typed statement signed by Sheppard: "I am not guilty of the murder of my wife, Marilyn. How could I, who have been trained to help people and devote my life to saving life, commit such a terrible and revolting crime?" We do not detail the coverage further. There are five volumes filled with similar clippings from each of the three Cleveland newspapers covering the period from the murder until Sheppard's conviction in December 1954. The record includes no excerpts from newscasts on radio and television but since space was reserved in the courtroom for these media we assume that their coverage was equally large.

II

With this background the case came on for trial two weeks before the November general election at which the chief prosecutor was a candidate for municipal judge and the presiding judge, Judge Blythin, was a candidate to succeed himself. Twenty-five days before the case was set, a list of 75 veniremen were called as prospective jurors. This list, including the addresses of each venireman, was published in all three Cleveland newspapers. As a consequence, anonymous letters and telephone calls, as well as calls from friends, regarding the impending prosecution were received by all the prospective jurors. The selection of the jury began on October 18, 1954.

The courtroom in which the trial was held measured 26 by 48 feet. A long temporary table was set up inside the bar, in back of the single counsel table. It ran the width of the courtroom, parallel to the bar railing, with one end less than three feet from the jury box. Approximately 20 representatives of newspapers and wire services were assigned seats at this table by the court. Behind the bar railing there were four rows of benches. These seats were likewise assigned by the court for the entire trial. The first row was occupied by representatives of television and radio stations, and the second and third rows by reporters from out-of-town newspapers and magazines. One side of the last row, which accommodated 14 people, was assigned to Sheppard's family and the other to Marilyn's. The public was permitted to fill vacancies in this row on special passes only. Representatives of the news media also used all the rooms on the courtroom floor, including the room where cases were ordinarily called and assigned for trial. Private telephone lines and telegraphic equipment were installed in these rooms so that reports from the trial could be speeded to the papers. Station WSRS was permitted to set up broadcasting facilities on the third floor of the courthouse next door to the jury room, where the jury rested during recesses in the trial and deliberated. Newscasts were made from this room throughout the trial, and while the jury reached its verdict.

On the sidewalk and steps in front of the courthouse, television and newsreel cameras were occasionally used to take motion pictures of the participants in the trial, including the jury and the judge. Indeed, one television broadcast carried a staged interview of the judge as he entered the courthouse. In the corridors outside the courtroom there was a host of photographers and television personnel with flash cameras, portable lights and motion picture cameras. This group photographed the prospective jurors during selection of the jury. After the trial opened, the witnesses, counsel, and jurors were photographed and televised whenever they entered or left the courtroom. Sheppard was brought to the courtroom about 10 minutes before each session began; he was surrounded by reporters and extensively photographed for the newspapers and telvision. A rule of court prohibited picture-taking in the courtroom during the actual sessions of the court, but no restraints were put on photographers during recesses, which were taken once each morning and afternoon, with a longer period for lunch.

All of these arrangements with the news media and their massive coverage of the trial continued during the entire nine weeks of the trial. The courtroom remained crowded to capacity with representatives of news media. Their movement in and out of the courtroom often caused so much confusion that, despite the loud speaker system installed in the courtroom, it was difficult for the witnesses and counsel to be heard. Furthermore, the reporters clustered within the bar of the small courtroom made confidential talk among Sheppard and his counsel almost impossible during the proceedings. They frequently had to leave the courtroom to obtain privacy. And many times when counsel wished to raise a point with the judge out of the hearing of the jury it was necessary to move to the judge's chambers. Even then, news media representatives so packed the judge's anteroom that counsel could hardly return from the chambers to the courtroom. The reporters vied with each other to find out what counsel and the judge had discussed, and often these matters later appeared in newspapers accessible to the jury.

The daily record of the proceedings was made available to the newspapers and the testimony of each witness was printed *verbatim* in the local editions, along with objections of counsel, and rulings by the judge. Pictures of Sheppard, the judge, counsel, pertinent witnesses, and the jury often accompanied the daily newspaper and television accounts. At times the newspapers published photographs of exhibits introduced at the trial, and the rooms of Sheppard's house were featured along with relevant testimony.

The jurors themselves were constantly exposed to the news media. Every juror, except one, testified at *voir dire* to reading about the case in the Cleveland papers or to having heard broadcasts about it. Seven of the 12 jurors who rendered the verdict had one or more Cleveland papers delivered in their home; the remaining jurors were not interrogated on the point. Nor were there questions as to radios or television sets in the talesmen's homes, but we must assume that most of them owned such conveniences. As the selection of the jury progressed, individual pictures of prospective members appeared daily. During the trial, pictures of the jury appeared over 40 times in the Cleveland papers alone. The court permitted photographers to take pictures of the jury in the box, and individual pictures of the members in the jury room. One newspaper ran pictures of the jurors at the Sheppard home when they went there to view the scene of the murder. Another paper featured the home life of an alternate juror. The day before the verdict was rendered—while the jurors were at lunch and sequestered by two bailiffs—the jury was separated into two groups to pose for photographs which appeared in the newspapers.

III

We now reach the conduct of the trial. While the intense publicity continued unabated, it is sufficient to relate only the more flagrant episodes:

1. On October 9, 1954, nine days before the case went to trial, an editorial in one of the newspapers criticized defense counsel's random poll of people on the streets as to their opinion of Sheppard's guilt or innocence in an effort to use the resulting statistics to show the necessity for change of venue. The article said the survey "smacks of mass jury tampering," called on defense counsel to drop it, and stated that the bar association should do something about it. It characterized the poll as "non-judicial, non-legal, and nonsense." The article was called to the attention of the court but no action was taken.

2. On the second day of *voir dire* examination a debate was staged and broadcast live over WHK radio. The participants, newspaper reporters, accused Sheppard's counsel of throwing roadblocks in the way of the prosecution and asserted that Sheppard conceded his guilt by hiring a prominent criminal lawyer. Sheppard's counsel objected to this broadcast and requested a continuance, but the judge denied the motion. When counsel asked the court to give some protection from such events, the judge replied that "WHK doesn't have much coverage," and that "[a]fter all, we are not trying this case by radio or in newspapers or any other means. We confine ourselves seriously to it in this courtroom and do the very best we can."

3. While the jury was being selected, a two-inch headline asked: "But Who Will Speak for Marilyn?" The front-page story spoke of the "perfect face" of the accused. "Study that face as long as you want. Never will you get from it a hint of what might be the answer . . ." The two brothers of the accused were described as "Prosperous, poised. His two sisters-in-law. Smart, chic, well-groomed. His elderly father. Courtly, reserved. A perfect type for the patriarch of a staunch clan." The author then noted Marilyn Sheppard was "still off stage," and that she was an only

child whose mother died when she was very young and whose father had no interest in the case. But the author—through quotes from Detective Chief James McArthur—assured readers that the prosecution's exhibits would speak for Marilyn. "Her story," McArthur stated, "will come into this courtroom through our witnesses." The article ends:

> Then you realize how what and who is missing from the perfect setting will be supplied.
>   How in the Big Case justice will be done.
>   Justice to Sam Sheppard.
>   And to Marilyn Sheppard.

4. As has been mentioned, the jury viewed the scene of the murder on the first day of the trial. Hundreds of reporters, cameramen and onlookers were there, and one representative of the news media was permitted to accompany the jury while they inspected the Sheppard home. The time of the jury's visit was revealed so far in advance that one of the newspapers was able to rent a helicopter and fly over the house taking pictures of the jurors on their tour.

5. On November 19, a Cleveland police officer gave testimony that tended to contradict details in the written statement Sheppard made to the Cleveland police. Two days later, in a broadcast heard over Station WHK in Cleveland, Robert Considine likened Sheppard to a perjurer and compared the episode to Alger Hiss' confrontation with Whittaker Chambers. Though defense counsel asked the judge to question the jury to ascertain how many heard the broadcast, the court refused to do so. The judge also overruled the motion for continuance based on the same ground, saying:

> Well, I don't know, we can't stop people, in any event, listening to it. It is a matter of free speech, and the court can't control everybody. . . . We are not going to harass the jury every morning. . . . It is getting to the point where if we do it every morning, we are suspecting the jury. I have confidence in this jury. . . .

6. On November 24, a story appeared under an eight-column headline: "Sam Called a 'Jekyll-Hyde' By Marilyn, Cousin To Testify." It related that Marilyn had recently told friends that Sheppard was a "Dr. Jekyll and Mr. Hyde" character. No such testimony was ever produced at the trial. The story went on to announce: "The prosecution has a 'bombshell witness' on tap who will testify to Dr. Sam's display of fiery temper—countering the defense claim that the defendant is a gentle physician with an even disposition." Defense counsel made motions for change of venue, continuance and mistrial, but they were denied. No action was taken by the court.

7. When the trial was in its seventh week, Walter Winchell broadcasted over WXEL television and WJW radio that Carole Beasley, who was under arrest in New York City for robbery, had stated that, as Sheppard's mistress, she had borne him a child. The defense asked that the jury be queried on the broadcast. Two jurors admitted in open court that they had heard it. The judge asked each: "Would that have any effect upon your judgment?" Both replied, "No." This was accepted by the judge as sufficient; he merely asked the jury to "pay no attention whatever to that type of scavenging . . . Let's confine ourselves to this courtroom, if you please." In answer to the motion for mistrial, the judge said:

Well, even, so, Mr. Corrigan, how are you ever going to prevent those things, in any event? I don't justify them at all. I think it is outrageous, but in a sense, it is outrageous even if there were no trial here. The trial has nothing to do with it in the Court's mind, as far as its outrage is concerned, but—

Mr. CORRIGAN: I don't know what effect it had on the mind of any of these jurors, and I can't find out unless inquiry is made.

The COURT: How would you ever, in any jury, avoid that kind of a thing?

8. On December 9, while Sheppard was on the witness stand he testified that he had been mistreated by Cleveland detectives after his arrest. Although he was not at the trial, Captain Kerr of the Homicide Bureau issued a press statement denying Sheppard's allegations which appeared under the headline: " 'Bare-faced Liar,' Kerr Says of Sam." Captain Kerr never appeared as a witness at the trial.

9. After the case was submitted to the jury, it was sequestered for its deliberations, which took five days and four nights. After the verdict, defense counsel ascertained that the jurors had been allowed to make telephone calls to their homes every day while they were sequestered at the hotel. Although the telephones had been removed from the jurors' rooms, the jurors were permitted to use the phones in the bailiff's rooms. The calls were placed by the jurors themselves; no record was kept of the jurors who made calls, the telephone numbers or the parties called. The bailiffs sat in the room where they could hear only the jurors' end of the conversation. The court had not instructed the bailiffs to prevent such calls. By a subsequent motion, defense counsel urged that this ground alone warranted a new trial, but the motion was overruled and no evidence was taken on the question.

IV

The principle that justice cannot survive behind walls of silence has long been reflected in the "Anglo-American distrust for secret trials." *In re Oliver,* 333 US 257. A responsible press has always been regarded as the handmaiden of effective judicial administration, especially in the criminal field. Its function in this regard is documented by an impressive record of service over several centuries. The press does not simply publish information about trials but guards against the miscarriage of justice by subjecting the police, prosecutors, and judicial processes to extensive public scrutiny and criticism. This Court has, therefore, been unwilling to place any direct limitations on the freedom traditionally exercised by the news media for "[w]hat transpires in the court room is public property." *Craig* v. *Harney,* 331 US 367. The "unqualified prohibitions laid down by the framers were intended to give to liberty of the press . . . the broadest scope that could be countenanced in an orderly society." *Bridges* v. *State of California,* 314 US 252. And where there was "no threat or menace to the integrity of the trial," . . . we have consistently required that the press have a free hand, even though we sometimes deplored its sensationalism.

But the Court has also pointed out that "[l]egal trials are not like elections, to be won through the use of the meeting-hall, the radio, and the newspaper." . . . And the Court has insisted that no one be punished for a crime without "a charge fairly made and fairly tried in a public tribunal free of prejudice, passion, excitement, and tyrannical power." . . . "Freedom of discussion should be given the widest range compatible with the essential requirement of the fair and orderly administration of justice." . . . But it must not be allowed to divert the trial from the "very purpose of a court system . . . to adjudicate controversies, both criminal and civil, in the calmness and solemnity of the courtroom according to legal procedures." . . . Among these "legal procedures" is the requirement that the jury's verdict be based on evidence received in open court, not from outside sources. Thus, in *Marshall* v. *United States,* 360 US 310, we set aside a federal conviction where the jurors were exposed "through news accounts" to information that was not admitted at trial. We held that the prejudice from such material "may indeed be greater" than when it is part of the prosecution's evidence "for it is then not tempered by protective procedures." At the same time, we did not consider dispositive the statement of each juror "that he would not be influenced by the news articles, that he could decide the case only on the evidence of record, and that he felt no prejudice against petitioner as a result of the articles." Likewise, in *Irvin* v. *Dowd,* 366 US 717, even though each juror indicated that he could render an impartial verdict despite exposure to prejudicial newspapers articles, we set aside the conviction holding:

With his life at stake, it is not requiring too much that petitioner be tried in an atmosphere undisturbed by so huge a wave of public passion. . . .

The undeviating rule of this Court was expressed by Mr. Justice Holmes over half a century ago in *Patterson* v. *State of Colorado ex rel. Attorney General,* 205 US 454:

The theory of our system is that the conclusions to be reached in a case will be induced only by evidence and argument in open court, and not by any outside influence, whether of private talk or public print.

Moreover, "the burden of showing essential unfairness . . . as a demonstrable reality," . . . need not be undertaken when television has exposed the community "repeatedly and in depth to the spectacle of [the accused] personally confessing in detail to the crimes with which he was later to be charged." . . . In *Turner* v. *State of Louisiana,* 379 US 466, two key witnesses were deputy sheriffs who doubled as jury shepherds during the trial. The deputies swore that they had not talked to the jurors about the case, but the Court nonetheless held that,

. . . even if it could be assumed that the deputies never did discuss the case directly with any members of the jury, it would be blinking reality not to recognize the extreme prejudice inherent in this continual association. . . .

Only last Term in *Estes* v. *State of Texas,* 381 US 532, we set aside a conviction despite the absence of any showing of prejudice. We said there:

It is true that in most cases involving claims of due process deprivations we require a showing of identifiable prejudice to the accused. Nevertheless, at times a procedure employed by the State involves such a probability that prejudice will result that it is deemed inherently lacking in due process.

And we cited with approval the language of Mr. Justice Black for the Court in *In re Murchison,* 349 US 133, that "our system of law has always endeavored to prevent even the probability of unfairness."

V

It is clear that the totality of circumstances in this case also warrant such an approach. Unlike Estes, Sheppard was not granted a change of venue to a locale away from where the publicity originated; nor was his jury sequestered. The Estes jury saw none of the television broadcasts from the courtroom. On the contrary, the Sheppard jurors were subjected to newspaper, radio and television coverage of the trial while not taking part in the proceedings. They were allowed to go their separate ways outside of the courtroom, without adequate directions not to read or listen to anything concerning the case. The judge's "admonitions" at the beginning of the trial are representative:

I would suggest to you and caution you that you do not read any newspapers during the progress of this trial, that you do not listen to radio comments nor watch or listen to television comments, insofar as this case is concerned. You will feel very much better as the trial proceeds. . . . I am sure that we shall all feel very much better if we do not indulge in any newspaper reading or listening to any comments whatever about the matter while the case is in progress. After it is all over, you can read it all to your heart's content. . . .

At intervals during the trial, the judge simply repeated his "suggestions" and "requests" that the jury not expose themselves to comment upon the case. Moreover, the jurors were thrust into the role of celebrities by the judge's failure to insulate them from reporters and photographers. . . . The numerous pictures of the jurors, with their addresses, which appeared in the newspapers before and during the trial itself exposed them to expressions of opinion from both cranks and friends. The fact that anonymous letters had been received by prospective jurors should have made the judge aware that this publicity seriously threatened the jurors' privacy.

The press coverage of the Estes trial was not nearly as massive and pervasive as the attention given by the Cleveland newspapers and broadcasting stations to Sheppard's prosecution. Sheppard stood indicted for the murder of his wife; the State was demanding the death penalty. For months the virulent publicity about Sheppard and the murder had made the case notorious. Charges and countercharges were aired in the news media besides those of which Sheppard was called to trial. In addition, only three months before trial, Sheppard was examined for more than five hours without counsel during a three-day inquest which ended in a public brawl. The inquest was televised live from a high school gymnasium seating hundreds of people. Furthermore, the trial began two weeks before a hotly contested election at which both Chief Prosecutor Mahon and Judge Blythin were candidates for judgeships.

While we cannot say that Sheppard was denied due process by the judge's refusal to take precautions against the influence of pretrial publicity alone, the court's later rulings must be considered against the setting in which the trial was held. In light of this background, we believe that the arrangements made by the judge with the news media caused Sheppard to be deprived of that "judicial serenity and calm to which [he] was entitled." . . . The fact is that bedlam reigned at the courthouse during the trial and newsmen took over practically the entire courtroom, hounding most of the participants in the trial, especially Sheppard. At a temporary table within a few feet of the jury box and counsel table sat some 20 reporters staring at Sheppard and taking notes. The erection of a press table for reporters inside the bar is unprecedented. The bar of the court is reserved for counsel, providing them a safe place in which to keep papers and exhibits, and to confer privately with client and co-counsel. It is designed to protect the witness and the jury from any distractions, intrusions or influences, and to permit bench discussions of the judge's rulings away from the hearing of the public and the jury. Having assigned almost all of the available seats in the courtroom to the news media the judge lost his ability to supervise that environment. The movement of the reporters in and out of the courtroom caused frequent confusion and disruption of the trial. And the record reveals constant commotion within the bar. Moreover, the judge gave the throng of newsmen gathered in the corridors of the courthouse absolute free rein. Participants in the trial, including the jury, were forced to run a gantlet of reporters and photographers each time they entered or left the courtroom. The total lack of consideration for the privacy of the jury was demonstrated by the assignment to a broadcasting station of space next to the jury room on the floor above the courtroom, as well as the fact that jurors were allowed to make telephone calls during their five-day deliberation .

VI

There can be no question about the nature of the publicity which surrounded Sheppard's trial. We agree, as did the Court of Appeals, with the findings in Judge Bell's opinion for the Ohio Supreme Court:

> Murder and mystery, society, sex and suspense were combined in this case in such a manner as to intrigue and captivate the public fancy to a degree perhaps unparalleled in recent annals. Throughout the preindictment investigation, the subsequent legal skirmishes and the nine-week trial, circulation-conscious editors catered to the insatiable interest of the American public in the bizarre. . . . In this atmosphere of a "Roman holiday" for the news media, Sam Sheppard stood trial for his life.

Indeed, every court that has considered this case, save the court that tried it, has deplored the manner in which the news media inflamed and prejudiced the public.

Much of the material printed or broadcast during the trial was never heard from the witness stand, such as the charges that Sheppard had purposely impeded the murder investigation and must be guilty since he had hired a prominent criminal lawyer; that Sheppard was a perjurer; that he had sexual relations with numerous women; that his slain wife had characterized him as a "Jekyll-Hyde"; that he was "a bare-faced liar" because of his testimony as to police treatment; and finally that a woman convict claimed Sheppard to be the father of her illegitimate child. As the trial progressed, the newspapers summarized and interpreted the evidence, devoting particular attention to the material that incriminated Sheppard, and often drew unwarranted inferences from testimony. At one point, a front-page picture of Mrs. Sheppard's blood-stained pillow was published after being "doctored" to show more clearly an alleged imprint of a surgical instrument.

Nor is there doubt that this deluge of publicity reached at least some of the jury. On the only occasion that the jury was queried, two jurors admitted in open court to hearing the highly inflammatory charge that a prison inmate claimed Sheppard as the father of her illegitimate child. Despite the extent and nature of the publicity to which the jury was exposed during trial, the judge refused defense counsel's other requests that the jury be asked whether they had read or heard specific prejudicial comment about the case, including the incidents we have previously summarized. In these circumstances, we can assume that some of this material reached members of the jury. . . .

VII

The court's fundamental error is compounded by the holding that it lacked power to control the publicity about the trial. From the very inception of the proceedings the judge announced that neither he nor anyone else could restrict prejudicial news accounts. And he reiterated this view on numerous occasions. Since he viewed the news media as his target, the judge never considered other means that are often utilized to reduce the appearance of prejudicial material and to protect the jury from outside influence. We conclude that these procedures would have been sufficient to guarantee Sheppard a fair trial and so do not consider what sanctions might be available against a recalcitrant press nor the charges of bias now made against the state trial judge.

The carnival atmosphere at trial could easily have been avoided since the courtroom and courthouse premises are subject to the control of the court. As we stressed in *Estes,* the presence of the press at judicial proceedings must be limited when it is apparent that the accused might otherwise be prejudiced or disadvantaged. Bearing in mind the massive pretrial publicity, the judge should have adopted stricter rules governing the use of the courtroom by newsmen, as Sheppard's counsel requested. The number of reporters in the courtroom itself could have been limited at the first sign that their presence would disrupt the trial. They certainly should not have been placed inside the bar. Furthermore, the judge should have more closely regulated the conduct of newsmen in the courtroom. For instance, the judge belatedly asked them not to handle and photograph trial exhibits laying on the counsel table during recesses.

Secondly, the court should have insulated the witnesses. All of the newspapers and radio stations apparently interviewed prospective witnesses at will, and in many instances disclosed their testimony. A typical example was the publication of numerous statements by Susan Hayes, before her appearance in court, regarding her love affair with Sheppard. Although the witnesses were barred from the courtroom during the trial the full *verbatim* testimony was available to them in the press. This completely nullified the judge's imposition of the rule. . . .

Thirdly, the court should have made some effort to control the release of leads, information, and gossip to the press by police officers, witnesses, and the counsel for both sides. Much of the information thus disclosed was inaccurate, leading to groundless rumors and confusion. That the judge was aware of his responsibility in this respect may be seen from his warning to Steve Sheppard, the accused's brother, who had apparently made public statements in an attempt to discredit testimony for the prosecution. The judge made this statement in the presence of the jury:

Now, the court wants to say a word. That he was told—he has not read anything about it at all—but he was informed that Dr. Steve Sheppard, who has been granted the privilege of remaining in the courtroom during the trial, has been trying the case in the newspapers and making rather uncomplimentary comments about the testimony of the witnesses for the State.

Let it be now understood that ir Dr. Steve Sheppard wishes to use the newspapers to try his case while we are trying it here, he will be barred from remaining in the courtroom during the progress of the trial if he is to be a witness in the case.

The Court appreciates he cannot deny Steve Sheppard the right of free speech, but he can deny him the . . . privilege of being in the courtroom, if he wants to avail himself of that method during the progress of the trial.

Defense counsel immediately brought to the court's attention the tremendous amount of publicity in the Cleveland press that "misrepresented entirely the testimony" in the case. Under such circumstances, the judge should have at least warned the newspapers to check the accuracy of their accounts. And it is obvious that the judge should have further sought to alleviate this problem by imposing control over the statements made to the news media by counsel, witnesses, and especially the Coroner and police officers. The prosecution repeatedly made evidence available to the news media which was never offered in the trial. Much of the "evidence" disseminated in this fashion was clearly inadmissable. The exclusion of such evidence in court is rendered meaningless when a news media makes it available to the public. For example, the publicity about Sheppard's refusal to take a lie detector test came directly from police officers and the Coroner. The story that Sheppard had been called a "Jekyll-Hyde" personality by his wife was attributed to a prosecution witness. No such testimony was given. The further report that there was "a 'bombshell witness' on tap" who would testify as to Sheppard's "fiery temper" could only have emanated from the prosecution. Moreover, the newspapers described in detail clues that had been found by the police, but not put into the record.

The fact that many of the prejudicial news items can be traced to the prosecution, as well as the defense, aggravates the judge's failure to take any action. . . . Effective control of these sources—concededly within the court's power—might well have prevented the divulgence of inaccurate information, rumors, and accusations that made up much of the inflammatory publicity, at least after Sheppard's indictment.

More specifically, the trial court might well have proscribed extra-judicial statements by any lawyer, party, witness, or court official which divulged prejudicial matters, such as the refusal of Sheppard to submit to interrogation or take any lie detector tests; any statement made by Sheppard to officials; the identity of prospective witnesses or their probable testimony; any belief in guilt or innocence; or like statements concerning the merits of the case. . . . Being advised of the great public interest in the case, the mass coverage of the press, and the potential prejudicial impact of publicity, the court could also have requested the appropriate city and county officials to promulgate a regulation with respect to dissemination of information about the case by their employees. In addition, reporters who wrote or broadcasted prejudicial stories, could have been warned as to the impropriety of publishing material not introduced in the proceedings. The judge was put on notice of such events by defense counsel's complaint about the WHK broadcast on the second day of trial. See p. 1513, supra. In this manner, Sheppard's right to a trial free from outside interference would have been given added protection without corresponding curtailment of the news media. Had the judge, the other officers of the court, and the police placed the interest of justice first, the news media would have soon learned to be content with the task of reporting the case as it unfolded in the courtroom—not pieced together from extra-judicial statements.

From the cases coming here we note that unfair and prejudicial news comment on pending trials has become increasingly prevalent. Due process requires that the accused receive a trial by an impartial jury free from outside influences. Given the pervasiveness of modern communications and the difficulty of effacing prejudicial publicity from the minds of the jurors, the trial courts must take strong measures to ensure that the balance is never weighed against the accused. And appellate tribunals have the duty to make an independent evaluation of the circumstances. Of course, there is nothing that proscribes the press from reporting events that transpire in the courtroom. But where there is a reasonable likelihood that prejudicial news prior to trial will prevent a fair trial, the judge should continue the case until the threat abates, or transfer it to another county not so permeated with publicity. In addition, sequestration of the jury was something the judge should have raised *sua sponte* with counsel. If publicity during the proceedings threatens the fairness of the trial, a new trial should be ordered. But we must remember that reversals are but palliatives; the cure lies in those remedial measures that will prevent the prejudice at its inception. The courts must take such steps by rule and regulation that will protect their processes from prejudicial outside interferences. Neither prosecutors, counsel for defense, the accused, witnesses, court staff nor enforcement officers coming under the jurisdiction of the court should be permitted to frustrate its function. Collaboration between counsel and the press as to information affecting the fairness of a criminal trial is not only subject to regulation, but is highly censurable and worthy of disciplinary measures.

Since the state trial judge did not fulfill his duty to protect Sheppard from the inherently prejudicial publicity which saturated the community and to control disruptive influences in the courtroom, we must reverse the denial of the habeas petition. The case is remanded to the District Court with instructions to issue the writ and order that Sheppard be released from custody unless the State puts him to its charges again within a reasonable time.

It is so ordered.

11. Rights of Juvenile Offenders

Re GAULT
387 US 1 (1967)

[A 15-year-old boy was committed as a juvenile delinquent to a state industrial school in Arizona for the period of his minority, after the boy had been taken into custody by the sheriff without notice to his parents. When his mother went to the detention home, she was told that there would be a hearing the next day in the juvenile court. Neither the boy nor his parents were shown the petition filed on the hearing day; the petition made no reference to the factual basis for the judicial action; at the hearing, no one was sworn and no complaining witness appeared; an officer stated that the boy had made certain admissions, but not in the presence of his parents and without counsel and without being advised of his right to silence; nor was the boy notified of his right to be represented by counsel. The boy's parents filed a petition for habeas corpus, which was dismissed by the state courts. On appeal, the Supreme Court reversed.

[In his opinion for five Justices, Justice Fortas held that the boy had been denied due process of law; that juvenile delinquency proceedings must measure up to the essentials of due process and fair treatment. The opinion details the more significant requirements of fair treatment. Justices Black and White wrote concurring opinions; Justice Harlan concurred in part and dissented in part; Justice Stewart wrote a dissenting opinion.]

Mr. Justice Fortas delivered the opinion of the Court:

This is an appeal under 28 U.S.C. § 1257(2) from a judgment of the Supreme Court of Arizona affirming the dismissal of a petition for a writ of habeas corpus. The petition sought the release of Gerald Francis Gault, petitioners' 15-year-old son, who had been committed as a juvenile delinquent to the State Industrial School by the Juvenile Court of Gila County, Arizona. The Supreme Court of Arizona affirmed dismissal of the writ against various arguments which included an attack upon the constitutionality of the Arizona Juvenile Code because of its alleged denial of procedural due process rights to juveniles charged with being "delinquents." The court agreed that the constitutional guarantee of due process of law is applicable in such proceedings. It held that Arizona's Juvenile Code is to be read as "impliedly" implementing the "due process concept." It then proceeded to identify and describe "the particular elements which constitute due process in a juvenile hearing." It concluded that the proceedings ending in commitment of Gerald Gault did not offend those requirements. We do not agree, and we reverse. We begin with a statement of the facts.

I

On Monday, June 8, 1964, at about 10 A.M., Gerald Francis Gault and a friend, Ronald Lewis, were taken into custody by the Sheriff of Gila County. Gerald was then still subject to a six months' probation order which had been entered on February 25, 1964, as a result of his having been in the company of another boy who had stolen a wallet from a lady's purse. The police action on June 8 was taken as the result of a verbal complaint by a neighbor of the boys, Mrs. Cook, about a telephone call made to her in which the caller or callers made lewd or indecent remarks. It will suffice for purposes of this opinion to say that the remarks or questions put to her were of the irritatingly offensive, adolescent, sex variety.

At the time Gerald was picked up, his mother and father were both at work. No notice that Gerald was being taken into custody was left at the home. No other steps were taken to advise them that their son had, in effect, been arrested. Gerald was taken to the Children's Detention Home. When his mother arrived home at about

6 o'clock, Gerald was not there. Gerald's older brother was sent to look for him at the trailer home of the Lewis family. He apparently learned then that Gerald was in custody. He so informed his mother. The two of them went to the Detention Home. The deputy probation officer, Flagg, who was also superintendent of the Detention Home, told Mrs. Gault "why Jerry was there" and said that a hearing would be held in Juvenile Court at 3 o'clock the following day, June 9.

Officer Flagg filed a petition with the Court on the hearing day, June 9, 1964. It was not served on the Gaults. Indeed, none of them saw this petition until the habeas corpus hearing on August 17, 1964. The petition was entirely formal. It made no reference to any factual basis for the judicial action which it initiated. It recited only that "said minor is under the age of 18 years and in need of the protection of this Honorable Court [and that] said minor is a delinquent minor." It prayed for a hearing and an order regarding "the care and custody of said minor." Officer Flagg executed a formal affidavit in support of the petition.

On June 9, Gerald, his mother, his older brother, and Probation Officers Flagg and Henderson appeared before the Juvenile Judge in chambers. Gerald's father was not there. He was at work out of the city. Mrs. Cook, the complainant, was not there. No one was sworn at this hearing. No transcript or recording was made. No memorandum or record of the substance of the proceedings was prepared. Our information about the proceedings and the subsequent hearing on June 15, derives entirely from the testimony of the Juvenile Court Judge, Mr. and Mrs. Gault and Officer Flagg at the habeas corpus proceedings conducted two months later. From this, it appears that at the July 9 hearing Gerald was questioned by the judge about the telephone call. There was conflict as to what he said. His mother recalled that Gerald said he only dialed Mrs. Cook's number and handed the telephone to his friend, Ronald. Officer Flagg recalled that Gerald had admitted making the lewd remarks. Judge McGhee testified that Gerald "admitted making one of these [lewd] statements." At the conclusion of the hearing, the judge said he would "think about it." Gerald was taken back to the Detention Home. He was not sent to his own home with his parents. On June 11 or 12, after having been detained since June 8, Gerald was released and driven home. There is no explanation in the record as to why he was kept in the Detention Home or why he was released. At 5 P.M. on the day of Gerald's release, Mrs. Gault received a note signed by Officer Flagg. It was on plain paper, not letterhead. Its entire text was as follows:

"Mrs. Gault:

"Judge McGHEE has set Monday June 15, 1964 at 11:00 A.M. as the date and time for further Hearings on Gerald's delinquency

/s/ Flagg"

At the appointed time on Monday, June 15, Gerald, his father and mother, Ronald Lewis and his father, and Officers Flagg and Henderson were present before Judge McGhee. Witnesses at the habeas corpus proceeding differed in their recollections of Gerald's testimony at the June 15 hearing. Mr. and Mrs. Gault recalled that Gerald again testified that he had only dialed the number and that the other boy had made the remarks. Officer Flagg agreed that at this hearing Gerald did not admit making the lewd remarks. But Judge McGhee recalled that "there was some admission again of some of the lewd statements. He—he didn't admit any of the more serious lewd statements." Again, the complainant, Mrs. Cook, was not present. Mrs. Gault asked that Mrs. Cook be present "so she could see which boy had done the talking, the dirty talking over the phone." The Juvenile Judge said "she didn't have to be present at that hearing." The judge did not speak to Mrs. Cook or communicate with her at any time. Probation Officer Flagg had talked to her once— over the telephone on June 9.

At this June 15 hearing a "referral report" made by the probation officers was filed with the court, although not disclosed to Gerald or his parents. This listed the charge as "Lewd Phone Calls." At the conclusion of the hearing, the judge committed Gerald as a juvenile delinquent to the State Industrial School "for the period of his minority [that is, until 21], unless sooner discharged by due process of law." An order to that effect was entered. It recites that "after a full hearing and due deliberation the Court finds that said minor is a delinquent child, and that said minor is of the age of 15 years."

No appeal is permitted by Arizona law in juvenile cases. On August 3, 1964, a petition for a writ of habeas corpus was filed with the Supreme Court of Arizona and referred by it to the Superior Court for hearing.

At the habeas corpus hearing on August 17, Judge McGhee was vigorously cross-examined as to the basis for his actions. He testified that he had taken into account the fact that Gerald was on probation. He was asked "under what section of . . . the code you found the boy delinquent?"

His answer is set forth in the margin.* In substance, he concluded that Gerald came within ARS § 8–201, subsec. 6(a), which specifies that a "delinquent child" includes one "who has violated a law of the state or an ordinance or regulation of a political subdivision thereof." The law which Gerald was found to have violated is ARS § 13–377. This section of the Arizona Criminal Code provides that a person who "in the presence of or hearing of any woman or child . . . uses vulgar, abusive or obscene language, is guilty of a misdemeanor. . . ." The penalty specified in the Criminal Code, which would apply to an adult, is $5 to $50, or imprisonment for not more than two months. The judge also testified that he acted under ARS § 8–201, subsec. 6(d) which includes in the definition of a "delinquent child" one who, as the judge phrased it, is "habitually involved in immoral matters."

Asked about the basis for his conclusion that Gerald was "habitually involved in immoral matters," the judge testified, somewhat vaguely, that two years earlier, on July 2, 1962, a "referral" was made concerning Gerald, "where the boy had stolen a baseball glove from another boy and lied to the Police Department about it." The judge said there was "no hearing," and "no accusation" relating to this incident, "because of lack of material foundation." But it seems to have remained in

---

* "Q. All right. Now, Judge, would you tell me under what section of the law or tell me under what section of—of the code you found the boy delinquent?

"A. Well, there is a—I think it amounts to disturbing the peace. I can't give you the section, but I can tell you the law, that when one person uses lewd language in the presence of another person, that it can amount to—and I consider that when a person makes it over the phone, that it is considered in the presence, I might be wrong, that is one section. The other section upon which I consider the boy delinquent is Section 8–201, Subsection (d), habitually involved in immoral matters."

his mind as a relevant factor. The judge also testified that Gerald had admitted making other nuisance phone calls in the past which, as the judge recalled the boy's testimony, were "silly calls, or funny calls, or something like that."

The Superior Court dismissed the writ, and appellants sought review in the Arizona Supreme Court. That court stated that it considered appellants' assignments of error as urging (1) that the Juvenile Code, ARS § 8–201 to § 8–239, is unconstitutional because it does not require that parents and children be apprised of the specific charges, does not require proper notice of a hearing, and does not provide for an appeal; and (2) that the proceedings and order relating to Gerald constituted a denial of due process of law because of the absence of adequate notice of the charge and the hearing; failure to notify appellants of certain constitutional rights including the rights to counsel and to confrontation, and the privilege against self-incrimination; the use of unsworn hearsay testimony; and the failure to make a record of the proceedings. Appellants further asserted that it was error for the Juvenile Court to remove Gerald from the custody of his parents without a showing and finding of their unsuitability, and alleged a miscellany of other errors under state law.

The Supreme Court handed down an elaborate and wide-ranging opinion affirming dismissal of the writ and stating the court's conclusions as to the issues raised by appellants and other aspects of the juvenile process. In their jurisdictional statement and brief in this Court, appellants do not urge upon us all of the points passed upon by the Supreme Court of Arizona. They urge that we hold the Juvenile Code of Arizona invalid on its face or as applied in this case because, contrary to the Due Process Clause of the Fourteenth Amendment, the juvenile is taken from the custody of his parents and committed to a state institution pursuant to proceedings in which the Juvenile Court has virtually unlimited discretion, and in which the following basic rights are denied:

1. Notice to the charges;
2. Right to counsel;
3. Right to confrontation and cross-examination;
4. Privilege against self-incrimination;
5. Right to a transcript of the proceedings; and
6. Right to appellate review.

We shall not consider other issues which were passed upon by the Supreme Court of Arizona. We emphasize that we indicate no opinion as to whether the decision of that court with respect to such other issues does or does not conflict with requirements of the Federal Constitution.

II

The Supreme Court of Arizona held that due process of law is requisite to the constitutional validity of proceedings in which a court reaches the conclusion that a juvenile has been at fault, has engaged in conduct prohibited by law, or has otherwise misbehaved with the consequence that he is committed to an institution in which his freedom is curtailed. This conclusion is in accord with the decisions of a number of courts under both federal and state constitutions.

This Court has not heretofore decided the precise question. In *Kent* v. *United*

States, 383 US 541, we considered the requirements for a valid waiver of the "exclusive" jurisdiction of the Juvenile Court of the District of Columbia so that a juvenile could be tried in the adult criminal court of the District. Although our decision turned upon the language of the statute, we emphasized the necessity that "the basic requirements of due process and fairness" be satisfied in such proceedings. *Haley* v. *State of Ohio,* 332 US 596, involved the admissibility, in a state criminal court of general jurisdiction, of a confession by a 15-year-old boy. The Court held that the Fourteenth Amendment applied to prohibit the use of the coerced confession. Mr. Justice Douglas said, "Neither man nor child can be allowed to stand condemned by methods which flout constitutional requirements of due process of law." . . . Accordingly, while these cases relate only to restricted aspects of the subject, they unmistakably indicate that, whatever may be their precise impact, neither the Fourteenth Amendment nor the Bill of Rights is for adults alone.

We do not in this opinion consider the impact of these constitutional provisions upon the totality of the relationship of the juvenile and the state. We do not even consider the entire process relating to juvenile "delinquents." For example, we are not here concerned with the procedures or constitutional rights applicable to the pre-judicial stages of the juvenile process, nor do we direct our attention to the post-adjudicative or dispositional process. We consider only the problems presented to us by this case. These relate to the proceedings by which a determination is made as to whether a juvenile is a "delinquent" as a result of alleged misconduct on his part, with the consequence that he may be committed to a state institution. As to these proceedings, there appears to be little current dissent from the proposition that the Due Process Clause has a role to play. The problem is to ascertain the precise impact of the due process requirement upon such proceedings.

From the inception of the juvenile court system, wide differences have been tolerated—indeed insisted upon—between the procedural rights accorded to adults and those of juveniles. In practically all jurisdictions, there are rights granted to adults which are withheld from juveniles. In addition to the specific problems involved in the present case, for example, it has been held that the juvenile is not entitled to bail, to indictment by grand jury, to a public trial or to trial by jury. It is frequent practice that rules governing the arrest and interrogation of adults by the police are not observed in the case of juveniles.

The history and theory underlying this development are well-known, but a recapitulation is necessary for purposes of this opinion. The juvenile court movement began in this country at the end of the last century. From the juvenile court statute adopted in Illinois in 1899, the system has spread to every State in the Union, the District of Columbia, and Puerto Rico. The constitutionality of juvenile court laws has been sustained in over 40 jurisdictions against a variety of attacks.

The early reformers were appalled by adult procedures and penalties, and by the fact that children could be given long prison sentences and mixed in jails with hardened criminals. They were profoundly convinced that society's duty to the child could not be confined by the concept of justice alone. They believed that society's role was not to ascertain whether the child was "guilty" or "innocent," but "What is he, how has he become what he is, and what had best be done in his interest and in the interest of the state to save him from a downward career." The child—

essentially good, as they saw it—was to be made "to feel that he is the object of [the State's] care and solicitude," not that he was under arrest or on trial. The rules of criminal procedure were therefore altogether inapplicable. The apparent rigidities, technicalities, and harshness which they observed in both substantive and procedural criminal law were therefore to be discarded. The idea of crime and punishment was to be abandoned. The child was to be "treated" and "rehabilitated" and the procedures, from apprehension through institutionalization, were to be "clinical" rather than punitive.

These results were to be achieved, without coming to conceptual and constitutional grief, by insisting that the proceedings were not adversary, but that the State was proceeding as *parens patriae*. The Latin phrase proved to be a great help to those who sought to rationalize the exclusion of juveniles from the constitutional scheme; but its meaning is murky and its historic credentials are of dubious relevance. The phrase was taken from chancery practice, where, however, it was used to describe the power of the State to act *in loco parentis* for the purpose of protecting the property interests and the person of the child. But there is no trace of the doctrine in the history of criminal jurisprudence. At common law, children under seven were considered incapable of possessing criminal intent. Beyond that age, they were subjected to arrest, trial, and in theory to punishment like adult offenders. In these old days, the State was not deemed to have authority to accord them fewer procedural rights than adults.

The right of the State, as *parens patriae,* to deny to the child procedural rights available to his elders was elaborated by the assertion that a child, unlike an adult, has a right "not to liberty but to custody." He can be made to attorn to his parents, to go to school, etc. If his parents default in effectively performing their custodial functions—that is, if the child is "delinquent"—the state may intervene. In doing so, it does not deprive the child of any rights, because he has none. It merely provides the "custody" to which the child is entitled. On this basis, proceedings involving juveniles were described as "civil" not "criminal" and therefore not subject to the requirements which restrict the state when it seeks to deprive a person of his liberty.

Accordingly, the highest motives and most enlightened impulses led to a peculiar system for juveniles, unknown to our law in any comparable context. The constitutional and theoretical basis for this peculiar system is—to say the least—debatable. And in practice, as we remarked in the *Kent* case, *supra,* the results have not been entirely satisfactory. Juvenile court history has again demonstrated that unbridled discretion, however benevolently motivated, is frequently a poor substitute for principle and procedure. In 1937, Dean Pound wrote: "The powers of the Star Chamber were a trifle in comparison with those of our juvenile courts. . . ." The absence of substantive standards has not necessarily meant that children receive careful, compassionate, individualized treatment. The absence of procedural rules based upon constitutional principle has not always produced fair, efficient, and effective procedures. Departures from established principles of due process have frequently resulted not in enlightened procedure, but in arbitrariness. The Chairman of the Pennsylvania Council of Juvenile Court Judges has recently observed: "Unfortunately, loose procedures, high-handed methods and crowded court calendars, either singly or in combination, all too often, have resulted in depriving some juveniles of fundamental rights that have resulted in a denial of due process."

Failure to observe the fundamental requirements of due process has resulted in instances, which might have been avoided, of unfairness to individuals and inadequate or inaccurate findings of fact and unfortunate prescriptions of remedy. Due process of law is the primary and indispensable foundation of individual freedom. It is the basic and essential term in the social compact which defines the rights of the individual and delimits the powers which the State may exercise. As Mr. Justice Frankfurter has said: "The history of American freedom is, in no small measure, the history of procedure." But, in addition, the procedural rules which have been fashioned from the generality of due process are our best instruments for the distillation and evaluation of essential facts from the conflicting welter of data that life and our adversary methods present. It is these instruments of due process which enhance the possibility that truth will emerge from the confrontation of opposing versions and conflicting data. "Procedure is to law what 'scientific method' is to science."

It is claimed that juveniles obtain benefits from the special procedures applicable to them which more than offset the disadvantages of denial of the substance of normal due process. As we shall discuss, the observance of due process standards, intelligently and not ruthlessly administered, will not compel the States to abandon or displace any of the substantive benefits of the juvenile process. But it is important, we think, that the claimed benefits of the juvenile process should be candidly appraised. Neither sentiment nor folklore should cause us to shut our eyes, for example, to such startling findings as that reported in an exceptionally reliable study of repeaters or recidivism conducted by the Stanford Research Institute for the President's Commission on Crime in the District of Columbia. This Commission's Report states:

> In fiscal 1966 approximately 66 percent of the 16- and 17-year-old juveniles referred to the court by the Youth Aid Division had been before the court previously. In 1965, 56 percent of those in the Receiving Home were repeaters. The SRI study revealed that 61 percent of the sample Juvenile Court referrals in 1965 had been previously referred at least once and that 42 percent had been referred at least twice before.

Certainly, these figures and the high crime rates among juveniles to which we have referred, could not lead us to conclude that the absence of constitutional protections reduces crime, or that the juvenile system, functioning free of constitutional inhibitions as it has largely done, is effective to reduce crime or rehabilitate offenders. We do not mean by this to denigrate the juvenile court process or to suggest that there are not aspects of the juvenile system relating to offenders which are valuable. But the features of the juvenile system which its proponents have asserted are of unique benefit will not be impaired by constitutional domestication. For example, the commendable principles relating to the processing and treatment of juveniles separately from adults are in no way involved or affected by the procedural issues under discussion. Further, we are told that one of the important benefits of the special juvenile court procedures is that they avoid classifying the juvenile as a "criminal." The juvenile offender is now classed as a "delinquent." There is, of course, no reason why this should not continue. It is disconcerting, however, that this term has come to involve only slightly less stigma than the term "criminal" applied to adults. It is also emphasized that in practically all jurisdictions, statutes provide that an adjudication of the child as a delinquent shall not operate as a civil disability or disqualify him for civil service appointment. There is no reason why the application of due process requirements should interfere with such provisions.

Beyond this, it is frequently said that juveniles are protected by the process from disclosure of their deviational behavior. As the Supreme Court of Arizona phrased it in the present case, the summary procedures of juvenile courts are sometimes defended by a statement that it is the law's policy "to hide youthful errors from the full gaze of the public and bury them in the graveyard of the forgotten past." This claim of secrecy, however, is more rhetoric than reality. Disclosure of court records is discretionary with the judge in most jurisdictions. Statutory restrictions almost invariably apply only to the court records, and even as to those the evidence is that many courts routinely furnish information to the FBI and the military, and on request to government agencies and even to private employers. Of more importance are police records. In most States the police keep a complete file of juvenile "police contacts" and have complete discretion as to disclosure of juvenile records. Police departments receive requests for information from the FBI and other law-enforcement agencies, the Armed Forces, and social service agencies, and most of them generally comply. Private employers word their application forms to produce information concerning juvenile arrests and court proceedings, and in some jurisdictions information concerning juvenile police contacts is furnished private employers as well as government agencies.

In any event, there is no reason why, consistently with due process, a State cannot continue if it deems it appropriate, to provide and to improve provision for the confidentiality of records of police contacts and court action relating to juveniles. It is interesting to note, however, that the Arizona Supreme Court used the confidentiality argument as a justification for the type of notice which is here attacked as inadequate for due process purposes. The parents were given merely general notice that their child was charged with "delinquency." No facts were specified. The Arizona court held, however, as we shall discuss, that in addition to this general "notice," the child and his parents must be advised "of the facts involved in the case" no later than the initial hearing by the judge. Obviously, this does not "bury" the word about the child's transgressions. It merely defers the time of disclosure to a point when it is of limited use to the child or his parents in preparing his defense or explanation.

Further, it is urged that the juvenile benefits from informal proceedings in the court. The early conception of the juvenile court proceeding was one in which a fatherly judge touched the heart and conscience of the erring youth by talking over his problems, by paternal advice and admonition, and in which, in extreme situations, benevolent and wise institutions of the State provided guidance and help "to save him from a downward career." Then, as now, goodwill and compassion were admirably prevalent. But recent studies have, with surprising unanimity, entered sharp dissent as to the validity of this gentle conception. They suggest that the appearance as well as the actuality of fairness, impartiality and orderliness—in short, the essentials of due process may be a more impressive and more therapeutic attitude so far as the juvenile is concerned. For example, in a recent study, the sociologists Wheeler and Cottrell observe that when the procedural laxness of the *"parens patriae"* attitude is followed by stern disciplining, the contrast may have an adverse effect upon the child, who feels that he has been deceived or enticed. They conclude as follows: "Unless appropriate due process of law is followed, even the juvenile who has violated the law may not feel that he is being fairly treated and may therefore resist the rehabilitative efforts of court personnel." Of course, it is not suggested that juvenile court judges should fail appropriately to take account, in their demeanor and conduct, of the emotional and psychological attitude of the juveniles with whom they are confronted. While due process requirements will, in some instances, introduce a degree of order and regularity to juvenile court proceedings to determine delinquency, and in contested cases will introduce some elements of the adversary system, nothing will require that the conception of the kindly juvenile judge be replaced by its opposite, nor do we here rule upon the question whether ordinary due process requirements must be observed with respect to hearings to determine the disposition of the delinquent child.

Ultimately, however, we confront the reality of that portion of the juvenile court process with which we deal in this case. A boy is charged with misconduct. The boy is committed to an institution where he may be restrained of liberty for years. It is of no constitutional consequence—and of limited practical meaning—that the institution to which he is committed is called an Industrial School. The fact of the matter is that, however euphemistic the title, a "receiving home" or an "industrial school" for juveniles is an institution of confinement in which the child is incarcerated for a greater or lesser time. His world becomes "a building with white-washed walls, regimented routine and institutional laws. . . ." Instead of mother and father and sisters and brothers and friends and classmates, his world is peopled by guards, custodians, state employees, and "delinquents" confined with him for anything from waywardness to rape and homicide.

In view of this, it would be extraordinary if our Constitution did not require the procedural regularity and the exercise of care implied in the phrase "due process." Under our Constitution, the condition of being a boy does not justify a kangaroo court. The traditional ideas of juvenile court procedure, indeed, contemplated that time would be available and care would be used to establish precisely what the juvenile did and why he did it—was it a prank of adolescence or a brutal act threatening serious consequences to himself or society unless corrected? Under traditional notions, one would assume that in a case like that of Gerald Gault, where the juvenile appears to have a home, a working mother and father, and an older brother, the Juvenile Judge would have made a careful inquiry and judgment as to the possibility that the boy could be disciplined and dealt with at home, despite his previous transgressions. Indeed, so far as appears in the record before us, except for some conversation with Gerald about his school work and his "wanting to go to . . . Grand Canyon with his father," the points to which the judge directed his attention were little different from those that would be involved in determining any charge of violation of a penal statute. The essential difference between Gerald's case and a normal criminal case is that safeguards available to adults were discarded in Gerald's case. The summary procedure as well as the long commitment were possible because Gerald was 15 years of age instead of over 18.

If Gerald had been over 18, he would not have been subject to Juvenile Court proceedings. For the particular offense immediately involved, the maximum punishment would have been a fine of $5 to $50, or imprisonment in jail for not more than two months. Instead, he was committed to custody for a maximum of six years. If he had been over 18 and had committed an offense to which such a sentence might apply, he would have been entitled to substantial rights under the Constitution of the United States as well as under Arizona's laws and constitution. The United States Constitution would guarantee him rights and protections with respect to arrest, search, and seizure, and pretrial interrogation. It would assure him of specific notice of the charges and adequate time to decide his course of action and to prepare his defense. He would be entitled to clear advice that he could be represented by counsel, and, at least if a felony were involved, the State would be required to provide counsel if his parents were unable to afford it. If the court acted on the basis of his confession, careful procedures would be required to assure its voluntariness. If the case went to trial, confrontation and opportunity for cross-examination would be guaranteed. So wide a gulf between the State's treatment of the adult and of the child requires a bridge sturdier than mere verbiage, and reasons more persuasive than cliché can provide. As Wheeler and Cottrell have put it, "The rhetoric of the juvenile court movement has developed without any necessarily close correspondence to the realities of court and institutional routines."

In *Kent* v. *United States, supra,* we stated that the Juvenile Court Judge's exercise of the power of the State as *parens patriae* was not unlimited. We said that "the admonition to function in a 'parental' relationship is not an invitation to procedural arbitrariness." With respect to the waiver by the juvenile court to the adult of jurisdiction over an offense committed by a youth, we said that "there is no place in our system of law for reaching a result of such tremendous consequences without ceremony—without hearing, without effective assistance of counsel, without a statement of reasons." We announced with respect to such waiver proceedings that while "We do not mean . . . to indicate that the hearing to be held must conform with all of the requirements of a criminal trial or even of the usual administrative hearing; but we do hold that the hearing must measure up to the essentials of due process and fair treatment." We reiterate this view, here in connection with a juvenile court adjudication of "delinquency," as a requirement which is part of the Due Process Clause of the Fourteenth Amendment of our Constitution.

We now turn to the specific issues which are presented to us in the present case.

III
NOTICE OF CHARGES

Appellants allege that the Arizona Juvenile Code is unconstitutional or alternatively that the proceedings before the Juvenile Court were constitutionally defective because of failure to provide adequate notice of the hearings. No notice was given to Gerald's parents when he was taken into custody on Monday, June 8. On that night, when Mrs. Gault went to the Detention Home, she was orally informed that there would be a hearing the next afternoon and was told the reason why Gerald was in custody. The only written notice Gerald's parents received at any time was a note on plain paper from Officer Flagg delivered on Thursday or Friday, June 11 or 12, to the effect that the judge had set Monday, June 15, "for further hearings on Gerald's delinquency."

A "petition" was filed with the court on June 9 by Officer Flagg, reciting only that he was informed and believed that "said minor is a delinquent minor and that it is necessary that some order be made by the Honorable Court for said minor's welfare." The applicable Arizona statute provides for a petition to be filed in Juvenile Court, alleging in general terms that the child is "neglected, dependent, or delinquent." The statute explicitly states that such a general allegation is sufficient, "without alleging the facts." There is no requirement that the petition be served and it was not served upon, given, or shown to Gerald or his parents.

The Supreme Court of Arizona rejected appellants' claim that due process was denied because of inadequate notice. It stated that "Mrs. Gault knew the exact nature of the charge against Gerald from the day he was taken to the detention home." The court also pointed out that the Gaults appeared at the two hearings "without objection." The court held that because "the policy of the juvenile law is to hide youthful errors from the full gaze of the public and bury them in the graveyard of the forgotten past," advance notice of the specific charges or basis for taking the juvenile into custody and for the hearing is not necessary. It held that the appropriate rule is that "the infant and his parents or guardian will receive a petition only reciting a conclusion of delinquency. But no later than the initial hearing by the judge, they must be advised of the facts involved in the case. If the charges are denied, they must be given a reasonable period of time to prepare."

We cannot agree with the court's conclusion that adequate notice was given in this case. Notice, to comply with due process requirements, must be given sufficiently in advance of scheduled court proceedings so that reasonable opportunity to prepare will be afforded, and it must "set forth the alleged misconduct with particularity." It is obvious, as we have discussed above, that no purpose of shielding the child from the public stigma of knowledge of his having been taken into custody and scheduled for hearing is served by the procedure appoved by the court below. The "initial hearing" in the present case was a hearing on the merits. Notice at that time is not timely; and even if there were a conceivable purpose served by the deferral proposed by the court below, it would have to yield to the requirements that the child and his parents or guardian be notified, in writing, of the specific charge or factual allegations to be considered at the hearing, and that such written notice be given at the earliest practicable time, and in any event sufficiently in advance of the hearing to permit preparation. Due process of law requires notice of the sort we have described—that is, notice which would be deemed constitutionally adequate in a civil or criminal proceeding. It does not allow a hearing to be held in which a youth's freedom and his parents' right to his custody are at stake without giving them timely notice, in advance of the hearing, of the specific issues that they must meet. Nor, in the circumstances of this case, can it reasonably be said that the requirement of notice was waived.

IV
RIGHT TO COUNSEL

Appellants charge that the Juvenile Court proceedings were fatally defective because the court did not advise Gerald or his parents of their right to counsel, and proceeded with the hearing, the adjudication of delinquency and the order of commitment in the absence of counsel for the child and his parents or an express waiver of the right thereto. The Supreme Court of Arizona pointed out that "[t]here is disagreement [among the various jurisdictions] as to whether the court must advise the infant that he has a right to counsel." It noted its own decision in *Arizona State Dept. of Public Welfare* v. *Barlow,* 80 Ariz. 249, 296 P.2d 298 (1956), to the effect "that *the parents* of an infant in a juvenile proceeding cannot be denied representation by counsel of their choosing." (Emphasis added.) It referred to a provision of the Juvenile Code which it characterized as requiring "that the probation officer shall look after the interests of neglected, delinquent and dependent children," including representing their interests in court. The court argued that "The parent and the probation officer may be relied upon to protect the infant's interests." Accordingly it rejected the proposition that "due process requires that an infant have a right to counsel." It said that juvenile courts have the discretion, but not the duty, to allow such representation; it referred specifically to the situation in which the Juvenile Court discerns conflict between the child and his parents as an instance in which this discretion might be exercised. We do not agree. Probation officers, in the Arizona scheme, are also arresting officers. They initiate proceedings and file petitions which they verify, as here, alleging the delinquency of the child; and they testify, as here, against the child. And here the probation officer was also superintendent of the Detention Home. The probation officer cannot act as counsel for the child. His role in the adjudicatory hearing, by statute and in fact, is as arresting officer and witness against the child. Nor can the judge represent the child. There is no material difference in this respect between adult and juvenile proceedings of the sort here involved. In adult proceedings, this contention has been foreclosed by decisions of this Court. A proceeding where the issue is whether the child will be found to be "delinquent" and subjected to the loss of his liberty for years is comparable in seriousness to a felony prosecution. The juvenile needs the assistance of counsel to cope with problems of law, to make skilled inquiry into the facts, to insist upon regularity of the proceedings, and to ascertain whether he has a defense and to prepare and submit it. The child "requires the guiding hand of counsel at every step in the proceedings against him." Just as in *Kent* v. *United States, supra,* 383 US, at 561–562, 86 S.Ct., at 1057–1058, we indicated our agreement with the United States Court of Appeals for the District of Columbia Circuit that the assistance of counsel is essential for purposes of waiver proceedings, so we hold now that it is equally essential for the determination of delinquency, carrying with it the awesome prospect of incarceration in a state institution until the juvenile reaches the age of 21.

During the last decade, court decisions, experts, and legislatures have demonstrated increasing recognition of this view. In at least one-third of the States, statutes now provide for the right of representation by retained counsel in juvenile delinquency proceedings, notice of the right, or assignment of counsel, or a combination of these. In other States, court rules have simliar provisions.

The President's Crime Commission has recently recommended that in order to assure "procedural justice for the child," it is necessary that "Counsel . . . be appointed as a matter of course wherever coercive action is a possibility, without requiring any affirmative choice by child or parent." As stated by the authoritative "Standards for Juvenile and Family Courts," published by the Children's Bureau of the United States Department of Health, Education, and Welfare:

> As a component part of a fair hearing required by due process guaranteed under the 14th Amendment, notice of the right to counsel should be required at all hearings and counsel provided upon request when the family is financially unable to employ counsel.

This statement was "reviewed" by the National Council of Juvenile Court Judges at its 1965 Convention and they "found no fault" with it. The New York Family Court Act contains the following statement:

> This act declares that minors have a right to the assistance of counsel of their own choosing or of law guardians in neglect proceedings under article three and in proceedings to determine juvenile delinquency and whether a person is in need of supervision under article seven. This declaration is based on a finding that counsel is often indispensable to a practical realization of due process of law and may be helpful in making reasoned determinations of fact and proper orders of disposition.

The Act provides that "At the commencement of any hearing" under the delinquency article of the statute, the juvenile and his parent shall be advised of the juvenile's "right to be represented by counsel chosen by him or his parent . . . or by a law guardian assigned by the court. . . ." The California Act (1961) also requires appointment of counsel.

We conclude that the Due Process Clause of the Fourteenth Amendment requires that in respect of proceedings to determine delinquency which may result in commitment to an institution in which the juvenile's freedom is curtailed, the child and his parent must be notified of the child's right to be represented by counsel retained by them, or if they are unable to afford counsel, that counsel will be appointed to represent the child.

At the habeas corpus proceeding, Mrs. Gault testified that she knew that she could have appeared with counsel at the juvenile hearing. This knowledge is not a waiver of the right to counsel which she and her juvenile son had, as we have defined it. They had a right expressly to be advised that they might retain counsel and to be confronted with the need for specific consideration of whether they did or did not choose to waive the right. If they were unable to afford to employ counsel, they were entitled in view of the seriousness of the charge and the potential commitment, to appointed counsel, unless they chose waiver. Mrs. Gault's knowledge that she could employ counsel is not an "intentional relinquishment or abandonment" of a fully known right.

V
CONFRONTATION, SELF-INCRIMINATION, CROSS-EXAMINATION

Appellants urge that the writ of habeas corpus should have been granted because of the denial of the rights of confrontation and cross-examination in the Juvenile Court hearings, and because the privilege against self-incrimination was not observed. The Juvenile Court Judge testified at the habeas corpus hearing that he had proceeded on the basis of Gerald's admissions at the two hearings. Appellants attack this on the ground that the admissions were obtained in disregard of the privilege against self-incrimination. If the confession is disregarded, appellants argue that the delinquency conclusion, since it was fundamentally based on a finding that Gerald had made lewd remarks during the phone call to Mrs. Cook, is fatally defective for failure to accord the rights of confrontation and cross-examination which the Due Process Clause of the Fourteenth Amendment of the Federal Constitution guarantees in state proceedings generally.

Our first question, then, is whether Gerald's admission was improperly obtained and relied on as the basis of decision, in conflict with the Federal Constitution. For this purpose, it is necessary briefly to recall the relevant facts.

Mrs. Cook, the complainant, and the recipient of the alleged telephone call, was not called as a witness. Gerald's mother asked the Juvenile Court Judge why Mrs. Cook was not present and the judge replied that "she didn't have to be present." So far as appears, Mrs. Cook was spoken to only once, by Officer Flagg, and this was by telephone. The judge did not speak with her on any occasion. Gerald had been questioned by the probation officer after having been taken into custody. The exact circumstances of this questioning do not appear but any admissions Gerald may have made at this time do not appear in the record. Gerald was also questioned by the Juvenile Court Judge at each of the two hearings. The judge testified in the habeas corpus proceeding that Gerald admitted making "some of the lewd statements . . . [but not] any of the more serious lewd statements." There was conflict and uncertainty among the witnesses at the habeas corpus proceeding—the Juvenile Court Judge, Mr. and Mrs. Gault, and the probation officer—as to what Gerald did or did not admit.

We shall assume that Gerald made admissions of the sort described by the Juvenile Court Judge, as quoted above. Neither Gerald nor his parents was advised that he did not have to testify or make a statement, or that an incriminating statement might result in his commitment as a "delinquent."

The Arizona Supreme Court rejected appellant's contention that Gerald had a right to be advised that he need not incriminate himself. It said: "We think the necessary flexibility for individualized treatment will be enhanced by a rule which does not require the judge to advise the infant of a privilege against self-incrimination."

In reviewing this conclusion of Arizona's Supreme Court, we emphasize again that we are here concerned only with proceedings to determine whether a minor is a "delinquent" and which may result in commitment to a state institution. Specifically, the question is whether, in such a proceeding, an admission by the juvenile may be used against him in the absence of clear and unequivocal evidence that the admission was made with knowledge that he was not obliged to speak and would not be penalized for remaining silent. In light of *Miranda* v. *State of Arizona,* 384 US 436, we must also consider whether, if the privilege against self-incrimination is available, it can effectively be waived unless counsel is present or the right to counsel has been waived.

It has long been recognized that the eliciting and use of confessions or admissions require careful scrutiny. Dean Wigmore states:

> The ground of distrust of confessions made in certain situations is, in a rough and indefinite way, judicial experience. There has been no careful collection of statistics of untrue confessions, nor has any great number of instances been even loosely reported . . . but enough have been verified to fortify the conclusion, based on ordinary observation of human conduct, that under certain stresses a person, especially one of defective mentality or peculiar temperament, may falsely acknowledge guilt. This possibility arises wherever the innocent person is placed in such a situation that the untrue acknowledgement of guilt is at the time the more promising of two alternatives between which he is obliged to choose; that is, he chooses any risk that may be in falsely acknowledging guilt, in preference to some worse alternative associated with silence. . . .
>
> The principle, then, upon which a confession may be excluded is that it is, under certain conditions, *testimonially untrustworthy.* . . . [T]he essential feature is that the principle of exclusion is a testimonial one, analogous to the other principles which exclude narrations as untrustworthy. . . .

This Court has emphasized that admissions and confessions of juveniles require special caution. In *Haley* v. *State of Ohio, supra,* where this Court reversed the conviction of a 15-year-old boy for murder, Mr. Justice Douglas said:

> What transpired would make us pause for careful inquiry if a mature man were involved. And when, as here, a mere child—an easy victim of the law—is before us, special care in scrutinizing the record must be used. Age 15 is a tender and difficult age for a boy of any race. He cannot be judged by the more exacting standards of maturity. That which would leave a man cold and unimpressed can overawe and overwhelm a lad in his early teens. This is the period of great instability which the crisis of adolescence produces. A 15-year-old lad, questioned through the dead of night by relays of police, is a ready victim of the inquisition. Mature men possibly might stand the ordeal from midnight to 5 A.M. But we cannot believe that a lad of tender years is a match for the police in such a contest. He needs counsel and support if he is not to become the victim first of fear, then of panic. He needs someone on whom to lean lest the overpowering presence of the law, as he knows it, crush him. No friend stood at the side of this 15-year-old boy as the police, working in relays, questioned him hour after hour, from midnight until dawn. No lawyer stood guard to make sure that the police went so far and no farther, to see to it that they stopped short of the point where he became the victim of coercion. No counsel or friend was called during the critical hours of questioning.

In *Haley,* as we have discussed, the boy was convicted in adult court, and not a juvenile court. In notable decisions, the New York Court of Appeals and the Supreme Court of New Jersey have recently considered decisions of juvenile courts in which boys have been adjudged "delinquent" on the basis of confessions obtained in circumstances comparable to those in *Haley.* In both instances, the State contended before its highest tribunal that constitutional requirements governing inculpatory statements applicable in adult courts do not apply to juvenile proceedings. In each case, the State's contention was rejected, and the juvenile court's determination of delinquency was set aside on the grounds of inadmissibility of the confession. . . .

The privilege against self-incrimination is, of course, related to the question of the safeguards necessary to assure that admissions or confessions are reasonably trustworthy, that they are not the mere fruits of fear or coercion, but are reliable expressions of the truth. The roots of the privilege are, however, far deeper. They tap the basic stream of religious and political principle because the privilege reflects the limits of the individual's attornment to the state and—in a philosophical sense —insists upon the equality of the individual and the State. In other words, the privilege has a broader and deeper thrust than the rule which prevents the use of confessions which are the product of coercion because coercion is thought to carry with it the danger of unreliability. One of its purposes is to prevent the State, whether by force or by psychological domination, from overcoming the mind and will of the person under investigation and depriving him of the freedom to decide whether to assist the State in securing his conviction.

It would indeed be surprising if the privilege against self-incrimination were available to hardened criminals but not to children. The language of the Fifth Amendment, applicable to the States by operation of the Fourteenth Amendment, is unequivocal and without exception. And the scope of the privilege is comprehensive. As Mr. Justice White, concurring, stated in *Murphy* v. *Waterfront Commission,* 378 US 52:

The privilege can be claimed in *any proceeding,* be it criminal or civil, administrative or judicial, investigatory or adjudicatory. . . . it protects *any disclosures* which the witness may reasonably apprehend *could be used in a criminal prosecution or which could lead to other evidence that might be so used.* (Emphasis supplied.)

With respect to juveniles, both common observation and expert opinion emphasize that the "distrust of confessions made in certain situations" to which Dean Wigmore referred in the passage quoted above, is imperative in the case of children from an early age through adolescence. In New York, for example, the recently enacted Family Court Act provides that the juvenile and his parents must be advised at the start of the hearing of his right to remain silent. The New York statute also provides that the police must attempt to communicate with the juvenile's parents before questioning him, and that a confession may not be obtained from a child prior to notifying his parents or relatives and releasing the child either to them or to the Family Court. In *In Matters of W. and S.,* referred to above, the New York Court of Appeals held that the privilege against self-incrimination applies in juvenile delinquency cases and requires the exclusion of involuntary confessions. . . .

The authoritative "Standards for Juvenile and Family Courts" concludes that, "Whether or not transfer to the criminal court is a possibility, certain procedures should always be followed. Before being interviewed [by the police] the child and his parents should be informed of his right to have legal counsel present and to refuse to answer questions or be fingerprinted if he should so decide."

Against the application to juveniles of the right to silence, it is argued that juvenile proceedings are "civil" and not "criminal," and therefore the privilege should not apply. It is true that the statement of the privilege in the Fifth Amendment, which is applicable to the States by reason of the Fourteenth Amendment, is that no person "shall be compelled in any *criminal case* to be a witness against himself." However, it is also clear that the availability of the privilege does not turn upon the type of proceeding in which its protection is invoked, but upon the nature of the statement or admission and the exposure which it invites. The privilege may, for example, be claimed in a civil or administrative proceeding, if the statement is or may be inculpatory.

It would be entirely unrealistic to carve out of the Fifth Amendment all statements by juveniles on the ground that these cannot lead to "criminal" involvement. In the first place, juvenile proceedings to determine "delinquency," which may lead to commitment to a state institution, must be regarded as "criminal" for purposes of the privilege against self-incrimination. To hold otherwise would be to disregard substance because of the feeble enticement of the "civil" label-of-convenience which has been attached to juvenile proceedings. Indeed, in over half of the States, there is not even assurance that the juvenile will be kept in separate institutions, apart from adult "criminals." In those States juveniles may be placed in or transferred to adult penal institutions after having been found "delinquent" by a juvenile court. For this purpose, at least, commitment is a deprivation of liberty. It is incarceration against one's will, whether it is called "criminal" or "civil." And our Constitution guarantees that no person shall be "compelled" to be a witness against himself when he is threatened with deprivation of his liberty—a command which this Court has broadly applied and generously implemented in accordance with the teaching of the history of the privilege and its great office in mankind's battle for freedom.

In addition, apart from the equivalence for this purpose of exposure to commitment as a juvenile delinquent and exposure to imprisonment as an adult offender, the fact of the matter is that there is little or no assurance in Arizona, as in most if not all of the States, that a juvenile apprehended and interrogated by the police or even by the juvenile court itself will remain outside of the reach of adult courts as a consequence of the offense for which he has been taken into custody. In Arizona, as in other States, provision is made for juvenile courts to relinquish or waive jurisdiction to the ordinary criminal courts. In the present case, when Gerald Gault was interrogated concerning violation of a section of the Arizona Criminal Code, it could not be certain that the Juvenile Court Judge would decide to "suspend" criminal prosecution in court for adults by proceeding to an adjudication in Juvenile Court.

It is also urged, as the Supreme Court of Arizona here asserted, that the juvenile and presumably his parents should not be advised of the juvenile's right to silence because confession is good for the child as the commencement of the assumed therapy of the juvenile court process, and he should be encouraged to assume an attitude of trust and confidence toward the officials of the juvenile process. This proposition has been subjected to widespread challenge on the basis of current reappraisals of the rhetoric and realities of the handling of juvenile offenders.

In fact, evidence is accumulating that confessions by juveniles do not aid in "individualized treatment," as the court below put it, and that compelling the child to answer questions, without warning or advice as to his right to remain silent, does not serve this or any other good purpose. In light of the observations of Wheeler and Cottrell, and others, it seems probable that where children are induced to confess by "paternal" urgings on the part of officials and the confession is then followed by disciplinary action, the child's reaction is likely to be hostile and adverse—the child may well feel that he has been led or tricked into confession and that despite his confession, he is being punished.

Further, authoritative opinion has cast formidable doubt upon the reliability and trustworthiness of "confessions" by children. This Court's observations in *Haley* v. *State of Ohio,* are set forth above. The recent decision of the New York Court of Appeals referred to above, *In Matters of W. and S.* deals with a dramatic and, it is to be hoped, extreme example. Two 12-year-old Negro boys were taken into custody for the brutal assault and rape of two aged domestics, one of whom died as the result of the attack. One of the boys was schizophrenic and had been locked in the security ward of a mental institution at the time of the attacks. By a process that may best be described as bizarre, his confession was obtained by the police. A psychiatrist testified that the boy would admit "whatever he thought was expected so that he could get out of the immediate situation." The other 12-year-old also "confessed." Both confessions were in specific detail, albeit they contained various inconsistencies. The Court of Appeals, in an opinion by Keating, J., concluded that the confessions were products of the will of the police instead of the boys. The confessions were therefore held involuntary and the order of the Appellate Division affirming the order of the Family Court adjudging the defendants to be juvenile delinquents was reversed.

A similar and equally instructive case has recently been decided by the Supreme Court of New Jersey. *In Interests of Carlo and Stasilowicz, supra.* The body of a 10-year-old girl was found. She had been strangled. Neighborhood boys who knew the girl were questioned. The two appellants, aged 13 and 15, confessed to the police, with vivid detail and some inconsistencies. At the Juvenile Court hearing, both denied any complicity in the killing. They testified that their confessions were the product of fear and fatigue due to extensive police grilling. The Juvenile Court Judge found that the confessions were voluntary and admissible. On appeal, in an extensive opinion by Proctor, J., the Supreme Court of New Jersey reversed. It rejected the State's argument that the constitutional safeguard of voluntariness governing the use of confessions does not apply in proceedings before the juvenile court. In pointed out that under New Jersey court rules, juveniles under the age of 16 accused of committing a homicide are tried in a proceeding which "has all of the appurtenances of a criminal trial," including participation by the county prosecutor, and requirements that the juvenile be provided with counsel, that a stenographic record be made, etc. It also pointed out that under New Jersey law, the confinement of the boys after reaching age 21 could be extended until they had served the maximum sentence which could have been imposed on an adult for such a homicide, here found to be second degree murder carrying up to 30 years' imprisonment. The court concluded that the confessions were involuntary, stressing that the boys, contrary to statute, were placed in the police station and there interrogated; that the parents of both boys were not allowed to see them while they were being interrogated; that inconsistencies appeared among the various statements of the boys and with the objective evidence of the crime; and that there were protracted periods of questioning. The court noted the State's contention that both boys were advised of their constitutional rights before they made their statemens, but it held that this should not be given "significant weight in our determination of voluntariness." Accordingly, the judgment of the Juvenile Court was reversed.

In a recent case before the Juvenile Court of the District of Columbia, Judge Ketcham rejected the proffer of evidence as to oral statements made at police headquarters by four juveniles who had been taken into custody for alleged involvement in an assault and attempted robbery. *In the Matter of Four Youths,* Nos. 28-776-J, 28-778-J, 28-783-J, 28-859-J, Juvenile Court of the District of Columbia, April 7, 1961. The court explicitly stated that it did not rest its decision on a showing that the statements were involuntary, but because they were untrustworthy. Judge Ketcham said:

Simply stated, the Court's decision in this case rests upon the considered opinion— after nearly four busy years on the Juvenile Court bench during which the testimony of thousands of such juveniles has been heard—that the statements of adolescents under 18 years of age who are arrested and charged with violations of law are frequently untrustworthy and often distort the truth.

We conclude that the constitutional privilege against self-incrimination is applicable in the case of juveniles as it is with respect to adults. We appreciate that special problems may arise with respect to waiver of the privilege by or on behalf of children, and that there may well be some differences in technique—but not in principle —depending upon the age of the child and the presence and competence of parents. The participation of counsel will, of course, assist the police, juvenile courts and appellate tribunals in administering the privilege. If counsel is not present for some permissible reason when an admission is obtained, the greatest care must be taken to assure that the admission was voluntary, in the sense not only that it has not been coerced or suggested, but also that it is not the product of ignorance of rights or of adolescent fantasy, fright or despair.

The "confession" of Gerald Gault was first obtained by Officer Flagg, out of the presence of Gerald's parents, without counsel and without advising him of his right to silence, as far as appears. The judgment of the Juvenile Court was stated by the judge to be based on Gerald's admission in court. Neither "admission" was reduced to writing, and, to say the least, the process by which the "admissions" were obtained and received must be characterized as lacking the certainty and order which are required of proceedings of such formidable consequences. Apart from the "admission," there was nothing upon which a judgment or finding might be based. There was no sworn testimony. Mrs. Cook, the complainant, was not present. The Arizona Supreme Court held that "sworn testimony must be required of all witnesses including police officers, probation officers and others who are part of or officially related to the juvenile court structure." We hold that this is not enough. No reason is suggested or appears for a different rule in respect of sworn testimony in juvenile courts than in adult tribunals. Absent a valid confession adequate to support the determination of the Juvenile Court, confrontation and sworn testimony by witnesses available for cross-examination were essential for a finding of "delinquency" and an order committing Gerald to a state institution for a maximum of six years.

The recommendations in the Children's Bureau's "Standards for Juvenile and Family Courts" are in general accord with our conclusions. They state that testimony should be under oath and that only competent material and relevant evidence under rules applicable to civil cases should be admitted in evidence. The New York Family Court Act contains a similar provision.

As we said in *Kent* v. *United States,* 383 US 541, with respect to waiver proceedings, "there is no place in our system of law for reaching a result of such tremendous consequences without ceremony. . . ." We now hold that, absent a valid confession, a determination of delinquency and an order of commitment to a state institution cannot be sustained in the absence of sworn testimony subjected to the opportunity for cross-examination in accordance with our law and constitutional requirements.

VI
APPELLATE REVIEW AND TRANSCRIPT
OF PROCEEDINGS

Appellants urge that the Arizona statute is unconstitutional under the Due Process Clause because, as construed by its Supreme Court, "there is no right of appeal from a juvenile court order. . . ." The court held that there is no right to a transcript because there is no right to appeal and because the proceedings are confidential and any record must be destroyed after a prescribed period of time. Whether a transcript or other recording is made, it held, is a matter for the discretion of the juvenile court.

This Court has not held that a State is required by the Federal Constitution "to provide appellate courts or a right to appellate review at all." In view of the fact that we must reverse the Supreme Court of Arizona's affirmance of the dismissal of the writ of habeas corpus for other reasons, we need not rule on this question in the present case or upon the failure to provide a transcript or recording of the hearings—or, indeed, the failure of the juvenile court judge to state the grounds for his conclusion. . . . As the present case illustrates, the consequences of failure to provide an appeal, to record the proceedings, or to make findings or state the grounds for the juvenile court's conclusion may be to throw a burden upon the machinery for habeas corpus, to saddle the reviewing process with the burden of attempting to reconstruct a record, and to impose upon the juvenile judge the unseemly duty of testifying under cross-examination as to the events that transpired in the hearings before him.

For the reasons stated, the judgment of the Supreme Court of Arizona is reversed and the cause remanded for further proceedings not inconsistent with this opinion. It is so ordered.

Judgment reversed and cause remanded with directions.

Appendix

UNIVERSAL DECLARATION OF HUMAN RIGHTS

[On December 10, 1948, the General Assembly of the United Nations adopted and proclaimed the Universal Declaration of Human Rights. Following this historic act, the Assembly called upon all member countries to publicize the text of the Declaration and "to cause it to be disseminated, displayed, read and expounded, principally in schools and other educational institutions, without distinction based on the political status of countries or territories." The United States and 47 other member nations voted for the Declaration; none voted against, but 8 nations—the U.S.S.R. and five other East European nations, and Saudi Arabia and the Union of South Africa abstained. Implementation waits upon a covenant that would need to be adopted, signed, and ratified.]

Preamble

Whereas recognition of the inherent dignity and of the equal and inalienable rights of all members of the human family is the foundation of freedom, justice and peace in the world,

Whereas disregard and contempt for human rights have resulted in barbarous acts which have outraged the conscience of mankind, and the advent of a world in which human beings shall enjoy freedom of speech and belief and freedom from fear and want has been proclaimed as the highest aspiration of the common people,

Whereas it is essential, if man is not to be compelled to have recourse, as a last resort, to rebellion against tyranny and oppression, that human rights should be protected by the rule of law,

Whereas it is essential to promote the development of friendly relations between nations,

Whereas the peoples of the United Nations have in the Charter reaffirmed their faith in fundamental human rights, in the dignity and worth of the human person and in the equal rights of men and women and have determined to promote social progress and better standards of life in larger freedom,

Whereas Member States have pledged themselves to achieve, in cooperation with the United Nations, the promotion of universal respect for and observance of human rights and fundamental freedoms,

Whereas a common understanding of these rights and freedoms is of the greatest importance for the full realization of this pledge,

Now, Therefore,

The General Assembly proclaims

This Universal Declaration of Human Rights as a common standard of achievement for all peoples and all nations, to the end that every individual and every organ of society, keeping this Declaration constantly in mind, shall strive by teaching and education to promote respect for these rights and freedoms and by progressive measures, national and international, to secure their universal and effective recognition and observance, both among the peoples of Member States themselves and among the peoples of territories under their jurisdiction.

Article 1. All human beings are born free and equal in dignity and rights. They are endowed with reason and conscience and should act towards one another in a spirit of brotherhood.

Article 2. Everyone is entitled to all the rights and freedoms set forth in this Declaration, without distinction of any kind, such as race, colour, sex, language, religion, political or other opinion, national or social origin, property, birth or other status.

Furthermore, no distinction shall be made on the basis of the political, jurisdictional or international status of the country or territory to which a person belongs, whether it be independent, trust, non-self-governing or under any other limitation of sovereignty.

Article 3. Everyone has the right to life, liberty and security of person.

Article 4. No one shall be held in slavery or servitude; slavery and the slave trade shall be prohibited in all their forms.

Article 5. No one shall be subjected to torture or to cruel, inhuman or degrading treatment or punishment.

Article 6. Everyone has the right to recognition everywhere as a person before the law.

Article 7. All are equal before the law and are entitled without any discrimination to equal protection of the law. All are entitled to equal protection against any discrimination in violation of this Declaration and against any incitement to such discrimination.

Article 8. Everyone has the right to an effective remedy by the competent national tribunals for acts violating the fundamental rights granted him by the constitution or by law.

Article 9. No one shall be subjected to arbitrary arrest, detention or exile.

Article 10. Everyone is entitled in full equality to a fair and public hearing by an independent and impartial tribunal, in the determination of his rights and obligations and of any criminal charge against him.

Article 11. (1) Everyone charged with a penal offence has the right to be presumed innocent until proved guilty according to law in a public trial at which he has had all the guarantees necessary for his defence.

(2) No one shall be held guilty of any penal offense on account of any act or omission which did not constitute a penal offence, under national or international law, at the time when it was committed. Nor shall a heavier penalty be imposed than the one that was applicable at the time the penal offence was committed.

Article 12. No one shall be subjected to arbitrary interference with his privacy, family, home or correspondence, nor to attacks upon his honour and reputation. Everyone has the right to the protection of the law against such interference or attacks.

Article 13. (1) Everyone has the right to freedom of movement and residence within the borders of each state.

(2) Everyone has the right to leave any country, including his own, and to return to his county.

Article 14. (1) Everyone has the right to seek and to enjoy in other countries asylum from persecution.

(2) This right may not be invoked in the case of prosecutions genuinely arising from non-political crimes or from acts contrary to the purposes and principles of the United Nations.

Article 15. (1) Everyone has the right to a nationality.

(2) No one shall be arbitrarily deprived of his nationality nor denied the right to change his nationality.

Article 16. (1) Men and women of full age, without any limitation due to race, nationality or religion, have the right to marry and to found a family. They are entitled to equal rights as to marriage, during marriage and at its dissolution.

(2) Marriage shall be entered into only with the free and full consent of the intending spouses.

(3) The family is the natural and fundamental group unit of society and is entitled to protection by society and the State.

Article 17. (1) Everyone has the right to own property alone as well as in association with others.

(2) No one shall be arbitrarily deprived of his property.

Article 18. Everyone has the right to freedom of thought, conscience and religion; this right includes freedom to change his religion or belief, and freedom, either alone or in community with others and in public or private, to manifest his religion or belief in teaching, practice, worship and observance.

Article 19. Everyone has the right to freedom of opinion and expression; this right includes freedom to hold opinions without interference and to seek, receive and impart information and ideas through any media and regardless of frontiers.

Article 20. (1) Everyone has the right to freedom of peaceful assembly and association.

(2) No one may be compelled to belong to an association.

Article 21. (1) Everyone has the right to take part in the government of his country, directly or through freely chosen representatives.

(2) Everyone has the right of equal access to public service in his country.

(3) The will of the people shall be the basis of the authority of government; this will shall be expressed in periodic and genuine elections which shall be by universal and equal suffrage and shall be held by secret vote or by equivalent free voting procedures.

Article 22. Everyone, as a member of society, has the right to social security and is entitled to realization, through national effort and international co-operation and in accordance with the organization and resources of each State, of the economic, social and cultural rights indispensable for his dignity and the free development of his personality.

Article 23. (1) Everyone has the right to work, to free choice of employment, to just and favourable conditions of work and to protection against unemployment.

(2) Everyone, without any discrimination, has the right to equal pay for equal work.

(3) Everyone who works has the right to just and favourable remuneration ensuring for himself and his family an existence worthy of human dignity, and supplemented, if necessary, by other means of social protection.

(4) Everyone has the right to form and to join trade unions for the protection of his interests.

Article 24. Everyone has the right to rest and leisure, including reasonable limitation of working hours and periodic holidays with pay.

Article 25. (1) Everyone has the right to a standard of living adequate for the health and well-being of himself and of his family, including food, clothing, housing and medical care and necessary social services, and the right to security in the event of unemployment, sickness, disability, widowhood, old age or other lack of livelihood in circumstances beyond his control.

(2) Motherhood and childhood are entitled to special care and assistance. All children, whether born in or out of wedlock, shall enjoy the same social protection.

Article 26. (1) Everyone has the right to education. Education shall be free, at least in the elementary and fundamental stages. Elementary education shall be compulsory. Technical and professional education shall be made generally available and higher education shall be equally accessible to all on the basis of merit.

(2) Education shall be directed to the full development of the human personality and to the strengthening of respect for human rights and fundamental freedoms. It shall promote understanding, tolerance and friendship among all nations, racial or religious groups, and shall further the activities of the United Nations for the maintenance of peace.

(3) Parents have a prior right to choose the kind of education that shall be given to their children.

Article 27. (1) Everyone has the right freely to participate in the cultural life of the community, to enjoy the arts and to share in scientific advancement and its benefits.

(2) Everyone has the right to the protection of the moral and material interests resulting from any scientific, literary or artistic production of which he is the author.

Article 28. Everyone is entitled to a social and international order in which the rights and freedoms set forth in this Declaration can be fully realized.

Article 29. (1) Everyone has duties to the community in which alone the free and full development of his personality is possible.

(2) In the exercise of his rights and freedoms, everyone shall be subject only to such limitations as are determined by law solely for the purpose of securing due recognition and respect for the rights and freedoms of others and of meeting the just requirements of morality, public order and the general welfare in a democratic society.

(3) These rights and freedoms may in no case be exercised contrary to the purposes and principles of the United Nations.

Article 30. Nothing in this Declaration may be interpreted as implying for any State, group or person any right to engage in any activity or to perform any act aimed at the destruction of any of the rights and freedoms set forth herein.

Library of Congress Cataloging in Publication Data

Konvitz, Milton Ridvas, date.   ed.
  Bill of Rights reader.

  (Cornell studies in civil liberty)
  1. Civil rights—United States—Cases. I. Title.
II. Series: Cornell University. Cornell studies in civil liberty.
KF4748.K6   1973   342'.73'085   73-8671
ISBN 0-8014-0783-4